MUSIC THERAPY
RESEARCH

SECOND EDITION

EDITED BY

BARBARA L. WHEELER

Barcelona PUBLISHERS

ISBN 1-891278-26-6

2 4 6 8 9 7 5 3 1

Distributed throughout the world by:
Barcelona Publishers
4 White Brook Road
Gilsum NH 03448
Tel: 603-357-0236 Fax: 603-357-2073
Website: www.barcelonapublishers.com
SAN 298-6299

Cover design:
© 2005 Frank McShane

Permissions

The editor thanks the following for permission to reprint materials in this book:

- Gudrun Aldridge, a table from *Die Entwicklung einer Melodie im Kontext improvisatorischer Musiktherapie.* Unpublished doctoral dissertation, Aalborg University/University Witten-Herdecke, Herdecke, Germany.
- The American Music Therapy Association, material from:
  - Adamek, M. S. (1994). Audio-cueing and immediate feedback to improve group leadership skills: A live supervision model. *Journal of Music Therapy, 31,* 135–164.
  - Bergstrøm-Nielsen, C. (1993). Graphic notation as a tool in describing and analyzing music therapy improvisations. *Music Therapy, 12,* 40–58.
  - Ford, S. E. (1999). The effect of music on the self-injurious behavior of an adult female with severe developmental disabilities. *Journal of Music Therapy, 36,* 293–313.
  - Hanser, S. B. (1974). Group-contingent music listening with emotionally disturbed boys. *Journal of Music Therapy, 21,* 220–225.
  - Kern, P., & Wolery, M. (2001). Participation of a preschooler with visual impairments on the playground: Effects of musical adaptations and staff development. *Journal of Music Therapy, 38,* 149–164.
  - Lee, C. (2000). A method of analyzing improvisations in music therapy. *Journal of Music Therapy, 37,* 147–167.
  - Spencer, S. L. (1998). The efficiency of instrumental and movement activities in developing mentally retarded adolescents' ability to follow directions. *Journal of Music Therapy, 25,* 44–50.
- Carl Bergstrøm-Nielsen, graphic notation of "Edward."
- *British Journal of Music Therapy*, a table from Baker, F., & Wigram, T. (2004). The immediate and long-term effects of singing on the mood states of people with traumatic brain injury. *British Journal of Music Therapy, 18,* 55–64.
- Kenneth E. Bruscia, *Improvisation Assessment Profiles—Abridged.*
- Erik Christensen, a figure from *The musical timespace: A theory of music listening.* Aalborg, Denmark: Aalborg University Press.
- Brian Gaines, Centre for Person-Computer Studies, RepGrid IV images.
- Hogrefe Verlag, figures from Wosch, T., & Frommer, J. (2002). Emotionsveränderungen in musiktherapeutische Improvisationen. *Zeitschrift für Musik-, Tanz- und Kunsttherapie, 13,* 107–114.
- Prof. H. Kächele, a table from Inselmann, U., & Mann, S. (1998). Auswertung von Musiktherapie. Einsatz von Adjektivskalen, Bestimmung der Interraterreliabilität, Darstellung von Spielmustern: Eine Einzellfallanalyse. In H. Kächele, U. Oerter, & N. Scheytt (Eds.), *Vortragssammlung 10 Ulmer Workshop für musiktherapeutische Grundlagen-forschung* (pp. 18–44), Ulm, Germany: Universität Ulm.
- Clifford Madsen and Contemporary Publishing Co., a table from Madsen, C. K., & Madsen, C. H. (1978). *Experimental research in music.* Raleigh, NC: Contemporary Publishing Co.
- Jennifer Marr, a table from *The effects of music on imagery sequence in the Bonny Method of Guided Imagery and Music.* Unpublished master's thesis, University of Melbourne, Melbourne, Australia.
- Thomas Muhr, ATLAS.ti Scientific Software Development GmbH, a figure from ATLAS.ti.
- *Nordic Journal of Music Therapy*, a figure from Bergstrøm-Nielsen, C. (1999). The music of Edward, session one, as graphic notation. *Nordic Journal of Music Therapy, 8,* 96–99.
- Sage Publications, a table from Lincoln, Y. S., & Guba, E. G. (1985). *Naturalistic inquiry.* Newbury Park, CA: Sage Publications.
- SPSS, Inc., figures and tables from SPSS 12.0.

Acknowledgments

There are many people to thank for helping to make this book possible. I am very grateful to the authors. Not only did they prepare 41 chapters, representing the organization and integration of a vast amount of information, but they worked to revise the chapters until they met all of our standards. This has been a challenging process but one that I think will show its worth in clear and stimulating reading.

A few people were instrumental in helping me to develop the concept for the book and at many points in the writing and editing. I am grateful to Kenneth Bruscia for having the vision to create Barcelona Publishers and encouraging the creation of this and other books that are important to the development of music therapy. I thank Kenneth Bruscia and Carolyn Kenny for unceasingly sharing their intellect and ideas and giving me feedback on various aspects of the book. This book would not be nearly as valuable had it not been for their help. I also thank Jane Edwards for her consistent support and input, and other colleagues who have shared ideas and helped me think things through.

A number of people have helped with portions of the book. Some of them are acknowledged in chapters throughout the book. I want to especially thank Douglas Keith for extensive assistance with German translations, Michael McGuire for sharing his editorial expertise, Cheyenne Mize and Elaine Abbott for proofreading, and Korin Kormick, Carolyn Nichols, and Michael Clark for help with computer problems. I also thank Patricia Coates for her care and expertise in indexing the book and her generosity in making the indexing available through a donation to the silent auction of the American Music Therapy Association.

Thank you also to Christopher Doane, Dean of the School of Music at the University of Louisville, and to Robert Amchin, Division Chair, for creating an environment that supports me in my scholarly and creative efforts. I am grateful to Herbert Koerselman, former Dean, for supporting me in coming to Louisville. I thank my current and past students for their work in music therapy and music therapy research courses, challenging me to find better ways to help them learn the concepts necessary to understand and do research and providing feedback on the ways that I have attempted to do this.

Finally, I would like to thank those who have nurtured me as a music therapist and researcher. Their knowledge, enthusiasm, and guidance have helped me to develop as a music therapist, researcher, and scholar. In addition to those acknowledged above, this includes those who have been my research mentors throughout my career, including Clifford Madsen, Carol Prickett, Art Sullivan, and Francis Crowley. I am grateful to the group of qualitative researchers from around the world with whom I have met on a regular basis over the past 10 years, with particular thanks to Mechtild Jahn-Langenberg, who has had the vision and the drive to make the meetings possible. These gatherings and the relationships formed through them have created a nurturing environment for qualitative researchers and promoted a sharing of ideas that is evident throughout this book.

Table of Contents

Contributors

Trygve Aasgaard, PhD
Associate Professor
Oslo University College
Oslo, Norway

Brian Abrams, PhD, MT-BC, LPC, FAMI
Assistant Professor and Director of Music Therapy
Immaculata University
Immaculata, PA

Kenneth Aigen, DA, MT-BC, NRMT
Co-Director, Nordoff-Robbins Center for Music Therapy
New York University
New York, NY

Dorit Amir, DA, ACMT
Head of Music Therapy Program
Bar Ilan University
Ramat Gan, Israel

Diane Austin, DA, ACMT
Director
Music Psychotherapy Center
New York, NY

Lars Ole Bonde, PhD, FAMI, MTL
Associate Professor, Head of Studies, Department of Music and Music Therapy
Aalborg University
Aalborg, Denmark

Joke Bradt, PhD, MT-BC
Assistant Professor and Coordinator of Music Therapy
Montclair State University
Upper Montclair, NJ

Kenneth E. Bruscia, PhD, MT-BC, FAMI
Professor of Music Therapy and Coordinator of the PhD Program
Boyer College of Music and Dance, Temple University
Philadelphia, PA

Debra S. Burns, PhD, MT-BC
Assistant Professor
Indiana University School of Music Program at Indiana University-Purdue University, Indianapolis
Indianapolis, IN

Anthony DeCuir, PhD, RMT
Associate Dean, College of Music
Loyola University
New Orleans, LA

Cheryl Dileo, PhD, MT-BC
Professor of Music Therapy and Director, Arts and Quality of Life Research Center
Boyer College of Music and Dance, Temple University
Philadelphia, PA

Jane Edwards, PhD, RMT
Sionna Academy of Music and Dance
University of Limerick
Limerick, Ireland

Joseph F. Fidelibus, DA, MT-BC, NRMT
Associate Clinical Director
Arts for Healing
New Canaan, CT

Michele Forinash, DA, LMHC, MT-BC
Associate Professor of Music Therapy and Coordinator of PhD in Expressive Therapies
Lesley University
Cambridge, MA

Denise Grocke, PhD, MT-BC, RMT, FAMI
Associate Professor and Head of Music Therapy
Faculty of Music, University of Melbourne
Melbourne, Victoria, Australia

Suzanne B. Hanser, EdD, MT-BC
Chair, Music Therapy Department
Berklee College of Music
Boston, MA

Prof. Dr. phil. Mechtild Jahn-Langenberg, Diplom-Musiktherapeutin
Director, Institute for Music Therapy
University of the Arts
Berlin, Germany

Carolyn Kenny, PhD, MT-BC, MTA
Professor of Human Development and Indigenous Studies
Antioch University PhD in Leadership and Change
Yellow Springs, OH

Joanne V. Loewy, DA, MT-BC
Director, The Louis Armstrong Center for Music and Medicine
Beth Israel Medical Center
New York, NY

Michael G. McGuire, MM, MT-BC
Professor of Music and Director of Music Therapy
Eastern Michigan University
Ypsilanti, MI

Cathy McKinney, PhD, MT-BC, FAMI
Professor and Director of Music Therapy
Appalachian State University
Boone, NC

Anthony Meadows, PhD, MT-BC, FAMI, LPC
Affiliate Faculty, Boyer College of Music and Dance
Temple University
Philadelphia, PA

James S. Musumeci, PhD
Assistant Professor of Management
Touro College
New York, NY

Carol A. Prickett, PhD, MT-BC
Professor of Music Therapy and Music Education
University of Alabama
Tuscaloosa, AL

Even Ruud, PhD, FAMI, Cand. Psychol
Professor
University of Oslo and Norwegian Academy of Music
Oslo, Norway

Henk Smeijsters, PhD
Associate Professor and Head of Research
KenVaK, Research Center for the Arts Therapies, Zuyd, Utrecht, and Saxion Universities
Sittard, The Netherlands

Alan L. Solomon, PhD, RMT
Dean and Professor of Music
The Crane School of Music
State University of New York at Potsdam
Potsdam, NY

Suzanne Nowikas Sorel, DA, NRMT, MT-BC
Assistant Professor of Music Therapy
Molloy College
Rockville Centre, NY

Brynjulf Stige, Dr. Artium
Associate Professor and Head of Studies in Music Therapy
Sogn og Fjordane University College
Sandane, Norway

Rosemarie Tüpker, Dr. phil., Diplom-Musictherapist-Psychotherapy (HP), Morphological Research
Music Therapy Training
University of Münster
Münster, Germany

Eckhard Weymann, Dr. sc. mus., Diplom-Musictherapist-Psychotherapy (HP), Morphological Research Professor
Music Therapy Institute, Hamburg University of Music and Drama
Hamburg, Germany

Barbara L. Wheeler, PhD, MT-BC
Professor and Director of Music Therapy
University of Louisville
Louisville, KY

Tony Wigram PhD, RMT
Professor and Head of PhD Studies in Music Therapy
Faculty of Humanities, Aalborg University
Aalborg, Denmark

Preface

Beginning to read *Music Therapy Research,* 2nd Edition, may be the beginning of a journey—a research journey and also a life journey. Reading this book may open up new ways of looking at research and at life. That is because there are ways in which research and life parallel one another—just as there are many ways to do research, there are also various ways to look at life. Much of how one chooses to do research reflects one's beliefs and the choices that one makes about life. This extends to questions of what we mean by truth, whether it is possible to be objective, and what knowledge we find to be meaningful.

The process of editing this book has been a journey in and of itself. This occurred also while preparing the first edition of the book, *Music Therapy Research: Quantitative and Qualitative Perspectives.* The challenge in the first edition was to pull together a large amount of information about music therapy research that had not been brought together before. The challenge in this edition has been to incorporate many changes in music therapy research, particularly in the growth of qualitative research, and also take into account what was learned from working with and hearing from others who used the first edition.

This book is arranged so that each part or section covers a different aspect of research. Part I, Music Therapy Research: Overview and Issues, addresses the diversity of music therapy practice and research and the complexity of music therapy research, including its many overlapping areas. It also deals with some considerations in making a distinction between quantitative and qualitative research. For those who want only a brief overview of music therapy research, this section can be read alone, using the overviews of quantitative and qualitative research rather than the more detailed coverage included in the remainder of the book.

Part II, The Research Process, is intended to cover all aspects of music therapy research and be the focus of reading for undergraduate music therapy research courses. Portions of Part I plus this section may be all that is read by some undergraduate students, as it is possible to read this section and understand much about research in general and also about quantitative and qualitative research.

Part III, Types of Quantitative Research, and Part IV, Types of Qualitative Research, provide detailed descriptions of numerous quantitative and qualitative research methods and include examples. Part V, Types of Other Research, includes chapters on Researching Music, Philosophical Inquiry, Developing Theory, and Historical Research. These final three sections provide a wealth of information on music therapy research employing 21 diverse methods and should be read by those wanting more information on any of them. Each chapter details an approach to research; many of them develop this information in ways that has not been done before in the music therapy literature.

I hope that people will find this book useful in continuing to develop and expand our models of music therapy research. Ultimately, it is through our research that our clinical practice will develop, leading to the best music therapy services for our clients.

Barbara L. Wheeler
Editor
University of Louisville
Louisville, Kentucky
March 2005

Part I

Music Therapy Research:

Overview and Issues

Chapter 1
Overview of Music Therapy Research[1]
Barbara L. Wheeler

Music therapy is a diverse field and music therapy research increasingly reflects that diversity. Many methods and approaches are used to examine the various facets of music therapy practice and theory. This chapter examines some salient features and issues of concern in music therapy research.

To do this, we first look at some definitions of music therapy research, including what distinguishes research from other professional tasks performed by music therapists. We then examine how research has developed as reflected through written work, placing music therapy research within a broader context of research in other disciplines. Then, distinctions and reciprocal relationships among research, theory, and practice in music therapy are examined. Following this, several divisions of music therapy research are defined and discussed: basic and applied; historical, experimental, descriptive, and philosophical; and quantitative and qualitative. Finally, the chapter concludes with observations about the diversity of music therapy research. We begin by looking at definitions of music therapy research.

Defining Music Therapy Research

What is *research?* It may be defined as "careful or diligent search" or "to search or investigate exhaustively" (*Merriam Webster's Collegiate Dictionary,* p. 992). Some take the parts of the word as a reminder that we must *re–search*—embark again and again on a journey of discovery and exploration (Charles T. Eagle, personal communication, June, 1982; Payne, 1993).

Research has been described as "a carefully organized procedure that can result in the discovery of new knowledge, the substantiation of previously held concepts, the rejection of false tenets that have been widely acclaimed, and the formal presentation of data collected" (Phelps, Ferrara, & Goolsby, 1993, p. 4). This organized plan, described by Gfeller (1995) as "a disciplined or systematic inquiry" (p. 29), is used to support or refute views held on "how and why things work the way they do" (Rainbow & Froelich, 1987, p. 10). Bruscia (1995a) has given the following definition of research: "a systematic, self-monitored inquiry which leads to a discovery or new insight, which, when documented and disseminated, contributes to or modifies existing knowledge or practice" (p. 21). Other authors suggest something that we might discern as we take time to study these definitions. They say that the process of research includes four basic steps: (a) the clear statement of purpose and the delineation of the specific aspects under investigation, (b) a methodology that is clearly described and justified, (c) a report of the results, and (d) conclusions that are subsequently related to existing knowledge (Rainbow & Froelich).

Any definition of research, including those given above, is grounded in beliefs of the researcher as to what is a legitimate object of study, the relationship between the knower and the known, the nature of causality, and what is meant by truth in research. These are *epistemological* questions, and the answers given to them have an impact on how that person views research. In fact, some definitions of research are steeped in a positivistic epistemology, lending themselves to a quantitative approach to research, and others in a nonpositivistic epistemology, leading to a qualitative approach. The consideration of such questions is part of the philosophy of science (see Chapter 3, Philosophy and Theory of Science) and an understanding of these questions will deepen music therapists' understanding of research and its meaning.

Music therapists undertake many professional tasks that are not research. Clinical work in and of itself is not research, although at times it shares some elements of the research process. When music therapists write progress notes on a client, it is not technically research because the purposes and outcomes of it are different, although it resembles the research process in some ways. And when we write about our work, or share our work so that others may learn from it, it is not necessarily research, although under certain conditions it may meet the criteria for research. To gain a better sense of what distinguishes these pursuits—clinical work,

---

[1] Portions of this chapter were adapted from the author's chapter by the same name (Wheeler, 1995a) in the first edition of this book (Wheeler, 1995b).

writing progress notes, and sharing our work—from research, we can look back to the definitions of research. The most important difference may be the goals: The goal of research is to modify the way that things are done or thought about, while the goals of the other pursuits mentioned are to perform clinical practice or communicate about it. We can also see differences in the systematic way in which we pursue a research question and the way in which we present the results of research.

Although many other definitions of research have been formulated, all suggest that it leads to the discovery of new things, the reaffirmation of what we already know, or changes in the way that we view what we already know. It is these possibilities of discovery and change that make research so exciting!

Music Therapy Research Reflected in Written Work

Music therapy research has grown and changed over the years. Much of this growth is reflected in music therapy journals and books. As Jane Edwards comments in the next chapter of this book when counting periodicals published in English with "music therapy" in their titles: "In 1970 there was one journal, in 1980 there were two, and in 1990 there were six" (p. 20). It should be noted that the journals contain varying amounts of research.

Another indicator of growth and change in music therapy research is the books that have been published. This may be seen in publications in the 10 years between the publication of the first edition of this book, *Music Therapy Research: Quantitative and Qualitative Perspectives,* in 1995, and the current edition. Prior to that time, the only books on research methods in music therapy were *Experimental Research in Music* by Madsen and Madsen, initially published in 1970 (reprinted in 1978), and an accompanying workbook (Madsen & Moore, 1978).[2] Although many books that included research related to music therapy, including some on research methods, were published in the intervening years (see Eagle, 1996; Payne, 1993), *Music Therapy Research: Quantitative and Qualitative Perspectives* (Wheeler, 1995b) was the next published book on methods in music therapy research. This was followed in quick succession by several books focusing on research methods in music therapy: *Music Therapy Research and Practice in Medicine* (Aldridge, 1996), *Qualitative Music Therapy Research: Beginning Dialogues* (Langenberg, Aigen, & Frommer, 1996), *Multiple Perspectives: A Guide to Qualitative Research in Music Therapy* (Smeijsters, 1997), and *Beginning Research in the Arts Therapies* (Ansdell & Pavlicevic, 2001).

Music Therapy Research in a Broad Context

The methods of music therapy research are generally part of a larger conception of research, with particular adaptations to the needs of music and music therapy. Many were developed by researchers in the social sciences, including psychology, education, and sociology. Some are used by researchers in the physical sciences such as biology and chemistry, while others have been developed by music and music psychology researchers. Similarly, trends toward newer research paradigms mirror and parallel trends in other fields. Some of the issues in music therapy research that will become apparent as you read this book are also issues in other disciplines.

It is important to keep this in mind as you study the concepts developed in this book. Many are similar to those that would be learned in a research course in psychology or education. Music therapy researchers can and should go to sources in those larger fields on which our research is based. New research techniques are being developed regularly in related disciplines, and these can add to the research knowledge in music therapy.

The distinctive thing about the field of music therapy, of course, is the use of music and musical relationships within an interpersonal context for purposes of therapy. The specific applications of research techniques that are necessary because of this combination are a unique

---

[2] There was also a series of British conferences focused on developing a research culture and research skills in music therapy and other arts therapies in London from 1987–1990, sponsored by the City University Music Department in conjunction with the Association of Professional Music Therapists. Proceedings were published for each conference (see Hoskyns & Clarke, 1987; Hoskyns, 1988; Gilroy, Hoskyns, Jenkyns, Lee, & Payne, 1989; Kersner, 1990).

and challenging aspect of research in this field. Indeed, the needs of music therapy research have led some to suggest that music therapists need to develop our *own* research methods—methods suitable for investigating the specific combination of factors inherent in music therapy.

Research, Theory, and Practice

The relationships among research, theory, and practice have been an ongoing concern in music therapy. As we seek to understand music therapy research, we will examine its relationship and relevance to theory and practice.

Distinctions

Bruscia (1995a, 1998) examined distinctions among research, theory, and practice. In differentiating research from practice, he points out that the goals are different, noting that research is intended to increase or modify the knowledge base of music therapy while practice is intended to help clients achieve health. He also says that knowledge is gathered for its own sake in research while it is gathered for the client's sake in practice. Further, he points out differences in roles and beneficiaries between research and practice, as well as a difference in who uses the knowledge that is gained. Bruscia goes on to distinguish research from theory, initially noting that quantitative and qualitative researchers view theory differently. He suggests that there is a clearer difference between theory and research in quantitative research, where research and theory are seen as continually adding to existing knowledge. In qualitative research, on the other hand, it is understood that research and theory increase understanding of our constructions, thus leading to reconstructions. Doing research is theorizing, and theorizing is an aspect of doing research. With these different views, it is clear that the distinctions between research and theory will be different in quantitative than in qualitative research.

The distinctions among research, theory, and clinical practice are not as clear as they once were, particularly in qualitative research. For example, in first-person, ethnographic, and participatory action research (as described in Chapters 30, 31, and 32, respectively), earlier distinctions are blurred as clients participate in the design and other aspects of the research process. The contributions of the participants are acknowledged, not just as those who participate in the research and to whom the findings may be applied, but also as creators of the research data and consequently of the findings as well.

Reciprocal Relationships

Research is an important aspect of the discipline of music therapy, along with practice and theory. The three areas have been linked together since Gaston (1968) suggested that theory, clinical practice, and research form a tripod, each necessary in order for the other to stand. In 1983, I encouraged music therapists to use the three areas together to form a progression in which: (a) Questions arise from the clinical practice of music therapy; (b) a theory is formulated to address those questions and tested through research; and (c) the results of the research inform and shape clinical practice (Wheeler, 1983). Research can also shape clinical practice or theory, or it can be shaped by them.

Bruscia (2005) speaks to the importance of theory for practice and its relationship to research, saying:

> Theory has a central place in music therapy—it shapes and is shaped by practice and research. Regardless of whether the theory has been clearly articulated by the therapist or theorist, theory provides a foundational structure for all clinical work. Conversely, practice is often the basis upon which a theory is developed. Similarly, research may be the foundation for theory, or it may be the result of theory. (p. 540)

Research and Practice

Several aspects of the relationships between research and the practice of music therapy have been considered. These views can be divided into concerns about the relevance of research to practice, possible reasons for lack of relevance, and the importance of integrating research and practice.

Concerns About Relevance. Several surveys of the attitudes of music therapy clinicians toward research, all done several decades ago, found that clinicians rated knowledge of research literature as low in importance (Braswell, DeCuir, & Maranto, 1980) or felt that the research that was published was not very relevant to their work (Nicholas & Gilbert, 1980). Gfeller (1995), after reviewing these and other studies, suggested that a problem in applying the results of research to the needs of clinicians might be that the research did not address the populations with which people work. To gather information on this possibility, Gfeller looked at the results presented by Nicholas and Gilbert in which 75% of the respondents felt that current research was irrelevant to their daily work and 64% felt that current research was not concerned with real-world problems. She calculated the percentage of people working in psychiatric music therapy (22% in 1994) and noted that content analyses of music therapy research showed that very little research had been conducted with people with emotional difficulties. She suggested that the problem might be that most of the studies failed to address those specialties most prominent in music therapy practice, so that a large percentage of therapists may have found little published research related to their daily practice.

Brooks (2003) analyzed nine music therapy journals containing a total of 1,521 articles, some of which were research and some of which were not research. She found the rate of publication of clinical articles to be rather low until about 1985, at which time she said, "a significant burst of activity and interest began" (p. 158). This is not directly applicable to the current discussion of the proportion of research articles that address various clinical specialties since articles were not considered clinical articles if they had already been classified as research. However, we might use Brooks' data as the basis for speculation that an increase in clinical focus that occurred in the mid-1980s may have also influenced how relevant clinicians at that time found publications to be. However, since we do not have formal data (from surveys) on this question, this is only speculation.

Gregory's (2002) analysis of 4 decades of the *Journal of Music Therapy (JMT)*, looking at articles that used behavioral research designs, gives information on clinical groups that have been addressed through research. She found that many of the studies that used those designs in the first 2 decades of her survey were primarily related to clients with mental retardation and emotional disturbances. During the 1980s, she found a wider range of people to be included, with the main increase in the inclusion of persons with physical disabilities. She found a large expansion of populations on which research was done in the 1990s, stating: "Clients with mental retardation or emotional disturbances are subjects in only 20% of the studies. Other populations during this period included infants, homeless children, and persons with Alzheimers and medical conditions" (p. 68).

Both the Brooks (2003) and Gregory (2002) content analyses indicate changes in the focus of publications in the 1980s. Since the information that we have of clinicians' attitudes toward research ends by 1980, we cannot know if the increased focus on clinical publications and broadened focus of (behavioral) research designs to a wider range of disabilities has had an effect.

The content analyses cited above (Gfeller, 1995; Gregory, 2002), as well as other similar analyses (Codding, 1987; Gfeller, 1987; Gilbert, 1979; James, 1985; Jellison, 1973) focused on articles in *JMT* and other music therapy journals. Only a portion of music therapy research is published in journals for which music therapy is the primary focus. Increasingly, music therapy studies are found in medical publications, including those devoted to nursing, rehabilitation, and neuropsychology. Music therapists also publish in education journals and books, including those on special education, in psychology and psychotherapy publications, and in other interdisciplinary areas. Numerous reviews and meta-analyses of research related to music therapy with varied populations have been published in recent years,[3] and music therapy

---

[3] For examples of meta-analyses and reviews, see meta-analyses by Standley, 2000; Whipple, 2004; Koger, Chapin, & Brotons (1999); Silverman (2003); Gold, Voracek, & Wigram, 2004; Dileo & Bradt, in

reviews are also being conducted and published as part of the Cochrane Reviews (see http://www.cochrane.org/reviews/index.htm). With all of the literature that is evident from these publications, it is difficult to make a case for research not being available in the areas in which music therapists work.

We have no information about the impact of increased published qualitative research, either. Although Brooks' (2003) study indicates that qualitative research is still among the least-published types of research, she says: "The publication rate of qualitative. . . articles has grown fairly steadily and significantly since about 1985" (p. 159). Brooks found 98 qualitative research articles. This indicates a change in the types of research that are being published and must be considered as we examine the relevance of music therapy research.

Without recent data on music therapists' views of the relevance of research, there is no way to know how music therapists currently view the relevance of research or whether there has been a change. It may be more useful to attempt to understand other reasons that these problems may have occurred over the years—why clinicians may not have viewed research as relevant or why they do not make the best use of the research that has been done.

Possible Reasons for Lack of Relevance. If it is still the case that clinicians have difficulty seeing the relevance of research to their work, we might wonder if it is because students are not prepared through the educational process to understand research and appreciate the need for it. Or perhaps they are prepared through the educational process but, as clinicians, they do not make the effort to read and understand research and apply it to their work. Or perhaps there is something about the research itself that makes it difficult to connect it to clinical practice.

The possibility that students are not learning through the educational process to read, understand, and apply research to their clinical work was suggested by Gfeller (1995), who said:

> It is possible that a reasonable proportion of research is, in fact, relevant to practice, but that clinicians, who through the educational process have been marginally prepared to understand and appreciate research, may fail to see connections between basic research and day-to-day clinical issues. Even the value of applied research may be underestimated if the reader lacks the tools to understand and interpret research outcomes. More music therapy programs providing better educational preparation regarding research methodology may be a partial remedy to the perceived split between research and practice. (p. 52)

There are reasons to wonder, though, if this is truly the case. In the United States, the *AMTA Professional Competencies* (American Music Therapy Association, 2003), which document the competencies that music therapists are expected to have, include various research skills. These include:

Interpret information in the professional research literature;
Determine if conclusions drawn in a study are supported by the results;
Demonstrate basic knowledge of the purpose and methodology of historical, quantitative, and qualitative research;
Perform a data-based literature search;
Apply selected research findings to clinical practice.

Additional support for the supposition that music therapy students are receiving training in music therapy research is that a large percentage of universities that teach music therapy in the United States use *Music Therapy Research: Quantitative and Qualitative Perspectives* (Wheeler, 1995b) for one of their courses. This is typically a psychology of music or music therapy research course.

Back in 1986, Madsen in his article, "Research and Music Therapy: The Necessity for Transfer," suggested that clinicians need to make the effort to read, understand, and apply research to their work. He said, "There is *always* something in the *Journal [JMT]* for every practicing music therapist, but sometimes it takes patience and imagination to make it relevant. The conscientious clinician will attempt to understand more fully the *Journal* and the many applications possible through reading and analyzing the research that it contains" (p. 51). Madsen went on to say, "The problem of research meaning and dissemination does not just rest with the research community, it also rests with each practitioner. Practicing music therapists

---

press; and reviews of music therapy literature including research on a number of topics in *Effectiveness of Music Therapy Procedures: Documentation of Research and Clinical Practice* (2000).

must learn to read, evaluate, and most importantly, *transfer,* from all information they receive, including research reports in whatever form" (p. 52).

Kenny raised questions about the focus of research and the suitability of quantitative methods as early as 1982, when she shared concerns about the prevailing behavioral views and attempts to predict behavior. Kenny (1982, 1989), Aigen (1991), and Smeijsters and Hurk (1993) concluded that the research methods traditionally used in music therapy are ineffective in answering the questions most relevant to clinicians. Aigen suggested that the lack of clinical relevance is due to reliance on research paradigms established in disciplines such as psychology and the biological sciences that may have limited usefulness in evaluating clinical music therapy techniques involving improvisation and the creative process. Aigen urged that new models of research be developed. Aigen (1991, 1993, 1995) advocated using various qualitative research models as a means of making the research that was done in music therapy more relevant to the clinical practice of music therapy. There is much more qualitative research today than in 1991 or 1995 when Aigen expressed these ideas, and it is possible that some clinicians are finding research to be more relevant. However, since no studies of attitudes have been done in these more recent years, we do not have this information.

Related to the points made by Aigen and the others, Asmus and Gilbert (1981) suggested that a "lack of a model for conceptualizing the therapeutic process" (p. 41) helps to explain why limited applied research has been conducted. Gfeller (1987) reached a similar conclusion in her review of articles from *JMT*. She found no single theory or philosophy that appeared central to music therapy practice. Gfeller recommended, "To devise a well-structured theoretical foundation of music therapy practice, music's function within external psychological or physiological theories should be clearly described in terms of its psychoacoustic properties, not simply administered in a global trial and error fashion" (pp. 192–193). In Chapter 40 of this book, Developing Theory, Bruscia explicates numerous theories that have been formulated about music therapy and aspects of it. We may need to question also, then, why music therapists have not applied the theories that are available to their research—but this is a somewhat different discussion.

Another influence on how relevant music therapists find research may be the kind of information that they find useful in their clinical practices. There are many approaches to music therapy (see Darrow, 2004, for an overview), reflecting different philosophies and needs of those who practice them. Bruscia (1987) suggested that research plays a different role in clinical practice depending upon the type of music therapy being practiced. He suggests that "in the more *technological* approaches, where music is used to directly influence the client's responses, and where the primary goal is to induce observable, measurable, *objective* changes, the therapist is more likely to base therapy on scientific data" (p. 25). Bruscia suggests, though, that in a more *psychotherapeutic* approach, "where music is used to facilitate the therapy *process,* and where the primary goal is to induce covert, unmeasurable, *subjective* changes, the practitioner is more likely to base therapy on the nature of the musical and interpersonal relationships that have emerged with the client" (p. 25). Therapists will find research methods that are congruent with the type of music therapy that they practice to be most useful for their clinical practice.

Integration of Research and Practice. Kenny's *The Field of Play: A Guide for the Theory and Practice of Music Therapy* (1989) presents an integration of clinical practice and research (as well as theory). She says, "The *Field of Play* offers a challenge to people interested in music therapy research. Can we begin to design our own research tools, which are informed by our direct experience in music therapy?" (p. 126).

More recently, Kenny (1998) has spoken of some of the tensions between practice and research, suggesting that good practitioners must also be good researchers within the context of practice. She gives as examples the need for a good practitioner to have observational skills and be able to evaluate programs in order to assess their effectiveness. Kenny says:

> Perhaps the most difficult role is that of the clinician/researcher who must sometimes make difficult choices between clinical goals and research goals. Is the clinical experience diminished by obtrusive methods such as videotaping, signing release forms, formal interviews? How can we as clinicians gain the trust necessary for clinical encounters if the patient feels they are being observed as a subject in a research project? (pp. 207–208)

It is evident that at least some music therapists are aware that research should be relevant to clinical work. Ansdell and Pavlicevic's (2001) book, *Beginning Research in the Arts Therapies: A Practical Guide,* is aimed at beginning researchers, arts therapists "researching their own work (rather than having it researched by professional researchers)" (p. 10). Another example is a Debate Day that was held in Aalborg, Denmark, in May 2004, in which researchers were specifically asked to present their research as it would be useful to clinicians. Such a focus is not unique but is an example of researchers trying to meet clinicians' needs for clinically relevant research. Along the same lines is a discussion in the web-based Forum of the *Nordic Journal of Music Therapy,* titled "The Relevance of Research to Clinical Work" (Trondalen & Wigram, 2005).

It is clear that the relationship between research and the clinical practice of music therapy is complex. This discussion suggests that both researchers and clinicians may have a contribution to make to the integration of research and practice. It also appears that the type of clinical work that people do may influence the extent to which they find research useful, with the possibility that different approaches to research may be suitable for different clinical approaches.

Research and Theory

There is also a relationship between research and theory, some of which is related to the earlier discussion of research and practice. This section will look at the importance of theory to music therapy and the integration of research and theory.

Importance of Theory. The importance of theory to music therapy and music therapy research may not have been fully appreciated for many years, although it was recognized by some. Gaston (1968) and Sears (1968) and others made theoretical contributions to the music therapy literature early in the development of music therapy. Ruud wrote his master's thesis, *Music Therapy and Its Relationship to Current Treatment Theories,* in 1973; it was published as a book in 1980. Ruud focused on the importance of music therapists understanding the relationship of music therapy to treatment theories within the mental health field. The suggestion that music therapists should base their work on theories from related fields was important, and some music therapists have continued to focus on it. Another move toward incorporating more theory into music therapy came with several meetings in the late 1970s that brought music therapists from various parts of the world together to consider the role of theory in music therapy.[4] These discussions often did not deal explicitly with the relationship of theory to research but provided some basis for these connections.

In spite of efforts by some to incorporate theory, Maranto (1988) suggested that music therapy research had, in many ways, developed faster than music therapy theory. She predicted:

> The enormous diversity that is now the discipline of music therapy will give rise to a movement that will seek a theoretical paradigm large enough to embrace it, yet specific enough to allow for a means to define it clearly and, at the same time, allow for possible growth. If this does not happen, the discipline may become fragmented into numerous specialties, organized around various populations, theoretical models, or clinical techniques. (p. 16)

As Maranto predicted, theory has gradually assumed a larger role in music therapy. Many music therapists now seem more able to locate their research approach within a broader approach to knowledge that evaluates epistemological and ontological positions (J. Edwards, personal communication, October 30, 2004). In addition to Ruud's (1998) continuing focus on theory, Kenny (1989), Aigen (1991), Bruscia (1995a, 1998), Edwards (1999), Stige (2002), and others have developed constructs and theories and incorporated theory into discussions of music therapy and music therapy research, helping to emphasize the importance of theory to music

---

[4] Following a symposium on music therapy education that was held in Herdecke, Germany, in 1978, a Theory of Music Therapy Group was formed and chaired by William Sears. This led to two further meetings seeking to examine theoretical bases for music therapy in 1979, one at Aalborg University in Denmark and the second, the International Study Group: Theory of Music Therapy, at Southern Methodist University in Dallas, TX. Theory was also a concern at the 1982 New York University Symposium, "Music in the Life of Man."

therapy research. Their writings speak of ways to integrate theory and research (and base these on the needs of clinicians). Some of their contributions to the integration of research and practice were suggested in the discussion above.

Brooks' (2003) survey of nine music therapy journals published in English found an increase since the 1990s in philosophical/theoretical articles. She attributes this largely to the *Nordic Journal of Music Therapy (NJMT)*, which, since its inception in 1992, has published a total of 32 philosophical/theoretical articles, or 33% of its content.[5] Brooks found that *NJMT* has published the largest percentage of theoretical articles (23.5%) of any of the journals (with *JMT* and *Music Therapy: Journal of the American Music Therapy Association* having the next largest percentages with approximately 21% each). She said of *NJMT*: "Because *NJMT* is a relatively young journal, it is quite remarkable that it has already exceeded much older journals in their publication of these kinds of articles" (p. 165). Wigram, Pedersen, and Bonde (2002), following a content analysis of several music therapy journals from 1998–2001, also found a leaning in the *Nordic Journal of Music Therapy* towards articles and discussion on music therapy theory, finding 46.9% of the articles to be concerned with theory. One of their observations after reviewing three European journals, *NJMT,* the *British Journal of Music Therapy,* and *Musiktherapeutische Umschau,* the primary German journal, was that "music therapy theory and research is under the influence of and inspired by the development within 'new musicology', anthropology and ethnography" (p. 235).

Bruscia provides a comprehensive survey of existing theory in music therapy in Chapter 40 of this book, Developing Theory. The chapter is the first to explicate the nature of theory in music therapy based on that survey and attests to the significance of theory since the very inception of music therapy.

Integration of Research and Theory. The role of theory is different in quantitative and qualitative research. Thus, we need to consider the type of research along with the role of theory.

Much quantitative research is done in an attempt to test a hypothesis, and many hypotheses come from theories. Often, the results of the research contribute to a theory. As Bruscia (2005) says, "In quantitative research, an empirical theory is an attempt to evaluate or explain a body of existing research findings, so that deductions can be made from them" (p. 544). As an example of how research and theory fit together from this perspective, Gfeller (1987) recommended, "To devise a well-structured theoretical foundation of music therapy practice, music's function within external psychological or physiological theories should be clearly described in terms of its psychoacoustic properties, not simply administered in a global trial and error fashion" (pp. 192–193).

Thaut (2000), also addressing quantitative research, developed a model upon which to base research, with theory occupying an important place in this model. He says:

> In order to do meaningful research, reasonable and testable hypotheses have to be developed, which requires the existence of good theory. That is, we need a valid prior understanding of input-output connections between stimulus input and therapeutic effect on a conceptual and empirical level. . . . It is the function of theory to provide explanatory models and help develop a dynamic understanding of cause and effect relationships for phenomena under observation. . . . Thus, the most useful theory of music therapy would be the one that provides the most persuasive and generalizable framework for explaining the translation process of music's therapeutic influence on psychological and physiological processes. (p. 4)

Aigen's (1991, 1993) plea for music therapists to develop an indigenous research paradigm has been heeded. Much of the qualitative research being done today is closely related to the practice of music therapy. Along with this, when appropriate, the theories informing the research are known and stated much more explicitly than they were in the past. Some qualitative research, though, is intentionally done without having a theoretical basis, thus allowing findings to emerge without the influence of prior theoretical assumptions. In addition, a purpose of some types of qualitative research is to build theories.

---

[5] Brooks' (2003) survey ended with 2001, so her figures reflect the content through that date.

Theory development for music therapy practice and research is in its early stages. As it continues, we can expect to see changes in the application of theory to music therapy research. Additional information on this area is contained in Chapter 40, Developing Theory.

Types of Research

There are several ways of classifying research in music therapy and related disciplines. Each serves a different purpose and may contribute in a different way to our understanding. We will look at basic and applied research; traditional divisions of research as historical, experimental, descriptive, and philosophical research; and distinctions between quantitative and qualitative research. Each conception of research that is presented here is informed by one's beliefs about "what constitutes the legitimate object of study; what is the relation between knower and known, that is, the problem of objectivity; how to approach the nature of causality; and what is meant by truth in research" (Ruud, 2005, p. 33). Epistemological issues are discussed as part of the philosophy of science in Chapter 3 of this book, Philosophy and Theory of Science.

Basic and Applied Research

In certain instances, it is useful to make a distinction between basic and applied research. In theory, there are clear differences between these two types of research, although in practice the distinctions are not always so clear.

Basic research, also called *pure* or *fundamental research,* is done primarily to increase knowledge without necessarily having in mind an application of the research findings. This type of research searches for knowledge for its own sake. The results may have little immediate practical use, although increases in knowledge brought about by basic research often lead to changes in practice. Some basic research involves the construction and testing of theories (Patton, 2002).

Applied research is performed to solve a practical problem. Its purpose is to test a hypothesis or model in a real situation of interest or to expand our understanding of an actual situation. The subjects of applied research are frequently the population of interest to the researcher. Research in many disciplines is most likely to be applied. Educational research, for example, generally has a particular goal in mind.

Basic research is done more often in some other disciplines than in music therapy. Much quantitative research in the physical sciences and psychology is done with no immediate practical goal in mind. Experiments on how cells divide or laboratory research on reinforcement of rats are examples of basic quantitative research. Basic qualitative research might involve looking at how people experience a particular phenomenon but without focusing on a practical application of that information.

Basic research, labeled by Bruscia (1995a) as *foundational,* provides the foundation for much of what music therapists do. It includes much of the research in the psychology of music. Studies of the elements of music (rhythm, melody, harmony), the perception of music, how the brain processes music, musical preference, and affective response to music are basic research.

At the point that results from basic research are applied to real problems, the research becomes applied. When scientists begin using the discoveries from research on cell division to seek treatments for cancer, the research is applied. Similarly, research on reinforcement provided the foundations of behavior modification; later research applying behavior modification to learning and therapy situations is thus applied. Basic research on people's experience of listening to music while surrounded by other people might become applied if this knowledge were applied to designing concert halls with special attention to how distance from and amount of contact with others could contribute to their experience of listening to music.

Because the purpose of music therapy is to help people, research in this discipline is generally applied. Music therapy assessment, treatment, and evaluation studies are all applied research. Further examples of applied research in music therapy include studies of musical preferences or surveys of the attitudes of music therapists, all of which focus on actual music therapy situations.

Some music therapists do basic research, intended to increase their knowledge of the area of interest without applying the results directly to clinical practice. The work of Thaut and his colleagues can provide insights as to the relationship between basic and applied research in music therapy. Thaut has been involved in a series of investigations of the effects of music on the muscles of the body. Thaut, Schleiffers, and Davis (1991), in "Analysis of EMG Activity in Biceps and Triceps Muscle in an Upper Extremity Gross Motor Task Under the Influence of Auditory Rhythm," provide a good example of basic research that employed subjects from a normal population and has no direct clinical application. Despite its classification as basic research, clinicians working with people with muscular problems might apply the results of this research to a clinical situation. A later study, "The Effect of Auditory Rhythmic Cueing on Stride and EMG Patterns in Hemiparetic Gait of Stroke Patients" (Thaut, Rice, McIntosh, & Prossas, 1993), has clinical applications and so would be considered applied research. It has elements of basic research and is an extension of the earlier area of study, but, because of the clear clinical applications, would most properly be categorized as applied research. Thaut's research is quantitative and the examples from his research are typical of quantitative research.

Qualitative research also may be basic. This chapter has already discussed the fact that one impetus for the increase in qualitative music therapy research was to make the research more relevant to clinical practice in music therapy, thus much qualitative research on aspects of music therapy clinical practice is applied research. There are, however, examples of basic qualitative research. Racette's (1989, 2004) study, "A Phenomenological Analysis of the Experience of Listening to Music When Upset," could be considered basic research. She was interested in people's experience of using music when they were upset. In its most basic form, this study did not purport to use the results to help people use music as a tool to overcoming being upset. A therapist who uses Racette's results to formulate clinical interventions that use music to help clients who are upset, and who then gathers information (possibly using the same phenomenological methods that Racette used), would be doing applied research. The lines between basic and applied research are not always clear. For example, since Racette made suggestions for practical uses of her results, some might suggest that her research was applied.

Traditional Divisions of Research

Many music therapists think of research as described by Madsen and Madsen (1970/1978) as philosophical, historical, descriptive, and experimental. Rainbow and Froehlich (1987) suggest that music educators have approached research from three different perspectives: philosophical, historical, and empirical inquiry. Phelps, Ferrara, and Goolsby (1993) divide research into six types: experimental/quasi-experimental, historical, philosophical, qualitative, aesthetic, and descriptive. Heller and O'Connor (2002) say that examples of research fall into "at least three general types: historical (mostly qualitative in technique), descriptive (qualitative or quantitative), and experimental (mostly quantitative)" (p. 1090). Historical, experimental, descriptive, and philosophical research will be described here.

Historical research in music therapy is "the systematic study of the past practices, materials, institutions, and people involved in therapeutic applications of music" (Solomon & Heller, 1982). It involves gaining knowledge by studying evidence from the past. Solomon (1995, see also Chapter 41 of this book) makes the point that history may refer to past events; things that have been written about the past; people's ideas, images, or memories of the past; a way of knowing about the past; or any combination of these.

Experimental research is generally thought of within a quantitative framework and is done to determine cause-and-effect relationships (Hanser & Wheeler, 1995, see also Chapter 21 of this book). In this type of research, the researcher manipulates the variables of interest to determine their effects. It is done under controlled conditions in which the experimenter determines the specific treatment techniques, how they will be administered, who will receive treatment, and when the treatment will occur. The researcher intends that only the variables of interest will vary systematically from condition to condition, so that changes that occur following the experiment are likely to be due to the experimental conditions. More broadly, experimental research may be thought of as research in which "the researcher engages participants in the phenomenon under study to produce the necessary data because the phenomenon will not present itself otherwise" (Bruscia, 1995c, p. 410). Experimental research within this broader definition may be applied within a nonpositivistic framework, as in participatory action research or in some case studies.

Descriptive research can refer to a broad range of research techniques. The focus is on describing the phenomena of interest, perhaps determining the "status or state of the art of a phenomenon such as examining process through surveys, case studies, trend studies" (Heller & O'Connor, 2002, p. 1089). Quantitative descriptive research may include survey research, ex post facto research (correlational or causal-comparative), case studies, and longitudinal studies. Descriptive research techniques are part of several qualitative research traditions, including ethnography, in which careful description is a primary characteristic, and case study research. In support of this, Schwandt (2001) discusses description, saying, "Careful, detailed factual description of people, objects, and action is said to be the empirical basis or foundation of ethnography and qualitative inquiry more generally" (p. 55).

Philosophical inquiry uses philosophical procedures to "analyze and contextualize theory, research, and practice within the history of ideas" (Bruscia, cited in Aigen, 2005, p. 526–527). This approach to research involves speculation, analysis, and criticism. Characteristic procedures are "clarifying terms, exposing and evaluating underlying assumptions of other philosophical and theoretical stances. . . relating ideas as a systematic theory and showing their connection to other conceptual and theoretical systems. . . [and] using argument as a primary mode of inquiry and a presentational device" (Aigen, p. 527).

These traditional divisions of research can be either quantitative or qualitative, depending upon the assumptions that underlie them and the procedures used to carry them out.

Quantitative and Qualitative Research

Quantitative research, which grew from a positivistic view of the world, has a long history in music therapy. Positivism refers to the view that "positive knowledge is based on natural phenomena and their properties and relations as verified by the empirical sciences" *(Merriam Webster's New Collegiate Dictionary,* 10th Edition, 2002, p. 906). The idea that the physical sciences followed patterns and could be investigated with the inductive-experimental method can be traced to the 17th century. One proponent of this method was Galileo, who, in 1632, held that "nature is consistent in its operations and is not random. . . . nature varies in a systematic way, and it is possible to discover and describe nature's patterns by using mathematical formulas" (Polkinghorne, 1983, p. 16). As early as 1637, Hobbes "was the first to comprehend and express the view that humans could be studied with the new methods of science" (Polkinghorne, p. 16). Then as now, an underlying belief of positivists was that truth exists and that it is possible to discover it or at least come closer to discovering it. Finding or coming closer to this truth, then, is the goal of research conducted within a positivistic framework, and the procedures outlined below are designed to accomplish that.

Research conducted within a positivistic paradigm is often quantitative research. Quantitative researchers use the empirical method to test theories through procedures for scientific objectivity, including careful observation of behavior, the isolation and manipulation of variables, and hypothesis testing. Inherent in the positivistic view is the expectation that, given appropriate methods, human behavior can be controlled and predicted in the same manner that the actions of inanimate objects are controlled and predicted by biologists, physicists, and other natural scientists. Positivists believe that findings can be generalized from one setting to another in a value-free manner. Much music therapy research has been within this tradition.

In contrast to positivists, nonpositivists believe that there is no truth, only multiple constructions or perspectives of a phenomenon. Thus, the knower and the known are inseparable. A central goal of research within nonpositivistic paradigms is, therefore, to understand more about these constructions.

Qualitative research is a term that has been applied to a broad category of research conducted by nonpositivists. This research reflects the belief of its followers that not all that is important can be reduced to measurements, it is essential to take into account the interaction between the researcher and the participant(s) being studied. Findings cannot be generalized beyond the context in which they are discovered, and values are inherent in and central to any investigation.

The roots of qualitative, as distinct from quantitative, research can be traced to an 18th century debate between Descartes, who spoke for the importance of mathematics and objectivity in the search for truth, and Kant, who suggested that human knowing is dependent upon what goes on inside the observer (Hamilton, 1994). Researchers in many fields, particularly the human sciences and the arts, have used qualitative methods over many years. Beginning in the 1980s, researchers in disciplines that had formerly employed quantitative methods almost exclusively—including education, psychology, and music therapy—began to use qualitative methods to answer some questions, and a debate arose as to whether quantitative research methods could actually meet the needs of these disciplines (Aigen, 1991; Campbell & Heller, 1980; Gage, 1989; Lincoln & Guba, 1985). Growing from that debate came a movement in music therapy toward the utilization of qualitative research methods.[6]

We can see that research conducted within a positivistic paradigm is concerned with finding truth, while research conducted within a nonpositivistic paradigm aims to increase understanding of people's multiple constructions of reality. Thus, one is concerned with objectivity and the other with subjectivity. These are very different positions and goals. This discussion shows that the distinctions between quantitative and qualitative research go far beyond the type of data with which they deal to encompass differences in philosophy, research interests, and methodology.

Bruscia (1995b) cautioned those who attempt to embrace both of these paradigms when he said:

> There is one unavoidable dilemma: Notwithstanding the possibility of collecting both quantitative and qualitative data in the same study, and combining the different interests and methodologies, the two *philosophical paradigms* cannot be integrated or combined. They are mutually exclusive ways of thinking about the world. (p. 73)

Bruscia went on to discuss several options that music therapists could follow in order to benefit from both quantitative and qualitative research, including studying some phenomena with one type of research and other phenomena with the other type; studying different aspects of the same phenomenon in independent studies, anchoring each in either the positivist or nonpositivist paradigm; or combining types of data and methods within the same study while anchored solidly in one paradigm or the other, with such combinations often referred to as triangulation (pp. 73–74).

Mixed methods research intentionally incorporates both quantitative and qualitative research methods, intending to use diverse perspectives, methods, and data to generate the information that is desired. Issues in combining methods occur on both pragmatic and philosophical/paradigmatic levels. Greene and Caracelli (1997a, 1997b) suggest that there are three main positions on mixing paradigms and methods:

> (1) The purist stance, in which people argue against mixing paradigms; (2) the pragmatic stance, in which people view paradigms as useful conceptual constructions but base practical methodological decision on contextual responsiveness and relevance, thereby often including diverse methods; and (3) the dialectical stance, in which people view paradigms as important guides for practice and regard the inevitable tensions invoked by juxtaposing different paradigms as potentially generating more complete, more insightful, even transformed evaluative understandings. (p. 1)

The feasibility and advisability of mixed methods research is a topic of discussion among many who write about and practice research. Robson (2002) advocates such a combination and suggests a number of ways of combining qualitative and quantitative methods and advocates utilizing more than one method. Kenny (2004) says, "Triangulating a study or using several methods to investigate the same phenomenon has the advantage of building on strengths and compensating for the weaknesses of various methods" (p. 32).

Some of the discussions of combining quantitative and qualitative research, or mixed methods research, take into account the differences in paradigms while others do not. It is unclear to me how researchers can discuss mixing methods without considering the differences in paradigms or belief systems. For example, the second position listed above by Greene and Caracelli (1997a, 1997b), labeled *pragmatic,* does not take paradigmatic differences into account. It is not clear how this would work—how do researchers make sense of their questions

---

[6] Additional information on both quantitative and qualitative research can be found throughout this book, with more detailed summaries of each in Chapter 4, Principles of Quantitative Research, and Chapter 5, Principles of Qualitative Research.

(or get answers that make sense) when they are not questions that can be asked within the paradigm in which they are operating?

It may be useful in discussions of the feasibility of combining quantitative and qualitative research to make a distinction between doing research using quantitative or qualitative methods and using quantitative or qualitative techniques but not subscribing to the corresponding worldview or paradigm. As used here, a technique refers to a specific means of working toward a goal, which, in this case, may be collecting data in a particular way (numerically or by interviews, for instance). A method is broader, in this case referring to the quantitative or qualitative method of doing research, and implies adopting the worldview taken by those who embrace that method. Thus, those who use techniques borrowed from the quantitative method (such as counting responses) may not necessarily embrace the positivist paradigm, while those who use techniques borrowed from the qualitative method (such as interviewing participants) may not necessarily accept the nonpositivist paradigm. Researchers who utilize quantitative techniques are not necessarily employing the quantitative method or accepting the positivist paradigm, therefore, and researchers who utilize qualitative techniques are not necessarily employing the qualitative method of research or adopting the nonpositivist paradigm.

While combining positivistic and nonpositivistic paradigms is fraught with problems due to the different belief systems, a number of music therapy researchers have combined quantitative and qualitative techniques. Many of these studies are conducted primarily within one method but incorporate elements of the other, often to provide additional information on the topic under study. Certainly a person who does a quantitative research study includes elements of qualitative research, or qualitative techniques, as he or she subjectively evaluates elements of the study, and one who does qualitative research may rely on numbers for a portion of the analysis, thus utilizing quantitative techniques. These might properly be referred to as using quantitative or qualitative techniques or including quantitative or qualitative information or data, rather than as true mixed methods research.

As an example of a study in which the paradigmatic issues are considered, Bonde (2004) carefully considers epistemological and methodological issues in a mixed methods study of the influence of 10 individual Bonny Method of Guided Imagery and Music sessions on mood and quality of life. He discusses some of these issues and reports the findings of the quantitative and qualitative investigations separately and in different formats and styles. Music therapists are encouraged to follow Bonde's lead in seeking to understand the philosophies underlying the methods that they use. Continued examination of these issues by music therapy researchers will no doubt result in better understanding of the issues and better ways of dealing with them, hopefully leading to better research.

All types of research, including historical, experimental, descriptive, and philosophical, can be conducted from either a positivistic or nonpositivistic perspective. Historical and philosophical research may be considered on a continuum of positivism to nonpositivism based on its ontological and epistemological positions. The core issue is the researcher's belief as to how one can arrive at useful knowledge and whether discovering truth is the goal of the research. The aim of positivistic historical research, for example, is to discover truth, while the aim of nonpositivistic historical research is not to find the truth but to develop a perspective on the past. Similar distinctions could apply to philosophical inquiry, with different types of philosophical inquiry existing at various points on a positivistic-nonpositivistic continuum.

Diversity in Music Therapy Research

From this overview, it is apparent that there is tremendous diversity in approaches to music therapy research. There is also diversity in how music therapists view the research literature, some finding it useful and others looking for something different. Music therapists also see several means of achieving the most useful results from research.

As we move from this chapter through the remainder of this book, we will have many opportunities to learn about this diversity in music therapy research. Many perspectives are included, some complementary and some with sharp differences. These different views are reflected in the chapters of this book, which cover issues with broad implications for research such as the philosophy of science; practical aspects of research such as funding research and designing research; and a broad spectrum of research methods, including their historical and theoretical underpinnings, questions considered in each, and examples of music therapy research in each approach.

These perspectives reflect the diversity that is music therapy and music therapy research. Readers of the book have an opportunity to learn about and examine the various viewpoints, then to carry this knowledge to their music therapy and music therapy research.

References

Aigen, K. (1991). The roots of music therapy: Towards an indigenous research paradigm. *Dissertation Abstracts International, 52*(6), 1933A. (University Microfilms No. DEY91-34717)

Aigen, K. (1993). The music therapist as qualitative researcher. *Music Therapy, 12,* 16–39.

Aigen, K. (1995). Principles of qualitative research. In B. L. Wheeler (Ed.), *Music therapy research: Quantitative and qualitative perspectives* (pp. 283–311). Gilsum, NH: Barcelona Publishers.

Aigen, K. (2005). Philosophical inquiry. In B. L. Wheeler (Ed.), *Music therapy research* (2nd ed., pp. 526–539). Gilsum, NH: Barcelona Publishers.

Aldridge, D. (1996). *Music therapy research and practice in medicine: From out of the silence.* London: Jessica Kingsley Publishers.

American Music Therapy Association. (2003). *AMTA Professional Competencies.* http://www.musictherapy.org/competencies.html

American Music Therapy Association. (2000). *Effectiveness of music therapy procedures* (3rd ed.). Silver Spring, MD: Author.

Ansdell, G., & Pavlicevic, M. (2001). *Beginning research in the arts therapies.* London: Jessica Kingsley Publishers.Asmus, E. P., & Gilbert, J. P. (1981). A client-centered model of therapeutic intervention. *Journal of Music Therapy, 18,* 41–51.

Bonde, L. O. (2004). *The Bonny Method of Guided Imagery and Music (BMGIM) with cancer survivors. A psychosocial study with focus on the influence of music therapy on mood and quality of life.* Unpublished doctoral dissertation, Aalborg University, Aalborg, Denmark.

Braswell, C., DeCuir, A., & Maranto, C. D. (1980). Ratings of entry level skills by music therapy clinicians, educators, and interns. *Journal of Music Therapy, 17,* 133–147.

Brooks, D. (2003). A history of music therapy journal articles published in the English language. *Journal of Music Therapy, 40,* 151–168.

Bruscia, K. (1987). Professional identity issues in music therapy education. In C. D. Maranto & K. Bruscia (Eds.), *Perspectives on music therapy education and training* (pp. 17–29). Philadelphia: Temple University.

Bruscia, K. E. (1995a). The boundaries of music therapy research. In B. L. Wheeler (Ed.), *Music therapy research: Quantitative and qualitative perspectives* (pp. 17–27). Gilsum, NH: Barcelona Publishers.

Bruscia, K. E. (1995b). Differences between quantitative and qualitative research paradigms: Implications for music therapy. In B. L. Wheeler (Ed.), *Music therapy research: Quantitative and qualitative perspectives* (pp. 65–76). Gilsum, NH: Barcelona Publishers.

Bruscia, K. E. (1995c). The process of doing qualitative research: Part II: Procedural steps. In B. L. Wheeler (Ed.), *Music therapy research: Quantitative and qualitative perspectives* (pp. 401–427). Gilsum, NH: Barcelona Publishers.

Bruscia, K. E. (1998). *Defining music therapy* (2nd ed.). Gilsum, NH: Barcelona Publishers.

Bruscia, K. E. (2005). Developing theory. In B. L. Wheeler (Ed.), *Music therapy research* (2nd ed., pp. 540–551). Gilsum, NH: Barcelona Publishers.

Campbell, W., & Heller, J. (1980). An orientation for considering models of musical behavior. In D. Hodges (Ed.), *Handbook of music psychology* (pp. 29–36). Lawrence, KS: National Association for Music Therapy.

Codding, P. (1987). A content analysis of the *Journal of Music Therapy,* 1977–1985. *Journal of Music Therapy, 24,* 195–202.

Darrow, A.-A. (Ed.). (2004). *Introduction to approaches in music therapy.* Silver Spring, MD: American Music Therapy Association.

Dileo, C., & Bradt, J. (Eds.) (in press). *Music therapy and medicine: A meta-analysis of the literature according to medical specialty.* Cherry Hill, NJ: Jeffrey Books.

Eagle, C. T. (1996). An introductory perspective on music psychology. In D. A. Hodges (Ed.), *Handbook of music psychology* (pp. 1–28). San Antonio, TX: Institute for Music Research.

Edwards, J. (1999). Considering the paradigmatic frame: Social science research approaches relevant to research in music therapy. *The Arts in Psychotherapy, 26*, 73–80.

Edwards, J. (2005). Developments and issues in music therapy research. In B. L. Wheeler (Ed.), *Music therapy research* (2nd ed., pp. 20–32). Gilsum, NH: Barcelona Publishers.

Gage, N. L. (1989). The paradigm wars and their aftermath: A "historical" sketch of research on teaching since 1989. *Educational Researcher, 18*(7), 4–10.

Gaston, E. T. (1968). *Music in therapy.* New York: Macmillan.

Gfeller, K. (1995). The status of music therapy research. In B. L. Wheeler (Ed.), *Music therapy research: Quantitative and qualitative perspectives* (pp. 29–63). Gilsum, NH: Barcelona Publishers.

Gfeller, K. (1987). Music therapy theory and practice as reflected in research literature. *Journal of Music Therapy, 24*, 178–194.

Gilbert, J. (1979). Published research in music therapy, 1973–1978: Content, focus, and implications for future research. *Journal of Music Therapy, 16*, 102–110.

Gilroy, A., Hoskyns, S., Jenkyns, M., Lee, C., & Payne, H. (Eds.). (1989). *Arts therapies research: Proceedings of the first arts therapies research conference.* London: Department of Music, City University.

Gold, C., Voracek, M., & Wigram, T. (2004). Effects of music therapy for children and adolescents with psychopathology: A meta-analysis. *Journal of Child Psychology and Psychiatry and Allied Disciplines, 45*, 1054–1063.

Greene, J. C., & Caracelli, V. J. (1997a). Editor's notes. In *Advances in mixed-method evaluation: The challenges and benefits of integrating diverse paradigms* (pp. 1–3). *New Directions for Evaluation* [series], No. 74. San Francisco: Jossey-Bass.

Greene, J. C., & Caracelli, V. J. (1997b). Defining and describing the paradigm issue in mixed-method evaluation. In *Advances in mixed-method evaluation: The challenges and benefits of integrating diverse paradigms* (pp. 5–17). *New Directions for Evaluation* [series], No. 74. San Francisco: Jossey-Bass.

Gregory, D. (2002). Four decades of music therapy behavioral research designs: A content analysis of *Journal of Music Therapy* articles. *Journal of Music Therapy, 39*, 56–71.

Hamilton, D. (1994). Traditions, preferences, and postures in applied qualitative research. In N. K. Denzin & Y. S. Lincoln (Eds.), *Handbook of qualitative research* (pp. 60–69). Thousand Oaks, CA: Sage Publications.

Hanser, S. B., & Wheeler, B. L. (1995). Experimental research. In B. L. Wheeler (Ed.), *Music therapy research: Quantitative and qualitative perspectives* (pp. 129–146). Gilsum, NH. Barcelona Publishers.

Heller, J. J., & O'Connor, E. J. P. (2002). Maintaining quality in research and reporting. In R. Colwell & C. Richardson (Eds.), *The new handbook of research on music teaching and learning* (pp. 1089–1107). New York: Oxford University Press.

Hoskyns, S., & Clarke, E. (1987). *Starting research in music therapy: Proceedings of the Third Music Therapy Day Conference.* London: Music Department, City University.

Hoskyns, S. (1988). *The case study as research: Proceedings of the Fourth Music Therapy Day Conference.* London: Music Department, City University.

James, M. (1985). Sources of articles published in the *Journal of Music Therapy*: The first twenty years, 1964–1983. *Journal of Music Therapy, 22*, 87–94.

Jellison, J. (1973). The frequency and general mode of inquiry of research in music therapy, 1952–1972. *Council for Research in Music Education, 35*, 351–358.

Kenny, C. B. (1982). *The mythic artery: The magic of music therapy.* Atascadero, CA: Ridgeview Publishing Co.

Kenny, C. B. (1989). *The field of play: A guide for the theory and practice of music therapy.* Atascadero, CA: Ridgeview Publishing Co.

Kenny, C. B. (1998). Embracing complexity: The creation of a comprehensive research culture in music therapy. *Journal of Music Therapy, 38*, 201–217.

Kenny, C. B. (2004). *A holistic framework for aboriginal policy research. Ottawa, Ontario, Canada: Status of Women Canada.* Available at http://www.swc-cfc.gc.ca/pubs/0662379594/index_e.html

Kersner, M. (Ed.). (1990). *The art of research: The Second Arts Therapies Research Conference, Proceedings.* London: Arts Therapies Research Committee.

Koger, S. M., Chapin, K., & Brotons, M. (1999). Is music therapy an effective intervention for dementia? A meta-analytic review of the literature. *Journal of Music Therapy, 36,* 2–15.

Langenberg, M., K. Aigen, K., & J. Frommer, J. (Eds.). (1996). *Qualitative music therapy research: Beginning dialogues.* Gilsum, NH: Barcelona Publishers.

Lathom-Radocy, W., & Radocy, R. (1995). Descriptive research. In B. L. Wheeler (Ed.), *Music therapy research: Quantitative and qualitative perspectives* (pp. 165–181). Gilsum, NH: Barcelona Publishers.

Lincoln, Y. S., & Guba, E. G. (1985). *Naturalistic inquiry.* Newbury Park, CA: Sage Publications.

Madsen, C. K., & Madsen, C. H. (1970). *Experimental research in music.* Englewood Cliffs, NJ: Prentice-Hall. (Reprinted 1978, Raleigh, NC: Contemporary Publishing Co.)

Madsen, C. K., & Moore, R. S. (1978). *Experimental research in music: Workbook in design and statistical tests* (Rev. ed.). Raleigh, NC: Contemporary Publishing Co.

Madsen, C. K. (1986). Research and music therapy: The necessity for transfer. *Journal of Music Therapy, 23,* 50–55.

Maranto, C. D. (1988). Music therapy: Present and future trends. *Journal of the International Association of Music for the Handicapped, 4*(1), 15–21.

Merriam Webster's collegiate dictionary (10th ed.). (2002). Springfield, MA: G. & C. Merriam.

Nicholas, M. J., & Gilbert, J. P. (1980). Research in music therapy: A survey of music therapists' attitudes and knowledge. *Journal of Music Therapy, 17,* 207–213.

Patton, M. Q. (2002). *Qualitative research and evaluation methods* (3rd ed.). Thousand Oaks, CA: Sage Publications.

Payne, H. (1993). Introduction to inquiry in the arts therapies. In H. Payne (Ed.), *Handbook of inquiry in the arts therapies* (pp. 1–6). London: Jessica Kingsley Publishers.

Phelps, R. P., Ferrara, L., & Goolsby, T. W. (1993). *A guide to research in music education* (4th ed.). Metuchen, NJ: Scarecrow.

Polkinghorne, D. (1983). *Methodology for the human sciences: Systems of inquiry.* Albany, NY: State University of New York Press.

Racette, K. (1989). *A phenomenological analysis of the experience of listening to music when upset.* Unpublished master's thesis. Temple University, Philadelphia.

Racette, K. (2004). A phenomenological analysis of the experience of listening to music when upset. In B. Abrams (Ed.), *Qualitative inquiries in music therapy* (Vol. 1, pp. 1–18). Gilsum, NH: Barcelona Publishers.

Rainbow, E. L., & Froelich, H. C. (1987). *Research in music education.* New York: Schirmer Books.

Robson, C. (2002). *Real world research: A resource for social scientists and practitioner-researchers* (2nd ed.). Malden, MA: Blackwell Publishing.

Ruud, E. (1973). *Music therapy and its relationship to current treatment theories.* Unpublished master's thesis, Florida State University, Tallahassee, FL.

Ruud, E. (1980). *Music therapy and its relationship to current treatment theories.* St. Louis, MO: MMB Music.

Ruud, E. (1998). *Music therapy: Improvisation, communication, and culture.* Gilsum, NH: Barcelona Publishers.

Ruud, E. (2005). Philosophy and theory of science. In B. L. Wheeler (Ed.), *Music therapy research* (2nd ed., pp. 33–44). Gilsum, NH: Barcelona Publishers.

Schwandt, T. A. (2001). *Dictionary of qualitative inquiry* (2nd ed.). Thousand Oaks, CA: Sage Publications.

Silverman, M. J. (2003). The influence of music on the symptoms of schizophrenia: A meta-analysis. *Journal of Music Therapy, 40,* 27–40.

Smeijsters, H. (1997). *Multiple perspectives: A guide to qualitative research in music therapy.* Gilsum, NH: Barcelona Publishers.

Smeijsters, H., & Hurk, J. van den. (1993). Research in practice in the music therapeutic treatment of a client with symptoms of anorexia nervosa. In M. Heal & T. Wigram (Eds.), *Music therapy in health and education* (pp. 235–263). London: Jessica Kingsley Publishers.

Solomon, A. L. (1995). Historical research. In B. L. Wheeler (Ed.), *Music therapy research: Quantitative and qualitative perspectives* (pp. 487–501). Gilsum, NH: Barcelona Publishers.

Solomon, A. L., & Heller, G. N. (1982). Historical research in music therapy: An important avenue for studying the profession. *Journal of Music Therapy, 19,* 161–178.

Standley, J. M. (2000). Music research in medical treatment. In *Effectiveness of music therapy procedures: Documentation of research and clinical practice* (3rd ed., pp. 1–64). Silver Spring, MD: American Music Therapy Association.

Stige, B. (2002). *Culture-centered music therapy.* Gilsum, NH: Barcelona Publishers.

Thaut, M. H. (2000). *A scientific model of music in therapy and medicine.* San Antonio, TX: Institute for Music Research.

Thaut, M. H., Rice, R. R., McIntosh, G. C., & Prossas, S. C. (1993). The effect of auditory rhythmic cueing on stride and EMG patterns in hemiparetic gait of stroke patients. *Physical Therapy, 73,* S107.

Thaut, M., Schleiffers, S., & Davis, W. (1991). Analysis of EMG activity in biceps and triceps muscle in an upper extremity gross motor task under the influence of auditory rhythm. *Journal of Music Therapy, 28,* 64–88.

Trondalen, G., & Wigram, T. (2005). The relevance of research to clinical work. *Forum: Nordic Journal of Music Therapy,* http://www.hisf.no/njmt/forum008list.html

Wheeler, B. L. (1995a). Introduction: Overview of music therapy research. In B. L. Wheeler (Ed.), *Music therapy research: Quantitative and qualitative perspectives* (pp. 3–15). Gilsum, NH: Barcelona Publishers.

Wheeler, B. L. (Ed.). (1995b). *Music therapy research: Quantitative and qualitative perspectives.* Gilsum, NH: Barcelona Publishers.

Wheeler, B. (1983). Prologue. *Music Therapy, 3,* 1–3.

Whipple, J. (2004). Music in intervention for children and adolescents with autism: A meta-analysis. *Journal of Music Therapy, 41,* 90–106.

Wigram, T., Pedersen, I. N., & Bonde, L. O. (2002). *A comprehensive guide to music therapy.* London: Jessica Kingsley Publishers.

Acknowledgments

I would like to thank Kenneth Bruscia and Carolyn Kenny for extensive assistance in developing this chapter, and Lars Ole Bonde, Jane Edwards, Wendy Magee, Even Ruud, and Brynjulf Stige for stimulating and useful feedback on earlier versions of the chapter. I would also like to thank Gene Ann Behrens, Nicki Cohen, Christian Gold, Suzanne Hanser, Cathy McKinney, and Henk Smeijsters for input on ways to conceptualize quantitative research; although the results of this conceptualization were not clear enough to become part of the chapter, the process was useful in helping to develop my ideas.

Chapter 2
Developments and Issues
in Music Therapy Research
Jane Edwards

This chapter provides an historical overview of aspects of the colorful threads woven into the fabric of music therapy research since the establishment of the first music therapy peer-reviewed journal in 1964. Major activities and outcomes in music therapy research work in music therapy research work are examined for general salient features and themes.

Music therapy research developments over time are characterized by fits and starts with individual effort playing the largest part in creating a whole, rather than a monolith called *music therapy research* directing the ebb and flow of research practice. Music therapy researchers in many parts of the world have taken their own individual paths that have, in turn, influenced greatly, partly, or inconsequentially the journeys of others. It is difficult to pinpoint unitary shared research goals in this field, so this chapter does not endeavor to find commonalities, lines, and threads that reflect some kind of cohesive and united history of music therapy research. Many individual stories have unfolded in different countries of the world, often in quite isolated circumstances; these, in their turn, have shaped the telling of the story of this chapter.

While it cannot be argued that music therapy research has distinguished itself as a force to be reckoned with in its closely related fields of musicology or music psychology research nor in the broader areas of humanities, science, or medicine, neither can we argue that our research efforts are ineffectual and underdeveloped. After 40 years, we have a discrete body of refereed literature, hundreds of studies using experimental or behavioral designs, published systematic reviews, and, more recently, the publication of a number of qualitative method investigations, as well as many in-depth clinical case descriptions and comprehensive reviews of literature, plus theories and models to guide and shape our practice. We are poised in this new century to use this body of knowledge to consolidate, refine, and further develop our approaches to research.

The Refereed Literature

The peer reviewed, or refereed, literature in music therapy is a useful resource to guide an historical overview of some of the characteristics and trends within the field. Since journals only publish papers that have been subjected to expert review, scrutinizing their content allows for a critical examination of what is accepted as research by the profession. As music therapy has a 40-year history of refereed publications, an examination of the journal literature is an important contributor to this historical overview.

Some of the refereed journals in music therapy and their dates of commencement, in chronological order, are listed in Table 1. Each of these journals continues to be published except for *Music Therapy: Journal of the American Association for Music Therapy (MT),* which ceased publication at the time of the unification of the American Association for Music Therapy (AAMT) and National Association for Music Therapy (NAMT) to form the American Music Therapy Association (AMTA).

Over the past 4 decades, and particularly in the most recent decade of this review, journals published in English with "music therapy" in their title have increased in number. In 1970 there was one journal, in 1980 there were two, and in 1990 there were six. For the past 10 years, six countries have regularly produced journals in English from which music therapists can select relevant research, clinical, and theoretical papers as a resource for their own professional development, as well as choose as destinations for their research efforts.

As the first refereed journal in the field, the *Journal of Music Therapy (JMT)* has set the standard for music therapy research since its establishment in 1964. In particular, *JMT* has provided a benchmark for the publication of outcome-based research that employs quantitative methods, whether from a positivist or postpositivist approach to knowledge building. In its more recent history, *JMT* has endeavored to include papers that use or discuss qualitative methods, and to this end a special issue was published on qualitative method research in 1998.

Table 1
Refereed Journals in Music Therapy Published in English*

Journal	Country of Publication	First Year of Issue
Journal of Music Therapy (JMT)	US	1964
Canadian Journal of Music Therapy (CAM)	Canada	1973
Music Therapy: Journal of the American Association for Music Therapy (MT)	US	1981(–96)
Music Therapy Perspectives (MTP)	US	1982
British Journal of Music Therapy (BJMT) †	UK	1987
Australian Journal of Music Therapy (AJMT)	Australia	1990
Nordic Journal of Music Therapy (NJMT)	Norway	1992
Annual Journal of the New Zealand Society for Music Therapy (NZ)	New Zealand	1994

* This list does not include the many creative arts therapy journals and bulletins published internationally nor online publications in music therapy. The *South African Journal of Music Therapy,* no longer in publication, was not consulted.

† Until 1994, this was titled the *Journal of British Music Therapy.*

Analysis of the content of music therapy journals has been presented in a number of publications including Jellison (1973), James (1985), Codding (1987), DeCuir (1987), Gfeller (1987), Wheeler (1988), Solomon (1993), Webster (1993), Wigram (1993), Wigram, Pedersen, and Bonde (2002), Gregory (2002), and Brooks (2003). Most of these studies examined papers published in *JMT* only, or reviewed *JMT* papers alongside those of other journals, with the exception of Webster who examined the first 5 years of the *British Journal of Music Therapy (BJMT).* Examining the content of journals can offer insights to music therapy's research history including trends, developments, and changes. The role of the refereed journal in both shaping and reflecting the approaches to knowledge in this discipline can then be observed over time.

The following section will provide a brief reflection on the way such evaluations of the journal literature have been approached and will also examine the conclusions of researchers when undertaking these analyses. For example, it was concluded from categorizing 499 articles from five of the music therapy journals into the groupings of clinical, research, and general that "Ninety-eight articles were identified as research, compared with 210 clinical papers and 191 general papers. This tells us that music therapists write more about their clinical work and music therapy theory than research" (Wigram et al., 2002, p. 230). These findings might also be used to suggest that more clinical work is undertaken than research or that there are fewer researchers than clinicians in music therapy or perhaps that research reports take longer to write because of time-consuming data analysis components, and therefore fewer of them are submitted to journals than clinical reports. Or it may be that journals and their reviewers favor the contribution of clinical reports for some reason, and it is therefore somewhat easier to get a clinical paper published. The point here is that, while it is quite difficult to come to definite conclusions or to assert a particular view simply from a description of the number of types of journal papers in a category, the findings of these reviews reveal some interesting phenomena, and, considered together, the reviews offer an historical overview of the field that is difficult to ascertain through any other approach.

The categories of clinical, research, and general as used by Wigram et al. (2002) were also used in an earlier examination of the content of four music therapy journals (Wheeler, 1988). Apart from *JMT,* which was indicated to have published mostly research papers, it was reported that the other journals demonstrated a balance between the three areas.

Previously, a study was published reviewing the content of articles appearing in *JMT* from 1964–1984 (Gfeller, 1987). This study responded specifically to a number of assertions made by Feder and Feder (1981) about music therapy. One of these statements was that music therapists mainly attributed the influences of music to physiological changes, however Gfeller's analysis found that *JMT* papers where physiological change was the measure of effect comprised only 9% of the total articles published over the 20-year period. This shows that while there may be some generally held beliefs about a profession, a close examination of the journal literature can provide evidence to support or refute assertions or generalizations.

An analysis of the content of nine refereed journals[1] was published in *JMT* (Brooks, 2003). This bibliographic study examined the English language journals in music therapy, creative arts therapy, and music imagery.[2] Brooks reviewed 1,521 articles from the journals and presented the outcomes in terms of historical trends and contributions to the field of music therapy. She assigned articles to six predetermined categories of type of publication as follows: (a) quantitative research, (b) qualitative research, (c) clinical reports, (d) philosophical and theoretical research, (e) historical research, and (f) professional articles. She found quantitative and clinical articles to be the predominant categories in terms of number of papers, together comprising over 1,000 of the papers in the review. Historical papers were the least in number with 55, 16 of which appeared in *Music Therapy Perspectives (MTP)* and 32 in *JMT*, and between 100 and 200 papers were published in each of the remaining categories of qualitative, philosophical, and professional.

The percentage contribution of each journal to the total number of articles within the categories was also reported. In the quantitative research category, 78.6% of the 542 articles were published in *JMT*, with the next highest percentage to the total number being *MTP*'s contribution of 10.7%. Apart from the U.S. journals of the AMTA, the remaining journals contributed around 10% of the total number of quantitative research articles published in the review period (Brooks, 2003). This dominance of *JMT* followed by *MTP* was explained by the greater number of years that the U.S. journals were published in comparison to the non-U.S. sources, which resulted in a greater proportion of the papers included in the review. Also, most of the journals that were included publish one or two issues per year whereas *JMT* has produced four yearly issues since its inception some 40 years ago, and so it has produced the largest number of music therapy papers of all the journals surveyed by Brooks.

Brooks (2003) concluded that the majority of the articles in most journals fell under one category type, with the exception of the *Nordic Journal of Music Therapy (NJMT)*, which was noted as having "the most even distribution of article types" across the six categories (Brooks, p. 163). For example, in the qualitative research category, *JMT* was recorded as contributing six articles of this type to the field since 1964, the fewest of all journals surveyed. By comparison, 31 qualitative research studies were reported to have appeared in *NJMT*, a journal in existence for less than a decade at the time the review was completed. Perhaps it is possible to suggest from this that authors may be more likely to submit qualitative studies to journals with a record of publishing this type of research.

Brooks (2003) also observed a number of patterns in the types of articles that appeared. Over the 4 decades, historical articles had a "steady, but low publication rate" (p. 158), whereas the number of quantitative research papers increased gradually every year until a much stronger increase was observed in the mid-1970s. The number of quantitative articles published each year since then has been between 15 and 20 papers. The increase observed in the number of articles in the clinical category that occurred around the mid-1980s was attributed to the introduction of *MTP* at that time. A similar observation is made for the philosophical and theoretical category where the increased number of papers in the 1990s was directly attributed to the introduction of *NJMT*. This supports the point made earlier that the introduction of a journal with a particular orientation can influence as well as reflect the profession in different ways.

James' (1985) review included comment on gender balance in the authorship of the journal literature in music therapy.[3] James reported that, since almost 10% more of the papers appearing in *JMT* in the 20-year period 1964–1983 were written by women than men, the music therapy literature reflected a gender balance. However, since the field of music therapy is so predominantly female, one would expect the literature to mirror the actual ratio of male music therapists proportionate to female.[4]

In further consideration of authorship issues, *JMT* (1964–2002) was examined to identify contributors who had published frequently in order to ascertain any characteristics of this cohort. Fourteen authors, eight women and six men, published six or more articles in the period 1964–2002. All of these authors had attained PhDs, and affiliations to 11 U.S. universities were noted

---

[1] *BJMT* is not clearly indicated as a refereed journal in Brooks' paper however it should be noted that the *BJMT* follows all procedures to meet criteria as a refereed journal publication.

[2] While Brooks' is the most comprehensive analysis of the journal literature in this field published to date, the *Canadian Journal of Music Therapy (CAM)* was not included.

[3] Only the names of first authors were included in the review.

[4] Thanks to Susan Hadley for informing this comment.

across the group. This indicates that those who publish the most papers over time are typically highly qualified university faculty, possibly because their employers funded, supported, and rewarded these efforts.

As a comparison, *BJMT* (1987–2003) was surveyed for characteristics of authors who contributed frequently. It was found there were six authors, four male and two female, who published three or more full articles during this period. All of these authors held academic appointments, three in universities outside of the United Kingdom, and five had attained a PhD or had a PhD near completion. This further supports the view that those who publish the most research papers over time are likely to have high-level research training and to be employed by institutions that enable and reward the publication of research.

Hands Across the Water

It is compelling to believe that historically there has been a community of international researchers working toward shared, congruent goals in this field, and certainly reviews of the refereed literature such as the ones above indicate that music therapy journals in various parts of the world share similar interests and concerns. A review of the frequency of citations of papers from music therapy journals over a number of years in the longest running journal in music therapy *(JMT)* and the oldest journal published in English in Europe *(BJMT)*, however, suggests that numbers of citations of papers published in journals from other countries, what can be called *cross citations,* perhaps do not yet achieve what might be expected within the music therapy research community internationally.

A review of reference lists in full articles published in *JMT* was undertaken using the searchable CD-ROM database for *JMT,* 1964–2003 (AMTA, 2004), and instances of citations of papers from music therapy journals published in English are presented in Table 2. Self-citations were not counted.[5] No papers from *NZ* or *CAM* were cited in *JMT* during the publication period reviewed here. It is notable that *BJMT* citations appeared in eight papers, five of which were authored by music therapists from countries outside the United States.

Table 2
References Appearing in Full Arti cles in *Journal of Music Therapy,* 1964–2003

	1994	1996	1998*	1999	2000	2001	2002	2003	Total
BJMT	2			3	6	4		3	18
AJMT		1		1	1	1			4
NJMT			1		1				2

* A bibliography that was published as part of the guest editorial for the 1998 issue included citation of 12 papers from *NJMT* and 7 papers from *BJMT.*

The 18 issues of the *BJMT* for the years 1995–2003 are indicated in Table 3. Reference lists of 53 full articles were scrutinized, and citations were noted of any papers from eight music therapy journals, *JMT, CAM, MT, MTP, BJMT, AJMT, NJMT,* and *NZ.* There were no references to *CAM* or *NZ.* Table 3 presents the incidence of citations from the journals listed.

Although 35 *JMT* citations appeared in the *BJMT* issues reviewed, resulting in an average of 0.66 for each paper published, in fact a total of 23 of these citations appeared in just three papers. When these three papers were removed, the average citation for a paper from *JMT* drops to 0.24 per full paper. The only *AJMT* citations appeared in a single 1999 article, written by an Australian. The two *NJMT* citations that appeared before 2001 were in a paper written by the editor of the *NJMT.* Since the time it ceased publication, the frequency of citations of *MT* was noted to steadily increase. In the first 6 years of the review undertaken, *MT* was cited three times and in the final 3 years it was cited a total of eight times, rivaled only by *JMT* for frequency of citations in the later period. This is perhaps due to the wider availability of the papers from this journal on the CD-ROM produced by AMTA (1999, 2004).

---

[5] Since authors are expected to be aware of the papers that they have written in other journals, self-citations are not indicators of the knowledge of other work internationally.

Table 3

References Appearing in Full Articles in *British Journal of Music Therapy,* 1995–2003

	1995	1996	1997	1998	1999*	2000	2001	2002	2003	Total
JMT	1		2		5	1	6†	5	15‡	35
MTP			1		5	2	3		2	13
MT	1			1	1		1	2	5	11
AJMT					4					4
NJMT				2§			4	2		8

* All citations from these journals appeared in a single paper.

† Five of these citations to *JMT* appeared in a single paper.

‡ Thirteen of these 15 citations to *JMT* appeared in a single paper.

§ Both of these citations are in a paper written by the editor of *NJMT.*

While some interest in the work of other scholars is evident here, this relatively low citation rate may suggest that many of those publishing in *BJMT* and *JMT* have not found that the research available in some of the other music therapy journals is relevant to their subject of inquiry. Or it might indicate that only a few of these authors have read the other journals in their field.

It must, of course, be noted that music therapy research articles have appeared in a wider range of peer-reviewed sources than in only the music therapy journals, including regular citations of papers from *The Arts in Psychotherapy.* For example, nine papers from this journal were cited in the 2000 volume of *JMT.*

Since one of the ways that newer researchers learn about the scope of related inquiry is by following up the reference lists of papers published by experts in their field, it is somewhat worrying to have found that the incidence of citations from journals published in English from other countries was somewhat limited in the *JMT* and *BJMT.* It might be assumed that this occurs because there are few similarities between the music therapy research and clinical approaches in these countries. However, a brief scrutiny of reference lists in 12 full papers that appeared in two issues of *AJMT* (2003, 2004) revealed that *JMT* was cited 30 times, *MTP* was cited 24 times, and *BJMT* was cited 5 times.[6] Although this is not a comprehensive comparison, it does suggest that there are topics of common interest between the journals of these English speaking countries, the United States, the United Kingdom, and Australia—countries that have had a history of providing music therapy service in a range of clinical, residential, and community settings for at least the past 4 decades.

It is possible therefore, that some claims of novelty in relation to the introduction of clinical or research ideas in the music therapy journal literature might need to be tempered, since there may have been previously undiscovered references to these ideas. As it might be argued that this has occurred because of the different orientations to the practice of music therapy in these various countries, it could be the case that some music therapy researchers are yet to develop the scholarly maturity to be able to include published research findings or methods where they do not agree with the premises of the paper and perhaps lack the confidence or skills to subject these to critical scrutiny in their writing. While it is not possible to draw definitive conclusions as to the origins of this phenomenon from the observations above, there could be better communication of the efforts of researchers across the world.

Comments about differences between approaches to research in the United States and Europe have appeared in the music therapy literature and are reported here briefly as a way to consider whether there are preexisting beliefs about the work of other countries that may lead some authors to dismiss the relevance of these sources. It has been claimed, for example, that in part because of the education structure within music therapy in the United States, "music therapy research. . . has often been polarized into two opposing camps: qualitative research versus quantitative research. The grounds for this polarization appear to be historically based in the establishment of a political professional identity within the field of practice" (Aldridge, 1996, p. 278). While some examples of this distinction are certainly evident in the music therapy

---

6 *AJMT* is the longest published music therapy journal in English in the Southern Hemisphere.

refereed literature and even in the structure of this book, it must be noted that the first music therapy research conference in the United Kingdom at City University in 1983 focused on the debate between choice of qualitative or quantitative methods for music therapy research (Darnley-Smith & Patey, 2003), suggesting that the debate over the use of one approach to method or the other has been engaged more broadly than just in U.S. teaching and literature. In a similar statement about the choices of methods, it has been claimed that, for music therapy research in the United States, "behaviorism and quantitative research predominated. . . for years," while in Europe, by contrast, qualitative research methods that had been in use for decades were "usurped by quantitative research" (Smeijsters, 1997, p. 3). Yet, it is the relatively recent *NJMT* that has been leading the way in publishing qualitative research studies in music therapy according to the findings of Brooks' (2003) review. The parochial tendencies observed in some of the journal literature surveyed above are possibly fuelled by ideas about the ways research is approached in different countries, and there may be some value in subjecting these ideas to more rigorous critique.

It is difficult to ascertain why journal editors and their reviewers have not taken more care to ensure that authors' reference lists reflect the contribution of authors in other music therapy journal sources. There have been a number of excellent initiatives over the past decade aimed at developing better access to journal sources, and these are outlined below. This suggests there is a wish, if not yet an established practice, that music therapy authors read and cite a wider range of music therapy journals.

Commencing in 1992, *MTP* embarked on an exercise to collate and regularly report all articles in music therapy published since 1985 in sources other than *MTP, JMT,* and *MT* in an annual reference review column. While the only articles included are those that appear on searchable electronic databases, music therapy studies published in languages other than English are included, as are dissertations. Similarly, *BJMT* has introduced a "text-watch" column since 2000 to document references to music therapy papers published in other sources.

The American Music Therapy Association produced a CD-Rom in 1999, updated in 2004, that includes, in full text, all articles from *JMT, MTP,* and *MT* through to 2003 (AMTA, 1999, 2004). In addition, the Witten-Herdecke searchable database of titles and abstracts from a number of the English language music therapy journals is an extraordinary contribution to music therapy scholarship. It will also be possible to search the proposed *Latin American Journal of Music Therapy* (Gilbertson & Aldridge, 2003), while the German journal *Musiktherapeutische Umschau* is currently indexed, and full-text articles from *AJMT* are available at www.musictherapyworld.net (Gilbertson & Aldridge, 2003).[7] This effort builds on some of the earlier work of the *European Research Register* (Smeijsters & Rogers, 1993; Smeijsters, Rogers, Kortegaard, Lehtonen, & Scanlon, 1995). In addition, some of the papers published in *NJMT* are available on the internet at www.njmt.no, and an online discussion forum encourages scholarly critical reflection on current published work. Each of these efforts is a tremendous boon to the communication of specialist research interests across the world. However, these efforts perhaps contribute further to the puzzle as to why the number of cross citations has not increased exponentially in response to this availability of information, since researchers and other authors of papers for music therapy journals have been able to access the work of colleagues across various bodies of water for at least the past decade.

The information garnered from the comparison and review studies above is important because it provides consideration of ways that knowledge in the field is developed and assists reflective consideration as to future research directions. For example, if a doctoral student wishes to undertake a research study for which qualitative method research would be most appropriate, it might be difficult for him or her to persuade a supervisor or panel that such research is justified if the proportion of published studies that have employed this method is used as a guide to the relevance of qualitative method within the field, or if the supervisor or panel only reads one journal not noted for inclusion of qualitative studies. Researchers might also heed that this historical survey shows that some sources may be more likely to result in citations of their publication efforts than others. In addition, the somewhat limited citation of music therapy journals outside one's own country demonstrated above presses the question as to whether editors and reviewers are actually aware of the contribution of researchers in other countries.

---

[7] A recent study found the database at www.musictherapyworld.net to be the most comprehensive search engine for articles from *JMT* (Gilbertson & Aldridge, 2003).

Resources

Essential resources are required to develop research and to create and foster a community of qualified researchers. In most countries it is considered the responsibility of universities and university programs to develop what might be termed *research capacity* in a particular discipline. The primary purpose of music therapy within institutions of higher education, however, is to provide for the professional training of enrolled candidates, and the work of developing clinical training and teaching core skills is often undertaken by academic faculty for whom research and publishing are not primary responsibilities. Thus, the ideal of developing a community of music therapy researchers simply through involvement in higher education institutions may be unrealistic. Efforts are also required from the wider community of practitioners to develop the research capacity in a particular location or country. This includes the important contribution of the relevant professional associations, especially where the development of the journal publications and other means for dissemination of research in music therapy is concerned.

A substantial body of published work, some of which is funded through the universities, has been produced by academics. Research may also develop through opportunities provided at a national level by government decisions and policies pertaining to research priorities and can be affected by changes in government priorities for funding.

As an example of this relationship between funding support and research outcomes, until the late 1990s music therapy training in the Netherlands was not established within the scientific universities. Apart from single research projects in music therapy, it was reported that there were no opportunities to conduct research in a highly scholarly research environment (Smeijsters & Vink, 2003). Now, however, research centers have been established at each of the five Universities for Professional Education (UPEs), and four of these centers include research projects for creative art therapies (Smeijsters & Vink). It is also notable that in *Music Therapy: International Perspectives* (Maranto, 1993), some countries reported that they were working on establishing basic library facilities and access. For those of us who have studied music therapy and then worked professionally with books and journals at our fingertips, it is difficult to imagine such a starting point, and it is almost certain then that research capacity is a long way from being established when even introductory literature resources are not available.

Also worthy of note are a number of research posts that have been established within various centers. The Nordoff-Robbins centers in both London and New York support research posts, and a number of individuals in various clinical institutions around the world have from time to time been engaged in research-only appointments. For example, the Royal Hospital for Neuro-Disability in London hosts a music therapy post with a primary focus on research activity, as does the Mental Health Trust Arts Therapies in Cambridge, although this post is not full time. Such research capacity may be able to be extended further and more comprehensively through research appointments outside of institutions of higher education.

Research Training

Music therapy research has changed its focus and shape over the past 40 years. While the journal literature both contributes to and reflects this, the increase in the number of music therapy journals may, to some degree, be attributed to the fact that more qualified practitioners have been trained in research competencies through the increasing number of masters, doctorates, and other research degree programs offered internationally. This increase in locally produced research studies has led to the expectation in an increasing number of countries that a peer-reviewed journal is a necessary adjunct to the professional discipline. The increase in music therapy journals can also be seen to directly reflect the introduction of or increase in number of training programs. Increasingly, opportunities have also developed in universities and training institutions to host and develop research capacity and degrees in the profession.

The section that follows seeks to highlight some of the research degree programs that are available internationally. A distinction is made here between degrees that are given for music therapy research qualifications and those that do not include music therapy qualifications, that is whether the term *music therapy* is used in the award of the degree or not. A distinction is also made between degrees that are primarily coursework degrees with a dissertation examined by experts within the university and those that are attained via an externally examined thesis/dissertation. There is no hierarchical perspective intended, but it is important to note the various ways of achieving research qualifications in music therapy in order to provide relevant and correct historical information for this chapter.

The route to attain research qualifications varies from country to country. In the United States, a coursework component is mandatory, followed by a dissertation. Doctoral awards apart from PhDs, such as a Doctorate of Arts (DA), are also given in the United States. In other English-speaking countries such as the United Kingdom, Ireland, and Australia, no doctoral studies in music therapy are currently available via coursework. PhDs are attained, in the main, via the submission of a substantial research thesis that is subjected to examination by international experts and then, in many cases but not always, defended before an external panel of these experts; this procedure is directly comparable with the broader European model for PhD programs.[8]

In the United States, Temple University awards a PhD in music therapy. New York University has offered a DA in music therapy for many years, with the research component of the degree focusing on qualitative music therapy research. At other universities, including Florida State University, the University of Kansas, and Michigan State University,[9] PhDs are awarded where candidates take music therapy specialist units of study and prepare doctoral theses on music therapy topics; however, the title of these awards is often music education rather than music therapy. Many music therapy educators in the United States are drawn from the graduates of these programs.[10]

In Europe, the only specialist PhD degree available in music therapy is offered at Aalborg University in Denmark. The development of the Aalborg PhD program commenced in the mid-1990s (Wigram et al., 2002). In the early years of the program, a close relationship was established with a clinically focused research group called the Nordic Research Network Group. This group obtained funding to host a series of twice-yearly research meetings focusing on the use of single-case study designs. Experts in music therapy and related research areas were invited to present papers at each meeting over a number of years (Wigram et al.). In 1997, an additional research grant offered funded places to doctoral students in the PhD program at Aalborg, substantially increasing the number of students participating in the program. This example offers further evidence as to how funding can lead to changes in music therapy research. In Norway, the University of Oslo and the Norwegian Academy of Music also support PhD research in music therapy and have begun awarding PhDs.

The first university in the United Kingdom to support doctoral level research in music therapy was City University, London, where the first PhD in a music therapy topic was awarded in the mid-1980s (Bunt, 1985). The establishment of a Research Fellowship to support postgraduate study funded by The Music Therapy Charity in 1980 made this specialized study possible. Music therapy PhDs have been awarded through the program at City University and through a number of other universities in the United Kingdom.

In Germany, two main centers have emerged for doctoral level study in music therapy: the University of Music and Theatre in Hamburg, which awards a Dr. rer. med., and the University of Witten-Herdecke, which offers a doctoral qualification either as a Dr. med., for medical practitioners, or Dr. rer. med. for graduates of other professions. The Witten-Herdecke program is offered through the medical faculty of the university.

A number of music therapists in Australia have attained PhDs. The University of Melbourne has been the main source of expertise to support music therapy research at the PhD level in that country. As is the case in many other countries, music therapists also have opportunities to study at the PhD level in a music therapy topic within a non-music department such as medicine, education, or allied health. In an exciting recent development, Massey University in New Zealand has enrolled PhD candidates in music therapy.

---

[8] It should be noted that masters programs often involve studying and conducting research. This is the case with many masters programs in the U.S. As another example, the masters program at the University of Melbourne in Australia, from which a number of students have graduated, is by research thesis alone.

[9] The American Music Therapy Association does not approve doctoral programs in music therapy, so there is no official list of universities offering PhD or other work. The universities listed here are not the only ones that grant PhDs to qualified music therapists.

[10] It would probably be accurate to say that most music therapy educators in the U.S. are drawn from these programs, but no data are available to substantiate this statement.

The opportunity for more students around the world to study at the PhD level with music therapy specialization rather than having to take PhD studies in a closely related field has allowed for the development of research communities in some countries. This has enhanced the prospect of increasing a sense of community and closeness between these researchers, as reflected in joint publications, co-presentations at conferences, and the publishing in a range of literature sources on similar topics by such groups.

A Wider View

Music therapy investigators have learned much about what we do by critically examining and reviewing research approaches of the past and by being open to changes in ways of researching. The ability of those within the profession to tolerate and respect different ways of knowing is a strength. This is exemplified in a number of statements that appear in the literature, such as that by Ruud (1998), who wrote, "Our profession will be forever populated with people and paradigms with competing claims of knowledge. The only answer is to learn from each other and communicate what we learn" (p. 114).

An historical perspective reveals that many of the more recent discussions and debates about research approaches in music therapy have focused on distinctions between research methods, in particular between qualitative and quantitative approaches or methods (Amir, 1993; Bruscia, 1998; O'Callaghan, 1996; Wheeler, 1995). The underlying theoretical and epistemological basis of these research methods has arguably received less attention. It is also the case that, apart from studies of professional aspects such as employment prospects and work satisfaction, most clinical studies focus on the needs and experiences of the client and do not involve neither scrutiny of the moment-by-moment work of the music therapist nor inclusion of the therapist's experiences and perspective about what it is that she or he does.

This may reflect arguments that have been made in music therapy about the theoretical informants for practice. For example, as Gfeller (1987) suggested,

> Because the music therapy profession is primarily concerned with successful treatment outcomes, theoretical considerations or a mental plan of principles may seem of secondary importance to the practicing music therapist. The value of theory, however, should not be underestimated. A coherent theoretical foundation provides a plan of action and a guideline for selection of approach. Without such a foundation, each therapeutic decision exists in isolation, with no connection to preceding or subsequent events. (p. 192)

A broader discussion of research approaches, to include what can be termed ontological and epistemological concerns, is present in some of the music therapy literature (e.g., Aigen, 1995, 1998; Edwards, 1999; Ruud, 1998). This area needs continued attention in order that distinctions between research approaches can be made in a way that relies less on overarching methodological considerations such as "quantitative" or "qualitative" (although these distinctions serve us well at present) and increasingly more on the inclusion of considerations of underpinning beliefs and their influence, or even bias, as to choice of method.

As the foundational epistemologies for music therapy methods receive greater attention and debate through such books as this one, and indeed in papers appearing in the wider refereed journal literature, it can only help in opening up possibilities in research as well as consolidating and refining the existing positions. It might even happen that "different epistemological frames can be run together in such a way that they create fresh understanding, rather in the manner that a good metaphor originates a meaning from several frames of reference" (Henzell, 1995, p. 185).

Kenny (1996) offered a useful historical insight into developments in music therapists' approaches to research when she described different categories of research traditions. She wrote, "Research in music therapy can be conducted in any of these categories [of research traditions]. And, in fact, the more categories the better to shine light on the research story" (p. 59). This music therapy story is evolving and maturing. This does not mean it has a definable, observable linear or logical flow that is easily traced directly to a primary unitary source but rather evidences an evolutionary process, one that involves change as its primary point of reference, rather than attention only to improvements or advancements.

In reference to Kenny's metaphor of story in the quote, a story must have a storyteller(s) but also listeners. With more refined listening to the wide scope of possibilities, the relevance and importance of fit between research ideas and research practice, as well as the continual grounding of these ideas in the reality of professional clinical practice, will undoubtedly contribute to the further maturing of our flourishing scholarship.

It has been suggested that:

> The practice of music therapy is marked by divergence between practitioners as to the way music therapy will be implemented to serve patient's needs, as well as by the perspective of the individual practitioner to the reasons why the responses of the patient occur. (Gfeller, 1995, p. 57)

The underlying theoretical approach of the researcher therefore inevitably influences the type of research undertaken (Gfeller, 1995). In support of this view, Peile (1988) cautioned that the choice of research methods in his field of social work research should not be made merely on the basis of epistemological arguments, but "should also be based on the compatibility of the research method with the researcher's own preferred paradigmatic assumptions or worldview, and these should be made explicit so that they can be challenged" (p. 8).

Historically, choices of research methods in music therapy have been proposed to have their origins in the fact that, "Therapists with an extensive musical background often felt more comfortable with research material rooted in artistic, social, aesthetic, cultural, musical or therapeutic perspectives" (Bunt, 2002, p. 276). That is, rather than music therapists being drawn to the methods of psychological research adapted from traditions in the physical or social sciences, it is suggested that the musicological and perhaps arts-based approaches to inquiry were considered more consistent with the sensibilities of many of the music therapy practitioners who have commenced research.

Kenny (1998) has, however, asserted that, in regard to choices of approaches to research at the foundation of music therapy in the mid-20th century, "The mainstream more or less accepted positivism, behaviorism, and the scientific method, which insisted on observable data as the grand narrative of the time in social behavioral research culture" (p. 203). In that case, as she recalled, music therapy research "joined the mainstream. We would hitch our star to the received view. We would prove our viability as a field by presenting studies in the scientific method" (p. 204). Music therapy, in her representation of its research history, became influenced by and adhered to the epistemology of the physical sciences.

Aigen (1998) has stated that those in the music therapy research community concerned with the further development of qualitative research have adopted a "liberal epistemology manifest in a recognition of multiple levels of knowing" (p. 152). This references ideas from what has been described as a constructivist paradigm or constructivist science. Lincoln (1990) has suggested that this view holds that "reality is a social, and, therefore, multiple, construction. . . the aim of constructivist science is to create idiographic knowledge, usually expressed in the form of pattern theories. . . expressed as working hypotheses, or temporary, time- and place-bound knowledge" (p. 77). This style or approach to research can be seen in some of the new methods of research emerging in music therapy publications.

Perhaps more controversially, Smeijsters (1997) concluded that, "If we think it is important to research effects as well as processes, then quantitative research is the right method for the former, and qualitative research, the latter" (p. 44). As Smeijsters himself points out, however, there has not been universal acceptance of this view from some researchers who use qualitative methods, since their research ontology does not necessarily support the gathering or incorporation of quantitative data into their research. Other music therapy researchers have noted the possibilities of mixed method research (e.g., Amir, 1993; Ridder, 2004). However, researchers are cautioned that the use of descriptive data is not necessarily evidence of the use of a qualitative method nor demonstrative of an ontological position outside that of the positivist paradigm.

Whatever the stance one takes in relation to the development and application of research methods and their service to the field of music therapy, historically it can be demonstrated that music therapists worldwide have been able to embrace a range of methods, sometimes eclectically, using these different methods to undertake a process of investigation or discovery, but more often demonstrating a pluralistic approach; that is, it is more clearly the case that individual researchers employ discrete methods that have been developed and refined as appropriate to the specific context of research. The breadth of research methods applied is a testament to the flexibility and openness in music therapy research with a range of benefits that, to date, have served the profession well.

Conclusion

While this overview has been able to highlight some of the characteristics and achievements of research in music therapy, one has the impression of an orchestra warming up rather than a full symphonic work underway. Music therapy's research history is perhaps poised at the start of a more cohesive, united era where previous distinctions and divisions between approaches are ready to give way to a more mature developed integration of knowledge and capacity. As research helps us to engage with the complexity of this thing we do called music therapy, we have the opportunity to refine our knowledge of the processes and outcomes and also to hold on to the uncertainty and complexity of what it is we do, as investigations into this work continue around the world.

Within this view to the future, perhaps we should be mindful of attempts to reject or deny any of the limiting aspects of our past history of research. Kenny (1982) has suggested that this tendency within music therapy to reject the past in order to idealize present developments is a cultural one:

> Within our culture we tend to think of development in hierarchical terms. When we have achieved a new stage, we discard the previous stages, or at least consider the latest acquisition of greatest value. . . . We often forget that our beginnings are an integrated and vital part of our now's. (p. 68)

Music therapy research has a rich and varied history with a number of trends and opportunities offering new flavors and colors to a vibrant mix of kaleidoscopic activity. At different times, certain ideas about ways we can research our work have had a dominant hold, and this may have isolated some research endeavors and approaches. As music therapy continues to consolidate its progress, it is hoped that the strengths of this history will prove a solid foundation contributing to emerging ideas that can excite and stimulate us to further develop and enhance our knowledge through research inquiry.

References

Aigen, K. (1995). Philosophical inquiry. In B. L. Wheeler (Ed.), *Music therapy research: Quantitative and qualitative perspectives* (pp. 447–484). Gilsum, NH: Barcelona Publishers.

Aigen, K. (1998). Creativity in qualitative research. *Journal of Music Therapy, 34,* 150–175.

Aldridge, D. (1996). *Music therapy research and practice in medicine: From out of the silence.* London: Jessica Kingsley Publishers.

American Music Therapy Association. (1999). *Music therapy research: Quantitative and qualitative foundations, CD-Rom I, 1964–1998.* Silver Spring, MD: Author.

American Music Therapy Association. (2004). *Music Therapy Research CD-ROM* (2nd ed.). Silver Spring, MD: Author.

Amir, D. (1993). Research in music therapy: Quantitative or qualitative? *Nordic Journal of Music Therapy, 2,* 3–10.

Brooks, D. (2003). A history of music therapy journal articles published in the English language. *Journal of Music Therapy, 40,* 151–168.

Bruscia, K. (1998). Standards of integrity for qualitative music therapy research. *Journal of Music Therapy, 35,* 150–175.

Bunt, L. (1985). *Music therapy and the child with a handicap: Evaluation of the effects of intervention.* Unpublished doctoral dissertation, City University, London.

Bunt, L. (2002). Some reflections on music therapy research: An example of collaborative enquiry. In L. Bunt & S. Hoskyns (Eds.), *Handbook of music therapy* (pp. 270–289). London: Routledge.

Codding, P. (1987). A content analysis of the *Journal of Music Therapy*, 1977–1985. *Journal of Music Therapy, 29,* 87–102.

Darnley-Smith, R., & Patey, H. (2003). *Music therapy.* London: Sage Publications.

DeCuir, A. (1987). Readings for music therapy students: An analysis of clinical and research literature from the *Journal of Music Therapy*. In C. D. Maranto & K. E. Bruscia (Eds.), *Perspectives on music therapy education and training* (pp. 57–70). Philadelphia: Temple University.

Edwards, J. (1999). Considering the paradigmatic frame: Social science research approaches relevant to research in music therapy. *The Arts in Psychotherapy, 26,* 73–80.

Feder, E., & Feder, B. (1981). *The expressive arts therapies.* Englewood Cliffs, NJ: Prentice-Hall.

Gfeller, K. (1987). Music therapy theory and practice as reflected in research literature. *Journal of Music Therapy, 24,* 178–194.

Gfeller, K. (1995). The status of music therapy research. In B. L. Wheeler (Ed.), *Music therapy research: Quantitative and qualitative perspectives* (pp. 29–63). Gilsum, NH: Barcelona Publishers.

Gilbertson, S., & Aldridge, D. (2003). Searching *PubMed/MEDLINE, Ingenta,* and the *Music Therapy World Journal Index* for articles published in the *Journal of Music Therapy. Journal of Music Therapy, 40,* 324–344.

Gregory, D. (2002). Four decades of music therapy behavioral research designs: A content analysis of *Journal of Music Therapy* articles. *Journal of Music Therapy, 39,* 56–71.

Henzell, J. (1995). Research and the particular: Epistemology in art and psychotherapy. In A. Gilroy & C. Lee (Eds.), *Art and music: Therapy and research* (pp. 185–205). London: Routledge.

James, M. R. (1985). Sources of articles published in the *Journal of Music Therapy:* The first twenty years, 1964–1983. *Journal of Music Therapy, 22,* 87–94.

Jellison, J. A. (1973). The frequency and general mode of inquiry of research in music therapy. *Council for Research in Music Education, 35,* 1–8.

Kenny, C. (1982). *The mythic artery: The magic of music therapy.* Atascadero, CA: Ridgeview Publishing Co.

Kenny, C. (1996). The story of the Field of Play. In M. Langenberg, K. Aigen, & J. Frommer (Eds.), *Qualitative music therapy research: Beginning dialogues* (pp. 55–80). Gilsum, NH: Barcelona Publishers.

Kenny, C. B. (1998). Embracing complexity: The creation of a comprehensive research culture in music therapy. *Journal of Music Therapy, 35,* 201–217.

Lincoln, Y. S. (1990). The making of a constructivist: A remembrance of transformations past. In E. Guba (Ed.), *The paradigm dialog* (pp. 67–87). London: Sage Publications.

Maranto, C. (Ed.). (1993). *Music therapy: International perspectives.* Cherry Hill, NJ: Jeffrey Books.

O'Callaghan, C. (1996). The relative merits of quantitative and qualitative research approaches in music therapy. *Australian Journal of Music Therapy, 7,* 28–36.

Peile, C. (1988). Research paradigms in social work: From stalemate to creative synthesis. *Social Service Review, 62,* 1–19.

Ridder, H. M. O. (2004). When dialogue fails. Music therapy with elderly with neurological degenerative diseases. *Music Therapy Today, 5*(4). Available at www. musictherapyworld.net

Ruud, E. (1998). *Music therapy: Improvisation, communication, and culture.* Gilsum, NH: Barcelona Publishers.

Smeijsters, H. (1997). *Multiple perspectives: A guide to qualitative research in music therapy.* Gilsum, NH: Barcelona Publishers.

Smeijsters, H., & Rogers, P. (Eds.). (1993). *European music therapy research register.* Utrecht, Netherlands: Werkgroep Onderzoek Musiktherapie/NVKT.

Smeijsters, H., Rogers, P., Kortegaard, H.-M., Lehtonen, K., & Scanlon, P. (Eds.). (1995). *European music therapy research register,* Vol. II. Castricum: Stichting Musiktherapie.

Smeijsters, H., & Vink, A. (2003). Music therapy in the Netherlands. *Voices: A World Forum for Music Therapy.* Available at http://www.voices.no/country/monthnetherlands_september2003.html

Solomon, A. (1993). A history of the *Journal of Music Therapy:* The first decade (1964–1973). *Journal of Music Therapy, 30,* 3–33.

Webster, J. (1993). Review of the *Journal of British Music Therapy:* 1987–1991. *Journal of British Music Therapy, 7,* 6–11.

Wheeler, B. L. (1988). An analysis of literature from selected music therapy journals. *Music Therapy Perspectives, 5,* 94–101.

Wheeler, B. L. (Ed.). (1995). *Music therapy research: Quantitative and qualitative perspectives*. Gilsum, NH: Barcelona Publishers.

Wigram, T. (1993). Music therapy research to meet the demands of health and education services: Research and literature analysis. In M. Heal & T. Wigram (Eds.). *Music therapy in health and education* (pp. 137–153). London: Jessica Kingsley Publishers.

Wigram, T., Pedersen, I. N., & Bonde, L. O. (2002). *A comprehensive guide to music therapy: Theory, clinical practice, research and training*. London: Jessica Kingsley Publishers.

Chapter 3
Philosophy and Theory of Science
Even Ruud

Contemporary research in music therapy is based upon attitudes, principles, and approaches prevailing in the human, social, and natural sciences. The nature of such scientific practice is a result of a long historical development shared among scientific disciplines. This history reflects a changing landscape in relation to basic philosophical questions. Some of these questions have particular relevance concerning research, and this chapter will demonstrate how different philosophical traditions may influence our ways of producing new knowledge or deciding what is true or false. From what is called *philosophy of science,* a number of topics are chosen and will be discussed under the heading of epistemological issues. Examples of such issues include what constitutes the legitimate object of study; what is the relation between knower and known, that is, the problem of objectivity; how to approach the nature of causality; and what is meant by truth in research.

Questions and Issues

Some of these questions or issues are *epistemological,* that is, they relate to questions of what is possible to know (Aigen, 1995, p. 465) and may concern how we gain access to reality, or what is the relation between reality and its representation in language and thought. Such issues may then lead into *ontological* questions, that is, questions about the nature of knowledge or reality itself, or what defines the essence or nature of a phenomenon. For instance, to ask questions like What is music? What is music therapy? is to deal with ontological questions. *Axiological* questions, that is to say questions concerning values and priorities, may also be involved in the theory of science.

The word *paradigm* appears in this chapter. Within the philosophy of science, this word has a certain meaning as used by the philosopher Thomas Kuhn (1962) in his book *The Structure of Scientific Revolutions.* According to Kuhn's theory, which is based upon the practice of natural science, one might find in the history of a science a pre-revolutionary phase and a post-revolutionary phase. The pre-revolutionary phase is characterized by contrasting models of understanding competing with each other. At a certain point in the development, this phase will be broken by a scientific revolution where one of the competing paradigms is established at the cost of all the others. This paradigm will become a model for science, and after this revolution we will meet a *real* scientific discipline going into the post-revolutionary phase. In this phase we will meet scientific activity in its *normal form,* that is, the articulation and specification of one model of understanding.

This development and situation will probably not happen in the sciences that have the individual as the object of study. It has been argued (see Ruud, 1980) that the prevailing variety of approaches reflects the individual's potential way of regarding him- or herself. If one model of understanding ever comes to establish itself at the cost of all the others (e.g., if we all believed in and practiced psychoanalysis or any other single model), it could mean that the individual's potential views of him- or herself would be decreased. This means that we have to accept a situation where different criteria may be counted as true. The challenge for music therapy, however, is to establish indigenous theories based upon research and practice rising from the clinical experiences of the music therapist (Aigen, 1995).

Contemporary approaches to music therapy are informed by various philosophies of science, as is demonstrated in the different quantitative and qualitative approaches to research. Due to the interdisciplinary nature of music therapy, the field may be characterized as a medical, psychological, and humanistic discipline. The music therapist, as both health worker and musician, will have to accept the multidimensionality of the field as a natural, a social, and a human science. Below, we will outline some of the most important underlying philosophies as they make up the foundations of our scientific activity.

Philosophies

Positivism

Music therapists are familiar with an understanding of science that emphasizes knowledge based upon objectivity in procedures and measurements, controlled experiments, and studies that can be replicated. These are ideals grounded in a philosophy of science called *positivism*.

Historical Background. Dating back to the middle of the 19th century, the French philosopher August Compte reacted against what he held as the speculative systems of thought in the romantic period (Kjørup, 1996). Compte understood the development of humankind based on three stages, the theological, the metaphysical, and the final positive stage in which the metaphysical forces eventually are substituted for natural laws. The term *positive* meant, for Compte, the real, the useful, the evident, and the precise.

Contemporary positivism is rooted in early 20th century Vienna, where a number of philosophers developed what is known as *logical positivism*. Among these philosophers were Rudolf Carnap, Otto Neurath, and (the early) Ludwig Wittgenstein. During the 1930s, many of these philosophers fled to the United States where they continued to have a major influence upon the Western conception of natural and social sciences.

Epistemological Issues. Austrian philosopher Ludwig Wittgenstein made the point that a meaningful statement is either *elementary,* or it can be analyzed logically in such a way that one can detect that it is composed of more elementary statements. Within empirical sciences, such elementary statements necessarily have to be based upon an observation. More complex statements, however, have to be traced back to or *reduced* to something more fundamental and observable. This standpoint developed into what we know as the *empirical thesis of meaning,* or the *thesis of verification*, meaning that language expressions only have meaning when they directly or logically can be traced back to an experience.

Logical positivism, or *empirical positivism*, is sometimes characterized through its three empirical dogmas. First, these philosophers insisted upon a divide between simple and complex statements. In scientific practice, this is demonstrated through the difference between direct statements about our experience and generalized formulations about lawfulness. This thought appears in the *reductionist* idea about how complex, generalizing statements have to be traced back to statements about particular observations. This is an idea that again is related to *falsification* as a scientific criterion, discussed below.

Second, empirical positivism made a split between *analytic* and *synthetic* statements. Analytic statements were considered to be true or false based on an analysis of the statements themselves. Synthetic statements could only be evaluated by confrontation with the experience itself. This led to a conviction that observations should be purified from all kinds of prejudgments or presumptions. In other words, this dogma insists upon the divide between empirical facts and theory. Consequently, we find in positivism a split between facts and values, in short, the dogma that science should be value free.

Third, we may also say that the idea that explanation should always be causal explanation is typical for positivism. Equally important is the idea of a unity of science, where physics resides as the ultimate scientific ideal. This means, for instance, that in music therapy we should rest our findings upon psychology, which again should be based upon chemistry and physics. As music therapists may recognize, research in music therapy sometimes aims towards this reductionistic and genuine positivist thought about how music influences our body and brain, and that, accordingly, our behavior can ultimately be explained by the chemical activity in the brain.

In the positivist paradigm, the concept of truth considers data to be in correspondence with reality in what is called the correspondence theory of truth. Another concept of truth found in much research upon the effects of treatment is the pragmatic point of view, which is concerned with the practical consequences and the usefulness of what is being measured.

Critical Issues. In a critique of positivism and the empirical thesis of meaning, Karl Popper made the point that any statements about lawfulness (e.g., natural laws) that made claims about *all* phenomena in question could in fact only account for a limited number of instances (Alvesson & Skölberg, 2000). We may always, in principle, find some instances in which things will not behave according to the prediction of this law. Popper thus suggested a *criterion of falsification* in order to decide what is scientific. Consequently, a scientific problem had to be of such a nature that it should be possible to refute or falsify it. If we look at some of the more exotic theories about the influences of music upon human behavior, for instance that we are subject to some kind of celestial influences by the universal harmonies inherent in music, we have a good example of a statement that is not possible to falsify. In other words, this kind of question cannot be handled scientifically.

Relevance to Music Therapy. Within medical music therapy and the prevailing scientific attitude in general, music therapists have to research their work according to the doctrines of experimental research where controlled experiments rank highest in the hierarchy of *evidence based practice* (EBP; Wigram, Pedersen, & Bonde, 2002). From behavioral music therapy, we find the idea of the importance of systematically recording observable behavior, in other words, relying upon synthetic statements about reality in order to establish lawfulness and causal explanations of behavior.

Examples of research within the positivist tradition are to be found in the *Journal of Music Therapy* and in Part III of this book, Types of Quantitative Research.

Phenomenology

Phenomenology has inspired music therapists to study experiences as they emerge from musical meetings with the clients. Phenomenology shares with positivism its close attention to the empirical material. This is also the case with other qualitative methods like *grounded theory* and *ethnomethodology* that may rely upon a phenomenological approach. In this sense, phenomenology takes a position both as a methodology and a philosophy.

Historical Background. Phenomenology was formulated as a philosophy by the German philosopher Edmund Husserl in the first half of the 20th century. Phenomenology was critical of natural science for having distanced itself too far from the basis in everyday life. The German slogan *Zu den Sachen selbst* (to the things themselves) signaled a return to the concrete, sensuous everyday lifeworld (Alvesson & Skölberg 2000, p. 36). It was thought that positivism had drained all substance and color from the observed reality, leaving behind only abstract formal structures. One may easily understand why this approach appeals to musicologists and music therapists, who want to reclaim the immediate and sensuous in musical expressions and interactions with clients.

Epistemological Issues. In the phenomenological approach, the experience becomes the point of departure. This implies disregarding the question of whether or not the experience has an objective counterpart. One is interested in the phenomenal world, which means that the researcher sets aside all preconceived experiences, as far as humanly possible. In other words, the real world is cut out or *bracketed* off. This is called the *phenomenological reduction*, which means that we abstract from real existing objects, confining ourselves to the world of ideas. In other words, the experience involves all active processes that include and form the different ideas and content that become present to awareness. It is claimed that the *intentional objects* of interest cannot be reduced to either the sphere of the mental or the sphere of the physical. Following such a methodology, one is supposed to perform various descriptions of the *essence*, to differentiate the unessential and particular from the essential elements and their relationships. Within such a phenomenological reduction comes an *eidetic reduction*. In this process there is a kind of comparative analysis of the elements in our thought process trying to reach something common, an *invariance* to a whole group of phenomena. A final reduction is reached through a process of *transcendental reduction* in order to investigate how these invariances are constructed.

Critical Issues. There is a certain tension between phenomenology and more interpretative approaches that are based upon epistemologies that claim that we only can gain access to our experiences as they are mediated by our language and placed within a larger cultural and political context.

Approaches that adhere to the correspondence theory of truth may be criticized for sometimes making naive assumptions about the possibility of defining essences and seeing things as if it were possible to define the world without a language. The historical character of language, as it has been transformed and infused by ideologies and cultural values, may make any effort to define the essence of something no more than a good representation, a good story. This problem may be met by establishing a broader interpretative approach, as within some hermeneutic traditions.

Relevance to Music Therapy. The phenomenological approach has opened the possibilities for a close examination of feelings, memories, expressions, and imaginations as they evolve in the here-and-now. A phenomenological approach to the analysis of music will allow experiences to be in the foreground of study, rather than musical structures as they may be examined in the scores.

Examples of phenomenological research are to be found in dissertations by Forinash (1990), Arnason (1998), Skewes (2001), and Trondalen (2003), and in Chapter 26 of this book, Phenomenological Inquiry.

Hermeneutics

Music therapists are often met with problems of understanding and interpreting creative musical processes, personal narratives, or cultural contexts framing the therapeutic processes. In this sense, the discipline of music therapy is more similar to other humanistic or social sciences than to natural sciences.

Historical Background. During the late 19th and early 20th century, *hermeneutics* was developed through the work of a number of outstanding philosophers, social scientists, and historians such as Wilhelm Dilthey, Georg Simmel, and Max Weber (Alvesson & Skölberg, 2000). A clear line was drawn between natural and cultural sciences. The opposition to positivism was clearly stated, and positivism was seen as more of a fit for the natural sciences than for the human sciences. *Understanding* (Verstehen) became the key word for doing research on human artifacts and agency. At the same time, the problem of objectivity and subjectivity in science was acknowledged within *objectivist hermeneutics*. This meant that these hermeneuticians saw the need for drawing a line between the subjectivity of the researcher and the object to be researched. Another school of hermeneutics is found in *alethic hermeneutics.* The basic idea of alethic hermeneutics concerns the revelation of something hidden, rather than the correspondence between subjective thinking and objective reality that was of principle interest to the objectivist hermeneuticians. There are three main fields within this alethic tradition, without sharp boundaries between them: *existential hermeneutics* (Martin Heidegger), *poetic hermeneutics* (Paul Ricoeur), and the *hermeneutics of suspicion* (Karl Marx, Sigmund Freud, and Friedrich Nietzsche). In a sense, all of them are preoccupied with uncovering something hidden.

Epistemological Issues. The duality between human and natural sciences was emphasized by the emerging hermeneutic tradition dating back to the Renaissance in European history. Originally, hermeneutics was applied in Protestant analysis of the Bible and in humanistic studies of the antique Greek texts. A main theme in this research was how the meaning of a part could only be understood when seen in connection with the whole. For instance, on the one hand, you can only understand a certain fragment of the Bible if you look at it in the context of the whole text. On the other hand, you can put it the other way around: Since the whole text is a composite of parts, you can only understand the whole through its parts. This led to the formulation of what is called the *hermeneutic circle.* Later, *circle* was changed to *spiral.* This means that one has to begin in some part of the text and tentatively try to connect the part with the whole text, which may give new meaning to the original part, and so on. Gradually we will arrive at a deeper understanding of both the parts and the whole.

There have been many suggestions in the literature about the nature of these circles, as well as a changing understanding of what is meant by a part and what should be defined as a whole. Originally, a part meant the same as a certain fragment of the Bible or an antique text. Throughout history, the hermeneutic method was applied to texts in general, spoken words, actions, or not least to aesthetic objects. As will be evident throughout this book, hermeneutic approaches prevail in many qualitative analyses in music therapy research, such as in understanding musical expressions, works, and improvisations; conversations; and experiences; as well as empirical data contained in case studies.

What constitutes the whole that frames a certain part has also been under debate. First, the author behind the text was drawn into the study, then the whole society, the cultural context, and the historical background were included.

In the first form of hermeneutics mentioned by Alvesson and Skölberg (2000), objectivist hermeneutics, the autonomy of the object of study is underlined. This means that what is to be understood must be understood in its own terms, from its own immanent standards and criteria or from the original intentions behind the object. It is also held that in any phenomenon under investigation, there is a coherent totality of meanings that is reflected in each part, as we saw in the description of the hermeneutic circle. Interpretation is also regarded as a creative, reproducing act. A researcher always produces meaning; it is not to be seen as a mechanical reflection. This is the reason that an interpretation always will be relatively objective, never absolute. This position is elaborated by alethic hermeneutics, in which our pre-understanding of phenomena always will inform our research. Another development was seen in the idea of *empathy* as a necessary prerequisite for the interpretation and understanding of a text. This meant that the researcher had to take the position of the agent behind the text and try to relive, or imagine, how the situation was felt.

The second form of hermeneutics takes its name from the Greek *aletheia*, which means uncoveredness, the revelation of something hidden. These hermeneuticians broke with the problem of the subject-object as well with the split between understanding and explanation. To the alethic hermeneutic, understanding is a basic way of existing for every human being, a precondition that orients us in the world. Both natural and cultural sciences are irrevocably marked by interpretations all the way down to the level of data. On this basis, a second hermeneutic circle emerged with its special relation between pre-understanding and understanding. In the concept of pre-understanding lies the formulation that our knowledge, language, or historical situatedness always will inform our perception of the world.

According to existential hermeneutics, one form of alethic hermeneutics, what is to be revealed constitutes an original structure of properties buried at the roots of our existence. In order to reveal the hidden meaning, we have to take these structures into consideration when we make our interpretations. This may be our basic situatedness in the world, as outlined for example in Heidegger's major work, *Being and Time*, and Sartre's concept of how we are "condemned to freedom."

Poetic hermeneutics, another form of alethic hermeneutics, is concerned with the role of language in our structuring of the world. What is important is not the logical and formal aspects of language but its rhetorical figures, its metaphors and narratives. To explore metaphors may help us to understand how meaning is transferred from one area of reality to another. For instance, to speak about music as a language is to create an identity between two different phenomena. In this way, we tend to search for characteristics in the music, which intends to reflect language-like traits.

What has remained hidden and is sought to be revealed by the hermeneutics of suspicion, the final form of alethic hermeneutics, can be regarded as something shameful and thereby suppressed. To put it simply, Marxists often tend to see economic interests as the motive of human agency. Nietzsche saw the *will to power* at the root of our struggles, and Freud postulated sexuality as a force in development and behavior.

In the positivist paradigm, we saw how the concept of truth considers data as being in correspondence with the reality in the correspondence theory of truth. Opposed to this, data in hermeneutic research are considered to be *constructed.* There is no way to know the reality directly, only through language and perception, which means that the hermeneutic effort aims to reveal some kind of meaning or significance in the data. This is in accord with the broader interpretative background, the hermeneutic concept of truth, or what is sometimes called the *coherence theory of truth.* The coherence criterion refers to the unity, consistency, and internal logic of a statement.

Critical Issues. Hermeneutic interpretation has sometimes been exercised too subjectively, as if the researcher had some kind of super perspective upon reality (or the client-music situation), an ability to speak for us all, regardless of cultural position.

Relevance to Music Therapy. A hermeneutic approach may be taken when we are confronted with a question like, "What meaning is conveyed?" We may say that interpretations can be made from different perspectives. In music therapy, these perspectives may in turn be informed, for example, by a particular philosophical position, a psychological theory, theories concerning metaphors and narratives, analytical theories in musicology, and indigenous conceptions of the nature of music therapy processes.

For example, music therapists may meet concepts from existential hermeneutics as their interpretations are informed by perspectives from existential psychotherapy (Medard Boss, Rollo May, and Irvin Yalom). Further, metaphors are unavoidable when we try to characterize music. In analyzing transcripts from clients, for instance from a GIM session, poetic hermeneutics and the identification of metaphors may help to reveal significant meanings behind the images of the client.

The hermeneutics of suspicion are relevant for the psychodynamic music therapists where Freud's metaphorical universe with its topographic and dynamic concepts inform their interpretation of the meaning behind musical and verbal expressions as well as interpersonal behavior. Analytic therapy does not necessarily deal with facts, but with clients' recollections and reinterpretations of their life stories. In revealing hidden meanings, possibilities arise to construct a new life narrative in cooperation with the therapist.

It is claimed that all research in some way has to involve interpretation and thereby implies hermeneutics. See examples in Chapter 27 of this book, Hermeneutic Inquiry. For research in the psychodynamic tradition, see Bruscia (1998b) and Eschen (2002). See Bonde (2000) for the use of theories from poetic hermeneutics.

Critical Theory

Music therapy will always need to understand itself within a larger cultural or social context. Music therapists work under different ideological circumstances, with material conditions as well as theoretical constructs informing their work. Critical theory may inform music therapists about the wider social and cultural contexts in which they are working. It may point to social issues behind the problems of clients, thus leading the focus of music therapy in a new direction.

Historical Background. Critical theory is a tradition within social science that includes the writers belonging to the Frankfurt school of philosophy. Among these authors, we find Theodor Adorno, Max Horkheimer, Erik Fromm, Herbert Marcuse, and Jürgen Habermas. Psychoanalysis and Marxism were influential theoretical sources for these authors.

Epistemological Issues. According to Alvesson and Skölberg (2000), critical theory is characterized by an interpretive approach with a pronounced interest in critically disputing actual social realities and ideologies. Critical theorists see the aim of social science as serving an emancipatory project. They held that social phenomena always have to be viewed in their historical context. Societal conditions are not natural and inevitable but rather created and influenced by power and special interests. Thus, they can be subjected to radical change. The task of critical social theory is to distinguish what is socially and psychologically invariant from what can be changed.

Habermas, one of the more outstanding critical theorists, has compared various views of knowledge in terms of what he calls *cognitive* or *human* interests (Alvesson & Skölberg, 2000). He differentiates between a *technical,* a *historical-hermeneutic,* and an *emancipatory* interest. Within a field such as music therapy, we will find that research may pursue all these kinds of interests. The first, technical interest, concerns the acquisition of knowledge used to develop resources for survival and is found in activities like the production and distribution of food and clothing, the treatment of disease, and so forth. This is an activity that presupposes that nature can be manipulated in a predictable way. This motivates research geared to the development of knowledge and methods for maintaining control over objective or objectified processes. We see this in research where objects are isolated and divided into dependent and independent variables in order to ascertain regularities and causalities. As we saw in connection with positivism, the prediction and establishment of reliable procedures for the confirmation or falsification of hypotheses are of pivotal importance (Alvesson & Skölberg).

Nevertheless, we also need research based upon the second type of interest, historical-hermeneutic, which is concerned with language, communication, and culture. The focus for this research lies in interhuman understanding within and between cultures as well as between different historical periods. As we saw in the hermeneutics section, actions, events, statements, texts, and gestures are interpreted, so the primary interest thus concerns significations and meanings.

The third knowledge interest is emancipatory, which is a sort of liberating activity aiming to negate pseudo-natural constraints. Focus is directed towards attempts to identify sources of misunderstandings and ideological notions. Critical theory looks at both structural and unconscious sources of social and psychological phenomena. Habermas cites Marx and Freud as examples of those working in emancipatory modes.

Critical Issues. One of the basic tenets of the critical school in the philosophy of science is that there is a correspondence between values and interests and how we perceive the world and act. The ideals of a value-free science have been met with a critique from the hermeneutically inspired critical tradition. We saw in the positivist conception of science that objectivity was held as one of the basic conditions of a scientific approach. According to this tradition, scientific results have to do with reducing possible sources of error, or being systematically open to critique in advance, by trying to reduce some of the most characteristic sources of errors.

Critical theorists would claim, though, that there are different types of errors. Our observations and theories may be influenced by personality or cultural, social, or political background. In addition, they may be influenced by the particular scientific tradition to which we belong. Objectivity addresses the possibility of dealing with such sources of errors. Scientific activity has developed procedures and methods in order to secure objective access to the phenomena we are studying. We call this type of objectivity *intersubjectivity*.

There is a type of *error* that we cannot handle in this manner. Researchers will always be informed by different interests or values that will influence their research activity. This pre-understanding concerns not only what we experience and describe as researchers, but also what we search for.

Relevance to Music Therapy. As we can understand, there is a close relationship between the three types of interests—technical, historical-hermeneutic, and emancipatory. In music therapy, we need knowledge about the human body and physiological functioning to develop procedures to handle the effects of music. We also need to understand culture and communication in order to understand how music is interpreted in a meaningful way. In addition, it is important to include the mode of *explanatory understanding* that helps us to look behind the categories of illness and disability to elucidate social structures or forces that maintain the individual in a limited role. In this way, critical theory may serve an important function in the development of music therapy as a complex discipline.

For works in music therapy influenced by critical theory, see Ruud (1998) and Stige (2002, 2003).

Systems Theories

As we saw in the discussion of hermeneutics, what should be counted as a *whole* surrounding what is being studied had changed throughout history. In the 20th century, as a result of influences from information theory and communication theory, the interrelationship of phenomena in the world, or in a field of study, gradually became understood. What has emerged under the label of systems theory is an approach within science that is concerned with how we interact with the world. Since systems theories attempt to deal with both complex systems and give explanations for multiple systems, they might be considered metatheoretical expressions (Lazlo, 1972).

Historical Background. The history of the development of systems theory begins in the Classical Period and is rooted in the worldview that developed through Greek contributions from Aristotle and Euclid over a period from 600 BC to 300 BC and lasted for approximately 2,000 years. Systems thinking continued through the Dynamic or Scientific Period, represented by theorists like Galileo, Newton, and Darwin, and continued to develop for 300 years. In the mid-1800s, the Dynamic Period began to break down when discoveries were made at the micro level that did not fit the models that had been suggested. The collective impact of new models in physics, such as quantum mechanics described by Max Planck, Niels Bohr, and Werner Heisenberg, was to break the assumption that the world is composed of discrete parts and focus on the importance of relationships. Systems theory became formalized as a complex interdisciplinary field when it was influenced by cybernetics, which is concerned with the regulation and control of movements within different types of systems. In the 20th century, systems theories were represented by communication theories, field theories, and evolutionary or transformational theories. Influential scientists were Nobert Wiener and Ludwig von Bertalanffy. Kurt Lewin should also be mentioned, who with his *field theory* helped to bring the natural and social sciences together. In psychiatry, Gregory Bateson and the Palo Alto Group made significant contributions to the study of ecological and family systems. Systems theory has greatly influenced social work where—instead of focusing upon the individual—families, groups, neighborhoods, and organizations are taken into consideration.

Epistemological Issues. Systems theories emerged in response to the classical or scientific model that imagined and studied factors in isolation. The primary epistemological principle in systems theory is that a set of elements is so related that a change in the state of any element induces changes in the state of other elements in the system as well as the system as a whole. As model makers, systems thinkers strive for a unity of science model, but one that can work with the complexity and paradoxes of diverse systems. String theory, for example, is a model that strives to combine Einstein's theory of relativity and quantum mechanics in order to provide a theory that gives one foundational model to explain all matter from macro to micro levels. The focus of study should be the whole system and its complexity as well as the interaction between parts, not isolated elements. Systems theory suggests dynamic and transformational mutual relationship as an alternative to the traditional cause-and-effect model within science. Causality is not considered in terms of linearity. Instead, a circular model of understanding how phenomena are interacting is proposed. In this sense, systems theories are similar to hermeneutic circles. Systems are changing because new knowledge and understandings must be integrated into any system to keep it relevant and alive.

Critical Issues. Systems thinkers advocate flexibility, but because of their natural science background, they are sometimes criticized for the unity of science imperative. Since systems theory holds that changes in one part of a system may influence other, even remote parts, the territory of exploration is vast. Sometimes these changes are difficult to perceive and to describe. How can we know that which we cannot perceive? Compared to more humanistic approaches in the theory of science, the role and responsibilities of the individual are reduced. The individual is not placed above nature within a systematic or ecological understanding of the individual in its relation to the world, but is seen on equal terms. This raises some axiological or ethical questions concerning the possible unique status of the individual within a larger ecological system.

Relevance to Music Therapy. William Sears introduced systems theories into the music therapy discourse in a collection of papers titled "Creativity Package" and "A Revision and Expansion of the Processes in Music Therapy" presented at the International Study Group on a Theory of Music Therapy (1979). This collection of models and summaries of theories dealing with complex problems represented a variety of disciplines including Erwin Laszlo's principles from *The Systems View of the World*. Systems theory clearly operates within *ecological music therapy* (see Kenny, 1989; Bruscia 1998a). Ecological music therapy, according to Kenny, who describes her model as the *field of play,* perceives music as an energy system in which the processes of music therapy reflect the processes of nature and interact with the relationship between the therapist and client to create a highly complex system. In *community music therapy* (Stige, 2003), the music therapist does not work on a traditional individual basis but tries to involve whole communities or engage different parts or participants in the system to interact. Therefore the role of the music therapist changes depending on the circumstances and needs of each community at different times and for different events.

Circular causality is clearly illustrated within improvisational music therapy, where we do not expect a single linear causality behind the production of music or communication of musical meanings. Rather, participants influence one another, much in the sense of a circular process, yet one that is in constant flux.

See Kenny (1985, 1989) for a discussion of systems theory and music therapy.

Semiotics and Structuralism

When it comes to the study of music and musical meanings, music therapists will need refined methods and conceptual systems designed to study human communication. Seen as a system of signs, music has many similarities with language.

Historical Background. Dating back to the ancient Greeks, the study of signs has been an important discipline throughout history. The Greek word *semeion* means *sign,* which has given the name to modern semiotics. Particularly influenced by Charles Sanders Peirce, semiotics developed a highly specialized terminology to study the meaning of signs. Peirce's definition of his concept of *sign* also became important when he stressed how a sign is something that stands for something to somebody in a certain regard.

The study of signs may also appear under the name of *semiology,* the name given to this field by the French linguist Ferdinand Saussure. Saussure stressed how a sign has two sides, expression and content, or in Saussure's terms, *signifiant* and *signifié*. Saussure's linguistics also became a model for *structuralism* as it emerged in the 1960s as a major theory of science. In short, structuralism meant a more *synchronous* approach in science. As Kjørup (1996, p. 333) writes, in the 19th century it was common to explain something by referring to its origin and development, in other words, a *diachronic* approach.

Epistemological Issues. *Semiotics* has had a particular influence in the study of musical meanings. Peirce introduced the *index, icons,* and *symbols* as important concepts when studying sign. An index has a causal relation to its object (such as a symptom), the icon is similar to what it stands for (such as a realistic painting), and the symbol is a kind of sign that has an arbitrary (and conventional) relation to its object (such as words). If we ask what kind of sign music is, we will easily enter a discussion about whether music can be a gestured reflection of an emotion (index or icon) or a cultural and coded representation (symbol). If we further consider how the sign always signifies something to somebody (in a particular context), we may need to seek assistance from music anthropology to entangle the meaning aspects of music.

Critical Issues. Structuralism maintains the old Western idea that there is a *real* reality behind the surface of the changing world. This more real reality is a kind of invariable formal structure. We can see this in the musicological approach to musical analysis that seeks to uncover deep structures underlying the surface of music.

Relevance to Music Therapy. We could imagine that music therapy could be described and explained by approaching music therapy as a system or structure of ideas and practices, models, and methods.

See Pavlicevic (1997) for an example.

Postmodern Currents

In a postmodern climate there is room for a variety of values and approaches. Postmodern theory has placed earlier philosophies of science in a new perspective. We are allowed to see how music therapy will need the pragmatic evaluation of the effects of music in therapy and efforts at making good essential descriptions of musical behavior, as well as a broader contextual interpretation of our symbolic interaction with music. There is no easy way out of a world seen as a single reality, where truth is reached through better measurements, more exact definitions, or deeper interpretations. As we will see, the postmodern approach asks for a greater concern about reflexivity, that is, a need to be more aware of the role of language in the construction of reality.

Historical Background. Since 1960, there has been a rich debate within the philosophy of science under the headlines of *postmodernism* and *poststructuralism*. In France, *structuralism* had become an important approach to the study of language, represented by thinkers such as Claude Lévi-Strauss, Jaques Lacan, and Roland Barthes. Prominent philosophers like Michel Foucault and Jacques Derrida broke with the conception of a dominating center in language that would govern the structure. The text became a *free play* with signs, without anchoring in either a producer of texts (subject) or an external world.

During the last decades, the term *postmodernism* has become increasingly more common. Within this broad field of ideas, not only structuralism is negated but also the metaphysical inheritance of ideas that pervades all Western tradition from Plato onwards. The idea that there are definite rational global solutions and explanations, some general principles that guarantee progress in the development of knowledge, has been challenged. Rather, postmodern thinkers see these principles as *grand narratives* and have thought to replace them by micro-histories, "local, always provisory and limited stories," as Alvesson and Skölberg (2000, p. 148) write.

Epistemological Issues. The different schools of science we have met so far all seem to rely on the value and possibility of doing empirical research. We have seen, though, that researchers may disagree upon how to approach the real world. However, they all assume an independent outer reality that can be perceived and accounted for. It is exactly this faith in data and empirical inquiry seen as a cornerstone in the development of knowledge that is being challenged by the many thinkers within the postmodern movement. The *interpretivist* perspective presents an example of this skeptical attitude. According to Alvesson (2002), this perspective emphasizes how our pre-understanding, paradigm, and metaphor pre-structure our basic conceptualization of what we want to study. Also, our approach to, perceptions of, and interpretations of our experiences are filtered through a web of assumptions, expectations, and vocabularies.

Within the postmodern movement, *feminism* occupies an important position. Feminism encompasses ideas ranging from liberal feminism striving for sex equality and neo-positivists' concerns for not taking gender as a variable seriously enough, to approaches that take a radical epistemological stand. Concerning the above problem of perception of reality, feminist advocates have pointed to how male domination and masculine standards influence dominant epistemology and methodology of science. As Alvesson writes, "male domination has produced a masculine social science built around ideals such as objectivity, neutrality, distance, control, rationality and abstraction. Alternative ideals, such as commitment, empathy, closeness, cooperation, intuition and specificity, have been marginalized" (2002, p. 3). It may be easily imagined, particularly in a field like music therapy, how research might have been radically different within a paradigm that allowed the latter values to come to the foreground.

Within the group of *constructivist* thinkers, it is held that science does not provide privileged access to the objective truth about the social worlds outside of language and the use of language. The language constructs rather than mirrors phenomena. It is argued that both outer reality, such as behavior, and inner reality, such as feelings or motives, are complex and ambiguous phenomena. They can never simply be captured, but, given the perspective, the vocabulary, and the chosen representation, reality emerges in a particular way. This means that any claim of truth says as much or more about the researcher's convictions and use of language as about the objects of study (Alvesson, 2002, p. 4).

We can understand that it might be naïve to think that it is possible to depict social realities in unequivocal terms. What people say in interviews, writings, or in everyday interaction may differ from what they really mean. Further, it may even be questioned if people have definite, unambivalent conceptions or values and attitudes that are explicitly expressed at all (Alvesson & Skölberg, 2000, p. 202). In order to be meaningful, utterances are necessarily context-dependent. This not only means that we may express ourselves differently in different social situations, but that the meaning of what is uttered may also be affected by what is said earlier in the conversation. *Discourse analysis* sees this as an empirical challenge and pays attention to variations in what is said. For instance, when dealing with interviews, we have to pay attention to the problem of *restriction*. This means that we as researchers tend to *lock in* our subjects by applying various techniques that force them into certain reaction patterns. We may also be misguided by preverbal *categorizations*, which may lead to the idea that important distinctions and variations within a certain category are being missed. Or, we may tend to *selective interpretation*, which means that we have a pre-structured understanding. Led by our theoretical framework and less conscious personal and cultural ideas and beliefs, we structure an account in such a way that a potential multiplicity of meanings is neglected in favor of what is regarded as a *primary meaning*.

A last approach to be mentioned under the heading of postmodernism stems from the French philosopher Michel Foucault, who is the leading name in research on social power and the relation between power and knowledge. In his *archeological* or *genealogical* method, Foucault tried to map out the overarching rule systems in the thought system of whole epochs. He wanted to track down the ordered fields of knowledge, which he called *epistemes*, which are common to discourses of a whole epoch. Foucault uses the word *discourse* in a different sense than it is used above. To Foucault, discourse is more of a framework and logic of analysis that, through its penetration of social practice, systematically forms its objects (Alvesson & Skölberg, 2000, p. 224). Foucault used the genealogical research program in many studies, for instance when dealing with the phenomenon and institutionalization of mental illness. Foucault is not interested in who exercises power over others due to office, knowledge, or a power base. Rather, power exists in relationships and when it is expressed in action.

Critical Issues. The postmodern turn in the philosophy of science has been criticized for its endless theoretical argument and for being too pessimistic about the possibility for doing actual research. However, postmodern ideas have opened new possibilities for reflexivity as well as providing new theoretical insights, which have then opened new possibilities for interpreting data.

Relevance to Music Therapy. First, if we accept the idea that we live in different subjective realities, differently informed by language, values, and cultural realities, there can be no general objective theories in music therapy. This means that it is impossible to make statements about music therapy or music that are generalizable to all patient populations or methodological approaches. Truth is local, and the best we can do is to give good interpretations and descriptions of what happened there and then. Second, our interpretations and descriptions are always communicated through language. This means a choice of metaphors and a narrative structure that is forced upon our descriptions of reality. If music is seen as communication, reward, symbol, sign, or whatever, our choice of metaphor is sought from other fields of language or other theoretical models. Of course, sometimes our choice of metaphors or our ways of enacting the music therapy situation may prove rhetorically efficient, particularly when our choice of narrative comes from an established theory in another field. Third, we should be aware that our ways of describing, interpreting, or performing music therapy is a kind of discourse that has the effect of creating the reality we believe in, and which we want other people to believe in. In therapy, this discourse must be felt to be true, otherwise we will meet with serious ethical and practical problems in dealing with clients. Fourth, scientific activity means a high degree of reflexivity. This may create a conflict between the music therapist as a researcher and as a clinician. As researchers, we always have to deal with the underlying values of our activity and our ways of conceptualizing and narrating our perceptions. This, in the end, will reveal the relativity of our ways of telling the story of our work, the arbitrary nature of our choice of communicative form.

See Ansdell (1999) for a reading example. Postmodern thinking has also influenced the field of musicology. For implications for music therapy, see Ansdell (2003).

Conclusion

This brief perspective on different philosophies of science is first of all meant as an overview of the field. The reader is referred to more extensive introductory texts as well as to more extensive literature within the different philosophies of science. The study of the philosophy of science may appear futile for students who want to find a method that is precise and easy to administer—a short route to the truth. As we have seen, there are major disagreements among different paradigms as well as inside each field. What we can learn from the study of the theory of science is to be more critical, aware, and reflexive concerning our own theorizing and understanding of our work. We may also learn to appreciate the many possibilities for doing research, or to learn from the various perspectives and interpretative possibilities given us. One could also claim that the multiple perspectives reflect our conditions as individuals, as a guarantee for not being locked into a one-dimensional existence.

References

Aigen, K. (1995). Philosophical inquiry. In B. L. Wheeler (Ed.) *Music therapy research: Quantitative and qualitative perspectives* (pp. 447–484). Gilsum, NH: Barcelona Publishers.

Alvesson, M. (2002). *Postmodernism and social research.* Buckingham, UK: Open University Press.

Alvesson, M., & Skölberg, K. (2000). *Reflexive methodology: New vistas for qualitative research.* London: Sage Publications.

Ansdell, G. (1999). *Music therapy as discourse and discipline: A study of 'music therapist's dilemma.'* Unpublished doctoral dissertation, City University, London.

Ansdell, G. (2003). The stories we tell: Some meta-theoretical reflections on music therapy. *Nordic Journal of Music Therapy, 12,* 152–159.

Arnason, C. (1998). The experience of music therapists in an improvisational music therapy group. (Doctoral dissertation, New York University, 1998). *Dissertation Abstracts International, 59*(09), 3386.

Bonde, L. O. (2000). Metaphor and narrative in Guided Imagery and Music. *Journal of the Association for Music and Imagery, 7,* 59–76.

Bruscia, K. E. (1998a). *Defining music therapy* (2nd ed). Gilsum, NH: Barcelona Publishers.

Bruscia, K. E. (Ed.). (1998b). *The dynamics of music psychotherapy.* Gilsum, NH: Barcelona Publishers.

Eschen, J. T. (Ed.). (2002). *Analytical Music Therapy.* London: Jessica Kingsley Publishers.

Forinash, M. (1990). A phenomenology of music therapy with the terminally ill. (Doctoral dissertation, New York University, 1990). *Dissertation Abstracts International, 51*(09), 2915A.

Kenny, C. (1985). Music: A whole systems approach. *Music Therapy, 5,* 3–11.

Kenny, C. B. (1989). *The field of play: A guide for the theory and practice of music therapy.* Atascadero, CA: Ridgeview Publishing Co.

Kjørup, S. (1996). *Menneskevidenskaberne. Problemer og traditioner i humanioras videnskabsteori.* [The Human sciences: Problems and traditions within the philosophy of human sciences]. Frederiksberg, Denmark: Roskilde Universitetsforlag.

Kuhn, T. S. (1962). *The structure of scientific revolutions* (2nd ed., enlarged). Chicago: University of Chicago Press.

Lazlo, E. (1972). *The systems view of the world.* New York: Braziller.

Pavlicevic, M. (1997). *Music therapy in context: Music, meaning and relationship.* London: Jessica Kingsley Publishers.

Ruud, E. (1980). *Music therapy and its relationship to current treatment theories.* St. Louis, MO: MMB Music.

Ruud, E. (1998). *Music therapy: Improvisation, communication, and culture.* Gilsum, NH: Barcelona Publishers.

Sears, W. (1979, November). *Creativity package.* Paper presented at symposium, International Study Group: Theory of Music Therapy. Dallas, TX: Southern Methodist University.

Sears, W. (1979, November). *A revision and expansion of the processes in music therapy.* Paper presented at symposium, International Study Group: Theory of Music Therapy. Dallas, TX: Southern Methodist University.

Skewes, K. (2001). *The experience of group music therapy for six bereaved adolescents.* Unpublished doctoral dissertation, University of Melbourne, Melbourne, Australia. Available at www.musictherapyworld.net

Stige, B. (2002). *Culture-centered music therapy.* Gilsum, NH: Barcelona Publishers.

Stige, B. (2003). *Elaborations toward a notion of community music therapy.* Unpublished doctoral dissertation, Faculty of Arts, Department of Music and Theatre, University of Oslo, Oslo, Norway.

Trondalen, G. (2003). *Klingende relasjoner. En musikkterapistudie av "signifikante øyeblikk" i musikalsk samspill med unge mennesker med anoreksi* [Sounding relations: A music therapeutic study of "significant moments" in musical interactions with young individuals suffering from anorexia]. Unpublished doctoral dissertation. Norwegian Academy of Music, Oslo.

Wigram, T., Pedersen, I. N., & Bonde, L. O. (2002). *A comprehensive guide to music therapy. Theory, clinical practice, research and training.* London: Jessica Kingsley Publishers.

Acknowledgments

Thank you to Ken Aigen, Ken Bruscia, Carolyn Kenny, Brynjulf Stige, and Gro Trondalen for comments and suggestions.

Chapter 4
Principles of Quantitative Research
Carol Prickett

Clinical music therapists, music therapy academicians, and music therapy undergraduate and graduate students are frequently asked, "Just what *is* music therapy?" We usually answer in terms of the clinical work we do, the populations we serve, and the goals and objectives we pursue. Nevertheless, looking back over the decades during which contemporary music therapy has established itself as a profession and an academic discipline, it becomes clear that a part of music therapy is the systematic documentation of people's responses to music and to musical situations. As accountability has become the watchword of the institutions and facilities we serve and as our long-standing ethical obligations to our clients and patients have become formal, legal responsibilities, this documentation of the effects of our practices and our clients' responses has established itself as an integral part of just what music therapy is. Music therapy is a clinical practice profession, but it is no less an exploration and documentation of the influences of music on behavior and of its unique usefulness in clinical practice.

A system for verifying the effectiveness of music therapy treatment becomes even more imperative when the treatment is innovative. When you ask, What would happen if I tried this new therapeutic technique with these clients? Would it be more effective than what I've been doing?, the stage is set for a clear decision. You may employ the technique, surmise if it was more effective, and be left to wonder if outside influences or your distinctive personal style may have contributed to or detracted from the results. Or you may follow the protocols of objective assessment and set up a way of assessing the technique's effectiveness ahead of time. On another day, you may wonder: Is my employment situation typical of that of other music therapists? Again, you may assume that you know the answer and look no further, or you may use systematic, objective techniques to gain the information. In both cases, your decision in favor of objective study is a decision to follow the protocols of research. While the choice of research strategy will vary based on the situation, several of the most frequently used systems fall under the heading of quantitative research.

Quantitative research attempts to answer important questions about music therapy practices and patients' responses by quantifying or ascribing importance to the number or size of reactions or results. Since there are times when quantification may clarify a situation, as well as times when it becomes a ludicrous parody of a search for understanding, we need to consider when it is appropriate and what it can and cannot offer in terms of music therapy theory and practice. Bruscia, in Chapter 7 of this book, Topics and Questions in Music Therapy, presents a number of thought-provoking criteria for deciding which research type best fits a given problem; Aigen (1995) has presented a stronger—even an unbridgeable—differentiation between music therapists who pursue quantitative or qualitative investigations. For the sake of a better understanding of the philosophical context from which the present chapter is written, I will discuss a few issues of concern to all who value the development of a knowledge base for music therapy practice and an improved dialogue between music therapists whose points of view differ.

The area of intellectual discourse that philosophers call *epistemology*—the human mind's attempt to understand how we come to know that which we think we know—is an ancient, honored, and multi-faceted discussion among thinking people. Across thousands of years, much has been learned; some ideas have been discredited, but no hard or fast answers have been cast in stone. At issue is the basic question: How can we best examine the workings of the human mind when the tool we are using for our examination is that same mind? The answers take the form of various protocols of investigation, and there are many more than just quantitative versus qualitative. These protocols have evolved and continue to evolve; their number, their varied objectives, and their weaknesses speak to the complexity of human experience and human nature. They complement each other and when we find ways to integrate them, they contribute to humanity's quest to understand human experience.

Some suggest that one or another protocol is universally superior for expanding our knowledge of musical experience. I disagree. Specifically, some suggest that quantitative researchers, characterized as *positivists,* only seek to reduce all human experience, including music therapy experiences, to numbers and statistical probabilities, deny cognitive or emotional verities, and generalize their findings to unrelated settings. Quantitative researchers do indeed attempt to apply scientific attitudes and concepts (discussed at length through the remainder of this chapter). Through several centuries of western civilization, those who have contributed to what is known as the philosophy of science have concluded that certain ways of doing things keep a researcher as objective as a human is capable of being (and, yes, objectivity is a goal of quantitative research). If any researcher, quantitative or otherwise, ever boasted of having established numerical predictive Truth (with a capital T) that applies to all situations, that person would have violated at least two of the basic tenets of the very scientific methodology espoused. While a list of contributors to the philosophy of science, and particularly to the tenets discussed here, would virtually reach to the stars, three very accessible internationally known English-language writers across the past century and a half are John Stuart Mill (1852), William Werkmeister (1940), and, in music research, Clifford Madsen (1985). Additional discussion of the philosophy of science is found in Chapter 3 of this book, Philosophy and Theory of Science.

One of these basic tenets is that the prevailing wisdom requires constant reevaluation of what we think we know when new evidence appears; researchers usually phrase this as scientific theory being *self-correcting*. Each exploration reveals a tiny piece of an enormous puzzle (for example, how people respond to musical experience) and, if the addition of new pieces transforms the picture originally formulated, so be it. Although the word *science* is bandied and battered about in every aspect of modern communication, at the heart of the mainstream of the scientific tradition is the idea that science never proves anything—each investigation merely adds another piece to the puzzle, which is a long way from being solved.

A second tenet that not only is not denied but is embraced is that the impact of the researcher's interaction with the people being studied can dramatically influence an outcome or conclusion. The constraints of validity testing, discussed later in this chapter, directly acknowledge this interaction. The quantitative researcher simply wants to know the extent to which various factors beyond the music itself account for an overall response. Obviously, clinical practitioners integrate human interaction, aesthetic response, and numerous other factors when working for the health of a person. From a quantitative researcher's point of view, understanding how each of these factors affects responses maximizes the therapist's ability to blend them for the person's immediate benefit.

Whether music therapists gravitate toward quantitative or qualitative research techniques, there should be no disagreement when it comes to rigorous adherence to the carefully developed (and continuingly evolving) protocols of either type of research. Sloppy thinking, careless documentation, conflating responses with unacknowledged biases on the part of the researcher—the list of infractions that demean any type of honest inquiry is long. Both qualitative and quantitative researchers have developed ways of doing things that counteract our human tendency to simply see that which we wish to see. And both protocols add new techniques when they catch themselves in a loophole (such as double-blind studies so that even the researcher doesn't know who received which treatment). As stated before, this self-correction is the very essence of clear, scientific thinking.

In trying to understand the wondrous tools we music therapists wield (music and therapeutic interaction), perhaps the most can be gained by adopting a pluralistic approach to methods of research, embracing quantitative and qualitative as best fits a situation. Most of us have become comfortable with pluralism in other important aspects of our lives. In a multicultural world, we rejoice in discovering and celebrating our own heritages, while at the same time we respect and want to know more about heritages that are unlike our own. When it comes to music, in the 21st century even once-stodgy university schools of music, who used to proclaim that composed art music of Western tradition was superior to any improvised or nontraditional music, have welcomed the study and performance of a large number of musics. Surely music therapy researchers sacrifice no integrity in acknowledging the worth of more than one method of discovering what we need to know to help those we serve as therapists.

Pros and Cons of Quantitative Research

The pros of quantitative research in music therapy are numerous. We may think we observe a difference in our clients' attentiveness when music therapy is employed compared with when it is not used. We may suspect that a particular patient's musical accuracy improves if we incorporate a certain reinforcement strategy. Or we may question whether music therapists' salaries are keeping pace with those of similar professions. To the extent that each of these areas may be meaningfully conceptualized in terms of quantities or numbers—attentiveness might be measured by counting off-task comments or the time that elapses between instructions and clients' responses; musical accuracy may be a count of the incorrect notes or rhythms; salaries are always stated as a quantity of dollars—and to the extent that these quantities or numbers can be compared, with integrity, to quantities or numbers from related situations, clear interpretations of what is happening will result. As we shall see later, each of these examples would use a different quantitative research technique (experimental, applied behavior analysis, descriptive/survey, respectively), but each answers a question based on a quantity. Quantification is one of the basic ways we make sense of and organize our perceptions of our world, and quantitative research, when fitting, generates pieces of knowledge that help us solve music therapy puzzles.

In addition, the protocols of this type of investigation, detailed later in this book, offer time-tested systems for careful scrutiny of events. These systems follow logical sequences and mandate important control of all the influences that can be anticipated. They incorporate deliberate measures to eliminate, as much as possible, any biases caused by the researcher's hopes and dreams. The history of scientific investigation stands behind quantitative research principles, setting stringent standards for testing and accepting or rejecting hypotheses. Procedures are described in such detail that they can and must be replicated by other investigators. Before a quantitative piece can be added to the puzzle, it must stand the test of replication.

Finally, but by no means of least importance, the results may be read and interpreted not only by music therapists but also by nonmusicians in related disciplines. When music therapy research questions lend themselves to quantitative investigation, and when those investigations are read by professionals in psychology, medicine, or sociology (to name only a few of the fields in which quantitative research is common), communication across disciplinary lines can take place. However much or little the reader may personally relate to musical phenomena, the language of quantitative research functions as a widely spoken common language and, as such, can communicate the effectiveness of music therapy to nonmusicians. The pieces of the music therapy puzzle can then be fitted into the larger puzzle of human behavior.

The cons of quantitative investigation must be considered. As other chapters in this book point out, some music therapy research questions are best approached by methods other than quantitative. Preliminary investigations in an area where the basic variables have yet to be identified or their effects hypothesized would be one example. Evaluations of intricate therapeutic processes are another case in point. No one quantitative study, or even a series of studies, can do more than chip away at establishing an outline of our full understanding of the effects of music on people. The very precision that gives this type of research its strength demands that only one or two questions be studied at one time. Indeed, it is often the case that the more questions a quantitative project attempts to address simultaneously, the more likely it is that all of the answers will be muddled. Complex issues, especially those that deal with deeply held values or that depend on fluctuating emotional responses, may become ridiculously simplistic when subjected to all but the most sophisticated quantitative research designs. Expertise in a variety of research techniques and the intellectual flexibility to envision more than one path to knowledge are essential prerequisites for music therapy research sophistication.

Scientific Attitudes

Much, if not most, of the published research in disciplines related to music therapy (psychology, special education, sociology, social work, and gerontology, to name but a few) is quantitative research in which the attitudes and methods of scientific investigation have been adapted to the study of human behavior. Since ancient times, scientific thinkers have attempted to establish ground rules for conducting investigations that contribute to knowledge about the world and the people who live in it. Following the path of the development and acceptance of these ground rules is worthwhile, and a few particularly useful and classic references can be found at the end of this chapter. Across time, several underlying basic principles, often referred to as *scientific attitudes*, have been so universally accepted that they now form the introductory lecture in most science-related undergraduate courses. These basic principles or attitudes determine both the way in which the research is conducted and the conclusions that will be considered legitimate, based on the results of the research. At the risk of oversimplifying, these underlying principles might be summarized as follows:

1. *Conclusions must be based on that which can be directly (that is, empirically) observed.* An example of following this principle might be setting up consistent criteria on which to base conclusions about the effectiveness of a therapeutic treatment strategy that can be counted, measured, rated on a scale of 1 to 10, or represented on a graph. The music therapist's intuitive perception that change has taken place is not a sufficient basis for affirming this conclusion; the change in the factor in question must be evidenced in a manner that is accessible to view by any trained observer. Some aspects of music therapy, such as the number or duration of behavioral episodes or the stated musical preferences of a certain group of people, easily lend themselves to *empirical verification*, or verification through observation or experimentation. Beginning researchers may find the challenge greater when the factor being studied is a mental or emotional one, but empirical evidence in these areas is increasingly accessible with modern technology, as two examples from the published music research literature illustrate.

   The Continuous Response Digital Interface (CRDI) is a specially designed computerized device to record ongoing responses to music without requiring a verbal response. The researcher sets up a continuum (such as like-dislike, exciting-calming, engaging-boring) and the rate at which responses will be sampled (from 1 to 10,000 times per second), and the listener manipulates a dial or mouse to reflect ongoing and fluctuating responses across time. Several explorations of musical responses using the CRDI have appeared in the *Journal of Music Therapy* (Madsen, Byrnes, Capperella-Sheldon, & Brittin, 1993; Madsen & Fredrickson, 1993; Walls, Taylor, & Falzone, 1992), but Madsen's 1997 study is perhaps the most complex investigation to date. A two-dimensional CRDI, which can track the interrelationship of two factors (in this case, dimensions of arousal and of affect) was used to assess the responses of 48 adult music majors to a 20-minute excerpt from Puccini's *La Boheme*. Madsen not only discussed the insights into individuals' responses—and their overall similarities and disparities—but explained how this type of investigation is of particular use to music therapists for diagnostic and treatment purposes. Another use of an emerging technology that allows covert cognitive musical responses to be empirically studied was put into play by Morrison, Demorest, Aylward, Cramer, and Maravilla (2003). Based on fMRI (Functional Magnetic Resonance Imagery) studies that have traced language and nonsense syllable processing by the brain, these researchers required subjects to listen to music from their culture (Western) and from an unfamiliar culture (Chinese) through specially designed headphones that excluded the extraneous noises associated with this machine while undergoing fMRI scanning. Activation of brain areas under the two music conditions was compared and correlated with the musical training of the individuals.

2. *Complex or complicated explanations of behavior phenomena are not to be adopted until all simpler explanations have been ruled out.* For example, this principle comes into play when a therapist postpones ascribing beneficial powers

to specific songs or musical rituals until the influences of all the other aspects of the suggestive context have been accounted for. Commercial manufacturers of musical tapes sometimes flout this principle by claiming that mysterious characteristics inherent in their tapes, such as subliminal messages, have almost miraculous powers to solve behavior problems.

In 1992, Staum and Brotons published a series of investigations that demonstrated empirically that commercial tapes that were marketed as having subliminal messages imbedded in music passages had no more effect on listeners' behavior than did placebo tapes. In terms of this scientific attitude or principle, the complicated explanation (that unheard messages overlaid with music can cause significant behavior changes in a person) cannot be accepted because a simpler, well-known psychological reaction (the power of suggestion, in this case, the tape's title) cannot be ruled out.

3. *For every effect, there is a cause.* To verify that a particular cause leads to a particular effect, there must be a controlled comparison to a situation where the assumed cause is not present or is substantially altered. As a researcher, you employ this principle when you devise a strategy to isolate a proposed music therapy treatment from other salient influences, such as your personality. If the treatment appears to have the same effect no matter which of two, three, or four different therapists uses it, the effectiveness of the treatment can be substantiated.

Various research techniques typical of quantitative research, discussed in upcoming pages, demonstrate this principle in differing scenarios. In Chapter 21, Hanser and Wheeler describe control factors in experimental research.

Applied behavior analysis demonstrates controlled comparisons to deduce cause and effect in another, equally conclusive manner. A classic study (McCarty, McElfresh, Rice, & Wilson, 1978) compared the fighting and out-of-seat behavior of a group of children with emotional disturbances riding their school bus. Identical tapes of the children's preferred music were prepared for each bus. The researcher counted the number of episodes of fighting and of children leaving their seats under alternating conditions of no music, noncontingent music, and music contingent upon appropriate behavior. By systematically reversing these conditions on all three buses, the researchers were able to demonstrate a clear cause-and-effect relationship between contingent music and appropriate behavior and illustrate these relationships graphically.

In descriptive research, this principle may, at first, seem to be a bit obscure. Since descriptive research must, first of all, describe, seeking a cause for an effect is not the main thrust. Nevertheless, it often comes into play in interpreting the data. In a study that has proved seminal for clinical practice and hundreds of subsequent investigations, Gibbons (1977) described the musical preference of older people, observing not only that different age segments of the elderly population liked different music, but that the differences were related to what was popular during a particular age span of the people's young adult years. Although control groups or reversal designs were not used, the cause for the effect (consistently differing preferences) could be deduced (although, as will be seen in later sections, other possible causes of their musical preferences were not ruled out with this design).

4. *Being able to make a reliable estimate of how likely it is that people will react in certain ways to particular events (in other words, being able to construct a probability statement) may be extremely useful in determining appropriate treatment procedures, but it will always be open to verification by replication and to newer methods of analysis.* Quantitative research cannot lock in truth for all times and all people. Keeping an open mind, replicating one's own work or that of others (and reporting results that are inconsistent), and facing the possibility that new techniques may yield new information are crucial.

The history of the investigation of physical and physiologic responses to stimulative and sedative music is a classic example of testing theories with ever more sophisticated technology, sometimes generating surprising results that alter music therapy theories and practices. Burns et al. (2002) and Knight and

Rickard (2001) offer thorough summaries of this area of research and excellent references for further reading; additional historical perspective may be gained from articles by Gaston (1951), Sears (1958), Taylor (1973), Jellison (1976), Hanser (1985), Davis and Thaut (1989) and Hurt, Rice, McIntosh, and Thaut (1998).

Types of Quantitative Research

When quantitative research is appropriate for a given music therapy question and when it is done competently, it can generate sorely needed information about the field of music therapy and its practices. The types of quantitative research to be described in succeeding chapters are experimental research, survey research, meta-analysis, and two types of single-subject designs: quantitative case studies and applied behavior analysis. These are described briefly in the paragraphs that follow. The possibilities for developing longitudinal research in music therapy are also described.

Several of these types of research are frequently classified as *descriptive research*. Descriptive research is just what the name implies. Using sophisticated methods for gathering numbers of respondents who fit into various categories, it pulls together specific features (such as the average or mean) for each category to outline a sort of numerical picture of a situation. Data for this kind of investigation may be reported as raw numbers, means, or percentages, or they may be statistically analyzed to evaluate whether correlations or trends exist.

Descriptive research may be thought of as an umbrella term for several quantitative protocols, most of which are discussed in succeeding chapters. Survey research, meta-analysis, and applied behavior analysis are among its categories, as are certain types of case study research and longitudinal research.

Experimental Research

Experimental research involves comparing two or more groups that are reasonably similar in all important ways except for one factor (the independent variable), which has been specifically identified as differing between or among the groups. For this type of investigation, statistical methods of analysis are used most often to help the researcher understand whether the results of the study were likely to have been due to the experimental conditions, or whether they more likely occurred by chance.

Experimental research can be used to study a variety of musical performance, learning, or reaction questions. For example, Brotons (1994) compared physiological, psychological, and behavioral factors of the performance anxiety of university students during applied music practice and during open versus blind juries. Response rates during juries were significantly higher than during practice, but there was no difference in the level of response between the two types of juries. Prickett and Moore (1991) videotaped 10 patients diagnosed with Alzheimer's disease as they sang long-familiar songs, sang a new song, recited long-familiar prose, and recited a new short verbal passage (there were four independent variables). Each patient was studied on three occasions. The investigators calculated the percentage of words recalled under each experimental condition.

In experimental research, the reactions of large groups of similar people can be compared under controlled conditions. Assessments can be made within a reasonable time frame. Music therapists who read experimental studies may look at the data and make treatment decisions based on the performance differences that have been quantified.

Survey Research

Survey research involves collecting information by asking a set of predetermined questions by means of a questionnaire to a sample of people who are selected to represent a particular population. In one survey, Choi (1997) surveyed mental health professional, patients, and professional music therapists, asking their opinions on music therapy's role, strengths, and weaknesses, as well as music therapists' feelings about their professional stature. In another, Darrow (1999) interviewed 35 professional music educators and analyzed the content of their responses to assess their attitudes about inclusion of students with severe disabilities in music classrooms. In both of these projects, answers were categorized and analyzed so that tendencies and trends could be detected. Survey methods cannot be casual if the survey results are to be valid.

Meta-Analysis

In recent years, a form of research called meta-analysis has come front and center in research in the social sciences. Meta-analysis is a statistical method by which numerous experimental investigations that have reported statistical analyses can be compared and overall trends may be seen. Specifically, the effect size (the amount of influence an independent variable has on the overall statistical result) can be computed and compared across a wide variety of related situations. Examples of meta-analyses that have advanced the credibility of music therapy interventions in the minds of many nonmusic health professionals are those by Standley (1986, 2000) and by Koger, Chapin, and Brotons (1999). Standley analyzed studies in which music interventions were used in an attempt to reduce pain during medical treatment; in the 2000 expanded citation, 233 variables were analyzed for effect size, and she found that "not all physiological measures respond consistently for the same individual within the same treatment condition. Such information is valuable to help identify those physiological measures which are most responsive to the effects of music" (p. 9). Koger, Chapin, and Brotons looked at 21 studies (336 total subjects) in which music therapy was employed to try to reduce troublesome symptoms of dementia; they found a significant effect of music therapy, a statistical verification of practitioners' perceptions.

Quantitative Case Study Research

Quantitative case study research, also called single-case designs, is one type of single-subject research. This type of research focuses on describing a specific case. The case study focuses on how and why questions in contemporary events without requiring control over behavioral events. Single-case designs can focus on the process and outcome in individuals or clinical groups, offering an opportunity to study the case in detail or in depth. They allow flexibility in treatment and duration as well as measurement. Quantitative single case designs may be hypothesis testing or hypothesis generating, and within a naturalistic or an experimental setting. They include applied behavior analysis as well as other models. In an example of a quantitative case study, Cohen (1995) examined the effects of vocal instruction and Visi-Pitch™ feedback on the speech of two persons with neurogenic communication disorders. Subjects' vocal intensity, fundamental frequency range, percentage of pause time, and verbal intelligibility were measured. Both received both treatments, thus serving as their own controls. The results were presented through tables and graphs.

Applied Behavior Analysis

Applied behavior analysis designs often involve only one person rather than groups and examine that person's behavior under differing circumstances. Typically, the differing circumstances will be some sort of sequential pattern of nontreatment-treatment segments. Applied behavior analysis investigations occur across time, and the results are usually depicted on graphs, with analysis and conclusions based on the interpretation of these graphs. In 1999, Ford tracked the incidence of three behaviors (teeth-grinding, mouth-scratching, and head-hitting) occurring for a 23-year-old woman with severe developmental disabilities including communication deficits, motor problems, and visual impairment.[1] Rates of the three self-injury behaviors were counted during alternating periods of baseline (the only intervention was to gently block the patient from hitting her head), a passive music activity (listening), baseline, a nonmusic activity (water play), baseline, an active music activity (keyboard playing), and a final return to baseline. This ABACADA structure is an example of a reversal design. The rates under each of these conditions are depicted in a series of graphs.

---

[1] This study is also described in Chapter 24, Quantitative Single-Case Designs.

At times, though, applied behavior analysis researchers study the reactions of more than one person. If the researcher repeats a behavioral process with several individuals, each person's results are reported discretely. Thomas, Heitman, and Alexander (1997) addressed the problem of counterproductive agitation of patients with dementia during necessary showering by presenting taped music during the procedure; nonmusic baseline rates and a return to baseline after music treatment were also observed. Summary graphs for the 14 people studied demonstrated that the music intervention had little or no effect on hiding, physical nonaggression, or verbal agitation, but dramatically reduced physical aggression, which is a major cause of disruption for dementia patients and their caregivers.

Longitudinal Research

To date, few examples of longitudinal research can be found in the music therapy literature. At least one reason for this lack quickly comes to mind: While it is obvious that longitudinal research is research that is conducted across time, no one pattern of research protocol has yet gained dominance. Ruspini (2000) gives three criteria for research to be considered longitudinal. First, data are collected for each item or variable for two or more distinct periods. Second, analysis of data is consistent from one period to the next. Finally, the analysis compares the data between or among periods. In the best established model, the same people are studied at different periods in their lives (for example, the National Institutes of Health's Framingham Heart Study, 1948–1998, or Women's Health Initiative, 1991–2007; National Longitudinal Surveys by the U.S. Department of Labor, Bureau of Statistics). Other systems (Ruspini; Schaie, 1997) may include repeated cross-sectional, prospective, and retrospective studies.

Using Ruspini's criteria, several studies related to music learning or music therapy have been published or presented in recent years, although there is great variation in the time spans across which observations were made. The briefest length of time denoted as longitudinal is 15 months (Gruhn, 2004), during which the researcher observed two groups of nine children each; one group received weekly music lessons and one group was a control group receiving only a standard daycare regimen. Gruhn concluded that the children who participated in music lessons were better able to coordinate movement and musical vocal production than the control group. McPherson and Renwick (2001) videotaped practice sessions of students twice per year across a span of 3 years, paying particular notice to specific practice behaviors (i.e., self-regulatory behaviors) that appeared to relate to higher musical achievement during this time. Wheeler and Stultz (2001, 2002) videotaped two normally developing children, beginning at the age of 1 month, at regular intervals across a 4-year period, comparing their musical development with that of children with multiple severe disabilities and relating their observations to the developmental frameworks of Greenspan (1992; Greenspan & Wieder, 1998) and others; their work can inform music therapists' understanding of children with disabilities. Brattström, Odenrick, and Kvam (1989) followed the effects of playing wind instruments on developing dental and facial structures from ages 6 through 15 years old; they found that those who studied the wind instruments had "a decreased anterior facial height and wider dental arches" (p. 179). Is a follow-up study 30 years later also longitudinal research? If so, Madsen's (2004) study, in which he contacted former collegiate applied music students whose practice time habits had been assessed in 1972 (Madsen & Yarbrough, 1975) and found that neither their recollection of how much they had practiced nor their subsequent achievement in musical performance correlated to the actual time reported 30 years earlier, adds to this genre.

Well done longitudinal research in music therapy would enhance understanding of our profession's impact. Nevertheless, Fernando (2004) has described potential hazards in longitudinal research in the social sciences that would seem to apply to music therapy also. Subject attrition is probably the most frequently encountered pitfall; it can prove difficult or expensive to maintain contact with subjects or to keep them motivated to participate. For example, in the work noted above, attrition was low for Gruhn's 15-month exploration but greater for McPherson and Renwick (of 27 who initially agreed to participate, only five completed the entire 3-year process). Maintaining subjects' confidentiality may also be a problem; data may be lost as Institutional Review Board protocols change over time. Finally, once an assessment measure has been adopted, modifications or updates of this measure for subsequent testing may invalidate results.

In summary, no matter which quantitative research model is adopted, certain basic concepts are common to all. These concepts must be fully considered before any data are collected. A hypothesis, whether formally stated or simply implied, is formed. Independent variables are identified and controlled. A reliable dependent variable must be selected, as well as the evaluation technique, for example, selection of the appropriate statistical test. And numerous issues concerning validity must be settled by thorough thought, review of related studies, discussion with research colleagues, and a possible pilot study or the project will be doomed at the outset.

Quantitative Research Concepts

Hypothesis

A hypothesis is an idea that will be tested in a research investigation. The results of the investigation either support or do not support the hypothesis and provide the framework for the research conclusions. Hanser and Wheeler, in Chapter 21, Experimental Research, discuss the hypothesis as it applies to experimental research.

Since every project, quantitative or qualitative, grows out of a research curiosity, in one sense every study is based on a hypothesis. Still, the concept of hypothesis testing is clearest in experimental research, which is sometimes referred to as hypothesis testing. The nature of experimental research and the statistical analysis through which it is interpreted incorporates formal hypotheses. When you read an article published a decade or more ago, you are likely to see the study's hypothesis clearly stated. "It was hypothesized that. . ." was often the phraseology. In more recent times, less formal phrases such as "the purpose of this study was. . ." or "this study investigated whether. . ." frequently introduce the comparison that will form the basis for statistical analysis. Other types of quantitative research, however, are not usually set up to statistically accept or reject hypotheses, so the underlying ideas are rarely labeled hypotheses in these types of projects.

Independent and Dependent Variables

Potential music therapy researchers must grasp a few concepts that apply to all types of quantitative research before they can devise a study. The first concept is the distinction between the two types of variables, independent and dependent. As the name suggests, a variable is something that changes or that can be changed. However, the ways in which independent and dependent variables change are quite disparate.

An independent variable may be thought of as what you, the researcher, deliberately sets up to vary. In experimental research, the criteria for an independent variable are: (a) It is the one difference between controlled, comparable situations; and (b) it is set by the researcher. In contrast, the dependent variable may be conceptualized as what you, the researcher, measure. The variation of the dependent variable is controlled by the independent variable, and the dependent variable yields information for analyses and subsequent conclusions; it is an outcome. Chapter 21, Experimental Research, gives additional details.

When an experimental group is compared with a control group, the two groups are assumed to be similar in every way but one; this one difference would be the independent variable. Sometimes, however, a group is studied under more than one condition, and the condition or parameter that differs between observations is the independent variable. Prickett and Moore (1991) observed the ability of patients diagnosed with Alzheimer's disease to recall the words to long-familiar songs versus long-familiar prose. For this portion of the study, music was the independent variable, because (at the risk of being redundant) it was the one difference between controlled, comparable situations, and it was set by the researchers. The dependent variable, the quantitative assessment, was the number of words recalled in each condition. In an applied behavior analysis example, the treatment procedure that is introduced in contrast to the baseline is considered the independent variable. In the study by Thomas, Heitman, and Alexander (1997), the baseline condition was a typical procedure for engaging a patient with dementia in taking a shower. During the treatment, which occurred between the baseline segments, taped music that was familiar to the patient and that had been indicated by a family member as being preferred was played in the shower area. In this case, it was the music plus the type of feedback, set up and controlled by the researchers, which was the definitive difference between the baseline and treatment segments of the study and, therefore, the independent variable. The number of incidents of physical aggression during baseline and the treatment condition was the dependent variable, as were hiding/hoarding, physical nonaggression, and verbal agitation.

To summarize, the independent variable is what you set up to vary, and the dependent variable is what you measure as an outcome. The variation in the independent variable is controlled by the researcher, while the variation in the dependent variable is controlled by subjects' responses to the independent variable.

Reliability

Selecting a suitable dependent variable is perhaps the most difficult aspect of designing a research investigation. What measurement will accurately represent what is really happening? Reliability refers to the need for a measure to be capable of giving consistent results under similar circumstances. A dependent variable that purported to measure musical aptitude, but which gave widely differing results when administered to the same person three consecutive times or when scored by several different people, would not be reliable, and to attempt to base a study on this measure would be foolish. Without a reliable measure, research cannot even begin, and, in fact, establishing the reliability of the dependent variable precedes considerations about validity.

Content, Criterion-Related, and Construct Validity

Our attempts to establish validity are responses to the nagging question in every researcher's mind: Is this research really addressing the issue it is supposed to be addressing, or is something extraneous tainting the results and leading me to an incorrect conclusion? In everyday vocabulary, you are already familiar with the word validity as it connotes believability and trustworthiness. Although there are several types of validity, keep in mind that in every case we are pursuing research findings that are believable and trustworthy, that is to say, that are valid.

Validity is a goal, but it is an elusive one that we can never be sure we have reached. We should, and do, make stringent efforts to design studies in such a way that we can insure we approach validity, but the humbling fact is that it is an intellectual ideal and even our best real-world attempts are no guarantee of achievement. Since validity asks the question, Can I believe this to be true?, discussions of the concept reflect the philosophical differences characteristic of all quests for understanding. It is, at one and the same time, one of the most exciting intellectual puzzles and one of the most perplexing. This area is complicated and controversial; the following section is an overview, a mere representation of the tip of the iceberg. The understanding of these concepts and their importance is evolving, and authors are not in perfect agreement.

Kerlinger (1986) and other writers describe three categories of validity: content, criterion-related, and construct validity. Each of these types of validity relates to the appropriateness of a given dependent variable.

Content validity concerns the extent to which the items on a test (a dependent measure) of knowledge or understanding reflect all the facets of the area being tested. In other words, does the test cover the waterfront sufficiently to sample broadly from all possible areas of knowledge? A music theory professor might emphasize melodic, harmonic, and rhythmic dictation throughout the course, as well as part-writing and sight-singing. However, if the sole test of music theory knowledge on the final examination were sight-singing, the content validity of the dependent measure (the final examination) would be considered low, since many critical aspects of music theory knowledge were not sampled.

Criterion-related validity comes into play when a test is supposed to serve as a predictor or describer of another established behavior, the criterion. For example, a set of questions designed to predict which patients will benefit the most from Guided Imagery and Music (GIM) would be subject to scrutiny for criterion-related validity. Can it be shown that the questions are believable assessors of the traits that facilitate GIM? This question touches the issues of criterion-related validity.

To insure construct validity, there must be a strong reason to believe that the dependent variable actually measures the quality or characteristic that it is supposed to be measuring. Judging construct validity requires a strong sense of logic, familiarity with other research, and knowledge of common research practices. Many health professionals would consider counting the number of self-derogatory statements that a patient makes to be one valid measure of low self-esteem, while a low income level would not be a valid measure of low self-esteem. The sensitivity of a dependent measure is another crucial element in construct validity. If you attempted to assess the musical preferences of a patient population, a simple dichotomous choice ("I like this music" vs. "I don't like this music") would not have the sensitivity to detect degrees of preference. The simplistic conclusions that followed would probably have little relevance to the variety of reactions the patients had to the musical selections. A good dependent measure is sensitive enough to detect meaningful differences, yet not so hypersensitive that it begins to introduce unrelated material.

Internal and External Validity

Another way of using the term validity is to consider internal validity versus external validity. In these concepts, validity connotes that what is being done is directly relevant to the question at hand. The integrity of any research study depends on the maintenance of both internal and external validity. In 1963, Campbell and Stanley published a succinct book called *Experimental and Quasi-Experimental Designs for Research*, in which they described these concepts and outlined 12 common threats to validity. Their book was not the first discussion of validity, but virtually every subsequent writer credits this as being a seminal work, and most of the later publications cited at the end of this chapter expand and elaborate on their ideas.

Internal validity is related to the care and good judgment the researcher uses in designing and carrying out a study. Internal validity is a reflection of your ability to anticipate factors or situations other than the independent variable that might influence the dependent variable or, in other words, to design an experiment with a high degree of control. To the extent that internal validity is strong in a given project, the results of that investigation may be credibly attributed to the independent variable. To the extent that it is compromised, an erroneous conclusion may be reached. The overall question a music therapy researcher must ask is: Are the design and procedures so tight that outside factors won't influence the results?

External validity relates to the extent to which the results of a research study can be generalized to people, settings, or experimenters beyond the research study. It is ever so tempting to expand the results of a necessarily limited investigation to encompass situations that are logically beyond the scope of the study; when this temptation wins out, external validity is lost. In formulating conclusions, you will want to ask yourself honestly and with as much objectivity as you can muster whether the results you observed would probably hold true for other patient populations, other therapy settings, other conditions of assessment, and so forth.

In an expansion of Campbell and Stanley's (1963) discussion of external validity, Bracht and Glass (1968) suggest that threats to external validity are of two major types: population validity and ecological validity. Population validity refers to questions about what population can be expected to behave in the way that the experimental sample did. Ecological validity refers to the conditions to which the results can be generalized; to what other settings, treatments, experimenters, and dependent variables they will apply.

An important concept in quantitative research, and one that is closely related to external validity (population validity), is sampling. This refers to the procedures employed by the researcher in selecting subjects for the study. In some types of quantitative research, efforts are made to select these subjects to be representative of another group, the population. The rationale for this is that, if the sample used in the research is representative, the results of the research can be applied to the larger population.

Considerations of internal and external validity are addressed most frequently by authors writing about experimental research, but actually they are not concepts that are limited to any one technique of research. Rather, they may be thought of as research values that transcend individual styles or structures of investigation. Being sure that you have accounted for all possible influences (internal validity) would seem to be relevant under any circumstances, and the way in which a researcher attempts to make sense of the investigation and to fit it into the larger body of knowledge (external validity) would not seem to be limited to a single style of research.

A Final Word

A final word about doing any sort of research in music therapy: It is hard. Subjecting our deeply held beliefs about the effectiveness of music therapy to the light of objective assessment is not for the squeamish. Following through on the rigid demands of objective investigation and never cutting corners is always a challenge. Still, the degree to which music therapists can look other professionals, our clients, and our reimbursers straight in the eye when we talk about the viability of our clinical practices is directly related to the level of objective, documented research that we can cite. Research may be difficult, but the effort is worthwhile. What is music therapy? It is a clinical practice profession, and it is a body of well-researched clinical knowledge.

References

Aigen, K. (1995) Principles of qualitative research. In B. L. Wheeler (Ed.), *Music therapy research: Quantitative and qualitative perspectives* (pp. 283–311). Gilsum, NH: Barcelona Publishers.

Bracht, G. H., & Glass, G. V. (1968). The external validity of experiments. *American Educational Research Journal, 5*, 437–474.

Brattström, V., Odenrick, L., & Kvam, E. (1989). Dentofacial morphology in children playing musical wind instruments: A longitudinal study. *European Journal of Orthodontics, 11*, 179–185.

Brotons, M. (1994). Effects of performing conditions on music performance anxiety and performance quality. *Journal of Music Therapy, 31*, 63–81.

Burns, J. L., Labbe, E., Arke, B., Capeless, K., Cooksey, B., Steadman, A., & Gonzales, C. (2002). The effects of different types of music on perceived and physiological measures of stress. *Journal of Music Therapy, 39*, 101–116.

Campbell, D. T., & Stanley, J. C. (1963). *Experimental and quasi-experimental designs for research.* Chicago: Rand McNally.

Choi, B. C. (1997). Professional and patient attitudes about the relevance of music therapy as a treatment modality in NAMT approved psychiatric hospitals. *Journal of Music Therapy, 34*, 277–292.

Cohen, N. S. (1995). The effect of vocal instruction and Visi-Pitch feedback on the speech of persons with neurogenic communication disorders: Two case studies. *Music Therapy Perspectives, 13*, 70–75.

Darrow, A. A. (1999). Music educators' perceptions regarding the inclusion of students with severe disabilities in music classrooms. *Journal of Music Therapy, 36*, 254–273.

Davis, W. B., & Thaut, M. H. (1989). The influence of preferred relaxing music on measures of state anxiety, relaxations, and physiological responses. *Journal of Music Therapy, 26*, 168–187.

Fernando, R. (2004). Course on longitudinal research. Department of Sociology, University of Western Ontario, Canada. Available at http://www.ssc.uwo.ca/sociology/longitudinal/course.htm

Ford, S. E. (1999). The effect of music on the self-injurious behavior of an adult female with severe developmental disabilities. *Journal of Music Therapy, 36*, 293–313.

Gaston, E. T. (1951). Dynamic music factors in mood change. *Music Educators Journal, 37*, 42–44.

Gibbons, A. C. (1977). Popular music preferences of elderly people. *Journal of Music Therapy, 14*, 180–189.

Greenspan, S. (1992). *Infancy and early childhood: The practice of clinical assessment and intervention with emotional and developmental challenges.* Madison, CT: International Universities Press, Inc.

Greenspan, S. I., & Wieder, S. (1998). *The child with special needs.* Reading, MA: Addison-Wesley.

Gruhn, W. (2004). Phases and stages in early music learning: A longitudinal study on the development of young children's musical potential. *Music Education Research, 4,* 51–72.

Hanser, S. B. (1985). Music therapy and stress reduction research. *Journal of Music Therapy, 22,* 193–206.

Hurt, C. P., Rice, R. R., McIntosh, G. C., & Thaut, M. H. (1998). Rhythmic auditory stimulation in gait training for patients with traumatic brain injury. *Journal of Music Therapy, 35,* 228–241.

Jellison, J. A. (1976). Accuracy of temporal order recall for verbal and song digit-spans presented to right and left ears. *Journal of Music Therapy, 13,* 114–129.

Kerlinger, F. N. (1986). *Foundations of behavioral research* (3rd ed.). New York: Holt, Rhinehart, and Winston.

Knight, W. E. J., & Richard, N. S. (2001). Relaxing music prevents stress-induced increases in subjective anxiety, systolic blood pressure, and heart rate in healthy males and females. *Journal of Music Therapy, 38,* 252–272.

Koger, S. M., Chapin, K., & Brotons, M. (1999). Is music therapy an effective intervention for dementia? A meta-analytic review of literature. *Journal of Music Therapy, 36,* 2–15.

Madsen, C. K. (1985). Developing a research agenda: Issues concerning implementation. In National Association of Schools of Music, *Proceedings: The 60th Annual Meeting* (pp. 37–43). Reston, VA: National Association of Schools of Music.

Madsen, C. K. (1997). Emotional response to music as measured by the two-dimensional CRDI. *Journal of Music Therapy, 34,* 187–199.

Madsen, C. K. (2004). A 30-year follow-up study of actual applied music practice versus estimated practice. *Journal of Research in Music Education, 52,* 77–89.

Madsen, C. K., Byrnes, S. R., Capperella-Sheldon, D. A., & Brittin, R. V. (1993). Aesthetic responses to music: Musicians vs. nonmusicians. *Journal of Music Therapy, 30,* 174–191.

Madsen, C. K., & Fredrickson, W. E. (1993). The experience of musical tension: A replication of Nielsen's research using the continuous response digital interface. *Journal of Music Therapy, 30,* 46–57.

Madsen, C. K., & Yarbrough, C. (1975). The effect of experimental design on the isolation of dependent and independent variables. In C. K. Madsen, C. H. Madsen, Jr., & R. D. Greer (Eds.), *Research in music behavior: Modifying music behavior in the classroom* (pp. 226–243). New York: Teachers College Press.

McCarty, B. C., McElfresh, C. T., Rice, S. V., & Wilson, S. J. (1978). The effect of contingent background music on inappropriate bus behavior. *Journal of Music Therapy, 15,* 150–156.

McPherson, G. E., & Renwick, J. M. (2001). A longitudinal study of self-regulation in children's musical practice. *Music Education Research, 3,* 169–188.

Mill, J. S. (1852). A system of logic ratiocinative and inductive: Being a connected view of the principles of evidence and the methods of scientific investigation. In J. M. Robson (Ed.) (1973–1974), *Collected works of John Stuart Mill* (Vols. 7 & 8). Toronto: University of Toronto Press.

Morrison, S. J., Demorest, S. M., Aylward, E. H., Cramer, S. C, & Maravilla, K. R. (2003). An fMRI investigation of cross-cultural music comprehension. *NeuroImage, 20,* 378–384

National Institutes of Health Framingham Heart Study 1948–1998. National Heart, Lung, and Blood Institute. Available at http://www.framingham.com/heart/index.htm

National Institutes of Health Women's Health Initiative 1991–2007. National Heart, Lung, and Blood Institute. Available at http://nhlbi.nih.gov/whi/

Prickett, C. A., & Moore, R. S. (1991). The use of music to aid memory of Alzheimer's patients. *Journal of Music Therapy, 28,* 101–110.

Ruspini, E. (2000). Longitudinal research in the social sciences [Electronic version]. *Social Research Update, 28.* Available at http://www.soc.surrey.ac.uk/sru/SRU28.html

Sears, W. W. (1958). The effect of music on muscle tonus. In E. T. Gaston (Ed.), *Music Therapy 1957* (pp. 199–205). Lawrence, KS: Allen Press.

Schaie, K. W. (1997). *Advances in longitudinal research methodology.* Keynote address, 1997 World Congress of Gerontology. Available at http://www.cas.flinders.edu.au/iag/proceedings/proc0028.htm

Standley, J. M. (1986). Music research in medical/dental treatment: Meta-analysis and clinical applications. *Journal of Music Therapy, 23,* 56–122.

Standley, J. M. (2000). Music research in medical treatment. In *Effectiveness of music therapy procedures: Documentation of research and clinical practice* (3rd ed., pp. 1–64). Silver Spring, MD: American Music Therapy Association.

Staum, M. J., & Brotons, M. (1992). The influence of auditory subliminals on behavior: A series of investigations. *Journal of Music Therapy, 29,* 130–185.

Taylor, D. B. (1973). Subject responses to precategorized stimulative and sedative music. *Journal of Music Therapy, 10,* 8–94.

Thomas, D. W., Heitman, R. J., Alexander, T. (1997). The effects of music on bathing cooperation for residents with dementia. *Journal of Music Therapy, 34,* 246–259.

U.S. Department of Labor, Bureau of Statistics (n.d.). *National longitudinal surveys.* Available at http://www.bls.gov/nls/home.htm

Walls, K., Taylor, J., & Falzone, J. (1992). The influence of subliminal suggestions and music experience on the perception of tempo in music. *Journal of Music Therapy, 29,* 186–197.

Werkmeister, W. H. (1940). *Philosophy of science.* New York: Harper and Brothers.

Wheeler, B. L., & Stultz, S. (April, 2001). The development of communication: Developmental levels of children with and without disabilities. European Music Therapy Congress, Naples, Italy. Available on *Info-CD Rom IV,* University of Witten-Herdecke (2002) and at http://www.musictherapyworld.net/

Wheeler, B. L., & Stultz, S. (July, 2002). Musical relatedness in infancy as a resource in understanding children with disabilities. 10th World Congress of Music Therapy. Oxford, UK. Available on *Info-CD ROM V,* University of Witten-Herdecke (2004) and at http://www.musictherapyworld.net/modules/wfmt/stuff/oxford2002.pdf

Additional Readings

Scientific Principles and Attitudes

Boring, E. G. (1950). *A history of experimental psychology* (2nd ed.). Englewood Cliffs, NJ: Prentice-Hall.

Cook, T. D., & Campbell, D. T. (1979). *Quasi-experimentation: Design and analysis issues for field settings.* Chicago: Rand McNally.

Madsen, C. K., & Moore, R. S. (Eds.) (1978). *Experimental research in music: Workbook in design and statistical tests.* Raleigh, NC: Contemporary Publishing.

Whaley, D., & Malott, S. (1971). *Attitudes of science.* Ann Arbor, MI: Behaviordelia.

Wolman, B. B. (1973). Concerning psychology and the philosophy of science. In B. Wolman (Ed.), *Handbook of general psychology* (pp. 22–48). Englewood Cliffs, NJ: Prentice-Hall. (extensive references for further reading)

Reliability and Validity

Agnew, N. M., & Pyke, S. W. (1982). *The science game: An introduction to research in the behavioral sciences.* Englewood Cliffs, NJ: Prentice-Hall.

Badia, P., & Runyon, R. P. (1982). *Fundamentals of behavioral research.* Reading, MA: Addison-Wesley.

Bausell, R. B. (1986). *A practical guide to conducting empirical research.* New York: Harper & Row.

Cherulnik, P. D. (1983). *Behavioral research: Assessing the validity of research findings in psychology.* New York: Harper & Row.

Cook, T. D., & Campbell, D. T. (1979). *Quasi-experimentation: Design and analysis issues for field settings.* Chicago: Rand McNally.

Kazdin, A. E. (1980). *Research design in clinical psychology.* New York: Harper & Row.

Leavitt, F. (1991). *Research methods for behavioral scientists.* Dubuque: Wm. C. Brown.

Madsen, C. K., & Madsen, C. H., Jr. (1996). *Experimental research in music* (3rd ed.). Raleigh, NC: Contemporary Publishing.

Chapter 5
Principles of Qualitative Research
Barbara L. Wheeler and Carolyn Kenny

Since the overall goal of qualitative research is the discovery of meaning, the qualitative research act is an intensely human act. Most qualitative researchers consider the researcher himself or herself to be the primary instrument of the research because meaning is assigned in human terms, within contexts of experience as a human being. The growing prevalence of qualitative research in music therapy and in the research culture at large reflects a collective sensibility and desire to locate and describe meaning in a variety of contexts in an increasingly complex world.

The qualitative researcher must create, as the primary instrument of the research, descriptions of phenomenon that make sense from the inside and are palpable to the outside, while adhering to a rigorous ethical code in which every aspect of the research, from the selection of the method to the presentation of the findings, is interpretive. In order for interpretive decisions and statements to be credible, the qualitative researcher must understand which of his or her premises inform the research. This understanding emerges from a reflection on the personal, professional, and philosophical underpinnings of the work. The principles of qualitative research assist the researcher in developing such an understanding.

Even in a simple qualitative research design, complexity is built into the study and must be explicitly considered, giving transparency to the interpretive process. What are the philosophical bases of the study? How does the researcher situate himself or herself within the context of the study? Why does the researcher believe that the methods chosen are a good fit between himself or herself and the context of the study?

Before we can define or examine qualitative research, we need to look at the history, philosophies, and underlying assumptions that lead to this approach. To go back to the most basic definition of qualitative research, we must look to the Latin root of the term quality, *qualis*, meaning "of what kind"? This definition suggests description.

Historical Roots

The story of the development of qualitative research as a formal research approach begins in the social sciences, particularly anthropology. Since the beginning of the 20th century, anthropologists have been gathering descriptive data in an attempt to understand tribal societies around the world. The primary method used in anthropological research has been ethnography. Ethnography involves the detailed gathering of what Clifford Geertz (1973) came to describe as thick description. Anthropologists would write elaborate descriptions of ceremonies and settings relying on *informers* to translate both the language and the meaning of cultural practices. The researcher would also take *field notes* on his or her impressions and interpretations of life in the host culture.

For decades, anthropologists, ethnomusicologists, and musicologists quietly gathered their data and reported results with little publicity. However, in the mid-1980s, several exposés about the flawed results and skewed interpretations of prominent anthropologists brought anthropology into the light of scrutiny in the larger world of scholarly discourse. Though much of the publicity could be considered a profound crisis of representation in anthropology (Denzin & Lincoln, 2000), another result was the education of scholars from many fields on the descriptive methods used in anthropology. Indeed the crisis of representation in anthropology traveled into a critique of problems with interpretation in all other sciences[1] and began to transform the way that we approach research in many disciplines, including music therapy. The term *bricoleur* came to describe the persona of the qualitative researcher, one in which researchers "struggled with how to locate themselves and their subjects in reflexive texts" (Denzin & Lincoln, p. 3).

At some point in history, music therapy was a new field of endeavor. It is difficult to locate the exact moment when music therapy emerged from an interdisciplinary set of converging fields into a separate and distinct professional and scholarly discipline. However, it is possible to

---

[1] Schwandt (2001) says of the crisis of representation: "Broadly conceived, the crisis is part of a more general set of ideas across the human sciences that challenge long-standing beliefs about the role of encompassing, generalizing. . . frameworks that guide empirical research within a discipline" (p. 41).

recount the history of how practicing music therapists recorded their work and what scholars in related disciplines wrote about music therapy.

Music therapists working in clinical settings created descriptions of music therapy sessions by writing in charts or keeping case notes. These descriptions, in the broadest sense, were a form of qualitative research, even though they usually did not become formalized into research texts. Case notes were and still are a way of monitoring treatment, sharing specific therapeutic events with therapeutic teams, and, generally, observing and assessing the effectiveness of music therapy sessions. It is the observing and interpreting aspects of case note writing that are particularly relevant in tracing the history of qualitative music therapy research.

Many music therapists choose qualitative methods precisely because these descriptive means of gathering data relate directly to their experiences with patients and clients. They become a type of field note, a method used in ethnographic research that easily translates into the more general qualitative practice of research, which includes both observing and interpreting.

Some of the early articles on music therapy were case studies, another descriptive method that is qualitative in nature. These include case studies written by Paul Nordoff and Clive Robbins (1971, 1977), by numerous authors in *Music in Therapy* (Gaston, 1968), and by many contributors to the yearly edited series of *Books of Proceedings* of the National Association for Music Therapy, published by Allen Press under the title *Music Therapy* between the years 1951 and 1963.

Early scholars from other disciplines used descriptive and interpretive methods in their attempts to understand music therapy. These early scholars included Pinchas Noy (1966–1967), a psychoanalyst who wrote about the psychodynamic meaning of music, and John Blacking (1973), an ethnomusicologist who wrote about the relationship of music to biology, psychology, dance, and politics.

In the United States in the 1940s and 1950s, as music therapy began to be used in hospitals and government-funded schools, behaviorism was in vogue in medical and educational research cultures. Naturally, music therapists adopted quantitative methods in their research practices. This was the socially constructed norm of the time, but practicing music therapists were still taking notes and thus continuing their descriptive practices.

However, the tide began to shift in the mid-1980s when music therapists began a critique of quantitative methods and their limitations in capturing important aspects of the music therapy experience. Many of the early researchers were interested in process, aesthetics, and philosophy, and eventually went deeper into epistemologies, ontologies, and other systems of thought to expand their understanding of music therapy. Perhaps the most comprehensive documentation of this exploration is Kenneth Aigen's (1991) doctoral dissertation, *The Roots of Music Therapy: Towards an Indigenous Research Paradigm*. Aigen considers historical influences on music therapy research from the philosophy and theory of science (with emphasis on ontology and epistemology) and describes the critique of what he calls "the received view" from a position of process, clinical realities, creativity, and research methodologies. He emphasizes the importance of the 1982 New York University Symposium, "Music in the Life of Man."[2] At this symposium, music therapy scholars from around the world began to develop a community in which a metacritique could begin to emerge. It is here that U. S. music therapists joined their European colleagues in an active debate on the efficacy of specific methodologies, their strengths and weaknesses, their meaningful applications, and their role in music therapy research.

---

[2] The invitation to this symposium said that it would "probe deeply into the musical experience and its effects on our bodies, minds, and spirits." Study groups focused on the following topics: Encountering the Self in the Musical Experience, Illness and Wellness in the Musical Experience, The Experience of Time and Rhythm in Music Therapy, and What Are Appropriate/Acceptable Approaches to Study Musical Experiences?

Philosophical Bases

Philosophy is the most general of the sciences. Often it is referred to as the "science of sciences." But if we look at the Greek roots of the term, we can understand that, from the beginning, philosophy also dealt with the problems of the human heart and, in general, the issues of human nature. The term *philosophy* comes from the Greek words *philein*, to love, and *sophia*, wisdom. So, when translated from the Greek, philosophy means *to love wisdom.*

The search for general principles under which all facts can be explained is the driving force underlying philosophical endeavors. Early in the history of philosophy, these general principles were assigned to metaphysical forces. Metaphysics can be described as "any scheme of explanation which transcends the inadequacies or inaccuracies of ordinary thought" (Runes, 1983, p. 212). Most ancient philosophy concerned itself with the activity of the gods. The Greek philosophers made many contributions to this body of knowledge. Early philosophy sought knowledge and understanding about the ultimate reality. Even today, with the complexities of contemporary philosophy, there is an occasional norm that seeks this ultimate wisdom, especially in theologically oriented philosophical practices. There are many references to Plato and his ideas about music in the music therapy literature, so music therapists are familiar with these early roots.

Philosophical ideas are often thought to be highly abstract, considering issues of metaphysics, or ontology and epistemology, logic, ethics, and aesthetics. But some philosophies, including aesthetics, can be concrete (or sensuous) and abstract. For example, *pragmatism* is a branch of philosophy particularly influential in the United States. William James and John Dewey are the main philosophers representing pragmatism in America. Pragmatism concerns itself with the practical issues of everyday life and getting things done. Music therapy researcher Kenneth Aigen has offered a well-considered treatment of the pragmatism of John Dewey (1991, 1995a). Certainly behaviorism, a strong early influence in music therapy practice and research, was very much influenced by pragmatic thinking.

Pragmatism is always an important issue when considering health and well-being. Suffering is an important theme in philosophy. And, as health care providers, music therapists must consider how to remediate health issues with efficacy and efficiency.

But the music part of music therapy invites the philosophies of Sartre and Merleau-Ponty, who consider the sensuous and aesthetic aspects of human life. In 1999, Lakoff and Johnson offered *Philosophy in the Flesh: The Embodied Mind and Its Challenge to Western Thought,* bringing together the latest developments in cognitive science with the philosophical ideas of Dewey and Merleau-Ponty. The authors use *metaphor* as the integrative phenomenon in bridging these schools of thought. The significance of metaphor in music therapy is developed more recently by music therapy researchers Lars Ole Bonde (2000) and Henk Smeisjters (2003, 2005).

In general, music therapists read and think about philosophical issues through discussions about ontology and epistemology in music therapy research. Some may wonder why it is helpful for music therapists to think about these issues.

Ontology asks: What is understood as reality? Ontology seeks to identify the essence of things, the fundamental principles or the ultimate philosophy, especially with the diversification of ideas and the continuing collaboration of discourses in our field and in the world of scholarship in general. However, it is part of human nature to seek coherence, and part of making sense out of our worlds is to find the connecting points in our ideas. Kenneth Bruscia (2000) and Rudy Garred (2001) have both reflected on ontology for music therapy.

Even more prevalent in music therapy literature is the branch of philosophy known as *epistemology.* Epistemology asks: What are the ways in which knowing can be achieved within the frame of this reality? Epistemology also has its roots in metaphysics, but it has become a central theme in the discourse on research practice in contemporary society because of the increasing complexity of ideas and crises of representation in virtually all disciplines. Epistemology is best understood as the science of knowledge. Goldstein (1978) wrote an important text in his area, titled *How We Know: An Exploration of the Scientific Process.* Another important text, *How We Know What Isn't So: The Fallibility of Human Reason in Everyday Life* (Gilovitch, 1991), describes how easily we can mislead ourselves about knowledge. This latter text is an accessible and palpable critique of the methods of inquiry. In general, epistemology covers the range of knowledge systems—from Belenky, Clinchy, Goldberger, and

Tarule's (1986) *Women's Ways of Knowing* that suggests an *embodied knowledge* based on the body's sensibilities, to Polanyi's *Personal Knowledge* (1958) that claims that we can only know what we have experienced, to claims that knowledge can only be gathered from mathematical formulas (a very old idea that can be traced back to ancient Greek philosophers). Lakoff and Johnson (1999), contemporary philosophers mentioned earlier in this section, attempt to bring the concrete and abstract ways of knowing together through current brain research, while Elliott (1991) suggests that music itself is a way of knowing.

In contemporary thinking about research, we tend to use a practical device to help us understand the vast territory of philosophy. In 1962, Thomas Kuhn introduced the generalized use of the term *paradigm*. This term has privilege in contemporary philosophical discourse and helps us to distinguish between positivist and postpositivist ways of thinking and naturalist or constructivist ways of knowing, as illustrated in Table 1 (see also Jane Edwards' [1999] discussion of paradigms and their relationship to music therapy research).

Table 1
Contrasting Paradigms: Positivist-Naturalist/Constructivist
Adapted from Lincoln & Guba (1985). Used with permission.

	Positivist	Naturalist/Constructivist
Nature of Reality	There is a single, tangible reality that can be broken apart into pieces that can be studied independently	There are multiple realities that can be studied only holistically
Relationship of Knower to Known	The observer can be separated from what is observed	The inquirer and the object of inquiry interact to influence one another
Possibility of Generalization	Time- and context-free generalizations are possible	Only time- and context-bound working hypotheses are possible
Possibility of Causal Linkages	Every action can be explained as the result of a real cause that precedes the effect (or is at least simultaneous with it)	All entities are in a state of mutual simultaneous shaping, so that it is impossible to distinguish causes from effects
Role of Values	Inquiry is value-free	Inquiry is value-bound

The philosophical roots of music therapy are deep and vast, particularly considering the ongoing discourse about the role of music in our human life. In Plato's world, music was prescriptive in the sense that particular music was believed to have very specific effects on people, thus reflecting what we would now call a positivist approach. Qualitative research in music therapy can be considered as more naturalistic or constructivist in nature. The goal of qualitative research is to gather descriptions of phenomena that are often ineffable. Qualitative researchers tend to be more phenomenological in nature. Phenomenology is complex and usually defies prescriptive methods. It looks at direct experience and seeks to authentically represent that experience.

In the mid-1980s, phenomenology and qualitative research began to influence music therapy research practice, as seen particularly in the work of Kenny (1983, 1987, 1989) and Forinash (1990; Forinash & Gonzalez, 1989). This influence has grown and may now be considered to be on equal footing with the positivistic/postpositivistic approaches to research, as reflected in this text and in many conferences and symposia on music therapy around the world. This philosophical shift in music therapy reflects the scholarly culture as a whole. The development of music therapy research parallels the development of scholarly research in many disciplines, including the consequences of the crisis of representation mentioned earlier.

Definition and Characteristics

It is difficult to define qualitative research as it has so many facets and there are so many ways of approaching it. There is no uniformly accepted definition of qualitative research, and many words are used to describe it.

In their introductory chapter in the *Handbook of Qualitative Research* (2nd Edition), Denzin and Lincoln (2000), while acknowledging that it is difficult for researchers to agree on a definition, provide the following definition of qualitative research:

> Qualitative research is an interdisciplinary, transdisciplinary, and sometimes counterdisciplinary field. It crosscuts the humanities and the social and physical sciences. Qualitative research is many things at the same time. It is multiparadigmatic in focus. Its practitioners are sensitive to the value of the multimethod approach. They are committed to the naturalistic perspective and to the interpretive understanding of human experience. At the same time, the field is inherently political and shaped by multiple ethical and political positions.
>
> Qualitative research embraces two tensions at the same time. On the one hand, it is drawn to a broad, interpretive, postexperimental, postmodern, feminist, and critical sensibility. On the other hand, it is drawn to more narrowly defined positivist, postpositivist, humanistic, and naturalistic conceptions of human experience and its analysis. Further, these tensions can be combined in the same project, bringing both postmodern and naturalistic or both critical and humanistic perspectives to bear. (p. 7)

Acknowledging the complexity of this definition, the authors go on to say that this means that qualitative research, as a set of practices, embraces within its own multiple disciplinary histories constant tensions and contradictions over the project itself, including its methods and the forms its findings and interpretations take. The field sprawls between and crosscuts all of the human disciplines, even including, in some cases, the physical sciences. Its practitioners are variously committed to modern, postmodern, and postexperimental sensibilities and the approaches to social research that these sensibilities imply (p. 4).

In the first edition of this book, *Music Therapy Research: Quantitative and Qualitative Perspectives,* qualitative research was described as "a process wherein one human being genuinely attempts to understand something about another human being or about the conditions of being human by using approaches which take full advantage of being human" (Bruscia, 1995b, p. 426).

Ruud (1998) has described the main characteristics of the qualitative approach as holistic, empirical and naturalistic, descriptive, interpretative, empathic, and says that it is sometimes based on grounded theory and that it emphasizes immediate observations and spontaneous interpretations (pp. 108–109).

Tesch (1990) has listed 46 terms used to describe what is broadly considered as qualitative research in the social sciences. Most of these terms are not synonymous but rather vary in what they describe. Some of the terms that she lists are action research, case study, clinical research, collaborative inquiry, content analysis, dialogical research, conversation analysis, Delphi study, descriptive research, discourse analysis, ecological psychology, ethnography, ethnomethodology, experiential psychology, field study, focus group research, grounded theory, hermeneutics, heuristic research, holistic ethnography, imaginal psychology, interpretive interactionism, life history study, naturalistic inquiry, oral history, participant observation, phenomenography, phenomenology, qualitative evaluation, symbolic interactionism, and transcendental realism (p. 58).

Patton (2002) has described design strategies, data collection and field characteristics, and analysis strategies of qualitative inquiry. These strategies and features will be used as a framework to describe qualitative research.

Characteristics of Qualitative Research

Design Strategies

Several general characteristics apply to the design of qualitative research. These include naturalistic inquiry, an emergent design flexibility, and purposeful sampling.

Naturalistic Inquiry. Much qualitative research takes place in natural or real-world settings, and the researcher does not attempt to manipulate or change the situation or phenomenon of interest. By occurring in a natural setting, the research is done on the same events and interactions that the researcher wishes to study. This is in contrast to some types of quantitative research in which the variables of interest are manipulated and which must be done outside of the natural setting. Even qualitative research that does not occur in a completely natural setting, such as interviews about one's experience of a phenomenon, attempts to capture the normally occurring thoughts, feelings, and interactions of the participants.

This means that music therapy clients and sessions may be studied as they are occurring and in the places where they naturally occur, rather than being re-created in a laboratory or experimental session. Qualitative researchers in music therapy believe that this ability to study music therapy as it occurs makes the research relevant to what music therapists actually do.[3]

Emergent Design Flexibility. An important aspect of qualitative research is that its design is not set and inflexible and may change based on the information that emerges and what the researcher learns during the research process. The researcher pursues new areas as they emerge so that the research evolves, taking advantage of what is learned in its earlier stages.

In music therapy research, this means that the researcher can take into account client and therapist responses as the research progresses and adjust the design accordingly. There may be an instance, for example, in which client responses that were unexpected emerge during the research process, and the researcher will therefore decide to move the research in the direction of the new material, either in addition to or in place of the previous focus. Aigen (1995b) describes a time in his research on the process of a music therapy group in which he decided to add interviews with the music therapists as an additional means of gathering data for his research; this decision was made part way through the research in response to the needs of the research.

Purposeful Sampling. In purposeful sampling, research participants are selected because of what their study may bring to the research question, not because they are necessarily typical of the group being studied. The purpose of selecting participants is not, therefore, so that the results may be generalized (as in quantitative experimental studies), but rather because there are things that can be learned from studying them.

Rather than using typical music therapy clients in a study, the qualitative music therapy researcher may select clients who have shown particular benefits from the music therapy. Similarly, the choice might be made to study a therapist who brings a unique perspective or specific strengths to the therapy situation, even though this person is not considered to be a typical therapist. The information gleaned from the research is not expected to apply to all similar situations, but rather is valued for what it can show about the instance under study.

Data Collection and Fieldwork Strategies

Data collection and fieldwork strategies commonly used in qualitative research include the use of qualitative data, the importance of personal experience and engagement, reliance upon empathic neutrality and mindfulness, and an acknowledgment that systems are dynamic.

Qualitative Data. This area is summarized by Patton (2002) as "observations that yield detailed, thick description; inquiry in depth; interviews that capture direct quotations about people's personal perspectives and experiences; case studies; careful document review" (p. 40). These descriptions provide the researcher with data to explore and analyze in depth, leading to meaningful results.

There are many examples of detailed descriptions of the situation under investigation and quotations from the participants in music therapy qualitative research. One is from *Playin'*

---

[3] Naturalistic inquiry is addressed more fully in Chapter 28 of this book.

in the Band (Aigen, 2002), a case study of a 7½-year music therapy experience with an adult who had developmental delays and was nonverbal, through which Aigen illustrates the use of improvisation in popular music styles. Aigen includes video segments of many musical examples, coordinated with descriptions in the book, one of which follows:

> The improvisation based on *Get Back* begins to near a musical climax unusual in Lloyd's sessions. Lloyd stops, looks at Alan who also stops, then looks down at his guitar and resumes strumming as Alan resumes playing. One minute and twenty seconds into the excerpt, we attempt to establish a "stop" rhythm. This rhythmic feel is stylistically related to the stop accents, but adds syncopation to them and builds a novel rhythmic feel based on these stops. This music is too jarring for Lloyd and he leaves the therapy room. (p. 41)

Personal Experience and Engagement. The qualitative researcher conducts the research largely through personal experience and engagement. Topics, areas of focus, and data for the research come largely from personal experiences. The researcher conducting the study becomes engaged with the participants, often going into the setting where they live or work and actually participating with them. These features, personal involvement and engagement, are part of the essence of qualitative research, which is intended to involve participants as fully and humanly as possible.

There are many examples of personal experience and engagement in the qualitative music therapy research. These include Wheeler's (1999) study of her experience of pleasure when working with children with multiple, severe disabilities, which is focused on understanding one aspect of her personal experience, the experience of pleasure. Similarly, Kenny's (1987, 1989) model of the field of play is based on her experiences with clients, and the book outlining the field of play includes a description of a session with a client, thus sharing the author's experiences that shaped the development of the theory.

Empathic Neutrality and Mindfulness. The qualitative researcher works to be empathic but not judgmental while conducting the research. In addition, the researcher strives to be fully present when observing or interviewing. These help in conducting research in an intentional, thoughtful manner that builds upon the researcher's relationship with the participants, while still allowing him or her to maintain the distance necessary to conduct the research in a trustworthy manner.

This was very important in Wheeler's (2002) study of music therapy students' experiences of music therapy practica. As she interviewed music therapy students to learn their perceptions, it was important to be able to listen to what the students said without judging. Since some of the students' perceptions were quite different than Wheeler, as a faculty member, had anticipated, this ability to be empathic but not judgmental was important.

Dynamic Systems. Qualitative researchers acknowledge the ever-changing nature of systems and attempt to build protocols into the research design that monitor these dynamics, enabling a shift in protocols as required. Qualitative research does not assume that things can remain static long enough to predict the continuing relevance of a set of protocols throughout the research, thus the research process must constantly adjust to these changes. One example of this process is the qualitative research method of *snowballing*. This method allows the researcher to add interviewees at any stage in the process of interviewing participants, based on social networks in the community. Thus, the qualitative researcher is aware of the evolving nature of human interactions and is sensitive to how the process must change to accommodate it in order to accurately reflect the research context.

Aigen (1991, 1993) advocated for qualitative research as most appropriate for music therapy research because process is important in both. The qualitative researcher's awareness of the changing dynamics and the process in the research does, indeed, reflect awareness of the same dynamics in the music therapy session and is an ideal way to study process.

Analysis Strategies

Some analysis strategies are important in qualitative research. These include treating each case as unique, employing inductive analysis and creative synthesis, taking a holistic perspective, being sensitive to context, and being mindful of the researcher's voice and perspective and the need for reflexivity in the research.

Unique Case Orientation. Each case is unique and important in qualitative research, thus the qualitative researcher analyzes and strives to understand each case. Comparisons are made only after careful understanding of the individual cases.

There are many examples of this in the qualitative music therapy research, where the researcher begins by understanding the individuals in the study, then later makes comparisons in an effort to form categories or draw conclusions. One example of this is Forinash's (1992) study of music therapists' experiences of clinical improvisation. Her research involved interviewing and understanding individual therapists' experiences, then developing categories that described experiences shared by a number of the therapists. In her presentation of the study, she provided quotations from individual therapists as a means of clarifying and supporting the categories.

Inductive Analysis and Creative Synthesis. The process of analyzing data for qualitative research generally requires the researcher to immerse himself or herself in the data, looking for patterns, themes, and relationships. There are few rules for this process, and the researcher must depend largely on his or her own ability to see these patterns. The process is guided by the principles underlying the research approach being used.

There are numerous examples of researchers' use of these strategies in qualitative music therapy research. One example is Bruscia's (1995a) study in which he sought to understand the music therapist's experience of "being there" for his client. Through his analysis of a Guided Imagery and Music (GIM) session, Bruscia discovered three experiential spaces and four levels of experience through which he moved his consciousness in the process of guiding a session. The procedures that he used in the research, and which he outlines in his article, involved inductive analysis and creative synthesis, as described here.

Holistic Perspective. Qualitative research studies its subjects from a holistic perspective. Qualitative researchers are skeptical about laboratory studies that attempt to isolate variables in human experience, and reason that it is virtually impossible to account for all potential variables because of the complexity of the referential totality of contexts. Although the phenomenon under study may be observed in pieces for some aspects of study and analysis, "the whole phenomenon under study is understood as a complex system that is more than the sum of its parts" (Patton, 2002, p. 41). This emphasis on the whole is an important feature of qualitative research.

New developments in the natural sciences influence the behavioral and social sciences, and, as the traditional physical sciences make movements toward holistic understandings, other disciplines follow. Developments in physics influenced several music therapists (Amir, 1995; Eagle, 1991; Kenny, 1985, 1989; Schmidt & Eagle, 1982), who considered principles from quantum physics and their potential application to music therapy, as metaphor or as experience. Concepts from field theory, in particular, emphasized principles of holism and maximum interdependence among the conditions in a context. These principles of physics supported qualitative researchers in their skepticism about isolating variables in artificially controlled laboratories. They also helped to introduce an orientation toward hermeneutic inquiry. Hermeneutics is the art and science of interpretation. Though hermeneutics is a very old type of research, having originated when monks took up the task of interpreting sacred texts, it has become extremely important, as well, in the postmodern climate of scientific research. The basic method for hermeneutic researchers is the hermeneutic circle, a formal expression of circular thinking. The elements of the hermeneutic circle are experiences, wholes, contextualizations, parts, integrations, and back to experiences. The hermeneutic circle gives due consideration to the temporal aspects of human inquiry. Each generation of researchers discovers new bodies of knowledge that must be taken into consideration, so that there is a never-ending stream of new and continuous knowledge that must be integrated into the whole. Hermeneutic inquiry is thus holistic in nature and is an unending circle of knowledge creation.

> The hermeneutic circle merely reflects the way in which the structure of human understanding is dictated by the temporal nature of our experience. It is *because* information becomes available to us only serially that it must be incorporated piecemeal into the synthetic vision which illuminates the meaning of the object of comprehension. (Bontekoe, 1996, p. 4)

Music therapists who incorporated the principles from new physics, holism, phenomenology, and hermeneutics represented a logical progression into the revision of criteria for research that had a dramatic impact on music therapy research (Eagle, 1991; Sears, 1979). A new type of empiricism emerged from this dialogue, allowing consciousness to emerge as a researchable phenomenon for music therapists who practiced GIM and other methods that accepted the ineffable or unobservable character of some experiences in music.

Context Sensitivity. One of the principles of qualitative research is that each situation is unique, and there is no possibility of generalization from one setting to another. When the results of qualitative research are applied to other areas, it is because of an understanding of the case that was presented, and thus an ability to apply it to a similar setting. Because of this, qualitative researchers are very sensitive to the context in which the observations and research occur.

Wheeler (1999) applied this as she studied her experience of pleasure in working with children with multiple, severe disabilities. While she did not assume that her results were generalizable to other music therapists, she described her experiences thoroughly so that others who could relate to them might be able to apply them to their own work because of the similarities or things that they prompted them to think about.

Voice, Perspective, and Reflexivity. The qualitative researcher recognizes that the experiences being investigated are seen through the researcher's eyes and heard through the researcher's ears, and thus that they are shared in the researcher's voice. Through reflexivity, the researcher maintains an awareness of these issues and takes steps to present the research fairly and as reflecting the researcher's perspective. One of the ways that qualitative researchers own their research is by what may be called the *stance of the researcher* or a *self-hermeneutic,* in which the researcher shares who he or she is in relation to the research, including the motivation for the research, prior ideas about probable results, and other things that might affect his or her perspective on the research. It is thought that, by stating these aspects clearly, the researcher can work to keep them from unduly influencing the research.

Ruud (1998) proposes reflexivity, or science as metacritique, and emphasizes the connection between our values, interests, and norms, and how we experience reality. For Ruud, "Reflexivity means taking into consideration not only that our categories of observation are theoretically biased but also that they determine what we hear and how we perceive or interpret those sounds, which in turn creates a basis for our choice of methods" (p. 105). Stige (2002) has also spoken of the need for reflexivity in music therapy research. Reflexivity is clearly seen in his many works and can be best represented in the exposition of his premises in *Culture-Centered Music Therapy.* In a comprehensive discussion of history and culture, he develops his understanding of the position of music therapy in the history of ideas with well-nuanced philosophical overtones, characteristic of many European music therapy researchers. An early example of such reflexivity in the United States is Kenny's (1982) "Reflexive Synthesis," the last chapter in *The Mythic Artery: The Magic of Music Therapy,* in which she creates a short commentary bringing together historical, clinical, political, cultural, and poetic elements, as well as critical questions upon which to reflect. In this reflection, she speculates about the future of music therapy and society-at-large within this context. Another example is "The Dilemma of Uniqueness: An Essay on Consciousness and Qualities," in which Kenny (1996) reflects on her own theoretical ideas and poses critical questions about the paradoxes contained in these concepts.

Criteria for Evaluating Qualitative Research

The purpose of criteria is to establish credible standards for scholarly research. Implementation of criteria is often the subject of private interactions between scholars who submit articles to peer-reviewed journals and the reviewers themselves. Authors are required to make revisions based on whatever criteria the reviewers are using for standards of the publication. Sometimes criteria are subjective and nonexplicit, while at other times they are explicitly stated in guidelines for submission that are published in the back of journals or in reviewer report forms, seen only by the reviewers. Articles in peer-reviewed journals represent the expression of criteria in practice.

But debates about criteria are a matter of public record and are particularly interesting as research practice becomes increasingly nonhierarchical, giving researchers a range of choice of methods. Debates over criteria can be summarized in the question, How do we judge research as good or flawed?[4] Such debates are elaborate and sometimes dramatic. One school of thought, for example, calls itself the realists and claims that the other school of thought represents the antirealists. The terminology in these debates reminds us of the ethical and political realities of scholarly practice. As does all research, qualitative research must address the issues of power. Ideally, the application of criteria will help to

- Safeguard professional codes of ethics;
- Develop a scholarly foundation in knowledge and understanding;
- Bring clarity to the author's treatment of subject matter;
- Emphasize the importance of discursive practice;
- Underscore the critical role of scholarly discourse in positive social change;
- Remind us about the important connections between research and practice;
- Ultimately, inform better practice.

As the possibilities for diverse approaches expand and qualitative research becomes more and more prevalent in fields previously dominated by quantitative research, dialectical critiques are apparent both across and within paradigms (Engel & Kuzel, 1992). This diversity is often in opposition to the principle of *unity of science*, advocated by many scholars in the philosophy and theory of science. This principle assumes that natural and social sciences must have the same set of criteria for judging the quality of research.

Regarding the unity of science principle, social and behavioral researchers question the ability of the hard sciences to establish appropriate methodology and subsequent criteria for studying the human condition. They often site Whitehead's (1919) *fallacy of misplaced concreteness,* or mistaking the abstract for the concrete. They assert that the human condition is not conducive to algorithmic analyses, interpretations, or study, and therefore the criteria for judging the quality of research cannot be the same.

In spite of convincing arguments to the contrary, there continues to be a propensity to apply the criteria of the experimental method, such as reliability and validity, to qualitative research practice. Qualitative researchers respond to this dilemma by attempting to qualify specific meanings of such criteria within the context of qualitative research, as opposed to quantitative. A good example of this type of qualification is Smeijsters's (1997) "Reliability and Validity in Qualitative Single-Case Research."

Many qualitative researchers, however, claim that establishing criteria for qualitative research is antithetical to the philosophical underpinnings of qualitative research practice. They assert that the discovery of meanings would be too limited by sets of preordained criteria. Kvale (1995) discusses validity within postmodern conceptions of knowledge, and claims that it is a socially constructed construct that can only have meaning within specifically defined contexts. Garratt and Hodkinson (1998) insist that it would be illogical and pointless to attempt to predetermine a definitive set of criteria against which all qualitative research should be judged. They argue that criteria can only be located in the interaction between research findings and the critical reader of those findings, who could be reviewers or readers of journals and other public documents.

Smith (as cited in Engel & Kuzel, 1992) argued that criteria for judging the quality of work in various traditions needs to be particular to the approach and might be markedly different across approaches. Aldridge (2002) concurs, stating,

> I see evaluative criteria as local and context specific according to the politic of the relationships involved—an ecosystemic paradigm. Trying to generalize is laden with difficulty and while necessary (perhaps) for a journal, the end result will be that many of us will agree to differ. (2002, ¶1)

The *Nordic Journal of Music Therapy* has hosted a debate on criteria for evaluating music therapy qualitative research (http://www.hisf.no/njmt/forumqualartlist.html). This debate offers music therapists an opportunity to understand the arguments and positions on criteria, as applied to music therapy as well as the activities of applying criteria to journal submissions. Stige (2003) proposed a set of criteria for evaluating qualitative research, summarized in an acronym, EPICURE. Stige explains the acronym:

---

[4] Chapter 20 of this book, Evaluating Qualitative Music Therapy Research, focuses on this question in more detail.

E   Empirical solidity
P   Presentational quality
I   Interpretational sensitivity
C   Critical awareness (self-critique and social critique)
U   Usefulness (in relation to real world problems)
R   Relevance (for the development of the discipline)
E   Ethical trustworthiness (p. 6)

Stige would like to establish criteria for the *Nordic Journal of Music Therapy* that are descriptive enough to guide the research as well as create the important standards of accountability required for scholarly excellence. This discourse is ongoing.

Another example of an attempt to encourage rigor in qualitative research in music therapy is Bruscia's (1998) work on standards. After a survey of the music therapy literature, he proposed four main areas of standards and described relevant categories within each. They are methodological integrity (responsiveness [including appropriateness of method and flexibility of method], fidelity, completeness), interpersonal integrity (situatedness, clarity of voice, respectfulness), personal integrity (authenticity, caring), and aesthetic integrity (creativity, enlightenment, relevance, structural beauty, expressive beauty). Though Bruscia does not propose criteria, as such, these standards can easily be translated into specific criteria for music therapy. Bruscia's standards expand the general categories of trustworthiness and authenticity used in music therapy and other disciplines. They also resemble criteria suggested by other scholars outside of music therapy, such as Alexander (1987), who recommends coherence, expansiveness, interpretive insight, relevance, rhetorical force, beauty, and texture of argument.

The discussion of criteria continues and will only get more complex. Criteria in music therapy qualitative research are interpretive in nature. Music therapy qualitative researchers will position themselves in these debates and implement criteria based on their roles in the music therapy community. But a thorough understanding of how criteria function in our research endeavors, and how they influence the principles of qualitative research, is very useful for music therapists who intend to conduct ethical research.

References

Aigen, K. (1991). The roots of music therapy: Towards an indigenous research paradigm. (Doctoral Dissertation, New York University, 1990). *Dissertation Abstracts International, 52*(6), 1933A. (UMI No. DEY91-34717)

Aigen, K. (1993). The music therapist as qualitative researcher. *Music Therapy, 12*, 16–39.

Aigen, K. (1995a). An aesthetic foundation of clinical theory: An underlying basis of creative music therapy. In C. B. Kenny (Ed.), *Listening, playing, creating: Essays on the power of sound* (pp. 233–257). Albany, NY: State University of New York Press.

Aigen, K. (1995b). Principles of qualitative research. In B. L. Wheeler (Ed.), *Music therapy research: Quantitative and qualitative perspectives* (pp. 283–311). Gilsum, NH: Barcelona Publishers.

Aigen, K. (2002). *Playin' in the band: A qualitative study of popular music styles as clinical improvisation.* New York: Nordoff-Robbins Center for Music Therapy.

Aldridge, D. (2002, May 3). The politics of qualitative research criteria: A local solution within an ecosystemic ecology. Message posted to forum topic, General Criteria for the Evaluation of Qualitative Research Articles, *Forum: Nordic Journal of Music Therapy*, http://www.hisf.no/njmt/forumqualart_3.html

Alexander, J. C. (1987). The centrality of the classics. In A. Giddens & J. Turner (Eds.), *Social theory today* (pp. 11–57). Stanford, CA: Stanford University Press.

Amir, D. (1995). On sound, music, listening, and music therapy. In C. B. Kenny (Ed.), *Listening, playing, creating: Essays on the power of sound* (pp. 51–57). Albany, NY: State University of New York Press.

Belenky, M. F., Clinchy, B. M., Goldberger, N. R., & Tarule, J. M. (1986). *Women's ways of knowing: The development of self, voice, and mind.* New York: Basic Books.

Blacking, J. (1973). *How musical is man?* Seattle, WA: University of Washington Press.

Bontekoe, R. (1996). *Dimensions of the hermeneutic circle.* Atlantic Highlands, NJ: Humanities Press International.

Bonde, L. O. (2000). Metaphor and narrative in Guided Imagery and Music. *Journal of the Association for Music and Imagery, 7,* 59–76.

Bruscia, K. E. (1995a). Modes of consciousness in Guided Imagery and Music (GIM): A therapist's experience of the guiding process. In C. B. Kenny (Ed.), *Listening, playing, creating: Essays on the power of sound* (pp. 165–197). Albany, NY: State University of New York Press.

Bruscia, K. E. (1995b). The process of doing qualitative research: Part II: Procedural steps. In B. L. Wheeler (Ed.), *Music therapy research: Quantitative and qualitative perspectives* (pp. 401–427). Gilsum, NH: Barcelona Publishers.

Bruscia, K. E. (1998). Standards of integrity for qualitative music therapy research. *Journal of Music Therapy, 35,* 176–200.

Bruscia, K. E., interviewed by Stige, B. (2000). The nature of meaning in music therapy. *Nordic Journal of Music Therapy, 9,* 84–96.

Denzin, N. K., & Lincoln, Y. S. (2000). The discipline and practice of qualitative research. In N. K. Denzin & Y. S. Lincoln (Eds.), *Handbook of qualitative research* (2nd ed., pp. 1–28). Thousand Oaks, CA: Sage Publications.

Eagle, C. (1991). Steps to a theory of quantum therapy. *Music Therapy Perspectives, 9,* 56–60.

Edwards, J. (1999). Considering the paradigmatic frame: Social science research approaches relevant to research in music therapy. *The Arts in Psychotherapy, 26,* 73–80.

Elliott, D. J. (1991). Music as knowledge. *Journal of Aesthetic Education, 25,* 165–175.

Engel, J. D., & Kuzel, A. J. (1992). On the idea of what constitutes good qualitative inquiry. *Qualitative Health Research, 2,* 504–510.

Forinash, M. (1990). A phenomenology of music therapy with the terminally ill. (Doctoral Dissertation. New York: New York University). *Dissertation Abstracts International, 51* (09), 2915A. (University Microfilms No. DEY91-02617)

Forinash, M. (1992). A phenomenological analysis of Nordoff-Robbins approach to music therapy: The lived experience of clinical improvisation. *Music Therapy, 11,* 120–141.

Forinash, M., & Gonzalez, D. (1989). A phenomenological perspective of music therapy. *Music Therapy, 9,* 35–46.

Garratt, D., & Hodkinson, P (1998). Can there be criteria for selecting research criteria: A hermeneutical analysis of an inescapable dilemma. *Qualitative Inquiry, 4,* 515–539.

Garred, R. (2001, Nov.). The ontology of music in music therapy—A dialogical view. *Voices: A World Forum for Music Therapy.* Available at http://www.voices.no/mainissues/ Voices1(3) Garred.html

Gaston, E. T. (1968). *Music in therapy.* New York: Macmillan.

Geertz, C. (1973). *The interpretation of cultures.* London: Fontana Press.

Gilovitch, T. (1991). *How we know what isn't so: The fallibility of human reason in everyday life.* New York: Free Press

Goldstein, M. (1978). *How we know: Exploration of the scientific process.* New York: Plenum Press.

Kenny, C. (1982). *The mythic artery: The magic of music therapy.* Atascadero, CA: Ridgeview Publishing Co.

Kenny, C. (1983, May). *Phenomenological research: A promise for the healing arts.* Paper presented at the Canadian Association for Music Therapy Conference, Toronto, Ontario, Canada.

Kenny, C. (1985). Music: A whole systems approach. *Music Therapy, 5,* 3–11.

Kenny, C. (1987). The field of play: A theoretical study of music therapy process. *Dissertation Abstracts International, 48*(12), 3067A. (UMI No. DEV88-02367)

Kenny, C. B. (1989). *The field of play: A guide for the theory and practice of music therapy.* Atascadero, CA: Ridgeview Publishing Co.

Kenny, C. B. (1996). The dilemma of uniqueness: An essay on consciousness and qualities. *Nordic Journal of Music Therapy, 5,* 87–96.

Kuhn, T. (1962). *The structure of scientific revolutions.* Chicago: University of Chicago Press.

Kvale. S. (1995). The social construction of validity. *Qualitative Inquiry, 1*(1), 19–40.

Lakoff, G., & Johnson, M. (1999). *Philosophy in the flesh: The embodied mind and its challenge to Western thought.* New York: Basic Books.

Lincoln, Y. S., & Guba, E. G. (1985). *Naturalistic inquiry.* Newbury Park, CA: Sage Publications.

Nordoff, P., & Robbins, C. (1971). *Therapy in music for handicapped children*. New York: St. Martin's Press.

Nordoff, P., & Robbins, C. (1977). *Creative music therapy*. New York: John Day.

Noy, P. (1966). The psychodynamic meaning of music, Part I. *Journal of Music Therapy, 3,* 126–134.

Noy, P. (1967). The psychodynamic meaning of music, Parts II–V. *Journal of Music Therapy, 4,* 7–23, 45–51, 81–94, 117–125.

Patton, M. Q. (2002). *Qualitative research and evaluation methods* (3rd ed.). Thousand Oaks, CA: Sage Publications.

Polanyi, M. (1958). *Personal knowledge: Towards a post-critical philosophy*. New York: Harper and Row.

Runes, D. D. (Ed.). (1983). *Dictionary of philosophy*. New York: Littlefield, Adams, and Company.

Ruud, E. (1998). *Music therapy: Improvisation, communication, and culture*. Gilsum, NH: Barcelona Publishers.

Schmidt, J. A., & Eagle, C. (1982, June). *Some implications of new physics for music therapy*. Symposium on Music in the Life of Man at New York University, New York, NY.

Schwandt, T. A. (2001). *Dictionary of qualitative inquiry* (2nd ed.). Thousand Oaks, CA: Sage Publications.

Sears, W. (1979, November). Paper presented at symposium, *International Study Group: Theory of Music Therapy*. Dallas, TX: Southern Methodist University.

Smeijsters, H. (1997). *Multiple perspectives: A guide to qualitative research in music therapy*. Gilsum, NH: Barcelona Publishers.

Smeijsters, H. (2003). Forms of feeling and forms of perception: The fundamentals of analogy in music therapy. *Nordic Journal of Music Therapy, 12,* 71–85.

Smeijsters, H. (2005). *Sounding the self: Analogy in improvisational music therapy*. Gilsum, NH: Barcelona Publishers.

Stige, B. (2002). *Culture-centered music therapy*. Gilsum, NH: Barcelona Publishers.

Stige, B. (2003, May). *EPICURE—Proposed criteria for evaluation of qualitative research articles*. Paper presented at the International Pre-Conference Seminar on Qualitative Music Therapy Research, Bergen, Norway.

Tesch, R. (1990). *Qualitative research: Analysis types & software tools*. New York: The Falmer Press.

Wheeler, B. L. (1999). Experiencing pleasure in working with severely disabled children. *Journal of Music Therapy, 36,* 56–80.

Wheeler, B. L. (2002). Experiences and concerns of students during music therapy practica. *Journal of Music Therapy, 39,* 274–304.

Whitehead, A. N. (1919). *An enquiry concerning the principles of natural knowledge*. Cambridge: University Press.

Acknowledgments

The authors wish to thank Kenneth Bruscia and Jane Edwards for feedback on an earlier version of this chapter.

Chapter 6
Funding Music Therapy Research
Jane Edwards and Debra Burns

For those who have made attempts and for those yet to make attempts to apply for research monies, this chapter seeks to clarify and demystify some procedures in the writing and submission of research grant applications. The application procedure for grants available for project funding or funding new services are undertaken somewhat differently from research grant monies, and the reader is directed elsewhere for support and advice for these other types of grants. While it is hoped that experienced research grant writers might find parts of this chapter useful, the chapter has been prepared with the novice applicant in mind. It is essential that applicants inquire about funding requirements and procedures from individual granting agencies, as this chapter provides an overview of processes generic to many types of grants. Some of the specific examples and procedures described below are from the National Institutes of Health (NIH), which is a major federal funding agency in the United States, as many federal and private research funding bodies in the U.S. and in other countries use procedures modeled after, or similar to, the NIH.

General Information

One of the most critical steps in achieving grant funding is to apply. This commonsense dictum needs reiteration, as success only comes in the repeated attempt to submit the best possible research grant application having undergone the key steps of researching the funding body; designing the project within the parameters of the types of research acceptable by the funding body; and submitting a well developed, concise, and well justified research program. Some of the more experienced researchers in music therapy will be aware of the way researchers sometimes describe their research grant funding success in terms of number of successes and numbers of rejections in the following way: "I am 3 for 17." That is, novice applicants should be aware that usually researchers have a few grant successes among a large number of proposals. Success depends upon repeated application attempts along with ongoing refining of the topic to fit the funding body's requirements.

It is important to note that each country, each university, and in some cases states and counties can have different procedures and requirements. International or European grant funding applications can require the applicant to read a vast amount of information particularly with reference to eligibility and procedures for applying. It is important to use time well to read, prepare, and research before writing the specifics of the grant proposal. Some grants have an initial application and review period followed by a time for feedback from the reviewers during which the applicants might have to modify or further explain the project. It is important to be aware of whether or not this will happen in the procedures of the specific grant body; if it will, then it is crucial to be able to be contacted during the feedback period.

Having access to information from previously successful grant recipients, staff who are trained in developing research proposals, and the details of the funding body and what they have previously supported can be essential supports in maximizing the return for the effort of applying. It can be quite demoralizing to be rejected for a small oversight that could have been picked up in the refining process.[1]

Success rates vary depending on the size of the grant and other factors. In the United States, for example, NIH post-doctoral fellowship proposals average a 40 per cent success rate (http://grants2.nih.gov/training/index.htm), while larger research proposals have much lower success rates ranging from 10 to 30 percent, depending upon the institute and the size of appropriations to the NIH from the federal government (http://grants1.nih.gov/grants/award/awardtr.htm#r).

---

[1] While there are books in every university library or bookshop that can advise about grant funding, please take care to note that the information is up to date. In addition, some books do not distinguish between the skills needed to write a research proposal or a funded project. In the opinion of the authors, the best sources for grant information are the granting bodies, your university research office, and experienced research grant recipients.

Partly because of the low success rate and partly because of the large amount of work required in developing a submission, it can be daunting to undertake the process of applying for research funding. To some extent, it is to be expected that not all processes and procedures will be made explicit or as clear as possible by the granting bodies. Demands on funds are so high that requiring a certain effort before written submission ensures that applications are well considered and appropriately progressed and refined by the time they have been received. With experience, the application procedures become less overwhelming; however, in starting out each applicant must give adequate consideration to the resources needed to prepare and write the best application possible.

Getting Started

One of the first questions new researchers may want to ask themselves is why they want to apply for research funding. Establishing a funded research program or a research study offers many benefits and is an exciting, albeit sometimes frustrating, career choice. Obtaining research funding can provide paid time to pursue areas of high research interest and passion.[2]

Obtaining research funding can also provide extra funds to the institution where the grantee works. These facilities and administration costs are sometimes termed indirects or on-costs and are calculated as a proportion of the total research grant. Usually these add-ons are between 20 and 50 per cent of the total amount. These provide funds to the institution where the research is to be conducted. These funds are not used for direct support of the proposed research project, but provide additional revenue for the institution to pay back to the institution their administrative time in processing the application and giving resources such as a desk or office space for use in the project and for funding of the university research office. It is important to note whether the granting agency allows these indirects to be funded, and whether the agency caps these costs, for example, at a percentage of the total.

The second question many beginning researchers ask is where they can find research grants. The Community of Science web page (www.cos.com) is an extensive resource of both private and funding agencies whose main mission is to fund research projects inside and outside of the United States. Other resources for potential research funds are the local university library or university-based research office. The purpose of offices within universities that support academics in applying for research is to promote success in obtaining funding to support the institution's research mission. It is therefore never a waste of their time to help with simple or complex questions or requests to find granting bodies that may support particular projects. Staff in research offices might not be academic researchers, but they are well trained in how to apply for grants and often are working to ensure that any grants available are brought to the attention of staff through such means as research bulletins, research open days, grant writing seminars, and workshops. While accessing these supports takes time, there is considerable gain in taking the trouble to attend such seminars, even for seasoned grant writers, given that aspects of grant procedure might change. In addition, attendance at such events provides an opportunity to make yourself known to research staff in order that they keep you in mind when new grant funds are announced.

When researching granting bodies for project funds, it is important to ensure that the proposed project falls within the guidelines of the funding body. In particular, making a distinction between proposals that are primarily research and proposals that are primarily for service delivery (even when there may be an important evaluation component) will help you to target your application to the most appropriate funding source. Research proposals must be submitted to research grant agencies, while program or project submissions must be made to other funding bodies.[3] When undertaking research into a funding source, it is important to identify from the outset whether the proposal has an orientation suitable to the granting guidelines.

---

[2] Some university promotion procedures only recognize research grants, not project funding, whereas others, in the authors' experience, recognize achievements across both types.

[3] In the U.S., the Foundation Directory Online, http://www.fconline.fdncenter.org/, is useful to look for general project funding. Many Australian universities have the SPIN database, which provides broad funding opportunities, including project funding.

Applicants should not be put off by the use of the term *science* or *scientific research* in the titles of some grant awards.[4] Read the granting guidelines carefully, as many grants use *science* as a descriptor for knowledge or research. It is important to check carefully whether the arts, health, or qualitative research come under the remit of the grant agency.

Private research funds are available from organizations such as the Leukemia Society, the American Cancer Society, and the Susan B. Komen Foundation. These agencies are focused on cancer research, but there are other foundations, such as the Alzheimer's Foundation, that provide research funds focusing on different diseases. The American Music Therapy Association gives the Arthur Flagler Fultz research award annually. The New Zealand Society for Music Therapy offers research awards through the McKenzie Music Therapy Hospice funds. These funds provide support for research that promotes the use of music therapy in palliative care (www.musictherapy.org.nz/grants.html).

. In the United States, public research funds are available through federal organizations such as the National Science Foundation, the Department of Defense, the Department of Education, and the National Institutes of Health (www.nih.gov). Canada also has a similar federal agency dedicated to research, the Canadian Institutes of Health Research (http://www.cihr-irsc.gc.ca). Most countries have similar agencies for research funding. Within Europe, the European Science Foundation is a starting point for seeking collaborative research funds (http://www.esf.org). A further source is the International Foundation for Music Research (http://www.music-research.org/Grants/guidelines.html) whose goal is to support scientific research to determine the relationship between music and physical and emotional wellness, with particular attention to the elderly population and the impact of music making on youth who are at risk.

Familiarization with the mission of these agencies is the key to seeking out the most relevant funding source. It cannot be emphasized enough how much time will be saved if you apply to the most suitable funding source for your type of research study.

National Institutes of Health

The National Institutes of Health (NIH) comprises 19 separate institutes, 8 centers, and 12 to 15 offices, part of the U.S. Department of Health and Human Services. The mission of the NIH is to discover new knowledge that leads to improved health for all people (http://www.nih.gov/about). To that end, the NIH offers both training awards to increase the number of scientists and research grant awards to support the discovery of new knowledge. The Institutes, Centers, and Offices of the NIH support the overall mission of NIH by focusing on specific disease (e.g., National Cancer Institute) or body systems (e.g., National Heart, Lung, and Blood Institute). While these institutes and centers provide similar research funding mechanisms, the reader is encouraged to examine the relevant mission statements and also to contact the corresponding program officers to seek guidance regarding potential submissions.

Training awards can offer excellent opportunities to begin a funded program of research. Typically, pre-doctoral awards (F series) are designed for students enrolled in doctoral programs. These funds pay a monthly stipend plus a small award for research costs. Post-doctoral awards are available for those who have completed doctoral work but do not have an academic appointment. They generally include both a research plan and a training plan, which may or may not include coursework. The proposals are evaluated on the applicant's training plan, research plan, and, sometimes more importantly, mentor. Another type of training award, a Career development award (K series), is for researchers who have an academic appointment.

There are awards within the NIH that are specifically for research proposals. These grants (R series) vary in duration and funding. For instance, the R03 is a small grant program that can be up to 2 years long with budget limits from $50,000 to $75,000 depending on the institute or center. The R21 Development/Exploratory grant mechanism is not available in all institutes or centers, but can be worth up to $150,000 per year for 2 years. The R03 and R21 are pilot study mechanisms that do not require pilot data before funding.

The traditional grant source, the R01, requires pilot data to accompany the submission before a proposal will be considered for funding. This mechanism is offered by most of the larger

---

[4] The European Science Foundation, http://www.esf.org/, has five areas of funding support, and these include Humanities and Social Sciences.

centers and institutes. The R01 maximum award is $500,000 a year for up to 5 years. Substantial preliminary work and pilot data are necessary to have a chance for success with this grant.

There are four mechanisms for proposing a research project within the NIH, (a) the Program Announcement (PA), (b) the Request for Applications (RFA), (c) the Request for Proposals (RFP), and (d) the Investigator-Initiated proposal. The researcher will need to have a research proposal started by the time a PA or RFA is released.

The NIH publishes *The Guide*, which announces the availability of funds and corresponding mechanisms (PA, RFP, or RFA). The Program Announcement indicates any increased research priority via particular funding mechanisms for specific areas of science as well as the standard dates for receipt of submissions. Request for Applications is a section devoted to defined areas for which one or more NIH institutes have set aside funds for awarding grants; it has one receipt date common to all institutes. The turnaround time for the RFAs is typically very quick (approximately 1 month), therefore, unless you have prior knowledge of an Institute's priorities, for example, through checking the consensus panel reports, it may be impossible to answer an RFA prior to the deadline. The Request for Proposals solicits proposals for a contract and also has one receipt date. Researchers can have *The Guide* e-mailed to them; it is published weekly and is released on Friday (http://grants1.nih.gov/grants/guide/index.html#desc).

Once the grant is submitted to the Center for Scientific Review (CSR) at the NIH, it goes through two series of reviews. The CSR assigns applications to a review group. After the review, the application is sent on to the assigned institute or center program. The Institute's Advisory Council then conducts another scientific review. The review process involves scrutiny of the skills of the proposed researcher, as part of the review process is to ascertain the perceived ability of the applicant to carry out the research. Therefore, the principal investigator (PI) must make sure to represent him- or herself in a positive light and give adequate information on previous research experience to instill confidence in the reviewers.

Proposals are assigned a priority score based on scientific merit. Scores range from 100 to 500 with lower scores indicating a more favorable review. The Advisory Councils make funding decisions based on priority scores or priority score percentiles. There are four other outcomes that are possible. The grant may be:

1. Rejected due to administrative problems such as wrong font size, human subject concerns, key elements not included;
2. Not recommended for further consideration, where there is considered to be inadequate protection against risks;
3. Unscored, where the grant is considered not competitive;
4. Deferred, will be reviewed at another time, meaning that additional information is needed from the applicant (http://grants1.nih.gov/grants/peer/peer.htm).

If the review is unscored, the PI will receive feedback from the reviewers. This can then help the PI determine (with assistance from his or her program officer) if the grant should be resubmitted. If the grant is scored, the PI will receive the score and then, 6 to 8 weeks later, the feedback forms. Again, the PI should contact the program officer of the review group to discuss resubmission. Generally, a grant can be resubmitted twice (depending on funding mechanism). It is very unlikely that a grant is funded on the first try, so plan on resubmitting!

Steps in Achieving a Successful Result

After determining the motivation for pursuing funding and determining possible funding agencies, the researcher must set a timeline for submitting the proposal. Typically, funded researchers allow 6 to 9 months to write a research proposal. Allowing adequate time for writing and feedback helps create a concise, well thought-out proposal. This timeline also allows the researcher to identify personal and research strengths and weaknesses. Remember that, once a grant is submitted, the review process and award notification can take an additional 9 months. So from research idea conception to the results of the first review can take up to 18 months.

While the NIH procedures are outlined as an example above, each funding body has its own process for accepting applications. Some require that a statement of intention to write a larger proposal be submitted, and so they ask for a bare outline. This is then either promoted to full submission or rejected at outline stage. It can be quite challenging to explain music therapy, describe the proposed project, and sell the method of the investigation in just a few hundred words. Some research funding bodies require that a full proposal be submitted, including detailed justified budget with goals and objectives. More detailed applications might also require that you include a large amount of information about your organization. In spite of the fact that it might be a well-known hospital or highly regarded university, it may be necessary to submit the philosophy of the organization, audited accounts for the last financial year,[5] and the targets and completions in areas relevant to the project.

Research grant funding is highly competitive. Preparation, research, and refinement of every aspect of the submitted proposal are key steps toward a successful outcome. A well-prepared application, however, only guarantees you will be in the running of the race, it will not guarantee a successful outcome. In order to ensure a well-prepared application, the investigator must keep a few key ideas of grant writing in mind:

1. Read all instructions carefully;
2. Tell a story;
3. Use pictures if appropriate;
4. Leave clear spaces on the page rather than cluttering up the proposal with word-filled pages.

The key step before writing the budget is to undertake research on the granting body guidelines for funding. Some bodies do not allow funding for certain types of capital equipment such as computers or musical instruments, others do not allow for administrative salaries. Some universities require that a proportion of any grant received be given over to central funding of the university, while some granting bodies do not allow any of their funding to be used for this purpose.[6]

Many granting agencies publish lists of previously funded programs, and sometimes these include details of the project undertaken. While this can be an excellent guide as to what is regularly funded, if possible also try to obtain copies of previously successful applications from those who submitted them. It is recommended that you be especially persistent in pursuing these if previous recipients are colleagues from the university where you work. If this is not possible, try to talk to previous recipients and gain an idea of the strengths of their proposal, and why, perhaps even anecdotally, they believe it was funded at that particular time.

When writing, make sure that the first page of the proposal is the best page in the entire grant. It is important to catch the reviewers' attention to keep them reading. Imagine a very tired reviewer sitting up late at night with a huge pile of research applications in front of them. Make sure your first piece of paper encourages them to read more. The page must be written in a concise, persuasive manner. Ensure that your writing does not rely on assumptions about what the reader should know, and avoid therapeutic or musical jargon. Until the music therapy profession experiences increased funding, it will be rare to have a music therapist review your grant proposal, so it is important that you show your draft grant proposal to non-music therapists to ensure that what you have prepared is readable as well as persuasive to someone who knows little or perhaps even nothing about music therapy.

As the proposal is being worked up and put together, it is important to clarify any questions you have with the granting agency. Most calls for submissions include a contact telephone number. While the contact person might not be a particularly senior person in the organization, he or she will usually ask someone more senior the question and pass on the reply to you, or in some cases will put you through to the person most experienced with your area of inquiry.

Getting the Grant

Parents have described what it is like when they take their baby home from the hospital—they take a look at the baby and each other and say, "What do we do now?" Similarities exist with the experience of gaining grant funding initially. After the euphoria, elation, and smug feeling of

---

[5] Sometimes these accounts are available in the organization's annual report that can be attached to the application document. If not, the accounts department should be able to provide a letter saying the accounts are in order and can be viewed on request.

[6] Different universities or research programs may have various requirements but usually a university would require that a certain percentage of the grant be given back to the central administration for the costs of managing and administering the research. Sometimes this requirement can be as high as 50 per cent.

success recede, it is important to review what was proposed in the project and how this might need modification in actually undertaking the project. Some granting agencies are absolutely strict about expenditure with separate categories for capital and salary expenses. Others give a lump sum and ask for a report on conclusion but are not overly concerned if computers cost less than anticipated and instead money is used to pay research assistants for additional hours. It is essential to understand how the funding body keeps track of expenditures, and how they expect the grant reporting to be done. It might be important to keep in touch with the grants office from the university where you work or the grants office from the funding body to ensure that you and your staff keep track of reporting dates. If any problems are encountered in undertaking the project, these should be relayed in a timely manner to the funding agency.

Dealing with Rejection

By all means be cross and disappointed. Let the paranoid fantasies run wild, give yourself time to sulk for at least a few days—then be prepared to take a look at the proposal again. What were the reasons given for refusal? What was the specific feedback, if any? How can you incorporate that feedback into refining your next proposal? The biggest deep breath you will have to take, however, is if someone else in your institution was awarded such a grant. Asking them for a copy of the grant proposal, or if they are reluctant, a discussion with them about the successful application may give you a few gems for the next time you apply.

Be aware that many granting agencies allow for a proposal to be submitted multiple times. In the United States, for example, the National Institutes of Health's policy on resubmission includes two resubmissions prior to major changes in the grant. The only reason not to resubmit a grant would be if the reviews were so negative that the program officer suggests a different idea or a substantial rewrite of the materials.

Summary and Top Tips

1. Research the funding body before applying.
2. Contact people who have previously received grants from the funding body even if outside your own area to seek advice or tips.
3. Write a convincing budget that is neither padded nor too sparse.
4. Have experienced grant writers check your application for consistency and coherence.
5. Anticipate announcement dates for grants and be prepared.
6. If in a university or research hospital, develop good working relations with the research officer or relevant designate. If outside a research center, develop links with a research center, whether in music therapy or a related field.
7. Build up a portfolio of smaller grant success as a means to convince larger grant authorities that you are a worthwhile investment who gets work in on time and publishes the outcomes the research efforts.
8. The R word is, of course, research, but R is also for rejection. If you are rejected, you are in good company the world over. If you are serious about being a funded researcher you will have to deal with rejection regularly. Remember R also stands for revise, refine, and resubmit.

Part II

The Research Process

Chapter 7
Research Topics and Questions in Music Therapy
Kenneth E. Bruscia

The purpose of this chapter is to provide an overview of the vast array of topics and questions that can be pursued in music therapy research. Three broad topical areas—discipline, profession, and foundational—are identified, and research interests appropriate for quantitative and qualitative research are presented. Prototypical questions are then identified for each type of research and topical area.

Broad Topical Areas

Most music therapy research can be categorized into three broad topical areas. *Discipline research* includes all those studies that examine the myriad facets of music therapy practice. As such, it deals with clinical topics such as assessment, treatment, and evaluation. *Profession research* includes all those studies that deal with music therapists and what they do collectively to establish and promote music therapy as a healthcare service. It deals with psychological, socioeconomic, political, legal, and educational aspects of music therapy as an organized profession. *Foundational research* includes all those studies that relate partially but not completely to the discipline or profession of music therapy. It deals with topics that emanate from related fields (for example, psychology, music, medicine, education) but have important implications for music therapy.

Discipline Research Topics

Research on the discipline of music therapy deals with three sub-areas: assessment, treatment, and evaluation.

> *Assessment research* studies are those aimed at gaining insights about individual clients or client populations served by music therapy—their clinical conditions and problems, their musical characteristics, their personal resources and experiences, and their therapeutic needs.
>
> *Treatment research* focuses on the clinical interventions used in music therapy, or the methods used by music therapists to induce change in clients. Included are topics such as the functions of music in therapy, the specific role of the various musical elements, how clients respond to different music interventions, the therapist's contribution to the therapeutic process, the way a particular method or technique is utilized with specific populations or problems, the effects of environmental conditions or interpersonal settings on the therapeutic process, the client-therapist relationship, the client-music relationship, the dynamics of therapy, and so forth.
>
> *Evaluation research* focuses on the resulting change in the client. Its main concern is demonstrating the outcomes or effects of music therapy. These outcomes may be musical or nonmusical changes made by the client as a result of music therapy. Essentially, evaluation research poses two basic questions: Were the methods used in music therapy effective? and, Did the client and his or her condition improve as result of these methods? Of course, evaluation studies can deal with a wide range of related topics such as: the sequence of changes made by clients during music therapy, a client's experience of his or her own change, and products resulting from therapy that reflect such changes (for example, songs or improvisations created by the client).

Profession Research Topics

Research on the profession covers a wide spectrum of interrelated topics, all dealing with music therapists as a group and the various contexts in which they work. Possible topics might be:

Employment practices: Investigating where music therapists work; trends in employment opportunities; job titles, salaries, and benefits; reimbursement; job duties and tasks in various settings; qualification requirements for employment; how music therapy services fit into various healthcare systems and institutions; policies and procedures for the provision of music therapy services; role of a music therapy administrator; accountability issues in music therapy.

Music therapists: Studying personality profiles of professionals and students; attitudes towards various matters related to clinical practice, employment, and so forth; values and orientations; motivation and burnout; professional self-esteem and identity issues; demographic information; and existing levels of education and competence.

Professional education and training: Examining academic requirements and curricula in music therapy at various levels; field training and internship requirements; methods of teaching and supervising and their effectiveness.

Professional standards: Studying standards for clinical practice in music therapy; rules governing the ethical conduct of music therapists; ethical issues and problems in practice, research, and theory; competency standards and procedural requirements for becoming registered or certified in the field; relevance of these standards and requirements to job analyses; accreditation and approval standards for academic and clinical training programs.

Legislation and public relations: Looking at how laws and regulations on the city, state, and federal levels impact music therapy; licensing issues; sociopolitical and contexts of music therapy practice; cultural factors in the advancement of music therapy; how music therapy relates to other disciplines and professions; cooperative ventures with other professionals or organizations.

History and culture: Including studies of historical accounts of the discipline or profession of music therapy; organizational history; biographies of music therapists; socioeconomic and cultural aspects of music therapy practice; meta-analyses and descriptions of the research literature.

Foundational Research Topics

Because music therapy is so interdisciplinary in nature, there are many areas of research that are of primary interest to another field, yet overlap or relate to the discipline and profession of music therapy. Such research can be considered foundational because the findings often provide empirical or theoretical support for practices, principles, or constructs used in music therapy, but, strictly speaking, were not originally focused on music therapy matters. Foundational research can pertain to the discipline or the profession of music therapy.

Foundational discipline research could include studies on music that do not pertain to health issues, clinical populations, or therapy. Such studies instead belong under the categories of psychology, physiology, sociology, or anthropology of music, acoustics or psychoacoustics, music learning, music education, and so forth, all of which can be regarded as musical foundations for music therapy. Foundational discipline research might also include studies on health-related issues, clinical populations, or therapy that do not pertain to music. This includes studies on the problems and needs of client populations without reference to music and studies on various forms of therapy that do not employ music. Such studies instead belong to health-related fields and provide important clinical foundations for music therapy.

Foundational profession research includes studies on health care or therapy and the socioeconomic, historical, political, or cultural factors that influence them. It could also include studies on other healthcare professions such as standards of practice, certification and licensing, education and training requirements, legislative agendas, and so forth. Finally, it might include studies on other healthcare professionals such as their personal and professional characteristics.

Quantitative Versus Qualitative Research Interests

Given the fundamental differences in philosophy and method between quantitative and qualitative research, it is not surprising that there are also fundamental differences in the topics and questions of interest.

Quantitative researchers seek to discover generalizable truths. They typically ask closed-ended, yes/no questions, aimed at determining whether something is true or false. These questions are pursued objectively by examining how operationally defined variables relate and interact with one another, within a defined population and under controlled conditions. Two types of variables are of prime interest:

Independent variables are those that are controlled or manipulated by the researcher in order to discover what effects they may produce. Usually included in this category are stimulus variables and organismic variables. Stimulus variables are those pertaining to inputs, tasks, treatments, or conditions that impinge on the subject and elicit a response. Organismic or subject variables are those pertaining to persons, including any physical, genetic, emotional, behavioral, social characteristic or trait that may affect how subjects respond to the stimulus variables.

Dependent variables are those that provide measures of the effects or reactions to the independent variables (that is, stimulus or organismic variables). Included in this category are response variables or measures of any output or reaction that subjects make to a stimulus.

In contrast to specifically defined variables in a controlled or laboratory setting, qualitative researchers are interested primarily in the lived world of human beings and how that world is subjectively constituted, construed, and made meaningful by individuals and groups. The specific focus may be human action, interaction, experience, language, art works, or combinations thereof, as these phenomena appear in individuals, groups, communities, or cultures. Given these interests, qualitative researchers tend to ask very open-ended research questions, which are unanswerable by a yes/no or true/false determination. Instead, qualitative researchers seek to describe, interpret, or critique the phenomenon being studied in a holistic way, emphasizing subjective differences, idiosyncrasies, complexities, and interdependencies.

Because of these differences in research interest, the types of questions posed in quantitative and qualitative research are quite different. What follows, then, are separate presentations of prototypical questions for quantitative and for qualitative research.

Quantitative Research Questions

While there are myriad questions that can be posed in quantitative research, most of them fall into one of the following prototypes.

Incidence Questions

Incidence questions are probably the most basic type posed in quantitative research. Essentially, they are concerned with describing a variable in terms of frequency distributions (ungrouped or grouped frequencies, proportions, percentages), central tendencies (mean, mode, and median), and variability (range, variance, standard deviation). The researcher may be asking how often a phenomenon occurs, how prevalent a certain characteristic is, how the frequencies of different phenomena or characteristics compare, what the average value or score is, or how much the values or scores differ from one another.

Examples of incidence questions in research on the discipline include:

- Assessment: How do individuals with IQs 55–70 score on the Doe Test of Rhythmic Abilities? What are the range, mean, and standard deviation?

- Treatment: When improvising with children, how often do improvisational therapists use empathic techniques such as reflecting, imitating, synchronizing? What is the rate per minute for any of these techniques among improvisational therapists trained in the Nordoff-Robbins approach?
- Evaluation: What percentage of clients reports a decrease in depression (Beck Depression Inventory) after 12 sessions of Guided Imagery and Music (GIM)? What is the average decrease in scores on the inventory?

Examples of incidence questions in research on the profession include: What percentage of music therapists pursues graduate study, and, of these, what percentages pursue degrees in music, music education, music therapy, or another field? What is the frequency of burnout among employed music therapists, as measured by the Maslach Burnout Inventory?

Examples of incidence questions in foundational research include: What is the incidence of cross-rhythms and syncopations in songs preferred by adolescents? Or, what percentage of musicians experiences performance anxiety, and, of these, what percentage seeks any form of treatment?

Measurement Questions

Measurement questions are concerned with finding the most accurate ways to evaluate and measure any type of variable, such as a stimulus, subject, task, treatment, or response variable. There are two main issues, reliability and validity. *Reliability* is the extent to which the measure or test yields the same results consistently. This is usually tested by comparing scores on matching versions or sections of the test. *Validity* is the extent to which the measure or test actually measures the variable in question. This is usually tested by comparing scores on the task or test with scores on other accepted or established measures of the same variable.

Examples of measurement questions on the discipline are:

- Assessment: How reliable are scores obtained on the Doe Test of Rhythmic Abilities when individuals with IQs of 55–70 are given two matched versions? Are the scores on the two versions related, or are they significantly different? How reliable are ratings of four music therapists on performance sections of the Doe test? How do scores on the Doe test compare with scores on other rhythmic tests? To what extent do scores on one test predict scores on the other?
- Treatment: Is rate per minute a reliable measure for determining the frequency of empathic techniques used in improvisational therapy? Is it a valid measure of therapist empathy, and, if so, is it musical or emotional empathy?
- Evaluation: How reliable are therapist ratings of the Client Improvement Scale in Music Therapy? Is this scale a valid measure of client progress in therapy or the effectiveness of therapy, as compared to other established tests or rating scales?

Examples of measurement questions on profession topics include: How reliable are ratings of clinical competence by trained professional observers, when based on two randomly selected 15-minute segments of a videotaped music therapy session? What is the test-retest reliability of the Certification Board for Music Therapists (CBMT) examination? Is the CBMT examination a valid measure of clinical competence when compare to professional ratings?

Foundational measurement questions might be: What is the most reliable measure of rhythmic complexity? What is a reliable and valid measure of performance anxiety? What are the most reliable measures of musical aptitude and achievement for children?

Correlation Questions

Correlation questions deal with the extent to which one variable fluctuates in relation to another variable or how closely two or more variables are interrelated. Three levels of complexity can be found in these types of questions: (a) Is change in one variable related to change in another (as in simple correlation)?, (b) Can changes in one variable be used to predict the amount and direction of change in another (as in regression)?, and (c) To what extent are several variables related (as in intercorrelations or multiple correlations)?

Examples of correlation questions on the discipline are:

- Assessment: Is there a relation between rhythmic ability and receptive vocabulary in individuals with IQs 55–70, as measured by the Doe Test and the Peabody Picture Vocabulary Test? To what extent do scores on one test predict scores on the other? Are there any inter-correlations among IQ, rhythmic ability, and receptive vocabulary?
- Treatment: Is therapist empathy related to the duration of client participation in improvisational therapy sessions? Is high therapist empathy predictive of longer client participation in each session? Can any relationships be found among number of sessions, frequency of empathic techniques, and duration of client participation?
- Evaluation: Do therapist ratings on the Client Improvement Scale relate to client satisfaction in music therapy? Is therapist rating of client improvement predictive of client satisfaction? Can any relationships be found among therapist personality, therapist ratings of client improvement, and client satisfaction?

Examples of correlation questions on profession topics include: To what extent are scores on the CBMT examination related to burnout scores on the Maslach Inventory? Do low scores on the CBMT examination predict high scores on the Maslach? Are there relationships among scores on CBMT examination, burnout, and job satisfaction?

Foundational correlation questions might be: Is adolescent preference for popular songs related to level of rhythmic complexity? Are scores on a performance anxiety scale related to scores on a self-esteem test? Are scores on the Quality of Life Scale predictive of scores on the Beck Depression Inventory?

Factor Questions

Factor questions are similar to those in correlation. They are concerned with determining what the constituent factors are of a particular stimulus, subject, task, treatment, or response variable, and the relative amount of influence of each variable.

Examples of factor questions on the discipline are:

- Assessment: To what extent can the performance of individuals with IQs 55–70 on the Doe test be attributed to Factors X, Y, or Z? What are these factors?
- Treatment: To what extent can the therapist's use of empathic techniques be attributed to Factors X, Y, or Z? What are these factors?
- Evaluation: To what extent can changes in depression resulting from 12 music therapy sessions be attributed to Factors X, Y, or Z? What are these factors?

Examples of factor questions on profession topics include: To what extent is longevity in the field attributable to Factors X, Y, or Z? What are these factors?

Foundational factor questions might be: What factors are implicated in rhythmic complexity measures? What factors determine prognosis for successful treatment of performance anxiety? What personality factors are predictive of depression?

Development Questions

Development questions are concerned with changes that take place as a function of time (or age) and the sequence and timing of these changes. Typical questions might be: To what extent does a stimulus, subject, or response variable develop or change as a function of time or age? What are the milestones, trends, or stages that can be found in such changes, and how are they timed? What similarities and differences can be found between Variables X and Y at two or more different stages of growth or development?

Examples of development questions on the discipline are:

- Assessment: Do individuals with IQs 55–70 obtain the same scores on the Doe test after 1, 2, or 3 years of time when given no formal training?
- Treatment: Do therapists use more empathic techniques as therapy progresses? Do therapists use more empathic techniques as they gain clinical experience?

- Evaluation: Does the level of client satisfaction with therapy increase over time after therapy has been terminated? Do improvements made in therapy increase with time after therapy has been terminated?

Examples of development questions on profession topics include: Does job satisfaction among music therapists increase with time working in the field? Do attitudes toward the effectiveness of music therapy change over time among music therapists?

Foundational development questions might be: How does age affect song preference? Does experience performing affect performance anxiety more than age?

Static Comparison Questions

Static comparison questions focus on whether two or more stimuli, groups, or response patterns are different along one or more variables before or without any experimental manipulation by the researcher. The comparisons are static because they examine the variables as they exist in the present, with no attempt to induce change through treatment of any kind.

Examples of static comparison questions on the discipline are:

- Assessment: Do individuals with higher IQs score differently on the Doe test than those with lower IQs? Do younger individuals score differently than older individuals with the same IQ?
- Treatment: Do improvisational therapists use empathic techniques more often (higher rate per minute) than redirective techniques (introducing change, modulating, differentiating)? Do improvisational therapists use empathic techniques more often with children than with adults?
- Evaluation: Do clients who score high on the client satisfaction survey exhibit greater changes in depression than those who score lower on satisfaction.

Examples of static comparison questions on profession topics include: Are the personality profiles of music therapists, as measured by the Myers-Briggs, different from those of occupational therapists? If so, how are they different? Are the personality profiles of music therapists with high burnout scores different from those with low burnout scores?

Foundational static comparison questions might be: Are songs preferred by adolescents more rhythmically complex than songs preferred by adults? Do dancers and musicians exhibit the same degree of performance anxiety?

Treatment Questions

Treatment questions focus on before-after comparisons in which the researcher has made an experimental manipulation of some kind. The basic question is: Does Treatment X produce change Y? Methodologically, this question can be answered in at least two ways, by comparing before-after conditions in one group of subjects or by comparing them in two groups, one that receives the treatment and one that receives a different or no treatment. The method affects the nature of the question. For example, in a one-group study, a typical question might be: Does a particular group of children with emotional difficulties exhibit fewer outbursts following 6 weeks of improvisational music therapy? In a two-group study (with one treatment and one no-treatment group), the question would be: Does a group of children with emotional difficulties who receive improvisational music therapy exhibit a larger decrease in outbursts than a matched group of children who do not receive it, or who receive an alternate treatment?

Examples of treatment questions on the discipline are:

- Assessment: What abreactions do psychotic adults exhibit in music therapy groups? Does the effectiveness of therapy vary according to age or gender? Does the effectiveness of music therapy vary according to diagnosis? Are adults with depression more responsive to receptive music therapy than those with anxiety?
- Treatment: Is music therapy effective in decreasing depression? What are the effects of song writing on self-esteem?
- Evaluation: Which of three methods of music therapy is the most effective in reducing depression? Is music therapy more effective than verbal therapy in building self-esteem in adolescents?

Examples of treatment questions on profession topics include: What effects do three different methods of clinical supervision have on intern self-confidence?

Foundational treatment questions might be: What effects do values clarification exercises have on song preferences among adolescents? What is the effect of cognitive therapy on performance anxiety?

Interaction Questions

Interaction questions deal with how variables interact in their effects. This may involve how subject, stimulus, treatment, or response variables interact with one another. For example, an interaction study might look at how two independent subject variables (high IQ, low IQ) interact with two dependent variables (memory and attention). Because this study looks at how two sets of scores interact with another two sets, it is called a 2 x 2 interaction study. Interaction studies can also be much more complex. For example, the study could examine how two subject variables (male-female) and two stimulus variables (easy-difficult) interact in their effect on two dependent or response variables (rhythmic memory, rhythmic motor skill). This would be a 2 x 2 x 2 interaction study.

Interaction questions on the discipline usually combine assessment, treatment, and evaluation topics. For example:

- Assessment: Does the effectiveness of three methods of music therapy vary according to whether the client has or does not have psychosis?
- Treatment: Does the effectiveness of active versus receptive music therapy vary according to therapist variables, such as personality, competence?
- Evaluation: Does the effectiveness of therapy vary according to client diagnosis and therapist variables?

Examples of interaction questions on profession topics include: When provided three methods of supervision, do interns with high self-confidence meet criterion measures for clinical competence more quickly than those with low self-confidence? If so, which method is the most effective with each group?

Foundational interaction questions might be: Does the effect of values clarification exercises on song preferences vary according to age and musical experience in adolescents? Does the effectiveness of cognitive versus psychodynamic therapy on performance anxiety vary according to age and performance and experience?

Qualitative Research Questions

Qualitative research questions have two primary components, a focus and a purpose. A *focus* is the phenomenon of interest, or what it is that the researcher wants to study. In practical terms, the focus reveals the kinds of data that the researcher wants to gather and analyze. A *purpose* is a statement about the kinds or levels of insight that the researcher wants to gain about the phenomenon. That is, the purpose describes what the researcher hopes to discover from studying the targeted data. The foci and purposes of qualitative research are discussed in detail below.

It should be kept in mind that, while every qualitative research study should begin with a question that specifies both the focus and purpose of the study, in reality, the focus, purpose, and research questions will continually evolve and change as the study progresses.

Qualitative Foci

The main foci for qualitative research are: events, actions, and interactions; experiences; written and spoken language; art works; and persons (individuals, groups, communities, or cultures).[1]

Events, Actions, and Interactions. Research on events, actions, or interactions focuses on anything observable that happens in-vivo within a defined, real-world context. This

---

[1] Artifacts—objects such as a chair or guitar that are related in some way to the other data sources but do not fall under the categories of language and art—may also be a focus, but because they have been researched so infrequently, they have been omitted from this chapter for the sake of brevity.

may include behaviors, actions, interactions, incidents, or happenings, as well as the occasions, environments, conditions, or circumstances of their occurrence.

In discipline research, the focus would be on what clients or therapists do in their work together. The core question is, What happens in music therapy? How do clients behave and interact with the therapist—musically, verbally, or nonverbally? Similarly, how does the therapist behave and interact with the client? Which actions lead to which results? How do circumstances and contexts affect client or therapist behavior? How do client and therapist find or make meaning in what they do? What theory of therapy might explain what happened? What do their actions mean or signify to each other? What is most meaningful about what took place?

In profession research, the focus would be on what music therapists do when interacting with other professionals. For example: What do music therapists do in the association? How do they interact with their supervisors or bosses? What do music therapists do at professional conferences? How do music therapists relate to communities and cultures?

In foundational research, a focus might be how patients with cancer verbally interact in support groups, or how children go about exploring a musical instrument they do not know how to play.

Experiences. Research on experience focuses on how a person apprehends, perceives, feels, and thinks about something. As such, it is concerned with covert or unobservable processes that occur in relation to an event, material object, or person. It bears mentioning here that an experience is considered to be more than an opinion, belief, or intellectual analysis. An experience encompasses many different layers and facets of the person, including body reactions and emotions as well as thoughts and perceptions. An experience also has both spontaneous and reflective components. The spontaneous components include all those things that take place from moment-to-moment while the person is having the experience; the reflective components include reactions, thoughts, and analyses that arise whenever the person makes observations about him- or herself or the experience, either during or after the experience itself. The difference is between actually experiencing what is happening with a free-floating consciousness, and observing what we are experiencing by reflecting upon this free-floating consciousness on another level. Thus, there is a direct spontaneous level of experiencing and a meta-level of reflecting on the experience.

In discipline research, the focus would be on what clients or therapists experience about each other and their work together. For example: What do clients experience when improvising alone versus when improvising with the therapist? What do therapists experience when listening to clients improvising versus improvising with them? Or, how do clients describe their experiences in a particular method of therapy, such as GIM?

In profession research, the focus is on what music therapists experience in their encounters with the profession and other professionals. For example: What is the experience of presenting at a conference? What is the experiencing of preparing an article for submission to a journal? What is the experience of being supervised? What is the experience of justifying music therapy to legislators?

In foundational research, an experience focus might be on how patients with cancer experienced their own diagnosis, or on how children experience music lessons.

Written and Spoken Language. Research on written and spoken language focuses on how people communicate and act upon one another through verbal means. The focus may be a speech or monologue, a dialogue or interview, written answers to a questionnaire, historical documents, medical charts, letters, diaries, technical writing, books, articles, literary prose, poetry, plays, and so forth. The research may be concerned with what was said or written, how it was said or written, and what the intent, meaning, and outcome might be.

In discipline research, the focus is on what clients and therapists say about their work together, how they communicate verbally, what linguistic structures or rules they apply, how they act upon one another through language, and what their utterances or statements might mean or signify (either intentionally or unintentionally). In profession research, the types of questions would be the same, except the focus would be on what, how, when, and why music therapists communicate through oral and written language when interacting with other music therapists, the association, colleagues in other fields, supervisors, educators, employers, and legislators, and so forth. In foundational research, the focus might be on how patients with cancer talk about their illness to doctors versus friends, or how children talk to other children about music.

Art Works. Research on art works focuses on the materials that result from participation in music, dance, or visual art activities. For example, in music the focus would be on compositions or improvisations; in dance, on choreographies or performances; in art, on paintings, drawings, or sculptures. These kinds of art works have been differentiated from prose, poetry, and drama (under spoken and written language) because they always require the researcher to describe, analyze, and interpret nonverbal forms of human expression, that is, those that depend upon the expressive or symbolic use of design, color, sound, gesture, and movement. Granted, the visual arts, music, and dance sometimes include verbal materials (as in songs, operas, ballets, picture books); however, when this is the case, the researcher still has to grapple with the problems of understanding the nonverbal components of the art form as well as the verbal ones.

In discipline research, the focus is on the music created or experienced by the client or therapist. For example: What characterizes the improvisations of a client? What are the myriad relationships between the therapist's and client's music in a certain case? What are the rhythmic characteristics of client improvisations on fear? What are the primary musical characteristics of a recorded music program used in GIM? In profession research, the focus is on the music created or experienced by music therapists in professional contexts such as jam sessions at conferences, performing jobs, supervision, and so forth. In foundational research, the focus might be on the art works of patients with cancer or the improvisations of 4-year-old children.

Persons. Research on persons focuses on understanding an individual, group, community, or culture within a defined setting or context—by studying how they constitute and find meaning through their actions, interactions, experiences, language, and art works. Here the focus shifts from understanding what is done, experienced, or communicated as an end in itself to understanding who the person or group is as doers, experiencers, or communicators.

In discipline research on persons, the focus would be on a particular client or group of clients or a particular therapist or group of therapists within a particular setting or context. The question is, What can we understand about the clients or therapists when we study what they do in music therapy and how they find meaning in it? In profession research, the focus would be on music therapists, individually or collectively, and what they do within professional circles and the communities within which they work, and how they find meaning in it. In foundational research, the focus might be on one patient with cancer, one child, or one musician or dancer.

It should be noted that research studies that focus on a particular individual or group have traditionally been referred to as case studies; however, technically speaking, a case in qualitative research may be any single example or instance of either an event, action, interaction, linguistic experience, material, or person.

Qualitative Purposes

The following are levels of understanding (or qualitative research purposes) that I have delineated, based on my own notions about music therapy research and on the qualitative research literature in other fields, particularly the work of Tesch (1990). Note that as these levels progress, they move from description to increasingly deeper levels of interpretation, from bracketing out the researcher's subjectivity to relying upon it almost entirely, and from data-bound conclusions to data-inspired constructions about the phenomenon.

Holistic Description. The researcher attempts to provide a composite picture of all findings of the study with a minimum of interpretation. A primary goal is to present how the phenomenon manifests itself—as comprehensively as possible—including its content (all manifestations, examples, and variations of the phenomenon), its structure (part-whole relationships, boundaries), and, where relevant, its process (the sequences in which it unfolds). Procedurally, this explication involves segmenting, labeling, grouping, and serializing the data; no attempts are made to infer what may be latent in the data or to search for rules, operational principles, causal relationships, and so forth. A key concept in holistic description is that the researcher compares the various sets of data gathered, not in a deductive, reductive, inductive, or interpretive way, but in an additive way—to capture as much as possible what belongs to the phenomenon. A holistic description gives the what, when, where, and how, without the whys. It is concerned with discerning what constitutes the phenomenon. The following are examples of holistic description questions dealing with a discipline topic: improvisational music therapy with clients who have psychiatric problems.

Events/Actions/Interactions: What happens in improvisational music therapy? What do clients with psychiatric problems and their therapists do in their session together?

Experiences: What do clients with psychiatric problems experience when they improvise music with their therapist?

Language: How do clients with psychiatric problems talk about what they do in improvisational music therapy? How do they verbalize the process or their own experience of it?

Art Works: What are the musical characteristics of improvisations created by clients with psychiatric problems? What will an analysis of their musical structure reveal?

Persons: What do the actions, reported experiences, and improvised music of a client with psychiatric problems reveal about his or her work in music therapy? How does improvisational music therapy unfold in two different ethnic groups?

Definition of Essence. The researcher seeks to identify those essential or defining properties that give the phenomenon its basic meaning, character, structure, or identity, and, in that process, to discover which of its elements must be minimally present for the phenomenon to exist and be defined as such.

Two procedures are commonly used to identify the essence of a phenomenon. In the first, various sets of data are compared to identify what is unique or different about each set, and what remains the same across all sets despite all the variations. The dual process of determining what is alike and different can be likened to the cognitive operation that Piaget called *conservation.*

In the second procedure, the researcher systematically imagines what the phenomenon would be like if each feature or element that has been observed is eliminated from it. If the phenomenon remains the same without the feature, it is not regarded as essential; when the phenomenon changes significantly without the feature, it is regarded as essential.

Note that the purpose and process of identifying essences is reductive instead of additive, as in holistic description. Here the myriad sets of what, when, where, and how in holistic description are reduced to the bare essentials required to define the phenomenon. In holistic description, the question is what constitutes the phenomenon in its entirety; in identification of essence, the question is what defines the phenomenon. The following are examples of essence questions, dealing with a discipline topic, Nordoff-Robbins Music Therapy (NRMT).

Events/Actions/Interactions: Are there certain therapist behaviors (musical or verbal) that are indigenous to NRMT?

Experiences: What defines the adult client's experience of NRMT?

Language: Are there common metaphors in the ways that NR therapists describe the progress of nonverbal clients?

Art Works: What are the essential musical devices that NR therapists utilize in their first improvisations with child clients?

Persons: Can an essential theme be discerned in the actions, interactions, and experiences of an adult client with cancer who has worked in NRMT for over 2 years? Is there a conceptual theme that characterizes the NR therapists in one center as compared to another?

Analysis. The researcher seeks to identify regularities, recurrent themes, relationships, and patterns embedded in the data, and, based on these, to offer meaningful explanations of the phenomenon. The prime questions are: In what ways is the phenomenon meaningfully configured, for example as part-whole and part-part relationships? And, what is intrinsically meaningful about the way the phenomenon is constituted?

The analysis process involves looking closer at what is already manifest about the phenomenon in order to detect what is latent but nevertheless detectable. The researcher does not go beyond what is overt or manifest but rather delves deeper into it to discover embedded content, structure, or process. The inferences made in analysis are always specific to the data at hand; no generalizations are made beyond the data, and no laws or theories are put forth about like phenomena. The following are examples of analysis questions on a profession topic—internet interactions of music therapists.

> *Events/Actions/Interactions:* Are there patterns of internet interaction among subscribers to the music therapy listserv? Are there sequential or temporal patterns in individual participation?
>
> *Experiences:* What recurrent experiences do subscribers report when interacting with others on the listserv? Are there any antecedent events to these experiences?
>
> *Language:* Are there patterns in how subscribers from different clinical orientations talk about their work?
>
> *Art Works:* What kind of songs would subscribers create to describe the emotions exchanged on the listserv forum?
>
> *Persons:* What are the range of interactions and experiences of a single subscriber? How do the forum interactions of European and American music therapists compare?

Theory Building. The researcher hypothesizes or speculates about the phenomenon in order to develop a schematic conceptualization of some kind. To build a theory is to formulate constructs, principles, laws, or conceptual schemes that explain the phenomenon in some way. The prime questions are: What meaning might these data have for the phenomenon in general? What is meaningful about the phenomenon in a generalizable way?

Theory building goes beyond analysis in two ways. First, it involves making hypotheses that extend beyond the given data. The data are thus regarded as representations of other sets and contexts and are used as a springboard for making statements of broader application.

Second, theory building involves higher-level conceptual schemes than analysis. Whereas analysis requires looking closer at the data, theory building requires stepping back and looking at the data from a broader and somewhat more distant perspective. The following are examples of theory building questions dealing with a discipline topic—what characterizes effective music therapy.

> *Events/Actions/Interactions:* What patterns of action, events, and interactions characterize sessions identified by therapists as effective work with clients? Can a general theory be developed on how these patterns lead to effective music therapy?
>
> *Experiences:* What are common features of therapist experiences of being effective with clients? What are common features of experiences of being ineffective with clients? Can a theory be developed of what constitutes the experience of being effective as a music therapist?
>
> *Language:* When describing experiences of being effective and ineffective, how do music therapists talk about their clients? What attitudes underlie the way therapists talk about clients in both conditions? Can a theory be developed of therapist attitudes that lead to effective music therapy?
>
> *Art Works:* What are the qualities and structures of the music used or created in effective and ineffective sessions? Can a theory be developed on what aspects of the music characterize effective music therapy practice?
>
> *Persons:* What patterns of action/interaction, experience, language, and music characterize the work of Mary Priestley, a leading pioneer in music therapy? Can a theory of music therapy be developed from an analysis of her work?

Interpretation. The researcher uses his or her own tacit understanding of the phenomenon, often in conjunction with relevant theories or previous interpretations by others, to derive or create meaning out of the data. Here the prime questions are: What does the phenomenon mean to the researcher after considering the data gathered and what is already known about this phenomenon? What meaning does the researcher propose about the phenomenon?

In this kind of research, the interpretation belongs to the researcher, or it is made in reference to the interpretations of others. That is, the researcher can attach meaning to the data, based either on his or her own personal experiences with or theories about the phenomenon or on various theories or interpretations already offered by others, including the participants themselves. In either case, to interpret is to *construe* or try out various *constructs* on the data until differences in meaning given to the phenomenon can be reconciled and a more inclusive understanding of its meaning can be offered.

Interpretation is different from theory building in two ways. A theory is a template that emerges from the data and is then tested and generalized to the entire phenomenon under study. An interpretation is an external template (either the researcher's or another person's theory) which is placed over the data in order to give an interpretation of its meaning. On the other hand, theory building usually involves creating or inventing constructs or conceptual schemes, whereas interpretation involves applying or adapting existing ones. The following are examples of interpretation questions on a profession topic—supervision.

Events/Actions/Interactions: Upon viewing the same videos of supervision sessions, how does the supervisee interpret what happened in the session, and how does the supervisor interpret the same session? How does another therapist interpret what happened in the session? Can the researcher compare these versions of the session to achieve an understanding of the supervisor's intention and style along with the supervisee's style of responding to supervision?

Experiences: Based on interviews of both supervisors and supervisees on what constitutes good and poor supervision, can the research identify the essential features of good supervision?

Language: How do supervisors talk to supervisees? How can the language used by the supervisor suggest an effort to dominate or oppress the supervisee? How can the supervisor's language imply gender or racial bias?

Art Works: When asked to do improvisations portraying oneself and the supervisor, what can be learned from the music about the supervisee's perception of the supervisor and the nature of the supervisory relationship?

Persons: In analyzing videos of supervisory sessions with one intern and interviews on each session, what can be discerned about what supervision means to the supervisor?

Artistic Re-Creation. The researcher gives his or her own rendering of the data or re-creates the phenomenon under investigation, based on an artistic interpretation of the data. More specifically, the researcher may: create a story or narrative that depicts how the phenomenon under investigation unfolds, based upon his or her interpretation of the data, or create an art work (poem, song, play, dance, improvisation, painting, etc.) that captures what the data meant to the researcher. Artistic re-creation is always based on the researcher's interpretations, but it goes beyond interpretative research by using artistic symbols and media to present the results. The following are examples of artistic re-creation questions dealing with a discipline topic—music therapy with children with autism.

Events/Actions/Interactions: What story could illustrate the events in a typical session with a child with autism, and what would the story disclose about my understanding of the child's therapeutic needs?

Experiences: Upon drawing mandalas to depict the relationship between each client with autism and his or her therapist, what will the drawings reveal about my understanding of their relationship? Is there a common theme?

Language: How can I use poetry to describe the way music therapists talk to children with autism, and what does the poetry reveal about how therapists think about their clients?

Art Works: How can I create improvisations that depict how children with autism improvise? How might these improvisations help therapists?

Persons: Can I present a song that depicts my understanding of the personality of each child with autism? What will the song reveal about my understanding of them?

Criticism. The researcher evaluates the data, phenomenon, or research study itself according to a particular value system, such as personal opinion or expertise, aesthetic standards, research criteria, logic, clinical efficacy, ethics, cultural or linguistic bias, politics, and so forth. The best example of this kind of research is called *critical theory.* The following are examples of criticism questions dealing with a profession topic—music therapy journals.

Events/Actions/Interactions: What is the nature of interactions between authors submitting an article for review and the editors of the journal, and what do these interactions disclose about the disparity of power between the parties? What ethical issues can be identified in the treatment procedures reported in research articles?

Experiences: How do experiences compare between male and female authors whose articles have been rejected, and what might these experiences reveal about gender biases within the profession?

Language: How does the language used in an American music therapy journal reflect philosophical biases of a capitalistic economy?

Art Works: What is the aesthetic quality of audio examples accompanying the journal?

Persons: What have been the contributions of the chief editor to the journal?

Self-Reflection. The researcher examines his or her own actions, interactions, experiences, language, or artworks, and then compares them to those of others. The purpose is to develop a broad but deeply personal understanding of the phenomenon that expands human consciousness with regard to it. This may involve studying one's own past encounters with the phenomenon or actively engaging the phenomenon to gain more current data. There are many variations of this type of research: It may involve the researcher being the only participant, serving as one of the participants (and either including or excluding the data), or being a co-participant with others. The following are examples of self-reflection questions dealing with a discipline topic—GIM.

Events/Actions/Interactions: How do I time my interventions when guiding clients? How do other guides time their interventions? How much time do I need between interventions when I am a GIM client? How much time do others need? What does the concept of *pacing* mean in GIM therapy?

Experiences: Are there any commonalities among the various *out-of-body experiences* that I have had as a GIM client? How do others describe their out-of-body experiences? What does it mean to be out of one's body when guiding male and female clients?

Language: What language rules do I follow when guiding a client? Are these rules followed by other guides? What are we seeking to do through the way that we word our guiding interventions? Are these intentions in the best interests of our clients?

Art Works: What do I learn about the process of GIM therapy if I draw mandalas after each session portraying how the client, the music, and I related to one another? What do I learn about myself, the client, and the music when I draw mandalas portraying how we interact in a typical session? What can mandala experts reveal to me about these drawings?

Persons: What do I learn about a GIM program from a music-focused and an imagery-focused listening in both alert and altered states of consciousness? What do I learn from others who are trained in these listening techniques? What can we, as a group, say about the nature of the musical and imaginal experiences that are possible with this program?

Conclusion

When considering the wide range of topics in the discipline, profession, and research, and the myriad kinds of questions typically posed in quantitative and qualitative research, it is clear that the possibilities for research in music therapy are endless. This chapter has provided only a few of those possibilities. It is hoped that readers will go beyond the prototypical questions presented here as well as the examples of research under each topical category to formulate and develop their own questions.

Reference

Tesch, R. (1990). *Qualitative research: Analysis types & software tools*. New York: The Falmer Press.

Chapter 8
Developing a Topic
Barbara L. Wheeler

The process of developing a topic frequently begins with a general area of interest and is refined through successive steps until it is focused on a specific question. The process clarifies many aspects of doing the research and leads naturally into designing the study, as discussed in Chapters 10 and 11, Designing Quantitative Research and Designing Qualitative Research, respectively. The process of developing a topic involves asking questions, reading, writing, and reflecting.

Identify a Broad Area of Interest

Every research study begins with a researcher's idea or a topic in which the researcher is interested. This idea is usually a question—about how something occurs, why it occurs, whether it occurs.

The first step in developing the topic, then, is to know what this idea is. It is usually helpful to write it down. At this point, it may be quite vague, such as "I wonder what I can do in music therapy practicum sessions to improve my students' learning?" or "I wonder how students feel about the music therapy clinical work that they did as part of their training?"

Once the question is written, the researcher can work with it until it becomes clearer. In the first question above, the researcher might wonder if a particular technique, say giving students immediate feedback during sessions, could be helpful. In the other question, which came from some research that I did (Wheeler, 2002), I began to realize that it was the students' experience of the clinical work in which I was interested.

The topic for a research study generally begins with a broad area in which the researcher is interested. This may have come from personal experience, reading, or questions that have arisen while doing clinical work. Although beginning researchers sometimes feel that they do not have any ideas or that every possible area which could be researched has already been studied, most people can come up with ideas if they think of their experiences or things they have read that interest them. Ely says:[1]

> In one sense, however, selecting an area or topic for study is already an answer to one essential question: "What topic interests or excites me as being worthy of study?" or "What do I want to contribute to others?" or "What do I feel I'd like to give myself to in the next year(s) of research work?" (Ely, Anzul, Friedman, Garner, & Steinmetz, 1991, p. 29)

If the research topic is of interest, you will probably find doing the study to be very stimulating. On the other hand, if you study an area in which you have little interest, the research may well become a chore rather than a pleasure. This is particularly important since, due to the complexity of the research process, even the most interesting research projects may at times become laborious!

At this point, the researcher should begin to think of whether the topic can be investigated most fruitfully through quantitative or qualitative means, or whether historical or some other type of research might be most appropriate. If the question has to do with whether something is effective or what is more effective, it is likely that the researcher is heading toward a quantitative study. On the other hand, if the question has to do with perceptions of a phenomenon or wanting to understand people's experience of something, it is likely to become a qualitative study. Similarly, a question having to do with the history of something would lead to a historical study. The question in which the researcher is interested will dictate the research approach that will be taken. It is important to be clear on this at this point as the assumptions

---

[1] Ely is writing about selecting a topic for qualitative research, but the comment is relevant for any type of research.

and steps to be taken for each type of research are different—the methodologies are based upon different epistemologies.[2]

Review the Literature

While reviewing the literature is covered in Chapter 9, Reviewing the Literature, it is important to mention it here also. Reviewing the literature provides the researcher with information about what others have learned about the topic and places it in the context of what others in the field are thinking and doing. This may include a theoretical or research context and a practical context.

In reviewing the literature, researchers will generally first read about the broad topic selected. From this reading, what is known and what is not known about the area should become clear. Unanswered questions will arise. Some will be questions that other writers have asked; others will occur to the researcher while thinking about the reading. It is a time for reading and reflecting, then writing a gradually more focused problem statement. The reading, reflecting, and writing generally occur in several cycles. The final result is that the research becomes focused enough to write a statement of the problem, reflecting an unanswered question or questions and specifying the focus of the study.[3] Even after this is done, additional review of the literature may lead to revisions and refinements of the focus and questions.

Formulate the Research Problem

In the next stage, the research will move from the broad area of interest to a more focused statement of the problem. Kumar (1996) says,

> The formulation of a research problem is the first and most important step of the research process. It is like the identification of a destination before undertaking a journey. As in the absence of a destination, it is impossible to identify the shortest—or indeed any—route, in the absence of a clear research problem, a clear and economical plan is impossible. (p. 35)

The research problem might also be called the "need for the study" (Creswell, 1998, p. 94).

The problem that the research seeks to answer should determine the approach that is to be taken in studying the problem. While some researchers choose the type of approach before stating their problem, researchers are encouraged to choose a problem and focus a question, then determine the type of study that will answer this question. Bruscia has suggested a number of questions appropriate for quantitative and a number of questions appropriate for qualitative research in Chapter 7, Research Topics and Questions in Music Therapy.

The two questions from above that deal with students' clinical training are from the music therapy literature and will be used in this chapter to illustrate the process of developing a topic. One leads naturally to a quantitative study, while the other leads to a qualitative study. Both studies focus on music therapy students' clinical experience. "The Use of an Auditory Device to Transmit Feedback to Student Therapists" by Charles Furman, Mary Adamek, and Amelia Furman (1992) is a quantitative study and answers a typically quantitative question about the effectiveness of this device. The other study, "Experiences and Concerns of Students During Music Therapy Practica" (Wheeler, 2002), looks at students' experiences and is thus a typical qualitative research topic.

The steps to follow in developing a topic will be presented separately for quantitative and qualitative research. There are some fundamental differences in the way the quantitative and qualitative research are approached and, although they may sometimes be more or less similar than is suggested here, this division should highlight the differences in the process.

---

[2] Epistemology is discussed in several chapters of this book. See Chapter 3, Philosophy and Theory of Science, for one such discussion.

[3] It should be noted that some approaches to qualitative research discourage researchers from reviewing the literature early in the study, believing that it is important that the focus of the research emerge from the research rather than being imposed by the literature or an outside theoretical framework.

Quantitative Research

Quantitative research follows a series of steps that are quite clear and are spelled out in many textbooks. Although they seem clear, do not be deceived—developing a topic in quantitative research can be difficult and the process can meander. It is presented here as it will eventually turn out, but be aware that this is not always such a straightforward process.

The Problem and Questions

A number of the initial steps in developing the topic for the research study help to focus the research and are essential at this stage. The order in which they are listed here is not always the order in which they are done. Indeed, some of the steps may not be needed in every situation. Although it may not be necessary to follow every step, the content of each must be covered in some form.

State the Problem and Research Question. The problem is exactly what it sounds like: the problem that the study addresses. A problem statement should state the questions that are to be investigated in the study, not what will be done.

In the study about the auditory device through which feedback can be given, the problem would be that there is normally a gap in timing between the therapist-in-training emitting a behavior and the time that he or she receives feedback about that behavior. The authors state, "Whether feedback is delivered through a live or a videotaped session, a time gap usually exists between the emission of teacher/therapist behavior and the feedback about that behavior" (Furman et al., 1992, p. 42).

The problem statement then leads to the research question. Kerlinger (1986) suggests three criteria that should be met: (a) It expresses a relation between two or more variables, (b) it is stated clearly in question form, and (c) it implies possibilities of empirical testing (pp. 16–17).[4]

Furman et al. (1992) state that the purpose of their study was "to evaluate the effects of an auditory device, similar to those worn by newscasters, to transmit feedback to student therapists during actual music therapy sessions" (p. 42). Their review of literature indicated that immediate feedback led to improvements in performance in other areas, so it is clear that they expect positive effects with the device. Their research question could thus be stated as, "Does the use of an auditory device to transmit feedback to student therapists during music therapy sessions. . . improve performance?" or "Does an auditory device to transmit feedback to student therapists during music therapy sessions. . . improve scores on the Standley (1991) Group Activity Leadership Skills Checklist?"

Develop Subordinate Questions. The researcher will normally have subordinate questions or problems as well as a main question. These subquestions may be formulated before or after the main question. Many aspects of the study, including the independent and dependent variables, the hypotheses, and the design, are contained in them. Although subordinate questions may not be spelled out in an article and may not always be formally devised by researchers, their use aids in focusing the research question. They are frequently detailed in theses and dissertations. Before determining the subordinate questions, the researcher must decide what the dependent variables are, and this is related to the literature review. At this point, the researcher has also determined the design. In other words, the subordinate questions reflect the design and the operational measures of the variables. All of these are aspects of designing a study and thus discussed in Chapter 10, Designing Quantitative Research.

Furman et al. (1992) used the Standley Group Activity Leadership Skills Checklist as their dependent measure. This test allows calculation of subscores that then become the outlines of the subordinate questions. Subordinate questions in the Furman et al. study are:

1. Does the use of an auditory device to transmit feedback to student therapists during music therapy sessions improve personal skills (such as voice quality and eye contact)?

---

[4] Kerlinger suggests these three criteria for a good problem statement, but, as used here, they actually address the research question.

2. Does the use of an auditory device to transmit feedback to student therapists during music therapy sessions improve general skills (such as preparation and implementation)?
3. Does the use of an auditory device to transmit feedback to student therapists during music therapy sessions improve music skills (such as note accuracy and cueing)?
4. Does the use of an auditory device to transmit feedback to student therapists during music therapy sessions improve client responses (such as on-task and enjoyment)?

Formulate Hypotheses. Researchers who will do an experimental study or (in some cases) an applied behavior analysis now formulate hypotheses. These usually follow the subordinate questions, with each subordinate question being addressed by a hypothesis. Research hypotheses, although more formal, are similar to those that we use every day to explain things that occur and to predict ways of changing them. They are predictions of what will occur, and they help to focus the research. Hypotheses can be stated with varying amounts of detail.

A hypothesis states the effect that one expects the independent variable(s) to have on the dependent variable(s) and is often stated in a form suggesting that X (independent variable) will have an effect (or no effect) on Y (dependent variable). Borg and Gall (1989) suggest four criteria of a good hypothesis: (a) It states an expected relationship between two or more variables; (b) it is based on either theory or evidence; (c) it is testable; and (d) it is as brief as possible, consistent with clarity (pp. 68–69).

A research hypothesis is appropriately used when the literature or the researcher's experience indicate that there will be a difference between two or more groups. The difference may be in a predicted direction (that one group will score higher or lower than the other), labeled a directional hypothesis, or an unpredicted direction (that there will be a difference but no statement as to the direction of the difference), labeled a nondirectional hypothesis. A null hypothesis is used largely for statistical purposes and predicts that no difference will occur. If a difference is found, the null hypothesis is rejected, and we assume that there is probably a real (not occurring by chance) difference between the groups. Although one use of the null hypothesis is for statistical purposes, it is also appropriately used when there is no indication from the literature or from the researcher's experience that a difference will occur.

The hypothesis or hypotheses are based directly on the research questions and subordinate questions asked above. While many researchers specify their hypotheses, the hypothesis is not always formally stated in a research study. Opinions differ in the psychological research literature about the use and usefulness of hypotheses (Wilkinson, 1999).

Furman et al. (1992) do not specify hypotheses. Since it is clear that they expect students to improve with use of the feedback device, a directional hypotheses could be stated: It is hypothesized that scores on the Standley Group Activity Leadership Skills Checklist will improve for student therapists who make use of an auditory device to receive feedback during music therapy sessions, compared with students who do not receive the feedback. A nondirectional hypothesis would be stated: It is hypothesized that scores on the Standley Group Activity Leadership Skills Checklist will be different for student therapists who make use of an auditory device to receive feedback during music therapy sessions than for students who do not receive the feedback. A null hypothesis would be stated: It is hypothesized that there will be no difference between scores on the Standley Group Activity Leadership Skills Checklist for student therapists who make use of an auditory device to receive feedback during music therapy sessions and students who do not receive the feedback.

The hypotheses could also be broken down into the subordinate questions with a separate hypothesis for each. Stated as a directional hypothesis, an example (based on the first hypothesis) would be: It is hypothesized that personal skills scores on the Standley Group Activity Leadership Skills Checklist will improve for student therapists who make use of an auditory device to receive feedback during music therapy sessions, compared with students who do not receive the feedback.

Definitions, Assumptions, and Delimitations

Definitions, assumptions, and delimitations are the next part of developing the topic. They are normally stated in the introductory material, perhaps along with the statement of the problem or the research questions.

Define Terms.[5] All terms being used should be defined. Clearly, the investigator has begun defining these terms earlier and utilized the definitions in establishing the questions, including subordinate questions. At this point, however, the definitions should be stated precisely. They may be taken from a dictionary or from the literature reviewed in preparing the study. Definitions serve to clarify the phenomenon under investigation and allow us to communicate with one another in an unambiguous manner (McGuigan, 1968).

One type of definition is an operational definition, which outlines a construct in observable terms. McGuigan (1968) says: "An operational definition is one that indicates that a certain phenomenon exists and does so by specifying precisely how (and preferably in what units) the phenomenon is measured" (p. 27). An operational definition is often stated as part of the method but may be stated earlier.

In a study that made use of several genres of music, the researchers (Gfeller, Christ, Knutson, Witt, & Mehr, 2003) operationally defined popular music as "music heard on radio stations that play predominately Top 40 Hits of a time period" (pp. 88).

Sometimes an operational definition is a verbal specification of exactly what behaviors will be considered examples of the construct. An example is a study of the effect of contingent background music on two inappropriate bus behaviors, fighting and being out of seat (McCarty, McElfresh, Rice, & Wilson, 1978). *Fighting* was operationally defined as "hitting, kicking, pulling hair, spitting, calling names, using profane language, and pulling on the clothes of another person on the bus. Any one or a combination of these behaviors was considered as fighting" (p. 152). And *being out-of-seat* was operationally defined as "standing up, sitting on knees, climbing over seats, and body parts protruding from the windows. Any one or a combination of these behaviors was considered as being out-of-seat" (p. 152).

In another example of operational definitions by specifying behaviors, Groene (2001) provided the following response definitions (only some of which are listed here) in a study of the responses of people with dementia to different presentation and accompaniment styles of music:

1. Singing: The percentage of participants singing the song presented at any time during the song, evident from movement of the lips of the mouth. . . .
2. Attention before: After the song title is announced, the number of participants facing the therapist with eye contact or head in the direction of the therapist, ready to sing, not head down or sleeping.
3. Leaving before: After the song title is announced, the number of participants who were present at the beginning of the session but have now left the group. Does not include doctor's appointments or the like.
4. Reading the lyrics: The number of participants joining the therapist in reading the lyrics before the song begins.
5. Nods before: After the song is announced, the number of participants nodding their heads (a form of affirmation). (pp. 40–41)

Another type of operational definition is performance on a test or other measure. In a review of test instruments used by authors in the *Journal of Music Therapy*, Gregory (2000) found that half of the experimental studies used a test instrument, including researcher-constructed tests, unpublished tests, and published tests, and that 40% of these were published tests. Although she did not determine how the tests were used, it can be assumed that many of these were used to measure dependent variables. This analysis found versions of Spielberger's State Trait Anxiety Inventory to be used more than any other test. Examples of the use of the anxiety inventory (Spielberger State Anxiety Inventory, see Spielberger, 1983) to measure state anxiety are found in research into the effects of several types of music and relaxation versus relaxing in silence (Strauser, 1997) and of subject-selected versus experimenter-chosen music on

---

[5] Portions of this section are adapted from Chapter 11 in the first edition of this book.

state anxiety and other variables (Thaut & Davis, 1993). In each of these cases, state anxiety is measured with this test, thus making the test scores the operational definition of state anxiety.

Both the independent and dependent variables require operational definitions. The operational definition of the independent variable details the areas to be manipulated or otherwise tested. One of the purposes of operationally defining the independent variable is so that the study can be *replicated*, or repeated as it was done originally. Results that can be replicated are less likely to have been due to chance. Another reason to operationally define procedures is so that they are clear enough to be applied to clinical work.

Operational definitions of independent variables in the music therapy research literature generally describe the procedures followed. An example is the list of what was done at each session provided by Hanser and Thompson (1994), who refer the reader to another article (Hanser, 1990) for details of the procedures followed. This is similar to what frequently occurs with theses and dissertations, where the researcher may put a complete *protocol* of procedures in the appendix. In articles, some researchers add a note that readers who are interested in complete procedures may write for them, while other investigators describe procedures in the article itself. As an example, Cofrancesco (1985) outlines in considerable detail the exact music therapy intervention procedures followed in her study with patients who had had strokes.

Some authors provide less detail, taking into account the variation of procedures that needs to occur in many clinical settings, even while trying to make procedures consistent for research purposes. An example of this is Hilliard's (2003) description of music therapy with patients in hospice care, in which he provides a general description of the music therapy that was provided, saying:

> Music therapists treated a variety of clinical needs of their subjects during the study and utilized a myriad of techniques. While needs and interventions varied, some themes emerged. Among these, most music therapists utilized one or more of the following music therapy techniques: song choice, music-prompted reminiscence, singing, live music listening, lyric analysis, instrument playing, song parody, singing with accompaniment using the iso-principle, planning of funerals or memorial services, song gifts, and music-assisted supportive counseling. (pp. 122–123)

As you read and evaluate examples of operational definitions of independent variables, it will be helpful to determine for yourself how much detail is necessary to understand what was done while still being realistic given the nature of clinical procedures.[6]

An operational definition of the dependent variable specifies what will be observed or how the effects of the manipulation of the independent variable will be measured. The out-of-seat bus behaviors (McCarty et al., 1978); the use of the State Anxiety Inventory (Strauser, 1997; Thaut & Davis, 1993); and the descriptions of behaviors of people with dementia (Groene, 2001) cited earlier are examples of operationally defined dependent variables.

It is important in the Furman et al. (1992) study to clarify the feedback that was given and the way that it was given. The authors say initially that the auditory feedback device is "similar to those worn by newscasters" (p. 42), and later that the instructor feedback was "delivered to the student therapists by way of an earpiece attached to a transmitter (Realistic No. 21-404, Two-Way Audionic Communication System), which was concealed under the student's clothing. The feedback consisted of approving verbal reinforcement (R+) for specific behaviors or general encouragement for session progress, directions for immediate action, and verbal disapproval" (p. 43). Because they use the Standley Group Activity Leadership Skills Checklist (Standley, 1991) to measure their dependent variables, their dependent measures are operationally defined (for practical purposes) as what this checklist measures. As stated above, this is divided into four subscales, personal skills, general skills, music skills, and client responses.

Clarify Assumptions. It is helpful at this point for the researcher to state the assumptions, or things that are being taken for granted, in designing the study. This includes assumptions that have been made about the nature of the behavior being investigated, the

---

[6] The lack of realism in being able to specify clinical procedures precisely and then follow them without variation is one of the criticisms made by qualitative researchers of the applicability of quantitative research to the needs of music therapists.

conditions under which the behavior occurs, the methods and measurements, and the relationship of the study to other persons and situations (Isaac & Michael, 1981).

Furman et al. (1992) do a thorough review of literature and state a number of assumptions that come from this literature. These include that it is desirable to train specific competencies and that the quality of feedback in preinternship music therapy experiences is important, videotape feedback is an effective means of developing these competencies, independent self-analysis of music therapy sessions can increase the desired therapist competencies, students trained using operationally defined definitions and videotape analysis develop skills most efficiently, videotape feedback is as effective in developing music therapy competencies as individual instructor-based feedback, and the use of a focusing mechanism such as a behavior checklist with videotape feedback enhances the desired feedback (pp. 42–43). It is taken for granted that these assumptions from the literature led to the researchers' assumptions that certain kinds of feedback, including positive reinforcement, would be useful for the students in the study.

State Delimitations. Delimitations are statements of what will and will not be included in the study. By delimiting, you focus the study on something that can be accomplished, being sure in the process that the topic does not become so narrow that it is trivial. The scope of the study must be realistic, given the time available to carry it out, the subjects who are available, any costs involved, and, of course, the variables under investigation. It is important to delimit the study during the planning stages, because researchers who try to study more than they are able to study—who have not properly delimited their studies—do not accomplish what they set out to accomplish.

Among the things that may be delimited are the number of subjects used, characteristics of subjects, number of independent variables to be investigated, number of dependent variables to be measured, time over which the study will extend, and so forth.

Delimitations in the Furman et al. (1992) study include the number of student therapists to be included in the study (a total of nine in two subexperiments), the number of settings (two, one for each subexperiment), that the research would take place in training sessions, and the number of sessions per week (two and three times a week, respectively).

Qualitative Research

There are many approaches to qualitative research, and most of them embrace an openness to a change and evolution as the research progresses. Thus, it is impossible to provide concrete steps to follow in developing a topic for all types of qualitative research. Some approach developing the topic in qualitative research as a completely different process than developing a topic in quantitative research. Bruscia (1995a) alludes to this when he says, "Qualitative research does not follow an established procedural sequence. . . . The research process is not always determined entirely through left-brain, deductive reasoning, or objective stances" (p. 391). The process of developing a qualitative research topic is without a doubt less straightforward than that of developing a quantitative research topic.

Indeed, there are so many types of qualitative research and so many approaches to developing a topic that there is no agreement on how to do this among those who write about qualitative research. Some authors suggest a process that is quite similar to that used in developing a topic in quantitative research; this will be satisfactory for some types of qualitative research and for some qualitative researchers. Others seem to suggest that the process of designing a qualitative study is so specific to a particular study that there is no process that can be followed by more than one researcher.

In describing the process of developing a topic for qualitative research in this chapter, an attempt has been made to make at least the outlines of the process similar to that for quantitative research, although what is done at each step is quite different for quantitative and qualitative research. The steps that are suggested must occur, although they often do not occur in the order that is described. In addition, many of them will need to be returned to at various stages of the process so they must be done more than once. The researcher should be aware of this cyclic nature of developing a topic in qualitative research.[7]

---

[7] See Bruscia (1995a, 1995b, 1995c) for a description of the process of doing qualitative research and illustration of its cyclic nature.

The Problem and Questions

The first steps will help the researcher to focus on and refine the problem of the study. These steps are to state the problem, focus on the research question, and develop subordinate questions.

State the Problem. Many authors emphasize the need to develop a problem statement at this point in the process. Bruscia (1995b) suggested that the focus of a qualitative research study might be quite different from a problem statement in more traditional research (p. 403). In some cases, though, a problem statement for a qualitative study may be quite similar to those found in quantitative or other types of research.

Erlandson, Harris, Skipper, and Allen (1993) said: "The problem statement in naturalistic research is not a question or even an objective, but rather. . . an expression of a dilemma or situation that needs to be addressed for the purposes of understanding and direction" (p. 49). They went on to say: "As a rule of thumb, the problem statement should be sufficiently broad to permit inclusion of central issues and concerns, and yet it should be narrow enough in scope to serve as a guide to data collection" (p. 49).

Creswell (1998) spoke of considerations in developing a problem statement in qualitative research when he said: "In addition to determining the source of the problem and framing it within the literature and concepts, qualitative researchers need to encode the problem discussion with language that foreshadows their tradition of inquiry" (p. 95). Different qualitative research traditions are based on different beliefs and assumptions and use different language in describing the assumptions, procedures, and so forth. Creswell's point is that there is a connection between the problem (and purpose) statement and the method chosen for the study, and the way that the study purpose is stated points to the tradition in which the study is conducted. The researcher is encouraged to clarify the ontological and epistemological underpinnings of the study as an aid in deciding on the type of study that she or he is pursuing. This decision will aid in some aspects of developing the topic and then designing the study.

In the study of the experiences and concerns of students during music therapy practica (Wheeler, 2002), the problem is stated as: "Although music therapy supervisors receive verbal and written input from students in narrative form, this input has not been studied systematically" (p. 277).

Focus on the Research Question. As the researcher works on developing the topic, he or she will focus on a question or questions. The research question will evolve from the more general topic of interest and will become the focus of the study. This question should be as clear as possible. Questions for many qualitative research studies are open-ended and reflect efforts to discover meaning or explore processes. Consistent with the emerging nature of qualitative research, the questions may evolve as the study develops. Qualitative researchers often ask questions rather than state hypotheses, and these questions are likely to deal with process or description. Many qualitative research questions will be open-ended and they are unlikely to be answered with yes or no answers. In a thesis or dissertation, the question and problem statement will be the core of a chapter titled Statement of the Problem.

While this area is being presented at the beginning of the steps here, it could also be presented later, or, more likely, should be presented first and again later. Keeping the research question in mind is important so that the study continues to be focused. But, as stated already, the question will change, evolve, be refined, be subdivided, and be asked again.

The research question in the Wheeler (2002) practicum study is: What concerns and experiences do music therapy students have during their preclinical experiences?

Develop Subordinate Questions. Subordinate questions help to further define what the research will look at. Again, some studies may not have subordinate questions, and, in those that do, they may evolve as the study goes forward. The researcher will begin with a general research question, and, as stated before, the nature of this question determines the type of study that is pursued. This question will become the focus of the study and is likely to become the core of the problem statement. Subquestions will be related to the question and may be asked before or after asking the question.

In the Wheeler (2002) study, the initial questions that were asked could be considered the subquestions:

1. What issues do students find pertinent in their practica?
2. What makes students anxious?

3. What strategies do they use to ease their anxiety?
4. What makes them comfortable?
5. What is useful in the supervision process, both by on-site and university faculty supervisors?
6. What are the challenges in doing practica?
7. What is useful and not useful in the practicum class?
8. How can the experience best be structured? (p. 278)

Definitions, Assumptions, and Delimitations

Definitions, assumptions, and delimitations help to clarify exactly what is included in the research. Clarifying them from the outset will facilitate designing and carrying out the study.

Define Terms. It is important to define terms used in the research. Clear definitions will keep you focused on what you intend to look at with the research.

Most terms in the Wheeler (2002) study were assumed to be clear and were not defined in the study. The study focused on preclinical or practicum experiences, and what these meant in the context of the particular students who were interviewed and the structure of the curriculum at their university was clarified in a section called Structure of Practica (p. 281).

Clarify Assumptions. Every researcher makes certain assumptions. These are things that are taken as is—they could be debated, but, for this study, they are accepted.

Assumptions made in the Wheeler (2002) study were stated as "the perception that students have thoughts and feelings about the practica that faculty never suspect, and that these thoughts and feelings influence both their experience of the practica and their wok in them" (p. 277). These were discussed as the "ontological view that guided the inquiry was that one can understand another's experience enough to be meaningful" (p. 277), "connected to the epistemological stance that this understanding can be obtained through what people say about their experiences" (p. 277). The discussion of the ontological and epistemological stances in the article reflects the importance of these views in understanding the assumptions made in the research. Assumptions are also evident in several of the questions that are asked and are stated above. The question, "What makes students anxious" assumes that something does, as does the question, "What makes them comfortable?" Had these assumptions not been made, the questions would have been, "What, if anything, makes students anxious?" and "What, if anything, makes them comfortable?" Similarly, "What is useful in the supervision process, both by on-site and university faculty supervisors?" assumes that some things are useful. A statement of that question without the assumption would have been, "What is useful *and* not useful in the supervision process. . . ?"

State Delimitations. Every study has things that it will and will not examine. In delimiting the study, the researcher decides how narrow or how broad the focus of the study will be. Bruscia (1995d) speaks of this as limiting the scope and focuses on how many sources of data are to be included—singular, idiographic, or collective. The qualitative research tradition followed in the study will determine some limitations, as will the design of the study. Discussion of these elements in the early stages of the proposal will help to remind the reader that the study has boundaries and is situated (as is all qualitative research) in a specific context and situation.

In the Wheeler (2002) study, delimitations included the fact that students were all from one university and that the structure of their practica, while having things in common with other practica, was specific to that university. The research was based on interviews with inherent limitations in that students were thus reporting retrospectively on their experiences, at least as they thought back to when they had been in their clinical setting or class in order to report these experiences. In addition, the researcher guided the interviews to some extent, even while attempting to do this as little as possible. In addition, it was acknowledged that the researcher's dual role as researcher and teacher would have an influence, and that she was not a student.

Summary

Developing a topic is the initial part of doing research. As has been outlined in this chapter, this process begins with a general area of interest, and the topic is then developed and refined through a series of steps. Fairly early in the process, the differences in developing a quantitative and a qualitative topic become clear, and, while the general steps toward these two types of research may have some similarities, their content is quite different.

Although it has not been covered in this chapter, the development of a topic for a different type of study, such as historical or philosophical, progress similarly. Some of the steps may be different, but the general progression is similar.

As the researcher develops the topic, he or she is also involved in reviewing the literature. When all of this is done, it is time to move on to designing the study. This will be covered separately for quantitative and qualitative research.

References

Borg, W. R., & Gall, M. D. (1989). *Educational research* (5th ed.). New York: Longman.

Bruscia, K. E. (1995a). The process of doing qualitative research: Part I: Introduction. In B. L. Wheeler (Ed.), *Music therapy research: Quantitative and qualitative perspectives* (pp. 389–399). Gilsum, NH: Barcelona Publishers.

Bruscia, K. E. (1995b). The process of doing qualitative research: Part II: Procedural steps. In B. L. Wheeler (Ed.), *Music therapy research: Quantitative and qualitative perspectives* (pp. 401–427). Gilsum, NH: Barcelona Publishers.

Bruscia, K. E. (1995c). The process of doing qualitative research: Part III: The human side. In B. L. Wheeler (Ed.), *Music therapy research: Quantitative and qualitative perspectives* (pp. 429–443). Gilsum, NH: Barcelona Publishers.

Bruscia, K. E. (1995d). Topics, phenomena, and purposes in qualitative research. In B. L. Wheeler (Ed.), *Music therapy research: Quantitative and qualitative perspectives* (pp. 313–327). Gilsum, NH: Barcelona Publishers.

Cofrancesco, E. M. (1985). The effect of music therapy on hand grasp strength and functional task performance in stroke patients. *Journal of Music Therapy, 22,* 129–145.

Creswell, J. W. (1998). *Qualitative inquiry and research design: Choosing among five traditions.* Thousand Oaks, CA: Sage Publications.

Ely, M., Anzul, M., Friedman, T., Garner, D., & Steinmetz, A. M. (1991). *Doing qualitative research: Circles within circles.* Bristol, PA: The Falmer Press.

Erlandson, D. A., Harris, E. L., Skipper, B. L., & Allen, S. D. (1993). *Doing naturalistic inquiry: A guide to methods.* Newbury Park, CA: Sage Publications.

Furman, C. E., Adamek, M. S., & Furman, A. G. (1992) The use of an auditory device to transmit feedback to student therapists. *Journal of Music Therapy, 29,* 40–53.

Gfeller, K., Christ, A., Knutson, J., Witt, S., & Mehr, M. (2003). The effects of familiarity and complexity on appraisal of complex songs by cochlear implant recipients and normal hearing adults. *Journal of Music Therapy, 40,* 78–112.

Gregory, D. (2000). Test instruments used by *Journal of Music Therapy* authors from 1984–1997. *Journal of Music Therapy, 37,* 79–94.

Groene, R. (2001). The effect of presentation and accompaniment styles on attentional and responsive behaviors of participants with dementia diagnoses. *Journal of Music Therapy, 38,* 36–50.

Hanser, S. B. (1990). A music therapy strategy for depressed older adults in the community. *Journal of Applied Gerontology, 9,* 283–298.

Hanser, S. B., & Thompson, L. W. (1994). Effects of a music therapy strategy on depressed older adults. *Journal of Gerontology: Psychological Sciences, 49,* P265–P269.

Hilliard, R. E. (2003). The effects of music therapy on the quality and length of life of people diagnosed with terminal cancer. *Journal of Music Therapy, 40,* 113–137.

Isaac, S., & Michael, W. B. (1981). *Handbook in research and evaluation* (2nd ed.). San Diego, CA: EdITS.

Kerlinger, F. N. (1986). *Foundations of behavioral research* (3rd ed.). New York: Holt, Rinehart & Winston.

Kumar, R. (1996). *Research methodology: A step-by-step guide for beginners.* Thousand Oaks, CA: Sage Publications.

McCarty, B. C., McElfresh, C. T., Rice, S. V., & Wilson, S. J. (1978). The effect of contingent background music on inappropriate bus behavior. *Journal of Music Therapy, 15,* 150–156.

McGuigan, F. J. (1968). *Experimental psychology* (2nd ed.). Englewood Cliffs, NJ: Prentice-Hall.

Spielberger, C. D. (1983). *Manual for the State-Trait Anxiety Inventory*. Palo Alto, CA: Consulting Psychologists Press.

Standley, J. (1991). *Music techniques in therapy, counseling and special education*. St. Louis, MO: MMB Music.

Strauser, J. M. (1997). The effects of music versus silence on measures of state anxiety, perceived relaxation, and physiological responses of patients receiving chiropractic interventions. *Journal of Music Therapy, 34,* 88–105.

Thaut, M. H., & Davis, W. B. (1993). The influence of subject-selected versus experimenter-chosen music on affect, anxiety, and relaxation. *Journal of Music Therapy, 30,* 210–223.

Wheeler, B. L. (2002). Experiences and concerns of students during music therapy practica. *Journal of Music Therapy, 39,* 274–304.

Wilkinson, L. (1999). Statistical methods in psychology journals: Guidelines and explanations. *American Psychologist, 54,* 594–604.

Acknowledgments

Thanks to Kenneth Bruscia and Carolyn Kenny for feedback on this chapter.

Chapter 9
Reviewing the Literature
Cheryl Dileo

"Research does not exist in isolation. Each research study is part of an existing body of knowledge, building on the foundation of past research and expanding that foundation for future research" (Gravetter & Forzano, 2003, p. 40). A literature review, as part of the research process, involves the reporting of previously published literature to define the state of knowledge on a given topic, including the gap in knowledge that the study at hand may fill.

Research textbooks do not provide guidelines for conducting a meaningful review of the literature often enough. The literature review may be one of the most difficult parts of the research process because of problems in delimiting, understanding, and organizing the large amounts of material that are often encountered. Thus, the purpose of this chapter is to provide specific guidelines for approaching and accomplishing this step in the research process, upon which all other components of research, such as design and method, rely.

The literature review is a necessary component of many types of research and serves several purposes. First, it provides a context for the current study. As such, it contains a description of the assumptions and theory underlying the study (Berg, 1989). In a sense, the related literature provides both a foreshadowing of what will be done and a history of what has been done to date on the topic. It provides information on how the study at hand fits into current theory and research and if the hypotheses being tested are consistent with accepted findings. It provides information to the researcher on whether the study duplicates another that has already been published or is an original approach to the problem.

Second, the review of literature identifies gaps in the literature and provides a rationale for the current study. It can be said that the related literature builds a case or justification for the research. By identifying and analyzing what has been done previously, the researcher can support the need for the current study more fully.

Third, the review of the literature assists the researcher in defining, delimiting, conceptualizing, or reconceptualizing the research question. By carefully studying past research, the investigator can avoid those approaches that have proven unsuccessful in the past, become aware of the scope of the current question or problem, gain insight into the problem, evaluate the freshness of the current approach, select the most appropriate designs and measurement techniques, and utilize recommendations from previous researchers.

Finally, the review of the research allows investigators to compare their findings with those of others. This occurs in the Discussion section of the paper.

Useful literature reviews: (a) present the topic with clarity, (b) include only relevant studies, (c) are comprehensive in nature, (d) are heterogeneous in their presentation of the diversity in the literature, and (e) are unbiased.

Generally speaking, there are two types of literature reviews, each taking a somewhat different approach to the summary of primary studies. The first, a *qualitative literature review,* is what is discussed in the present chapter and involves a narrative presentation of the relevant published literature in the field. The second, a *systematic review,* is a more formalized and explicit scientific research technique in its own right that is intended to provide the information needed for making clinical decisions. The Cochrane Library (www.cochrane.org) contains a database of systematic reviews in the field of medicine; these provide excellent examples for conducting this type of review.

Conducting the Literature Review

Because of the perceived ambiguous and overwhelming nature of the literature review, it is sometimes postponed in the research process—researchers sometimes avoid completing this section until after the data have been collected. In doing this, the purpose of the related literature review is defeated; the researcher cannot benefit from previous research in the conceptualization and design of the study.

Thus, it is strongly recommended that the review of the literature process be initiated as soon as a general area for research is identified. The review can provide ideas for a study focus as well as details regarding methodological issues. A major risk in not completing a review at the initial stages of the study is that the researcher may be duplicating previous efforts, a potentially devastating finding for the researcher who thinks he or she is conducting original research.

Although the steps in the review process may vary according to the experience and expertise of the researcher, the following steps are relevant to the beginning music therapy researcher:

1. Identifying keywords;
2. Consulting the indices and searching the literature;
3. Limiting the scope of the review;
4. Retrieving the articles and developing the bibliography;
5. Outlining the related literature section;
6. Abstracting articles;
7. Organizing and classifying abstracts and articles;
8. Writing the related literature section.

Step 1: Identifying Keywords

After the music therapy research topic has been identified (see Chapter 8, Developing a Topic), the researcher may begin the review of literature process. As most information relevant to music therapy and related areas can be retrieved only through correct terms or keywords, those relevant to the topic at hand must be identified.

The first step in the process is to identify the variables in the research study. For example, if the researcher is studying the use of music to reduce anxiety in children undergoing tonsillectomy procedures, the variables are: music, anxiety, children, tonsillectomy (surgery). This list of variables is important because it will also be used in outlining the entire related literature section.

The next step is to identify synonyms, broader terms, and narrower terms related to each of these variables. As large a list as possible of keywords should be initially generated; it is likely that this list will be modified or expanded as one continues with the search, that is to say, keywords will vary depending on the keywording system used with each index.

Using the current example, synonyms, broader terms and narrower terms for each of the variables may be as follows:

Music: music therapy, sedative music, new age music, music listening, vocal music, instrumental music, sound,

Anxiety: relaxation, fear, relaxation training, stress, psychological patterns, phobia, emotional problems, state anxiety, trait anxiety, emotional problems, anxiety disorders,

Children: hospitalized children, pediatrics, young children, preschool children, elementary school students, youth, child,

Tonsillectomy: medical problem, otolaryngology, surgery, anesthesia, local anesthesia, general anesthesia, anesthesiology, diseases, hospital, patients, physical health.

Additional sources of help in generating keywords are published thesauri such as the *Thesaurus of Eric Descriptors* (Houston, 2001); *Thesaurus of Psychological Index Terms* (Gallagher, 2004); *Medical Subject Headings (MeSH)*; and National Library of Medicine, National Institutes of Health, n.d.). These are available in the reference sections of libraries.

Step 2: Consulting the Indices and Searching the Literature

After a list of keywords has been generated, various indices and databases should be consulted to identify literature that has been written in each of the areas. There are large numbers of computerized databases available online and in libraries, and the list of these grows daily. Based on the topic, the researcher will select one or more of these databases for searching the literature.

Because of the interdisciplinary nature of music therapy, as well as its breadth of clinical applications, literature relevant to music therapy may be spread out among many databases. Moreover, different journals are indexed in the various databases. Thus, the use of more than one database is recommended. Researchers are strongly advised to consult reference librarians prior to attempting searches, as their expertise is often invaluable in identifying appropriate databases and in implementing search short cuts. In addition, some databases provide the full texts of articles that are indexed, whereas others provide only the reference information of the article and an abstract.

A list of some databases used frequently in music therapy is provided below. It is noted that each of these databases is used differently, and information regarding their use should be obtained from the index itself or from the library. Likewise, lists of additional databases should be obtained from the researcher's library, as libraries often subscribe to different ones.

CINAHL
Dissertation Abstracts
Education Abstracts
ERIC
Health and Psychosocial Instruments
HealthSTAR
International Index to Music Periodicals
MEDLINE
Music Index
OVID Gateway
Project MUSE
PsycINFO
PubMed Central
Social Sciences Abstracts
Social Work Abstracts
Sociological Abstracts

Music therapy researchers should also own or have access to the CD-Rom, *Music Therapy Research* (2nd Edition, AMTA, 2004). This full-text resource contains the complete collection of the *Journal of Music Therapy, Music Therapy,* and *Music Therapy Perspectives* from 1950 through 2003.

Researchers may also conduct online searches for information, although the risk of retrieving inaccurate information is high in some Internet resources. There are some reputable Internet sites specifically for music therapy information. These include the website of Temple University's music therapy program (www.temple.edu/musictherapy), also containing databases of master's theses in music therapy, qualitative research in music therapy, and other unique sources of information. A second resource is the searchable music therapy database from the University Witten/Herdecke in Germany (www.musictherapyworld.net), which contains a variety of music therapy databases, manuscripts, and conference proceedings and also access to the *Australian Journal of Music Therapy.*

A last source of literature is the *gray literature,* that which is not identifiable or available through database searches. This literature includes books and book chapters as well as conference presentations. Searching for books and book chapters can be done through library catalogs; searches for conference presentations can be done by hand searches through published conference proceedings and abstracts.

Once the various relevant databases have been identified, keywords are searched, either singly or in combination, to find the most appropriate and relevant literature. What will result from the searching process will be a list of titles of journal articles (sometimes books as well), most containing abstracts and some containing full texts. Some of this information will be directly related to the study at hand, some will be irrelevant. When the results of the search have yielded very few references, a search involving broader terms should be used. Conversely, when a search has resulted in an unwieldy number of articles, the search has been too broad, and more specific keywords should be used.

Step 3. Limiting the Scope of the Review

The next step involves the discrimination of what is and is not relevant to the proposed study. The amount of literature retrieved from the indices will vary greatly from study to study; for some studies, there will be copious amounts of literature, while, for other studies, there will be very little. In either event, the researcher must decide what is and is not appropriate to include in the related literature section. Several guidelines may be used in making this decision.

Content: Obviously, the most important factor in determining the relevance of an article to the research topic is its content. It is likely that a perusal of the references and abstracts will allow the researcher to place references in three general categories: (a) research that is clearly relevant, (b) research that is clearly irrelevant, and (c) research that may be relevant if more information is obtained. To facilitate decision-making, the researcher should first look over every title as the first step in the screening process. Based only on the title, it is possible to eliminate a large percentage of the articles. The abstract of the article is then used as the second screening method. By reading the abstract closely, the researcher can find more detail on the specifics of the article, and whether it is indeed relevant. It is advised that decision-making for clearly irrelevant literature be done at this stage; it will save the researcher valuable time and money, as the third stage of the screening process involves retrieving the articles themselves. This is facilitated in databases that include the full text of articles. If the full text is not included, the researcher will need to obtain a copy of the article, available in the library itself or requested through Interlibrary Loan.

Date of publication: Another criterion that may help the researcher decide the relevance of articles is the date of publication. Thus, the researcher may decide to include only literature published after a certain year (for example, within the past 10 years). This is particularly helpful when there is an abundant amount of literature, and some limits need to be imposed. If few articles have been identified in the search, however, it is not recommended that this be done.

Availability of articles: Depending on the size and content of the library the researcher is using, there will inevitably be articles that the researcher cannot locate, even through Interlibrary Loan. This will be another factor in limiting the scope of the search. Related to this is the language of article. Articles in a foreign language should be eliminated if the researcher has no means of translating them.

Use of review studies: When the literature on a topic is extremely broad, it is sometimes useful to rely on recently published review studies rather than on a multitude of very specific studies. This strategy is helpful when summarizing information outside the field of music therapy (see subsequent section).

Step 4: Retrieving the Articles and Developing the Bibliography

After developing a meaningful list of articles relevant to the study, the researcher should locate these articles, either within the library or through Interlibrary Loan, and make a copy of the article itself, if needed.

When hard copies of the articles have been obtained, the researcher should carefully check the list of references in the articles to determine if there are other related articles that were not identified in the search process, as is often the case. If these are found, the researcher should attempt to locate these also. This process provides a valuable way of checking on the validity of the search procedures employed and also allows the researcher to extend the reference list.

It is very useful for the researcher at this stage to enter the list of articles alphabetically into a word-processing program using the correct style, for example, APA style (American Psychological Association, 2001). In this way, the reference list is not created at the last minute. Also, this allows the researcher to keep track of which articles have and have not been located and also to add and eliminate articles based on relevance. Researchers who do this early in the research process save time at the end because the reference list is already complete.

Step 5: Outlining the Related Literature Section

It is helpful to draft an outline of the related literature section prior to abstracting articles. In following this sequence, the researcher can abstract the article and categorize it in the appropriate section simultaneously. This may also help the researcher make decisions about ambiguous articles—if they do not neatly fit into a section of the related literature, they are probably not relevant to the study.

It should be remembered that the outline, once developed, may be fairly flexible in terms of order of presentation. At this stage, it is most important to determine what the sections will be. The order can always be changed at a later stage (and this can be done easily with the assistance of a word-processing program), based on the amount of literature that is found and the logic of the writing.

The basic procedure used in outlining the related literature section is to develop specific sections based on the pairing of variables studied. Recall the variables isolated in the example above: Music, Anxiety, Children, Tonsillectomy (Surgery). If these variables are paired, the following six categories will result: Music and Anxiety; Music and Children; Music and Surgery; Anxiety and Children; Anxiety and Surgery; Children and Surgery. Additional categories may be created by combining more than two variables: Music, Anxiety, Children; Music, Anxiety, Surgery; Anxiety, Children, Surgery; Music, Anxiety, Surgery, Children.

These 10 categories should then be organized and sequenced in outline form, progressing from general to specific, to allow a logical flow of thought. The outline should end with the consideration of all four variables. These 10 categories should be sequenced as major categories or subcategories of each other. Some categories ultimately may be eliminated to avoid redundancy. For example, the following arrangement may be a useful outline for related literature:

I. Anxiety and Surgery
    a. Children and Surgery
    b. Children, Anxiety, and Surgery (Children and Anxiety)
(II. Music and Children)
III. Music and Anxiety
    a. Music, Anxiety, and Children
    b. Music and Surgery
        1. Music, Anxiety, and Surgery
        2. Music, Anxiety, Children, and Surgery

Once the connections between the variables have been made and a tentative outline established, the overall outline should be reviewed for logic, relevance, and practicality. For example, in this particular outline, the combination of the variables Children and Anxiety produces a very broad topic, one that may not be as relevant as Children, Anxiety, and Surgery. Thus these two categories are combined. Similarly, Category II (Music and Children) may be eliminated, as it is very broad and somewhat irrelevant to the study. Additionally, in this outline, several other categories, such as Music and Anxiety, Music and Surgery, Children and Surgery, and Anxiety and Surgery are very broad. These areas will need to be limited for the literature review, perhaps with the use of larger review studies rather than a multitude of specific studies.

Step 6. Abstracting Articles

The purpose of an abstract is to provide a summary of the article in a concise manner. An original abstract should be written for each relevant article retrieved. The following information should be included in abstracts of experimental and descriptive studies:

1. Title of study, author, volume, year, issue, and page numbers,
2. A brief description of the purpose of the study,
3. A concise description of subjects,
4. A concise description of the method, including independent and dependent variables, experimental groups, and so forth,
5. A brief description of the results of the study,
6. A concise statement of the conclusions of the study.

Several points should be kept in mind when writing abstracts:

1. Never use direct quotations or exact language contained in the article or the author's abstract; instead, paraphrase;
2. Abstracts should be kept short (fewer than 250 words); writing concise abstracts requires practice; this skill will improve over time;
3. Related literature, statistics, equipment, and discussion are generally excluded from an abstract, unless absolutely essential to understanding it (for example, if the purpose of the study was to test specific equipment);

4. Select several abstracts from a journal to use as a guide in writing;
5. Use concise, scientific language; be factual and to the point.

An example of an abstract is provided in Table 1.

Table 1
Sample Abstract

The purpose of this study was to examine the effects of music on reducing anxiety in children undergoing tonsillectomy procures. Thirty subjects (ages 6–10 years) scheduled for nonemergency tonsillectomy procedures were randomly assigned to one of two groups: (a) music listening or (b) play therapy. Subjects in the music listening group listened to prerecorded tapes of preferred music for 30 minutes prior to surgery; subjects in the play therapy group engaged in preferred play therapy activities with a trained therapist for 30 minutes prior to surgery. Dependent measures included the Spielberger State-Trait Anxiety Scale, administered before and after both treatments and following surgery; heart rate monitoring before and during treatment and during surgery; and behavioral observations of anxiety. Similar anesthesia and surgical protocols were used for all subjects. Results indicated significant differences between the groups ($p < .05$) on all three measures during treatment. Post-hoc analyses showed significantly lower heart rates, anxiety scores, and behavioral observations for the music listening group. It was concluded that music listening may be effective in reducing anxiety of children prior to surgery.

Step 7. Organizing and Classifying Abstracts and Articles

A useful procedure that may be employed in organizing abstracts involves the use of large index cards or appropriate word-processing software. For each article that is consulted, one index card is used or a computer file is made. On this, the researcher should include the complete bibliographic citation (including this simultaneously in the appropriate computer bibliography file as mentioned previously) and the original abstract. Any material that is quoted from the article should also be included on the index card or file, making sure that it is correctly recorded with the corresponding page number. Also, the researcher may make comments about the article (a critique of the article, etc.) on the card for future reference. Finally, the article should be classified using a number, color, or other system identifying its section of the related literature outline. For example, all articles dealing with music and anxiety would have the number III or designated color. If the bibliography of the article has not already been checked for additional references, it should be done at this point. If an article fits under more than one category, a duplicate index card or file can be completed.

After the researcher has compiled this information for each article, the original article can be filed, as all of the necessary information has been obtained from the article.

Index cards or computerized information should then be separated and arranged according to various sections of the related literature outline.

Step 8. Writing the Related Literature Section [1]

Using the method described above, various sections of the related literature outline may be written independently. It has been the author's experience that the most difficult part of the related literature (Introduction) section to write is the first paragraph. Therefore, it is recommended that the student begin the writing process with the smallest subsection of related literature; the introductory paragraphs can, in fact, be written last.

Once a section has been selected, the index cards or computer files should be arranged in a logical sequence, for example, from general to specific or from least recent to most recent. The studies that are similar should be grouped together with a paper clip or pasted together in one computer file. The researcher can then discuss these simultaneously, summarizing their results

---

[1] More extensive information on writing the related literature section can be found in Chapter 16, Writing the Quantitative Research Report, and Chapter 17, Writing the Qualitative Research Report.

or indicating that the results of these studies were similar. The researcher may then proceed to write the section, using the information that has already been written on the index cards. At this stage, this is a very simple process, because each abstract has already been written. Thus, the researcher simply types information from the index cards or rearranges the information on the screen of the computer.

When writing, the researcher should rely heavily on the use of transitions so that there is a clear, logical progression in thought. In general, each sentence and paragraph should relate to the previous one; gaps in thought or logic should be avoided. Thus, the flow of the writing should be natural, effortless, and seamless. Also, the researcher should avoid merely stringing abstracts together; transitions are needed to make the writing engaging and readable.

Flowery, nonscientific language should be avoided in the related literature section (as in all types of scientific writing).[2] Conciseness, clarity, and economy of words are the goals.

At the end of each section, a very brief summary should be provided. The summary should indicate the major (or perhaps inconclusive) findings of that section. For example: "In summary, music appears to be influential in reducing anxiety in a number of situations."

It is important to remember that in the related literature section, the researcher is building a rationale for the study. It should be problem-oriented, for instance: "Because this information on the topic is unknown, the current research is justified."

After each section has been written with its brief conclusions, the conclusions from all the sections may be summarized. This should then lead to (and provide support for) the problem statement (purpose) of the study. For example:

> Because the research indicates that surgery is anxiety-provoking, especially for children, and that music has been successful in reducing anxiety in both surgical and nonsurgical situations, it is logical to assume that music may be helpful in reducing anxiety in children undergoing the very common tonsillectomy procedure. Thus, the purpose of this study. . . .

Conclusion

A review of literature is a key component in the research process, as it is used to provide a rationale and context for the study as well as important methodological information. A review of literature need not be intimidating to the researcher, if undertaken in an organized, step-by-step, detailed manner. In fact, it is likely to be a very rewarding and educational experience in and of itself. It may also stimulate the researcher with many research ideas for the future.

References

American Music Therapy Association. (2004). *Music therapy research CD-ROM* (2nd ed.). Silver Spring, MD: Author.

American Psychological Association. (2001). *Publication manual of the American Psychological Association* (5th ed.). Washington, D.C.: Author.

Berg, B. L. (1989). *Qualitative research methods for the social sciences.* Needham Heights, MA: Allyn & Bacon.

Gallagher, L. A. (2004). *Thesaurus of psychological index terms: 30th anniversary 1084–2004* (10th ed.). Washington, D.C.: American Psychological Association.

Gravetter, F. J., & Forzano, L. B. (2003). *Research methods for the behavioral sciences.* Belmont, CA: Thomson-Wadsworth.

Houston, J. E. (2001). *Thesaurus of Eric descriptors* (14th ed.). Phoenix, AZ: Oryx Press.

National Library of Medicine, National Institutes of Health (n.d.). *Medical subject headings.* http://www.nlm.nih.gov/mesh/

---

[2] Some approaches to qualitative research have expanded the notion of what constitutes a legitimate focus of scholarly inquiry. The way that these reports are written can therefore include narrative devices and uses of language that would not be appropriate in strictly scientific reports as traditionally conceived. See Chapter 17, Writing the Qualitative Research Report, and some of the chapters in Part IV, Types of Qualitative Research.

Chapter 10
Designing Quantitative Research[1]
Barbara L. Wheeler

After you have developed your topic and reviewed the literature, you have already made progress toward designing the study. Following the steps presented in this chapter will help to insure that the study is designed and implemented in such a manner that you can satisfactorily answer the problems that were posed.

The steps outlined in the *Publication Manual of the American Psychological Association* (5th Edition, American Psychological Association [APA], 2001) for writing the Method section of the report provide useful guidelines for designing and implementing the study. They are presented here in a format adapted from Cone and Foster (1993). This chapter outlines the areas that must be addressed, provides information as to considerations under each, and gives examples of how some of the steps have been followed by music therapy researchers.

Select Design

The research problem and questions guide the researcher toward a particular design. The *design*[2] of a study refers to the way that the researcher structures the study in order to answer the questions that he or she is asking; thus, the researcher who chooses to do a quantitative study will select a design and type of research to answer the questions of interest. There are many ways to design a study, but they can be divided into categories that share basic features.

The chapters in which these types of research are discussed provide details on appropriate designs for each category. Chapter 4, Principles of Quantitative Research, provides an overview of quantitative research as well as some examples of longitudinal research. Chapter 21, Experimental Research, discusses several types of experimental designs, including pre-experimental, true experimental, and quasi-experimental designs. Important questions in these designs are how the groups into which people are placed to test the experimental conditions are formed and the characteristics of the members of these groups, with each set of circumstances suggesting different ways of designing the study. Chapter 22, Survey Research, provides information on different ways of designing surveys. Chapter 23, Meta-Analysis, discusses meta-analytic procedures for summarizing and understanding the results of multiple related studies. Various types of case-study and single-subject designs are discussed in Chapter 24, Quantitative Single-Case Designs, and Chapter 25, Applied Behavior Analysis. Each of these terms designates a different way of designing the research study to answer the questions asked.

The choice of design is based on the questions or problems posed by the researcher. To follow this process, we will examine studies that follow several of these designs. To look at an experimental design, we will examine a study by Hanser and Thompson (1994), "Effects of a Music Therapy Strategy on Depressed Older Adults," that addresses questions about the impact of three treatment strategies on the depression, distress, mood, and self-esteem of older adults with depression. Their study employed three independent groups, with pretest, midtest, and posttest observations plus follow-up observations for the treatment groups after 9 months. We will look at "Gender Differences Among Newborns on a Transient Otoacoustic Emissions Test for Hearing" (Cassidy & Ditty, 2001) as an example of an ex post facto study, a type of quasi-experimental design.[3] It is ex post facto because the comparison involves a variable—gender—that has already occurred and thus cannot be manipulated. Finally, to examine the design of a survey study, we will look at "Music Therapy Practicum Practices: A Survey of Music Therapy Educators," where I (Wheeler, 2000) surveyed music therapy educators to answer questions about how various universities structure their music therapy practica.

---

[1] Portions of this chapter are taken from the chapter by the same name in the previous edition of this book.

[2] Many of the terms used in this chapter were defined in Chapter 4, Principles of Quantitative Research, and many will be defined and used in later chapters.

[3] See Chapter 21 for explanation of quasi-experimental and ex post facto studies.

The researcher must decide among the available designs, based on which one best addresses the questions to be answered or the hypotheses posed. From there, the steps to carry out the study are selected based on the research questions and type of design.

Determine Criteria for Selecting Participants[4]

Who will participate, how they will be selected, and how many there will be are questions that need to be answered as the study is designed. The answers are interrelated and apply to the most important consideration: The information that you obtain should be relevant to those to whom you wish to apply the results of your research.

Who Will Participate?

The quantitative researcher is generally interested in doing research on people who will help to increase the understanding of those who are similar on some characteristics. In general, the participants or *sample* should be people from whom you are interested in gaining information and will often be those who possess the important characteristics of those to whom you hope to apply the results of your research. The way that they are selected and how many are selected follow from your decision about whom you wish to learn.

How Will Participants Be Selected?

There are two primary considerations in selecting participants or subjects. The generalizability of the findings from the research is the first consideration, while the second has to do with practical aspects of doing the study.

Generalizability. The primary consideration in selecting participants is to select the people about whom you desire information. A goal in many types of quantitative research is to discover something that can be applied to people beyond those who are studied but who share many of the same characteristics. In order to do that, the sample should be representative of your population, or the larger inclusive group of those to whom you wish to apply, or generalize, your findings.

In experimental research, the best way to be sure that you can generalize your findings is to randomly select your sample from the group to whom you plan to generalize. To *randomly select* or *randomly sample* means to select your sample so that each member of the population has an equal chance of being selected. For example, if you are interested in the effects of your experimental treatment on children with learning disabilities, ages 7 to 9, you should randomly select a group of children with learning disabilities for your sample. You might do that by selecting 30 children at random from 200 children ages 7 to 9 who have been identified by a school district as having learning disabilities. The assumption here is that children who are randomly selected will represent the population from which they were drawn and enable generalization of the results from the sample to that population. This is the ideal situation and one for which we should aim.

There are also other methods of sampling. One of these is *purposive sampling*, in which a deliberate effort is made to obtain a representative sample by selecting people who have characteristics presumed to be typical of those in the population of interest. In *stratified sampling*, the population is divided into strata (such as men and women) from which random samples are then drawn.

From the music therapy literature, the people in Hanser and Thompson's (1994) study were volunteers who had agreed to participate in the study. As such, they were not randomly selected and may have had particular characteristics that led them to volunteer; this selection bias may therefore have confounded the results of the study (for example, the authors mention that the participants had received short-term psychotherapy and were highly educated). This

---

[4] Although in the past all research participants were called *subjects,* it is now most appropriate to label them with a term that actually describes them such as participants, students, clients, individuals, and so forth. Several terms will be used interchangeably in this chapter to refer to those who participate in the study.

leads to a less than ideal situation in terms of generalizing the results, and the authors do not suggest that the results can be generalized on the basis of this study but rather that they provide support for future study.

Survey research intends to describe a situation as it exists. It is most useful if the sample for a survey is representative of others so that the responses will be of interest and applicable to a larger group. It is possible in survey research, though, that people who are particularly interested in the topic or have other characteristics that make them not representative of those sampled may tend to return the survey at higher rates than more typical recipients, thus limiting the generalizability of the results. In addition, the lower the return rate, the less representative the respondents are likely to be.

Applied behavior analysts and single-subject researchers, who normally utilize only one or a few participants or one group, do not intend for their results to be generalized to a larger population. Part of the rationale for applied behavior analysis is that, in order to understand the behavior of an individual or group, that individual or group must be studied. On a practical level, however, these researchers expect that people will apply what they discover about their participants to others. And when applied behavior analysts find similar results in several situations, their findings are more likely to be applicable beyond the people on whom they have done their research than when they have only found those results on only one subject.

Even when formal generalizations are not made from a study, the research is most valuable if the situation that it describes is similar to a situation in which readers of the study are interested. Thus, the more representative the sample selected for most types of quantitative research, the more useful the research will be to those reading it.

Cassidy and Ditty (2001) randomly selected their newborns from all infants born at a particular hospital in a 3-month period of time. I (Wheeler, 2000) sent a survey about how various aspects of the music therapy practica were structured to the director of every music therapy education program in the United States. Thus, I sent it to all the members of the population in which I was interested.

Practical Considerations. Researchers frequently must modify the way they carry out their experiments for practical reasons. If it is not practical to randomly select the sample, you may choose to use an available sample such as an intact classroom, which is not randomly selected. In this situation, it is important to: (a) Try to find a classroom of children whose characteristics closely resemble what you think those of a randomly selected sample would be; (b) describe these characteristics in great detail; and (c) be clear as you analyze, interpret, and report your results that you did not use a randomly selected sample and thus must be particularly cautious in applying the results.

Another consideration has to do with the practicality of doing research with large numbers of people. Since much music therapy research involves direct treatment of participants, a process that can be time consuming, the size of groups must generally be limited. Difficulties in gaining the participation of subjects may also restrict the number, as may obtaining parental permission, access to a setting, or permission to administer an experimental treatment. Another practical consideration has to do with people who drop out of the research or do not return surveys. You may decide to include more participants than are actually needed to allow for this to occur.

How Many Will Participate?

There are a number of considerations in determining sample size, some related to research design and method and others practical. Those discussed here are applicable to experimental research. First of all, the size of the sample must be adequate to support generalization to people beyond the sample. If only five people are part of the research study, it is less likely that they are representative of the larger population than if there are 30; 30 people are less likely to be representative than are 75. Second, in experimental research, the sample must be large enough so that variability due to individual differences does not outweigh variability due to the experimental treatment. Third, the underlying assumptions for many commonly used statistical tests require at least moderately large groups. For these reasons, very small groups are not generally ideal for experimental research studies.

There are reasons also for avoiding an unduly large sample. Not only is a sample that is larger than necessary a waste of time and resources, but very small treatment effects are likely to be statistically significant but have little practical significance. However, because of the nature of what we do, music therapists seldom need to be concerned with their research including too many subjects.

Computations of *power* and *effect size* should be done for experimental studies. Power means the ability to detect real differences between the experimental variable and a control variable when such a difference exists. The computation of power is a statistical procedure that helps to determine the size of the sample that is needed, based on a number of factors (Cohen, 1992). It takes into account the statistical test being used, the probability level chosen, the size of the sample, and the size of the effect that is being studied (Rosenthal & Rosnow, 1984). An effect size is a standardized measure of the direction and strength of relationship between the variables in a study. According to Dileo and Bradt in Chapter 23 of this book, Meta-Analysis, the two types of effect sizes most often employed by researchers are Cohen's *d* and the Pearson product moment correlation *r*. The *Publication Manual of the American Psychological Association* (APA, 2001) supports the use of the computation of power and effect size, stating: "You should routinely provide evidence that your study has sufficient power to detect effects of substantive interest" (p. 24), and "For the reader to fully understand the importance of your findings, it is almost always necessary to include some index of effect size or strength of relationship" (p. 25).[5]

Hanser and Thompson (1994) selected 30 older adults for their study. They do not say how they chose this number but assigned 10 participants to each of three conditions. This number allowed them to examine their conditions on a reasonable number of older adults without having individual variability outweigh variability due to treatment condition. Cassidy and Ditty (2001) randomly selected 350 newborns (from 1,685 infants born in a 3-month period of time) as their sample. I (Wheeler, 2000) mailed my survey to 69 people (all of the directors of music therapy education programs in the United States) and received 40 responses for a 58% response rate; thus the sample size was 40.

Determine Formation of Groups

People are assigned to groups or conditions in experimental research, with the design of the experiment determining the formation of the groups. Participants will be placed into the number of groups called for by the design. The design will also determine whether they are placed into groups randomly or matched to one another.[6]

The least satisfactory way of placing participants into groups is using already existing groups such as individual classrooms, since this may add confounding variables to the experiment. If you must form your groups in this manner, care should be taken to equalize the groups in all other ways except your experimental treatments and to take this into account when interpreting the results.

Hanser and Thompson (1994) randomly assigned people to one of three conditions. Cassidy and Ditty's (2001) groups were based on gender, male and female. The fact that gender is a given and thus cannot be randomly assigned is the reason that their study is classified as an ex post facto study. Wheeler's (2000) survey had no groups.

Select Setting and Apparatus

Setting

The site of the experiment must be big enough to accommodate the research study. The acoustics in the room must be adequate for the experiment, and the room must be soundproof so that sounds from the outside do not interfere with the treatments that are being administered. As with much of what occurs in music therapy, it is important to insure that others are not bothered by the music coming from the room.

Care must be taken that space does not become a confounding variable in experimental and single subject research, including applied behavior analysis. As an example of a problem, if

---

[5] See Chapter 12, Statistical Methods of Analysis, for an explanation of statistical power and effect size.

[6] See Chapter 21, Experimental Research, for further discussion of experimental designs and their implications for assignment of subjects to groups.

different rooms are used for treatments in an experimental study, a difference in the groups could occur due to variations in the rooms rather than because of the experimental treatments. For example, one group might use artwork along with music therapy and meet in a sunny room with a nice view, while another might use movement along with music therapy and meet in a dark room with an ugly view. If the art and music therapy group showed more positive mood change (assuming that mood was the dependent variable) than the movement and music group, it would not be clear if this change was due to the fact that art and music therapy are actually more effective in influencing mood or whether being in a sunny room with a good view led to the difference.

Hanser and Thompson's (1994) research was done in participants' homes; since participants were randomly assigned to conditions, it is assumed that there was no systematic variation due to the space in which treatment was done. Cassidy and Ditty (2001) conducted their research with newborns in the hospital where they were born. Space was not a consideration in the Wheeler (2000) survey.

Apparatus

Apparatus or equipment must also be planned in advance. Equipment to play music must be of good quality and able to be regulated precisely. If several types of music are played as levels of an independent variable, it is important that their decibel levels be comparable and that they be reported. Musical instruments must be of good quality and comparable for all conditions.

With recent advances in recording technology, music therapists have more control in the recordings that they make. Computers provide easy access to recording and editing and allow for consistency in recording. Editing can now be done digitally, and CD-ROMs and DVDs provide for easy access and efficient storage. This technology gives researchers the ability to separate vocal tracks and change tempo or keys, all of which can be used to keep variables constant and insure the accuracy of the variables that are manipulated.

In an earlier article, Hanser (1990) described the apparatus used as "a cassette, record, or compact disc player with a music collection composed of pieces of the patient's and the therapist's choices" (p. 285); the later article (Hanser & Thompson, 1994) refers to the earlier protocol. It can be assumed from this description that these pieces of equipment were those found in participants' homes. Cassidy and Ditty (2001) describe the transient evoked otoacoustic emissions tests (TEOAE), a test that is given to all newborns to screen for peripheral hearing loss:

> Sudden click-type noises are presented through a probe placed in the ear canal. In the TEOAE, very brief sounds produced by the probe almost instantaneously trigger movement in the outer hair cells of the cochlea (i.e., transiently evoked, or TE). This movement produces mechanical energy within the cochlea that is transmitted back through the middle ear and tympanic membrane. There it is converted to an acoustic signal in the ear canal. This acoustical signal is an otoacoustic emission (OAE). (p. 30)

Describe Independent Variables

The *independent variable* is the variable that is independent of the dependent variable, or the variable that the researcher controls. In experimental and many single-subject designs, the independent variable is manipulated in order to see its effects. The independent variable often has several levels; for instance, type of music might be an independent variable with rock, classical, and no music (the control condition) as its three levels. The description of the independent variables may be an operational definition or an exact description of the behavior under consideration.

Typically, the independent variable is labeled concisely, and a protocol or description of procedures is provided. The precision with which these procedures are described may vary. One of the difficulties of doing experimental and descriptive research in music therapy is that what is done in a music therapy session varies so much depending upon the person, the situation, the music, and so forth, that it is difficult to describe independent variables precisely and still be realistic as to the content of music therapy. The independent variable in Hilliard's (2003) study of the effects of music therapy on the quality and length of life of people diagnosed with terminal cancer was music therapy. His description of music therapy allows for a variety of procedures to be followed. He describes the music therapy as follows:

> The philosophical foundation of the music therapy program at Big Bend Hospice is a cognitive-behavioral approach where music therapy interventions are designed to treat identified problems and allow for the expression of emotions while respecting the process inherent within the live musical dialogue. All music therapy interventions in this study utilized live music, and all music selected was subject-preferred. Each subject received at least two music therapy sessions. During the course of the study, subjects died at varying intervals. Therefore, some subjects received only two sessions while one subject received thirteen sessions.
>
> Music therapists treated a variety of clinical needs of their subjects during the study and utilized a myriad of techniques. While needs and interventions varied, some themes emerged. Among these, most music therapists utilized one or more of the following music therapy techniques: song choice, music-prompted reminiscence, singing, live music listening, lyric analysis, instrument playing, song parody, singing with accompaniment using the iso-principle, planning of funerals or memorial services, song gifts, and music-assisted supportive counseling. (pp. 122–123)

Hilliard's description can be contrasted with the description provided by Hanser and Thompson (1994), whose independent variable was type of treatment for an 8-week period, with the following levels: (a) home-based music therapy in which participants "received eight weekly one-hour home visits with the music therapist in which they learned and practiced the eight techniques"; (b) self-administered music therapy, which included the "initial interview and . . . written instructions with recommendations for music therapy to accompany each technique," in addition to speaking with the music therapist for 20 minutes a week by telephone to discuss their experiences and responses; and (c) a wait-list control group whose members did not receive any type of therapy during this period (p. P266). Home-based music therapy was described with an outline of the protocol that was followed in their two music therapy conditions. The eight sessions consisted of:

1. Gentle exercise to familiar, energetic music;
2. Facial massage to familiar, relaxing music;
3. Progressive muscle relaxation to specially designed music interspersed with instructions by the therapist;
4. Guided imagery to programmatic music, where relaxing images incompatible with depressed mood and dysfunctional thinking were suggested before the music segment was played;
5. Special imagery to music where the individual created a structured visualization of some positive action to solve a problem or improve mood;
6. Slow, repetitive music to enhance falling asleep or deep relaxation;
7. Rhythmic music to enhance energy; and
8. Music listening in conjunction with drawing, painting, or other art forms to identify talents and interests. (p. P266)

A similar independent variable may be operationally defined in different ways for different studies. An example of this occurs in two studies that examine complexity as an independent variable. In one study (Gfeller, Christ, Knutson, Witt, & Mehr, 2003), music along a continuum of complexity was presented. The authors say:

> All test stimuli were excerpts (12–17 seconds) of the main themes of recordings heard in "real-life" that include various combinations of melody (sequential pitch patterns), harmony (simultaneous presentation of different pitches), rhythm, and timbre (tone quality). The items represented a continuum of vertical (harmonic) complexity, with some examples using solo instruments or vocalists, while others include complex combinations (blends) of instruments and/or voices. These complex songs reflect to a considerable extent the sorts of musical stimuli heard in everyday life. (p. 94)

Groene (2001) examined a different aspect of complexity in a study that looked at the responses of people who had been diagnosed with dementia to live or recorded music that had simple or complex accompaniment styles. He operationally defined simple and complex accompaniment styles as follows:

> The Simple Accompaniment style consisted of all song melodies sung on the beat with little or no syncopation, along with a guitar accompaniment of blocked chord strumming once per beat in duple or triple meter, depending upon the song. Harmonically, the Simple Accompaniment style was relegated to a minimum number of chord changes, usually three (I, IV, V7) and if necessary four (added V7 of V). The Complex Accompaniment style consisted of the following: syncopating the live song melody; performing the following guitar techniques: playing an introduction pattern (primarily of the last phrase) melodically and harmonically before leading the song syncopating the chordal structure; playing a ragtime/stride style (tonic, chord, 5th, chord) for songs in duple meter; adding bass runs between chords; playing improvisatory passages in the interim time between lyrics within the song; and employing percussive "shuffle"-type strum patterns. Harmonically, the Complex Accompaniment Style provided a richer chord palette than the Simple Style, including dominants of the basic harmonic structure (V or V7 of ii, iii. IV, V, etc.), 9th chords, suspended chords, substitution (e.g., ii/m7th for IV chord, e.g., diminished and augmented chords where appropriate), and two-part harmonic improvisatory passages. (pp. 39–40)

Some independent variables will have technical descriptions. An advantage of musical stimuli that are created through computer-based technologies such as the Musical Instrument Digital Interface (MIDI) is that they allow for precise description and also for re-creation, transposition, and so forth.

The independent variable in Cassidy and Ditty's (2001) study was gender and did not need to be described beyond the label. Wheeler's (2000) survey did not include independent variables.

Determine Measures of Dependent Variables

The *dependent variable* is what is measured to determine the effects (if any) of the independent variable. In other words, the dependent variable is dependent upon the independent variable. It is important to measure the dependent variable accurately—if the measurements are not accurate, there is nothing on which to base decisions in a quantitative study.

The first concerns in this area are the reliability and validity of the scores from a measure. As you know from earlier chapters, *reliability* deals with the consistency and accuracy of recording, while *validity* deals with the meaningfulness of the data, or whether it measures what it is supposed to measure. Both are important considerations in deciding how to collect data. If you are utilizing an instrument that has been designed and validated by others, levels of reliability will generally be reported, and you should include those levels in your report. If you are using an observational technique or other method in which the reliability of an instrument has not been determined previously, you will need to compute and then report the reliability.

After you have read the literature dealing with your topic, it is likely that you will have seen data collection instruments that other researchers have used. Whenever possible, it is recommended that you utilize these instruments that have already been tested, found to be reliable and valid, and used by others in research similar to yours.

However, there will be times when an instrument used by others is not available or is too complex to administer in your situation, or when nothing that you find in the literature exactly suits your needs. These considerations may make it necessary for you to design a means of data collection specifically for your study. In this case, you will need to determine the reliability and validity of your instrument. In addition, you will probably want to *pilot test* the instrument that you design. This means that you will use it prior to your actual study to be sure that it is satisfactory and, if not, work out the problems prior to using it.

In surveying the test instruments used by authors in the *Journal of Music Therapy (JMT)* from 1984–1997, Gregory (2000) found 115 different test instruments used in research studies. Of these, 25% were constructed by the researcher, 35% were constructed by someone else but unpublished, and 40% were published. Very few of the tests were of musical responses: Only 2 of the 46 published tests and 6 of the 40 unpublished tests measured musical responses.

A brief overview of some of the testing instruments that are available is given here along with examples from the music therapy literature.

Nonmusical Test Instruments

Nonmusical test instruments have been developed for a range of uses. They include such well-known and widely used standardized tests[7] as the Wechsler Intelligence Scale for Children® (Edition 4; WISC-IV; Wechsler, 2003) and other tests of cognitive functioning, the Minnesota Multiphasic Personality Inventory (Edition 2; MMPI-2; Butcher, Dahlstrom, Graham, Tellegen, & Kaemmer, 1989), and the Child Behavior Checklist and other Achenbach scales (Achenbach, 2004). New measures are developed regularly, described in the psychological literature, and available through companies that sell psychological tests. Reviews of tests are provided regularly in a series of publications through the Buros Institute of Mental Measurements (see www.unl.edu/buros). It is recommended that you consult one of these references prior to adopting a psychological test or inventory for your research. Some of these tests can be obtained and administered only by people with certain qualifications, such as a psychologist; if your measure falls into this category, you will need to work with a qualified person in order to utilize the test.

Test instruments that Gregory (2000, pp. 85–86) found to be used in three or more studies, listed in descending order by frequency of use, include:

- State and Trait Anxiety Inventory
- Global Deterioration Scale
- Mini-Mental Status Examination
- Peabody Picture Vocabulary Test
- Vineland Social Maturity Scale
- Multiple Affect Adjective Checklist
- Hamilton Rating Scale for Depression

Several psychological tests and inventories were used in Hanser and Thompson's (1994) study of older adults who were depressed. These included the Geriatric Depression Scale (GDS) and the Brief Symptom Inventory (BSI) to measure depression and distress, the Self-Esteem Inventory (SEI) to assess self-concept, the Profile of Mood States-Bipolar Form (POMS) to examine changes in mood, and the Beck Depression Inventory (BDI) to monitor levels of depression.

Musical Test Instruments

A number of standardized tests have been developed to measure various aspects of musical response,[8] of which musical aptitude and musical ability are frequently of interest in music therapy research. The Seashore Measures of Musical Talents (Seashore, Lewis, & Saetveit, 1960) was one of the earliest tests of musical aptitude (the 1960 edition is a revision of a 1939 test). This test may be used in its entirety, or, as is more frequently done, particular subtests may be used to measure specific aptitudes. A more recently developed test that has a high degree of validity is the Gordon Musical Aptitude Profile (MAP; Gordon, 1995). This test is divided into three major divisions, each of which has subtests. They include Tonal Imagery (Melody, Harmony), Rhythm Imagery (Tempo, Meter), and Musical Sensitivity (Phrasing, Balance, Style). The Seashore Measures of Musical Talents and the Gordon MAP are intended for children in grades 4–12. The Primary Measures of Music Audiation (PMMA; Gordon, 1986) is suitable for children in kindergarten through third grade and includes a Tonal and a Rhythm test, while the Intermediate Measures of Music Audiation (IMMA; Gordon, 1982) is useful for grades one to six.

As mentioned, Gregory (2000) found only a small number of test instruments that measured musical responses to be used in research in *JMT*. She found the Primary Measures of

---

[7] *Standardized tests* are tests that have been given to many people whose scores are compiled so that norms can be established. A *norm* is a set of scores derived from the average achievement of a large group; the scores of an individual can be located on this distribution and compared with others with similar characteristics.

[8] See *Measurement and Evaluation of Musical Experiences* (Boyle & Radocy, 1987) for additional information on these and other measures of musical experiences.

Music Audiation and Standley Group Activity Leadership Skills Checklist (Standley, 1991) each to be used by two researchers. The PMMA was used by Darrow (1987) to compare the musical aptitude of children with hearing losses in Grades 1–3 to that of children with normal hearing in the same grades. The PMMA was also used by Gibbons (1983a) to examine the musical aptitude of elderly people of various ages who were institutionalized. Gibbons (1983b) used the tempo portion of the MAP to determine the aptitude for rhythm discrimination of a group of children with emotional disturbances.

Observational Methods

The same methods that music therapists utilize to assess and evaluate sessions may be used as measures in research studies. Tallying, duration and latency recording, checklists, rating scales, and interval recording are some of the methods that may be used. These same means of measuring responses are also utilized in some of the more formal assessments and tests that were presented above. When using any observational method, it is crucial that an operational definition be included. You will recall that an operational definition is an exact description of the behavior under consideration. A good operational definition is likely to increase both interobserver and intraobserver reliability.[9]

Tallying, also called *frequency* or *event recording,* is when the observer marks every time that a discrete behavior occurs. This may be done with pencil and paper or a mechanical counter. The important thing is that each incidence of the behavior in question is recorded.[10] Waldon (2001) used frequency counts of participant-completed music therapy objectives and of "the number of 'cohesive gestures' or 'cohesive statements'" (p. 227) in a study of the effects of group music therapy on mood states and cohesiveness in adult oncology patients.

Duration recording measures the length of time during which something occurs. This is most accurately done with a stopwatch or, even more accurately, with a direct electrical connection that measures the time.[11] Related to duration is *latency recording,* which measures the length of time before a behavior occurs. Latency recording was used by Stratton and Zalanowski (1984) when they analyzed tapes of group discussions to measure the amount of time that each of several groups took to reach a consensus.

A *checklist* is a list of behaviors to be checked off when they occur. Cartwright and Cartwright (1984) suggest that the use of a checklist is appropriate when the behaviors of interest are known in advance and when there is no need to indicate their frequency or quality. A checklist developed by Standley (1991), the Group Activity Leadership Skills Checklist, has been used by several researchers to study the responses of practicum students to feedback (Adamek, 1994; Furman, Adamek, & Furman, 1992). Cripe (1986) utilized a checklist to collect information on the behavior of children who were hyperactive while hearing rock music or no music.

A *rating scale* consists of statements that are then rated on some kind of scale. It may be used when the degree or quality of the behavior, trait, or attitude is of interest. The scale may be numerical, with lower numbers indicating more or less of the statement. It is sometimes assumed that there are equal distances between each number. Such a scale is called a *Likert scale.* Rating scales are used often in music therapy studies. One area in which they are frequently used is in the measurement of pain, with the person experiencing the pain rating the degree of pain that he or she is experiencing. An example of this is a study by Rider (1985) in which level of pain and music preference were indicated by marking points on horizontal lines. The Improvisation Assessment Profiles (IAPs) developed by Bruscia (1987) are based on musical analyses organized into six areas (profiles), each of which utilizes a series of rating scales to evaluate improvisations on various dimensions. Ratings on the IAP scales correspond to verbal descriptors but are not

---

[9] Interobserver reliability is the amount of agreement among several observers of a situation while intraobserver reliability is the amount of agreement among various observations/recordings by the same observer.

[10] Interobserver agreement (reliability) for tallying is calculated by "dividing the lower frequency count by the higher frequency count and multiplying by 100" (Hall & Van Houten, 1983, p. 18).

[11] Interobserver agreement for duration recording is calculated by "presenting the average. . . difference between the two observers' durations on days that both observers recorded the behavior along with the range of the differences. . . . The average difference between the durations reported by the two observers is equal to the sum of the differences. . . divided by the number of times both observers recorded the behavior" (Hall & Van Houten, 1983, pp. 19–20).

correlated with any numerical values. Among many other uses of rating scales are studies by Burns et al. (2002) where participants rated their levels of relaxation; Browning (2001) where women rated their expectation of personal control during labor; and de l'Etoile (2002) where participants rated their mood.

Since they measure the degree or quality of something, it is important to realize that rating scales are by nature less objective than many other forms of measurement. Qualities are simply not as objective as behaviors.

Interval recording is an observational method that requires the complete attention of an observer. In interval recording, the observational time is divided into small intervals (e.g., 15 seconds). Within these intervals, the observer is normally instructed (often via earphones audible only to that person) to observe and then to record whether or not the behavior of interest occurred.[12] This measurement technique is called *time sampling* by some researchers (see Robb, 2003).[13] Hall and Van Houten (1983) divide interval recording systems into whole or partial interval recording. In whole interval recording, the behavior of interest must occur during the entire interval in order to be counted; in partial interval recording, it is scored if it occurs at all during the interval. Other authors (Madsen & Madsen, 1983) suggest that behavior be observed during an initial interval and recorded during the next interval (10-second intervals are recommended).

More complex interval recording techniques utilizing codes to enable observers to record many different behaviors of teachers and students have been used (Madsen & Madsen, 1983; Medley, 1982). In an application of the system developed by Madsen and Madsen to a music therapy setting, Cunningham (1986) recorded the number of vocalizations of residents with mental retardation under several volume levels of background music. Robb (2003) measured attentive behavior using a form developed by Madsen and Madsen, and she measured following one-step directions, remaining seated, facing the central speaker, and functional object manipulation using a time sampling form that she designed.

Physiological Measures

Many physiological observation methods, or ways to measure the functioning of a person or other living organism, have been developed. These measures are used under the assumption that physiological changes reflect changes (such as emotional state) in other parts of the person. Although the anticipated correlations have not always been found, physiological measures are still of great interest to researchers.

Some methods have been used for many years to study the effects of music. The measurement of skin conductance (galvanic skin response, GSR), heartbeat, gastric motility (related to digestion), muscle tension (electromyography, EMG), and blood pressure was popular for studying the effects of music on responses in the middle part of the 20th century and later. Some of these methods are still used today, frequently in conjunction with biofeedback systems. Recent examples of music therapy studies that use physiological measures are by Rüütel (2002), who used measures of blood pressure, pulse rate, and muscle oscillation frequency to study the effects of music and vibroacoustic stimulation; Lem (1998), who used electroencephalogram (EEG) measures to examine ongoing relationships between characteristics of the music and categories of imagery; and Burns et al. (2002), who measured skin temperature, frontalis muscle activity, and heart rate to study the effects of different types of music on perceived and physiological measures of stress.

When people receive auditory or visual feedback to mirror their physiological functions and thus provide feedback on them, it becomes biofeedback. The concept behind biofeedback is that, when people are given feedback as to what is going on inside their bodies, including their brains, they can learn to have some control over these physiological processes (Olson & Schwartz, 1987). Biofeedback monitors and measures physiological processes and aims to present what is monitored as meaningful information (Peek, 1987). The measurement of the monitorings may serve as a dependent measure in a research study. According to Scartelli (1989), the most

---

[12] Interobserver agreement for interval recording is calculated by dividing the number of agreements by the number of agreements plus disagreements (Hall & Van Houten, 1983).

[13] Although some authors use *time sampling* synonymously with interval recording, it is defined differently by Hall and Van Houten (1983).

popular biofeedback mechanisms monitor GSR, skin temperature, brain waves, blood pressure, and muscle tone. An example of a research study that utilizes biofeedback is by Scartelli (1984), examining the effects of sedative instrumental music on EMG biofeedback.

A newer physiological measure is of salivary secretions, used as a measure of immune system response. This is of interest because immune system function is related to health. One study utilizing salivary secretions is by Lane (1991), who measured the production of salivary immunoglobulin A (IgA) by children with cancer following a music therapy session. Bartlett, Kaufman, and Smeltekop (1993) looked at the effects of music listening and perceived sensory experiences on Interleukin-1 and Cortisol. Hirokawa and Ohira (2003) measured the effects of music listening after a stressful task using secretory IgA (S-IgA) and several other measures.

As music therapists work more closely with medical researchers, it is expected that additional physiological measures will be utilized. In addition, more sophisticated theories and research designs, combined with these and other measures, are yielding new information.[14]

Electronic Musical Measures

With technological advances in recent years, electronic musical measures have changed dramatically and will continue to do so. MIDI, high-speed photography, infrared light-emitting diodes (LEDs), traditional instruments modified to accept sensors, and computers allow researchers to examine increasingly subtle aspects of musical performance (Wilson & Roehmann, 1992). In some cases, measures developed to measure areas such as speech production can be used to measure aspects of musical production.

The PITCH MASTER™ performs both treatment and data collection functions; it provides feedback on pitch while also collecting data as to the pitches produced. Darrow and Cohen (1991) utilized the PITCH MASTER™ to improve the accuracy of vocal reproduction by two children who did not hear well.

Visi-Pitch™ was designed to provide immediate visual feedback and statistical analysis of speech and voice characteristics (Cohen, 1995). Cohen examined the effect of Visi-Pitch™ feedback in conjunction with vocal instruction on the speech of people with neurogenic communication disorders.

Baker (2004; Baker, Wigram, & Gold, 2005) used Cool Edit 2000™, a digital audio recorder, editor, and mixer, to study the effects of song singing on affective intonation in people with traumatic brain injury. She used this program to prepare musical material for various parts of the research study. She also used a software analysis program, Multi-Speech™ Model 3700 with its Real Time Pitch 5121 module. She describes this as:

> A windows-based speech analysis program that uses standard multimedia
> hardware to capture, analyse and play speech samples. The program includes
> displays for analysis, including wave form, spectrum, spectrogram, more than
> twenty voice parameters, pitch, palatogram, motor speech protocols and
> measurements, audio synchronisation, digital filtering and formant values.
> (Baker, p. 112)

Another device that combines treatment and data collection is the Music Vibration Table (MVT™; Chesky & Michel, 1991). The MVT™ "consists of a base table, a sound system, a vibrating membrane (tabletop), and a computerized vibration feedback processing system that measures and controls the transmission of the vibrations as they affect a subject's body" (p. 34).

Some music and sound measures have been used for many years; most have been or will be updated with computer technology. They include chromatic tuners and stroboscopes to measure pitch, decibel meters to measure loudness, and spectrograms or oscilloscopes to display sounds. While details on the many computer applications available for gathering musical data are beyond the scope of this chapter, overviews of applications of technology in psychomusicology research (Webster, 1989), for music education (Williams & Webster, 1999; Webster, 2002), and for music therapy (Crowe & Rio, 2004; Krout, 1987, 1997, 1998; Krout, Burnham, & Moorman, 1993; Krout & Mason, 1988) may be useful.

---

[14] See *A Scientific Model of Music in Therapy and Medicine* (Thaut, 2000) and "Neuropsychological Processes in Music Perception and Their Relevance in Music Therapy" (Thaut, 2002) for examples of connections between theory and research.

Other Electronic Measures

Modern technology has made many other measures available to the music researcher. Among the most common are analog and digital audio- and videotapes. Taping something allows the researcher to study the responses repeatedly and to obtain reliability measures, leading to greater accuracy as well as potentially deeper levels of understanding. Analysis of tapes has been made much more efficient with the use of computer technology. An example is from a study of infant preferences of auditory stimuli (Standley & Madsen, 1990) in which videotapes were made of the sessions and elapsed milliseconds were recorded on the videotape. According to Gregory (1989), "It soon became apparent that the changes from one condition to the other were often too quick to be captured by the traditional timed behavioral observation methods" (pp. 131–132). Gregory goes on to say: "Computerized direct observation appeared to be the best available alternative for measuring durations of complex infant responses to 'individualized' sequences of sound conditions" (p. 132). With these considerations in mind, a computer program was adapted to assist trained observers in categorizing the behaviors, after which it compiled the percentages of responses for each variable. The use of the computer in this situation allowed for a much more detailed level of analysis than could have been achieved without it.

The use of computer technology in music therapy research has grown in recent years and has incorporated the use of both commercially available products and researcher-designed applications. The ongoing miniaturization of equipment and technology from the 1980s (Greenfield, 1985; Hunter, 1989; Krout, 1989) and 1990s (Krout, 1997; Reilly, 1997) through to the present (Ingber, 2003; Rickson, 2004; in press) has allowed for its use in a variety of settings.

An example is the Continuous Response Digital Interface (CRDI), which was developed to measure ongoing and fluctuating musical responses while people are listening to music. It consists of a dial or a slide that can be manipulated by the listener as the listener's responses or perceptions vary, even subtly (Gregory, 1989; Madsen, 1990), and is connected to a computer. The software includes the means of receiving, manipulating, and saving information about subjects' responses; storing subjects' summary data, and displaying it on tables and graphs. The CRDI has been used to measure participant responses in a number of dependent areas such as emotional responses (Madsen, 1997a, 1997b; Madsen & Frederickson, 1993), mood (Goins, 1998), attention (Gregory, 2002), relaxation (Staum & Brotons, 2000), attitudes toward people with disabilities (Gregory, 1998), listener preferences (Brittin, 1996), and listener tension (Madsen & Frederickson, 1993), and as a reliability measure of other physiological variables (Gregory, 1995). Additional information on the CRDI and a bibliography of studies that have used it can be found at http://otto.cmr.fsu.edu/memt/crdi.

Neurologic Music Therapy (NMT) was developed by Thaut and his colleagues from laboratory studies of the effects of rhythm and music on movement into a clinical technique with broad application for people with various neurological problems. The laboratory studies use a variety of electronic measures to measure responses. The NMT technique of Rhythmic Auditory Stimulation (RAS), geared to the maintenance and rehabilitation of functional behavior through sensorimotor training, is one of the most researched in both laboratory and clinical settings (Clair & Pasiali, 2004). A number of studies have measured changes in EMG patterns as dependent variables in a variety of areas such as synchronization of finger tapping (Thaut, Rathburn, & Miller, 1997; Thaut, Tian, & Azimi-Sadjadi, 1998), gait cycle profiles (Miller, Thaut, McIntosh, & Rice, 1996), and gastrocnemius muscle amplitude (Thaut, McIntosh, & Rice, 1997). One typical study (Thaut, McIntosh, Prassas, & Rice, 1993) used a multichannel EMG system, consisting of a power unit and two amplifier processor modules, to collect raw EMG signals as a subject walked with and without a rhythm stimulus. "Temporal stride data were collected via an 8m long dual walkway consisting of voltage coded pressure-sensitive switch mats with a rubber surface. EMG equipment and walkway were interfaced via a DMA interface board with a 386 computer for data collection" (p. 10). Numerous references to the extensive research on NMT can be found at http://www.colostate.edu/depts/cbrm/references.htm.

Other researchers have designed procedures and adapted technology for specific studies. In a recent example, Rickson (2004; in press) designed and used a computer-based synchronized tapping task (STT) as a dependent measure in comparing the effects of instructional versus improvisational models of music therapy on the motor impulsivity of adolescents with attention deficit hyperactivity disorder (ADHD). The STT involved participants tapping the space bar of a laptop computer in time with rhythmic beats presented at two speeds, both visually on the laptop monitor and played simultaneously through a speaker. Data were captured by the computer and then analyzed for regularity of tapping and tapping errors.

Plan for Data Collection, Scoring, and Analysis

Data Collection

Once you have selected the instruments for collecting your data, you need to be sure that it is administered correctly. The best data collection instrument is of no use if it is not properly administered.

This may involve training people to administer the instrument you have selected or learning to administer it yourself. As part of this process, you will want to insure that people who administer your instrument have a high level of intra- and interobserver reliability. To develop this, they will probably need to practice administering the instrument repeatedly with feedback until they have a developed a high degree of agreement (with themselves on repeated observations and with other observers). The level of interobserver reliability is commonly reported as part of a research report, when applicable.

As mentioned earlier, only people with certain qualifications can administer some psychological tests; if you use one of these, you will need to enlist a qualified person to administer it. Other types of data collection may also require people with special skills to administer or assist in the administration of the instruments.

Scoring

Data must also be scored correctly. If you are using a psychological test or inventory, procedures for scoring and interpretation are provided in the manual that accompanies the test. Computerized scoring and analysis may be available.

Analysis

The data analysis is tied to the research question and the design of the research. A particular question and design often calls for a certain kind of inferential, descriptive, or visual data analysis. Some designs and types of quantitative research require statistical analysis while others utilize graphic illustration. Quantitative case studies frequently utilize graphs to facilitate understanding of the results. Therefore, the particulars of any study must be taken into account in determining appropriate methods of data analysis. See Chapter 14, Statistical Methods of Data Analysis, for further information on this subject.

Ethical Review

After the research study has been designed, it must go through an ethical review process. This is the case with research involving human subjects and may apply to some other studies. This process normally involves presenting the proposal to an institutional review board (IRB). The IRB, along with the researcher, has the responsibility for insuring that ethical considerations are met. See Chapter 18, Ethical Precautions in Music Therapy Research, for additional information on these important procedures.

Implement Procedures

When the study has been properly conceived and designed, the next step is to implement the procedures. An advantage of proper planning in quantitative research is that implementing the study does not involve continuing to plan the study but is rather a matter of carrying out the procedures as planned.

One way to increase the chances of your study running smoothly is to do a pilot study. As you do this smaller, preliminary study to try out your procedures, measurement devices, and so forth, unanticipated problems in the procedures will appear and can be worked out so that the final study runs more smoothly.

It is an unfortunate fact that, in spite of the best planning, things do not always go as expected during the study itself. Many of the things that may go wrong are because people do not always do as we expect. Some of our participants may move or drop out of the study. The room that we planned to use for the experiment may develop a leak. Children may go on a field trip during the time that we are scheduled to observe them. Problems in carrying out the research arise in spite of proper planning—the researcher's task is to minimize the problems so they have the least possible effect on the study. With experience, the ability to anticipate and proactively solve problems increases dramatically.

Further Steps

Following the collection of the data, the data will be analyzed, conclusions drawn based on the research questions and results, and the research report written. Chapter 14 provides information on statistical analysis of the data, while information on writing the research report is covered in Chapter 16, Writing the Quantitative Research Report.

References

Adamek, M. S. (1994). Audio-cueing and immediate feedback to improve group leadership skills: A live supervision model. *Journal of Music Therapy, 31,* 135–164.

Achenbach, T. M. (2004). *Achenbach System of Empirically Based Assessment.* Burlington, VT: ASEBA Research Center for Children, Youth, and Families. Available at www.ASEBA.org

American Psychological Association. (2001). *Publication manual of the American Psychological Association* (5th ed.). Washington, DC: Author.

Baker, F. (2004). *The effects of song singing on improvements in affective intonation of people with traumatic brain injury.* Unpublished doctoral dissertation, Aalborg University, Aalborg, Denmark. Available at http://eprint.uq.edu.au/view/person/Baker,_Felicity.html

Baker, F., Wigram, T., & Gold, C. (2005). The effects of a song singing programme on the affective speaking intonation of people with traumatic brain injury. *Brain Injury, 19,* 519–528.

Bartlett, D., Kaufman, D., & Smeltekop, R. (1993). The effects of music listening and perceived sensory experiences on the immune system as measured by interleukin-1 and cortisol. *Journal of Music Therapy, 30,* 194–209.

Boyle, J. D., & Radocy, R. E. (1987). *Measurement and evaluation of musical experiences.* New York: Schirmer Books.

Brittin, R. V. (1996). Listeners' preference for music of other cultures: Comparing response modes. *Journal of Research in Music Education, 44,* 328–340.

Browning, C. A. (2001). Music therapy in childbirth: Research in practice. *Music Therapy Perspectives, 19,* 74–81.

Bruscia, K. E. (1987). *Improvisational models of music therapy.* Springfield, IL: Charles C. Thomas.

Burns, J. L., Labbé, E., Arke, B., Capeless, K., Cooksey, B., Steadman, A., & Gonzales, C. (2002). The effects of different types of music on perceived and physiological measures of stress. *Journal of Music Therapy, 39,* 101–116.

Butcher, J. N., Dahlstrom, W. G., Graham, J. R., Tellegen, A., & Kaemmer, B. (1989). *Minnesota Multiphasic Personality Inventory-2.* Minneapolis, MN: University of Minnesota Press.

Cartwright, C. A., & Cartwright, G. P. (1984). *Developing observation skills* (2nd ed.). New York: McGraw-Hill.

Cassidy, J. W., & Ditty, K. M. (2001). Gender differences among newborns on a transient otoacoustic emissions test for hearing. *Journal of Music Therapy, 38,* 28–35.

Chesky, K. S., & Michel, D. E. (1991). The Music Vibration Table (MVT™): Developing a technology and conceptual model for pain relief. *Music Therapy Perspectives, 9,* 32–38.

Clair, A. A., & Pasiali, V. (2004). Neurologic Music Therapy. In A.-A. Darrow (Ed.), *Introduction to approaches in music therapy* (pp. 143–157). Silver Spring, MD: American Music Therapy Association.

Cohen, J. (1992). A power primer. *Psychological Bulletin, 112,* 155–159.

Cohen, N. S. (1995). The effect of vocal instruction and Visi-Pitch™ feedback on the speech of persons with neurogenic communication disorders: Two case studies. *Music Therapy Perspectives, 13,* 70–75.

Cone, J. D., & Foster, S. L. (1993). *Dissertations and theses from start to finish.* Washington, DC: American Psychological Association.

Cripe, F. F. (1986). Rock music as therapy for children with attention deficit disorder: An exploratory study. *Journal of Music Therapy, 23,* 30–37.

Crowe, B. J., & Rio, R. (2004). Implications of technology in music therapy practice and research for music therapy education: A review of the literature. *Journal of Music Therapy, 41,* 282–320.

Cunningham, T. D. (1986). The effect of music volume on the frequency of vocalizations of institutionalized mentally retarded persons. *Journal of Music Therapy, 23,* 208–218.

Darrow, A.-A. (1987). An investigative study: The effect of hearing impairment on musical aptitude. *Journal of Music Therapy, 24,* 88–96.

Darrow, A.-A., & Cohen, N. (1991). The effect of programmed pitch practice and private instruction on the vocal reproduction accuracy of children with hearing impairments: Two case studies. *Music Therapy Perspectives, 9,* 61–65.

de l'Etoile, S. K. (2002). The effect of a musical mood induction procedure on mood state-dependent word retrieval. *Journal of Music Therapy, 39,* 145–160.

Furman, C. E., Adamek, M. S., & Furman, A. G. (1992). The use of an auditory device to transmit feedback to student therapists. *Journal of Music Therapy, 29,* 40–53.

Gfeller, K., Christ, A., Knutson, J., Witt, S., & Mehr, M. (2003). The effects of familiarity and complexity on appraisal of complex songs by cochlear implant recipients and normal hearing adults. *Journal of Music Therapy, 40,* 78–112.

Gibbons, A. C. (1983a). Primary Measures of Music Audiation scores in an institutionalized elderly population. *Journal of Music Therapy, 20,* 21–29.

Gibbons, A. C. (1983b). Rhythm responses in emotionally disturbed children with differing needs for external structure. *Music Therapy, 3,* 94–102.

Goins, W. (1998). The effect of moodstates: Continuous versus summative responses. *Journal of Music Therapy, 35,* 242–258.

Gordon, E. E. (1982). *Intermediate Measures of Music Audiation.* Chicago: G.I.A. Publications.

Gordon, E. E. (1986). *Primary Measures of Music Audiation.* Chicago: GIA Publications.

Gordon, E. E. (1995). *Musical Aptitude Profile* (rev.). Chicago: GIA Publications.

Greenfield, D. (1985). The evaluation of a computer system for behavioral observation training and research. *Journal of Music Therapy, 22,* 95–98.

Gregory, D. (1995). Research note: The Continuous Response Digital Interface: An analysis of reliability measures. *Psychomusicology, 14,* 197–208.

Gregory, D. (1989). Using computers to measure continuous music responses. *Psychomusicology, 8,* 127–134.

Gregory, D. (1998). Reactions to ballet with wheelchairs: Reflections of attitudes toward people with disabilities. *Journal of Music Therapy, 35,* 274–283.

Gregory, D. (2000). Test instruments used by *Journal of Music Therapy* authors from 1984–1997. *Journal of Music Therapy, 37,* 79–94.

Gregory, D. (2002). Music listening for maintaining attention of older adults with cognitive impairments. *Journal of Music Therapy, 39,* 244–264.

Groene, R. (2001). The effect of presentation and accompaniment styles on attentional and responsive behaviors of participants with dementia diagnoses. *Journal of Music Therapy, 38,* 36–50.

Hall, R. V., & Van Houten, R. (1983). *Managing behavior 1: Behavior modification: The measurement of behavior.* Austin, TX: Pro-Ed.

Hanser, S. B. (1990). A music therapy strategy for depressed older adults in the community. *Journal of Applied Gerontology, 9,* 283–298.

Hanser, S. B., & Thompson, L. W. (1994). Effects of a music therapy strategy on depressed older adults. *Journal of Gerontology: Psychological Sciences, 49,* P265–P269.

Hilliard, R. E. (2003). The effects of music therapy on the quality and length of life of people diagnosed with terminal cancer. *Journal of Music Therapy, 40,* 113–137.

Hirokawa, E., & Ohira, H. (2003). The effects of music listening after a stressful task on immune functions, neuroendocrine responses, and emotional states in college students. *Journal of Music Therapy, 40,* 189–211.

Hunter, L. L. (1989). Computer-assisted assessment of melodic and rhythmic discrimination skills. *Journal of Music Therapy, 26,* 79–87.

Ingber, J. (2003). Using MIDI with adults who have developmental disabilities. *Music Therapy Perspectives, 21,* 46–50.

Krout, R. (1987). Evaluating software for music therapy applications. *Journal of Music Therapy, 24,* 213–223.

Krout, R. (1989). Microcomputer use in college music therapy programs. *Journal of Music Therapy, 26,* 88–94.

Krout, R. (1997). *Music technology for music therapists* (rev. ed.). Coralville, IA: West Music.

Krout, R. (1998). *Designing digital success in music therapy and education.* Coralville, IA: West Music.

Krout, R., Burnham, A., & Moorman, S. (1993). Computer and electronic music applications with students in special education: From program proposal to progress evaluation. *Music Therapy Perspectives, 11,* 28–31.

Krout, R., & Mason, M. (1988). Using computer and electronic music resources in clinical music therapy with behaviorally disordered students, 12 to 18 years old. *Music Therapy Perspectives, 5,* 114–118.

Lane, D. L. (1991). The effect of a single music therapy session on hospitalized children as measured by salivary Immunoglobulin A, speech pause time, and a patient opinion Likert scale. *Pediatric Research, 29* (4, Pt. 2), 11A.

Lem, A. (1998). EEG reveals potential connections between selected categories of imagery and the psycho-acoustic profile of music. *Australian Journal of Music Therapy, 9,* 3–17.

Madsen, C. H., Jr., & Madsen, C. K. (1983). *Teaching/discipline: A positive approach for educational development* (3rd ed.). Raleigh, NC: Contemporary Publishers.

Madsen, C. K. (1990, November). Research in the music classroom. *Music Educators Journal, 77*(3), 26–28.

Madsen, C. K. (1997a). Emotional response to music. *Psychomusicology, 16,* 59–67.

Madsen, C. K. (1997b). Emotional response to music as measured by the two-dimensional CRDI. *Journal of Music Therapy, 34,* 187–199.

Madsen, C. K., & Fredrickson, W. E. (1993). The experience of musical tension: A replication of Nielsen's research using the Continuous Response Digital Interface. *Journal of Music Therapy, 30,* 46–63.

Medley, D. M. (1982). Systematic observation. In H. E. Mitzel (Ed.), *Encyclopedia of educational research* (5th ed., pp. 1841–1851). New York: Free Press.

Miller, R. A., Thaut, M. H., McIntosh, G. C., & Rice R. R. (1996). Components of EMG symmetry and variability in Parkinsonian and healthy elderly gait. *Electroencephalography and Clinical Neurophysiology, 101,* 1–7.

Olson, R. P., & Schwartz, M. S. (1987). An historical perspective on the biofeedback field. In M. S. Schwartz (Ed.), *Biofeedback: A practitioner's guide* (pp. 3–16). New York: Guilford.

Peek, C. J. (1987). A primer of biofeedback instrumentation. In M. S. Schwartz (Ed.), *Biofeedback: A practitioner's guide* (pp. 73–127). New York: Guilford.

Reilly, J. F. (1997). LIGHTNING strikes: A correlational study of the gesturo-musical responses of in-patients with acute manic or depressive symptomatology using the LIGHTNING module. *Journal of Music Therapy, 34,* 260–276.

Rickson, D. J. (2004). *Instruction and improvisational models of music therapy with adolescents who have attention deficit hyperactivity disorder (ADHD): A comparison of the effects on motor impulsivity.* Unpublished master's thesis, Massey University, Wellington, New Zealand.

Rickson, D. J. (In press). Instructional and improvisational models of music therapy with adolescents who have attention deficit hyperactivity disorder (ADHD): A comparison of the effects on motor impulsivity. *Journal of Music Therapy.*

Rider, M. S. (1985). Entrainment mechanisms are involved in pain reduction, muscle relaxation, and music-mediated imagery. *Journal of Music Therapy, 22,* 183–193.

Robb, S. L. (2003). Music interventions and group participation skills of preschoolers with visual impairments: Raising questions about music, arousal, and attention. *Journal of Music Therapy, 40,* 266–282.

Rosenthal. R., & Rosnow, R. L. (1984). *Essentials of behavioral research: Methods and data analysis.* New York: McGraw-Hill.

Rüütel, E. (2002). The psychophysiological effects of music and vibroacoustic stimulation. *Nordic Journal of Music Therapy, 11,* 16–26.

Scartelli, J. P. (1984). The effect of EMG biofeedback and sedative music, EMG biofeedback only, and sedative music only on frontalis muscle relaxation ability. *Journal of Music Therapy, 21,* 67–78.

Scartelli, J. P. (1989). *Music and self-management methods.* St. Louis, MO: MMB Music.

Seashore, C. E., Lewis, L., & Saetveit, J. G. (1960). *Seashore Measures of Musical Talents.* New York: Psychological Corporation. (Originally published, 1939)

Standley, J. (1991). *Music techniques in therapy, counseling and special education.* St. Louis, MO: MMB.

Standley, J. M., & Madsen, C. K. (1990). Comparison of infant preferences and responses to auditory stimuli: Music, mother, and other female voice. *Journal of Music Therapy, 27,* 54–97.

Staum, M. J., & Brotons, M. (2000). The effect of music amplitude on the relaxation response. *Journal of Music Therapy, 37,* 22–39.

Stratton, V. N., & Zalanowski, A. (1984). The effect of background music on verbal interaction in groups. *Journal of Music Therapy, 21,* 16–26.

Thaut, M. H. (2000). *A scientific model of music in therapy and medicine.* San Antonio, TX: Institute for Music Research.

Thaut, M. H. (2002). Neuropsychological processes in music perception and their relevance in music therapy. In R. F. Unkefer & M. H. Thaut (Eds.), *Music therapy in the treatment of adults with mental disorders* (pp. 2–32). St. Louis, MO: MMB Music.

Thaut, M. H., McIntosh, G. C., Prassas, S. G., & Rice, R. R. (1993). Effect of rhythmic auditory cuing on temporal stride parameters and EMG patterns in hemiparetic gait of stroke patients. *Journal of Neurological Rehabilitation, 7,* 9–16.

Thaut, M. H., McIntosh, G. C., & Rice, R. R. (1997). Rhythmic facilitation of gait training in hemiparetic stroke rehabilitation. *Journal of Neurological Sciences, 151,* 207–212.

Thaut, M. H., Rathburn, J. A., & Miller, R. A. (1997). Music versus metronomic timekeeper in a rhythmic motor task. *International Journal of Arts Medicine, 5,* 4–12.

Thaut, M. H., Tian, B., & Azimi-Sadjadi, M. R. (1998). Rhythmic finger tapping to cosine-wave modulated metronome sequences: Evidence of subliminal entrainment. *Human Movement Science, 17,* 839–863.

Waldon, E. G. (2001). The effects of group music therapy on mood states and cohesiveness in adult oncology patients. *Journal of Music Therapy, 38,* 212–238.

Webster, P. R. (Ed.). (1989). Microcomputers in psychomusicology research [Special issue]. *Psychomusicology, 8.*

Webster, P. R. (2002). Computer-based technology and music teaching and learning. In R. Colwell & C. Richardson (Eds.), *The new handbook of research on music teaching and learning* (pp. 416–439). New York: Oxford University Press.

Wechsler, D. (2003). *Wechsler Intelligence Scale for Children®* (4th ed.). San Antonio, TX: PsychCorp.

Wheeler, B. L. (2000). Music therapy practicum practices: A survey of music therapy educators. *Journal of Music Therapy, 37,* 286–311.

Williams, D., & Webster, P. (1999). *Experiencing music technology* (2nd ed.). New York: Schirmer Books.

Wilson, F. R., & Roehmann, F. L. (1992). The study of biomechanical and physiological processes in relation to musical performance. In R. Colwell (Ed.), *Handbook of research on music teaching and learning* (pp. 509–524). New York: Schirmer Books.

Acknowledgments

The author wishes to thank Robert Krout for input into technological applications as well as feedback on the chapter and Gene Ann Behrens for feedback on the chapter.

Chapter 11
Designing Qualitative Research[1]
Kenneth E. Bruscia

The purpose of this chapter is to describe the basic tasks involved in the process of designing qualitative research. It is important to understand from the onset that these tasks may be done in a variety of ways and in various sequences, and that the methodological process of doing qualitative research varies from study to study, depending on the researcher and the phenomenon being studied.

Characteristics of the Process

The reason for the wide variability in methodologies is that the process of doing qualitative research has three defining characteristics. First, qualitative research is an emergent process rather than a determined sequence of step-by-step procedures. Qualitative researchers do not begin with a specific design or method and then impose it on the phenomenon; instead, they begin by focusing on the phenomenon, approaching it in a exploratory way, and then figuring out how the phenomenon will reveal itself in its own way or with the least amount of interference. The design of a qualitative study is not fully decided and known beforehand; it emerges through a process of discovery. As such, the research process is not predictable or linear, rather it unfolds in ways that are unique to the phenomenon under study. The researcher tries one method of approaching the phenomenon, evaluates its effectiveness in providing data, and then adjusts or changes the method until it yields rich, relevant, and meaningful data. For this reason, the present chapter equates *designing* research to actually *doing* it. Designing a study begins with establishing a focus and purpose and continues through data collection, data analysis, data interpretation, and presenting the results in a scholarly forum. Thus, every phase of doing a qualitative study involves designing and redesigning some aspect of the study.

Second, qualitative research is inextricably a personal process. Every study is rooted in the values and beliefs of the researcher and how these are implicated in studying and making discoveries about the phenomenon. There are no sharp delineations between knower (researcher) and known (phenomenon). The knower or researcher is revealed within the context of the phenomenon to be known, and the phenomenon to be known is revealed within the context of the knower or researcher. In qualitative research, the entire study can be seen as a personal creation of the researcher. Everything about the study—its focus, its design, its methods of gathering data, its approach to data analysis, its findings and conclusions—is determined or implemented by the researcher, not according to pre-established rules of science but on the basis of the researcher's values, beliefs, and pre-understandings being uncovered from moment to moment as she or he studies the phenomenon.

Third, qualitative research is also an inextricably interpersonal process. It is a way that human beings study other human beings and the condition of being human. As such, qualitative research always focuses on and requires human interaction and inter-experience—between researcher and participant, between participants and the phenomenon, among participants, and between researcher and audience. Hence, in addition to being a personal creation of the researcher, it is also a co-creation of researcher, participant, and audience. Thus, everything about the study—its focus, its design, its methods of gathering data, its approach to data analysis, its findings and conclusions—is created by the researcher inter-responsively, that is, as these elements influence and are influenced by all those involved in the research.

These three characteristics of qualitative research are implicated in every task described below, and, for this reason, each task can be reframed according to which characteristic is most relevant at any time during the research process. Also, note that, although presented in a quasi-logical or chronological sequence, a researcher may do these tasks in any order, work on several at the same time, and repeat them throughout the study.

---

[1] This chapter is a reworking of Chapters 20, 21, and 22 in the first edition of this book.

Basic Design Tasks

Journaling

Once the focus and purpose has been set, even tentatively, the qualitative researcher should begin a reflexive journal. Lincoln and Guba (1985) describe the journal as "a kind of diary in which the investigator on a daily basis, or as needed, records a variety of information about *self* (hence the term 'reflexive') and *method*"(p. 327). They also suggest that the journal

> consist of separate parts that include the following: (1) the daily schedule and logistics of the study; (2) a personal diary that provides the opportunity for catharsis, for reflection upon what is happening in terms of one's own values and interests, and for speculation about growing insights; and (3) a methodological log in which methodological decisions and rationales are recorded. Entries should be made on a daily basis in the daily schedule and diary, and as needed in the methodological log. (p. 327)

As will be explained below, the researcher's journal is the place to record outcomes of self-inquiry, consultation, collaboration, and most other tasks involved in implementing the study as described in this chapter.

Self-Inquiry

Self-inquiry is any attempt of the researcher to bring into awareness or to understand his or her own personal and professional perspective with regard to any aspect of the study. In this context, a researcher's perspective may include myriad personal and professional experiences, concerns, needs, reactions, thoughts, feelings, values, beliefs, and so forth that may influence the study in any way, along with the researcher's educational background, culture, language, and philosophy (such as ontology, epistemology, axiology).

Given the personal nature of qualitative research, self-inquiry is absolutely essential to the process—it is something that the researcher must do before, during, and after every phase of the research study, with regard to every participant, every data set, every major event or interaction, every consultation, every analysis or interpretation, every finding, and every conclusion. Here are a few typical questions that might guide such self-inquiries:

- What beliefs do I bring to this study, about the nature of the world (ontology), how knowledge is gained (epistemology), and what has value (axiology)?
- How does my location in a particular culture, country, professional landscape, and workplace influence my conception of this study? How is the study already embedded in my own language?
- Why am I doing a study with this particular focus and purpose? How do the research questions reflect my own personal, professional, and cultural perspectives?
- Why have I designed the study in this way? How does the method reflect my own personal, professional, and cultural perspectives?
- What expectations do I have for the outcome of this study, and how are they related to my personal, professional, and cultural biases?
- How have my biases influenced how I analyze and interpret the data? Am I truly open to discover something I did not expect?
- How are my perspectives and biases implicated in how I writing up this study?

Self-inquiry can be accomplished in various ways. The most common is making reflective entries in the journal about one's own personal and professional experiences and reactions as they occur during the research. Other ways may include dialoguing with a consultant, a coresearcher, or a participant. In all cases, material uncovered from the various self-inquiries should be recorded in the journal.

When a researcher uses self-inquiry effectively and remains aware of how his or her own perspective and biases are implicated in the research process, the researcher is said to demonstrate the quality of reflexivity (Stige, 2002). When one is being reflexive, one is bringing into awareness how one's own position in the world bears upon the research task at hand.

Of course, being reflexive is not enough—it is the beginning of the self-inquiry process, not the end. What does the researcher do with the reflexivity or awareness that she or he has acquired? Generally, a qualitative researcher may take two approaches to dealing with the material uncovered through self-inquiry. The first is called *bracketing* or making an *epoché*. To bracket is to suspend or hold in abeyance any perspectives or biases the researcher might have in order to minimize their effects on the study. Here the researcher puts aside or suppresses the bracketed material.

In contrast, the second approach is to acknowledge and incorporate material from the self-inquiry into the research study. Here the researcher openly admits to using his or her own perspectives and biases to color and shape all aspects of the study, including the findings. This second approach is what is characteristically done in heuristic or hermeneutic studies. Note that bracketing can be seen as an effort to maintain some degree of *objectivity*, while incorporating the reflexive material into the research study is an effort to utilize one's own *subjectivity*. Thus, the two approaches may sometimes reflect variations in paradigm and epistemology.

Regardless of which approach to reflexivity is taken, the most important discoveries gleaned from self-inquiry should appear somewhere in the final report. Sometimes the introduction to the study can include a narrative on how and why the researcher got involved in the topic and where the researcher was coming from in designing the study. Discoveries made later in the research process can appear in other sections (for example, Method, Results, Discussion, Conclusions), depending on which section of the study is affected by the discovery.

Consulting

To consult is to seek the guidance of an expert who is knowledgeable about the topic being researched and the process of doing qualitative research. It is most helpful to work with the same consultant throughout the entire study and, if necessary, to consult with others around specific issues.

The role of a consultant is threefold: (a) to guide the researcher's decision-making with regard to the design, implementation, and final presentation of the study; (b) to facilitate the self-inquiry process; and (c) to help relate materials uncovered from the self-inquiry process with what the researcher is actually doing at each phase of the study. In short, the consultant helps the researcher to integrate self and method.

Identifying Data Sources and Settings

Before data collection procedures are designed, the researcher must identify the kinds of data that will be needed to answer the research question while also determining how to gain access to that data. As outlined in Chapter 7, Research Topics and Questions in Music Therapy, most qualitative studies focus on the following kinds of data:

Events/actions/interactions: behaviors, incidents, or any observable happening,

Experiences: a person's perception, interpretation, or understanding of a particular phenomenon,

Written and spoken language: texts and discourses of all kinds,

Art works: materials that result from participation in music, dance, or visual art activities (for example, composition, recorded improvisation),

Artifacts: objects that are related in some way to any of the other data sources but do not fall under the categories of language and art (for example, chair, guitar),

Persons: individuals, groups, communities, or cultures as revealed through any or all of the above kinds of data.

A qualitative study may focus on one or more of these data sources, depending upon the type of research. For example, phenomenological research focuses almost entirely on experience while discourse analysis focuses on language; in contrast, ethnography and action research may focus on events, experiences, language, art works, or various combinations thereof.

Once the data types are selected, the next questions are: How can the researcher gain access to these data? And, in what situations will the targeted phenomenon occur or be accessible? Researchers can gain access to data at three levels of engagement. In experimental studies, the researcher engages participants in a particular task, situation, or activity in order to produce data on the phenomenon under study. Usually, this is necessary if the phenomenon does not present itself naturally, that is, without the participant being engaged in a specific way by the researcher. In naturalistic studies, the researcher studies or observes participants in their everyday lived worlds where the phenomenon being studied occurs naturally, without intervention or manipulation by the researcher. In ex post facto or retrospective studies, the participants have already encountered or engaged the phenomenon being studied, and their engagement has already been recorded, so the researcher only needs to gather data that are already available.

Designing Data Collection Procedures

Once data sources and settings have been identified, the researcher is ready to design data collection procedures. Two questions are fundamental: Will the researcher engage the participant in specific interactions, dialogues, or music activities? and, Will the data be gathered through observations, interviews, or the examination of documents, artworks, and artifacts? Returning to the above kinds of data:

Data on events, actions, and interactions: These are best gathered through some type of observation. The researcher may observe the participants while engaging them in a particular activity, while they are being engaged by someone else, or while they are behaving and interacting within a naturalistic setting without any intervention or direction.

Data on experiences: Such information is best gathered through some type of verbal inquiry. Verbal inquiry may include a variety of techniques. The researcher may question participants in formal or informal interviews, ask them to write about their experiences, or enter into various types of dialogue where the participants can co-construct their description of the experience with the researcher or with other participants. Here again, the researcher may have to engage the participant in the experience, have someone else engage them in the experience, wait until the experience occurs naturally, or search the participant's past for previous occurrences of the experience.

Data on spoken language: Speech can be gathered in-vivo, that is, while the researcher is engaging the participants in a discussion or while participants talk to one another. Or, the participants' use of language may have already been recorded. Usually spoken language is converted to a written transcript. Written language may be solicited through verbal inquiry, or it may exist already as a text and only needs to be collected.

Data on art works: These can be gathered by engaging participants in an art activity and then making some kind of recording of it, or the participants' art works may already exist and only need to be collected.

Data on artifacts: Artifacts usually exist already and only need to be identified and procured.

Data on persons: People can be observed in various configurations (individual, group) and settings (real world, created), using any combination of data collection procedures described above.

Gathering data involves many different layers of human interaction. Thus, an important part of the design is to define the roles of each party involved in the research, including the researcher, the participants, and any coresearchers, consultants, therapists, or agency staff involved. Considering all of the parties involved and the various steps to be taken, the following questions are important to answer: Who will participate in planning how data will be gathered? Who will engage participants in the phenomenon being studied? Who will gather and record the data? And, who will analyze and interpret the data?

The final step in designing data collection is to determine how the data will be recorded and stored. When the researcher engages or observes participants directly, audio or video recordings are usually necessary to capture the data. Sometimes it is also helpful to take notes during the data collection process. When the data are primarily verbal in nature, the discussions are tape-recorded and usually transcribed into written text. The text serves as the second format for the raw data. When the data are taped music, the researcher has to decide whether to transcribe or notate the music in some way or to leave it in the audio-temporal format. The taped music can also be translated into a moment-by-moment verbal description of it. Taped dances or dramas pose the same questions of recording and transcribing as does music. Other kinds of data, such as written texts, artworks, and artifacts, usually already exist and therefore need only be selected and stored.

Altogether, data from a qualitative study may have to be stored in several formats, including audio or video recordings, paper transcripts, and computer files. Methods for storing data have to be worked out carefully, not only to prevent data from being destroyed or lost but also to insure anonymity and confidentiality. There are three primary considerations. First, make sure that all data are labeled with all the necessary details, using pseudonyms rather than real names. Second, make sure to back up essential data with extra copies or duplicate files. Third, for purposes of confidentiality, keep all data in a secure and locked place where only appropriate individuals have access.

Selecting Participants

Lincoln and Guba (1985) outline some important considerations in selecting participants for qualitative research. First, rather than specifying all desired characteristics of the participants before doing the study, qualitative researchers are encouraged to select a few participants at a time and then wait to select the next batch until after data from the previous sample have been analyzed, even partially. This allows the researcher to change the criteria for selection as the study progresses and as previous sets of data indicate the kinds of sampling needed to obtain the most relevant information. Thus, qualitative research involves continuously adjusting and redefining criteria for participation as the selection process continues throughout the study. As for determining the ideal number of participants, Lincoln and Guba advise researchers to continue seeking new participants until the data become redundant and very little or no new information is forthcoming from new participants.

Patton (1990) provides specific strategies for selecting participants that are quite useful. To understand them, let's create a hypothetical study aimed at discovering the most effective ways of improving the rhythmic skills of individuals with schizophrenia. Based on Patton's strategies, here are the kinds of cases that a researcher might seek at different phases of the study.

Typical case: Select a participant that is likely to give information that will be also given by other participants. An example would be finding an individual with schizophrenia that has average rhythmic skills, being neither superior nor inferior to most of his peers. Typical cases provide homogeneity of data.

Critical case: Select a participant that will give dramatic evidence of the phenomenon being studied. An example would be finding an individual with schizophrenia that is most likely to respond very acutely and positively to a rhythm instruction program. Critical cases or prime exemplars help to identify key factors that may not be evident in typical or deviant cases.

Deviant or extreme case: Select a participant that is likely to give information that is very different from other participants. An example would be finding an individual with schizophrenia that has extremely low or high rhythmic skills prior to instruction. Deviant or extreme cases provide heterogeneity of data, or maximal variation.

Snowball or chain case: Ask participants to recommend other participants or other criteria to use in selecting them. An example would be asking an individual with schizophrenia to identify another individual with schizophrenia that might respond well to the rhythmic instruction program.

Criterion case: Select a participant who meets certain requirements, or has certain characteristics. An example would be selecting only adult individuals with schizophrenia and only those who have not had prior music instruction and who have not participated previously in music therapy. Here the purpose is to delimit the focus and purpose of the study and to limit participation to those who fit within the parameters established.

Confirming or disconfirming case: Select a participant who is likely to give data that support or contradict emergent patterns in the data already gathered. Sometimes a disconfirming case is called a *negative case.* An example would be selecting an individual with schizophrenia who is unlikely to benefit from rhythmic instruction, after all previous participants have given evidence of its effectiveness.

Political case: Select a participant who will enhance the possibility that the research study will lead to some kind of social change. An example would be selecting a well-known or famous individual with schizophrenia who wants to pursue a degree in music.

Convenience case: Select a participant that is most readily available, and not for any reason or purpose described above. An example would be selecting a group of individuals with schizophrenia in the same institution where the researcher is working.

Contextualizing

To contextualize is to identify and take into account the many different frameworks, systems, environments, and conditions operating within a research study and potentially affecting the participants, the researcher, and implementation of the study itself. To contextualize, then, is to understand the *situatedness* of all parties operating in the study as well as all aspects of the study itself. The following contexts are most essential to situate:

Situatedness of the researcher: This involves examining all the personal and professional contexts in which the researcher is operating. This context is explored through self-inquiry (see above).

Situatedness of participants: This involves examining the personal, cultural, and institutional contexts in which participants are operating prior to and during the study and taking them into account in designing the study. To situate the participants is to understand how their own lived worlds outside of the study relate to the phenomenon under investigation. It also includes how the research study fits into their lives, and whether it will be meaningful, relevant, or helpful to them. Where are the participants coming from when entering this study, and how will the study affect their lives?

Situatedness of researcher and participants: This involves examining the myriad physical, emotional, and interpersonal contexts in which the study takes place and taking them into account in implementing the study. The aim is to situate the researcher, participant, and phenomenon in relation to one another within the shared ecological context of the study itself.

Situatedness within the discipline: This involves examining how the topics and questions addressed in the study relate to existing research, theory, and practice in the field. This is usually accomplished through a comprehensive review of the literature.

Situatedness within sociopolitical and economic contexts: This involves examining how the results of the study and the medium in which they will be communicated may potentially affect the social, political, and economic worlds of the participants. Will the study lead to some kind of change in the worlds in which participants live?

This step is a crucial one in qualitative research, for the way in which a researcher contextualizes these elements of the study will have a profound effect on the focus, purpose, ethical safeguards, method, data interpretation, and presentation and publication of the findings. It is best accomplished through self-inquiry, consultation, and collaboration as defined above, and the results can be communicated in any section of the study, depending on where the context is most relevant.

Ethical Review

Once the method has been outlined in sufficient detail and before data gathering begins, the entire research study must be reviewed by an ethical review board or committee. The purpose of the review is to insure that the research and researcher will not violate the human rights of participants in any way. See Chapter 18, Ethical Precautions in Music Therapy Research, for further information on this essential step in doing any kind of research.

Two ethical issues are of particular concern in qualitative research. First, because the method of gathering data may often shift and change during the study, the researcher must inform the ethical review board of all possible variations in method. The best rule of thumb is to try to describe what the participant will be doing or experiencing, taking into account all possible methods of data gathering appropriate to the study; report all those methods in the ethical review; and then, if approved, stay within the limits of those methods.

Second, dual relationships can pose many ethical dilemmas. Of particular relevance is when a therapist does research using his or her own clients as participants, or when a teacher or supervisor does research with his or her own students. When the study involves these kinds of relationships, it is helpful to consult with an expert on research ethics, as there are satisfactory ways of resolving certain ethical issues of this kind.

Collaborating

To collaborate is to involve the research participants in the design and implementation of the study. This can be done at different levels, depending on the nature of the research and the capabilities of the participants. For example, in *action research*, the participants provide continuous feedback and direction to the researcher—while the researcher collects data from them. The feedback may pertain to the focus, purpose, method, and findings of the study. In *collaborative research,* the participants are coresearchers and take a major role, equal to the primary researcher, in designing and implementing the study. In this type of study, the participants are often the main beneficiaries of the research. In other types of studies, the researcher will gather data from participants, then, after summarizing and interpreting it, give it back to the them for correction and comment. This is sometimes called *member checking* (Lincoln & Guba, 1985).

Collaboration is considered by many to be the cornerstone of qualitative research. In clinical disciplines like music therapy, however, certain precautions must be made when the participant is a client. The participant's (client's) well-being should never be in any way threatened by any aspect of collaboration. This is most likely to happen when a researcher's interpretations of data from a client might be harmful or detrimental to the client or therapeutic process. Collaboration should also never interfere with or jeopardize the relationship between client and therapist. This is likely to happen when the roles of participant and researcher are imposed upon an already existing client-therapist relationship. One of the dangers is that, when a client participates in a research project at the request of his or her therapist-researcher, the roles of helper and helped can be distorted or even reversed. The client can easily become the helper by helping the therapist to do the research, and the therapist becomes the one in need of help because she or he needs the client to participate in the research. In short, collaboration with participants who are clients of a therapist-researcher can create ethical problems that must be carefully avoided or at least closely monitored. This is a central issue that must be presented to an ethical review board.

Appraising

To appraise is to continuously evaluate and refine every aspect of the research process—the focus, context, selection of participants, identification of data sources and settings, design of data collection procedures, consultation, and collaboration plan.

Ongoing appraisal is at the very heart of the qualitative approach to research. It is this continuous appraisal that allows the focus, context, and method, to emerge in a way that will allow the phenomenon under investigation to unfold and reveal itself in its own way. As frequently noted, the concept of an emergent research process is the cornerstone of qualitative methodology. It allows the qualitative researcher to affirm or revise the overall direction of the research according to whatever is discovered during each step of the process—from the participants, the data, the consultants, and the self-inquiries. Through continuous evaluation of the process, the researcher can discern which questions are relevant and meaningful and which are not, which methods work and which do not, and which stances aid understanding and which do not.

Appraisal goes hand in hand with self-inquiry. While appraisal helps the researcher to design and implement the best methodological strategies, self-inquiry helps the researcher to be aware of all factors that influence those practical decisions. Thus, appraisal is the methodological counterpart to personal self-inquiry.

What is required of the researcher during the many appraisal periods is an openness and sensitivity to whatever presents itself—failures as well as successes, doubts as well as certainties, questions as well as answers or solutions—along with a willingness to change or retain as needed. A researcher can err in either direction, that is, in being hypersensitive or oblivious and by affirming the direction too often or revising it too often. For example, retaining the same focus too rigidly may reflect a bias, or it may take data collection nowhere; changing the focus too often will prevent the best design from emerging and will yield highly scattered data. Retaining the same context too rigidly may reflect an inability to take different perspectives on the participants or data and may result in biased outcomes; changing it too often may reflect an inability to make the commitment necessary to draw meaningful conclusions. Retaining the same design may produce data that are meaningless or irrelevant to the focus; changing it too often may distort the focus of the study and produce unnecessary or useless data. Sticking to one's first impressions of the data or to initial hypotheses or expectations may lead to biased and unfounded conclusions; allowing one's interpretations to change too often may render the entire study pointless and the findings untrustworthy. Ultimately, then, the appraisal step is the basis for insuring the quality of the study and the integrity of its findings.

Qualitative researchers have several specific techniques for appraising their studies. The first is the pilot study. It is difficult to imagine any study that would not benefit from a pilot study, when carried out on the very first participants, immediately after the study has been approved by the ethical review board. While a pilot study can permit experimentation with different approaches to gathering the data, the researcher is limited to using only those already approved by the ethical review board. This is why it is best to include as many different strategies as possible in the ethical review proposal. If, as a result of the pilot, the researcher decides that a procedure or method not already approved by the ethical review board should be used, the researcher must return to the review board to seek approval for changing the method.

Other ways of appraising a study include consultation and collaboration (as described above) and two approaches recommended by Lincoln and Guba (1985), *stepwise replication* and *audits*. A stepwise replication involves having another qualified colleague gather data using the same procedures as the main researcher and then comparing the results. An audit involves having qualified colleagues go over every phase of the research study and every piece of data, evaluating both the trustworthiness of the process and the integrity of the findings. It is important to remember that any transaction that involves the participants, including all plans for consultation, collaboration, stepwise replication, or audits, must be approved by the ethical review board.

Conclusion

Rather than summarize the details of the chapter, it seems important to bring some closure by offering a few comments that may help the reader to put all of these details into a larger context. First, qualitative research is intrinsically a developmental process. As described here, qualitative research is a complex process that unfolds moment to moment, proceeding one step at a time with each step flowing unpredictably from the previous one and leading just as unpredictably to the next step. While such a process can appear to the outsider as rather serendipitous or arbitrary, in reality, qualitative research unfolds in quite an orderly, developmental way. In fact, a researcher goes about doing qualitative research in much the same way that children go about learning about the world. Children learn and develop by experimenting and interacting with the world while continually observing the outcomes and modifying their approaches as they go along, until they are able to achieve their objectives. Similarly, qualitative researchers make discoveries about the world by experimenting with and interacting with the participants and data while continually analyzing the results and modifying the design, until the purpose of the study has been achieved. This leads to the next big point.

Second, the real challenge of doing qualitative research is not so much in the *doing* as it is in the *being*. To do qualitative research, one must be a qualitative researcher. Qualitative research is not a method to be mastered—it is an approach to human inquiry and discovery that can only emerge from a particular way of being in the world. That way of being is that of a discoverer who is exploratory, observant, open, flexible, creative, and committed to learning. More to the point, that way of being is intrinsically human. Paraphrasing and expanding a definition of qualitative research provided by the author in the first edition of this book (Bruscia, 1995):

> Qualitative research is a process wherein one human being genuinely attempts to understand something about another human being or about the very condition of being human, by using approaches that take full advantage of being human. To deny being who we are in order to understand who we are simply makes no sense. One must be fully human to understand other humans in their myriad ways of being. (p. 426)

References

Bruscia, K. E. (1995). The process of doing qualitative research: Part II: Procedural steps. In B. L. Wheeler (Ed.), *Music therapy research: Quantitative and qualitative perspectives* (pp. 401–427). Gilsum, NH: Barcelona Publishers.

Lincoln, Y., & Guba, E. *Naturalistic inquiry.* Thousand Oaks, CA: Sage Publications.

Patton, M. (1990). *Qualitative evaluation and research methods* (2nd ed.). Thousand Oaks, CA: Sage Publications.

Stige, B. (2002, April 26). Do we need general criteria for the evaluation of qualitative research articles, and if we do, how could such criteria be formulated? *Forum: Nordic Journal of Music Therapy*, http://www.njmt.no/forumqualart_1.html

Chapter 12
Statistical Methods of Analysis
Anthony A. DeCuir[1]

This chapter provides an overview of what is needed to understand the use of statistics in music therapy research. It includes information on scales and measurement and on descriptive and inferential statistics, including parametric and nonparametric statistics.

In the past several years, access to computers and computer programs has dramatically changed how data are analyzed. The Statistical Package for the Social Sciences (SPSS) and its adaptations such as SPSS for Windows (SPSS, 2003), for example, allows the researcher to perform both sophisticated and simple operations in seconds (Argyrous, 2000; Hinton, 1995). The calculation of selected statistical tests will be presented as paper and pencil operations and in SPSS format.

In preparation for this chapter, the *Journal of Music Therapy (JMT)* was surveyed from 1995 to 2002 in order to determine how data were being analyzed. The results indicated that the most common statistical operations cited in *JMT* were the one-way analysis of variance and the *t* test, followed by analysis by percentages, frequency data, and means. Simple and multiple correlation analyses were also prevalent. Analysis of covariance, multiple analyses of variance, and meta-analysis also appeared in the music therapy literature but with much less frequency. Among the nonparametric statistical tests cited in order of frequency were chi-square, Mann-Whitney *U*, Wilcoxon matched-pairs signed-ranks test, and the Kruskal-Wallis one-way analysis of variance of rank. These results are similar to those found in previous analyses of statistical tests found in *JMT* (DeCuir, 1980).

Scales and Measurement

Assigning numbers to people, objects, events, or occurrences is measurement. The manner in which these numbers are assigned is called the scale. The four levels of measurement are: (a) nominal, (b) ordinal, (c) interval, and (d) ratio.

Nominal or naming is the most fundamental and involves assigning numbers in order to differentiate objects or events. For example, nominal data might be numbers on a team uniform; responses coded as yes (1) or no (2); or musical instruments identified by number where autoharp = 1, piano = 2, and guitar = 3. Numbers assigned using this scale are suited only for use with certain nonparametric statistical techniques developed for nominal levels of measurement.

The next level of measurement is the ordinal scale. Measurement on an ordinal scale permits the ordering or ranking of events, objects, and so forth by the magnitude of some characteristic. For example, a music therapist might be asked how frequently she uses five types of therapy strategies. She might respond with the following rank order of use, from least to most used: sing-a-along, drum circle, music and imagery, clinical improvisation, and music psychotherapy. These scores would then be ranked from smallest to largest as 1 = sing-a-long, 2 = drum circle, 3 = music and imagery, 4 = clinical improvisation, and 5 = music psycho-therapy. Or, a professional panel of music therapists might rank the clinical performances of interns from 1 to 10. Numbers assigned using this scale give no indication of the distance between them, only relative magnitude. The ordinal scale is suited for nonparametric statistics appropriate for ordinal data.

The interval scale indicates equal distance (intervals) between points, so that fundamental arithmetic functions such as addition, subtraction, multiplication, and division can be performed. For example, the distance between scores of 10 and 20 is equal to the distance between 90 and 100. Most standardized tests are based on interval data. The interval scale is suited for parametric statistics.

The ratio scale has all of the characteristics of the interval scale but, in addition, has an absolute zero point. Because of this absolute zero point, values can be compared to other values as proportions or ratios. An example of the ratio scale is a stroboscopic tuning device used by bands and wind ensembles that measure *cent* deviations from some target pitch.

---

[1] The SPSS examples in this chapter were provided by Anthony Meadows.

Descriptive and Inferential Statistics

Statistical tests are divided into two categories: descriptive and inferential. These two categories of tests have different characteristics and different uses.

Descriptive Statistics

A researcher might be interested in summarizing large groups of numbers for the purpose of identifying characteristics of a population or sample. Descriptive statistics generally are used for this type of study. As the name implies, descriptive statistics describe data.

Collectively, the most fundamental of the descriptive statistics are referred to as measures of central tendency, central value, or centrality. Individually, they are the mean, mode, and median. The mean or arithmetic average is computed by first adding a set of numbers and then dividing that sum by the number of entries in the set. The mean is defined as $\sum X$, or the sum of all scores divided by N the number of scores. Given five numbers 5, 5, 8, 9, 13, for example, the mean would be calculated as follows:

$$\frac{5+5+8+9+13}{5} = \frac{40}{5} = 8$$

The mode is the most frequently occurring score. In the above set of numbers, the most frequently occurring number is 5; it appears twice and would therefore be the mode. The last measure of centrality is the median or midpoint of a distribution. In this ordered distribution, 8 is the middle score (third score from the top, third score from the bottom), so the median equals 8.

Variability or dispersion is another type of descriptive measure. It describes how the scores are dispersed, or how closely they are grouped around the mean. If numbers in a set are grouped close together or are homogeneous, variability is low; conversely, if the numbers are far apart or are varied and heterogeneous, variability is high. (These concepts are called homogeneity of variance and heterogeneity of variance, respectively.) Measures of variability are the range, standard deviation, and variance. The range is the difference (distance) between the highest score and the lowest score. The standard deviation (s.d. or s.), a measure of how varied the numbers in a set are, is determined by the formula:

$$s.d. = \sqrt{\frac{\sum X^2 - \frac{(\sum X)^2}{N}}{N-1}}$$

where $\sum x^2$ is the sum of all squared scores and $(\sum x)^2$ is the sum of all scores squared. There are other formulas that produce the same result. The variance (s^2), another measure of variability, is the square of the standard deviation.

Correlation is the final descriptive statistic, and it deals with association among variables. As the name implies, correlation measures the degree of relatedness between two or more quantities. It is important to keep in mind that correlation examines relatedness and not causation. Correlation coefficients are usually abbreviated with the letter r. Correlation is expressed as a number between +1.00 and –1.00. A perfect positive correlation is $r = +1.00$, where the absolute value of the coefficient (0.00 through 1.00) expresses the strength of the relationship, and the sign (+ or –) expresses whether the two variables covary in the same or opposite directions. The graphs in Figure 1 illustrate a positive and then a negative correlation.[2] Note that, in the first example, as the numbers on the horizontal axis increase so do the numbers on the vertical axis, leading to a positive correlation and the ascending line.

---

[2] In these examples, the data points would be plotted on the graphs corresponding to the X and Y axes (e.g., X = 5, Y = 6). The correlation coefficient then represents the degree to which changes in X coincide with changes in Y.

In the second example, as the numbers on the horizontal axis increase the numbers on the vertical axis decrease, leading to a negative correlation and the descending line.

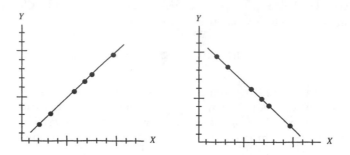

Figure 1. A Positive and a Negative Correlation

Inferential Statistics

Frequently, the purpose of research is to go beyond merely describing data in order to infer or estimate certain population characteristics based on a sample of the population. The preciseness of the inference depends on how well the sample mirrors the population. Statistical inference is a set of procedures that the researcher follows in order to make decisions about an *unknown* population from studying a *known* sample. Inference involves: (a) formulating a hypothesis, (b) choosing a probability level, (c) selecting a statistical test, (d) predicting the direction of the difference, (e) calculating a statistical value, (f) comparing the statistical value to a critical value in the appropriate statistical table, and (g) accepting or rejecting the null hypothesis.

Formulating a hypothesis: For theoretical reasons, the hypothesis is usually stated in a negative or null form. Its statement can be a helpful step in the organization of the project, even though one can find countless research articles where the null hypothesis is not formally stated. The null hypothesis (Ho) states that there is no difference between the sample means. The alternate or research hypothesis states what the researcher actually expects to find.

For example, a music therapist might be interested in finding out to which of two types of music juvenile offenders responded. In the null form, the hypothesis might be stated as: There will be no difference in clients' responses to the two types of music. The alternate or research hypothesis would be: Clients will respond more positively to one type of music than the other. If the null hypothesis (no difference) can be rejected based upon the results of the statistical test (and the other steps detailed in this section), then the alternate hypothesis—that the clients respond more positively to one type of music than the other—is likely to be the correct answer.

Choosing a probability level: Probability level is defined as the likelihood that the data collected occurred by chance. That is, in the battle against the forces of a chance occurrence, the researcher believes that his or her results could occur by chance fewer than *five* times out of 100 ($p < .05$) or fewer that *one* time out of 100 ($p < .01$). Traditionally, a significance level of $p < .05$, occasionally $p < .01$, has been used by music therapy researchers and those in related fields. There may be instances in which a researcher would choose probability levels $p < .005$ or $p < .001$, depending on the need for greater certainty that the results did not occur by chance. The selection of a confidence or probability level is an a priori decision—it is decided as part of the design of the study. The terms *probability level, alpha (α) level, confidence level, level of confidence, level of significance*, and *significance level* are used interchangeably in the literature.

Selecting a statistical test: Whether the research is a dissertation, thesis, or classroom project, the period of time prior to data collection is the last opportunity the researcher has to correct any procedural problems in the study, including problems in the planned data analysis. Statistical tests are selected to fit the data and the experimental design. The best time to select the statistical test is during the formulation of the proposal, and definitely before collecting data.

Predicting the direction of the difference: Generally, after the design issues have been resolved and the statistical test or tests have been selected, the researcher predicts the direction of the difference. As an example of a directional hypothesis (also called a *one-tailed prediction, one-tailed test,* or *directional hypothesis of predictable difference*), the researcher may predict that one group will do better or worse than the other. For example, a music psychologist comparing the effects of a progressive muscle relaxation program with and without music may know from the literature that progressive muscle relaxation combined with music is more effective than progressive muscle relaxation alone and thus may be interested in only the magnitude of a positive effect. In this case, a one-tailed prediction would be appropriate because the researcher knows the direction of the expected difference.

A two-tailed test or two-tailed prediction, also called a *nondirectional hypothesis,* is appropriate if unknown variables are being compared, and the researcher hypothesizes that there will be a significant difference in the effects but does not know the direction of the difference. The two-tailed test is appropriate for variables on which previous research has not been done or on which research has been inconclusive, thus precluding a prediction of the direction of the difference. A two-tailed test is used in most experimental research in music therapy.

The same statistical test is used for both one-tailed and two-tailed predictions, but the calculated value is interpreted differently based on the statistical tables. The choice made at this point becomes critical to the interpretation of the results.

Calculating a statistical value:[3] After the appropriate preparations for the statistical analysis have been made and the data collected, the data are then analyzed by means of the statistical test. The value that is calculated is known as the statistic.

Comparing the value to a critical value: Comparing the calculated value (the statistic) with a critical value is the next step. The critical value is the value that would be obtained if chance alone were operating. Tables of critical values for selected significance levels, along with instructions on how to read the tables, can be found in most statistics books. The researcher compares the statistic obtained through the statistical analysis with the critical value found in the table.

Generally, the degrees of freedom *(df)* must be known in order to use the table of critical values. Degrees of freedom might be defined as the number of observations in a linear distribution that are allowed to vary. For example, if we know that the sum of five scores equals 10, and we know that four of the scores are 1, 2, 3, 2, then the remaining score is not free to vary—it must be 2. Therefore, the degrees of freedom for this example equal 4, because, once we know the four values, the fifth is not free to vary.

Accepting or rejecting the null hypothesis: The decision to accept or reject the null hypothesis is based on the comparison of the calculated value with the critical value, as described in the previous step. A calculated value that is larger than the critical value will allow the null hypothesis to be rejected, while a smaller calculated value will not allow the researcher to reject the null hypothesis. In research language, the researcher does not *accept* the null hypothesis, but rather *fails to reject* the null hypothesis.

The process just described is referred to as *hypothesis testing.* Remember, the researcher is inferring population characteristics from a sample, and there is the possibility that the researcher will accept the null hypothesis (Ho) when it should be rejected—a miss—or reject Ho when it should be accepted. Failing to accept (or rejecting) the null hypothesis (Ho) when it should be accepted is a Type I error, while accepting Ho when it should be rejected is a Type II error. If there is concern about committing a Type I error, the confidence level should be set lower, for example, at .01 or .001. Conversely, to avoid a Type

---

[3] These steps are normally performed by a statistical computer program, such as SPSS.

Hypothesis of No Difference (two-tail)

Hypothesis of Predictable Difference (one-tail)

Area of rejection when p = .05

	One-Sample			Two-Sample					Multiple-Sample				
				Equivalent			Independent		Equivalent			Independent	
	Post-test only	Post-test only	Pre-test-Post-test	Post-test only	Pre-test-Post-test	Post-test only	Pre-test-Post-test	Post-test only	Matching by Counterbalance	Temporal	Counterbalance	Pre-test-Post-test	Temporal

DESIGNS

XO	X_1X_2O	O_1XO_2	M XO / M O	M O_1XO_2 / M $O_1 O_2$	XO / O	O_1XO_2 / $O_1 O_2$	M XO / M O	$X_1OX_2OX_3O$ etc.	$MO_1X_1O_2X_2O$ / $MO_1 O_2X_1O_3$ / $M O_1 O_2 X O$	$O_1X O_2XO_3$ / $O_1XO_2 O_3$	$O_1X O_2$ / $O_1 O_2$	$O_1X O_1O_2O_3$

RESEARCH

Classification or ranking — Subjects as own control

NOMINAL MEASUREMENT

$O_1O_2O_3O_4$ etc. — $O_1XO_2XO_3$ — M X_1O / M X_2O — O,M — XO_1 / O_2 — X_1O / X_2O — O_1 / O_2 — XO_2 / O_3

χ^2 *One-Sample Test.* Goodness of fit for testing expected vs. observed frequencies (e.g., preferences among defined categories on questionnaire, performance rating scale, etc.). *Binomial Test.* Goodness of fit for testing (two discrete categories (e.g., flat-soft, loud-soft, correct-incorrect).

McNemar Test for Significance of Changes. Used when the two categories are not related in measurement levels i.e., when one or both categories achieve only nominal level (e.g. comparing musical judgments good-bad with rank order judgments). Excellent when subject acts as own control.

Fisher Exact Probability Test. Used with small N to test differences between samples on basis of central tendency in a 2 × 2 table. χ^2 *Test for Independent Samples.* Used to test differences between samples on basis of any discrete differences between the two populations.

Cochran Q Test. Used to test whether three or more matched sets differ significantly among themselves on the basis of dichotomous data (e.g., yes-no, flat-sharp, correct-incorrect). Matching may be between different subjects or on different observations for each subject.

χ^2 *Test for Multiple Independent Samples.* Used to test significant differences among samples.

Table 1.
Selected Research Designs and Statistical Tests
Madsen & Madsen (1978). Used with permission.

ORDINAL MEASUREMENT	*Kolmogorov-Smirnov One-Sample Test.* Goodness of fit for testing ranked data (e.g., pre- vs. post-test measures, questionnaire, performance rating scale). Preferred to χ^2 if sample is small.	*Wilcoxon Matched Pairs.* Used when measurements achieve ordinal level both *between* and *within* pairs. *Sign test.* Used when ordinal measurements achieved only within pairs.	*Mann-Whitney U.* Used to test differences in samples on basis of central tendency. Most powerful alternate to the parametric *t* test. *Kolmogorov-Smirnov Two-Sample Test.* Used to test significance between samples on basis of any differences between populations (two-tail) or central tendency (one-tail).	*Friedman Two-Way Analysis of Variance.* Used to test whether three or more matched sets differ significantly among themselves on basis of mean ranks for each set.	*Kruskal-Wallis One-Way Analysis of Variance.* Used to test significant differences among samples on basis of ranks. This test is always preferred to χ^2 if data quality.
INTERVAL OR RATIO MEASUREMENT	*t Test.* Used to test significance between the sample mean and theoretical distribution or of different scores.	*t Test.* Used to test significance between related sample means or of different scores. *Welsh Test.* Used to test significance between samples of ranked differences when N is less than 15.	*t Test.* Used to test significance between independent sample means. *Randomization Test for Two Independent Samples.* Used to test significance between independent sample means. Should be used with small N.	*Analysis of Variance.* Used to test whether three or more matched samples differ significantly among themselves on basis of variance between sample means.	*Analysis of Variance.* Used to test whether three or more independent samples differ significantly on basis of variance between sample means.

X = Experimental Variable (treatments)
O = Observation (measurements)
M = Matching on basis of known attributes or pre-test by pairs of subjects, groups, or by using each subject as own control

II error, the confidence level should be set higher, for example, at .05 or .10. Unless the study is replicated repeatedly, the researcher seldom knows if a Type I or Type II error has been committed.

Inferential statistical tests go beyond a general description of the data and make certain inferences from the data. Statistical tests are divided into parametric and nonparametric tests. In selecting a test, the researcher makes certain assumptions about the data.

The assumptions for the use of parametric statistics are: (a) Data have a normal distribution, (b) groups have equal variance (similar variability in the data), and (c) data are on an interval or ratio scale. If there are many subjects and if the subjects have been randomly selected, the data are frequently assumed to be distributed normally. Equal variance is often thought not to be crucial (Minium, King, & Bear, 1993), although its existence can be determined through a statistical test. Parametric statistics have been found to be quite robust, meaning that these assumptions can be violated to a certain extent without harming the ability of the test to detect differences among groups (Boneau, 1970; Kerlinger, 1973). While researchers seem to agree that minor violations of the assumptions are not crucial, they do caution that small sample sizes can affect the outcome of research (Minium, King, & Bear).

Nonparametric statistics, or so-called distribution-free tests, are useful for research in music therapy and other behavioral sciences, because samples in these areas are often small and the data are nominal or ordinal. It should be noted that the actual data (numbers) are not used, but that the data are ranked. There are advantages in using nonparametric statistical tests: (a) They are distribution-free, making no assumptions about population characteristics; (b) nominal and ordinal scales of measurement are adequate; (c) they are amenable to nonnumeric data and small samples; and (d) computation is relatively simple.

Nonparametric statistics are sometimes substituted for the more powerful parametric statistics when the assumptions for using parametric tests cannot be met. When possible, though, it is generally a good idea to use parametric rather that nonparametric tests, as they are more powerful.

Power, in statistical terms, means the ability to detect real differences between the experimental variable and a control variable when such a difference exists. However, this is a bit of an over simplification. Power is a multifaceted concept that is affected by sample size, alpha level, statistical test, and effect size (Lipsey, 1998). While increasing the size of the sample is a sure fire way to increase power, increasing the sample size can be very difficult in music therapy research. A less difficult maneuver to increase power is to increase the alpha level. Convention dictates $p < .05$, but, depending upon the seriousness of the research question, $p < .10$ might be more realistic. In terms of human subject research, institutional research boards consider the cost-risk ratio. In music therapy research, the question is not likely to carry the weight of life or death. In terms of statistical tests, the reader is advised to select carefully. For example, parametric tests are generally considered to be more powerful than nonparametric tests. However, in the case of small samples, a nonparametric test might yield similar results. The last factor to be considered when assessing power is effect size. Briefly, effect size is the difference between the mean of the sample and the mean of the population divided by the standard deviation. Lipsey refers to effect size as a signal-to-noise ratio. In order to maximize the effect of the independent variable on the dependent variable, the researcher will need to decrease the standard deviation (the denominator) or increase the difference between the experimental and control variables (the numerator).

See Table 1, Selected Research Designs and Statistical Tests, for a list of experimental designs and appropriate statistical tests to be used with each design.

Parametric Statistical Tests

t Test

The *t* test is the most extensively used test for comparing differences between two means. It is a parametric statistic. We will preview three versions of the *t* test, one for comparing a sample and population mean, another for comparing related or correlated means, and a third for comparing independent means.

t Test for Sample and Population Means

This *t* test is used to compare a sample mean and a population mean when the researcher knows both the population mean (or theoretical value of the population mean) and the mean of the sample. The hypothesis that the researcher is testing is whether a sample that has been drawn is significantly different from the population.

t Test for Related Samples or Means

Correlated or related indicates that the subjects either acted as their own controls or that they were matched on one or more variables, such as gender, race, socioeconomic status, or age, and are therefore related. The assumption is that the groups are equivalent or similar rather than being randomly assigned. The *t* test for related means determines whether the means of the two related samples differ significantly.

t Test for Independent Samples or Means

The calculations for the *t* test for two independent means are similar to the other two versions of the *t* test. In the case of two independent means, however, the comparison is between two separate and independent samples rather than between a sample and a population. The researcher is attempting to determine whether the means of two samples differ significantly. Experimental-control group studies are normally analyzed with this test. Having randomly assigned subjects to experimental and control groups, it does not matter whether the control group is treated as a control group or a second experimental group.

Example: *t* Test for Independent Samples

A researcher is interested in determining whether cent differences exist between the pitch reproduction abilities of a random sample of clients with developmental delays who participate in planned music therapy activities and those who did not. She collects the data shown in Table 2, representing cent differences from a standard pitch.

Table 2
Cent Differences in Pitch Reproduction

	Clients in Therapy			*Clients Not in Therapy*		
Subject	Cents	x^2	Subject	Cents	x^2
S1	5	25	S16	9	81
S2	4	16	S17	10	100
S3	6	36	S18	11	121
S4	3	9	S19	12	144
S5	2	4	S20	13	169
S6	6	36	S21	14	196
S7	7	49	S22	15	225
S8	4	16	S23	10	100
S9	3	9	S24	11	121
S10	8	64	S25	8	64
S11	5	25	S26	9	81
S12	6	36	S27	10	100
S13	4	16		132	1502
S14	2	4			
S15	5	25			
	70	370			

Step 1.   Arrange the scores as shown above.

Step 2.   Sum the scores in Sample 1.
$(5 + 4 + 6 \ldots) = 70$

Step 3.   Square each score in Sample 1 and sum the squares.
$(25 + 16 + 36 \ldots) = 370$

Step 4.   Square the result of Step 2 and divide by the number of scores in Sample 1.
$70^2 = 4900/15 = 326.67$

Step 5.   Subtract the result of Step 3 from Step 4.
$326.67 - 370 = -43.33$

Step 6.   Repeat Steps 2 through 5 for Sample 2.

Step 6a.   Sum the scores in Sample 2.
$(9 + 10 + 11 \ldots) = 132$

Step 6b.   Square each score in Sample 2 and sum the squares.
$(81 + 100 + 121 \ldots) = 1502$

Step 6c.   Square the result of Step 6a and divide by the number of scores in Sample 2.
$132^2 = 17,424/12 = 1452$

Step 6d.   Subtract the result of Step 6b from Step 6c.
$1452 - 1502 = -50$

Step 7.   Add Steps 5 and 6d.
$(-43.33) + (-50) = -93.33$

Step 8.   Divide the result of Step 7 by the quantity $(N_1 + N_2) - 2$.
$$\frac{-93.33}{(15 + 12) - 2} = \frac{-93.33}{25} = -3.73$$

Step 9.   Multiply the result of Step 8 by $1 + 1 \over N_1 \; N_2$

$1/15 + 1/12 = .15$
$.15 (-3.73) = -.56$

Step 10. Compute the square root of the absolute value of Step 9.

$\sqrt{.56} = .75$

Step 11. Compute the means of Samples 1 and 2.

$70/15 = 4.67$

$132/12 = 11$

Step 12. Subtract the mean of Sample 2 from the mean of Sample 1.

$4.67 - 11 = -6.33$

Step 13. To obtain t, divide the value of Step 12 by Step 10.

$t = -6.33/.75 = -8.44$[4]

The formula with the necessary substitutions is as follows:

$$t = \frac{\overline{X_1} - \overline{X_2}}{\sqrt{\left[\Sigma X_1^2 - \frac{\frac{(\Sigma X_1)^2}{N_1} + \Sigma X_2^2 - \frac{(\Sigma X_2)^2}{N_2}}{(N_1 + N_2) - 2}\right]\left[\frac{1}{N_1} + \frac{1}{N_2}\right]}}$$

$$= \frac{4.67 - 11}{\sqrt{\left[\frac{3\,70 - \frac{4900}{15} + 1502 - \frac{17\,,424}{12}}{(15 + 12) - 2}\right].07 + .08}}$$

$$= \frac{4.67 - 11}{\sqrt{\left[\frac{-93.33}{25}\right](.15)}}$$

$$= \frac{6.33}{\overline{).56}}$$

$$= \frac{6.33}{.75}$$

$$= 8.44$$

Step 14. To determine the significance of t, first compute the degrees of freedom (df).

$df = N_1 + N_2 - 2$

$df = (15 + 12) - 2 = 25$

The obtained $t = 8.44$ is significant beyond the .05 level of confidence for the two-tailed test. Therefore, we can say that the music therapy activities that were used appear to have been effective in improving the pitch reproduction abilities of the clients with developmentally delays. More technically, we can say that fewer than 5 times out of 100, these results would have occurred by chance.

---

[4] A negative value for t is of no consequence as only the absolute value is used in determining the significance of t.

Example: *t* Test for Independent Samples Using SPSS[5]

Because SPSS operates in a slightly different fashion than do hand calculations, you will need to make a small change to the data that appear in Table 2. SPSS will need to recognize the different groups (those in music therapy and those not in music therapy) in order to understand if there is any difference in pitch reproduction abilities. This is achieved very simply, by using a different numerical value to identify each group.

Data entry. When you begin entering the data in SPSS, you will need to create three columns, one for each variable. The first column will be used to identify each client (variable 1), using the numbers 1 to 27. The second column will be used to identify each group (variable 2), using the number 1 or 2 with 1 representing the music therapy group (subjects 1 to 15) and 2 representing those subjects who did not receive music therapy (subjects 16 to 27). The third column will be used for the client's actual pitch reproduction score (variable 3), measured in cents. Follow the procedure outlined in Chapter 13 to label the columns and enter the data. You want to label the columns Subject, Group, and Cents.

Computation. Once the data are entered into SPSS, the procedure for calculating the *t* test is very simple. Select Analyze on the menu bar, then choose Compare Means. From this menu, choose Independent-Samples T Test. This produces a dialogue box that looks like Figure 2. In this box, your list of variables will appear in the box to the left, and you must (a) move one (or more) of the variables into the box labeled Test Variable(s), and (b) move one of the variables into the box labeled Grouping Variable to identify the groups to be compared.

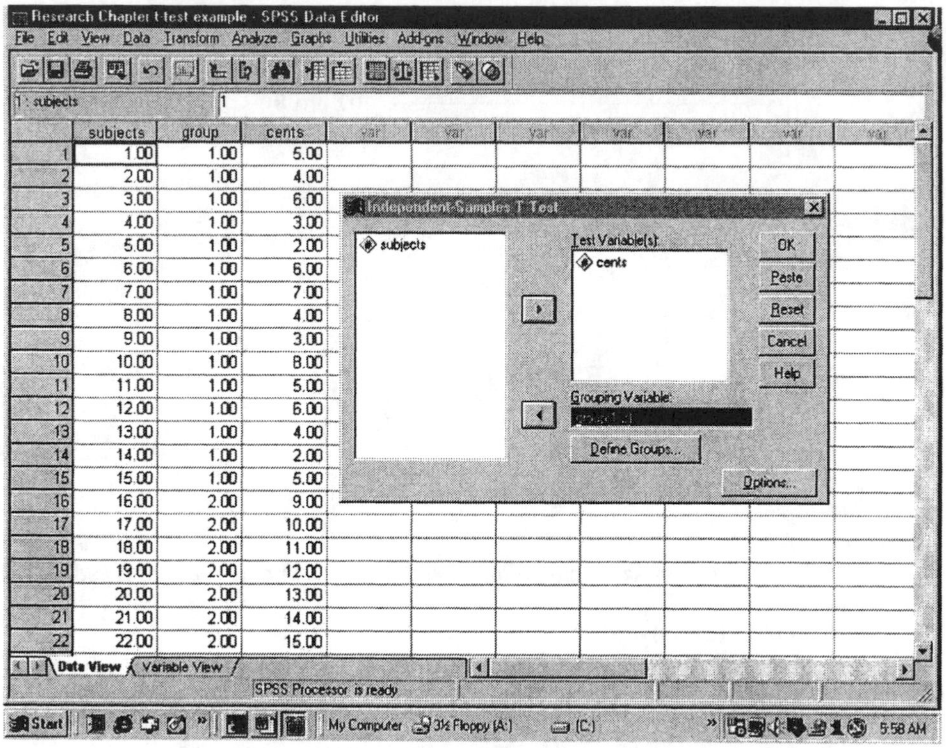

Figure 2. Data Window and *t* Test Dialogue Box

Depress the Cents variable (the word Cents) and use the arrow key next to the Test Variable(s) box to move it into the box. Next depress the group variable and click the arrow key next to the Grouping Variable box. Once you have entered group into this box, click on the box titled Define Groups, which is immediately underneath. This will allow you to differentiate between the music therapy and non-music therapy groups. For group 1 enter the number 1, and for group 2, the number 2. After this, depress "Enter," and SPSS will complete the calculation. The output will look like Figure 3.

---

[5] It may be necessary to consult the next chapter, Computer Programs for Quantitative Data Analysis, which gives instructions for using SPSS, in order to understand the SPSS examples in this chapter.

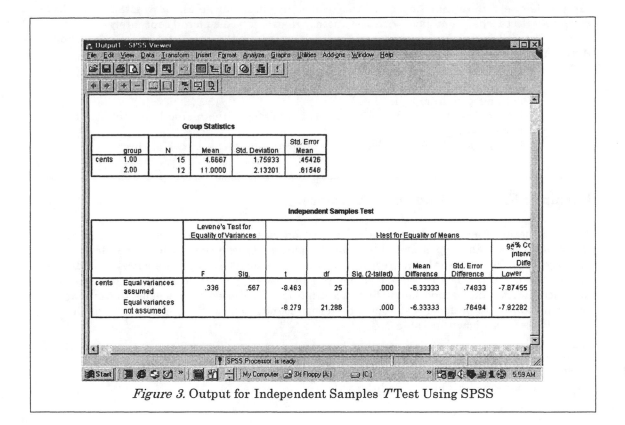

Figure 3. Output for Independent Samples *T* Test Using SPSS

Analysis of Variance

Simple One-Way Analysis of Variance

The most frequently cited statistical tests in the literature are the analyses of variance (ANOVAs). The simple one-way ANOVA is one type of ANOVA and is similar in computation and use to the *t* test. As a matter of fact, this test is an extension of the *t* test except that the means of two or more groups are compared. Where the *t* test produces a *t* statistic, the ANOVA produces an *F* statistic. As with the *t* test, the analysis of variance is computed by dividing the difference between the groups by an error term. The simple one-way ANOVA requires interval or ratio data and must meet the other assumptions required by other parametric statistical tests. It is necessary that there be only one score per subject; each subject is measured only one time. It is desirable, although not required, that there be an equal number of subjects in each group.

Factorial Analysis of Variance

The factorial analysis of variance is a statistical technique that assesses the effects of several independent treatments, variables, or factors and their interaction effects (Kerlinger, 1973; Minium, King, & Bear, 1993) on a single dependent variable. Since the number of factors or treatment variables involved differentiates factorial designs, the appropriate factorial analysis of variance is sometimes designated accordingly. The analysis of variance for a two-factor design is designated as a two-way analysis of variance, two-factor analysis of variance, or sometimes simply as a factorial ANOVA.

Unlike the simple analysis of variance, which involves only one factor or independent variable, the factorial ANOVA (and the factorial design with which it is used) helps to answer three research questions, corresponding to the two main effects and the one interaction. One main effect question deals with the influence of the first independent variable (or factor), while the other deals with the effect of the second independent variable. The interaction effect represents the differential impact of the two main effect variables, or whether they have different effects when combined with one another than when considered separately.

The following things need to be kept in mind in the computation of the factorial ANOVA:

1. Only one score per subject can be used. If more than one score is taken, these scores must be combined (combining data is permitted in this case because we are dealing with intervallic data).
2. Optimal sample size is 10–15 subjects per group with an equal number of subjects in each group.
3. It is preferable to keep the number of groups per factor to two or three.

Example: Factorial Analysis of Variance

A music therapist employed in a special education classroom is interested in the effects of sound intensities and types of lighting on the pattern recognition skills of children whose primary disability is visual. The researcher selects continuous sound intensities of 60dB and 100dB for the first factor, sound intensity, and two types of lighting, fluorescent and incandescent, for the second factor, lighting condition. The researcher wishes to examine the children's ability to perform a standard pattern recognition task, the dependent variable. The data collected are shown in Table 3.

Table 3
Sound Intensity and Lighting Conditions

| | | Sound Intensity Level | | | | |
| | | 60 dB | | | 100dB | |
	Subject	X	X^2	Subject	X	X^2
Fluorescent	S_1	5	25	S_6	3	9
	S_2	6	36	S_7	7	49
	S_3	7	49	S_8	5	25
	S_4	8	64	S_9	8	64
	S_5	4	16	S_{10}	6	36
		30	190		29	183
Incandescent	S_{11}	6	36	S_{16}	8	64
	S_{12}	5	25	S_{17}	4	16
	S_{13}	7	49	S_{18}	5	25
	S_{14}	5	25	S_{19}	3	9
	S_{15}	3	9	S_{20}	4	16
		26	144		24	130

Step 1. Arrange the scores as in Table 3, sum the scores in each group, and total the sum of each group.
$$(30 + 26 + 29 + 24) = 109$$

Step 2. Square each score and sum the total squared scores for each group, them sum the results.
$$(5^2 + 6^2 + 7^2 + 8^2 + 4^2) = 190 + (3^2 + ...) = 183 + ...$$
$$190 + 183 + 144 + 130 = 647$$

Step 3. Having summed the scores in each group (see Step 1), square the total and divide by the total number of scores in the study.

$\dfrac{109^2}{20} = \dfrac{11,881}{20} = 594.05$

This determines the correction factor.

Step 4. To find the total sum of squares (SS_t), subtract the correction factor from the sum of all the squared scores (Step 2).

$SS_t = 647 - 594.05 = 52.95$

Step 5. To find out the effect of the *first* factor (here, sound intensity), add the sum of the two sound intensity groups, ignoring the lighting condition factor.

$30 + 26 = 56$ (60 dB)

$29 + 24 = 53$ (100 dB)

Next, square each of the totals and divide the result by the number of scores in the overall group.

$56^2/10 + 53^2/10 = 3136/10 + 2809/10 = 594.5$

To find the sum of squares for the first factor, subtract the correction factor from the above quantity.

$SS_{sound} = 594.5 - 594.05 = .45$

Step 6. To obtain the effect of the *second* factor (here, lighting condition), add the sums of the two lighting condition groups, this time ignoring sound intensity.

$30 + 29 = 59$ (fluorescent lighting)

$26 + 24 = 50$ (incandescent lighting)

Again, square each of the totals and divide the result by the number of scores in the overall group.

$59^2/10 + 50^2/10 = 3481/10 + 2500/10 = 598.1$

To determine the sum of squares for the second factor, subtract the correction factor from the above quantity.

$SS_{lighting} = 598.1 - 594.05 = 4.05$

Step 7. To compute the *interaction* effect, square the sum of each cell and divide by the number of scores in the cell.

$30^2/5 + 26^2/5 + 29^2/5 + 24^2/5 =$

$900/5 + 676/5 + 841/5 + 576/5 = 598.6$

Now, determine the sum of squares for the interaction by subtracting the correction factor, SS_{sound}, and $SS_{lighting}$ from this number.

$SS_{sound \times lighting} = 598.6 - 594.05 - .45 - 4.05 = .05$

Step 8. To compute the error sum of squares (SS_{error}), subtract SS_{sound} (Step 5), $SS_{lighting}$ (Step 6), and $SS_{sound \times lighting}$ (Step 7) from SS_t (step 4).

$SS_{error} = 52.95 - .45 - 4.05 - .05 = 48.4$

Step 9. To compute the mean square, the total degrees of freedom (df for SS_t or df_{total}) and degrees of freedom for SS_{sound}, $SS_{lighting}$, $SS_{sound \times lighting}$, and SS_{error} must first be obtained.

df_{total} = total number of scores $- 1 = 20 - 1 = 19$

df_{sound} = number of sound conditions $- 1 = 2 - 1 = 1$

$df_{lighting}$ = number of lighting conditions $- 1 = 2 - 1 = 1$

$df_{sound \times lighting}$ = df sound x df lighting = $1 \times 1 = 1$

df_{error} = df total $-$ df_{sound} $-$ $df_{lighting}$ $-$ $df_{sound \times lighting}$ = $19 - 1 - 1 - 1 = 16$

Step 10. The mean square values are computed by dividing each SS by its corresponding degrees of freedom.

MS_{total} (not required)

$MS_{sound} = SS_{sound}/1 = .45/1 = .45$

$MS_{lighting} = SS_{lighting}/1 = 4.05/1 = 4.05$

$MS_{sound \times lighting} = SS_{sound \times lighting}/1 = .05/1 = .05$

$MS_{error} = SS_{error}/16 = 48.4/16 = 3.025$

Step 11. To compute the F ratios, divide

$MS_{sound}/MS_{error} = .45/3.025 = .1488$

$MS_{lighting}/MS_{error} = 4.05/3.025 = 1.34$

$MS_{sound \times lighting}/MS_{error} = .05/3.025 = .01653$

Step 12. A necessary and required part of the analysis of variance is the Summary Table (Table 4).

Table 4 [6]
Analysis of Variance Summary Table

Sources	SS	df	MS	F	p
Total	52.95	19	—	—	—
Sound	.45	1	.45	.15	n.s.
Lighting	4.05	1	4.05	1.34	n.s.
Sound x Lighting	.05	1	.05	.02	n.s.
Error	48.4	16	3.03	—	—

The table of F ratios indicates that none of the F ratios is significant, so we conclude that neither the sound intensity levels nor the lighting conditions affected the performance of the students with learning disabilities, nor was the Sound x Lighting interaction significant. They are labeled as *nonsignificant* (n.s.) under probability level *(p)* on the table.

Example: Factorial ANOVA Using SPSS

The factorial ANOVA is called the Two-Way Between Groups ANOVA in SPSS.

Data entry. Follow the procedure outlined in Chapter 13 or in the *t* test example described earlier. Briefly, you will need to create four columns: one for the subject number, one for light level (group 1 or 2, where 1 is the fluorescent lighting and 2 the incandescent lighting), one for the listening level (group 1 or 2, where 1 is the 60dB level and 2 is the 100dB level), and one for the actual score on the pattern recognition test. Make sure you label each column clearly so that you can select the appropriate variables when completing the analysis. For this example, we will label column 1 Subject, column 2 Lighting, column 3 Soundint, and column 4 Score.

Computation. Once the data entry is completed, depress Analyze on the main menu bar, choose General Linear Model from the pull-down menu, and then choose Univariate. This produces a dialogue box that looks like Figure 4. This dialogue box looks very similar to the *t* test and one-way ANOVA boxes presented previously. In this box, you need to move your variables into the Dependent Variable and Fixed Factor(s) sections.

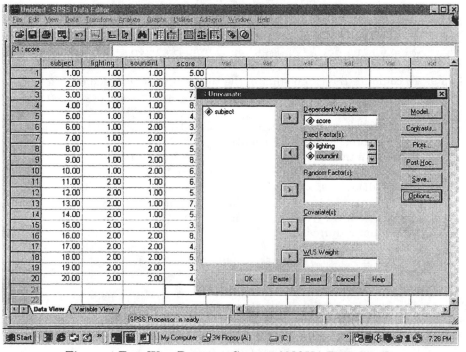

Figure 4. Two-Way Between Groups ANOVA Dialogue Box

---

[6] Note that 3.025 is rounded off in the Summary Table to two decimal points as 3.03; .149 is rounded to .15; and .0165 is rounded to .02.

First, move the score (the dependent variable in this example) into the Dependent Variable box. You do this by highlighting the word Score and then using the arrow next to the Dependent Variable box to move it. Next, highlight Lighting and move it into the Fixed Factor(s) box, using the same process just described. Finally, highlight Soundint and move it into the Fixed Factor(s) box.

You may wish to see descriptive statistics for these variables. If you do, depress the button Options in the Univariate window, and you will be presented with a window offering numerous output options. Check the Descriptive statistics box, and then click on Continue. You are now ready to complete your analysis, which you do simply by clicking on "OK." The results are presented in Figure 5.

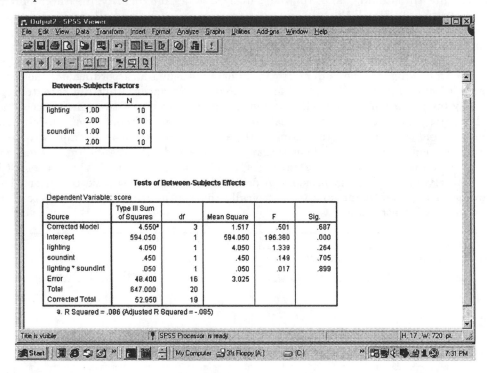

Figure 5. Two-Way Between Groups ANOVA Output Window

Mixed Effects Analysis of Variance

The mixed effects ANOVA is used for a design in which there are at least two factors, at least one of which represents different groups of subjects and at least one of which involves repeated measurements on the same subjects. The mixed effect ANOVA combines the simple one-way ANOVA with a repeated measures design. There are many variations of the mixed effects ANOVA, each of which is used for a different form of factorial designs. An experimental design book should be consulted for more information on these designs.[7]

---

[7] Experimental design books by Dayton (1970), Edwards (1985), Keppel (1991), Keppel and Zedeck (1989), Kirk (1995), and Myers and Well (1991) are recommended.

Example: Mixed Effects ANOVA Using SPSS

A music therapy researcher read an article describing the effects of severity of cancer diagnosis on self-reported fatigue ratings in adults with cancer. The article found that those patients who had the perception that their cancer diagnosis was imminently life threatening tended to have higher fatigue ratings during treatment. Finding the results intriguing, the researcher hypothesized that a music-relaxation intervention may improve these patients' perceptions of their treatment and reduce the amount of fatigue they experience. For this study, the researcher recruited 30 women who had recently been diagnosed with breast cancer: 10 who perceived their diagnosis as not life threatening, 10 who perceived it as moderately life threatening, and 10 who perceived it as imminently life threatening. The researcher proposed that all the women would experience fatigue and all would respond to the music-relaxation intervention. However, he proposed that women who perceived their cancer is imminently life threatening would experience the greatest reduction in their fatigue rating after the music-relaxation sessions.

  The following is the summary data for each subject according to the patient's perception of her diagnosis (1 = not life threatening, 2 = moderately life threatening, 3 = imminently life threatening) and self-reported fatigue ratings under two conditions. Condition 1 is the rating at the end of 1 week of chemotherapy without the music-relaxation intervention, and condition 2 is the rating at the end of 1 week of chemotherapy with a music-relaxation session during each chemotherapy treatment day. Patients rated their fatigue scores using a Likert scale, with a rating of 1 being no fatigue and a rating of 10 being overwhelmingly fatigued. It is possible to derive data under these two conditions because women undergoing treatment for cancer typically come in multiple weeks, with rest periods between weeks of treatment.

Table 5
Cancer Ratings and Music Conditions

Subject	Cancer Rating	Condition 1-No Music	Condition 2-Music
1	1	7	5
2	1	6	5
3	1	5	5
4	1	9	4
5	1	8	8
6	1	5	5
7	1	9	5
8	1	10	6
9	1	4	4
10	1	6	5
11	2	8	4
12	2	7	6
13	2	5	5
14	2	6	5
15	2	5	4
16	2	7	4
17	2	6	2
18	2	5	3
19	2	6	6
20	2	4	2
21	3	8	6
22	3	10	7
23	3	9	4
24	3	8	5
25	3	9	7
26	3	5	5
27	3	6	4
28	3	10	5
29	3	6	5
30	3	7	3

In this example, we are conducting a two-way mixed analysis of variance with one within-subjects factor and one between-subjects factor. Fatigue is a within-subjects factor because each subject's fatigue level was monitored in the presence or absence of music relaxation sessions. Patient perception of her diagnosis is a between-groups factor because it subdivides the sample into three discrete groups.

As in any two-way analysis of variance, three different null hypotheses (two main effects and an interaction) are tested. The three null hypotheses that we are testing are:

1. There is no main effect for perception of cancer diagnosis. That is, there is no difference in the fatigue scores for the three different populations of not life threatening, moderately life threatening, and imminently life threatening.

2. There is no main effect for fatigue scores. That is, there is no difference in the fatigue scores of patients in the presence or absence of music-relaxation sessions; subject experience the same amount of fatigue in the presence or absence of these sessions.

3. There is no interaction (perception of cancer diagnosis x fatigue scores). The effect of perception of cancer is independent of fatigue. The effects of the perception of cancer are consistent across all levels of fatigue

Data entry. Following the procedure outlined in Chapter 13 (and previously in this chapter), enter the data into the first four columns of the Data Editor and label the variables `Subject`, `Percept` (perception of cancer, labeled Cancer Rating in Table 5); `Fatigue1` (no music condition, labeled Condition 1 in Table 5; and `Fatigue2` (music condition, labeled Condition 2 in Table 5).

Computation. To begin the analysis, you will need to specify the within-subjects (repeated measures) independent variable. To do this, depress <u>A</u>nalyze on the menu bar, then choose <u>G</u>eneral Linear Model, and then choose <u>R</u>epeated Measures.

With the window open, begin your selections by specifying your Within-Subject Factor Name to be `Fatigue`, specify 2 as the number of levels, and depress Add. Then press Define, which takes you to a new screen. On this screen, define the Within-Subject factor by choosing `Fatigue1` and `Fatigue2` by moving them from the left-hand box to the right-hand box.

Because this is a mixed design, we still need to specify a between subjects independent variable. Below the Within-Subject Variables box is a smaller one labeled Between-Subjects Factor(s). As you may have guessed, you specify this variable by choosing the appropriate variable from the list to the left, in this case `Percept`, and then depressing the arrow key pointing to the Between-Subjects Factor(s) box.

If wanted, you can also get descriptive statistical data such as cell means and standard deviation by selecting Options and then choosing Descriptive Statistics from the resulting dialogue box. Then click on Continue to return to the main dialogue box and depress "OK" to run the analysis.

Interpreting the analysis. Don't be alarmed when you see the output viewer. A number of tables are presented, of which only two are essential for understanding the relationships between the variables. These tables are titled Tests of Within-Subjects Effects and Tests of Between-Subjects Effects, and we will discuss these in a moment. The other tables (for example, *Multivariate Tests* and *Mauchly's Test of Sphericity*) provide analyses that are typically only examined by advanced users, along with various tables that reaffirm the actual variables that have been examined. This is helpful when you are examining the relationships among a selected number of variables from a larger variable set.

Let's now look at the Tests of Within-Subjects Effects table, which is shown in Figure 6. In this table you will see the variables Fatigue and Fatigue*Percept listed in the left hand column, followed by a series of computations. These are all *F* tests, computed in a number of different ways to assure that the assumptions made about the sample are correct. Notice that all four calculations are the same, so we can assume that the sample is representative of a larger population from which it is drawn (sphericity assumed). Notice that the *F* test for Fatigue $F = 44.468$ is significant, $p < 0.0001$. In this case, we can reject the null hypothesis that there is no effect for the music condition on fatigue. The music relaxation condition positively affected the fatigue scores of these patients with cancer. The second row combines the Fatigue and Perception variables and examines these simultaneously. In this case, the *F* test found no effect, $F = 1.053$, $p > 0.05$. The effectiveness of the music relaxation intervention did not change according to the extent to which patients perceived their illnesses as life threatening.

Source		Type III Sum of Squares	df	Mean Square	F	Sig.
Fatigue	Sphericity Assumed	64.067	1	64.067	44.468	.000
	Greenhouse-Geisser	64.067	1.000	64.067	44.468	.000
	Huynh-Feldt	64.067	1.000	64.067	44.468	.000
	Lower-bound	64.067	1.000	64.067	44.468	.000
Fatigue * Percept	Sphericity Assumed	3.033	2	1.517	1.053	.363
	Greenhouse-Geisser	3.033	2.000	1.517	1.053	.363
	Huynh-Feldt	3.033	2.000	1.517	1.053	.363
	Lower-bound	3.033	2.000	1.517	1.053	.363
Error (Fatigue)	Sphericity Assumed	38.900	27	1.441		
	Greenhouse-Geisser	38.900	27.000	1.441		
	Huynh-Feldt	38.900	27.000	1.441		
	Lower-bound	38.900	27.000	1.441		

Figure 6. Tests of Within-Subjects Effects

Figure 7 shows the second table of importance, Tests of Between-Subjects Effects. In this case, there is only one effect, for Percept, which distinguishes the three groups: patients' perceptions of their illness as 1 = not life threatening, 2 = moderately life threatening, and 3 = imminently life threatening. (You will also see a significant F value for something called Intercept, but this is not relevant and should be ignored.) This indicates that there were differences between these patients according to the extent to which they perceived their cancer as life threatening. When combined with the results of the Tests of Within-Subjects Effects, this indicates that although there were differences between each of these three groups (low, moderate, and imminent perception of their cancer as life threatening), the music relaxation intervention was equally effective in reducing fatigue.

Source	Type III Sum of Squares	df	Mean Square	F	Sig.
Intercept	2041.667	1	2041.667	657.032	.000
Percept	22.433	2	11.217	3.610	.041
Error	83.900	27	3.107		

Figure 7. Tests of Between-Subjects Effects

Multiple Regression and Multivariate Analyses

The statistical devices covered in each of the previous sections have been easy tasks for a pocket calculator or a microcomputer. Even the mixed designs, however lengthy and tedious, can be calculated using either of the two. Multiple correlation is not easily computed on either of the small devices, and the discriminant function analysis can be computed only on a computer.

There are many similarities between multiple correlation and discriminant function analysis. The mathematician will note that the two approaches have virtually identical mathematical bases, except that the multiple correlation analysis uses a continuous criterion variable while discriminant analysis uses a categorical criterion variable. Several new terms, *criterion variable* and *predictor variable,* are used with these two designs. In the literal sense, the criterion or criterion variable is a behavioral measure of future performance to be predicted using a set of variables that presently are being measured. For example, the criterion measured might be success as a therapist (a categorical criterion variable, coded with two numbers for successful or unsuccessful) or job satisfaction (a continuous criterion variable, rated on a scale of 1 to 10). The predictor variables are those variables chosen to statistically predict the criterion variable, such as the gender of the therapist, number of years of practice, age, or annual salary.[8]

Despite these similarities between multiple correlation and discriminant function analysis, there is at least one major difference: They are used with different research designs. Multiple correlation is a correlational technique used when there is a single criterion and multiple predictors measured from a single group of subjects. It is essentially correlational, attempting to determine a relationship between variables or possibly attempting to predict the criterion because of this relationship. The discriminant function analysis, on the other hand, is used with quasi-experimental or experimental designs that have several groups of subjects, where the researcher wants to test whether the groups are different in terms of the set of predictor variables. The research question underlying discriminant function analysis is one of significant difference between groups, even though the researcher using this technique may later want to predict the group membership of certain subjects.

Since the multiple correlation and multiple regression techniques in this unit are advanced correlational techniques, it is necessary to be thoroughly familiar with simple correlation and regression. Correlation, as discussed earlier in the chapter, refers to relationship or the extent to which variables go together (covary) or measure the same thing. The most common correlational test is the Pearson product-moment correlation, expressed as r; this test is used when the variables are represented by intervallic data. The nonparametric counterpart to the Pearson product-moment correlation is the Spearman rank-order correlation or the Spearman rank-order correlation coefficent (rho), appropriate for ordinal data. Simple, or bivariate, correlation describes the most elementary model in which two variables are related. In bivariate correlation, one variable is correlated with another; if these two are related, one can be predicted from the other (see the discussion of regression below).

Multiple correlation is a model in which one variable (the criterion) is correlated with a set of variables (the predictors). It should be emphasized that the predictors are a set of variables or, more accurately, a weighted set of variables that are being treated as a whole unit correlated with the single variable, the criterion. Multiple correlation produces a single statistical measure of relationship, the multiple correlation coefficient, usually written as an upper case R (that is, $R = .86$). The coefficient of determination, identified as r^2 or R^2, describes the amount of common or shared variance among variables, or how much of the variability in the criterion variable is accounted for by all predictors. Since the purpose of multiple correlation is to predict the criterion as well as possible, or account for as much variance in it as possible, multiple predictors are more effective than a single predictor.

Regression is an extension of correlation when the aim is to develop an equation that actually *predicts* values of the criterion variable. Simple regression (bivariate regression) aims to predict one variable from another: The larger the coefficient, the more accurate the prediction. We say that we wish to study the regression of Y scores on X scores, meaning that we wish to study how the Y scores go back to, or depend upon, the X scores (Kerlinger, 1973).

Graphically, correlation and regression might be expressed as shown in Figure 1 (p. 140), where X and Y scores are plotted and regression line a is drawn through the plotted points. In the case of correlation, the scores X and Y are known and the regression line illustrates their relationship. However, in regression, where the scores are not known, the aim is to predict a score based on known data.

A simple regression equation is expressed as $Y' = a + bX$, where a is a constant and b is the slope of the line. As scores become more dispersed, represented by a low absolute value of r, it becomes more difficult to draw a line to represent the scores or to make an accurate prediction based upon the scores.

Multiple regression uses the same principles as simple regression, but with a set of predictor variables, to predict a criterion. Regression analysis is performed after correlation analysis, but only when there is a significant relationship and the aim is prediction. Regression equations can be used to predict actual values of a criterion variable if the researcher knows the values of the predictor variables. They also can be used to compare the relative importance of each variable in the equation.

---

[8] Note that all variables used in correlation and multiple correlation are represented numerically.

Example: Multiple Regression Using SPSS

Previous research in Guided Imagery and Music (GIM) has suggested that there may be a relationship between mental health and responsiveness to this method of music therapy. There is also some indication that responsiveness to the music used during GIM sessions may be a predictor of mental health, although this relationship has not been adequately explored. Understanding this relationship more fully would be of benefit to GIM therapists, in particular, because it would underscore the importance of engaging their clients fully in the music experiences typical of GIM, as this may lead to increased mental health.

In order to examine this relationship more fully, 30 GIM clients were asked to complete the Sense of Coherence Scale (SOC; Antonovsky, 1993) prior to completing a series of 15 individual GIM sessions. At the end of these sessions, the GIM therapist completed two scales for all clients, one measuring their overall responsiveness to the music used during sessions and another indicating their overall responsiveness to the series of sessions. Responsiveness to the music was rated between 1 and 50 and overall responsiveness to GIM rated between 1 and 100. Scores on the SOC vary between 29 and 207 with a mean of approximately 142 for a general, nonclinical population. The results are found in Table 6.

Table 6
Sex, Sense of Coherence, Musical Responsiveness, and Overall Responsiveness

S	Sex	SOC	Music	Overall	S	Sex	SOC	Music	Overall
1	1	138	37	82	16	2	127	25	59
2	1	119	28	27	17	2	139	36	66
3	1	151	43	56	18	2	143	44	78
4	1	119	45	19	19	2	118	25	44
5	1	165	44	78	20	2	150	40	80
6	1	100	32	50	21	2	128	36	71
7	1	128	36	65	22	2	141	35	72
8	1	129	25	44	23	2	156	41	79
9	1	138	39	59	24	2	119	29	67
10	1	128	28	55	25	2	155	45	83
11	1	154	43	78	26	2	140	33	71
12	1	149	41	81	27	2	137	39	65
13	1	124	30	76	28	2	136	37	69
14	1	149	45	88	29	2	149	41	79
15	1	139	33	72	30	2	152	42	80

Data entry. Following the procedure outlined in Chapter 13, enter the data into the first five columns of the Data Editor and label the variables Subject, Sex (male or female), SOC (Sense of Coherence Scale), Musicres (musical responsiveness), and Therares (overall therapeutic responsiveness).

Computation. To begin the analysis, go to <u>A</u>nalyze on the menu bar, then choose <u>R</u>egression. For the resulting menu, choose <u>L</u>inear and in the resulting dialogue box move the variable Musicres into the <u>D</u>ependent box and the variables SOC and Therares into the <u>I</u>ndependent(s) box. To get the <u>D</u>escriptive statistics, check the <u>S</u>tatistics button and select <u>D</u>escriptives in the resulting dialogue box. Click on Continue to close the box, and then click "OK" to run the analysis.

Output. The output produced by SPSS is shown in Figures 8 and 9 (other information will also be included if descriptive statistics have been requested). Figure 8 gives information on the variables entered and removed as well as the model summary. This provides a confirmation of the actual analysis undertaken and includes the multiple correlation coefficient (R) and adjusted R^2 and the standard error of the estimate. In this example, 68% of the variance in music responsiveness scores can be accounted for by overall responsiveness and SOC scores.

Figure 9 provides two summary tables of the ANOVA and Coefficients. The ANOVA table represents a test of the null hypothesis that multiple R in the population equals 0. This variance is partitioned into two sources: the part predictable from the regression equation (Regression) and the part not predictable (Residual or error). Here, the F is significant.

In the final section of the output (Figure 9), information is provided so as to construct a least-squares regression (prediction) equation. The column labeled B lists the regression coefficients for each independent variable and for the *constant* term. Thus, in this example, the least squares prediction equation is: Predicted MUSICRES = −12.892 + (.273)*(SOC) + (.165)*(THERARES).

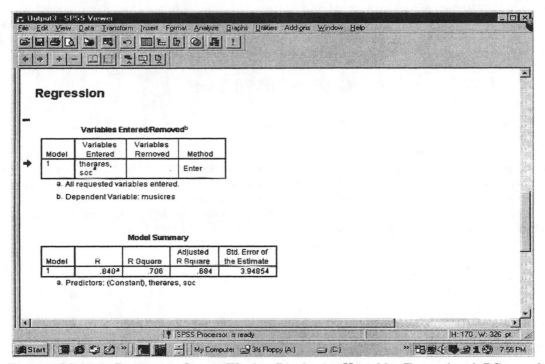

Figure 8. Multiple Regression Output Window Display ing Variables Entered and *R* Squared

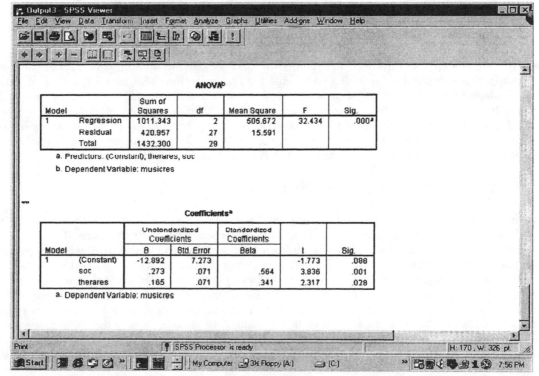

Figure 9. Multiple Regression Output Window Displaying the Least Squares Regression Equation

Nonparametric Statistical Tests

As mentioned earlier, nonparametric statistics may be useful in music therapy research because samples are generally small, and the data are nominal or ordinal. The following nonparametric statistical tests appear in the music therapy literature: chi-square, one-sample runs tests, Kolmogorov-Smirnoff, Mann-Whitney U, Wilcoxon matched-pairs signed-ranks test, McNemar test for significance of change, Kolmogorov-Smirnoff two-sample test, chi-square for two independent samples, Friedman Two-way analysis of variance, chi-square for k independent samples, and the Kruskal-Wallis one-way analysis of variance.

Goodness-of-Fit-Test

Chi-Square (X^2) One-Sample Test

One-sample, or goodness-of-fit, tests attempt to determine whether a particular sample was actually drawn from a particular population. The chi-square, one of the most versatile tests, attempts to determine whether there are significant differences between an observed number of responses and an expected number. It is used with nominal data.

In order to test whether the observed frequency is different from the expected frequency, the following formula is used:

$$\chi^2 = \sum_{i=1}^{k} \frac{(O_i - E_i)^2}{E_i}$$

Where O_i = observed number of cases
E_i = expected number of cases

The larger the value of χ^2, the more likely it is that the sample in question was not drawn from the population.

Nonparametric Tests for Independent Samples

As with parametric tests, there are nonparametric statistical techniques appropriate for comparing two independent samples (see Table 2). Test selection is based on the type of data used. Independent groups or samples may be defined as groups or samples selected separately, in other words, from separate populations or from populations whose characteristics are unknown. The nonparametric tests appropriate for independent samples are chi-square for two independent samples (nominal) and Mann-Whitney U (ordinal). Also appropriate, although not discussed here, is the Kolmogorov-Smirnoff (ordinal).

Chi-Square for Two Independent Samples

Researchers are often faced with comparing two independently drawn samples on a variable that is measured on a nominal scale. This comparison attempts to determine if there is a significant difference between the two samples, as, for example, in a situation where a music therapist is interested in comparing the rhythmic perception abilities of girls and boys.

The advantages of the chi-square for two independent samples are: (a) Computation is simple, (b) only nominal data are required, (c) a researcher is capable of setting the expected frequency on an a priori basis on a sample with which he or she is familiar. It must be emphasized, however, that chi-square tests are limited to situations in which the categories are all independent. The occurrence of data from the same subject in two or more places in the analysis would violate the assumption of independent observation; this is probably the most frequent error in the use of chi-square tests.

As with the one-sample chi-square, the chi-square for two independent samples is calculated as:

$$\chi^2 = \sum \frac{\left(\text{Observed - Expected}\right)^2}{\text{Expected}}$$

This formula requires that the expected frequency be calculated. The expected frequency can be calculated by multiplying the sum of the rows by the sum of the columns and dividing by the total number of cases, N.

Example: Chi-Square for Two Independent Samples

In a study of the success or failure of men and women on a musical task, each subject's performance is evaluated. The numbers of men and women succeeding or failing on the task are then placed in the appropriate quadrant and compared with the expected frequency. The table is called a *contingency table* (see Table 9).

Table 9
2 x 2 Contingency Table

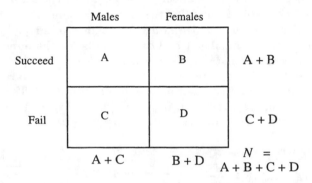

In Table 10, Quadrant A's expected frequency would be (A + B) x (A + C)/N, or (13 x 15)/25 = 7.8. Therefore, the expected frequency of 7.8 is placed in the upper left-hand corner of Quadrant A (in italics), as shown in Table 10. The expected frequencies for the other quadrants are calculated in the same manner. Actual scores are entered in the center of the quadrant in regular print.

This formula requires that the expected frequency be calculated. Multiplying the sum of the rows by the sum of the columns and dividing the total number of cases, N, can calculate the expected frequency.

Table 10
Males and Females Succeeding and Failing on a Musical Task

	Males	Females	
Succeed	A *7.8* 7	B *5.2* 6	13
Fail	C *7.2* 8	D *4.8* 4	12
	15	10	25

This example yields the following calcula tions:

$$\chi^2 = \frac{(7-7.8)^2}{7.8} + \frac{(6-5.2)^2}{5.2} + \frac{(8-7.2)^2}{7.2} + \frac{(4-4.8)^2}{4.8}$$

$$= .427$$

$$df = 1$$

$$p > .05$$

Since the χ^2 of .427 was not significant, the data from this example fail to support the hypothesis that gender influences success or failure on a musical task.

Example: Chi-Square Using SPSS

Data entry. It is relatively easy to apply the same basic ideas to data input using SPSS for Windows as in the hand calculations given above. You do not need raw scores but simply code each variable differently. In the above case of sex differences on a music task, you will need to create three columns, as follows. To begin, open the data editor window as previously described. Once open, you can begin entering the data with the first column being a number of each subject, 1-25. In the second column, labeled Sex, give the first 15 subjects the number 1 for male and subjects 16–25 the number 2 for female. In the third column, labeled Musictest, you can see from Table 10 that 7 of the males succeeded in the test and 8 failed the test. Similarly, 6 females succeeded and 4 failed. In column 3, simply give those males and females who passed the test the number 1 and those who failed the number 2. You will then have created the same information in the 2x2 table of Table 10.

Computation. With the data entered, you can now begin the chi-square analysis. Depress <u>A</u>nalyze, then choose <u>D</u>escriptive <u>S</u>tatistics from the pull-down menu. Then, depress Crosstabs, which will produce the dialogue box shown in Figure 10. You will also notice that you can see much of how the data were entered into the data editor in Figure 10.

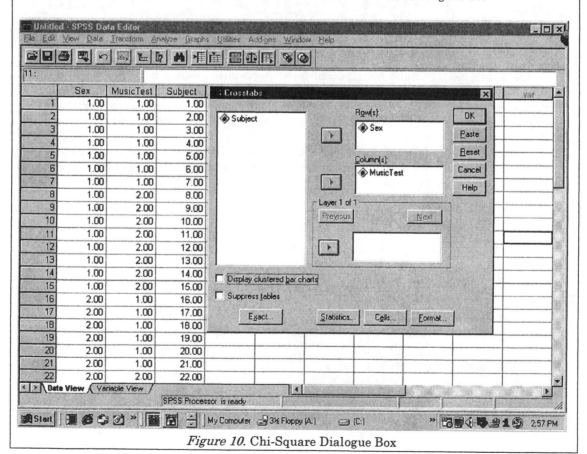

Figure 10. Chi-Square Dialogue Box

With the dialogue box open, you can begin specifying your analyses. Click on Sex and place it in the row(s) section of the dialogue box. Then, click on Musictest and place it in the column(s) section of the dialogue box. Next, you must click on the Cells button at the bottom of the dialogue box and open it. This produces a new dialogue box that allows you to specify your analysis and additional information that will be helpful once your analysis is complete. In our case, we want to choose Row and Column, as this will give the percentages for each cell, much in the same way as Table 10 provides information on sex and music test scores.

Output. After closing this window, click on the Statistics tab at the bottom of the main dialogue box and choose Chi-Square. You will see from that window that there are many analyses available, but we will only need Chi-Square. Click on the key in this box, then on Continue. Once back in the Crosstabs window, click on "OK," and the analysis will be provided. It will give you several different outputs, the most important of which is the Pearson Chi-Square of .427, shown in Figure 11 below.

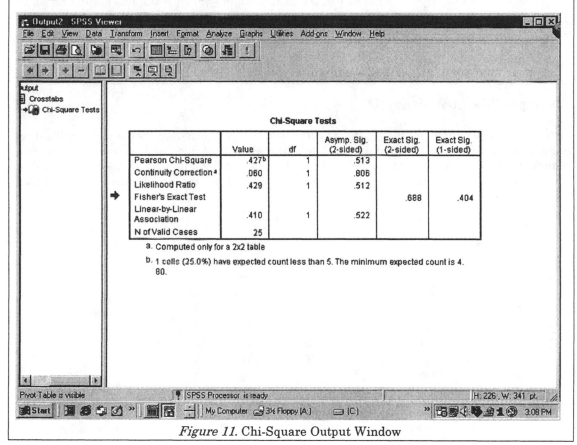

Figure 11. Chi-Square Output Window

Mann-Whitney U

The Wilcoxon Mann-Whitney U test was first devised by Wilcoxon in 1945 and modified by Mann and Whitney in 1947. Most sources indicate the U test as a suitable alternative to the t test for independent samples. The Mann-Whitney U requires only ordinal data, while the t test requires at least interval data and possesses a number of other assumptions.

Many researchers suggest the use of the U test instead of the t test when the assumptions underlying the t test cannot be met. Still others refrain from using the U test, fearing that it is a weak alternative to the t test. Boneau (1970), in his article: "A Comparison of the Power of the U and t Test," examined both tests according to homogeneity and heterogeneity of variance of normal and non-normal distributions. The results of this study indicated that the t test is no less robust with minor violations of the assumptions than U, but also that the use of U should not be avoided on the assumption that is less powerful than t. As a matter of fact, Sawilowsky and Blair (1992) reported that Mann-Whitney U is more powerful then t when the sample is small and asymmetrical.

The Mann-Whitney U uses ranked data, that is, the actual raw scores are ranked from 1 to N. The assumption being that the two samples is drawn from different populations. The null hypothesis states that there will be no significant difference between the two samples.

The formula for the Mann-Whitney U follows:

$$U_1 = n_1 n_2 + \frac{n_1(n_1 + 1)}{2} - R_1$$

$$U_2 = n_1 n_2 + \frac{n_2(n_2 + 1)}{2} - R_2$$

The Mann-Whitney U is calculated with the above formula, where n_1 = the number of scores in sample one, n_2 = the number of scores in sample two, R_1 = the total of the ranks in the first sample, and R_2 = the total of the ranks in the second sample. Two steps are required to get the numbers for the formula: (a) Rank all of the scores from both groups together, from smallest to largest; and (b) sum the ranks. When ranking, tied scores are handled by averaging the ranks for each tie.

Example: Mann-Whitney U

A researcher wishing to judge the effectiveness of two different behavior modification programs compares the total number of tokens received by clients from programs in two different cottages. These data, shown in Table 11, represent the number of tokens awarded to clients in Cottage A, using one behavior modification program, compared with different clients in Cottage B, using another program.

Table 11
Number of Tokens Per Cottage

Cottage A			Cottage B		
Subject	Tokens	Rank	Subject	Tokens	Rank
S_1	10	5.5	S_7	10	5.5
S_2	12	8	S_8	12	8
S_3	9	4	S_9	15	12
S_4	8	3	S_{10}	17	13
S_5	7	2	S_{11}	12	8
S_6	6	1	S_{12}	13	10
			S_{13}	14	11
	$R_1 = 23.5$			$R_2 = 67.5$	

$$U_1 = n_1 n_2 + \frac{n_1(n_1 + 1)}{2} - R_1$$

$$= (6)(7) + \frac{6(6+1)}{2} - 23.5$$

$$= 42 + 21 - 23.5$$

$$= 39.5$$

$$U_2 = n_1 n_2 + \frac{n_2(n_2 + 1)}{2} - R_2$$

$$= (6)(7) + \frac{7(7+1)}{2} - 67.5$$

$$= 42 + 28 - 67.5$$

$$= 2.5$$

$$p < .05$$

It is necessary to compute both values of U, as most tables are computed on the smaller of the two values.[9] Since our groups of $n = 6$ and $n = 7$ are a small sample, we must consult a table of critical values of U that includes small values. From such a table (Siegel, 1956), our smaller U of 2.5 yields an exact probability of $p = .003$, or $p < .05$, suggesting that the difference in number of tokens awarded in the two cottages is dues to differences in the behavior modification programs rather than to chance.

Nonparametric Tests for Dependent Samples

Correlated, related, and *dependent* are terms used to describe samples or groups matched on some extraneous variables (gender, age, IQ, etc.) or because a pretreatment-posttreatment design has been used. The McNemar Test, although not presented here, is useful for evaluating data from before and after experiments; it utilizes nominal data.

Wilcoxon Matched-Pairs Signed-Ranks Test

The Wilcoxon was mentioned previously as the counterpart of the Mann-Whitney U, with the exception that the Wilcoxon is uses matched samples. It is suitable for comparing pretest and posttest scores. The Wilcoxon also uses ordinal data. It is a nonparametric alternative to the t test for related means.

Nonparametric Statistics for More Than Two Groups

Researchers are frequently interested in studying variables across groups of three or more. The advantages of studying three or more groups simultaneously are that the tedium of comparing each group to the other is avoided, it frequently provides linear information about the independent variable, and the researcher is able to examine variables in a more natural state. In addition, repeatedly comparing groups increases the chance that significant results will be achieved due to chance alone, an example of a Type I error or alpha build-up.

The tests reviewed here are appropriate for determining whether three or more dependent or independent samples were drawn from the same population. The chi-square for three or more samples (or for k samples; nominal) is suited for independent samples, while the Kruskal-Wallis one-way analysis of variance is useful for independent samples and the Friedman two-way analysis of variance is useful for matched samples.

---

[9] An alternative (and simpler) way to compute the second value is with the following formula:

$$U_2 = n_1 n_2 - U_1$$
$$= 42 - 39.5$$
$$= 2.5$$

Kruskal-Wallis One-Way Analysis of Variance

The Kruskal-Wallis one-way analysis of variance is appropriate for determining whether three or more independent samples were drawn from the same population. It is the nonparametric counterpart of the simple one-way analysis of variance (Huck, Cormier, & Bounds, 1974). The Kruskal-Wallis uses the procedure of ranking the data, similar to the Mann-Whitney *U*.

Friedman Two-Way Analysis of Variance

The last nonparametric test to be discussed is the Friedman two-way analysis of variance. The Friedman is a repeated measures test suitable for determining whether three or more correlated samples are drawn from the same population. In spite of its name, it is more similar to the parametric one-way ANOVA than to the two-way ANOVA. The Friedman is particularly useful for testing the same subject (repeated measures) under a number of different conditions. For example, subjects' performances might be analyzed according to three or more different teaching approaches.

Summary

The purpose of this chapter was to introduce and perhaps reacquaint the reader with research concepts. It is hoped that discussions of scales, descriptive and inferential statistics, and parametric and nonparametric statistics will demystify some of these concepts found in music therapy research.

Research in the *Journal of Music Therapy* cites statistical tests presented in this chapter. The *t* tests and ANOVAs continue to be the most popular statistical tests used by researchers in music therapy. The nonparametric tests are still very popular especially with the small samples found in much music therapy research. Of course, clear communications can still be accomplished using frequency tables and percentages.

It should be noted that the manual computations presented are in no way meant to discourage the use of computer based statistical packages, but are intended to inform the reader of how results are derived. The researcher still has to make decisions relative to the appropriateness of the statistic selected and interpret the meaning of the results. However, anyone interested in quantitative research and statistics is urged to become familiar with SPSS or any of the other menu-driven statistical packages for the computer, as described in Chapter 13, Computer Programs for Quantitative Data Analysis.

References

Antonovsky, A. (1993). *Unraveling the mystery of health: How people manage stress and stay well.* San Francisco: Jossey-Bass.

Argyrous, G. (2000). *Statistics for social and health research with a guide to SPSS.* London: Sage Publications.

Boneau, C. A. (1970). The effects of violations of assumptions underlying the *t* test. In A. Haber, R. P. Runyon, & P. Badia (Eds.), *Readings in statistics* (pp. 231–254). Reading, MA: Addison-Wesley.

Dayton, C.M. (1970). *The design of educational experiments.* New York: McGraw-Hill.

DeCuir, A. A. (1980, November). *A survey of statistical course offerings in music therapy.* Paper presented at the conference of the National Association for Music Therapy, Minneapolis, MN.

Edwards, A. L. (1985). *Experimental design in psychological research* (5th ed.). New York: Harper & Row.

Hinton, P. R. (1995). *Statistics explained: A guide for social science students.* New York: Routledge.

Huck, S. W., Cormier, W. H., & Bounds, W. G. (1974). *Reading statistics and research.* New York: Harper & Row.

Keppel, G. (1991). *Design and analysis: A researcher's handbook* (3rd ed.). Englewood Cliffs, NJ: Prentice Hall.

Keppel, G., & Zedeck, S. (1989). *Data analysis for research design.* New York: W.H. Freeman.

Kerlinger, F. N. (1973). *Foundations of behavioral research* (2nd ed.). New York: Holt, Rinehart and Winston.

Kirk, R. E. (1995). *Experimental design: Procedures for the behavioral sciences* (3rd ed.). Belmont, CA: Brooks/Cole.

Lipsey, M. W. (1998). Design sensitivity: Statistical power for applied experimental research. In L. Bickman & D. J. Rog (Eds.), *Handbook of applied social research methods* (pp. 39–68). Thousand Oaks, CA: Sage Publications.

Madsen, C. K., & Madsen, C. H. (1978). *Experimental research in music.* Raleigh, NC: Contemporary Publishing Co.

Minium, E. W., King, B. M., & Bear, G. (1993). *Statistical reasoning in psychology and education.* New York: John Wiley & Sons, Inc.

Myers, J. L., & Well, A. D. (1991). *Research design and statistical analysis.* New York: Harper Collins.

Sawilowsky, S. S. & Blair, R. C. (1992). A more realistic look at the robustness and type error properties of the *t*-test to departure from population normality. *Psychological Bulletin, 3,* 352–360.

Siegel, S. (1956). *Nonparametric statistics for the behavioral sciences.* New York: McGraw-Hill.

SPSS Inc. (2003). SPSS for Windows. Chicago: SPSS Inc.

Additional Readings

Anderson, N. H. (1970). On teaching *F* instead of *t.* In A. Haber, R. P. Runyon, & P. Badia (Eds). *Readings in statistics* (pp. 106–110). Reading, MA: Addison-Wesley.

Bruning, J. L., & Kintz, B. L. (1987). *Computational handbook of statistics* (3rd ed.). Glenview, IL: Scott, Foresman and Co.

Cochran, W. G. (1954). Some methods for strengthening the common X^2 tests. *Biometrics, 10,* 417–451.

Acknowledgments

The author wishes to thank Anthony Meadows for the SPSS examples in the chapter and Cheyenne Mize for her assistance in proofreading and correcting formulas.

Chapter 13
Computer Programs for
Quantitative Data Analysis
Anthony Meadows

The purpose of this chapter is to describe the basic functions and uses of the Statistical Package for the Social Sciences (SPSS), commonly used in the social sciences for teaching and research purposes. SPSS uses a pull-down menu system of commands that allows for both simple (such as descriptive statistics) and complex (such as regression, factor analysis) analyses as well as a broad range of options for the presentation of findings (such as graphics, tables). A brief description and comparison of SPSS with SAS and Minitab will precede the introduction to SPSS.

Background and Overview

Computer programs for quantitative data analysis were used as far back as the 1960s, when packages such as SPSS were developed at academic institutions to meet the needs of students and faculty who wished to compute large data sets that had traditionally taken a significant amount of time to compute by hand. With the advent of mainframe computers, statistical programs were handwritten using punch cards that were filled out and fed or run through the computer. As these techniques were developed and refined, programs were written that allowed researchers to perform analyses on mainframe computers using *Syntax* language in the Unix operating system. Syntax is a shorthand statistical language that allows a user to identify variables and compute complex statistical procedures using a command system. While very powerful, Syntax is often intimidating to the novice user because of the unusual way in which the analytic language operates. Furthermore, unless the student or researcher regularly works with Syntax language, it is easy to forget, requiring relearning the language before engaging in the actual statistical analyses.

Recently, statistical packages such as SPSS, SAS, and Minitab developed versions of their software that operate in a pull-down menu system, with all the necessary commands built into the various windows. This gives greater access to these rather complex programs because users no longer have to rely on syntax yet can complete very complex statistical analyses with large data sets. A brief description of these packages follows.

Overview of SPSS, Minitab, and SAS

SPSS, Minitab, and SAS are essentially commercial competitors in providing the means for conducting a range of statistical analyses on the personal computer. SPSS is perhaps the most widely used program in psychology and education for conducting data analyses, whereas Minitab is commonly used in statistics departments as a teaching and research tool and SAS is commonly used in sociology research (R. Goren, personal communication, July 14, 2003). However, each package is used by a diverse group of clientele. While each program offers a common pool of statistical procedures that are frequently used in quantitative research, such as ANOVA, regression, factor analysis, and time series, each also offers unique methods of data analysis that may attract certain users over others. For example, while SPSS and Minitab offer nearly identical options at the basic and intermediate level of statistical analyses, Minitab offers some very complex statistical analyses, such as exploratory data analysis, that SPSS does not, unless additional modules are purchased. While SAS is perhaps the most complex of the three packages because it relies on Syntax commands, it is also generally seen as having the best options for data manipulation. So, while it might be easy to ask the question, Which program is best?, a better way of asking such a question is, Which program best suits my research needs? While SPSS is likely to meet most of the needs of a beginning and intermediate user, the needs of the advanced user may be better met by another statistical package.

If you were to examine SPSS, SAS, and Minitab simultaneously, you would notice that all have certain similarities and some unique qualities. The first thing that you will notice about all of the programs is that they use windows to display information about the programs and their various functions, such as how to enter data and show the outcome of analyses. Each program varies in the way this information is presented. SPSS and Minitab present a single window of information, with other windows popping up based on the choices made with data. SAS is very different in that the main screen actually comprises three screens: one that overviews all the commands the user has made, another for entering data and analysis commands, and a third for output. Herein lies the first very important distinction between the three programs: While SPSS and Minitab use pull-down menus to operate all of the data entry and statistical procedures, SAS uses the Windows format but operates only in Syntax language. As previously mentioned, Syntax is a shorthand command language that allows the user to complete all of the tasks offered in the program. For example, to enter data into SAS you must begin by typing the word DATA, then define the data set and the various variables, which will be listed in columns. So, for a set of three variables, subject, sex, and score, the commands would appear as follows:

```
DATA scores;
INPUT subject sex score;
1    1    25
2    1    75
3    2    50 etc.
```

Notice the use of semicolons, spaces, and discrete lines for information. These are all important for the presentation of information to the program, because the absence of a colon, space, or period could produce an error message and the need to rerun the command.

In SPSS and Minitab, you do not need any of these commands if you are working in the windows and pull-down menu system. The option to enter data will be presented in the first window of the program. If you choose this option, you will be presented with a grid of rows and columns (similar to programs such as Microsoft Excel), with each cell representing a discrete piece of data (see Figure 1 for the SPSS window). To enter data, you simply point and click on the cell and begin entering your data. At some later point, you can label the variable (or subject) however you wish, but it is not a prerequisite to enter or save data.

The next level of comparison comes in the ways that data can be analyzed, that is, the actual statistical procedure. In both SPSS and Minitab, this is done through a system of pull-down menus that give the user numerous options in conducting analyses. In SPSS, you would move your mouse to the pull-down menu labeled Analyze. In Minitab you would go to the pull-down menu labeled Stat. Once you click on the desired statistical analysis (for either package), you are given a series of options for conducting the analysis. If you select the desired statistical procedure, the program will guide you through all the options, such as selecting variables for completing the analysis.

SAS is very different in the way it conducts data analyses. Using Syntax, all analyses begin with the PROC command. For example, to find the mean of the scores presented in the previous SAS syntax example, the command would be as follows:

```
PROC Means;
Var score;
Run
```

Notice the simplicity of the commands. So, while Syntax can be intimidating, it often is very simple, even elegant, in its design. Writing and running Syntax can actually be faster than using the pull-down menu system. It may help you to gain a better understanding of the actual statistical procedure because it requires you to construct the analysis language rather than rely on the computer program to move you through the various windows.

While SPSS and Minitab operate with pull-down menus, both also offer the option of operating in syntax. In SPSS, this is achieved by enabling the *Syntax Editor* and then typing the necessary commands into the Syntax Editor window. In Minitab, syntax is called command language or session commands and is enabled by clicking on the Session Windows button and typing into this window. It is important to know that the syntax language in each of the programs (SPSS, Minitab, and SAS) is different, as are the procedures for opening data files, running analyses, and presenting findings.

In terms of saving files, SPSS and Minitab are very similar. To save a file, simply click on the File pull-down menu and select Save As. You will then be given options on where to save your data and what name to give the file. Minitab offers a very interesting option in saving data. While SPSS will only allow you to save data and the output of analyses, Minitab will allow you to save the entire set of analyses you conduct, which is called a *project.* That is, Minitab allows you to save all of the analyses you conduct, as you conduct them. This is very helpful in reviewing the output of analyses, especially when you are manipulating data, such as selecting certain subjects rather than the entire *N,* because you can review the precise way in which you conduct your analysis. You are not able to do this in SPSS.

In SAS, you actually create the name and save the file at the very beginning of the *session* (as it is called in SAS). You do this through the SAV (save) command that allows you to identify variables, enter data, and run analyses. When you open a saved file, you may not actually see the raw data (as you always would in SPSS and Minitab), but through another series of commands you can see the data.

This brief comparison of SPSS, Minitab, and SAS presents some basic information as to the similarities and differences in these programs. In the following sections, you will now have the opportunity to learn, in detail, how to enter data, run statistical analyses, and save data and output using SPSS for Windows. For a thorough introduction to using Minitab see *Minitab Handbook* by Ryan and Joiner (2001). For an introduction to using SAS, see *The Little SAS Book: A Primer* by Delwiche and Slaughter (1998).

SPSS for Windows[1]

This overview of SPSS for Windows[2] relates to version 12.0. Earlier versions have some differences in the main window, but the basic principles of the Windows operating system apply. Student packages (commonly called student versions) are also offered by SPSS Inc. and have the same basic operational features but offer fewer options for statistical analysis, particularly complex analyses.

When you first open SPSS and view the main Data Editor screen, you may feel overwhelmed by the sheer number of options available to you in all of the pull-down menus. Don't be alarmed! SPSS operates rather like Microsoft Word in that there are several menus you will use frequently, while others will be less commonly used. By following the instructions below, you will be able to begin entering data almost immediately and, by following the examples in Chapter 12, Statistical Methods of Analysis, complete a range of statistical analyses by following the instructions. You are encouraged to consult one of several texts dedicated to understanding how to use SPSS, such as Cramer (1998) to fill out your understanding of using SPSS.

Remember that the information contained in this chapter, while comprehensive in its intent, is merely a beginning in the use of SPSS. Below are instructions on how to use SPSS using the pull-down menu system. It is also possible to operate SPSS using Syntax language, which has certain advantages over the pull-down menu system. How to use Syntax is not included in this chapter, although the reader is encouraged to develop a basic understanding of Syntax.

A Quick Overview of the Main Screen

SPSS is usually started from Windows by double clicking the SPSS icon, or by choosing it from the menu of options (Windows —> Programs —> SPSS). Once the program is loaded, your screen should look like Figure 1 (there will be variations in the main screen or data editor window depending on the version of SPSS you are using). When SPSS first starts up, Figure 1 may be partly covered by a small box asking "What do you want to do?" and listing several options. If this happens, click on Type in Data, then click on OK, and your screen should return to Figure 1.

---

[1] While this chapter gives basic information, it was necessary to provide some guidance in using SPSS in the previous chapter in order to illustrate basic statistical analysis procedures. Therefore, many readers will have already discovered some of what is presented here.

[2] SPSS is also made for use with Apple computers. The basic principles of operation are the same.

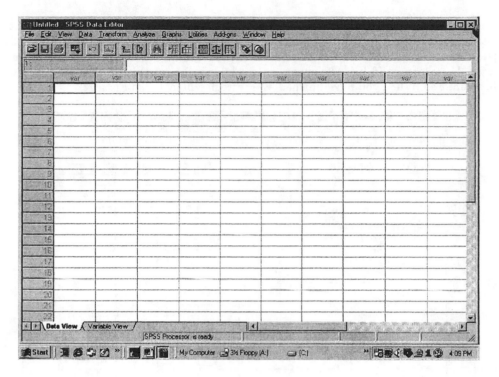

Figure 1. SPSS Data Editor Window

We will start by taking a short tour of the screen, because you will move in and out of this screen when working in SPSS. At the very top you will see SPSS Data Editor and on the second line, the words File, Edit, View, and so on. This is the *menu bar* and works like any Windows pull-down menu. By clicking on each word, several options are presented. The third line, containing a row of pictures or icons, is known as the *tool bar*. These buttons provide shortcuts to tasks otherwise accomplished through the menu bar. File, Save, and Print are three of the most helpful shortcuts here, although you will find the others useful as you become more familiar with the program. The rest of the screen is taken up by one or more windows for entering data, writing syntax (if you choose this option), displaying output, and so forth.

Step 1: Entering Data

The Data Editor is the starting point for everything you do in SPSS. It is a spreadsheet interface made up of rows and columns. The columns are used for variables and the rows for subjects (or whatever the elements under examination are).

When you start, the first thing you need to do is to enter your data into the SPSS Data Editor and tell the program what these data represent. To give an example of this, consider that data have been collected for *in-seat behavior* for a group of children who have autism. Each child has a value on each of three variables: (a) an identification number; (b) sex, coded 1 for male and 2 for female; and (c) a score for total in-seat behavior, where 1 represents no time seated during a 15-minute music therapy session and 100 represents seated throughout the session.

Client	Sex	Score
1	1	55
2	1	25
3	2	76
4	2	100
5	2	20

Entering these data into the Data Editor proceeds as you might imagine. Begin by double clicking (clicking the mouse twice in quick succession) in the upper left cell, after which you will see the vertical flashing bar inside the box. Simply type in the number 1 to represent the first child's identification number, then click on the "Enter" key. Now move the right arrow key to move one cell to the right (you can also use the "Tab" key or the mouse and double click on the cell), and enter a 1 again, this time representing the child's sex. Next, move to the right again and enter the child's score for in-seat behavior, 55, into the third cell. Now that the first row is completed, use the arrow keys or mouse to move to the beginning of the second row and enter the values for the second child into the appropriate columns. Repeat this process until all five rows have been entered. When you have finished, your screen will look like Figure 2.

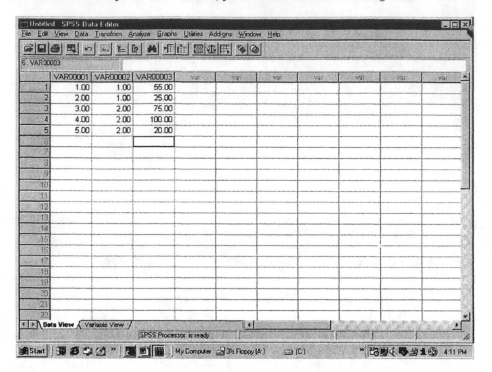

Figure 2. Raw Data Entered Into Data Editor Screen

Step 2: Naming the Variables

As soon as you enter data into SPSS, you should decide upon names for the variables and tell SPSS what names these are so that you can always refer back to them. You can use any name, number, or combination, as long as it is between one and eight characters and makes sense to you. (Using complex letter-number combinations or abbreviations can make it difficult to remember what variable you are referring to, so while being brief may be best, don't overdo it!) SPSS doesn't distinguish between upper and lower case letters and, in general, tends to convert upper case into lower case letters.

The way in which variables are labeled varies for earlier versions of SPSS and may vary for later versions, too. The next section illustrates SPSS version 12.0.

Example of Data Entry

In the example, there are three columns of data representing each child (child, sex, and in-seat behavior score). To begin, click on the window tab at the bottom of the window labeled Variable View. This looks like Figure 3. In the screen that is shown, the first variable is named VAR00001; this is the name that SPSS gives by default (each variable will have this default, with variable 2 being VAR00002, variable 3 being VAR00003, and so on). To change the variable name, double click on VAR00001 and edit the contents of the box so that it contains the variable name you wish to use. The best way to do this is to depress "Backspace," although you can also highlight the box and depress "Delete." Enter the name you wish to use, in our case child. Then depress "Enter" or use the arrow keys to move to the next variable name and repeat the above process. Once you have labeled all your variables (in our case, we will use child for variable 1, sex for variable 2, and in seat for variable 3, click on Data View in the lower left of the screen to return to the Data Editor window.

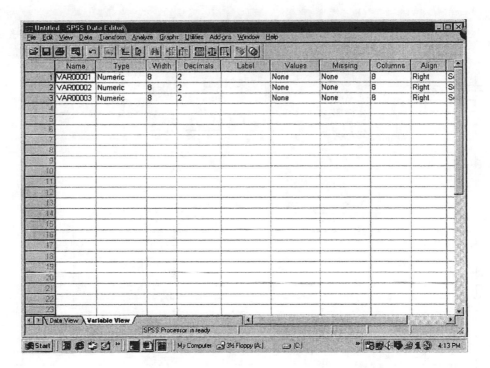

Figure 3. SPSS Data Editor Variable View Window

Step 3: Undertaking Analyses

As soon as you've entered the data and labeled the variables, you're ready to tell SPSS what kind of analysis (or analyses) you'd like to run. In the Chapter 12, Statistical Methods of Analysis, you were given various statistical examples and shown how to complete these using SPSS. In the forthcoming section, you'll be introduced to the basic procedures in completing data analyses using the point and click method.

To undertake analyses using the point and click method, you should begin by clicking Analyze on the menu bar, which produces a pull-down menu listing all the statistical procedures available. As you will see, these have been divided into various categories, including Descriptive Statistics, Compare Means, Correlate, Regression, Classify, Scale, and Nonparametric Tests. Within each of these menus is a choice of statistical procedures. For example, as you can see in Figure 4, within the Compare Means window are the options of comparing Means, One-Sample T Test, Independent-Samples T Test, and so on. Each of the windows within the Analyze menu offers a series of statistical options that can be selected by simply scrolling to the exact procedure required and clicking on it. Once you click on the actual statistical procedure, a dialogue box will appear in which you can specify the parameters of your analysis and identify the variables you wish to examine and choices concerning what information is to be included in the output. Once you have made all these choices, click OK, and SPSS will do the rest. It's that simple.

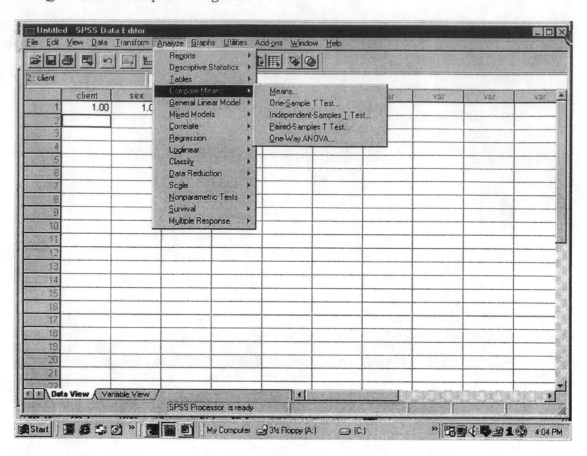

Figure 4. Statistical Options Presented in the Analyze Menu

Step 4: Viewing and Editing Output

When you complete any analysis, your output will appear in a new window called an Output Viewer. This window contains a report of the results of your analysis and will look something like Figure 5. In this figure, you will see the results of an independent sample *t* test for the data I have referred to throughout this chapter. In an actual analysis, you would not use such a small data set, but it suffices for this particular example.

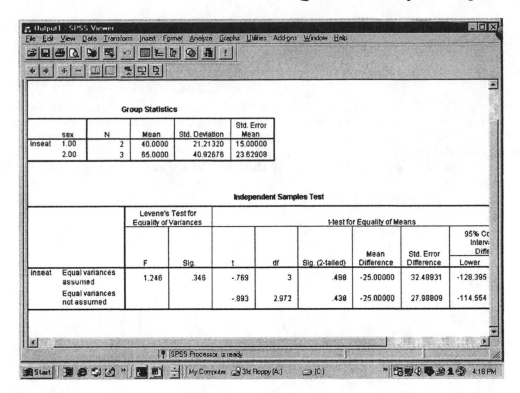

Figure 5. Output Viewer Window

Clearly, the first thing you want to do is to look at the results. You can move around the window using the mouse to manipulate the scroll bars along the window's right and bottom edges. For an alternate view, try clicking on File on the menu bar at the top of the screen, then click on Print Preview on the pull-down menu. This gives you a preview of your output just as it would appear if you printed it.

You may want to delete unwanted sections of output. In many procedures, SPSS prints information that may not be needed, and you can delete these sections prior to printing and saving. This is where the chart on the left hand side of the viewer comes in handy. If you click on an item in the viewer, say Title or Statistics, two things happen: (a) The word you clicked on is selected (it appears highlighted), and (b) the specified section of the output appears in the large window surrounded by a box identifying what it is. You can delete the entire section simply by depressing the "Delete" key on your keyboard.

Step 5: Printing Output

Printing the output of a statistical procedure is quite straightforward. From the main output viewer window (see Figure 5), click on File on the menu bar and choose Print from the pull-down menu. A dialogue box appears on screen and is quite similar to those you see in word-processing packages. With this window open, simply check that you have selected the number of copies you want and click OK. This will print the entire output window.

Step 6: Saving Output and Retrieving Files

Saving a file proceeds as you might expect it to. While in the main SPSS window, click on the File menu and scroll down to Save As. This produces a dialogue box that allows you to specify the file name and save it into a particular area of your hard drive (or removable disc). It is recommended that you create a specific SPSS data folder and keep all your information there. This aids greatly in retrieval and helps to organize different output files for the same data set into an easily accessible display.

While there are several different ways to retrieve files, the easiest is to open the SPSS program and, once in the main window, click on File on the menu bar and then scroll down to

Open. Once open, select the file you wish to open, either double click on the file name or highlight the file name, and click OK in the dialogue window.

Using SPSS: An Example

Let us now work through an example using SPSS. We will complete an analysis of the relationships between two variables, scores on an IQ test and scores on a music competency test (MCT). To find if there is a relationship between IQ and music competence, we will need to compute a correlation coefficient, or Pearson *r*.

Let's take the following data set for 10 children who are attending a school for children with special needs.

Subject	IQ Score	Music Competency Test Score (MCT)
1	95	30
2	100	37
3	80	24
4	67	23
5	92	28
6	55	19
7	75	24
8	100	40
9	60	21
10	88	31

Following the directions previously outlined in this chapter, enter the data into the Data Editor window and label each variable. Once you have done this, save the data as Correlation. Your SPSS screen should look like Figure 6.

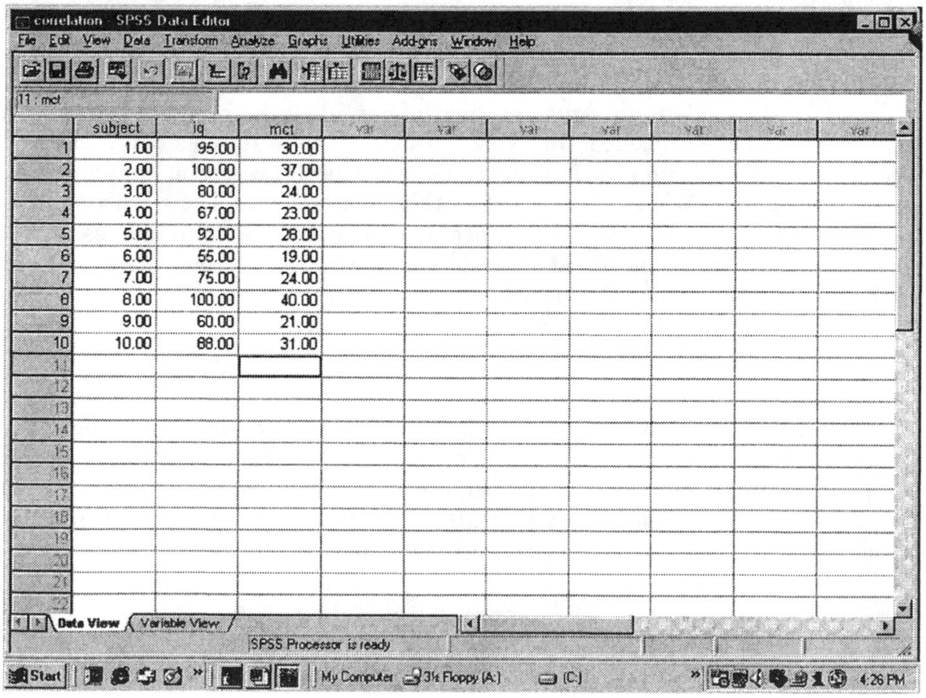

Figure 6. Data Editor Window for Correlation Example

To perform the analysis, click on <u>A</u>nalyze, then <u>C</u>orrelate, and then <u>B</u>ivariate. This will present a window similar to that in Figure 7.

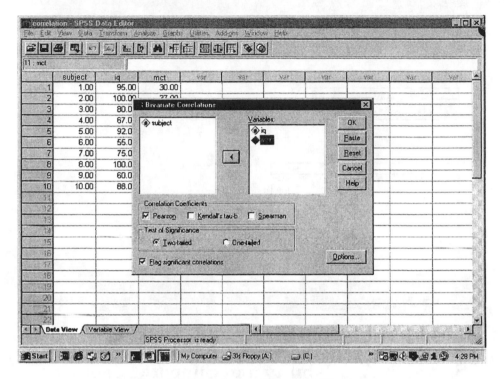

Figure 7. Correlation Command Window

From this Window, select the variables you wish to compare. In this case, you will select IQ and MCT and use the arrow in the middle of the window to move these two variables into the variable box (as shown in Figure 7). Once you have done this, you can click OK and see your results, which will be presented in a manner similar to Figure 8. Notice that you will actually get a number of tables in your output. You will get some descriptive statistics and the results of the Pearson r correlation. You may also get t test information, depending on the options you checked in the correlation window. In this case, you can see that the correlation between IQ and music competency, when measured by the MCT, is $r = 0.91$ (you see this correlation as 0.912 in the output viewer window), $p < 0.01$. That is, there is a high positive correlation between IQ and MCT for this group of children.

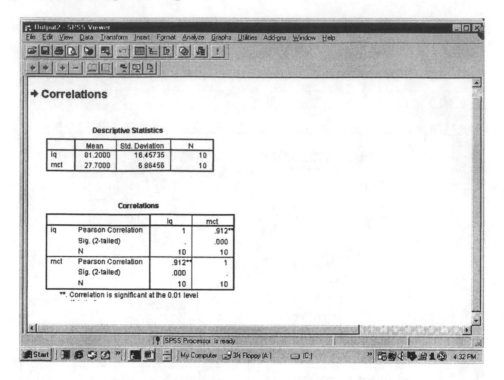

Figure 8. Output Screen for Correlation Analysis

Software Availability and Support Resources

SPSS is available directly from SPSS Inc. Go to www.SPSS.com and follow the prompts. SPSS is also available from various online stores and can usually be found at university bookstores. Please note that there are several different versions of SPSS. The full version, which is the most expensive, is the most powerful version of SPSS and includes manuals and customer support to answer questions about the program. There are also less expensive versions, usually called *student versions,* which are suitable for the novice or intermediate user. These versions do not usually include manuals or customer support but offer inexpensive ways of gaining access to the program.

References

Cramer, D. (1998). *Fundamental statistics for social research: Step-by-step calculations and computer techniques using SPSS for Windows.* New York: Routledge.

Delwiche, L. D., & Slaughter, S. J. (1998). *The little SAS book: A primer* (2nd ed.). Cary, NC: SAS Institute.

Ryan, B., & Joiner, B. L. (2001). *Minitab handbook* (4th ed.). Pacific Grove, CA: Duxbury Thomson Learning.

Chapter 14
Data Analysis in Qualitative Research
Kenneth E. Bruscia

The purpose of this chapter is to provide an overview of the various tasks that may be involved in analyzing data gathered in a qualitative research study. Since the design of every qualitative study varies according to focus, purpose, method and epistemology, procedures for analyzing the data also cannot be standardized. For example, a study that focuses on action or interaction might involve different data analysis tasks than one focusing on music or language; a study aimed at describing a phenomenon may involve different tasks than one aimed at developing a theory; an ethnographic study may involve different tasks than a phenomenological study; a study steeped in one epistemology may involve different tasks than a study steeped in another. Thus, each task described in this chapter may or may not be relevant to every study but rather will vary widely from study to study and researcher to researcher. An attempt has been made, however, to examine those tasks that are most commonly employed.

Preparing for Data Analysis

Before starting to analyze the data, it is a good idea for the researcher to review the entire journal that he or she has kept as the study as progressed. Then once data analysis begins, particular attention should be paid to the methodological log. Briefly described in Chapter 11, Designing Qualitative Research, a methodological log is a day-to-day record of any thoughts or insights the researcher has had during the course of the study about how to gather and analyze the data. Ely et al. (1991) describe entries in this log as "conversations with oneself about what has occurred in the research process, what has been learned, the insights this provides, and the leads these suggest for future action" (p. 80). Data analysis requires complex decision-making, and logging one's thought process can be very helpful not only to the researcher but also the reader after the study has been completed.

Define the Case

Data from a single qualitative study are often of various types, and this has myriad implications for analyzing them. In music therapy, the researcher may gather verbal, nonverbal, or musical data that may have been recorded, transcribed, translated, or notated through various methods. For example, if a researcher is studying what happens in an improvisational music therapy session, the session may be videotaped and then turned into various kinds of data, such as a verbal description of the moment-to-moment actions and interactions of client and therapist, a transcript of the verbal dialogues between client and therapist, and a notated score of the improvisation itself. Thus, when it comes time for data analysis, the researcher has to find ways of understanding, relating, and synthesizing these different data streams.

The first task in preparing these different data streams is to define the case and its boundaries. Important questions are: What constitutes the fundamental set of data to be analyzed as a whole? Where does this set of data begin and end, and what are the various kinds of data that are to be included in each set? Perhaps the best way to answer these questions is to return to the focus of the study. If the focus is on action, interaction, or experience, a case may be defined as each occurrence of the same, whether involving one participant or several; or, with these same foci, the case may be defined as each participant involved in the action, interaction, or experience. Similarly, if the focus is on text, artifacts, or artworks, a case may be defined by each separate example of it, or a case may be each participant who produced an example. Finally, if the focus is on a person, group, community, or culture, each case is defined as such, regardless of the multifarious kinds of data that are gathered about each one.

Take Inventory of the Data

Once the case is defined, the next step is to take inventory of the data that have been gathered to date. Two kinds of inventories are useful. The case summary sheet lists all the data that have been gathered about each case, noting the date of contact, method of data collection, researcher who gathered the data, the formatting of the data (video, audio, transcripts), the completeness of each data set, notes about possible follow-ups, and any comments that the researcher has about the case, including preliminary ideas about how to analyze or interpret the data (Miles & Huberman, 1994). The master inventory is a summary of all case summary sheets completed to date. This list should give the pseudonym or number of the case, contact dates, types of data gathered, location for where each type of data is store, back-ups of the data made and not made, what kinds of other data might be needed, and the planned date for analyzing each case (Miles & Huberman). Obviously, both inventories can be designed and formatted in various ways depending on the researcher and the nature of the study. In any case, these inventories should be kept up to date to the very end of data collection.

All data should be stored in a locked, safe place, with access limited only to the researchers. This is necessary to maintain confidentiality of the data.

Define Roles and Responsibilities

Because qualitative research includes many different layers of human interaction, it is important that the roles and responsibilities of each party involved in the study be clearly defined. With regard to the data analysis, who will take primary responsibility for analyzing which sets of data? Will a consultant be involved and, if so, at what junctures in the analysis process? What will be the role of participants in analyzing the data? Will they check the accuracy of the researcher's reports and findings? Will they help in interpreting the results? Will other colleagues or experts participate in the data analysis? (See Chapter 11, Designing Qualitative Research, for a description of self-inquiry, consultation, and collaboration.)

Schedule the Analysis of Cases

One of the most important steps in analyzing the data is scheduling. Selecting which data to process first can shape the researcher's mental set for the rest of the data. Also, following a sequence without a particular rationale can often make data processing more difficult and time-consuming. The two primary questions are: In what order should the cases be analyzed, and in what order should each data set within each case be analyzed? For example, if the data include a solo and a duet improvisation for each of three participants and six accompanying discussions for each improvisation, the researcher could analyze all the improvisations first then the discussions, each of the solos with corresponding discussions, each of the duets with the discussions, or all the data of each participant, one at a time. Thus, data analysis can proceed by case or by data set within each case and in any order therein. The differences will be surprising, and the researcher will then have to decide which schedule is more efficient and trustworthy given the purpose of the study. There is no single way of proceeding—if one way does not work, do it another way, in a different sequence.

Another aspect of scheduling is how to time data analysis with respect to other phases of the study. Qualitative data analysis is a cyclic process that moves back and forth between analyzing the data and reconsidering every other aspect of the study. Specifically, data analysis should alternate with data collection which, in turn, should alternate with reconsideration of the focus and purpose of the study, which then has implications for revising procedures for collecting and analyzing the data. This cycling back and forth between different components or phases of the study insures responsiveness to the phenomenon being investigated while also allowing procedures for gathering and analyzing the data to adapt to the way the phenomenon is unfolding. It is also a way of insuring that the data are complete and relevant to the purpose of the study.

In most cases, data analysis should proceed case by case, preferably two to four cases at a time. Specifically, the researcher should gather data on two to four cases and analyze these cases before proceeding with the next two to four cases, then continue in this vein until all the data have been gathered. Meanwhile, after analyzing sufficient cases, the researcher may also change the methods of data collection or go back and gather additional supplementary data from all the cases analyzed so far. Data analysis should never be done after all the data have been gathered, unless the nature of the study specifically dictates such an approach.

Focusing the Analysis

Because qualitative research typically produces large and rich streams of data, it is very easy to lose the focus and purpose of the study as originally envisioned. For this reason, it is essential for the researcher to return to the problem statement and research questions and focus and refocus on them frequently throughout the data analysis process. At this point, it is important to decide: (a) whether the focus of the analysis will be on the content or form of the data; (b) whether focus will be on each case separately (within-case) or all the cases together (cross-case); and (c) whether the analysis is case-oriented or variable-oriented.

Content Versus Form

Upon return to the problem statement and research questions, the researcher should ask whether the study is concerned with the content or the form of the data, that is, on the substantive or the structural aspects of the data. For example, in narrative inquiry the researcher may focus on the story itself (e.g., what happened to whom and why) or on its form (for example, plot structure, sequencing, complexity, coherence; Lieblich, Tuval-Mashiach, & Zilber, 1998). In discourse analysis, the researcher may focus on what the text says or means (content) or what grammatical or linguistic structures were used in the text (form; Wood & Kroger, 2000). In music analysis, the researcher may focus on the musical content (for example, melodic or rhythmic motifs, chords) or the musical form or structure (how the musical elements are organized in relation to one another).

Case and Variable Analysis, Within and Cross Cases

In a case-oriented analysis, the researcher focuses on describing or explaining each case as a whole entity in itself, giving attention to its own particular context, history, and idiographic details (Miles & Huberman, 1994). The researcher looks at configurations, dynamics, sequences, and themes that occur within each case, one at a time, and only in reference to itself. Once every case has been understood on its own terms through this within-case analysis, the researcher may then opt to do a cross-case analysis. In a cross-case analysis (that is case-oriented), the researcher uses each case as a building block in creating some kind of synthesis of cases. More will be said of this later.

In a variable-oriented analysis, the researcher focuses on describing and explaining the relationship among variables, either within each case or across cases (Miles & Huberman, 1994). Here the building blocks are variables within and across cases, rather than entire cases. The researcher looks at the data from each case to identify variables, and then compares cases to identify common variables and thematic relationships among these variables.

Thus, altogether, a researcher has the following options for focusing the analysis:

1. *Case-oriented analysis using a within-case approach:* Each part of data within a case is described or explained in terms of other parts of data within the same case.
   a. Content
   b. Form
2. *Case-oriented analysis using a cross-case approach:* Each case is a whole in itself that is described or explained in terms of other cases, also seen as wholes.
   a. Content
   b. Form
3. *Variable-oriented analysis using a within-case approach:* Parts of the data within each case are identified as variables, and these variables are used to describe and explain what is happening within each case separately.
   a. Content
   b. Form
4. *Variable-oriented analysis using a cross-case approach:* Common variables across cases are used to describe and explain what is happening acro ss all cases.
   a. Content
   b. Form

These options may also provide sequences wherein the research combines case- and variable-oriented analysis using both within and cross case approaches.

Preliminary Processing of Each Case

Get a Sense of the Whole

Once the case and its boundaries have been defined, a schedule is in place, and the focus has been clarified, it is time to actually start processing the data. The first step is to go through all the data pertaining to the case to get a sense of the whole. This may involve, for example, reading all the transcribed data, looking at the videotape in its entirety, listening to the audiotape in its entirety, and then beginning to get an overview of all the various kinds of data comprising the case. Whatever the data and format, the main idea is to get an overall picture of what gives each particular set of data set its coherence, meaning, character, or distinctiveness. At the same time, the researcher will be beginning to identify the unique properties of each type of data comprising the case (such as interview, improvisation, and drawing).

Make Case Notes

While developing an overall impression of each data set, the researcher invariably will be struck by parts of the data that are particularly interesting. The researcher may also begin to develop preliminary ideas about what themes or regularities may be inherent in the data. It is essential to make case notes on these overall impressions or insights and record them on the contact summary sheet. Because data analysis may extend over a long period, these little gems may be easily forgotten, so this step may save considerable time and energy. These notes are different from the methodological log, as they pertain to a particular set of data rather than to general issues with regard to the entire study.

Cull the Raw Data

Once the researcher has a sense of the whole case, the next step may be to cull the data, that is, to delete all parts of the data that are either redundant or irrelevant to the purpose of the study. For example, in interview data, this may involve eliminating the "uhs" or any repetitive phrases or cutting out any side comments or discussions about a topic not pertaining to the research (such as the weather). Culling is not necessarily something to be done in every study or with every type of data. In some research studies, every unit of data is regarded as essential, even if seemingly irrelevant, whereas in others, only certain units are considered essential or relevant to the study. The most important benefit of culling is that it prevents the researcher from being overwhelmed with the sea of details of qualitative data. Culling may be done before data analysis begins, or it may be done after a few cases have been analyzed, and the researcher has a better idea of what parts of data may be irrelevant or unwanted.

Segment

To segment is to divide each set of data into the most appropriate and meaningful units. A segment or unit is any part, element, layer, or structural entity that "is comprehensible by itself and contains one idea, episode, or piece of information" (Tesch, 1990, p. 116). The nature of the unit depends upon the type of data being segmented. For example, actions and interactions can be segmented into behavioral acts, their antecedents and consequents, or complete interactional episodes. A spoken or written text can be segmented according to topical, structural or semantic units. Experiences can be segmented into foci of consciousness, or layers (physical, emotional, cognitive, and so forth). Music can be segmented according to beats, measures, chord changes, phrases, motifs or themes, sections, movements, and so forth. Obviously, the size and nature of the unit has pervasive effects on how efficient and meaningful data processing will be. How to define a segment is a crucial decision because it will determine the ease with which each set of data can be analyzed and then compared with other sets. At the same time, like other data processing tasks, segmenting is not always desirable or appropriate. Much depends upon whether the data are divisible, whether the data retain their meaning when divided into parts, and whether the study is concerned with part-part, part-whole, or whole-whole relationships.

Format

The culled, segmented data now need to be put into the appropriate format for further processing. If a case-oriented approach will be taken, the researcher will condense the culled, segmented data into a synopsis or condensation of the case. This synopsis should stay as close to the raw data as possible, and include actual words and phrases from the raw data. At the same time, the purpose of a synopsis is to summarize and thereby reduce the raw data to its essential components. The synopsis, then, may be significantly shorter than the raw data.

If a variable-oriented approach will be taken, the researcher will create a transcript of the data. In interview studies, a transcript consists of a written record of the culled, segmented discussion. In studies involving audio or video recordings, the transcript may be a verbal description of each unit of the recording or a notated score or chart of the main events heard or seen. If a combined variable-case-oriented approach will be taken, the researcher should create both a transcript and a case synopsis.

Collaborate

At this point, it is usually advisable to check the accuracy of the case synopses with each participant, or to collaborate. Lincoln and Guba (1985) call this kind of collaboration with participants member-checking. Essentially, the researcher shows each participant a synopsis of his or her case data and asks for corrections, additions, or revisions.

Identifying Variables

This section of the chapter provides information on how to identify variables operating in each case. As such, it is relevant when taking a variable approach. The subsequent section, Synthesizing, is relevant for a case approach.

Code the Data

After the raw data have been culled and segmented and the appropriate transcripts have been made, it is time to code the data. To code is to fix a label or title on each unit of data that best describes or represents the unit. Miles and Huberman (1994) describe a code as a category label. A category is a meaningful unit of data. A label is a title, which may consist of a word, phrase, number, color, design, or musical symbol.

Various kinds of codes can be used, and they are named and defined differently by various authors. A descriptive code is one that very closely matches the raw data. It is created without the researcher making any inferences or interpretations about the data (Miles & Huberman, 1994). In fact, the label is often lifted directly out of the data. Strauss and Corbin (1990) use the term *open coding* for ascribing descriptive codes to the data. Descriptive or open codes are both created inductively, that is, they emanate directly from the data.

An interpretive code requires the researcher to make inferences or interpret the raw data in some way (Miles & Huberman, 1994), based either on the researcher's insights into the data gathered so far or on an outside theory or research study. An interpretive code may be created inductively (based on the researcher's understanding of what the data mean), or it may be created a priori (based on outside theory or research findings). Thus, an inductive interpretive code involves the researcher giving his or her interpretation of the data themselves, while an a priori interpretive code involves the researcher imposing an outside construct or idea on the data.

A provisional code is one that the researcher creates prior to data collection, based on the problem statement and research questions specific to the study. Though originally emanating from the researcher's questions and expected answers, provisional codes are usually modified by whatever emerges in the raw data (Miles & Huberman, 1994). Thus, provisional codes involve both inductive and a priori coding.

A standard code is one that that is not content specific to the data but has general categories that can be applied to most data (Miles & Huberman, 1994). In this case, each unit of data is fit into predetermined categories. A standard code, then, is similar to an a priori interpretive code, except that the standard code is even more general in scope. Standard codes may be applied directly to the raw data or they may be used to aggregate data that have already been coded descriptively. An example of a standard code applied to already coded data is what Strauss and Corbin (1990) call axial codes. Axial codes are categories that are used to further organize open or descriptive codes. The categories are standard in that they follow what Strauss and Corbin call a coding paradigm, consisting of the following categories: conditions, context, action/interaction, and consequences.

When any of the codes are fit into larger abstractions, the process may be called either pattern coding (Miles & Huberman, 1994) or categorizing. In both cases, the initial or first-level codes are further abstracted into larger concepts or ideas (second-level codes), which in turn can be abstracted into themes or variables in the data (meta-codes). Thus, codes can exist on different levels of abstraction, starting from the raw data and gradually moving more and more interpretively and abstractly to the main variables or themes of the data.

Whenever a researcher creates codes to fit the data, several steps should be followed. One can begin by coding each unit of data separately based on content or by scanning all the units to identify similarities that might serve as initial codes. Whether coded separately or in aggregates, each unit of data must eventually be compared with every other unit in the data so that similar units can be assigned the same codes. When all units have been assigned a code, the researcher should begin to look for similarities and differences among the codes. At this point, the question is whether any of the initial codes can be combined. Ideally, each code should subsume homogeneous units of data, and each code should be different from the next. In other words, each code should have very clearly defined boundaries. The number of data units subsumed under each code is not important. Codes representing only one unit of data may be just as significant as those representing several units. Once the codes for the first set of data have been established, the researcher should give them preliminary definitions.

The researcher then moves to the second set of data and repeats this coding process. When the second data set has been coded, codes assigned to the first and second sets need to be compared and adjusted so that each code subsumes like units of data while also being significantly different from other codes. Based on this comparison, the codes are defined again, this time with greater specificity and detail. This entire process continues until all data sets are coded, and a set of codes has been clearly defined and differentiated.

So far, the codes used at the first level of abstraction are essentially descriptive. They are very close to the raw data. At this point, the researcher may begin to look at the relationship between the codes on the next level of abstraction. More specifically, can different codes be subsumed under the same process, condition, property, or dimension? The purpose at this level of coding is to move upward from the descriptive details of each case to larger themes that might resolve superficial differences between cases. This is where pattern coding or categorizing begins. Once again, the same process of constant comparison of codes is used until the second level of codes are clearly defined and differentiated; if necessary, a third level is also defined. The second or third levels of codes are attempts to identify variables.

During the entire process of coding, the researcher should be making methodological log entries. Glaser (1978) calls log entries about the coding process a memo, which he defines as "the theorizing write-up of ideas about codes and their relationships as they strike the analyst while coding. . . it can be a sentence, a paragraph, or a few pages. . . it exhausts the analyst's momentary ideation based on data with perhaps a little conceptual elaboration" (p. 83–84).

Ultimately, the coding process culminates in the creation of a glossary that gives each code and its definition. The glossary may or may not be included in the final research report.

Displaying the Data

Qualitative data are multi-faceted and complex and can be easily overwhelming. A good way to deal with these complexities is to make displays of the data. Since it is beyond the scope of this chapter to go into any great detail regarding displays, the reader is referred to Miles and Huberman (1994) for a comprehensive discussion of how to display various kinds of data in the most effective ways.

There are basically two kinds of displays: a graphic representation and a matrix. A graphic representation is a drawing that visually displays the relationships between parts of a case or among variables. The drawing usually includes words and phrases that are connected with arrows in various configurations. A matrix is a text table that shows the relationships between and among cases and variables. A text table can be organized with cases going down on the left and variables going across to the right, or with cases going down and across, or with variables going down and across.

These kinds of displays can be made for data within each case, or data across cases. Thus, a researcher may want to do a graphic display of data within each case or synthesize the cases into a graphic display of all cases; or a researcher may do a text table of data within each case or synthesize the cases into a text table for all cases.

Musical data can be charted or graphed in various ways, and, because there is no standard way, researchers most often develop their own way of displaying the music.

Synthesizing

Reviewing the data analysis process so far, the researcher begins with analytic tasks, which involve breaking the data down and examining the details, and then moves to synthetic tasks, which involve putting the data back together again based upon what was discovered through analysis. Thus, the process goes from part to whole, from analysis to synthesis, and from description to interpretation and explanation. This section deals with the various ways that the researcher can synthesize within-case findings and cross-case findings.

Within-Case Synthesis

To determine how to synthesize within-case findings, the researcher must return once again to the problem statement and, more specifically, to the purpose of the study. Based on these purposes, within-case findings may be presented in various formats, each representing a different mode or level of interpretation and each requiring a different communication skill, depending on the media in which the findings are to be presented. The following are some examples of how case findings can be presented. Notice how they move from being descriptive to being more and more interpretive.

> *Descriptive Case Study:* The researcher presents a condensed version of the most pertinent data within each case. An effort is made to stay as close as possible to the data, without making any interpretations. Words of the participants are important to include. This type of description includes the particulars of each case, including all those aspects that make the case idiographic or unique.
>
> *Coded Case Study:* The researcher presents a condensed version of the raw data pertinent to each case, including the codes assigned to the data in parentheses. This type includes the particulars of each case, while also showing how the particulars have been cast into codes shared with other cases. A coded case study may also include a graphic display of the codes (or variables).
>
> *Linguistically Transformed Case Study:* The researcher presents the data of each case by transforming the raw data (in first person) into technical terminology of the discipline relevant to the study (in third person). Here the researcher puts the data into his or her own professional language, with the purpose of making explicit what is implicit in the raw data. A prime example is Giorgi's (1985) method for transforming data on human experiences into psychological language and, in the process, defining the essential structures of the experience.
>
> *Hermeneutic Case Study:* The researcher interprets the data of each case from different horizons (or perspectives), showing similarities and differences.
>
> *Artistic Case Study:* The researcher presents the data of each case by creating an art form (for example, poem, story, play, improvisation, and so forth).
>
> *Critical Case Study:* The researcher critiques each case using a particular point of view (such as feminism, psychoanalysis), sometimes using the raw data as examples.
>
> *Explanatory Case Study:* The researcher gives explanations of the intentionality, dynamics, contingencies, event sequences, or cause-effect relationships found in the data.

Cross-Case Synthesis

Whereas some studies end with a presentation of within-case findings, others go on to compare or synthesize the individual cases. This is a matter of choice for the researcher, and depends entirely upon the problem statement. The two most commonly used approaches are:

Synthetic Case Study: The researcher aggregates and synthesizes all of the individual cases into one all-inclusive description, using the same method employed in constructing the individual cases (see above). Thus, a synthetic case may be: descriptive, coded, linguistically transformed, hermeneutic, artistic, critical, or explanatory. Notice that it is case oriented rather than variable oriented.

Theory: The researcher explains the relationships between and among all the variables operating across cases and develops a theory. This approach is variable-oriented and essentially does away with the individual cases, except for their use in grounding the theory.

Conclusion

Because the tasks used in qualitative data analysis can vary so widely among researchers and studies and from one stage of research to the next, successful analysis requires the researcher to have some higher-order abilities in addition to being able to implement the tasks efficiently. First, the researcher has to respect the data, which requires not only organizing and preserving it carefully but also making sure that all parts of the data are accepted and accounted for in the findings. Second, the researcher has to be clearly focused on the purpose of the research at all times, even if the purpose shifts during the study. Ultimately, a researcher analyzes and interprets data to answer the basic questions posed in the study. Thus, successful data analysis depends upon a constant unswerving focus on the fundamental questions in the study. Do the questions focus on content or form, case or variable, within or cross cases? Third, the researcher has to be flexible procedurally. Whenever something does not work, the key to success is to do it differently or to do something else entirely.

Qualitative research is an emergent process. The researcher learns how to do the research while doing it, and to adapt to what is happening from moment to moment. Lastly, the researcher has to be able to take different perspectives, looking at the data up close and then stepping back and looking again from a distance, looking at one case from one vantage point and then looking from another. Qualitative research is an attempt to honor the multiple perspectives that humans can take when studying themselves and the worlds in which they live.

References

Ely, M., Anzul, M., Friedman, T., Garner, D., & Stenmetz, A. (1991). *Doing qualitative research: Circles within circles.* Philadelphia: Falmer Press.

Giorgi, A. (Ed.) (1985). *Phenomenology and psychological research.* Pittsburgh, PA: Duquesne University Press.

Glaser, B. G. (1978). *Theoretical sensitivity: Advances in the methodology of grounded theory.* Mill Valley, CA: Sociology Press.

Lieblich, A., Tuval-Mashiach, R., & Zilber T. (1998). *Narrative research: Reading, analysis, and interpretation.* (Applied Social Research Method Series, Vol. 47). Thousand Oaks, CA: Sage Publications.

Lincoln, Y., & Guba, E. (1985). *Naturalistic inquiry.* Newbury Park, CA: Sage Publications.

Miles, M., & Huberman, A., (1994). *Qualitative data analysis* (2nd ed.). Thousand Oaks, CA: Sage Publications.

Strauss, A., & Corbin, J. (1990). *Basics of qualitative research.* Newbury Park, CA: Sage Publications.

Tesch, R. (1990). *Qualitative research: Analysis types & software tools.* Philadelphia: Falmer Press.

Wood, L., & Kroger, R. (2000). *Doing discourse analysis: Methods for studying action in talk and text.* Thousand Oaks, CA: Sage Publications.

Chapter 15
Software Tools for Music Therapy Qualitative Research
James S. Musumeci, Joseph F. Fidelibus, and Suzanne N. Sorel

There is a story about a sculptor working hard with his hammer and chisel on a large block of marble, being watched by a little boy who saw only large and small pieces of stone falling away left and right. He had no idea what was happening. When the boy returned to the studio a few weeks later, he saw to his great surprise a large, powerful lion sitting in the place where the marble had stood. With great excitement the boy ran to the sculptor and said, "Sir, tell me, how did you know there was a lion in the marble?"

The art of sculpture is, first of all, the art of seeing. In one block of marble, Michelangelo saw a loving mother holding her dead son on her lap; in another, he saw a self-confident David ready to hurl his stone at an approaching Goliath; and in a third, he saw an irate Moses at the point of rising in anger from his seat. Visual art is indeed the disciplined art of making visible what had only been seen by the imagination.

Like the work of the sculptor, qualitative research is an art. As researchers, we need to see and hear the stories of others in particular settings and make their meaning visible and concrete. Just as the creative eye and skilled hands of the sculptor bring life to a block of marble, our own experience, intelligence, emotions, and creativity enliven collected data and give it meaning. Each of us has our own self-as-instrument who collects and analyzes data. The process of qualitative research is no mystery, but the unveiling of meaning creates a sense of wonder and awe even within the seasoned researcher.

In this chapter, we discuss qualitative research in music therapy through the use of computer software and describe how such software enhanced our ability to extract powerful insights from collected data. We review the literature and provide examples of programs that store and permit easy access to print, audio, and video data, as well as annotated musical scores used in the clinical session.

After the music therapy research topic is decided, the design of the study completed, approval by the human subjects committee obtained, the gatekeeper met, and the consent of the participants acquired, the qualitative researcher enters the field to collect data. The data, collected in a variety of ways, may include observation notes, field logs, interview transcripts, analytic and personal memos, musical scores, drawings, pictures, videotape, audiotape, books, and articles. These descriptive records are then analyzed to help us understand the phenomena, and from these data, categories and themes are developed. In the process of analysis, additional categories may emerge that force the researcher to ask further questions about the data and check tentative hunches against new and different log entries. Thus, from a continual and recursive analysis of the data, particular themes and important concerns emerge that symbolize an understanding of the research subject matter. This is the creative work of the qualitative researcher.

Just as the sculptor works with marble and chisel, we researchers have data, pen, paper, word-processing programs, and qualitative software tools to help make visible the insights, connections, and meanings from the data. Computer-assisted qualitative data analysis software, or CAQDAS, is one tool that can assist us to organize and think about the data.

Although CAQDAS cannot do the analysis for you, it can provide the information needed to explore the meaning your data offer. In both academic and consulting environments, it is not uncommon to hear the question, "Are you aware of how CAQDAS was used in an ethnographic study?" or "Please tell me how interviews can be analyzed using a particular software package."

In fact, the basic functions of CAQDAS are the same regardless of the type of qualitative research conducted. CAQDAS helps you, the researcher, to examine your data, code and retrieve select passages, and store your memos. It provides a variety of ways to search your data for specific text strings or data associated with a specified code. It allows a flexibility to compare data across multiple documents or locate co-occurrences of several codes from different sources. Some packages can hyperlink data or help you to visually represent relationships between specified data. However, CAQDAS demands that you be in command of your research. You are responsible for knowing the qualitative process, being keenly aware of your data, exploring its meaning, and asking questions about what you have discovered thus far. CAQDAS provides tools that are helpful once you know how you want to organize and examine your data. If you have no clue how to analyze an interview, no software program is going to be of much help to you. Learning qualitative method is the indispensable starting point. Learning and using software for qualitative research is not a method. It is a tool, one that is used and respected by qualitative researchers.

A full review of literature on the use of computer data analysis software programs and the existing software is addressed in several books and articles. Here we want to briefly sketch some highlights from this literature.

Tesch (1990, 1991), an early proponent of CAQDAS, argued that the research analyst can benefit from the mechanical tasks of data management offered by these specialized software programs. Locating words and phrases, obtaining word use frequency, creating indexes, attaching codes to data segments, and connecting codes are some helpful operations facilitated by the use of computers.

Computer use can assist the researcher in the rigorous detailing of analytic procedures and enabling team-based studies (Fielding & Lee, 1998). Many software programs designed for qualitative research offer unique tools to create an audit trail by helping the researcher organize and view data according to the dates and times that files were created or edited. There are also ample ways to record one's actions, thoughts, and feelings throughout the research process. Although the memo features are most useful to capture concerns about data, codes, and the analytic process, Fielding and Lee suggest that this feature might also help make replication possible.

Several researchers can work on a shared project even though they might be physically separated from each other. For example, a health study can be conducted in Africa and North America simultaneously. Data from individual researchers are merged into one project file to which all team members have access. A common codebook is developed, and memo sharing helps keep team members informed about each other's thinking and questioning. Concerns about the use of CAQDAS for qualitative research as to its accessibility and availability, exaggerated benefits, homogenization of qualitative method, keeping researchers from staying close to their data, and encouraging researchers to mimic survey research are well addressed by several authors (Coffey, Holbrook, & Atkinson, 1996; Fielding & Lee, 1998; Seidel, 1991). Fielding and Lee also noted that CAQDAS seemed to enhance the credibility of qualitative research findings within the academic social science community.

Weitzman and Miles (1995) have comprehensively discussed methodological features and principal characteristics of CAQDAS software. More recently, Richards and Richards (1998) and Fielding (2001) have suggested how the differing architectural types of CAQDAS are useful in the analytic process, and how they might affect methodology. Creswell and Maietta (2002) offer useful criteria for assessing current software programs. They review seven software programs for ease of integration into one's qualitative analysis approach; use of different data types; ease of reading and reviewing text; memo-writing capability; coding capabilities and applications; conceptual tools and mapping resources; transfer of tables for statistical analysis; and ability to merge projects.

There is no one-size-fits-all software for qualitative research. Weitzman and Miles (1995) suggest that one's comfort in using a computer, the type of project to be undertaken, the type of data to be analyzed, and the method to be used are all useful areas to consider when choosing appropriate software.

Uses in Music Therapy Research

Music therapy qualitative research relies heavily on the use of transcripts of interviews, field observation logs, musical scores, and audio-visual recordings. Software that is referred to as *theory-building software* (Richards & Richards, 1998) is useful for these types of analyses. Theory-building software, at the cutting edge of CAQDAS, includes features that help you make connections between codes, develop categories, and formulate theories. These features will be discussed below, using examples from our experience. Three theory-building programs will be described later in the chapter.

Joe explains his decision to use software tools for qualitative research:

As I conducted and transcribed interviews for my dissertation study, the volume of words and music began to grow. My Word document files, electronic pages of interview text, and descriptions of music were tucked away behind Word file icons in the computer's memory. Similarly, musical excerpts were compactly stored in cassette tapes and mini-discs. These neatly wrapped packages of data contained the therapist-participants' music, thoughts, impressions, perceptions, feelings, and insights into their experiences in music therapy clinical improvisation, the focus of my study. However, it was both an exciting and overwhelming prospect to know that these packages would need to be unwrapped, and I would need to sort through the mountain of words and notes, analyzing and ultimately creating meaning from this rich and voluminous store of data. As I began to dig into the data, there were preliminary decisions to make—codes, categories, potential themes, and larger concepts somehow lifted from the words and music.

As I continued in this qualitative research process, I found that I was looking for an integration of analytical and creative thinking while maintaining organization, without either one precluding the other. I wanted to be as clear as possible about where I was in my thinking and where things were. I did not wish to be enslaved or confused by an organizing tool or system that limited opportunities for insight and creativity. What seemed potentially inhibiting to a thinking process was searching through countless piles of paper with color codes and sticky labels, flipping between computer files, or ultimately getting buried in whatever schemes I might design that were originally intended to maintain balance between creative thinking and organization. Hoping to find this balance, I decided to use a qualitative research software program that I had recently learned in a semester-long course.

Suzanne's experience is helpful in understanding how the use of CAQDAS, and specifically her use of ATLAS.ti, is of special interest in music therapy qualitative research.

In previous music therapy research projects, I relied heavily on color-coding to delineate codes and themes in my data. When I studied a case, for example, I color-coded my index sheets (a moment-by-moment documentation of a recording of the musical improvisation) to refer to specific ideas. For example, the code *awakening music* was indicated by the color yellow. As I continued my analysis, I sometimes changed the coding of passages originally coded as awakening music and at other times added sub-codes such as *musical surprises.* When I added musical surprises as a sub-code of the yellow awakening code, I bracketed the selected passages with a star. If I later added another code such as affirmation in the music and realized that some of the examples I identified as awakening music really belonged under this new heading, I had to change the color-coding in the document. I found myself rifling through the data in search of the chameleon-like codes I utilized to interpret the musical interventions and exchanges. As a result, my pages of data became messy, and the procedure was confusing.

ATLAS.ti eliminated this confusion and allowed me to analyze my data in a more flexible and fluid way. As new ideas became apparent by sifting and re-sifting the data, I could easily reshape my analysis by revising or establishing new codes that reflected a deepening understanding of my data.

I also needed to re-listen to the audiotapes in order to stay close to the primary data source. This was convenient to do since I had immediate access to the audio file from within the project. I reflected on what I heard and then verbally described what was taking place musically. I found myself writing memos about significant themes in the therapeutic process and translating musical notation into descriptive linguistic phrases, so they could be coded as well. I appreciated the convenient function for writing and coding memos that ATLAS.ti provided.

Of high value to me was the ability to introduce scanned images of musical scores into ATLAS.ti and then code directly onto the score itself. The program also allowed me to listen to complete audiotapes and to code different sections from it as easily as textual or graphical segments. This feature enabled me to remain as close as possible to the music—the primary data source.

Programs for Use in Music Therapy

Only three CAQDAS packages, as identified by Creswell and Maietta (2002), provide researchers with the ability to manage, store, and analyze text, image, audio, and visual data. These software packages are ATLAS.ti 5.0, HyperRESEARCH 2.5, and NVivo 2.0. They have the ability to manage, store, and analyze text, image, audio, and visual data. Each program does this with a different degree of flexibility.

HyperRESEARCH 2.5 is the only one of these three software packages that is available on both Windows and MAC platforms. ATLAS.ti 5.0 and NVivo 2.0 are designed for the Windows platform. All the programs read TXT files, which can be created by using your word processor and saving the file in ASCII or TXT format. In addition, ATLAS.ti 5.0 can use data saved as rich text format, RTF, as well as the dynamic Word, Works, HTML, and WordPerfect formats. Although NVivo also can read rich text formats, with ATLAS.ti, you can have in-place activated embedded objects such as Excel tables, video passages, and audio bits within the document. All the programs allow character-based coding, which means that you can choose to code from the smallest unit, a character, to the largest unit, the entire document.

The use of image data is similar in ATLAS.ti 5.0 and HyperRESEARCH 2.5. Both programs allow you to use images as data, portions of which can be discretely coded. A scanned image of a musical score, for instance, can be viewed in its entirety with the first measure coded as *Introduction* while the last measure might be coded *coda*. When you view the code Introduction, you can then see the entire score with the first measure highlighted within a border. Similarly, when viewing the code coda, only the last measure would be highlighted.

ATLAS.ti 5.0 converts more than 20 raster file formats. The use of image files with HyperRESEARCH is limited to a handful of formats. The WIN version will accept BMP, GIF, JPG, and PNG file types. Mac file types include BMPf, GIFf, JPEG, PNGf, and PICT.

NVivo manages image data differently from ATLAS.ti and HyperRESEARCH. You will need to make proxy documents to represent these data, as they cannot be imported directly into NVivo. From the proxy document, you can link to any image file, which only can be coded in its entirety. Discrete segments of the file cannot be coded. Thus, an image of a musical score can be coded but not any particular measure of the score.

NVivo also does not convert images for viewing. Any image file type linked to a proxy document, however, can be viewed provided that you have the image-viewing software required to view that particular file type. A complete listing of image and multimedia file types used by these programs appears in Table 1.

ATLAS.ti and HyperRESEARCH 2.5 allow the user to assign to the project entire files of a wide variety of popular audio and video data. Both programs use underlying technologies in a seamless way, making it appear that the audio or video application is working within the program. This feature allows working with the data and creating data segments from the larger file, which can then be coded.

In ATLAS.ti, selecting an audio file will open a MediaControl window. If you select a video file, another window will open that displays the video material. Clicking on the play/pause button can play the file. When the beginning of the segment you wish to code is reached, click the Start Segment Marker. Clicking on the End Segment Marker button will mark the end of the segment.

Figure 1 shows the MediaControl window for a segment from the *Theme from Summer of '42* being played. Information fields display the start position, end position, and length of the current segment in minutes: seconds: milliseconds format. The trackbar indicates the current position of the file segment. You can control the trackbar by moving backward or forward in order to mark the ends of the segment with greater accuracy.

In HyperRESEARCH you can shift-drag over the portion of the audio or video file you wish to select. A video file is treated in the same way; it simply has a playback controller with a video track.

Table 1
Graphic, Audio, and Video File Types for Use in ATLAS.ti, HyperResearch, & NVivo

	Format	Win filetype	Mac filetype	ATLAS.ti	Hyper Research	NVivo*
Images	Windows Bitmap	.bmp	BMPf	W	WM	W
	Graphics Interchange Format (89a)	.gif	GIFf	W	WM	W
	Joint Photographic Experts Group	.jpg	JPEG	W	WM	W
	Portable Network Graphics	.png	PNGf	W	WM	W
	Tagged Image File Format	.tif	TIFF	W	WM	W
	PC Paintbrush	.pcx		W		W
	Truevision TarGA Bitmap Image	.tga		W		W
	Kodak Photo CD	.pcd		W		W
	MacPaint	.mac		W		W
	Fuzzy BitMap	.fbm		W		W
	Sun Raster Bitmap Image	.ras		W		W
	CMU Window Manage (WM) Bitmap	.cmu		W		W
	Portable Bit Map	.pbm		W		W
	Faces Project Bitmap Image	.fac		W		W
	Utah RLE	.rle		W		W
	X Window Dump	.xwd		W		W
	McIDAS areafiles	multiple		W		W
	Group 3 FAX format	.g3		W		W
	Digital Research GEMmetafile	.gem		W		W
	X11 Windows XpixMap (color)	.xpm		W		W
	X Windows System Bitmap (B/W)	.xbm		W		W
	Macintosh PICT Format	N/A	PICT		M	NA
Audio	Audio Interchange File Format	.aif	AIFF	W	WM	W
	Sun Audio File Format	.au		W		W
	MPEG-1 Layer-3	.mp3	MPG3	W	WM	W
	Sound Generic Name	.snd		W		W
	QuickTime Audio	.mov	MooV	W	WM	W
	Windows WAVE	.wav	WAVE	W	WM	W
Video	Video for Windows	.avi	VfW	W	WM	W
	Motion Picture Experts Group	.mpg	MPEG	W	WM	W
	QuickTime	.mov	MooV	W	WM	W
	Shockwave Flash animation	.swf	SWFL	W	WM	W
	Animated GIF 89a files	.gif	GIFf	W	WM	W
	QuickTime	.qt		W	WM	W
	1 Layer III Audio Stream	.mp3		W	WM	W

W = Win file type can be used; M = Mac file type can be used
*Image-viewing, audio, and video software is required to view these file types while using NVivo

ATLAS.ti and HyperRESEARCH allow the user to assign or import the entire audio and video file from which any number of selected segments can be coded. The Windows MCI interface used in ATLAS.ti supports 28 multimedia file extensions. Users of NVivo can code only imported segments or *databites* of the original recording. In other words, whatever file or file segment is linked to the proxy document can only be coded once. No discrete marking of segments is allowed. An advantage of using NVivo for audio or video work is that one is not limited to specific file types, as with ATLAS.ti or HyperRESEARCH. You must, however, have the correct device drivers and software needed to listen to or view these files.

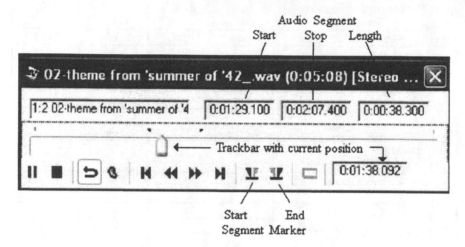

Figure 1. The MediaControl Window in ATLAS.ti

While the ability to store, code, retrieve, and use audio and video data in the analytic process is of great interest to the qualitative music therapy researcher, there are limitations of what may be expected. At present, no software package produces a text transcription of a recorded audio or video interview. Links between the multimedia data and its transcribed equivalent must be done manually.

There are few data concerning the analysis of audiotapes without a transcription. Reports of users' experiences in this area will be a helpful addition to the qualitative research literature. There is also a lack of literature describing how these various software packages were used in music therapy qualitative research, the features that were most useful, and how the software supported the qualitative method used. We encourage researchers to describe the integration of CAQDAS in their music therapy qualitative research.

CAQDAS, and in particular ATLAS.ti, HyperRESEARCH, and NVivo, are tools that can be quite helpful to music therapy qualitative researchers, but not a substitute for a rigorous thinking process. Researchers are held accountable for and are required to be acutely aware of their analytical decisions and insights. The software programs help one to navigate through the complex interaction between data and an ever-evolving analytical process. Pointing, clicking, and visual representations are only tools that help move the mountains, boulders, and stones of the data, so that the researcher can do the human thinking, imagining, and visualizing that are necessary to try to convey the qualities of lived experiences in music therapy clinical improvisations.

Demonstration versions of these software packages are available at these web addresses:

ATLAS.ti 5.0: http://www.atlasti.com/demo.shtml

HyperRESEARCH 2.5: http://www.researchware.com/hr/downloads.html

NVivo: http://www.qsrinternational.com/DemoReg/DemoReg1.asp

Advantages

From our experience teaching and using software tools for qualitative research and the reported experience of students and users, several themes emerge that may be helpful in understanding how CAQDAS can be of assistance to music therapy qualitative researchers. These themes that have emerged from our collective experience are captioned in bold and described below.

"I can analyze a wide variety of qualitative data types"

Qualitative data include text materials such as transcriptions of therapy sessions; interviews or focus groups; field observations; newspaper, magazine, or journal articles; and legal, historical, or literary documents. Data may also consist of photographs, pictures, drawings, maps, musical scores, and audio or video recordings. ATLAS.ti 5.0, HyperRESEARCH 2.5, and NVivo assist the researcher in the management and retrieval of these data throughout the analytic process. A powerful feature of these software programs is the ability to use textual, graphical, audio, and visual data that can be coded, sorted, and linked. An illustration of using the software in this way is given later in this chapter.

Suzanne explains how this feature was helpful to her.

My challenge in tackling my dissertation was to find a way to code data that came from different types of primary sources. ATLAS.ti can effectively manage multimedia projects and make it quite suitable for a music therapy research project. I was able to scan in musical scores, download excerpts of audiovisual sessions, and transfer written documents, such as interview transcripts, to the software so that I could work with them.

"I can have easy access to all my data"

Even a small project of 30 documents, each 20–25 pages in length, would take a 4-inch three-ring binder to keep the project together. Flipping back and forth within the binder is not an impossible task, but CAQDAS provides almost instant access to text (transcriptions), graphical (musical scores), and audiovisual (taped sessions) data.

Suzanne's music therapy doctoral dissertation was a study that included 22 sessions of a mother and her high-functioning son with autism who were seen at an outpatient music therapy center by a team of two therapists. Particular interest focused on how improvised songs helped the mother and son communicate with each other, express emotions, and work through conflicts. The data included selected material from the 22 videotaped sessions as well as musical scores, interview transcriptions, and therapist reports. The amount of data for any large project like this can seem overwhelming. CAQDAS provides a rigorous file management, storage, and retrieval facility. All data are placed in a project folder from which a backup can safely be made. Data, codes, and memos can be dated and sequentially arranged, codebooks can be produced, and all materials can be easily retrieved.

"I can code and re-code text and retrieve the text I have coded"

Each document can be analyzed line by line, and, when appropriate, the events, statements, and observations may be coded or binned or categorized. For example, the coding may relate to the interplay between words, musical intervals, improvised melodies, melodic harmonization, and particular musical structures such as the 12-bar blues form. As the project continues the coded data are re-read or re-listened to, allowing the researcher to notice new ideas about the data. These new insights may result in adding, revising, or deleting a code. CAQDAS assists you as you code documents by enabling you to see on the screen, at all times, the text, the code name, and data coded. With a simple mouse click, you can choose to code selected data, rename code names, delete codes, or view all passages associated with a particular code.

Joe comments about this feature:

As I sifted through the data, I came up with preliminary codes and told the program to store the data under a name I had chosen. I could attach a memo that fleshes out my current thinking about this code. This memo stayed attached and was easily retrieved with a simple click. I could now move on, read, listen to, and think about another piece of data. If I found that there was more than one idea embedded in this one chunk of textual or musical data, I was able to sort this chunk under multiple codes with a simple click. The ability to double- or triple-code a section allowed me to let go of trying to hold in my mind multiple ideas and helped me to remain nearly unfettered by any physical consideration of how to organize these ideas in a way that would be easily retrieved and available for further analysis. In this program, I could easily return to these coded sections and rethink and recode them.

"I can easily review my coding for adequacy and quality"

The qualitative process is a recursive one. New coding categories are created as new ideas and ways of looking at the issues become apparent from examining the observation logs and interviews. The emergence of new nodes leads the researcher to reread and rethink previously coded data. CAQDAS provides researchers with the facility to review codes and share coded material with members of a research team or dissertation support group.

For example, when you want to see the passages coded as *frustration,* NVivo gives you the ability to click on frustration in the node (code) explorer. Each instance of text that is coded as frustration is immediately available for further exploration. You can also view the coded passage in the context of the document within which it is found. In the same way, when reading any given passage from a document, you can simultaneously view all the codes assigned to that text segment of the document.

Joe comments on this feature:

> I made my way through each interview after it had been transcribed and imported into the program, coding and thinking, thinking and coding, watching the codes grow both in number and in the amount of text and music under each. What helped me at this point is the program's capacity to keep track of many codes, where these chunks of coded text and music came from, how I saw them relate to one another, and, most important, my thinking about the process, my discoveries, wonderments, questions, and hunches. The words of the researcher and the words and music of the participants were then simply attached and related to one another, readily retrievable. The program actually enabled me to be more conscious of my thinking process. In a way, I needed to teach the program what I was thinking, and that added step clarified and highlighted my thinking. It also gave me a visual representation of my current thinking while giving me the flexibility to make changes as the study evolved.

"I can write analytic memos for the document, code, or project"

In his insightful monograph, *Writing Up Qualitative Research,* Wolcott (1990) instructs us that "writing is thinking" (p. 21). Reflecting on and writing about your thinking becomes an important way of thinking. Putting your thoughts about an interview into print, doubts about that observation, questions about the focus group, hunches concerning where the data were leading, are all part of the analytic process. Each of the software programs mentioned above offers the means to capture these important analytical musings. Memos can be written and attached to text segments, images, audio or video segments, and codes. The programs also store analytic memos that detail the analytic process, concerns about method, or thinking about theory.

In a past study, Suzanne wrote the following comment about the project she was undertaking. She was able to save this project memo and had easy access to it throughout the study.

> This is a study of a dance class of 3½ to 4 year-old girls. The documents include observations and interviews with the teacher. My research questions include: How does Eileen negotiate her role as boss and teacher? How does she reconcile her philosophy with her actual teaching style? How is Eileen able to attend to individual strengths and needs of girls in the group? How does Eileen handle unanticipated events and what does that say about her need for control?

"I can search for words or phrases in any or all of my data in a matter of seconds"

When reading one of the interviews of a therapist-participant, the researcher was struck by the therapist's use of the word *discontent* to describe feelings about the musical interactions with a patient. The researcher remembered that the therapist had used discontent in other interviews describing musical improvisations with other patients. The researcher had a hunch that it might be important to look at these other instances of the therapist's use of the word discontent in describing musical interactions with patients. The researcher proceeded with the data analysis and wondered if those parts of the interviews might provide additional insight into this therapist's clinical work. But where, in the 1,000 pages of data, were those phrases? How could they ever be found? CAQDAS makes this search quite easy. Searching through the entire data, multiple places where discontent was used by the therapist were found in less than two seconds! Try doing that search by hand.

"I can copy and paste quotes and analytic memos into Word when writing my report"

Rich and juicy quotes from data can help anchor your findings when writing an analytic memo or final report. ATLAS.ti, HyperRESEARCH, and NVivo allow you to copy passages from your data and paste them into your memo or report.

"I can bring together materials under one idea that I previously treated separately"

ATLAS.ti, HyperRESEARCH, and NVivo all have powerful interface capabilities that allow you to visually represent connections or networks between codes, memos, documents, or quotations. They offer you the ability to explore these relationships and develop concepts in much the same way the mind processes memory and thought. For example, if you wanted to think deeply about the concepts of improvising clinical themes, words, and musical interplay, you could visually represent them by their code name and link them under an umbrella code, *qualities of participation*. The representation of that relationship in a two-dimensional image enables the user to refine her thinking about the commonality between three seemingly unrelated ideas.

"I can compare text segments attributed to specific persons, settings, or selected attributes from all data"

In a study examining the drug compliance of 10 patients, a researcher wanted to compare interview text segments of all patients coded as *medication always taken properly, medication rarely taken properly*, and *medication usually taken properly*. These specialized software packages can retrieve coded texts in a matter of seconds. This powerful feature saves the researcher the drudgery of retrieving certain coded text units, thus allowing more time to do the far more important work of analyzing the text.

"I can ask many different types of questions about my data"

Depending on how well the material is coded, these software programs can facilitate the retrieval of text segments that guide formulation of questions about the data. For example, to study the impact of music therapy on children's abilities and difficulties in communication, social interaction, and emotional development, questions asked of the data might focus on each of those topics. CAQDAS can help locate data coded not only under the discrete codes of *abilities, difficulties, communication, social interaction,* and *emotional development,* but also locate data segments coded with combinations of these categories. The software provides powerful search engines to locate the co-occurrence of data coded as *abilities* and *communication,* or finer searches to identify data coded as *abilities* and *social interaction* but not *emotional development*.

These theory-building features were helpful to Joe:

As categories and higher conceptual levels arose, I could work on a new level of analysis while staying in close contact with the raw data. An asset of a computer program is its ability to keep track of mundane minutia, to be minding the store as I worked in more abstract levels of analysis. I found that the program not only allowed me to move from the raw data of text and music to higher levels of analysis, but I could move readily between a more microscopic analytical view of notes and words and a more macroscopic stage of analysis—a characteristic tenet of the qualitative research process. I was able to stay aware of the connection between the participants' words and music while I formulated ideas, relationships, and concepts about them. The raw data remained alive throughout the analysis, since the program kept track of how and what I was doing and where I could find it all.

In the hands of a researcher who thinks critically, CAQDAS provides a powerful tool to explore the collected qualitative data in depth. The findings will be useful to the extent that the questions asked of the data help lift meaning from the captured words and sounds.

References

Coffey, A., Holbrook, B., & Atkinson, P. (1996). Qualitative data analysis: Technologies and representations. *Sociological Research Online.* Available at http://www.socresonline.org.uk/1/1/4.html

Creswell, J. W., & Maietta, R. C. (2002). Qualitative research. In D. C. Miller & N. J. Salkind (Eds.), *Handbook of research design and social measurement* (6th ed., pp. 143–184). Thousand Oaks, CA: Sage Publications.

Fielding, N. G. (2001). Computer applications in qualitative research. In P. Atkinson, A. Coffey, S. Delamont, J. Lofland, & L. Lofland (Eds.), *Handbook of ethnography* (pp. 453–467). Thousand Oaks, CA: Sage Publications.

Fielding, N. G. & Lee, R. (1998). *Computer analysis and qualitative research.* Thousand Oaks, CA: Sage Publications.

Richards, T. J., & Richards, L. (1998). Using computers in qualitative research. In N. K. Denzin & Y. S. Lincoln (Eds.), *Collecting and interpreting qualitative materials* (pp. 211–245). London: Sage Publications.

Seidel, J. (1991). Method and madness in the application of computer technology to qualitative data analysis. In R. Lee & N. G. Fielding (Eds.), *Using computers in qualitative research* (pp. 107–116). Thousand Oaks, CA: Sage Publications.

Tesch, R. (1990). *Qualitative research: Analysis types & software tools.* London: The Falmer Press.

Tesch, R. (1991). Software for qualitative researchers: Analysis needs and program capabilities. In N. G. Fielding & R. Lee (Eds.), *Using computers in qualitative research* (pp. 16–37). Newbury Park, CA: Sage Publications.

Weitzman, E. A., & Miles, M. B. (1995). *Computer programs for qualitative data analysis: A software sourcebook.* Thousand Oaks, CA: Sage Publications.

Wolcott, H. F. (1990). *Writing up qualitative research.* Newbury Park, CA: Sage Publications.

Chapter 16
Writing the Quantitative Research Report
Michael G. McGuire

The essence of all research originates in curiosity.

Fraenkel and Wallen[1]

Human research has a history that extends back to at least to the 1st century, when the physician Celsius conducted experiments on human participants (Drug Study Institute, n.d.). Although it is not known if he collected quantitative data, one certainly can imagine that he might have. The development of quantitative human research in Europe can be traced back to Andreas Vesalius who published, in 1543, *De humani corporis fabrica (On the Fabric of the Human Body*, commonly referred to as *De fabrica)*. Vesalius stressed describing natural facts accurately (Williams, 2002). This emphasis on accuracy undoubtedly was influenced by the work of philosopher-scientists in the physical and biological sciences who contributed to the scientific revolution and led to the development of the scientific method. Experimental research in psychology was an outgrowth of this progression.

Experimental psychology (and thus quantitative music therapy research) had its origin in the 19th century. Wilhelm Wundt conducted research studies as early as 1857 and created the first experimental laboratory in psychology at the University of Leipzig in the late 1870s (Freedheim, 2003). Quantitative research in music therapy is built upon the foundation created by those who contributed to the development of the scientific method and experimental psychology. The generally accepted order of the scientific method is: (a) Observe a phenomenon or identify a question, (b) describe the phenomenon or clarify the problem, (c) create a hypothesis, (d) make predictions based on the hypothesis, (e) test the predictions, (f) modify the hypotheses or predictions and retest them (if the results are not consistent with the original observation), or (g) accept the observations based on the findings.

Research was among the earliest goals developed by the music therapy profession, and it still is among its top priorities. Quantitative studies, specifically experimental research, are highly regarded by the research community (Bordens & Abbott, 1996). In addition, quantitative data are consistently expected by a wide variety of funding sources and human services agencies (Department of Health and Human Services, 2002).

Some of the reasons that quantitative research is highly regarded are that it has a consistent structure (Creswell, 2002), its results are based on data that often have measurable validity (Bordens & Abbot, 1996), and it is replicable (American Psychological Association [APA], 2001). The consistent structure (introductory material and review of literature, hypothesis, purpose, method, results, and discussion) of quantitative reports has advantages. It is used for student papers, theses and dissertations, refereed articles, and conference papers. It provides a framework that can be utilized to assist researchers who are developing their skills. The consistency in structure also helps the reader to comprehend more easily what the researcher has done and thus be able to evaluate the report more efficiently (Creswell). Measurable validity is often a mainstay of quantitative research. This is as true today as it has been since the beginning of the scientific revolution. Its structure and validity allow quantitative research to be replicated, which validates previous findings and produces new research questions to be examined that will add to the corpus of knowledge.

Within the structure of quantitative music therapy research, the researcher demonstrates creativity in how the study is planned and implemented, how the data are analyzed, and how the results are used to draw implications for clinical music therapy. Clinical music therapists who conduct research in their treatment settings have to be particularly ingenious in order to respect both the treatment and research aspects of their work. They develop unique procedures in order to conduct their research, using especially their skills in problem solving. Most data can be analyzed in multiple ways. Consequently, researchers make sure that, however they decide to analyze their data, the results provide answers to the original research questions and hypotheses.

---

[1] This quotation is from Fraenkel and Wallen (2003), p. 7.

Writing the quantitative research report is a common experience for music therapists. These reports are written by undergraduate, master's, and doctoral students, as well as professional music therapists. Because people are likely to encounter it so frequently, it is important that music therapists understand how to write and present quantitative research.[2] The ultimate goal is to disseminate their methods and findings to others—peers, professors, or the music therapy community. The purposes of this chapter are to describe the content and format of quantitative research reports, to provide a brief discussion of the research proposal, and to present information to help in understanding and using the *Publication Manual of the American Psychological Association* (5th Edition, APA, 2001), herein referred to as the *Manual.*

Content and Format

The most commonly specified style manual in music therapy is the *Publication Manual of the American Psychological Association* (5th Edition, APA, 2001). It is referred to in the publication guidelines of most of the music therapy journals published in English.[3]

This section provides information regarding the content and format of the report, with elements presented in the order in which they appear in a manuscript using the *Manual* (APA, 2001), with reference to section numbers in the *Manual.* See Table 1 for an outline of a typical quantitative research report. The information in this section is based on common information found in several sources (Bell, Staines, & Michell, 2001; Creswell, 2002; Drotar, 2000; Fraenkel & Wallen, 2003; Kantowitz, Roediger, & Elmes, 2001; Kirscht & Schlenz, 2002; Salkind, 2000).

Two frequent expectations of authors of quantitative research reports are the following:

1. Write clearly and concisely. The primary objective of the written report is to communicate, to convey efficiently all aspects of your research.
2. Write with enough detail (but not too much) so that others can replicate your study.

Further advice is given in the *Manual* on three major characteristics of the report: length, headings, and tone. To determine the appropriate length, compare your manuscript to published reports or follow word count guidelines that may be provided. Headings serve as an outline for your ideas as well as the report. They also help provide focus to the author and the reader (see the *Manual,* section 3.30). Considering tone: "Although scientific writing differs in form from literary writing, it need not and should not lack style or be dull" (APA, 2001, p. 10). Authors are encouraged to be direct, interesting, and compelling.

Title and Abstract

Because the title and abstract of the quantitative report, if written well, will attract potential readers, their importance cannot be overestimated. Some suggest writing both of them early in the process to help maintain focus. They can be refined before the final draft is submitted.

Title. The title of the report is descriptive and should be able to stand alone. The title informs readers about the study and is used by information retrieval databases such as *PsycINFO* (APA ONLINE, n.d.) and *RILM Abstracts of Music Literature* (RILM International Center, n.d.) to index the report. The *Manual* recommends a title length of 10 to 12 words (section 1.06). An example of a title that meets the *Manual's* criteria is: "The Impact of Music Therapy on Language Functioning in Dementia" (Koger & Brotons, 2000, p. 183).

Abstract. An abstract that is well written can serve as one of the most essential paragraphs of your report. It is one of the first parts of the study that potential readers review to decide whether or not they will access it and use it. The abstract provides a summary of the report and is used by database retrieval services to index the published article. It is restricted

---

[2] It is important for researchers who are interested in writing philosophical or historical papers, or those who are serious writers, to know the rubrics of *The Chicago Manual of Style* (2003) and the very similar *A Manual for Writers of Term Papers, Theses, and Dissertations* (Turabian, revised by Grossman & Bennett, 1996).

[3] Some of the journals modify their use of APA style. The *Journal of Music Therapy* also accepts philosophical and historical manuscripts that use the Chicago (Turabian) style manual.

Table 1
Outline for a Typical Quantitative Research Report

I. Introductory Material (This section is not labeled [APA, 2001, p. 16].)
    A. Clear Statement of the Research Problem: Indicate the importance of the problem
        1. Lack of previous research
        2. Inconclusive evidence from previous research
    B. Review of Literature. This is related to the research problem and ends with a brief summary.
    C. Theoretical Rationale
    D. Specific Statement of Purpose (This subsection is sometimes labeled.)
II. Hypotheses, Specific Research Questions, or Research Objectives (To be developed based on the research problem and information presented in the Review of Literature.)
    A. State clearly
    B. For each hypothesis, identify the variables or phenomena under investigation.
        1. Independent
        2. Dependent
    C. Define terms related to the variables or phenomena under investigation
III. Method
    A. Sample: The sample is to represent the population from which it is chosen.
        1. State how the sample is selected
            a. randomly
            b. conveniently
        2. State the sample size
        3. Describe the sample using relevant demographic characteristics
            a. age
            b. sex
            c. diagnostic category
            d. level of functioning
            e. race
            f. geographic location
        4. Provide rationale for the size of the sample
    B. Participants
        1. If participants are assigned to groups, state the method of assignment used
            a. random assignment
            b. matched by
                i.   characteristics
                ii. treatment received
                iii. other
        2. If participants are not assigned to groups, describe the testing conditions
        3. Report participation rate
        4. Report ethical precautions taken
    C. Procedure
        1. Describe the treatment or intervention
            a. who implements
            b. testing site
            c. frequency and duration
            d. equipment and materials used

2. Describe the data-collection method
   a. apparatus and materials
      i. state the type of measurement used
      ii. describe how data are recorded
   b. report reliability
   c. report validity
      i. internal
      ii. external
3. Describe control measures

IV. Results
   A. Statistical Tests
      1. Identify the tests used
      2. Provide a rationale for the use of these tests
   B. Presentation of the Results
      1. Report the results for each objective, specific research question or hypothesis in the same order as they are presented in the introductory material
         a. use tables and figures when appropriate (APA, pp. 21, 147–175, 176–201)
         b. provide "informationally adequate statistics" (APA, p. 23)
         c. consider statistical power (APA, p. 24)
         d. report statistical significance
         e. include "effect size and strength of relationship" (APA, p. 25)

V. Discussion
   A. Content is related directly to the information presented in the introductory material
   B. State clearly whether or not the hypotheses (objective or specific research questions) are supported
   C. Relate your finding to previous research
   D. Evaluate and interpret the implications of the results
   E. "Examine, interpret, qualify," and draw inferences from the results (APA, p. 26)
   F. Provide theoretical consequences
   G. Provide practical consequences
   H. Support the validity of your conclusions
   I. Indicate the limitations of the study
   J. Importance of the Findings (included "when appropriate and justified" (APA, p. 26)
      1. Problem choice
      2. Levels of analysis
      3. Application and synthesis
   K. Specific suggestions for further research

VI. References

VII. Appendix

VIII. Author note

by the *Manual* to 120 words (section 1.07). Write the abstract so that it (a) is accurate, (b) is self-contained, (c) is concise and specific, (d) is nonevaluative, (e) is coherent and readable, and (f) its content parallels the text (section 1.07). Emphasize the study's research problem and content rather than the method. The elements of an abstract for an empirical study are: (a) the problem; (b) the subjects or participants and their characteristics; (c) the research method; (d) "the findings, including statistical significance levels" (APA, 2001, p. 14); and (e) the conclusions, applications, or implications (section 1.07).

Introductory Material

The main purposes of the introductory material are to: (a) State the research problem and its importance; (b) provide supporting information through the review of literature; (c) discuss the theoretical implications; (d) identify the purpose of and the rationale for the study; (e) present the hypotheses to be tested, objectives to be met, or the specific questions to be answered and relate these to the research problem; and (f) define terms. Authors frequently include more introductory material than is necessary; make it as brief as possible while still conveying the necessary information.

Research Problem. The research problem, which is the primary focus of the research, sets the boundaries of the study (see Chapter 8 in this book, Developing a Topic). It may be defined as a phenomenon that needs a solution that can be described, explained, or predicted (Gillis & Jackson, 2002). In support of the research problem, the author should address the theoretical basis of the problem and present how the information in the study adds to the body of knowledge. In other words, the importance of the problem is to be made clear. The clarity of the problem also assists readers in the evaluation of the study. An example of a clearly stated problem is, "Are. . . pleasure and distraction benefits of music listening available to people with cognitive impairments?" (Gregory, 2002, p. 245). Note that the research problem can be written in the interrogatory or declarative form. Some prefer the interrogatory form because it clearly implies that an answer to the problem is necessary (Gillis & Jackson, 2002).

Review of Literature. The review of literature provides supporting information for the study. It should be restricted to the most relevant and recent previous studies. The review helps to establish the framework, provide a theoretical base, and place the context of the research into previously reported work. Often the findings, conclusions, and deficiencies of each study are presented in one or two sentences. In organizing the review, present the least-related studies first and the most related last (see Chapter 9 of this book, Reviewing the Literature). Conclude with a brief summary, including implications (Isaac & Michael, 1995).

It is the responsibility of all writers to document their sources of information accurately and consistently. Since much of the introductory material is based on the work of others, it is necessary to be careful in giving credit to the authors whose ideas and information are used. This is true for paraphrased as well as quoted material. The American Music Therapy Association's *Code of Ethics* (2003) provides a clear statement for crediting authors: "Acknowledgment through specific citations will be made for unpublished as well as published material that has directly influenced the research or writing" (section 8.7.4). The *Manual* gives excellent examples of how to credit sources within the body of the paper in the section on Quotations (section 3.34) and Reference Citations in Text (sections 3.94–3.103). Be absolutely sure throughout the report that credit is given where credit is due.

Purpose. The importance of purpose cannot be overemphasized. It is a succinct statement that provides the framework for the study (Fraenkel & Wallen, 2003). This clear declarative statement helps readers keep the purpose in mind, and it helps them evaluate the study. An example of a purpose statement is, "The purpose of this study was to investigate the effect of actively participating in music making versus passively listening to live music on the production of SIgA" (Kuhn, 2002, p. 33).

Hypotheses, Objectives, and Specific Questions. End the introductory material with the hypotheses to be tested or a clear statement of objectives to be met or questions to be answered. An example of a hypothesis is, "There will be a significantly greater increase in SIgA concentrations for the active [music] group over the control group" (Kuhn, 2002, p. 33).

Examples of research objectives are, "This study was designed to (a) provide additional evidence for the effectiveness of a musical mood induction procedure and (b) further explore mood state-dependent effects on the encoding and free recall of internally-generated words" (de l'Etoile, 2002, p. 150).

Lipe (2002) provides an example of specific research questions:

1. What is the content of the literature?
2. What types of articles exist?
3. What are the credentials of the authors?
4. How does this literature define or describe spirituality?

5. How does this literature define or describe health or healing?
6. How does music function in relation to spirituality and health? (p. 213)

Definition of Terms. It is important to define the terms used in the dependent variable. There are three ways to define dependent variables: (a) a *constitutive definition,* (b) examples, or (c) *operational definitions* (Fraenkel & Wallen, 2003). A constitutive definition uses words to define other words, much like a dictionary does. This type of definition is limited; it can still be ambiguous. This is also true with examples; they may not add clarity. Operational definitions define the term by providing actions (operations), characteristics, or behaviors that can be observed reliably by multiple observers. Fraenkel and Wallen suggest the use of operational definitions in combination with a constitutive one.

Kern and Wolery (2001) use a combination of operational and constitutive definitions:

> *Social interaction with peers* was defined as initiating or responding to a peer by talking, giving/taking an object, reaching for or touching a peer. . . *Play and engagement* was defined as actively manipulating a material (e.g., digging in the sand, bangs with a stick), riding a trike, pulling—but not riding in—a wagon, climbing on an apparatus, walking purposefully to a given location, pushing a cart or other toy. . . . (pp. 153–154)

Method

The Method section is a description of how the study was conducted (APA, 2001). This description enhances the readers' understanding of the results, provides a basis for the readers' evaluation, and supplies sufficient information for possible replication (APA; Bell et al., 2001; Fraenkel & Wallen, 2003). The *Manual* cautions against including irrelevant details.

The information included most often in the Method section is on the (a) participants; (b) apparatus, instrumentation, or materials; and (c) procedure and data collection methods (APA, 2001; Kantowitz, Roediger, & Elmes, 2001). Creswell (2002) suggests further detail, indicated by subsections: (a) a description of the sample and the site of the experiment; (b) access to and permissions from or for the participants; (c) instruments used in the study, including their reliability and validity; interventions utilized with the experimental groups; and (d) procedures for data collection. The *Manual* suggests the use of labeled subsections within the Method section. Refer to published articles to see how authors use the various levels of headings.

Participants. The information on participants includes: (a) relevant demographics, (b) the number of participants, (c) the selection criteria, and (d) their assignment to groups (if applicable) (APA, 2001, pp. 18–19). Characteristics that are commonly given are the participants' (a) gender, (b) age range (including the mean and standard deviation), (c) ethnicity, (d) level of intellectual functioning, and (e) diagnostic category. The *Manual* provides the rationale for a well-described participant pool. "Appropriate identification of research. . . clientele is critical. . . particularly for assessing the results; generalizing the findings; and making comparisons in replications, literature review, or secondary data analyses" (APA, p. 18). An example:

> Participants were 60 undergraduate students recruited from psychology courses. . . . Fifty-one percent were male ($n = 31$) and 48% female ($n = 29$). Participants ranged in age from 18 to 49 years ($M = 21.6$, $SD = 6.50$). . . . The sample was 85% Caucasian ($n = 51$), 7% African-American ($n = 4$), and 8% other ($n = 5$); other includes Indian, Asian and Hispanic. (Burns et al., 2002, p. 104)

When participants are used, include a report on the ethical precautions that were taken. Attention to this aspect of music therapy is emphasized by Dileo (see Chapter 18 of this book, Ethical Precautions in Music Therapy Research, and Dileo, 2000). When a manuscript is submitted, the author must indicate in one of three ways that participants were treated ethically: (a) in a cover letter submitted with the manuscript; (b) within the text of the report when describing participants; or (c) upon request of an editor, signing a form verifying ethical treatment of the participants (APA, 2001, p. 355). Authors are expected to adhere to accepted ethical practices of the profession, such as those in the *Code of Ethics* of the American Music Therapy Association (AMTA, 2003).

Apparatus and Materials. In this part of the Method section, provide a description of all apparatus, instruments, and materials used in the study (APA, 2001, p. 19). Keep in mind that someone may later wish to replicate the research being reported, thus detail is important. Describe fully all items used in eliciting responses from the participants and how these responses were measured. Acoustic instruments are to be described by type, manufacturer name, and model number, as are any electronic instruments or sound equipment. All measurement devices, which may be a paper-and-pencil test, an automatic measuring device (such as a computer or biofeedback apparatus), video equipment, or an observation recording sheet, must be described enough to make replication of the study possible. For example,

> A Toshiba lap top computer with a *Biotech Component 4.65* software package was used to record levels of music activity, skin temperature, and heart rate. Music activity was measured by a J&J EMG Module. . . with silver-silver electrodes; . . . temperature was measured by a J&J Model T-68. . . with a thermistor; . . . and heart rate was measured by a J&J Module P-401 with a plethysmograph. . . . (Burns et al., 2002, p. 105)

Procedures and Data Collection. The procedures and data collection information are presented in the order in which they occur (APA, 2001). Describe how the treatment or independent variables were presented to the participants. In a survey study, this would include how the survey document was distributed, the return (response) rate, and follow-up procedures used with nonrespondents (Isaac & Michael, 1995). It is equally important to describe the data collection method—how the participants' responses were recorded or documented. If a published test was used, report its reliability and validity. If the test was revised for the study, report how this affected reliability and validity. If the test is newly developed, report how it was developed, how the items used in the study were extracted, and its reliability and validity (Drotar, 2000).

One common remark from readers of music therapy research is that they do not know what music was used or how it was presented. This is important information, especially when one considers that different music and types of music will elicit considerably different responses. It is not just that music was presented, but that specific music was presented in predetermined ways to create the experimental conditions.

The Method section is to be precise yet concise. For the purposes of replication, "remember that the Method section should tell the reader *what* you did and *how* you did it" (APA, 2001, p. 20). If nonessential details are given, clarity is lost. Give the details that had an impact on the study's final results. Read the method sections of published research studies to determine the kind of detail that is common.

Results

The Results section presents the statistical analysis of the collected data for each objective or hypothesis. State whether or not the objective was met or whether the hypothesis was supported or rejected. This information is presented in a narrative, with tables or figures used to supplement the text, if appropriate. Tables present numerical data or words, while figures are "any type of illustration other than a table" (APA, 2001, p. 176). Because they are expensive to print, tables and figures should be used judiciously. Consider using them if they present data more efficiently than could be presented with text only. When tables are used, state what information the tables or figures present but do not interpret or explain them. (See section 1.10 of the *Manual* for specific details of the content for the Results section. For general information about tables and figures, see p. 21 of the *Manual*. For more specific information, see sections 3.62–3.74; for figures, sections 3.77–3.86.)

Regarding statistical presentation of the results, the *Manual* is detailed and explicit. See "informationally adequate statistics" (p. 23), "statistical power" (p. 24), "statistical significance" (p. 24), and "effect size and strength of relationship" (p. 25).

Discussion

One could consider the closing material to be the most important part of the report. This can be a difficult section to write. Drotar (2000) indicates that writing this section is problematic in terms of (a) avoiding the reiteration of results by presenting all findings; (b) being dynamic and creative, yet specific; (c) including only the most important contributions; and (d) relating the study to theoretical models and other related research findings—but not for each finding.

In the Discussion section, the researcher-writer reviews, explains, and describes the results, evaluating and interpreting the findings in relationship to the research problem. The objective of the Discussion section is to provide logical support for the researcher's position. This section opens with a "clear statement of the support or nonsupport of your original hypothesis" (APA, 2001, p. 26). The focus should be on the contributions made by the study, the degree to which the original problem was resolved, and what reasonable judgments and implications can be made. The conclusions are based on the data and supported by comparing the study to previous research. The writer should make new points rather than repeating points already made. When writing the Discussion section, be careful not to confuse results with conclusions. A result is "something obtained by calculation or investigation," such as a test of significance (Merriam-Webster, n.d.). "A conclusion is an interpretation of [the] result especially as it relates to the objectives of the study" (Burnett, 1991, p. 12).

Other important considerations for the Discussion section are: All generalizations made must be data specific, and overgeneralizations are to be avoided; the limitations are discussed without overemphasis; and applications or implications for music therapy practice or theory are given. It is common to provide recommendations for further research.

References

The References section provides the publication information of all sources cited in the text; these must correspond exactly. It is crucial that all citations are referenced, and that no reference is given for information not cited. The References section informs readers of the materials used in writing the paper, and it is often used to help readers further their own knowledge. It is important that all references be listed accurately.

Appendixes

Place detailed information or material that draws attention away from the content of the report in an appendix. Although publishers often discourage the use of appendixes because of space and cost, instructors may encourage their inclusion for quantitative research reports written by students. Include researcher-developed tests, surveys, questionnaires, cover letters, extensive procedural statements, and the like in appendixes. (See APA, 2001, section 1.14, sections 3.90–3.93, and pp. 299–300 for further details.)

The Research Proposal

Some academic and clinical training programs require students to prepare a research proposal. It is common practice for graduate programs to require master's and doctoral students to write proposals for the thesis or dissertation. The proposal contains all aspects of a research study up to data collection. It is written in either the present or future tense. For more detailed information on research proposals, the reader is referred to Fraenkel and Wallen (2003) and Salkind (2000).

Getting to Know the APA *Publication Manual*

The purposes of this section are to help you become familiar with the organization of the *Manual* (APA, 2001), to identify some of the APA rubrics (rules) that frequently confound authors, and to provide a systematic approach to finding the answers to questions about these rubrics.

Using the *Manual's* consistent presentational style and format provides structure for authors so that they present information in the long tradition of scientific publication. This consistency helps you organize your writing and assists those who will read the report to focus on content. Before you begin to write, it is recommended that you become familiar with the contents of the *Manual* so it will be used in the most efficacious manner. The Introduction to the *Manual* (pp. xxiii–xxviii) provides the initial information with which you should become familiar. It will help you understand the *Manual*, which will then help you be successful in writing a research report in APA style.

One particularly useful section is How to Use the *Manual* (pp. xxvi–xxviii). Three resources in becoming more adept with this *Manual* are (a) the APA website http://www.apa.org/; (b) *Mastering APA Style: Instructor's Resource Guide* (Gelfand, Walker, & APA, 2002a); and (c) *Mastering APA Style: Student's Workbook and Training Guide* (Gelfand, Walker, & APA, 2002b). The website presents changes that took place between the Fourth and Fifth editions of the *Manual*. Additionally, future changes will be placed there.

Sections Useful to Writers

The authors of the *Manual* recommend the sections given below as being particularly useful to writers who are not familiar with its rubrics:

> Quotations (sections 3.34–3.41), Examples of Reference Citations (chap. 4), Manuscript Preparation Instructions (chap. 5), Sample paper and Outlines (Figures 5.1–5.3, chap. 5), Bibliography (section 9.03, suggested reading), Theses, Dissertations, and Student Papers (chap. 6), Manuscript Checklists (Appendixes A and B). (APA, 2001, p. 383)

To use the *Manual* successfully and prepare a manuscript in APA style, it is important to understand the distinction between editorial style and manuscript preparation. *Editorial style* (see Chapter 3) consists of "the rules or guidelines a publisher observes to ensure clear, consistent presentation of the printed word" (APA, 2001, p. 77). *Manuscript preparation* (see Chapter 5) provides "the mechanical details of producing a typical paper manuscript" (APA, p. 283). Consequently, when you have a question about how to do something, it is helpful to know if the question is presentational (style) or mechanical (preparation). For many of these questions, the answers are found in more than one place within the *Manual*. To find where these various answers are, it is necessary to use the Index to the *Manual*. It is also indispensable to be familiar with the contents of Chapter 3, APA Editorial Style (pp. 77–88) and Chapter 5, Manuscript Preparation and Sample Papers to be Submitted for Publication (pp. 283–320).

Selected Rubrics and Common Errors in APA Style

As you write, many questions will be encountered regarding the presentation of material. The subsections that follow cover many of those concerns, in addition to common errors. They are presented in alphabetical order, with guidelines as to where to find the answers in the *Manual*.

> *Abbreviations:* Suppose that you need to know the APA-approved abbreviation for Alaska. Go to the Index, and you find that *abbreviations* is the first item listed. You also see there is a long list of abbreviation rules. It is necessary to read the list to find the exact rule, *states and territories*, which applies to your question. Note that most of the rules are in Chapter 3, which deals with style (presentation).
>
> *Abstract:* Start the abstract on page 2. It is presented as a non-indented paragraph of no more than 120 words. The label Abstract is typed at the top of the page, centered, in lower- and upper-case letters. Create the abstract page by inserting a page break after the last line of the title page. Do not use the return key multiple times on the title page to create a page break. Create the first page of text by inserting a page break after the last line of the abstract.
>
> *Authors' names in parenthetical citations:* In the Index, see *Reference citations,* then go to "two or more works within the same parentheses" (APA, 2001, p. 432) to determine the order of authors' names when parentheses are used.
>
> *Authors' surnames:* Do not use authors' first names in the text or reference list. This is detailed under *Reference citations,* where section 3.94 indicates, "use. . . the surname of the author" (APA, 2001, p. 207).
>
> *Bias-free language:* It is important to present relevant, bias-free information regarding the participants. The *Manual* provides guidelines used to "reduce bias in language" (APA, 2001, p. 61). It presents specific caveats to be taken into consideration about gender, sexual orientation, racial and ethnic identity,

disabilities, and age. The *Manual* provides many examples of problematic language and preferred language to ameliorate the use of biased language. (See Guidelines to Reduce Bias in Language, pp. 61–76, including sections 2.13–2.17 and Table 2.1 in the *Manual*.)

Body of the paper: Text: The primary section of the manuscript begins on page 3. The title of the report is typed in upper- and lower-case letters at the top of the page, centered and double-spaced. The text of the report is continuous; there are no breaks between sections or when a new heading is used. The header and page number is to appear automatically in the upper right-hand corner of the page. Use the word-processing header function to accomplish this.

Books included in the Reference List: See *Books* in the Index for specific rules; see also *General Forms* in section 4.07. It is helpful to review the list provided under *B. Books, brochures, and book chapters.* Consult also *Elements and Examples of References in APA Style.*

Co., Ltd., Inc., and other publisher abbreviations: See *Publication information, nonperiodicals* in the Index.

Divided words: This is found under *Manuscript preparation* in the Index, under *line length and alignment* (p. 287, section 5.04) in the *Manual*. The rule indicates not to divide words at the end of a line.

Double-spacing: This is perhaps the most consistent of all the rubrics: Double-space everything (p. 286, section 5.03).

Electronic media in references: Consult the list *I. Electronic media* on p. 236 and the electronic media section that begins on p. 268 in the *Manual*.

Et al., use of: See the Index to determine where the two rubrics are for the correct use of this abbreviation.

Figures: It is common for figures to not be designated or presented correctly; there are several rubrics regarding figures. It is important to be familiar with these rules if you intend to use figures in your research report. Note that the placement of figures in the manuscript is different for theses, dissertations, and student papers than it is for manuscripts submitted to journals.

Header on the manuscript pages: Pages from a manuscript may become separated, consequently a header is used to identify each page. Create the header by using the first two or three descriptive words from the title of your paper. These words are placed to the left of the page number, separated by five spaces. (The page header may also be above the page number.) To create a header, view the header in your word-processing program. With the cursor placed flush to the left margin, type the header, insert 5 spaces, indicate the page number by using the automatic page numbering function of the word processor (never do this manually), then move the header and page number to the upper right-hand corner by using the *align right* function of the word-processing program.

Headings: Use headings consistently. "Levels of heading establish. . . the hierarchy of sections to orient the reader" (APA, 2001, p. 111). Common sections given headings in a quantitative report are: Method, Results, and Discussion; subsection headings are Materials and Procedure. See *headings* in the Index. The rules frequently referred to are *levels of headings, organizing manuscripts,* and *selecting the levels.*

Issue numbers: The rubric indicating when to include the issue number of a journal in the references is found in the Index under *Publication information* and then *periodicals.* An example can be found by referring in the Index to *Periodicals* and then *paginated by issue.*

Journal articles included in the reference list: See *Periodicals* in the Index for specific rules; see also *General Forms* in section 4.07. Also review the list provided under *A. Periodicals.* Consult *Elements and Examples of References in APA Style.*

Margins: The *Manual* mandates uniform margins (section 5.04). Individual instructors and sponsors of theses and dissertations may have their own requirements regarding margins. Their requirements supercede the *Manual*, which recommends at least a 1-inch margin on all edges of the manuscript.

Numbers, expression of: There are more than 40 rules for numbers; see the Index for specifics. The most common question regarding numbers is: Which ones are spelled out and which ones are typed using numbers? The answer to this question is found by referring to the numbers section of the *Manual*. Note also that there are different rules for the abstract and the body of the paper.

Page numbers: Place page numbers in the header using Arabic numbers. The title page is page 1, and all other pages are numbered automatically (using the header function) and consecutively except artwork for figures. It is acceptable for the page number header to be ½ inch from the top edge of the paper, but it must be at least 1 inch from the right edge.

Pages, order of: Before determining the final order of the manuscript pages, it must be decided whether the manuscript is a copy manuscript, which will be submitted for publication, or a final manuscript, such as a dissertation or other student paper. The *Manual* is written specifically for the preparation of copy manuscripts. To determine the correct order of pages for your manuscript, see Chapter 6. If you prepare the report to meet course or graduation requirements, clarify which type of manuscript is required.

Paragraph indentation: Use the tab key to create consistent indentation. The default in most word-processing programs is ½ inch. All subsequent lines are typed flush to the left margins. See the exceptions to these requirements on p. 289, section 5.08.

Punctuation: There are both presentational (style) and mechanical (word-processing) rules regarding punctuation. Most of the necessary rubrics are found in the *punctuation* section in the Index.

Quotations: It is important to know the rules regarding quotations, especially to avoid plagiarism. These rules are, like many others, both presentational and mechanical. Most of the rules for quotations and quotation marks are concentrated on a few pages of the *Manual*. Find these pages by referring to the Index.

Reference list: Be sure that all sources given in the References appear in the text of the report, and that all citations included in the text are acknowledged in the References. It is especially important to check for accuracy after each revision of the manuscript. The reference list begins on a new page that is created by inserting a page-break after the last line of the text. Do not use the return key multiple times after the last line of text to create a page break. Type the label References (or Reference if only one source is used) at the top of the page, centered, in upper- and lower-case letters. The reference list of a manuscript submitted for publication is double-spaced. For theses, dissertations and other student papers, it may be single-spaced. The sponsoring authority of the paper determines this. References are formatted using a hanging indent, which can be created automatically using word-processing functions. Usually the second and subsequent lines of a hanging indent are .5 inch from the left margin.

References: Some of the most common errors found in the References section and in textual citations related to it are author's names are misspelled; dates of publication are incorrect; titles are inaccurate; and volume, issue, or page numbers are incorrect. This information must be presented accurately so that readers can refer to your sources. It is also imperative to compare textual citations with the reference list to assure accuracy. One of the most bothersome aspects of creating the reference list is finding the format and example for particular items listed in it. The *Manual* provides assistance in this area by including an extensive list of types of referenced works. This list begins on p. 232. It is divided into three categories: (a) print, (b) audiovisual, and (c) electronic media. Also within this section (pp. 236–237) can be found variations on the elements of a reference. Additionally, there are no fewer than 95 examples given for items within each of these categories. (References, section 1.13; Reference Citations, sections 3.94–3.103; Chapter 4: Reference List, pp. 215–281 in the *Manual*.)

Statistical results, format of: There are over 30 rubrics listed under *Statistical and mathematical copy* in the Index, along with cross-references to additional rules. Consult the rubrics to determine the required format.

Tables and table titles, notes, and rules: Tables are used to present quantitative data efficiently. There are several complexities regarding tables; see sections 3.62–3.74 in the *Manual*. The examples provided are particularly helpful. Some common errors are for the tables that are presented to not summarize the data, not referring to the tables in the text, and repeating information given in the tables in the text.

Titles of books and articles: To ascertain the rules for word-processing titles within the reference list, see *Capitalization* in the Index.

Widowed and orphaned lines: When the last line of a paragraph appears at the top of a page, it is called a *widow.* An *orphan* is the first line of a paragraph, or a heading, that appears by itself at the bottom of a page. Avoid these two types of lines when submitting student papers. Word processing programs can be set to control widowed and orphaned lines.

Title page: The title page includes (a) the header, with the page number 1 inserted automatically; (b) the running head (section 1.06); (c) the title (section 1.06), (d) the author's name or byline, and (e) the author's institutional affiliation.

Word-processing/manuscript preparation: Chapter 5 of the *Manual* is dedicated to manuscript preparation. This chapter should be reviewed thoroughly. An excellent part of this chapter is the Sample Paper and Outlines (pp. 305–320), which gives the user the visual answer to many questions.

References

American Music Therapy Association. (2003). *Code of ethics.* Available at http://www.musictherapy.org/ethics.html

APA ONLINE. (n.d.). *PsycINFO.* Available at http://www.apa.org/psycinfo/

American Psychological Association. (2001). *Publication manual of the American Psychological Association* (5th ed.). Washington, DC: Author.

Bell, P. B., & Staines, P. J., with Michell, J. (2001). *Evaluation, doing and writing research in psychology: A step-by-step guide for students.* London, UK: Sage Publications.

Bordens, K. S., & Abbott, B. B. (1996). *Research design and methods: A process approach* (3rd ed.). Mountain View, CA: Mayfield.

Burnett, M. F. (1991, November). Manuscript preparation. In D. H. Redman (Organizer), *Getting published in journals and conference proceedings* (pp. 10–13) (Report No. CS-213-096). Symposium conducted at the annual meeting of the Mid-South Educational Research Association, Lexington, KY. (ERIC Document Reproduction Service No. ED340023)

Burns, J. L., Labbé, E., Arke, B., Capeless, K., Cooksey, B., Steadman, A., et al. (2002). The effects of different types of music on perceived and physiological measures of stress. *Journal of Music Therapy, 39,* 101–116.

Chicago manual of style (15th ed.). (2003). Chicago: University of Chicago Press.

Creswell, J. W. (2002). *Educational research: Planning, conducting, and evaluating quantitative and qualitative research.* Upper Saddle River, NJ: Pearson Education.

de l'Etoile, S. (2002). The effect of a musical mood induction procedure on mood state-dependent word retrieval. *Journal of Music Therapy, 39,* 145–160.

Department of Health and Human Services. (2002). *Research, demonstration and evaluation activities FY2003 plan and budget: February 2002.* Available at http://www.aspe.hhs.gov/progsys/rde/3_2.htm

Dileo, C. (2000). *Ethical thinking in music therapy.* Cherry Hill, NJ: Jeffrey Books.

Drotar, D. (2000). Writing research articles for publication. In D. Drotar (Ed.), *Handbook of research in pediatric and clinical child psychology: Practical strategies and methods* (pp. 347–374). New York: Kluwer Academic/Plenum.

Drug Study Institute. (n.d.). Human research training: A historical perspective. In *Industry resources.* Available at http://www.drugstudy.md/resource3.html

Fraenkel, J. R., & Wallen, N. E. (2003). *How to design and evaluate research in education* (5th ed.). New York: McGraw-Hill Higher Education.

Freedheim, D. K. (Ed.). (2003). *History of psychology.* In I. B. Weiner (Editor-in-Chief), *Handbook of psychology* (Vol. 1). Hoboken, NJ: John Wiley.

Gelfand, H., Walker, C. J., & American Psychological Association. (2002a). *Mastering APA style: Instructor's resource guide.* Washington, DC: American Psychological Association.

Gelfand, H., Walker, C. J., & American Psychological Association. (2002b). *Mastering APA style: Student's workbook and training guide.* Washington, DC: American Psychological Association.

Gillis, A., & Jackson, W. (2002). *Research for nurses: Methods and interpretation.* Philadelphia: F. A. Davis.

Gregory, D. (2002). Music listening for maintaining attention of older adults with cognitive impairments. *Journal of Music Therapy, 39,* 244–264.

Isaac, S., & Michael, W. B. (1995). *Handbook in research and evaluation* (3rd ed.). San Diego, CA: EdITS.

Kantowitz, B. H., Roediger, III, H. L., & Elmes, D. G. (2001). *Experimental psychology: Understanding psychological research.* Belmont, CA: Wadsworth.

Kern, P., & Wolery, M. (2001), Participation of a preschooler with visual impairments on the playground: Effects of musical adaptations and staff development. *Journal of Music Therapy, 38,* 149–164.

Kirscht, J., & Schlenz, M. (2002). *Engaging inquiry: Research and writing in the disciplines.* Upper Saddle River, NJ: Prentice-Hall/Pearson Education.

Koger, S. M., & Brotons, M. (2000). The impact of music therapy on language functioning in dementia. *Journal of Music Therapy, 37,* 183–195.

Kuhn, D. (2002). The effects of active and passive participation in musical activity on the immune system as measured by salivary immunoglobulin A. *Journal of Music Therapy, 39,* 30–39.

Lipe, A. W. (2002). Beyond therapy: Music, spirituality and health in human experience: A review of the literature. *Journal of Music Therapy, 39,* 209–240.

Merriam-Webster. (n.d.). *Merriam-Webster online dictionary.* Available at http://www.m-w.com/

RILM International Center. (n.d.). *Répertoire international de Littérature musicale.* Available at http://www.rilm.org/about.html

Salkind, N. J. (2000). *Exploring research* (4th ed.). Upper Saddle River, NJ: Prentice-Hall.

Turabian, K. L. (revised by Grossman, J., & Bennett, A.). (1996). *A manual for writers of term papers, theses and dissertations* (6th ed.). Chicago: University of Chicago Press.

Williams, L. P. (2002). The history of science. In *The new encyclopaedia Britannica* (Vol. 27, pp. 32–41). Chicago: Encyclopaedia Britannica.

Acknowledgments

The author thanks Suzanne R. Burns, Associate Editor, *Journal of Music Therapy,* and Brian L. Wilson, Editor, *Music Therapy Perspectives,* for their assistance.

Chapter 17
Writing the Qualitative Research Report
Kenneth Aigen

The key for qualitative researchers is to breathe into our words the life we have experienced.

Margot Ely[1]

Unlike quantitative work, which can carry its meaning in its tables and summaries, qualitative work depends upon people's reading it. Just as a piece of literature is not equivalent to its "plot summary," qualitative research is not contained in its abstracts. Qualitative research has to be read, not scanned; its meaning is in the reading.

Laurel Richardson[2]

The great variability in the form and content of qualitative research reports reflects the fact that there are different views on the nature of qualitative research.[3] Qualitative researchers who believe that qualitative and quantitative research differ primarily in the type of data gathered tend to write reports similar to quantitative reports in their function, structure, and content. Researchers who believe that qualitative research is a fundamentally different mode of inquiry write reports with pronounced differences in these areas. In all cases, however, qualitative research reports make demands upon the researcher's writing skills because data and the results of their analysis are most often in the form of words

Because there are many different forms of qualitative research, each with its own ideas about the appropriate form and content of research reports, it is not possible to discuss the elements and functions of a generic qualitative research report. There just is no such thing. The variability in research reports exists on many levels: between quantitative and qualitative research, among the different qualitative research traditions, and within each tradition as well. Just as one cannot make blanket statements about how qualitative writing differs from quantitative writing, it is similarly not possible, for example, to make general statements about how phenomenology reports differ from hermeneutic reports, or even about what characterizes a phenomenologically based qualitative research report. Compounding this difficulty is that researchers tend to blend methods and narrative styles in their reports.

Because there is such variability among the various approaches and among researchers, the best that one can do is examine how qualitative researchers write and what they say about their writing. The advantageous part of this state of affairs is that there are many choices for qualitative researchers to make in compiling their reports; the disadvantage is that there are many choices for qualitative researchers to make in compiling their reports.

Freedom in writing empowers authors while also presenting challenges. Each researcher must determine the writing form that best suits the findings of a particular study. The form of the report can reflect the sequence of activities of the researcher, as in most quantitative writing, or it can reflect the content of the findings. Just as this variability presents opportunities and challenges to qualitative researchers, it presents similar difficulties in trying to write about writing in qualitative research.

The variability of structure and content in qualitative reports, taken together with the idea that the form of the report should mirror its content, means that it is not possible to make context-free recommendations on how to write qualitative research. However, while it is not possible to make recommendations about what a given report should include without taking into account its specific purpose, focus, and findings, it is possible to examine what qualitative research reports look like and discuss the rationales given for various structural and content-related decisions made by their authors.

---

[1] This quotation is from Ely et al. (1997), p. 1.
[2] This quotation is from Richardson (1994), p. 517.
[3] Refer to discussion of various views on qualitative research in Chapter 5, Principles of Qualitative Research, and elsewhere in this book.

Fortunately, there is a tradition of writing about writing among qualitative researchers (Atkinson, 1990; Ely, Vinz, Downing, & Anzul, 1997; Wolcott, 1990). This is partly because the flexibility in qualitative research writing leads researchers to overtly discuss the rationale for their choices. It also stems from qualitative research activities that frequently involve an intense examination of the way that people use words to both express and construct their personal social realities.

In many qualitative research traditions, verbal expression is seen not just as something that reflects reality, but as something that helps determine our realities. In other words, the words available to us and the permitted ways of using them help determine our experiences as human beings. Qualitative researchers who practice self-reflexivity understand that their beliefs about the interaction of language and reality apply not only to the way that research participants express themselves in interviews, for example, but to the way that researchers express themselves through research reports. This self-awareness about the construction of research reports means that there is ample material from researchers themselves about the nature of writing and the interaction between writing choices and how research findings are conveyed.

Qualitative research reports are found in all forms of scholarly and professional publications. The recommendations in the present chapter are not equally applicable to all of these forms, as the requirements of each vary.

Options in Writing Qualitative Research Reports

The great majority of articles in scholarly research journals share a similar format, including an Introduction, Method, Results, and Discussion sections. Some qualitative researchers choose to follow this format; doing so may increase the likelihood of an article being accepted for publication in certain journals. However, because writing in that format is well covered in many other publications, including Chapter 16 of this text, the present chapter will focus more on those reports that differ in fundamental ways from such reports.

Here are some of the ways that qualitative reports may depart from this format:

- The reports can be written in first person, second person, or third person, or a multiplicity of writing voices can be employed in a layered fashion;
- Related scholarly literature can be in a literature review section or it can be sprinkled liberally throughout the study;
- The focus of a study can be contextualized in scholarly concerns, practical professional concerns, inherent human concerns, or the life of the researcher;
- Method can be discussed in a introductory section, in a section labeled *method* in an appendix, or not at all;
- Results can be expressed in music, pictures, diagrams, images, and, of course, words, although the words may take a variety of narrative forms more commonly associated with literature than with science;
- Inference, interpretation, and theory can appear throughout the research document;
- The report can take the form of a distanced, technical publication, or it can be a vital expression of particular people who are portrayed in detail as individuals. This last consideration goes for those who participate in the research as well as for those who conduct it and write about it.

As mentioned, some qualitative research reports, such as Amir (1993) and Wheeler (2002), follow a standard format of beginning with a brief discussion of the research problem or question and follow this with sections on method, results, and discussion. While their content may be quite different from quantitative research, they are similarly structured, following the sequence of activities engaged in by the researcher. Other reports are more of a blended nature, such as Aigen (2002) and Bruscia (1998), and incorporate some of the sections just mentioned with others either omitted or placed in a different sequence, such as putting a discussion of method into an appendix. Some of the more unconventional reports have the outward form of a traditional report but weave into their structure narrative devices and content not typically associated with research reports, such as themes or stories, as examples of the former, and personal information about the research or in-depth examinations of the researcher's experience, as examples of the latter. And the most innovative research reports assume a narrative structure more typical of literary forms. In this last type of report, for example Aigen (1997) and Kenny (2002), the literary devices are not woven in but form the very structure of the report.

The various choices available to the authors of qualitative research reports are summarized in Table 1.

Table 1
Narrative and Structural Options in Qualitative Research Reports

Writing Voice
Third person
First person/researcher's voice
First person/participant's voice
Second person
Multiple voices

Writing Tone
Distanced technical report
Technical with limited narrative
or personal elements
Predominantly Personal

Context of Research Focus
Related scholarly research
Practical professional concerns
Participant's needs
Researcher's life and interests
Inherent human concerns

Explication of Method
In introduction
In method section
Throughout report
In appendix
Not provided

Related Literature
In literature review section
Used throughout document
Employed minimally

Results Expressed Through
Analytic verbal descriptions
Diagrams (tables, grids, and so forth)
Pictures
Images
Music (recording or notation)
Literary narrative forms

Source and Placement of Theory
Presented initially prior to data analysis
Generated from data
Drawn from literature after data analysis
Not employed (or minimally employed)

Structure of Report
Technical report structured by method
Technical with some nontraditional aspects
Narrative with some traditional aspects
Narrative, minimal scholarly conventions

With so many areas of writing to address and so many variations within each area, it is clear why there is such variability in published qualitative reports. The conceptual organization represented in Table 1 can provide a means for understanding the construction of qualitative research texts and generating new ones.

Functions of Qualitative Research Reports

Functions of qualitative research reports are summarized in Table 2.[4] As you might infer from much of the preceding discussion, some of the functions of a qualitative report are similar to quantitative research and some are quite different. These functions constitute the next section of this chapter. While it is not possible to sequence the topics in the way that they appear in a typical report because there is no such thing, it is possible to take them up in a sequence that is close to how they are often encountered by researchers.

---

[4] The term *function* is used in the heading of this section rather than *purpose*. Contrary to popular usage in research studies (The purpose of this study is. . .), people have purposes, studies do not. However, the prohibition on first-person writing in quantitative research means that individuals cannot write about their purposes. This leads to the awkward grammatical construction of attributing purpose to an inanimate, immaterial object, that is, the study. So in describing research studies it is more accurate to refer to the purposes people possess for writing the reports as they do.

Table 2
Functions of Qualitative Research Reports

Summarize Areas of Inquiry	Convey Findings
Research problems or questions	*Describe*
General topic/focus	Establish research setting
	Report data
Present Context of Research	Illustrate interpretations, ideas, theory
Scholarly context	Create a vicarious experience
Content area	*Interpret*
Methodological area	Essences, themes, patterns, qualities,
Researcher's context	categories, motifs, bins, codes
Existential context	*Theorize*
Participant's context	Present theory
	Generate theory
Describe Method	Import theory
Establish trustworthiness	Evaluate theory
Make method publicly available	
Critique method	**Trace Evolution and Process of Study**
Establish inquiry as research	Evolution of focus
Facilitate evaluation of study	Evolution of method
	Development of conceptual elements
	Change in researcher
	Have Social Impact
	Indirectly through conveying findings
	Directly through embracing activist role

Summarize Areas of Inquiry

The first thing most readers want to know about a research study is what it is about. Qualitative reports are often not amenable to such a direct or single statement of purpose. Qualitative research is often oriented to gaining insight and understanding. Open and unpredictable environments, people, and experiences that have a multitude of constantly shifting variables are studied. The people, experiences, systems, and environments studied can be spontaneously generated ones, thus defying the type of researcher control that contributes to the articulation of tightly focused research questions.

Research Problems or Questions. The traditional way of labeling the focus of a research study is to talk about the research problem or the research question. Such terminology evolved both from the protocols for creating doctoral dissertations and proposals and as a convention imported from research in the physical and biological sciences. However, for many types of qualitative studies, conceiving of the focus as a problem or a question is not accurate. Many qualitative studies are multidimensional and are given to multiple interpretations of the significance of their descriptions and findings. Thus, to fix the meaning of a study as answering a specific problem or question is counter to the spirit in which much qualitative research is undertaken.

It is not unusual for the qualitative researcher to simultaneously work on data gathering, data analysis, interpretation, and theorizing, all the while making adjustments to the very focus of the study based on what is being learned through all of the other activities. Thus, the traditional notion of research as solving a structured sequence of problems does not apply to many qualitative research studies.

In addition, the idea of research as problem-centered or as providing a singular solution to a readily described problem is not an apt descriptor of many qualitative projects. The entire realm of human experience in music therapy is considered a legitimate focus for research, regardless of whether a particular problem can be articulated.

Some authors argue that a researcher really does not know what questions will be answered by the research until the research is over and the final report written. Because qualitative research involves discovering the unexpected, and because research focuses often evolve over the course of a given study, it is disingenuous to articulate a set of questions as motivating a study when they were not actually present at its origins.

None of this is to say, in cases where a researcher begins a study with a set of unambiguous questions and the research activities do not alter these questions substantially, that it is not appropriate to articulate these questions at the start of the study. The point is that this is not a required part of a qualitative research report.

General Topic/Focus. Qualitative researchers do present the overall focus of their writings in ways that are characteristic of any good piece of writing. Providing a conceptual overview allows the reader to establish internal lines of thought into which the material presented can be aggregated. When the reader can develop an internal schema that parallels that of the publication, it becomes easier to absorb the material and be influenced by it. It is also important to articulate the different purposes behind the study as they each establish different contexts for understanding the research. Articulating these various contexts is an essential aspect of a qualitative research report, and there are significant differences from quantitative research in this area.

Present Context of Research

Qualitative researchers often recognize that meaning depends on context and is not an objective property perceived universally. Qualitative researchers consider a variety of contexts of meaning in their research reports.

Scholarly Context. An important characteristic of scholarly research is that it occurs within a particular tradition or area of inquiry. The more conventional qualitative reports establish this scholarly context through a discussion of related literature, thus identifying unresolved questions that the researcher hopes to answer. Establishing the context of research through this exploration of the related literature is so important that it is usually the first topic addressed and no study is considered to be fully legitimate without this supportive framework.

As is illustrated in Tables 1 and 2, qualitative research studies do not exist within a single context but are located at a variety of intersecting ones. Because qualitative studies can have many legitimate sources and contexts, aspects other than related literature and supportive theory are used to locate them in a scholarly context. Since it does not have to contain the rationale for the study, related literature can be brought in at places in the report when relevant to the content.

Also, because research findings can and should be unforeseen, the researcher can often locate related literature after much of the data analysis has been completed. Used in this way, the literature functions not to legitimize the initial focus but to provide theoretical, conceptual, and practical contexts in which to place the findings. And a more fluid and better integrated publication can result when "theoretical elements. . . [are] woven in a more organic way in the overall fabric of the discussion" (Ely, Vinz, Downing, & Anzul, 1997, p. 232).

For a variety of reasons, discussions of method are more essential in qualitative research than in quantitative research. These discussions are different from the description of method that will be taken up in the next section of the present chapter, and they concern how the method for a given study is arrived at, the origins of its elements, and how it impinges upon the research findings.

Most qualitative research methods were developed outside of music therapy and were created to examine fundamentally different kinds of phenomena (and for different purposes) from those investigated by music therapists. Moreover, some approaches, such as phenomenology, originated in philosophy and have given rise to quite different methods that go by the same label. By discussing its originating context, authors give readers information useful in assessing the appropriateness of the method used and determining if the conceptual and philosophical roots of the method are consistent with the conceptual underpinnings of the study.

Additionally, many researchers use an eclectic approach as they construct individualized methods suited to specific inquiries. This is appropriate in a discipline that incorporates musical, psychological, and social processes that must be studied in unique combinations. Providing the originating elements of a method, along with other studies that have used its elements successfully, assists readers in judging the appropriateness of the method while also providing some insight into the aspects of the phenomena that the method will bring to light and those that it may not be suited to illuminating.

Researcher's Context. Many qualitative researchers choose to discuss the personal source of a study, thus establishing another context in which to understand it. This is done to varying degrees and with different purposes within different qualitative traditions. Placing the origins of a study within the researcher's personal experiences and interests is part of the broader methodological stance of contextualizing the entire study, including the findings, as the result of a particular individual with a specific life history.

In general, information about the researcher is offered because of a fundamental epistemological belief that knowledge results from an interaction between the knower and the known. Qualitative approaches typically operate under the assumption that inquiry is value bound, necessitating the public disclosure of elements of the researcher's value system that may have a bearing on the research. In some forms of qualitative research, it is the researcher's self that is the primary instrument of data collection, analysis, and interpretation. It thus makes sense that the characteristics of this self must be articulated in order for the reader to know the idiosyncratic factors bearing on a particular inquiry.

In the various qualitative research approaches, different labels are used and different uses for this information are emphasized. Naturalistic inquiry refers to the *stance of the researcher;* in phenomenology, this is called an *epoché;* in hermeneutic research, one offers a *self hermeneutic;* and, although it lacks a simple term to describe the procedure, all heuristic inquiry originates in concerns "strongly connected to one's own identity and selfhood" (Moustakas, 1990, p. 40). These elements of the researcher's biography can be reported in a specific section with one of the headings noted above, or they may be subsumed into an introduction, general discussion of method, or methodological appendix.

What the researcher chooses to report in this area is influenced by the scope and focus of the study as well as by the precepts of the particular research approach. These elements include a variety of personal characteristics: (a) the researcher's motivation for conducting the study; (b) prior experiences and beliefs which have shaped the area of inquiry and which influence data collection and analysis; (c) the researcher's group memberships, including gender, ethnicity, socioeconomic status, position of employment, and so forth, offered so that the political and social forces that may have been active in the study can be considered openly; (d) possible biases, blind spots, or personal difficulties that may distort the findings or render them incomplete; (e) the nature of the relationship between the investigator and the research participants; (f) intuitions and expectations about what the findings may be prior to beginning the study; and (g) ways in which the researcher was changed by the process of research.

Presenting this information is important for a few reasons: First, it helps the researcher by forcing a level of self-reflection needed to ensure the integrity of the research document. When one is aware of preconceptions, expectations, and prejudices, it is possible to take steps to minimize their influence. Second, being forthcoming about one's motivation as a researcher helps the reader by providing additional information with which to assess a research document. The reader has the right to know whether the researcher is a disinterested observer or has a vested interest in a particular outcome. Third, providing the personal context from which the focus of a particular study emerges may engage readers and help to involve them more deeply in the research report.

Existential Context. In disciplines where qualitative research methods have a longer history than in music therapy, such as education or sociology, the range of legitimate research topics has expanded in scope. There is a trend to regard all aspects of human activity and experience as worthy of systematic inquiry, whether or not such inquiry can be closely connected to a problem-centered line of investigation.

As one way of ensuring the value and relevance of research reports, it is legitimate in qualitative research to formulate research topics based on their value in addressing questions of inherent human interest. In their seminal article applying a phenomenological method to music therapy, Forinash and Gonzalez (1989) analyzed the experience of a music therapist working in a hospice whose client died during the session being studied. In this instance there was no need to justify the inquiry based on anything extrinsic to the study other than the desire to find a way to describe music therapy processes without distorting their essence. The authors rightly assumed that the human encounter with death is of such inherent meaning to human beings that any inquiry into its nature is self-justifying.

Participant's Context. Because there is often a great degree of equality and mutuality between researchers and participants in qualitative research, the context provided by the participants themselves is often included in the research report. In contrast to the researcher's context, the information relevant to the participants' contexts is subsumed into other areas of a report. There are a few ways in which the considerations originating in participants' concerns come into play.

One is through the presence of participant profiles. These are descriptions of research participants that provide information that goes beyond the narrow parameters of the research focus. The phenomena and processes investigated by music therapists through qualitative methods should always be contextualized within the lives of the particular people who participate in the study, because what is learned about the object of study is influenced by who those people are.

Another way that the phenomenon being researched is connected to research participants is through procedures that involve the participants reacting to and assessing the accuracy of the researcher's descriptions and interpretations. Sometimes these processes can have a significant impact on a study and alter its fundamental assumptions and focus. Because the research focus evolves throughout the course of a qualitative study, this participant information can influence the way the focus is described in the final research report.

The idea of collaborative inquiry[5] takes participant involvement one step further. In this research model, research participants are involved at all levels of a research project, from initial formulation of the topic, through selection of method, data gathering and analysis, and putting the findings into a reporting form. The key here is that research participants help select the focus of the study; it therefore must be contextualized within the concerns that are important to them.

Describe Method

There are important reasons to describe method in qualitative research. Some of these will be detailed below.

Establish Trustworthiness. The concept of *trustworthiness* originates in naturalistic inquiry (Lincoln & Guba, 1985). It was put forth as an alternative to the traditional notions of validity, reliability, and objectivity, which the authors felt were inappropriate criteria to apply to their form of inquiry, given its philosophical foundations. Because it is formulated in quite general terms, it can stand in as a criterion relevant for many qualitative approaches in the present discussion. Very simply, trustworthiness criteria are addressed to the following question: "How can an inquirer persuade his or her audiences (including self) that the findings of an inquiry are worth paying attention to, worth taking account of?" (Lincoln & Guba, p. 290).

In qualitative research, method is neither a guarantor nor an arbiter of truth. In other words, faithfully following a recognized method will not necessarily lead to significant, interesting, or novel findings. It is then up to the researcher to persuade the reader that the findings faithfully represent the phenomena under study. By describing their method in detail, researchers attempt to convince readers that their method allowed for insight and interpretation and that the researcher enacted the method with the open-mindedness, thoroughness, and attention to detail that characterizes good scholarly inquiry.

Make Method Publicly Available. One of the biggest challenges facing qualitative researchers is the choice of appropriate method, whether this is a specific one or an eclectically constructed one. Part of the reason for this is that many qualitative methods were formulated within other academic disciplines and must be altered when applied outside the discipline. Music therapy studies often involve looking at a unique constellation of products, processes, people, and phenomena and require specially tailored research methods.

Qualitative research has only been applied in music therapy since the late 1980s, and it is just beginning to establish a foothold in the profession. Music therapists are only now generating a sufficient number of qualitative studies for researchers to be able to choose from a variety of methodological designs and approaches that have actually been used in music therapy

---

[5] Collaborative inquiry is discussed as part of Chapter 32, Participatory Action Research.

studies. By describing method in detail, researchers provide a foundation for other researchers who may wish to use the same design.

Critique Method. Be cause qualitative methods are still relatively new in music therapy, two levels of analysis are relevant in critiquing method. The first is specific to the study in which it was used; the second relates more globally to methodological analyses that will advance the overall conduct of qualitative research in music therapy.

In the first area, one of the problems with qualitative research in music therapy is that researchers learn a particular approach and apply that approach without a strong enough consideration of its suitability for the topic and focus of a particular study. It is essential to match the philosophical and methodological foundations of a given approach with the area of study. For example, phenomenology is oriented towards distilling the essences of experience and thus may not be suitable for studying group therapy processes that incorporate multiple perspectives on events. And grounded theory was developed to study social processes and is probably less than suitable for analyzing notations of musical improvisations. Describing the underlying conceptual foundation and the specific activities of the method used is essential in helping readers determine for themselves the suitability of the design. This, in turn, helps them to evaluate the value of the research findings.

In the second area, it is only now that there are beginning to be enough qualitative music therapy studies to enable us to begin the methodological task of assessing the value of different types of methods for different types of investigations. It is only by providing detailed descriptions of method that they can be used and evaluated by other researchers. Thus, the detailed recounting of method provides an important function for the communal development of qualitative methods in music therapy that goes beyond their value for the study in which the method was used.

Establish Inquiry as Research. What earns an inquiry the designation of *research*? The answer to this question for qualitative research is not always clear. Is qualitative research a form of scientific inquiry or is it a form of scholarly inquiry similar to that characterizing the humanities? And, closer to home for most music therapists, what is it, for example, that actually distinguishes a clinical case study from a research case study?

While a consideration of these questions is beyond the scope of the present chapter, suffice it to say that including a description of the research method within a qualitative research publication is one of the most important considerations in influencing whether or not a particular publication is considered to be an example of research.

The amount of detail required for the description of method varies according to type of publication, with more detail generally being required for theses, dissertations, and journal articles. Authors for other types of publications tend to have more latitude in determining how the method should be presented. These authors can describe the method in as much or as little detail as suits their needs and may place this description at a point in the publication that reflects the importance they want the reader to place on it.

Facilitate Evaluation of Study. Some of the previously mentioned functions contribute to the evaluation of the study in a general sense. Yet, determining appropriate criteria for evaluation is a very thorny issue in qualitative research, where the research topic rules.[6] Method is subservient to content rather than dictating content.

Because they are built on different philosophical foundations, and because they make different kinds of knowledge claims, qualitative methods have different evaluation standards from quantitative research. And within the family of qualitative research methods there are also differences significant enough to preclude the development of universal evaluation criteria. Compounding the difficulty is that many researchers draw from more than one research approach in designing their studies. In these cases of eclectic design, it is even more difficult to determine appropriate evaluation standards.

Nevertheless, if qualitative researchers want their work to be considered a form of serious scholarship, or even scientific in nature, it is essential that readers are provided with tools to assess the value of their findings. In some types of qualitative research, methodologists have taken pains to specify evaluation criteria appropriate for their methods; in other types, standards must be inferred from the nature of the knowledge claims made. A detailed explication

---

[6] See Chapter 20, Evaluating Qualitative Music Therapy Research, for more extensive discussion of the evaluation of qualitative research.

of method allows readers to evaluate the research document using whatever standards are available.

Convey Findings

The single most important function of a research report is to communicate findings in three primary areas: (a) describing people, their experiences, social settings, music, and therapy processes; (b) interpreting described elements into essences, themes, patterns, qualities, or categories; and (c) theorizing through presenting, generating, and evaluating theory.

The three activities of describing, interpreting, and theorizing are not as formally or procedurally distinct as might be assumed. Philosophers of science have long agreed that there is no such thing as theory-neutral observation. Consider the activities of a researcher observing a music therapy group and describing the events in a written log. The researcher will not be able to record everything that happens, so there is a constant selection process over what represents significant events. Every decision to ignore an event or include it in the description reflects some conceptual or theoretical commitment on the researcher's part. In labeling a particular finding as descriptive, interpretive, or theoretical, it should be kept in mind that these are relative rather than absolute judgments.

Describe. Far from being a mere tool for developing concepts and theories, description in qualitative research reports can be an end in and of itself. While some researchers and scholars will not consider a research study to be complete without significant theory attached to it, others recognize that, for certain topics, careful, sensitive, thorough, and nuanced description can be a valuable research result, regardless of whether it is contextualized within a theoretical framework. This is particularly true when the research is grounded within an existential context of inherent human interest, when the milieu being described is not well known or has not been previously researched, or when the primary goal of the research is to create a vicarious experience in the reader.

Description has at least four primary functions in a qualitative research report: to establish the research setting; to report data; to illustrate and support interpretations, ideas, and theory; and to create a vicarious experience in the reader. These functions are implemented through multiple levels, multiple perspectives, critical incidents, thick description, and visual displays.

Establish research setting: In establishing the setting, the writer creates a context in which the data, interpretations, and theory can be understood. If one studies a particular model of therapy, a particular type of intervention, or clinical work with a particular client group, for example, it is done within a particular local context inhabited by real people with their customs, predilections, and values. Description of the research setting is integral to those qualitative approaches that emphasize the local nature of all knowledge and the idea that knowledge acquisition is an interactive process. Generalization is enabled by this description of the research setting, as readers are able to determine how similar it is to contexts into which they may wish to apply the findings.

Report data: By definition, data in qualitative research are nonnumerical, and, although this does not mean that data are always in the form of words, in practice verbal information is the most typical form of data. Common forms of qualitative data include interview transcripts, archival manuscripts, the responses of a research panel to information presented by the researcher, clinical session notes compiled by a therapist participating in a research project, and observation logs created by the therapist. These are all different forms of descriptive data because they represent relatively uninterpreted materials.

Illustrate interpretations, ideas, theory: These descriptive materials play a crucial role in illustrating and lending credibility to all aspects of the researcher's analysis, from interpretive statements of a relatively restricted scope to broadly formulated theories. Readers need to be persuaded of the value and accuracy of the conclusions of the research, and descriptive materials are the evidence upon which the researcher's interpretive and theoretical statements depend. Well-chosen and well-written descriptions support the researcher's conclusions and provide an important link in the chain of evidence for readers for whom assessing this is important.

Create a vicarious experience: The final function of description is to create a vicarious experience in the reader. The qualitative researcher wants the reader to know that the researcher has *been there* and wants the reader to have the experience of having been there as well. There are two primary reasons for this: First, the more deeply involved in a text a reader becomes, the greater the likelihood that the text will have a significant impact on the reader. Second, some researchers believe that readers should be in a position to construct their own meanings from a qualitative research document. Thus, a text with ample description and multiple types of description can support the reader's main task of constructing a personalized meaning from the text.

Qualitative research reports often make use of the technique of *layering*. This is the blending of different voices, stances, epistemological positions, presentational devices, and sources of information to create a more complete portrait of a phenomenon or milieu of study. Multiple perspectives are offered in a number of ways: gaining input from research panels; incorporating research participants' points of view; including information from clients, their families, and other health professionals; and having a research team contribute to a publication. Multiple levels of perception and knowing are offered through combining different sources of information, such as objective observations, intuitive understandings, affective reactions, musical forms of knowledge, images, and body reactions. Multiple layers and sources of description lead to the multilayered understandings that characterize the important criterion of thick description often applied to qualitative research reports. Drawing information from a multitude of sources maintains the interest of readers while also facilitating their ability to apply the information they glean from research reports.

Graphic devices such as graphs, tables, figures, and diagrams perform an essential function in qualitative research reports that are so heavily dependent on words. Researchers who write about writing frequently observe that, in qualitative research, limiting words is a bigger challenge than generating them. As Ely et al. (1997) attest,

> even as winnowing out is necessary, so at times are strategies that help us "crowd more in." Within a research paradigm that relies so heavily on words, displays can often reduce a great deal of data and make them more readily graspable and memorable. (p. 194)

Displays of various types make a complex process or body of knowledge more intelligible and more easily assimilated. Iconic or diagrammatic representations operate by increasing understanding through providing a metaphoric representation of process. There are many examples of these types of devices in the qualitative research literature, often illustrating a variety of processes in music therapy practice.

Charts and tables organize information for presentation. A good table is more than a summary device because conceptual relationships can be revealed that may not otherwise be obvious and questions can be answered in an immediate fashion. Conveying the findings in this way allows for many types of analysis and allows readers to ask their own questions of the data, some of which may not have even been considered by the author.

Interpret. Many qualitative research approaches have their own terms for describing their basic units of interpretation or inference. Some common ones are *essence, theme, pattern, quality, code, motif, bin,* and *category*. The primary function of these units of conceptualization is to elevate the discourse of a report from the descriptive level to the interpretive level. So, for example, phenomenological approaches can provide a set of essences as the culmination of a research study, and naturalistic inquiry projects may summarize findings through a set of themes.

However, one of the most crucial decisions that an author of a qualitative report has to make is the disposition of these devices. At times, they function as organizational and conceptual tools for the researcher in analyzing data and need not appear in the final report. At other times, they represent important findings and should be prominent parts of the final report. A third option is that they appear in the final report, but are integrated into a discursive narrative presentation rather than being labeled as important themes or categories. The thoughts of Ely et al. (1997) on this matter show how themes can be illustrated, exemplified, and tacitly expressed rather than explicitly stated:

> Some researchers have found numerous ways to present and illustrate their themes, some that do not involve directly writing theme statements. We think of a powerful novel—*War and Peace* for example. Surely its themes are evident,

yet Tolstoy did not write them out for us. Whether and how thematic statements will be effective in the final document is a decision each researcher must make. (p. 210)

In addition to delineating findings directly through themes or essences, qualitative researchers use a variety of narrative devices typical of dramatic writing, such as constructs, poems, plays, and stories. This reflects a change in academia in the status of such literary tools. Increasing numbers of people are recognizing that narrative represents an eminently human form of conveying and assimilating information. The use of these devices has a number of functions: to embody findings through dialogue rather than explaining them; to express the poetic truth of an area of study or human experience; to make a particular milieu come alive; and to present information and knowledge through forms that will enhance their applicability.

The content of these literary writing forms represents extensive analysis and interpretation on the part of the researcher, even though it is presented in a descriptive guise. The different poems, plays, stories, and constructs represent composite portraits of the milieu and people participating in the research project. The value of the portrait is directly related to the degree in which it represents the important themes and essences revealed through the analysis of data. And awareness of these central themes comes about only through the interpretive skills of the researcher.

None of these literary devices should be employed in a research report in an automatic or casual manner. These devices are not ends in and of themselves, and those devices should be deliberately chosen that best convey the central findings of a given study.

Discovering how and what to write is a problem to be solved through the research activities. Because one is discovering meanings through the research, articulating the appropriate forms and content of the writing cannot be done in advance. In fact, if one is drawn to particular narrative forms, this can be used in a retroductive way to gain insight into the nature of one's findings. That is, if one is drawn to include a poem in a research report, then that suggests that some of the important findings have poetic qualities that can best be conveyed through that form.

Theorize. While some qualitative research is conducted within a theoretical context, theory does not always have a privileged place in qualitative research. The reasons for this vary in being epistemological, methodological, and even political in origin. Some qualitative research methods are built on philosophies whose view of knowledge acquisition requires the suspending of previously-held beliefs and preconceptions. The idea is to gather observational and experiential data in as pure a form as is possible, uncolored by a complex belief system, as is embodied in a theory. Other methods stress this type of more pure perception but do so not because of a particular epistemological stance but because of a methodological belief that one can gather better data this way, data that lend themselves to a more detailed and comprehensive understanding of a particular milieu. And last, some researchers see the purpose of their work as primarily conveying the meanings and experiences of the people they study without overlaying this experience with theory. This can lead to a reluctance to interpret and analyze the behavior and experience of research participants through theory.

When theory is written about in a qualitative research study, it can be in the form of presenting and elaborating existing theory, generating theory, importing existing theory, or less commonly, evaluating theory.

Present theory: When the primary purpose of report is to present and elaborate upon existing theory, the theory is usually presented early in the document. The study is designed with this purpose in mind, and data are analyzed according to the concepts constituting the theory. This type of report is normally structured in one of two ways: either in a procedural way according to the steps of the research, or in a conceptual way that is patterned after the structure of the theory.

Generate theory: Some qualitative research approaches, such as grounded theory, do place a high value on theory but assert that theory should be developed from research activities rather than imported from other sources. It is believed that theory generated in this way will be more applicable to the domain of study, and the purpose of the research is to create theory. Authors have three primary options in terms of where to place such grounded theory. First, if the primary purpose of the report is to present and support the theory, it is possible to place it at the outset of the report. This can be helpful to the author in suggesting a structure for the report and to the reader who will have a conceptual template in mind in reading the report. Second, the author can present the theory incrementally. This can be done either because it can best be conveyed in this way, or because there is a desire for the reader to recapitulate the researcher's process in gradually forming the theory. And last, the theory can be presented as one of the final elements of the report. This is a preferred option when the descriptive elements of the report are of such value that the author does not want to obscure the reader's experiencing of them by intruding upon their presentation with the more abstract form of understanding embodied in theory.

Import theory: In some studies, researchers neither begin with a pre-existing theory nor create a new one, but instead discover an already existing theory, either as the study proceeds or after the major data gathering and analysis have been concluded, and then apply this theory in a new context. Because theory discovered in this way will usually be more limited in applicability to the study than theory that serves as the source of the study or theory generated from a study, it is generally not presented at the outset of a report. To do so would probably create an inaccurate impression of the effect of the theory on the research activities. There are two options here that are chosen based on the author's intent. If the theory was discovered after the majority of the data gathering and analysis has been concluded and did not affect these activities significantly, it may be appropriate to place such theory near the end of a report. The other choice is for the theory to "be woven in a more organic way in the overall fabric of the discussion" (Ely et al., 1997, p. 232). This option is preferable when the author wants to help illuminate the meaning of the descriptive elements as they are presented, or if the theory is a relatively complex one that would be more easily presented in conjunction with the data that support it.

Evaluate theory: In studies oriented toward evaluating theory, it is obvious that the theory should be presented at the outset of the report. The theory is known before the research begins, and it serves as the rationale for the study.

Trace Evolution and Process of Study

To repeat an oft recurring theme in the present chapter, while some qualitative research studies have a specific focus, detailed method, and predetermined conceptual context that does not change from initial conceptualization through compiling the final report, it is more common that one or more of these elements changes as a study is enacted and written up. It is often expected that these types of changes will be discussed in the final report.

Evolution of Focus. Although the focus of a research study can change, it is not always necessary to write about it. Changes that reflect a developing or refining of interest on the researcher's part may not need to be shared with readers. However, when changes reflect discoveries or insights made by the researcher that bear on the substance of study, it can be useful for readers to have this information. It helps them to understand the rationale for the particular focus, thus providing an important context for the study. Another reason to write about the change in focus is that it contributes to establishing the trustworthiness of the research findings. When a researcher comes in to a study with a particular focus and empirical discoveries lead to a change in the focus, this attests to the open-mindedness of the researcher in assimilating information that does not conform to prior expectations over the salient elements of a study.

Evolution of Method. Certain qualitative research projects employ predetermined research protocols and others allow the researcher to develop the method as the study proceeds. Many of the preceding comments regarding the evolution of focus apply to the evolution of method as well. In those approaches that sanction design changes, it is generally important to write about them for two reasons: First, it is important to be forthcoming about method as readers have the right to know which elements of a design were specified in advance and which ones were added and why. Second, when investigators write about the considerations that lead them to make such changes, it can by very helpful for other researchers who encounter similar challenges in their own research.

Development of Conceptual Elements. The conceptual elements of a study range in scope from specific categories or themes relevant to small portions of data to broadly formulated theories. And much like the focus and method, these elements can undergo broad changes over the course of a study. Often, data analysis involves the progressive elucidation and refinement of conceptual categories. Typically, when an author believes that it is important to demonstrate how the analysis proceeded—such as for studies performed to earn academic degrees and in articles submitted to refereed journals—it can be important to illustrate this analysis through detailing how the basic units of analysis and interpretation evolved. Also, when the categories represent important findings, rather than just being tools of data analysis, writing about the way they developed can provide substantive insights in a research report. When the change is primarily relevant to the substance of the ideas presented, the discussion should be in a prominent place. When the evolution of conceptual elements is written about primarily to illustrate data analysis or to address questions of trustworthiness, it can be placed in an appendix or other methodologically focused section of a report.

Change in Researcher. The last item to be discussed in this section is specific to qualitative research. This is the way that the research changed the researcher. Just as some forms of psychotherapy emphasize that the therapist is changed by therapeutic encounter, in some forms of qualitative research it is acknowledged that the researcher can undergo important changes as well. At times these changes come about because the research topic has great personal meaning for the researcher. Sometimes the researcher develops open and trusting relationships with research participants who share profound aspects of their experience and these relationships can have significant impact on the researcher.

As the activity and challenges of writing qualitative research have a profound impact on the researcher, the "deepened understanding of a Self deepens a text" (Richardson, cited in Ely et al., 1997, p. 329). Ely et al. also discuss how qualitative research writing enhances the researcher's self-awareness and has the power to change them in profound ways.

> Through the process of writing. . . qualitative researchers developed a heightened sensitivity to their language and what their words disclosed of their biases, assumptions, glib categorizations of people and situations. Having set aside labels—poor people, prisoners, AIDS victims, Alzheimer patient, autistic child—to pursue the understanding of real people and their life experience, qualitative researchers report that they have come to question facile classifications, simplistic phrases, and premature generalizations, their own and other people's. (Ely et al., 1997, p. 371)

When do personal insights that have been gained through the research bear public reporting? Although this is really a matter of personal choice, it is possible to offer some guidelines here. First, when writing about the researcher's personal changes helps to illuminate the focus of the research in a unique way it is certainly a legitimate part of a research report. Second, when the changes in the researcher have a level of inherent human interest, this can be valuable and compelling information to provide to readers, regardless of whether or not the personal changes directly address some aspect of the research focus. And last, many qualitative researchers acknowledge how difficult, challenging, and rewarding their work can be. Detailing some of these personal encounters can provide a valuable service to other researchers who may gain encouragement from the personal difficulties and challenges engaged in by published researchers.

Have Social Impact

There are two primary ways in which research publications have social impact: indirectly through conveying findings that challenge convention and directly as when the researcher overtly embraces an activist role. In addition there are (at least) two spheres of influence in which social impact occurs: the professional, scholarly realm and the communities to which research participants belong.

Indirectly Through Conveying Findings. Politically aware researchers acknowledge that writing defines a domain as it determines whose voices speak and what those voices say. To write is to be engaged politically, socially, morally, and ethically. Every kind of writing represents a choice of who and what to include and exclude. Every piece of writing has political and social consequences. Every act of writing involves bowing to some authority, some notion of what is right, what is appropriate, and thus serves to validate that authority and its message.

Directly Through Embracing Activist Role. Qualitative researchers working in more progressive models endeavor to have their research participants speak directly to the reader, unmediated by interpretive frameworks. This alone can have social impact as it brings the thoughts, feelings, and perspectives of those studied to professional audiences often charged with acting in the best interests of those participating in research.

This consideration is directly relevant for educators, anthropologists, and sociologists who traditionally have studied marginalized members of society. Some researchers now argue that it is not ethical to merely study these people for the researcher's own ends, but instead the activity, focus, and final write-up of the research must benefit those studied in some direct or tangible way in order to be valid and ethical research. Certain trends in music therapy that are congruent with these values are emerging. The effort to have clients speak directly in public presentations and publications is oriented to giving them a voice in the professional discourse. And the effort of many qualitative researchers to create research that originates in the concerns of practicing clinicians and that is relevant to their work is motivated by similar concerns.

The writing of qualitative research reports has had a profound impact on the nature of scholarly exchange as it challenges many of its traditional conventions. These traditional conventions, once seen as necessary components of scholarly writing, are now recognized as vehicles to reinforce the hegemony of particular worldviews, ideologies, and theoretical frameworks. All research reports utilize particular rhetorical and narrative devices to make their points. What differentiates the authors of qualitative research from quantitative research is not the use of such devices, but the acknowledgment that such devices are being used consciously and deliberately.

Paul Atkinson (1990) has noted that even the impersonal writing voice of the traditional experimental report in which the first person voice is completely absent is itself a rhetorical device. The impersonal voice of this writing suggests that the knowledge claims have greater authority because they are not the product of a fallible human being, an imperfect "I," but instead are the pronouncements of an impersonal, faceless authority. Atkinson's main point is that all publications utilize narrative strategies to make their arguments and influence the understanding of the realities they represent and he argues that all writing reflects epistemological biases. As an example, he cites Bazerman's (1987) analysis of the *APA Publication Manual* in which

> he shows how a set of behaviourist assumptions have become increasingly taken for granted and inscribed in the required formats of APA style. . . . The APA style. . . is one of the restricted range of acceptable styles that place constraints—in some cases quite severe—on what is to count as a well-formed scholarly representation. (p. 50)

Different scholarly conventions affect and control content. They are a way of enforcing certain views because competing ideas that require alternate formats for expression are not publishable within the conventions of dominant scholarly, academic traditions. Richardson (1994) takes up this point and addresses how discouraging the use of footnotes reinforces the idea of legitimate scholarly inquiry as linear and problem focused, a conception discussed previously in the present chapter:

> How we are expected to write affects what we can write about. The referencing system in the social sciences, for example, discourages the use of footnotes, a place for secondary arguments, novel conjectures, and related ideas. Knowledge is constituted as "focused," "problem" (hypothesis) centered, "linear," straightforward. Other thoughts are extraneous. Inductively accomplished research is to be reported deductively; the argument is to be abstracted in 150 words or less. . . . Each of these conventions favors . . . a particular vision of what constitutes sociological knowledge. (p. 520)

Ely et al. (1997) concur that discouraging the use of footnotes inhibits complex theoretical discussions that are the hallmark of scholarly inquiry. They go on to observe why the very subject matter of qualitative research entails changes not just in academic writing but in what is considered to be legitimate areas of academic inquiry:

Qualitative research writing . . . emphasizes subjectivities as an integral part of the research process. It follows that totally cool, distanced and distancing research writing would be alien to what qualitative research is all about. It is our task to write in order to communicate people's emotions, their life cycles, and how researchers face what they learn about themselves and others in the process of the research. This is not to say that qualitative research writing focuses solely on emotions. Indeed, useful products present data and interpretations through a variety of lenses—from the very intimate to the very abstract. It is the inclusion of the personal and emotional that is sometimes difficult in the world of academia where emotional and intuitional aspects of research have long been denied, suppressed and considered suspect if not unworthy. (p. 53)

Closing Words

A common theme among writers who discuss qualitative research writing is that reading qualitative reports should be more than just an abstract process of gleaning information on the reader's part. Part of the meaning of qualitative research findings lies in the experience of the researcher and research participants and it is important for readers to have this experience in a vicarious way, not just read about it. The purpose of a qualitative text is to engage the reader in the text much in the way the researcher was engaged in the area of study. Providing the vicarious experience allows the reader to engage in the same cognitive strategies of making judgments and coming to understandings that the researcher did. This is what is ultimately convincing to the reader and what allows the reader to internalize the findings of the report and relate them directly to his or her own life.

The "authenticity" of the text is thus provided not by the "scientific" canons of evidence, but by the active involvement of the reader in the construction of the text. . . . In this way, the ethnographic text parallels the forms of life it reports. . . . The ethnographer's understanding is warranted not by accumulation of "facts", but through his or her active involvement in an interpretation of the social world. Likewise, therefore, the reader's understanding of the social world is to be furnished by his or her active involvement with the text and deployment of interpretive strategies of everyday life. (Atkinson, 1990, p. 91)

Another common value is that qualitative research writing should be interesting, even compelling, reading. The individuals, groups, cultures, and institutions that qualitative researchers study are fascinating, multifaceted, complex entities. Qualitative reports should not just say that, but rather they must exemplify it. This integration of form and content is necessary because form and content are ultimately inseparable.

References

Aigen, K. (1997). *Here we are in music: One year with an adolescent creative music therapy group.* St. Louis, MO: MMB Music.

Aigen, K. (2002). *Playin' in the band: A qualitative study of popular music styles as clinical improvisation.* New York: Nordoff-Robbins Center for Music Therapy, New York University.

Amir, D. (1993). Moments of insight in the music therapy experience. *Music Therapy, 12,* 85–100.

Atkinson, P. (1990). *The ethnographic imagination: Textual constructions of reality.* New York: Routledge.

Bazerman, C. (1987). Codifying the social scientific style: The APA *Publication Manual* as a behaviorist rhetoric. In J. S. Nelson, A. Megill, & D. N. McCloskey (Eds.), *The rhetoric of the human sciences* (pp. 125–144). Madison, WI: University of Wisconsin Press.

Bruscia, K. E. (1998). Modes of consciousness in Guided Imagery and Music: A therapist's experience of the guiding process. In K. E. Bruscia (Ed.), *The dynamics of music psychotherapy* (pp. 491–525). Gilsum, NH: Barcelona Publishers.

Ely, M., Vinz, R., Downing, M., & Anzul, M. (1997). *On writing qualitative research: Living by words.* Bristol, PA: The Falmer Press.

Forinash, M., & Gonzalez, D. (1989). A phenomenological perspective of music therapy. *Music Therapy, 8,* 35–46.

Kenny, C. B. (2002). Blue Wolf says goodbye for the last time. *American Behavioral Scientist, 45,* 1214–1222.

Lincoln, Y. S., & Guba, E. (1985). *Naturalistic inquiry.* Newbury Park, CA: Sage Publications.

Moustakas, C. (1990). *Heuristic research.* Newbury Park, CA: Sage Publications.

Richardson, L. (1994). Writing: A method of inquiry. In N. K. Denzin & Y. S. Lincoln (Eds.), *Handbook of qualitative research* (pp. 516–529). Thousand Oaks, CA: Sage Publications.

Wheeler, B. L. (2002). Experiences and concerns of students during music therapy practica. *Journal of Music Therapy, 39,* 274–304.

Wolcott, H. F. (1990). *Writing up qualitative research.* Newbury Park, CA: Sage Publications.

Additional Readings

Aigen, K. (2003). *A guide to writing and presenting in music therapy.* Gilsum, NH: Barcelona Publishers.

Ansdell, G., & Pavlicevic, M. (2001). *Beginning research in the arts therapies: A practical guide.* London: Jessica Kingsley Publishers.

Atkinson, P. (1992). *Understanding ethnographic texts.* Newbury Park, CA: Sage Publications.

Chapter 18
Ethical Precautions in Music Therapy Research
Cheryl Dileo

Ethical issues are now, more than ever, considered an essential part of the critical training of researchers (Kimmel, 1996). Ethical issues must be considered throughout the research process. Research ethics dictate subject recruitment and selection, treatment interventions and study implementation, research designs, measurement tools, data analysis, and research reporting (Gravetter & Forzano, 2003). The ethical obligations of researchers extend to the subjects of their studies as well as to the larger scientific community to whom they report (Gravetter & Forzano).

Researchers must comply with their respective professional codes of ethics (American Music Therapy Association, 2003; Canadian Music Therapy Association, 2005; Certification Board for Music Therapists, 2001) along with a growing number of federal and state regulations regarding the protection of human subjects in research. The purpose of this chapter is to familiarize readers with these requirements as they prepare to submit their research for institutional review board review. As the general scope of ethical issues in research and publication is much broader than the confines of this chapter, the reader is encouraged to review additional sources of information, such as *Ethical Thinking in Music Therapy* (Dileo, 2000).

If readers have never participated as subjects in research, they might begin thinking of how it might be to participate personally in a research study. What would be important to know about the research before agreeing to participate? What would be involved, and how long would it take? Would there be risks or inconvenience involved? What is the likelihood that there would be personal benefits? How would it feel to be deceived about the purpose of the study? How would one feel if assigned to a control instead of treatment condition? With whom would one's personal information be shared? Would it be possible to withdraw from the study if it did not feel right, and what would the consequences of withdrawal be? Would the monetary compensation for participating be too good to pass up? To whom would one go if discomfort, injury, or emotional distress were experienced? Personal sensitization to some of these issues may provide an important start to ethical thinking as a researcher (Dileo, 2000).

The Ethical Principles of Research

The following three principles are essential information for any person involved in human subjects research at any level and are set forth in the landmark *Belmont Report* (The National Commission for the Protection of Human Subjects of Biomedical and Behavioral Research, 1979): (a) *respect for persons* (respect for individual autonomy and protection for individuals with reduced autonomy); (b) *beneficence* (maximizing benefits and minimizing harm); and (c) *justice* (fairness in distribution of research burdens and benefits). The application of these principles in research necessitates the following research procedures: *informed consent, privacy,* and *confidentiality* (respect for persons); *risk/benefit analysis* and *evaluation of scientific merit* (beneficence); and *review of subject selection* (justice) (Hicks, 2003).

Laws Governing Research with Human Subjects

There are two primary sources for governmental regulations regarding the protection of human subjects. The first, the Federal Policy for the Protection of Human Subjects (Common Rule) (1991) covers research conducted, supported, or regulated by 16 federal agencies, including the Department of Education, the National Science Foundation, and the Department of Health and Human Services. Until 1991, these 16 departments and agencies used varying policies and procedures regarding human research. To provide uniformity, an overarching federal policy was thus implemented. The provisions of the Common Rule are identical to the second source, DHHS Regulations (45 CFR 46, Subpart A; Department of Health and Human Services, 2001). There are additional subparts of the DHHS regulations that detail additional protections for vulnerable populations (such as pregnant women, fetuses, neonates, prisoners, and children). Both sources of regulations require the monitoring of research by institutional review boards and the use of informed consent in research activities. Each of these topics is discussed below in more detail.

New legislation, the HIPAA Privacy Rule (U.S. Department of Health and Human Services, Protecting the Privacy of Patients' Health Information, 2003), will be discussed in more detail later in this chapter.

Institutional Review Board

The institutional review board (IRB) is a committee established to protect the rights and welfare of human research subjects involved in research activities conducted under the auspices of the institution within which it operates. Comprised of individuals with expertise in various fields and disciplines, the IRB is responsible for reviewing all research involving human subjects at a particular institution. For example, university IRBs typically review all student research, all faculty supported and unsupported research, all university-initiated research, and all staff research. The IRB has the authority to approve, disapprove, or require modifications in the research protocols it receives. No research may be implemented until IRB approval is received. Furthermore, the IRB continues to monitor approved research at regular intervals and has the authority to suspend or terminate previously approved research if its guidelines are not upheld or if unexpected harm to subjects occurs. There are three types of IRB review: (a) a full-IRB review, conducted by the regularly convened meeting of its full committee; (b) an expedited review, conducted by several committee members working independently; and (c) a continuing review of approved research. When a vulnerable population is included in a research protocol, often a full review is required.

The IRB has numerous responsibilities. These include: (a) to ascertain that informed consent is obtained and documented according to regulations; (b) to assure that all risks to subjects are minimized, and that risks are proportional to benefits; (c) to assure that subject selection is equitable; (d) to ascertain that subject confidentiality and privacy are protected; (e) to assure that adequate provisions are in place for monitoring safety; (f) to assure that, when other research sites or institutions are involved, appropriate authorization has been obtained; and (g) to require additional safeguards for the protection of vulnerable populations. Populations that may be considered vulnerable include: students, employees, the elderly, minorities, persons with cognitive impairment, traumatized or comatose patients, and people with terminal illnesses (Hicks, 2003).

Some research protocols may be considered exempt from IRB monitoring and approval; however, this decision is determined by the IRB and not by the individual conducting the research. Research that may qualify for IRB exemption may include: (a) that which is conducted in established educational settings involving normal educational practices; (b) that which involves educational tests (for example, cognitive, diagnostic, aptitude, achievement), survey procedures, interview procedures, or observations of public behavior; or (c) that which involves existing data or documents that are publicly available or data recorded by the investigator in a manner that human subjects cannot be directly identified or through identifiers linked to the subjects (Temple University, 2003).

Informed Consent

Adequate and appropriate informed consent is at the heart of an ethical research study and achieving this requires a thoughtful, careful, and thorough approach. Informed consent refers to the voluntary choice of a person to participate in a research study after having received full information regarding its purposes, procedures, risks, benefits, and any other factors that may influence his or her decision. There are many issues that can influence effective informed consent, and it is helpful if the researcher approaches informed consent as an educational process rather than as a single event or a standard form that simply needs to be signed. Informed consent is always obtained prospectively, that is, before a subject is enrolled in a study. Unless specifically waived by the IRB, all human research subjects must be afforded the opportunity to provide informed consent, and this consent must be documented in writing. Adequate and complete informed consent relies on: (a) the capacity of the individual to comprehend the information provided, (b) the freedom with which the individual makes the decision, and (c) the completeness of the information conveyed (Dileo-Maranto, 1995).

Capacity and Comprehension

An individual's capacity to consent may be compromised by age and by cognitive, physical, and/or emotional functioning (Dileo, 2000). Individuals under the age of 18 (or according to state law) are not legally eligible to provide informed consent, and a parent or guardian must provide consent for them. Adults who are considered incompetent, including those with severe developmental disabilities, who have cognitive impairments such as Alzheimer's disease, who are in comas, who are in extreme emotional distress, who have been traumatized, or who are inebriated are also incapable of providing true informed consent. Only legally authorized representatives of these individuals (according to state law) can provide consent. Decisions regarding a subject's capacity to consent must often be made on a case-by-case basis.

However, even when a person's capacity to provide true informed consent is diminished for the reasons stated above, the individual's *assent* should be obtained whenever possible. Assent procedures involve providing sufficient information about the study in language simple enough for the individual to understand (either verbally or in writing) and ascertaining the willingness of the subject to participate (either verbally or in writing). In cases where subject assent as well as parent or guardian consent are solicited, it is advisable to stipulate in both documents that approval from both individuals is required, that is, if one person refuses assent or consent, the subject will not be eligible to participate. Thus, participation in research is a shared decision of both parties.

In situations where potential subjects have limited fluency in English, informed consent documents must be translated into the individual's native language, and both versions of the consent form must be submitted to the IRB.

The researcher has the sole responsibility of assuring that subjects can comprehend all information provided them. The information in the consent form should be explained to subjects verbally using lay terminology, as well as provided in written form. In other words, the written consent document should serve as a script for the verbal explanation of the study to the subject, while also being as brief as possible. The language used in the consent form must be nontechnical and simple; usually, consent forms geared to a sixth grade reading level are satisfactory. The visual appearance and format of the consent form should also be accessible; for instance, subheadings may be used to organize content, sufficient margins and white space on the page will aid readability, and larger print will help those with visual difficulties.

Assuring that subjects comprehend the information may be difficult to achieve in actual practice. For example, the majority of potential subjects in music therapy research may not be well informed about what research entails and may confuse it with clinical practice, especially when it is the researcher who provides both. Cultural differences and anxiety levels of subjects, among other things, may interfere with the amount of information an individual may be able to take in at any given time. Therefore, the researcher must develop good skills in communicating this information, including establishing eye contact, active listening, empathy, appropriate tone of voice, and professional demeanor (Beach, 1996; Dileo, 2000). The verbal information regarding the research should be provided to subjects as many times as they require, and the researcher should allow sufficient time to answer any and all questions from the subject. It may be helpful to ask subjects to explain the study in their own words so that the researcher may assess their level of comprehension (Sales & Folkman, 2000).

Voluntariness

Researchers must provide subjects with the opportunity to decide about their participation based on their own free will; an adequate amount of time should be allowed for subjects to make this decision. Researchers may also encourage subjects to ask the advice of others (Sales & Folkman, 2000). Furthermore, all subjects in research studies must have the freedom to withdraw their consent to participate at any time during the study without consequence.

Several factors may compromise a subject's free choice. Besides impaired capacity or age, issues involving the researcher's power may exert undue influence upon a subject's decision. For example, the potential subject may be intimidated by the researcher's education, status, knowledge, or job title and, because of this, be reticent to refuse participation. Individuals who are receiving treatment at a facility may fear that a decision not to participate may incur recrimination from persons at the facility and may compromise the quality of services they are receiving. Power issues are exacerbated by the existence of dual relationships between subject and researcher. For example, if the researcher is also the client's music therapist, this factor may unduly influence the subject to participate in the study. In a similar manner, university students who are recruited to participate in a research study by their course professor may feel compelled to volunteer because of fears of their grades being affected if they refuse. Friends, family members, or employees of researchers may experience similar feelings of being required to participate in research studies to help. In all of these situations, the subject is not able to make a free choice to participate or to be a true volunteer.

Coercion of potential research subjects can be both obvious and subtle (Dileo, 2000). Excessive financial or other incentives to participate (such as grades) are considered coercive and may constitute "an offer they can't refuse" because of financial or other types of neediness (Dileo, p. 177). On the other hand, it is not unethical to offer subjects a reasonable compensation for their time or reimbursement for their travel expenses to the research site. Material incentives, such as CDs, tee shirts, free meal coupons, and so forth, are also acceptable if they are not excessive. Financial or material compensation for participation should be given to subjects for various tasks of the research and should be proportional to the amount of time and energy invested. For example researchers may pay a subject $5 for participation in a pretest and $5 for participation in each treatment condition. Subjects should be compensated as they complete each of the study tasks. It is considered overly coercive to withhold the entire compensation for participation in all aspects of the study until the end of the study or to stipulate that only subjects who complete all aspects of the study will be compensated. This approach diminishes the subject's right to withdraw from the study at any time because of financial reasons.

Researchers may often provide more subtle coercion of subjects to join a study or to remain in a study. This is likely to happen when the researcher is under pressure to complete a study, for example, to complete a degree requirement (Dileo-Maranto, 1995) or to meet the demands of a funding source. For example, promising a class party for students whose parents return a signed consent form can be considered a coercive strategy. Thus, researchers need to be aware of subtle and indirect ways in which they may convey coercion, as well as their inherent power as a researcher.

Subjects who are vulnerable require additional provisions by the researcher to assure that their participation is voluntary. For example, individuals who are in a great deal of pain may feel compelled to try a new experimental procedure to ameliorate their condition. Parents of children with disabilities may seek out any new procedure to try to help their child. In these and other situations, the researcher has the responsibility to clearly explain alternative procedures to participation in the study that may be of potential benefit. In addition, it is the responsibility of the researcher to clearly and accurately describe the possible benefits of participation (as described in the following section) so as not to promise beneficial results for the subject.

Some researchers are beginning to rely upon the strategy of *passive consent*. In these situations, subjects are informed that they will be included in a study unless they specifically decline, usually through written means. There are a myriad of ethical issues inherent in this approach, and passive consent, or active refusal to consent, cannot be used as a substitute for active, informed consent (Sales & Folkman, 2000).

The perceived power of the researcher may be deleterious to a true informed consent process. To address this issue, it has been suggested that researchers establish more balanced relationships with subjects and view them as collaborative rather than vertical. "A collaborative relationship would be one in which both the researcher and subjects work together as equals on mutually interesting behavioral research questions" (Kimmel, 1996, p. 234).[1] Rosnow and Rosenthal (1997) further suggest that researchers view their subjects as an additional *granting agency* insofar as subjects, in reality, grant researchers their time, energy, and cooperation.

Completeness of Information

To provide true consent for participation, subjects must receive a full disclosure of the nature of the research and their participation in it. The federal regulations give specific elements of information that must be provided to each subject. These elements are detailed below:

---

[1] See Chapter 32, Participatory Action Research, for discussion of collaborative approaches to research.

1. *Heading.* The first page of the consent form is typed on the letterhead of the institution where it is carried out.[2] The heading should indicate that it is an informed consent document. The title of the research and the names, titles, phone numbers, and e-mail addresses of the researchers and his or her research advisor (if the research is done as a student project) should appear at the top of the form. If there are funding agencies or sponsors of the research, this information should also appear at the top of the first page. Subsequent pages of the consent form should be on plain paper, with the title of the research appearing on each page.

2. *An invitation to participate.* Beginning the consent form with an invitation to participate helps establish the role of the subject as voluntary.

3. *The purpose of the study.* The reasons the subject is asked to participate and the number of subjects included should be stated. Subject inclusion and exclusion criteria should be detailed in this part of the form. Subjects who do not meet study criteria may screen themselves from the study.

4. *A description of research procedures.* Subjects should be informed of all that the study involves and what is expected of them, including where and when the study will take place, what their time commitment will be, how long the study will last, who will be involved, what the treatment will be, what the assessment or measurements will involve, and what follow-up participation is required. If subjects have the possibility of being assigned to a control group, they should be informed of this in advance, as it may influence their decision to participate. In any event, it is important for subjects to understand that the procedures being used in the study are indeed research procedures.

5. *All foreseeable risks, inconveniences, and discomforts associated with participation.* To make an informed decision about participating in research, subjects need to know not only the potential risks, discomforts, and inconveniences involved (including severity), but also the likelihood of their happening. Risks in a study may be physiological, psychological, intellectual, economic, social, and legal, and include possible side effects, discomforts, stresses, lack of effects, distress, and potential future effects (Dileo, 2000). Inconveniences can include the time needed to travel to the research site and time involved for participation. In addition, costs (financial or otherwise) to subjects may be involved in study participation. For example, subjects who participate in a music therapy treatment study may be required to refrain from participation in other therapies. Researchers should describe all reasonably anticipated risks, costs, and so forth clearly and specifically (not glossing over them) and also include a statement in the consent form that unforeseeable risks may be possible. It is the responsibility of the researcher to take precautions to minimize these risks (Fischman, 2000). If the researcher is unsure of the potential for risks, it is often a very good idea to conduct a pilot study to assess risk factors prior to implementing the study (Koocher & Keith-Spiegel, 1994). The IRB will carefully review potential risks to subjects to make sure that all precautions have been taken to minimize risks and may suggest additional precautions, if necessary.

   If more than minimal risks are possible, the researcher must describe how potential injury will be addressed. These include any physical, psychological, social, financial, or other types of harm. For example, if psychological distress is experienced as a result of the study, the researcher must detail how this distress will be dealt with, for example, through additional interventions by the music therapist or by referral to another therapist or counseling center. The researcher must also indicate if he or she will assume financial responsibility for this additional treatment or provide compensation to the subject for injury. In no way should the consent form convey that subjects are relinquishing their legal rights by signing it. If additional risks involved in participation are identified during the

---

[2] University students may conduct research at another facility (governed by a different IRB). In these cases, it is usually required that the research protocol be reviewed by both IRBs (in whatever sequence is determined), or one IRB may accept the decision of the other. It is up to the IRBs involved to decide which institution's letterhead is used.

course of the research, the consent process and documentation will require revisions to inform subjects as they are contacted again or newly contacted.

6. *All possible benefits that may reasonably result from the study to the subject or others.* Benefits (something of positive value) for the subject may be psychological, physical, social, or monetary in nature. The researcher should indicate the magnitude and probability of such benefits. Detailed information regarding the financial compensation of subjects should be included as well. Benefits to others may include the advancement of scientific knowledge in the field or the advancement of information that may be helpful to society at large. Not all studies provide a benefit for the individual subject. In these cases, it is important to state this in the consent form, and not overestimate the benefits to a particular subject. In reviewing research, IRBs will attempt to determine if the benefits to the individual or society outweigh the risks to an individual subject (risk/benefit analysis). If the risks of the study outweigh its possible benefits, the study will not receive approval by the IRB.

   It is important to note that IRBs will look carefully at all methodological aspects of a study to determine the study's possible benefits. If a study is poorly constructed and is not likely to achieve its scientific aims, then it will likely not be approved. In these instances, the study may be considered a waste of the subject's time.

7. *Available alternative procedures.* In this section of the consent document, the researcher informs the subject of possible alternative treatment options that might be advantageous to the subject besides participation in the study, particularly when an experimental intervention is being tested (Fischman, 2000). The researcher should provide specific information about these alternatives.

8. *Assurance of confidentiality.* Confidentiality assures that any information obtained about the subject in the research process will be kept private, and that the identity of the subject will not be revealed in the reporting of results. Thus, it is important for subjects to be informed in the consent document regarding who will have access to the data; how the data will be used; to whom the data will be disclosed; and if the results of the study, including the subject's individual data, will be provided to the subject following the study. All individuals having access to the study data must be accountable for protecting the subject's confidentiality, and the researcher is responsible for assuring that this is done (Dileo, 2000).

   Some data collected in research are more sensitive than others. Some data, such as sexual preference or drug use, are sensitive under any circumstances, whereas other data, for example, musical preferences, may not be. However, it is not the right of the researcher to make this determination for his or her subjects; it is up to the subjects to decide this for themselves (Dileo-Maranto, 1995).

   The researcher must implement a variety of procedures to protect the confidentiality and anonymity of subjects. Researchers should not include any names or identifying information on any study materials. Instead, subject codes are generally applied to any data (and no subject is identified directly). If it is necessary to connect codes with individual subjects' names, a separate list of subjects' codes and names is maintained. This must be kept in a secure, locked location, and only the researcher (and key persons involved in the research) may have access to this list. When preparing research for publication, only aggregate data are presented, and no subject's individual information may be identified.

   All other research materials, such as audiotapes, videotapes, and pictures, must receive similar precautions to preserve the subject's anonymity and confidentiality. They should also be coded, and care should be taken not to include the subjects' names or any other personal information. As pictorial data do reveal the identity of the subject, these materials need special care regarding storage and who may have access to them. When analyzing audiotapes and videotapes to extract data, the researcher must be careful to do this in a secure location so that they are not heard or seen by others.

   Detailed procedures regarding how the researcher will protect the subject's anonymity and confidentiality need to be included in the consent form. A separate consent form may also be required when audiotaping, videotaping, and photographing are used.

In research it is sometimes impossible to guarantee complete confidentiality to the subject because of legal requirements and financial issues (for example, when subjects are paid and checks issued, a subject's anonymity is compromised).

Laws governing confidentiality in research vary by state, and the IRB monitoring the study is usually aware of these laws. Many complicated issues can arise regarding confidentiality in research, and laws may require the researcher to breach the subject's confidentiality. The researcher may become privy to confidential information, for example, where the subject or others may be at risk for harm or are in violation of the law (to mention just a few issues). These are often present when subjects are children; when there is a suspicion of child or elder abuse; when subjects have AIDS or HIV; when there is a potential for suicide; when criminal acts, present or future, are revealed; and so forth.

As a member of Temple University's IRB for many years, the current author has seen numerous instances where there are very thorny issues present for both researcher and subjects. One example, which has occurred repeatedly, involves the measurement instruments that researchers use, in this case the Beck Depression Inventory. An item on this inventory directly solicits information concerning the subject's intent to commit suicide. When researchers use this inventory as a tool, and a subject responds positively to this particular item, the researcher is presented with a significant ethical dilemma: What are his or her responsibilities as far as reporting this (and in determining if the subject answered this question authentically)? What does his or her state law require? What are the liability issues involved for the researcher in reporting or not reporting? And, on a more practical level, how will the researcher accomplish this? If the law requires the researcher to report this information, details of this requirement and procedures for how this will occur must be included in the consent form. In any event, if the subjects used may present the opportunities for these types of issues to arise, it would be important for the researcher to indicate to the subject in the consent form that there are limits to the confidentiality of data gathered in the study according to the existing regulations. In addition, sponsors, funding agencies, regulatory agencies, and the IRB may also review research records, and this information should also be included in the consent form.

New governmental privacy regulations, the HIPAA Privacy Rule (U.S. Department of Health and Human Services, 2003), which went into effect on April 14, 2003, protects the privacy of individually identifiable health information by establishing conditions for its use and disclosure by a health plan, healthcare clearinghouse, and certain healthcare providers (Kutkat, 2003). This legislation expands upon the existing Common Rule and requires an individual's written authorization for use or disclosure of his or her private health information and an accounting and reporting of these disclosures (Kutkat). The Privacy Rule (as it relates to researchers) primarily influences medical researchers or researchers in hospitals who transmit identifiable health information electronically or maintain it in any form. The Privacy Rule defines 18 identifiers that must be removed by researchers (see http://privacyruleandresearch.nih.gov/pr 02.asp for further information). The Privacy Rule requires that an individual's written authorization be obtained before the use and disclosure of personal health information. The authorization must be for a specific research study, and the authorization form must be reviewed by an IRB only if it is combined with an informed consent document. All personal health information must be de-identified (according to the 18 identifiers) if it is used in research without express authorization of the subject (Kutkat). As there are many additional requirements involved in the Privacy Rule, researchers who plan to use personal health information in their studies should obtain additional information at http://privacyruleandresearch.nih.gov/ and http://www.hhs.gov/ocr/hipaa/.

9. *Whom to contact.* Specific clauses in the consent form should provide direct information (names, local telephone numbers, and e-mail addresses) to the subject regarding persons that can be contacted regarding the study to obtain varying

types of information. Subjects should be given the name and contact information of the researcher that they can contact for further information about the study. They should also be given the name and contact information of the IRB manager who can be contacted concerning their rights as a research subject. Finally, subjects should be given the name and contact information of a person (if different from the researcher) who can be contacted in the event of a research-related injury.

10. *Voluntariness and right to refuse or withdraw.* Subjects should be informed directly that that participation in the study is on a voluntary basis. In addition, subjects need to know that they may refuse to participate or withdraw from the study at any time without any penalty or loss of benefits to which the subject may be entitled otherwise. Procedures for withdrawing should also be mentioned. The researcher should also state that there may be circumstances that cause the researcher to terminate the subject's participation in the study or ask for additional consent from the subject, even if consent has been provided. These circumstances may include, for example, new information obtained during the study that might influence the subject's willingness to continue to participate, health reasons, risk of injury, inadequate participation of the subject, or early termination of the study (Dileo, 2000; Fischman, 2000).

11. *Closing statements and signatures.* An explicit statement should be included that indicates that the subject has been informed of the study; has had the opportunity to ask questions; is cognizant of the risks, benefits, and alternate treatment options; has received a copy of the consent form; and freely grants consent to participate in the study (Dileo, 2000). This is followed by dated signatures of the subject, the researcher, a witness, and the interpreter (if relevant). The subject and the researcher each retain a copy of the consent form. Consent forms are retained according to the policy of the institution at which the research takes place. Signed consent documents and IRB research records must be retained for at least 3 years past completion of the research activity.

Investigator Responsibilities and Informed Consent

According to legal regulations, investigators are responsible for promptly reporting to the IRB any changes in previously approved research protocols, and the IRB must approve any and all changes to these protocols. Researchers must also report progress on their research to the IRB at regular intervals (to be determined by the IRB during its review of a protocol, but not less than once a year). Lastly, researchers are required to promptly report any unanticipated problems, injuries, adverse events, or risks of the research to the subjects or to others.

Waiver of Written Consent

IRBs may waive requirements for the written documentation of consent in situations where: (a) Signing the consent document represents a potential breach of the subject's confidentiality concerning his or her participation in the research; the consent document may be the only record that links the subject with his or her data; or (b) the research itself is of very low risk and does not require consent procedures when performed outside of the research setting. An example of the former is survey research. In this situation, where survey responses are not coded in any way, a letter containing all elements of informed consent is attached to the survey, and subjects indicate their implied consent to participate by returning the survey. If a consent form were returned with the survey, the subject's identity would be revealed.

Use of Deception in Research

Deception occurs when an investigator deliberately withholds information relevant to a study, either actively through the presentation of misinformation (usually about the study's purpose) or passively by omitting information that would be necessary to understand the study (Gravetter & Forzano, 2003). Deception can be detrimental by embarrassing the subject, making the subject anxious, or reducing self-esteem, and this may be in addition to a loss of respect for the researcher, the study, and the discipline in general. It is obvious that the use of deception in research severely compromises informed consent. Deception may be used only: (a) when the benefits of its use outweigh its risks, there are no other alternatives available, and its use is approved by an IRB; (b) all significant aspects of the study that would influence the subject's willingness to participate, such as risks, are not withheld; and (c) a debriefing of subjects is implemented immediately following the study. Debriefings include a complete description of the true intent of the study, including why deception was used (Gravetter & Forzano), and serve to minimize possible negative effects of the deception or harm to the subject.

Alternatives to deception may include the provision of partial, general, and non-erroneous information to subjects prior to the study and a debriefing immediately following (Dileo, 2000). It is possible to inform subjects in the consent form that deception may be used in the study; this is often the case in drug research, in which placebos are used. In this way, the subject provides his or her consent to be deceived. In any event, because deception is a practice contrary to true informed consent, it should be used only with the utmost caution in research.

Conclusion

The purpose of this chapter was to familiarize readers with some of the legal and ethical requirements for research and to assist them in preparing an informed consent document for IRB review. This is just one aspect of the role of ethics in the research process, although often a very stressful aspect indeed. Nevertheless, ethics must be considered in every phase of research, and the reader is encouraged to continue to explore and learn about ethics, as each and every subject in research is certainly worth this effort.

References

American Music Therapy Association. (2003). *Code of ethics.* http://musictherapy .org/ethics.html

Beach, D. (1996). *The responsible conduct of research.* New York: VCH Publishers.

Canadian Music Therapy Association. (2005). *Code of ethics.* http://www.musictherapy.ca/

Certification Board for Music Therapists. (2001). *Code of professional practice.* http://www.cbmt.org

Department of Health and Human Services 45 CFR 46 (2001). *Protection of human subjects.* http://www.hhs.gov/ohrp/humansubjects/guidance/45cfr46.htm

Dileo, C. (2000). *Ethical thinking in music therapy.* Cherry Hill, NJ: Jeffrey Books.

Dileo-Maranto, C. (1995). Ethical precautions. In B. L. Wheeler (Ed.), *Music therapy research: Quantitative and qualitative perspectives* (pp. 79–96). Gilsum, NH: Barcelona Publishers.

Federal Policy for the Protection of Human Subjects; Notices and Rules. *Federal Register* 56 (June 18, 1991): 28002–28032.

Fischman, M. W. (2000). Informed consent. In B. D. Sales & S. Folkman (Eds.), *Ethics in research with human participants* (pp. 35–48). Washington, DC: American Psychological Association.

Hicks, S. J. (April, 2003). *OHRP top ten investigator responsibilities when conducting human subjects research.* Presentation at Temple University Medical School.

Gravetter, F. J., & Forzano, L. B. (2003). *Research methods for the behavioral sciences.* Belmont, CA: Wadsworth/Thomson Learning.

Kimmel, A. J. (1996). *Ethical issues in behavioral research: A survey.* Cambridge, MA: Blackwell Publishers.

Koocher, G. P., & Keith-Spiegel, P. (1994). Scientific issues in psychosocial and educational research with children. In M. A. Grodin & L. H. Glanz (Eds.), *Children as research subjects: Science, ethics and the law* (pp. 47–80). New York: Oxford University Press.

Kutkat, L. (April, 2003). *The HIPAA Privacy Rule and research.* Presentation at Temple University Medical School.

The National Commission for the Protection of Human Subjects of Biomedical and Behavioral Research. (1979). *Ethical principles and guidelines for the protection of human subjects of research.* http://www.hhs.gov/ohrp/humansubjects/guidance/belmont.htm

Rosnow, R. L., & Rosenthal, R. (1997). *People studying people: Artifacts and ethics in behavioral research.* New York: W. H. Freeman and Co.

Sales, B. D., & Folkman, S. (2000). *Ethics in research with human participants.* Washington, DC: American Psychological Association.

Temple University. (2003). *Protection of human subjects in research.* http://www.research .temple.edu/irb

U.S. Department of Health and Human Services. (2003). *Protecting the privacy of patients' health information.* http://www.hhs.gov/news/facts/privacy.html

Chapter 19
Evaluating Quantitative Music Therapy Research
Cathy McKinney

Quantitative researchers employ a variety of criteria and methods to monitor and evaluate the integrity of the research study. This chapter will explore some of these, with particular attention to their relation to music therapy research. Among the criteria that will be discussed are theoretical grounding and the validity of research and statistical hypotheses; reliability and validity in data collection procedures; the integrity of data analysis, including the limitations of statistical significance testing; and drawing evidence-based conclusions. Finally, three ultimate criteria for evaluating the integrity of quantitative research—replicability, conflicts of interest and biases, and clinical importance—are considered.

Criteria for Evaluation

Theoretical Grounding and Hypothesis Validity

In effective quantitative research design, theory generates research hypotheses that lead to congruent statistical hypotheses that, in turn, reveal the results of the study. Reversing the process, inference from the results leads to decisions about the statistical hypotheses (such as whether or not to reject the null hypothesis or how to assess the magnitude of effect), which indicate whether the research hypotheses are verified. In this way, the theory is corroborated or falsified (Wampold, Davis, & Good, 2003). Thaut (2000) emphasized the importance of grounding music therapy studies in theory, asserting that "studies need to be preceded by an epistemological structure of valid scientific theory that will help us understand how the data contribute to an understanding of music in therapy" (pp. 7–8). He noted that data not rooted in underlying theory are subject to misinterpretation and may create a disjunct and confusing *data puzzle* rather than contribute to an understanding of the phenomena in question. Thus, evaluation of quantitative research begins with the theory and research hypotheses being tested by the research study.

Wampold et al. (2003) employed the phrase "*hypothesis validity* to refer to the extent to which research results reflect theoretically derived predictions about the relations between or among constructs" (p. 390). The greater the hypothesis validity, the more a research study will contribute to the advancement of theory. Conversely, studies with low hypothesis validity may actually result in ambiguity about the relations among constructs and hinder the development of underlying theory (Wampold et al.). Their chapter provides a comprehensive discussion of potential threats to hypothesis validity. These threats include inconsequential or ambiguous research hypotheses, incongruence between research and statistical hypotheses, and diffuse statistical hypotheses and tests.

Heller and O'Connor (2002) emphasized the need for each researcher to undertake a critical review of the previous literature prior to the formulation of research hypotheses and design of the methodology. Without such an examination, research may be based on poorly designed studies, lead to false conclusions, and, ultimately, hinder the development of music therapy.

Reliability and Validity in Data Collection

The integrity of data collection procedures in quantitative research contributes substantially to the quality of the body of the research and the applicability of the results. Girden (2001) identified three issues central to the evaluation of the integrity of data collection in quantitative research: controlled observation, reliability, and validity. Problems in any of these three areas can compromise the study, rendering the results useless, misleading, or even harmful.

"*Controlled observation* refers to the precision under which the data are collected" (Girden, 2001, p. 2). Every effort is made to minimize sources of extraneous variance so that the observed variance in the dependent variables results from the independent variables and not from *noise* arising from individual differences among human begins, the experimental environment, or too diverse a sample.

One of the primary techniques for equally distributing the extraneous variance resulting from individual differences in human participants is randomized assignment of experimental condition to each participant (Hsu, 2003). In addition to equal distribution of variance, true randomization eliminates selection bias, the differential assignment of participants with respect to anticipated response to the intervention (Altman et al., 2001). Detailed reporting of randomization procedures in outcome studies is essential to the accurate evaluation of the results, since inadequate reporting may result in bias in estimating treatment effectiveness (Moher, Schulz, & Altman, 2001). Because achieving true equivalence among experimental conditions is based on mathematical probability and, therefore, particularly challenging with small samples (Hsu), the outcome of the randomization is generally confirmed and reported by statistically testing for differences among groups in potentially confounding variables.

In quantitative research, controls also are applied to the experimental procedure itself. Potential controls include administering identical instructions under identical conditions to all groups or individuals and sequencing the procedure the same way for each administration. Although some considerations are true for many studies involving human participants, such as room temperature, lighting, type of seating or other furniture arrangement, type and extent of interaction with the researcher, there are additional considerations for music therapy studies. For example, in music therapy studies employing recorded music, controls may include specification of the range of decibel levels or the peak decibel level of any music played; the specific pieces played; the specific recording, including the performers and the format; and the equipment used to play the music, including any use of headphones. In studies of active music therapy, the specific instruments available, their arrangement in the room, and the participants' access to them may need to be specified.

In order to observe under sufficiently controlled conditions, it may be necessary to apply controls to the participant sample. Controls may be applied through selection or exclusion criteria or through measurement of potential confounding variables relevant to the dependent variables of interest. For example, in a study of a specific music therapy procedure for adults undergoing treatment for cancer, some potential sources of extraneous variance might include the age range and gender of the participants; type, location, and stage of the cancer; time since diagnosis; type of treatment; whether adjuvant treatment is ongoing or completed; and level of social support. If the number of participants in the study is large, these factors may be controlled through collecting the relevant data and using statistical procedures to assure equality among subgroups prior to any intervention. If the number of participants is small (as in most music therapy studies), it may be impossible to examine subgroups. In this case, it is necessary to narrow the selection criteria, recognizing that doing so will limit the generalizability of the findings to others with the same characteristics as the participants in the study.

A second criterion by which the integrity of quantitative data collection may be evaluated is the *reliability* of the measures employed in the study. Reliability refers to the consistency with which an instrument or method of measurement will reveal the same result for the same participant under the same conditions. Therefore, reliability of the observations collected is a function of both the precision of the instruments or observational methods used and their appropriate use. The more precise the instrument or method, the more likely it is to yield the same result. For example, a calibrated metronome will provide more reliable data concerning the tempo of a client's playing or her or his walking speed than the music therapist's unaided ear or eye. The reliability of the measures employed is reported in the form of correlation coefficients. Girden (2001) recommend a coefficient of at least .65 to establish the reliability of a measure.

Validity is the extent to which an instrument or other measurement procedure allows the researcher to draw useful and valid conclusions about the variable of interest. Instruments are devised and validated based on constructs considered to be meaningful at the time. However, the validity of the construct itself is heavily affected by societal beliefs and professional opinions, among other factors. For example, writing in the *New Orleans Medical and Surgical Journal* in 1851, physician Samuel Cartwright described a mental disorder among slaves, drapetomania, which caused slaves to run away from their masters (Leavitt, 2001; Whitaker, 2002). While observation of the population of slaves could certainly confirm the presence of this disorder with reliability, the false validity of the construct itself was firmly rooted in perceptions based on the belief system prevailing in the American South at the time. For further information on the types and nature of validity, the reader is referred to the clear and concise table offered by Haynes (2003).

Leavitt (2001) urged researchers to thoroughly search for an existing instrument before constructing a new one, since "good measures are refined and standardized over time, while less satisfactory ones are winnowed out" (p. 62). A second advantage is that use of the same measure facilitates comparisons among studies (Gold, Voracek, & Wigram, 2004). However, as Haynes (2003) noted, a test that was valid when developed some years ago may no longer be valid today because the understanding of the construct that it was designed to measure may have evolved. "The validity of an assessment instrument can diminish over time, and past validity indices should not be presumed to be generalizable to contemporaneous applications of the instrument" (Haynes, p. 250).

One major challenge to quantitative researchers is to devise meaningful operational definitions of highly abstract constructs. For example, defining what constitutes *improvement* in the client as a result of a therapeutic intervention is a highly subjective task, and the range of possible correct definitions is broad, even for a given diagnosis or disorder. Nevertheless, without clear operational definitions, systematic, replicable observation is impossible; conversely, definitions may be so narrowly defined as to be meaningless for practical purposes or even absurd. For example, Freeman and Watts (as cited in Whitaker, 2002), the pioneers of the contemporaneously acclaimed prefrontal lobotomy, wrote a book in 1950 describing 623 individuals with mental illness on whom they had operated, reporting that 80% had been helped by their new therapy, consistent with the glowing outcome studies reported in the medical literature. A closer examination of their definition of *helped,* however, reveals a disturbing picture. They reported that about 25% of patients never recovered beyond "surgically induced childhood" and therefore required lifelong hospitalization, and about 25% of those discharged could be "considered as adjusting at the level of a domestic invalid or household pet" (Freeman & Watts, as cited in Whitaker, p. 124). The loss of creativity, imagination, feelings, and spiritual yearnings were seen as positive outcomes (Whitaker).

This need to balance operational definitions with practical meaningfulness also applies to the selection of measurement procedures in quantitative studies. Any instrument, no matter how reliable and well validated, measures only an aspect of the broader construct. Kazdin (1995) notes that this fact underscores the need for employing multiple assessment procedures related to the construct. "A weakness of many studies is using a single measure to assess a central construct of interest" (p. 295). The use of multiple measures more broadly represents the construct and may increase the relevance to the clinical world. Reliance on a single measure may be viewed as a limitation in the interpretation of the results (Kazdin).

Integrity of Data Analysis

Beyond the issues of sample selection and data collection, several criteria are essential to the evaluation of the integrity of data analysis in quantitative research. These include use of appropriate statistical tests given the levels of measurement, confirmation of underlying assumptions for statistical tests, and recognition of the limitations of statistical significance testing.

As was noted in Chapter 12, Statistical Methods of Analysis, parametric statistical tests require that the data be of an interval or ratio scale. Ordinal or nominal data are appropriately analyzed using nonparametric statistics. For example, while a parametric test may be used to determine if there is a significant difference between groups in the ratio scale variables of age or years of formal music training, a nonparametric test would be used to ascertain differences between groups in nominal scale variables, such as the number of string players versus wind players in each.

A second requirement of all parametric statistics is that certain assumptions regarding the data must be met. All uses of analysis of variance require that observations be random samples independently drawn from normally distributed populations and that the variances of the sets of scores from the groups represent estimates of the same population variance (Kirk, 1982). Written accounts of quantitative studies, therefore, should include a description of the sampling techniques (recruitment procedures), as well as statistical confirmations of the assumptions. Ideally, in quantitative studies involving analysis of variance, these confirmations include tests of homogeneity of variance as well as appropriate statistical tests demonstrating that the groups are equivalent prior to any intervention. In addition, a detailed description of attrition is needed to ascertain whether the results may be skewed by withdrawal from the study.

One well-documented but seldom-acknowledged challenge to the integrity of quantitative research lies in the limitations of statistical significance testing and the failure of researchers to recognize those limitations (Cohen, 1994, 2003; Falk, 1998; Falk & Greenbaum, 1995; Gold, 2004a; Heller & O'Conner, 2002; Kirk, 1996; Schmidt, 2003; Tunks, 1978; Wampold et al., 2003). As Cohen wrote, significance testing of the null hypothesis "does not tell us what we want to know" (p. 997). What researchers seek to know is the "probability that the null hypothesis is true given that we have obtained a set of data" (Kirk, p. 747). Instead, the procedure tells us the "probability of obtaining these or more extreme data if the null hypothesis is true" (Kirk, p. 747). Unfortunately, finding a low probability value for the latter does not indicate that the probability of the former is also low.

Through generally adopted research conventions, quantitative researchers assume that if the p value associated with a given test statistic is low, then the null hypothesis is probably false (Cohen, 1994, 2003; Falk, 1998; Falk & Greenbaum, 1995; Schmidt, 2003; Wampold et al., 2003). Cohen (1994) demonstrated the deductive fallacy that is at the core of the researcher's thinking. He presented the following syllogism that is reflected in most of the quantitative music therapy literature:

> If the Ho [null hypothesis] is true, then this result (statistical significance)
>   would probably not occur.
> This result has occurred.
> Then Ho is probably not true and therefore formally invalid. (p. 998)

He elucidates the error inherent in this reasoning by substituting an example from Pollard and Richardson (cited in Cohen, 1994):

> If a person is an American, then he is probably not a member of Congress.
>   (True, right?)
> This person is a member of Congress.
> Therefore, he is probably not an American. (p. 998)

Falk and Greenbaum (1995) have termed this form of deduction the "illusion of probabilistic proof by contradiction" (p. 76).

Further complicating our unquestioning adoption of this illogic in research practice are two widespread erroneous beliefs: (a) That a low p value indicates the probability that replication will result in a similarly significant result (Cohen, 1994; Kirk, 1996; Thompson, 1996), and (b) that a low p value signifies that the effect is important or large (Cohen, 2003; Thompson). About the former, Falk (1998) has acknowledged the compelling nature of the faulty assumption of replicability, suggesting that it is based on "a sound intuitive need to answer the natural and most pressing questions: 'Could this be a coincidence?' and 'Will the finding recur in similar circumstances?'" (p. 315). However, Rosenthal (1993) has shown that in three replications of a study, given the typical level of power for medium effect sizes (.50) employed by many researchers, only one study in eight would have significant results in all three replications.

Concerning the assumption of association between statistical significance and the importance of an effect, Thompson (1996) noted that the importance of findings cannot be determined by statistics, but only by subjective judgment. Contrary to the objectivist roots out of which quantitative methods arose, he maintained "empirical science is inescapably a subjective business" (p. 28). As to the relation between p values and effect size, the p value simply says that the effect probably exists and indicates nothing about the size of the effect (Cohen, 2003).

Ultimately, the focus on p values and the rejection of the null hypothesis leads the researcher away from the goal of research, which is discovering whether the findings support the hypothesis and have practical applicability (Cohen, 1994). Kirk (1996) has pointed out that such a focus has turned "a continuum of uncertainty into a dichotomous reject-do-not-reject decision" (p. 748). He noted that, under current practice, two researchers could obtain the same treatment effects yet draw diametrically opposed conclusions. For example, a researcher whose study yields a p value of .06 would be likely to choose not to reject the null hypothesis, while another researcher who has a few more participants would find $p = .05$ and reject the null hypothesis. These contradictory actions could result from identical treatment effects. In the small sample sizes often employed in music therapy studies, this hypothetical scenario is quite likely. Gold (2004a) has demonstrated how the small sample size of a music therapy study may yield no statistically significant difference despite a medium effect size of the intervention and, thus, a clinically significant result.

Kirk (1996) has declared that testing the significance of the null hypothesis is a trivial exercise. He and others (Cohen, 2003; Körlin & Wrangsjö, 2002) have noted that the null hypothesis is always false if the sample is sufficiently large or the variance is sufficiently low. More importantly, he has asserted that the preoccupation with p values coupled with failure to consider practical significance has often led to ignoring the real question of whether or not the data support the research hypotheses and are useful. He has gone so far as to lament "our science has paid a high price for its ritualistic adherence to null hypothesis significance testing" (Kirk, 1996, p. 756). Kirk is not alone in his dismay over the misuse of p values. Participants in a symposium at the 1996 conference of the American Psychological Association (APA) discussed the idea of banning significance tests from articles published in APA journals. Subsequently, the APA formed a Task Force on Statistical Inference, which issued guidelines in 1999 (Morgan & Morgan, 2003).

Meanwhile, many research methodologists have recommended the use of confidence intervals to replace the use of the p value (Cohen, 1994; Kirk, 1996; Schmidt, 2003). Confidence intervals have three advantages over significance testing:

1. Rather than indicate an absolute decision to reject or not, confidence intervals indicate the range of values within which the real difference is likely to occur.
2. Confidence intervals reveal relationships among the results of different studies of the same measure that are not revealed by significance testing (Schmidt). As noted above, significance testing sometimes would lead one to believe that the results of two studies are contradictory when in fact they are not.
3. "Unlike the significance test, the confidence interval does hold the error rate to the desired level" (Schmidt, p. 447), thereby reducing Type II errors.

Despite the fact that statisticians have implored researchers since 1925 to employ measures of practical significance in addition to significance tests in analysis of variance, reports of such measures are not routinely made (Kirk, 1996). More recently and more closely related to the music therapy literature, music psychologist Tunks (1978) and Bonny Method of Guided Imagery and Music therapists/researchers Körlin and Wrangsjö (2002) have advocated that researchers test not only statistical significance but also strength of association or effect size. As a harbinger of increasing awareness of this issue among music therapists, Gold (2004a) has articulated clearly this issue for the music therapy community. Prentice and Miller (2003) noted that effect sizes confer many benefits.

1. They indicate the degree to which a phenomenon is present in a population on a continuous scale, with zero always indicating that the phenomenon is absent. . . .
2. They come with conventions for what values constitute a small, medium, and large effect.
3. They provide some indication of the practical significance of an effect. . . .
4. They can be used to compare quantitatively the results of two or more studies.
5. They can be used in power analyses to guide decisions about how many subjects are needed in a study. (p. 128)

Prentice and Miller (2003) observed that "many researchers have suggested that effect sizes should be reported routinely for all significant and nonsignificant results" (p. 129). The Consolidated Standards for Reporting Trials, developed by an international group of medical editors and researchers to improve the quality of reports of clinical outcome studies, require both effect size and a measure of precision, such as confidence intervals (Moher et al., 2001). A survey by this author of the studies that employed inferential statistics and were published in the *Journal of Music Therapy* between 2000 and 2003 revealed that this is not yet the case in music therapy. Fewer than 5 of more than 35 articles reported any measure of effect size or strength of association for any variable. Gold (2004a) reviewed several of the most commonly used measures of effect size. Kirk (1996) provided a list of 40 different measures of effect magnitude and guidelines for interpreting several of the most used measures.

Evidence-Based Conclusions

The last point of threat to the integrity of a quantitative research study lies in the conclusions drawn by the researcher. Heller and O'Connor (2002) noted that "often the conclusions reported in published research articles are not appropriate to the evidence provided" (p. 1093). A common error is the overgeneralization of the results of the study. To be externally valid, the findings of a particular study may be generalized only within the limits of the design of the study, including both the population studied and the statistical results. As described above, a small sample size may require that the population parameters be narrowly defined in order to control for extraneous variance in the variables of interest. However, in so doing, the researcher limits generalization of the findings to the same narrowly defined population. For example, the music therapy researcher who tests a music therapy intervention in preschool children hospitalized to treat cancer cannot assume that the results of the study will apply to school age children hospitalized for cancer or to preschoolers hospitalized for disorders other than cancer.[1]

Findings of a study also may be generalized only within the limits of the statistical results of the study. If inferential statistics were not used, the researcher cannot generalize the results beyond the present sample. The researcher may discuss the present data and their possible implications, but may draw no conclusions about anyone except those included in the study. Similarly, when a statistical test is not significant, no difference may be predicted in the population (Heller & O'Connor, 2002). For example in a study of the effects of different types of music on relaxation, if post hoc tests find that there is no statistically significant difference among types, the researcher who proceeds to discuss that one type is more effective than the others has generalized the results beyond the evidence.

Ultimate Criteria

Three additional factors contribute to the ultimate evaluation of the integrity of quantitative research in music therapy. The first is the replicability of the study, since replication is the only way to increase certainty in the results; the second is real or potential conflicts of interest and research biases of the researcher; and the third is the clinical importance of the findings.

Replicability

In the final analysis, the only way to determine whether an observed effect is due to chance sampling error is through replication of the study (Cohen, 1994; Falk, 1998; Kirk, 1996; Thompson, 1996). Falk noted that the essential role of replication in scientific advancement is one point of agreement among statisticians and research methodologists. "Every successful demonstration of the effect predicted by a hypothesis adds to our confidence in the truth of the hypothesis" (Falk, p. 319). Yet, the common practice of viewing statistical significance as the final word in research may discourage replication attempts (Falk).

The music therapy literature contains few replications. Moreover, many articles contain insufficient information to allow replication. Careful documentation of the circumstances of each aspect of the data collection process is necessary for another researcher to recreate the conditions of the experiment in order to replicate the study. This has not always been done in music therapy research. For example, an examination of the numerous studies that have investigated physiological effects of music will show that, while some researchers specified the musical selections used, many neglected to document even the piece of music used, instead employing descriptive terms such as *agreeably exciting, beautiful music,* or *anxiolytic music.* A researcher attempting to understand the body of literature or preparing to replicate the study needs to know not only the specific piece, but also the particular recording used. A comparative journey through the first 16 bars of 10 different recordings of Pachelbel's *Canon in D* will illustrate clearly that

---

[1] It should be noted, though, that it is appropriate and often necessary for a clinician to apply the most closely related research available. (As Sackett, Richardson, Rosenberg, and Haynes [1997] noted, applying research results to an individual patient from a similar population by a clinician is a basic tenet of evidence-based practice.) However, it would be inappropriate for the researcher to extend the conclusions to a population beyond that sampled for the study.

specific recordings may vary in many dimensions that may affect the research outcome, including tempo, instrumentation, motion, style, and other aspects.

Since inferential statistics are based on probability, a single replication of an effect cannot achieve certainty. To achieve certainty would require that one reach infinite probability. Since infinity cannot be reached, certainty cannot be achieved, only approached (Falk, 1998). Nevertheless, successful replication can increase confidence in theories of music therapy and the underlying mechanisms, and in the ability to predict outcome.

Conflicts of Interest and Biases

Many choices are exercised in the decision-making process leading to quantitative research, including what to research, how to approach the problem, what interpretations to make of the data, which results to publish, and how to disseminate the findings. These decisions are influenced by a number of factors, both intrinsic and extrinsic to the researcher. These factors may converge to create conflicting pressures on the researcher, leading to conflicts of interest that may bias the individual research study and ultimately the body of published research (Bradley, 1995).

One potential source of conflict of interest is the funding source of a research study, especially when the funding agent has a commercial interest in the subject of the research. Such a conflict may introduce a direct or indirect effect upon the findings (Bradley, 1995). For example, in research studies of new drugs, only 13% of studies funded by sources without obvious bias favored the new drug over traditional therapies versus 43% of studies funded by the drug company (Davidson, cited in Leavitt, 2001). While this source of conflict has been less often present in music therapy research because of the historical lack of corporate funding, recent increased interest shown by commercial sources in funding research may present dilemmas for the music therapist-researcher. Whether or not the funding agent makes any overt statements of desirable outcome, the therapist-researcher may experience real or perceived pressure to obtain findings that will please the funding source and thus increase the likelihood of future financial support. Research in which the funding source has an obvious financial interest must be carefully considered.

A second way that corporate funding sources and clinical agencies sometimes introduce bias into the published literature is through control of the dissemination of research results. Because of their financial interest in the outcome of research studies, some corporations suppress the publication of unsatisfactory results through clauses in the grant contract that require approval of any results prior to submission for publication (Bradley, 1995; Leavitt, 2001; Whitaker, 2002). This trend has been recognized as a violation of academic freedom, and some university systems have adopted policies precluding the universities from entering into any agreement, including accepting a grant that restricts the rights of faculty or students to publish (D. Cole, personal communication, June 13, 2001). Entering into a contractual agreement with any party that restricts the right to publish may place the music therapist/researcher into an uncomfortable ethical dilemma.

Clinical Importance

In music therapy, the connection between research and clinical practice has at times been tenuous. Music therapy clinicians (and other professionals in clinical practice) sometimes claim that the research studies are unrelated to their work with clients, that they fail to contribute to their clinical decisions, and that they are jargon-laden and hard to comprehend. The result of this uneasy relationship between research and practice may be that ineffective methods continue to be used and effective methods are slow to be adopted (Reynolds, 2000).

One process first developed in medicine and later applied to psychotherapy in an effort to strengthen the research-practice relationship is evidence-based practice (Reynolds, 2000; Sackett, Richardson, Rosenberg, & Haynes, 1998). Evidence-based practice encourages the clinician to combine the best of personal experience and external evidence, including professional guidelines and research studies, in making clinical decisions about individual clients (Sackett et al.). Evaluation of external evidence consists of both establishing the validity of the results and deciding whether the results are clinically important. Establishing the validity of a single study is accomplished through examination of many aspects of the research already considered in this chapter, including randomization, accounting for attrition, and controlling for extraneous sources of variance.

In evidence-based practice, the concept of statistical significance is replaced with the concept of clinical importance. Clinical importance is determined by calculations of the number needed to treat (NNT) and the number needed to harm (NNH). NNT and NNH convert the results of studies of a treatment procedure into quantitative indicators of "how many patients would have to be treated with the treatment method in order to bring about one good outcome or one harmful outcome" (Reynolds, 2000, pp. 260–261). In addition, the size of the treatment effect on clinically important outcome measures is a major factor in determining whether a given treatment is worth the cost and effort of treatment. The results of a quantitative meta-analysis of more than one randomized controlled trial is seen as the optimal source of evidence and a randomized controlled trial with definitive results as next best (Guyatt, Sackett, Sinclair, Hayward, Cook, & Cook, 1995). Combining the evaluation of research evidence, the clinical importance of the treatment, and the size of the treatment effect with the personal experience, expertise, and judgment of the clinician allows the clinician to determine whether or not the treatment may be appropriate for an individual client.

Music therapy recently has begun to appear in *The Cochrane Library,* a series of systematic reviews prepared according to exacting standards set by the international Cochrane Collaboration, an independent, not-for-profit organization that disseminates reviews of clinical outcome research in healthcare (Cochrane Collaboration, 2004). Each review is based on randomized, quasi-randomized, and clinical controlled trials and includes a meta-analysis, if sufficient high-quality studies are available. As of the end of 2004, protocols had been developed and reviews were underway concerning music therapy in several areas of music therapy clinical practice, including schizophrenia and schizophrenia-like illnesses, pain relief, autism spectrum disorders, and depression (Cochrane Collaboration). To date, the only published review in music therapy is for dementia (Vink, Birks, Bruinsma, & Scholten, 2004). In an indictment of music therapy research, the authors stated, "The methodological quality of the studies was generally poor and the study results could not be validated or pooled for further analysis" (p. 1). The reviewers found that no useful conclusions could be drawn.

Some music therapists have decried the demand for quantitative evidence of clinical efficacy of music therapy, citing concerns for the applicability of evidence-based practice methods to music therapy (Edwards, 2004) and for the potential that misapplication will impair clinical services (Aldridge, 2003). Others have stressed the importance of evidence-based data in securing funding for services (Wigram, Pedersen, & Bonde, 2002) and justifying positions (Edwards, 2002). Researchers have begun to report the evidence base for music therapy with specific populations using the more stringent inclusion criteria of evidence-based methods (Gold, 2004b; Gold, Vorzcek, & Wigram, 2004). Despite the concerns voiced by music therapists, it appears that the criteria of evidence-based methods will continue to influence the evaluation of quantitative research in music therapy for some time to come.

Summary

Quantitative researchers have a number of criteria and methods at their disposal for monitoring and evaluating the integrity of research studies. In music therapy, researchers have attended to some of these, such as controlled observations and the reliability of measures. However, they have given less attention to others, such as the reporting of effect sizes and confidence intervals, and some methods, such as replication, are rarely observed in the music therapy literature. If music therapy is to advance in its clarity and understanding of the efficacy of and indications for its various clinical methods, researchers will need to embrace every means available for building a body of knowledge that meets the highest standards of integrity.

References

Aldridge, D. (2003, November). Staying close to practice: Which evidence, for whom, by whom. *Music Therapy Today, 4*(5). Available at http://musictherapyworld.net

Altman, D. G., Schulz, K. F., Moher, D., Egger, M., Davidoff, F., Elbourne, D., Getzsche, P. C., & Lang, T. (2001). The revised CONSORT statement for reporting randomized trials: Explanation and elaboration. *Annals of Internal Medicine, 134,* 663–694.

Bradley, S. G. (1995). Conflict of interest. In F. L. Macrina (Ed.), *Scientific integrity: An introductory text with cases* (pp. 161–187). Washington, DC: ASM Press.

Cochrane Collaboration. (2004). *What is the Cochrane Collaboration?* Available at http://www. cochrane.org/ index0.htm

Cohen, J. (1994). The earth is round (*p* < .05). *American Psychologist, 49,* 997–1003.

Cohen, J. (2003). Things I have learned (so far). In A. E. Kazdin (Ed.), *Methodological issues and strategies in clinical research* (3rd ed., pp. 407–424). Washington, DC: American Psychological Association.

Edwards, J. (2002). Using the evidence based medicine framework to support music therapy posts in health care settings. *British Journal of Music Therapy, 16,* 29–34.

Edwards, J. (2004, August). Can music therapy in medical contexts ever be evidence-based? *Music Therapy Today, 5*(4). Available at http://musictherapyworld.net

Falk, R. (1998). Replication—A step in the right direction: Commentary on Sohn. *Theory and Psychology, 8,* 313–321.

Falk, R., & Greenbaum, C. W. (1995). Significance test die-hard: The amazing persistence of a probabilistic misconception. *Theory & Psychology, 5,* 75–98.

Girden, E. R. (2001). *Evaluating research articles: From start to finish* (2nd ed.). Thousand Oaks, CA: Sage Publications.

Gold, C. (2004a). The use of effect sizes in music therapy research. *Music Therapy Perspectives, 22,* 91–95.

Gold, C. (2004b, November 17). *The evidence base on music therapy for ASD.* Presentation for the Institute on Autism Spectrum Disorders, American Music Therapy Association, Austin, TX.

Gold, C., Voracek, M., & Wigram, T. (2004). Effects of music therapy for children and adolescents with psychopathology: A meta-analysis. *Journal of Child Psychology and Psychiatry, 45,* 1054–1063.

Guyatt, G. H., Sackett, D. L., Sinclair, J. C., Hayward, R., Cook, D. J., & Cook, R. J. (1995). Users' guide to the medical literature. IX. A method for grading health care recommendations. Evidence-based medicine working group. *Journal of the American Medical Association, 274,* 1800–1804.

Haynes, S. N. (2003). Clinical applications of analogue behavioral observation: Dimensions of psychometric evaluation. In A. E. Kazdin (Ed.), *Methodological issues and strategies in clinical research* (3rd ed., pp. 235–264). Washington, DC: American Psychological Association.

Heller, J. J., & O'Connor, E. J. P. (2002). Maintaining quality in research and reporting. In *The new handbook of research on music teaching and learning* (pp. 1089–1107). New York: Oxford University Press.

Hsu, L. M. (2003). Random sampling, randomization, and equivalence of contrasted groups in psychotherapy outcome research. In A. E. Kazdin (Ed.), *Methodological issues and strategies in clinical research* (3rd ed., pp. 147–161). Washington, DC: American Psychological Association.

Kazdin, A. E. (1995). Preparing and evaluating research reports. *Psychological Assessment, 7,* 228–237.

Kirk, R. E. (1982). *Experimental design: Procedures for the behavioral sciences* (2nd ed.). Pacific Grove, CA: Brooks/Cole Publishing.

Kirk, R. E. (1996). Practical significance: A concept whose time has come. *Educational and Psychological Measurement, 56,* 746–759.

Körlin, D., & Wrangsjö, B. (2002). Treatment effects of GIM therapy. *Nordic Journal of Music Therapy, 11,* 3–15.

Leavitt, F. (2001). *Evaluating scientific research: Separating fact from fiction.* Upper Saddle River, NJ: Prentice-Hall.

Moher, D., Schulz, K. F., & Altman, D. (2001). The CONSORT statement: Revised recommendations for improving the quality of reports of parallel-group randomized trials. *Journal of the American Medical Association, 285,* 1987–1991.

Morgan, D. L., & Morgan, R. K. (2003) Single-participant research design: Bringing science to managed care. In A. E. Kazdin (Ed.), *Methodological issues and strategies in clinical research* (3rd ed., pp. 635–654). Washington, DC: American Psychological Association.

Prentice, D. A., & Miller, D. T. (2003). When small effects are impressive. In A. E. Kazdin (Ed.), *Methodological issues and strategies in clinical research* (3rd ed., pp. 127–137). Washington, DC: American Psychological Association.

Reynolds, S. (2000). Evidence based practice and psychotherapy research. *Journal of Mental Health, 8,* 257–266.

Rosenthal, R. (1993). Cumulating evidence. In G. Keren & C. Lewis (Eds.), *A handbook for data analysis in the behavioral sciences: Methodological issues* (pp. 519–559). Hillsdale, NJ: Erlbaum.

Sackett, D. L., Richardson, W. S., Rosenberg, W., & Haynes, R. B. (1998). *Evidence-based medicine: How to practice and teach EBM.* New York: Churchill Livingstone.

Schmidt, F. L. (2003). Statistical significance testing and cumulative knowledge in psychology: Implications for training of researchers. In A. E. Kazdin (Ed.), *Methodological issues and strategies in clinical research* (3rd ed., pp. 437–464). Washington, DC: American Psychological Association.

Thaut, M. H. (2000). *A scientific model of music in therapy and medicine.* San Antonio, TX: IMR Press.

Thompson, B. (1996). AERA editorial policies regarding statistical significance testing: Three suggested reforms. *Educational Researcher, 25*(2), 26–30.

Tunks, T. (1978). The use of omega squared in interpreting statistical significance. *Council for Research in Music Education Bulletin, 57,* 28–34.

Vink, A. C., Birks, J. S., Bruinsma, M. S., & Scholten, R. J. S. (2004). Music therapy for people with dementia (Cochrane review) [Abstract]. Available at http://www.cochrane.org/cochrane/evabstr/AB003477.htm

Wampold, B. E., Davis, B., & Good, R. H. (2003). Hypothesis validity of clinical research. In A. E. Kazdin (Ed.), *Methodological issues and strategies in clinical research* (3rd ed., pp. 389–406). Washington, DC: American Psychological Association.

Whitaker, R. (2002). *Mad in America: Bad science, bad medicine, and the enduring mistreatment of the mentally ill.* Cambridge, MA: Perseus Books.

Wigram, T., Pedersen, I. N., & Bonde, L. O. (2002). *A comprehensive guide to music therapy: Theory, clinical practice, research and training.* London: Jessica Kingsley Publishers.

Chapter 20
Evaluating Qualitative Music Therapy Research
Brian Abrams

The value of a given qualitative research study depends upon the rigor and integrity with which it is designed, conducted, and documented, as well as the richness, meaningfulness, relevance, and sophistication of the new knowledge it produces. Many of the criteria used to evaluate such properties of qualitative research are considered analogous to those utilized for evaluating quantitative research (Cobb & Hagemaster, 1987; Lincoln & Guba, 1985; Smeijsters, 1996a, 1996b; Stiles, 1993). While certain parallels may exist, there are a number of ways in which qualitative evaluation differs radically from quantitative evaluation. Unlike quantitative research, qualitative research evaluation is based upon nonpositivist tenets such as relative truth, multifaceted meanings, and realities composed of multiple, co-constructed, intersubjective realities. Qualitative research studies must therefore be evaluated according to how well they enlarge constructions of the world and help create individual meanings therein (Bruscia, 1998). They must also be evaluated according to *truthfulness*, or the honesty and trustworthiness of their methods and discoveries, as opposed to *truth*, or how well they generate independently verifiable fact (Wilber, 1997). Thus, as Bruscia has stated: "One simply cannot impose standards for quantitative research onto qualitative research, no matter how intellectually tempting or convenient that would be" (p. 177).

Because of the multifaceted nature of qualitative research, delineating standards for evaluating qualitative research is no simple matter. In its typical usage, the term *qualitative research* denotes the myriad forms of nonpositivist research, collectively encompassing a diversity of perspectives on purposes, values, and processes (Bruscia, 1998). Therefore, with respect to evaluation standards, Bruscia has stated: "There are as many qualitative standards as there are nonpositivistic epistemologies. This is certainly not a problem to be avoided or resolved—it is a fundamental condition of research" (p. 178). Furthermore, the specific nature of the evaluation process depends upon who does the evaluation (such as members of the editorial staff of a professional journal, scholars or academic instructors, research experts of various kinds, peers, readers, members of the public, research participants, or the researchers themselves), and the evaluator's orientation within one or more specific cultures embodying certain perspectives (or worldviews) and sets of values concerning research.

To a certain extent, distinct sets of evaluation criteria have been developed within specific, established methodological traditions of qualitative research such as phenomenology, hermeneutics, heuristics, grounded theory, historical inquiry, and ethnography. Certain scholarly journals that publish qualitative research, such as *Action Research International, Educational Action Research, The Journal of Occupational and Organizational Psychology*, and *Qualitative Research in Psychology,* have also specified evaluation criteria in the context of publication guidelines.

Qualitative research within music therapy involves its own pluralistic set of epistemologies and methodologies concerning music, health, and therapy, in unique combination. As a result, sets of guidelines have emerged (Aldridge, 2002; Bruscia, 1998), some of which have been developed expressly for appraising the integrity of research submitted to scholarly journals (Stige, 2002b) or monographs (Bruscia, 2003).

The purpose of this chapter is to summarize major themes of qualitative research evaluation relevant to the field of music therapy, based upon the current literature. In certain cases, terminology denoting these themes appears explicitly in the literature; in other cases, the present author has selected terminology to represent implicit ideas and constructs. The intent is not to establish a master set of standards or procedures but rather to present a synthesis of existing guidelines. Moreover, the reader should understand each theme as a general category only, not to be utilized as a substitute for the many case-specific considerations involved in the actual evaluation process.

The themes are:

- Reflexivity
- Contextualization
- Groundedness
- Durability

- Usefulness
- Comprehensibility
- Aesthetic depth
- Congruence
- Ethical integrity
- Intersubjectivity

Following summaries of the themes, a model for organizing the interrelationships among these themes will be proposed and concluding thoughts will be offered.

Themes in Qualitative Research Evaluation

Reflexivity

In qualitative research, the researcher is the primary instrument of the research (Aigen, 1995, 1996a; Stiles, 1993) and everything produced through a research study is the result of the researcher's interpretations on some level (Stige, 2002a). Therefore, the qualitative researcher's personal, professional, and cultural identities are inextricably a part of the research (Aigen, 1995; Ansdell, 2002; Bruscia, 1995a). From a nonpositivist, qualitative standpoint, it is falsely dichotomous to presume that a research study can be disembedded from the living context of the researcher, as research constructions "do not exist outside of the persons who create and hold them; they are not part of some 'objective' world that exists apart from their constructors" (Guba & Lincoln, 1989, p. 143). Thus, as Aigen (1995) has stated, "What you do as a qualitative researcher directly reflects who you are" (p. 296).

The researcher's role in qualitative research requires the researcher to self-inquire conscientiously and to disclose her or his relationships to the research. This combination of self-inquiry and disclosure is known as *reflexivity* (Rennie, 1995), which represents a core element by which qualitative research may be evaluated. Certain methodological traditions within qualitative research have adopted specific terminology for reflexivity, including *epoché* in phenomenology; *stance of the researcher* in naturalistic inquiry; *self-hermeneutic* in hermeneutic research; and *movement between personal and public* in heuristic research (Aigen, 1995, 1996b).

Through reflexivity, the researcher takes ownership of and responsibility for her or his perspectives, assumptions, motives, values, and interests that inform the process of doing the research (Bruscia, 1996, 1998; Elliot, Fischer, & Rennie, 1999). This extends to anything conscious or unconscious about the researcher's personal identity (Bruscia, 1995a, 1996, 1998), the researcher's relationship to research participants (Cobb & Hagemaster, 1987), and the researcher's philosophical, theoretical, paradigmatic, and conceptual presuppositions (Edwards, 2002; Stige, 2002a; Stiles, 1993). It also extends to the researcher's own honest perceptions of both virtues and constraints of the method and of both desirable and undesirable aspects of findings (Bruscia, 1996). In addition, reflexivity includes a researcher's consideration of her or his social, cultural, political, historical, and linguistic realities, as each of these inform her or his expectations, values, and ways of making meaning (Stige). To promote reflexivity during the research process, the researcher may record her or his personal thoughts, feelings, reactions, and concerns in a reflexive journal (Aigen, 1995; Bruscia, 1995c; Lincoln & Guba, 1985) and then communicate any emergent revelations in a forthright, explicit manner within the research report (Aigen; Bruscia, 1996).

To illustrate the concept of reflexivity, consider an example of a study investigating musical and lyrical themes in group song writing with persons recovering from chemical dependency. For reflexivity, the researcher may begin by considering her or his own relationship to and experiences of chemical dependency in both personal and professional contexts. The researcher may also consider any assumptions and value judgments about persons with chemical dependency as informed by her or his personal or cultural background. The researcher may then consider how any of the foregoing illuminates her or his personal motives and cultural pretexts for conducting the study, for involving the participants, and for posing the research question. In the course of implementing the study, the researcher might maintain a reflexive journal. Finally, the researcher would document the reflexive process and any resulting discoveries in a clear, forthright manner.

Qualitative research in music therapy requires musical self-inquiry on the part of the researcher in order to reveal her or his personal relationship to the musical experiences, processes, and products that are typically at the heart of the research. The researcher must consider these relationships in terms of individual and cultural dimensions, past personal and professional experiences, associations relating to the music or a particular instrument, and specific reactions and preferences. Thus, in the chemical dependency study example, the researcher might consider the meaning of songs and song writing in her or his life, including significant song writing experiences or specific approaches to song writing. Moreover, the researcher may consider the role of song writing that she or he has observed in the recovery processes of clients or in her or his own life (if applicable).

It is arguable that total reflexivity can never be achieved, as one cannot be fully aware of oneself in relation to research and cannot fully communicate that which is in awareness. In a research report, however, it is necessary to communicate the internal processes of investigation only to the extent that awareness permits (Stiles, 1993), and that they are relevant (Bruscia, 1996). Moreover, some reflexivity is always preferred over no reflexivity. As Rennie (1995) has stated on this topic, "A half loaf is better than none" (p. 49).

Contextualization

A concept related to reflexivity is contextualization, yet another major basis for qualitative research evaluation. Contextualization means inquiring into and disclosing the contexts of the research participants, the phenomenon being studied, and the research study itself. According to Bruscia (1995b), "To contextualize is to identify the many different frameworks, orientations, systems, environments, and conditions in which a research study is taking place" (p. 404).[1]

Contextualizing the participants (or sample) entails working to observe, study, and understand participants according to their own personal identities, life experiences, and cultural backgrounds. It further entails an understanding of the participants' relationships to the researcher within the shared, lived world in which the study takes place (Bruscia, 1998).

An extension of contextualizing the participants is clarity of voice (Bruscia, 1998). Clarity of voice is the degree to which the researcher explicitly acknowledges the specific identity, role, and lived experience of each individual involved in the study (researcher, participant, consultant, and so forth). Even when the role boundaries of researcher and participant are not absolutely distinct (such as in participant observation research), striving toward maximal clarity of voice helps explicate sources of data and distribution of roles, thereby deepening the integrity of the research.

Contextualizing the research phenomenon entails understanding and disclosing the biographical, historical, cultural, and other factors pertaining to the phenomenon being studied. In research about the arts, this means explicating the contexts surrounding the art (Wilber, 1997). Specifically in qualitative music therapy research, it means examining the ways in which the music being studied is created, expressed, and experienced by those involved in the study.

Contextualization of the research study itself is yet another basis for research evaluation. Stige (2002a) has emphasized the significance of contextualizing the research purpose and agenda, data, processes, interpretations, and outcomes in terms of their historical, sociocultural, political, and ideological contexts. For Aldridge (2002), this type of contextualization is particularly important with respect to understanding the values of the community within which the study is conducted and how those values may or may not legitimize the study. In large part, it is the related literature that represents the primary resource for this form of contextualization, as it embodies much of the history and values of a given research community or culture.

In the example chemical dependency study, contextualizing the participants might involve inquiring into participants' life experiences pertaining to drug use and song writing. To help ensure clarity of voice, the researcher could identify the specific roles of participants and researcher in shaping the group process and the songs written in the group. Contextualizing the research phenomenon would require a close examination of how study participants create, express, and experience writing songs, both as individuals and as part of a group. Finally, the

---

[1] For Bruscia (1995b), contextualizing includes the kinds of self-inquiry on the part of the researcher that have been described under the description of reflexivity above; here, it specifically refers to the various relationships surrounding the research study itself.

researcher could contextualize the study by considering its role and value within the existing music therapy research literature, as well as any historical, sociocultural, and ideological implications of the study with respect to the research community, such as motives for research on chemical dependency and song writing or attitudes on the research topic within the surrounding culture.

Groundedness

Qualitative researchers often strive to *accommodate* the multiple realities of participants and phenomena under study, as opposed to *assimilating* them into preconceived theories, methods, and research agendas (Bruscia, 1996, 1998; Stiles, 1993). Yet the potential for forced, contrived, or inauthentic constructions by the researcher warrants attention (Stige, 2002b). Thus, qualitative research is often evaluated according to its groundedness (Glaser & Strauss, 1967), meaning the extent to which the researcher orients research processes, data, and findings around the participants and phenomena in their original, living contexts. In a well grounded study, the researcher's constructions of research phenomena are consonant with the way these phenomena were originally expressed and experienced (Ansdell, 2002; Glaser & Strauss; Lincoln & Guba, 1990; Smeijsters, 1996a).

Groundedness should be distinguished from positivistic concepts of accuracy and bias. Given the tenet of multiple realities underlying qualitative research, there is no singular reference point concerning the way things really are and thus no way to determine accuracy versus inaccuracy or bias versus neutrality.[2] Groundedness does relate directly to a qualitative study's trustworthiness, however, as the more clearly the researcher's constructions are linked to the original data, the more solid the foundations of those constructions tend to be.

The elements underlying groundedness are achieved through a logical and systematic means of interacting with the research data (Stige, 2002b), usually organized as a sequence of purposive steps extending all the way through the research process (Stiles, 1993). Two procedures that are commonly employed when collecting and analyzing data are prolonged engagement, or the observation and study of research participants and phenomena over an scope of contexts and periods of time, and persistent observation, or the researcher's intensive involvement with research participants and phenomena (Lincoln & Guba, 1985). In addition to enriching and intensifying the collection and analysis of data, these procedures also help develop rapport between study participants and the researcher (Aigen, 1995).

In the midst of data collection, triangulation, or consulting multiple perspectives and data sources concerning the study phenomenon (Aigen, 1995; Elliot, Fischer, & Rennie, 1999; Lincoln & Guba, 1985; Stiles, 1993), helps ensure that resulting constructions are grounded in the sense of being as well-informed and holistic as possible (Bruscia, 1995b; Rennie, 1995; Stiles, 1993). Specific procedures can be employed for the purpose of triangulation, such as stepwise replication (Guba, 1981), in which another researcher applies the same research method with different samples so that emerging themes might be compared and contrasted between groups.

As the researcher begins to analyze the data, alternation between data collection and data analysis (i.e., formulation of categories, meanings, theories, etc.), or iterative cycling, promotes well-grounded research through balanced and fair representations of participant perspectives and experiences (Stiles, 1993). Moreover, the researcher can monitor the analysis process for signs of saturation, or when enough data on a particular aspect of the study have been processed so that additional data yields nothing significantly new concerning that aspect (Glaser & Strauss, 1967).

Throughout implementation of the research method, the researcher should promote fidelity, or the faithful accommodation of the study phenomenon as it unfolds in the lived world, as reported by participants and experienced by researcher in relation to that world (Bruscia,

---

[2] This misattribution of positivistic constructs to nonpostivist thinking applies to other areas of qualitative research as well. Naturalistic inquiry, which means noninterference with persons and processes in the many ways they express themselves and can be experienced by others, can be misconstrued as observing things in the one true way that they are. Likewise, the phenomenological practice of bracketing, or the researcher's purification of her or his research focus and intent through a reflexive consideration of her or his perspectives and motives with respect to the research phenomenon, can be misunderstood as dispelling biases and distortions concerning some singular truth of the research phenomenon.

1996, 1998). In this sense, fidelity means collecting and analyzing data in a manner that is analogous in form and process to the nature of the living process being studied.

Finally, communicating the study's groundedness in the research report requires fair and thorough conveyance of both the data and their links to findings. In part, this is accomplished through thick description, in which the researcher conveys the study phenomenon with sufficient depth and detail to illustrate all of its unique, individual qualities (Lincoln & Guba, 1985) while simultaneously proposing possible meanings of the phenomenon based upon the situational and cultural contexts in which it unfolds (Geertz, 1993). It is also accomplished through illustration-by-example, or citing specific instances of collected data and their transformation into findings through analysis (a common practice in phenomenology).

In the chemical dependency study example, the researcher could establish prolonged engagement with participants by spending extended periods of time with them throughout the course of the group process, and accomplish persistent observation through ongoing work with group participants on a particular issue. As data are collected, the researcher could triangulate by making comparisons among various lyrical and musical structures relating to particular elements or phases of drug use or addiction recovery, across different participants and songs. At the same time, the researcher might practice iterative cycling by constructing musical and lyrical themes in the midst of the group process itself while seeking evidence of saturation. Throughout data collection and analysis, the researcher could help ensure fidelity by striving to gather data in a way that supports and mirrors the natural unfolding of the group song writing process for participants and by analyzing the musical data through some form of musical process. In the research report, the researcher could help ensure groundedness through a thick description of participants' song writing experiences, as well as through illustration-by-example of how the researcher processed these experiences (as originally conveyed by participants) into findings.

Durability

Qualitative research findings are often evaluated according to their durability. One sense of durability is what Lincoln and Guba (1985) term dependability, or the consistency and stability of findings throughout repeated applications (stepwise replication) of the research method. This sense of durability may also include testing the strength of the findings amidst the rigors of shifting modes of data collection (Bruscia, 1995b), as well as shifting approaches to interpreting the data.

A second sense of durability is persistence of the meaningfulness and value of findings when considered in contexts beyond the original scope of the research study. Durability in this regard indicates a kind of resilience or robustness of the findings that accommodates reformulation in response to factual variations (Wertz, 1986) and contextual variations (Glaser & Strauss, 1967). To denote this sense of durability, Stiles (1993) has used the term *permeability*, whereas Lincoln and Guba (1985) have used the term *transferability*.

Yet a third sense of durability is the endurance of findings in the face of disconfirmatory evidence known as negative cases (Guba & Lincoln, 1989; Lincoln & Guba, 1985). Negative cases are instances of the study phenomenon that do not fit into any of the researcher's category schemes, theories, or other conceptual frameworks in the findings. Because qualitative research findings are not based upon statistical support of a hypothesis concerning causal, predictive relationships between variables, negative cases can actually help strengthen findings, as they shed additional light upon the specific nature of study phenomena and establish more secure boundaries around a conceptual framework or theory (by defining its limits).

With respect to the chemical dependency study, durability of findings might be demonstrated through compatibility with findings in a related study on improvisation and chemical dependency. Findings in this study could also be rendered more durable through the incidence of a negative case in which a participant lyrically expresses a sense of power connected with acquiescing to his cravings for a drug, in spite of the researcher's categorization of this kind of phenomenon as powerlessness.

Usefulness

A qualitative research study can also be appraised according to its applied value (Polkinghorne, 1983), or its usefulness. Qualitative research methods should generate data of variation, breadth, and depth sufficient to enlarge the constructions and potentials of the participants and researcher (Bruscia, 1998). Research findings should contribute to practical knowledge within a discipline (Cobb & Hagemaster, 1987; Polkinghorne; Stige, 2002a) and should be applicable to real life contexts (Stiles, 1993).

One specific way in which qualitative research can be useful is in its promotion of theory development (Cobb & Hagemaster, 1987), particularly theory that fits the substantive area within which it will be applied and is applicable to real-life situations (Glaser & Strauss, 1967). For example, the chemical dependency study might lead to a theory concerning stages of recovery as expressed through song themes that, in turn, might provide a unique model of recovery for use by music therapists or other creative arts therapists working in community-based drug rehabilitation programs.

Qualitative research can also be useful by empowering participants, researchers, members of disciplines, and society to meaningful and constructive action through a raised awareness (Guba & Lincoln, 1989; Stige, 2002a; Stiles, 1993). The chemical dependency study, for example, might empower clients, clinicians, and society by promoting a better understanding of and hence a more proactive stance on drug addiction and recovery.

Comprehensibility

Qualitative research can also be evaluated according to how comprehensible it is; that is, the extent to which the research report is accessible and understandable both to those directly involved in the research and to others interested in learning about the research and its findings (Glaser & Strauss, 1967). Comprehensibility also concerns how well the report is understood by those both within and outside of the discipline addressed by the research.

For comprehensibility in a research report, the researcher must make the study purpose clear (Cobb & Hagemaster, 1987), make theoretical frameworks explicit (Glaser & Strauss, 1967), adequately address sampling procedures and sample characteristics (Cobb & Hagemaster), and present data in an organized and accessible manner (Cobb & Hagemaster; Stige, 2002b). Essentially, the report must carefully and deliberately accommodate the reader. As Aigen (1996b) has stated: "Instead of establishing the necessary connections to readers in an oblique or unconscious way, we recognize the importance of directly and overtly accessing our readers' body of assumptions and common experiences in order to make the full meaning of the research document available to them" (p. 12).

In the chemical dependency study, for example, comprehensibility might be expressed in the form of the researcher helping the reader to understand and appreciate the essence of the participants' song writing experiences as well as the resulting themes. As part of this, comprehensibility would also be apparent in the care with which the researcher employs jargon concerning chemical dependency, psychological processes, and music.

Aesthetic Depth

Qualitative research involves an artistic, as opposed to scientific, way of knowing (Bruscia, 1998). It is composed of emotional, intuitive, and value-centered dimensions (Aigen, 1996b) and, when art is the topic of the research, integrally involves sensual and creative realms of expression (Keen, as cited in Polkinghorne, 1983). Thus, qualitative research is often evaluated according to the rigors of art; that is, the rigors that demand aesthetic depth. Qualitative music therapy research poses the unique problem of conveying aesthetic music experiences in words (Stige, 2002b) while avoiding reductionistic and contrived verbal descriptions that fail to do justice to the richness of these experiences (Ansdell, 2002). Thus, a qualitative music therapy research report must be evaluated according to how beautifully it conveys experiences and processes, not just how factually it does so.

Research reports with aesthetic depth convey research phenomena through artistic, creative expressions that uniquely represent experiences and meanings (Keen, cited in

Polkinghorne, 1983). These reports disclose the essence of research phenomena with elegance, grace, poignancy, and economy of expression. They are compelling and convincing to the reader (Glaser & Strauss, 1967) and are appealing to others due to richly detailed descriptions and meaningful presentation of topics, foci, findings, and theories (Aigen, 1995). They resonate with readers, thereby clarifying and expanding their appreciation for the phenomenon being investigated (Elliot, Fischer, & Rennie, 1999).

Bruscia (1998) has proposed a number of standards specifically concerning the aesthetic dimension of qualitative research, three of which relate directly to the construct of aesthetic depth. One is *creativity*, or the degree to which the researcher generates new possibilities for being in participants, audience, and self, as well as new possibilities for manifestations of the study phenomenon. Another is *structural beauty*, or the economy, clarity, cohesion, harmony, balance, and wholeness of the research. A third is e*xpressive beauty*, or the poignancy and imagination of the research report, including the effective use of creative media. As an extension of this third standard, Stige (2002b) has suggested the need for nonconventional journal manuscript format guidelines for qualitative research reports due to the highly individual, creative nature of these reports (particularly when addressing the arts).

Aesthetic depth in the chemical dependency study example could be evaluated in a number of ways. Creativity might be expressed as new perspectives on the meaning of chemical dependency in the lives of participants, new possibilities for empathy with persons struggling with chemical dependency on the part of the audience, new insights about what it means to experience the worlds of persons with chemical dependency through music, and new ways of expressing and working with the phenomenon of chemical dependency in clinical settings. Structural beauty would require a clear and consistent study purpose on the part of the researcher, a meaningfully organized set of methods and materials employed throughout the session series with participants, a plan of intervention that is both well-prepared and flexible to the evolving needs of the participants, continuity and integrity in the researcher's management of the research process, and so forth. Finally, for expressive beauty, the researcher might communicate certain elements of the purpose, method, process, data, findings, or conclusions through poetic verse, graphic illustration, written scores of music, audio recordings of music, video recordings, and so forth.

Congruence

Qualitative research studies are also evaluated according to congruence, or the degree to which all of the various components within a given study align, so that the study is in harmony with itself. Essentially, congruence is how consistently and meaningfully a study's purpose, methodology, findings, and report, along with the researcher's own understandings, values, and paradigmatic orientation, fit together as a cohesive, well-integrated whole.

One aspect of congruence concerns alignment between the qualitative research study and the researcher (Bruscia, 1996, 1998). A study that is congruent in this sense must resonate with a coherent framework of meanings and assumptions (Stiles, 1993) and must be consistently guided by the researcher's clear and secure sense of her or his own intentions, values, and ideals (Bruscia, 1998). In congruent research studies, the researcher's intentions are well formed and manifest purely and consistently throughout the research process, findings, and report. Likewise, congruence means that the researcher avoids duplicity, diffusion, and obfuscation of intent or purpose as well as use of incompatible paradigms or theoretical frameworks.

Another aspect of congruence concerns methodological appropriateness. Qualitative method should accommodate the study purpose (Aigen, 1995; Bruscia, 1996; Cobb & Hagemaster, 1987; Elliot, Fischer, & Rennie, 1999) and should never be contrived or predetermined, but should be purposively designed for the specific aims of the research (Bruscia; Stige, 2002b). Lincoln and Guba (1985) have used the term *credibility* to denote the appropriateness of a qualitative research method for investigating that which the researcher has targeted. For example, ethnographic analysis might be a more appropriate method than phenomenological interviewing for the chemical dependency study, as the central purpose of the study is to explore the various ways in which participants express their therapeutic (and life) experiences through their songs, as opposed to participants' verbal reflections upon their own experiences.

Ethical Integrity

The fair and trustworthy treatment of participants is generally regarded as a core concern in qualitative research and has thus been given careful consideration (Guba & Lincoln, 1989, 1994). Likewise, the American Music Therapy Association has established its own professional *Code of Ethics* (2003) that includes specific guidelines for ethical conduct in music therapy research. In the interest of protecting the welfare of research participants in accordance with such guidelines, the question of ethical integrity in music therapy research has been given significant attention (Dileo, 2000).

According to Bruscia (1998), in ethical qualitative research, the researcher maintains a genuine concern for the welfare of all persons involved in the study throughout all phases of research. This concern consists of honoring the human rights of others by avoiding any form of harm to their humanity, such as manipulation, coercion, exploitation, abuse, gratuitous or malevolent critique, or misuse of researcher privilege. Ethical research also requires a concern for the well being of other elements of the research, such as the phenomenon being studied and the study itself. Finally, the ethical researcher must take responsibility for her or his actions throughout the research process (Bruscia, 1996, 1998). This level of responsibility requires conscientiousness, or a combination of ethical care and self-awareness (an extension of reflexivity, as described previously).

In the chemical dependency study example, ethical integrity might be upheld through a number of careful measures implemented by the researcher. For example, ensuring that participant involvement is voluntary, that participants are not harmed in any way through the exploration of issues related to their personal struggles, that participants are not dehumanized through objectification of their experiences, that all personal disclosure is kept confidential and anonymous, and that active steps are taken on the researcher's part to remain aware of her or his own impact upon the well-being of participants.

Intersubjectivity

Although much of the accountability for ensuring the integrity of a qualitative research study rests with the researcher, the researcher has only limited access to the inner experiences of participants. Moreover, the researcher has only her or his own individual set of perspectives, with all of its limits and blind spots. Involving others in the research process helps mediate these limitations by providing communal, consensual viewpoints. Thus, qualitative research can also be evaluated according to its intersubjectivity, or the degree to which the researcher integrates the perspectives of others throughout the various stages of the research.

One way of promoting intersubjectivity in a research study is through collaboration with research participants. Perhaps the most common form of collaboration is member checking (Aigen, 1995; Elliot, Fischer, & Rennie, 1999), or asking participants to compare their own experiences and meanings (as they intended to convey these to the researcher) with the way the researcher has recorded and represented these experiences and meanings as research data. Thus, member checking in the chemical dependency study would entail asking participants to compare their own experiences of the song writing process with the ways in which the researcher has recorded and represented these experiences as data (such as descriptive summaries).

Another means to intersubjectivity is consultation with knowledgeable authorities or experts regarding research processes and practices. The terms *auditing* and *peer debriefing* (Aigen, 1995; Elliot, Fischer, & Rennie, 1999; Stiles, 1993) have been used to denote this process. This is not simply a one-way appraisal of the researcher's findings by peers, but an elaborate process of support, guidance, feedback, scrutiny, dialogue, uncovering, and arrival at insights. Smeijsters (1996a) has emphasized that consultation helps reduce negative ramifications of the researcher's preconceptions about the research. Furthermore, a research consultant can help promote the ethical integrity (as discussed above) of a researcher's practices.

With respect to consultation, Lincoln and Guba (1985) have used the term *confirmability* to signify that other researchers can uphold the data and findings in a study. Similarly, Bruscia (1995b) has used the term *neutrality* for research findings that are meaningful to persons beyond the researcher. In the chemical dependency study, for example, the researcher might help ensure confirmability by collaborating with those who have some working orientation to persons with chemical dependency, song writing, and the research method.

In consultation, a peer does not evaluate the researcher's work strictly according to the peer's own ideas about what the research should be (Aigen, 1995) but according to how well the researcher has done what she or he intended to do within the scope and context of the study, in addition to how faithfully she or he has honored established guidelines within the research community, where applicable. Furthermore, the researcher must be an expert in her or his own right regarding the qualitative paradigm, general research strategies, and the particular method being implemented (Cobb & Hagemaster, 1987). Therefore, the evaluator does not necessarily have access to a more exclusive, privileged understanding of the study's value, nor does the expertise of peer evaluators supplant the researcher's own expertise. Rather, peers contribute additional perspectives on the researcher's already well-informed understandings of participants' experiences, research methods, and constructed findings.

A Model of Qualitative Research Evaluation

While the above themes represent important components in understanding qualitative research evaluation, a single model expressing the interrelationships among these themes may serve to deepen understanding of the topic through a singular, cohesive framework. The *integral model of qualitative research evaluation* illustrated in Figure 1 is intended to represent such a framework. This model is based upon Wilber's (1997) integral model of consciousness.

Each evaluation theme discussed here concerns internal perspectives (experiences, meanings, and contexts pertaining to research phenomena and processes), external perspectives (expressions, practices, and constructions pertaining to research phenomena and processes), or both. Likewise, each theme concerns individual perspectives (those of a researcher, of a participant, or those represented in a particular set of findings), collective perspectives (those of groups or communities of researchers, groups or communities of participants, and cultures in which the research takes place), or both. Together, the internal versus external and individual versus collective dimensions produce four possible combinations, each of which can be represented as one of four quadrants in a subdivided square diagram, and each of which represents a particular perspective on qualitative research evaluation.

The *internal-individual* (upper left), or *I*, perspective concerns the first-hand (personal) experiences, meanings, and contexts of an individual participant, researcher, research peer, audience member, research report reader, member of the larger society, and so forth. A prime example of a theme that relates to this quadrant is reflexivity, as it concerns how an individual researcher self-inquires and discloses about any aspects of herself or himself (personal and cultural) that relate to the research. It is therefore an I matter.

The *internal-collective* (lower left), or *We*, perspective concerns the experiences, meaning systems, and contexts shared among participants, researchers, members of the larger society, and so forth, that culturally situate the research and all of the persons involved. A theme that may be positioned within this quadrant is contextualization, specifically with respect to research participants. Given that the qualitative researcher considers the research experience to be shared with the research participants, the matter of how these experiences are informed by the participants' biographical backgrounds, life experiences, and cultural backgrounds would be a We matter. This extends to clarity of voice, as it requires that the researcher and participants collectively identify contrasting points of view regarding experiences of the research phenomenon. Intersubjectivity is another We theme, as it concerns shared perspectives between the researcher and one or more participants or researchers/consultants.

The *external-individual* (upper right), or *It*, perspective concerns the expressions and practices of an individual participant or researcher, as well as procedures involved in and constructions emerging from a single research study. This also includes the ways in which a research peer, audience member, research report reader, or member of the larger society expresses her or his reactions and relationship to any aspect of the research. One theme that fits well into this quadrant is groundedness, which concerns the degree to which the researcher's practices, data, and findings align with the study phenomenon as expressed in its original context. Groundedness is a question of the study's integrity as an object and is hence an It matter. Congruence is another theme that belongs within this quadrant, as it concerns evaluation of the study according to its internal consistency.

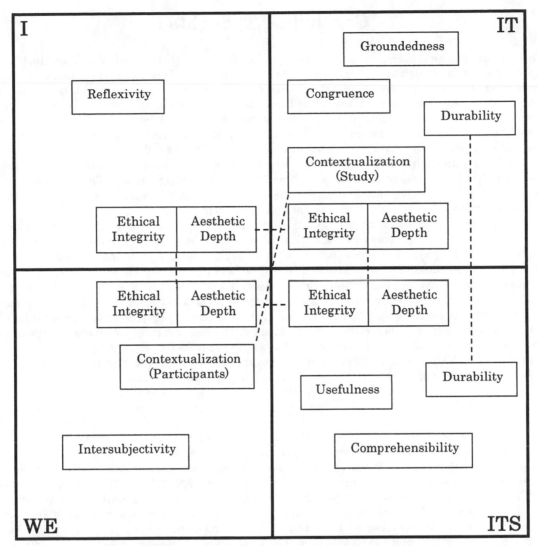

Figure 1. Integral Model of Qualitative Research Evaluation

The *external-collective* (lower right), or *Its,* perspective concerns the practices and products of participant communities, researcher communities, and society as a whole. These may manifest in various ways, including as patterns and systems within the research literature. Comprehensibility, concerning alignment between research constructions and expressions and practices of the greater community, and well as usefulness, concerning the practical implications of a study with respect to the research community and society as a whole, are examples of Its matters that belong within this quadrant.

Although each evaluation theme tends to fit into one particular quadrant more clearly than into any of the others, certain themes relate meaningfully to more than one quadrant. For example, contextualization can involve either participants, a We matter, or the study, an It matter. Likewise, durability might be considered an It matter, as it can involve evaluating the stability of the research constructions with respect to that study, or an Its matter, as it can also involve evaluating how well the research constructions align with collective constructions resulting from related research. Still other themes might relate more equally to all four quadrants. For example, aesthetic depth can involve subjective or objective components of beauty on either individual or collective levels. This is likewise the case with ethical integrity with respect to matters such as authorship, peer review, and institutional review (Dileo, 2000).

Concluding Thoughts

The various themes concerning evaluation of qualitative music therapy research identified here raise a number of questions and carry a number of implications. One question concerns whether evaluation of qualitative music therapy research can be based upon general qualitative research standards, or whether it should always be based upon standards indigenous to music therapy. For example, if we grant that music therapy is centrally defined by the promotion of health through music experiences within a therapeutic relationship, one could argue that reflexivity in qualitative music therapy research must always include the researcher's self-awareness about her or his relationships to health, to music, and to people. Likewise, one could argue that aesthetic depth (concerning constructs such as beauty, art, and creativity) should apply to all evaluations of qualitative music therapy research, as the music experience component that partially defines music therapy is an aesthetic phenomenon.

Another issue concerns the question of who exactly has the authority to evaluate qualitative music therapy research. According to Bruscia (1995a, 1996), it is the researcher who appraises the design and implementation of the research, makes revisions if needed, and is ultimately responsible for how consistently and coherently she or he has maintained and expressed her or his intentions and values through the research. For Aigen (1996a), this intrasubjective perspective "relieves us from the impossible task of becoming 'authenticity police' judging fellow researchers" (p. 169). In contrast to intrasubjective perspectives on accountability, culture-centered, or intersubjective, perspectives hold that integrity in research must be understood according to how integrity is situated within the collective set of values in a culture as a whole (Stige, 2002a, 2002b). Thus, the most relevant concern regarding this issue might be the fit between a given approach and the culture in which it is being applied.

A final issue concerns the establishment of comprehensive standards for evaluation of qualitative music therapy research. While such a set of guidelines might be helpful in conveying a spectrum of criteria through which a given study can be appraised, the potential context insensitivity would fail to acknowledge the complexity and multifaceted nature of the study. Thus, to the extent that such standards represent overly general, fixed methods of evaluation, these may threaten the credibility of the evaluation process and impede potentially meaningful discoveries. As a result of considerations such as these, Bernstein (1976, 1983) argued some time ago for nonfoundational ways of evaluating research, or evaluation without fixed sets of standards. To avoid the perils of utter relativism, however, such an endeavor would require an active, dynamic dialogue among all those responsible for the appraisal of a given study, in which each member would consider the study (and the intentions of the researcher) on its own intrinsic terms yet still strive for some form of collective consensus. Simultaneously, perhaps various evaluation models and metacriteria can help guide and organize this process in general, nonrestrictive ways. Moreover, it is conceivable that evaluating qualitative research (particularly when concerning the arts) may require certain unconventional modes of awareness on the part of the evaluator. Braud (1998), for example, has suggested modes of awareness such as emotions, intuition, bodily wisdom, and other nondiscursive impressions. In any event, it is the author's hope that further exploration through dialogue and practical application will lead to more integrated, well-informed, and sophisticated understandings of qualitative music therapy research evaluation.

References

Aigen, K. (1995). Principles of qualitative research. In B. L. Wheeler (Ed.), *Music therapy research: Quantitative and qualitative perspectives* (pp. 283–311). Gilsum, NH: Barcelona Publishers.

Aigen, K. (1996a). The researcher's cultural identity. In M. Langenberg, K. Aigen, & J. Frommer (Eds.), *Qualitative music therapy research: Beginning dialogues* (pp. 165–176). Gilsum, NH: Barcelona Publishers.

Aigen, K. (1996b). The role of values in qualitative research. In M. Langenberg, K. Aigen, & J. Frommer (Eds.), *Qualitative music therapy research: Beginning dialogues* (pp. 9–33). Gilsum, NH: Barcelona Publishers.

Aldridge, D. (2002, May 3). The politics of qualitative research criteria: A local solution within an ecosystemic ecology. Message posted to forum topic, General Criteria for the Evaluation of Qualitative Research Articles, *Forum: Nordic Journal of Music Therapy*, http://www.hisf.no/njmt/forumqualart_3.html

American Music Therapy Association. (2003). *Code of ethics.* http://musictherapy .org/ethics.html

Ansdell, G. (2002, May 27). Goethe's response: On qualifying the qualifiers. Message posted to forum topic, General Criteria for the Evaluation of Qualitative Research Articles, *Forum: Nordic Journal of Music Therapy*, http://www.hisf.no/njmt/forumqualart_3.html

Bernstein, R. J. (1976). *The restructuring of social and political theory.* Philadelphia: University of Pennsylvania Press.

Bernstein, R. J. (1983). *Beyond objectivism and relativism: Science, hermeneutics, and praxis.* Philadelphia: University of Pennsylvania Press.

Braud, W. (1998). An expanded view of validity. In W. Braud & R. Anderson (Eds.), *Transpersonal research methods for the social sciences: Honoring human experience* (pp. 213–237). Thousand Oaks, CA: Sage Publications.

Bruscia, K. E. (1995a). The process of doing qualitative research: Part I: Introduction. In B. L. Wheeler (Ed.), *Music therapy research: Quantitative and qualitative perspectives* (pp. 389–399). Gilsum, NH: Barcelona Publishers.

Bruscia, K. E. (1995b). The process of doing qualitative research: Part II: Procedural steps. In B. L. Wheeler (Ed.), *Music therapy research: Quantitative and qualitative perspectives* (pp. 401–427). Gilsum, NH: Barcelona Publishers.

Bruscia, K. E. (1995c). The process of doing qualitative research: Part III: The human side. In B. L. Wheeler (Ed.), *Music therapy research: Quantitative and qualitative perspectives* (pp. 429–443). Gilsum, NH: Barcelona Publishers.

Bruscia, K. E. (1996). Authenticity issues in qualitative research. In M. Langenberg, K. Aigen, & J. Frommer (Eds.), *Qualitative music therapy research: Beginning dialogues* (pp. 81–107). Gilsum, NH: Barcelona Publishers.

Bruscia, K. E. (1998). Standards of integrity for qualitative music therapy research. *Journal of Music Therapy, 35,* 176–200.

Bruscia, K. E. (2003). Editorial review form, *Qualitative inquiries in music therapy* [research monograph series]. Unpublished manuscript.

Cobb, A. K., & Hagemaster, J. N. (1987). Ten criteria for evaluating qualitative research proposals. *Journal of Nursing Education, 26,* 138–143.

Dileo (2000). *Ethical thinking in music therapy.* Cherry Hill, NJ: Jeffrey Books.

Edwards, J. (2002, June 4). Another contribution to the forum. Message posted to forum topic, General Criteria for the Evaluation of Qualitative Research Articles, *Forum: Nordic Journal of Music Therapy*, http://www.hisf.no/njmt/forumqualart_3.html

Elliot, R., Fischer, C. T., & Rennie, D. L. (1999). Evolving guidelines for publication of qualitative research studies in psychology and related fields. *British Journal of Clinical Psychology, 38,* 215–229.

Geertz, C. (1993). *The interpretation of cultures.* London: Fontana Press.

Glaser, B. G., & Strauss, A. L. (1967). *The discovery of grounded theory: Strategies for qualitative research.* New York: Aldine De Gruyter.

Guba, E. G. (1981). Criteria for assessing the trustworthiness of naturalistic inquiries. *Educational Communication and Technology Journal, 29,* 75–92.

Guba, E. G., & Lincoln, Y. S. (1989). *Fourth generation evaluation.* Newbury Park, CA: Sage Publications.

Guba, E. G., & Lincoln, Y. S. (1994). Competing paradigms in qualitative research. In N. K. Denzin & Y. S. Lincoln (Eds.), *Handbook of qualitative research* (pp. 105–117). Thousand Oaks, CA: Sage Publications.

Lincoln, Y. S., & Guba, E. G. (1985). *Naturalistic inquiry.* Beverly Hills, CA: Sage Publications.

Lincoln, Y. S., & Guba, E. G. (1990). Judging the quality of case study reports. *Qualitative Studies in Education, 3,* 53–59.

Polkinghorne (1983). *Methodology for the human sciences: Systems of inquiry.* Albany, NY: State University of New York Press.

Rennie, D. L. (1995). Plausible constructionism as the rigor of qualitative research. *Methods: A Journal for Human Science, Annual Edition,* 42–58.

Smeijsters, H. (1996a). Qualitative research in music therapy: New contents, new concepts, or both? In M. Langenberg, K. Aigen, & J. Frommer (Eds.), *Qualitative music therapy research: Beginning dialogues* (pp. 179–188). Gilsum, NH: Barcelona Publishers.

Smeijsters, H. (1996b). Qualitative single-case research in practice: A necessary, reliable, and valid alternative for music therapy research. In M. Langenberg, K. Aigen, & J. Frommer (Eds.), *Qualitative music therapy research: Beginning dialogues* (pp. 35–53). Gilsum, NH: Barcelona Publishers.

Stige, B. (2002a). *Culture-centered music therapy.* Gilsum, NH: Barcelona Publishers.

Stige, B. (2002b, April 26). Do we need general criteria for the evaluation of qualitative research articles, and if we do, how could such criteria be formulated? Message posted to forum topic, General Criteria for the Evaluation of Qualitative Research Articles, *Forum: Nordic Journal of Music Therapy,* http://www.hisf.no/njmt/forumqualart_3.html

Stiles, W. B. (1993). Quality control in qualitative research. *Clinical Psychology Review, 13,* 593–618.

Wertz, F. J. (1986). The question of the reliability of psychological research. *Journal of Phenomenological Psychology, 17,* 181–205.

Wilber, K. (1997). *The eye of spirit: An integral vision for a world gone slightly mad.* Boston: Shambhala.

Part III

Types of Quantitative Research

Chapter 21
Experimental Research
Suzanne B. Hanser and Barbara L. Wheeler

*Does music therapy cause changes in immune system function in patients
who have cancer?*

*Does music therapy result in improved quality of life for older adults in
nursing homes?*

*Is music therapy responsible for increased self-esteem in children with social
adjustment problems?*

These questions and many more like them are the subjects of experimental research performed
by music therapists. But why choose experimental research over other types of designs?

There are many advantages to experimental designs, especially in an evolving scientific
endeavor such as music therapy. Early in the development of any science, theories emerge and
hypotheses abound. Clinicians design new approaches, techniques, and models, while they
discuss their implications and test them out with small groups of people. As more and more
protocols are developed for different therapeutic purposes, researchers become more adept at
articulating hypotheses, considering the reliability and validity of their practices, and fine-tuning
the variables of interest. After this initial groundwork is done, music therapy researchers are
ready to test methods with single subjects and small groups. Following all of these steps, they are
in a position to identify specific treatments for particular populations using controlled
experimental designs.

In experimental research in music therapy, researchers determine and control the
precise conditions and factors of interest, including the specific treatment techniques, how they
will be administered, who will receive treatment, and when the treatment will occur. They are
able to repeat their observations and develop replicable protocols, treatment that may be tested
with other samples and in other settings. Controlled experiments give them the opportunity to
vary treatment conditions and systematically observe the changes that take place.

The purpose of using a true experimental design is to determine cause and effect, an
advantage unique to experimental research. Because the experimenter takes pains to manipulate
variables, the data that are generated may be highly reliable, making it easier to interpret
results and generalize the findings from one setting to another.

Types of Experimental Research

Several terms are used to describe experimental research. *Basic* or *pure research* is usually
performed in a laboratory or other setting in which all conceivable variables are controlled. This
type of research, exemplified by much of the genetic research that seeks to find a cure for
illnesses, may not have an immediate application. Similarly, laboratory experiments that study
the effect of an auditory stimulus on evoked potentials in our brains may not have obvious impact
on clinical music therapy practice with patients with Alzheimer's disease today, but eventually
music therapists will need to adapt their methods if it is shown that these patients' brains
respond differently than do the brains of patients who do not have Alzheimer's disease. In
contrast, applied research has a direct and immediate application to the problems that music
therapists face in the real clinical settings in which they work.

Exploratory experiments, or *pilot studies,* are performed to test previously untested
hypotheses or to investigate areas that lack a strong foundation in theory or background
research. A *confirmatory experiment,* as implied in the name, tests a more developed hypothesis
that is able to predict more precise outcomes and confirm previous findings. Both of these are
experimental research models in which the experimenter controls all possible factors in order to
isolate the true source of observed variation.

Principles of Experimental Research

Independent and Dependent Variables

Whether basic or applied, exploratory or confirmatory, experiments are designed to test the effect of an experimentally manipulated variable, the *independent variable,* on the variable that is free to vary, the *dependent variable.* Under ideal conditions, true experiments allow the researcher to determine whether this manipulation is the cause of an observed change in the variable of interest. In the examples opening this chapter, we are investigating the effect of music therapy (the independent variable) on immune function, quality of life, and self-esteem, respectively (the dependent variables). Experimental group designs compare two or more independent variables, conditions, or groups, often represented by types of therapies, styles of music, or forms of treatment. They enable the researcher to determine, after analyzing the results with statistical tests, whether changes in the dependent variable are due to the independent variable. When the variability between groups is significantly greater than the variability within each group, a statistically significant difference between groups may be established, within the boundaries of a selected probability level. This results in the isolation of the independent variable as the most probable cause of changes in the dependent variable.

Control

If we have managed to *control* the experiment well, only the variables that we have intended to vary (the independent variables) have changed from condition to condition. Random assignment of subjects to groups or conditions ensures that there is an equal probability that an individual will be assigned to one condition as opposed to any other condition. All other known extraneous variables, such as setting, time of day, therapist, and other factors that may influence the outcome, are kept constant. If an extraneous variable is inadvertently allowed to affect the independent variables, it is called a confounding variable. Consideration is given to the validity and reliability of measures of the dependent variable and the integrity of the independent variable. In music therapy research, this may translate into standardized or tested assessment instruments borrowed from other scientific disciplines and a music therapy protocol or music technique that already has been pilot studied with smaller samples. Since another name for control is *internal validity,* if we have a well-controlled experiment, we may also say that our experiment has high internal validity.

Generalizability

We want to generalize the results of a true experimental design to the population from which random sample was drawn. When we *generalize,* it means that we apply our results to people outside of those used in our experiment; the people to whom we hope to apply those results are considered the population. *Random selection* of subjects ensures that the sample represents the population at large; a sample selected in this manner is called a *random sample.* Other things that influence the ability to generalize the findings are the size of the sample (generally, the larger it is, the more likely it is to be representative of the population), and whether it has a normal distribution. If it is normally distributed, it is likely that it is representative of the population. *External validity* is another term for the generalizability of the results. The ability to generalize from the sample to a larger population is important; if we cannot generalize, there is no carryover from the experiment to clinical or other situations. If we are unable to select subjects randomly for our experiment, it is important to select subjects in such a way that they are likely to represent the population of interest.

Experimental Design

An *experimental design* is a way to structure conditions in scientific inquiry. The scientific method attempts to draw inferences from observing relationships amongst phenomena.

Experimental designs help researchers test hypotheses by controlling certain variables and allowing others to change so that they can be observed. Various experimental designs are presented later in this chapter.

Hypotheses

Before designing an experimental research study, the researcher states a prediction in the form of a *hypothesis.* An example of a hypothesis is: A structured approach to music listening and relaxation administered by a music therapist will decrease depression and anxiety in elderly depressed people, as opposed to the same treatment without the presence of a music therapist or to no treatment. Frequently, hypotheses are stated in the null form, predicting that no difference will be found; if a difference is found, the null hypothesis is rejected.

Evolution of a Study: An Example

The more established the theory underlying an experiment, the greater the justification for applying a given approach. The greater the body of exploratory evidence behind a hypothesis, the better the likelihood of confirming that hypothesis. One way to understand the evolution of research process from theory to a sophisticated, true experimental design is to follow the progress of one music therapy experimenter, namely the first author, Hanser.

Based on many years of experience as a music therapist, Hanser had developed a set of methods and procedures that she had found to be effective with individuals who were anxious. When the latest experiment was proposed, she already had investigated the theoretical foundation for the therapeutic model, a cognitive behavioral approach to coping with anxiety. She had published and presented descriptive studies of successful cases and tested adaptations of music therapy techniques in controlled experiments with women in childbirth (Hanser, Larson, & O'Connell, 1983) and dental patients and patients awaiting in-office medical procedures (Hanser, Martin, & Bradstreet, 1982).

The next step was to test this music therapy protocol with individuals who had been referred to therapy for anxiety and depression. Furthermore, it was desirable to select a population that had the greatest need for these services, but limited access. She identified the population of older adults who were homebound and unable to receive psychotherapy for anxiety and depression because it was difficult for them to leave their homes for regular therapy appointments. Previous experience and research using other treatments with this population gave indications about the minimum treatment period necessary to expect clinically significant changes.

Because she could not randomly select depressed and anxious people, she defined the population of interest as specifically as possible and recruited eligible participants. She formulated the details of a protocol, a music listening and relaxation strategy. She decided to compare a weekly home visit administered by a music therapist with a wait-list control group who agreed to delay any treatment until after the 8-week experimental period. Realizing that this experimental-control group design had not controlled a very critical variable, the presence of a therapist in the client's home, she instituted a third condition, an additional control group that received the same music listening and relaxation strategy without the therapist's presence. Individuals in this condition were given written instructions and music cassettes specifying how to use the strategy, but received a weekly telephone call by the music therapist in place of the home visit. She tested depression and anxiety in all subjects in all three conditions; they were tested pretreatment, at midtreatment (after 4 weeks), and posttreatment (at the end of the 8 weeks) in an effort to compare the outcome of the three conditions (Hanser & Thompson, 1994).

Individuals in the two music therapy conditions scored significantly better than the controls on measures of depression, distress, mood, and self-esteem. Their improvement was clinically significant and sustained over a 9-month follow-up period. Hanser published the clinical protocol, suggesting its potential with residents of long-term care facilities (Hanser, 1996) and pursued still another application, to women with metastatic breast cancer. She began clinical work at Dana-Farber Cancer Institute, adapting and extending these music therapy techniques for use alongside chemotherapy treatment. She developed a new clinical program, this time using live music, improvisation, and songwriting, and observed its efficacy in several cases. She developed a simple scale to measure changes in comfort, relaxation, and contentment, and began to examine pulse and blood pressure before and after each session. After reporting these results in descriptive studies, Hanser identified additional standardized tests of quality of life, anxiety, and depression, and instituted an experimental design to compare women who participated in music therapy sessions (experimental group) with those who did not (control group). Seventy women participated in a randomized groups design whose findings indicated that, while statistically significant pre- to post-session differences were found in heart rate, comfort, relaxation, and contentment, there were no significant differences between the music therapy and control groups on the standardized measures after the completion of the treatment period and at follow-up. Small sample size and high attrition rates, probably due to the intensity of their illness, may have contributed to the lack of statistical significance (Hanser, Bauer-Wu, Kubicek, Healey, Bunnell, & Manola, 2005).

Designs for Experimental Research

As you can see, designing an experiment is a matter of structuring conditions so that the independent and dependent variables are defined clearly, and extraneous variables are controlled to the greatest degree possible. Music therapy researchers use a variety of designs that may be classified as pre-experimental, true experimental, and quasi-experimental designs (Campbell & Stanley, 1963). The *pre-experimental designs* consist of single groups observed under controlled conditions. The *true experimental designs* involve comparisons of two or more groups that are either independent or related. The *quasi-experimental designs* are not set up to determine cause-and-effect relationships but involve structured observations under controlled conditions.

Pre-Experimental Designs

We will look at two examples of pre-experimental designs in music and music therapy research, both of which employ systematic observations of a single group. Obviously, when investigating the responses of one group, there is no basis for comparison, limiting the ability to determine cause and effect. Without a control group, it is difficult to determine whether observed changes are the result of the selected treatment. However, for certain experimental questions, pre-experimental designs provide an appropriate format for hypothesis testing. Pre-experimental designs are actually a type of descriptive research.

Consider the following case. A music therapist is interested in determining whether clients will choose to participate in music therapy as opposed to three other available therapy programs. Is music therapy the treatment of choice, according to incoming clients at Clinic X? The null hypothesis states that the four therapy programs will be equally popular. The therapist sets up an experiment whereby new clients select from the available therapy programs at the clinic. If music therapy is the most frequent program choice, the therapist is able to reject the null hypothesis in favor of the alternative hypothesis that music therapy is more popular than one would expect by chance.

This example is similar to a study conducted by Heaney (1992) in which he looked at how hospitalized psychiatric patients evaluated music therapy, art therapy, recreation therapy, traditional therapies, and other aspects of care provided during their hospitalization. Therapies were rated on the following semantic differential scales: *good-bad, important-unimportant, pleasurable-painful,* and *successful-unsuccessful*. He found music therapy to be rated significantly higher than art or recreation therapy on the pleasurable-painful scale, but there were no other significant differences among music therapy and the other activity therapies.

Another pre-experimental design examines clients attending a 6-month music therapy program to determine whether it affects their adaptive styles. The therapist administers a standardized psychological test of adaptive styles to each member of the group before therapy begins and then again after the 6-month period. Pretreatment and posttreatment scores are compared to test the null hypothesis that there will be no change in adaptive styles from pretest to posttest. It is clear that the generalizability of these results is limited without a comparison or control group, but this single case study offers good exploratory evidence.

One example of this design uses music notation to improve the speech prosody of children with hearing problems (Staum, 1987). In this study, children of varying ages and from several schools who had hearing problems learned a visual notation system to match words or word sounds with notation of the appropriate rhythmic and inflectional structure. They were evaluated throughout the treatment on program objectives. The improvement shown by the children led the experimenter to conclude that music notation written below printed words could be effective in improving verbal, rhythmic, and intonational accuracy in reading tasks with the older children.

All of these examples employ designs in which inferences are made from a single group of observations. Despite gross limitations in generalizability, these pre-experimental designs are appropriate for testing certain hypotheses and pilot testing others.

True Experimental Designs: Independent Groups

In general, the most rigorous way to test a hypothesis is to control as many variables as possible by using random assignment to groups. These investigations include examinations of music versus silence, music therapy versus no therapy, auditory stimuli versus no stimuli, or an experimental condition versus a condition with everything but the experimental variable itself. These pairs of conditions constitute the independent variables of a classic experimental-control group design.

The simplest design for implementing these controls uses two randomly assigned groups, comparing an experimental to a control group. These designs include a randomized groups design, where subjects are randomly assigned to conditions; an independent groups design, where two or more randomly assigned groups are compared; a pretest-posttest control group design, where assessment or observation of the dependent variable occurs before the conditions begin (pretreatment) and after the conditions end (posttreatment) in both the experimental and control groups; and a posttest-only control group design, which eliminates the pretest.[1] In all designs, the experimenter uses statistics to compare the central tendency and variability of the two conditions and determine whether the null hypothesis may be rejected.

An example of an independent groups design and a pretest-posttest control group design is a study by Knight and Rickard (2001) in which they investigated the effects of what they considered relaxing music (Pachelbel's *Canon in D Major*) on stress-induced increases in subjective anxiety, heart rate, and systolic blood pressure, as well as several other measures. The study is an independent groups design because people were assigned to two independent conditions and is a pretest-posttest design because they were tested before the introduction of the stressor and again after the stressor had been introduced. The control group (condition) experienced greater stress reactions than those who listened to music.

Sometimes using a control group that removes the experimental variable is inappropriate or not feasible. For instance, when a researcher tests the efficacy of music therapy with patients in crisis or trauma, it is unethical to withhold treatment from a control group. In this case, a more advisable comparison condition might consist of therapy with the same therapist, for the same duration, in the same setting, and with the same content, except including verbal techniques in place of music therapy techniques. This design tests the more specific independent variable, music therapy techniques, as opposed to studying music therapy versus no therapy.

In fact, this is the design of choice for the therapist who wanted to test the hypothesis at the beginning of the chapter that music therapy causes changes in immune function in patients with cancer. He identified cancer patients who met specific medical criteria, ensuring that this sample would be relatively homogenous with regard to diagnosis and prognosis. He selected patients in a similar age bracket and from the same community to limit socioeconomic and other environmental and demographic variables. He reviewed the literature to find the latest, most reliable, and most valid measurement of immune system function. Then, he randomly assigned each selected patient to either the music therapy condition or to one in which the therapist met with the patient and kept all conceivable conditions constant, except that he did not use any music or music therapy techniques. He measured immune system function posttreatment in both groups and compared the results. When controlled effectively, this design yields considerable assurance that changes observed between the conditions are due to music therapy as opposed to other factors.

---

[1] See Campbell and Stanley (1963) or an experimental design textbook for more complete descriptions of these designs and the other designs presented in this chapter.

So that she would not have to withhold treatment from any of her participants, Burns (2001) used a wait-list control group. She wanted to see if Guided Imagery and Music (GIM) would have an effect on the mood and quality of life of women who had cancer. She randomly assigned the women in her sample to two groups, then pretested them before giving the women in the GIM (experimental) group 10 weekly GIM sessions. They were tested again after the treatment period, and 6 weeks later. The GIM sessions were found to be helpful in improving mood and quality of life. Having a wait-list control group means that those women were offered GIM sessions following the conclusion of the research and provides another option to ensure the ethical treatment of participants.

Designs that compare three or more randomly assigned groups are also classified as randomized group designs. These designs have the advantage of being able to decipher the relative value of multiple levels or types of treatment. Consider the experiment cited earlier with depressed and anxious older adults (Hanser & Thompson, 1994). Adding the third group with no direct access to the music therapist controlled for the presence of the therapist so that conclusions could be drawn regarding whether the music therapy protocol itself contributed to the outcome. The results demonstrated that both the home visit and minimal therapist contact groups had significantly better outcomes than the wait-list control group.

In this experiment, using pretests and posttests allowed Hanser, the first author of the present chapter, to determine whether the three groups had equivalent levels of depression and anxiety before the experiment began. When we randomly assign subjects to groups, we assume that all subject characteristics will be equally distributed across the groups. However, when we have less than ideal conditions, for example, sources of uncontrolled bias, a small sample, or any experimental error, it is advisable to determine whether the groups perform similarly on the critical dependent variable prior to treatment. This check often takes the form of a pretest. Not only is the pretest useful for experimental control, but it also allows the experimenter to test the magnitude of changes from pretest to posttest. In this experiment, the advantage of a midtest 4 weeks into treatment was that it provided additional information regarding the feasibility of detecting a significant treatment effect in a shorter period of time. In fact, the results confirmed that the longer, 8-week treatment period was necessary to identify significant differences among the conditions.

Sometimes delivering a pretest may influence subjects' posttest performances or be inappropriate in the context of the experiment. Often, subjects may be biased if they are aware of the purpose of the experiment or the intentions of the experimenter. A posttest-only control group design, with all possible controls and random assignment to groups, may be the most appropriate choice.

A posttest only design was employed by Cordobés (1997) to examine the effects of group songwriting on the level of group cohesion in patients who were HIV-seropositive or had AIDS and who were diagnosed with depression. Her volunteer subjects participated in one of three groups: writing a song using emotion topics, participating in a game of *Gay Monopoly®*, or no treatment control. Following each activity, subjects filled out a questionnaire intended to measure group cohesion. She also included a content analysis of the language used in the sessions and counted the number of emotion words used in the session. While she did not find any differences in group cohesion between the groups, the number of emotion words used was greater for the songwriting condition than for the game playing condition. She suggested that using more subjects and randomly selecting them might make it more likely that differences in group cohesion might be detected.

Another important research question asked by music therapists concerns the interaction of a music therapy condition with different groups of subjects. A factorial design handles this question nicely. Suppose the music therapist is interested in different levels of music therapy with three different samples. The therapist wishes to determine the intensity of treatment necessary to make a difference in inpatients with three psychiatric diagnoses: chronic schizophrenia, manic depression, and personality disorder. She compares intensive, daily music therapy (Condition A) with weekly music therapy (Condition B) and hospital programming without music therapy (Condition C). She randomly assigns one third of each diagnostic group to one of the three different levels of therapy. The design allows the experimenter to examine the various interrelationships between levels of treatment and diagnosis. The experimenter asks: Is there an overall effect for certain therapy conditions regardless of diagnosis? Is there an overall effect for one or more of the diagnostic groups regardless of therapy condition? Alternatively, are certain levels of therapy more effective for one or two diagnostic groups as opposed to the others?

Factorial designs are more complicated to set up but offer the researcher the opportunity to test many more specific subhypotheses and to obtain much more information about interactions between variables.

Hurt, Rice, McIntosh, and Thaut (1998) used a factorial design with repeated measures to investigate the effects of Rhythmic Auditory Stimulation (RAS) with variations in two variables, tempi (fast and normal) and cuing (no rhythm and rhythm), on velocity, cadence, stride length (meter), and swing symmetry of people with traumatic brain injuries. While the first experiment looked at immediate effects of rhythmic cuing on gait, the second experiment examined training effects. Statistically significant changes were found in the second experiment.

True Experimental Designs: Related Groups

In some cases, it is desirable for subjects to act as their own controls rather than be compared to other subjects. This experimental design is known as a repeated measures or within subjects design. In this design, every subject is observed under all of the conditions. This design holds advantages when great variability is expected.

One challenge to music therapy researchers is the tremendous amount of individual difference, or variability, that exists in special clinical populations. Recall that, in all types of experimental research, it is the variability between treatment conditions compared with the variability within each condition that determines whether an observed difference is statistically significant. Large individual differences mean large variability within each treatment condition and, subsequently, little power to detect a difference when one really exists.

In this event, the repeated measures design offers a viable alternative to randomly assigned groups. Hanser found this useful in planning research on the effect of background music on tension in women in labor and childbirth (Hanser, Larsen, & O'Connell, 1983). The individual differences in women's tension observed during labor were so tremendous that it would have taken an extremely large sample to detect treatment effects as a function of music listening. However, with each woman acting as her own control, all subjects experienced conditions of background music and no background music, alternately, throughout the course of labor. Because each woman was compared to herself, there was complete control over individual characteristics across the two conditions. However, there was a limitation to this design in that, with repeated conditions, the order of the conditions could have affected the results. In other words, participating in the background music could have influenced subsequent participation without background music, and vice versa. In spite of this possibility, significant differences between music and no music conditions were observed in this experiment.

Baker (2001) conducted a research study in which subjects served as their own controls when she examined the effects of live, taped, and no music on people who were experiencing posttraumatic amnesia. Each of her subjects was exposed to each of her three conditions, with the exposure occurring twice over six consecutive days. Her comparisons, therefore, were of each subject under all of the conditions, with the subjects' responses being compared over the three conditions. She found that music decreased agitation and enhanced orientation, but that there were no significant differences in the effects of live and taped music.

When order of conditions is of concern, there is a way to control this. Counterbalancing the conditions means that the experimenter allows each group to experience the conditions in a different order.[2] In the nursing home example at the start of the chapter, in order to test the quality of life hypothesis, the music therapist decided to compare three conditions: (a) music therapy, (b) a structured reminiscence approach with no music, and (c) traditional programming without music therapy or structured reminiscence. Using a counterbalanced design, the therapist rotated the nursing home patients through the three conditions. He randomly assigned them to Groups A, B, or C. Group A experienced 4 weeks of music therapy, 4 weeks of reminiscence, and 4 weeks of traditional programming. Group B started with reminiscence for 4 weeks, then participated in 4-week blocks of traditional programming and then music therapy. Group C began with 4 weeks of traditional programming, then music therapy, then reminiscence. If all groups showed significantly greater improvement on the therapist's measures of quality of life after the 4 weeks of music therapy than after the other 4-week-long conditions, the therapist may

---

[2] It should be noted that counterbalancing can be used in designs in which the groups are not related as well as in those in which they are related.

reject the null hypothesis and conclude that music therapy is the most effective treatment. If all groups performed significantly better after the last condition, no matter what it was, then the cumulative effect of the therapies or passage of time may have been responsible for the changes. Other combinations of results allow researchers to draw different conclusions, but all would provide a good deal of data from which to make inferences about a number of subhypotheses and continue the search for the best method to enhance quality of life.

An example of a counterbalanced design is by Rüütel (2002), in which she examined the psychophysiological effects of music alone and of vibroacoustic therapy (the same music with the addition of low frequency sound vibration), each at two levels of intensity, on healthy people. In this repeated measures design, Rüütel counterbalanced the order of presentation so that each of 12 different trial plans (orders of conditions) was completed by one female and one male participant. By counterbalancing, she could be sure that both men and women were studied in each combination of conditions. She found significant decreases in blood pressure, pulse rate, and muscle oscillation frequency for all subjects. She also found differences in subjective feeling of health and comfort for both music and vibroacoustic conditions compared with those who did not hear music.

Still another option utilizing related groups is the matched pairs design. Subjects are matched on relevant characteristics such as gender, age, socioeconomic status, intelligence, and grade in school. Some researchers pair or match subjects with the same pretest scores, assigning one to the experimental group and the other to the control group. Matching has the advantage of making the treatment groups equivalent on certain relevant characteristics. However, the matching process actually may introduce bias because other unknown characteristics of the group will not be randomly assigned across the conditions.

Take the example of self-esteem posed at the beginning of the chapter. The therapist had evidence that academic achievement and socioeconomic status may affect self-esteem. She limited her sample to children with social adjustment problems between the ages of 14 and 16 who attended a special education class. For those whose parents gave informed consent to participate in the research, she calculated a score based on parental income to define socioeconomic status and examined their grade point averages. She matched the subjects who had the most similar scores on these two indices and assigned one to music therapy and the other to a condition that involved discussion with the music therapist without using music therapy techniques. Just to be sure, she summed the number of boys and girls in each condition and the number of ethnic minorities in each group. They were not significantly different. She administered a standardized test of self-esteem to everyone before the experiment began and compared these pretest scores across subjects in the two conditions. Fortunately, the mean scores of subjects in each condition were nearly equal, and statistical tests revealed no significant differences between the groups. At the end of the experiment, she examined the subjects' self-esteem scores once again (the posttest) and compared each subject with the matched pair. If statistically significant differences existed between the subjects who experienced music therapy and those who did not, the therapist could be somewhat assured that those differences are due to music therapy.

Malone (1996) used a matched pairs design to investigate the benefits of live music on the behavioral distress levels of pediatric patients. The children in her experimental group received a variety of age-appropriate children's songs, led by the experimenter and with guitar accompaniment, as they experienced a variety of needle insertions. She matched pediatric patients in her experimental group to those in the control group on the basis of age, site of procedures, and type of needle insertion. Matching these children allowed her to be confident that she had children with similar traits in each group, thus lending credence to the differences that she found as a result of her experiment. She found that the music group, particularly those children in the music group who were 1 year old and younger, exhibited less behavioral distress.

Because the repeated measures and matched pairs designs depart from the principle of random assignment, some consider them to be quasi-experimental. While there may be limitations when compared with randomized group designs, these widely used and accepted designs have a great deal to offer music therapy researchers.

Quasi-Experimental Designs

Quasi-experimental designs cannot determine cause and effect but can point to relationships that exist. In the real clinical world, it is difficult to control the environment, and there are many sources of experimental error that are beyond the experimenter's control. Sometimes we want to study situations that have already occurred. Indeed, to answer some experimental questions, random assignment, matching, or using subjects as their own controls simply cannot be done. The many varieties of quasi-experimental designs use the most controlled conditions possible to answer the research question.

In many clinical settings, assignment to treatments is based on the best interests of the client, the feasibility of staffing patterns, and other practical considerations. Clients are probably assigned to music therapy without regard to controlling variables. Often, the music therapy researcher must deal with a convenience sample, that is, a limited number of people who meet entrance criteria for a particular group or who can attend certain scheduled sessions. Even in this scenario, given the obvious limitations in generalizing to other samples, it is possible to design an experiment using nonequivalent groups. An excellent pilot test may be accomplished by comparing two or more convenience samples in different conditions and pretesting them to determine how equivalent they are on variables known to be critical in predicting outcome. Then, given a positive result, confirmatory research will give the experimenter greater confidence in this outcome as the effect of music therapy alone.

A study by Nayak, Wheeler, Shifflet, and Agostinello (2000), investigating the use of music therapy as an aid in improving mood and social interaction among people who had had traumatic brain injuries or strokes, illustrates some of these considerations. Although the original intention was to randomly assign participants to the experimental group (music therapy), a control group that would receive art therapy, and a no contact control group, this goal was not achieved. Due to problems finding enough participants who met the criteria, it was not possible to randomly assign people to either the music therapy or the no contact control group and also see people as a group for music therapy, and the plan for the art therapy group was dropped because it proved impossible to get enough subjects. Nevertheless, the information that was gained provided support for the use of music therapy in reaching some of the goals. The article includes a discussion of these problems and suggestions for rectifying them in a later study that would be better controlled.

Many quasi-experimental designs are classified as *ex post facto research*. This type of research was discussed by Lathom-Radocy and Radocy (1995), and much of what follows is adapted from their writing.[3] Ex post facto research refers to research in which the researcher does not have direct control of the independent variables because they have either already occurred or are inherently not manipulable (Kerlinger, 1973). Variables that have already occurred include such things as gender, diagnosis, and age. A classic example of variables that are inherently not manipulable, and thus must be investigated through ex post facto research, is the relationship between smoking and the development of lung cancer.

Correlational and *causal-comparative research* are both types of ex post facto research and look at relationships. Conceptually, they are quite similar; it is in the statistical treatment where the distinctions sometimes are made. Busch and Sherbon (1992) maintain that correlational methods are utilized when the independent variables is continuous, while causal-comparative research is used when the independent variable is categorical.[4] Other authors do not distinguish between causal-comparative and correlational research.

In correlational research, the researcher examines two or more data sets to note the degree of relationship. In simple correlational studies, researchers do not manipulate independent variables. Correlation does not show causality; what happens with one data set does not cause changes in another set with which it is correlated. The researcher does not decide group membership or arrange for events to happen but rather studies existing relationships between naturally occurring events, without any experimental control of variables.

---

[3] The chapter by Lathom-Radocy and Radocy (1995) provides more detail and should be consulted for additional information on these distinctions.

[4] In a continuous variable, the numbers are on a continuum; in a categorical variable, the numbers identify separate categories. An example of a continuous variable is IQ; using a number to identify a musical instrument that someone has studied (for example, 1 = violin, 2 = piano) is an example of a categorical variable.

In simple correlational studies, the emphasis is on accurate description of data sets at a given time. Simple correlational studies examine the relationship between two variables. Multiple correlation studies the relationship of a set of variables to another variable. Simple and multiple regression extend these correlational methods to prediction. In these methods, the ability of one or more variables to predict a criterion variable is examined.

The music therapy literature includes simple correlational studies and multiple regression studies. A study by Allen (1996) provides examples of both. Allen investigated a theory that suggests that occupational achievement and satisfaction can be predicted from the interaction of the personality and the work environment and its relevance to music therapy majors. He used simple correlation in looking at the relationships of academic achievement, educational satisfaction, and the constructs of congruence, consistency, differentiation, and identity. He used multiple regression to determine the variables that predicted educational satisfaction among music therapy majors.

Causal-comparative research is concerned with probable causation of different effects and may sometimes also be correlational research. Causal-comparative studies identify factors or variables and then try to account for why these factors occurred at a given point in time.

In a classic example of causal-comparative research, Darrow (1987) administered Gordon's Primary Measures of Music Audiation to 28 children with hearing impairments. She then compared their scores to the norms published for children with normal hearing in the same grades and found that the hearing impaired children's tonal, rhythm, and composite scores were significantly lower than the scores of the children in the normative group.

A study by Wheeler (1987) also exemplifies causal-comparative research. In order to validate suggestions that music therapy procedures could be categorized into three levels, music therapy as activity therapy, insight music therapy with reeducative goals, and insight music therapy with reconstructive goals, Wheeler sent a questionnaire to clinicians working with adults with psychiatric problems. She found that goals for each level were consistently used together, supporting the theory that music therapy procedures could indeed be categorized into the three levels. She also found that client diagnosis could predict the level of therapy being used, lending credence to the suggestion that each level of procedures was used with clients with particular diagnoses. Multiple regression was used to answer the question about whether client diagnosis could predict the level of therapy.

Conclusion

While no one experiment determines definitively that music therapy *causes* a particular outcome for all people everywhere, repeated experiments with different samples yield greater certainty that music therapy is a viable treatment. As the body of experimental literature supporting the impact of music therapy expands, the scientific community becomes more and more convinced of the efficacy of music therapy.

Frequently, attention to experimental control is able to transform a clinical session into an experimental one, offering the therapist and the scientist objective documentation of the effects of music therapy. We hope that this brief sampling of experimental designs has encouraged the reader to attempt to test hypotheses with the rigors of experimental research.

References

Allen, M. L. (1996). Dimensions of educational satisfaction and academic achievement among music therapy majors. *Journal of Music Therapy, 33,* 147–160.

Baker, F. (2001). The effects of live, taped, and no music on people experiencing posttraumatic amnesia. *Journal of Music Therapy, 38,* 170–192.

Burns, D. S. (2001). The effect of the Bonny Method of Guided Imagery and Music on the mood and life quality of cancer patients. *Journal of Music Therapy, 38,* 51–65.

Busch, J. C., & Sherbon, J. W. (1992). Experimental research methodology. In R. Colwell (Ed.), *Handbook of research on music teaching and learning* (pp. 124–140). New York: Schirmer Books.

Campbell, D. T., & Stanley, J. C. (1963). *Experimental and quasi-experimental designs for research.* Chicago: Rand McNally.

Cordobés, T. K. (1997) Group songwriting as a method for developing group cohesion for HIV-seropositive adult patients with depression. *Journal of Music Therapy, 34,* 46–67.

Darrow, A.-A. (1987). An investigative study: The effect of hearing impairment on musical aptitude. *Journal of Music Therapy, 24,* 88–96.

Hanser, S. B. (1996). Music therapy to reduce anxiety, agitation, and depression. *Nursing Home Medicine, 4,* 286–291.

Hanser, S. B., Bauer-Wu, S., Kubicek, L., Healey, M., Bunnell, C., & Manola, J. (2005). Effects of a music therapy intervention for women with metastatic breast cancer (Abstract). *Oncology Nursing Forum, 32,* 184–185.

Hanser, S. B., Larson, S. D., & O'Connell, A. S. (1983). The effect of music on relaxation of expectant mothers during labor. *Journal of Music Therapy. 22,* 50–58.

Hanser, S. B., Martin, P., & Bradstreet, K. (1982, November). *The effect of music on relaxation of dental patients.* Paper presented at the Annual Conference of the National Association for Music Therapy, Baltimore, MD.

Hanser, S. B., & Thompson, L. W. (1994). Effects of a music therapy strategy on depressed older adults. *Journal of Gerontology: Psychological Sciences, 49,* P265–P269.

Heaney, C. J. (1992). Evaluation of music therapy and other treatment modalities by adult psychiatric inpatients. *Journal of Music Therapy, 29,* 70–86.

Hurt, C. P., Rice, R. T., McIntosh, G. C., & Thaut, M. H. (1998). Rhythmic Auditory Stimulation in gait training for patients with traumatic brain injury. *Journal of Music Therapy, 35,* 228–241.

Kerlinger, F. N. (1973). *Foundations of behavioral research* (2nd ed.). New York: Holt, Rinehart & Winston.

Knight, W. E. J., & Rickard, N. S. (2001). Relaxing music prevents stress-induced increases in subjective anxiety, systolic blood pressure, and heart rate in healthy males and females. *Journal of Music Therapy, 38,* 254–272.

Lathom-Radocy, W. B., & Radocy, R. E. (1995). Descriptive quantitative research. In B. L. Wheeler (Ed.), *Music therapy research: Quantitative and qualitative perspectives* (pp. 165–181). Gilsum, NH: Barcelona Publishers.

Malone, A. B. (1996). The effects of live music on the distress of pediatric patients receiving intravenous starts, venipunctures, injections, and heel sticks. *Journal of Music Therapy, 33,* 19–33.

Nayak, S., Wheeler, B. L., Shiflett, S. C., & Agostinelli, S. (2000). The effect of music therapy on mood and social interaction among individuals with acute traumatic brain injury and stroke. *Rehabilitation Psychology, 45,* 274–283.

Rüütel, E. (2002). The psychophysiological effects of music and vibroacoustic stimulation. *Nordic Journal of Music Therapy, 11,* 16–26.

Staum, M. J. (1987). Music notation to improve the speech prosody of hearing impaired children. *Journal of Music Therapy, 24,* 146–159.

Wheeler, B. L. (1987). Levels of therapy: The classification of music therapy goals. *Music Therapy, 6,* 39–49.

Chapter 22
Survey Research
Tony Wigram

This chapter focuses on survey research using questionnaire-based methods, one form of descriptive research. This is a common and very relevant form of enquiry used in music therapy for descriptive quantitative research. It can address issues relating to the education of music therapists and the publication of research and clinical activities, as well as explore the attitudes and perceptions of both music therapists and people from outside the field. Data collected from surveys and questionnaire-based research can be analyzed and presented through descriptive statistics and also through correlational and inferential statistics. Surveys fulfill an important role in presenting demographic and other information that informs the profession as a whole and provides supportive evidence to underpin the current and future deployment of music therapy services. Surveys can highlight the prevalence of different forms of research studies in the literature (DeCuir, 1987; Gregory, 2002; Jellison, 1973, 2000; Wheeler, 1988; Wigram, 2002) or demonstrate the extent to which clinical music therapists give time to supervision in their every day clinical work (Lathom, 1982). For most professions and commercial enterprises, surveys can provide either a general overview or a microscopic analysis of the impact of that organization within society. As music therapists face up to the challenges of evidence-based practice in order to develop and focus services, the information gathered through surveys can be incorporated as one part of the hierarchy of evidence to support intervention criteria.

Undertaking a survey is a typical method for obtaining information from people about their ways of thinking; their feelings, plans, and beliefs; and their working methods, as well as aspects of their social, educational, and professional backgrounds. It is also a means of analyzing available information regarding the methods by which music therapy is commissioned from educational and healthcare agencies and how music therapy procedures are implemented and reported. A survey involving questionnaires, interviews, or analysis of available data is a common method of gathering information in order to plan future music therapy services, or of investigating the potential of music therapy for a population, reporting on the working practices of music therapists, and considering the available literature and the areas that it covers.

Survey research is "the method of collecting information by asking a set of pre-formulated questions in a predetermined sequence in a structured questionnaire to a sample of individuals drawn so as to be representative of a defined population" (Hutton, 1990, p.8).

Fink (1995a) suggests the following most important features in defining the best and most systematic way of undertaking a survey:

- Specific measurable objectives,
- Sound research design,
- Sound choice of population sample,
- Reliable and valid instruments,
- Appropriate analysis,
- Accurate reporting of survey results. (p. 1)

Clarity in defining the objectives of the survey is critical in order to ensure that the tools that will be used to obtain information and the way in which that information is analyzed do in fact achieve what the survey sets out to explore.

In music therapy, many surveys are concerned with collecting information from qualified practitioners, students in training, and others associated with the profession in order to analyze and highlight important information. Most surveys rely on obtaining a sample of the target population, or the group of people in whom interest is expressed in the survey. In marketing research, surveys are usually associated with asking groups of people questions to explore market attitudes and consumer interest in products, or attitudes about important issues in society and politics (Blaxter, Hughes, & Tight, 1996). In the social sciences, surveys are used to collect information for analysis of objects and processes rather than subjects. For example, an international survey undertaken in 1993 sought documentation from accredited courses in music therapy throughout the world on behalf of the World Federation of Music Therapy. This survey was subsequently published (Grocke, 1996), with the publication including the information submitted about courses in music therapy as well as analyses of the content and status of these courses. Surveys of the literature are often undertaken in order to focus on the style and content of publications over a period of time; these surveys have been published both in journals and in books reviewing music therapy literature.

Applications of Survey Research

One of the characteristics of clinical practice and research in music therapy is the wide diversity that one observes worldwide when attempting to define and apply common standards of clinical practice and research outcome. There are relatively few surveys in music therapy literature when compared with clinical articles, research studies, and philosophical papers. Those surveys that have been undertaken tend to focus on reviewing published literature to see what is being published, reviewing published literature in specific clinical areas, exploring methods and attitudes in the training of music therapists, and exploring professional attitudes.

Publication trends in different journals have provided a rich source of data for survey research and alerted the profession to strengths and weaknesses in emphasis and content. Surveys of journals are important as they provide insight into where research is actually happening and also how that research is divided among various clinical fields. There have been quite regular reviews examining the content of the *Journal of Music Therapy,* including those by Jellison (1973), Madsen (1978), Gilbert (1979), James (1985), Codding (1987), DeCuir (1987), Gfeller (1987), Wigram, 1993 and Gregory (2002). Gfeller's study was particularly helpful in identifying how the theory and practice of music therapy are reflected in the research literature as practiced in the United States, highlighting the prominence of behavioral and psychoanalytic theories influencing clinical practice and the socializing and energizing effects of rhythm in music, a lack of studies with elderly and people with physical disabilities, and also a very low instance of articles on work in adult psychiatry. Wheeler (1988) undertook an analysis of the literature of music therapy journals, including the *Journal of Music Therapy (JMT), Music Therapy,* and *Music Therapy Perspectives,* as well as *The Arts and Psychotherapy,* following the model used by DeCuir in 1987. This survey categorized the available literature into 17 different areas by topic and classified articles as research, clinical, or general, depending on the mode of inquiry. Using the same broad categories, an overview of the literature was undertaken by the author (Wigram, 1993), concentrating on the type of articles written. Publications in clinical areas from five journals of music therapy were compared, looking at articles between 1987 and 1991 and sustaining DeCuir and Wheeler's use of the three discrete categories, clinical, research, and general. A subsequent survey evaluating three music therapy journals between 1998 and 2001 (Wigram, Pedersen, & Bonde, 2002, p. 231), including the *JMT,* the *British Journal of Music Therapy (BJMT),* and the *Nordic Journal of Music Therapy (NJMT),* identified *JMT* as having the highest proportion of research articles, with most of those being quantitative research (34%). The articles classified under nonclinical research in *JMT* (34%) are also predominantly quantitative studies. The *BJMT* demonstrated a significant number of articles on general theory and music therapy theory (37.5%); in the same area, the *NJMT* also had a high proportion of theoretical articles (46.9%). In the clinical categories, 26.5% of the articles in *NJMT* were dedicated to purely clinical articles compared with 24.8% in the *BJMT.* Only 2% of the *JMT* articles in this period were purely clinical papers (Wigram, Pedersen, & Bonde).

Clinical surveys consider aspects of clinical practice, attitudes from both professionals and patients regarding the relevance and benefits of music therapy, and information about where people work (Braswell, Maranto, & DeCuir, 1979a, 1979b; Choi, 1997; Merker, Bergström-Isaacson, & Engerström, 2001). Methods of intervention and effectiveness of music therapy have been documented in the fields of physical rehabilitation (Staum, 2000), correctional and forensic settings (Codding, 2002), people who are blind and have severe visual impairments (Codding, 2000), children and youth with disabilities (Jellison, 2000), older people and psychogeriatrics (Brotons, Koger, & Pickett-Cooper, 1997; Gibbons, 1988; Koger, Chapin, & Brotons, 1999; Prickett, 2000; Ridder, 2002), and in hospice and palliative care (Krout, 2000).

Several surveys on the training of music therapy students in the United States have been carried out and published in the *Journal of Music Therapy,* in particular evaluating what goes on in music therapy practica (Wheeler, 2000); exploring backgrounds, attitudes, and experiences of music therapy students (Clark & Kranz, 1996); assessing the effectiveness of clinical training (Gault, 1978); and, for qualified therapists, exploring multicultural training (Toppozada, 1995) evaluating undergraduate academic curricula (Petrie, 1993), and competency requirements for music therapy practice (Braswell, Maranto, & DeCuir 1980; Taylor, 1987).

Advantages and Disadvantages

At one time or another, most people have been asked to participate in some sort of survey, and obtaining information directly through this method remains the most common method of collecting quantitative data. The potential advantages of surveys are summarized by Hutton (1990):

- Questions are designed so that answers from individual interviews can be added together to produce results which apply to the whole sample;
- The research is based on interviews with a representative sample of respondents;
- Questions are designed to be unbiased;
- Surveys lend themselves to future replication;
- Large surveys can often be broken down. (pp. 11–13)

The following problems can be found in using questionnaires, especially through postal surveys (Gillham, 2000):

- Motivating respondents may be difficult;
- Questions must be brief and relatively simple;
- Misunderstandings cannot be corrected;
- Questionnaire development is often poor;
- Wording of questions can have a major effect on answers;
- Respondents may have literacy problems;
- People talk more easily than they write (or read);
- It is impossible to check the seriousness or honesty of answers.

Survey Methods

Descriptive surveys are designed to portray accurately the characteristics of particular individuals, situations, or groups, while analytical surveys are concerned with testing hypotheses about the relationships between variables in order to understand and explain a particular social phenomenon (Bulmer, 1984, p. 54). All forms of survey research involve identifying a population and, when necessary, drawing a representative sample to take part in the investigation.

There are many different methods of undertaking surveys, including postal surveys, personal and structured interviews, telephone surveys, self-administered surveys, panels, and omnibus studies (Blythe, 2001), with the first three being most likely to be used in music therapy research. Survey methods may be divided into two main models, questionnaire-based and interview-based.

Questionnaire-Based Surveys

The primary type of questionnaire-based survey is a postal survey. In this model, questionnaires are sent in the mail to those in the selected sample who are asked to fill in the answers and send the survey back. It has the advantage of being inexpensive, avoiding the bias and influence of an interviewer, and being able to contain information on a broad range of issues. Response rate is typically low (20–25%), which is one of the disadvantages, together with a lack of researcher control over the respondent and even the possibility that somebody other than the identified respondent may influence the completion of the questionnaire (despite clear instructions to the subjects invited to participate). Return rates of less than 50% are usually suspect, unless drawn from a smaller sample that is considered representative (Lathom-Radocy & Radocy, 1995).

A questionnaire consists simply of a list of preset questions. The same questions are usually given to respondents in the same order so that the same information can be collected from every member of the sample (Haralambos & Holborn, 1995). Blythe (2001, p. 85) defines the criteria for writing survey questions as follows:

- Questions need to be short, simple, and unambiguous;
- Questions should not be leading; they should not direct the respondent towards a particular answer;

- The questionnaire's introduction should be persuasive and must qualify the respondent as belonging in the sample;
- The answers must be capable of being analyzed, preferably by computer;
- Questions must be necessary and relevant to the study;
- The respondent must have the information needed to answer the question;
- Respondents must be willing to answer the questions; if the questions are too personal, people will not respond;
- Questions must be specific; avoid asking two questions at once (for example, Was your therapy pleasant and helpful? Therapy can be helpful without being pleasant!)
- Hypothetical questions should be avoided; they require guesswork on the part of respondents and also can rarely be worded in such a way that respondents have enough information to answer.

A questionnaire can be designed or a survey undertaken for any area of interest or target population to elicit relevant and specific information. Therefore, it is important to establish that the questionnaire is going to produce data that are both reliable and valid. Many researchers choose to do a pilot study for their questionnaire, meaning that they test the first draft with a group of typical respondents that fit the criteria for inclusion in their sample, and analyze the results. This makes it more likely that errors and bias can be corrected or eliminated before the final version is administered to the complete sample.

A reliable questionnaire will reap consistent information, and a valid tool will also reap accurate information.[1]

Interview-Based Surveys

Interview-based surveys allow for more flexibility than questionnaire-based surveys in the questions that are asked. There are two primary types of interview-based surveys.

Personal structured interviews include a face-to-face meeting, with the researcher leading the subject through the questions. There is a high degree of control over the process, particularly the order in which the questions are asked, but the disadvantages include the high cost and refusal rate for participation, as well as the recognizable element of researcher influence as the interviewer is present.

Telephone surveys are often used in market research and are very quick and easy to administer, allowing one to achieve a high response rate whilst still allowing the researcher to control the process. However, responses may be negatively affected by that degree of control unless pre-interview arrangements have been made for a convenient time for the interview to take place.

Sampling

Sampling refers to obtaining a balanced and representative sample from a large population. In the case of studying music therapy practitioners, the small size of the profession may lead surveyors to consider it more efficacious to simply include all of the qualified practicing music therapists listed in the directory of a particular country, thus incorporating the entire population as the selected sample. The disadvantages in this approach are that the likelihood of a lower response rate is much greater, as well as finding that the people who have been chosen to be included in the sample do not necessarily fit the defined sample group. For example, Register (2002) achieved a return of 42.8% from a total of 2,039 surveys sent in a recent study looking at collaboration and consultation among Board Certified Music Therapists in the United States. However, of the 873 responses, 60 were excluded because their responses indicated that they were no longer employed as music therapists, and only 350 or 44% of the remaining respondents indicated that they acted as music therapy consultants, a focus of the study.

While within the small field of music therapy the viability of including a whole population or selection of material without sampling is feasible, more typically a form of

---

[1] For information on reliability and validity see Chapter 4, Principles of Quantitative Research.

sampling takes place in order to limit the amount of data that has to be handled and analyzed in more detail.

Two means of selecting people to participate in a survey, probability and nonprobability sampling, are typically used (Fink & Kosekoff, 1985). A wide variety of sampling strategies can be used in both types of sampling.

Probability Sampling

Within probability sampling, one can employ simple random sampling, which involves the selection of subjects at random from a population. This is probably the most well-known and well-understood model of obtaining a clear cross-section that can represent a particular population, where each individual in the population at large has an equal chance of being included in the sample. It is easy to conduct and both statistical textbooks and computers give ready-to-use tables or methods for drawing a random sample. However, there are disadvantages to random sampling for survey-based research. For example, the respondents cannot be broken down into subgroups or strata (such as by identifying an equal number of males and females). Sometimes it is almost impossible to achieve random sampling, and so-called random samples can be seriously biased. If there is wide diversity in the population from which the sample is being drawn, random sampling might in fact create a sample that is not truly representative of that whole, diverse population.

In systematic sampling, every 10th or 20th person in the population is selected for inclusion. Stratified sampling involves sampling within groups of the population; this could be more appropriate where the diversity and hierarchy within a population means that one wishes to draw on people at different levels or strata within the whole population. Finally, cluster sampling relies on surveying whole clusters of the population sample at random. Cluster sampling is like random sampling except that groups, such as a clinical population or multidisciplinary team, rather than individuals, are selected at random.

In selecting the sample, one is confronted with the question of how large that sample should be. Statistical methods are available to help sample representatively, and in using statistics a degree of confidence is necessary that the sample and population only differ by some specified amount (or sampling error). Given the size of a sample, there is also concern regarding the requirements as to how high a response rate should be. Simply put, a response rate is supposed to be as high as possible, and, if you lose responses when using random sampling, there is an inevitable influence of bias. However, if you do not use random sampling methods, the response may lack credibility.

Nonprobability Sampling

In this category, one can use convenience sampling, sampling those that are most convenient for the study; voluntary sampling, where the sample is self-selected; quota sampling, a form of convenience sampling within groups of the population; purposive sampling, hand-picking interesting cases thought to be typical; multidimensional sampling, involving a multidimensional form of quota sampling; and snowball sampling, building up a sample through informants. In quota sampling, the researcher draws up a quota for each category in the population; when those quotas are met, the sample is considered complete. The advantage of this is that it produces a clear cross section of opinion, provided the basis for the quota is correctly set and the researcher rejects respondents that do not meet pre-set criteria for the quota.

Blaxter, Hughes, and Tight (1996) argue that nonprobability sampling approaches are used when the researcher lacks a sampling frame for the population in question, or where a probability approach is not judged to be necessary. They refer to a situation in which the study of an issue is potentially quite sensitive—such as the incidence of sexual abuse in a psychiatric population—and to achieve the required sample, the subject pool has to be built up confidentially through known and trusted contacts.

Blythe (2001) reports that there has recently been a move away from probability sampling towards quota sampling and a growing use of databases for sampling. The reasons for this are that quota sampling is easier and more reliable, and databases provide a quick and easy way of sampling for postal surveys. Surveying a sample is obviously not a perfect substitute when compared with surveying the entire population. The sample obtained from random, stratified, or cluster sampling is likely to be different from the population by some margin of error. It is important to ensure that a sample is as accurate as possible, and the margin of error should be kept small. This will rely on measuring the accuracy of a particular sampling method by computing the standard error (*SE*) of the mean of that particular sample.

Response rate is a critical issue in survey research, as a poor response rate will reduce that survey's credibility. Fink and Kosekoff (1985) offer sensible suggestions for improving the response rate:

1. Use a technique that usually has a high response rate. Face-to-face interviews produce better results than mailed questionnaires.
2. Plan in advance to replace nonrespondents. If only half of the subjects have been randomly selected to be included in a survey of attitudes in working in multidisciplinary teams in psychiatry, the other half could serve as replacements. Sometimes it is worth over-sampling: selecting more people than the researcher really intends to use so that dropouts can be replaced relatively easily. The researcher should not wait until the survey has begun to replace these dropouts; it is administratively more complex and adding people at this time will probably introduce bias.
3. Provide evidence that the loss of data from nonresponse does not harm or bias the survey's findings. This might be done by showing that no obvious differences exist among respondents and nonrespondents in factors such as age, education, experience, professional background, and so forth. (p. 46)

Gathering Survey Data

For quantitative analysis, most of the data that are gathered should be numerical or be responses that can be categorized and placed as numerical data into categories.

Given an example where a survey is intended to find out how helpful and beneficial the research studies in music therapy journals are to everyday clinical work, one could imagine a variety of questions that would elicit numerical, categorical, and visual data.

Preliminary questions might be the following:

1. Identify which of the following music therapy journals you regularly receive and read.
2. Identify the clinical population with which you work for the majority of your clinical practice from the following lists.

Both of these questions elicit categorical data, placing the participants in the survey into categories both in the journals they read and the clinical populations they serve.

Likert scales are used to elicit a rating from respondents to a particular question such as the following:

How often do you search the literature in the journals to find research to support your clinical work?

1	2	3	4	5
Almost never	Rarely	Occasionally	Often	Almost always

Constructing categories in the Likert scale needs careful consideration. In the above example, for instance, if one had placed *never* and *always* at each end of the Likert scale, it is quite likely that most of the respondents would never use them. However, putting *almost always* and *almost never* catches people who feel that they fall into that category. Likert scales are ordinal,[2] and there is no defined numerical value in the gap between 1 and 2 or 2 and 3. Therefore, data can only be analyzed through nonparametric (rank ordering) forms of statistical analysis.

Asking respondents to identify how useful they find research articles for their particular clinical area on a 1–10 scale of *not useful at all* to *very useful* is also based on an ordinal scale, because of the lack of precision about the difference between the numerical intervals on the scale.

---

[2] See definitions of ordinal and other types of data and also discussion of nonparametric statistics in Chapter 12, Statistical Methods of Analysis.

Conversely, if you want more precise information about how many articles people read from research journals in relation to their clinical field over the last year, you could ask a more specific question:

How many articles in each journal have you found that specifically relate to your clinical area?

Ansdell and Pavlicevic (2001, pp. 211–217) give well thought through examples of data collection within these different models based on a hypothetical analysis of whether arts therapists in the United Kingdom think that social science research methods (SSRM) are useful for their own research projects. In one question, they try to determine whether people included in the survey would have consulted SSRM over a 12-month period using the criteria:

Never   1–2 times/yr.   3–4 times/yr.   Monthly   Weekly   All the time

This gives a range of categories into which most people would be able to place their current practice.

Confidentiality needs to be assured to participants in both postal and interview-based surveys. With postal surveys, it is important to enclose a cover letter assuring confidentiality and explaining what coding will be used in place of names so that the identification of the participant will not be revealed on publication. Ethical standards also require that informed consent is obtained, and the cover letter should also explain the purpose of the research and how the information obtained will be used. Participants are then asked to sign a form giving consent.[3]

Statistical Analysis

The data collected in survey research are numerical and, for the purpose of analysis through descriptive statistics, can be converted into percentages. The normalization of data through this process allows one to prepare histograms, bar graphs, and pie charts to illustrate the outcomes of surveys. While descriptive statistics do not allow generalizability through the calculation of probability, the value of simple display analysis is in revealing frequencies and proportions and identifying further relevant research questions. Displays where the incidence of data is ranked in bar graphs are helpful, but the temptation to calculate averages must be avoided where the data are not interval. The other weakness in drawing assumptions and conclusions from percentages is that the absolute numbers are not specified, raising the question, a percentage of what? Knowing the original scores and totals from which the percentages have been calculated is relevant in understanding the implications of the calculations.

Where the data from a survey can be assigned to categories, the differences between the numbers falling into categories can be analyzed to determine whether those differences are significant and meaningful. The chi-square test of probability is designed to analyze how far the obtained frequencies falling into categories differ from the expected frequencies, thus calculating the probability of whether these results would occur by chance. The limitation of chi-square is that the expected frequency falling into any category (cell) needs to exceed 10. When cells contain fewer than 10 occurrences, a Yates' correction needs to be applied, and, if expected frequencies are found to be less than five, chi-square should not be applied as a test of statistical significance. Fisher's test of exact probability should also be used where obtained frequencies are fewer than 12 (Gillham, 2000).

Resources

There are many pitfalls and potential areas of weakness in a badly planned or poorly designed survey. There are some excellent guidelines in the literature that can help the researcher through the process of both designing a good quality survey and formulating and developing a questionnaire. One of the most helpful sequences of texts for the methodology of survey research is *The Survey Kit,* developed by Arlene Fink. She has developed a handbook on survey methods, and the topics in a series of books include how to ask survey questions, how to conduct self-administered mail surveys and telephone interviews, the design of surveys, and the importance of sampling, as well as how best to measure survey reliability, validity, and the analysis of survey

---

[3] Additional information on ethical standards and informed consent is found in Chapter 18, Ethical Precautions in Music Therapy Research.

data. Fink and Kosekoff (1985) also provide a useful and basic step-by-step guide on how to conduct surveys, introducing in a compact text aspects of the method found in *The Survey Kit* (Fink 1995b). Gillham (2000) has produced a well-structured text designed to help develop a questionnaire and this is an excellent guide to questionnaire-based survey methods.

Summary

Survey research continues to provide periodic and valuable analysis of clinical and professional issues in music therapy. The accessibility of data presented through descriptive statistics informs the promotion and provision of music therapy services and, where relevant detail is presented, a more precise focus on the modality of intervention. Attitudes within the profession are highlighted through surveys, and the literature surveys of articles in the research and clinical journals identify trends in publication. The tangible result is the provision of evidence towards the clinical and professional development of music therapy as a discipline.

References

Ansdell, G., & Pavlicevic, M. (2001). *Beginning research in the arts therapies: A practical guide.* London: Jessica Kingsley Publishers.

Blaxter, L., Hughes, C., & Tight, M. (1996). *How to research.* Buckingham, UK: Open University Press.

Blythe, J. (2001). *Essentials of marketing.* London: Prentice Hall.

Braswell, C., Maranto, C., & DeCuir, A. (1979a). A survey of clinical practice in music therapy, Part 1: The institutions in which music therapists work and personal data. *Journal of Music Therapy, 16*, 2–16.

Braswell, C., Maranto, C., & DeCuir, A. (1979b). A survey of clinical practice in music therapy, Part 2: Clinical practice, educational and clinical training. *Journal of Music Therapy, 16*, 50–69.

Braswell, C., Maranto, C. D., & DeCuir, A. (1980). Ratings of entry skills by music therapy clinicians, educators, and interns. *Journal of Music Therapy, 17*, 133–147.

Brotons, M., Koger, S. M., & Pickett-Cooper, P. K. (1997). Music and dementias: A review of the literature. *Journal of Music Therapy, 31*, 220–233.

Bulmer, N. (1984). *Sociological research methods: An introduction* (2nd ed.). Basingstoke, UK: Macmillan.

Choi, B. (1997). Professional and patient attitudes about the relevance of music therapy as a treatment modality in NAMT approved psychiatric hospitals. *Journal of Music Therapy, 34*, 277–292.

Clark, N. E., & Kranz, P. (1996). A survey of backgrounds, attitudes, and experiences of new music therapy students. *Journal of Music Therapy, 33*, 124–146.

Codding, P. (1987) A content analysis of the *Journal of Music Therapy*. *Journal of Music Therapy, 24*, 195–202.

Codding, P. (2000). Music therapy literature and clinical applications for blind and severely visually impaired persons: 1940–2000. In *Effectiveness of music therapy procedures: Documentation of research and clinical practice* (3rd ed., pp. 159–198). Silver Spring, MD: American Music Therapy Association.

Codding, P. (2002). A comprehensive survey of music therapists practicing in correctional psychiatry: Demographics, conditions of employment, service provision, assessment, therapeutic objectives, and related values of the therapist. *Music Therapy Perspectives, 20*, 56–69.

DeCuir, A. (1987). Readings for music therapy students: An analysis of clinical and research literature from the *Journal of Music Therapy*. In C. Dileo Maranto & K. Bruscia (Eds.), *Perspectives on music therapy education and training* (pp. 57–70). Philadelphia: Esther Boyer College of Music, Temple University.

Fink, A., & Kosekoff, J. (1985). *How to conduct surveys.* Newbury Park, CA: Sage Publications.

Fink, A. (1995a). *How to design surveys.* London: Sage Publications.

Fink, A. (1995b) *The survey kit.* London: Sage Publications.

Gault, A. W. (1978). An assessment of the effectiveness of clinical training in collegiate music therapy curricula. *Journal of Music Therapy, 15*, 36–39.

Gfeller, K. (1987). Music therapy theory and practice as reflected in research literature. *Journal of Music Therapy, 24*, 178–194.

Gibbons, A. C. (1988). A review of literature for music development/education and music therapy for the elderly. *Music Therapy Perspectives, 5*, 33–40.

Gilbert, J. P. (1979) Published research in music therapy, 1973–1978: Content, focus and implications for future research. *Journal of Music Therapy, 16*, 102–110.

Gillham, B. (2000). *Developing a questionnaire.* London: Continuum.

Gregory, D. (2002). Four decades of music therapy behavioral research designs: A content analysis of *Journal of Music Therapy* articles. *Journal of Music Therapy, 39*, 56–71.

Grocke, D. E. (1996). *Directory of music therapy training courses worldwide: World Federation of Music Therapy.* Melbourne, Australia: Faculty of Music Publications, University of Melbourne.

Haralambos, M., & Holborn, M. (1995). *Sociology: Themes and perspectives.* London: Collins Educational Harper Collins.

Hutton, P. (1990). *Survey research for managers: How to use surveys in management decision-making* (2nd ed.). Basingstoke: Macmillan.

James, M. R. (1985) Sources of articles published in the *Journal of Music Therapy:* The first twenty years, 1964–1983. *Journal of Music Therapy, 22*, 87–94.

Jellison, J. (1973) The frequency and general mode of enquiry of research in music therapy, 1952–1972. *Council for Research in Music Education, 35*, 351–358.

Jellison, J. (2000). A content analysis of music therapy research with disabled children and youth (1975–1999): Applications in special education. In *Effectiveness of music therapy procedures: Documentation of research and clinical practice* (3rd ed., pp. 199–264). Silver Spring, MD: American Music Therapy Association.

Koger, S. M., Chapin, K., & Brotons, M. (1999). Is music therapy an effective intervention for dementia? A meta-analytic review of the literature. *Journal of Music Therapy, 36*, 2–15.

Krout, R. E. (2000). Hospice and palliative music therapy: A continuum of creative caring. In *Effectiveness of music therapy procedures: Documentation of research and clinical practice* (3rd ed., pp. 323–411). Silver Spring, MD: American Music Therapy Association.

Lathom, W. B. (1982). Survey of current functions of a music therapist. *Journal of Music Therapy, 19*, 2–27.

Lathom-Radocy, W. B., & Radocy, R. E. (1995). Descriptive quantitative research. In B. L. Wheeler (Ed.), *Music therapy research: Quantitative and qualitative perspectives* (pp. 165–181). Gilsum, NH: Barcelona Publishers.

Madsen, C. K. (1978). Research on research: An evaluation of research presentations. *Journal of Music Therapy, 15*, 67–73.

Merker, B., Bergström-Isacsson, M., & Engerström, I. W. (2001). Music and the Rett disorder: The Swedish Rett Center survey. *Nordic Journal of Music Therapy, 10*, 42–53.

Petrie, G. E. (1993). An evaluation of the National Association for Music Therapy undergraduate academic curriculum: II. *Journal of Music Therapy, 30*, 158–173.

Prickett, C. A. (2000) Music therapy for older people: Research comes of age across two decades. In *Effectiveness of music therapy procedures: Documentation of research and clinical practice* (3rd ed., pp. 297–321). Silver Spring, MD: American Music Therapy Association.

Register, D. (2002). Collaboration and consultation: A survey of Board Certified music therapists. *Journal of Music Therapy, 39*, 305–321.

Ridder, H. M. O. (2002). Music therapy with older adults. In T. Wigram, I. N. Pedersen, & L. O. Bonde (2002), *A comprehensive guide to music therapy theory, clinical practice, research and training* (pp. 188–196). Philadelphia: Jessica Kingsley Publishers.

Staum, M. J. (2000). Music for physical rehabilitation: An analysis of the literature from 1950–1999 and applications for rehabilitation settings. In *Effectiveness of music therapy procedures: Documentation of research and clinical practice* (3rd ed., pp. 65–111). Silver Spring, MD: American Music Therapy Association.

Taylor, D. B. (1987). A survey of professional music therapists concerning entry level competencies. *Journal of Music Therapy, 24*, 114–145.

Toppozada, M. R. (1995) Multicultural training for music therapists: An examination of current issues based on a national survey of professional music therapists. *Journal of Music Therapy, 32,* 65–90.

Wheeler, B. L. (1988). An analysis of literature from selected music therapy journals. *Music Therapy Perspectives, 5,* 95–101.

Wheeler, B. (2000). Music therapy practicum practices: A survey of music therapy educators. *Journal of Music Therapy, 37,* 286–311.

Wigram, T. (1993) Music therapy research to meet the demands of health and education services: Research and literature analysis. In M. Heal & T. Wigram (Eds.), *Music therapy in health and education* (pp. 137–153). Philadelphia: Jessica Kingsley Publishers.

Wigram, T. (2002) Indications in music therapy: Evidence from assessment that can identify the expectations of music therapy as a treatment for autistic spectrum disorder (ASD); Meeting the challenge of evidence based practice. *British Journal of Music Therapy, 16,* 11–28.

Wigram, T., Pedersen, I. N., & Bonde, L. O. (2002). *A comprehensive guide to music therapy theory, clinical practice, research and training.* Philadelphia: Jessica Kingsley Publishers.

Chapter 23
Meta-Analysis
Cheryl Dileo and Joke Bradt

Why Meta-Analysis?

With the explosion of the scientific literature on music therapy during the past 20 years, it has become increasingly difficult for the typical music therapist to stay abreast of the research literature in the multitude of clinical areas in which music therapy is practiced. A recent literature search by the authors in the area of music and medicine revealed several thousand published articles (100 plus pages of references) that needed to be summarized and evaluated. The breadth of the area of music and medicine alone was astounding, and 12 categories for the literature were identified according to medical specialty. With such a wealth of information on this and other topics in music therapy, there is an urgent need for reliable summaries of primary research. Even more pressing is the need to understand what all this research means. Thus, in basic terms, we need to be able to answer the simple question: Is music therapy an effective intervention? More importantly, music therapists need to be able to answer this question for potential employers, third-party payers, clients and their families, grant providers, and governmental and regulatory agencies.

All music therapists know in their hearts that music therapy is effective; they have observed its effectiveness many times. However, this may not be enough to convince the individuals who are asking this question. Even if one diligently searches the research literature in an attempt to provide studies that support music therapy's effectiveness, one discovers that the literature is not at all homogeneous, and results differ. So how does one make sense of this literature as a whole? How can one accurately summarize music therapy's effects across so many different studies? Meta-analysis has become a widely accepted technique for exploring both the direction and magnitude of relationships among variables from various primary research studies (Cooper & Hedges, 1994) and can be very useful in this situation.

Meta-analysis can be likened to a form of survey research in which research studies, rather than individuals, are surveyed. A form for coding the data (protocol) is designed, research studies are identified, and each research report is "interviewed" by a researcher, who examines it and codes the data according to its findings. These data are then statistically analyzed using specially adapted statistical methods, and the patterns of results are described (Lipsey & Wilson, 2001). Meta-analysis is becoming an increasingly popular and very flexible method that "makes research synthesis an explicit scientific activity" (Cook, et al., 1992, p. 5). Usable with large bodies of literature, meta-analysis may be looked upon as a type of research in its own right, with its own techniques and methods, which uses the results of other studies as its raw data (Feldman, 1971). In essence, meta-analysis allows for "combining the numerical results of studies with disparate, even conflicting, research methods and findings; it enables researchers to discover the consistencies in a set of seemingly inconsistent findings and to arrive at conclusions more accurate and credible than those presented in any one of the primary studies" (Hunt, 1997, p. 1). This research method can be used as a means for conducting a quantitative, objective literature review, or as a design to test hypotheses, even those that were not tested in the primary studies (Arthur, Bennett, & Huffcutt, 2001). Furthermore, meta-analysis is being used with greater frequency to determine *why* studies differ in their results through the examination of moderator and mediating variables (Hunt).

In very simple terms, meta-analysis provides a bird's eye view of a landscape (in this case, various research studies). By studying the landscape from an aerial view, one can discern patterns and make conclusions not possible when viewing the landscape from the ground.

The key feature to meta-analysis that allows it to accomplish the above is the concept of a standard *effect size,* a measure that gives an indication of the size and variability of the phenomenon under investigation. For example, when researchers evaluate the effects of music therapy on depression, a number of measurement tools may be used: depression inventories, mood scales, behavioral observations, or other tools. Meta-analysis statistics compute a standard effect size for each of these types of data, so that they can be compared numerically among themselves in a consistent fashion across all measures and variables (Lipsey & Wilson, 2001). Thus, the effect size allows for a common language among many tongues.

Advantages and Disadvantages

Advantages and Strengths

There are a number of advantages in using meta-analysis as a tool to summarize and analyze a body of literature, as compared to traditional literature reviews. First, meta-analysis is a rigorous research method in its own right, and each step of its process is documented and available for review and scrutiny, thus enhancing its validity as a process (Lipsey & Wilson, 2001).

Second, meta-analysis uses a much more sophisticated approach than descriptive or qualitative methods of literature review. Because the calculated effect size provides information on both the magnitude and direction of the effect, it is sensitive to the strength of findings from study to study. Furthermore, because an effect size is calculated and these calculations are pooled across various studies (weighting results according to sample size), meta-analysis calculations provide more statistical power than those used in primary studies (Lipsey & Wilson, 2001).

Third, when working with large numbers of studies, taking notes or coding on index cards often becomes unmanageable, even after just a few studies. The systematic procedures used for coding in meta-analysis and the use of a computerized database to store this information allows the procedures to be done even with massive amounts of information (Lipsey & Wilson, 2001).

Fourth, meta-analysis can help clarify areas in which future research will be most productive (Dileo & Bradt, in press). Whereas meta-analysis procedures serve a retrospective function by providing a view of the literature published to date, they also serve a prospective function (Hedges, 1990).

Disadvantages and Weaknesses

Meta-analysis procedures are somewhat controversial, even though they are being used with greater frequency. There are, though, some disadvantages. Meta-analysis is much more labor-intensive and time-consuming than a traditional literature review and requires expertise in selecting appropriate statistics for calculating effect sizes and in computing and interpreting the statistics (Lipsey & Wilson, 2001).

Another criticism of meta-analysis is that it is mechanistic in its coding procedures and does not lend itself to the more subtle and complex aspects of a primary study. It is clear that meta-analysis cannot do everything one would like to do, and it is quite possible to combine meta-analysis with qualitative literature reviews to address this issue (Slavin, 1995).

A third criticism of meta-analysis concerns sampling and publication bias. This refers to the tendency of authors to submit, and journals to accept, those studies with statistically significant findings. Studies with findings that are not significant may not be submitted or accepted, and this may produce skewed results in the meta-analysis. Furthermore, not enough data are reported in some published studies to permit them to be included in the meta-analysis. An additional problem involves restricting literature searches to one language (Tower of Babel bias)[1] (Gregoire, Derderian, & LeLorier, 1995). There is no one solution to these problems, although many suggestions have been made. It is imperative that the literature review used in the meta-analysis attempts to include unpublished as well as published studies, although the unpublished studies have not been subject to peer review, which presents another controversy. Another suggestion involves maintaining research registries of all trials (Simes, 1986), which would ensure that there would be a record of studies done, published and unpublished, and some way of tracking studies with neutral or negative results (Priebe & Slade, 2002).

A fourth and very common criticism of meta-analysis is the *apples and oranges* issue. Although it may seem ideal to combine results of studies, this procedure may not always be appropriate. When disparate studies (such as those with different measuring instruments, different definitions of variables, and different subjects) are pooled together, the results may be meaningless (Eysenck, 1994). In dealing with this issue, it is necessary to ascertain that the

---

[1] *Tower of Babel bias* refers to the common practice of not including research literature from foreign countries because translation is not available.

studies involved examine the same clinical or research question. Furthermore, criteria for including or excluding studies from the meta-analysis must be clearly delineated (Geddes & Carney, 2002). Finally, the meta-analyst needs to apply a homogeneity test. This test examines whether the variability of effect sizes produced by a group of studies is greater than that expected from sampling error alone. If the test produces a significant Q or homogeneity statistic, the effect sizes are inconsistent across studies, and factors other than subject-level sampling error are responsible for the heterogeneous distribution of the effect sizes. For example, it could be that in a given meta-analysis, studies using self-report resulted in higher effect sizes than studies using observational measurement. The audience should always be informed about the level of variability of the effect sizes.

A related criticism concerns the variation in methodological quality of primary studies included in a meta-analysis. To avoid this problem, it is considered important to evaluate the primary studies included qualitatively according to their internal validity (Geddes & Carney, 2002).

Meta-Analyses in Music Therapy

Meta-analysis research is making its way into the music therapy literature. The following is a summary of the meta-analysis research thus far.

Standley (1986, 1992, 1996, 2000) published the first of her pioneering series of meta-analyses of the literature on music in medical and dental treatment in 1986. In this landmark study that included 30 studies, an average effect size of .98 for music treatment was found across all 55 dependent variables. Sources of variability in effect sizes included: patient diagnosis and symptoms, sample size, type of study design, function and type of music, and type of dependent measure. No information on homogeneity was reported.

Standley's 1992 meta-analysis (54 studies and 129 dependent variables) and her 1996 and 2000 studies (92 studies and 232 dependent variables) updated the original study. Of interest in the 1996 and 2000 publications were analyses of the generalized effects of music according to gender, age, level of pain, type of dependent measure, diagnosis, and type of music. Also included in the 2000 study were specific topical meta-analyses of the research concerning music in surgery (13 studies, 26 dependent variables) and music with premature infants (11 studies, 21 dependent variables). The mean effect size (Cohen's $d = 0.38$) of the surgery studies was significant, however, the effect sizes were inconsistent across studies as indicated by the significant homogeneity statistic (Q; $p < .003$). The mean effect size ($d = .75$) of the premature infants study was also statistically significant, but, here too, a statistically significant Q value indicated inconsistent results.

Standley (2002) also performed a meta-analysis of the literature (with 10 studies included) on the effectiveness of music with premature infants in neonatal intensive care units. Results indicated a positive overall effect size ($d = 0.83$). It was concluded that music has significantly positive effects that remains consistent across a number of variables, including birth weight, method of music delivery, volume of the music, gestational age, behavioral state, physiological measures, and stay in the hospital.

Koger, Chapin, and Brotons (1999) conducted a meta-analysis to determine the effectiveness of music therapy treatment for patients with dementia. Twenty-one studies were included in the analysis. A highly significant mean effect size ($d = 0.7879$) was obtained; however, the effect sizes were not consistent across the studies analyzed, and the source of variability could not be determined according to the different independent or dependent variables used in the studies including type of music therapy intervention; length of treatment; training of the therapist; or behavioral, cognitive, or social outcomes.

Silverman (2003) examined the effects of music therapy on the symptoms of psychosis. His meta-analysis of this literature included 19 studies. A positive, significant effect size ($d = 0.71$) was found, although homogeneity in effect sizes across the studies was not observed. Effects were consistent, however, for type of intervention (live versus recorded music and structured groups versus receptive listening). It was also found that classical music was less effective than non-classical music in influencing symptoms of psychosis.

The current authors (Dileo & Bradt, in press) conducted a meta-analysis of the literature involving music in medical treatment, including 184 studies. Only studies that employed a no-music control group were included. Studies without a control group comparison, such as pretest-posttest treatment studies, were not included in this meta-analysis. Furthermore, we only included those dependent variables for which two or more study results were available. In addition, many dependent variables were grouped together under a common denominator, as they were believed to measure the same phenomenon. This close examination of available dependent variables resulted in the inclusion of 47 dependent variables. Effects of music and music therapy were reported for each dependent variable, grouped according to 11 medical specialty areas: premature infants, fetal responses to music, pediatrics, obstetrics/gynecology, cardiology/intensive care, oncology and terminal illness, general hospital, surgery, rehabilitation, dementia, and dentistry. The overall study-level mean effect sizes, grouped by population, are reported in Table 1. Combining study-level effect sizes, however, led to heterogeneous results in several populations. This could be expected as many studies within one population group examined different outcome measures and had diverse study characteristics.

Table 1
Combined Effect Sizes
Dileo and Bradt (in press)

Population	k	N	r_u	95% c. i.	p	Q
Across populations	184	7934	.31	+.26 to +.35	.00	640.48*
Surgery	50	2779	.26	+.18 to +.35	.00	246.86*
Cardiac/ICU	14	666	.27	+.14 to +.40	.00	36.50*
Cancer/HIV/Terminal illness	19	651	.24	+.16 to +.33	.00	20.40
Fetal	4	81	.57	+.34 to +.74	.00	4.31
General hospital	11	703	.12	+.05 to +.19	.00	9.67
Neonatal	17	895	.21	+.10 to +.32	.00	35.63*
OBGYN	7	638	.23	+.06 to +.39	.01	10.59
Pediatrics	11	291	.39	+.20 to +.56	.00	29.60*
Dental	6	311	.16	−.01 to +.32	.06	9.92
Gerontology	26	547	.56	+.42 to +.67	.00	89.75*
Rehabilitation	18	372	.38	+.25 to +.49	.00	22.67

k = sample size, N = number of subjects, r_u = unbiased effect size, 95% $c.i.$ = 95% confidence interval, p = significance level, Q = homogeneity value[2]
* $p < .05$, indicating that the sample is not homogeneous

We listed detailed results (in a similar fashion as Table 1) for each dependent variable included in our study. Moreover, we reported the results of our search for moderator variables, or factors that could account for the variance in outcomes. For example, the role of music preference, level of treatment, and level of randomization was examined and reported. Finally, we also included a separate meta-analysis of experimental studies examining the effect of music on stress in non-medical populations (41 studies). A statistically mean effect size ($r = .21$) was found. However, the results were inconsistent across studies, as indicated by a significant Q value.

Pelletier (2004) conducted a meta-analytic review of the research concerning the effects of music therapy on stress reduction. Based on the results of 22 studies, the author found significant effects of music and music-relaxation approaches in reducing the arousal attributable to stress ($d = 0.67$). The significant Q value indicated that the effect sizes were heterogeneous.

In a similar manner, Whipple (2004) examined the meta-analytic effects of music interventions with children and adolescents with autism. This analysis included 9 studies and 12 dependent variables. Results revealed an overall significant effect size of $d = 0.77$ and presence of homogeneity, thus supporting the benefits of music therapy for individuals with autism.

Gold, Voracek, and Wigram (2004) examined the effects of music therapy on children and adolescents with psychopathology in 11 studies. This analysis showed a medium to large positive effect size of music therapy ($ES = 61$; $p < .001$) on clinical outcomes, and results were homogeneous. Larger effects were noted for: clients with behavioral and developmental disorders (compared to emotional disorders); eclectic, psychodynamic, and humanistic treatment music therapy approaches (compared to behavioral models); and behavioral and developmental outcomes (compared to social skills and self-concept).

---

[2] These statistical terms are explained later in the chapter.

Several additional meta-analyses have been published or are in press. These include studies by Gold, Heldal, Dahle, and Wigram (in press) on music therapy and schizophrenia; Gold and Wigram (2005) on music therapy and autism spectrum disorder; and Maratos and Gold (2005) on music therapy and depression.

As the overall results of these studies provide strong, objective evidence for the effectiveness of music therapy as a treatment intervention, it is highly likely that meta-analysis procedures will be used with much greater frequency in the future. In the next section of this chapter, details are provided on how to conduct a meta-analysis.

Conducting a Meta-Analysis

The basic steps involved in conducting a meta-analysis follow:

1. Determine the focus of the study;
2. Identify appropriate studies;
3. Code the studies that meet the inclusion criteria;
4. Calculate the effect size (if not reported by the author);
5. Deal with heterogeneity;
6. Compare and combine effect sizes;
7. Evaluate the importance of the obtained effect sizes.

After the focus of the meta-analysis has been determined, inclusion criteria should be established by the meta-analyst. Relevant research studies can then be located by conducting computerized database searches. In addition, the reference lists of all obtained studies should be read to locate additional studies. To help avoid publication bias, correspondence with the contributors to the specific research area can assist in obtaining unpublished manuscripts. Four major classes of documents are traditionally included in a meta-analysis: (a) books, including authored books, edited books, and chapters in edited books; (b) journals, including professional journals, published newsletters, magazines, and newspapers; (c) theses, including doctoral, master's, and bachelor's theses; and (d) unpublished work, including technical reports, grant proposals, grant reports, convention papers, ERIC reports, films, cassette recordings, and other unpublished materials (Rosenthal, 1991, p. 37).

Once the studies to be included in the meta-analysis have been located, the meta-analyst needs to develop a coding protocol that outlines the information to be extracted from each study. Crucial information to make calculation of effect sizes possible is: (a) all statistics, if provided, on the dependent variables, including means, standard deviations, t tests, F ratios, correlations, chi-squares, degrees of freedom, and significance levels; (b) sample sizes (total N as well as n of each group); (c) types of dependent variables reported; and (d) treatment conditions for each group. In addition, the coding protocol should include information about study characteristics such as: (a) research design, (b) level of randomization, (c) measures, (d) type of treatment, and (e) demographic information. One should carefully select the study descriptors to be extracted. Coding information that is not reported in most studies is useless, as it cannot be compared in a meaningful way in the data analysis (Lipsey & Wilson, 2001). Finally, one should also record the complete reference and the author's full name and contact information, if available.

It is of utmost importance that the meta-analyst read each study report very carefully. Careful reading of these reports will often reveal errors made by the authors. Fortunately, these errors can often be corrected before the meta-analytic computations begin. In addition, the meta-analyst needs to carefully review his or her own data input, as he or she, also, will most likely make errors in coding and inputting the data.

Calculating Effect Sizes

An effect size is a "standardized measure of the direction and strength of relationship [between two variables] in a study" (Schafer, 1999, p. 43). It informs one about the extent of the effect on subjects of having been assigned to the experimental or the control group (Rosenthal, Rosnow, & Rubin, 2000). This common metric is always accompanied by an indication of the accuracy of the estimated effect size. It is important to understand that estimated effect sizes are very different from traditional probability (p) levels. A research finding that has a statistically significant p value is not necessarily meaningful or even clinically relevant. To accurately interpret the research finding, one needs information on the magnitude of the observed effect in addition to information on the statistical significance (Gold, 2004).

Most researchers do not yet routinely report effect size estimates along with their tests of significance. In music therapy research reports, effect size estimates are seldom reported (Gold, 2004).[3] Therefore, the meta-analyst must compute the effect size from the tests of significance that have been provided. Extracting effect sizes from primary research findings may be easy or may be a daunting challenge, depending on the information the author has provided. Researchers frequently provide numerical information not needed by the meta-analyst but fall short in providing crucial information for computing effect size estimates.

The two types of effect sizes that are often employed by researchers are the Pearson Product Moment Correlation *r* and Cohen's *d*. The correlation coefficient *r* is typically used when relationships between variables are assessed and, therefore, when the study characteristics and the outcomes are continuous in nature. Cohen's *d* is typically used when the impact of treatments or interventions is assessed (Durlak, Meerson, & Foster, 2003). Rosenthal (1991) provides several arguments for the use of *r* over *d*. It is, for example, impossible to compute *d* accurately if authors fail to report the sample sizes of the experimental group as well as the control group; unfortunately, this negligence is commonly encountered in the literature. For discussion on additional reasons for preferring *r* over *d*, the reader is referred to Rosenthal (1991).

To begin the meta-analytic calculations, an effect size is calculated for each dependent variable included in the study. The correlation coefficient *r* value can range from −1.00 to +1.00. Interpretation of the statistic is straightforward. A positive number indicates that the experimental or treatment group performed better than the control group on the variable of interest, whereas a negative number reflects that the control group showed greater improvement on the outcome measure. The index *d* is reported in standard deviation units. This means that if the treatment resulted in an effect size of .25, the treatment led to a quarter of a standard deviation increase in the outcome. When reporting effect sizes, it is important to provide a sign. A positive value indicates that the effect is in the predicted direction (as set forth by the hypothesis); a negative sign reflects an effect in the direction that was not predicted. The following interpretation of effect size has been proposed by Cohen (1977) and is widely accepted:

Small	Medium	Large
$r = .10$	$r = .30$	$r = .50$
$d = .20$	$d = .50$	$d = .80$

Rosenthal (1991) provides helpful guidelines for converting various statistics into the effect size *r*. The effect size *r* can be easily computed from *t* statistics and from *F* statistics with 1 degree of freedom *(df)* in the numerator using the following formula:

$$r = \sqrt{\frac{t^2}{t^2 + df}}$$

where $df = n_1 + n_2 - 2$ (the same as adding the sample sizes of the experimental group and the control group minus 2);

$$r = \sqrt{\frac{F}{F + df_{error}}}$$

where *F* indicates any *F* with $df = 1$ in the numerator. *F* tests with $df > 1$ in the numerator cannot be included in the meta-analytic calculations.

---

[3] The *Publication Manual of the American Psychological Association* (5th Edition; APA, 2001), says, "Take seriously the statistical power considerations associated with your tests of hypotheses. Such considerations relate to the likelihood of correctly rejecting the tested hypotheses, given a particular alpha level, effect size, and sample size" (p. 24).

The effect size *r* can also be computed from chi-square:

$$r = \sqrt{\frac{\chi^2}{n}}$$

In the event that none of these test values has been reported, an effect size *r* can be computed from a *p* level as long as the size of the study *(N)* is reported. Two steps are involved in this computation. First, the one-tailed *p* value needs to be converted to its standardized normal deviate equivalent, called *Z*. This can be done by using a table of *Z* values (available in most quantitative research books) or by using a statistical calculator (many of which are available free of charge online). A word of caution: In most studies, a two-tailed *p* value is reported. To obtain a one-tailed *p* value, simply divide the two-tailed value by 2 (for example, a two-tailed *p* = .05 becomes a one-tailed *p* = .025). The effect size *r* can then be calculated using the following formula:

$$r = \frac{Z}{\sqrt{N}}$$

In case the only statistical information given is *p* < .05, the meta-analyst should use the most conservative *p* value, *p* = .05, and employ the equation above. In some instances, the report of research findings is limited to statements such as "the independent variable had no significant effect on the dependent variable" or "no significant difference was found." In this case, the meta-analyst must assign a *Z* = 0 to the variable in this study; this will result in *r* = .00. This is unfortunate as it most likely results in an underestimate of the effect size. However, such a conservative approach is necessary (Rosenthal, 1991).

To compute Cohen's *d*, one needs to subtract the mean of the control condition from the mean of the treatment condition at posttest and divide this by the pooled standard deviation of the two groups at posttest.

$$d = \frac{\overline{X}_t - \overline{X}_c}{S_p}$$

where $\overline{X}_t$ is the mean of the treatment group, $\overline{X}_c$ is the mean of the control group, and S_p is the pooled standard deviation.

The pooled standard deviation can be derived as follows:

$$S_p = \sqrt{\frac{(n_t - 1)s_t^2 + (n_c - 1)s_c^2}{(n_t - n_c - 2)}}$$

where *S* is the standard deviation, *n* the number of subjects, and $_t$ and $_c$ indicate the treatment group and control group, respectively.

Some meta-analysts have used only the standard deviation of the control condition to calculate the effect size. However, in small samples, this gives an inaccurate estimate due to sampling error (Gold, 2004) and this should be avoided.

Finally, Cohen's *d* can be easily converted into *r* by using the following formula:

$$r = \sqrt{\frac{d^2}{d^2 + 4}}$$

The *d* to *r* conversions are listed below:

d	*r*	*d*	*r*	*d*	*r*
2.0	.707	1.3	.545	0.6	.287
1.9	.689	1.2	.514	0.5	.243
1.8	.669	1.1	.482	0.4	.196
1.7	.648	1.0	.447	0.3	.148
1.6	.625	0.9	.410	0.2	.100
1.5	.600	0.8	.371	0.1	.050
1.4	.573	0.7	.330	0.0	.000

Many of the studies used in a meta-analysis will have more than one test of significance relevant to the hypothesis of the meta-analysis, leading to multiple effect size estimates. For example, a study might look at the effect of active music making on level of anxiety, perceived level of control, and pain levels in pediatric oncology patients. If there are many studies that use the same dependent variables, a separate meta-analysis can be performed for each different type of dependent variable involved (Rosenthal, 1991). When using the study as the unit of analysis (rather than one dependent variable), it is of crucial importance that multiple effect sizes within each study be averaged, so that each study contributes the same number of data points to the analysis (Durlak et al., 2003).

Identifying Outliers

After the effect sizes have been obtained, it is important to look at their variability. In an attempt to achieve homogeneity, the distribution of the effect sizes is examined to determine whether outliers, or deviant effect sizes, exist. Effect sizes are considered outliers when they are located two or more standard deviations from their respective means (Durlak et al., 2003). Removing these outliers from the statistical analyses increases the chance of obtaining homogeneity. This procedure should be done before computing the meta-analysis. Some researchers, however, opt to conduct and report analyses with and without the outliers. Durlak et al. rightly point out that outliers should never be ignored. Outliers could be the result of an error in the data, but they could also point at important phenomena that possibly have influenced the results. It could be, for example, that a certain music therapy intervention is very effective with one population but less effective with another.

Comparing and Combining Effect Sizes

Comparing Studies

When looking at two studies examining the same research question, a researcher is usually interested in finding out whether the results are consistent with or significantly different from each other. For example, upon a first look, the following two studies appear to have obtained very different results:

Study 1: $t(78) = 2.21$, $p < .05$

Study 2: $t(18) = 1.06$, $p > .30$

However, when computing the effect size for each study, both studies result in an effect size of $r = .24$ (Rosenthal, 1991, p. 61).

When comparing two research studies, an effect size r is calculated for each study. For each r, an associated Fisher Z_r is identified. Conversion tables for r to Z_r are available in most research textbooks. The following formula can then be used to calculate Z, reflecting the difference between the two effect sizes:

$$Z = \frac{Z_{r1} - Z_{r2}}{\sqrt{\dfrac{1}{N_1 - 3} + \dfrac{1}{N_2 - 3}}}$$

with N_1 and N_2 representing the sample size of each study.

Finally the p value associated with the computed Z needs to be identified (again, tables for this are available in research textbooks). A two-tailed p value $< .05$ reflects a significant difference between the two effect sizes, meaning that the two studies disagree significantly on their estimates of the size of the relationship between the independent and dependent variables (Lipsey & Wilson, 2001; Rosenthal, 1991).

The following example described by Rosenthal (1991) provides an idea of how careful the meta-analyst must be when comparing significance levels and effect sizes:

> Studies A and B yield effect size estimates of $r = .00$ ($N = 17$) and $r = .30$ ($N = 45$), respectively. [Using the above formula], a $Z = -1.00$ with an associated two-tailed p value of .32 was obtained, meaning that these two studies do not differ significantly from each other. (p. 64)

Thus, although the studies might appear at first to have achieved very different results, they do not actually differ significantly from each other.

Combining Studies

The mean effect size for a group of studies is computed by weighing each effect size by the inverse of its variance or w_i. This results in an unbiased effect size because it weights larger samples whose effect sizes are generally considered to be more reliable more heavily (Rind, Tromovitch, & Bauserman, 1998).

The general formula for the weighted mean effect size is:

$$\overline{ES} = \frac{\sum (w_i ES_i)}{\sum w_i}$$

When using the correlation coefficient r, the meta-analyst first needs to identify the associated Fisher Z_r for each effect size. The weighted Z_r is then computed with the following formula:

$$\text{Weighted } \overline{Z_r} = \frac{\sum w_j z_{rj}}{\sum w_j}$$

This mean Z_r is then converted back to a corresponding mean weighted effect size r, referred to as the *unbiased effect size estimate (r_u)* (Rosenthal, 1991).

After obtaining the mean effect size, the confidence interval needs to be determined. This confidence interval portrays the range of effects one might expect at a predetermined p level (for example, $p = .05$). When the confidence interval does not include zero, the estimated effect size is considered significant.

Finally, a homogeneity test needs to be performed. This test results in a Q statistic which is based on a chi-square with $df = k - 1$ (with k representing the number of effect sizes). When this Q statistic is statistically significant ($p < .05$), the distribution of the effect sizes is considered heterogeneous or inconsistent. In other words, the variability of the effect sizes is greater than would be expected from sampling error alone and there are other factors, moderator variables, influencing the results, such as type of treatment, level of randomization, musical preference. It is, of course, important for the meta-analyst to try to identify these moderator variables. This can be done by applying the fixed effects, random effects, or mixed effects model (Durlak, et al., 2003) to the data. The reader is referred to Lipsey and Wilson (2001) for a detailed discussion on the different assumptions and the statistical features of these models.

Most meta-analysis software programs will automatically perform the above statistical calculations when combining or comparing studies. Unfortunately, few comprehensive meta-analytic software programs are available. A program that has been widely used is DSTAT (Johnson, 1989). It comes with a useful manual but is, unfortunately, MS-DOS based. Lipsey and Wilson (2001) have developed SPSS macros for meta-analysis. Their book, *Practical Meta-Analysis,* takes the reader through all the steps involved in meta-analysis and offers explanation for the use of the macros.

Conclusion

As has been described in this chapter, meta-analysis may provide a useful method to examine the effects of music therapy on various outcomes, important information for music therapists themselves and for persons who use or fund services. In a growing discipline such as music therapy, results of meta-analysis research may provide a helpful means to develop future research agendas. Although meta-analysis is still growing as a research method, refinements in its methods will continue to support its valuable place in the quest for better ways of knowing.

References

American Psychological Association. (2001). *Publication Manual of the American Psychological Association* (5th ed.). Washington, DC: Author.

Arthur, W., Bennett, W., & Huffcutt, A. I. (2001). *Conducting meta-analysis using SAS.* Mahwah, NJ: Lawrence Erlbaum Associates.

Cohen, J. (1977). *Statistical power analysis for the behavioral sciences* (2nd ed.). New York: Academic Press.

Cook, T. C., Cooper, H., Cordray, D. S., Hartmann, H., Hedges, L. V., Light, R. J., Louis, T. A., & Mosteller, F. (1992). *Meta-analysis for explanation: A casebook.* New York: Russell Sage Foundation.

Cooper, H., & Hedges, L. V. (Eds.). (1994). *The handbook of research synthesis.* New York: Russell Sage Foundation.

Dileo, C., & Bradt, J. (Eds.). (in press). *Music therapy and medicine: A meta-analysis of the literature according to medical specialty.* Cherry Hill, NJ: Jeffrey Books.

Durlak, J. A., Meerson, I., & Foster, C. (2003). Meta-analysis. In J. Thomas & M. Hersen (Eds.), *Understanding research in clinical and counseling psychology* (pp. 243–270). Mahwah, NJ: Lawrence Erlbaum Associates.

Eysenck, H. J. (1994). Meta-analysis and its problems. *British Medical Journal, 309,* 789–792.

Feldman, K. A. (1971). Using the work of others: Some observations on reviewing and integrating. *Sociology of Education, 44,* 86–102.

Geddes, J., & Carney, S. (2002). Systematic reviews and meta-analyses. In S. Priebe & M. Slade (Eds.), *Evidence in mental health care* (pp. 72–80). New York: Bruner-Routledge.

Gold, C. (2004). The use of effect sizes in music therapy research. *Music Therapy Perspectives, 22,* 91–95.

Gold, C., Heldal, T. O., Dahle, T., & Wigram, T. (in press). Music therapy for schizophrenia and schizophrenia-like illnesses [Cochrane Review], *The Cochrane Library, 2, 2005.* Chichester, UK: John Wiley & Sons, Ltd.

Gold, C., Voracek, M., & Wigram, T. (2004). Effects of music therapy for children and adolescents with psychopathology: A meta-analysis. *Journal of Child Psychology and Psychiatry and Allied Disciplines, 45,* 1054–1063.

Gold, C., & Wigram, T. (2005). Music therapy for autistic spectrum disorder. [Protocol]. *Cochrane Database of Systematic Reviews,* Issue 1.

Gregoire, G., Derderian, F., & LeLorier, J. (1995). Selecting the language of the publications included in a meta-analysis: Is there a Tower of Babel bias? *Journal of Clinical Epidemiology, 48,* 159–63.

Hedges, L. V. (1990). Directions for future methodology. In K. W. Wachter & M. L. Straf (Eds.), *The future of meta-analysis* (pp. 11–26). New York: Russell Sage Foundation.

Hunt, M. (1997). *How science takes stock: The story of meta-analysis.* New York: Russell Sage Foundation.

Johnson, B. T. (1989). *DSTAT: Software for the meta-analytic review of the research literature.* Hillsdale, NJ: Lawrence Erlbaum Associates.

Koger, S. M., Chapin, K., & Brotons, M. (1999). Is music therapy an effective intervention for dementia? A meta-analytic review of the literature. *Journal of Music Therapy, 36,* 2–15.

Lipsey, M. W., & Wilson, D. B. (2001). *Practical meta-analysis.* Thousand Oaks, CA: Sage Publications.

Maratos, A., & Gold, C. (2005). Music therapy for depression. [Protocol]. *Cochrane Database of Systematic Reviews,* Issue 1.

Pelletier, C. L. (2004). The effect of music on decreasing arousal due to stress: A meta-analysis. *Journal of Music Therapy, 41,* 192–214.

Priebe, S., & Slade, M. (Eds.). (2002). *Evidence in mental health care.* New York: Bruner-Routledge.

Rind, B., Tromovitch, P., & Bauserman, R. (1998). A meta-analytic examination of assumed properties of child sexual abuse using college samples. *Psychological Bulletin, 124,* 22–53.

Rosenthal, R. (1991). *Meta-analytic procedures for social research* (Rev. ed.). Applied social research methods series, Vol. 6. Newbury Park, CA: Sage Publications.

Rosenthal, R., Rosnow, R. L. & Rubin, D. B. (2000). *Contrasts and effect sizes in behavioral research: A correlational approach.* Cambridge, UK: Cambridge University Press.

Schafer, W. D. (1999). An overview of meta-analysis. *Measurement & Evaluation in Counseling & Development, 32,* 43–61.

Simes, R .J. (1986). Publication bias: The case for an international registry of clinical trials. *Journal of Clinical Oncology, 4,* 1529–1541.

Slavin, R. E. (1995). Best evidence synthesis: An intelligent alternative to meta-analysis. *Journal of Clinical Epidemiology, 48,* 9–18.

Silverman, M. J. (2003). The influence of music on the symptoms of schizophrenia: A meta-analysis. *Journal of Music Therapy, 40,* 27–40.

Standley, J. (1986). Music research in medical/dental treatment: Meta-analysis and clinical implications. *Journal of Music Therapy, 23,* 56–122.

Standley, J. (1992). Meta-analysis of research in music and medical treatment: Effect size as a basis for comparison across multiple dependent and independent variables. In R. Spintge & R. Droh (Eds.), *MusicMedicine* (pp. 364–378). St. Louis, MO: MMB Music.

Standley, J. (1996). Music research in medical/dental treatment: An update of a prior meta-analysis. In C. Furman (Ed.), *Effectiveness of music therapy procedures: Documentation of research and clinical practice* (2nd ed., pp. 1–60). Silver Spring, MD: National Association for Music Therapy.

Standley, J. (2000). Music research in medical treatment. In *Effectiveness of music therapy procedures: Documentation of research and clinical practice* (3rd ed., pp. 1–64). Silver Spring, MD: American Music Therapy Association.

Standley, J. M. (2002). A meta-analysis of the efficacy of music therapy for premature infants. *Journal of Pediatric Nursing, 17*(2), 107–113.

Whipple, J. (2004). Music in intervention for children and adolescents with autism: A meta-analysis. *Journal of Music Therapy, 41,* 90–106.

Chapter 24
Quantitative Single-Case Designs
Henk Smeijsters

This chapter focuses on single-case designs, about which Hilliard (1993) says: "Little systematic attention has been given to describing what single-case research actually is" (p. 373). Single-case designs will be compared to group designs, more particularly randomized controlled trials (RCTs). The positivistic framework, which underlies positivistic group designs and positivistic single-case designs, will be described, examples of several types of single-case designs will be given, reliability and validity in positivistic single-case research will be discussed, and finally examples of different types of quantitative single-case studies will be provided. This chapter does not focus on applied behavior analysis, which may be considered a type of single-case design, as it is addressed in another chapter of this book.

What Is Single-Case Research?

Yin (2003) defines a single-case study as an empirical inquiry that differs from a history, an experiment, and a survey. The case study differs from a history because it occurs in a real-life context. It differs from an experiment because it does not divorce a phenomenon from its context and does not split up the phenomenon into variables. The case study differs from the survey because it can investigate the context more deeply. Moreover, the case study focuses on *how* and *why* questions in contemporary events without requiring control over behavioral events. Yin's examples are not therapeutic; for instance, he uses the decision-making process during the Cuban missile crisis as an example. However, Yin's characteristics for the case study show that this type of explanatory research can be very useful for therapy.

In therapy, questions as to why decisions on indications for therapy, goals, and treatment are made are of interest. What is more, the question of how treatment works is very important but cannot be answered easily by controlling experimental conditions since treatments in their essence are individually oriented. The nonexperimental nature of the case study makes it useful for research on therapy. As we shall see, and as Yin (2003) puts forward, case-study research is not identical with the exploratory stage of some other type of research, nor is it typically qualitative or naturalistic. Therefore, a case study can use quantitative data and a clear theoretical model. We shall see also that there can be levels of experimentation between the laboratory experiment and the nonexperimental real life case study as described by Yin.

Hilliard (1993), who focuses on psychotherapy research, defines single-case research as a subclass of intrasubject research. In intrasubject research there is variation within individual subjects over time and thus repeated measures over time within the subject. This is different from intersubject research where measures between subjects are used and aggregation across cases takes place. Intrasubject research can be quantitative or qualitative.

This brings us to the conclusion that, when discussing research, we have quantitative and qualitative methods and intrasubject and intersubject methods, and their interconnections such as intrasubject-quantitative, intrasubject-qualitative, intersubject-quantitative, and intersubject-qualitative research. Questions about the appropriateness of quantitative or qualitative research should not be confused with the intrasubject-intersubject positions.

To begin to illustrate these points, RCTs, the prototype of the intersubject position, will be compared with single-case designs, which are part of the intrasubject position.

Single-Case Designs Versus Randomized Control Trials

The Positivistic Research Paradigm

First let us summarize the characteristics of the positivistic research paradigm:[1]

Sampling from population and generalizing from the sample to the population: The data from a small group of persons are representative of a large group of persons;

Randomization or matching between groups: Groups are equalized by putting persons at random in one of both groups or putting in each group persons who have the same value on several variables (age, education, sexes, disturbance, and so forth);

The use of an experimental and control group: The experimental group equals the control group, except for the treatment; thus any change in the experimental group can be attributed to treatment only;

The focus on independent and dependent variables: Life's complexity is reduced to a limited set of variables;

The use of standardized measuring instruments: Standardized measuring instruments are used to quantify values of the dependent variables;

A hypothesis is deduced from a theory: A theory is used that predicts a causal relationship between two or more variables;

A fixed research design and treatment: Design and treatment cannot be changed during research because it would obscure the value of the independent variable;

The use of statistics: Statistics such as mean, standard deviation, t test, analysis of variance, multiple regression analysis, and so forth, are used.

In conclusion, one can say that the positivistic paradigm makes phenomena equal (personal variables, group variables, treatment variables, outcome variables) to make it possible that many similar events can be compared and that differences can be computed statistically. The positivistic paradigm gives us same or similar data that occur often because phenomena are reduced to comparable figures by means of standardization. Because these figures are comparable, means, standard deviations, t tests, analyses of variance, multiple regression analyses, and so forth can be computed. Thus the standardization is a condition for statistical analysis. If you do not standardize, you get unique phenomena, and it will not be possible to compute statistics.

In medical research, RCTs stand out as the best way of researching treatment effects. RCTs have many characteristics that reflect the positivistic paradigm: random assignment, control groups, standardized treatment, a fixed number of sessions, operationalized final terms (goals), blind assessment, no comorbidity, and follow-ups.

This research design is put forward as the *gold standard.* Wessely (2001) tells us: "If we had not done clinical trials we would still be giving insulin coma to schizophrenics" (p. 49). By means of RCTs, we not only are able to show that treatment has some benefit compared to placebo, but we also are able to detect when a treatment does more harm than no treatment.

However, there have been many critics of this research design. Most critics combine comments on the intersubject design and on experimental and quantitative procedures.

Seligman (1995) concludes that RCTs cannot show the effects of psychotherapy because many crucial factors are left out. Clients are very complex, no two clients are alike, no two interventions can be the same, and therapeutic outcomes are difficult to standardize (see also Rustin, 2001). As a result of this complexity, the interaction between clients and therapy will also be very complex. In Seligman's opinion the so-called strong aspects of the randomized clinical trial (random assignment, standardized treatment protocol, fixed duration, standardized outcome measures) give insufficient insight in the specific process that unfolds within the client and between the client and the therapist. In line with this, one of the most important criticisms is that RCTs are nonrepresentative because the standardization of persons and treatment leads to a lack of comorbidity within clients and thus a lack of clinical validity of the treatment (Slade & Priebe, 2002).

---

[1] See Chapter 4, Principles of Quantitative Research, for an additional perspective on the positivist research paradigm.

Marshall (2002) mentions that RCTs do not tell us how treatment works. Statistically aggregating across cases results in mean scores and statistical significance, which do not give much information about the client's individual process. RCTs are not process oriented or person oriented. Outcome research on groups can tell you that there has been a change in a group of clients that is determined through statistical analysis not likely to have been due to chance. It tells you that an averaged treatment leads to an averaged effect, but it does not tell how the process of change took place in the individual clients. Reducing complexity to a limited set of variables and averaging scores across subjects leads to pseudoparsimony. Because it is an artifact for therapists, this pseudoparsimony has little meaning.

When researching medicine, the process over time in the individual may be less important, but in psychotherapy research the smaller changes that result from client and therapist interaction are very important.

Single-Case Designs

Turpin (2001) says: "Single-case experimental designs have been developed in an attempt to provide proof of effectiveness within the individual" (p. 93). While he focuses on the single-case experimental design, thereby limiting the scope of single-case designs, I advocate that quantitative (and qualitative) experimental and nonexperimental single-case designs all come forward with some type of evidence. Thus we should ask ourselves what we define as *evidence based*. One must conclude that evidence is not only a result from RCTs. Instead of an evidence-based medicine, we need an evidence-based mental health in which scientific practitioners evaluate their clinical practice by means of generating and testing hypotheses; monitoring treatment goals, interventions, and results; and submitting findings to panels of experts (Hutschemaekers, 2003; Smeijsters, 2003).

As a conclusion, one can say that from the perspective of intrasubject versus intersubject research, the single-case design is the counterpart of the RCT. The strength of the RCT (internal validity) is the weakness of the single-case design, and the weakness of the RCT (external validity) is the strength of the single-case design. The benefits of single-case designs can be:

- Focus on the process and outcome in individuals (or clinical groups),
- Inclusion of comorbidity,
- Flexibility in treatment and duration,
- Flexibility in measurement.

The benefits that come forward depend on the particular type of single-case design: on its quantitative or qualitative and its experimental or nonexperimental aspects.

Reliability and Validity

The criteria that hold for positivistic group designs also hold for those single-case designs that are based on the positivistic paradigm. The criteria of reliability (test-retest reliability, interrater reliability, and internal consistency) are the same. These same reliability criteria are needed when measuring instruments are used in quantitative single-case designs. Using measuring instruments implies that the dependent variables are standardized. At each time, at each place, and for each person the same data are collected. The difference with quantitative group designs is that, in the single-case design, no means between persons are calculated. Take, for instance, a multiple baseline design in which numerical data for several individual persons are collected. If the researcher should decide to calculate a group mean, then it no longer is a single-case design.

Because measuring instruments are standardized, they can provide numerical data of phenomena. These numerical data suggest that a value in one case has the same meaning as a value in another case. The quantitative single-case design shares the idea with the quantitative group design that phenomena easily can be abstracted and compared.

In quantitative single-case designs the criteria of validity also are the same as in quantitative group designs. Content, criterion-related, and construct validity are of concern when a measuring instrument is used. These criteria make sure that a measurement instrument measures what it supposes to measure. For example, when a measurement is thought to measure depression, it should not measure verbal fluency.

In experimental group designs, internal validity refers to the question of whether one can be sure that the independent variable (the treatment) and not some other variable causes the effect. As described before, this is solved in the RCT by using randomization and an experimental and control group. If an effect occurs in the experimental group only, the researcher knows that, because all other things between the experimental and control group were equal, the effect is a result of the treatment.

In quantitative single-case designs, there is no control group. The changes occur within the single subject. Without a control group, it seems difficult to control for variables like spontaneous recovery, placebo effects, and other threats to internal validity. But even then, the researcher wants to know if effects are a result of treatment.

In the experimental single-case design, these flaws are countered by means of variations of treatment and control periods over time. If treatment and control periods are varied over time and the effect occurs only when there is treatment, it is supposed that the effect is because of treatment. It is not likely that there is another variable that happens precisely parallel to the treatment periods. Take, for instance, maturation. If there are several treatment periods and baselines over time, and each time the effect is only there when there is treatment, then maturation cannot be the cause. Other competing variables that might influence internal validity can be controlled in the same way. Take, for instance, the client finding a job during the course of therapy. This job will be there when there are treatment periods and nontreatment periods. If the job causes a positive change in the client's mood, then this mood will not be affected by the alternation of treatment and nontreatment periods. But when it is not the job that affects his mood, but rather the music therapy, then his mood will vary parallel to the treatment and nontreatment periods.

Thus, whereas in the experimental group design the treatment group is compared to a nontreatment group, in the experimental single-case design the treatment periods within the individual are compared to the nontreatment periods of the same individual.

In positivistic single-case designs the idea of external validity is the same as in the positivistic group design. The individual case is meant to be a sample from a population.

Objectivity, referring to the use of standardized measuring instruments with observable, understandable items that exclude interpretation, and the use of blind conditions, insuring that the observer does not know whether the excerpt is from a treatment or control period, can be arranged in quantitative single-case designs.

Types of Single-Case Designs

From the writings of Aldridge (1993, 1996), two criteria can be deduced: the *level of experimentation* and the *level of formality*. The level of experimentation refers to the rigor that is used when treatment and baseline periods are alternated. The level of formality refers to the explicitness of the research design and assessment procedures, both of which result in the transparency of interpretation. These criteria can be used when discriminating among the three approaches that have been described by Aldridge: randomized single-case designs, single-case experimental designs, and case-study research

In randomized single-case designs ($N = 1$ studies) there is a baseline period during which the client's symptom is measured, then treatment is randomly assigned. This type of research can easily be used when, for instance, alternating the use of a drug and a placebo. When the symptoms decrease in several trials during periods where the drug has been used, the effect of the drug is evident. However, the usefulness of this type of design is disputable when such a linear causal biological connection between treatment and effect does not exist, and when the effects of treatment are steady and thus do not reverse during baseline. Turpin (2001) puts forward that the reasoning behind this design is based on a certain (limited) theory about learning. This can be relevant for some effects in music therapy. However, many times learning and other change has occurred, thus there is an influence on the client's musical behavior and psyche that is not likely to go back to the baseline when the treatment is interrupted or when a placebo musical activity is used. When there is such a development in this research design, the internal validity is difficult to guarantee.

The single-case experimental design is much more an experiment. As in group designs, the experimental and control phases are set out before the start, and, like other experiments, there is a more artificial and less naturalistic context. The single-case experimental design can have the form of an AB, ABAB (the reversal design), multiple baseline design with concurrent measures, or small *N* design in which the single-case experimental design is repeated across a small series of individuals. When large amounts of data are collected daily over several months, these designs are often called *time-series designs*. Turpin (2001) and Alderman (2002) suggest the following characteristics of the single-case experimental design:

Stable baseline: When baselines are unstable, there is too much fluctuation in nontreatment phases.

Single, well-specified, and well-defined treatment methods with minimized variability: This can be a combination of methods. External therapeutic factors should be held constant or should be evaluated.

Systematic manipulation of the independent variable: This is done by means of reversibility or time-lagged introduction. When there is a nonreversible treatment one should use *therapeutic holidays* in which the client is invited to make a break and put aside what has been learned in therapy.

Repeated measurement: At least three baselines and three treatment measures should be taken.

Measurement of the dependent variable:[2] This is done quantitatively.

Development of cause-effect relationships. These are done between the independent and the dependent variable.

Generalizability: This can be achieved through a series of *N* = 1 designs across clients.

As with randomized single-case designs, the internal validity in reversal designs is not easy to guarantee when there is a development process along baselines and treatment phase. This problem can be coped with by means of a multiple baseline design.

Case-study research differs from traditional *case histories* because there is a well-defined research method, and although case-study research is not experimental, it scores high on the criterion of formality. In a traditional case history there are ad hoc descriptions and interpretations that are not formalized or tested for trustworthiness, or there are post hoc descriptions and interpretations that are even less trustworthy.

Hilliard (1993) differentiates single-case designs along three dimensions: *quantitative or qualitative, manipulative or nonmanipulative, hypothesis-testing or hypothesis-generating*. By combining these three distinctions you get eight interesting types of single-case designs:

1. *Quantitative-experimental hypothesis-testing* single-case design: numerical data, manipulation, hypothesis testing,
2. *Quantitative-naturalistic hypothesis-testing* single-case design: numerical data, no manipulation, hypothesis testing,
3. *Quantitative-experimental hypothesis-generating* single-case design: numerical data, manipulation, no hypothesis,
4. *Quantitative-naturalistic hypothesis-generating* single-case design: numerical data, no manipulation, no hypothesis,
5. *Qualitative-experimental hypothesis-testing* single-case design: qualitative data, manipulation, hypothesis testing,
6. *Qualitative-naturalistic hypothesis-testing* single-case design: qualitative data, no manipulation, hypothesis testing,
7. *Qualitative-experimental hypothesis-generating* single-case design: qualitative data, manipulation, no hypothesis,
8. *Qualitative-naturalistic hypothesis-generating* single-case design: qualitative data, no manipulation, no hypothesis.

The case history has not been included when describing the different types of single-case designs. I agree with Hilliard that a case study as such is not research. As Soldz (1990) suggested, we should develop and use research-informed case studies. To be trustworthy, individual case studies should be carried out using sound research techniques.

For the integration of quantitative and qualitative knowledge in case-study research, see Scholz and Tietje (2002).

---

[2] A problem with statistics in quantitative single case designs is *serial dependency,* meaning that a measure influences the next measure, violating the assumptions of statistical tests (Aldridge, 1993, 1996; Turpin, 2001; Wampold, 1988). That is why graphic time-series designs and clinical significance (Jacobson, 1988) are used.

Music Therapy Examples

There are many examples of single-case designs. This section will include examples of the four types of single-case designs that all are quantitative but are combined with hypothesis-testing or hypothesis-generating within a naturalistic or an experimental setting. The first example comes close to applied behavior analysis (reversal and multiple baseline designs), described in Chapter 25.

A Quantitative-Experimental Hypothesis-Testing Single-Case Design

The research by Kern and Wolery (2001) with a 40-month old boy with congenital blindness is a single-subject design in which three conditions are used. The boy's general development (motor functioning, language, play skills, socialization, and so forth) was delayed. He was fearful on the playground. There were few peer interactions and low play activities. Because of his blindness, he was unable to find play objects. The boy had developed stereotypic behaviors such as shaking his head, bumping his head on objects, and rocking. All of these behaviors can be integrated into a diagnostic schema: Because of his blindness, he could not find and manipulate objects and persons adequately. Therefore, his learning and playing abilities did not improve. The lack of involvement in activities resulted in stereotypic behaviors.

Because his withdrawn, unplayful, and stereotyped behavior was exhibited on the playground, this playground was used as the experimental context. The three experimental conditions were as follows:

Baseline: In the morning, no playground adaptations and no instructions to the teachers were used.

Playground adaptations: Six musical stations were added to the playground at meaningful locations (at the entrance of the playground, near the sandbox, near the tricycle track that could increase social interactions, near a tree with a wooden bench where teachers and children interacted, near a second tree, in another sandbox). Each musical station consisted of easy playable musical instruments. A drainage pipe (with ridges on it like a guiro) connected all musical stations to each other. The boy could navigate the path by means of a pushcart with a rubber flat that created a sound when it was pushed along the drainpipe.

Staff development activities: Teachers were encouraged to use recorded songs for each musical station, and were instructed how to help the boy at each musical station and how to move from one to the next musical station.

Many music therapists will argue that this conditional procedure without any interaction between the boy and the music therapist is not music therapy as it is conceived nowadays, but this will not be discussed in this chapter. What I would like to describe is the research design.

Data were gathered using 30-second time samples in which an observer recorded a judgment on five behavioral categories: social interaction with peers, social interaction with adults, play and engagement with materials, movement on the playground, and stereotypic behavior.

Percentages of intervals were computed on the three conditions (baseline, playground adaptations, and staff development activities) for the dependent variables. Figure 1 gives the results of the interaction with peers. Figure 2 gives the results of play/engagement with materials.

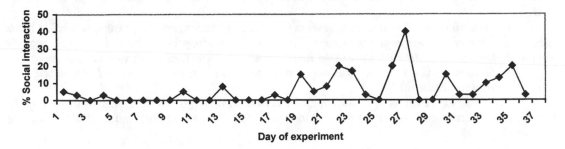

Baseline: Days 1–12; Playground adaptations: Days 13–19; Staff development: Days 20–36

Figure 1. Percentage of Intervals of Social Interaction Across Three Conditions
Kern & Wolery (2001). Used with permission.

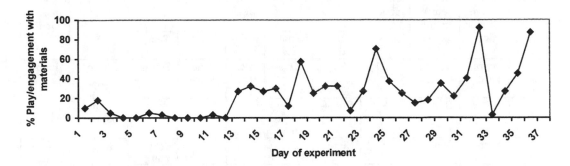

Baseline: Days 1–12; Playground adaptations: Days 13–19; Staff development: Days 20–36

Figure 2. Percentage of Intervals of Play/Engagement with Materials Across Three Conditions
Kern & Wolery (2001). Used with permission.

As can seen in Figure 1, the staff development condition resulted in more social interactions with peers. The playground adaptations in Figure 2 show a sharp increase in the play/engagement with materials. The staff development condition gave the highest scores for play/engagement with materials but also increased the variability. Additional effects are described in the article (Kern & Wolery, 2001).

A Quantitative-Naturalistic Hypothesis-Testing Single-Case Design

Inselmann and Mann (1998) used rating scales to research the therapy course of one female client who was treated with 65 sessions of analytically oriented music therapy. Each session included zero to three improvisations, and all sessions were videotaped. The client improvised most of the time in interaction with the music therapist. A combined quantitative-qualitative (naturalistic) design was used. Rating scales focusing on emotional expression, interpersonal communication, musical expression, and musical interaction were used.

Basic to all scales was the hypothesis that more health will be reflected in a greater range of (emotional and musical) expressive and communicative possibilities. The scales for emotional expression and interpersonal communication included adjectives (attributes) that could be rated 1–5. The adjectives were modified from studies by Timmermann, Scheytt-Hölzer, Bauer, and Kächele (1991) and Timmermann, Bauer, Scheytt-Hölzer, Schmidt, Kächele, and Baitsch (1992). Interrater reliability (Cohen's kappa) was calculated for all scales. Factor analysis of the scales with adjectives, emotional expression and interpersonal communication, resulted in five condensed scales with high internal consistency (Cronbach's alpha): self-conscious, harmonic, joyful/turning towards, depressive, and aggressive. The values on each scale were then dichotomized as *low* or *high* based on a cut-off point between 1 and 5 for use in the session evaluations.

For the analysis of musical expression (rhythm, dynamics, melody, range, tempo), a list of three codes for each parameter was used. For instance, melody could be coded as *no melody, simple melody,* or *melody with developed motif.* Musical interaction was rated on a scale of 1–6, from *no interaction* (1) to *synchronously or in sequence incorporating and developing the partner's musical theme* (6).

The analysis of the single case yielded the results shown in Table 1, which illustrates the way that the condensed scales were used to typify the client's and the therapist's play during episodes.[3]

Table 1
Musical Expression and Musical Parameters in the Treatment of One Client With Improvisational Music Therapy
Inselmann & Mann (1998). Used with permission.

Episode (session #)	Client's emotional expression	Therapist's emotional expression	Musical interaction	Musical expression					Client's instruments	Therapist's instruments
				Rhythm	Dynamics	Melody	Range	Tempo		
1 (10)	Depressive	Depressive	3 / 1	Simple	One	No/simple	One octave	Similar	Bongos, xylophone	Piano
2 (10)	Secure	Secure	3	Simple	One/variation	-	-	Varying	Tambourine	Sounding dish
3 (11)	Aggressive	Depressive	2	Simple	One	-	-	Varying	Bongos	Tambourine
4 (11)	Depressive	Secure	4 / 3	Simple	One	No	One octave	Similar	Xylophone	Piano
5 (11)	Depressive	Secure	4 / 1	Simple	Variation/one	No/simple	Whole tone space	Varying	Xylophone	Piano
6 (12)	Secure	Secure	1 / 2	Simple	Variation/one	Simple	Whole tone space	Varying	Xylophone	Piano
7 (12)	Aggressive	Joyful/turning towards	3	Simple	Variation	-	-	Varying	Sounding dish	Piano
8 (14)	Aggressive	Secure	4	Simple	One	-	-	Varying/transitions	Wooden bars	Bongos
9 (14)	Harmonic	Aggressive and joyful/turning towards	3	Simple	One	Simple	Whole tone space	Varying	Metallophone	Bongos
10 (14)	Joyful/turning towards	Joyful/turning towards	4	Variation	Variation	-	-	Transitions/varying	Bongos	Bongos

---

[3] When there are two numbers in the musical interaction scale, it is because of a lack of interrater agreement (the two numbers are the ratings of two raters). We see that there is more agreement between raters near the end of the episodes on levels 3 and 4 (on the scale 1–6). As with musical interaction, lack of agreement between raters can be seen on dynamics, melody, and tempo, where two codes are written within a cell.

If Table 1 is read horizontally, the interconnections of the psychological and musical parameters can be seen. In episode 1, for instance, the expression of the client's play, or emotional expression, is depressive and her music is without variation. In episode 4, the client's expression still is depressive, which is sounded in the musical parameters, but the musical interaction has improved to 4/3 (on the scale 1–6). In episodes 9 and 10, the client's emotional expression has changed into harmonic, her communicative possibility is joyful/turning towards, the musical interaction is 3 and 4, and rhythm, dynamics and tempo are varied.

Reading the table from top to bottom (episode 1 through episode 10), it can be seen that the client's expression, her musical play, and the musical interaction all improved and thus can be triangulated with each other.

A Quantitative-Experimental Hypothesis-Generating Single-Case Design

This type of research design is rare because generally when there is a quantitative and experimental procedure there is also a clear hypothesis that is tested. However, in several cases the hypothesis is not so clear-cut. There is not a sophisticated theory from which the hypothesis is deduced, and the outcome can be predicted, verified, or falsified.

This is the case in an example by Ford (1999), a single-case research study with an experimental design and quantitative data. The single case is about a 23-year old woman with a developmental level between 3 and 12 months. She could not walk and was unable to use verbalizations. She showed three self-injurious behaviors: teeth grinding, mouth scratching, and head hitting. The frequency at which these three behaviors occurred was measured. (This was done by means of 30 10-second intervals during two randomized 5-minute periods. The number of intervals in which the behavior occurred was divided by the total number of intervals and multiplied by 100.)

Three therapeutic interventions were exchanged with a baseline period (A) in a reversal ABACADA format. During the baseline period, there was no intervention except the contingent blocking of head-hitting behavior. Then there was a phase of music listening (B). After another baseline period there was water play (C) and music playing (D). All interventions except blocking the head-hitting behavior were used as noncontingent stimuli. Music listening occurred by means of listening by earphones to Scott Moulton's *Tropical Dreams* and Mood Scapes' *Savanna Night*. There was no interaction with the music therapist during music listening. Music playing meant playing on an electronic keyboard. There was interaction with the music therapist during water play and musical playing. During the water play, the music therapist talked to the client and squeezed water from a sponge over the client's hands. During the music playing, the music therapist imitated what the client played, added musical parameters (rhythm, harmony, form), and hummed at the same frequency to the client's vocalizations. Interventions (B, C, D) took place for 7 days for 30 minutes each day. The A periods varied between 4 and 9 days.

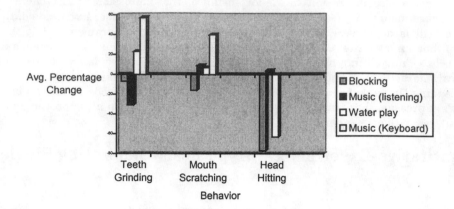

Figure 3. Average Percentage of Change in Behavior from Preintervention to Postintervention Ford (1999). Used with permission.

There was not a straightforward hypothesis. The researcher wanted "to investigate the effects of music on self-injurious behavior [SIB] in an adult with severe developmental disabilities. Specifically, the study was designed to determine if there was a difference in the rate of SIB following a passive music activity, an active music activity, and a nonmusic activity" (Ford, 1999, p. 297). Thus, there is no hypothesis that predicts that the passive or active music activity will have more effect.

It can be seen in Figure 3 that contingent blocking had an effect on all behaviors, especially head hitting, as blocking was used to stop head hitting. Music listening was the only intervention that showed a considerable decrease in teeth grinding (31%). Water play decreased head hitting (63%). Interestingly there is no reduction of self-injurious behavior when music playing is used. This is the case with head hitting because there was no head hitting during presession observation and during interventions, so there could have been no reduction. However, an increase in teeth grinding and mouth scratching can be seen during keyboard playing.

These results suggest that music listening is effective with specific types of self-injurious behavior, and that music playing is not. A theory can be developed and hypothesis can be deduced to explain how this type of music listening positively influences neurological, psychological, and behavioral patterns, and why this type of keyboard playing does not. Variables like preference, novelty, and complexity might be important theoretical concepts.

A Quantitative-Naturalistic Hypothesis-Generating Single-Case Design

Wosch and Frommer (2002) refer to the fact that outcome research should be preceded by research on the specific characteristics of the treatment process and the development of treatment methods. They made use of a quantitative single-case design in a naturalistic setting. There were no clearly specified hypotheses beforehand. Their research focused on changes in emotions as a result of music therapy improvisations.

The *resonator function*, which refers to the music therapist being touched by the client's music play (Langenberg, Frommer, & Tress, 1995), is used as a research instrument. When using the resonator function, independent observers listen to the music therapy improvisations and write down their associations that are content analyzed and developed into motifs. Different from the original resonator function, Wosch and Frommer used a questionnaire about emotions for micro-episodes in the improvisation instead of the complete improvisation. The questionnaire was presented in a computer program that also played the sounds of the improvisation. The observers could click on a label of an emotion each time in the improvisation when their emotional state changed. The improvisations lasted 2–8 minutes. The answers of the observers were statistically analyzed.

The improvisations were taken from one single case; the statistics were used on the group of observers. A cluster analysis resulted in time values that showed emotional changes during an episode in which the client and music therapist improvised

Triangulation by sources and data collecting techniques was used. Client, music therapist, and observers were involved. Client and music therapist gave open descriptions; the observers filled in two questionnaires and also gave open descriptions. The first questionnaire for the observers was about the changes in emotions, the second addressed the validity of the emotional answers (looking at whether the emotions were connected to the improvisation or to the personality of the observer).

The case is about a 32-year old female client with bulimia and a depressive personality. From the total treatment of 24 individual music therapy sessions (3 months, two sessions each week), four improvisations were chosen (from sessions 1, 12, 16, 24). Observers were university students.

The cluster analysis of each improvisation showed statistically significant emotional episodes. The validity of the answers was high, which means that there was openness to the music improvisation; thus, the emotions reflected the music and not the observer's personal emotional state. It appeared that there were five emotions: interest, fear, anger, grief, and joy.

The improvisation of session 12, illustrated in Figure 4, shows that in the beginning, interest was the strongest emotion shown by the client. In the second episode, there is a succession of interest and anger (anger by the client and the music therapist). In the third episode, the anger of the client is the strongest emotion. Finally, there is a mix of emotions in the client.

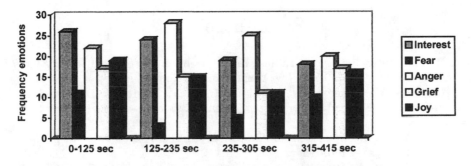

Figure 4. Emotional Profile of Improvisation in Session 12
Wosch & Frommer (2002). Used with permission.

The emotional development of the client over all sessions is shown in Figure 5. In session 1, there is fear and joy; in session 12, interest and anger; in session 16, grief, joy, and grief; and in session 24, grief and interest.

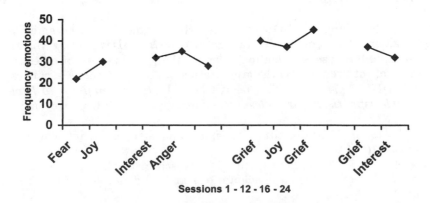

Figure 5. Emotional Changes of the Client in Improvisations Over All Sessions
Wosch & Frommer (2002). Used with permission.

One can say that this type of research shows how emotions fluctuate within sessions and between sessions. In this particular case, there is a pattern in which joy and interest go up and down during the course of treatment, whereas fear and anger occur at the start of treatment, and the process of grieving comes up in the second part of treatment. It seems that anger has to be worked through before grieving is possible. This is in line with the general theory of grieving.

Conclusion

This chapter has shown how single-case designs can have their roots in the positivistic paradigm but also offer solutions for the problem we encounter when using positivistic group designs. Having roots in the positivistic paradigm means that single-case research results in the same type of reductionistic evidence that is characteristic of positivistic research and that limits the clinical scope because client, therapist, and treatment are standardized and manipulated. Nevertheless, we also need this type of evidence. If we combine quantitative and qualitative, experimental and naturalistic, hypothesis-testing and hypothesis-generating aspects, we get metatriangulation.

In conclusion, it may be stated that each researcher should specify the design as follows:

1. Intersubject or intrasubject,
2. Quantitative or qualitative,
3. Experimental or nonexperimental,
4. Hypothesis-testing or hypothesis-generating,
5. Formal or informal.

References

Alderman, N. (2002). Individual case studies. In S. Priebe & M. Slade (Eds.), *Evidence in mental health care* (pp. 142–157). New York: Brunner Routledge.

Aldridge, D. (1993). Single case research designs. In G. T. Lewith & D. Aldridge (Eds.), *Clinical research methodology for complementary therapies* (pp. 136–168). London: Hodder & Stoughton.

Aldridge, D. (1996). *Music therapy research and practice in medicine: From out of the silence.* London: Jessica Kingsley Publishers.

Ford, S. E. (1999). The effect of music on the self-injurious behavior of an adult female with severe developmental disabilities. *Journal of Music Therapy, 36,* 293–313.

Hilliard, R. B. (1993). Single-case methodology in psychotherapy and outcome research. *Journal of Consulting and Clinical Psychology, 61,* 373–380.

Hutschemaekers, G. (2003, February). *De kunst van het hulpverlenen. Over de professionalisering van vaktherapieën in de gezondheidszorg* [The art of helping. About the professionalization of arts therapies in health care]. Paper presented at the inauguration of KenVaK, the Centre of Expertise for the Arts Therapies. Sittard, Netherlands: Universities of Professional Education Zuyd, Utrecht, and Saxion Enschede.

Inselmann, U., & Mann, S. (1998). Auswertung von Musiktherapie. Einsatz von Adjektivskalen, Bestimmung der Interraterreliabilität, Darstellung von Spielmustern: Eine Einzelfallanalyse [Evaluation of music therapy. The use of adjective scales, the calculation of interreliability, the presentation of play patterns: A single-case analysis]. In H. Kächele, U. Oerter, & N. Scheytt (Eds.), *Vortragssammlung 10 Ulmer Workshop für musiktherapeutische Grundlagenforschung* (pp. 18–44). Ulm, Germany: Universität Ulm.

Jacobson, N. S. (1988). Defining clinically significant change: An introduction. *Behavioral Assessment, 10,* 131–132.

Kern, P., & Wolery, M. (2001). Participation of a preschooler with visual impairments on the playground: Effects of musical adaptations and staff development. *Journal of Music Therapy, 38,* 149–164.

Langenberg, M., Frommer, J., & Tress, W. (1995). From isolation to bonding. A music therapy case study of a patient with chronic migraines. *The Arts in Psychotherapy, 22,* 87–101.

Marshall, M. (2002). Randomized controlled trials—Misunderstanding, fraud and spin. In S. Priebe & M. Slade (Eds.), *Evidence in mental health care* (pp. 59–71). New York: Brunner Routledge.

Rustin, M. (2001). Research, evidence and psychotherapy. In C. Mace, S. Moorey, & B. Roberts (Eds.), *Evidence in the psychological therapies* (pp. 27–45). New York: Brunner Routledge.

Scholz, R. W., & Tietje, O. (2002). *Embedded case study methods: Integrating quantitative and qualitative knowledge.* London: Sage Publications.

Seligman, M. E. P. (1995). The effectiveness of psychotherapy: The *Consumer Reports* study. *American Psychologist, 50,* 965–974.

Slade, M., & Priebe, S. (2002). Conceptual limitations of randomized controlled trials. In S. Priebe & M. Slade (Eds.), *Evidence in mental health care* (pp. 101–108). New York: Brunner Routledge.

Smeijsters, H. (2003, February). *Een polyfonie van innovatie* [A polyphony of innovation]. Paper presented during the inauguration of KenVaK, the Centre of Expertise for the Arts Therapies. Sittard: Universities of Professional Education Zuyd, Utrecht, and Saxion Enschede.

Soldz, S. (1990). The therapeutic interaction. In R. A. Wells & V. J. Gianetti (Eds.), *Handbook of brief psychotherapies* (pp. 27–53). New York: Plenum Press.

Timmermann, T., Bauer, S., Scheytt-Hölzer, N., Schmidt, S., Kächele, H., & Baitsch, H. (1992). The musical dialogue in music therapy process research. In R. Spintge & R. Droh (Eds.), *MusicMedicine* (pp. 350–363). Saint Louis, MO: MMB Music.

Timmermann, T., Scheytt-Hölzer, N., Bauer, S. & Kächele, H. (1991). *Musiktherapeutische Einzelfall-Prozessforschung. Entwicklung und Aufbau eines Forschungsfeldes* [Music therapy single-case process research. Development and construction of a research field]. *Psychother. Psychosom. med. Psychol., 41,* 385–391.

Turpin, G. (2001). Single case methodology and psychotherapy evaluation: from research to practice. In C. Mace, S. Moorey, & B. Roberts (Eds.), *Evidence in the psychological therapies* (pp. 91–113). New York: Brunner Routledge.

Wampold, B. E. (1988). Special mini-series on autocorrelation. *Behavioral Assessment, 10,* 227–297.

Wessely, S. (2001). Randomized controlled trials: The gold standard? In C. Mace, S. Moorey, & B. Roberts (Eds.), *Evidence in the psychological therapies* (pp. 46–60). New York: Brunner Routledge.

Wosch, T., & Frommer, J. (2002). Emotionsveränderungen in musiktherapeutische Improvisationen [Emotional changes in music therapeutic improvisations]. *Zeitschrift für Musik-, Tanz- und Kunsttherapie, 13,* 107–114.

Yin, R. K. (2003). *Case study research: Design and methods.* London: Sage Publications.

Chapter 25
Applied Behavior Analysis
Suzanne B. Hanser

Student: Mickey

Setting: *Individual Education Plan (IEP) Team Meeting*

Problem: *Mickey has been acting out in school and at home, throwing temper tantrums, becoming easily annoyed by others, and, in turn, yelling and cursing at those around him. After the birth of his sister, Mickey became verbally abusive toward his parents and avoided the baby, disturbing his parents deeply. In addition, teachers report that he has been extremely emotional and moody, cries for no apparent reason, is unwilling to talk about these problems, and angers his peers.*

Everyone on the team is concerned about these alarming changes in Mickey, and they explore different strategies to help him. Mickey does not seem to be confiding in anyone, but his parents comment that playing the guitar has a very calming influence on him. The group agrees that music may be the most appropriate medium to help him communicate and express his feelings. The school psychologist suggests that Mickey be referred to Mrs. T., the music therapist, and music therapy is added to his IEP.

Solution seeking: *As with every new client, the music therapist must evaluate several things. What is Mickey's problem? What can music therapy do for him? What will be the most effective music therapy strategy? Will this strategy be effective at home and school? If one behavior is affected, will others also change? These questions require an analysis of his behavior, both under present conditions without the benefit of music therapy and under treatment with the prescribed music therapy strategy. If the music therapist makes an effort to structure these conditions over time, it may be possible to test the hypothesis that music therapy is an effective intervention for Mickey.*

The subject of this chapter is applied behavior analysis, specifically single-subject research designs as they are applied in behavioral research. Single-subject designs are used when the purpose of an investigation is to test hypotheses about the behavior of a single individual or group and examine the effect of a particular strategy on this entity. As opposed to experimental group designs, where the intent is to compare subjects or groups by examining the central tendency and variability of many observations, single-subject research applies the same rigorous standards to examining intrasubject changes over time under different conditions.[1] In other words, instead of looking at the average response of many individuals to music therapy, it focuses on multiple observations of one subject or group with and without music therapy. Like so many other music therapists, Mrs. T. will be able to develop, test, and retest hypotheses regarding the most effective music therapy strategy, using a variety of single-subject designs.

Introduction to Applied Behavior Analysis

Why Choose a Single-Subject Design?

When testing a hypothesis regarding the effectiveness of music therapy, experimental control helps the therapist determine whether observed changes are due specifically to music therapy as opposed to other factors. With a large pool of available, representative subjects and the feasibility of control and comparison groups, experimental group designs are extremely useful in controlling variables and drawing conclusions and generalizations from a data set. However, in clinical settings, the use of control groups may yield questions about the ethics of such practices.

---

[1] Additional information on these and related designs may be obtained from Kazdin (2003), Pierce and Epling (1995), and Sulzer-Azaroff and Mayer (1991).

Additionally, in most clinical environments, the number of subjects who share the same diagnosis and demographic characteristics is limited. Aside from these practical difficulties, when the experimenter finds no statistically significant differences between groups, it is difficult to make meaning of the data. Why did the treatment affect some individuals and not others? Applied behavior analysis, with its emphasis on the single subject, attempts to address these concerns.

It is common for music therapists and other psychological researchers to find no statistically significant differences between treatments. Differences between individuals often exceed the differences observed between treatment groups, resulting in a finding of no statistically significant difference between music therapy and the comparison or control group without music therapy, even when the treatment seems efficacious.[2] Indeed, the clients served by music therapy have many individual differences. One might say that, in general, they consist of the most challenging and difficult cases who have failed to respond to traditional methods. Given this scenario, experimental group designs will require a tremendous number of subjects in order to have the power to detect any real differences between treatments.

Single-subject designs may test the same types of hypotheses about the effectiveness of music therapy as do experimental designs. But single-subject designs do so by examining the functional relationships between music therapy or other treatments and the particular behavior(s) of interest. They apply rigorous controls to observing behaviors over time and under changing conditions, thereby bringing the laboratory into the field where actual problems exist. The accountable music therapist is able to determine the factors that are controlling behavior and test the impact of music therapy on these behaviors.

This chapter will present three types of applied behavior analysis, single-subject designs: the reversal, multiple baseline, and multiple treatment or multi-element design. After identifying the ways in which Mrs. T. implements these designs to determine the effectiveness of treatment, examples of applied behavior analysis in the music therapy research literature will be given.

Step One: At the Baseline

Mrs. T. has been informed about the details of Mickey's case and the discussion that led to his referral. Clearly, there are many ways in which emotional outbursts manifest themselves. Crying, tantrums, bouts of anger, yelling, shouting, and cursing are all problems in Mickey's repertoire that are observable in the classroom and at home. In order to target the problem and develop a potentially effective strategy, Mrs. T. decides to start by observing these behaviors in the classroom setting. Several questions come to mind: How often do these behaviors occur? When do they occur? Where do they occur? Do these behaviors still constitute a problem, or have they stopped or decreased already?

Mrs. T. enlists the assistance of Mickey's classroom teacher to count the number of emotional outbursts, as identified above. Because Mickey's first appointment with the music therapist is next week, the teacher will be able to record the number of emotional outbursts per day for 5 days before they meet. The teacher is asked to do nothing more than she has done previously to change these behaviors. Mrs. T. prepares a behavioral checklist for the teacher to use as she counts emotional outbursts in the classroom and at recess. The graph shown in Figure 1 allows Mrs. T. to summarize these events on a daily basis.

---

[2] For background on the role of variability in experimental research, see the discussion of variability within versus variability between conditions in Chapter 21, Experimental Research.

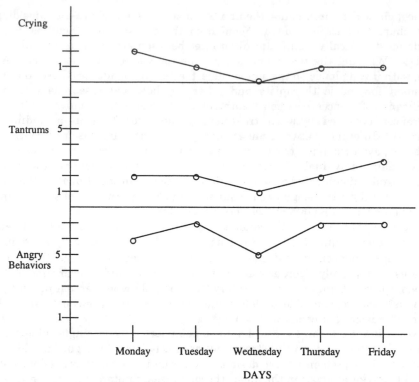

Figure 1. Baseline of Mickey's Emotional Outbursts by Type of Behavior

These data will help answer all of Mrs. T.'s questions except, Where do they occur? Mrs. T. calculates the sum of the number of checked behaviors in the classroom and in the schoolyard during recesses and plots these on the graph in Figure 2.

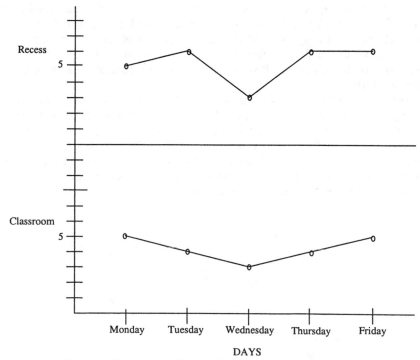

Figure 2. Baseline of Mickey's Emotional Outbursts by Setting

Figures 1 and 2 present baseline observations for Mickey's emotional outbursts by category of behavior and by setting, respectively. Baseline is the term in applied behavior analysis referring to the level or strength of a behavior before any intervention is introduced. When a stable level of behavior is evident through a relatively flat slope on the graph, this serves as a basis for comparison when a new treatment or technique is introduced.

These graphs of Mickey's behavior demonstrate that emotional outbursts are still problematic, that they occur both in the classroom and at recess, and that angry behavior is the most frequent. Relatively stable graphs are displayed; in the case of crying, there is a low frequency overall.

Introducing Treatment: The AB Design

The appointment has come, and Mrs. T. is ready to institute the first music therapy strategy. She begins with a simple approach in the classroom. Treatment I is a guitar intervention in which the music therapist meets with Mickey at lunch time every day for 15 minutes. During this time, Mickey selects his favorite songs and the music therapist coaches him on the correct chords and strumming technique. They talk about the meaning of the songs and play together. Afterward, Mickey may use additional time to practice the guitar on his own. His teacher continues to chart behaviors in the classroom and at recess (see Figure 3).

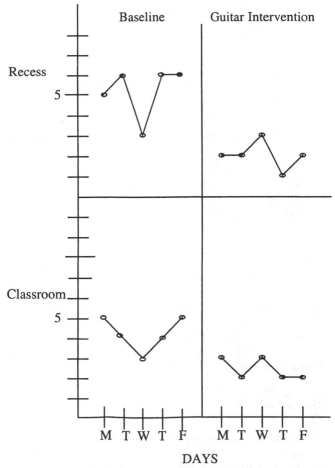

Figure 3. Mickey's Emotional Outbursts During Baseline and Music Therapy

Applied Behavior Analysis Designs

Reversal Design

As shown in the graph, Mickey's behavior is somewhat improved during Treatment I, the guitar intervention. The music therapist is encouraged and she informs Mickey's parents of his progress. Mickey's father has an alternate explanation for the changes observed in Mickey. He says that he took Mickey to a ball game just before music therapy began, and that it was this time that they spent together that accounts for the change. To test this assumption, the music therapist decides to reverse the music therapy treatment for a short period and then reinstitute the guitar intervention. If the father is correct, the cessation of music therapy should have little or no effect on Mickey's behavior. If, on the other hand, there is a functional relationship between music therapy and behavioral change, the graph should display differences between baseline and treatment conditions.

Figure 4 shows Baseline (A), Treatment I–guitar intervention (B), reversal to baseline with no structured intervention (A), and a return to Treatment I–guitar intervention (B). This design is known as a reversal, complete reversal, or ABAB design.

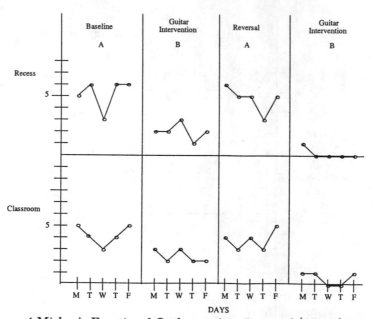

Figure 4. Mickey's Emotional Outbursts in a Reversal (ABAB) Design

Indeed, there is a clear change in behavior when music therapy is reintroduced in the fourth phase shown on the graph. This offers documentation that there is a functional relationship between music therapy and Mickey's behavior.

Multiple Baseline Design

While Mickey's teachers are tracking his progress at school, his parents are recording the same targeted behaviors at home. Despite the good results in the school setting, they still have complaints about his behavior at home. They decide to contract with the music therapist to offer the same treatment in their home.

Mickey's parents are collecting baseline data during the reversal phase and second treatment condition at school. If changes are observed at home as soon as music therapy begins in the home environment, the therapist has some assurance that it is the music therapy-guitar intervention that makes a difference. The results are shown in Figure 5.

The results demonstrate that, after music therapy begins at home, immediate changes are observable. The multiple baseline design offers considerable evidence that music therapy is responsible for behavior change at home as well as at school.

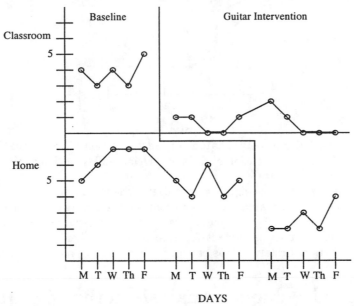

Figure 5. Mickey's Emotional Outbursts in the Classroom and at Home As a Function of Music Therapy

When baseline data are recorded like this under two separate environmental conditions, and the beginning of treatment is staggered across the two settings, the resulting design is known as a multiple baseline design. In this case, treatment is offered in turn across two different settings. Sometimes the same treatment is given to two or more individuals or for at least two different behaviors. The characteristic staggering of the baseline constitutes the unique element of the multiple baseline design.

Multiple Treatment or Multi-Element Design

While Mickey's behavior, specifically his crying and emotional behavior, has improved at home, his parents want to see more of a difference in his verbally abusive behavior. They agree to continue music therapy sessions with the therapist on Monday, Wednesday, and Friday, while they try a new family oriented music therapy strategy on Tuesday, Thursday, and Saturday. They are instructed to listen to Mickey playing the guitar, sing along, and discuss the music while offering encouragement and praise. This second type of treatment is contrasted with the results of the after-school music therapy on the same behavior, namely, the number of occurrences of yelling or cursing. When two or more treatments or conditions are implemented during the same period of time, this creates another way of observing differences between treatments. This design is known as the multiple treatment or multi-element design. Figure 6 displays the results of the two music therapy conditions, therapist-led sessions versus family oriented sessions, on verbally abusive behavior. For this behavior, the family oriented music therapy approach appears to hold a distinct advantage.

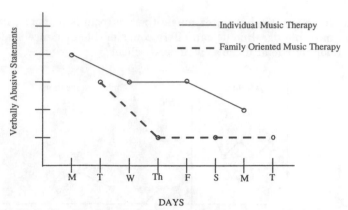

Figure 6. Mickey's Verbally Abusive Statements as a Function of Individual Music Therapy-Guitar Intervention and Family Oriented Music Therapy

The multiple treatment design is appropriate when a baseline condition or reversal to baseline is inadvisable. The researcher is able to contrast the effects of two or more conditions on a given behavior without first observing a stable pretreatment rate of behavior. When an identifiable pattern of behavior is evident for each condition, then it may be possible to draw conclusions about functional relationships between behavior and experimental treatments.

Applied Behavior Analysis in the Literature

Applied behavior analysis designs are prevalent in the music therapy literature. Although they are particularly appropriate when behavioral techniques are being tested, they are useful to study the effects of any number of therapeutic approaches. Because they examine behavioral change as a function of a therapeutic stimulus or condition, these designs are conducive to investigating many music therapy research questions.

Gregory (2002) performed a content analysis of behavioral research designs in *Journal of Music Therapy* articles from 1964 to 1999. She found that 96 out of the 607 total articles used behavioral designs. Most common was the reversal, although there were creative variations of this model. While there were only 10 behavioral designs applied in research from 1964 to 1969, there were 27 in the 1970s, 33 in the 1980s, and 26 in the 1990s. The most recent research included a wide variety of populations, including people who were physically frail; persons diagnosed with mental retardation, with brain-injury, and with Alzheimer's disease; caregivers; college students; and patients receiving bone marrow transplants. The articles examined diverse behaviors including self-injury, gait, purposeful responses, communication, aggression, picture recognition, and physiological reactions.

One excellent example of an ABAC reversal design is a study of the use of musically adapted stories with children with autism, such as Peter (Brownell, 2002). Peter's echolalia manifested in repetitive phrases and sound effects from movies and television. The words were often violent and aggressive, and he would utter them when he was unhappy or frustrated. The music therapist developed social stories that addressed the potential consequences of this behavior and alternative behaviors. Phrases included messages, such as "My friends like it when I talk about other things with them." An observer counted Peter's TV and movie words and sounds during baseline (A), after the therapist read social stories (B), without intervention (A), and after the therapist sang the stories (C). Figure 7 displays observable changes in behavior as a function of the stories and even more so, after the songs.

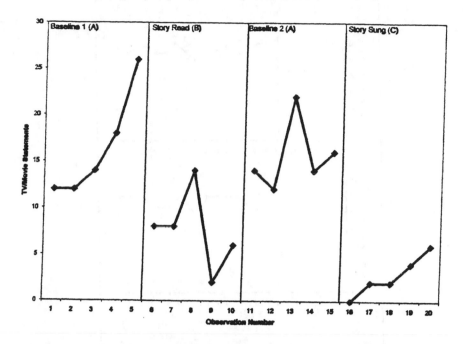

Figure 7. Frequency of TV/Movie Statements Made by Peter by Condition
Brownell (2002). Used with permission.

Adamek (1994) applied a multiple baseline design to investigate the effect of immediate verbal feedback from a supervisor on the group leadership skills of four student music therapists. Students heard the supervisor's comments through an earpiece as they worked with adults who have mental retardation. Adamek observed changes in student performance on a checklist developed to assess group leadership skills on a 0 to 100 scale (Standley, 1991). Figure 8 shows the results of four student therapists, A through D, in the first phase without immediate feedback; in the second phase using the earpiece; and in the third phase, again without the earpiece. Note the start of the intervention at the 8th, 10th, 12th, and 14th sessions for the students. At the 21st session, Adamek added the reversal to baseline as another test of the feedback technique.

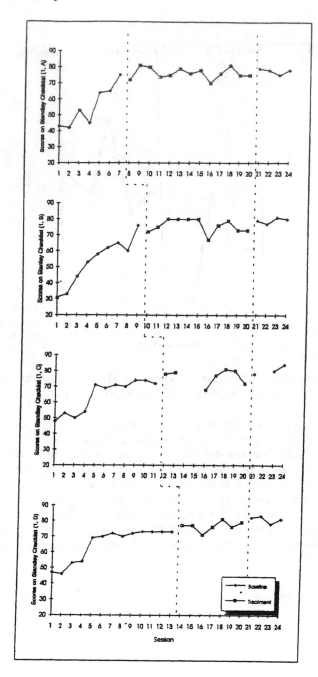

Figure 8. Student Music Therapist Performance on
Leadership Checklist as a Function of Immediate Feedback
Adamek (1994). Used with permission.

A combination of reversal and multiple baseline designs was used by the author to test a music reinforcement technique with boys with emotional disturbance during a study period in school (Hanser, 1974). After baseline observations (Phase I) were completed, the boys were instructed that whenever any of them talked out of turn, the background music that they had selected would be turned off. In Phase II, this music contingency was applied to inappropriate verbal behavior, while baseline continued for inappropriate motor behavior. As shown in Figure 9, talking out decreased, but acting out did not. In Phase III, the music contingency was applied to inappropriate motor behavior but removed for verbal behavior, and the behavior changed accordingly. Lastly, in Phase IV, the music contingency was applied to both verbal and motor behavior, and changes were observed in both types of behavior.

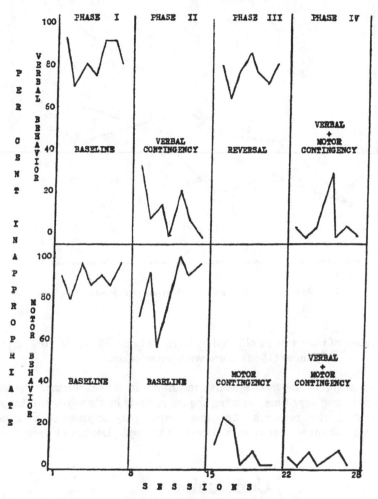

Figure 9. Mean Percent Inappropriate Behavior as a Function of Sessions
(Combined Reversal and Multiple Baseline Designs)
Hanser (1974). Used with permission.

In still a different setting, Spencer (1988) compared the effects of active instrumental and movement activities with passive music listening (the control condition) on the ability of adolescents with mental retardation to follow directions. Spencer matched the adolescents on the basis of a pretest and employed an experimental design. However, because the researcher used posttests of several sessions over time and graphed these results, this may also be conceived of as a multiple treatment design (see Figure 10).

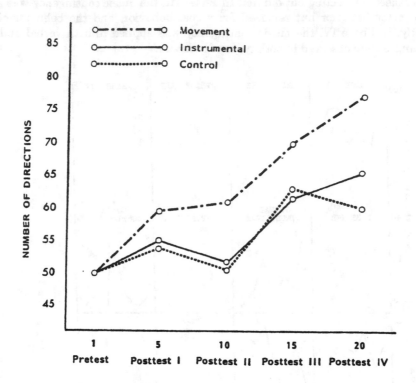

Figure 10. Total Number of Directions Followed by Each Patient (Multiple Treatment Design) Spencer (1988). Used with permission.

Not only was movement the most effective technique in this experiment, but there also appeared to be a widening gap over time, favoring the gains made by those performing movement activities. As is evident in this research, the experimenter may implement an experimental design, but, in evaluating changes over time, the graphic multiple treatment design is useful in interpreting results.

Conclusion

The music therapy researcher has access to a variety of design approaches that may assist in answering a research question. Applied behavior analysis offers rigor in examining the effects of treatment over time in single subjects or small groups of individuals. The focus is on identifying the factors or treatments that are most efficacious for a single individual or sample. While the results may not be generalizable to other groups, the researcher is most interested in studying the behavior of an identified sample in the greatest detail possible. Researchers may not be able to definitively determine cause and effect using these designs, but they learn a great deal about the effects of any number of manipulations on the single subject. Clearly, applied behavior analysis designs are a useful adjunct to the clinical music therapist's armamentarium of research designs.

References

Adamek, M. S. (1994). Audio-cueing and immediate feedback to improve group leadership skills: A live supervision model. *Journal of Music Therapy, 31,* 135–164.

Brownell, M. D. (2002). Musically adapted social stories to modify behaviors in students with autism: Four case studies. *Journal of Music Therapy, 39,* 117–144.

Gregory, D. (2002). Four decades of music therapy behavioral research designs: A content analysis of *Journal of Music Therapy* articles. *Journal of Music Therapy, 39,* 56–71.

Hanser, S. B. (1974). Group-contingent music listening with emotionally disturbed boys. *Journal of Music Therapy, 11,* 220–225.

Kazdin, A. E. (2003). *Research design in clinical psychology* (4th ed.). Boston: Allyn & Bacon.

Pierce, W. D., & Epling, W. F. (1995). *Behavior analysis and learning.* Englewood Cliffs, NJ: Prentice-Hall.

Spencer, S. L. (1988). The efficiency of instrumental and movement activities in developing mentally retarded adolescents' ability to follow directions. *Journal of Music Therapy, 25,* 44–50.

Standley, J. (1991). *Music techniques in therapy, counseling and special education.* St. Louis, MO: MMB Music.

Sulzer-Azaroff, B., & Mayer, G. R. (1991). *Behavior analysis for lasting changes.* Ft. Worth, TX: Holt, Rinehart & Winston.

Part IV

Types of
Qualitative Research

Chapter 26
Phenomenological Inquiry
Michele Forinash and Denise Grocke

Phenomenological inquiry in music therapy has a rich history that will be explored in this chapter. But first, what is phenomenology? What are the central tenets of this approach to research, and what are the philosophical traditions from which phenomenology emerged?

Overview and Definition

Phenomenology is an approach that allows researchers to study phenomena, such as human experience, as "unified wholes" (Aldridge, 1989, p. 92) rather than dissecting phenomena into separate fragments to be studied. The phenomenologist studying human experience or beingness would study *human experience in the world* or *being in the world*. Being in the world needs to be embraced as a whole rather than fragmented into *being* and *in the world*.

Phenomenologists examine what is called the *lived experience*. This refers to experiences that we, as humans, have in relation to any event that we experience. Phenomenologists can study our lived experience of emotions such as grief, love, or anger; existential concepts such as aloneness or being effective as a therapist; as well as other human experiences such as intuition, listening to music, or improvising music.

For the phenomenologist there is no one correct way to experience any of the events listed above—one person's experience is not true and another person's false. Human experiences simply exist and therefore are worthy of investigation.

Theoretical Premises and Historical Roots

Theoretical Premises

There are several concepts central to phenomenological inquiry. First is *complexity,* referring to the idea that humans are complex beings, so it stands to reason that human experiences are equally complex. The phenomenologist embraces this complexity because of a belief that there are many aspects that contribute to any human experience and that to eliminate any of these aspects is to lose the essence and thus not fully comprehend the event. Bruscia (1995) stated

> Human beings are complex organisms. We are not merely objects that can be reduced to one or two dimensions, and then explained in deterministic terms. What makes us unique as a species is our subjectivity—and the ability to experience ourselves as subjects. The challenge of the human condition, then, is to fully grasp the complexity of subjective experience. (p. 196)

Ihde (1976) echoed this idea. Phenomenology is a "style of thinking which concentrates an intense examination upon experience in its multifaceted, complex, and essential forms" (p. 17).

A second concept is *intentionality*. Simply stated, this implies that human consciousness is consciousness directed toward something whether it is an object (book, music, etc.) or a concept (feeling, state of mind, or even transcendent consciousness). The awareness or reality of an "object, then, is inextricably related to one's consciousness of it. Thus, reality. . . is not divided into subjects and objects" (Creswell, 1998, p. 53).

A third concept is *bracketing* or *epoché*. This refers to the researcher's ability to suspend or bracket his or her beliefs about the phenomenon being studied. The researcher must let go of preconceived notions and beliefs and be fully present with the experience as it is being revealed. Rather than having a preconceived idea of what will happen, the researcher "lets the unfolding of the phenomenon itself guide the logic of his inquiry" (Giorgi, 1975, p. 72).

A fourth concept is the search for the *essential structure* or *essence* of experience (Creswell, 1998, p. 55). This implies that there is a fundamental structure within an experience that allows us to recognize it for what it is. It does not mean that everyone experiences the phenomenon in exactly the same way; it simply means there are necessary elements in an experience that let us know that experience and differentiate it from other types of experience.

Let us examine these concepts in an example: Intuition is not necessarily a universal human experience, yet certainly those who have experienced it could provide a description of their lived experience of it (even if at times the experience is ineffable). It is a complex and multifaceted experience that for some may include bodily sensations, emotions, or images. Using phenomenology, we can examine intuition without having to omit any aspects of the experience.

As researchers, we can direct our consciousness towards the experience of intuition and recognize that it puts us in a dance together. Intuition is not a tangible object that exists outside of our awareness; it does not exist *out there,* rather it exists in our consciousness. When we choose to study it, it becomes the intention of our consciousness. While we are familiar with our own experiences of and beliefs about intuition, as researchers we must bracket those beliefs so that we may be fully present with how others relate their experiences of intuition. We must become available to learn something new about intuition through our research. By studying intuition, we would be looking for essential structures in the experience of intuition which, when described, would make it recognizable and meaningful to others.

In addition to the publications cited so far, there are many useful resources for the serious student of phenomenology. Don Ihde, quoted above, published a book, *Experimental Phenomenology: An Introduction* (1986), which can serve as a workbook for learning to do phenomenology. Moustakas' *Phenomenological Research Methods* (1994) also provides step-by-step instruction of the analysis process. Max van Manen's website, http://www.phenomenologyonline.com, provides information on traditions in phenomenology, scholars of phenomenology, publications and sources, and websites and organizations. While no published music therapy research is included, there is a wealth of information in this site that readers will find valuable. Van Manen's book *Writing in the Dark: Phenomenological Studies in Interpretive Inquiry* (2002) is also very accessible and useful to those interested in pursuing phenomenology.

Historical Roots

The early roots of phenomenology are found in the writings of Goethe (1749–1832) and Franz Brentano (1838–1917) as they began to write about how humans experience events as wholes rather than as separate parts that make up a whole (Aldridge, 1989, p. 92). Edmund Husserl (1859–1938) is generally considered to be the father of modern day phenomenology. Hegel (1779–1831) had used the term previously, but Husserl was the one to articulate phenomenology as a philosophic viewpoint. In general, this viewpoint holds that "the phenomena of experience are products of the activity and structures of our consciousness" (Lavine, 1984, p. 393). In other words, Husserl's basic starting point is that anything that we experience is directly related to our consciousness of the experience. There is no separate event unrelated to human consciousness.

This is in direct opposition to philosophies that hold that there is some reality or certainty that lies beyond the grasp of human consciousness. It follows that it is only by examining our consciousness that we can understand phenomena and, as discussed previously, consciousness is consciousness of something, not nothing.

Husserl's phenomenology also rejects science that attempts to predict and control nature, and scientifically based understandings of the world that exclude the role of consciousness in perceiving the world. Husserl's view of phenomenology is "that it seeks to describe the structures of our daily life experience, our common experience in the life-world (lebenswelt) of everyday affairs" (Lavine, 1984, p. 395).

Later philosophers including Heidegger, Sartre, Merleau-Ponty, and Ricour further developed the philosophical viewpoint of phenomenology. In particular, Heidegger and Sartre brought existentialism into phenomenology as they began to focus on our existence as conscious beings and the necessary absurdity, anguish, and despair that accompany existence (Lavine, 1984, p. 396). Serious students of phenomenology are encouraged to delve into the writings of the great philosophers to deepen their understanding of this philosophical perspective.

Applied phenomenology was introduced to the field of psychology by Adrian van Kaam (1959), who is recognized as the founder of the phenomenological school at Duquesne University in Pittsburgh, PA. Van Kaam and Amedeo Giorgi went on to formulate a phenomenological methodology in psychology (Tesch, 1990, p. 34). In recent years phenomenology has been applied to research in the social sciences, education, and psychology.

Music therapists began considering phenomenology as a promising approach to research in the early 1980s. One of the topics discussed at the 1982 New York University Symposium,

Music in the Life of Man, was the relationship of phenomenological and introspective methods to the study of musical experience (unpublished proceedings, June 1982). This discussion was influenced by some of the Scandinavian and European symposium participants' knowledge of phenomenology.

In May of 1983, Carolyn Kenny presented a paper titled "Phenomenological Research: A Promise for the Healing Arts" at the Canadian Association for Music Therapy Conference and articulated ways that phenomenological research could address issues of importance to music therapists and other creative arts therapists. Lawrence Ferrara, a musicologist, originated an application of reflexive phenomenology in 1984. Even Ruud first adapted Ferrara's method in his doctoral dissertation, *Music as Communication and Interaction* (1987), completed at the University of Olso and written in Norwegian. Forinash and Gonzalez (1989) adapted Ferrara's method utilizing seven steps to study the experience of a music therapy session with a hospice patient. Ferrara's method and the adaptation by Forinash and Gonzalez are discussed below, as are some of the phenomenological research methods in psychology, music, and music therapy.

Methodology

Phenomenological Research in Psychology

Phenomenological research allows data to be collected from a number of different perspectives: by self-reflections (heuristic descriptions); by interviewing other people about their experience of the phenomenon under study; by gathering writings about the topic; or by depictions of the topic in question as expressed in works of art, in dance, or in poetry (Polkinghorne, 1989). Phenomenological studies are of necessity retrospective and recollective (van Manen, 1990) since participants are required to reflect on the experience.

Among the phenomenological methods that have been applied to research in the social sciences, education, and psychology is reflexive phenomenology, which applies to studies where researchers use their own experience of the phenomenon and write descriptively from that perspective (Ferrara, 1984; van Kaam, 1959; van Manen, 1990). Duquesne University developed another method, the empirical phenomenological school, the proponents of which were van Kaam, Giorgi, and Colaizzi. Many of the early studies in empirical phenomenology focused on the lived experience of situations that are common occurrences in life—the experience of being angry (Stevick, 1971), the phenomenology of suspicion (deKoning, 1979), the phenomenology of self-esteem (Mruk, 1983), and the phenomenology of being criminally victimized (Fischer & Wertz, 1979). Reflexive phenomenology, then, focuses on one's own experience, while empirical phenomenology focuses on others' experiences.

More recently, transcendental phenomenology has emerged through the writings and research of Moustakas (1994). Moustakas recognized Husserl as the founder of transcendental phenomenology, in which an experience is studied and understood through a process of intuition and reflection. Experiences are viewed from two perspectives: what was experienced (the textural description, or noema) and how it was experienced (the structural description, or noesis).

Other forms of phenomenology have emerged as researchers have adapted the phenomenological process for their respective research studies. For example, Lett (1993) used an experiential phenomenology in a study of professional supervision of four trained therapists. The modalities used in this research were multimodal forms of dance, drama, drawings, and improvised sound.

In clarifying phenomenology as a human scientific study, van Manen (1990) says it is

systematic in that phenomenology uses a practiced mode of questioning, reflecting and focusing;

explicit in that it articulates the meaning embedded in the lived experience;

self-critical in that it continually examines its own goals and methods;

intersubjective in that it needs co-researchers to develop a dialogue relationship with the phenomenon, and thus validate the phenomenon; and

a human science in that the subject material is always human experience. (pp. 11–12)

Phenomenology does not deal in facts, cause-effect relationships, generalization, or speculation. Instead it aims to "transform lived experience into a textual expression of its essence" (van Manen, 1990, p. 36). For this reason, phenomenology lends itself well to studies of complexities and mysteries of life that require thoughtful, reflective approaches.

A common method of gathering data in phenomenology is through the interview. Phenomenological interviews are open-ended and seek to understand the depth of the experience. The objective is to gather descriptions of the interviewee's lifeworld in order to interpret the meaning of the described phenomena (Kvale, 1983).

Interviews may be semi-structured. The researcher draws up a list of questions that need to be addressed during the interview, leaving the exact phrasing of the question open to suit the interviewee. As the participants describe their experience, the interviewer seeks further detail and understanding about the experience by asking questions about their feelings at the time or greater detail about the event. The purpose of the interview is to gather the fullest description of the experience itself.

As discussed earlier, in order that the researcher's own biases do not influence the interview procedure, the researcher undertakes a process of bracketing assumptions about the experience being explored, also known as an epoché. It is important also for the researcher to be experienced in phenomenological interviewing and to be open to diverse descriptions, since it is through the diversity of the participant's experience that the researcher gains a richer understanding.

The steps involved in analyzing the interview transcripts (called protocols) differ from one researcher to the next, although the process is fundamentally the same. Polkinghorne (1989) summarizes the process as:

> (a) The original protocols are divided into units [of meaning], (b) the units are transformed by the researcher into meanings that are expressed in psychological and phenomenological concepts [sometimes called *imaginative variation*], and (c) these transformations are tied together to make a general description of the experience [called *the essence*]. (p. 55)

There are differences however in how phenomenologists explain each part of the process. Table 1 compares the terminology used by four researchers and traces the development in procedures over a 25-year period. Van Kaam (1969), for example, used a positivist concept in step 1 in that he calculated the percentage of protocols in which a category occurred. Giorgi (1975) and Colaizzi (1978) used similar terminology for their analytical procedures, whereas Moustakas (1994) introduced new terminology such as *invariant constituents* to explain his process. While this might be confusing for the novice researcher, the common thread across all researchers is that the interview protocols are distilled to a statement or essence that authentically reflects the experience.

Ferrara's Method

Ferrara (1984), a musicologist, applied reflexive phenomenology to the analysis of music. He identified five stages in analyzing a contemporary piece of music on first hearing. This seminal work has inspired a number of music therapy researchers to adapt his protocol to varying degrees for use in music therapy. His original protocol is paraphrased as follows:

> *Open listening-subjective response:* On the first listening the person writes down the subjective response, including any impressions that stand out;
>
> *Listening for syntactical meaning—describing the sound as it is heard:* In this stage the listener writes down all the musical sounds that are heard, including instruments, embellishments, dynamic changes, melodic, rhythmic, and harmonic features;
>
> *Listening for semantic meaning:* On the third hearing the listener describes what the meaning of the music is thought to be, what mood it suggests, and how the listener feels;
>
> *Listening for ontological meaning—the lifeworld of the composer:* In the fourth hearing the listener puts the music into the lifeworld of the composer and tries to understand what the composer is saying;

Open listening—the meaning dimension of all the hearings of the music: In the final stage of listening, all the impressions and perceptions from the previous four hearings are synthesized and integrated to create a final description of the work.

Relationship to Other Types of Research

Phenomenology shares some commonalities with many other qualitative research approaches. First and foremost, most phenomenology comes from a constructivist stance, which holds that there is no absolute reality. Rather, reality is constructed by those experiencing it, so it becomes important to examine reality through our shared experiences with others (Edwards, 1999).

Data analysis is another area where phenomenology shares similarities with other qualitative models. The search for meaning units or descriptions comes about not necessarily through a rigid protocol, but rather by allowing the natural unfolding of data to guide the research steps.

One can also find many aspects of phenomenology in other studies. The reason for this is that phenomenology is a philosophical approach as well as a research method. So when one examines a study such as Amir's (1993) "Moments of Insight in the Music Therapy Experience," it becomes apparent that, while this is a study that can be categorized as grounded theory research, she focused on the participants' experiences of meaningful moments. She used the philosophy of phenomenology and applied it to a grounded theory study. However, Amir did not work toward an essence of the experience, which is the cornerstone of phenomenology, and this differentiates her study from a phenomenological one.

This holds true with many studies. Aigen's (1997) study, *Here We Are in Music: One Year With an Adolescent Creative Music Therapy Group,* focused on the process of the adolescent group. It is a naturalistic music therapy study, but its focus on providing a voice for the adolescents' experiences aligns it with the philosophy of phenomenology. Heuristic research, which is essentially the study of one's personal experience, also overlaps with phenomenological philosophy in its focus on trying to understand personal experience.

Those looking for clear boundaries and distinctions may be frustrated by these overlaps, yet once again embracing complexity becomes paramount.

Music Therapy Examples

Phenomenology was first used in music therapy in the early 1980s. As it had been used in the study of psychology (van Kaam, 1959) and music (Ferrara, 1984), it seemed a natural fit to music therapy. In looking at the music therapy studies, one can see two general approaches: Ferrara's method and its adaptations and other forms including reflexive, empirical, transcendental, and experiential approaches.

Studies Influenced by Ferrara's Method

As stated earlier, Ruud (1987) first adapted Ferrara's method in his doctoral dissertation. Forinash and Gonzalez (1989) adapted Ferrara's method utilizing seven steps to study the experience of a music therapy session with a hospice patient who died during the session. Those steps were: (a) background information on the client; (b) a phenomenological description of the session; (c) a description of the musical syntax or formal music elements—meter, tonality, song form, and so forth; (d) a description of the *sound as such* which referred to the entire sound event of the session, including environmental sounds such as the rhythm and sound of the oxygen machine; (e) a description of the semantic or referential meaning found by the therapists, including images, such as a waning tide, that the therapists had while witnessing the transition from life to death; (f) a description of the ontological lifeworld of the client as brought to stand in the session, including an existential awareness and appreciation for life and death; and (g) a meta-critique which summarized and critiqued the process. This research approach allowed them

Table 1. Stages of Analyzing Phenomenological Interview Protocols: A Comparison of Approaches*

In each approach the researcher carefully reads the interview transcripts (protocols) to get a sense of the participants' experience

Step	Van Kaam's 1969 Study	Giorgi's 1975 Study	Colaizzi's 1978 Study	Moustakas (1994)	Moustakas (based on Stevick, Colaizzi, Keen)
1	Researcher classifies data from random sample into *categories*, calculates percentage of protocols in which each category occurred.	Researcher highlights key statements that describe the experience.	Researcher extracts *the phrases or sentences* that directly pertain to the experience.	Researcher creates *individual textual-structural descriptions* of the experience.	Researcher extracts significant statements: invariant horizons or meaning units.
2	Researcher makes a *reduction and linguistic transformation* of selections of text into more precise language.	Researcher groups similar statements into self-contained *meaning units*.	The meaning of each statement/ phrase is transformed into the researcher's words (individual themes).	Redundant statements eliminated through reduction of the descriptions, the invariant constituents.	Relate and cluster invariant meaning units into themes.
3	Elimination of the reduced statements that are not inherent in the phenomena being studied.	Researcher transforms the meaning unit, retaining the context of the experience.	Individual themes are clustered to produce a further reduction of general themes common to all participants' experiences.	Invariant constituents are clustered and transformed into core themes of the experience.	Synthesize the invariant meaning units and themes into a description of the textures of the experience.
4	The first hypothetical identification and description of the experience is explicated.	Meaning units and trans-formations are placed within study's question, described in psychological terms.	The essential structural definition is distilled.	Identification of the invariant constituents and themes (validation against the complete transcript).	Through imaginative variation, researcher constructs description of the structure of the experience.
5	The hypothetical description of step 4 is applied to a number of randomly selected protocols. This step is carried out several times.	Researcher synthesizes meaning units into descriptive statement of essential psychological meanings (global meaning units/themes).	Researcher asks participant(s) how descriptive results compare with experiences and if aspects of experience were omitted (verification).	Construction of individual textural description.	Construct a textural-structural description of the meanings and essences.
6	Hypothetical description is then viewed as a valid identification until new cases of the experience are shown to not correspond with the constituents contained in the formula.	Researcher moves from situated descriptions to create general structural descriptions of experience.	Any relevant new data that emerges are worked into the final description.	Construct individual structural description.	Do above steps for all transcripts.
7		Researcher develops a general description (essence of the experience).		For each participant construct a textural-structural description.	Construct a composite textural-structural description of meaning and essences of the experience.
8				Develop composite description.	

*Columns 1, 2 and 3 are adapted from Polkinghorne, 1989, pp. 52–56; columns 4 and 5 are from Moustakas, 1994

to focus on the existential complexity of witnessing the transition from life to death while also allowing them to gain a new awareness of the role of music and sound in this session.

Kasayka (1988, 1991), working with Forinash and Gonzalez's adaptation, analyzed a Bonny Method of Guided Imagery and Music (BMGIM) session. Using the same seven steps, she analyzed each of the five pieces on the BMGIM *Peak Experience* program. Having undertaken the analysis of the five pieces, Kasayka completed a qualitative meta-critique comparing the interrelationship of the music with the imagery sequences of the client's BMGIM sessions. In order to link the music with the imagery sequences of her client, Kasayka analyzed each piece in the *Peak Experience* program according to sections in the music and groupings of the measures within the sections. For example, the slow movement of Beethoven's *Piano Concerto, No. 5,* is divided into the three sections, indicating the ternary form of the movement, followed by a fourth section, the coda. Kasayka matched the imagery sequences of the client alongside the descriptive accounts of the music, providing a grid of music description, imagery experiences by the client, and comments about the interrelationship of the two. In the semantic analysis, Kasayka identified key elements in the music that may have triggered the sequences in imagery. For example, she noted that a sequence of imagery relating to a ritual began at the point in the Beethoven *Piano Concerto* where trills were featured. In Vivaldi's *Et in terra pax* (from the *Gloria*), Kasayka noted that the client seemed to respond at the point where the female voices entered. In the ontological analysis, she described the meaning of the client's imagery in relation to the client's issues—her search for her cultural roots.

Amir (1990) used the same seven-step adaptation as Forinash and Gonzalez. Amir studied two music therapy sessions conducted with a 20-year old man who had become quadriplegic as a result of an automobile accident. He improvised song lyrics as the therapist improvised music. Amir provided a deeper look into the subtle nuances of human experience in the music therapy session.

Forinash (2000) later used the method with music therapy students as she sought to teach them new ways of listening to clinical music. She returned to Ferrara's original five-step method and had students listen to the tape of Edward from *Creative Music Therapy* (Nordoff & Robbins, 1977). In addition to providing an intense listening experience, this method provides students with an awareness of the different levels of the clinical event (musical syntax, semantic, and so forth). It also provides students with insights into which levels of listening are easiest or most comfortable, as well as which levels are most challenging or difficult.

Arnason (2002) adapted Ferrara's method and developed six levels of reflection in listening to group improvisations. The levels include open listening; a description of thoughts, emotions, and moods; a more specific account of the musical elements; a description of the referential nature of the improvisation, including images and metaphoric aspects of the music; becoming more aware of the client's world; and a return to the open listening.

More recently, Trondalen (2002, 2003) utilized Ruud's (1987) initial adaptation. She offered a seven-step method that includes the following levels: (a) contextual, referring to the "client's personal, social, biological, music and clinical history"; (b) structural, including the sound as such and Grocke's (1999) *Structural Model for Music Analyses (SMMA);* (c) semantic, describing what the music means or refers to and describing the music as metaphor of being in the world; (d) pragmatic, referring to the effects of outcomes of the music therapy process; (e) phenomenological horizonalization, listing and giving equal value to "important issues, musical cues, and events"; (f) phenomenological matrix, including a descriptive summary of the music and potential meaning and the possible effects of "the improvisation within the treatment process of music therapy"; (g) meta-discussion, including the "client's comments and behavior, the interview with the client after finishing music therapy, and the therapist's self-reflexive notes" (pp. 6–7).

Studies Using Other Forms of Phenomenological Analysis

Other phenomenological studies in music therapy used a variety of approaches. Carolyn Kenny's study of the *field of play* was first her doctoral dissertation (1987) and later presented in a book (1989). Kenny was the first to articulate that one's philosophical stance or burning question should precede the actual research method. She uses Husserl's concept of "free phantasie variation" (Kenny, 1996, p. 61) as a way to uncover the essence of experience as to share the results of the research. Free phantasie variation refers to the idea of uncovering essences through reflective thinking during which one imagines the experience being studied in different forms or situations until the essences are revealed. Method and results necessarily become entwined, thus making the method impossible to describe separately from its results (Colaizzi, 1978). Kenny (1996) summed it up this way:

> I could not communicate our story [the research] in a method, per se, nor could I invent any method which could do this. But approaching the research task phenomenologically through free phantasie variation, I could tell the story in an imaginative way, staying close enough to our experience to still be art. I could hope to communicate the essence of the experience to others, thus offering a template of the referential totality, looking not for "facts" or causes or effects or proof, but rather for experience and meaning in an aesthetic and philosophical approach. (p. 62)

Kenny's initial foray into phenomenology set the stage for many other researchers.

Other music therapy research followed in the late 1980s. Racette (1989, 2004) studied the experience of listening to music when upset. She interviewed eight people and analyzed the protocols by (a) categorizing significant statements, (b) creating individual case synopses, (c) developing an essential description of the phenomenon that comprised the significant characteristics or *essences* from the eight participants, and (d) providing illustrated descriptions of each essence across all the participants. Aldridge (1989) used phenomenology in a comparison of the organization of music to the self. He proposed that one could see the "identity of a person as a musical form that is continually being composed in the world" (p. 91). His endeavor "is to view people as 'symphonic' rather than 'mechanic'" (p. 91).

Forinash (1990) completed her dissertation on a phenomenological study of music therapy with terminally patients in which she provided phenomenological descriptions of key music therapy sessions. She recorded 10 sessions with hospice clients to uncover the essential structures of the music therapy experience. In a later study, Forinash (1992) examined the lived experience of clinical improvisation in the Nordoff-Robbins model of music therapy. She interviewed eight Nordoff-Robbins music therapists and sat with them as together they watched a video segment chosen by the therapist to represent his or her clinical work. Forinash asked each interviewee about his or her experience of clinical improvisation and arrived at 12 *meaning units* that described their experiences.

Comeau (1991, 2004) studied the experience of being effective as a music therapist. Through interviews with music therapists, he provided a thorough description of the experience, containing essences as well as unique individual aspects of the experience. Gonzalez (1992) used phenomenology to create an essential description of the process of mythopoeic music therapy. Beck (1995) used phenomenology in her dissertation titled *The Role of Music in the Deepening of the Disposition of Compassion*. This study, based on van Kaam's work, sought to understand the role of music listening in the formation of compassion in therapists.

Four phenomenological studies were completed at the University of Melbourne in Australia. Hogan (1999) conducted a phenomenological study of nine patients in palliative care and their experiences of music therapy. Fourteen themes emerged: an altered state of well-being; an emotional experience; memories; spiritual experiences; preparing for funeral; positive transference to the music therapist; the impact of others on the music therapy experience; awareness of the music's inherent qualities; and the lasting effect of the music therapy experience. Dun (1999) studied the experience of music therapists working with children in comas. She interviewed five music therapists about their clinical experiences of working with these children. The themes she found included: feelings of inadequacy, the Hero's Journey, feelings of doubt, feelings of joy, gratification, inner conflict, staff impact, and pressure from the child's family. *A Phenomenological Study of Pivotal Moments in Guided Imagery and Music (GIM) Therapy* was completed by Grocke (1999). This study is presented in additional detail later in this chapter. Skewes (2001) examined group music therapy for six bereaved adolescents over 10 music therapy sessions using song sharing (sharing a favorite CD followed by group discussion) and improvisation. The participants were interviewed. Results showed that fun, freedom, control, and achievement were core experiences of music therapy, and that improvisations allowed more self-expression than recorded songs. Forty-one group improvisations were analyzed and verified by independent raters. There were increasing levels of cohesion in the improvisations over time, reflected in rhythmic structure and group leadership roles.

Bruscia (2001) offered a "qualitative approach to analyzing client improvisations" (p. 7) in which he examined different perspectives in analysis. He provided methodological stages that can be used in analysis and discussed the decisions and issues involved in each stage. These stages apply to a variety of qualitative approaches including phenomenology, which he described as an "interest in how the music is experienced by those involved. . . and the development of analytic methods based on the essential nature of the musical phenomenon to be studied" (p. 8).

Wheeler (2002) studied the experiences and concerns of music therapy students during their practicum training. This study is described in the next section.

Detailed Music Therapy Examples

Two examples of phenomenology applied to music therapy will be presented in greater detail.

Grocke's Phenomenology of Pivotal Moments. Grocke's study of pivotal moments in Guided Imagery in Music (1999) emerged from her interest in the life-changing experiences she had gone through in her own GIM therapy, as well as those moments she observed in her GIM clients. In the first part of the study, she interviewed seven clients and asked them to recall a session that had been pivotal for them. *Pivotal* was explained as "an intense and memorable experience that stands out as distinctive or unique" (p. 69). The interview protocols of each participant were analyzed and a horizontal analysis[1] across all participants was completed to determine composite themes and the composite essence:

1. Each interview transcript was read through to gain a sense of the overall experience.
2. The transcript was read again, and key statements were underlined.
3. The key statements were placed together and grouped into units of meaning, termed meaning units. Each unit was given a category heading.
4. The meaning units for each transcript were transformed into a distilled essence of the participant's experience.
5. The interview transcript (with key statements underlined), the meaning units, and the distilled essence were sent to the participant for verification with the question "does my final distilled description capture the essence of your experience? Is there any aspect of your experience that has been left out?"
6. When the participant had returned the material, any changes or omissions were noted.
7. When all seven participants had verified the distilled essence of their experience, I undertook a horizontal distilling process, whereby the common meaning units across all seven interviews were laid side by side and composite categories were developed.
8. Composite themes were distilled from the categories and distilled further into the composite essence.
9. The distilled composite essence was then transformed into a final global description of the experience of pivotal moments in GIM. (Grocke, 1999, pp. 61–62)

In the second part of the study, Grocke interviewed the GIM therapists who had facilitated the sessions with the clients. She asked the therapists about their recollections of the session and what stood out for them, then applied the same process of analysis to the interview protocols of the therapists.

In the third part of the study, Grocke made phenomenological descriptions of the music program that had been chosen by the therapist for the session that the client identified as pivotal. She divided sections of each music selection according to points of change in themes, modulation points, and dynamic shifts, and grouped these as *music meaning units*. She placed the imagery experiences of the client alongside the phenomenological descriptions to draw out the elements of the music most likely to have stimulated the imagery experience. The depiction of the full music program for one client was described as follows:

---

[1] The word *horizonal* is similar to *horizontal,* but horizonal is intended here—as if looking to the horizon to capture the wider view.

Depiction of the Music

The music of the Inner Odyssey program is characterised by wide contrasts. The 1st movement from Brahms *3rd Symphony* is strong in character but there are contrasts in the pastoral theme, waltz movement and sections of playfulness. The movement of Nielsen's *5th Symphony* is dissonant, and there are striking contrasts in the orchestration. In one section there are four competing elements that eventually resolve and climax. The ending however is tranquil. There is a sense of stability in the slow movement of Beethoven's *Violin Concerto*, underpinned by consonant harmonies and repetitious themes. The solo violin often extends to high register, so that the texture is thin and ethereal. The second theme is quite beautiful with long held notes and a secure accompaniment. The Corelli *[Concerto Grosso]* movement by contrast is very structured and exact. (p. 164)

Depiction of the Imagery

Although the music selections are contrasting in mood and structure, David's imagery was quite focussed. The image of himself as a three year old child appeared in the first piece of music and returned in the third and fourth. David explored his relationship with the child. During the Brahms' movement, the three-year old was a happy child, content and chubby in appearance. David was delighted to be with him. He wanted to "be one with" this child, and to enter his world of play. He then started questioning "Where have you gone, how do I connect with you?" There is a sense of wanting to get closer and more involved. The three year old puts out his hand and David walks beside him, but the three year old is in his own world. During the excerpt from the Nielsen symphony, the imagery becomes embodied and David feels a gnawing emptiness in his abdomen. A distant wave appears; it is night-time on a beach; it is cold and windy. Compared to the little boy David feels hollow and empty. He is formless. During the slow movement of Beethoven's violin concerto, the little boy returns. There is a warm welcome and a sense of feeling connected. There is physical contact as the little boy grasps his finger (this is the pivotal moment). During the Corelli movement from the concerto grosso, there is a bonding (like father and son) and David has a sense of his body filling out and expanding. (p. 165)

The essences from the seven clients, two therapists, and the music analyses were then integrated into the final distilled essence of pivotal moments in GIM:

A pivotal moment in GIM is an intense and memorable GIM experience which stands out as distinctive or unique. The pivotal moment may be an embodied experience and may come from feelings or images which are uncomfortable and distressing. The moment of the pivotal change occurs as something is transformed or resolved, so that there is a feeling of freedom, or a resolution of a struggle. The therapist's intervention or presence may facilitate this process, but the therapist's silence or non-intervention may be helpful to the client at the precise pivotal moment. The music which underpins the pivotal moment may prolong the moment or provide momentum for it. Typically the music is composed in a structured form within which there is repetition of themes. It is predominantly slow in speed, predictable in melodic, harmonic and rhythmic elements, and features dialogue between instruments.

The pivotal moment may be experienced at different points in the GIM session, and the imagery of the pivotal moment is rich in meaning. The mandala may depict the feelings of the pivotal moment. The essential component of the pivotal moment is that it is one of change. It stands out from other GIM sessions or GIM experiences. It is a shift in the person's perspective on their life that may include how they relate to themselves or others, and this may lead to a permanent change in the pattern of their life experience. (p. 220)

Wheeler's Phenomenology of Experiences of Music Therapy Students.

Wheeler (2002) used a phenomenological method to investigate the "experiences and concerns that music therapy students have during their preclinical or practicum experience" (p. 274). As an educator, Wheeler became interested in this topic when a student suggested a hypothetical research topic that focused on "dealing with criticism" (p. 277) from one's supervisor. This led her to think that students have "thoughts and feelings about practica that faculty never suspect, and that these thoughts and feelings influence both their experience of practica and their work in them" (p. 277).

The students, all undergraduate music therapy majors and students of the researcher, were interviewed over the course of a year, most of them having three interviews. The interviews were conducted in an open-ended manner "designed to elicit as much of the students' experiences and as many of their feelings as possible" (p. 279). The first interview was conducted halfway through the semester in the first practicum. The second interview took place near the end of the first semester and the final interview took place near the end of the second semester of practicum.

Wheeler discussed the various roles she had with the students and how she worked with the students so that these multiple roles did not negatively impact the study. In particular, she contacted the students in a follow-up communication when she was no longer working at the university where they were students. This provided the students with more freedom for honesty as she was no longer involved in their training.

For data analysis, Wheeler used followed these steps:

1. Interviews were transcribed.
2. Summary statements of segments of the interviews were made.
3. Transcriptions and summary statements were sent to the students for their input; at the same time, students were asked to share any reflections that they had at that time, during the academic year following the interviews, and were also asked to share any thoughts that they had as to how the interviewer being a faculty member, including at times their supervisor and/or practicum class teacher, influenced their responses.
4. Changes in summary statements were made based on students' feedback.
5. Summary statements were divided into categories and subcategories.
6. After reviewing the data analysis and its usefulness, subcategories were placed under the initial questions that had guided the research.
7. Comments were regrouped under areas of interest and explanatory statements from the transcriptions added. (pp. 283–284)

Categories and subcategories emerged during the analysis, yet Wheeler felt that these were not based on the "types of experiences that emerged from what the students had said" (p. 284) but rather on the questions that she had asked. She then organized them under "areas of interest" (p. 284) that she felt were more useful in both understanding the experiences as well as presenting them.

The six main areas were: "challenges encountered by students, means of dealing with challenges, involvement with clients, areas of learning, supervision issues, and structure of practicum" (p. 284). Wheeler provided examples for each area that included the students' actual words along with Wheeler's summary of the experience. For the area of *challenges encountered by students,* five specific examples were: fear of new experiences, session planning, needs of clients, music skills, and concerns about grades. Session planning was described thus:

> Students had many concerns about planning sessions. The primary one was what to do in the sessions—what activities to use. Patricia, a student in the upper level practicum (but only beginning her clinical experience with children/adolescents), said:
>
> > My biggest anxiety at this point is that I don't know enough activities to do, and I don't know any resources where I can find activities for adolescents. We seem to have a lot of things for young children, but I don't see anything for adolescents.
>
> This theme, the difficulty of planning what to do, occurred repeatedly with several students. (pp. 285–286)

Under the main area of *means of dealing with challenges,* Wheeler had five specific examples: self-devised strategies to ease discomfort, involvement, knowledge of clients, music progress, and applications of experiential learning.

Applications of experiential learning. One student, Rebecca, was at a placement in which interns and practicum students were part of an experiential music therapy group. This was a special experience to have, and must have been personally challenging in her very first practicum. She appeared to benefit from the experience, and spoke of applying the knowledge:

> In the student group, I'm learning a lot about myself and I'm learning a lot about music therapy at the same time. I like going to it, even though I'm a little apprehensive because I don't know what we're going to do. It's OK. I like the fact that I'm pushed to jump in and try things and learn things. I think it's a good experience.
>
> The student group, which was just myself and the other interns, got me to realize that different people have different perspectives, and then once I got into the patient group, I was able to apply it, see how they dealt with it. . . . That brings up a lot of questions. Was this spur of the moment or was this planned, what the music therapist decides to do? When a client yells something out do you go with it, or do you ignore it? It was pretty interesting since they each have their own interpretation. (pp. 289–290)

Wheeler went on to present the remaining four main areas (involvement with clients, areas of learning, supervision issues, and structure of practicum) and provided specific examples for each area quoting from the actual transcripts.

In her discussion Wheeler shared new awareness that she gained through this research. In true qualitative fashion, the burden of applicability of the results is on the reader. In our case, as music therapy educators, these results do resonate and provide meaning. As Wheeler stated:

> My understanding, as a faculty member, of students' experiences has also increased, and this will influence my approach to certain aspects of the students' clinical experience. One of these changes has to do with taking care to be sure that I do not make assumptions about what students are thinking or feeling. One of the things that struck me as I did these interviews was that there were times in which I simply did not think as the students did. Beyond that, I couldn't imagine why they thought the way that they did. (p. 301)

The awareness that the experience of another—in this case, a student—can be so dramatically different than what one experiences is an important finding for educators to reflect on.

Conclusions

Phenomenology has a rich history and an exciting future. It has been applied in numerous ways to study a variety of experiences in music therapy over the past 20 plus years. The flexibility and openness of this research approach allow the phenomenologist to study the complexity of these experiences in a way that deepens our understanding of the events in our clinical work. We look forward to continued application phenomenological methods in music therapy.

References

Aigen, K. (1997). *Here we are in music: One year with an adolescent creative music therapy group.* St. Louis, MO: MMB Music.

Aldridge, D. (1989). A phenomenological comparison of the organization of music and the self. *The Arts in Psychotherapy, 16,* 91–97.

Amir, D. (1990). A song is born: Discovering meaning in improvised songs through phenomenological analysis of two music therapy sessions with a traumatic spinal-cord injured adult. *Music Therapy, 9,* 62–81.

Amir, D. (1993). Moments of insight in the music therapy experience. *Music Therapy, 12,* 85–101.

Arnason, C. (2002). An eclectic approach to the analysis of improvisations in music therapy session. *Music Therapy Perspectives, 11,* 4–12.

Beck, D. M. (1995). The role of music in the deepening of the disposition of compassion (Doctoral dissertation, Duquesne University, 1995). *Dissertation Abstracts International, 56*(05), 1571.

Bruscia, K. E. (1995). Modes of consciousness in Guided Imagery and Music (GIM): A therapist's experience of the guiding process. In C. B. Kenny (Ed.), *Listening, playing, creating: Essays on the power of sound* (pp. 165–197). Albany, NY: State University of New York Press.

Bruscia, K. E. (2001). A qualitative approach to analyzing client improvisations. *Music Therapy Perspectives, 19,* 7–21.

Colaizzi, P. F. (1978). Psychological research as the phenomenologist views it. In R. S. Valle & M. King (Eds.), *Existential-phenomenological alternatives for psychology* (pp. 48–71). New York: Oxford University Press.

Comeau, P. (1991). *A phenomenological investigation of being effective as a music therapist.* Unpublished master's thesis, Temple University, Philadelphia, PA.

Comeau, P. (2004). A phenomenological investigation of being effective as a music therapist. In B. Abrams (Ed.), *Qualitative inquiries in music therapy* (Vol. 1, pp. 19–36). Gilsum, NH: Barcelona Publishers.

Creswell, J. W. (1998). *Qualitative inquiry and research design: Choosing among five traditions.* Newbury Park, CA: Sage Publications.

deKoning, A. (1979). The qualitative method of research in the phenomenology of suspicion. In A. Giorgi, R. Knowles, & D. Smith (Eds.), *Duquesne studies in phenomenological psychology* (Vol. 3, pp. 122–134). Pittsburgh, PA: Duquesne University Press.

Dun, B. (1999). *The experience of music therapists working with children in coma.* Unpublished master's thesis. University of Melbourne, Melbourne, Australia.

Edwards, J. (1999). Considering the paradigmatic frame: Social science research approaches relevant to research in music therapy. *The Arts in Psychotherapy, 26,* 73–80.

Ferrara, L. (1984). Phenomenology as a tool for musical analysis. *The Musical Quarterly, 7,* 355–373.

Fischer, C., & Wertz, F. (1979). Empirical phenomenological analyses of being criminally victimized. In A. Giorgi, R. Knowles, & D. Smith (Eds.), *Duquesne studies in phenomenological psychology* (Vol. 3, pp. 135–158). Pittsburgh, PA: Duquesne University Press.

Forinash, M. (1990). A phenomenology of music therapy with the terminally ill. (Doctoral dissertation, New York University, 1990). *Dissertation Abstracts International, 51*(09), 2915A.

Forinash, M. (1992). A phenomenological analysis of Nordoff-Robbins approach to music therapy: The lived experience of clinical improvisation. *Music Therapy, 11,* 120–141.

Forinash, M. (2000). Dialogues on the study of Edward. *Nordic Journal of Music Therapy, 9*(1), pp. 83–89.

Forinash, M., & Gonzalez, D. (1989). A phenomenological perspective of music therapy. *Music Therapy, 9,* 35–46.

Giorgi, A. (1975). Convergence and divergence of qualitative and quantitative methods in psychology. In A. Giorgi, C. T. Fisher, & E. L. Murray (Eds.), *Duquesne studies in phenomenological psychology* (Vol. 2, pp. 72–79). Pittsburgh, PA: Duquesne University Press.

Gonzalez, D. (1992). Mythopoeic music therapy: A phenomenological investigation into its application with adults. *Dissertation Abstracts International, 53*(8), 4371B. (UMI No. DA92037753)

Grocke, D. E. (1999). *A phenomenological study of pivotal moments in Guided Imagery and Music therapy.* Unpublished doctoral dissertation, University of Melbourne, Melbourne, Australia. Available at www.musictherapyworld. net

Hogan, B. (1999). The experience of music therapy for terminally ill patients. In R. R. Pratt & D. E. Grocke (Eds.), *MusicMedicine 3* (pp. 242–252). Melbourne: Faculty of Music, University of Melbourne.

Ihde, D. (1976). *Listening and voice: A phenomenology of sound.* Athens, OH: Ohio University Press.

Ihde, D. (1986). *Experimental phenomenology: An introduction.* New York: State University of New York.

Kasayka, R. E. (1988). *To meet and match the moment of hope: Transpersonal elements of the Guided Imagery and Music experience.* Unpublished paper. Savage, MD: Institute for Music and Imagery.

Kasayka, R. E. (1991). To meet and match the moment of hope: Transpersonal elements of the Guided Imagery and Music experience. *Dissertation Abstracts International, 52*(06), 2062A. (UMI No. DEY9134754)

Kenny, C. B. (1983, May). *Phenomenological research: A promise for the healing arts.* Paper presented at the meeting of the Canadian Association for Music Therapy, Toronto, Ontario, Canada.

Kenny, C. B. (1987). The field of play: A theoretical study of music therapy process. *Dissertation Abstracts International, 48*(12), 3067A. (UMI No. DEV88-02367)

Kenny, C. B. (1989). *The field of play: A guide for the theory and practice of music therapy.* Atascadero, CA: Ridgeview Publishing Co.

Kenny, C. B. (1996). The story of the field of play. In M. Langenberg, K. Aigen, & J. Frommer (Eds.), *Qualitative music therapy research: Beginning dialogues* (pp. 55–78). Gilsum, NH: Barcelona Publishers.

Kvale, S. (1983). The qualitative research interview: A phenomenological and a heuristic mode of understanding. *Journal of Phenomenological Psychology, 14,* 171–196.

Lavine, T. Z. (1984). *From Socrates to Sartre: The philosophic quest.* New York: Bantam Books.

Lett, W. R. (1993). Therapist creativity: The art of supervision. *The Arts in Psychotherapy, 20,* 371–386.

Moustakas, C. (1994). *Phenomenological research methods.* Thousand Oaks, CA: Sage Publications.

Mruk, C. (1983). Toward a phenomenology of self-esteem. In A. Giorgi, A. Barton, & C. Maes (Eds.) *Duquesne studies in phenomenological psychology* (Vol. 4, pp. 137–149). Pittsburgh, PA: Duquesne University Press.

Music in the Life of Man (1982, June). Unpublished symposium proceedings. New York: New York University.

Nordoff, P., & Robbins, C. (1977). *Creative music therapy.* New York: John Day.

Polkinghorne, D. E. (1989). Phenomenological research methods. In R. S. Valle & S. Halling (Eds.). *Existential-phenomenological perspectives in psychology* (pp. 41–60). New York: Plenum Press.

Racette, K. (1989). *A phenomenological analysis of the experience of listening to music when upset.* Unpublished master's thesis. Temple University, Philadelphia, PA.

Racette, K. (2004). A phenomenological analysis of the experience of listening to music when upset. In B. Abrams (Ed.), *Qualitative inquiries in music therapy* (Vol. 1, pp. 1–18). Gilsum, NH: Barcelona Publishers.

Ruud, E. (1987). *Musikk som kommunikasjon og samhandling* [Music as communication and interaction]. *Institutt for musikk og teate.* Unpublished doctoral dissertation, Oslo, Norway: Oslo University.

Skewes, K. (2001). *The experience of group music therapy for six bereaved adolescents.* Unpublished doctoral dissertation, University of Melbourne, Melbourne, Australia. Available at www.musictherapyworld.net

Stevick, E. (1971). An empirical investigation of the experience of anger. In A. Giorgi, W. F. Fischer, & R. von Eckartsberg (Eds.), *Duquesne studies in phenomenological psychology* (Vol. 1, pp. 132–148). Pittsburgh, PA: Duquesne University Press.

Tesch, R. (1990). *Qualitative research: Analysis types & software tools.* New York: Falmer.

Trondalen, G. (2002). En fenomenologisk inspirert arbeidsprosedyre for analyse av improvisasjoner I musickkterapeutishk praksis. Et narrativt perspektiv [A phenomeno-logically inspired working procedure for analysis of improvisations in music therapy: A narrative perspective]. In E. Neseim (Ed.), *Flerstemmige innspill.* NMHs Skriftserie, No. 2. Oslo: Norges Musikkhogskole.

Trondalen, G. (2003). Self-listening in music therapy with a young woman suffering from Aznorexia nervosa. *Nordic Journal of Music Therapy, 12,* 3–17.

van Kaam, A. L. (1959). Phenomenal analysis: Exemplified by a study of the experience of "really feeling understood." *Journal of Individual Psychology 15*(1), 62–72.

van Manen, M. (1990). *Researching lived experience: Human science for an action sensitive pedagogy.* Albany, NY: State University of New York Press.

van Manen, M. (2002). *Writing in the dark: Phenomenological studies in interpretive inquiry.* London, Ontario, Canada: University of Western Ontario.

Wheeler, B. L. (2002). Experiences and concerns of students during music therapy practica. *Journal of Music Therapy, 39,* 274–304.

Chapter 27
Hermeneutic Inquiry
Carolyn Kenny, Mechtild Jahn-Langenberg, and Joanne Loewy

Everywhere the claim of hermeneutics seems capable of being met only in the infinity of knowledge, in the thoughtful fusion of the whole of tradition with the present. We see it based on the ideal of perfect enlightenment, on the complete limitlessness of our. . . horizon.

Gadamer[1]

Overview and Definition

"The ideal of perfect enlightenment, of course, is unattainable. But it can be approached, and insofar as we genuinely desire to understand our circumstances and conditions, there is no stopping place short of this ideal of perfect enlightenment that will fully satisfy us" (Bontekoe, 1996, p. 236). Hermeneutics is the art and science of interpretation *(Kunst des Verstehens)*. Although early use of hermeneutics is associated with the Delphic oracles, the term finds its primary roots in the name of the Greek god Hermes, messenger of the gods. Unfortunately, Hermes was killed when he delivered a bit of news that the community did not want to hear. The phrase "don't kill the messenger" comes from this story. Hermeneutics came into general usage when theologians began to interpret sacred texts. It originated as a way to come to terms with the gaps in history between when texts were written and how they should be applied to the context of readers in a different historical period. "Hermeneutics makes us aware that, in a reciprocal interpretive process, the present is interpreted in terms of the texts of the past and their historical context, although those texts and that context are themselves interpreted in terms of the present" (Bentz & Shapiro, 1998, p. 106). Hermeneutics is a very complex science and art.

In contemporary social science, and especially in disciplines such as anthropology, sociology, and cultural studies, hermeneutics is used to interpret not only texts but also other expressions that need interpreting like conversations, nonverbal interactions, and even clothing and fashion. Debates about what can constitute *text* and therefore what is eligible for the hermeneutic process are ongoing. Some research methodologists believe that hermeneutics is an everyday process and that all understanding is hermeneutical. Hermeneutics is one of the ways we make sense of our lifeworlds (Bentz & Shapiro, 1998).

Music therapists are particularly interested in hermeneutic inquiry because of its close association to the arts. When we study music, we are always interpreting the music. How would Bach want us to play his *Goldberg Variations?* Bach lives today through his music, but he is not living in our historical time. We have experienced the variety of interpretive expressions on the work of Bach through thousands of concerts and recordings with a great deal of variety. In addition to being musicians, music therapists have another layer of interpretive practice in their relationships with clients. How do we interpret the expressions of our clients in terms of their needs? A fascinating area for research is music psychotherapy, which can bring another theoretical layer of interpretation or hermeneutics into the process of psychoanalysis or other theoretical stances.

The quality and accuracy of the interpretation offered by the researcher in this method is determined by his or her proximity to the phenomenon being studied. Hermeneutics is an important type of qualitative research. So in hermeneutics, just as in all forms of qualitative research, the researcher is the primary instrument of the work.

Situating the Authors

"The way I research is who I am" (Watson, 1999). In a postmodern research climate, the researcher must situate him- or herself or provide the story of how he or she comes into the

---

[1] This quotation is from Gadamer (1960), pp. 341–342.

research or the study. Situating oneself satisfies the qualitative research criteria of trustworthiness, transparency, and authenticity.

From the Authors

Each of the chapter authors came to hermeneutic inquiry in her own way. Their stories reflect their unique paths to hermeneutics.

Carolyn Kenny. I first heard about hermeneutics when I was an undergraduate at Loyola University where my Jesuit education gave me an early exposure to interpretive processes, especially in our philosophy and theology classes. Even though at that time (as an 18 year old), I could not possibly have coped with the complexities of hermeneutics, a few seeds were planted there, especially in terms of how hermeneutics relates to another interest of my Jesuit professors, phenomenology. But when I became a music therapist at age 23, the seeds began to sprout and, as a clinician, I was fascinated by the interpretive process.

Many years later, after having reflected on my clinical practice with patients and clients from ages 3–102 with many different life circumstances, and after traveling to observe other music therapists on two continents, I designed theoretical concepts to help in understanding music therapy processes. That theory is called the *field of play* and is described in my book *The Field of Play* (1989). The field of play can be described as a hermeneutic circle (or circles). Each of the seven fields keeps circling back into itself as the process of music therapy moves along in an ever-expanding expression. Each time the expressions and understandings come around again, more layers of complexity are introduced. The process becomes so complex that it is difficult to articulate, which is how I see music therapy. We can only articulate fragments and constantly recontextualize these thought fragments into our understandings. During this period, I studied under Jeremy Shapiro, one of Theodor Adorno's students. He had translated several works of Adorno and of Jürgen Habermas, so I became familiar with the Frankfurt School of Critical Theory.

Even though I am very interested in general theory for music therapy, I also understand that my interpretations are seen through my own lifeworld, especially my Native American ancestry. So, the field of play is also an historical and cultural expression. This became obvious to me when one of my articles was published in the *Journal of Music Therapy* (Kenny, 1998) and I used the image of a tree to represent research in music therapy. The tree was a metaphor. But it was a predictable metaphor, given my Native American worldview. It was also a hermeneutic circle because it described how data are the leaves that fall to the ground and nurture the roots of the tree, which are the philosophies that inform us. And the philosophies change based on the new knowledge. This is also a picture of a hermeneutic process.

I still practice hermeneutics in my clinical work. And after so many years of this practice, I truly believe that knowledge and understanding is a never-ending process that is alive.

Mechtild Jahn-Langenberg. Once I experienced a great challenge at a workshop with music therapy students in a masters program in Vancouver. We had to stay in a lively interaction in order to find the meaning of a psychotherapeutic process while being confronted not only with the unknown inner world of the patients but also with different languages. Creative use of words brought up a humorous search for meaning using the variety and playfulness of the power of a group that dared to work with the unknown. I had the sense that we were circling in and out of a hermeneutic circle of understandings. And the students were open to the process and certainly eager to embrace qualitative research and hermeneutics.

When my specialization as a psychoanalytically informed music therapist and qualitative researcher was developing within the context of psychosomatic medicine and psychotherapy in the early 1990s, there was an intense resistance to qualitative approaches in German psychotherapy research from psychotherapy researchers. The main arguments were that such a method lacked scientific methodology and did not meet the same criteria as other empirical research methods.

Innovative projects started in our Psychosomatic Clinic in Düsseldorf, integrating qualitative approaches into the field of medicine within the specialty of psychosomatic medicine and psychotherapy. We began to integrate arts-based psychotherapy into the overall treatment plan for patients. This clinical approach was accompanied by research strategies to identify a qualitative, inductive methodology that was derived directly from the practical field (Langenberg, Frommer, & Tress, 1992). Our team of clinicians believed strongly that interpersonal interactions such as verbal and musical communication warranted qualitative judgments. We knew that the use of the symbolically transmitted process of social interaction between individuals contained hermeneutic and contextualized processes of interpretation (Faller & Frommer, 1994).

Joanne Loewy. I have specialized in assessment and in the building of medical music psychotherapy programs in the United States and abroad. The essence of these two specialties involves the ability to describe and uncover a method of music therapy that defines the possibilities of music. This occurs by means of description through words.

In the first instance, the description of music psychotherapy is in the interest of the patient. The clinical music therapy assessment sits in a written medical file, sandwiched in between a host of medical reports. The music therapy assessment may be the sole report that reflects a patient's human condition. The words assigned to this evaluation must crystallize the opportunity of the experience in a way that will enhance future recommendations made for the patient psychologically and physically (Loewy, 1995).

In the second instance, the description of music psychotherapy is in the interest of a potential program. As I consult with staff who are seeking to understand what music therapy is and whether or not it could benefit a particular institution, and to encourage investment in funding a program, my task is delicate. I need to be able to describe how music therapy works: What are its values? Why would it be effective to invest in this service?

Video recordings illustrate a great deal and our scientific music therapy data reflect compelling potential for music therapy. However, the most effective means of validation, which highlights the essences of what music therapy can offer, lies within the words we assign to describe the process. Words and reports, and spoken description are the *lingua franca* of patient protection and program building. As music therapists, it seems that we are auditorily and intuitively focused. This is not surprising as music involves attentive listening and the process of becoming a therapist beckons us to look within. Many music therapists do their work in the music. What often gets left behind in this process is the ability to help non-music therapists understand what we do. Our field is lacking in its ability to precisely define a clinical music therapy process. As a researcher, I came into hermeneutic inquiry seeking to define and refine the language of our field. This is a process in which I am still actively involved. Hermeneutic inquiry is the way I choose to study the process of music therapy that will be later described in this chapter.

Historical Roots and Theoretical Premises

Hermeneutics is an ancient tradition that began as Greek and Judaic interpretation of legal and religious texts. In this tradition are Moses, Jesus, Paul, Origine, Augustine, and others, and also humanistic studies of philosophy, poetry, rhetoric, and history.

However, hermeneutics began to take off as a formal type of inquiry with Friedrich Ast (1778–1841) and his *Basic Elements of Grammar, Hermeneutics, and Criticism*, published in 1808. We can see that the focus on language and text remains. Ast (1990) developed his hermeneutics into a dialectical circle of romantic idealism with constant attention to a mystical principle, which he called *world spirit (Geist)*. The next significant development in hermeneutics occurred with Friedrich Daniel Ernst Schleiermacher (1768–1834). Though Schleiermacher published nothing on hermeneutics in his lifetime, upon his death three sets of lecture notes on hermeneutics were published (Schleiermacher, 1990). When these notes were published, Wilhelm Dilthey (1833–1911) took up a continuation of the work of Schleiermacher. At the turn of the 20th century, Dilthey published a paper titled "The Rise of Hermeneutics" (Dilthey, 1990), which identified Schleiermacher as the founder of what we now know as modern hermeneutics.

Palmer (1969) suggested six modern definitions of hermeneutics:

1. The theory of biblical exegesis,
2. General philological methodology,
3. The science of all linguistic understanding,
4. The methodological foundation of Geisteswissenschaften,[2]
5. Phenomenology of existence and of existential understanding,

---

[2] *Geisteswissenschaften* was used by Dilthey to suggest that the human sciences should not be modeled on the natural sciences but rather required different methodology (Polkinghorne, 1983, pp. 283–284).

6. The systems of interpretation, both recollective and iconoclastic, used by man to reach the meaning behind myths and symbols. (p. 33)

In the modern period, additional theorists emerged in the elaboration of the uses of hermeneutics, and hermeneutics became a subject of interest in many schools of thought. After Schleiermacher, Dilthey proposed a theory of hermeneutics as the foundation of the Geisteswissenschaften, building on the work of Schleiermacher and his forerunners. Martin Heidegger, in *Being and Time* (1962), developed *phenomenological hermeneutics.* Over the course of his life, Heidegger took a specific interest in the literary aspects of hermeneutics and today he is closely associated with narrative forms. Heidegger's contribution is a deep reflection over the course of his life on the mysterious process of disclosure in which being comes into manifest existence. Like Nietzsche, Heidegger took up the work of calling the whole of Western metaphysical tradition into question. Hans-Georg Gadamer, in his 1960 publication, *Wahrheit und Methode. Grundzüge einer philosophischen Hermeneutik* (translated in 1975 to English and titled *Truth and Method: Elements of a Philosophical Hermeneutics*), brought hermeneutics into a decidedly aesthetic dimension. Gadamer's interest in aesthetics gives him privilege in the research of artists and creative arts therapists. Not only does he help us to understand the relationships between interpretation and art, but he also addresses the importance of play.

As a contemporary philosopher, Paul Ricoeur has contributed a great deal to the understanding of hermeneutics. Until the 1960s he framed his work as philosophical anthropology. But in the mid-1960s he took a linguistic turn, focusing on the importance of signs and symbols in human communication and expression. Ricoeur (1971/1991) liberated hermeneutics from the bounded application in texts with his important essay, "The Model of the Text: Meaningful Action Considered as a Text." Later he developed his ideas further in *From Text to Action* (1991). In these two works, Ricoeur helps us to develop a deeper understanding of discourse as expressed not only in text but also in action. This is not surprising since the source of much of Ricoeur's thinking came from Heideigger's and Marcel's concepts of *care.* How do we relate to each other in meaningful ways, as human beings, given our fragile human condition? This is the underlying question of much of Ricoeur's work.

Many philosophical problems are addressed with the introduction of this type of hermeneutic reflection. In research, the immediate dilemma is the existence of competing claims on knowledge through different or opposing interpretations. In referring to both interpretation of text and the interpretation of action, Ricoeur (1991) wrote:

> If it is true that there is always more than one way of construing a text, it is not true that all interpretations are equal. . . . The text is a limited field of possible constructions. The logic of validation allows us to move between the two limits of dogmatism and skepticism. It is always possible to argue against an interpretation, to confront interpretations, to arbitrate between them and to seek for an agreement, even if this agreement remains beyond our reach. (p. 160)

In this statement, Ricoeur expressed one of the fundamental principles of qualitative research of any type. So-called hypotheses are generated and proven valid based on the strength of their logical interpretation, not necessarily through the presentation and analysis of empirical data.

Richard Addison (1989) considered understanding of an event as the key element in hermeneutic research. This would include the circular relationships between understanding and interpretation. In addition, the aspect of considering one's background in interpreting actions is essential. What distinguishes the qualitative methodology of hermeneutic inquiry from other research methods is an emphasis on the researcher's interest and preliminary understanding of a text or *text analog.* This preliminary understanding provides "an essential. . . access to understanding and a starting place for interpretation" (Packer & Addison, 1989, p. 5).

Of course, many other hermeneutic theorists have made contributions to our understanding of the art and science of interpretation throughout history. The contributions of only a few have been discussed here.

Hermeneutics and Psychoanalysis

Qualitative psychotherapy research has been influenced by historical and sociological developments in psychiatry, psychosomatic medicine, clinical psychology, and the social sciences. Thinking about the ontological and epistemological contexts of research methods brings about a necessary reflection about traditions involving both the sociological context of the researcher and the stance of the researcher.

For example, the subject of one hermeneutic empirical study within psychoanalysis is the relationship between patient and therapist with the main questions being the following: What is going on in the therapeutic relationship? What can be experienced consciously and unconsciously? What is wished, perceived, and wanted? What is communicated, what is acted out? (Tress, 1994).

Qualitative Psychotherapy Research: Methods and Methodology by Jörg Frommer and David Rennie (2001) brought together the European and Canadian-American efforts to bridge historical differences in the use of qualitative research in psychotherapy. This work detailed variations in current, state-of-the-art qualitative psychotherapy research. Rennie (2001) focused on an integration in the qualitative field:

> Hermeneutics thus is a common thread that weaves together the many diverse strands constituting these methods. Still, the resulting fabric has no clear pattern. This is because there are different forms of hermeneutics, and these different forms have different implications for methodology and method. (p. 185)

Rennie (2004) presented an overview of Anglo-American counseling and psychotherapy qualitative research in terms of three dualities: realism versus relativism, rationalism versus empiricism, and demonstration versus rhetoric. He described the application of method to hermeneutics, or *methodical hermeneutics,* as the most essential path to follow because it more than any other methodology provides a way of reconciling the dualities, and of closing the gap between research and practice.

Since hermeneutic inquiry adheres to the coherence theory of knowledge, we can understand how hermeneutics and psychoanalysis work well together in making knowledge claims. Hermeneutic understanding underscores the integration of mind and emotion in psychoanalysis, emphasizing the discovery of animation that is critical to hermeneutic knowledge claims. In psychoanalysis, patient and therapist alike undergo a shared process in understanding biographical material in a patient's life and identifying areas for change. This mutual understanding is, indeed, at the core of hermeneutics. Some researchers believe that hermeneutics is, in fact, the study of understanding itself. The imperative to understand the stories or narratives of patients and how we interact in these stories with our own stories is the context for studies oriented toward hermeneutics and psychoanalysis.

Hermeneutics, Symbolic Interactionism, and Cultural Studies

The application of hermeneutics to psychoanalysis finds its origins in psychology and moves to sociological implications. The fields of symbolic interactionism and cultural studies begin with sociology and often move to psychology. Symbolic interactionism is a social psychological and sociological theory with

> roots in American pragmatism. . . . Many of the shared assumptions of this school of thought derive from the work of Herbert Blumer, who was in turn was influenced by the philosopher and social theorist George Herbert Mead. The Blumer-Mead version of symbolic interactionism rests on three premises. First, humans act toward the objects and people in their environment on the basis of the meanings these objects and people have for them. Second, these meanings derive from the social interaction (communication, broadly understood) between and among individuals. . . . Finally, meanings are established and modified through an interpretive process undertaken by the individual actor. (Schwandt, 2001, pp. 244–245)

Over the years, the field of symbolic interactionism has attracted a long list of luminaries. Many theorists identify George Herbert Mead as the father of symbolic interactionism, beginning with his 1910 essay "What Social Objects Must Psychology Presuppose?" (1910/1964). Others claim that William James' 1890 work *Principles of Psychology* established the field (1890/1950). These founding theorists planted a paradoxical construct into the nature of the discipline. "On the one hand. . . they argued for the interpretive, subjective study of human experience. On the other hand, they sought to build an objective science of human conduct, a science which would conform to criteria borrowed from the natural sciences" (Denzin, 1992, p. 2).

Regardless of individual scholarly debates to secure the best intellectual position, symbolic interactionists are interested in the same contexts for study. Denzin (1992) characterized the field as:

> Constantly preoccupied with the daily, ritual, and enforced performances of stigmatized identities (race and gender), the interactionists speak always to those persons who occupy powerless positions in contemporary society. These interests set interactionism apart from other points of view. This includes those perspectives which stress attribute-like properties of systems, their identities and actions, rational choice, exchange, structural, ritual chain, role-guided, and lifeworld/system theories of communicative competence. (p. 20)

A new interdisciplinary field began to emerge, largely influenced by symbolic interactionism, with the founding of the Centre for Contemporary Cultural Studies in Birmingham, United Kingdom, in 1964. Like many emerging schools of thought at this time, including the Frankfurt School in Germany, British academics in cultural studies were attempting to come to terms with the constraints of the *grand narrative* of Marxism. In the early stages, the works of Antonio Gramsci (Forgacs, 2000) provided the basis for the *problematic* of Marxist thought. The driving force behind the Birmingham School was Stuart Hall (Hall & Whannel, 1965) and the work of cultural studies seemed to take off nicely from where symbolic interactionism left off as an academic field, using hermeneutics as its primary mode of research. Cultural studies preferred to be characterized as a grassroots movement and concerned itself with popular culture, racism, feminism, issues of identity, and politics.

Both symbolic interactionism and cultural studies are concerned with *the politics of interpretation* and both focus on the critique of hegemony as an embedded power system. Particularly interesting to many music therapists is the focus of cultural studies on the arts as instruments of identity formation and social change.

Cultural studies scholar Simon Frith (1988) has written extensively about popular music and influenced European music therapists like Even Ruud, who published an article titled "Music in the Media: The Soundtrack Behind the Construction of Identity" (1995). Ruud conducted and reported on an ethnographic study of a rock band, with the analysis and interpretation of the data leading to the following conceptual categories: music as a map of reality, everyday aesthetics as necessary symbolic work, music as a soundtrack for life, and music as an organizer of social life. This is an example of the interdisciplinary exchanges between cultural studies and music therapy.

The concept of *the band* has been the subject of other interpretive works. In his book, *Playin' in the Band* (2002), Kenneth Aigen adapts Charles Keil's (1994, 1995) theoretical construct of *participatory discrepancies* to interpret music therapy sessions with a client at the Nordoff-Robbins Music Therapy Center. Though Keil is a musicologist, his study of contemporary bands also positions him in the field of cultural studies, as it does Aigen's work about the band in music therapy.

As this sampling of applications illustrates, the possibilities for applying hermeneutics are vast and complex. It can be applied to the examination of sacred texts, the intimate details of the individual psyche in psychoanalysis, the contemporary context of rock bands, or the practice of music therapy.

Methodology

In these preliminary discussions of hermeneutic methodology, it is important to remember that the concept of *knowledge claims* is the bridge between such a philosophical research approach and its methodology. Hermeneutic inquiry is sometimes criticized as a method that simply reflects a vicious circle that goes nowhere. Criteria are always important in judging the value of research and the knowledge claims accessed by our methodology of choice. As is evident in the brief introduction to hermeneutics in the last section, the practice of hermeneutic methods is largely intersubjective. The intent of the research is to understand through a dynamic interaction between texts, people, history, insight, and any other conditions that might influence our understanding. The challenge of current hermeneutic research is the issue of validity, a criterion often borrowed from quantitative research. Ricoeur argues that verstehen (to understand) is in actuality a matter of guessing and that erklären (to explain) is a matter of validation (as cited in

Brown, Tappan, Gilligan, Miller, & Argyris, 1989). These scholars suggest that we are, in fact, misinterpreting the term validity or limiting ourselves in its application. There is an entire field devoted to *verificationism* and *falsificationism* (Misak, 1995) that illuminates the debates on these concepts. However, as one reads a text, both of these processes are involved. Since the stance of the hermeneutic researcher is intersubjective by nature, the researcher must use methods of self-discovery and reflection to position him- or herself in the research in order to keep the integrity of the research in place.

The Self-Hermeneutic

A self-hermeneutic, or stance of the researcher (Aigen, 1995, p. 294), is commonly reported in research and sets forth one's personal, social, and philosophical beliefs prior to reporting findings. A self-hermeneutic implies that the researcher's biases will be reported accurately. In an intersubjective space, the researcher must establish a set of checks and balances that provide diverse perspectives through which to view the phenomenon under study. No matter which perspective is selected, however, all must go through the eyes of the researcher him- or herself in terms of the writing of the text that will represent the research. The self-hermeneutic is a method that helps us to stay within the coherence theory of knowledge, insuring that there is integrity in the methods informing the study.

The Hermeneutic Circle

The hermeneutic circle is a way of thinking about how one derives meaning for an experience. Interpretation is not simply understanding and interpreting words and texts, nor is it only gaining insight into how the text fits into the history of its context or the cultural reference of the reader. The circle is the way in which access to the phenomenon is achieved, and there is always a deeper meaning assigned and uncovered. These meanings, understood through text, must then be resynthesized and brought back to the original source, where new insights are illuminated. The hermeneutic circle is as much a way of working through our own translations as it is the insights that then are uncovered and renamed, which in turn take us back to the text: "We must come into the circle the right way. . . leaping into it primordially and wholly. In the circle, there is a positive possibility of the most primordial kind of knowing" (Heidegger, 1962, p.195).

It is essential that this circle include the part that is one's own understanding to the whole of understanding that is uncovered through assigning words to help the interpretation (Hoy, 1978). "In practice though, as readers, we move, however gropingly and uncertainly, toward a deeper understanding of a text as we struggle with it" (Valle, King, & Halling, 1989, p. 15). These authors note the importance for the reader of returning to the top of the spiral, yet they note that the place of return, which is the primary inquiry or *place of origin,* is always returned to at a deeper level as the awareness expands.

In the context of social sciences, we focus on our subject of music therapy as a field of human agency, where people are already interpreters of their experiences of themselves. This double hermeneutic is the center of psychotherapy research. Processes of understanding take place in everyday life. The scientific interpreter works in a state of hermeneutic reflection, using hermeneutics as an attitude and action. Such a person seeks to reflect upon internal methods of understanding. In this sense, understanding is systematic and controlled and serves also for teaching and learning. In hermeneutics, understanding is actually discovered in a circle in that a single experience is contextualized in a whole, which in turn is influenced by knowledge of the single experience, referred to as the hermeneutic circle. Hermeneutic operation stays in contrast to the validation of a hypothesis as a process of falsification (Popper, 1965). Karl Popper was known for his deep and thorough critique of positivism and influenced the development of a perspective of skepticism regarding knowledge claims emerging from this school of thought. There are basic differences in the process, the theory, and the subjects of research. Comparing the issues, we can affirm that in hermeneutics, the search for meaning in expressions of life are not hypothetically deductive but provide for the participants to be systematically involved.

Martin Packer and Richard Addison (1989) devoted several chapters to the perspective of *entering the circle* in a collection of studies in hermeneutic investigations in psychology:

Interpretive accounts are not undisciplined guesses and do not shoot beyond the available evidence in a speculative way. They are ordered and organized by the fore-structure of the projection, the fore-structure guide's interpretation. The guidance is not automatic. . . . We have a responsibility to prepare so that we "enter the circle" with an appropriate fore-structure, and so conduct our interpretation in a proper manner. . . . Entering the circle is mostly the manner of inquiry. . . which requires self-disclosure on the part of the researcher. (p. 4)

If one is attempting to enter the circle, the role of culture cannot be overlooked. Heidegger's (1962) temporal accounts are useful. Cultural realms are embedded in the constructs of time. The very language and, furthermore, the assignment of words employed as descriptive headers to an experience carry historical and current societal composites. This is why many qualitative researchers forecast their findings with a self-hermeneutic that reveals not only their conscious biases but their place in the history of ideas as well as the methods in which the climate of their inquiry prevailed.

The understanding of each part, in turn, influences the understanding of the whole. This circling from part to whole and back again results in progressive understanding that, in principle, is unending, although hopefully it reaches a kind of stability, at least within the horizon of the particular hermeneut (Packer& Addison, 1989; Rennie, 2001).

The JAKOB Method

Another example of hermeneutic methods, Brigitte Boothe's narrative analytic method called JAKOB illustrates methods taken from linguistics and literary studies in which the narrative process is seen as a dramatic act. The acronym *JAKOB* means the dramaturgical analysis of *OBJects* and *ACtions* (Boothe, Wyl, & Wepfer, 1999, p. 261).

Narratives are linguistic stage productions. The storyteller directs the scene and assigns dramatic roles and degrees of involvement to the speaker-listener group. Thus, conflict-laden experience becomes something that can be articulated, and finds emotional acceptance in the social sphere. (Boothe et al., 1999, p. 258)

Relationship to Other Types of Research

Hermeneutics is closely related to phenomenology. We see this in the writings of both Heidegger (1962) and Gadamer (1975/1989), and we also experience it in the reading of studies using each method. In fact, some might say that it is virtually impossible to separate hermeneutics from phenomenology, since the practice of phenomenology also requires a deep reflexivity on the part of the research. Like hermeneutics, phenomenology keeps returning to the subject of the study and continues to reanalyze and reinterpret data until essences have been discovered, or, as some might say, the essence of consciousness has been revealed. Both methods tend to be process-oriented and seek understanding circling back into new knowledge in the service of the research process.

Ethnography is another method that is closely associated with hermeneutics. Since Clifford Geertz published his *Interpretation of Cultures* in 1973, the influence of anthropology and anthropological methods has been pervasive in the social sciences and, in the post-modern context, has started to influence the physical sciences as well. In the crisis of representation, all scholarly expressions are considered interpretive. Geertz' approach to ethnography as *thick description* has had a pervasive influence not only on anthropology in the many forms of interpretive ethnography and critical ethnography, but across all fields in the social and behavioral sciences (Scott & Keates, 2001).

Semiotics and morphology are also related to hermeneutics because they focus on symbols, language, words, and signs. Umberto Eco (1979), in his study of semiotics, wrote extensively about the significance of understanding signs, language, and communicative interchanges. His recommendation in processing sign-function coding is that we recognize how we seek to "justify systems of attraction and repulsion" (p. 124). He carefully but creatively encouraged interpreters to recognize that these two processes are at work all the time.

And, of course, narrative inquiry is very closely related to hermeneutics because it is concerned with the telling of stories and texts, which are then analyzed and interpreted.

Examples in Music Therapy

The way in which the therapist notates a music therapy experience is extremely important. Within the work of any symbolic modality, it has become increasingly evident that there must be a basis of understanding about how meaning is derived from the clinical experience. This occurs through the assignment of words or text.

With an emphasis on interpretation, hermeneutic methodology provides a means of processing and refining the way an artistic experience is thought about and ultimately reported through writing. The final outcome of such processing lies within the notations and words that clinicians use to describe the experience. Carl Bergstrøm-Nielsen's (2005) Intuitive Music and Graphical Notation and Michael Langenbach's musico-graphic perspective (Langenberg, Frommer, & Langenbach, 1996) are examples of notation systems.[3]

The Resonator Function

A collaboration began at Düsseldorf University in 1990, integrating a music therapist trained in music psychotherapy into a team consisting of a psychiatrist and a psychoanalyst who participated in clinical work in the Department of Psychosomatic Medicine and Psychotherapy (Langenberg et al., 1992). The focus of this clinical medical collaboration was in-depth hermeneutics based on psychoanalytic understanding and use of qualitative methods for research. Langenberg's (1988) theoretical concept of the resonator function created the foundation for integrating music therapy research into the interdisciplinary qualitative research program at the university.

Langenberg's psychoanalytically informed music therapy is based on a therapeutic model of psychoanalysis and a specific definition of music as free improvisation (see Priestley, 1975). Emerging material in the active relationship between patient and therapist is worked out in the improvisation and through conversations before and after the playing. An oscillating process, intrapsychic and interpersonal, creates the therapeutic experience, a mutual exchange of thought, feelings, and fantasies in the transference relationship. The *resonator function* is the personal instrument of relating and understanding by which the therapist resonates to the latent content of the music, allowing this content to become conscious and inspire clinical interventions (Langenberg, Frommer, & Tress, 1993).

Attempting to integrate perspectives and approaches of qualitative social research into music therapy, these researchers took advantage of the fact that the descriptions they received consisted of relatively unstructured verbal material, similar to narrative interviews (Mishler, 1986; Schütze, 1983), allowing for interpretive and comparative evaluation. It was assumed when interpreting texts that the material for interpretation consisted of subjective viewpoints and experiences of the individuals being researched (Bergold & Breuer, 1987), and that the categories into which the material is organized should be drawn from the research material itself, becoming more abstract at each step (Strauss, 1987). The interpretation stems from the comparing data from various perspectives (Denzin, 1970; Flick, 1991). Methods borrowed from the field of comparative case studies (Jüttemann, 1990) are also used for comparing data.

Using this model, both therapist and patient write down descriptions of the improvisation, following the instruction: "Describe in a frank manner the associations that arise in you upon hearing the music. You can report feelings, thoughts, images, mental pictures, and stories, even if they seem chaotic" (Langenberg, Frommer, & Langenbach, 1996, p. 136). The same recording and instructions are then sent to independent observers who write their own descriptions of the improvisation. In addition, a musical analysis of the improvisation was carried out, using an individual system of signs similar to those used in the notation of contemporary

---

[3] Additional information on the notation systems developed by Bergstrøm-Nielsen and Langenbach is available. They are among 13 models of musical analysis in improvised music therapy that Mahns (2004) surveyed. The section of this work, "Die musiktherapeutische Improvisation als Forschungsgegenstand" [Musical improvisation as an object for research], is a comparative discussion of 13 models of analysis of improvised music in music therapy. See also Langenbach (1998).

music (Karkoschka, 1966). Lastly, these results were analyzed in a process of hermeneutic circling in relation to the clinical data from the patient's case history.

Two general categorical dimensions of qualities and motifs were developed. Qualities describe the subjective responses of the listeners and three levels of qualities were defined to differentiate from an outer to an inner emotional character. Motifs describe the character of the music and are thematic categories that are methodically summarized in a process of content analysis (Mayring, 1983) and open coding (Strauss, 1987) in a hermeneutic process of analysis.

Similar statements from various texts and graphic notation of the music were placed in relation to each other. The hermeneutic analysis, using the psychoanalytical way of understanding and taking into consideration the dialectic nature of human conditions, illustrated the connections between motifs found in the text and aspects in the patient's biography, psychodynamics, and treatment. The musico-graphic perspective was developed further by Michael Langenbach in a case analysis of a patient with a narcissistic personality disorder (Langenberg et al., 1996) and in later work (Langenbach, 1998).

The concept of resonator function (Langenberg, 1988) was developed further and elaborated in the university context of psychosomatic medicine and psychotherapy. This development used the standards of qualitative psychotherapy research, primarily methodology from the social sciences, adapted to music therapy (Langenberg et al., 1992; Langenberg, Frommer, & Tress, 1995; Langenberg et al., 1996).

Using a hermeneutic approach, case studies were analyzed to gain a deeper insight into the problems of affect regulation with psychosomatic patients. Affective motifs that occurred in the understanding process between patient and therapist could be found in the interpretation of verbal and nonverbal, graphic signs were a translation of the inner processes of experience. This phenomenon revealed openness as dialectic movement of moments of surprise and newness as the roots of healing processes (Jahn-Langenberg, 2003; Langenberg, 1999). In-depth hermeneutic investigation provides a means that can close the gap between research and practice. Psychoanalytically informed music therapy tends to be genuinely hermeneutic in its scientific discourse.

Finding Language to Describe Music Therapy

In an effort to understand how music therapists assign words to a music therapy process, Loewy (1995) asked five established music therapists, with 10 or more years of evaluating experience, to view and write an assessment of a single music therapy assessment session. She conducted this session via video with an emotionally disturbed boy. Upon receiving and organizing the language used in each of these reports, Loewy then interviewed and recorded the discussions of the same five therapists. This further refined the language, specifically, the words that these therapists used in discussion and in writing that related to the music therapy behaviors seen in the videotaped assessment. This study illuminated what is essential for these therapists to consider in the music therapy assessment process.

The findings were surprisingly succinct and led to the endorsement of language, description, and words that are acceptable, easily understood (such as "symbolic association of musical instruments" and "rhythmic synchrony"). There were other terms that were negotiable and less understood (such as "singing in tune" and "cognition").

What surprised most readers of this study was that what seemed easily definable and quantifiable (such as singing in tune, cognition) was variable and open for debate. One would think, for instance, that singing in tune would be an area in which music therapists (with broad backgrounds in music and musical theory) would agree. This was not the case. This area caused a large amount of disagreement among the five distinguished music therapists. Through hermeneutic inquiry, the study showed that the meaning assigned to the language, this preconceived, well-known phrase that is used in the field to describe many aspects of a person's music-self, had serious discriminating variances based on the therapist's definitions and perceptions of what they had pre-conceived singing in tune to mean (Loewy, 1995, p. 103). Their bases were related to "a perception of melodic gestalt," "sense of pitch" (as an inborn trait, in this case a lack of physical ability), an ability that would be developed "if one was sung to as a young baby or child," a problem related to self-esteem, or a "vocal response to the environment," which could reflect confidence or fear, and so forth.

The descriptions noted above are in and of themselves interesting. Perhaps more critical, however, is that the actual nuance of the phrase singing in tune is not understood and warrants detailed interpretative stance. Of the five panelists, two felt that the child sang in pitch or had a good sense of pitch. One noticed that the child would only sing in tune when the therapist had sung with him. The other two panelists felt that he did not sing in tune. Thus, hermeneutic investigation may point toward a variance in the words assigned to the experience. Refining differences between singing in pitch and singing in tune may be an important distinction. Variances such as this reflect the importance of examining description and deriving information that seeks to promote the development language. Hermeneutic investigation will reflect how succinctly or poorly the words music therapists use on a daily basis crystallize or admonish the importance of meaning at-hand. In writing further about music therapy assessment in the medical domain, Loewy (2000) used hermeneutic inquiry a second time, only this time she interviewed staff (MDs, RNs, teachers, and paraprofessionals) to gain insight about how the music therapy descriptive language was understood in terms of the child.

Collaborative Hermeneutic Inquiry in Music Therapy

A working group to design the next meeting of the International Symposium on Qualitative Research in Music Therapy engaged in an innovative collaborative hermeneutic research process in Sauen, Germany, in October 2000. Hosted by the University of the Arts in Berlin, members of the group included Mechtild Jahn-Langenberg, Dorit Amir, Carolyn Kenny, Wolfgang Mahns, Barbara Wheeler, and Gabriele Dorrer. The focus of the research was a transcript from a panel presentation on qualitative research at the 1999 World Congress of Music Therapy in Washington, DC (Kenny et al., 1999). In a sense, this was a research process about research.

The purpose of this collaborative research was to study the themes of the presenters at the Washington, DC, meeting, all of whom were associated in one way or another with the community of qualitative researchers in the ongoing symposium group. Through an interpretation of the ideas and expressions of panel members, they hoped to discover core discursive components that could help to guide the next meeting of the symposium in April 2002. The research question was: Where do we go next in our qualitative research discussions, based on the last meeting and also on the collective sensibilities of the symposium group since 1994?

Each group member studied the transcript, which included the presentations of 10 panel members from the Washington conference. The first step in the research process was to interpret the texts individually by analyzing the material for themes. Sixty-five themes were found when the findings of all six of the working group members were combined.

The second stage of the hermeneutic process was imagining the broader music therapy research community as a whole. Members of the working group, in a dialogical process, made a group list of themes that were implied in the transcripts but not explicitly stated, significant in the broader culture of music therapy research but not stated in the transcripts, or important to each of the members of the working group but also not stated in the transcript. Seventeen themes were created through this process.

A third stage was the collapsing of the themes from the first two stages into a list of emergent themes that had come out of an engagement in the hermeneutic circle of understanding by reflecting on both lists, the individual list of 65 themes, and the collective list of 17 themes. A third list, including 30 emergent themes, was generated from this process.

In the fourth stage of the process, members of the group once again worked individually and created a list of five more emergent themes that were meant to be interpretive categories of the previous stages and processes, based on a deep reflection on what was most significant to each individual member in the culture of music therapy qualitative research. Stated another way, each individual member was to make a list of five categories that he or she believed to be important in the ongoing discourse in music therapy that would maintain the connection between past work in the symposium group and future work, in particular, for the next gathering of the symposium group in 2002.

After individual group members articulated five preferred themes, the next stage of analysis and interpretation was a discursive negotiation, forcing the members to create preferences among the themes for ultimate collective selection. Each of the six members presented his or her five choices and provided an explanation about why these themes were important in the music therapy qualitative research culture. In a sense, each group member became an advocate for his or her individual set of themes, adding a rhetorical component to the research.

The group agreed on the following lists of emergent themes:

1. Meaning, metaphor, symbol, affect/emotion, stories, music, images,
2. Theoretical foundations, boundaries, and definitions; form, function, content, and standards; and ethics,
3. Past, present, and future; history, change, intergenerational, and culture and cultural identity; community, sharing, resources, cultural communication, and biography.

The final result of this process was the discerning of three core themes for the next meeting: meanings, foundations, and histories (sharing stories). The focus question would be: How do we find meaning and provide a theoretical foundation for music therapy within the cultural and social context?

If one is not familiar with the hermeneutic circle or the principles of hermeneutic inquiry, it might be surprising that, after 2 days of working on a research team, the team came up with a total of 22 words as the outcome of their research. Since the purpose of hermeneutics is a serious analysis of texts and an understanding which involves histories and different languages and professional issues, these 22 words are embedded in a collective process of understanding and deep reflection. In such a collaborative inquiry, participants were able to reach a sophisticated level of understanding of the material and a deep feeling of connection to a community of scholars who share the same interests in the society. In this case, the themes that emerged and the question that was formulated from these themes produced a very provocative set of topics for discussion and helped to establish professional collaborations between music therapy scholars at the next symposium. The discourse at the 2002 International Symposium on Qualitative Research in Music Therapy encouraged the elaboration of important concepts for music therapy that continue to be expressed in articles, books, and conference presentation, as well as influence clinical practice around the world.

Additional Examples

Three important German doctoral dissertations, all written in 1988, provide a historical foundation for in-depth hermeneutics in qualitative music therapy research (Langenberg, 1988; Niedecken, 1988; Tüpker, 1988). The work of these pioneers paved the way for further hermeneutic investigation.

Rosemarie Tüpker (1988) laid the foundation for morphological music therapy as a treatment model and concept of understanding. Morphological music therapy is based on morphological psychology (Salber, 1965), a way of thinking that is rooted in Goethe's scientific concepts, psychoanalysis, and gestalt psychology (Tüpker, 2001). In morphological music therapy, specific phenomena of the therapeutic musical action are analyzed in an arts-based approach, utilizing a process of hermeneutic description and reconstruction.Academic studies in addition to publications of case studies and theoretical articles came from this morphological group, including an analysis of group processes from a morphological point of view (Grootaers, 2001) and a concept of understanding the meaning of improvisations (Weymann, 2002).

The work of Dietmut Niedecken, a professionally trained music therapist and psychoanalyst, was very important in integrating music therapy into the psychoanalytic practice of music therapy, based upon the theories of Adorno and Lorenzer. She was the first to practice, research, and publish about psychoanalytically informed music therapy with people with mental disabilities (Niedecken, 1988, 1989).

Isabelle Frohne-Hagemann (1998) embodied Paul Ricouer's (1971/1991) principle of *meaningful action considered as text,* in which he argued that social action can be fruitfully approached as text. Frohne-Hagemann used both a 70-page transcript text and group improvisations in her study of East Berlin women with the purpose of understanding differences between East and West Germany. She felt that her findings helped to develop universally valid statements on the problems of East and West Germans.

Sally McKnight (1998) looked for meaning in responses of Alzheimer's patients using multiple data sources including videotape from actual music therapy sessions, session notes that preceded the session as well as audiotaped descriptions of family members' reactions to the session videos. She analyzed and derived meaning from the responses to music therapy sessions conducted with an elder diagnosed with Alzheimer's disease. McKnight's analysis reflected how a person with serious difficulties with verbal communication, significant memory loss, and uncertain capacity for processing receptive language responded to music therapy, the therapist conducting the therapy, and a family member. Through hermeneutic analysis, the study attempted to extrapolate meaning for both verbal and musical responses. A major assumption of the study concerned the existence of a self-concept and how meaning can be attributed through music. Since Alzheimer's disease is often associated with the loss of self, the study provided clarity to our understanding of a patient with Alzheimer's sense of self in the context of the response to music therapy.

Wolfgang Mahns (1998, 2002, 2004) developed a hermeneutic process of understanding with an emotionally disturbed boy and, more generally, with patients with emotional disturbances using psychoanalytically based music therapy. His method is a multifaceted analysis of improvisation with the focus on finding the very early signals of symbolization in children's inner worlds, called the *birth of a symbol.* Mahns' work is rooted in in-depth hermeneutic inquiry.

Gudrun Aldridge (1998) focused on interpretation of music therapy traces, which refers to the process of understanding as hermeneutics. Her clinical context was creative music therapy with the importance of musical analysis, in this case the meaning of melody.

From a humanistic psychology background, Lars Ole Bonde (2000) also wrote about the hermeneutic framework for understanding GIM sessions. This framework includes the core metaphor, the hidden meaning that emerges through imagery; the ego and self-metaphors, the discovery of the client's personal voice; and the narrative level of interwoven images, the emergence of the client's ongoing self-understanding. In thinking about these three levels, Bonde acknowledges the importance of metaphoric language in the GIM process. This study demonstrated an effective means for therapists-in-training to use a hermeneutic (self-graphic and therapeutic) to deepen their level of understanding of the therapeutic process.

Aigen (1995) wrote that, in hermeneutic research, "primacy is given to accumulating data through direct observation of human practices, rather than through examining beliefs and attitudes through interviews, for example" (p. 292). The essential task of hermeneutics is the assignment of meaning through multiple means of interpretation. Arguably, the direct observation and examination of attitudes through the mechanism of interpretation and how these meanings are derived through words are the elements with which hermeneutic researchers are most concerned. It is for the distinct concern of the very beliefs and attitudes Aigen refers to that hermeneutic researchers collect multiple means of data, seeking through discourse, text, and action, an understanding that will enable the text to have a life of its own (Ricoeur, 1981).

Summary and Conclusions

Hermeneutic research is not the type of inquiry that offers proof of the existence of any phenomenon, unless, of course, we want to say that we exist because we understand. It is an open-ended and circular process that can be marked by diversity and creativity as well as increasing levels of understanding. It also reflects the profound complexity of our human condition and encourages examining these dilemmas through a variety of interpretations. For this reason, hermeneutic researchers have an opportunity to express their intellectual acuity and compassion for the complexities of human situations and societies. Because hermeneutics is literary in nature, it is also aesthetic. As music therapists we are always concerned with aesthetic processes because music is one of the defining elements of our work.

Hermeneutics is characterized by deep reflection. In order to be a competent researcher in hermeneutics, one must understand that such reflection is multidimensional. It takes into account our personal histories, our time in history and the history of ideas, the precision and meanings of words, phrases, melodies, rhythms, the history of our works and fields, and, generally, as many conditions as we possibly can reveal before we create our interpretations. This is a long and rich tradition of research that has themes and variations and a nuanced history. Certainly in the emergence of the culture concept and the sociology of knowledge that challenged 19th century theory, represented by thinkers like Dewey, Benedict, Levi-Strauss, Geertz, Horkheimer, Adorno, Kuhn, MacIntyre, and Ricoeur, this turn to interpretation has become very elaborate. And with the emergence of post-modern thought, thinkers like Foucault, White, Derrida, Rorty, and others have continued to place hermeneutics in the center of their thinking.

In a sense, we are always interpreting our experience and making attempts to understand. Modern hermeneutics focuses on text and other concrete expressions, and actions. But we must not forget that the slow, reflective, and thorough processes demanded of this research method had their origins in the oracles of Delphi. Through a careful examination of the complexities of hermeneutics, we have an opportunity not only to understand the past and present but also to anticipate the future.

References

Addison, R. (1989). Grounded interpretative research: An investigation of physician socialization. In M. Packer & R. Addison (Eds.), *Entering the circle: Hermeneutic investigation in psychology* (pp. 39–59). Albany, NY: SUNY Press.

Aigen, K. (1995). Principles of qualitative research. In B. L. Wheeler (Ed.), *Music therapy research: Quantitative and qualitative perspectives* (pp. 283–311). Gilsum, NH: Barcelona Publishers.

Aigen, K. (2002). *Playin' in the band: A qualitative study of popular music styles as clinical improvisation.* New York: Nordoff-Robbins Center for Music Therapy, New York University.

Aldridge, G. (1998). *Die Entwicklung einer Melodie im Kontext improvisatorischer Musiktherapie* [The development of a melody in the context of improvisational music therapy]. Unpublished doctoral dissertation, University Witten/Herdecke, Herdecke, Germany. Available at http://www.musictherapyworld.net/modules/archive/dissertations/list_all.php

Ast, F. (1990). Hermeneutics. (D. Van Vranken, Trans.). In G. L. Ormiston & A. D. Schrift (Eds.), *The hermeneutic tradition: From Ast to Ricoeur* (pp. 39–56). Albany, NY: State University of New York Press.

Bentz, V., & Shapiro, J. J. (1998). *Mindful inquiry in social research.* Thousand Oaks, CA: Sage Publications.

Bergold, J., & Breuer, F. (1987). Methodologische und methodische Probleme bei der Erforschung der Sicht des Subjekts [Methodological and methodical problems in researching the view of the subject]. In J. Bergold & U. Flick (Eds.), *Einsichten. Zugänge zur Sicht des Subjekts mittels qualitativer Forschung* (pp. 20–52). Tübingen, Germany: DGVT-Verlag.

Bergstrøm-Nielsen, C. (2005). Intuitive Music homepage. http://hjem.get2net.dk/intuitive

Bonde, L. O. (2000) Metaphor and narrative in Guided Imagery and Music. *Journal of the Association for Music and Imagery, 7,* 59–76.

Bontekoe, R. (1996). *Dimensions of the hermeneutic circle.* Atlantic Highlands, NJ: Humanities Press International.

Boothe, B., Wyl, A. von, & Wepfer, R. (1999). Narrative dynamics and psychodynamics. *Psychotherapy Research, 9,* 258–273.

Brown, L., Tappan, M., Gilligan, C., Miller, B., & Argyris, D. (1989). Reading for self and moral voice: a method for interpreting narratives of real-life moral conflict and choice. In M. Packer & R. Addison (Eds.), *Entering the circle: Hermeneutic investigation in psychology* (pp. 141–164). Albany, NY: SUNY Press.

Denzin, N. K. (1970). *The research act.* New York: McGraw-Hill.

Denzin, N. K. (1992). *Symbolic interactionism and cultural studies.* Oxford, UK: Blackwell.

Dilthey, W. (1990). The rise of hermeneutics. F. Jameson (Trans.). In G. L. Ormiston & A. D. Schrift (Eds.), *The hermeneutic tradition: From Ast to Ricoeur* (pp. 101–114). Albany, NY: State University of New York Press.

Eco, U. (1979). *A theory of semiotics.* Bloomington, IN: Indiana University Press.

Faller, H., & Frommer, J. (1994). *Qualitative Psychotherapieforschung: Grundlagen und Methoden* [Qualitative psychotherapy research: Foundations and methods]. Heidelberg, Germany: Asanger.

Flick, U. (1991). Triangulation. In U. Flick, E. v. Kardoff, H. Keupp, L. v. Rosenstiel, & S. Wolff (Eds.), *Handbuch Qualitativer Sozialforschung* (pp. 432–435). Munich, Germany: Psychologie Verlags Union.

Forgacs, D. (2000). *The Antonio Gramsci reader: Selected writings, 1916–1935.* New York: New York University Press.

Frith, S. (1988). *Music for pleasure: Essays in the sociology of pop.* New York: Routledge.

Frohne-Hagemann, I. (1998). The "musical life panorama" (MLP): A facilitating method in the field of clinical and sociocultural music therapy. *Nordic Journal of Music Therapy, 7,* 104–112.

Frommer, J., & Rennie, D. L. (Eds.). (2001). *Qualitative psychotherapy research: Methods and methodology.* Lengerich: Pabst Science Publishers.

Gadamer, H.-G. (1960). *Wahrheit und Methode. Grundzüge einer philosophischen Hermeneutik* [Truth and method: Foundations of philosophical hermeneutics]. Tübingen: J. C. B. Mohr (Paul Siebeck).

Gadamer, H.-G. (1989). *Truth and method* (2nd ed., rev.). New York: Crossroad. (Original work published [translated] 1975)

Geertz, C. (1973). *The interpretation of cultures.* New York: Basic Books.

Grootaers, F. (2001*). Bilder behandeln Bilder—Musiktherapie als angewandte Morphologie* [Images treat images—Music therapy as practical morphology]. Münster: LIT-Verlag.

Hall, S., & Whannel, P. (1965). *The popular arts.* New York: Pantheon Books.

Heidegger, M. (1962). *Being and time.* New York: Harper & Row.

Hoy, D. (1978). *The critical circle: Literature, history, and philosophical hermeneutics.* Berkeley, CA: University of California Press.

Jahn-Langenberg, M. (2003). Harmony and dissonance in conflict: Psychoanalytically informed music therapy with a psychosomatic patient. In S. Hadley (Ed.), *Psychodynamic music therapy: Case studies* (pp. 357–373). Gilsum, NH: Barcelona Publishers.

James, W. (1950). *The principles of psychology* (Vols. 1–2). New York: Holt. (Original work published 1890)

Jüttemann, G. (Ed.) (1990). *Komparative Kasuistik* [Comparative case studies]. Heidelberg: Ansanger.

Karkoschka, E. (1966). *Das Schriftbild der neuen Musik* [The notation of modern music]. Celle, Germany: Moeck Verlag.

Keil, C. (1994). Motion and feeling through music. In C. Keil & S. Feld, *Music grooves* (pp. 53–76). Chicago: University of Chicago Press.

Keil, C. (1995). The theory of participatory discrepancies: A progress report. *Ethnomusicology, 39,* 1–20.

Kenny, C. (1989). *The field of play: A guide for the theory and practice of music therapy.* Atascadero, CA: Ridgeview Publishing Company.

Kenny, C. (1998). Embracing complexity: The creation of a comprehensive research culture in music therapy. *Journal of Music Therapy, 35,* 201–217.

Kenny, C. et al. (1999, November). *Music therapy qualitative research: How music therapy research can influence social change.* Panel presentation at the 9th World Congress of Music Therapy, Washington, DC.

Langenbach, M. (1998). "Nervenmesser"—Zur körperlichen Qualität von Musik und Musiktherapie und der Angemessenheit ihrer graphischen Notation [Emotional measure—On the bodily quality of music and music therapy and the appropriateness of its graphic notation]. *Musiktherapeutische Umschau, 19,* 15–28.

Langenberg, M. (1988). Vom Handeln zum Be-Handeln. Darstellung besonderer Merkmale der musiktherapeutischen Behandlungssituation im Zusammenhang mit der freien Improvisation [From "dealing" to treating: Music therapy—Specific characteristics in the context of free improvisation]. Heidelberger *Schriften zur Musiktherapie,* Band 3. Heidelberg: Herausgegeben von der Stiftung Rehabilitation.

Langenberg, M. (1999). Music therapy and the meaning of affect regulations for psychosomatic patients. In T. Wigram & J. DeBacker (Eds.), *Clinical applications of music therapy in psychiatry* (pp. 232–244). London: Jessica Kingsley Publishers.

Langenberg, M., Frommer, J., & Langenbach, M. (1996). Fusion and separation: Experiencing opposites in music, music therapy, and music therapy research. In M. Langenberg, K. Aigen, & J. Frommer (Eds.), *Qualitative music therapy research: Beginning dialogues* (pp. 131–160). Gilsum, NH: Barcelona Publishers.

Langenberg, M., Frommer, J., & Tress, W. (1992). Qualitative Methodik zur Beschreibung und Interpretation musiktherapeutischer Behandlungswerke [Qualitative method of describing and interpreting works created in music therapy treatment]. *Musiktherapeutische Umschau, 13,* 258–278.

Langenberg, M., Frommer, J., & Tress, W. (1995). From isolation to bonding: A music therapy case study of a patient with chronic migraines. *The Arts in Psychotherapy, 22,* 87–101.

Langenberg, M., Frommer, J., & Tress, W. (1993). A qualitative approach to Analytical Music Therapy. *Music Therapy, 12,* 59–84.

Loewy, J. V. (1995). A hermeneutic panel study of music therapy assessment with an emotionally disturbed boy (Doctoral dissertation, New York University, 1994). *Dissertation Abstracts International, 55*(09), 2631.

Loewy, J. V. (2000). Music psychotherapy assessment. *Music Therapy Perspectives, 18,* 47–58.

Mahns, W. (1998). *Symbolbildungen in der analytischen Kindermusiktherapie: Eine qualitative Studie über die Bedeutung der musikalischen Improvisation in der Musiktherapie mit Schulkindern* [Symbol development in analytical music therapy with children: A qualitative study of the meaning of improvisation in music therapy with school children]. Unpublished doctoral dissertation, Aalborg University, Denmark.

Mahns, W. (2002) The psychodynamic function of music in Analytical Music Therapy with children. In J. Eschen (Ed.), *Analytical Music Therapy* (pp. 95–103). London: Jessica Kingsley Publishers.

Mahns, W. (2004). Symbolbildung in der analytischen Kindermusiktherapie: Eine qualitative Studie über die Bedeutung der musikalischen Improvisation in der Musiktherapie mit Schulkindern [Symbol development in analytical music therapy with children: A qualitative study of the meaning of improvisation in music therapy with school children]. Series: *Materialien zur Musiktherapie* (Vol. 6). Münster: Lit-Verlag.

Mayring, P. (1983). Einführung in die qualitative Sozialforschung [An introduction to qualitative social research]. Munich: Psychologie Verlags Union.

McKnight, S. (1998). *Music therapy and an elder with probable Alzheimer's disease—Looking for meaning in responses: A hermeneutic analysis.* Unpublished master's thesis, Lesley University, Cambridge, MA.

Mead, G. H. (1964). What social objects must psychology presuppose? In A. J. Reck (Ed.), *Selected writings: George Herbert Mead* (pp. 105–113). Indianapolis, IN: Bobbs-Merrill Co. (Reprinted from *Journal of Philosophy, Psychology, and Scientific Methods,* 1910, *7,* 174–180)

Misak, C. J. (1995) *Verificationism: Its history and prospects.* London: Routledge

Mishler, E. (1986). *Research interviewing: Context and narrative.* Cambridge, MA: Harvard University Press.

Niedecken, D. (1988). *Einsätze. Material und Beziehungsfigur im musikalischen Produzieren* [Cues: Material and relationship figure in the production of music]. Hamburg, Germany: VSA.

Niedecken, D. (1989). *Namenlos. Geistig Behinderte verstehen* [Nameless: Understanding the mentally handicapped]. Munich: Verlag Piper.

Packer, M., & Addison, R. (1989). *Entering the circle: Hermeneutic investigation in psychology.* Albany, NY: SUNY Press.

Palmer, R. (1969). *Hermeneutics.* Evanston, IL: Northwestern University Press.

Polkinghorne, D. (1983). *Methodology for the human sciences: Systems of inquiry.* Albany, NY: State University of New York Press.

Popper, K. (1965). *Conjectures and refutations: The growth of scientific knowledge.* New York: Basic Books.

Priestley, M. (1975). *Music therapy in action.* London: Constable.

Rennie, D. L. (2001). Reflections. In J. Frommer & D. L. Rennie (Eds.), *Qualitative psychotherapy research: Methods and methodology* (pp. 185–200). Lengerich: Pabst Science Publishers.

Rennie, D. L. (2004). Anglo-American counselling and psychotherapy: Qualitative research: Critique and call for a middle path. *Psychotherapy Research, 14,* 37–55.

Ricoeur, P. (1981). Appropriation. In P. Ricoeur & J. B. Thompson (Ed. & Trans.), *Hermeneutics and the human sciences: Essays on language, action, and interpretation* (pp. 182–193). Cambridge, MA: Cambridge University Press.

Ricoeur, P. (1991). The model of the text: Meaningful action considered as a text. In P. Ricoeur, *From text to action: Essays in hermeneutics II* (K. Blamey & J. B. Thompson, Trans., pp. 144–167). Evanston, IL: Northwestern University Press. (Reprinted from *Social Research,* 1971, *38,* 529–562)

Ricoeur, P. (1991). *From text to action: Essays in hermeneutics II* (K. Blamey & J. B. Thompson, Trans., pp. 144–167). Evanston, IL: Northwestern University Press.

Ruud, E. (1995). Music in the media: The soundtrack behind the construction of identity. *Young 3*(2), 34–45.

Salber, W. (1965). *Morphologie des seelischen Geschehens* [The morphology of the emotional life]. Ratingen, Germany: Henn.

Schleiermacher, F. D. E. (1990). The hermeneutics: Outline of the 1819 lectures. (J. Wojcik & R. Haas, Trans.). In G. L. Ormiston & A. D. Schrift (Eds.), *The hermeneutic traditions: From Ast to Ricoeur* (pp. 85–100). Albany, NY: State University of New York Press, 1990.

Schütze, F. (1983). Biographische Forschung und narratives Interview [Biographical research and narrative interviews]. *Neue Praxis, 3,* 283–293.

Schwandt, T. A. (2001). *Dictionary of qualitative inquiry* (2nd ed.). Thousand Oaks, CA: Sage Publications.

Scott, J. W., & Keates, D. (Eds.). (2001). *Schools of thought: Twenty-five years of interpretive social science.* Princeton, NJ: Princeton University Press.

Strauss, A. L. (1987). *Qualitative analysis for social scientists.* Cambridge, UK: Cambridge University Press.

Tress, W. (1994). Forschung zu psychogenen Erkrankungen zwischen klinisch-hermeneutischer und gesetzeswissenschaftlicher Empirie: Sozialempirische Marker als Vermittler [Researching psychogenic illness between clinical-hermeneutical and juristic empiricism: Social-empirical markers as mediators]. In H. Faller & J. Frommer (Eds.), *Qualitative Psychotherapieforschung. Grundlagen und Methoden* (pp. 38–52). Heidelberg: Roland Asanger Verlag.

Tüpker, R. (1988). *Ich singe, was ich nicht sagen kann. Zu einer morphologischen Grundlegung der Musiktherapie* [I sing, what I cannot say. A morphological foundation for music therapy]. Bosse, Germany: Regensburg.

Tüpker, R. (2001). Morphologisch orientierte Musiktherapie [Morphologically oriented music therapy]. In H. H. Decker-Voigt (Ed.), *Schulen der Musiktherapie.* Munich: Ernst Reinhardt Verlag.

Valle, R. S., King, M., & Halling. S. (1989). An introduction to existential-phenomenological thought in psychology. In R. S. Valle & S. Halling (Eds.), *Existential-phenomenological perspectives in psychology* (pp. 3–16). New York: Plenum Press.

Watson, K. (1999) *The way I research is who I am: The subjective experience of qualitative researchers.* Unpublished master's thesis, York University, Toronto, Canada.

Weymann, E. (2002). *Psychologische Untersuchungen zur musikalischen Improvisation* [Psychological studies of music improvisation]. Unpublished doctoral dissertation, Institute for Music Therapy at the Hamburg University of Music and Drama, Hamburg. Available at http://www.sub.unihamburg.de/disse/841/dissertation.pdf

Chapter 28
Naturalistic Inquiry
Kenneth Aigen

The interest in qualitative research among music therapists has been motivated by a desire to generate research results more applicable to clinical work than have been generated by quantitative methods. In the human sciences, the impetus behind naturalistic research methods is to provide insight into how and why people act in their natural environment. The idea of studying people in their natural settings came about because of a belief that knowledge about how and why people act in laboratories does not generalize well into other settings. Because it puts such a priority on knowledge that is not constrained by experimental protocols, naturalistic inquiry is well suited to meet the need in music therapy for a clinically relevant research approach. More specifically, there is congruence between the practices and precepts of creative, improvisational music therapy methods and naturalistic approaches to qualitative research (Aigen, 1993) that illustrates the value of illuminating the processes of the former through the methods of the latter.

Overview and Definition

Norman Denzin (1971) defined naturalistic inquiry as

> the studied commitment to actively enter the worlds of native people and to render those worlds understandable from the standpoint of a theory that is grounded in the *behaviors, languages, definitions, attitudes* and *feelings* of those studied. Naturalistic behaviorism attempts a wedding of the covert, private features of the social act with its public, behaviorally observable counterparts. . . . The naturalist is thus obliged to enter people's minds, if only through retrospective accounts of past actions. (pp. 166–167)

First identified as naturalistic research, then as naturalistic inquiry, and currently as constructivism, this approach to research has multiple historical roots and contemporary applications. In this chapter, the origins of naturalistic inquiry will be described as they were discussed in Denzin (1971, 1978). The full development of naturalistic inquiry as presented through the writings of Egon G. Guba and Yvonna S. Lincoln will occupy the largest portion of the chapter, and the contemporary developments promoted by authors such as Lincoln and Guba, Margot Ely, and David Erlandson will then be reviewed. And last, a few examples of naturalistic music therapy studies will be discussed with one study examined in detail.

Theoretical Premises and Historical Roots

Historical Overview

The compilation *Naturalistic Viewpoints in Psychological Research,* edited by Edwin P. Willems and Harold L. Raush (1969), represents one of the earliest publications on naturalistic research. While the origins of the approach in the area of psychology may seem surprising to some because of a common belief that naturalistic inquiry originated in educational research, William Gephart observed that naturalistic inquiry "has its root in ethnography and phenomenology" (cited in Tesch, 1990, p. 43), methods indigenous to anthropology and psychology, respectively.

The term *naturalistic inquiry* was first used by Denzin (1971), who presented its original methodological and philosophical framework. It was taken up in 1978 by Guba, who, together with Lincoln, presented it as a comprehensive research approach in Guba and Lincoln (1981) and Lincoln and Guba (1985). In the latter publication, they observed that while there exists a variety of conceptions of naturalism, Willems' (1969) version was most influential on them.

However, Lincoln and Guba (1990) eventually abandoned the term, preferring the label of *constructivism* for their ideas about research. Subsequently, Erlandson, Harris, Skipper, and Allen (1993) further specified the methodological guidelines of naturalistic inquiry. Guba seems to have demonstrated that while he has chosen to emphasize different aspects of research by using the term *constructivism,* he nonetheless remains fully supportive of methodological advances taken in the name of naturalistic inquiry as indicated by his enthusiastic foreword to the text by Erlandson et al. (1993).

Naturalistic inquiry was introduced into music therapy primarily through the qualitative research activities of the music therapy program at New York University (NYU), where the teaching and publications of Margot Ely (Ely, Anzul, Friedman, Garner, & Steinmetz, 1991; Ely, Vinz, Downing, & Anzul, 1997) have been instrumental. Ely has been an important influence over the work of the present author in guiding the research of the Nordoff-Robbins Center for Music Therapy at NYU, and she has been similarly influential in a number of qualitative doctoral research studies undertaken at NYU that have employed naturalistic principles to varying degrees, for example, Amir, 1992; Arnason, 1998; Austin, 2004; Hammel-Gormley, 1996.

Origins of Naturalistic Inquiry

Denzin (1971, 1978) first introduced the term *naturalistic inquiry,* and his publications provide the basis for the characterization of the early formulation of the approach in this section. Most people who have studied this approach would agree with Renata Tesch (1990) that "the nature of naturalistic inquiry is difficult to describe" (p. 43). Is it an all-encompassing approach to knowledge that includes qualitative research, or is it a more specific type of qualitative research? Tesch acknowledged that one can make a case for either formulation: Its philosophical foundations are explicitly stated and its tenets do not preclude the use of quantitative data, thus supporting the former characterization, and yet specific methodological guidelines have been delineated for its implementation to an extent that would not be expected of a broad intellectual framework, thus supporting the latter. However, naturalistic inquiry is not alone in bearing formulations that exist at different conceptual levels. Other types of qualitative research, such as phenomenology, hermeneutics, and symbolic interactionism, can also be considered as both philosophies and research approaches.

While the writings of its primary proponents support a characterization of naturalistic inquiry as being broader than just a particular qualitative approach, many researchers see it and use it as an approach to qualitative research. One solution is to differentiate between the broader characterization of naturalistic inquiry as *the naturalist paradigm,* containing a set of five foundational axioms, and *operational naturalistic inquiry,* a more narrowly construed formulation of naturalistic inquiry that comprises specific characteristics of research (Lincoln & Guba, 1985, p. 39). The axioms will be examined briefly because they form the foundations from which the specific beliefs and practices are derived, although the majority of the chapter focuses on the more narrow formulation as an approach to research.

From the outset, naturalistic inquiry was put forth as a means for gaining insight into social situations by revealing patterns of interaction. Behavior and inner experiences were the objects of study, with theory development as the goal of research. The perspectives and meaning-making activities of those studied were essential to research focused on everyday life. The idea was to generate understandings of how people functioned in the real world, not in the laboratory. To this end, a number of researcher practices were valued from the outset: participating in the social setting being studied; making efforts to gain the perspectives of those being studied; investigating all aspects of the affective inner life of humans; and maintaining a broad definition of data that includes pictures, images, and verbal descriptions.

The necessity for the researcher to be embedded within the system being studied has directly led to developing relationships with participants, seeing them as equals, and developing methodological maneuvers to handle this level of personal involvement. The researcher's self becomes the primary tool of data gathering and analysis. This practice necessitates discussions in research reports of how the researcher's stance interacted with the field to produce the unique findings.

Generally, the research focus has personal relevance to the researcher and reflects his or her unique stance. The focus is not hypothesis- or problem-centered. The researcher does not enter the field with preconceptions about what will be discovered and what interpretive categories will be most suitable. Instead, the researcher begins by studying the routine, nonproblematic features (Denzin, 1971, p. 177) of settings. By gaining familiarity with the normal, unproblematic functioning of people, problematic areas will emerge within a context that will give them greater meaning. The contents of the researcher's experience gained by introspection are an essential source of data as "the researcher becomes both object and subject in his studies" (Denzin, p. 167).

The researcher's role was articulated by Denzin (1978) in a way that should seem familiar to therapists. Keeping a record of one's actions permits the researcher to be objective and subjective. Researchers should participate with the peers in a way that parallels that of clinical supervision: "By probing his own motives and inclinations and by discussing them with his fellows he can reconstruct the covert dialogues with self that produced the behavior just observed" (p. 7). The individual human self is highly valued, and taking account of individual perspectives is necessary in gaining a full understanding of social behaviors. The observation of public behavior is the starting point, but naturalistic researchers are required to work their way back into the private worlds of research participants.

The flexible approach to method in contemporary naturalistic inquiry and its lack of specificity have its roots in this initial formulation. A role for quantitative data was carved out, and Denzin also emphasized the importance of rigorous and transparent approaches to data analysis. The use of formal interviews is allowed but preference is given to the direct observation of behaviors as they are naturally engaged in. Research participants are respected for their native knowledge of the realities the researcher hopes to understand; they are seen as the experts.

This led Denzin (1978) to encourage the use of research participants (called *native persons*) to check on theory as it develops and to serve as consultants on method. Because it is recognized that different informants may have different perspectives and motivations, he recommended the use of multiple viewpoints that may lead to contradictory accounts and which it is the researcher's task to reconcile through the concept of triangulation. This involved the combining of "multiple data sources, research methods, and theoretical schemes" (p. 21) in order to continually evaluate the interpretations arising from data analysis. Denzin asserted that in the naturalistic perspective no single event is considered to be the "the product of one variable process" (p. 25), thus planting the seed for the theory of causation later developed by Lincoln and Guba (1985) known as *mutual simultaneous shaping*.

In Denzin's (1971) original formulation of naturalism, there were novel elements that have remained part of the approach to the present day (the emphasis on studying living organizations, the use of naturalistic indicators, observing and keeping a record of researcher's actions in the setting), elements that were later abandoned (use of standards of reliability, repeatability, and validity), and elements that straddled the divide (using purposive rather than random sampling, but with the goal of selecting representative examples).

The Full Development of Naturalistic Inquiry

Axioms of the Naturalist Paradigm

The foundations of naturalistic inquiry as a paradigm consist of five axioms found in Lincoln and Guba (1985). They support the practices and beliefs that constitute its research method and bear a brief explication. In order to illustrate that these are of more than esoteric interest, I will provide a brief illustration of how each axiom might come in to play in a hypothetical study of a music therapy group.

1. *There is no single objective reality*. Instead, there are multiple realities constructed by the people who experience them. This means that systematic inquiry will not yield a unified portrait of a particular domain and that insight and understanding, rather than prediction and control, are the goals of research. In studying the process of a music therapy group from the perspectives of its members, for example, the research focus would not be to distill the various impressions into a single account of what *really* happened, but merely to report the various members' constructions of what occurred in order to draw as complete a portrait as is possible.
2. *There is an inseparable and interactive relationship between the knower and the known*. There is no need for the researcher to stand apart from the area of study in order to avoid influencing it because there is no such thing as the undisturbing observer of a social situation. In our music therapy study, if the researcher wanted to interview group members at the conclusion of the therapy process, there would

be no need to utilize a predetermined, structured interview. Instead, the researcher could interact with the participants, using individual insight to engage in a spontaneously directed interview.

3. *It is not possible to make time- and context-free generalizations.* Research leads to findings of a more limited nature that have the character of "working hypotheses" (Lincoln & Guba, 1985, p. 38) rather than of general laws. In studying a particular music therapy group, then, one would not be warranted in extrapolating the findings to another music therapy group in an unqualified way. Generalization can occur, but it must be done tentatively and only if grounded in the similarities between the original group studied and the specific group to which one would like to apply the findings.

4. *There is no strict cause-and-effect relationship as all entities that researchers study are in processes of mutual simultaneous shaping.* Human beings do not act in a deterministic fashion. In studying human domains "everything influences everything else. . . . Each element interacts with all of the others in ways that change them all" (Lincoln & Guba, 1985, p. 151). So, for example, in explaining the specific nature of the process in a music therapy group, it would not be necessary (nor even possible) to attribute the development of group members solely to specific interventions made by the therapists.

5. *Human values are necessarily implicated in research activities—there is no such thing as value-free inquiry.* Researchers make choices guided by values in a number of areas that influence inquiry. Inquirer values are reflected in basic considerations such as the choice of problem, paradigm, and theory that guide an inquiry. The values of the context being studied influence the inquiry as well. In our hypothetical example, if a researcher is also a music therapist, then the entire study will be affected both by the researcher's clinical philosophy and by the degree to which this philosophy is congruent with the philosophy of the therapists participating in the study.

Characteristics of Naturalistic Inquiry

Lincoln and Guba (1985) present 14 characteristics of operational naturalistic inquiry.

1. *Natural setting.* Research is carried out in the settings that researchers would like to better understand. Laboratory research cannot possibly replicate all the important variables that exist in such settings, and the social context of particular settings provides the framework in which findings become intelligible.

2. *Human instrument.* The researcher's self is the primary vehicle for data-gathering and analysis. The use of tools such as questionnaires, personality inventories, and mechanical devices is eschewed because of a belief that none can be as flexible as the human being to adjust to research findings as they emerge. Only human beings are complex and multi-leveled enough to grasp the multitude of factors that influence people in social settings.

3. *Tacit knowledge.* Human beings use all types of knowledge in conducting their daily affairs, not just that which can be stated formally in verbal language. Therefore, all these types of knowledge are used by researchers to gain a more complete understanding of a particular setting, group, or phenomenon.

4. *Qualitative methods.* These methods are preferred because they are more suitable to grasp complex realities and because they better allow researchers to examine the idiosyncratic effects of their own stances upon the research process.

5. *Purposive sample.* Because they are not constrained by the requirements of statistical analysis, researchers are not required to draw random samples. Researchers can study a wider range of individuals and phenomena and select particular entities to study because they are more likely to hold the answer to specific research questions, concerns, or interests.

6. *Inductive data analysis.* Because knowledge is a human construction, not a reflection of a single, objective reality, researchers can use inductive and interpretive forms of data analysis. These strategies are used because researchers

are not seeking unchanging, universal truths but instead are forming flexible working hypotheses for use in specific settings.

7. *Grounded theory.* The complexities of multiple, human realities are not easily captured by preexisting theories. In order to be able to examine a particular setting or phenomenon most comprehensively, it is preferred that the researcher not enter the field with a predetermined theory that will constrict or prematurely focus perceptions, observations, and interpretations. The theory that will be most suited to a particular setting will be theory generated from that setting. Naturalistic inquiry is similar to grounded theory research in emphasizing the value of creating theory grounded in data. However this notion is not as central in the former approach as it is in the latter in which the creation of theory is the ultimate goal of research.

8. *Emergent design.* The findings and structure of a given research project will unfold spontaneously as a result of the unique interaction between the researcher and the setting at a particular time. The knowledge gained as the research unfolds should be actively used by the researcher in guiding the emerging design of the study.

9. *Negotiated outcomes.* The researcher is not the sole or primary authority and instead seeks to share interpretive outcomes with research participants in order to enlist their assistance in making the material better reflect their experiences, feelings, and beliefs. The researcher attempts to reconstruct the realities as experienced by participants and examine the forces that influence these realities; it is thus natural that respondents are in the best position to evaluate such reconstructions and descriptions of the forces that shape their experience.

10. *Case study reporting mode.* This refers not to sample size but to the form and content of the research report. This mode of report is better suited to describing multiple realities and communicating the researcher's interaction with the site or phenomenon of study. Moreover, these nontechnical reports are better suited to being generalized by readers because they parallel the forms of report to which readers are more accustomed.

11. & 12. *Idiographic interpretation and tentative application.* Research findings are portrayed within the specifics of the research setting rather than being formulated as general laws. Local realities contain many factors not replicated in other contexts. Interpretive statements are therefore more accurately considered as a portrait of conditions in a specific locale. Human settings vary extensively and generalizing findings from one setting to another must be done with a great deal of caution.

13. *Focus-determined boundaries.* Just as is it not possible to select the theory or specific methodological steps for a study prior to generating some of the findings, it is similarly recommended to let the boundaries of a study be determined in a fluid manner by the focus as it emerges from the research activity itself.

14. *Special criteria for trustworthiness.* Trustworthiness is how naturalistic inquirers define the criteria for evaluating their studies. Because the conceptual foundations of the naturalistic paradigm are so different from the positivist paradigm (the foundation for quantitative research), the research method of naturalistic inquiry demands different criteria from the traditional ones of internal and external validity, reliability, and objectivity. Because this is such an important topic, it will be taken up later in the present chapter.

Methodology

The Form of a Naturalistic Inquiry

Although naturalistic studies are not designed in the traditional sense with a predetermined method, they do incorporate typical steps that follow each other in spontaneously determined ways. For a flow chart that illustrates these steps, see Lincoln and Guba (1985, p. 188, Figure 8.1). The present discussion is based on their explication of the elements of this figure.

The *natural setting* is the source of the study because the context it provides is necessary to establish the meaning and significance of its findings. The specific, salient characteristics of the context cannot be known beforehand, so the presence of the human instrument is required to adapt to the unknown situation. The researcher uses all forms of knowledge, including tacit knowledge, to become more familiar with the people and setting being studied. Qualitative tools such as direct observations, interviews, and analyzing documents and other artifacts are all used in this process. At this stage, four processes are employed in succession and they constitute a cycle that is engaged in repeatedly: (a) Purposive sampling leads the researcher to engage specific locales, people, or objects which generate data; (b) inductive analysis of the data leads to (c) the construction of grounded theory, which may consist of interpretive statements that form the foundation for theory; the tentatively formulated theoretical statements suggest (d) alterations of the emergent design that lead back to (a) purposive sampling. These steps are repeated until redundancy is reached, as indicated by a decreasing amount of new data and the stabilizing of the theoretical components.

Although the researcher interacts with research participants throughout the study, once the primary activities of data gathering and analysis are nearing completion, this activity becomes more prominent as descriptive and interpretive materials are provided to the participants to see how well the researcher's view of their social world matches that of the participants themselves. The researcher then negotiates the outcomes with the participants, meaning that the researcher either adapts findings to reflect these views or presents information to the readers that some participants disagreed with the conclusions of the researcher. The entire research process is written up in a case study report and the research findings are idiographically interpreted, meaning they are considered to be relevant primarily to the context of study, and they are only tentatively applied to other settings within the research document. The trustworthiness of the study is under constant scrutiny throughout all stages of the research. Those who participate in procedures to ensure trustworthiness can include peers of the researcher, research participants, academic research advisors, contracted research consultants, research auditors, and, of course, the researcher himself or herself.

Considerations on Design, Implementation, Data Gathering, Storage, and Analysis

Each of the topics in this section is typically addressed through a complete chapter in research texts; indeed, a complete book could be written about each one. In the present chapter, it is only possible to make a few comments on each area as it is viewed from the perspective of naturalistic inquiry.

Design. In traditional, quantitative research, a study is completely designed before it is begun. In naturalistic inquiry the design emerges through the activity of the research. "It does not follow, however, that because not *all* of the elements of the design can be prespecified in a naturalistic inquiry, *none* of them can. . . . Design in the naturalistic sense. . . means planning for certain broad contingencies without, however, indicating exactly what will be done in relation to each" (Lincoln & Guba, 1985, p. 226). The authors mention 10 broad areas in which planning can be fruitfully done, although there are no prohibitions on departing from the planning when there is a reason for doing so. Some of these areas include determining a focus, determining where and from whom data will be collected, planning data collection and recording modes, and planning for trustworthiness.

Implementation. Four concerns require attention in the early phases of a study: "making contact and gaining entree to the site; negotiating consent; building and maintaining trust; and identifying and using informants" (Lincoln & Guba, 1985, p. 252). We will briefly examine the establishment of trust between the researcher and research participants, both because it is a defining characteristic of naturalistic study and because it represents one of the clearest departures from quantitative research.

In quantitative research, the relationship between the participant and the researcher is generally one of neutrality. In contrast, in naturalistic inquiry it is recognized that research participants are more likely to provide honest, detailed, and in-depth information to researchers when there is a bond of trust between the two and when participants "respect the inquirer and believe in his or her integrity" (Lincoln & Guba, 1985, p. 256). The establishment of trust does not automatically result in data that are credible, but without this trust data clearly become more suspect.

Data Gathering. Data can be collected from human and nonhuman sources. Human sources of data include interviews, both structured and unstructured, and direct observation. Unstructured interviews are more prevalent at the initial stages of a study, while structured interviews are more prevalent at its concluding stages. While interviews allow the researcher to pursue a directed exploration of the phenomena of study, observation provides the advantage of offering a direct experience of them.

Nonhuman sources of information include documents and records, and unobtrusive informational residues. The latter group includes physical traces of human activity that can be observed and recorded by researchers. This could include the condition of songbooks or musical instruments examined to ascertain frequency of use. Session notes and treatment summaries are examples of documents used by music therapy researchers.

Data Storage. The research log is the repository of all information gathered during a naturalistic study. The contents of the log can be divided into three areas: (a) raw data such as interview transcripts and field observations; (b) analytic memos that include the researcher's speculations about data analysis, including the establishment of categories, connections among categories, emerging ideas about changes in focus and research design, and initial ideas about theory; (c) a reflexive journal in which the researcher records reflections pertaining to the researcher as the instrument of the research. This is an essential part of the log in which the researcher examines any and all emotional reactions to the research for their implications about the interaction between the researcher's self and the milieu of study. The reflexive, self-monitoring that takes place through this type of writing provides insight into the research study and helps to counterbalance the researcher's use of subjective feelings as a source of research data.

Data Analysis. Naturalistic inquiry does not employ a unique mode of data analysis. Instead, the constant comparative method used in grounded theory research, first presented in Glaser and Strauss (1967) and later elaborated in Strauss (1987), is employed because it was created for the study of social processes and because it allows for the "simultaneous collection *and* processing of data" (Lincoln & Guba, 1985, p. 335), an important component of naturalistic inquiry. Because the details of this method are readily available elsewhere, including Chapter 29, Grounded Theory, of the present text, rather than describing it I will instead discuss a few considerations relating to its use within naturalistic inquiry.

In creating categories that emerge from data, it is characteristic of naturalistic inquiry to use labels that primarily reflect how participants in a study conceptualize or construct the nature of their own experience. In adapting Glaser and Strauss's data analysis method into naturalistic inquiry, there are two important differences to keep in mind between the two approaches. First, in grounded theory the purpose of research is to highlight the causative factors operative in social processes in order to be able to predict and explain behavior. This focus on prediction and control is alien to naturalistic inquiry. Second, the entire function of data analysis in the grounded theory approach is to generate theory and, again, this is not true of naturalistic inquiry which is focused instead on creating (re)constructions of the experience of research participants. The fact that naturalistic inquiry borrows important data analysis procedures from grounded theory should not obscure the fundamental differences between the two approaches.

Criteria for Evaluation: Establishing Trustworthiness

Lincoln and Guba (1985) asserted that all researchers are concerned with the trustworthiness of their findings. In order to persuade their audiences of the value of their research results, quantitative researchers concern themselves with questions of truth value, applicability, consistency, and neutrality. They have devised standards of internal validity, external validity, reliability, and objectivity, respectively, to address these concerns.

While qualitative researchers have concerns in the same areas as quantitative researchers, the standards of quantitative research are unsuitable for naturalistic inquiry because quantitative research possesses different conceptual foundations and research methods and therefore makes very different knowledge claims. Lincoln and Guba (1985) proposed the standards of credibility, transferability, dependability, and confirmability as more appropriate to naturalistic inquiry, and they offered procedures to address each standard, some of which will be described below.

Three activities that support the generation of credible findings are prolonged engagement, persistent observation, and triangulation. Prolonged engagement means that the researcher stays engaged with the research study and milieu long enough to establish trust with participants, learn the milieu of study well enough to grasp the context of the culture in which the meaning of events and experiences is found, and filter out intentional and unintentional distortions and examples of selective perceptions reported by research participants. While prolonged engagement provides breadth to a researcher's perceptions and analyses, persistent observation provides depth to them. It makes it possible for a researcher to discern those elements arising in a study that are of greater importance by providing criteria, explicit or implicit, for focusing a researcher's attention on elements of greater saliency. Triangulation is the use of multiple "sources, methods, investigators, and theories" (Lincoln & Guba, 1985, p. 305). The rationale is that when we find a convergence of results generated in different ways and by different individuals, those results become more credible.

Peer debriefing "is a process of exposing oneself to a disinterested peer in a manner paralleling an analytic session and for the purpose of exploring aspects of the inquiry that might otherwise remain only implicit within the inquirer's mind" (Lincoln & Guba, 1985, p. 308). These meetings, which are very close to the process of clinical supervision as employed by psychotherapists, have a variety of functions. The colleagues who participate in this process function like devil's advocates and investigate the researcher's bias and grounds for interpretations, challenging the researcher to support interpretive statements through evidence in the data. Tentative hypotheses can be explored with supportive colleagues in this way, as can possible design decisions. And last, qualitative research can be a lonely and difficult endeavor that challenges the researcher in many ways. The peer support groups in which debriefing processes take place can be a place for the researcher to obtain emotional release and support as well as inspiration.

In conducting member checks, researchers share "data, analytic categories, interpretations, and conclusions" (Lincoln & Guba, 1985, p. 314) with the participants in the research. If researchers want to claim that their constructed interpretations of the realities experienced by their participants are credible, it is important for these participants to have the opportunity to comment upon them.

Contemporary Developments

Naturalistic Inquiry or Constructivism?

Different qualitative research approaches often share some basic characteristics, and the name for a given approach is often a reflection of which of those characteristics is most important. Hence, the name *naturalistic inquiry* reflects the value this approach places on studying people in their natural settings rather than in laboratories.

In publications after 1985, Guba and Lincoln (1989) began using the term *constructivism* to describe their research approach, a choice that reflected their belief that the study of social reality is the study of how people mentally construct the nature of their experience as social beings. They did not create the term *constructivist* or the philosophy it represents, instead adapting it from existing writings on the nature of reality and cognition.

This change on their part illustrates the fact that they are constantly reflecting on their ideas and the nature of their experience and that they continue to further develop and refine the implications of ideas spelled out in previous publications. Does the way that they are articulating constructivism differ in fundamental ways from the way that naturalistic inquiry is portrayed? To my mind, all of the developments are consistent with the original axioms, and in the present chapter we can briefly look at a few of these changes.

Changes in Trustworthiness Criteria

In Lincoln and Guba (1985), the process of triangulation is presented as a credibility check because of a belief that a convergence of findings on a particular construction makes it more credible. In subsequent work, they abandon this function of triangulation because they have more thoroughly thought through its implications. If realities are multiple and are constructed, there is no single objective reality that all people experience so researchers should not expect to find convergences. Divergent findings are equally credible as convergent ones.

In Guba and Lincoln (1989), the authors note that their previously articulated evaluation criteria were exclusively methodological in character. That is, they were based on assessing how well the researcher implemented certain procedures. They observed that this was overly positivistic in character and not well suited to their alternative paradigm. As a result, they developed five authenticity criteria of fairness, and ontological, educative, catalytic, and tactical authenticity, all of which "spring directly from constructivism's basic assumptions" (p. 245). As a group, they are oriented to ensuring that researchers actively seek to illuminate the constructions and values of research participants, enhance these constructions within the minds of participants, and stimulate and empower participants to action based on their enhanced constructions.

Writing the Report

Throughout their writings, Guba and Lincoln expressed the idea that the case study is the preferred mode of report in naturalistic inquiry. By this they did not mean that the study is just of a single person, organization, or community, but that the report is fundamentally different from the type of scientific report that characterizes quantitative research. Naturalistic inquiry methodologists who write about writing assert that there is no single form and that determining the form and content of a report is part of the researcher's task. Erlandson et al. (1993) summarized the function of the report as communicating "a setting with its complex interrelationships and multiple realities to the intended audience in a way that enables and requires that audiences interact cognitively and emotionally with the setting. Such communication is always a work of art and as such may take many forms" (p. 163).

Margot Ely fully embraced this idea of the case study report as a work of art and many of the important ideas about writing in naturalistic inquiry, including the importance of the use of literary narrative devices, have come from her publications (Ely et al., 1991; Ely et al., 1997). The primary rationale for the use of these devices is that they demonstrate that the researcher has lived through the experiences being reported, and they give the reader the same sense of living through something. The idea is to "construct stories in ways that bring readers into the settings, characters, actions, dialogue and events of the research story using many of the same devices that other writers of narrative employ. . . . The narrative aspects of story help us as research writers to create vicariously lived and realistically comprehended stories of what was researched" (Ely et al., 1997, p. 64). In conveying the findings of studies, researchers can use traditional literary forms such as poems, plays, and stories. In addition to these forms are some particular ones adopted by researchers such as vignettes, constructs, themes, pastiche, and layered presentations all of which are described in detail in the two texts by Ely et al. (1991, 1997).

Writing is a central activity in the naturalistic approach. There is a circular relationship that the researcher participates in that implicates the researcher as a whole person. The researcher's self shapes the research, the research activities shape the writing, and writing as an activity can profoundly shape the researcher's self as it is simultaneously an act of self-discovery and discovery about the research findings. Ely et al. (1997) nicely summarized the writer's task: "Through imagination and craft, the researcher tries to penetrate the dimensions of experience below surface appearances and to represent these in compelling words that make the essence come alive" (p. 368).

Music Therapy Examples

In the first section below, three studies are discussed that utilized aspects of naturalistic inquiry combined with elements of other compatible research approaches. The focus of each of these studies will be highlighted along with the aspects of naturalistic inquiry of which they made use. In the second section, a study that is more of a pure example of naturalistic inquiry will be described in more detail in order to show how the conceptual elements of naturalistic inquiry are implemented in practice.

Studies Employing Aspects of Naturalistic Inquiry

Dorit Amir (1992) interviewed music therapists and clients in order to study meaningful moments in the music therapy process. Her research revealed 12 categories of experience on an intrapersonal level and 3 on an interpersonal level. Some examples of the former include moments of freedom, wholeness, and beauty; in the latter category were experiences such as moments of musical intimacy. In addition, the analysis of data revealed the factors that enabled the emergence of these experiences as well as the contributions they made to the participants' lives.

Amir combined aspects of naturalistic inquiry with the data analysis method of grounded theory. She used the idea of the researcher-as-instrument in utilizing her "insights, hunches, feelings, intuitions, and thoughts" (p. 38) in analyzing data, gaining an understanding of the meanings behind the data, and in establishing interpersonal rapport in her interviews. Purposive sampling was used as Amir selected clients and therapists to study based on specific characteristics they possessed that she felt were relevant in answering the questions that she was interested in researching. She also employed the idea of trustworthiness in setting the standards for research, utilizing process of triangulation, peer debriefing, negative case analysis, and member checks. A portion of her results are reported in Amir (1993).

Henk Smeijsters and Hans Storm (1996) used aspects of action research and naturalistic inquiry in illustrating how research is woven into their clinical treatment through a case study of music therapy treatment of a young girl with enuresis and her mother. In this model, a research team works together with the clinical team in using research methods to enhance the ongoing process of therapy.

Member checking was used when transcripts of the therapy sessions were provided to the mother who commented on how well they represented her experiences in the sessions. Triangulation was used in the application of a variety of theoretical models to gaining a greater understanding of the therapy process. Multiple perspectives were employed through combining the ideas and perceptions of the therapist, the researcher, and an outside observer in analyzing the data. And last, peer debriefing was employed as the research conclusions were presented to neurologists and psychotherapists whose role it was to challenge the conclusions of the research and clinical team.

Carolyn Arnason (1998) blended many characteristics of naturalistic inquiry with a formal musical analysis of improvisations in her study of the experience of professional music therapists in an improvisational music therapy group. In studying the therapy group in which she was the therapist, Arnason utilized the natural setting in which she was a participant-researcher. In addition, the focus of her study changed as it broadened from a focus on improvisation to the experience of the group process as a whole. In her report of the research, Arnason used a variety of novel narrative devices such as "anecdotes, layered stories, plays, poems, metaphors, and textual juxtapositions" (p. 46). She also employed techniques for trustworthiness by checking her interpretations with the group members (participant checking) and being a member of an ongoing research support group. This support group is a form of peer debriefing that functions similarly to a clinical supervision group for therapists. Members of the group share their data, interpretations, and personal struggles, and they offer each other support in addition to challenging the researcher's interpretations of the data.

A Detailed Examination of a Naturalistic Study

This study (Aigen, 1997) was one undertaken by the present author. It involved studying the music therapy process of a group of adolescents at the Nordoff-Robbins Center for Music Therapy for one year and it exemplifies some of the primary aspects of naturalistic inquiry.

The *natural setting* was a music therapy group that was conducted as it would have been had it not been the object of research. I did nothing to constrain the interventions of the therapists or to limit them to a set of predetermined protocols. Because all of the sessions at this facility are videotaped, I did not introduce a novel element by recording the sessions. The *human instrument* was the only means for data analysis, as I used no psychological tests or evaluation tools to assess outcomes.

Purposive sampling was illustrated by my criteria for selecting this group for study. The clients were among the oldest and most verbally skilled individuals at this facility, and I assumed that this meant that there would be more sources of information for a researcher than would be the case with a group of nonverbal clients. Also, the relative maturity of the group members suggested that there would be more of a group process to study, as I assumed that the therapists would give more latitude to them than to a group of small children. Last, my familiarity with the two therapists suggested that the clinical work would be interesting to study and that they would participate in the study in a way that would enhance it. In sum, rather than choosing the most representative group to study, I chose a group that would provide a rich and detailed example of the full spectrum of clinical-musical processes that characterize Nordoff-Robbins work.

Prolonged engagement and persistent observation were illustrated by the fact that I observed the entire year of therapy and that I viewed the sessions repeatedly. In fact, some of the sessions were viewed three times: first as I videotaped it, second as I analyzed it alone, and third as I participated in the therapists' indexing session in which they viewed the recording and noted salient events to be taken up in future sessions.

The interaction of knower and known can be seen in terms of the different levels of engagement I had in the phenomena under study. As the person operating the camera, I had control over which events were recorded and how they were framed. The therapists used this record of the session to effect ongoing treatment evaluation and planning. Thus, the clinical process that I was studying was affected by my participation in it, and I was intimately involved in the creation of the phenomena I was studying.

An *emergent design* can be seen in two aspects of the study. First was my participation in the therapist's indexing sessions as described above. At a midpoint in the year, I decided that it would be helpful to see the clinical events through the eyes and ears of the therapists, and so I sat passively in their indexing sessions and observed as they watched the tape and discussed the events. This broadening of the scope of the study led me to interview the therapists in order to get more information about the group process while it was occurring. Neither of these sources of data gathering was planned at the outset of the study.

Negotiated outcomes were employed in that I provided the two therapists with drafts of the study to ascertain how well my impressions of the group members, group process, and therapeutic interventions matched theirs. Although as the author and researcher I was ultimately responsible for the contents of the study, I modified my own descriptions and interpretations in certain instances to accommodate the therapists' perceptions.

The *case study format* of the final report embodied some additional important aspects of naturalistic inquiry and included some *characteristic narrative structures*.

The group members were introduced through the narrative device of *constructs*. A construct is an "inferred soliloquy based on the content of repeated observation and an interpretive composite of. . . characteristic thought and behavior" (Garner, cited in Ely et al., 1991, p. 153) of participants in research studies. I put myself in the mind of the group participants and wrote about what I inferred their thoughts and feelings to be, based on my year of close observation of them. In this way, I wanted the group members to have a voice in the final report and for the reader to have a vicarious experience in getting to know the research participants as people.

Extensive musical notations of improvised songs were provided throughout the text. They were integrated into the narrative so that the reader could switch from reading words to playing music and singing lyrics. By having the reader live through the therapists' music, the *tacit knowledge* embodied in the therapists' skills was made available to the reader to experience.

Additionally, the nature of the music that the clients lived through was as important as any verbal description in providing an accurate portrayal of the group's process for the year. And last, all of the songs were created cooperatively together with the clients. For the reader to live in the music is to more directly experience the unique creative and expressive capacities evoked from the clients by the particular music therapy approach that was studied.

Conclusion

Is a Therapy Session a Natural Setting?

The foundational premise of naturalistic inquiry is that if we want to gain insight into how human beings function in the world, construct their inner realities, and experience others, it is necessary to study them in the contexts that we would like to understand. Psychology laboratories were considered to be bereft of both the social context that renders human actions intelligible and the multitude of factors that influence these actions. In music therapy, most quantitative studies do not examine actual therapy sessions. And those that do often place constraints on the therapist's protocols in a way that does not model how therapists act in sessions that are not being researched. For both of these reasons, the generalizability of many quantitative studies is questionable.

According to naturalistic precepts, to generate research findings that are applicable to actual music therapy sessions, it is essential to study music therapy sessions as they exist in their natural state, that is, without artificial constraints placed them because of research protocols. Of course this does not mean that the therapy sessions are unaffected by the fact of being researched. In the example above, the fact that I was videotaping the sessions that formed the basis for the therapists' ongoing treatment planning, and that I interviewed them during the course of therapy, clearly influenced the therapy process. This is why in a naturalistic study that includes participant-observation and the researcher as instrument, it is essential to speculate upon the effect of the research process on the milieu of study and the overall findings.

In sum, a therapy session is as natural as is any other setting studied by naturalistic methods, such as school classrooms, political meetings, or public social gatherings. What defines an appropriate natural setting is that it shares enough salient characteristics with the domains into which one would like to import the research findings. The judgment that a particular setting is a natural setting, or one that could legitimately accommodate the use of naturalistic inquiry, is context-dependent, with the relevant context consisting of the researcher's aims for the study and the anticipated realm of application.

References

Aigen, K. (1993). The music therapist as qualitative researcher. *Music Therapy, 12*, 16–39.

Aigen, K. (1997). *Here we are in music: One year with an adolescent creative music therapy group.* St. Louis, MO: MMB Music.

Amir, D. (1992). Awakening and expanding the self: Meaningful moments in the music therapy process as experienced and described by music therapists and music therapy clients. (Doctoral dissertation, New York University, 1992). *Dissertation Abstracts International, 53*(08), 4361.

Amir, D. (1993). Moments of insight in the music therapy experience. *Music Therapy, 12*, 85–100.

Arnason, C. (1998). The experience of music therapists in an improvisational music therapy group. (Doctoral dissertation, New York University, 1998). *Dissertation Abstracts International, 59*(09), 3386.

Austin, D. (2004). When words sing and music speaks: A qualitative study of in depth psychotherapy with adults (Doctoral dissertation, New York University, 2003). *Dissertation Abstracts International, 64*(11), 3895.

Denzin, N. (1971). The logic of naturalistic inquiry. *Social Forces, 50*, 166–182.

Denzin, N. (1978). The logic of naturalistic inquiry. In N. K Denzin (Ed.), *Sociological methods: A sourcebook* (2nd ed., pp. 6–29). New York: McGraw-Hill.

Ely, M., Anzul, M., Friedman, T., Garner, D., & Steinmetz, A. M. (1991). *Circles within circles: Doing qualitative research*. London: The Falmer Press.

Ely, M., Vinz, R., Downing, M., & Anzul, M. (1997). *On writing qualitative research: Living by words*. London: The Falmer Press.

Erlandson, D. A., Harris, E. L., Skipper, B. L., & Allen, S. D. (1993). *Doing naturalistic inquiry: A guide to methods*. Newbury Park, CA: Sage Publications.

Glaser, B., & Strauss, A. (1967). *The discovery of grounded theory*. Chicago: Aldine Publishing Co.

Guba, E., & Lincoln, Y. (1981). *Effective evaluation: Improving the usefulness of evaluation results through responsive and naturalistic approaches*. San Francisco: Jossey-Bass Publishers.

Guba, E., & Lincoln, Y. (1989). *Fourth generation evaluation*. Newbury Park, CA: Sage Publications.

Hammel-Gormley, A. (1996). Singing the songs: A qualitative study of music therapy with individuals having psychiatric illnesses as well as histories of childhood sexual abuse. (Doctoral dissertation, New York University, 1995). *Dissertation Abstracts International, 56*(10), 5768.

Lincoln, Y., & Guba, E. (1985). *Naturalistic inquiry*. Newbury Park, CA: Sage Publications.

Lincoln, Y. (1990). The making of a constructivist: A remembrance of transformations past. In E. Guba (Ed.), *The paradigm dialog* (pp. 67–87). Newbury Park, CA: Sage Publications.

Smeijsters, H., & Storm, H. (1996). Becoming friends with your mother: Techniques of qualitative research illustrated with examples from the short-term treatment of a girl with enuresis. *Music Therapy, 14*, 61–83.

Strauss, A. L. (1987). *Qualitative analysis for social scientists*. Cambridge, UK: Cambridge University Press.

Tesch, R. (1990). *Qualitative research: Analysis types & software tools*. London: The Falmer Press.

Willems, E. P. (1969). Planning a rationale for naturalistic research. In E. P. Willems & H. L. Raush (Eds.), *Naturalistic viewpoints in psychological research* (pp. 44–71). New York: Holt, Rinehart and Winston.

Willems, E. P., & Raush, H. L. (Eds.). (1969). *Naturalistic viewpoints in psychological research*. New York: Holt, Rinehart and Winston.

Additional Readings

Guba, E. (1967). The expanding concept of research. *Theory into practice, 6*, 57–65.

Guba, E. (1978). *Toward a methodology of naturalistic inquiry in educational evaluation*. Los Angeles: Center for the Study of Evaluation.

Lofland, J. (1967). Notes on naturalism in sociology. *Kansas Journal of Sociology, 3*, 45–61.

Lofland, J., & Lofland, L. H. (1971/1984). *Analyzing social settings: A guide to qualitative observation and analysis* (2nd ed.). Belmont, CA: Wadsworth Publishing Company.

Chapter 29

Grounded Theory
Dorit Amir

Grounded theory methodology and methods are now among the most influential and widely used modes of carrying out qualitative research when generating a theory is the researcher's principal aim. This mode of qualitative study has spread from its original use by sociologists to the other social science and practitioner fields. . . . What this reflects is a great desire for theoretical explanations and, of course, the increasing use of qualitative materials and their analysis.

Strauss and Corbin[1]

Overview and Definition

Grounded theory is a general approach of comparative analysis linked with data collection that uses a systematically applied set of methods to generate an inductive theory about a substantive area. Its purpose is to "discover theory from data" (Glaser & Strauss, 1967, p. 1). The researcher focuses on one area of study, gathers data from a variety of sources such as interviews and field observations, and analyzes the data using coding and theoretical sampling procedures. That leads to producing a well-constructed theory (Glaser & Strauss, pp. 22–23). Grounded theory was developed by Glaser and Strauss in 1967 in social science and was reshaped and further developed by Strauss (1987), Strauss and Corbin (1990), and Glaser (1998).

The process of analysis through which theory emerges is called *coding* (Strauss & Corbin, 1990). This process requires the researcher's total immersion in the data, becoming intimately acquainted with the data and developing a detailed knowledge of it. This knowledge assists the researcher in shaping and reshaping categories, generating themes, and coming up with grounded theory—a comprehensive description, analysis, and interpretation of data that explains the properties, dimensions, and connections among categories.

Glaser (1998) described the method of grounded theory as trying to "understand the action in a substantive area from the point of view of the actors involved" (p. 115). The analysis consists of three levels: (a) data, (b) conceptualization of the data into categories and their properties, and (c) a conceptual perspective analysis (p. 136).

Theoretical Premises and Historical Roots

Grounded theory was developed within the field of sociology to study social processes. According to Tesch (1990), grounded theory was inspired by phenomenology and was invented as a reaction against an overemphasis on theory verification. Even though grounded theory is generally seen as a qualitative approach to research, Corbin and Strauss (1998) claimed that grounded theory is a general method that can be used in both qualitative and quantitative studies. Its procedures are neither statistical nor quantitative. It does not start with hypotheses or strict questions as do quantitative methods. Tesch (1990) claimed that grounded theory is a research approach that has features in common with positivistic approaches and that its research interest is in the discovery of regularities. However, since grounded theory is both a descriptive and an interpretive type of research, it has to do with reflection and elaboration of meaning as well. The coding process used in grounded theory calls for the discovery of meaning units and requires reflection and conceptualization throughout the analysis.

The epistemology of grounded theory is post-positivist (Strauss & Corbin, 1990), since "one project could yield several different ways of bringing it together" (p. 117). In addition, the multiple testing of explanatory models is one of the hallmarks of post-positivism, placing grounded theory firmly within this research framework (Edwards, 2000).

---

[1] This quotation is from Strauss and Corbin (1997), p. vii.

Grounded theory was originally developed by Barney Glaser and Anselm Strauss, two sociologists with different philosophical backgrounds who worked in a close collaboration. Glaser and Strauss (1967) emphasized that only sociologists can generate sociological theory. Later on, differences built up between the two and they split. Glaser continued by himself to reshape the approach. While his approach is rather formal and rigid, Strauss and Corbin (1990) described grounded theory in a more flexible way. They encouraged researchers from other disciplines to use grounded theory when they say, "One need not be a sociologist or subscribe to the interactionist perspective to use it" (p. 26).

Glaser and Strauss (1967) viewed grounded theory as a whole method. Their basic theme was "the discovery of theory from data systematically obtained from social research (p. 2). In his 1987 book, Strauss took a different approach and called grounded theory a particular style of qualitative analysis of data. He did not refer to it as a complete method. This may mean that grounded theory is a more limited approach to research than are naturalistic inquiry or phenomenology, for example. This allows us to view grounded theory as a "data analysis method focused upon generating theory of social processes that could be fit into any one of many other more general qualitative research approaches" (K. Aigen, personal communication, February 20, 2003). Indeed, historical review shows that grounded theory is used either as a specific methodological paradigm that aims to generate an inductive theory, or as one aspect of research that is usually combined with other qualitative methods. Very few studies represent a complete grounded theory research study, meaning using the specific coding paradigm advocated by Strauss and Corbin, focusing primarily on social processes, and generating a theory[2] (K. Aigen, personal communication, February 20, 2003). Most of the studies take grounded theory as a general outline and a basic set of principles and use specific aspects of its method of analysis. Grounded theory h as been successfully applied in sociology, education, nursing (Strauss & Corbin, 1997), psychology (Tesch, 1990), information systems (Smit, 1999), and music therapy (Amir, 1992; O'Callaghan, 1996).

Methodology

Features of Grounded Theory

Grounded theory follows steps and has features that have been clearly delineated in the literature. They are described below.

Open Coding. The researcher begins to collect the data. Data sources can be transcriptions of interviews, participant observations, protocols, letters, documents, and video and audio material. Once initial data are collected and the researcher starts to become familiar with them, the researcher begins to have a general feel of the data and to dissect patterns, processes, relationships, concepts, and categories (Glaser & Strauss, 1967).

Open coding means that the researcher divides the data into "concepts, concepts into categories, assigning properties to categories, dimensions of properties along a continuum, and breaking properties into dimensions" (Hueser, 1999, p. 61). The researcher then writes a memo to document the coding process. Out of this process, additional questions need to be asked and the data need to be further examined (Strauss & Corbin, 1990). The researcher writes a summary of the findings for each interview or document reviewed.

There are two approaches to open coding: inductive and deductive. Strauss and Corbin's (1990) approach is more inductive—they recommend that codes be developed from the analysis of the data as they are collected—while Miles and Huberman's (1994) approach is more deductive. They encourage the researcher to develop a list of codes before collecting the data, based on the conceptual framework that was developed to design the research questions (pp. 57–58). Either approach is legitimate as long as the researcher is open to adding codes that emerge from the study as it develops (Hueser, 1999).

An initial and general structure of categories can initially be set up based on research questions and expected themes. This early structure changes as the actual themes develop from the data. The data are coded and recoded several times. Open coding is essentially interpretive rather than just providing summaries (Robson, 2002).

---

[2] Examples of complete grounded theory studies can be found in Strauss and Corbin's (1997) *Grounded Theory in Practice.*

Theoretical Sampling and Saturation. Theoretical sampling is "a means whereby the analyst decides on analytic grounds what data to collect next and where to find them. . . this process of data collection is controlled by the emerging theory" (Strauss, 1987, pp. 38–39). An "adequate sample" is "determined by the researcher and occurs when further sampling fails to reveal additional categories, properties, or interrelationships" (Glaser & Strauss, 1967, p. 63. Then the researcher stops collecting data and proceeds to the next research step. Repeated data collection "only adds bulk to the coded data and nothing to the theory" (Glaser & Strauss, p. 111). Once theoretical saturation has occurred, the researcher begins determining the relationships between categories using a process called axial coding.

Axial Coding. Axial coding involves procedures for connecting categories found in open coding. Coding processes concern matching "conditions, context, action/interactional strategies and consequences" (Strauss & Corbin, 1990, p. 96). The object is to uncover causal conditions for phenomena observed in the data analysis and to determine the dimensions of the phenomena, as well as to determine dimensions of categories found in the open coding with additional data gathering. In order to explain and document the data and the coding, an axial coding memo about the phenomena, categories, dimensions, and conditions is prepared.

Selective Coding. Selective coding is the process of identifying core categories from the analysis and relating them in a systematic way to other categories found in the analysis. This process allows the researcher to find additional categories. The researcher organizes the categories in groups and grounds the theory by constantly comparing it against the data. If there are gaps in the data, the researcher goes back to the categories and fills in missing details (Strauss & Corbin, 1990, p. 141).

Process. Process is the action and interaction sequences associated with the category and phenomenon uncovered by the analysis. It covers the sequencing of changes in actions and interactions over time and the responses to those changes.

Memos and Diagrams. Memos are the means of documenting the findings in a grounded theory investigation. They are prepared as the study progresses and follow each of the coding sessions of the raw data. One can use diagrams to demonstrate the relationships between the phenomena documented in the memos (Strauss & Corbin, 1990).

Theoretical Sensitivity. Theoretical sensitivity is the ability to recognize what is important in the data and to give it meaning (Strauss & Corbin, 1990). Its four sources are: (a) the literature, gaining familiarity with various publications on theory and research; (b) professional experience, the knowledge one has gained throughout years of practice; (c) personal experience; and (d) the analytic process, all of which provide insight and understanding concerning the phenomenon under study. It is important to state that all these steps and features are not necessarily sequential but likely to overlap.

Synthesis Throughout the analysis, theory is built through constant interaction with the data, constant comparison, and asking questions of the data (Robson, 2002). After the categories are integrated and synthesized into a core set of categories, the researcher develops a narrative in which the properties, dimensions, and circumstances under which they are connected are explained. This narrative of the phenomenon under investigation is the grounded theory. The researcher tells the story of the specific area of study from the point of view of the actors involved as understood and interpreted by the researcher (Glaser, 1998). Strauss and Corbin (1990) gave four central criteria as applicable to theory generated by the grounded theory process: "fit, understanding, generality and control" (p. 23).

Trustworthiness

Inductive methods must be thoroughly grounded in the data after the researcher has reached theoretical saturation of the sample selected for analysis. One needs to evaluate theoretical sampling, depth of research, and clarity of methods in order to assure validity, reliability, and credibility of the research.

Liu (1996) suggested the following methods for verification of both internal and external validity. For internal validity, triangulation (multiple data collection methods), informant verification, and explicit clarification of the researcher's bias are used. Grounded theory is an example of interpretive research and therefore it is important that the researcher clearly states his or her biases, values, and judgments about the data (Hueser, 1999). For external validity, rich description of the data, multiple methods of data collection and data analysis, and expert and peer review are important.

Computer Programs

It is not always necessary to use a computer program to do grounded theory research, but this can help to collect and analyze the data. These programs relieve much of the tedious manual labor associated with this kind of research and allow the researcher to make sense of much more data in a reduced amount of time.

Computer programs that are used for qualitative research were described in Chapter 15, Software Tools for Music Therapy Qualitative Research. NUD*IST and ATLAS.ti have been found to be particularly useful for analyzing grounded theory data.

Relationship to Other Types of Research

Many qualitative approaches to research have similar procedures to the grounded theory method of analysis, such as the importance of grounding findings in the data and analyzing data systematically and intensively into sets of categories and themes (see Bogdan & Biklen, 1982; Ely et al., 1991; Lincoln & Guba, 1985). In its philosophical perspective, grounded theory is closely related to phenomenology, since it takes an explicitly phenomenological stance (Glaser & Strauss, 1967). Both phenomenology and grounded theory ask the researcher to bracket existing notions about a phenomenon (Tesch, 1990). This is done by reflecting again and again on the data during analysis. An example of this can be seen in Forinash's (1990) study, *A Phenomenology of Music Therapy with the Terminally Ill*. Forinash recorded 10 sessions with terminally ill patients. While she bracketed her preexisting notions about this phenomenon, she made several rounds of reflections in which she uncovered the essential structures of the music therapy experience with the terminally ill. Amir (1992) did similar rounds of reflection in her grounded theory study of meaningful moments. She went back and forth from the data to the analysis and vise versa, reflecting at each step and trying to uncover the meaning of the data without the use of preexisting knowledge.

The main difference between grounded theory and phenomenology is the primary concern of the researcher. While grounded theory researchers are primarily concerned with theory building and follow specific predetermined procedures of data analysis, phenomenologists are less concerned with building a theory and tend to take more freedom in establishing procedures for analysis (Aigen, 1995b; Tesch, 1990). Some phenomenological approaches that have been used in music therapy have systematic approaches to analyzing data (see Amir, 1992; Forinash, 2000; Forinash & Gonzalez, 1989; Kasayka, 1991). These approaches have more in common with grounded theory than with less systematic approaches, although they do not aim towards building a theory.

A common method of gathering data in many types of qualitative research is the interview. Both phenomenological inquiry and grounded theory use interviews that are open ended (and may also be semi-structured) and seek to understand the deep meaning of the phenomena under study. An example of a study that shares elements of grounded theory and phenomenology is this author's study of musical and verbal interventions in music therapy (Amir, 1999). Six experienced music therapists were interviewed by the researcher, who utilized *dialogal interviews* (Colaizzi, 1978; Forinash, 1995) as the method of data gathering for the purpose of *imaginative listening*. In a dialogal interview, the researcher interviews the participant about the experience she or he is interested in studying and is able to extract the content as well as nonverbal cues (Colaizzi, p. 62). Two models of qualitative analysis served as a basis for this research: Colaizzi's first phenomenological method, *protocol analysis*, and Ely's model (Ely et al., 1991), which consists of the discovery of core categories and themes. A core category is one that is related to as many categories and subcategories as possible and is central to the integration of the findings; a theme is a statement of meaning that runs through all or most of the categories or a category in the minority that carries meaningful impact (Ely et al.). Even though this study does not follow the steps of grounded theory analysis in an exact manner, it does arrive at a theory that is grounded in the data. This part of the study can thus be considered as a modified grounded theory approach.

There are research studies in music therapy that developed a theory but did not follow a grounded theory method. For example, in his study of the therapist being there for his client, Bruscia (1995) developed a theoretical model that is totally grounded in his data. However, he did not use grounded theory procedures or techniques.

Heuristic research also grounds findings in the data. Wheeler's (1999) research in which she investigated her experience of pleasure in working with children with severe disabilities is an example of heuristic research, in which the researcher studied her own feelings. Even though she did not aim towards theory building, she came up with categories (intentionality, emotionality, communication, and mutuality) that can be considered as "building blocks to generalizations" (Aigen, 1995a, p. 336) concerning the therapist's sources of pleasure when working with children with severe disabilities. Therefore, it can be argued that this study created a small theory that is grounded in the data, so, while it would not be classified as a grounded theory study, it contains elements of grounded theory. The same can be argued concerning data analysis. Although the researcher did not follow the exact steps of grounded theory, she formulated categories and subcategories, reflected again and again on her data, revised categories, and added to the descriptions until she came up with her small theory. This process of analysis has elements of grounded theory, such as open, axial, and selective coding. Tesch's (1990) map of qualitative research types placed grounded theory with other types of qualitative research that aim at the discovery of regularities, such as ethnography, content analysis, phenomenography,[3] and naturalistic inquiry (p. 63). Naturalistic inquiry also grounds findings in the data and can employ a grounded theory method of analysis although it does not aim towards generating a theory. Instead, naturalistic inquiry puts an emphasis on studying people in their natural environments.

Aigen's study of an adolescent creative music therapy group, *Here We Are in Music* (1997), is a naturalistic music therapy study that has purposive sampling, natural setting, prolonged engagement, and negotiated outcomes in common with grounded theory. Aigen wanted the group members to be heard in the final report and accomplished this through methods such as written constructs of what participants might be thinking and feeling and musical notations of improvised songs sung by the participants. This is similar to the method of grounded theory that is described by Glaser (1998) as trying to "understand the action in a substantive area from the point of view of the actors involved" (p. 115).

Grounded theory, symbolic interactionism, and action research are concerned with theory building. The goal of symbolic interaction research is to formulate propositions about relationships among categories of data and weave them into a theoretical scheme (Tesch, 1990). The goal of action research is to generate theories of practice (McNiff, 1988). In carrying out grounded theory research, the researcher is expected to go back and forth to the field to collect data. The data are analyzed between visits (interviews). "This movement back and forth. . . is similar to the 'dialogic' process central to the hermeneutic tradition" (Robson, 2002, p. 193).

> The text is returned to time and time again. Initial understandings are refined through interpretation; this then raises further questions, calling for a return to the text and revision of the interpretation. Throughout the process, one is trying to understand what it means to those who created it and to integrate that meaning with its meaning to us. (Robson, pp. 197–198)

---

[3] Phenomenography is:

> The empirical study of the limited number of qualitatively different ways in which we experience, conceptualize, understand, perceive, apprehend, etc., various phenomena in and aspects of the world around us. These differing experiences, understandings, etc., are characterized in terms of categories of description, logically related to each other, and forming hierarchies in relation to given criteria. Such an ordered set of categories of description is called the outcome space of the phenomenon, concepts in question. . . . The categories of description corresponding to those differing understandings and the logical relations that can be established between them constitute the main results of a phenomenographic study. (Marton, 1994, p. 4424)

Music Therapy Examples

When reviewing the music therapy literature, one notices that there are some grounded theory studies where the researcher uses the grounded theory data analysis method, focuses on social processes, and creates a theory. In most of these studies, researchers use modified versions of grounded theory (see Edwards, 2000; O'Callaghan, 1996; Ruutel, Ratnik, Tamm, & Zilensk, 2004) and sometimes mix aspects of grounded theory with other kinds of qualitative (and sometimes quantitative) research (see Ala-Ruona, 2002; Moe, 2002; O'Callaghan & Colegrove, 1998; Ramsey, 2003). In other words, these researchers use aspects of grounded theory but do not follow every detail of the method or do not create a full theory.

This brings up two important questions: First, why are there so few grounded theory studies in music therapy? And second, why do we almost never see a full application of the grounded theory approach? These questions are related.

A general reason for not finding many grounded theory studies is because the profession of music therapy is still young in performing qualitative research in general and grounded theory in particular. Even though grounded theory research methods have been around since the 1960s, the first grounded theory study in music therapy was published in 1992 (Amir). Thus, grounded theory research in music therapy is still relatively new, and each researcher has to adapt or modify its methods to music therapy.

If we look at the nature of grounded theory, we see that Glaser and Strauss (1967) intended their approach to be applicable for studying social processes. Music therapy researchers are interested in studying musical and psychological processes as well, which may mean that the researcher has to adapt parts of grounded theory and supplement its ideas with those from other authors (K. Aigen, personal communication, February 20, 2003). There are difficulties in theory building, both practical and ideological. Practical difficulties include the amount of time necessary to complete a grounded theory study, and access to potential data and participants, both of which mean that theoretical sampling may need to be compromised and the researcher may need to impose a limit on the data collection (C. O'Callaghan, personal communication, February 19, 2003). In the postmodern era, where theories are being reconstructed and deconstructed according to changeable life circumstances, researchers stop short of theory development. "We realize that there will always be new potential data, so that theories can only be viewed as tentative and in a state of evolution" (C. O'Callaghan, personal communication, February 19, 2003).

Another problem is that researchers do not have the knowledge, experience, or financial resources to conduct complete grounded theory studies. There are no specific grounded theory courses in music therapy training programs, unlike fields like nursing and sociology in which students are required to take courses in grounded theory (D. Aldridge, personal communication, January 26, 2003). There are governmental or institutional constraints on funding such long research projects. Therefore, it is easier for researchers to use a modified version of grounded theory—it takes less time and one can study a smaller number of informants.

As a result, many music therapy researchers prefer to view grounded theory as one aspect of qualitative research instead of seeing it as a complete method. This view allows researchers the freedom to mix grounded theory with other kinds of qualitative research and not to feel obliged to do a pure grounded theory study.

Examples of published and unpublished music therapy research studies are described below. This includes studies that use a complete or modified version of grounded theory, are informed or inspired by grounded theory, or mix aspects of grounded theory with other methods.

Grounded Theory Studies

I would like to use my own study on meaningful moments in music therapy as an example of a grounded theory study. In order to illuminate how music therapists and clients experienced meaningful moments in the music therapy process, I used a qualitative method of grounded theory for both data gathering and analysis (Amir, 1992, 1993, 1996). My study was concerned with social, musical, and psychological processes. I followed Glaser and Strauss' coding method (1967) and developed a grounded theory of 15 meaningful moments, conditions under which these moments may occur, and the contribution of these moments to the participants' lives. Even though I consider this study to be grounded theory, I was also influenced by the writing of others such as Ely et al. (1991), Bogdan and Biklen (1982), and Lincoln and Guba (1981) and used some of their concepts and methods in the study. The reasons for using other models were two: I view grounded theory as a specific method, and I was influenced by my teacher, Margot Ely, who explained that different terms are being used in a "roughly synonymous way" (Ely et al., p. 2) and uses *qualitative research* as an umbrella term.

In this study the research instrument was an open interview. I interviewed four experienced music therapists and four clients who provided the data I needed in order to formulate a theory *(theoretical sampling)*. When I realized that the categories start repeating themselves, I stopped collecting data and proceeded to the next research step *(saturation)*. The actual analysis consisted of nine steps:

1. All interviews were audiotaped and transcribed verbatim. After I finished transcribing each interview, I added comments about my own feelings, thoughts, and impressions throughout the interview.

2. I started to become familiar with the content of each interview through listening to the tapes and reading the transcribed material, and created an initial organization of data into categories for each interview *(open coding)*. For example, the organization of each interview suggested at this point categories such as client's and therapist's background information; examples of meaningful moments; and feelings, images, reactions, and explanations about the meaning of the experience for them.

3. I read the transcriptions and listened to each interview for the second time, started to connect categories that were found in the open coding *(axial coding)*, and came up with further lists of categories, such as client's or therapist's emotional reactions, physical reactions, and spiritual feelings and meanings. Description of the music and the context were also included.

4. I again read each transcription and the analysis of each interview and started to refine the categories by finding core categories and subcategories for each interview *(selective coding)*. This was done by cross-analysis of the different examples in each interview. For example, client's emotional, physical, spiritual reactions were organized as subcategories in a new core category for all the examples: client's intrapersonal experience. The same was done for the therapist. In addition, new core categories, such as conditions that allowed the client and the therapist to have these intrapersonal experiences, were discovered. This category included subcategories such as clients' and therapists' perceptions of themselves; clients' readiness and commitment; and clients' and therapists' perception of music and music therapy, trust, and the client-therapist relationship.

5. I wrote profiles for each participant that included three main parts: basic information about the participant, description and analysis of each example of client's or therapist's meaningful experience, and a cross-analysis of all the examples together. This analysis included three core categories: (a) the components and characteristics of all the examples, (b) the conditions that spawned these experiences, and (c) the contribution of these experiences to the clients' lives.

6. By this stage, I had four profiles of clients and four profiles of music therapists. This step included a second level analysis: cross-analysis of all the clients' profiles together and all the therapists' profiles together. I compared the three core categories of the cross-analysis in each profile and organized them all together *(selective coding and process)*. For example, all the clients' intrapersonal experiences were put together and became a core category, while each component and characteristic of these experiences became subcategories. These subcategories included a sense of freedom, a sense of spirituality, a sense of intimacy, insight, a sense of integration, and a sense of being whole. The same was done with the other two core categories, conditions and contributions.

7. At this time, I had two sets of analysis, one pertaining to clients' profiles and the other including therapists' profiles. I read again what I did in step 5 and started to see that each component was, in fact, a meaningful moment in the process of music therapy as described by clients and therapists. Now the subcategories changed to moments of insight, moments of freedom, moments of spirituality, and

moments of intimacy. I compared the moments that emerged in the clients' cross-analyses with the moments of the music therapists' cross-analyses and saw that, out of 15 moments, 12 were the same.

8. I organized all the moments, the conditions, and the contributions of these moments of both clients and therapists together and further refined the categories. For example, in the clients' analysis I had moments of accomplishment. The music therapists talked about their clients' moments of achievement and their own moments of feeling proud after their clients had a strong moment. It became clear that all three could be organized under the same category: moments of completion and accomplishment. Throughout steps 1–8, I documented the findings and followed each of the coding sessions of the raw data *(memos)*. I also used a diagram to demonstrate the relationships between the core and subcategories of meaningful moments documented in the memos *(diagrams)*.

9. At this final stage, I wrote up and presented the theory *(synthesis)*. I organized the findings in two sections: The first section consisted of eight profiles, four clients and four music therapists. Each profile included some background information about the participant and two to three vignettes. All the vignettes were organized by me and consisted of the participants' verbatim descriptions. The second section consisted of the second level analysis that stemmed from the previous step. This section included meaningful moments, the factors that allowed these moments to come to birth (categories of conditions that influence meaningful moments), and the contribution of these moments to the participants. *Theoretical sensitivity* was used in order to recognize what was important in the data and give it meaning.

To ensure internal and external validity (trustworthiness of the study), I used several methods. For internal validity I had *intensive contact* with the participants and the phenomenon under study. With all the participants I conducted intensive interviews until I felt that no additional material was surfacing in spite of probing. I also became thoroughly familiar with the content of the interviews by repeatedly listening to the tapes and reading the transcriptions and the process notes. In addition, I made sure that I had *informant verification* when, while conducting second interviews with my participants, I checked some of the findings with each of them. When the profiles were ready, I gave six participants their personal profiles and asked them to check the categories against their own experience. This was done to ensure that I understood meanings as participants intended to convey them. A few of the participants corrected some of the findings, and these corrections were included in the final analysis. For external validity, I used *peer debriefing*. Throughout the study I participated in a peer support group consisting of three doctoral students doing qualitative studies. I reported and shared with the group some of the interviews and all of my analysis throughout the process. The group members assisted me in developing and checking categories and emerging theory and gave me support whenever I needed it. At the same time I gave other profiles to two of my music therapy colleagues in order to get their opinions, which helped me to reshape and refine my theory. I incorporated *expert review* when, as an inexperienced researcher doing my dissertation, I worked under the guidance and supervision of an experienced qualitative researcher.

The grounded theory that was constructed out of the data had a descriptive portion (profiles of participants and types of moments) and an interpretative portion (the conditions that give rise to each type of moment and the contributions of the moments to the participants' lives). All 15 moments were organized in two sections: moments that occurred on an intrapersonal level and moments that occurred on an interpersonal level. Twelve of the moments occurred on an intrapersonal level: moments of awareness and insight; acceptance; freedom; wholeness and integration; completion and accomplishment; beauty and inspiration; spirituality; intimacy with self; ecstasy and joy; anger, fear, and pain; surprise; and inner transformation. Three moments occurred on an interpersonal level: moments of physical closeness between therapist and client; musical intimacy between therapist and client; and close contact between the client and a significant person in his or her life. It is important for the reader to realize that these moments were not experienced as linear: They did not have only one dimension and did not come one after the other. All were experienced as multidimensional and some of them were experienced simultaneously.

Factors that allowed these moments to come to birth were organized in four categories: (a) environmental factors: music and being a part of a music therapy group; (b) therapist's intrapersonal factors: knowledge and experience; listening to inner impulse, instinct, and intuition; listening and exploration of the client's needs; trust; perception of therapist-client relationship; and a set of beliefs that influenced the work; (c) client's intrapersonal factors: meaning of music; view of self; readiness, inner motivation, and commitment to the work; courage in taking risks; perception of music therapy as a special place; perception of the music therapist and the relationship between client and therapist; and client's trust; and (d) process. The process made the moments possible; likewise, the moments made the process successful. The process bred familiarity and fueled the trust. The clients were motivated to be more involved in the process, allowing them to take more risks and to experience success and delight. The contribution of these moments to the participants' lives ranged from improved self-esteem, emotional and physical health, and interpersonal relationships to no improvement outside of therapy. The contribution of these moments to the therapists' work and lives included improved therapeutic skills and personal growth.

The following additional examples of research studies in music therapy use grounded theory as a method of analysis and result in grounded theory.

Nagler (1993) employed a method based on grounded theory procedures and techniques in his study, *A Qualitative Study of Children in Crisis: Interventions Through Music Therapy and Digital Music Technology.* The purpose of the study was to determine if music created by children using digital technology was appropriate for addressing their issues. Participants were children in crisis who used electronic musical instruments in their music therapy sessions. Nagler explained that he chose to use the grounded theory method because of the nature of the data in his research. Reduction of the participants' responses to the numbers necessary for statistical analysis would not have allowed for the richness of the children's experiences to come forth. The analysis followed grounded theory procedures of open, axial, and selective coding. The categories were then formulated into a taxonomy that was reshaped and redefined until it reached its final presentation. The analysis led to the formulation of two grounded theories: (a) The therapeutic process in which the three core categories that comprise this theory and represent three stages of therapy were trust, awareness, and internalization; and (b) transparent technology where the two core categories that comprise this theory were musical structures (improvisation: solo, duet, and trio; directed musical activities; music-making using precomposed music and songwriting) and the participants' relationships to the digital music technology (imagery associated with digital music technology, instrument, preset rhythm patterns, and timbre choices). The purpose of the second theory, transparent technology, was "to explain and clarify the interaction between the participants and the digital music technology under study" (p. 53).

In his study "Music and Identity," Ruud (1997) used musical and verbal forms of autobiography to examine how 60 music therapy students constructed their identities. He asked the first group of 20 students to make a tape of 10 to 15 pieces of music that were significant to them and then interviewed each student about the tape. He asked the second group of 40 students to write a 10-page commentary on the music selected in addition to making the tape. The verbal data were analyzed according to the guidelines of Strauss and Corbin's (1990) version of grounded theory. The task of the analysis was "to make explicit the main theme of this study, that is 'music and identity' through constructing some core categories out of the material. Further, it was intended to give these categories a richer description through identifying relevant subcategories or dimensions in each category" (Ruud, p. 4). Ruud developed a theory of four core categories, ways in which music helps to construct a person's identity: (a) music and personal space, (b) music and social space, (c) the space of time and place, and (d) the transpersonal space.

Moe (2002), in "Restitutional Factors in Receptive Group Music Therapy Inspired by GIM," examined nine patients diagnosed with schizophrenia or schizotypical disorders who participated in a GIM music therapy group that lasted for 6 months. In order to study the effect of music therapy on the patients' levels of functioning and their own evaluations of the music therapy, Moe used the Global Assessment of Functioning Scale (GAF), a questionnaire administered after termination of therapy, a semi-structured interview that included questions based on cards with written qualities, and additional questions concerning the patients' views of the therapy (p.156). A qualitative analysis that was inspired by grounded theory was used to analyze the experiences and images of four out of nine patients.[4] The analysis included both individual and characteristic patterns of all four patients. The patients' experiences of important

---

[4] Only the results of the qualitative analysis are reported here.

issues concerning the group were also categorized. The analysis confirmed the patients' overall positive view of the therapy. The researcher developed eight categories in which restitutional factors occurred and formulated a theory concerning the relationships between self-objects, psychological defensive maneuvers, and restitutional factors.

Modified Grounded Theory Studies

Some researchers used a modified version of grounded theory in order to either systematically develop a full description of the phenomenon under study or to generate more information about a phenomenon, but did not aim to come up with a theory. Some studies also combine elements of grounded theory with other methods. Examples of such studies follow.

O'Callaghan (1996), in "Lyrical Themes in Songs Written by Palliative Care Patients," used modified grounded theory and content analysis to discover and analyze lyrical themes in 64 songs written by 39 patients in palliative care. The aim of the study was to systematically develop descriptions that encompassed all of the phenomena expressed in the lyrics. The researcher imposed a limit on the data collection and did not come up with a theory. The steps that guided the lyric analysis of the songs included open coding, axial coding, and alternations between open and axial coding (Strauss & Corbin, 1990). The researcher added two more stages: verification and finding the frequencies of the categories and themes in the songs. Eight themes emerged: messages, self-reflections, compliments, memories, reflections upon significant others (including pets), self-expression of adversity, imagery, and prayers (O'Callaghan, 1996, p. 74).

In another study, "Effect of the Music Therapy Introduction When Engaging Hospitalized Cancer Patients," O'Callaghan and Colegrove (1998) researched the relationships between styles of music therapy introductions made by music therapy students when trying to engage patients hospitalized with cancer, and the comfort levels of the patients. The researchers used both modified grounded theory and content analysis to analyze the written descriptions of the music therapy students' introductions. The researchers found that some styles of offering music therapy were associated with patients agreeing to receive music therapy. O'Callaghan (2001) researched experiences of patients, visitors, and staff members involved in a music therapy program in a cancer hospital during 3 months in order to find out the relevance of music therapy for the patients. The participants of the study provided written feedback about the program anonymously by answering open-ended questions. These answers, together with the music therapist researcher's reflective journal, were analyzed in a thematic analysis based on grounded theory. ATLAS.ti software was used to assist with the data management and analysis. First, codes were generated by the researcher to denote text fragments from the transcripts of the written responses and researcher's journal (open coding; O'Callaghan, 2001, p. 157). Then "the codes were compared and similar coded phenomena were grouped into categories" (axial coding; p. 157). Third, "similar categories informed the descriptive thematic labels" (selective coding; p. 157). The researcher constantly compared the data until the themes and the categories adequately described the text and were grounded in the data. All 128 patients who responded to the questionnaire indicated that music therapy was a positive experience.

Edwards (2000), in her study "Keeping Things Going': Techniques Used by the Music Therapist with Children in a Hospital-Based Rehabilitation Service," used a modified grounded theory method as described by O'Callaghan (1996) to identify and categorize the techniques used by the music therapist in working with children in a pediatric rehabilitation service. After transcribing and analyzing music therapy sessions with three patients, the researcher identified eight categories of techniques: cuing, synchrony, choices, orientation, preparation, feedback, incorporation, and humor. Outcomes clarified aspects of the practice of music therapy in pediatric rehabilitation, a relatively new area of music therapy research, and therefore contributed to the development of music therapy practice and research in music therapy with children in a rehabilitation service. Edwards used the method of grounded theory to generate categories and themes in order to inform the work of the music therapist in a new program. In order for a grounded theory to be developed, these categories and themes would need to be further explored, and the researcher would need more data, such as an examination of these categories and themes in different contexts such as work in other centers or work with clients of different ages and genders who are in rehabilitations services (J. Edwards, personal communication, August 17, 2004).

Ruutel, Ratnik, Tamm, and Zilensk (2004) utilized the principles of grounded theory to study the experience of vibroacoustic therapy[5] in the treatment of 10 adolescent girls who suffered from high anxiety combined with low self-esteem and/or poor body image. The research goals were to study the role of vibroacoustic therapy in reducing tensions and psychological discomfort and promoting self-acceptance, and to describe the girls' experiences and the outcome of the intervention. The reason for using grounded theory as the method of data analysis was "to develop interrelated concepts that can describe reality as well as possible and describe phenomena without preconceptions" (p. 37). The findings consisted of three categories that described the meaning of the girls' experiences: balancing self-discovery, tension release, and interesting and beneficial experience. These results confirmed that vibroacoustic therapy can be considered as an important therapy in reducing tension and promoting self-acceptance.

Some researchers used the method of grounded theory together with another qualitative approach in their research projects. Ramsey (2003), in *The Restoration of Communal Experiences During the Group Music Therapy Process with Non-Fluent Aphasic Patients,* utilized a research approach that combined features of naturalistic inquiry with grounded theory. This mixed method allowed him to look at his own work as a music therapist and develop a language to describe findings related to what he perceived as essential provisions for patients with aphasia. The goals of the research were: (a) to discover the function of singing and the use of familiar songs for patients who have lost their ability to speak, (b) to find out more about the therapist's role in group process, and (c) to understand what is an appropriate model of music therapy intervention consistent with humanistic principles for these patients. The research procedures followed guidelines posed by Lincoln and Guba (1985) and Aigen (1995a). Data were coded, categorized, and analyzed according to a four-dimensional coding paradigm posed by Strauss and Corbin (1998): (a) the conditions of the phenomena, (b) the interaction among the participants in the phenomena, (c) the strategies necessary to sustain or diminish the phenomena, and (d) the consequences of the strategies to the phenomena. Ramsey appears to have viewed a naturalistic paradigm as the larger conceptual framework for his study, using grounded theory as a specific method of analysis in this paradigm. This may explain why a theory did not emanate from his research.

In many qualitative studies, the researcher has an initial idea of the research approach but, as the study goes on, develops a more specific research method. Also, a researcher may have a clear idea of the specific method he or she wants to utilize but later discovers that it is not sufficient so needs to add another method in order to make a more complete study. Ala-Ruona (2002) studied music therapists' views on procedures and applications of initial assessment of psychiatric patients. Because of his interest in studying and clarifying this concept, his starting point was phenomenographic. As the process proceeded, he decided that phenomenography did not have enough depth to investigate all aspects of his data. In order to be able to make causal connections and interpretations, he adopted grounded theory as the main method of analysis. First, he studied different concepts that the interviewees used and defined. After that, he organized the data into categories. Finally, he analyzed the data once more, created a qualitative synthesis of categories, and found the core category that tells the story of the collected data. This core category served as a scheme that was written as a story line that answers the research questions and describes and conceptualizes the process of an initial nonstructured assessment in music therapy. Ala-Ruona (2002) adapted Strauss and Corbin's (1990) version of grounded theory, mainly because of its flexible application (E. Ala-Ruona, personal communication, August 24, 2004).

Summary and Conclusions

The obvious advantage of grounded theory is that it can be used to derive theory from within the context of the data collected. When done well, it can supply the basis and develop the sensitivity and harmony that are needed in order to create a rich, well-constructed theory that is close to the reality being described. Since grounded theory is considered to be theory-building research, the results can be seen as "building blocks to generalizations" (Aigen, 1995a, p. 336). That means

---

[5] Vibroacoustic therapy was developed by Skille (1989). The client lies on a vibroacoustic bed with six built-in loudspeakers, enabling the body to perceive sound vibrations. In this case the therapist used a CD recording of low frequency sound vibration of 56.7 Hz, suggested for stress release.

that other music therapists who become familiar with the categories can use them to describe their own work, and researchers can use these already existing categories to investigate their own areas of interest and add more categories to the theory.

In general, carrying out a pure grounded theory is more difficult than other methods, and a more experienced researcher is bound to produce better theory than a beginner (Pandit, 1996). The beginning researcher often does not have the research judgment to know when the data are theoretically saturated and as a result becomes bogged down in mountains of data with no clear plan or data analysis infrastructure to analyze the data. It is recommended that the inexperienced researcher work under the guidance and supervision of a consultant who is an experienced qualitative researcher (Hueser, 1999). Grounded theory requires more time than methods that begin with more structured research questions and may include a long period of ambiguity and uncertainty due to the lack of a priori hypotheses or definite research questions.

As we have seen, there are a few grounded theory studies in music therapy. Most music therapy researchers are inspired by grounded theory method and use a modified version of it. Some music therapy researchers use other research methods as well in order to get a more holistic picture within a reasonable period of time. Strauss and Corbin (1990) themselves do not necessarily urge researchers to do pure grounded theory research, but encourage them to get inspiration and to modify the method according to their needs. As seen in the quotation at the beginning of the chapter, Strauss and Corbin (1997) see grounded theory methods as modes of carrying out qualitative research when generating a theory is the researcher's principal aim. The rationale of what methods to combine depends upon the researcher's views about epistemology, ontology, and methodology. Edwards (1999) and O'Callaghan (2001) both advocate putting forth the researcher's conceptual frames in order to clarify their views to themselves and to the reader.

Can we consider the music therapy studies that were described in this chapter grounded theory studies? It depends on our perception of grounded theory. If we look at it as a particular style of qualitative analysis of data (Strauss, 1987) rather than refer to it as a complete paradigm, I suggest that the answer is yes.

References

Aigen, K. (1995a). Interpretational research. In B. L. Wheeler (Ed.), *Music therapy research: Quantitative and qualitative perspectives* (pp. 329–366). Gilsum, NH: Barcelona Publishers.

Aigen, K. (1995b). Principles of qualitative research. In B. L. Wheeler (Ed.), *Music therapy research: Quantitative and qualitative perspectives* (pp. 283–312). Gilsum, NH: Barcelona Publishers.

Aigen, K. (1997). *Here we are in music: One year with an adolescent creative music therapy group.* St. Louis, MO: MMB Music.

Ala-Ruona, E. (2002). *Initial assessment of psychiatric clients in music therapy: Music therapists' views on procedures and applications of initial assessment.* Unpublished master's thesis, University of Jyväskylä, Jyväskylä, Finland.

Amir, D. (1992). Awakening and expanding the self: Meaningful moments in the music therapy process as experienced and described by music therapists and music therapy clients. (Doctoral dissertation, New York University, 1992). *Dissertation Abstracts International, 53*(8), 4361B.

Amir, D. (1993). Moments of insight in the music therapy experience. *Music Therapy, 12*, 85–100.

Amir, D. (1996). Experiencing music therapy: Meaningful moments in the music therapy process. In M. Langenberg, K. Aigen, & J. Frommer (Eds.), *Qualitative music therapy research: Beginning dialogues* (pp. 109–130). Gilsum, NH: Barcelona Publishers.

Amir, D. (1999). Musical and verbal interventions in music therapy: A qualitative study. *Journal of Music Therapy, 36*, 144–175.

Bogden, R., & Biklen, S. (1982). *Qualitative research for education.* Boston, MA: Allyn & Bacon.

Bruscia, K. E. (1995). Modes of consciousness in Guided Imagery and Music: A therapist's experience of the guiding process. In C. Kenny (Ed.), *Listening, playing, creating: Essays on the power of sound* (pp. 165–197). Albany, NY: State University of New York Press.

Colaizzi, P. F. (1978). Psychological research as the phenomenologist views it. In R. S. Valle & M. King (Eds.), *Existential-phenomenological alternatives for psychology* (pp. 48–71). New York: Oxford University Press.

Corbin, J., & Strauss, A. (1998). *Basics of qualitative research: Techniques and procedures for developing grounded theory* (2nd ed.). Thousand Oaks, CA: Sage Publications.

Edwards, J. (1999). Considering the paradigmatic frame: Social science research approaches relevant to research in music therapy. *The Arts in Psychotherapy, 26,* 73–80.

Edwards, J. (2000). "Keeping things going": Techniques used by the music therapist with children in a hospital-based rehabilitation service. In *Developing a platform for research to inform music therapy practice with hospitalised children.* Unpublished doctoral dissertation, University of Queensland, Brisbane, Australia.

Ely M., with Anzul, M., Friedman, T., Garner, D., & Steinmetz, A. M. (1991). *Doing qualitative research: Circles within circles.* New York: The Falmer Press.

Forinash, M. (1990). A phenomenology of music therapy with the terminally ill (Doctoral dissertation, New York University, 1990). *Dissertation Abstracts International, 51*(09), 2915A.

Forinash, M. (1995). Phenomenological research. In B. L. Wheeler (Ed.), *Music therapy research: Quantitative and qualitative perspectives* (pp. 367–387). Gilsum, NH: Barcelona Publishers.

Forinash, M. (2000). On listening to Edward. *Nordic Journal of Music Therapy, 9,* 83–89.

Forinash, M., & Gonzalez, D. (1989). A phenomenological perspective of music therapy. *Music Therapy, 8,* 35–46.

Glaser, B. G. (1998). *Doing grounded theory: Issues and discussions.* Mill Valley, CA.: Sociology Press.

Glaser, B. G., & Strauss, A. L. (1967). *The discovery of grounded theory: Strategies for qualitative research.* Chicago, IL: Aldine Publishing Co.

Hueser, N. G. (1999). *Grounded theory research: Not for the novice. Grounded theory as a research methodology.* Retrieved February 3, 2003, from http://www.users.uswest.net/~nhueser/grounded.html. Cited in http://rms46.vlsm.org/citations-h.html

Kasayka, R. E. (1991). To meet and match the moment of hope: Transpersonal elements of the Guided Imagery and Music experience. (Doctoral dissertation, New York University, 1990). *Dissertation Abstracts International, 52*(06), 2062A.

Lincoln, Y., & Guba, E. (1985). *Naturalistic inquiry.* Beverly Hills, CA: Sage Publications.

Liu, D. (1996). *Teaching chemistry on the Internet.* Unpublished paper. University of Nebraska, Lincoln, NB. Available at http://dwb.unl.edu/Diss/DLiu/ROM.html

Marton, F. (1994). Phenomenography. In T. Husen & T. N. Postlethwaite (Eds.), *The international encyclopedia of education* (2nd ed., Vol. 8, p. 4424). Oxford, UK: Pergamon Press.

McNiff, J. (1988). *Action research: Principles and practice.* London: Routledge.

Miles, M. B., & Huberman, A.M. (1994). *Qualitative data analysis: An expanded sourcebook* (2nd ed.). Thousand Oaks, CA: Sage Publications.

Moe, T. (2002) Restitutional factors in receptive group music therapy inspired by GIM. *Nordic Journal of Music Therapy, 11,* 152–166.

Nagler, J. C. (1993). A qualitative study of children in crisis: Interventions through music therapy and digital music technology. *Dissertation Abstracts International, 54*(07), 2502A (UMI No. 9333953)

O'Callaghan, C. (1996). Lyrical themes in songs written by palliative care patients. *Journal of Music Therapy, 33,* 74–92.

O'Callaghan, C. (2001). Bringing music to life: A study of music therapy and palliative care experiences in a cancer hospital. *Journal of Palliative Care, 17,* 155–160.

O'Callaghan, C., & Colegrove, V. (1998). Effect of the music therapy introduction when engaging hospitalized cancer patients. *Music Therapy Perspectives, 16,* 67–74.

Pandit, N. R. (1996). The creation of theory: A recent application of the grounded theory method. *The Qualitative Report 2*(4), 1–16. Available at http://www.nova.edu/ssss/QR/QR2-4/pandit.html

Ramsey, D. (2003). The restoration of communal experiences during the group music therapy process with non-fluent aphasic patients. (Doctoral dissertation, New York University, 2002). *Dissertation Abstracts International, 63*(07), 3266.

Robson, C. (2002). *Real world research* (2nd ed.). Oxford, UK: Blackwell Publishers.

Ruud, E. (1997). Music and identity . *Nordic Journal of Music Therapy, 6*, 3–13.

Ruutel, E., Ratnik, M., Tamm, E., & Zilensk, H. (2004). The experience of vibroacoustic therapy in the therapeutic intervention of adolescent girls. *Nordic Journal of Music Therapy, 13,* 33–46.

Smit, J. (1999). Grounded theory methodology in information system research: Glaser versus Strauss. *South African Computer Journal, 24,* 219–222.

Skille, O. (1989). Vibroacoustic therapy. *Music Therapy, 8,* 61–67.

Strauss, A. L. (1987). *Qualitative analysis for social scientists.* Cambridge, UK: Cambridge University Press.

Strauss, A., & Corbin, J. (1990). *Basics of qualitative research: Grounded theory procedures and techniques.* Newbury Park, CA: Sage Publications.

Strauss, A., & Corbin, J. (1997). (Eds.). *Grounded theory in practice.* Thousand Oaks, CA: Sage Publications.

Tesch, R. (1990). *Qualitative research: Analysis types & software tools.* Bristol, PA: The Falmer Press.

Wheeler, B. L. (1999). Experiencing pleasure in working with severely disabled children. *Journal of Music Therapy 36,* 56–80.

Chapter 30
First-Person Research
Kenneth E. Bruscia

The purpose of this chapter is to provide an overview of first-person research, including an examination of its history and theoretical roots, its basic premises, and the diverse methods that have been developed for gathering and analyzing data.

Overview and Definition

First-person research is defined here as any method in which researchers or participants gather data from themselves, using processes such as introspection, retrospection, self-perception, self-observation, self-reflection, self-inquiry, and so forth. It is called first-person research because, grammatically speaking, it includes all the relational options for researchers and participants to be data collectors and informants, for example: I study me; I study us; we study me; or we study us.

Within this book, a distinction is needed between first-person research and the kinds of self-inquiry that qualitative researchers regularly do as an integral part of studying others (or third-person research). In first-person research, researchers or participants study themselves to provide the primary sources of data; in third-person research, researchers may use self-inquiry to monitor the integrity of the study itself (such as its method, findings, and presentation), but data from the self-inquiry are not included in the analysis. This chapter deals only with first-person research; the role of self-inquiry in third-person research is covered in Chapter 11, Designing Qualitative Research.

Historical Roots and Theoretical Premises

Historical Roots

While the idea of self-inquiry can be traced back to the writings of St. Augustine in the 5th century, it was Brentano who first introduced the notion of introspection as a research method. He did this by proposing that the core subject matter for psychology is mental phenomena and that the most appropriate method of study was inner perception (Lyons, 1986). Other contemporaries, such as Wundt, Titchener, and James also believed in the need for some kind of introspection in experimental psychology, but each had different views on how one should proceed and what aspects of the mind are accessible to self-study. They also used different terms for it (Lyons).

Since the early 1900s, introspection has had a long and cyclic history in psychological research, moving from periods of acceptance to periods of almost complete disparagement and abandonment to enthusiastic revivals around new applications (Lyons, 1986). Meanwhile, over the last century, sociology and anthropology have also been wrestling with the limitations of third-person research and the possibilities of first-person research. In sociology, questions have arisen about whether first-person research is more appropriate than third-person research in studying the emotions of both researcher and participant encountered in fieldwork. In anthropology, questions have arisen about whether first-person research might be a solution to the colonialism and Eurocentrism that pervades third-person, Western research on other cultures. At the same time, the entire philosophy of science has been shifting toward postmodernism, and nonpositivistic paradigms of research have been increasing and expanding. Of crucial significance in all areas of human research has been a growing uneasiness with the truth claims of third-person, positivistic research, along with the growing interest in constructivism, feminism, and value-laden research methodology. Thus, within this intellectual climate, it has been inevitable that the research community return to the values inherent in first-person research. The broad spectrum of methods described in this chapter attests to the significance that has been given to first-person research in nonpositivistic paradigms, and to its potential for providing relevant and meaningful information about the human condition.

Theoretical Premises

First-person research is a spectrum of practices that have been used in the human sciences of psychology, sociology, and anthropology, as well as in the humanities, education, the arts, and the arts therapies. Because of this varied disciplinary background, its theoretical roots are numerous and complex. In fact, each practice has its own epistemological foundations, based not only on the field of the research but also on the focus of the inquiry. Thus, there is not one set of theoretical premises that is common to all practices; rather there are premises that are variously shared by different researchers. What follows, then, is a presentation of premises that may apply to one practice but not another. The premises are concerned with different epistemological problems. They are:

Individual self-knowledge (How I know myself). The inner subjective space of a person can only be directly accessed and known by that person, through various forms of self-inquiry. When the integrity of such *individual self-knowledge* is evaluated for its *truth* value, it may be considered arguable, privileged but fallible, or largely unreliable; when integrity is evaluated for its *meaning* value, such knowledge is acknowledged as idiographic, situated, interpreted, and perhaps even fictional.

Co-constituted knowledge of other in relation to self (How we know one another). The inner subjective space of one person is not directly accessible to or fully knowable by another person; only indirect access and partial knowledge of another person is possible. Knowledge of other arises out of a dialectical relationship between self and other. When persons dialogue with one another about their inner beings, they co-constitute knowledge of and about one another.

Collective self-knowledge (How we know ourselves). The inner subjective space of a group, society, or community can only be directly accessed and known by members of the group, either individually or as a group, through various forms of self-inquiry or dialogue. The integrity of such knowledge is a function of intersubjective agreement, or the extent to which members of the group accept one another's constructs of themselves.

Self-knowledge of object world (How I know within myself about the world of objects). Every human being has an implicit or tacit knowledge of the object world (all physical and behavioral aspects of the world) gained from one's life-long experience of *being-in-the-world*. That is, the reality of the outer world is already known to us internally, regardless of whether *it* really exists out there independent of our knowledge of it, or it is entirely constructed by us. In both cases, to study it, we have to in some way deal with what we already know about it. In the former case, one would follow the path of Husserl, who advocated focusing on the object, bracketing one's own tacit knowledge, and allowing the object to reveal itself through appearances that are uncluttered by one's own self-knowledge of it. For him, the purpose of research is to return to the things themselves. In contrast, in the latter case, one would follow the path of Heidegger, who proposed focusing on one's own tacit knowledge of the object vis-à-vis our already being-in-the-world with it, physically, interpersonally, or psychologically. For him, the purpose of research is to explicate what we already know about the object.

When the inquiry proceeds by observing the object without considering one's own relationship to it, the knowledge is third-person singular: *It appears to behave this way to anyone who observes it similarly.* When the inquiry proceeds by focusing on one's relationship with the object, the knowledge is first-person singular or plural: *I know it to behave in this way. We know it to behave in this way.* The integrity of first-person versus third-person knowledge of *it* is a function of one's philosophy of science. Positivists give primary value to third-person knowledge; nonpositivists give primary value to first-person; and post-positivists (or integrationists) give primary value to linking together first-person and third-person knowledge.

Methodology

Based on the above, first-person research may involve any of the following interpersonal options: (a) I study the inner me, (b) You and I study the inner you and me, (c) I study the inner us, (d) We study the inner us, and (e) I study my construction of it. As these are applied to how researchers and participants might study themselves, four methodological streams can be identified. They are self-study by (a) participants only, (b) researchers and participants, (c) researchers only, and (d) co-researchers.

Participants Study Themselves

In this type of first-person research, participants study their own encounters with the phenomenon of interest, with various kinds of help from the researcher; then the researcher analyzes and interprets the data relatively independently. In most cases, the researcher trains the participants in self-study. The various models of this type are described below.

Introspection, generally speaking, involves asking participants to observe something about their own inner processes in an objective way; that is, as if another person was doing the observation. The earliest examples were: Wundt's notion of active observation of perceptual processes, Brentano's notion of passive apperception of perceptual processes, James' notion of retrospecting on one's thought processes after completing a mental act, and Titchener's notion of self-description of the contents of one's consciousness (Lyons, 1986; Titchener, 1912).

In the *Think-Aloud* technique, the researcher engages the participant in a particular task or experience with the instruction to verbally report what the participant is thinking or experiencing moment-to-moment while engaged in the task or experience (Aanstoos, 1983). A spin-off of this method is called *constructive interaction*, which involves two participants thinking aloud with one another (O'Malley, Draper, & Riley, 1984).

Phenomenological Self-Description is a term given by the present author to an untitled method developed by Petitmengin-Peugeot (1999). Three steps comprise the method: First, self-descriptions are gathered from participants by having them live or relive the experience being studied, then helping them slowly think through each part of the experience so that it can be verbalized clearly. Second, the descriptions are reduced by the researchers, and various models are developed to describe how the different elements of the experience are interrelated. Third, the models developed for each participant are synthesized into a structural description, then the structural descriptions are integrated across all participants.

Neurophenomenology is a method that involves gathering first-person phenomenological data on the participant's experience of a phenomenon, along with neural measurements during their experience (see Lutz, Lachaux, Martinerie, & Varela, 2002). The purpose is to explicate the embodied structure of human experience by using the two different data sets as *mutual constraints* (Varela, 1996).

Systematic Self-Observation (SSO) is a method developed by Rodriguez and Ryave (2002) to study those everyday experiences that are essentially covert, hidden, elusive, or intensely personal (such as telling lies, keeping secrets, withholding compliments, feeling envy) and therefore more amenable to self-observation than observation by another party. In SSO, participants are trained by the researcher to observe and record their own everyday experiences of the event or phenomenon under investigation. Once trained, the participants are told to "go about their daily life as they normally do and in no way to act differently as a result of the assignment" (p. 16). When the event or phenomenon occurs, participants are told to write a field note about it as soon as possible. Once the field notes are gathered from all the participants, the researcher compares the data sets across participants according to the form of the field notes. Based on this comparison, the researchers write a general description of the phenomenon, noting important themes as well as exceptions to them.

Dialogal Introspection is any form of self-study that involves dialoguing about the inner process or experience under study. It may also be called *Dialogal Phenomenology*. The dialogue may be among participants or between the participants and researcher. The practice of participant dialogue is found in the "Hamburg Approach to Qualitative Heuristic Research," (Kleining, 1982), which uses experimentation, observation, and dialogal introspection as integrally related techniques of data collection.

Experiential Research is a method of participant self-study developed by Barrell and his coworkers (Barrell, Aanstoos, Richards, & Arons, 1987; Barrell & Barrell, 1975). It begins by having participants repeatedly engage in the experience under study, taking notes on each occasion. After producing several protocols, each participant analyzes his or her own data to identify the commonalities across the multiple protocols. Thus, each participant synthesizes his or her own final description of the experiences. The participants then meet in a group to share and discuss their experiences and to find some commonalities across the individual descriptions. As a result, a consensual group description of the experience is formulated. Finally, the researcher makes operational definitions of elements of the group description, often so that a quantitative study of the experience can be done.

Experiential Self-Knowing (Lett, 1993, 1995, 1998) is an approach to group supervision that can be used for research purposes. The supervisor (researcher) facilitates the self-study of a group of supervisees (participants), engaging them in various art activities and discussions, aimed at helping them to access, re-experience, and reflect upon their way of being as therapist with clients.

Autobiography is an entire genre of story-telling methods used to help participants examine their experiences and lives. It may include longer self-narratives about one's entire life history, in-depth narratives about a particular context or situation in one's own life, narratives about different events or periods in one's life related to a particular issue, or narratives about others at a particular time in one's own life (Denzin, 1989). For example, Denzin (1987a, 1987b) collected *self-stories* spontaneously told by alcoholics at AA meetings and analyzed them using different interpretive strategies. Ginsburg (1989a, 1989b) studied the life stories of 35 women in a community who had different views on abortion. Related to music therapy, Ruud (1997) used musical forms of autobiography to examine how his students constructed their identities. He asked one group to make a tape of 10 to 15 pieces of music that were important to them and then interviewed each student about the tape. He asked another group to make a tape, following the same instructions, but to write a 10-page commentary on the music selected. Using a grounded theory strategy to analyze the verbal data, Ruud came up with four ways in which music helps to construct a person's identity. Music helps to define one's own personal (psychological) space, one's social space, the time and place of significant life events, and one's transpersonal realm.

Hibben (1999) gathered together 33 self-stories in music therapy. Some of the stories were written by the clients themselves with minimal help from the therapist, some stories were written by the clients' parents, some were constructed by the therapist or researcher based on interviews with the clients, and some were stories told by therapists on behalf of their clients.

Researcher Studies Self and Participants

In this form of self-study, the researcher studies his or her own individual encounters with the phenomenon of interest, gathers data from participants, and works independently to analyze and interpret the data.

Heuristic Research is the first and most comprehensive method of this type, developed by Clark Moustakas (1990). In his landmark study, Moustakas (1961) spent several years exploring the human experience of loneliness. The study began when Moustakas had to make a life-death decision as to whether his daughter should undergo heart surgery. His feelings of utter aloneness in making such a decision sensitized him to others faced with similar feelings and, in particular, the terrible loneliness of hospitalized children separated from their parents. After observing and talking to the children and hearing their experiences, he began to recognize that other examples of loneliness in his own life, and in the lives of others, added greater breadth and depth to his understanding. This led him to extend his research to interviewing other people who had experienced loneliness of all kinds and to the study of writings on the topic, including writings in psychology and literary works such as autobiographies, biographies, novels, poems, and so forth. After years of gathering these data, he synthesized all of the findings with the aim of shedding light on the meaning of loneliness as a human experience.

Moustakas (1990) formulated several techniques that are indigenous to his research method. They include identifying with the phenomenon through empathic experience, dialoguing with self, searching for what one already knows tacitly, using one's intuition, *indwelling* in the experience with unwavering attention, clearing oneself to focus, and relating to an internal frame of reference. These techniques are used throughout the six phases of the heuristic research process identified by Moustakas. They are:

Initial engagement: Discovering and framing the research topics and questions that are of personal significance to the researcher;

Immersion: Living the research question continuously, during waking and sleep hours, keeping it in the forefront of everyday awareness;

Incubation: Retreating from the intense, concentrated focus of the previous phase and allowing what has been encountered and learned to integrate and emerge anew;

Illumination: The breakthrough into consciousness when the researcher begins to recognize the core component of the experience;

Explication: The researcher develops a more complete apprehension of the phenomenon by examining the various components of the experience in relation to its core;

Creative synthesis: All discoveries, findings, intuitions, and awareness are integrated into a composite description of the meaning of the experience.

Moustakas (1990) gave many examples of heuristic research, showing its applicability to a wide range of topics including growing up in a fatherless home, the experience of shyness, the experience of synchronicity, the androgynous male, and the experience of unconditional love. A particularly relevant study for this chapter is Shaw's (1989) study on the nature of rhythmic interaction. Shaw began his investigation by tracing his own fascination for interacting rhythmically with others, starting from his earliest memories and moving into his present. As a result, he identified many different examples in sports, social activities, games, dancing, music, and playing with his children. He also interviewed eight men and women to further discern its qualities, themes, and essences. In addition to these rather psychological topics, Moustakas' ideas have been particularly useful in studying phenomena that are intensely personal, internal, and subjective, such as the arts, imagery, fantasy, and dreams.

Dialogal Phenomenology is a method developed by Strasser (1969). It involves the researcher reflecting on his or her own encounters with the experience under study, making multiple descriptions of it, having internal dialogues about the experience, and then dialoguing with others. These descriptions are then used as the basis of internal dialogues. Studies in this vein by Fischer and von Eckartsberg can be found in Giorgi, Fischer, and von Eckartsberg (1971).

Organic Inquiry is a feminist approach developed by four women (Clements, Ettling, Jenett, & Shields, 1998). The fundamental technique of gathering data is for the researcher and co-researchers to be continually telling and listening to one another's stories. Analysis of these stories is also a collaborative venture between researcher and co-researchers, and ultimately the results of the study are presented in story form, always voiced in the first-person. Topics for organic inquiry always come from the researcher's life stories. Examples of topics pursued by the authors are: (a) beauty, body image, and the feminine; (b) how sacred images, stories, and rituals in India inform their social and political decisions; (c) women's experiences of living on the U.S.-Mexico border; and (d) women's experiences of menopause. No matter what topic is pursued, the primary goal is "personal transformation for the reader of the study, the co-researchers, and the researcher" (p. 125).

Arts-Based Research includes any method of inquiry wherein the researcher uses an art form or art experience as a means of producing or presenting insights about a phenomenon. The researcher may study only his or her own artwork or experience, or collaborate with participants in studying their works or experiences jointly. McNiff (1998) explained the essence of this approach: "In art, the self is a major participant, but there is always the goal of making expressions that are able to speak for themselves. . . . When the process of research recognizes objects as full participants, there is a decided shift away from one-sided autobiography and toward the examination of an interplay" (pp. 54–55). In short, researchers and participants gain insights not only from the experience or process of creating the art works themselves but also from what the works of art communicate back to them. It is a dialectical process of the artist producing knowledge by making art, and the artwork producing knowledge by communicating something back to the artist and the audience. See Chapter 36 in this book, Arts-Based Research, for further discussion of this area.

Heuristic Music Analysis (Bruscia, 1999) is an adaptation of Moustakas' heuristic approach that has been used to analyze classical music programs used in Guided Imagery and Music (GIM). GIM is a form of music psychotherapy in which the client spontaneously images to specially designed classical music programs while in a deeply relaxed state and while dialoguing with the therapist. Given the centrality of the music programs in shaping the client's experience, the characteristics of the music selections used in each program, and the way the selections are sequenced are of considerable interest to both practitioners and researchers. For this reason, several methods of analysis have been developed (B. Abrams, 2002).

The present author's method of analysis is aimed at understanding the programs as they are experienced by the client and therapist during an actual GIM session—in both imaginal and musical ways. The basic premise is that to understand what the client experiences in GIM, therapists and researchers must experience GIM as the client does. Thus, the analysis involves the researcher experiencing the music in four experiential spaces: (a) an alert state focused on the music, (b) a deeply relaxed state being guided to focus on the music, (c) a deeply relaxed state being guided to allow images to arise spontaneously to the music, and (d) an alert state focused on the imagery potentials of the music (as the therapist does when guiding the client's images). These four experiential states parallel the client-therapist interactions during a GIM session. The client is in a deeply relaxed state listening to the music and allowing images to arise spontaneously (spaces a and c) while the therapist, though often in an alert state listening to the music and imagining its potentials (spaces a and d), also moves into a deep state with the client (spaces b and c) to empathize with what the client is experiencing.

After gathering data on his or her own responses in all four experiential spaces, the researcher gathers data from participants (clients) in the third experiential space, that is, by guiding the participants while imaging to the music in a deeply relaxed state. Transcripts are taken. The results of the many analyses are then presented as a synthesis of all four spaces, using data from the researcher and the participants. Several studies have been done using this method including those by Swanson (1999), Sakadjian (2000), J. Abrams (2000), Soderhielm (2001), Brookens (2002), and Knechtel (2002). Also, a similar method for heuristically analyzing imaginal music was independently developed by Booth (1998–1999).

Empathic Participatory Research is a method of inquiry developed by Skolimowski (1994), defined by its reliance upon the researcher's efforts to empathize with participants as fully as possible. To do this, the researcher studies each participant on his or her own terms, from the participant's point of view, using his or her own language. By indwelling in this empathic position, the researcher enters into a communion with each participant, allowing the researcher to experience and understand what the participant is revealing about the phenomenon being studied. Thus, empathy serves as the primary source of understanding both self and other in relation to the phenomenon, which in turn helps to reveal the phenomenon under investigation. In music therapy, this approach can be found in several case studies in Hibben (1999) where the therapist, because of a client's inability to communicate, has empathically recreated what he or she imaginatively felt the client experienced.

Sociological Introspection is a model of self-study proposed by Ellis (1991) for sociological research in the area of lived emotions, or what she called *emotional sociology*. Within this context, introspection is the active thinking about one's own thoughts and feelings as they relate to the thoughts and feelings of others, while interacting in a particular social setting. Ellis proposed four different kinds of introspection that can be used separately or in combination: (a) The researcher asks participants to introspect on emotions through diaries, journals, and free-writing; (b) the researcher introspects about his or her own emotional process during the research; c) the researcher and participant introspect interactively through conversations aimed at understanding the emergent experiences of both parties; and (d) the researcher introspects in response to interactions with the participants and the data that come from these interactions.

Autoethnography is a combination of studying the ethnography of one's own group and writing an autobiography within an ethnographic context. Ellis and Bochner (2000) defined autoethnography as follows:

> An autobiographical genre of writing and research that displays multiple layers of consciousness, connecting the personal to the cultural. Back and forth autoethnographers gaze, first through an ethnographic wide-angle lens, focusing outward on social and cultural aspects of their personal experience; then, they look inward, exposing a vulnerable self that is moved by and may move through, refract, and resist cultural interpretations. . . . As they zoom backward and forward, inward and outward, distinctions between the personal and cultural become blurred, sometimes beyond distinct recognition. (p. 739)

Examples of autoethnography abound in Bochner and Ellis (2002), where several authors present literary and artful autoethnographies on a wide range of topics such as father-son relationships, erotic mentoring, research-based theater, torch singing, and more.

An autoethnography in music therapy can be found in the story told by the author (Bruscia, 1996) about how he experienced himself and his international colleagues during the First International Symposium of Qualitative Research in Music Therapy. The symposium, held in Düsseldorf in 1994, was the beginning of a new culture of research in music therapy. As each participant presented his or her own work and listened to the work presented by others and as the dialogues unfolded during and after the symposium, interactional roles and relationships formed, patterns of value evolved, meanings were shared, norms of behavior appeared, and the reciprocal contributions of individual and group became evident. In the book of proceedings, each participant wrote a monologue based on the original presentation and then, after reading the presentations of all the other participants, wrote a reaction to them. The author's story was his reaction to the monologues and presentations of his fellow participants, but, more broadly, it was his way of explicating the social structure of this culture of researchers. Based on the myth of Daedalus and the labyrinth, the story details the character of each presenter (in his or her own voice, as well as the voice of the storyteller), the unique gifts and limitations that they brought to the culture (in the voice of the King), and how they all related to one another in their shared quest to find the center of the labyrinth, where all knowledge resided.

Researcher Studies Self

In this type of first-person inquiry, the researcher studies his or her own encounters with the phenomenon of interest, then analyzes and interprets the data. There are several approaches.

Reflexive Phenomenology is a term used by Paul Colaizzi (Tesch, 1990) for a form of phenomenology where, instead of gathering data from subjects (empirical phenomenology), the researcher uses his or her own experience as data. Early examples of this approach are a study of dreams by Craig (1987) and a study of imaginative experiences by Giorgi (1987).

Reflexive Neurophenomenology is a method where the researcher uses systematic self-observation combined with physical measurements. An example is a set of four studies by Nielsen (1995) aimed at examining hypnogagic imagery (those occurring in the drowsy period preceding sleep). By stimulating and studying 250 hypnogagic images of his own, Nielsen found a systematic way of comparing self-observed events in consciousness with quantitative measures of neuromuscular correlates (limb jerks, head tilts) and recordings of EEG and other physiological activities. Based on these data, Nielsen identified a way to study the memory sources of hypnogagic imagery.

Embodied Phenomenology is an approach based on Merleau-Ponty's premise that humans are fundamentally embodied beings—our primary way of being-in-the-world is first and foremost bodily. Moreover, the body encounters and understands the world independently and prior to the symbolizing functions of consciousness. Thus, Merleau-Ponty's approach to understanding a phenomenon as it appears directly to us (the very purpose of phenomenology) is to return to what the body already knows about it. Embodied phenomenology, then, is any form of self-reflection that relies upon the body as a primary source of implicit or explicit knowledge. Examples of this approach include Shapiro's (1985) self-study of ambivalence and Sudnow's (2001) account of how he learned to improvise jazz at the piano. It also bears mentioning that Priestley's (1994) method of analyzing her own countertransference was a form of embodied phenomenology in that she relied upon what her body was revealing to her to understand her own experience of the client, as well as the client's experience of him or herself.

A music therapy version of embodied phenomenology can be found in Bonny's (1993) method of *affective-intuitive listening,* which she developed to gain an experiential understanding of the music programs used in Guided Imagery and Music (see description above). Here is how she proceeded:

> Before the music I sit quietly and engage in a meditation that clears my mind of its busy pre-occupations. I find that quiet place within. I then arise with my mind only on my body and in appreciation of its functions and ability to express through movement any feelings that might arise. As relaxation, I stretch the muscles of my body, first from a standing position, then from a sitting and lying position. Then I start the music and lie on the floor. To prepare myself to receive the vibrational elements of the music with closed eyes, I visualize my body lying prone and relaxing on the floor. . . . The final step is movement, which I initiate only in response to the vibrations of the music. I move only when the music suggests movement. My mind is solely on the music and its effect in and through my body. (p. 6)

After moving to the entire program (usually lasting 25–40 minutes), the researcher writes notes describing the music and what it was like to experience the various parts of it. Bonny found that the discoveries she made about the program (which she knew extremely well) were "quite astonishing." She said: "I came away from that experience with new understandings of the music which arose from places inside me not explored before" (Bonny, p. 7).

Researcher Autobiography is the use of the researcher's own life narratives as a primary source of data. Probably the earliest example in music therapy was an unpublished paper presented at the New York University Symposium, titled "Music in the Life of One Man: Ontogenetic Foundations for Music Therapy" (Bruscia, 1982). The study had two parts: a musical autobiography that described and analyzed how the author related to music at different periods of his life, and a set of 14 *working hypotheses* derived from this musical self-analysis. The first hypothesis, which established the basic premise for all that followed, was that "every individual has a relationship to music." The remaining hypotheses dealt with what defines this relationship, its essential characteristics, how it develops, and the various ways that it can reflect wellness as well as illness.

Clinical Retrospection is a term created here for research on one's own clinical work that was completed in the past. Several examples can be found in music therapy. The first was a retrospective study on what it means for a therapist to *be there* for a client (Bruscia, 1995) when using GIM. The study began by a self-inquiry into what it meant to the author to be there for a client in GIM, which led to a set of provisional constructs on how a therapist can expand, center, and shift his or her own consciousness while guiding a client. These provisional constructs were then used to analyze an actual transcript of the music and imagery portion of a GIM session that he led for one of his clients. The session was one that presented real challenges for the author and therapist to be there. The analysis proceeded section by section, interrogating each image reported by the client and each verbal response made by the author. The interrogation consisted of asking questions, such as: "Where was my consciousness focused at this point?" "What was my experience at that moment?" After analyzing the first section of the transcript using the provisional constructs, the author then adjusted the constructs and created new ones to account for those experiences that were not adequately covered in the first set of constructs. This process of formulating and testing constructs and then inventing new constructs as necessary continued until all elements of the transcribed session had been accounted for. As a result of the study, "a new form of reflective self-inquiry for analyzing clinical work had been developed, a methodology for theory development had emerged, a clinical theory had been put forth on what it means to be there for a client in GIM, and theoretical constructs had been proposed for classifying transference and countertransference manifestations" (Bruscia, 1998b, p. 528).

One of the important side-discoveries of this study was how easy it was for the therapist to identify countertransference issues by analyzing his own reactions to a client's images. It was therefore interesting to find that, some years earlier, Ross and Kapp (1962) had analyzed the imagery evoked by their patient's dreams and discovered unexpected countertransference issues; similarly, Kern (1978) analyzed the spontaneous background (or screen) images that he created in his own imagination when listening to his patients talk and free-associate.

To delve more deeply into the process of explicating countertransference in therapist imagery, the author did two follow-up studies (Bruscia, 1998a, 1998b), both addressing issues that emerged from the original study on being there. While the original study used a reflective form of self-inquiry where the researcher reconstructed a past experience from memory, the follow-up studies used an experiential method for gathering new data on similar experiences (that is, re-imaging); while the purpose of the original study was to develop a theory on being there, the follow-up studies aimed at understanding transference and countertransference phenomena in GIM, both of which were implicated in being there for the client; while the original study analyzed experiences that were accessible to the author's conscious mind, the follow-up studies aimed at uncovering unconscious material about the same kind of experiences.

The experiential method used in gathering data for both follow-up studies was the *re-imaging technique* in which the therapist has a short GIM experience focused on an image created by a client. Specifically, with a colleague guiding the experience, the therapist revisits a client image in an altered state of consciousness while listening to the same music experienced by the client. The therapist lets his or her own imagination go deeper into the events and characters in the client's image, allowing them to develop freely. The purpose is to allow the therapist's unconscious to disclose itself in relation to the client's unconscious. After the experience, the therapist/researcher analyzes the written transcript of the experience, using specific procedures for identifying transference, countertransference, and projective identification (Bruscia, 1998a, 1998b). Meashey (1998) followed these procedures and also found them helpful in illuminating countertransference issues. The re-imaging technique has also been applied in clinical supervision (Grocke, 2002).

As a result of all these studies, two new directions in self-reflexive research have been established, particularly in the areas of music, imagery, dreams, and therapies that involve them. First, they suggest that for a researcher to understand the experiences of participants, it may be helpful to actually experience what they are experiencing. Put another way, it may be helpful for a researcher to serve as a participant in his or her own study. Thus, if the study requires the informant to improvise under certain conditions, the researcher should also improvise under those conditions. Notice that in both of these imagery studies, the researcher/therapist explored what it was like to experience the client's image under the same conditions. This not only enhances empathy but also establishes a definite boundary between the researcher and the informant. Specifically, the researcher/therapist's images of the client image now stand in direct comparison to the client's original image so that consistencies and inconsistencies can be quickly identified. Second, these studies suggest that one way to explore the researcher's hidden suppositions and biases may be to examine his or her unconscious responses to the participants and the experiences they are reporting. Perhaps projective techniques that tap the researcher's unconscious may be a useful addition to existing techniques for *bracketing* presuppositions and biases that are already at the conscious level.

Returning to other approaches to clinical retrospection, a different twist was taken by Pellitteri (1998) and Hadley (1998) in understanding the client's experience of transference in music therapy. Both authors are music therapists who received music therapy as a client over an extended period. Pellitteri analyzed one of his own past GIM sessions to examine where and how the music, the imagery, and the therapist were experienced as objects of transference, and how the transferences were handled. Hadley compared the kinds of transferences she experienced in two different forms of improvisational music therapy. Other studies involving therapists' study of their own work as clients can be found in Hibben (1999).

Meadows (1995) used self-retrospection to examine his music therapy work with clients with profound, multiple disabilities. Given the inability of his clients to communicate verbally or sometimes even physically what they were experiencing, Meadows questioned how he went about understanding what they needed moment-to-moment in the music therapy setting while also wondering what the basis was for his understanding. To answer these questions, Meadows analyzed a videotape of one music therapy session with a client, wrote his own observations and interpretations of what he and the client were experiencing, and then interviewed the client's teacher as she viewed the same videotape. He found that, while both of them had the same general impressions of what was happening in the session (that is, the events and behaviors), the teacher did not attempt to describe the feelings that were apparent to Meadows. Meadows concluded that observing and being with the client are very different experiences that lead to similarly different perceptions of the same session. He also concluded that, in working with noncommunicative clients, the therapist's experience of the client's experience is a primary, if not the only, source of data.

Hintz (1995) did a self-exploration of her own spiritual experiences as a GIM client. As data, she used the written transcripts of 15 GIM sessions that she had experienced over a period of a little over 2 years. Going over each transcript, Hintz searched for all the images she had generated that contained a *spiritual symbol* of some kind, and then categorized them. She also analyzed the sequence of each spiritual experience, noting what situations preceded the experience, how the spiritual symbol manifested itself, and what effects the symbol had within the image.

Fenner (1996), an art therapist, used Moustakas' method as a basis for designing a study of her own drawings. The purpose was to determine the value of the drawings and reflections upon them in producing self-knowledge and change.

Wheeler (1999) used self-retrospective methods to gain a better understanding of what made her music therapy work with children with severe disabilities so pleasurable to her. In her approach, she studied transcribed videotapes of herself working with eight children in seven different sessions per child, along with her logs of the session. She then identified incidents in the sessions that were particularly pleasurable for her and began coding and categorizing them according to what was happening. After re-checking her codes and categories with the data, she reflected upon her experience working with each child. Wheeler found that all the data could be accounted for in four pleasurable events: when the child acted intentionally, when the child displayed emotions, when the child tried to communicate, and when the child displayed mutuality. Upon further reflection on why these four responses might be rewarding, Wheeler found two interdependent factors: the child's responsiveness and her own expectations as therapist. Specifically, she concluded: "The experiences that I found enjoyable are those where the children altered my expectations by their responsiveness" (p. 75).

Co-Researchers Study Themselves

This category differs from the preceding ones in three significant ways. First, the researcher and participants have equal roles and status as co-researchers, rather than being separated into hierarchical roles. Second, rather than involving only one researcher, collaborative self-study involves an entire group of researchers studying themselves through both individual and group means. Third, the entire research process is created by the co-researchers through continuous dialogue—about the topic and purpose of the study, the method, the sampling, organization, and analysis of the data, interpretation, and presentation. Different approaches can be taken.

Cooperative Inquiry is a participatory form of research developed by Heron (1996) "in which all involved engage together as co-subjects and in a democratic dialogue as co-researchers" (Heron, 1998, p. 240). Crucial to the method is a repeated cycling through four basic research activities, each of which leads to a different mode of knowing. The four activities are: (a) reflection and dialogue, leading to propositional knowing; (b) applying propositions in the everyday world, leading to practical knowing; (c) finding new ways to engage the phenomenon, leading to experiential knowing; and (d) finding themes, patterns, and meanings, leading to presentational knowing.

Collective Autobiography is a new method of sociological research developed by Konopásek (2000) and his colleagues. In their book, *Our Lives as Database: Doing a Sociology of Ourselves,* author-participants conducted sociological research on changes in Czech society after the fall of Communism by writing their own autobiographies and dialoguing about them. Several Czech sociologists participated over a period of 4 years. The participants varied in age, gender, and theoretical orientation to sociology. The book presents a description of the project, eight life narratives, and interpretive and analytic texts created through participant dialogues about their own narratives.

Collaborative Heuristic Analysis of Music is currently being done by the author and six co-researchers (Elaine Abbott, Dena Condron, Andi McGraw Hunt, Laura Thomae, Nadine Cadesky, Dawn Miller), who are doing a collaborative self-inquiry aimed at analyzing a music program (*Imagery*) used in GIM. The purpose of the analysis is to gain an understanding of the musical and imaginal experiences that are potentially evoked by this program. The Heuristic Method of Music Analysis (Bruscia, 1999) is being used (see above); however, it has been expanded into a collaborative format. That is, instead of having one researcher studying self and several participants, the collaborative approach involves all seven researchers serving as researchers and participants with one another, continually guiding and traveling to the program with one another, and analyzing the results.

Conclusion

The interdisciplinary nature of music therapy is a very significant advantage for researchers. This chapter has presented a rich palette of research methods from psychology, sociology, anthropology, the humanities, education, the arts, and the other arts therapies—all which can be implemented in and adapted for music therapy. The task ahead for music therapy is to establish its own research direction and to create its own methods, being informed by the many approaches already being used.

References

Aanstoos, C. (1983). The think aloud method in descriptive research. *Journal of Phenomenological Psychology, 14,* 243–266.

Abrams, B. (2002). Analyzing music programs used in the Bonny method. In K. E. Bruscia & D. E. Grocke (Eds.), *Guided Imagery and Music: The Bonny method and beyond* (pp. 317–335). Gilsum, NH: Barcelona Publishers.

Abrams, J. (2000). *An analysis of Elegy: A Guided Imagery and Music program.* Unpublished master's project, Temple University, Philadelphia.

Barrell, J., Aanstoos, C., Richards, A., & Arons, M. (1987). Human science research methods. *Journal of Humanistic Psychology, 27,* 424–457.

Barrell, J. J., & Barrell, J. E. (1975). A self-directed approach for a science of human experience. *Journal of Phenomenological Psychology, 6,* 63–74.

Bochner, A., & Ellis, C. (2002). *Ethnographically speaking: Autoethnography, literature, and aesthetic.* Walnut Creek, CA: AltaMira Press

Bonny, H. (1993). Body listening: A new way to review the GIM tapes. *Journal of the Association for Music and Imagery, 2,* 3–10.

Booth, J. (1998–1999). The Paradise program: A new music program for Guided Imagery and Music. *Journal of the Association for Music and Imagery, 6,* 15–36.

Brookens, R. (2002). *An analysis of the Guided Imagery and Music program "Creativity III."* Unpublished master's project, Temple University, Philadelphia.

Bruscia, K. E. (1982, June). *Music in the life of one man: Ontogenetic foundations of music therapy.* Paper presented at Symposium on Music in the Life of Man at New York University, New York, NY.

Bruscia, K. E. (1995). Modes of consciousness in Guided Imagery and Music: A therapist's experience of the guiding process. In C. Kenny (Ed.), *Listening, playing, creating: Essays on the power of sound* (pp. 165–197). Albany NY: State University of New York Press.

Bruscia, K. E. (1996). Daedalus and the labyrinth: A mythical research fantasy. In M. Langenberg, K. Aigen, & J. Frommer (Eds.), *Qualitative music therapy research: Beginning dialogues* (pp. 205–212). Gilsum, NH: Barcelona Publishers.

Bruscia, K. E. (1998a). Re-imaging client images: A technique for exploring transference and countertransference in Guided Imagery and Music. In K. E. Bruscia (Ed.), *The dynamics of music psychotherapy* (pp. 527–548). Gilsum, NH: Barcelona Publishers.

Bruscia, K. E. (1998b). Re-imaging client images: A technique for uncovering projective identification. In K. E. Bruscia (Ed.), *The dynamics of music psychotherapy* (pp. 549–560). Gilsum, NH: Barcelona Publishers.

Bruscia, K. E. (1999). A method of analyzing music programs in GIM. In *Manual for GIM training.* Unpublished manuscript. Philadelphia: Author.

Clements, J., Ettling, D., Jenett, D., & Shields, L. (1998). Organic research: Feminine spirituality meets transpersonal research. In W. Braud & R. Anderson (Eds.), *Transpersonal research methods for the social sciences* (pp. 114–127). Thousand Oaks, CA: Sage Publications.

Craig, P. E. (1987). Dreaming, reality, and allusion: An existential–phenomenological inquiry. In F. Van Zuuren, F. Wertz, & B. Mook (Eds.), *Advances in qualitative research: Theme and variations* (pp. 115–136). Amsterdam: Swets & Zeitlinger.

Denzin, N. (1987a). *The alcoholic self.* Newbury Park, CA: Sage Publications.

Denzin, N. (1987b). *The recovering alcoholic.* Newbury Park, CA: Sage Publications.

Denzin, N. (1989). *Interpretive biography.* Thousand Oaks, CA: Sage Publications.

Ellis, C. (1991). Sociological introspection and emotional experience. *Symbolic Interaction, 14*(1), 23–50.

Ellis, C., & Bochner, A. P. (2000). Authoethnography, personal narrative, reflexivity: Researcher as subject. In N. Denzin & Y. Lincoln (Eds.) *Handbook of qualitative research* (2nd ed., pp. 733–768). Thousand Oaks, CA: Sage Publications.

Fenner, P. (1996). Heuristic research study: Self-therapy using the brief image-making experience. *The Arts in Psychotherapy, 23,* 37–51.

Ginsburg, F. (1989a). *Contested lives: The abortion debate in an American community.* Berkeley, CA: University of California Press.

Ginsburg, F. (1989b). Dissonance and harmony: The symbolic function of abortion in activists' life stories. In Personal Narrative Group (Ed.), *Interpreting women's lives: Feminist theory and personal narrative* (pp. 59–84). Indianapolis, IN: Indiana University Press.

Giorgi, A., Fischer, W., & von Eckartsberg, R. (Eds.) (1971). *Duquesne studies in phenomenological psychology* (Vol. 1). Pittsburgh, PA: Duquesne University Press.

Giorgi, A. (1987). Problems in self-descriptive research as exemplified in a phenomenological analysis of imaginative experiences. In F. Van Zuuren, F. Wertz, & B. Mook (Eds.), *Advances in qualitative research: Theme and variation* (pp. 41–51). Amsterdam: Swets & Zeitlinger.

Grocke, D. (2002). Re-imaging in GIM supervision. *Nordic Journal of Music Therapy, 11,* 178–181.

Hadley, S. (1998). Transference experiences in two forms of improvisational music therapy. In K. E. Bruscia (Ed.), *The dynamics of music psychotherapy* (pp. 249–286). Gilsum, NH: Barcelona Publishers.

Heron, J. (1996). *Cooperative inquiry: Research into the human condition.* London: Sage Publications.

Heron, J. (1998). *Sacred science: Person-centred inquiry into the spiritual and subtle.* Ross-on-Wye, UK: PCCS Books.

Hibben, J. (Ed.) (1999). *Inside music therapy: Client experiences.* Gilsum, NH: Barcelona Publishers.

Hintz, M. (1995). *Empowerment through spiritual experiences in Guided Imagery and Music: A self-exploration.* Unpublished master's project, Temple University, Philadelphia.

Kern, J. (1978). Countertransference and spontaneous screens: An analyst studies his own visual images. *Journal of American Psychoanalytic Association, 26,* 21–48.

Kleining, G. (1982). Umriss zu einer Methodologie qualitativer Sozialforschung [Outline of a methodology of qualitative social research]. *Kölner Zeitschrift für Soziologie und Sozialpsychologie, 34,* 224–253.

Knechtel, S. (2002). *An analysis of the Mournful program in GIM.* Unpublished master's project, Temple University, Philadelphia.

Konopásek, Z. (Ed.). (2000). *Our lives as database—Doing a sociology of ourselves: Czech social transitions in autobiographical research dialogues.* Prague, Czech Republic: Karolinum Press.

Lett, W. (1993). Therapist creativity: The arts of supervision. *The Arts in Psychotherapy, 20,* 371–386.

Lett, W. (1995). Experiential supervision through simultaneous drawing and talking. *The Arts in Psychotherapy, 22,* 315–328.

Lett, W. (1998). Researching experiential self-knowing. *The Arts in Psychotherapy, 25,* 331–342.

Lutz, A., Lachaux, J. Martinerie, J., & Varela, F. (2002). Guiding the study of brain dynamics by using first-person data: Synchrony patterns correlate with ongoing conscious states during a simple visual task. *Proceedings of the National Academy of Science, U.S.A., 99,* 1586–1591.

Lyons, W. (1986). *The disappearance of introspection.* Cambridge, MA: The MIT Press.

McNiff, S. (1998). *Art-based research.* London: Jessica Kingsley Publishers.

Meadows, A. (1995). *How do I understand a child's experience in music therapy?* Unpublished master's project, Temple University, Philadelphia.

Meashey, K. (1998). *Re-imaging: A trainee's experience in Guided Imagery and Music (GIM).* Unpublished master's project, Temple University, Philadelphia.

Moustakas, C. (1961). *Loneliness.* Englewood Cliffs, NJ: Prentice Hall.

Moustakas, C. (1990). *Heuristic research: Design, methodology, and applications.* Thousand Oaks, CA: Sage Publications.

Nielsen, T. (1995). Describing and modeling hypnagogic imagery using a systematic self-observation procedure. *Dreaming, 5,* 75–94.

O'Malley, C., Draper, S., & Riley, M. (1984). Constructive interaction: A method for studying human-computer-human interaction. *Proceedings of INTERACT 84* (pp. 269–274). Amsterdam: North-Holland.

Pellitteri, J. (1998). A self-analysis of transference in Guided Imagery and Music (GIM). In K. Bruscia (Ed.), *The dynamics of music psychotherapy* (pp. 481–490). Gilsum, NH: Barcelona Publishers.

Petitmengin-Peugeot, C. (1999). The intuitive experience. In F. Varela & J. Shear (Eds.), *The view from within: First-person approaches to the study of consciousness* (pp. 43–77). Bowling Green, OH: Imprint Academic. (Also published in *Journal of Consciousness Studies, 6*(2–3), 43–77)

Priestley, M. (1994) *Essays on Analytical Music Therapy.* Gilsum, NH: Barcelona Publishers.

Rodriguez, N., & Ryave, A. (2002). *Systematic self-observation: Qualitative research methods* (Vol. 49). Thousand Oaks, CA: Sage Publications.

Ross, W., & Kapp, F. (1962) A technique for self-analysis of countertransference. *Journal of the American Psychoanalytic Association, 10,* 643–657.

Ruud, E. (1997). Music and identity. *Nordic Journal of Music Therapy, 6,* 3–13.

Sakadjian, H. (2000). *An analysis of the GIM program, Gaia.* Unpublished master's project, Temple University, Philadelphia.

Shapiro, K. (1985). *Bodily reflective modes: A phenomenological method of psychology.* Durham, NC: Duke University Press.

Shaw, R. (1989). The heartbeat of relationships: A heuristic investigation of interaction rhythms. (Doctoral dissertation, Union Institute, 1989). *Dissertation Abstracts International, 50,* 5334.

Skolimowski, H. (1994). *The participatory mind: A new theory of knowledge and of the universe.* New York: Penguin, Arkana.

Soderhielm, A. (2001). *A Guided Imagery and Music program analysis: Solace.* Unpublished master's project, Temple University, Philadelphia.

Strasser, S. (1969). *The idea of dialogal phenomenology.* Pittsburgh, PA: Duquesne University Press.

Sudnow, D. (2001). *Ways of the hand: A rewritten account.* Cambridge, MA: The MIT Press.

Swanson, L. (1999). *An analysis of the Consoling program in GIM.* Unpublished master's project, Temple University, Philadelphia.

Tesch, R. (1990). *Qualitative research: Analysis types & software tools.* Philadelphia: The Falmer Press.

Titchener, E. (1912). The schema of introspection. *American Journal of Psychology, 23,* 485–508.

Varela, F. (1996). Neurophenomenology: A methodological remedy for the hard problem. *Journal of Consciousness Studies, 3,* 330–350.

Wheeler, B. L. (1999). Experiencing pleasure in working with severely disabled children. *Journal of Music Therapy, 36,* 56–80.

Chapter 31
Ethnography and
Ethnographically Informed Research
Brynjulf Stige

To see ourselves as others see us can be eye-opening. To see others as sharing a nature with ourselves is the merest decency. But it is from the far more difficult achievement of seeing ourselves amongst others, as a local example of the forms human life has locally taken, a case among cases, a world among worlds, that the largeness of mind, without which objectivity is self-congratulation and tolerance a sham, comes. If interpretive anthropology has any general office in the world it is to keep reteaching this fugitive truth.

Clifford Geertz[1]

To study music therapy practice, where two or more people interact and communicate, is to study a social practice. Since humans are cultural by nature, a social practice is necessarily also a cultural practice. This suggests that there is a relationship between music therapy research and ethnography.[2]

Overview and Definition

Ethnography may be understood as a scholarly approach to the study of culture as lived, experienced, and expressed by a person or a group of people. Although there are currently few if any examples of full-scale ethnographic studies in the music therapy literature, it is possible to argue that ethnography is what music therapy researchers are doing all the time since human life, including therapy, is embedded in culture. This argument provides us with a rather vague conception of ethnography, so the purpose of this chapter is to provide a more accurate idea of what music therapy researchers can learn from the practices and texts of ethnographers. The term *ethnography* is a compound where *ethno* is borrowed from Greek, meaning race, people, or culture. The latter meaning is central, and it is no longer assumed that culture is linked to race or discrete ethnic groups in any simple or straightforward way.[3] The second element in the compound, *-graphy,* of course refers to the recording, representing, and writing that is needed for the study of culture.

Several subtraditions of ethnography exist. There are empirical (fact-oriented) approaches, and there are more interpretive approaches including critical, postmodern, and feminist ethnography (Alvesson & Sköldberg, 2000; Atkinson, Coffey, Delamont, Lofland, & Lofland, 2001; Hammersley & Atkinson, 1983/1995; Naples, 2003). In this chapter I will focus upon insights developed within interpretive perspectives, without neglecting the need for solid empirical material as a foundation for interpretation and critique. The *primacy of interpretation* that this choice indicates is illuminated well by Anthony Giddens' well-known comment about social research:

---

[1] This quotation is from Geertz (1983), p. 16.

[2] Some sections of this chapter are revised arguments from Chapter 10 of *Culture-Centered Music Therapy* (Stige, 2002). The two chapters supplement each other: In the former chapter, more space is given for discussion of the writing aspects of ethnography, including problems of representation. In the present chapter, I have simplified these aspects in order to give space for more illumination of ethnography's relevance for music therapy.

[3] This contention relates to a broad and complex debate, which can be illuminated with a few examples: The term race is usually considered meaningless in contemporary science, since evolutionary biologists have found that all humans probably share common ancestors and therefore are genetically very similar (Barrett, Dunbar, & Lycett, 2002, p. 16). The term ethnicity, however, is central in much cultural theory but is usually not used to denote a stable given, rather to describe a relational and changeable construction of symbolic boundaries (Eriksen, 1995). Ethnicity, then, in most cases could not be conceived as rigid group identity. Developments in late modern societies, where culture is individualized, strengthen this tendency (Nielsen, 1993).

First, all social research has a necessarily cultural, ethnographic or "anthropological" aspect to it. This is an expression of what I call the double hermeneutic which characterizes social science. The sociologist has as a field of study phenomena which are already constituted as meaningful. The condition of "entry" to this field is getting to know what actors already know, and have to know, to "go on" in the daily activities of social life (Giddens, 1984, p. 284).

Music therapy researchers have as a field of study phenomena that are already constituted as meaningful by clients, therapists, and other involved agents. In order to be able to understand what is going on in music therapy, we need to understand how the participants understand this. Giddens' comment about double hermeneutics and the ethnographic aspect as foundational therefore comes into play. In fact, music therapy researchers are involved in *multiple hermeneutics,* including the interpretations of the interpretations that the interpreted make of the interpreters, and so on.

Culture is an inescapable resource and restriction when humans try to make sense of events and experiences. Inevitably, though, culture is a complex term, defined in a multitude of ways.[4] Any scholars using the term thus need to clarify their usage, while acknowledging the limitation of this clarification. My own definition of the term is: "Culture is the accumulation of customs and technologies enabling and regulating human coexistence" (Stige, 2002, p. 38). A central premise for this definition is that human existence may be understood as basically dialogic and communicative, even in societies cultivating individualism. Customs and technologies are therefore not only characteristics of the outside or collective world but are internalized by the individual as personal resources and restraints. Personal habits, for instance, relate to cultural customs in a multitude of ways. Similarly, sign systems such as language and music may be viewed as shared technologies of expression and communication.

From this brief excursion to theoretical issues on the primacy of interpretation and culture, it follows that ethnographic research in this chapter will not be discussed as a research method or type of research only, rather as an orientation to research where the cultural is used as an analytic and interpretive resource. Ethnography is then not only relevant for the study of the practices of *others* (which for many music therapists could be, for instance, the healing rituals of indigenous people). It is also relevant for the self-reflective and critical study of clinical and community practices as they exist in modern music therapy all over the world.

Most music therapy researchers are not ethnographers, so how could they possibly do ethnography? When I propose a close relationship between music therapy research and ethnography, I am not suggesting that all music therapy researchers should or could be professional ethnographers. I am rather suggesting that music therapy research needs to be informed by ethnography, and I also suggest that music therapists should take interest in other relevant ethnographically informed research, such as ethnomusicology.[5]

Historical Roots and Theoretical Premises

Historical Roots

Ethnography grew out of the European colonial powers' need to describe and understand the natives of their colonies, and ethnographers have therefore been criticized for serving colonial powers. The once quite common Eurocentric division of peoples with and without history could be seen in this perspective. Only people constituted with a history were in colonial times considered to have the right to establish nations. This division of political power was in fact, if indirectly, also connected to a division of labor among academic disciplines. The prehistoric and historic development of nations was studied by archeologists and historians, while the indigenous people of, for instance, Africa, Australasia, or America were studied by ethnographers. These people

---

[4] As O'Sullivan, Hartley, Saunders, Montgomery, and Fiske (1994, p. 190) suggest, culture is a multidiscursive term, that is, a term that can have significantly different meanings according to its use within different discourses.

[5] Related scholarly traditions may be of relevance in similar ways. An example is cultural studies, which is a (often radical and critical) branch of learning focusing upon subjectivity and contemporary culture, including the cultural study of music (see Clayton, Herbert, & Middleton, 2003).

were then constructed as living in timeless stable traditions, and ethnographers thus in some ways contributed to the political processes that made repression of the *others* possible (Clifford & Marcus, 1986; Denzin & Lincoln, 1998). This not so respectful history of ethnography reminds us of the relationship between power and knowledge and also serves as a backdrop for understanding the strong focus upon self-criticism and reflexivity in current ethnography.

Some of the late 19th and early 20th century pioneers of modern ethnography, such as Franz Boas and Bronislaw Malinowsky, tried to break the servile tradition of earlier ethnography. Malinowsky is also often considered the pioneer of *prolonged field observation* as the preferred method of research in anthropology. In the 19th century, armchair ethnographers studying and comparing documents produced by others were common. Malinowsky considered this approach to be unsatisfactory because it so easily led to ethnocentric judgments. He emphasized participant observation and detailed description and also advocated that the researcher's task was to understand the world as it was seen by the others. From this perspective, the goal of ethnography was to grasp the native's point of view and relation to life; in other words, to realize the native's vision of the world (Eriksen, 1995).

This ideal of giving primacy to insider perspectives has been much discussed among ethnographers.[6] The tradition of hermeneutics teaches us that any understanding is colored by the researcher's pre-understanding. To grasp the native's point of view could then be considered an ideal, but strictly speaking an unattainable ideal. This situation requires reflexivity and awareness about the situated character of any perception and judgment. One central development in 20th century ethnography relates to this indirectly and is of specific interest to this presentation: There has been an expansion of contexts studied by ethnographers, from a focus restricted to remote pre-modern contexts to inclusion of modern everyday contexts closer to the researcher's own background.

The expansion of contexts studied has contributed to the current relatively common assumption that ethnography is an interdisciplinary research tradition rather than a subfield of anthropology alone. In the 1930s, for instance, sociologists of the Chicago School started to use ethnographic techniques to study urban subcultures. The work of the scholar Erving Goffman in the 1940s and onwards exemplifies the next step. In Goffman's work, ethnographic approaches are no longer restricted to the study of a specific culture or to a subculture linked to a given locality. Instead, broader cultural themes are examined. Goffman, who did fieldwork examining the communication conducted in a community in the Shetland Islands, used the same observations as part of a more general argument about the dramaturgical principles of social life (Goffman, 1959/1990). Similarly, after 1 year of participant observation at St. Elizabeth's Hospital in Washington, DC, his agenda when writing *Asylums* (Goffman, 1961/1991) was not to describe the specific culture of this specific place, but to discuss it as an example of total institutions and closed communities comparable to monasteries, prisons, army camps, and boarding schools.

Recent developments within ethnography include the growth of feminist and postcolonial perspectives. Among contemporary ethnographers there are continuous debates on issues such as the researchers' self-presentations in the fields they study and their self-representations in the texts they produce (Atkinson, 1990; Clifford & Marcus, 1986). Criticisms of ethnocentric perspectives in scholarly works have flourished, and the relationships between insider perspectives and outsider perspectives have been examined carefully, particularly by feminist and third world ethnographers (Naples, 2003).

Ethnography may now be described, then, as an interdisciplinary research tradition relevant in any setting where people interact and thus are embedded in culture. For instance, ethnographic studies have been conducted within education, where researchers have studied the social life of the classroom, the staff room, the schoolyard, and so forth. So far, ethnographic perspectives have not been very influential in music therapy, but I expect this to change in the future. It may change if and as culture-centered perspectives get a stronger foothold in the discipline. It may change if and as community music therapy develops, and it may change if and as music therapy expands in new cultural settings around the world (Kenny & Stige, 2002; Pavlicevic & Ansdell, 2004; Stige, 2002, 2003).

---

[6] This discussion is often termed as the tension between emic (insider) and etic (outsider) perspectives, as discussed later.

Theoretical Premises

The basic ethnographic question is, What does it mean to be human? A common attitude toward this question among ethnographers is described by Anthony P. Cohen (1989):

> Instead of asking, "What does it look like to us? What are its theoretical implications?," we ask, "What does it appear to mean to its members?" Rather than describing analytically the form of the structure from an external vantage point, we are attempting to penetrate the structure, to look *outward* from its core. (p. 20)

Ethnographers seek to describe patterns and regularities in processes of human social life as found in habits and practices and in more objectified forms such as various artifacts. How are things said and sung, done and made? What roles, rituals, rationales, and relationships support these habits and practices? Sometimes the answers concentrate on what it means to be human in a specific context. At other times, answers are generalized to broader contexts. To examine what it means to be human requires the inclusion of biological, psychological, and social perspectives, and ethnography therefore relates to a complex interdisciplinary theoretical field. In a short chapter like this, there would be no sense in trying to represent the breadth of relevant theoretical roots. Instead, I will try to demonstrate how ethnography can operate as a crystallizer for theoretical debates that are relevant for broader perspectives on human and social research.

As the epigraph to the chapter indicates, ethnography can be represented as narratives about the meeting of life worlds. A classic dilemma in ethnography, therefore, is the tension between *etic* and *emic* perspectives. The etic perspective is the outsider view that the researcher brings, while the emic perspective is the native view, the insider way of seeing and understanding. As Cohen's statement above illuminates, emic description is seen as the ideal to pursue in much contemporary ethnography. The problem, of course, is that the researcher will never be a native and will not be able to see the world as the native sees it. In addition, there are usually serious problems of translation involved when doing ethnography. The translation from vernacular oral statements into written accounts is quite often given in a different language than the original oral statements. A common research strategy among ethnographers is to try to establish some kind of *emic-etic dialectic,* that is, to let different perspectives inform each other in a dialogical search for understanding and meaning. This is sometimes approached through use of the active interplay of descriptions and interpretations in a research text, where descriptions are given in a language as close to the emic perspective as possible, while interpretations include scholarly terms and relate to theoretical frameworks and therefore explicitly are given in an etic perspective.

The value of letting different perspectives inform each other dialogically will be better understood in light of the comparative approach advocated by anthropologists: "If, say, one chooses to write a monograph about a people in the New Guinea highlands, one will always choose to describe it with at least some concepts (such as kinship, gender, and power) that render it comparable with aspects of other societies" (Eriksen, 1995, p. 9). A basic assumption about humans and humankind informs this approach: Humans share a biological origin, they relate to groups and communities, and they live unique individual lives. Any human is then similar to all other humans in some respects, similar to some and different than others in some respects, and unique compared to all others in some respects.[7]

Universal versus local aspects of culture are therefore among the key issues to discuss and consider when doing ethnography. Late modern ethnographers have opposed some claims about universal patterns and processes that can be found in a number of positivistic social research studies, where what is typical in the Western world may be considered universal. In return, some of these ethnographers have frequently been counted as relativists. An interpretive ethnographer such as Clifford Geertz has, for instance, been a major target of criticism when

---

[7] The simplified summary given in this paragraph does not, of course, suggest that all ethnographers share a concept of humankind. On the contrary, ethnographies may be read as a continuous debate about this concept. To what degree and in which ways do humans share a nature, and how does this influence cultural developments? How local is local culture, and are there any universal cultural elements and processes? The debate is complicated by the fact that biological, sociocultural, and idiosyncratic elements hardly exist as observable and separated layers, but rather as intertwined processes.

biologically informed researchers have discussed evolutionary foundations of culture (see Tooby & Cosmides, 1992). This criticism is not necessarily accurate, however, since Geertz (1973/2000) and many other ethnographers have grappled with the issue of integrative and synthetic theory, that is, the linking of biological, psychological, social, and cultural perspectives.[8]

Methodology

Ethnography in practice is usually understood as the detailed study of a delineated social environment. Participant observation in the milieu of subjects is therefore essential to this tradition of research. Ethnographers *join in* or *hang around*; they take part in and/or observe the activities of other people in order to understand more of their way of life. In short, then, it is possible to describe ethnography as *fieldwork and interpretation*, that is, as the gathering of empirical material through prolonged presence in the field supplemented by analyses and interpretations informed by relevant theory (Eriksen, 1995).

Ethnographic accounts are therefore interpretive, since ethnographers search for the meaning of what they observe. At the same time they are descriptive, because interpretations need to be based on some kind of evidence.[9] Sometimes quite detailed information about a culture might be necessary as a foundation for interpretations. Ethnography is, however, hardly a well-defined and prescriptive set of techniques for collection and analysis of empirical data. Such a set of techniques would in fact be counterproductive to the sensitivity for context that is a basic asset of any ethnographic endeavor. Ethnography is very much about judgment in context, and preconditions for good research include solid training in theory as well as development of the everyday sensitivity of social communication that we all possess (Hammersley & Atkinson, 1983/1995). Such criteria may seem vague, but given the complexity of the situations that ethnographic researchers meet, it would be unhelpful, to say the least, to produce fixed research procedures. One ideal sometimes conveyed is that ethnographers do not study people but rather try to learn from them. While the researcher has some specific interests that differ from those of a student or learner in general, this ideal communicates some of the respect and humility for other ways of life that is a necessary precondition for productive ethnography. Put this way, ethnographers learn from what people do, what they say and sing, and what they make and use. The three main ethnographic techniques are therefore often considered to be participant observation, interviews, and interpretation of texts and artifacts. In addition, the use of field notes—usually used as an integrative tool—is the most widespread method among ethnographers throughout the ethnographic process.[10]

Participant observation through prolonged participation and observation in the setting of interest is often considered to be the main approach to ethnography. An ethnographic account should include concrete observations as well as appropriate quotations of spontaneous dialogues in relevant situations. This means that ethnographers need to visit their sites often or stay at them for a long time. A researcher in music therapy could use participant observation, for instance, by studying a therapy process over time and by following clients or therapists in daily life activities. Settings differ in how they allow access to empirical material and also because they regulate the possible roles a researcher may take in different ways. Social roles in a setting are, of course, not something that researchers choose freely. They are established in negotiation with the other agents of the setting. Among possible roles, at one extreme is the complete participant while at the other is the complete observer. A clinician researcher studying his or her own therapy may be close to being a complete participant, a researcher behind a one-way mirror closer to being a complete observer. As different as these roles seem, they paradoxically share some of the same advantages and disadvantages. They may minimize the subject's reactivity to being studied, but they also limit what can be studied and how, since these roles are not very flexible and give little room for role extension (Hammersley & Atkinson, 1995, p. 107). Usually, therefore, an ethnographically informed researcher would do well to supplement such roles with

---

[8] For a discussion of this, see Stige (2002, Chapter 1).

[9] Ethnographers often concentrate on qualitative evidence, but quantitative evidence may also be relevant.

[10] The format of this chapter only allows for a brief discussion of techniques and methodology. I refer readers who want to learn more about ethnography to textbooks and handbooks (see Atkinson et al., 2001; Hammersley & Atkinson, 1983/1995).

variants of participant as observer or observer as participant, in such a way that it is possible to extend and modify roles to serve research needs (a clinician researcher may supplement the study of sessions with research interviews of the client, etc.)

Interviews give the researcher access to insider accounts and may be of utmost importance for an ethnographically informed researcher. As with participant observation, to conduct an interview demands negotiation of roles. How formalized and structured should the interview be? At one extreme, interviews are conducted in separate and protected settings and are structured and focused by the researcher; at another extreme, interviews are not much different from any spontaneous conversation and come close to participant observation. Interviews give information on both the phenomena under scrutiny and the subjects presenting the accounts (what they say and how they say it). Music therapy researchers may have interest in having insider accounts from clients, family members, therapists, and other professionals, as well as from people of the community, depending upon the research question and the approach to therapy. Some music therapy researchers may be skeptical about the idea of conducting such interviews, either because it is considered impossible to describe music experiences in words or because it is suggested that such descriptions require specific competencies that most lay people do not have. From an ethnographic perspective, one would argue that, while it may be impossible to translate music to words, it is still meaningful to talk about music. It is essential for the understanding of humans' relationship to music to understand how music and narratives are linked together (Berkaak, 1993).

Interpretation of texts and artifacts is the third main ethnographic technique to be mentioned here. In music therapy, this may include analysis and interpretations of music as recorded or the study of musicking as memorized activity.[11] Other options are analysis and interpretation of diaries, lyrics, and drawings produced by clients, therapists, and other agents. Such cultural artifacts must be understood in the context of their social use, and the interpretation must be examined in the light of the researcher's own pre-understanding, which obviously influences the interpretation. These issues illuminate how ethnographic interpretation is related to hermeneutics.

The three techniques described here—participant observation, interviews, and interpretation of texts and artifacts—are usually integrated through the use of field notes. In field notes, the researcher's impressions, ideas, and provisional interpretations are outlined. Field notes could therefore be viewed as the fourth (some would say the first) central technique in ethnography. Alternatively, their use may be viewed as the major strategy for integrating the information gained through use of other techniques. Field notes typically include a mix of personal information, raw data, and sketches for future steps in the research process.

The techniques mentioned above are the most common among ethnographers. There is no reason for not using other techniques, though, such as questionnaires, polls, and even projective tests. One advantage of surveys is that they may provide the researcher with information from more informants, and sometimes it is important for the researcher to have responses from a representative sample. While a representative sample is an obvious requirement in much empirical research, this is not necessarily so in ethnography, however. Just as often, it is important to choose informants strategically. One looks for informants that are willing and able to give information, and subjects that are more interesting than others because they may be especially insightful, because their role and history may be especially rich and multifaceted, or for other reasons.

The possibility of using several techniques when conducting ethnography invites the researcher to explore triangulation and to develop a multi-perspective understanding of the phenomenon under scrutiny (Hammersley & Atkinson, 1995, pp. 230–232).[12] Sensitivity in the process of interpreting data is crucial. Ethnographic fieldwork involves the disciplined study of what the world is like to people who have learned to see, hear, think, speak, and act in ways that are different from our own. This world does not present itself for the ethnographer in ready-made concepts. Rather, what the researcher usually has is a messy heap of empirical material, such as field notes, interview transcripts, and recordings of various sorts. Some kind of order and

---

[11] The term *musicking,* as coined by Christopher Small (1998), refers to the idea of music as a situated activity rather than as an object. As situated activity, musicking allows for the performance of a multitude of personal, social, and cultural relationships.

[12] Some researchers advocate that triangulation does not necessarily give a more complete picture of one phenomenon, but that different techniques illuminate different aspects.

structure will be cultivated from or superimposed upon this heap. To some degree, ethnography may be understood as the textual construction of reality (Atkinson, 1990). The writing aspect of doing ethnography (including awareness of the fact that to write is to privilege certain perspectives) therefore has been given serious consideration by several ethnographers (see for instance Clifford & Marcus, 1986; Geertz, 1988/1997; Naples, 2003).

Geertz's (1973/2000) concept of *thick description* is illustrative of the interaction of description and interpretation typical in ethnographic methodology. Imagine you see someone contracting the eyelids of his right eye. How should you interpret this? It could be an involuntary twitch, a wink as a signal to a friend, a parody of another wink, or a rehearsal of a parody. "Complexities are possible, if not practically without end, at least logically so" (Geertz, 1973, p. 7). When researching culture, it is not enough to give descriptions of what is seen or heard, and to add details to such descriptions does not automatically add to our understanding. You need to add descriptions of contexts (situations of use) in which events can be understood. This is not to say that details are irrelevant. In the example above, for instance, very frequent twitches are more likely to be interpreted as involuntary than less frequent ones. However, a detailed description of this, with the frequency counted and means and variation calculated, would still be a thin description. Contexts of use must be added in order to make a sound interpretation.

Geertz (1973/2000) borrowed the term thick description and the example to illuminate it from the Oxford philosopher Gilbert Ryle. If I should create a music therapy example, it could be: Imagine you hear a client playing synchronically with the therapist. How should you interpret this? It could be synchrony by intention, or it could be an unconscious and unreflective coordination of playing. It could be an expression of immediacy, or it could be lack of differentiation. It could be a parody of the therapist's way of playing or a rehearsal of something. A long series of complexities is possible, and a thick description through sensitivity to the context of practice will be required for interpretation of the event. To give a thick description is to capture as many possible or relevant contexts of use as can be found, and to draw on these as a basis for the process of guessing meanings and assessing the guesses. For music therapists, this suggests that analysis and interpretation of music as heard is insufficient. The meaning of music cannot be understood if isolated from the meaning game that it is part of.[13]

If to give a thick description is to try to capture possible meanings through examination of our own constructions of other people's constructions, how could we ever find a way through all the layers of possible meanings? Thick descriptions must be given some kind of specification, not through reliance on general or context-independent theories of meaning but through *situating* the process of guessing meanings and assessing guesses. In other words, the meaning of music could not be derived from musical analysis if this analysis is separated from descriptions and interpretations of the roles, rituals, relationships, and rationales of the music therapy context (Stige, 2002).

The researcher's subjectivity is essential in the process of interpretation. Broadly speaking, there have been two main ways of dealing with this among ethnographers (the problem is shared with many other qualitative researchers also). One strategy is to minimize subjectivity, the other is to acknowledge it and reflect upon its role in the research process. The first strategy has been characteristic of approaches labeled as *naturalistic*. Based upon a criticism of dominant positivistic traditions of social research, naturalistic inquirers have advocated the relevance of the study of particular phenomena in their natural contexts. The possible confusion created by the use of the term naturalistic (which also is used in the natural sciences) may be illustrative, since practices of naturalistic inquiry often inherited some of the presuppositions from the positivists they criticized, one of them being the idea of minimizing subjectivity. The alternative is to acknowledge that the researcher necessarily influences the informants in some way or another. If this perspective is taken, reflexivity throughout the research process is what is asked for, not techniques of minimizing subjectivity (see Hammersley & Atkinson, 1983/1995; Naples, 2003).

---

[13] This may be considered in relation to Wittgenstein's (1953/1967) notion of language game, suggesting that meaning in language is not given independently of human activities and the contexts they belong to (see Stige, 2002, for discussion of this).

Relationship to Other Types of Research

While quantitative researchers may aim at telling stories about the effect of music therapy, qualitative researchers may be concerned about being able to tell an effective story. The value of both approaches depends on the researcher's ability to acknowledge that his or her account is partial. Who speaks? Who writes? When and where? With or to whom? In which way? For what reasons? Under what structural and historical constraints? Interpretive ethnographers have developed an awareness of the partiality of truths and have explored the possibilities and limitations of rigorous partiality. They may offer valuable and challenging insights for other approaches to the study of humans.

This illuminates how ethnography relates to a broad range of other research traditions. At the level of technique, there are obvious links between ethnography and, say, case studies, where participant observations, interviews, and analysis of artifacts are central. At a more theoretical level, relationships exist with other approaches to the study of human beings, such as biography and historical research, which may support ethnographic investigations by ensuring the inclusion of individual experiences and time dimensions (and which in return may be informed by ethnographic descriptions of culture and context). At the epistemological level, ethnographic research shares problems of description and interpretation with, say, the hermeneutic tradition. It is possible to conceive such relationships as complementary. Some say that ethnographers do *philosophy with people in it*. Whether or not this is an exact description, ethnography shares with several other approaches to research an interest in what it means to be human, and it contributes perspectives due to characteristics such as its basis in fieldwork and its focus upon comparative interpretations.

Some central dilemmas of ethnography, such as conflicts between insider (emic) and outsider (etic) perspectives and gaps between experience and description, have been discussed in this chapter. Contemporary attempts to grapple with such dilemmas also illuminate how there are mutual relationships between research traditions such as ethnography, discourse analysis, and participatory action research. For instance, feminist researchers (see Naples, 2003) have argued that taking insider perspectives seriously requires that researchers and informants meet each other with mutual respect and a dialogic attitude. In other words, they become involved in the research process with comparable roles and responsibilities, thus building bridges between ethnography and participatory action research. Similarly, to examine gaps between experience and description requires that the categories of the ethnographic account be examined carefully and critically. In other words, ethnography and discourse analysis become linked.

Music Therapy Examples

There is a long way to go before we can speak of a solid tradition of ethnography and ethnographically informed research in music therapy. This is so even though the first North American pioneers of music therapy demonstrated interest in ethnography. In the 1950s, the *Books of Proceedings* of the National Association for Music Therapy included several contributions on ethnography and ethnomusicology. One example was written by Bruno Nettl (1956), today one of the grand old men of ethnomusicology. He described how music in "primitive and simple"[14] cultures hardly is used for therapeutic purposes alone. Instead music is part of ritual and ceremony, with an integration of music, words, and movement. In short, what he described is music as situated mode of communication rather than as separate stimuli. Nettl contrasted this to the more limited study of the direct effect of music upon behavior, which he understood was the focus of modern U.S. music therapy. He underlined how music and ritual could be a way of giving individuals with adjustment difficulties a possibility of regaining their proper place in the community, through participation:

> In modern music therapy, listening is a frequent way for the patient to experience music. This reflects our basic musical culture, in which most people listen, a few perform, and even less compose. But in many primitive cultures the picture is different. Almost everybody participates in performing

---

[14] We will have to excuse him for using such derogatory terms, still common in the scholarship of the 1950s.

music. . . . Consequently the therapeutic aspects of music tend to be concentrated in the creative side of musical activity. No doubt this is something which might be taken to the heart by modern music therapists. (p. 39)

Similar ideas to those advocated by Nettl have probably been taken to heart by many music therapy practitioners, but, despite the interest in the pioneering years, ethnography seems never to have been properly accepted as part of the music therapy research palette. I argue that this is unfortunate and that ethnographic research could contribute insights about music therapy as discipline, profession, and practice. Based upon this tripartite conception of music therapy (see Stige, 2002), I suggest that ethnographically informed research could contribute to the discipline of music therapy through exploration of a broad range of practices and discourses on music and health in context (including indigenous healing rituals, modern music therapy, and everyday uses of music in modern societies). The profession of music therapy could be informed through the study of institutions and communities where music therapists work, and the practice of music therapy could be enhanced through fieldwork on and interpretations of music therapy approaches in action, ranging from medical music therapy to music psychotherapy to community music therapy.

Although the list of ethnographically informed studies in the music therapy literature is currently relatively short, I will not attempt to present a comprehensive overview of it. Instead I will mention a few examples that may demonstrate the range of possibilities. The writing of Chava Sekeles (1996) and Joseph Moreno (1995) have for years reflected a strong interest in culture and indigenous healing rituals, and Michael Rohrbacher (1999) has argued that it is about time that music therapists again take more interest in the tradition of ethnomusicology. Ethnographic awareness is present in Carolyn Kenny's (1982, 1989) discussions of music therapy theory, and she has in the last few years developed this further as a research scholar in indigenous studies (see Kenny, 2002). Another pioneer, who has expanded the focus to include everyday uses of music in late modern societies, is Even Ruud (2002). An interesting observation is that music therapy recently has been included in some recent ethnographic studies of music (DeNora, 2000; Gouk, 2000; Horden, 2000; Weisethaunet, 1999). Still, there are, to my knowledge, very few ethnographic studies of institutions and communities where music therapists work, although some ethnographically informed studies of music therapy practices have been conducted (see for instance Forrest, 2002; Stige, 2003). While the list of examples could certainly be made longer, I contend that there are potentials in ethnography that have not been explored by music therapists. To illuminate some of the possibilities, I will close this chapter by presenting briefly one ethnographic study.

Ruud (1973/1980, 1990, 1998) has for many years included sociological and anthropological perspectives in his texts on music therapy theory, and he has also illuminated the relevance of ethnographic studies. It is probably not correct to propose that Ruud has as yet conducted a full-scale ethnographic study of music therapy practices, but he did conduct an ethnographic popular music study together with an anthropologist (Berkaak & Ruud, 1994) that in several ways may function as a model for music therapists.[15] The object of study is the rock band Sunwheels and its relationships to the local community as well as to the international music industry. The subtitle of the book describing the project is *Stories about a Rock Band.* These stories are presented in a way that allows room for several perspectives. First, the musicians in the band (who all came from the same suburb) have different interests informed by different ideas and ideologies, so that they tell quite different stories. Second, the researchers add extra layers of stories as they interpret the band members' stories through giving them a context of cultural theory. In the research text, Berkaak and Ruud manage to separate the different voices through establishing distinctions between empirical material (including field notes, interview statements, and quotations from various written sources) and the authors' comments. At the same time, the different perspectives interact closely; comments and interpretations follow descriptions and quotations in a close weave.

Berkaak and Ruud (1994) tell stories about Sunwheels, from modest beginnings as a local band of young boys, to growing success in a national context, to somewhat less success in Los Angeles some years later. The weave of descriptions and interpretations that the text

---

[15] I am referring to the original Norwegian book about the study, first published in 1994. The book is not translated into English, but, in a later publication in English, Ruud (1998, Chapter 6) has given an abbreviated presentation of some elements of the study.

represents provides the reader with a rich understanding of values, practices, and conditions in a certain segment of the rock world. In an epilogue, the authors sum up some of the insights the study has given them. They stress how rock music is established in a social and cultural field where views and values are contested and where certain power hierarchies are established. At the same time, they underline how rock may be attractive for young people as it may provide them with tools for making themselves heard in diverse contexts. Rock music may then be described in an ambiguous way: It may be a commodity for the international rock industry, but it may also be a tool for the establishment and maintenance of community and social networks in a given local context. A central point in the epilogue is thus how Sunwheels could often operate as a cultural meeting point, that is, as mediator between the local and the global, dreams and reality, conflict and concord, individuality and community. In developing these points, the researchers draw on their extensive knowledge about cultural theory (see Berkaak & Ruud, 1992). They are, however, careful not to kill the stories with theoretical elaborations. The general points that they make in the epilogue are therefore relatively short. Much of what can be learned from the stories of and about this rock band is to be found in the stories themselves, not in the meta-reflections of the epilogue. Or it may be more precise to suggest that it is the interplay among stories, interpretations, and meta-reflections that provides researchers and readers with insight.

How can this study function as a model for future music therapy studies? In line with the closing argument of the previous paragraph, I believe that the lessons we may learn from ethnographic studies are only rarely or at least only partly to be found in the conclusion sections of these studies. In the complex whole of an ethnographic study, different readers may learn different lessons. Four possibilities linked to Berkaak and Ruud's (1994) text could be the following: First, music therapy researchers may learn something about the value of interdisciplinary collaboration (in this case between an anthropologist and a musicologist/music therapist). Or, they may learn from the authors' reflexivity in presenting their own roles as researchers (their knowledge of the field as well as their limitations, including the danger of *home-blindness*) or from the careful weaving of descriptions and interpretations in the research report. Second, music therapy practitioners may learn from this study by comparing their own values and assumptions with those of the rock world that is presented. For instance, reflections upon the various roles of parents, teachers, and youth workers in the early years of Sunwheels could be used as a starting point for reflections on how the roles of a music therapist could vary in different stages of a community music therapy project. Third, theoretically inclined readers may learn from this study through comparison with existing music therapy theories. The work may be taken as an anthropologically informed contribution to the ongoing debates within the discipline of music therapy in relation to central notions such as the concept of music, the nature of health, and so forth.[16] Fourth, socially and politically engaged readers may learn from how this study illuminates how musicking can enable individuals and empower them in social and cultural contexts.

In conclusion, this example may illuminate how ethnographically informed studies could have a double edge in future developments of music therapy theory, practice, and research: They could remind us about the local quality of human experience and they could illuminate how culture is universally present in the study of humans. In the future it will, in my judgment, be helpful for music therapists to include ethnography in the research palette and to be able to locate themselves within interdisciplinary fields of study where the cultural aspects of music, human health, and development are seen in relationship.

References

Alvesson, M., & Sköldberg, K. (2000). *Reflexive methodology: New vistas for qualitative research.* London: Sage Publications.

Atkinson, P. (1990). *The ethnographic imagination: Textual construction of reality.* London, Routledge.

Atkinson, P., Coffey, A., Delamont, S., Lofland, J., & Lofland, L. (Eds.). (2001). *Handbook of ethnography.* Thousand Oaks, CA: Sage Publications.

---

[16] This is, by the way, how Ruud (1998) himself has interpreted this project when exploring music as a map of reality (pp. 85–99) and health as linked to identity and the quality of life (pp. 31–67).

Barrett, L., Dunbar, R., & Lycett, J. (2002). *Human evolutionary psychology*. New York: Palgrave.

Berkaak, O. A. (1993). *Erfaringer fra risikosonen. Opplevelse og stilutvikling i rock* [From the zone of risks. Experience and the development of style in rock]. Oslo, Norway: Universitetsforlaget.

Berkaak, O. A., & Ruud, E. (1992). *Den påbegynte virkelighet. Studier i samtidskultur* [Emerging reality. Studies in contemporary culture]. Oslo: Universitetsforlaget.

Berkaak, O. A., & Ruud, E. (1994). *Sunwheels: Fortellinger om et rockeband* [Sunwheels. Stories about a rock band]. Oslo: Universitetsforlaget.

Clayton, M., Herbert, T., & Middleton, R. (2003). *The cultural study of music: A critical introduction*. London: Routledge.

Clifford, J., & Marcus, G. E. (1986). *Writing culture: The poetics and politics of ethnography*. Berkeley, CA: University of California Press.

Cohen, A. P. (1989). *The symbolic construction of community*. London: Routledge.

DeNora, T. (2000). *Music in everyday life*. Cambridge, UK: Cambridge University Press.

Denzin, N. K., & Lincoln, Y. S. (Eds.). (1998). *The landscape of qualitative research: Theories and issues*. Thousand Oaks, CA: Sage Publications.

Eriksen, T. H. (1995). *Small places, large issues. An introduction to social and cultural anthropology*. London: Pluto Press.

Forrest, L. C. (2002). Addressing issues of ethnicity and identity in palliative care through music therapy practice. In C. Kenny & B. Stige (Eds.), *Contemporary* Voices *in music therapy: Communication, culture, and community* (pp. 67–82). Oslo: Unipub forlag.

Geertz, C. (1983). *Local knowledge: Further essays in interpretive anthropology*. New York: Basic Books.

Geertz, C. (1997). *Works and lives: The anthropologist as author*. Stanford, CA: Stanford University Press. (Original work published 1988)

Geertz, C. (2000). *The interpretation of cultures*. New York: Basic Books. (Original work published 1973)

Giddens, A. (1989). *The constitution of society: Outline of the theory of structuration*. Cambridge, UK: Cambridge University Press. (Original work published 1984)

Goffman, E. (1990). *The presentation of self in everyday life*. London: Penguin Books. (Original work published 1959)

Goffman, E. (1991). *Asylums: Essays on the social situations of mental patients and other inmates*. London: Penguin Books. (Original work published 1961)

Gouk, P. (2000). *Musical healing in cultural contexts*. Aldershot, UK: Ashgate.

Hammersley, M., & Atkinson, P. (1995). *Ethnography: Principles in practice* (2nd ed.). London: Routledge. (1st ed. published 1983)

Horden, P. (2000). *Music as medicine: The history of music therapy since antiquity*. Aldershot, UK: Ashgate.

Kenny, C. B. (1982). *The mythic artery: The magic of music therapy*. Atascadero, CA: Ridgeview Publishing Company.

Kenny, C. B. (1989). *The field of play: A guide for the theory and practice of music therapy*. Atascadero, CA: Ridgeview Publishing Company.

Kenny, C. (2002). Keeping the world in balance—Music therapy in a ritual context. In C. Kenny & B. Stige (Eds.), *Contemporary* Voices *in music therapy: Communication, culture, and community* (pp. 157–170). Oslo: Unipub forlag.

Kenny, C., & Stige, B. (Eds.). (2002). *Contemporary voices in music therapy: Communication, culture, and community*. Oslo: Unipub forlag.

Moreno, J. (1995). Candomblé: Afro-Brazilian ritual as therapy. In C. B. Kenny (Ed.), *Listening, playing, creating: Essays on the power of sound* (pp. 217–232). Albany, NY: State University of New York Press.

Naples, N. A. (2003). *Feminism and method: Ethnography, discourse analysis, and activist research*. New York: Routledge.

Nettl, B. (1956). Aspects of primitive and folk music relevant to music therapy. In E. T. Gaston (Ed.), *Music therapy 1955: Fifth book of proceedings of the National Association for Music Therapy* (pp. 36–39). Lawrence, KS: National Association for Music Therapy.

Nielsen, H. K. (1993). *Kultur og modernitet* [Culture and modernity]. Aarhus, Denmark: Aarhus University Press.

O'Sullivan, T., Hartley, J., Saunders, D., Montgomery, M., & Fiske, J. (1994). *Key concepts in communication and cultural studies.* London: Routledge.

Pavlicevic, M., & Ansdell, G. (Eds.). (2004). *Community music therapy.* London: Jessica Kingsley Publishers.

Rohrbacher, M. (1999, November). Music therapy and ethnomusicology revisited. Paper presented at the 9th World Congress of Music Therapy, Washington, DC.

Ruud, E. (1980). *Music therapy and its relationship to current treatment theories.* St. Louis, MO: MMB Music. (Originally [1973] a master's thesis, Florida State University, Tallahassee, FL).

Ruud, E. (1990). *Musikk som kommunikasjon og samhandling. Teoretiske perspektiv på musikkterapien.* [Music as communication and interaction. Theoretical perspectives on music therapy]. Oslo: Solum.

Ruud, E. (1998). *Music therapy: Improvisation, communication, and culture.* Gilsum, NH: Barcelona Publishers.

Ruud, E. (2002). Music as a cultural immunogen—Three narratives on the use of music as a technology of health. In I. M. Hanken, S. Graabæk, & M. Nerland (Eds.), *Research in and for higher music education. Festschrift for Harald Jørgensen* (2002: 2; pp. 109–120). Oslo: NMH (Norwegian Academy of Music).

Sekeles, C. (1996, July). *Music in the traditional healing rituals of Morocco.* Paper presented at the 8th World Congress of Music Therapy, Hamburg, Germany.

Small, C. (1998). *Musicking: The meanings of performing and listening.* Hanover, NH: Wesleyan University Press.

Stige, B. (2002). *Culture-centered music therapy.* Gilsum, NH: Barcelona Publishers.

Stige, B. (2003). *Elaborations toward a notion of community music therapy* (doctoral dissertation, University of Oslo). Oslo: Unipub forlag.

Tooby, J., & Cosmides, L. (1992). The psychological foundations of culture. In J. Barkow, L. Cosmides, & J. Tooby, J. (Eds.), *The adapted mind: Evolutionary psychology and the generation of culture* (pp. 19–136). New York: Oxford University Press.

Weisethaunet, H. (1999). Critical remarks on the nature of improvisation. *Nordic Journal of Music Therapy, 8,* 143–155.

Wittgenstein, L. (1967). *Philosophical investigations.* Oxford: Blackwell. (Original work published 1953)

Acknowledgments

I want to express my thanks to Carolyn Kenny and Even Ruud for their roles as pioneers in the field and for the valuable feedback they gave to an earlier version of this chapter.

Chapter 32
Participatory Action Research[1]
Brynjulf Stige

The investigation of thematics involves the investigation of the people's thinking—thinking which occurs only in and among men seeking out reality together. I cannot think for others, nor can others think for me. Even if the people's thinking is superstitious or naïve, it is only as they rethink their assumptions in action that they can change.

Paulo Freire[2]

What is true knowledge? Arguments in response to such a question are often supported by reference to a theory of truth. Two of the more widespread of these are the *correspondence theory,* suggesting that truth is defined by the correspondence between a statement and the facts of the world, and the *coherence theory,* suggesting that truth is defined by the coherence between a belief and an existing system of beliefs. Participatory action researchers approach the question of true knowledge from a somewhat different angle. Their main concern is not whether research is the accumulation of facts or the discovery and construction of meaning. Instead, their basic premise is that power and knowledge are linked. Therefore, they take interest in who knows what and in where, when, how, and why they know what they know. In other words, they explore the reciprocal relationships between knower, knowledge, and sociocultural context. Participatory action research therefore addresses issues of social critique and change. Participatory action research is more (and less) than a method; it may be considered an orientation to research, supported by specific attitudes and assumptions. It may also be considered a central example of a paradigm that challenges many established ideas about what knowledge is.

Overview and Definition

Participatory action research obviously involves the elements of participation, action, and research. Questions such as the following then surface: Who is participating, how, and why? What kind of action? What type of research? Participatory action research usually involves active lay participation throughout the research process and thus leads to shared ownership of the research. It therefore goes beyond the practice of studying others to include more collaborative approaches; it aims at solving problems as they are experienced by a group or a community. The term *participatory action research* has come into use to denote situated research advocating the primacy of the voices and goals of the participants themselves. A broad range of labels is commonly used to denote some related practices of research, including *action research, participatory research, thematic research, collaborative research, mutual inquiry, community-driven research,* and *emancipatory research.* The term *action research* is probably the most established of these terms, but it is increasingly and somewhat confusingly used very broadly to cover all kinds of research aimed at informing or improving practice.[3]

In this chapter, I will focus upon the potentials of a collaborative and democratic conception of the research process linked to concerns about social justice and change. Currently,

---

[1] This chapter relates to a previous chapter with the same title: Chapter 11 of *Culture-Centered Music Therapy* (Stige, 2002). While there are of course some overlaps between the two chapters, I have tried to produce two texts that complement each other. The previous chapter gives a more thorough presentation of some theoretical issues (such as Kurt Lewin's contribution and the legacy of critical theory) as well as some methodological issues (such as the cyclic process and the problem of participation). The present chapter adds more explicit reference to issues such as the extended epistemology (theory of knowledge) and the postcolonial beginnings of participatory action research. It also includes a figure that illuminates aspects of the communal and cyclic process of doing participatory action research, and clarifies the relevance for music therapy.

[2] This quotation is from Freire (1972), p. 80.

[3] This broad use of the term *action research* is applied in the first edition of *Music Therapy Research: Quantitative and Qualitative Perspectives,* where action research is treated as synonymous with clinical research (Bruscia, 1995).

one of the most recognized English terms for research practices informed by such a perspective is participatory action research.[4] Four of the dimensions central to this tradition are: (a) active lay participation in the research process; (b) empowerment of participants and sociocultural change as part of the research agenda; (c) linkage of theory, practice, and research; and (d) application of a broad conception of knowledge when evaluating research processes and outcomes.

When a person faces a problem, he or she may think about the situation, talk about it, or do something about it. Participatory action research could be said to bring these possibilities together in a collaborative approach where local knowledges are challenged by more general knowledges and vice versa.[5] It is a communicative approach, where collective reflections for identification of problems and solutions are essential. But the process does not stop with thinking and talking; practical actions are implemented and evaluated as a basis for new collective reflection. Participatory action research is therefore characterized by a specific cyclic approach that will be discussed later in the chapter.

Practical actions are inevitably linked to concrete contexts (although influences and implications may go well beyond the context in question). For this reason, participatory action research projects and local contexts reciprocally shape each other. Such projects therefore may take a variety of forms. I do not aim in this chapter to give a categorical definition or a comprehensive overview of the multitude of approaches that currently go under the label participatory action research. Instead I will attempt to present some premises and perspectives that have informed many participatory action researchers and to outline some implications for music therapy.

Theoretical Premises and Historical Roots

Theoretical Premises

The impetus for participatory action research could be said to be based in the assumption that knowledge has the ambivalent potential of nurturing and suppressing people. Two concurrent questions—What counts as knowledge? and Whose knowledge counts?—intimate some of the ground that nourishes the theoretical roots of participatory action research. These roots are multiple, and I think it is accurate to use an image that I used earlier when discussing the ancestry of community music therapy. Instead of thinking of roots as a single system with a given origin, we could think of them as compound and emerging (Stige, 2003, p. 401). With this image in mind, we can examine some of the theoretical roots that have influenced current theories and practices of participatory action research.

The first question, What counts as knowledge? has been explored by numerous thinkers. Participatory action research is informed by concerns for popular knowledge, that is, the knowledge of the people. From this follows interest for *personal knowledge* (Polanyi, 1958/1998) and *local knowledge* (Geertz, 1983), and many participatory action researchers explicitly elaborate different ways of knowing (see for example Susan Smith's discussion of six ways of knowing [Smith, Willms, & Johnson, 1997]). While the philosophical quality of some of these elaborations could be disputed, it is noticeable that the idea that knowledge is a product of the rational mind only has been seriously challenged. The later work of the philosopher Ludwig Wittgenstein (1953/1967) has been influential in this development, since Wittgenstein delivered convincing arguments about how the meaning of language is linked to contextualized activities, including activities that involve acts of *knowing how* more than *knowing that*. From this foundation, more general arguments about the connection between knowledge and social action have been developed. For participatory action researchers, this involves going beyond disputes on the validity of an objective world versus subjective worlds to focus more on the legitimacy of *collective worlding*, that is, going beyond objectivism and relativism (Bernstein, 1983) to take

---

[4] Another term that has been established lately is *community-based participatory research* (Minkler & Wallerstein, 2003). Use and meanings of terms vary over time and between countries and languages. In my own Norwegian language, for instance, the equivalent to action research (aksjonsforsking) is usually used in a more restrictive way than what is typical in the United States, closer to what is labeled participatory action research in this chapter.

[5] For a discussion of the term *knowledges*, or what different people make of the world, see Worsley (1997).

interest in knowledge as performed expressions of relationships. Knowledge is then not considered in abstract terms, but as emerging and embodied processes situated in a context of shared practice.[6]

 This leads to the second question referred to above: Whose knowledge counts? An important contribution to the understanding of this question has been given by the critical theory of the Frankfurt School. Critical theory may be seen as a revision and criticism of Marxism, with influences from both humanist thinking and psychoanalysis. Compared to some orthodox readings of Marx, the critical theorists strongly emphasize the possibility of human agency. Such agency is, however, conditioned by restraints of the natural and the sociocultural world. Of specific importance to critical theory is the oppressive function of ideology. Groups and classes in social and economic power will, according to the Frankfurt School, strongly influence what counts as knowledge and reason. The term *ideology* is used to conceptualize the result of such a process. While the term in the vernacular may denote the body of myth or doctrine of a group of people, ideology in critical theory refers to *repressive trains of thought*. Ideology is also sometimes called *false consciousness*. What is socially constructed to serve certain groups in a society has been given an air of naturalness. Ideology is what makes it possible for subordinates to accept their social position as inevitable; they have accepted the worldview of those who are in power. People in dominating roles and positions seek to communicate that things are necessary and normal; they are simply the way they need to be and should be. Ideology thus conceals the power relations involved and the exploitation connected to that. The oppressed persons start to define themselves in ways first defined by their masters. In this perspective the critical theorists advocate that the main task of the social researcher is social critique of ideology.

 In his influential work, *Knowledge and Human Interests*, Jürgen Habermas (1968/1971) explores the relationships between thought and action.[7] Habermas argues against positivist ideas on research as an objective and neutral search for knowledge based on a straightforward correspondence conception of truth. Habermas is not convinced that *apolitical hermeneutics* is a satisfying alternative for the social sciences, however. He suggests that social research should be political and critical, guided by an emancipatory interest. By focusing strongly upon communication and emancipation, Habermas avoids presenting a social theory where the individual primarily is counted as a member of a class. Habermas is thus critical of any reading of Marx in such a direction, and he is critical of Marx's own neglect of the difference between work and interaction (Habermas, p. 62).

 Habermas has been an influential thinker among participatory action researchers. There are several other important roots to consider, however, and many of these have much more southern origins. Some authors argue that participatory action research is an intellectual and practical creation of the peoples of the third world (Smith et al., 1997, p. 175). In support of such an argument, the liberationist ideas of the Brazilian educator and thinker Paulo Freire are important to consider. In his influential work, *Pedagogy of the Oppressed*, Freire (1968/1972) advocates a dialogic and democratic approach to education and inquiry, aiming to restore to oppressed peoples the ability to create knowledge and practice in their own interests. Several participatory action researchers, including Hall (1997), refer to Freire's thinking as an important influence.

 Hall (1997) also highlights another southern influence that is held highly by many contemporary participatory action researchers, the philosophy of Tanzania's first president, the late Julius Nyerere. In several of his speeches and books, Nyerere (1968; 1974/1976) advocated an African way to people-centered development. Focusing upon Swahili terms such as *uhuru* (liberty), *umoja* (unity), and *ujima* (cooperation and mutual aid), Nyerere explicitly argued against Western ideas about knowledge and challenged the conventional role of academics as experts. With the integrative notion *ujamaa* (fellowship), he envisioned a society of solidarity, including collaborative projects where academics would work together with the people in order to promote development in context. While Nyerere's vision of ujamaa remains unfulfilled, he

---

[6] The way participatory action research involves processes of learning may therefore be described as related to the tradition of *situated learning* (for explication of this term, see Lave & Wenger, 1991).

[7] In the context of participatory action research, a specific notion of *action* is relevant: The term is not used synonymously with behavior, but "refers to acts that one consciously wills, usually to pursue goals and to realize values. In this perspective the term action is closely linked to terms such as intention and reflection" (Stige, 2002, p. 325). This is not to communicate that action may not have subconscious elements, but to underline the political dimension of the term.

inspired several researchers to explore more participatory approaches to inquiry, and his influence is still considerable. A notable feature of Nyerere's work is that it expresses awareness of intellectual and ethical dilemmas linked to collaborative approaches to education, inquiry, and development.

A striking characteristic of texts exploring the theoretical roots of participatory action research is an explicit interest in contributions indigenous to the context of the author in question. Naturally, some North American scholars, such as Schubert and Lopez-Schubert (1997), therefore have explored other roots than those outlined above, such as the pragmatic humanism in the work of John Dewey and William James. In sum, the range of theoretical influences is broad indeed. Some of the roots are clearly radical and political. Other roots are linked to extended views on knowledge and development, with less focus upon large political questions and more concern about the everyday challenges of building inclusive and self-critical communities.

In order to build a genuine music therapy tradition of participatory action research, roots need to be grown in relation to music therapy theory and practice. No comprehensive overview can be given here, but a few possible starting points can be mentioned. In the American context, Carolyn Kenny's (1985, 1989) introduction of systems theory and field theory to music therapy would be important. In Europe, powerful arguments for a social approach to music therapy have been developed by Christoph Schwabe and Ulrike Haase (1998). Also, Even Ruud's (1998, pp. 51–53) sociologically inspired discussion of health problems as limited *possibilities for action,* with the concurrent proposal that music therapy should be linked to theories that explore relationships between individuals and their sociocultural contexts, would be highly significant. Theoretical perspectives on music therapy as collaborative and cultural practice have recently been developed by the present author (Stige, 2002, 2003), and currently there is an international awakening of initiatives for community music therapy (Pavlicevic & Ansdell, 2004). These texts may count as examples of possible roots in future developments of a tradition of participatory action research in music therapy. It must be noted, however, that participatory action research is a bottom-up approach. When it comes to concrete projects, the goals, resources, and communicative skills of the involved participants will be essential.

Historical Roots

As there are many theoretical roots to participatory action research, there are also complex and multifaceted histories of use. For matters of simplification, I will briefly outline the histories under the two labels, action research and participatory research, before illuminating some contemporary trends integrating these traditions.

Kurt Lewin (1946/1948) is often credited as having coined the term *action research.* He was quite certainly not the first to use this term—his contribution was rather to give it a definition and a theoretical content. Lewin developed his ideas on action research on the foundation of his field theory and his strong interest in group dynamics, and explored the approach in his work with inter-group relations. In the mid-1940s, he constructed a theory of action research that described it as proceeding in a *spiral of steps,* guided by an overall idea and specific goals that may be reformulated in the course of the spiral. He also argued that in order to understand and change social practices, researchers must include practitioners from the real social world in all phases of inquiry. Lewin, then, clearly articulated his vision of bridging social action and social theory through social research. This construction of action research contributed to its acceptance as a method of inquiry and has influenced later action researchers. Some authors, however, suggest Jacob Moreno as the true pioneer of action research, and he might indeed have been one of the first to use terms such as *interaction research* and *action research.* As early as 1913, when working with a community project with prostitutes in a Vienna suburb, he thought of group participants as co-researchers. Moreno insisted on principles such as field-based research, participant observation, participation of concerned lay people, and improvement of social situations as an aim of the research (Altrichter & Gstettner, 1997, p. 48).

Some important postcolonial initiatives for *participatory research* were mentioned in the previous section, with reference to the work of Paulo Freire and Julius Nyerere. In the 1970s, new ways of doing research emerged in several southern countries. Some researchers in Tanzania and elsewhere in Africa began to object to research that started with an idea in the head of an academic with the goal of discovering information about others. Instead, they explored more democratic and situated approaches where ideas and goals were collectively discussed and the empirical material collectively produced, analyzed, and interpreted. Similar initiatives were made in India and in Latin America (Hall, 1997). Central to these initiatives has been the intention of countering what is considered colonizing aspects of western scholarship, with the concurrent goal of breaking the monopoly of occident elites in relation to knowledge production (Minkler & Wallerstein, 2003, p. 7).

The 1970s also fostered a heightened interest in politically informed action research and participatory research in the western world. After strong growth, partly due to the politically radical climate of the decade, action research in many scholars' judgment had outplayed its role by the early 1980s. Many commentaries argued that action researchers were too keen on action and too relaxed on the obligation to produce knowledge. Authors of textbooks on social research again stated that the only value central to research is truth, and disapproved of action researchers' preoccupation with social justice. Throughout the 1980s, however, there were signs of new beginnings. Fresh approaches to action research, some of which were informed by the extended epistemology mentioned in the beginning of the previous section, started to gain strength.[8] These approaches to action research often had less overt and systematic critical and theoretical baggage than those of the preceding decades. Instead, other elements were emphasized, such as practical judgment in context, the problem of participation, and the influence of factors such as gender and ethnicity. Such tendencies were fueled by developments in feminism and a variety of alternative movements, and were often also informed by postmodern sensitivities.

Gradually, action research has grown to a broad range of practices and is no longer linked exclusively to radical practice and leftist politics. Many commercial companies, for instance, have started to try out action research in order to improve their services. In the present context, it is more important to observe that several health, education, and community development professions have developed traditions of action and participatory research as alternatives to traditional and less context-sensitive approaches to research (Banks & Mangan, 1999; Greenwood & Levin, 1998; McTaggart, 1989, 1997a; Minkler & Wallerstein, 2003; Morton-Cooper, 2000; Reason & Bradbury, 2001; Smith et al., 1997). Government-initiated evaluation and community projects also commonly are framed as action research projects.

Thus today there is a confusing variety of action research approaches. If we use Habermas' (1968/1971) conception of interests of knowledge as a departure point, it may be reasonable to suggest that there are three main traditions: technical action research aimed at scientific problem solving; collaborative action research aimed at communicative exploration of shared concerns; and emancipatory action research aimed at liberation, social critique, and social change. Or, if we want to express this in a simpler way, we could say that there is a continuum of collaborative research practices with goals ranging from practical problem solving to societal transformation. The term participatory action research is usually used to denote the scholarship of engagement typical of the emancipatory end of this continuum, but this author acknowledges that the line between problem solving and emancipation is often difficult and somewhat meaningless to draw. I maintain, however, that the challenge of producing *dangerous knowledge*—"the kind of information and insight that upsets institutions and threatens to overturn sovereign regimes of truth" (Kincheloe & McLaren, 1998, p. 260)—remains central to participatory action research.

Methodology

In line with the emphasis on participatory action research as emancipation and empowerment informed by extended epistemologies, it is common to argue that specific research methods take second place to emerging processes of collaboration and communication. A participatory action research project may involve the use of diverse techniques of inquiry, for example, quantitative surveys assessing the distribution of needs and attitudes in a community and qualitative interviews exploring meanings of certain practices. Participatory action research therefore cannot be described as a specific method or set of methods. The community is the method, so to

---

[8] As explained under Theoretical Premises, the extended epistemology referred to goes beyond a conception of knowledge as an abstract body of statements to include embodied, personal, and social ways of knowing.

say, with communal action-reflection cycles as central elements. With the use of community meetings and events of various kinds, participatory action research is about giving marginalized people voice and about listening to the voices of others. The process may thus be described as a self-reflective spiral through the building of creative and self-critical communities.

McTaggart (1997b, p. 34) argues that the realistic alternative to academic researchers acting as *visiting strangers,* taking their own values for granted and imposing them upon the context of the study, is not to have self-effacing idealists serving the people with no personal interests whatsoever. It is more credible to argue that participatory action research projects by nature are *polyphonic* and that people participate with different perspectives and ambitions. The central question, then, is how and to what degree the negotiated goals and procedures serve the interests of all participants. Methodological implications of this argument include the need to pay more attention to communal and critical interpretations than is common in more conventional empirical-analytical traditions of research. These elements are already important in choice of research question, since any question supports and reflects certain values. Researchers, no less than others, struggle with the problem of uncritically adopting conventional views, and participatory action researchers try to pay attention to the problem of ideology when choosing research questions. This links to the request for *reflexivity* in late modern culture (Stige, 2002).

The above argument requires clarification of the term *participatory action researcher.* While equality and collaboration are central values in this tradition of inquiry, it would be inaccurate and naïve to assume that all participants contribute in equal ways and in equal roles. Earlier in the chapter, I proposed that participatory action research usually involves active lay participation throughout the research process. This indirectly indicates that many different roles are involved in a participatory research project. In order to be able to distinguish between academic researchers and other participants, various terms have been proposed. For instance, Durham (2001) speaks of lead researchers and co-researchers, while McTaggart (1997b) speaks of academics and workers. To the present author, the term *lead researcher* is somewhat confusing in the basic structure of a collaborative approach, while the term *worker* is too narrow to include the range of participants that would be typical or at least possible in a music therapy project (music therapists, colleagues from other professions, clients, and community members). I therefore suggest that *academic researchers* and *lay researchers* is a more suitable pair of terms.

Let us now look at the process of doing participatory action research. This process may be described as steps toward social change through a series of collaborative action-reflection cycles.[9] In these collaborative action-reflection cycles, the different participants should be given the possibility of contributing with their specific perspectives and resources. The process starts with some regulating values and ideas that give direction to the work, while the concrete steps in the process could be depicted as recurring cycles of assessment, planning, action, evaluation, and reflection. The objectives and plans for action are based on the original values and ideas, but through assessments of the situation the available means to reach the objective are examined. The making of plans goes beyond concrete action planning to include necessary modifications of the original ideas. The action may then be seen as the first step of an overall plan and leads to the next step, evaluation, which could serve multiple functions: to learn, to gain information for planning the next step, and to create a basis for future modifications of the overall plan. All this is achieved through various forms of collective discussion and reflection.

An attempt to describe the steppingstones that may lead into the reflexive spiral sought for in participatory action research is given in *Culture-Centered Music Therapy* (Stige, 2002, pp. 290–296). In Figure 1 the process is illuminated, with an outline of these steps and the cyclic relationships involved.

Starting with shared values and visions, the process of participatory action research is guided by collective reflections on the results of actions. These actions are informed by plans incorporating facts and beliefs based upon continuous assessments of the situation at hand, as well as evaluations of processes and outcomes. In Figure 1, the steps of the process are all

---

9 The following description of the participatory action research process is a variation of the process as originally described by Kurt Lewin (1946/1948). Lewin's description included the following sequences: (a) definition of objective, (b) fact-finding, (c) making of overall plan, (d) action, and (d) evaluation. What I try to offer is a reformulation that illuminates the value of communication and collective reflection in the process. The process of reciprocal communication necessary to establish the relationships that are required for collective identification of community issues is described well by Minkler and Wallerstein (2000).

given in their plural forms (assessments, plans, actions, and so forth). This is to communicate that participatory action research is a cyclic and ongoing process, with spirals of assessments, plans, actions, evaluations, and reflections. These cyclic steps are continuously informed by some basic values and visions, which in turn may be changed by the process.

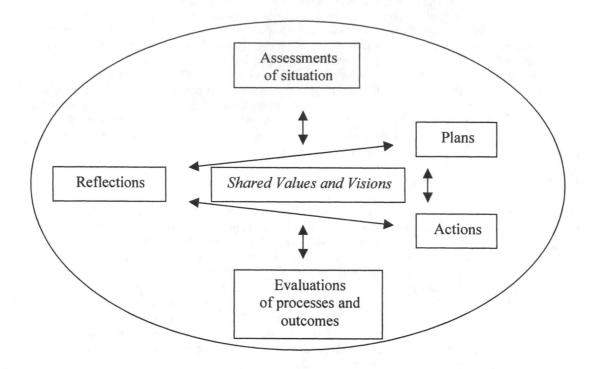

Figure 1. Illustration of the Cyclic Character
of the Process of Participatory Action Research

To suggest that values and visions are shared does not necessarily mean that all participants have the same values and visions. Usually they do not, but the term *shared* suggests that values and visions are communicated publicly and that the community is able to handle the differences involved. It should also be noted that values and visions may be articulated at different levels, and not necessarily in refined verbal ways. Sometimes, for instance, visions are vague dreams only, and part of the research process is to clarify realistic goals.[10] The research process is polyphonic, then: Several values, visions, and perspectives will inform it. This requires the development of *meeting places* in the shape of team meetings as well as more open forums for performance, discussion, and development. The process thus requires tolerance for multiple perspectives. Given the collaborative nature of participatory action research, the research process is necessarily also a *group process* and therefore cannot be planned in detail in advance; it will involve conflict and resistance and ways of negotiating and resolving such problems. The main virtue of a good participatory action researcher may therefore be said to be willingness to listen and ability to learn from the mistakes made. Interpersonal qualifications and ethical concerns are crucial in the research process.[11]

To sum up the description so far, the process of doing participatory action research may be conceptualized as a cycle of collaborative activities that starts with a thematic concern. There is a problem situation that needs to be understood and transformed. The research process maintains a purposeful change focus, committed to the social context under scrutiny rather than the researchers' enthusiasm for particular research methods or theoretical problems. Team

---

[10] In music therapy research there may be huge differences among participants as to their ability to articulate their values and visions verbally, but ideas that are evident in some participants' body language or other aspects of music-making may of course also influence the research process.

[11] As Durham (2001) clarifies, the requirements of research ethics committees may paradoxically counteract the ethos of participatory action research by demanding that the academic researcher give an outline of goals and procedures before the other participants have been involved.

building and development of arenas for reflection and discussion may continue throughout the research process. Collective evaluations and reflections based upon negotiated role definitions are continuous elements in the process and form the basis for refined diagnosis of the situation of concern and for the development of new plans of action.

Outcomes are defined by the characteristics of the process: empowerment of participants, collaboration and participation, social change, and acquisition of knowledge. While there is a continuous commitment to the social context of scrutiny, knowledge and experiences that might be transferred to other contexts are also of interest. Knowledge diffusion and replication of ideas that work are therefore important elements. This also illuminates the value of Lewin's (1946/1948) suggestion that action research involves the integration of social action, research, and training and supervision.

I will conclude this section on methodology with a note on the *problem of participation*. There are two main dilemmas from a power perspective: First, one or several of the participants may try to use the research project to promote their own ideas and values in ways that lead the other participants to believe that these are actually their own when they are not. In other words, we are back to the issue of ideology in the critical theory meaning of that term. There is of course no easy way out of this. Subtle mechanisms of power are ubiquitous in human interaction. I can see no other option than paying serious attention to the legacy of critical theory. While this does not mean that all participatory action research projects should be leftist, the term participatory at least implies a commitment to values supporting a minimal version of critical research; the research should be actively monitored with the aim of at least not contributing to dominance (Alvesson & Sköldberg, 2000). Second, some of the participants may experience serious barriers to participation, for instance lack of cognitive capabilities or communicative skills. If this problem is not given attention, these participants may end up being marginalized in the research project in spite of the ethos of empowerment. To acknowledge extended epistemological positions so that musical and other nonverbal performances and expressions may be taken into consideration could be one of the ways out of this dilemma and should be highly relevant for music therapists.

Relationship to Other Types of Research

From the above discussion, it should be clear that participatory action research is a blurred genre. Relationships may be defined with other types of qualitative as well as quantitative research, and with certain theories and practices of music therapy. Relationships with critical theory, feminism, and postcolonial perspectives, as well as with sociocultural perspectives to music therapy, have been mentioned above and will not be reiterated here.

A participatory action research project may include elements of biography, ethnography, and case study, or as McTaggart (1997b, p. 38) expresses it, a project may simultaneously aim at the articulation of biography (individual identity) and the making of history (group culture). The extended epistemology typical of some participatory action research projects also suggests that there are relationships both to narrative inquiry (Rappaport, 1995; see also Chapter 33, Narrative Inquiry, in this book) and to the emerging tradition of arts-based research (McNiff, 1998; see also Chapter 36, Arts-Based Research, in this book). What is shared is the idea that knowledge is creative and takes many forms, and that there must be a breadth of inquiry. Both research forms also acknowledge the value of new ways of telling stories, to include performance and nonverbal expressions. There is an integration of thought and image, of knowledge and art, and of theory and practice. One of the differences is that participatory action researchers usually stress the communal aspects of knowledge production more than what is typical in arts-based research.

The tradition of participatory action research also challenges some of our established assumptions about distinctions among practice, theory, and research. While Bruscia's (1995) argument about the need for boundaries between these practices is not necessarily invalidated, the theories and practices of participatory action research indicate that these boundaries will be fluid and variable, and that such questions must be discussed in relation to specific contexts and situations of social practice.

Music Therapy Examples

Currently, there is no established tradition of participatory action research in music therapy. Some examples that demonstrate aspects of the approach will be given here. When taken together, they may illuminate some of the future potentials of participatory action research in music therapy.

One music therapy researcher who has used the label *action research* is Henk Smeijsters (1997, pp. 152–165), whose work is on the problem-solving end of the previously described continuum of collaborative research practices.[12] In a discussion of *researchers as co-actors,* Smeijsters describes the work of a research team consisting of a music therapist, a researcher, and an observer, and he outlines a method in which the research team members are able to improve and develop the therapist's goals and interventions in relation to specific clinical problems through procedures such as member checking and peer debriefing.

While Smeijsters' project stresses collaboration between researcher and therapist, other music therapy scholars have stressed collaboration between researcher and client. Some British arts and music therapy scholars have conducted studies that usually would not be labeled action research but which may demonstrate one very important aspect, the willingness to let clients be participants who influence the formulation of research questions as well as the analysis and interpretation of findings. In a chapter titled "From Practitioner to Researcher," Helen Payne (1993) describes a historical process that during the 1980s brought practice and research together for British arts therapists and underlines how this has opened up the possibility of learning from the client. In line with this argument, some British music therapy researchers, such as Penny Rogers (1993) and Colin Lee (1996), have developed various ways of learning from the client.

The above projects illuminate participatory aspects in fascinating ways, but the action aspect is not prominent; that is, the element of social change in a given context is not included. A project that includes this element is the work with Upbeat, a group of people with mental challenges (Kleive & Stige, 1988; Stige, 2002, Chapter 5).[13] In this project the initial shared values were linked to principles about equality and justice and the guiding vision was the development of a more inclusive musical life in the local community. For the members of Upbeat, this vision was articulated as a dream of being able to play in the local marching band. I will briefly outline the first cycle of action-reflection in this project in the next paragraph. As described above, a central idea of participatory action research is that a project consists of a series of such action-reflection cycles, with continuous refinement of plans and actions through assessments, evaluations, and collective reflections. In this specific project the original vision was realized (in a modified form) after 3 years of work and a long series of cycles, but because of space limitations I will only outline the first cycle of the first months of the project.

First the collaborators were identified and brought together. In addition to Upbeat, they included music therapists and music educators, amateur musicians, and community members, as well as administrators and local politicians. These collaborators then engaged in a process of examining the original values and visions more carefully in order to refine and specify them in the direction of more concrete goals in relation to the sociocultural situation of the local community. We learned that, on a general level, the legitimacy of social integration and mainstreaming was acknowledged by all musical organizations of the community, but that there was resistance to engaging in concrete projects of collaboration and that this resistance was higher among the marching band than among the choirs of the community. Based upon this assessment of the situation, a more refined understanding of the vision emerged, and a plan for action was made. The first plan included continued work with the musical and sociocultural competence of Upbeat, short-term collaborative work with a choir, and long-term work with attitudes in the local community. This plan was then put into action. Songs were chosen,

---

[12] As described in the section Historical Roots, this continuum is based upon Habermas' (1968/1971) conception of different interests of knowledge.

[13] While the project referenced explicitly was informed by values and procedures typical of participatory action research, the research value of the project could be challenged as it initially was not framed as a research project and procedures for production of empirical material therefore were somewhat loose (for discussion of this, see Stige, 2003). In the absence of other examples in the literature available for this author at the time of writing, I have still chosen to include this project as an example in this section.

arranged, and rearranged for Upbeat. Articles about the project were written for the local newspaper, and a series of shared rehearsals with the choir (including sequences of mutual improvisation) was established. After some weeks, the songs were performed for the first time in a semi-public concert. This phase immediately led into the next, that of evaluation, where the collaborators assessed the results of these actions. In dialogue with the different participants, the main conclusion of this first phase of evaluation was that short-term collaboration was a promising strategy to pursue for development of more inclusive attitudes and practices in this particular community. Some concrete modifications were then suggested for future collaborations so that new plans and new actions could be developed in the direction of Upbeat's original vision. This vision, as mentioned above, was realized after 3 years of hard work. The steps in the cycle described above initiated two interacting processes: For the members of Upbeat, it led to realization of some specific goals they had articulated for their community membership; for this author it also led to an emerging understanding of how music therapy theory and practice need to take community into consideration (Stige, 2002, 2003). This interaction of local and more general themes is typical of participatory action research.

Other examples of participatory action research projects in music therapy may also exist, but there is yet no solid and established tradition within the discipline. Recently, signs of a new awareness about collaborative and participatory research in music therapy have become evident (see for instance Bunt, 2002; Durham, 2001; Warner, 2004), and I believe that there are several current cultural tendencies that suggest that participatory action research could be fruitful for the discipline and profession and, not least, for the people that we are supposed to serve. In conclusion I will outline three such tendencies: the emergence of community music therapy, the growth of modern music therapy in the third world, and the appearance of feminist and postmodern critique within the discipline.

Community music therapy (Ansdell, 2002; Bruscia, 1998, Chapter 28; Pavlicevic & Ansdell, 2004; Stige, 2002, 2003) involves seeing health as a relationship between individual and community. Health disparities in a society must then be examined and countered, and to nurture and support underserved and oppressed communities can then be defined within the range of music therapy practice. Music therapists also often work with clients and groups who are disempowered and who experience major barriers in their life spaces, and the relevance of empowerment through participatory action research should be self-evident, at least if the therapist subscribes to values of equality and justice. In addition, music therapists often work with clients with a high degree of context-dependency, and the context-transforming power of music-making will be relevant to explore.

The current growth of modern music therapy in the third world and other nonwestern contexts (see Kenny & Stige, 2002) establishes a new challenge for the discipline. If music therapy is cultivated and researched in what have become the conventional ways of Europe and North America, this may serve the elites of third world countries only. Participatory action research may provide practitioners with tools for developing knowledge and practice sensitive to needs as identified by the communities in which they work.

As a young modern profession, music therapy has not yet developed a strong tradition of critique (Ansdell, 2003), and feminist and postmodern perspectives have so far had a relatively weak position within the discipline of music therapy (see Hadley & Edwards, 2004; Rolvsjord, 2004). Participatory action research may turn out to be a constructive and context-sensitive alternative for music therapists who want to explore and document the value of their work and to combine this with a self-critical awareness about how value is linked to perspective. Contemporary social and intellectual developments such as postcolonialism and feminism will probably become more influential in music therapy in the future, and this will certainly increase the relevance of participatory action research.

References

Altrichter, H., & Gstettner, P. (1997). Action research: A closed chapter in the history of German social science? In R. McTaggart (Ed.), *Participatory action research: International contexts and consequences* (pp. 45–78). Albany, NY: State University of New York Press.

Alvesson, M., & Sköldberg, K. (2000). *Reflexive methodology: New vistas for qualitative research.* London: Sage Publications.

Ansdell, G. (2002). Community music therapy and the winds of change—A discussion paper. In C. Kenny & B. Stige (Eds.), *Contemporary* Voices *of music therapy: Communication, culture, and community* (pp. 109–142). Oslo, Norway: Unipub forlag.

Ansdell, G. (2003). The stories we tell: Some meta-theoretical reflections on music therapy. *Nordic Journal of Music Therapy, 12,* 152–159.

Banks, C. K., & Mangan, J. M. (1999). *The company of neighbours. Revitalizing community through action-research.* Toronto, Canada: University of Toronto Press.

Bernstein, R. J. (1983). *Beyond objectivism and relativism: Science, hermeneutics, and praxis.* Philadelphia: University of Pennsylvania Press.

Bruscia, K. (1995). The boundaries of music therapy research. In B. L. Wheeler (Ed.), *Music therapy research: Quantitative and qualitative perspectives* (pp. 17–27). Gilsum, NH: Barcelona Publishers.

Bruscia, K. (1998). *Defining music therapy* (2nd ed.). Gilsum, NH: Barcelona Publishers.

Bunt, L. (2002). Some reflections on music therapy research: An example of collaborative enquiry. In L. Bunt & S. Hoskyns (Eds.), *The handbook of music therapy* (pp. 270–289). Hove, UK: Brunner-Routledge.

Durham, C. (2001, October). *Whose research is it? Using action research design in music therapy.* Paper presented at the British Society for Music Therapy Research Convivium, London, UK.

Freire, P. (1972). *Pedagogy of the oppressed* (M. B. Ramos, Trans., 1970). [Original title: Pedagogia do oprimido]. Middlesex, UK: Penguin Books. (Original work published 1968)

Geertz, C. (1983). *Local knowledge: Further essays in interpretive anthropology.* New York: Basic Books.

Greenwood, D. J., & Levin, M. (1998). *Introduction to action research: Social research for social change.* Thousand Oaks, CA: Sage Publications.

Habermas, J. (1968). *Knowledge and human interests* (J. J. Shapiro, Trans., 1971). [Original title: Erkenntnis und Interesse]. Boston: Beacon Press.

Hadley, S., & Edwards, J. (2004). Sorry for the silence: A contribution from feminist theory to the discourse(s) within music therapy. In *Voices: A World Forum for Music Therapy.* Available at http://www.voices.no/mainissues/mi40004000152.html

Hall, B. L. (1997). *Reflections on the origins of the International Participatory Research Network and the Participatory Research Group in Toronto, Canada.* Available at http://www.anrecs.msu.edu/research/hallpr.htm

Kenny, C. B. (1985). Music: A whole systems approach. *Music Therapy, 5,* 3–11.

Kenny, C. B. (1989). *The field of play: A guide for the theory and practice of music therapy.* Atascadero, CA: Ridgeview Publishing Company.

Kenny, C., & Stige, B. (Eds.). (2002). *Contemporary* Voices *in music therapy: Communication, culture, and community.* Oslo: Unipub forlag.

Kincheloe, J. L., & McLaren, P. L. (1998). Rethinking critical theory and qualitative research. In N. K. Denzin & Y. S. Lincoln (Eds.), *The landscape of qualitative research: Theories and issues* (pp. 260–299). Thousand Oaks, CA: Sage Publications.

Kleive, M., & Stige, B. (1988). *Med lengting, liv og song* [With longing, life, and song.] Oslo: Samlaget.

Lave, J., & Wenger, E. (1991). *Situated learning: Legitimate peripheral participation.* Cambridge, UK: Cambridge University Press.

Lee, C. (1996). *Music at the edge: The music therapy experiences of a musician with AIDS.* London: Routledge.

Lewin, K. (1948). Action research and minority problems. In K. Lewin, *Resolving social conflicts: Selected papers on group dynamics* (pp. 201–216). New York: Harper & Brothers. (Reprinted from *Journal of Social Issues, 2,* 1946, 34–46.)

McNiff, S. (1998). *Art-based research.* London: Jessica Kingsley Publishers.

McTaggart, R. (1989). 16 tenets of participatory action research. *The Caledonia Centre for Social Development.* Available at http://www.caledonia.org.uk/par.htm#1

McTaggart, R. (Ed.). (1997a). *Participatory action research: International contexts and consequences.* Albany: State University of New York Press.

McTaggart, R. (1997b). Guiding principles for participatory action research. In R. McTaggart (Ed.), *Participatory action research: International contexts and consequences* (pp. 25–44). Albany: State University of New York Press.

Minkler, M., & Wallerstein, N. (Eds.). (2003). *Community-based participatory research for health.* San Francisco, CA: Jossey-Bass.

Morton-Cooper, A. (2000). *Action research in health care.* Oxford: Blackwell Science.

Nyerere, J. (1968). *Uhuru na ujamaa* [Freedom and socialism]. Nairobi, Kenya: Oxford University Press.

Nyerere, J. (1974). *Fattigdom og frigjering* (S. Grotmol & A. Olsnes, Trans., 1976). [Original Title: Poverty and liberation]. Oslo: Samlaget.

Pavlicevic, M., & Ansdell, G. (Eds.). (2004). *Community music therapy.* London: Jessica Kingsley Publishers.

Payne, H. (1993). From practitioner to researcher: Research as a learning process. In H. Payne (Ed.), *Handbook of inquiry in the arts therapies: One river, many currents* (pp. 16–37). London: Jessica Kingsley Publishers.

Polanyi, M. (1998). *Personal knowledge: Towards a post-critical philosophy.* London: Routledge. (Original work published 1958)

Rappaport, J. (1995). Empowerment meets narrative: Listening to stories and creating settings. *American Journal of Community Psychology, 23,* 795–807.

Reason, P., & Bradbury, H. (Eds.). (2001). *Handbook of action research: Participative inquiry and practice.* Thousand Oaks, CA: Sage Publications.

Rogers, P. (1993). Research in music therapy with sexually abused clients. In H. Payne (Ed.), *Handbook of inquiry in the arts therapies: One river, many currents* (pp. 197–217). London: Jessica Kingsley Publishers.

Rolvsjord, R. (2004). Music as a poetic language. In *Voices: A World Forum for Music Therapy.* Available at http://www.voices.no/mainissues/mi40004000138.html

Ruud, E. (1998). *Music therapy: Improvisation, communication, and culture.* Gilsum, NH: Barcelona Publishers.

Schubert, W. H., & Lopez-Schubert, A. (1997). Sources of a theory for action research in the United States of America. In R. McTaggart (Ed.), *Participatory action research: International contexts and consequences* (pp. 203–222). Albany: State University of New York Press.

Schwabe, C., & Haase, U. (1998). *Die Sozialmusiktherapie (SMT)* [Social music therapy]. Wetzdorf, Germany: Akademie für angewandte Musiktherapie Crossen.

Small, C. (1998). *Musicking: The meanings of performing and listening.* Hanover, NH: Wesleyan University Press.

Smeijsters, H. (1997). *Multiple perspectives: A guide to qualitative research in music therapy.* Gilsum, NH: Barcelona Publishers.

Smith, S. E., Willms, D. G., & Johnson, N. A. (Eds.). (1997). *Nurtured by knowledge: Learning to do participatory action-research.* New York: Apex Press.

Stige, B. (2002). *Culture-centered music therapy.* Gilsum, NH: Barcelona Publishers.

Stige, B. (2003). *Elaborations toward a notion of community music therapy.* Doctoral dissertation, University of Oslo. Oslo: Unipub forlag.

Warner, C. (2004). *Music therapy with adults with learning difficulties and 'severe challenging behaviour.' An action research inquiry into the benefits of group music therapy within a community home.* Unpublished doctoral dissertation, University of the West of England, Bristol, UK.

Wittgenstein, L. (1967). *Philosophical investigations.* Oxford: Blackwell. (Original work published 1953)

Worsley, P. (1997). *Knowledges: What different people make of the world.* London: Profile Books.

Acknowledgments

Thanks to Mette Kleive who first introduced me to the tradition of action research and to Randi Rolvsjord who contributes with insights on how awareness and action may be linked in feminist thought.

Chapter 33
Narrative Inquiry
Carolyn Kenny

Once, flying over the American Midwest, I was struck by the contrast between the straight and direct lines of the plowed fields, and the curved, indirect meanderings of the rivers crossing these fields. My initial reaction was to denigrate the linear, "shorter distance between two points," logically produced lines, and to elevate the "natural," curved lines that seemed to follow the whims of the river, unguided by any utilitarian purpose.

Yet, as I recalled that geologists have actually devised formulae for describing the various curves and paths of rivers, I realized that the lines described by the flow of the rivers were themselves guided by an inner logic. The river is also guided by logic, although it is not a logic that is rigidly linear, but is instead one that molds to the quality of the land in shaping and transforming the contours in which the river flows.

The structure of this article follows the meandering logic of the river, subsuming our capacity for linear reasoning to the "contour of the land" I wish to explore, comprising the connection between my clinical experience as a music therapist and the deep feelings of reverence for music and nature that I possess and notice in other music therapists. Although this exploration takes us through a variety of areas that may seem only peripherally related, in fact each step along the way is guided by and integral to the effort to gain a greater understanding of the phenomenon of music, our tool of choice as music therapists.

Aigen[1]

Narrative inquiry invites the reader into a story. This short example illustrates the complex nature of the narrative method of research. The goal of narrative research is not to isolate and simplify. It is to elaborate complexities and relationships in the service of understanding human life. Narrative inquiry is hermeneutic in nature because it is contingent upon the perception and interpretation of the researcher. The writer/researcher selects aspects of a narrative to highlight elements of a research context in order to portray a holistic picture of research participants, issues, and settings.

In the above example, we can see the critical role played by the writer and researcher in framing the issues he will subsequently explore in the research. Aigen creates a theoretical work that poses concepts for music therapy theory and uses narrative inquiry to help us understand his position regarding these concepts.

Overview and Definition

Story is the simplest and most direct way to define a narrative. Narrative inquiry creates an intersubjective space that reflects a dynamic relationship between researcher, the context of research, and the reader. Narrative mediates between an inner world of thought-feeling and an outer world of observable actions and states of affairs (Bruner, 1986). Narrative form implies that something happened to particular subjects in a given life world (Bentz & Shapiro, 1998). Narrative is a fundamental way of giving meaning to experience (Mattingly & Garro, 2000). Narrative inquiry attempts to formalize the nature and character of narratives to communicate dynamic elements of our worlds and our experiences that would be lost without a story.

Narrative inquiry is increasingly used in the fields of psychology, gender studies, education, anthropology, sociology, linguistics, law, history, and the creative arts therapies. Narrative studies are flourishing as a means of understanding the personal identity, lifestyle, culture, and historical world of the narrator (Lieblich, Tuval-Mashiach, & Zilber, 1998).

---

[1] This quotation is from Aigen (1991), pp. 77–78.

Lieblich et al. (1998) provide one of the more formal definitions:

> Narrative research, according to our definition, refers to any study that uses or analyzes narrative materials. The data can be collected as a story (a life story provided in an interview or a literary work) or in a different manner (field notes of an anthropologist who writes up his or her observations as a narrative or in personal letters). It can be the object of the research or a means for the study of another question. It may be used for comparison among groups, to learn about a social phenomenon or historical period, or to explore a personality. (pp. 2–3)

After a thorough examination of the many proposed criteria for qualitative research, Lieblich et al. (1998) also suggest specific criteria for evaluating narrative inquiry:

> *Width:* the comprehensiveness of evidence,
>
> *Coherence:* the way different parts of the interpretation create a complete and meaningful picture,
>
> *Insightfulness:* the sense of innovation or originality in the presentation of the story and its analysis,
>
> *Parsimony:* the ability to provide an analysis based on a small number of concepts, and elegance or aesthetic appeal.

Mishler (1990), on the other hand, attempts to maintain simplicity and accessibility to narrative inquiry by suggesting only two criteria: trustworthiness, which refers to the evaluation of a community of researchers; and authenticity, which focuses on the believability and integrity of the story.

Historical Roots and Theoretical Premises

Historical Roots

Narrative inquiry may be the oldest type of research. Stories were the way people shared information, compared aspects of their lives, and engaged in debates long before written texts were even imagined. In oral traditions, facts and figures were embodied in memory and passed down to generations of new knowledge keepers through oral traditions.

Literary narratives have always been important. Plato offered the *Dialogues*, which were stories. Aristotle offered the first elaborated theory of narrative in his *Poetics*. These were the formal academic expressions of their time, and they have spawned academic fields such as literature, literary criticism, and literary studies. Later in this chapter, we will see how these early roots have influenced the practice of contemporary narrative inquiry.

When the possibility of documenting narratives in written text emerged, there were many expressions of narrative form that were academic. Certainly the Greek historian Herodotus (ca. 485–425 BC) was prolific in the gathering of stories about the lands and people surrounding Greece. The Age of Exploration produced thousands of texts used to document the discovery of new lands and new peoples around the world.

However, the contemporary use of narrative as an academic method goes hand in hand with the blossoming of the formal academic discipline of anthropology a little over 100 years ago. Franz Boas was considered the father of anthropology, but scholars like Frank Hamilton Cushing, Bronislaw Malinowski, and Ruth Benedict initiated cultural anthropology in the mid-20th century. These early scholars in anthropology gathered descriptions, called *field notes,* of settings, events, and people from their observations of tribal societies. Field notes were narratives telling the stories of the scholars' experiences and interpreting aspects of community life through their own eyes. As well, anthropologists gathered stories from community members and made use of *informants* to translate and interpret these narratives.

Another strong historical influence on narrative inquiry is the literary tradition. With the liberation of the novel from structural composition associated with form, narrative became the construct of analytical choice in literary criticism (Martin, 1990). The spirit of liberation and the crisis of representation expressed in a postmodern climate and the discourse on the power of text in critical theory encouraged the proliferation of many forms of narrative inquiry including story, life history, and autoethnography.[2]

Narrative inquiry has also emerged as a method of inquiry called *narrative psychology*. Lieblich et al. (1998) report an increase in the number of narrative-related research studies in databases from 10 studies in 1979 to 371 studies in 1995. A comprehensive source for investigating narrative inquiry is online at www.narrativepsych.com. In psychology, narratives are used in basic and applied research and also to diagnose and treat. Restoration, or development of the life story through psychotherapy, is considered the core of the healing process.

Theoretical and Philosophical Foundations

As we have seen from the historical framework, narratives have been with us since antiquity. In contemporary society, we think of narratives as constructed, so theoretically they belong in the meta-methodological frame of constructivism. The narrative inquirer is concerned with the style of representation. According to Pamphilon (1999), some of the styles characteristic of narrative inquiry are: a story that places the character as central to a heroic trajectory, the epic, the Romanesque, and the picaresque. Other styles include the fantasy form, mythological forms, and minimalist.

Clandinin and Connelly (2000) offer one of the most comprehensive texts on the use of narrative inquiry to date. They take the following position, when it comes to theory: "The place of theory in narrative inquiry differs from the place of theory in formalistic inquiries. . . formalists begin inquiry in theory, whereas narrative inquirers tend to begin with experience as lived and told in stories" (p. 128).

Many disciplines have influenced the development of narrative inquiry. Hermeneutics, anthropology, literary criticism, postmodernism, and cultural psychology are the primary contributors. Hermeneutics, the art and science of interpretation, became a scholarly field with the invention of written texts. Monks would take the sacred texts and attempt to interpret their meanings beyond their historical contexts. Interpretation of texts includes not only historical and cultural contexts, but the contexts of language and linguistics, the sacred and the secular, and a myriad of other contextual influences, including resources and technology.

Music therapy researchers have been interested in hermeneutics as a philosophical influence and also as a theory. Ruud (1998) states:

> Life becomes human through narrative articulation. In creating plot and coherence in our unclear understanding of everyday life we change/transform it in a more comprehensible literary configuration. The narratives we create about our lives will change it and give it a specific form—just like in a hermeneutic circle. (p. 198)

Because text is so important in narrative inquiry, literary configurations, linguistics, and the use of language in general, it is important in the understanding of this method of inquiry and in narrative analysis.

Bonde (2000) has related Ricouer's theory of narrativity and metaphor to the Bonny Method of Guided Imagery and Music (GIM). In a paper titled "Metaphor and Narrative in Guided Imagery and Music," Bonde uses Ricouer's theory to help us understand GIM.

Paul Ricouer, often considered the most distinguished philosopher in recent times, followed in the footsteps of Martin Heideggar and Gabriel Marcel. Though Ricoeur has written extensively on a broad range of issues, his three-volume work *Time and Narrative* (1984–1988) is the work most considered by music therapy theorists like Bonde. Certainly, the nature of the stories or narratives produced in the GIM experience has inspired this connection to Ricoeur's work.

Ricoeur (1984–1988) is sensitive to the role of history in present-time human action. He considers narrative to be the primary agent for the transmission of knowledge across time and

---

[2] Autoethnography is a method in narrative inquiry that situates the researcher within the context of the culture being studied. The researcher tells his or her own story as an insider, providing an important emic position within, and therefore creating trust in the teller, diminishing the problems of representation from the outside. An example of such an autoethnography in music therapy is Kenneth Bruscia's story about his experience at the First International Symposium for Qualitative Research in Music Therapy in Düsseldorf, Germany (Bruscia, 1996). See Chapter 30, First-Person Research, for additional information on this method.

human experience. For Ricoeur, narrative is a discourse, not something fixed and flat. It is in constant motion, shifting and changing in a dialogue between history and our current existential lives. Historical time becomes embedded in the immediacy of our human moments "to the extent that it is articulated through a narrative mode, and narrative attains its full significance when it becomes a condition of temporal existence" (Ricoeur, 1984, Vol. 1, p. 52). In fact, for Ricoeur, history is only significant within the context of now. How do the stories of our past influence our present and future? As a fallible species, how can we reflect and compare our experiences across time and allow those reflections to influence our day-to-day actions?

There is a strong relationship in Ricoeur's philosophy between narrative and identity. It is in the movement of the story or narrative that identity is constructed. This, too, is a dynamic process that engages in a dialectic between order and disorder. Narratives are not always clean and clear. They are alive, just as human beings are alive. This ambiguity is what makes the narrative form particularly suited to human expression and communication.

It is important to note that Marcel's philosophy advocated *presence, commitment, and communion* and Heidegger advocated the importance of *care,* all important concepts for music therapists. Ricouer emphasizes the fragility of the human condition and considers the narrative unity of a person's life. He rejects a purely structured theory for the analysis of narratives and embraces a combination of structural analysis of texts and reflection on the discursive partners involved in texts, including writers, readers, and characters in the story itself. In any story, whether fiction, nonfiction, chronicle, or historical account, *coherence* is an important theoretical element. If analysis includes too many isolating categories, the categories themselves and not the story become dominant. Coherence and style are compromised. The story is perceived not as a unified whole but as fragmented and nonrelational.

We know that all research, since the crisis of representation,[3] has hermeneutic components. However narrative inquiry is more explicitly hermeneutic than many other types of research because a storyteller manipulates the facts through interpreting the best possible order, style, semantics, and other literary components so that the story can be told in a purposeful way.

Hans-Georg Gadamer, a hermeneutic theoretician, also had a strong influence on the creation of narrative inquiry, and his ideas are attractive to music therapists because they take on the issues inherent in aesthetic experiences. In *Truth and Method* (1989), he considers truth as it emerges in the experience of the arts. Gadamer also describes the significance of play. Play is nondirective. It continues without resolution because of infinite possibilities in the realm of the imagination. Such an infinite realm of possibilities also pertains to a popular notion in hermeneutics called the *hermeneutic circle* (Bontekoe, 1996). Gadamer (1989) also reminds us that narrative inquiry creates text that places the reader, the text, and the author in relationship:

> In fact the horizon of the present is continually in the process of being formed because we are continually having to test all of our prejudices. An important part of this testing occurs in encountering the past and in understanding the tradition from which we come. Hence the horizon of the present cannot be formed without the past. Understanding is always the fusion of these horizons supposedly existing by themselves. . . . In a tradition this process of fusion is continually going on, for the old and the new are always combining into something of living value. (p. 306)

The final theorist we will consider in this chapter is M. M. Bakhtin (1981). Toward the end of the 20th century and the beginning of the 21st century, his treatment of the issues of language, discourse, and narrative has been core reading material in the lives of intellectuals who are concerned with narrative and text across disciplines. Bakhtin's great contribution to narrative discourse is his ability to embrace the paradox of human existence as a struggle between the forces that attempt to bring us together and the ones that drive us apart. He understands that language is at the core of this struggle and presents a theory or model for narrative and discourse that validates this struggle and helps us to rise above it.

There is no shortage of theoretical ideas when it comes to narrative inquiry. And there are many theorists to explore, if one chooses to learn about the various theories.

---

[3] See discussion of the crisis of representation in Chapter 5, Principles of Qualitative Research.

Methodology

There are two general categories of narrative method: (a) the use of narrative form and (b) the analysis and interpretation of texts. The first, *the use of narrative form,* means that the style of texts themselves constitutes a method. For example, life histories; stories about an experience; stories that make use of metaphor, fantasies, diary entries, autobiographies, autoethnographies; and other narrative expressions can be used. The general criteria for research narratives are literary forms. One of the most eloquent examples of the use of style to communicate knowledge in narrative inquiry in anthropology is Julie Cruikshank's *Life Lived Like a Story* (Cruikshank, Sidney, Smith, & Ned, 1992), an anthropological study of three Yukon elders.

In an effort to blend my own interests in music therapy and indigenous stories, I wrote "Blue Wolf Says Goodbye for the Last Time" (2002). The article begins with a classic technique in narrative inquiry, one that locates the reader in a place: "The road to Skidegate is dangerous at the best of times" (p. 1241). In the context of a ceremonial headstone moving and feast in the Haida Gwaii, the Queen Charlotte Islands of British Columbia, I describe the importance of the aesthetic experience in traditional societies.

Journals for narrative inquiry, especially in narrative psychology, are full of examples of the narrative style as method. The music therapy examples later in this chapter will provide additional examples.

The second category of narrative method is concerned with *analysis and interpretation of texts.* Some studies in the human and social sciences focus on the content of the stories. Some favor process and the constant negotiations in the ongoing relationships between researchers and participants. Others can be mechanical and transcribe stories strictly for the purpose of content analysis, seeking emergent or critical themes. These approaches parallel standard research methods in qualitative research.

Most narrative inquirers reject computer-based analysis and tend to consider the story as a gestalt, believing that the whole is greater than the sum of its parts (Holloway & Jefferson, 2000). Wengraf (2001) follows a strict schedule of asking a single open-ended question, such as "tell me the whole story of your life," and then a follow-up session where topics are revisited in the precise order in which the respondent raised them:

> No question can be asked which not a story-eliciting one is; no question can be raised about a topic not raised by the interviewee in the initial narration. Nor can a question about a "raised topic" be put out of sequence. There is "directionality" given by the interviewer in this subsection, but it is highly restricted. (Wengraf, p. 120)

Wengraf describes his approach as *SQUIN-BNIM,* or *S̲ingle QU̲estion aimed at I̲nducing N̲arrative and B̲iography-N̲arrative-I̲nterpretation M̲ethod.*

There is a natural tension between maintaining the integrity of the style of narrative itself through coherence, and the research mandate to analyze elements, thus fragmenting the text. Lieblich et al. (1998) suggest specific approaches to reading, interpreting, and analyzing life stories and other narrative materials that attempt to mediate this dilemma. These authors accept the diversity of approaches to narrative research. In general, they acknowledge that there is a continuum between holistic versus categorical approaches and content versus form (p. 12). In the former approach, the *coherence* of the story is privileged, while in the latter, the analysis of the *contents* of the story is privileged. Maxwell (1996) also addresses this dilemma when he notes the distinctions between *contextualization* and *categorization.* For Maxwell, contextualization attempts to maintain the integrity of the relationships of the various elements in the story or text by consistently referring to context, whereas categorization refers to coding practices that tend to fragment the narrative.

Clandinin and Connelly (2000) take a less formal approach to methods. Their model is a three-dimensional inquiry space, a type of inquiry inspired by John Dewey's view of experience as situation, continuity, and interaction. Their three-dimensional inquiry concept of space is particularly interesting because they describe it as ambiguous, complex, difficult, and filled with uncertainty—the uncertainty of doing narrative inquiry. They also provide some straightforward field methods that help to classify types of narrative inquiry including interwoven field texts and teacher stories, autobiographical writing; journal writing; field notes; letters; conversation; research interviews; family stories and stories of families; photographs, memory boxes, and other personal-family-social artifacts; and life experience as sources of field texts.

Relationship to Other Types of Research

Phenomenology is at the foundation of many qualitative research practices, but perhaps is most easily recognized in narrative inquiry. In a story, we are able to learn about life in context and therefore gain knowledge about direct experience through the voices of the participants. Voice plays an important part in this type of research. There is a great deal of debate about how voices serve as an interpretive tool in narrative inquiry, able to elaborate or inhibit the nature and quality of the story. How can the reader know things that are not in the telling, things that might be articulated by a different storyteller?

Van Manen (1990) asserts that hermeneutic phenomenological research is fundamentally a writing activity and that when we construct narratives, we are engaging in hermeneutic activity by the way we construct our story, the elements we choose to reveal, the style of writing, and various factors involved in the writing.

In empirico-analytic research, we rely on laboratories for our research, or at least the metaphor of the laboratory. Naturalistic inquiry is an alternative to the laboratory. *Natural* implies a situation of context that is not possible to control in the way we control variables in a laboratory setting. Narrative inquiry is naturalistic because it is framed within the context of a life or a setting that cannot be captured in a laboratory.

In order to emphasize the aesthetic dimension of narrative inquiry, we can remember that stories are art forms, thus sharing elements of arts-based research. In *The Art and Science of Portraiture*, Sara Lawrence-Lightfoot and Jessica Hoffman Davis (1997) emphasize the power of narrative as art to paint a picture of a research situation.

Narrative inquiry is related to grounded theory because the stories we tell are given primacy. From the analysis of these stories, constructs may rise up from the ground of being and bring a distinctive human character to our research.

The power of the story is more prevalent in critical theory research than in any other form of research because stories are invested not only with primacy, but with power. In fact, in critical theory, empowerment through the stories of the people is essential.

Often the core of ethnographic research is the stories of the research participants and the researcher. Modern variations on ethnography, for example, autoethnographies, are even more obviously narrative in character.

Qualitative case studies provide information about clients, patients, and settings through the articulation of details, similar to stories found in narrative inquiry.

Music Therapy Examples

Numerous examples of narrative inquiry are scattered throughout the music therapy literature. Many of these are in the first category of narrative inquiry, the use of narrative form, favoring an adherence to Maxwell's contextualizations. By presenting research stories or fragments of stories, these researchers provide the reader with a context in which to understand the inherent principles of holism within their music therapy practice or observations of practice without isolating aspects of the story in analytical categories.

We can read narratives but we also can read about the categories the researcher has created to analyze the text or experience, adding a second layer of formalized research practice.

Music therapists tend toward story because they have a natural affinity with it on two counts. First, story is also an art form, like music. Second, as clinicians, we record clinical notes that often have the style of story. This affinity with story and narrative form is certainly apparent in transcripts from GIM sessions.

Narratives offer history, and history is certainly a legitimate form of research. So, when music therapists use the first type of narrative inquiry, choosing to favor contextualization, we must judge these works by asking ourselves if these narratives fulfill the basic requirements of research. Research must be systematic, rigorous, ask questions (implicit or explicit), original, and contribute something to the body of knowledge. Though much scholarly work is involved in the creation of categories, we must take some caution regarding the assumption that research must include an analysis and the creation of categories to qualify as research.

Systematic, rigorous, questioning (implicitly or explicitly) original contributions to the body of knowledge can be made through a formalized research approach through literary devices.

Is the story coherent? Does it have a beginning, a middle, and an end? Does it give the reader a sense of history, of place, of human circumstance? Is it believable? Is it transferable?

The purpose of the following examples is to provide a context for narrative style, expressed by music therapists in a variety of circumstances.

Example One: The Story of Adele

An early example of narrative inquiry used in music therapy, prior to the use of extensive narrative inquiry in psychology, is the case study presented by Gillian Stephens (1981) titled "Adele: A Study in Silence."

> This is the story of Adele.
>
> Adele gave me the opportunity to examine my work in a very special way. All my work was as if done for the first time. I could take nothing for granted. I had to dig deep into myself to understand what I was seeing, to discover how I could make decisions, and how, as a music therapist, I could begin to work.
>
> I wish to share this process, this struggle, and, through the silence. . . Adele. (p. 25)

After this short introduction, the format of the article continues to some degree as a traditional case study. However, the author does continue her initial purpose to examine the dynamics of the relationship with Adele, including dialogue and literary style:

> She puts her hand in mine and lightly lifts and drops my hand against the strings. I brush her fingers across the strings sometimes softly, sometimes firmly, sometimes slowly, sometimes quickly. (p. 30)

In her final statement, Stephens writes: "I see Adele. And I know why I am here" (p. 31).

This is an example of the emotional and relational character of clinical music therapy. Though the methods of narrative inquiry had not yet been formalized in 1981, Stephens demonstrates the relation between case study research and narrative inquiry. This could be considered a mixed genre example.

Example Two: The Story of a GIM Therapist in GIM Therapy

One of the important elements of GIM is the gathering of the story reported to the therapist while the client is on a journey with the music. The therapist faithfully records a transcript of the music therapy journey, which usually includes prompts from the therapist while the client is in a deeply altered state. In the next example, we have a rare opportunity to read the narrative of a GIM therapist describing how the music has an effect on her while she is in a GIM session. Connie Isenberg-Grzeda (1999), speaking as a client in this section of the narrative, writes:

> How does the music act on me as I listen to it in a state of relaxed preparedness? Sometimes it envelops me, holding me, caressing me. I sink into the music as a baby would sink into its mother's arms and I allow it to rock me, to cradle me, and to help me feel safe. The more I let go, the closer I get to a state of blissful fusion with the music, a sleeplike state of total repose. The music is now all that exists for me; the therapist recedes into the background. Memory fragments sometimes emerge for me in this state: memories of early but verbal life, memories of preverbal life, muscle memories, visceral memories. . . . At other times, the music acts in a far less nurturing manner. It sweeps over me in turgid waves, engulfing me, scaring me, and threatening to drown me. Barely able to breathe, I seek to fight it, to escape, or, alternatively, I succumb to the power of the onslaught. (pp. 62–63)

We see once again, how the narrative invites the reader into the story. Literary descriptions bring emotional texture. This is an insider's portrait of the GIM experience.

Example Three: A Story Fragment from a Music Therapist

Suzanne Nowikas (1999) provides us with another narrative from the clinician's perspective. Her narrative fragment is offered within the context of a case study on music therapy:

> I am always struck each time I see her. She is angelic-looking—beautiful curly blond hair to her shoulders and a peaches-and-cream complexion. As she enters, I hear her hum. Yes! She wants to be here. She looks tired today and a little pale. I watch her sit down in a chair that is approximately 6 feet away from the piano. To see her, I must crane my neck and turn around while continuing to play. A little smile comes over her face, a cue for me to begin singing our greeting song. She seems to be anticipating something. (p. 210)

A similar quality of narrative is communicated in this short segment. Through the use of present tense and first person voice, we enter the world of the therapist and the client. We can examine the setting for the work. We can feel the anticipation of the therapist and the aesthetic interpretations about the visual image of her client.

Example Four: The Story of Ken and Ariane

Aigen (1990) provides an example of reflective practice. In the midst of descriptions similar in literary quality to the examples cited above, Aigen inserts this narrative reflection:

> It is hard to know where to begin this story that has so recently ended. I feel compelled to document somehow the depth and quality of the relationship Ariane and I have shared. Partly, this is because of my inability to be completely detached from the fruits of our mutual labor. I am invested in Ariane's continued growth—though our relationship has ended—because I genuinely care about her. I am not sure if committing these thoughts and feelings to paper is my way of finding closure or is serving only to maintain my connection to this silent woman. (p. 48)

Aigen writes that he is *compelled,* indicating the important role of the researcher as primary instrument of this mixed genre article, which is a combination of case study, philosophy, evaluation research through reflective practice, and narrative inquiry.

Example Five: The Blue Room

In this example, we have excerpts from a piece titled "The Blue Room." Like Aigen's excerpt in the introduction to this chapter, this is an example of Ricouer's theory of narrativity and metaphor. I offer a prose piece, representing a fantasy of how it feels to be a music therapist, at the end of my theoretical work, *The Field of Play* (Kenny, 1989). Though Ricouer distinguishes between fiction and nonfiction, I chose to leave the ambiguity in place so that the reader can experience the fluid boundaries between imaginary and concrete worlds. After a theoretical work that is primarily denotative, this connotative piece uses poetic and metaphoric language suggesting an *inner space* for the music therapist:

> I took my place in the Blue Room. . . . The Blue Room is a temple of another time. Does it come to me in a dream or as a memory deep in the center of a Sacred Journey I left so long ago? I am always waiting here with calm anticipation. The temple is full of silent sound. I guard the space. . . . Everything is blue and the air is pregnant. It is a container for loving and creating. Any healing sound, which needs to be made, lives here in these walls. . . . Within this room can be heard the sound of the stars and planets as they make their journey through space. There are sounds of children laughing. The rustling of leaves in the wind. There is the sound of tears from the pool of grief. There is the sound of great anger as it rises out of the belly of the Earth herself. Even the sound of a rainbow is heard within these walls. The ancient drums and chants. The water. The Blue Room is. . . a healing space in the landscape of my imaginings. Grandmother has told us that it is a dream and many other

things as well. . . . In the Blue Room we believe that Music is taking care of Sound. (pp. 142–143)

This narrative reads simply. But it strives for immediate access to the reader's consciousness through a minimalist style and combines many elements of my personal and professional identity, including my Native American ancestry and my sense of the sacred in the music therapy experience.

Example Six: The Story of a Player Who Can't Play

In his master's thesis, *When Players Can't Play: Musicians' Experiences of Playing-Related Injury*, Martin Howard (2003) offers an example of yet another mixed-genre analysis of narrative texts using Moustakas' (1994) phenomenological method. In his study he presents his research with both narrative style and phenomenological/qualitative analysis. He begins his thesis with a narrative:

> The sound of one ensemble merges into the next as I walk down the hallway of the music department where I teach guitar. Music is all around: jazz, blues, Celtic fiddle, a choir rehearsing. I'm between lessons and heading to the bathroom. The hall is crowded and I weave between students who carry guitars, horns, drums, a double bass. The mood here is upbeat; students are laughing and joking, guitar players trade licks, someone is singing part of a jazz tune. It's a thriving place, alive with sound and energy.
>
> Entering the bathroom I see only one other person. He's hunched over the sink, motionless, head resting on the counter, cold water running over his arm. The water gushing from the tap fills the room with white noise; a stark contrast to the bustling soundscape I have just walked through. The sight before me is not unfamiliar; in a glance I know what's happening with this fellow, and I know he's in a kind of a private hell. I recall that he's a student from the jazz program, a guitar player. I go about my business and wash my hands in the neighboring sink. When I finish he hasn't moved at all. The static sound of the running water drones on.
>
> "Hey man, tendonitis?" I venture.
>
> He looks up, anguish on his face, eyes cloudy, "Yeah, it's a total drag man. I can barely play. I'm going nuts."
>
> I sigh and shake my head slowly, "Well, hang in there," I offer, feeling more empathy than I can convey.
>
> I leave the bathroom and again am engulfed by the sounds of people playing music. (p. 1)

The narrative frames his study and again, invites the reader into a story about overuse injury. Howard's research question is what is the experience of a musician whose ability to play music is compromised by an overuse injury? Later he continues his use of narrative style with an autoethnography detailing how his own overuse injury influenced his life and was a factor in his decision to become a music therapist.

Howard also embarks on a time-consuming phenomenological analysis of the essential elements of overuse injury for three participants, analyzing texts according to Moustakas' method, and identifies critical themes and a model for process and recovery.

Example Seven: A Therapist's Experience of the Guiding Process

Kenneth Bruscia's (1995) work, "Modes of Consciousness in Guided Imagery and Music (GIM): A Therapist's Experience of the Guiding Process," provides a classic example of the combination of contextualization and categorization with a focus on the creation of categories. In this piece, Bruscia employs narrative style, expressed in dialogue and reflection on modes of consciousness of the therapist, and adds a second layer of analysis, actually coding the transcripts from his narrative descriptions in a systematic way. He calls this work a self-inquiry, and his intent is to investigate the concept of *being there* for the client. Bruscia uses what can be understood as a narrative inquiry to explore a case with a young man with the AIDS virus.

Bruscia presents his data in a split page. The left side of the page gives us fragments of dialogue from his client. The right side of the page provides us with Bruscia's reflective comments on how he is being there for his client. These are his coding abbreviations:

C = Client's World   1 = Sensory
P = Personal World   2 = Affective
T = Therapist's World   3 = Reflective
                            4 = Intuitive

Here is an example from the 10th music therapy session:

Dialogue

Modes of Consciousness

Tom: The flowers are azaleas bright magenta—the grass is very green and lush. I see myself kneeling on the ground, digging into the earth with my hands.

T1: His breathing is regular; his face is calm. *T4:* He may use this scene to dig up his past. *T3:* The music offers the right support for this. Let him explore without any influence.

Ken: mm—hmm.

Tom: I feel bones down there. They seem to be cracked into several pieces. I found a skull. It's broken in two. The edges are real jagged.

C2: I can feel him getting nervous about what he's digging up. *P2:* I don't want this skeleton to be him. *T1:* His body is tensing.

Ken: How are you feeling?

Tom: Confused. Why am I digging up Such bones in such a beautiful place?

In this short example, we see narrativity and metaphor. We get a sense of place, of circumstance, of life story, even from a small excerpt. We also can perceive the reflective process of the therapist in exploring being there for his client. Bruscia has included both important elements of narrative inquiry, the narrative style and the analysis, with a focus in this case on the analysis. He has invented his own creative categories for coding the GIM transcript for analysis and these categories offer him a frame of reference for his discussion of the case.

In the theoretical discussion that follows this transcript analysis, he states:

A therapist must have freedom to move his consciousness wherever needed or desired. Within understandable limits of personal and professional boundaries, he should have no major problems or limitations in moving—at will—anywhere within the worlds, levels, and media. In the example above, I had to be able to move away from the music, away from my world of images, and center myself squarely on Tom's world—his physical responses, his feelings, and his images. (p. 191)

Bruscia's research methods assisted him in answering his explicit research question, which was about locating his modes of consciousness while functioning as a therapist in the GIM session. He wanted to learn more about being there for his client.

Comments on Examples

In the previous examples of narrative inquiry, the research questions are embedded between the lines and words of the narratives. These narrative examples favor the story and narrative style and thus represent contextualization more than categorizations.

In all of the examples above, we can see that narrative inquiry also offers an opportunity for music therapists to experience reflective practice. There is something about the telling of a story that helps us to examine our practices and to express elements of our work that would be lost to our readers without such tellings, whether those tellings convey a narrative history, a narrative sense of place and context, or our analysis of holistic texts through categories.

Critique of Narrative Inquiry

Narrative inquiry does not fit into a positivist frame of reference where codification, reduction, and isolation are required. The core premise of narrative inquiry is that a story communicates what other forms of inquiry cannot and that there is integrity to a whole story that must be considered if research is to be real. The complexities of the method are not easily grasped. Life is more like a story than a laboratory in which we can exert some control over variables. There are many invisible intervening variables in life. Many social sciences, with the exceptions of anthropology and psychology, have been reluctant to embrace this method of inquiry. However, the elements of the method that make it attractive for holistic purposes are the same ones that create problems because life is not always like the stories we read in texts. And texts themselves are interpretive works that select specific aspects of the stories to be told. The choice of style for representation is an interpretive act in itself. We admire stories that are coherent. But lives are not always coherent. They do not always have tidy beginnings, middles, and ends. And often, the literary influences of the narrative create fictions and illusions that must be considered within their literary context and not taken literally.

Narratives are embedded within the sense-making processes of historically and culturally situated communities (Bruner, 2002). Many elements of stories are therefore idiosyncratic. Critiques of this method focus on the problems of transferability, historical and cultural relativism, and the singularity of the subject of the narrative. Though stories are examples of lives lived, their power rests in their ability to communicate life circumstances to others who do not always recognize the details of those life circumstances, but who can glean a sense from the telling. The goal of narrative inquiry is to elaborate our understanding of life worlds. Their power to convince is somewhat rhetorical. And as some critics say, "That's a good story. But is it really research?" (Ceglowski, 1997).

As expressions of narrative inquiry increase over time, basic questions emerge in terms of their capacity to serve the research imperative. The first question is: How will experimental textual forms be evaluated? And the second one is: How will various disciplines respond to researchers who use experimental writing genres? (Ceglowski, 1997).

Jerome Bruner (2002), one of the great theorists in narrative inquiry, in a self-critique of the method, states:

> There may be something more than the subtlety of narrative structure that keeps us from making the leap from intuition to explicit understanding, something more than that narrative is murky, hard to pin down. Is it that storytelling is somehow not innocent, surely not as innocent as geometry, that it even has a wicked or immoral penumbra? We sense, for example, that too good a story is somehow not to be trusted. It implies too much rhetoric, something fake. Stories, presumably in contrast to logic or science, seem too susceptible to ulteriority—to special pleading and particularly to malice. (p. 5)

Perhaps the answer to some of these critics is the steady dialogue between art and science, as we experience the discourse of the early 21st century. Foucault (1991a) argues that the work of individuals in modernity is to produce themselves as works of art. "Art is something which is specialized or which is done by experts who are artists. But couldn't everyone's life become a work of art? Why should the lamp or the house be an art object but not our life?" (p. 350). Bruner (2002) confesses: "In time, life comes not so much to imitate art as to join with it" (p. 89).

Even Ruud (1998), in proposing *science as narrative,* emphasizes the strengths and weaknesses of the narrative approach for music therapy. His suggestion is that we consider all of the possibilities, but use our critical analysis to temper our acceptance of each one.

References

Aigen, K. (1990). Echoes of silence. *Music Therapy, 9,* 44–61.

Aigen, K. (1991). The voices of the forest: A conception of music for music therapy. *Music Therapy, 10,* 77–98.

Bakhtin, M. M. (1981). *The dialogic imagination.* Austin, TX: University of Texas Press.

Bentz, V. M., & Shapiro, J. J. (1998). *Mindful inquiry in social research.* Thousand Oaks, CA: Sage Publications.

Bonde, L. O. (2000). Metaphor and narrative in Guided Imagery and Music. *Journal of the Association for Music and Imagery, 7,* 59–76.

Bontekoe, R. (1996). *Dimensions of the hermeneutic circle.* Atlantic Highlands, NJ: Humanities Press International.

Bruner, J. (1986). *Actual minds, possible worlds.* Cambridge, MA: Harvard University Press

Bruner, J. (2002). *Making stories.* New York: Farrar, Straus and Giroux.

Bruscia, K. E. (1995) Modes of consciousness in Guided Imagery and Music (GIM): A therapist's experience of the guiding process. In C. B. Kenny (Ed.), *Listening, playing, creating: Essays on the power of sound* (pp. 165–197). Albany, NY: State University of New York Press.

Bruscia, K. E. (1996). Daedalus and the labyrinth: A mythical research fantasy. In M. Langenberg, K. Aigen, & J. Frommer (Eds.), *Qualitative music therapy research: Beginning dialogues* (pp. 204–211). Gilsum, NH: Barcelona Publishers.

Ceglowski, C. (1997). That's a good story, but is it really research? *Qualitative Inquiry, 3,* 188–201.

Clandinin, D. J., & Connelly, F. M. (2000). *Narrative inquiry: Experience and story in qualitative research.* West Sussex, UK: Jossey-Bass Publications.

Cruikshank, J., Sidney, A., Smith, K., & Ned, A. (1992). *Life lived like a story: Life stories of three Yukon elders.* Lincoln, NE: University of Nebraska Press.

Foucault, M. (1991a). On the genealogy of ethics: An overview of work in progress. In P. Rabinow (Ed.), *The Foucault reader* (pp. 340–372). London: Penguin.

Gadamer, H.-G. (1989). *Truth and method.* New York: Crossroad.

Holloway, W., & Jefferson, T. (2000). *Doing qualitative research differently: Free association, narrative and the interview method.* Thousand Oaks, CA: Sage Publications.

Howard, M. (2003). *When players can't play: Musicians' experiences of playing-related injury.* Unpublished master's thesis, Simon Fraser University, Burnaby, British Columbia, Canada.

Isenberg-Grzeda, C. (1999). Experiencing the music in Guided Imagery and Music. In J. Hibben (Ed.), *Inside music therapy: Client experiences* (pp. 61–65). Gilsum, NH: Barcelona Publishers.

Kenny, C. B. (1989). *The field of play: A guide for the theory and practice of music therapy.* Atascadero, CA: Ridgeview Publishing Co.

Kenny, C. B. (2002). Blue Wolf says goodbye for the last time. *American Behavioral Scientist, 45,* 1214–1222.

Lawrence-Lightfoot, S., & Davis, J. H. (1997). *The art and science of portraiture.* San Francisco, CA: Jossey-Bass.

Lieblich, A., Tuval-Mashiach, R., & Zilber, T. (1998) *Narrative research: Reading, analysis, and interpretation.* Thousand Oaks, CA: Sage Publications.

Martin, W. (1990). *Recent theories of narrative.* Ithaca, NY: Cornell University Press.

Mattingly, C., & Garro, L. (Eds.). (2000). *Narrative and the cultural construction of illness and healing.* Berkeley, CA: University of California Press.

Maxwell, J. A. (1996). *Qualitative research design: An interactive approach* (Applied Social Research Methods Series, Vol. 41). Thousand Oaks, CA: Sage Publications.

Mishler, E. G. (1990). Validation in inquiry-guided research: The role of exemplars in narrative studies. *Harvard Educational Review, 60,* 415–442.

Moustakas, C. (1994). *Phenomenological research methods.* Thousand Oaks, CA: Sage Publications.

Nowikas, S. (1999). Discovering meaning in Kelly's nonverbal expressions. In J. Hibben (Ed.), *Inside music therapy: Client experiences* (pp. 209–230). Gilsum, NH: Barcelona Publishers.

Pamphilon, B. (1999). The zoom model: A dynamic framework for the analysis of life histories. *Qualitative Inquiry, 5,* 393–410.

Ricoeur, P. (1984–1988). *Time and narrative* (Vols. 1–3; K. McLaughlin & D. Pellauer, Trans.). Chicago: University of Chicago Press.

Ruud, E. (1998). *Music therapy: Improvisation, communication, and culture.* Gilsum, NH: Barcelona Publishers.

Stephens, G. (1981). Adele: A study in silence. *Music Therapy 1,* 25–32.

Van Manen, M. (1990). *Researching lived experience.* London, Ontario: The Althouse Press.

Wengraf. T. (2001). *Qualitative research interviewing: Biographic narratives and semi-structured methods.* Thousand Oaks, CA: Sage Publications.

Additional Readings

Chamberlain, M., & Thompson, P. (1998). Introduction: Genre and narrative in life stories. In M. Chamberlain & P. Thompson (Eds.), *Narrative and genre* (pp. 1–22). London: Routledge.

Ezzy, D. (2002). *Qualitative analysis: Practices in innovation.* London: Routledge.

Denzin, N. K., & Lincoln, Y. S. (Eds.). (2000). *Handbook of qualitative research* (2nd ed.). Thousand Oaks, CA: Sage Publications.

Foucault, M. (1991b). What is enlightenment? In P. Rabinow (Ed.), *The Foucault reader* (pp. 32–50). London: Penguin.

Gergen, K., & Gergen, M. M. (1997). Narratives of the self. In L. P. Hinchman & S. K. Hinchman (Eds.), *Memory, identity, community: The idea of narrative in the human sciences* (pp. 161–84). Albany, NY: State University of New York Press.

Kenny, C. B. (1996). The story of the field of play. In M. Langenberg, K. Aigen, & J. Frommer (Eds.), *Qualitative music therapy research: Beginning dialogues.* Gilsum NH: Barcelona Publishers.

Lincoln, Y. S., & Guba, E. G. (1985). *Naturalistic inquiry.* Newbury Park, CA: Sage Publications.

Polkinghorne, D. E. (1991). Narrative and self-concept. *Journal of Narrative and Life History, 1*(2 & 3), 135–154.

Tonkin, E. (1992). *Narrating our pasts: The social construction of oral history.* Cambridge: Cambridge University Press.

Smith, L. T. (1999) *Decolonizing methodologies: Research and indigenous peoples.* London: Zed Books, Ltd.

Van Manen, M. (2002). *Writing in the dark: Phenomenological studies in interpretive inquiry.* London, Ontario, Canada: The Althouse Press.

Acknowledgments

I would like to express my appreciation to Even Ruud, Lars Ole Bonde, Ken Aigen, Jane Edwards, Barbara Wheeler, and Mechtild Jahn-Langenberg for comments and suggestions.

Chapter 34
Morphological Research
Eckhard Weymann and Rosemarie Tüpker

Müsset im Naturbetrachten
immer eins wie alles achten.
Nichts ist drinnen, nichts ist draussen,
denn was innen, das ist außen.
So ergreifet ohne Säumnis
Heilig öffentlich' Geheimnis.

Erfreuet Euch des wahren Scheins,
Euch des ernsten Spieles
denn nichts Lebendiges ist eins,
immer ist's ein Vieles.

You must, when contemplating nature,
Attend to this, in each and every feature:
There's nought outside and nought within,
For she is inside out and outside in.
Thus will you grasp, with no delay,
The holy secret, clear as day.

Take joy in true appearance,
And in serious play,
For no living being is singular,
But always a plurality.

Goethe—"Epirrhema" (1821)

Morphology (from Greek *morphe,* meaning form, shape) refers to the study or knowledge of forms or shapes. The objects of morphological research are investigated from the perspective of their formation, their structure, and their changes of form (metamorphosis). Today the term *morphology* is used in disciplines as diverse as psychology, geology, biology, and linguistics. Occasionally the term is used in a limited way to refer only to set structures or the results of a process of formation. At other times, as in this chapter, the formation process itself is examined and may even be the focus of interest.

In music therapy the entire therapeutic process (music, conversations, emotions, behavior, and so forth) can be thought of as a *gestalt* formation and be related to other relevant gestalt formations in the patient (biography, organization of daily life, symptoms, and so forth). This is primarily a psychological perspective, since it is related to formations of the psyche, but it includes musicological perspectives also. To think about music as a psychological object means above all to investigate it from an experiential aspect, that is, to understand it as a *gestalt of effects.*

Historical Roots and Theoretical Premises

Under the premise that psychological data can only be obtained through the reflected subjectivity of the researcher, *experiential description* became the most important instrument of knowledge in morphology, integrated into varied methodological contexts such as the in-depth interview and the experiential record. "The description of complete contexts becomes the basic method of psychological morphology because no isolated facts or data as such exist outside of the object-oriented living context" (Salber, 1991, p. 52). "Description seeks to grasp the movement of phenomenal forms"[1] (Salber, 1969, p. 63), which then have to be transformed into explanatory reconstructions through several intermediate steps. Aside from developing and reflecting upon

---

[1] The sources for this and other quotations are in German but have been translated to English as cited here. The original German is given only when it provides information that is not apparent in the translation.

therapeutic concepts, the main foci of morphological psychological research are psychological factors of everyday life, psychology of the arts and the new media, and commercial and business psychology. Research results are published in the journal *Zwischenschritte* (Intermediate Steps) and elsewhere.

Some music therapists became interested in morphological psychology in the 1970s because of its affinity with art and the psychology of the arts. In 1980, Frank Grootaers, Tilman Weber, and the authors of this chapter established a research group for the morphology of music therapy and then later, in 1988, the Institute for Music Therapy and Morphology (IMM). In this institute, the basic ideas of morphological music therapy were developed as an integration of research and practice. The initial goal was to use concepts from morphological psychology to make description of the music therapy process possible, and to develop music therapy-specific procedures to enable their scientific reconstruction. In this context, the investigation of improvisation in music therapy is of special significance. The results were disseminated through numerous professional conferences, courses, and publications, as well as in a series called *Materialien zur Musiktherapie* (Studies of Music Therapy). Morphological music therapy is taught at the University of Münster and the Hamburg University of Music and Drama.

The term *morphology* goes back as far as the German poet and scientist J. W. Goethe (1749–1832), who proclaimed a scientific view expressly set against the (then current) mainstream of positivist and reductionist positions. He turned against the prevailing opinion that the knowledge of nature was to be found only by dissection and analysis, by an identification of ever-smaller pieces. Instead, he sought to understand characteristic features of "organic natures" in a holistic manner, using principles such as formation and transformation, including both spatial and temporal dimensions. In this way he tried to gain "insight into the context of their essence and actions"[2] (Goethe, 1954, p. 6). He described these contexts, derived by thorough observation of individual cases, as types or formation principles (*ur* or primeval phenomena). With these ideas, Goethe placed himself in the tradition of Aristotle's empirical (based on experience) philosophy of nature, according to which living forms are subject to growth and loss. This philosophy views living forms as historical phenomena, emphasizing aspects of development and process. Thus, Goethe (as well as Aristotle) could be called a forerunner of modern qualitative research strategies (see Harlan, 2002; Mayring, 1986).

Goethe developed his concept of morphology beginning in 1790 in different scientific subjects (anatomy, botany, theory of colors, and so forth). He characterized it distinctly in his programmatic introduction *About Morphology*, written in 1817, as the science of "formation and transformation of organic natures" (Goethe, 1954, p. 2).[3] These living organic natures were always regarded both as having/being form and being changeable.

The morphologist attempts to graphically convey the experience of and create a systematic reconstruction of whatever phenomenon or living object is the focus of interest and perception. According to Goethe, theory develops from unmediated vivid experience and is not found behind or beyond the level of phenomena. In the process of perception, we already actively begin to theorize and systematize—or, more to the point, we form, shape, or reorganize. The gestalt concept connects phenomenon, perception, and theoretical reconstruction: All are understood both to be and to have form. In Goethe's (1965) terms: "Gestalt is something that moves, becoming and diminishing. Knowledge of gestalt is the knowledge of metamorphosis" (p. 128). In this definition of the gestalt concept, the developmental approach of morphology becomes clear.

Morphological psychology, established by Wilhelm Salber in the 1950s, takes up this gestalt concept against a background of considerations from gestalt psychology and psychoanalysis. In morphological psychology, the psyche and its essence are conceptualized as a gestalt formation and at the same time as a transitory event between gestalt and transformation. Experience and behavior are functions of this overall process. Within the flow of the reality of formations of the psyche, morphological psychology strives for principles of organization, for blueprints and inherent laws. It attempts to work out the *moving system* of the life of the psyche. The life of the psyche resembles a *traveling figure*[4] (Salber, 1991), a guiding metaphor of morphological psychology. This view attributes to the life of the psyche a special affinity towards the arts. "The marriage of science and art sets a cognitive process in motion where art und science can learn from each other" (Tüpker, 2001, p. 57).

---

[2] Original: Einsicht in den Zusammenhang ihres Wesens und Wirkens
[3] Bildung und Umbildung organischer Naturen
[4] Gestalt auf Reisen

Methodology

The decision to use a specific methodology is based on preconceived notions about the type, composition, and limitations of the object of research. An object with a certain prescientific or everyday meaning becomes a scientific object.[5] Using the instruments and procedures of morphological psychology, diverse phenomena are viewed and conceptualized as psychological phenomena, as productions of the psyche. Therefore, the main objective of morphological research is the exploration of psychological processes as they emerge from experience and behavior. One approach involves structural analysis of verbalizations of different (self-) observations. These are then reconstructed in several interrelated hermeneutic steps. The objective in each case is to reconstruct the interplay of those *gestalt factors* or structures of experience involved in the experiential situation under investigation. The psychological event is reconstructed as a dramatic interplay, as an interlocking of several polarities within the process.

The morphological research process unfolds its object suspended between phenomenon and interpretation. A constant shifting of perspectives is characteristic. Every data collection is the result of choosing (and excluding), sorting, or forming. It is motivated by a specific search, a vague pre-knowledge or preconception of the whole. Neither pure facts nor complete objectivity exist. Morphological research always involves reconstruction.

Four Versions or Perspectives

A typical morphological course of research can be demonstrated from four different versions or perspectives that organize the process. The method of the steps is based on the general idea that a psychological wholeness[6] can only be represented (reconstructed) in a sufficiently complete and complex way if it is described repeatedly and from different perspectives. These four perspectives can be equally applied to the therapy process and case descriptions as to the research process in a modified form (for more detail see Tüpker, 2001, pp. 60–70; Tüpker, 2004).

1. *Wholeness—Gestalt Logic.* What is seen as a psychological unit or whole is determined through experience on the one hand and scientific investigation (or treatment objectives) on the other. Here, the goal is to discover which stories or images hold the experiences of a given situation together meaningfully, what is the unfolding gestalt of effects and what is the case.
2. *Form Development—Gestalt Construction.* Forms (Gestalten) are structured units. They are made up of parts that are related to each other and to the whole, and they unfold in a dynamic order. This second version tries to work out the system, the inherent order of the individual gestalt of effects, and thus to find some initial explanation for the impact of the whole.
3. *Formation and Reformation—Gestalt Refraction.* The individual gestalts of effects have their own histories; they have precursors; and they affect others. *Gestalt refraction* alludes to this mutual influencing of gestalts. While observing the developmental aspect of our research subject, we learn of the possibilities for transformation and intervention.
4. *Interplay/Cooperation—Gestalt Paradox.* In psychological morphology the gestalt formation is understood as an interplay of factors of the psyche. This interplay always has to cope with polarities and paradoxical circumstances. The fourth version tries to reconstruct phenomena based on a general theory and thus to explain their effects in a way native to the phenomena themselves.

Morphology offers several systems that make this theoretical orientation possible. For research in music therapy, the system of the six *gestalt factors* (Tüpker, 1988/1996a) and the concept of primary and secondary figuration (for example, Grootaers, 2001; Weymann, 2004) have been used.

As an illustration of two possible perspectives that morphological research can bring to understanding treatment and research processes, one example of treatment steps and one of

---

[5] Gegenstandsbildung (formation of the scientific object)
[6] Ganzheit

research steps are presented below. These are only two of many possible examples of how these perspectives can be applied.

Treatment Steps

As steps or aspects of treatment, the system of the four versions or perspectives can be used on two levels: (a) to help to structure the treatment or to develop a special treatment concept, or (b) to analyze and evaluate a course of treatment after it is completed (as might be done for research purposes). Going through all four steps is the qualitative criterion, with its specific application being based on the individual project that is being researched as well as its general set up. The treatment steps can be used either to describe the entire development of a treatment or to analyze an individual session.

Step 1. Leiden-Können[7] or Treatment Objectives. The first treatment step represents treatment objectives and thus corresponds to diagnosis in music therapy. However, whereas in medicine diagnosis and indication formally precede treatment, in psychotherapy they are part of treatment and may develop and change in the course of treatment. The technical term from morphological psychology, Leiden-Können, refers to several things simultaneously. It refers to what the patient complains about as the source of emotional and physical suffering, but also under what circumstances she or he suffers. In the same way, we are interested in the patient's skills, abilities, and resources and in what she or he likes and dislikes.[8] We also go on the assumption that the patient might possibly like what she or he complains about even more than that from which she or he must protect him- or herself through the emotional constructions. All this is explored in both the patient's narrations and the music. In order to do this, the description and reconstruction that are described below may be applied as a diagnostic instrument. Leiden-Können changes within the course of treatment, not just as progress is made in treatment but also as deeper layers of suffering become apparent.

Step 2. Methodifying. The second treatment step refers on the one hand to the therapist following methodical principles of treatment. On the other hand, we assume that patients will follow a method as well in the sense that they treat the treatment situation, the therapeutic relationship, and the music in the same way that they deal with themselves and the world. In this way patients transfer their *method of living* to the treatment situation and also involve the therapist in this event. This is all the more so when the therapist gets involved in the interplay of transference and countertransference. Like modern psychoanalysis, morphological music therapy assumes that it is part of the therapist's methodological task to become empathically involved by being moved. Then, by again acquiring some distance, the therapist's empathy leads to understanding. This understanding may then be communicated to the patient, either symbolically (in music or play) or by means of verbal interpretation. Thus becoming methodological connects the participants and speeds up the development of treatment.

Step 3. Changing. With the concept of changing (transformation), we look for changed experiences in treatment, a new viewpoint, a different tone in the music, a new way of expression. Through these, transformation and restructuring within the patient's method of living may announce themselves. Such turning points can become evident when connected with an *aha* experience, a sudden insight, a jolt in the psyche. Changes can also take place almost unnoticed and become more evident in retrospect. Changing is the internal criterion for the effects of the treatment, such as the effects of therapist's interpretations or of musical interventions. If those elements are missing, we must ask ourselves what must be changed methodologically and why the methodological procedures have not worked so far.

---

[7] To suffer, to be able to

[8] The German word leiden not only means to suffer but also to like something. Etymologically it is linked to the meaning of traveling and gaining experience.

Step 4. Implementation.[9] In the last step we look at the changes that reach beyond the treatment setting: What does the patient put into action in her or his everyday life? What is he or she able to implement? How is he or she able to deal with daily life differently? Part of this is, of course: How do her or his symptoms, complaints, and suffering improve, or how does the treatment improve her or his quality of life?

Methodological Steps: Description and Reconstruction

A scientific procedure called *Description and Reconstruction,* originally developed for analyzing improvisations in music therapy (Tüpker, 1996a), is frequently used. It enables us to focus on the musical part of music therapy as the center and starting point for scientific (as well as musical) considerations. Diagnosis and the evaluation of therapy can consequently be done in a music-centered way (Weymann, 2000b).

It is our aim to work out the *gestalts of effects* in improvisations. Assuming that their musical structures correspond to those of the psyche, we wish to explore those characteristic patterns in improvisations, which, as psychic structures (method of living), are also connected to the patient's disorder or dilemma.

Through these four methodological steps, the above-mentioned versions can be clearly identified. This procedure may be applied to different subjects and contexts of research and is based on the effect of the musical experience. In this regard, it is similar to other comparable methodological approaches from the sphere of in-depth hermeneutic procedures (see also Langenberg et al., 1996; Metzner, 2000).

As part of the first step, *experiential descriptions* of the music are made. This is done by a group of trained experts who listen to the audio recording without having any other case information. The subsequent steps are then developed by the researcher, who usually also is the therapist of the case study, along the guidelines of the summarized text.

The four methodological steps (which on the whole perform a hermeneutic spiral), summarized in Table 1, will subsequently be illustrated through excerpts from a case study. (For a detailed example that uses all the steps in a case study see Irle, 1996.)

Table 1
Methodological Steps: Description and Reconstruction

Step	Perspective	Procedure
1	Wholeness	Listening, written descriptions, exchange/discussions of texts, summarized text
2	Internal regulation	Investigation of musical structures, possibly by notating the music
3	Transformation	Comparison with other relevant observations and data from the patient's biography and medical history
4	Reconstruction	Description of the gestalt of effects on a general and a more abstract level (theoretical orientation), for example, by means of the gestalt factors or the concept of primary and secondary figurations

Step 1. Wholeness. The describers focus their attention on the phenomenon with an unprejudiced attitude and a willingness to be moved by it. They are asked to write notes in a simple and comprehensible language. The descriptions are read aloud and compared with an eye to common factors or differences. The discussion within the describer's group aims at the formulation of a summarized text, which should also include possible contradictions and countertendencies and thus often

---

[9] The German word Bewerkstelligen, containing the word Werk, emphasizes the product character of this last step as well as the process.

represents something like a formulation of the problem. The following excerpt from the description of one person provides an example:

> Something must be done very fast. No pauses. Stillness is dangerous, on and on. I cannot stop. There is a stumbling somewhere inside there. I've got to get away. I'm running, but something always holds me back; shouldn't I rather stay? No, I have no time to linger. . . almost unbearable longing.

Common to all descriptions was the symptom of restlessness, a restless movement that has no ending and therefore seems without purpose. In a counter-movement, the existence of obstacles is emphasized: stumbling, something holds me back, and so forth. Everything seems to be kept in suspension, although this becomes *almost unbearable*. After some discussion the group finally agreed on the following summarized sentence:

> Something that's being driven is continuously held up and never arrives. The result is a tormenting suspense.

Step 2. Internal Regulation. Working from the summarized text, we develop questions and follow up with a selective detailed analysis of the music. We investigate relevant examples on the basis of the recording and possibly the notation, as to how the described impression is created in sound. Through this, particular features of the musical structure are worked out. These may then be used as evidence and specification of the experiential gestalt and moreover as an indication of the (subconscious) method of its production. Here, the relationship of part-to-whole is investigated, in the sense of a hermeneutic approach. For example:

> How is the impression of suspense achieved, of being driven and at the same time being stopped? What constellation of musical parameters creates the image of not-arriving?
>
> This can be demonstrated in the example through the rhythmic features. From the very beginning, the impression of the unexpected, the unpredictable, is created. The rhythms seem to be put together from many snippets. The first three notes seem to establish the pulse, but the fourth comes too early by comparison. This could be a syncopation, if the connection to the pulse were reestablished at some point. Instead, more breaks follow, but always just missing what is expected, creating an impression of suspense.

Step 3. Transformation. In the third step the research unit is broadened, again along the guideline of the theme gained so far, by including data from other sources: notes from the therapy process, from the case history, the patient's biography, the patient's everyday narrations and dreams. Thereby the picture is enriched but is also corrected. But most of all we discover indications about the importance and the *secret meaning* of the observed gestalt formation within the patient's life context. Through the variation, the structural element is also emphasized. For example:

> The patient, a 24-year-old man, suffers from a severe compulsion with obsessive washing and control compulsions. He feels constantly tormented by doubts, rendering him almost completely incapable of making decisions in his daily life. For instance, he cannot just sit down in a chair but hesitates for a while between a standing and a sitting position, as if in suspense. He tries to avoid leaving any traces or feeling impressed by anything.

Step 4. Reconstruction. The reconstruction seeks to lead the gestalt that was found back to basic conditions of emotional life, for instance the interplay of factors of the psyche. Thus, on a structural level, the internal logic of the phenomenon can be represented as a kind of moving pattern from which indications about the patient's subconscious life organization, or about his individual gestalt formation, can be deduced. For example:

> The gestalt factors of *arrangement* and *effect* do not form a complementary relationship with each other but create a short circuit, as it were. The beginnings of formation are incessantly subjected to sorting procedures; these seem unachievable by any other limiting tendency. Thus, actions are initiated

but then inhibited and cannot be completed. At the same time, the sorting tendency does not unfold because no distinctive gestalt is formed, leading to disorganization.

Relationship to Other Types of Research

The methods resulting from the above-mentioned fundamental ideas of morphology show numerous factors common to other types of qualitative research. These factors include reflexivity, an idiographic approach, and the interpretive paradigm that takes its starting point from the researcher's reflected subjectivity.

Methodologically, the affinity to the hermeneutic approach is particularly noticeable. The postulate of an experiential moving along together[10] with the living research object determines a procedural and somewhat phenomenal approach to reality. Through several intermediate steps, this approach approximates the level of theory and thus also the possibility of understanding and explaining the phenomena. Since unconscious determinants are also included, one could also call it an *in-depth hermeneutic* approach in the sense of Lorenzer (1986). A synthesizing basic feature is characteristic of a morphological research process: the search for a context substantiated by analytical working steps. In this we recognize similarities with the heuristic procedures of art, a connection that in morphology is termed *psycho-aesthetics* or an *art-analogous* procedure.

Apart from psychoanalysis and gestalt theory, we also recognize a special affinity with *systemic thought* (Watzlawick, 1976) on the level of models and theories (gestalt factors, versions, part-whole relationship, gestalts, and transformation).

Examples in Music Therapy

Morphological music therapy research includes practical and methodological questions, as well as broader questions that are concerned with music, therapy, health, illness, and society. More specialized areas are classified into: (a) individual case and group studies, (b) comparative studies, and (c) music psychology. A selective overview of studies and results to date on the basis of this classification follows.

Individual Case and Group Studies

The morphological scientific procedure Description and Reconstruction, described above, is applied most frequently. There are about 100 examples of this diagnostically oriented research procedure (in some cases as yet unpublished). Almost the whole scope of music therapy is found wherever free improvisation, in the broadest sense, is used. For other areas, some partly modified procedures have been developed (Spliethoff, 1994), and a specially modified form for group analysis may be found in Grootaers (2001). Apart from analysis on the basis of gestalt factors, other reference systems, such as psychoanalytic pathology or developmental psychology (Irle & Müller, 1996), may be chosen for the theoretical orientation. On a pragmatic level, it is possible to apply morphological procedures without fully understanding principles of morphology. This is of special interest because we have found that description itself (included in step 1 of the Description and Reconstruction procedures), even in nonscientific contexts such as supervision or practice-related quality assurance, allows a more in-depth and elucidating view of the individual case, which improves the treatment. The music therapist is thus in the position to make an important contribution to the treatment team toward understanding the patient by translating the results of musical communication with the patient into psychological language.

Naturally the results of such individual case studies can only be summarized in a very general way. The results of these studies allow us to state: Irrespective of the patient's musical background and under certain preconditions with regard to the therapeutic setting, fundamental structures of the psyche can be expressed by improvising with the therapist. These are also related to the patient's disorder or conflict situation. They can be described and objectified by independent observers through their manifestation as musical structures, thus contributing to

---

[10] Mitbewegung

the comprehensive psychological understanding of the patient by complementing the language-limited approach to patient care.

The method of analyzing the course of treatment presented here (treatment steps) has been used in about 30 case studies or short presentations to verify the sequence of events in treatment. The results differ from case to case because of different treatment conditions that make comparison difficult. Not only do the very diverse reasons for therapy play a role, but external conditions beyond the control of the music therapist also make a difference. These include such factors as financial restrictions on treatment, legal restrictions on outpatient music therapy, and a lack of options for patients. We can state, though, that in those music therapy treatments that were not too heavily restricted by exterior conditions, a complete cycle of the four steps of treatment was achieved, which methodologically could be considered a successful treatment. Individually, the respective preconditions are too diverse for us to formulate an overall result. One exception is the study by Grootaers (2001) in which 13 individual and 2 group studies in psychosomatic care, based on the four treatment steps, show in detail the success of a music therapy treatment in favorable and comparable inpatient conditions. There the relevant turning figure is worked out for every patient individually, so that the success of the treatment is oriented toward and measured by the individual patient's method of living, disorder, and living situation.

Comparative Studies

Comparative studies include papers in which morphological methods themselves are reviewed and further developed by means of comparative observation.

In one study (Mömesheim, 1999), the 171 texts created through Description and Reconstruction procedures were investigated using methods from literary studies. The researcher developed criteria for text analysis that were then used for further comparative research. She found that in all 26 descriptions there was a verifiable connection between the established gestalt of effects of the improvisation (research step 1) and the musical formation of forms (step 2). In addition, the researcher made detailed recommendations as to the formulation of the gestalt of effects as well as the development of the gestalt formation. These recommendations were made on the basis of qualitative differences within the comprehensibility of individual contexts, the summary generalization, and internal regulation.

Hülsmann (2002) compared two morphological descriptive procedures, one with an external group of describers (Tüpker, 1988/1996a) and the other with a description by patients (Grootaers, 2001), on the basis of examples of music in group music therapy. Certain clearly discernable common factors emerged, and these are regarded as proof of the validity of both procedures. The obvious differences may be psychologically explained on the grounds of individual perspectives (self-involvement/distance, awareness/lack of awareness of temporal developments, and other events in the group) and constitute a supplementary relationship.

Another group of studies includes studies in which patients' initial improvisations are compared to comparable diagnoses in terms of their psychological gestalts of effects and their musical gestalt formation. To this date, comparative studies of patients with chronic pain (Krapf, 2001; Tüpker, 2002, pp. 56–67), borderline personality disorder (Tönnies, 2002), and anorexia (Erhardt, 2003; Kang-Ritter, 2003) are available. To varying degrees, common factors were demonstrated in the way these groups of patients expressed themselves. For instance, many more common factors emerged with patients with pain than with those with borderline personality disorder or anorexia. However, new insights were gained about the understanding of these disorders as well as some clues for music therapy treatment.

On the basis of the four treatment steps, Haubitz (1999) compared the development of two group treatments with depressive patients. In the music, as well as in transference and countertransference, the differences between one group of patients with more neuroses and another group with psychoses were clearly observed.

Other issues are worked out in comparative studies that relate to general aspects of treatment. Methodologically, these studies overlap to some degree with the aforementioned area. Based on interviews, Mönter (1998) compared the proportions of verbal conversations in music therapy and systematized the results using the four versions (based on 12 explorative expert interviews). Music therapy publications are the subject of two other comparative studies investigating the beginning (Krückeberg, 2000) and the ending (Stihl, 2000) of music therapy treatment. Wältring-Mertens (1999) compared 40 case histories based on the question of the practical significance of music in music therapy with children. This study shows a multitude of music-related event forms, emphasizing flexibility and openness as characteristic features of music therapy with children.

Music Psychology

By means of the methodological evaluation of qualitative interviews (in-depth interviews, explorative expert interviews) and other qualitative interview methods (such as semi-structured questionnaires), general questions related to music therapy such as the experience of music therapy supervision (Schmutte, 2002; Tüpker, 1996b) can be explored, as well as basic issues about the psychology of musical experience and activity outside of the therapy context. Studies to date are concerned with questions of improvisation (Domnich, 1995; Leikert, 1990; Weymann, 2004), singing (Wachwitz-Homering, 1993), the relationship between player and instrument (Meyer, 1992), or practicing an instrument (West, 1992). There are no clear-cut differences between those papers with a morphological orientation and other related psychological approaches.

As one example, we will examine more closely the dissertation of Weymann (2004). It deals with the question of "how life's work and the activity of improvisation are related to one another. How does the *method of living* manifest in dealing with improvisation? How does this indicate specific characteristics and implications of the improvisation activity?" (p. 53). For this purpose, 12 in-depth interviews were conducted with musicians in whose lives improvisation plays an emotionally significant role. The basic conditions were first worked out individually. These may be described as different forms of a polarity around the central theme of *transformation versus identity* (p. 192). As soon as the transformation became evident as the primary figuration (in the form of: stimulating, dissolving, delimiting, shifting, going beyond, letting go, being swept along in an intoxicated way, united/going beyond one's own space, rough/unfinished), the opposite pole appeared in the secondary figuration (as anchoring, unifying, securing, framing, integrating, controlling, being opposite, different, developed/elaborated; pp. 189–191). By contrast, in a second group, aspects of finding one's identity through improvisation were initially emphasized with these words: assertion, alone, finding oneself. Here too, the opposite pole appeared in the secondary figuration (canceling, united, sharing).

The final typical solutions that were worked out with regard to the established polarity in the sense of a self-treatment through music "represent. . . examples in the sense of pre-images or prototypes which may serve as guideposts for the concrete gestalt formation in real-life practice of music therapy" (Weymann, 2004, p. 207).

Summary

Morphological Music Therapy is an approach that has been developed in Germany for 25 years. It is based on old European scientific traditions, especially on the scientific approach of Goethe. In its modern form, it includes insights from psychoanalysis and Gestalt psychology and has developed methods for qualitative research in music therapy (Tüpker 2002, Weymann 2000a). In Germany this approach is taught at several university music therapy trainings and a number of books and articles have been published.

References

Domnich, C. (1995). *Untersuchung zur freien musikalischen Improvisation als Gestaltungsversuch des Seelischen* [An exploration of free music improvisation as emotional gestalt]. Unpublished music therapy diploma thesis, Münster University, Münster, Germany.

Erhardt, C. (2003). *Hunger nach Weniger. Vergleichende Untersuchung musiktherapeutischer Erstimprovisationen magersüchtiger Patienten* [The hunger for less: A comparison of initial improvisations of anorexic patients in music therapy]. Unpublished music therapy diploma thesis, Münster University, Münster.

Goethe, J. W. von (1954). *Bildung und Umbildung organischer Naturen. Die Schriften zur Naturwissenschaft* (Leopoldina-Ausgabe). Erste Abteilung, Band 9 [Formation and transformation of organic natures. Writings on natural science (Leopoldina Edition). 1st section, Vol. 9]. Weimar, Germany: Böhlau.

Goethe, J. W. von (1965). *Die Schriften zur Naturwissenschaft* (Leopoldina-Ausgabe). Erste Abteilung, Band 10 [Writings on natural sciences (Leopoldina Edition). 1st section, Vol. 10]. Weimar: Böhlau.

Grootaers, F. G. (2001). *Bilder behandeln Bilder: Musiktherapie als angewandte Morphologie* [Images treat images: Music therapy as applied morphology]. Münster: Lit-Verlag.

Harlan, V. (2002). *Das Bild der Pflanze in Wissenschaft und Kunst* [The image of plants in science and art]. Stuttgart, Germany: Mayer.

Haubitz, S. (1999). *Vergleichende Untersuchung zweier Musiktherapiegruppen in der Psychiatrie* [Comparative study of two music therapy groups in psychiatry]. Unpublished music therapy diploma thesis, Münster University, Münster.

Hülsmann, M. (2002). *Vergleichende Untersuchung von zwei morphologischen Beschreibungsverfahren* [Comparative study of two morphological descriptive processes]. Unpublished music therapy diploma thesis, Münster University, Münster.

Irle, B. (1996). Der Spielraum Musiktherapie als Ergänzung des padagogischen Auftrages in einem Internat [The music therapy playroom as an educational augmentation in boarding school]. In B. Irle & I. Müller (Eds.), *Raum zum Spielen—Raum zum Verstehen. Musiktherapie mit Kindern* (pp. 10–102). Münster: Lit-Verlag.

Irle, B., & Müller, I. (1996). *Raum zum Spielen—Raum zum Verstehen. Musiktherapie mit Kindern* [Room to play—room to understand. Music therapy with children]. Münster: Lit-Verlag.

Kang-Ritter, A. (2003). *Musiktherapie mit essgestörten Kindern und Jugendlichen. Eine vergleichende Untersuchung von Beschreibungstexten musiktherapeutischer Improvisationen* [Music therapy for children with eating disorders: A comparative study of descriptions of initial improvisations in music therapy]. Unpublished music therapy diploma thesis, Münster University, Münster.

Krapf, J. M. (2001). *Auf den Schmerz hören. Vergleichende Untersuchung der musikalischen Erstimprovisationen von chronischen Schmerzpatienten* [Listening to the pain: A comparative study of initial music improvisations by patients with chronic pain]. Unpublished music therapy diploma thesis, Münster University, Münster.

Krückeberg, W. (2000). *Zum Beginn musiktherapeutischer Behandlungen* [Beginning music therapy treatment]. Unpublished music therapy diploma thesis, Münster University, Münster.

Langenberg, M., Frommer, J., & Langenbach, M. (1996). Fusion and separation: Experiencing opposites in music, music therapy, and music therapy research. In M. Langenberg, K. Aigen, & J. Frommer (Eds.). *Qualitative music therapy research: Beginning dialogues* (pp. 131–160). Gilsum, NH: Barcelona Publishers.

Leikert, S. (1990) Die Lust am Zuviel—Der Wirkungsraum der Instrumentalimprovisation [The pleasure in overabundance—The "effect area" of instrumental improvisation]. *Zwischenschritte, 2,* 27–39.

Lorenzer, A. (1986). Tiefenhermeneutische Kulturanalyse [In-depth hermeneutic cultural analysis]. In A. Lorenzer (Ed.), *Kultur-Analysen* (pp. 11–98). Frankfurt, Germany: Suhrkamp.

Mayring, P. (1986). *Einführung in die qualitative Sozialforschung* [An introduction to qualitative social research] (2nd ed.). Weinheim, Germany: Beltz.

Meyer, B. (1992). *Instrument und MusikerIn—Psychologische Aspekte einer Beziehung* [Instrument and musician: Psychological aspects of a relationship]. Unpublished music therapy diploma thesis, Münster University, Münster.

Metzner, S. (2000). Ein Traum: Eine fremde Sprache kennen, ohne sie zu verstehen. Zur Evaluation von Gruppenimprovisationen [A dream: to know a foreign language, without understanding it. Evaluating group improvisations]. *Musiktherapeutische Umschau, 21,* 234–247.

Mömesheim, E. (1999). *"Wer verschweigt das letzte Wort?"—Vergleichende Untersuchung von Beschreibungstexten aus der Morphologischen Musiktherapie* [Who conceals the last word? A comparative study of descriptive texts in morphological music therapy]. Unpublished music therapy diploma thesis, Münster University, Münster.

Mönter, U. (1998). *Das Gespräch in der Musiktherapie* [Discussion in music therapy]. *Musiktherapeutische Umschau, 21,* 5–22.

Salber, W. (1969). *Wirkungseinheiten* [Effect units]. Cologne, Germany: Moll und Hülser.

Salber, W. (1991). *Gestalt auf Reisen* [Traveling figure]. Bonn: Bouvier.

Schmutte, M. (2002). *Supervision in der Musiktherapie—Erlebensweisen, Erfahrungen und Einschätzungen von Supervisanden* [Supervision in music therapy: Experiences and estimations of supervisors]. Unpublished music therapy diploma thesis, Münster University, Münster.

Spliethoff, G. (1994). *Untersuchung seelischer Gestaltbildungen auf dem Hintergrund musiktherapeutischer Erfahrungen mit geistig Behinderten* [An exploration of emotional gestalt formations on the background of music therapy experiences with the mentally handicapped]. Unpublished music therapy diploma thesis, Münster University, Münster.

Stihl, C. (2000). *Die letzte Musiktherapiestunde—Abschied und neuer Anfang* [The last music therapy session: Closure and new beginning]. Unpublished music therapy diploma thesis, Münster University, Münster.

Tönnies, F. (2002). *Erstimprovisationen von Borderline-Patienten. Eine vergleichende musikalisch-psychologische Untersuchung* [Initial improvisations of borderline patients. A comparative music-psychological exploration]. Unpublished music therapy diploma thesis, Münster University, Münster.

Tüpker, R. (1996a). *Ich singe, was ich nicht sagen kann. Zu einer morphologischen Grundlegung der Musiktherapie* [I sing what I cannot say. A morphological foundation of music therapy] (2nd ed.). Münster: Lit-Verlag. (1st edition published 1988).

Tüpker, R. (1996b). Supervision als Unterrichtsfach in der musiktherapeutischen Ausbildung [Supervision as a course in music therapy education]. *Musiktherapeutische Umschau, 17,* 242–251.

Tüpker, R. (2001). Morphologisch orientierte Musiktherapie [Morphologically oriented music therapy]. In H-H. Decker-Voigt (Ed.). *Schulen der Musiktherapie,* 55–77. Munich, Germany: E. Reinhardt.

Tüpker, R. (2002). Forschen oder Heilen. Kritische Betrachtungen zum herrschenden Forschungsparadigma [To research or to heal. Critical observations of the dominant research paradigm]. In P. Petersen (Ed.), *Forschungsmethoden künstlerischer Therapien* (pp. 33–68). Stuttgart: Mayer

Tüpker, R. (2004). Morphological Music Therapy. *Nordic Journal of Music Therapy, 13,* 82–92.

Wachwitz-Homering, (1993). *Untersuchung zur Wirkungseinheit des Singens* [An exploration of the "effect unit" of singing]. Unpublished music therapy diploma thesis, Münster University, Münster.

Wältring-Mertens, B. (1999). *Zur Bedeutung der Musik in der Musiktherapie mit Kindern* [The meaning of music in music therapy with children]. Unpublished music therapy diploma thesis, Münster University, Münster.

Watzlawick, P. (1976). *Wie wirklich ist die Wirklichkeit? Wahn—Täuschung—Verstehen* [How real is reality? Illusion—deception—understanding]. Munich: Piper.

Weymann, E. (2000a). Sensitive suspense: Experiences in musical improvisation. *Nordic Journal of Music Therapy, 9,* 38–45.

Weymann, E. (2000b). Indications of the new: Improvisation as a means of inquiry and as an object of research. *Nordic Journal of Music Therapy, 9,* 55–66.

Weymann, E. (2004). *Zwischentöne. Psychologische Untersuchungen zur musikalischen Improvisation* [Intermediate tones. Psychological explorations of music improvisations]. Gießen, Germany: Psychosozial Verlag.

West, U. (1992). *Psychologische Untersuchung über Einübungsprozesse beim Musizieren* [A psychological exploration of practice processes in making music]. Unpublished diploma thesis, Cologne University, Cologne.

Acknowledgments

This chapter was translated by Susanne Albrecht. The Editor wishes to thank Douglas Keith for additional assistance with translation.

Chapter 35
Qualitative Case Study Research
Henk Smeijsters and Trygve Aasgaard

This chapter offers theoretical premises and methodological criteria for qualitative case study research.[1] It also gives a historical overview that shows the development from the use of case histories to qualitative case study research in music therapy. Finally, three examples of qualitative case study research are described. "Although 'case study' itself is a catch-all term, the case study has regained stature in qualitative research and particularly amongst clinical practitioners" (D. Aldridge, 2005a, p. 14).

Overview and Definition

The Case

A *case* denotes something unique: The Latin noun *casus* means an individual object. Health workers commonly refer to a client or patient as a case, sometimes even as a *difficult case* or a *hopeless case*. However, there is no universal agreement as to what a case is or how a case becomes an integral part of a research strategy.

Stake describes a case as a "specific, complex functioning thing" (1995, p. 2). *Specific* means that a case is something particular, it is not a sample from a population, and it is not an aggregation across cases. Saying that a case is a *complex functioning thing* means that it has working (functioning) parts, a *self*. Stake refers to Smith, one of the first educational ethnographers, in defining a case as a "bounded system" (Stake, p. 2). *Bounded system* refers to the boundary between the case and its environment and the working parts of the case (the system). This can be a boundary in time or space: A boundary in time refers to a process that lasts several weeks or months, while a boundary in space means that something happens in a particular setting. Another characteristic of a case is that it is *real-life grounded*, related to contemporary events.

Thus a case may be defined as a particular thing with functioning parts that is differentiated from its environment by boundaries and unfolds in the present. Single events and processes that do not meet these criteria would not be cases. On first sight there seems to be a difference between this distinction and the definition that a case is "any single example or instance of either an event, experience, material, or person" (Bruscia, 1995c, pp. 318–319) given in the first edition of this book. However, there is no difference when you realize that events, experiences, materials, and certainly persons can be very complex things with functioning parts, differentiated from their environments.

This definition seems to be clear-cut, but the difficulty in defining a case is that an accepted level of complexity must be present in order for something to be classified as a case. We suggest that a researcher should thus make it clear that there is a sufficient level of complexity and that there are functioning parts. The same holds true for boundaries. The system can be bounded by time and place, but there are no clear rules as to how long the period of time and the maximum or minimum setting must be to fulfill the requirements to be a case. Similarly, the distinction between present and history is not so evident as it seems, because today's present is tomorrow's past.

From the above discussion, we can summarize a case as being:

- Specific and particular, not a sample from a population and not an aggregation across cases,
- Complex in its functioning, with working parts,

---

[1] At times, a topic has been developed more deeply in either this chapter, Qualitative Case Study Research, or Chapter 24, Quantitative Single-Case Designs. For instance, the definition of a case and the difference between a case history and case study research are more fully explored in this chapter. Other chapters in this book that focus on qualitative research designs will be referred to in order to show the link between qualitative case study research and qualitative research designs in general.

- A bounded system, differentiated from the environment,
- Real-life grounded, related to contemporary events.

In music therapy, a case can be a client, a therapist, a group, a course of treatment, or a method of treatment in a particular real-life context within a period of time and in a particular setting. When there are enough functioning parts, one session or one improvisation within one session can also be a case. General themes, such as the methodological paradigm of a certain music therapist or simply *improvisation,* lack specificity and real-life context and thus should not be considered a case. The criteria mentioned above can help to differentiate between an occurrence that can be considered a case and one that cannot.

Case Histories, Case Vignettes, Case Examples, and Case Study Research

Case histories, case vignettes, or case examples (all of which are sometimes called case studies) have been common ways of presenting music therapy practice. The case is almost always a single client or client group, and the study is an account of music therapy sessions in which the therapeutic process, including problems, goals, interventions, and outcomes, is described. Until now, there has been no agreement as to whether the term *case study* should be reserved for a specific research method.

Bruscia (1995a) distinguished between the clinical use of a case study and the use of a case study as research, suggesting that in the case study as research, the goal is to develop the body of knowledge by using a systematic method of inquiry. Traditional case studies have some characteristics of research in that they are written for the professional rather than the client and are disseminated among the professional community. However, these characteristics do not fulfill the requirements for definition as research. Smeijsters (1996, 1997) distinguished between the *nonscientific case study* and the *scientific case study*, with the systematic method of inquiry being typical for the scientific case study. Ansdell and Pavlicevic (2001) said, "it depends in a way what you do with a case study as to whether it qualifies as research or not" (p. 142).

In this chapter we distinguish between the case study as a study not ruled by a research method and case study research, which does follow a research method. Descriptive accounts of music therapy, not fulfilling standards of scientific research, can be case studies, but should not be called case study research. Case studies can be case histories, where the chronological dimension is important, or case examples or case vignettes, where a particular instance or event is highlighted for illustration. This chapter will consider qualitative case study research and how it is applied in music therapy research.

Yin claims that case study research and case histories have similarities, including similar research questions *(how* and *why)* and lack of control over behavioral events. In his view, the two strategies differ in their relationship to contemporary events (Yin, 2003). A case history in Yin's opinion describes a case after it has happened, for instance, studying the decision-making process during the Cuban missile crisis of 1962 in 2004, whereas case study research is researching the event as it happens. However, as we said in the definition of a case, in our opinion, the contemporary and near history perspectives are closely interwoven in case study research, where it is difficult to draw a strict boundary between studying present and history.

As we shall see, the essential aspects of case study research are the following:

- The use of a research method that requires all data to be observed and analyzed;
- The use of various forms of data collection and analysis;
- Data analyses that are checked by members and peers;
- Data analyses that are informed by multiple perspectives.

In case study research, the case is considered an *object of research* (Stake, 1995). Case study research is most commonly applied when one knows little about the object of study. We can research a case because we need to learn about that particular case, or we want to develop more general knowledge by studying one particular case. Stake differentiates between intrinsic and instrumental case study research. When the researcher has an intrinsic interest in the case and wants to understand the particular case for its own benefit, then he or she performs *intrinsic case study research. Instrumental case study research* starts with a particular interest, question, or puzzlement, with the case study research being performed to gain insight into that theme. Stake's distinction between intrinsic and instrumental case study research may not be absolute, because to a certain extent there can be transferability in intrinsic case study research, which makes the findings in one particular case of interest for other cases. A field-focused researcher, during the process of studying a particular subject, oscillates his or her attention between exceptional entities and themes that might be of general importance.

Case study research can include several cases when we believe that this will provide a better, broader, or multifaceted insight than through researching one case only. This kind of case study research is both instrumental and *multiple* (or *collective*) (Stake, 1995). However, to be case study research, each case should be researched and presented individually. It is not case study research if there is aggregation of data over cases and the particular case is no longer reflected.[2]

If we combine the characteristics of the case and research, we can summarize case study research as having the following characteristics:

- Focuses on the case, which is a specific, complex functioning thing with boundaries, and is real-life grounded;
- Uses a systematic method of inquiry;
- Can be intrinsic or instrumental;
- Can be multiple but is not an aggregation of data over cases.

Qualitative Case Study Research

When the method of research by which the case is researched is qualitative, then we have qualitative case study research. As was discussed in the chapter on quantitative single-case designs, there are three dimensions that describe case study research: the quantitative versus qualitative dimension, the experimental versus naturalistic dimension, and the hypothesis testing versus hypothesis/theory generating dimension. This makes it possible to distinguish among four types of qualitative case study research:

1. *Qualitative-experimental hypothesis-testing single-case design*: qualitative data, manipulation, hypothesis testing,
2. *Qualitative-naturalistic hypothesis-testing single-case design*: qualitative data, no manipulation, hypothesis testing,
3. *Qualitative-experimental hypothesis-generating single-case design*: qualitative data, manipulation, no hypothesis,
4. *Qualitative-naturalistic hypothesis-generating single-case design*: qualitative data, no manipulation, no hypothesis.[3]

In the *qualitative-experimental hypothesis-testing single-case design,* the researcher[4] has an idea of how events are related and introduces an event to see if another event is influenced in the way that was predicted. For instance: The music therapist alternates several times between singing and playing on instruments with an individual client to research the hypothesis that playing on instruments helps the client to stabilize his feelings.

When the *qualitative-naturalistic hypothesis-testing single-case design* is used, the researcher has an idea of relationships between events but does not influence practice by experimentation. He or she describes the events as they happen naturally. For instance: The music therapist does not experimentally alternate between singing and playing on instruments, rather the researcher researches his hypothesis by analyzing the natural flow of treatment.

In the *qualitative-experimental hypothesis-generating single-case design,* the researcher does not have a preliminary idea of relationships between events but nevertheless uses experimentation to see what happens. For instance, without a clear idea of the effect of singing or playing on instruments, the music therapist might alternate between them. In assessment

---

[2] As was suggested in Chapter 24, Quantitative Single-Case Designs, there is a distinction between intrasubject research and intersubject research.

[3] We prefer to write *hypothesis* (or theory) *generating* for the two last options. We do not use these words in a traditional way that refers to general laws that go beyond cases. In our opinion every local and specific idea about a particular case can be called hypothesis or theory.

[4] The researcher can be a therapist/researcher or a researcher who works closely with a therapist in a type of *action research* in which the dialogue between the researcher and the therapist influences the course of therapy.

procedures, we often see that music therapists use a standard set of musical activities to see how the client reacts. One could say that the therapist is experimenting without a hypothesis.

In the *qualitative-naturalistic hypothesis-generating single-case design*, there is no hypothesis and no experimentation.

These four designs have been written from the perspective of researching a single case. Remember that case study research can include more cases (multiple, collective case study research) as long as there is not an aggregation across cases.

Qualitative is used in some of these designs to refer to type of data only, which can be words or music but not figures. The experimental and naturalistic hypothesis-testing designs would not be classified as qualitative research in a true conception of qualitative research, as described in other chapters of this book.[5] A researcher who works within a paradigm based on ontological and epistemological beliefs that are congruent with naturalistic inquiry or constructivism uses a research method that is non-experimental and hypothesis/theory-generating in character. Combining the naturalistic/constructivist and hypothesis/theory-generating characteristics leads to an integrated research paradigm that comes very close to the clinical process. In ontological terms, this paradigm refers to reality as multiple, local, specific, mental intangible constructions, which are not true but more or less informed (see Lincoln & Guba, 1985, 2000; Guba & Lincoln, 1994). In epistemological terms the relationship between knower and what can be known is transactional and subjective, based on interaction and dialogue in which findings are created. When qualitative research is done within a paradigm consistent with these beliefs, there can be no experimentation and no hypothesis or theory at the beginning because hypotheses and theories are constructed in the dialogue between researcher and participants. In this chapter the examples of qualitative case study research will thus focus on this type of research design.

Theoretical Premises and Historical Roots

Theoretical Premises

The qualitative-naturalistic hypothesis-generating single-case design integrates principles from several qualitative research methods. These include the following:

- Contexts are described as specific and not representative;
- There is an open research attitude (for theory, respondents, research technique);
- The focus is on wholeness;
- Hypotheses are generated from the naturalistic context;
- There is no focus on general laws;
- There is no manipulation of the context;
- The focus is on intrasubjective and interpersonal experiences and meanings;
- Meaning is constructed in an act of communication with respondents and researchers;
- The person is the research tool.

Interpretation is a general feature in the various stages of the research process in qualitative case studies. In the course of the case study, the researcher oscillates between analysis—detaching data from its place or context—and interpretation—constructing and expressing the meaning of data. Naturalistic settings (where variables cannot be well controlled) do not produce data suitable for analysis of causal relationships between selected variables but are ideal for developing dialogues between subjects and multi-voiced texts. From a constructivist stance, one neither collects nor gathers data as though data are just out there waiting to be discovered or harvested. Data sources simply are the building stones for the researcher's constructions. *Raw data* always emerge from a process of selecting (such as choosing what may be considered to be relevant data and what may not) and are then transformed into a shape that the researcher is able to handle. In a broad sense, "There is no particular moment when data analysis begins" (Stake, 1995, p. 71).

---

[5] See Chapter 5, Principles of Qualitative Research, for a more complete discussion.

Historical Roots

Qualitative case study research developed within the disciplines of sociology and anthropology during the first decades of the 20th century. A major center was the Chicago School of Sociology, associated with the University of Chicago, which employed fieldwork and empirical study presented in the form of case study research. Researchers in the social sciences developed case study research during the 1970s, 1980s, and 1990s, including Argyris and Schön (1974) in management, Yin (2003) in social policy, Stake (1995) in education, and others. Case study research is also widespread in political science, economics, and anthropology.

The term *case study* was probably first applied in psychiatry to give an account for pathology in a client (Andersen, 1997). Since the beginning of the 20th century, qualitative research methods have been used to research individual cases in psychiatry and psychology. Freud and many other psychoanalysts, psychotherapists, psychologists, and neurologists (including Piaget, Bühler, Vygotski, and Luria) used these methods.

However, the quantitative, experimental, hypothesis-testing research design became established as the gold standard for research in psychotherapy so that, today, there is the strong demand to use evidence-based medicine (EBM), which has been very useful in medicine.[6] However, psychotherapists often feel uneasy with the experimental design and between group comparisons of EBM. In the 1960s and 1970s, Allport, Maslow, and Rogers criticized the positivistic paradigm, saying that research should begin with the individual (Allport, 1962) and describe the individual person holistically (Maslow, 1966, 1974). A textbook by Bromley (1986) showed the ongoing interest in case studies. Even quantitative researchers like Campbell (1975) and Cronbach (1975) reached the conclusion that single-case studies are needed to give a *thick description* of complex interactions in a natural context.

Because of this, qualitative research methods like phenomenology (Giorgi, 1985), symbolic interactionism (Blumer, 1969), humanistic psychology (Maslow, 1966, 1974; Moustakas, 1990; Rogers, 1945, 1968), and social constructivistic psychology (Shotter & Gergen, 1989) remained influential in psychotherapy research.

Similar developments occurred in music therapy. Decades ago, music therapy researchers suggested that the positivistic research design is just one way of looking at things, resulting in an inability to assess the essence of phenomena. In addition to the music therapy research methods that have already been mentioned, methods like grounded theory (a further development of symbolic interactionism, by Glaser & Strauss, 1967), naturalistic inquiry (Lincoln & Guba, 1985), hermeneutics (Gadamer, 1975), and morphology (Salber, 1965) became influential. All of these qualitative research methods provided input for qualitative case study research.

Qualitative case study research is an alternative to the positivistic paradigm and quantitative research. Qualitative and naturalistic research traditions and theories are particularly valuable from this perspective. The textbooks by Glaser and Strauss (1967), Bogdan and Biklen (1982), Lincoln and Guba (1985), Lamnek (1989), Tesch (1990), Miles and Huberman (1993), Silverman (1999), Denzin and Lincoln (2000), and others were landmarks. Some books, such as Faller and Frommer (1994), dealt exclusively with qualitative and naturalistic research in psychotherapy.

Methodology

The first important question that needs to be addressed concerns the scientific value of qualitative case study research. To answer this we will focus on the concept of trustworthiness which, in our opinion, makes qualitative case study research different from but equal to quantitative experimental research in terms of scientific integrity.

---

[6] For more complete critique on EBM see Chapter 24, Quantitative Single-Case Designs.

Trustworthiness

What, then, is the scientific value of qualitative case study research applied as a qualitative research method? Yin (2003), perhaps the most influential and frequently quoted author on case study research wrote:

> The case study has long been (and continues to be) stereotyped as a weak sibling among social science methods. Investigators who do case studies are regarded as having downgraded their academic disciplines. Case studies have similarly been denigrated as having insufficient precision (i.e., quantification), objectivity, or rigor. (p. xiii)

Qualitative case study research represents the opposite pole from quantitative experimental research. In a 1941 article, "Case Studies vs. Statistical Method—An Issue Based on Misunderstanding," Lundberg concluded that when (qualitative) case study research obtained a more rigorous set of symbols and rules, the argument that it is a weak scientific method would disappear (Andersen, 1997).

We suggest that this does not imply that the closer qualitative case study research is to traditional quantitative research, the greater its scientific value. Qualitative case study research uses a different set of techniques and criteria to insure that it is scientific. It is agreed that insight and understanding are no guarantee for good research if there is not a sound research strategy that guides the birth of insight and understanding.

Trustworthiness in qualitative research can be divided into four areas that differ from the criteria of validity, reliability, internal validity, and external validity as applied in quantitative research. Many of these criteria, which are applicable to quantitative research, are fruitless in naturalistic cases. On the other hand, some checks are needed to keep the researcher from falling back to mere subjectivity. Generally speaking there are several ways to do this: (a) The researcher checks his or her own data production, (b) the respondents check it, or (c) other researchers check it. Lincoln and Guba (1985, Ch. 11) suggest that subjectivity should be checked as follows:

> *Credibility:* Are the researcher's reconstructions credible to the constructors of the original multiple realities?
>
> *Dependability:* Have all data been accounted for and all reasonable areas been explored?
>
> *Confirmability:* Can an independent auditor check the chain of evidence that has led to the research findings?
>
> *Transferability:* Are data described in a way that other researchers in other cases can see if there is any similarity or not?

To fulfill these requirements, research techniques such as thick description, analytical memos, repeated analysis, member checking, auditing and peer debriefing, triangulation, using different types of data, and using different theoretical perspectives can be used. These and other research techniques are part of qualitative research designs that have been described in other chapters of this book. Now these techniques are used in a single case. A researcher can use one specific qualitative research method and adjust it to the single case, or may integrate techniques from several qualitative methods.

Research Steps

With the previous criteria in mind we can schedule the following research steps:

1. The researcher selects a bounded system to be researched: an activity, event, or one or several individuals during a certain period of time.
2. The researcher defines the research goal as an in-depth analysis and understanding of the chosen case, meant to develop the body of knowledge of the discipline.
3. The researcher selects a qualitative research method that is linked to the research goal.
4. The researcher describes techniques to fulfill criteria of trustworthiness, for instance, checks such as repeated analysis, member checking, and peer debriefing.

5. The researcher makes use of triangulation by collecting data from multiple sources (respondents) and documents (written/audio/video materials, physical artifacts, and so forth), and applies multiple methods of data collection (archival records, interviews, observations) and multiple theoretical perspectives.

6. Data are analyzed using methods of qualitative content analysis. The researcher codes data; a categorical aggregation takes place when data with the same code are put into one category. Sensitizing concepts and themes are developed within and between categories. The analysis may also establish certain patterns between themes. The researcher may draw conclusions about latent aspects through in-depth interpretation.

7. The researcher describes and justifies the research method, research techniques, and research rationales through an ongoing process so that an auditor can check the chain of evidence.

8. The researcher selects an appropriate narrative form to present the case in context through a transcript that can present a chronology or a categorization of events. Thick description is employed to secure transferability.

9. The research closes with the researcher's conclusions or assertions in which the researcher does not try to hide subjective elements in the process of performing qualitative case study research. Experiential notes may conclude the written product.

Progression of Music Therapy Research: From Case History to Qualitative Case Study Research

In the first edition of the current book, Lathom-Radocy and Radocy (1995) said that they regretted that relatively few case studies in music therapy had been published although "music therapy interns or practicing clinicians frequently compile case studies" (p. 173). This conclusion, of course, depends upon what is meant by "relatively few."

In the last decade, many case histories have been published. We also see a gradual increase of qualitative case study research as shown through the examples that follow.

Edward

Aigen (1995) presented and discussed the classic account of Edward by Nordoff and Robbins (1977) as one of four examples of *interpretive-descriptive studies*. Aigen commented on the study by saying that it "predates the development of an explicit qualitative research paradigm for music therapy" (p. 339). It is appropriate to mention the study of Edward here because it contains elements characteristic of early qualitative research in music therapy. Aigen called it "a seminal case study" (p. 339), and we quote from his comments to show some of its central properties:

> The presentation of Edward's clinical process contains traditional components of case study presentations. These include background information on Edward's developmental levels and pathology, a roughly chronological presentation of his course of therapy, explanations of the therapists' rationale for various interventions, periodic observations of areas where progress had been noted, and illustrations of general clinical techniques and theories based on his treatment.
>
> There are also novel elements to this presentation which recommend it as an important study, apart from its significance in documenting a particular child's development. These include detailed transcriptions of the music generated during Edward's sessions; detailed verbal descriptions of music, paying special attention to the manner in which the tonality, placement, and form of his vocalizations revealed the presence of an otherwise opaque communicative process; and the inclusion of audiotaped examples from each stage of Edward's process.

Although it might seem that inclusion of musical transcriptions and recorded examples would be standard elements of music therapy texts, journals, and reports, in fact *Creative Music Therapy* is the only major music therapy text of which this author is aware that includes an audiotape. Not only is this tape of unique instructional value in conveying the formal aspects and quality of the music used, but the tape captures the power and impact of the work in a way that no verbal description can. The fact that music therapy authors in general have as yet to follow the precedent established by Nordoff and Robbins only recommends their work as one still at the forefront of how to capture and present clinical music therapy work.

In addition, there are many important aspects of the clinical elements of Nordoff-Robbins music therapy that are illustrated perfectly by Edward's therapy; in fact, this is one of this study's primary functions. (p. 344)

The music therapy in the example above related directly (and solely) to what goes on within the regular music therapy sessions. The single client, the therapist, and the cotherapist constituted the actors. An important characteristic was that it was based on regular clinical practice. The author stressed written transcriptions and detailed verbal descriptions plus audiotaped examples of the music generated during the sessions. However, these aspects do not fulfill the requirements of qualitative case study research. There was no explicit use of a qualitative research method such as naturalistic inquiry, phenomenology, or hermeneutics.

Book: *Case Studies in Music Therapy*

Bruscia (1991) edited *Case Studies in Music Therapy*, presenting "42 case histories, each describing the process of music therapy over an extended period of time" (page ix). All the histories followed the same basic format, and the authors expressed diverse theoretical orientations, primarily qualitative eclectic, humanistic, and psychotherapeutic. This book presented case studies (case histories), classified as such because the research method and the research process were not described. Most cases were presented as the therapist's accounts of a series of music therapy sessions. Some of the 42 authors, however, also included information about their communication with people who were outsiders in relation to the music therapy sessions or how clients used their musical skills to present themselves and to communicate outside actual music therapy sessions (see Boone, 1991; Robbins & Robbins, 1991). Sharing information with outsiders resembles the qualitative research technique of peer debriefing, but it is still not qualitative research because the process of sharing is not used as a systematic technique of research.

Book: *Case Studies in Psychodynamic Music Therapy*

Hadley (2003) also applied case studies (case histories) to present music therapy practice. "I chose the format of case studies for this book because their engaging narrative flow allows readers to feel as though they are right there, watching the process unfold. Case studies have a personal dimension that profoundly touches those who read them" (p. xx).

As in the Bruscia (1991) book, each author utilized a more or less uniform case format. None of the many interesting narratives of psychodynamic music therapy in this book focused on research method. Thus, they are not qualitative case study research.

Qualitative Case Study Research

Qualitative case study research has developed gradually in the last 2 decades. It can be seen in the examples that follow that this type of research has been based on qualitative research methods. When a qualitative research method has been used to study or explicate a single case, we have an example of qualitative case study research.

Each of the following examples of qualitative case study research uses an explicit research method. Although the authors have not always presented them explicitly as examples of qualitative case study research, each has the features of case study research: The study is about a case, the research methods and techniques are made explicit by the researcher, and several criteria of trustworthiness have been fulfilled. This does not imply that they employ a rigid method of research. In qualitative case study research, as in other qualitative research, the aims and research method often are adjusted during the process of investigation.

The number of qualitative case study research examples is growing. We will select some examples to show that this type of research has become a strong force within music therapy research.

Tüpker (1988) used a morphological research design with a *resonating panel* in her qualitative case study research, which showed how a client's *life method* is expressed in his inhibition of musical development on the one hand and taking over leadership from the music therapist on the other hand. Both behaviors reflected a need for omnipotence as well as a need to compensate inhibition. Since that time, many qualitative case study research projects have been developed within the morphological school of music therapy (see for instance Tüpker, 1996, and also Chapter 34 in this book, Morphological Research).

Forinash and Gonzalez (1989) used phenomenology in their qualitative case study research with a woman who died during the session. In a reflexive and heuristic form of phenomenology, they describe their personal thoughts, feelings, and images to give us an awareness of dying. By means of intuition they try to become aware of the client's experience of dying.

In "A Song Is Born," Amir (1990) researched the meaning of improvised song in the treatment of a man with traumatic spinal cord injury caused by an automobile accident. She used perceptual description and phenomenological reflection. The songs expressed the client's despair and mourning, but also the experience of freedom and energy.

Lee (1992, 1995, 1996, 2000) developed a method of collaborative inquiry for the analysis of improvisations of a client with HIV. The analysis used feelings of the therapist and comments of the client and of several experts as to when and how they were moved during listening. This led to clinically significant musical segments that were notated, verbally described, and submitted to an in-depth analysis by means of the hermeneutic circle.

Frohne-Hagemann (1999) developed a similar hermeneutic method to perceive, differentiate, connect, and explain experiences during the phases of the process of music therapy. This method can also be used as a method of qualitative case study research. It progresses from holistic perception (What is now?); followed by the intuitive connection of perception with moods, scenes, feelings, thoughts, and images (Do I know this?); to the development of patterns of meaning (Do I understand this?); and finally the explanation of what has been understood (Can I explain to you what I understand?).

Langenberg and her colleagues (Langenberg, Frommer, & Tress, 1993, 1995; Langenberg, Frommer, & Langenbach, 1996) used the *resonator function* in several studies as a method of qualitative case study research. Their works shows how members of a panel are able to translate the musical expression of a client and therapist into thoughts, feelings, images, fantasies, and stories. These descriptions are content analyzed and motifs are developed to describe the client's psychic and social condition in the music.

Rogers (1993) developed a method of collaborative research, which she described as research *with* people rather than *on* people. She involved the clients in investigating the factors that were important. In the process of action and reflection, clients became co-researchers who themselves gave meaning. She also included an inquiry group of former clients, the staff, and the music therapists. Her research showed that clinical improvisation in music therapy is one of the most useful means of therapy with people who have been sexually abused.

In "Modes of Consciousness in Guided Imagery and Music (GIM): A Therapist's Experience of the Guiding Process," Bruscia (1995b) researched his shifts of consciousness while working with a client in GIM. By means of self-inquiry, similar to reflexive phenomenology and hermeneutics, he developed a clinical theory about levels of experience, levels of distance to the client's experiences, and the media of transport between therapist and client.

Kenny (1996), when researching a case, uses free fantasy variation as a technique of reflective phenomenology and calls it an *intramember check*. She calls it an *intermember check* when she works with a panel. The panel is a research tool that is used often in qualitative case study research, as seen in Kenny's work as well as that of Tüpker and Langenberg.

Smeijsters and Storm (1998) used case study research based on naturalistic inquiry to show how a controversy between parent and child can be resolved by forming a musical coalition, while Smeijsters and Van den Hurk (1999) illustrated how melodic development can help to establish a feeling of new identity. Smeijsters' qualitative case study research led to the development of his *theory of analogy* (connected to the work of D. Aldridge, 1989; Pavlicevic, 1997; Tüpker, 1988) and tried to work out the isomorphism of musical and psychic patterns, based on Stern's developmental psychology (see Smeijsters, 1999b, 2003a, 2003b, 2003c, 2005). Smeijsters and Van den Hurk's study, summarized below, showed that qualitative case study research provides the opportunity to use several different qualitative research methods. Smeijsters (1999a) used a phenomenological analysis of the same data to discover the client's essential psychological themes.

Aigen's (2002) qualitative case study *Playin' in the Band* was an exploration into a particular manner of relating through musical improvisation in rock and other contemporary music styles. Aigen's primary research goal was to create a vicarious experience in the reader who then could obtain some form of experiential knowledge of the milieu of study. He accomplished this though a project combining elements of both an intrinsic and an instrumental case study:

> Through this case study, I portray the long-term process of a course of individual music therapy that integrates different levels of functioning: motoric, cognitive, and affective. I also highlight the changes in the musical relationship(s) which are used as indicators of clinical growth. As much as this is a case study of an individual, it is also an exploration into a particular manner of relating through musical improvisation in rock and other contemporary music styles. Thus, I hope to represent some of the unique features of these types of music, including their experiential foundations and their stylistic attributes. So within one publication I am attempting to portray the story of an individual while also explaining a particular tool in music therapy. (p. 22)

Data sources in this project consisted of video documentation and the detailed research log written by the primary therapist and the cotherapist. In addition to other analytic and interpretational procedures, the entire study was situated within the musical biography, interests, and predilections of the researcher.

Grocke (2005) presented an overview of four different types of qualitative case studies applied to investigate phenomena related to the Bonny Method of Guided Imagery and Music (BMGIM): the individual case study, the collective case study, the negative case study, and the heuristic case study.

One important element in Stige's (2003) doctoral thesis, *Elaborations Toward a Notion of Community Music Therapy*, is an instrumental case study related to the theme of *hypertextuality* in music therapy:

> The case study that I will present here is based upon an ethnographically informed qualitative investigation of my own clinical practice in a psychiatric clinic, and the main sources of data are field observations combined with qualitative interviews with the client. The original focus when the study was initiated was to investigate the client's experience of meaning and meaning-making in music therapy. . . . While clarity of voice is searched for, and the perspective of the client is of high interest, the case is presented as an instrumental case study and not as an intrinsic case study. (p. 286)

Qualitative research including case study research is a major focus of the PhD program at Aalborg University, Denmark.[7] Some of the Aalborg students whose dissertations were based on various models of qualitative case studies are:

- G. Aldridge (1996, 1998) did phenomenological case study research on the development of melody as an isomorphic form of a new identity with two patients with breast cancer.
- Ridder (2003, 2005) applied data from video-recordings, staff's day-to-day accounts of clients' states of health and behavior, and the music therapist's own case descriptions and chronological logbook. This flexible design resulted in six examples of case study research and multidimensional analytic procedures. The study included elements of quantitative research (for example, heartbeat

---

[7] For additional information, see Wigram, Pedersen, and Bonde (2002).

measures and psychological tests). Ridder's research demonstrated that singing songs may regulate arousal and promote dialogue.

- Hannibal (2000) followed general principles of case-based research as he investigated methods to describe transference processes in the music therapeutic context in general and in the musical interaction specifically.

Aasgaard's (2002) dissertation, which will be discussed later, was also done through the Aalborg program.

Many other qualitative case study researchers have used types of analysis as listed above. One difference lies in the way in which the musical and the personal aspects have been worked out. These aspects can be analyzed separately and connected later (for example, Forinash & Gonzalez, 1989; Lee, 1992, 1995, 1996, 2000; and Langenberg, Frommer, & Tress, 1993, 1995; Langenberg, Frommer, & Langenbach, 1996), or they can be integrated from the beginning where the musical is the personal and vice versa (for example, Tüpker, 1988, 1996; Smeijsters & Storm, 1998; Smeijsters & Van den Hurk, 1999; Smeijsters, 1999a). An integration of the musical and personal methods of analysis offers a strong methodical assessment tool for qualitative case study research. What is more, the analogy between the musical and the psychological can be described; thus this type of research can show that indeed psychological changes take place in the musical parameters and forms.

An important point, illustrated in the above examples, is that the explicit intra- and intermember checks done by the clinician/researcher transform case studies into qualitative case study research. It should be noted that these research methods do not intrude on the clinical situation. The object of research is the case as it occurs during regular clinical treatment, and the research tools are built around the case and not the other way around. What is important also is that the persons (observers, music therapists, and clients themselves) are the research tools. Although evidence-based medicine excludes the human person as a valid and reliable research tool, qualitative case study research respects the tacit knowledge and the observational and evaluative skills of good practitioners who make inferences every day based on the comparison of gestalts among client, treatment program, and treatment effect (see also Duncker, 1963; Kenny, 1998; Kienle et al., 2003).

Another trend in contemporary case study research is to combine qualitative and quantitative approaches. Smeijsters and van den Berk (1995) developed a qualitative naturalistic hypothesis and theory generating single-case research project focusing on a client suffering from musicogenic epilepsy. In addition to the use of qualitative naturalistic research techniques (for example, open coding, different forms of triangulation, and content analysis), the number of seizures and the number of minutes of musical playing, quantitative measures of results, were tabulated. The researchers found that it is possible to find musical structures that can be used by a client with musicogenic epilepsy.

Book: *Case Study Designs in Music Therapy*

Case Study Designs in Music Therapy was the first book to deal specifically with case study *designs* in music therapy research. David Aldridge (2005b) edited a collection of works by nine music therapy practitioners and researchers from Europe, Israel, Australia, and the United States. All the projects related to various forms of case study research methodologies with quantitative or qualitative foci. The majority of the chapters presented doctoral theses (or parts thereof). Aldridge (2005a) emphasized the closeness of case studies to practice:

> We need an approach to music therapy research that stays close to the practice of the individual clinician; that is, the musician as therapist. Each therapeutic situation is seemingly unique. Yet we compare our cases and share our knowledge with each other. Research methods are means for formalizing our knowledge so that we can compare what we do. . . . it is the very context-related feature of case studies that make the approach important for music therapy. Case studies relate what is being studied to real life situations and allow us to use a multiplicity of variables. (pp. 10–11)

Aldridge discussed several important issues: What data may count as evidence? What kind of data do anecdotes represent? Why is a pluralist stance necessary to express and understand the life of human beings? Most interestingly, he also looked into questions about relationships between the researcher and his or her field of study, patients, and health care systems, and between *research as advocacy* and biases. In this section Aldridge acknowledged his deep respect to the early sociological studies that used qualitative case study methods. The final pages of this book presented "Guidelines for Case Study Design Research in Music Therapy," where the author asks and give the grounds for fundamental theoretical and practical questions for the potential case study researcher.

Case Study Research Where the Cases Are Not Individual Clients

There are relatively few examples in music therapy literature where the cases are not individual clients. Aigen's (1997) monograph *Here We Are in Music* was an example of qualitative case study research in which the case is a group of four adolescents with autistic features. In our opinion the research method included characteristics of Colaizzi's (1978) method of *perceptual description*, meant to observe and describe events that are difficult to conceptualize. The researcher's monologues, grounded in observation, are used to describe the role of music as a means to support interpersonal contacts with wide emotional variety.

The Danish music therapist Roer's (2001) account of performance in music therapy, containing many similarities with qualitative case study research, was totally outside the frame of *sessions*. We learned about a New York tour of the band Chock Rock, whose members were long-term psychiatric clients and hospital staff. The author consistently focused on relationships between music therapy and performance. He described a time-limited interplay between the musicians and communication with other people in different contexts: preparations in Århus, Denmark; the New York tour; return to the local hospital. Here, the tour to New York can be considered the case, a phenomenon bounded in time and place. Roer's narrative, including substantial video material, fell in the gray zone between science and not science.

Aasgaard (2002, 2005), in his doctoral dissertation, performed naturalistic case study research of 19 *life-histories* of songs made by children with cancer. A constructivist paradigm formed the basis for ontological, epistemological, and methodological considerations of a multiple, instrumental qualitative case study research. This example is summarized below.

Music Therapy Examples

Three examples of qualitative case study research are presented here. The form of presentation demonstrates that qualitative case study research can be analyzed by means of a format that shows the main characteristics of the design and techniques. We analyzed one of each of our own studies and a piece of qualitative case study research that was undertaken by another researcher. Each has a different research background. The first is strongly *research-informed*, meaning that the design and techniques were developed in line with existing research methods. Researcher and music therapist are two different persons. The second, Schumacher's, is *practice-informed* and shows how a music therapist added research to her clinical work. The third, similar to Schumacher's study, is research-informed since the music therapist and researcher is the same person. We believe that many of the previous mentioned examples of qualitative case study research can be analyzed with this or a similar format.

Example 1
"Music Therapy Helping to Work Through Grief and Finding a Personal Identity" by Smeijsters & Van den Hurk (1999) and follow-up analysis by Smeijsters (1999a)

Case: A 53-year old woman with depression as a result of unresolved grief.

Focus of study: 23 sessions of individual music therapy using melodic vocal improvisation. The music therapist supported the client with chords on the piano and stimulated her to break through melodic stereotypes and to explore unknown melodic material. Indications, goals, play forms, and techniques were developed through an open treatment and an open research attitude. Gradually, the focus of the study became whether it is possible for the client to find a new sense of identity through melodic vocal improvisation.

Research type: Qualitative-naturalistic hypothesis-generating design.

Type of case study research: Case study research based on research techniques from naturalistic inquiry and grounded theory (see analysis and criteria for quality).

Data sources: Audiovisual recordings, interviews with music therapist and client.

Role of researcher: An observer of audiovisual recordings and interviewer who contributes to the music therapy process through his analyses.

Case presentation (narrative form): A description of all themes, of the treatment method, and of critical sessions within three therapy phases. The improvisations of client and therapist during three sessions are listed in tables that are segmented in sequential parts and show how the client's interaction and musical exploration increases during improvisation. Personal statements of the client are included to corroborate the researcher's analysis.

Analysis: Making transcripts; content analysis based on grounded theory, leading to categories and themes linked to diagnosis, indication, goals, play forms, treatment techniques, and rationales. Analytical memos support the analysis.

Assertions (results): It is shown that by means of music therapy the client's defense of rationalization is lessened, that blocked feelings are expressed, and that self-esteem and identity as well as the balance in the client's social behavior is increased. These changes are *sounded* in the music. A suppressed part of the client found expression in the music by extending and varying her vocal melody. The client discovered analogies between her musical and nonmusical motoric, emotional, and social behavior. This supports the premise of the theory of analogy, which states that the vitality affects of the psyche are expressed in musical parameters and psychic processes change when the musical expression changes.

Criteria for quality of the research project: Based on criteria for trustworthiness (credibility, dependability, confirmability) and techniques to fulfill them (member checking, peer debriefing, triangulation; see Lincoln & Guba, 1985).

Example 2

"Assessing Qualities of Relating in the Musical Expression of an Autistic Child" by Schumacher (1999)

Case: A boy with autism. The child was 7 years old at the beginning of the therapy and research.

Focus of study: Based on 6 years of videotaped sessions of active individual music therapy in which the music therapist focused on the assessment of the quality of relating in musical expression.

Research type: Naturalistic inquiry.

Type of case study research: Longitudinal qualitative case study research.

Data sources: Audiovisual recordings from 6 years of therapy with additional descriptions of experiences of countertransference of the therapist/researcher.

Role of researcher: The researcher is therapist as well as researcher who analyzes, together with a developmental psychologist, the audiovisual recordings and by means of this analysis improves the therapy process.

Case presentation (narrative form): Musical analyses of sessions by the musician and comments made by the music therapist researcher for all modes of relating. The comments focus on the musical and psychic abilities of the child, the mode of relating, the music therapist's attitude, and the therapy goal and therapeutic techniques. Audiovisual tapes illustrate the modes of relating.

Analysis: Repeated analysis of all sessions by music therapist/researcher and musician, developing modes of relating.

Assertions (results): This case study research shows the development of the process of relating in the treatment of a child with autism, by means of seven levels of contact (the first being the no contact level). The assessment scale is linked to Daniel Stern's concept of development of self.

Criteria for quality of the research project: Peer debriefing was used to insure credibility.

Example 3
"Song Creations by Children with Cancer—Process and Meaning" by Aasgaard (2002, 2005)

Cases: The life-histories of the 19 songs made by five hospitalized children with leukemia or aplastic anemia.

Focus of study: Based on 5 years of music therapy practice in two pediatric hospital departments. The processes of making and using the children's own songs were investigated in various arenas within the hospital environments as well as in the patients' homes and schools-kindergartens. (Regular music therapy sessions form a small part of the song-related activities in this study.) The focus is on how, where, when, and by whom the songs were created, developed, performed, and used; the songs' lyrics and musical elements and what the song activities (understood as *musicking*) meant to the child in the pediatric oncology ward. To promote health is the primary goal of the music therapy described. Health is related to experiencing well-being and ability (Nordenfelt, 1987).

Research type: Based on a constructivist paradigm, originally discussed by Guba and Lincoln (1994) under the heading naturalistic inquiry.

Type of case study research: Qualitative multiple instrumental case study research. Different cases are studied to obtain diverse and multi-faceted study material. Each client is presented through her or his song creations—both the individual song history and each of the five young clients may be understood as a case.

Data sources: Documentation and archival records, interviews, observations, and physical artifacts (in order to make thick, detailed descriptions).

Role of researcher: The researcher is both a participant and an observer. The project records ordinary music therapy related activities.

Case presentation (narrative form): Each song case is edited in four-column tables providing contextual information, accounts of song-related events, and commentaries from interviewees and the music therapist researcher. The study also presents the original lyrics and melodies. Each song is represented with at least one audio document.

Analysis/Interpretation: Three major themes are constructed and discussed: expression, achievement, and pleasure. Analytic/interpretational strategies include highlighting specific constructions or findings, displaying constructions, comparing cases, extending the analysis and turning to theory to discuss the three basic themes from different theoretical perspectives, and connecting with personal experience (see also Wolcott, 1994, pp. 23–48).

Assertions (results): When expression, achievement, and pleasure are prominent in the song cases, the related activities seem to foster, at least momentarily, expanded social roles for the young clients. Well-being and ability are properties related (in different proportions) to these roles. The creation and performance of their own songs adds new elements of health to the lives of the children during the long and complicated process of being treated for serious blood disorders.

Criteria for quality of the research project: Data source triangulation, methodological triangulation, member checking (Stake, 1995).

Summary

Because qualitative case study research is related to several other qualitative research methods and traditions, examples of this type of research can be found in other chapters of this book that describe qualitative research methods. Case study research, be it quantitative or qualitative, is perhaps the most promising form of inquiry to counter the quantitative experimental group design as advocated by evidence-based medicine. The power of its research method and its grounding in clinical practice gives case study research a high level of trustworthiness. Qualitative case study research in particular respects the tacit knowledge of clinicians, which can be codified. Increasing credible evidence is our goal for the future.

References

Aasgaard, T. (2000). 'A Suspiciously Cheerful Lady': A study of a song's life in the paediatric oncology ward, and beyond. . . . *British Journal of Music Therapy, 14,* 70–82.

Aasgaard, T. (2002). *Song creations by children with cancer—Process and meaning.* Unpublished doctoral dissertation, Aalborg University, Aalborg, Denmark.

Aasgaard, T. (2005). Song creations by children with cancer—Process and meaning. In D. Aldridge (Ed.). *Case study designs in music therapy* (pp. 67–96). London: Jessica Kingsley Publishers.

Aigen, K. (1997). *Here we are in music: One year with an adolescent creative music therapy group.* St. Louis, MO: MMB Music.

Aigen, K (1995). Principles of qualitative research. In B. L. Wheeler (Ed.), *Music therapy research: Quantitative and qualitative perspectives* (pp. 283–311). Gilsum, NH: Barcelona Publishers.

Aigen, K. (2002). *Playin' in the band: A qualitative study of popular music styles as clinical improvisation.* New York: Nordoff-Robbins Center for Music Therapy, New York University.

Aldridge, D. (1989). A phenomenological comparison of the organization of music and the self. *The Arts in Psychotherapy, 16,* 91–97.

Aldridge, D. (2005a). A story told from practice: The reflective inquirer in an ecology of ideas. In D. Aldridge (Ed.), *Case study designs in music therapy* (pp. 9–30). London: Jessica Kingsley Publishers.

Aldridge, D. (Ed.). (2005b). *Case study designs in music therapy.* London: Jessica Kingsley Publishers.

Aldridge, G. (1996). "A walk through Paris": The development of melodic expression in music therapy with a breast-cancer patient. *The Arts in Psychotherapy, 23,* 207–223.

Aldridge, G. (1998). *Die Entwicklung einer Melodie im Kontext improvisatorischer Musiktherapie* [The development of a melody in the context of improvisational music therapy]. Unpublished doctoral dissertation, Aalborg University/University Witten-Herdecke, Herdecke, Germany. Available at http://www.musictherapyworld.net/modules/archive/dissertations/list_all.php

Allport, G. W. (1962). The general and the unique in psychological science. *Journal of Personality, 30,* 405–422.

Amir, D. (1990). A song is born: Discovering meaning in improvised songs through phenomenological analysis of two music therapy sessions with a traumatic spinal-cord injured young adult. *Music Therapy, 9,* 62–81.

Andersen, S. S. (1997). *Case-studier og generaliseringer* [Case studies and generalizations]. Bergen–Sandviken, Norway: Fagbokforlaget.

Ansdell, G., & Pavlicevic, M. (2001). *Beginning research in the arts therapies: A practical guide.* London: Jessica Kingsley Publishers.

Argyris, C., & Schön, D. (1974). *Theory in practice: Increasing professional effectiveness.* San Francisco: Jossey-Bass.

Blumer. H. (1969). *Symbolic interactionism: Perspective and method.* Englewood Cliffs, NJ: Prentice-Hall.

Bogdan, R, C., & Biklen, S. K. (1982). *Qualitative research for education: An introduction to theory and methods.* Boston: Allyn & Bacon.

Boone, P. (1991). Composition, improvisation and poetry: The psychiatric treatment of a forensic patient. In K. E. Bruscia (Ed.), *Case studies in music therapy* (pp. 433–449). Gilsum, NH: Barcelona Publishers

Bromley, D. B. (1986). *The case-study method in psychology and related disciplines.* Chichester, UK: John Wiley & Sons.

Bruscia, K. E. (Ed). (1991). *Case studies in music therapy.* Gilsum, NH: Barcelona Publishers.

Bruscia, K. E. (1995a). The boundaries of music therapy research. In B. L. Wheeler (Ed.), *Music therapy research: Quantitative and qualitative perspectives* (pp. 17–27). Gilsum, NH: Barcelona Publishers.

Bruscia, K. E. (1995b). Modes of consciousness in guided imagery and music (GIM): A therapist's experience of the guiding process. In C. B. Kenny (Ed.), *Listening, playing, creating: Essays on the power of sound* (pp. 165–197). Albany, NY: State University of New York Press.

Bruscia, K. E. (1995c). Topics, phenomena, and purposes in qualitative research. In B. L. Wheeler (Ed.), *Music therapy research: Quantitative and qualitative perspectives* (pp. 313–327). Gilsum, NH: Barcelona Publishers.

Campbell, D. T. (1975). Degrees of freedom and the case study. *Comparative Political Studies, 8,* 178–193.

Colaizzi, P. F. (1978). Psychological research as the phenomenologist views it. In R. S. Valle & M. King (Eds.), *Existential-phenomenological alternatives for psychology* (pp. 48–71). New York: Oxford University Press.

Cronbach, L J. (1975). Beyond the two disciplines of scientific psychology. *American Psychologist, 30,* 116–127.

Denzin, N. K., & Lincoln, Y. S. (Eds.). (2000). *Handbook of qualitative research* (2nd ed.). Thousand Oaks, CA: Sage Publications.

Duncker, K. (1963). *Zur Psychologie des produktiven Denkens* [The psychology of productive thinking]. Berlin, Germany: Springer.

Faller, H., & Frommer, J. (Eds.). (1994). *Qualitative Psychotherapieforschung: Grundlagen und Methoden* [Qualitative psychotherapy research: Fundamentals and methods]. Heidelberg, Germany: Asanger.

Forinash, M., & Gonzalez, D. (1989). A phenomenological perspective on music therapy. *Music Therapy, 8,* 35–46.

Frohne-Hagemann, I. (1999). Zur Hermeneutik musiktherapeutischer Prozesse. Metatheoretische Überlegungen zum Verstehen [The hermeneutics of music therapy processes. Metatheoretical reflections on understanding]. *Musiktherapeutische Umschau, 20,* 103–113.

Gadamer, H. G. (1975). *Truth and method.* New York: Seabury Press.

Giorgi, A. (Ed.). (1985). *Phenomenology and psychological research.* Pittsburgh, PA: Duquesne University Press.

Glaser, B. G., & Strauss, A. L. (1967). *The discovery of grounded theory.* Chicago: Aldine.

Grocke, D. (2005). A case study in the Bonny Method of Guided Imagery and Music (BMGIM). In D. Aldridge (Ed.), *Case study designs in music therapy* (pp. 97–117). London: Jessica Kingsley Publishers.

Guba, E. G., & Lincoln, Y. S. (1994). Competing paradigms in qualitative research. In N. K. Denzin & Y. S. Lincoln (Eds.), *Handbook of qualitative research* (pp. 105–117). Thousand Oaks, CA: Sage Publications.

Hadley, S. (2003). *Psychodynamic music therapy: Case studies.* Gilsum, NH: Barcelona Publishers.

Hannibal, N. (2000). *Praeverbal overforing i musiktherapie – kvalitativ undersogelse af overforingsprocessor i den musikalske interaction* [Preverbal transference in music therapy—A qualitative investigation of transference process in the musical interaction]. Unpublished doctoral dissertation, Aalborg University, Aalborg, Denmark.

Kenny, C. B. (1996). The story of the field of play. In M. Langenberg, K. Aigen, & J. Frommer (Eds.), *Qualitative music therapy research: Beginning dialogues* (pp. 55–78). Gilsum, NH: Barcelona Publishers.

Kenny, C. B. (1998). Embracing complexity: The creation of a comprehensive research culture in music therapy. *Journal of Music Therapy, 35,* 201–217.

Kienle, G. S., Karutz, M., Matthes, H., Matthiessen, P., Petersen, P., & Kiene, H. (2003). Evidenzbasierte Medizin. Konkurs der ärztlichen Urteilskraft? [Evidence-based medicine. Bankrupt of the physician's judgment?]. *Deutsches Ärzteblatt Sonderdruck, 100*(33), 1–7.

Lamnek, S. (1989). *Qualitative Sozialforschung Band 2, Methoden und Techniken* [Qualitative social research. Vol. 2, Methods and techniques]. Munich, Germany: Psychologie Verlags Union.

Langenberg, M., Frommer, J., & Langenbach, M. (1996). Fusion and separation: Experiencing opposites in music, music therapy and music therapy research. In M. Langenberg, K. Aigen, & J. Frommer (Eds.), *Qualitative music therapy research: Beginning dialogues* (pp. 131–160). Gilsum, NH: Barcelona Publishers.

Langenberg, M., Frommer, J., & Tress, W. (1993). A qualitative research approach to analytical music therapy. *Music Therapy, 12,* 59–84.

Langenberg, M, Frommer, J. & Tress, W. (1995). From isolation to bonding. A music therapy case study of a patient with chronic migraines. *The Arts in Psychotherapy,* 22, 87–101.

Lathom-Radocy, W. B., & Radocy, R. E. (1995). Descriptive quantitative research. In B. L. Wheeler (Ed.), *Music therapy research: Quantitative and qualitative perspectives* (pp. 165–181). Gilsum, NH: Barcelona Publishers.

Lee, C. A. (1992). *The analysis of therapeutic improvisatory music with people living with the virus HIV and AIDS.* Unpublished doctoral dissertation, City University, London, UK.

Lee, C. (1995). The analysis of therapeutic improvisatory music. In A. Gilroy & C. Lee (Eds.), *Art and music: Therapy and research* (pp. 35–50). London: Routledge.

Lee, C. (1996). *Music at the edge: The music therapy experiences of a musician with AIDS.* London: Routledge.

Lee, C. (2000). A method of analyzing improvisations in music therapy. *Journal of Music Therapy, 37,* 147–167.

Lincoln, Y. S., & Guba, E. G. (1985). *Naturalistic inquiry.* Newbury Park, CA: Sage Publications.

Lincoln, Y. S., & Guba, E. G. (2000). Paradigmatic controversies, contradictions, and emerging confluences. In N. K. Denzin & Y. S. Lincoln (Eds.), *Handbook of qualitative research* (pp. 163–188). London: Sage Publications.

Maslow, A. (1966). *The psychology of science.* New York: Harper & Row.

Maslow, A. (1974). *Motivation and personality.* New York: Harper & Row.

Miles, M. B., & Huberman, A. M. (1993). *Qualitative data analysis: A sourcebook of new methods.* Newbury Park, CA: Sage Publications.

Moustakas, C. (1990). *Heuristic research: Design, methodology, and applications.* Newbury Park, CA: Sage Publications.

Nordenfelt, L. (1987). *On the nature of health: An action-theoretic approach.* Dordrecht, The Netherlands: D. Reidel Publishing Co.

Nordoff, P., & Robbins, C. (1977). *Creative music therapy.* New York: John Day & Co.

Pavlicevic, M. (1997). *Music therapy in context: Music, meaning and relationship.* London: Jessica Kingsley Publishers.

Ridder, H. M. O. (2003). *Singing dialogue. Music therapy with persons in advanced stages of dementia.* Unpublished doctoral dissertation, Aalborg University, Aalborg, Denmark.

Ridder, H. M. O. (2005). Music therapy with the elderly: Complementary data as a rich approach to understanding communication. In D. Aldridge (Ed.), *Case study designs in music therapy* (pp. 191–209). London: Jessica Kingsley Publishers.

Robbins, Clive, & Robbins Carol. (1991). Creative music therapy in bringing order, change and communicativeness to the life of a brain-injured adolescent. In K. E. Bruscia (Ed.), *Case studies in music therapy* (pp. 231–249). Gilsum, NH: Barcelona Publishers.

Roer, S. (2001). Performance as therapy: Chok-Rock New York Tour 1997. In *Book of abstracts, The 5th European Music Therapy Congress,* Naples, Italy. In G. diFranco, E. Ruud, T. Wigram, & D. Aldridge (Eds.), *Music therapy in Europe: The 5th European Music Therapy Congress* (p. 78). Rome: ISMEZ.

Rogers, C. R. (1945). The nondirective method as a technique for social research. *The American Journal of Sociology, 50,* 279–283.

Rogers, C. R. (1968). Some thoughts concerning the pre-suppositions of the behavioral sciences. In W. R. Coulson & C. R. Rogers (Eds.), *Man and the science of man* (pp. 55–72). Columbus, OH: Charles E. Merrill.

Rogers. P. (1993). Research in music therapy with sexually abused clients. In H. Payne (Ed), *One river, many currents: Handbook of inquiry in the arts therapies* (pp. 197–217). London: Jessica Kingsley Publishers.

Salber, W. (1965). *Morphologie des seelischen Geschehens* [The morphology of the psychic process]. Ratingen, Germany: Henn.

Schumacher, K. (1999). *Musiktherapie und Säuglingsforschung. Zusammenspiel. Einschätzung der Beziehungsqualität am Beispiel des instrumentalen Ausdrucks eines autistischen Kindes* [Music therapy and infant research: Interplay, assessment of relational qualities illustrated by the example of the instrumental play of an autistic child]. Frankfurt, Germany: P. Lang.

Shotter, J., & Gergen, K. J. (Ed.). (1989). *Texts and identity.* London: Sage Publications.

Silverman, D. (1999). *Doing qualitative research. A practical handbook.* London: Sage Publications.

Smeijsters, H. (1996). Qualitative single-case research in practice: A necessary, reliable, and valid alternative for music therapy research. In M. Langenberg, K. Aigen, & J. Frommer (Eds.), *Qualitative music therapy research: Beginning dialogues* (pp. 35–53). Gilsum, NH: Barcelona Publishers.

Smeijsters, H. (1997). *Multiple perspectives: A guide to qualitative research in music therapy.* Gilsum, NH: Barcelona Publishers.

Smeijsters, H. (1999a). Feelings of doubt, hope, and faith. In J. Hibben (Ed.), *Inside music therapy: Client experiences* (pp. 277–294). Gilsum, NH: Barcelona Publishers.

Smeijsters, H. (1999b). *Grundlagen der Musiktherapie. Theorie und Praxis zur Behandlung von spezifischen psychischen Störungen und Behinderungen* [Fundamentals of music therapy. Theory and practice of the treatment of psychic disturbances and handicaps]. Göttingen, Germany: Hogrefe.

Smeijsters, H. (2003a). Analogie als Kernkonzept der Musiktherapie. Eine psychologische und empirische Betrachtung [Analogy as a core concept of music therapy. A psychological and empirical reflection]. *Zeitschrift für Musik-, Tanz- und Kunsttherapie, 14,* 9–18.

Smeijsters, H. (2003b). Forms of feeling and forms of perception: The fundamentals of analogy in music therapy. *Nordic Journal of Music Therapy, 12,* 71–85.

Smeijsters, H. (2003c). *Handboek creatieve therapie* [Handbook of creative arts therapies]. Bussum, The Netherlands: Coutinho.

Smeijsters, H. (2005). *Sounding the self: Analogy in improvisational music therapy.* Gilsum, NH: Barcelona Publishers.

Smeijsters, H., & van den Berk, P. (1995). Music therapy with a client suffering from musicogenic epilepsy: A naturalistic qualitative single-case research. *The Arts in Psychotherapy, 22,* 249–263.

Smeijsters, H., & Hurk, J. van den. (1999). Music therapy helping to work through grief and finding a personal identity. *Journal of Music Therapy, 16,* 222–252.

Smeijsters, H., & Storm, H. (1998). Becoming friends with your mother: Techniques of qualitative research illustrated with the short-term treatment of a girl with enuresis. *Music Therapy, 14,* 61–83.

Stake, R. E. (1995). *The art of case study research.* Thousand Oaks, CA: Sage Publications.

Stige, B. (2003). *Elaborations toward a notion of community music therapy.* Doctoral dissertation, University of Oslo. Acta Humaniora Nr. 175. Oslo, Norway: Unipub.

Tesch, R. (1990). *Qualitative research: Analysis types & software tools.* New York: The Falmer Press.

Tüpker, R (1988). *Ich singe was ich nicht sagen kann. Zu einer morphologischen Grundlegung der Musiktherapie* [I sing what I cannot say. A morphological foundation of music therapy]. Regensburg, Germany: Gustav Bosse Verlag.

Tüpker, R. (Ed.). (1996). *Konzeptentwicklung musiktherapeutischer Praxis und Forschung* [Concept development in music therapy practice and research]. Münster, Germany: Lit Verlag.

Wigram, T., Pedersen, I. N., & Bonde, L. O. (2002). *A comprehensive guide to music therapy.* London: Jessica Kingsley Publishers.

Wolcott, H. F. (1994). *Transforming qualitative data: Description, analysis, and interpretation.* Thousand Oaks, CA: Sage Publications.

Yin, R. K. (1983). *The case study method: An annotated bibliography* (1983–1984 ed.). Washington, DC: COSMOS Corporation.

Yin, R. K. (2003). *Case study research: Design and methods.* Thousand Oaks, CA: Sage Publications.

Chapter 36
Arts-Based Research
Diane Austin and Michele Forinash

Arts-based research is perhaps the newest and least explored of the qualitative research approaches. While still in early development, it holds great promise as a research method due to its emphasis on using music and other art forms as the research instruments. As we hold music and other art forms at the center of our clinical practice, it follows that music can also be the foundation of our research methods.

Overview and Definition

Arts-based research has been described in a variety of contexts (Bagley & Cancienne, 2002; Blumenfeld-Jones & Barone, 1997; Diaz, 2002; Hervey, 2000; Jenoure, 2002; Jipson & Paley, 1997; Lawrence-Lightfoot & Davis, 1997; McNiff, 1998; Olsen, 1995). These authors offered various descriptions of the connection of art to research, how arts-based research has been carried out, and how it might be used in future studies. Diaz (2002), referring to her artistic form as writing, stated:

> In searching for a way of describing what we do, I have arrived at this place between art and inquiry to dig for details, notice nuances, and engage in the creative process of writing. I create inquiry as I do art, and know art as inquiry. (p. 147)

Jenoure (2002), summarizing her research culminating in a dance and music performance (discussed more fully below), wrote:

> There is no demarcation indicating where the research ended and the performance began, since each facet was always related to the other. For simplicity's sake, one might say that it began with the phenomenological interview study, evolved to the stage when the conversational "riffs" were developed, then metamorphosed into a musical performance. (p. 87)

A description of the book *Daredevil Research* (Jipson & Paley, 1997) stated:

> This book seeks to transform thinking about analytic practice and the construction of research knowledge. By experimenting with alternative models of representation unconstrained by the weight of traditional research protocols, the authors create multiple spaces for imagining how to differently identify issues for inquiry, select modes of analysis, and inscribe "data" into transmittable form. [This book] suggests the possibilities of analytical practice in imaginative, independent space. (back cover)

Perhaps the most comprehensive exploration of arts-based research comes from Hervey (2000). Her seminal book provided a thorough exploration of what she terms *artistic inquiry* in dance and movement therapy. She gave the following tripartite definition of artistic inquiry:

1. Artistic inquiry uses artistic methods of gathering, analyzing and/or presenting data;
2. Artistic inquiry engages in and acknowledges a creative process;
3. Artistic inquiry is motivated and determined by the aesthetic values of the researcher(s). (p .7)

While we resonated with Hervey's definition, we believe there is an additional step in which the arts can play a role—that of formulating the research question.

Most recently the *Journal of Pedagogy, Pluralism and Practice* devoted an entire issue (Fall 2004) to the topic of arts-based research (http://www.lesley.edu/journals/jppp/9/index.html). It contained philosophical perspectives as well as practical applications of research.

Based on these various descriptions from the literature along with our own experiences, we offer the following definition: *Arts-based inquiry* is a research method in which the arts play a primary role in any or all of the steps of the research method. Art forms such as poetry, music, visual art, drama, and dance are essential to the research process itself and central in formulating the research question, generating data, analyzing data, and presenting the research results.

Arts-based research emphasizes an artistic response to the raw data (interview, music, and so forth) as part of the data-generating process. It requires the researcher to tolerate the ambiguity of not knowing and to trust that the creative flow of images, music, movement, poetry, and story telling will evolve into recognizable patterns of meaning that bring together and integrate primary processes with cognitive thinking.

While many forms of qualitative research use artistic methods to enhance research methods, arts-based research holds the art form (whether it be music, art, poetry, or another artistic medium) at the center of the research process. We argue that the artistic process can provide information at each step of the research study that is unique and is not knowable by other means. While this may at first seem radical, this basic belief about the primacy of music is also at the center of some philosophies of music therapy. Music and the arts can provide us with access to information about our clients that is not available in any other way—essential information that is unknowable through other means can be gained in music making with clients. Arts-based research places a primacy on the arts at any step of the research process as a way of gaining information that would otherwise be unavailable.

Many music therapy studies incorporate music and other art forms to varying degrees, yet it is important to recognize that simply having music or other art forms in any of the research steps does not necessarily qualify a study as arts-based research. If inclusion of music in a study made it arts-based, then many music therapy studies would be arts-based and there would be no need to articulate arts-based research as a distinct qualitative research approach. We are creating a distinction between arts-based research and research that uses various artistic methods or examines the arts, such as studies of clinical improvisation. As defined, the arts are primary to the research process in arts-based research. Other research approaches can include artistic approaches yet not be considered arts-based research. Aigen's (1998) book, *Paths of Development in Nordoff-Robbins Music Therapy*, contained music of session material on CD, yet is not arts-based research because the music is included as examples to deepen the reader's experience of the music therapy sessions. The music is the raw data but is not essential to any other aspect of the research process. Likewise, studies of improvisation (Forinash, 1992; Lee, 1996), while including or focusing on improvisation, are not arts-based as they are not using the arts in response to the raw data to create new data or lift the analysis to another level or to gain access to otherwise unavailable material. As Hervey (2000) stated:

> Simply using an art object as data does not make research artistic. Interpretation or analysis of an art object also does not constitute artistic inquiry. In addition, artistic inquiry is not the use of types of analysis developed in relation to an art form, but which are not part of the art-making process. Both art objects and the interpretation of art may be *part* of artistic inquiry, but are not sufficient alone to warrant its identification as such. (p. 44)

Theoretical Premises and Historical Roots

Theoretical Premises

The theoretical premises of arts-based inquiry lie in creativity and the use of arts for personal exploration. McNiff (1998) described a series of experiences he had while teaching research to students in expressive therapies in the 1980s. He found that his students naturally began to "integrate their personal creative expression with the production of a master's thesis or doctoral dissertation" (p. 22). His students seemed to find the task of research inseparable from the artistic process. Describing one student's early use of arts-based inquiry, McNiff wrote:

> One of the first art-based masters thesis projects that I supervised involved a woman who did a series of paintings of female bodies. Rather than write about what women told her about their body images or what she saw in their drawings and paintings, my student (Jenkins, 1988) chose to spend the school year investigating the female body through paintings of large human figures. The finished work included the presentation of the paintings in the thesis, an

exhibition of the works, and a written text reflecting on the process of making the series of paintings and its effects upon the artist. (p. 23)

Thus it appears that early arts-based research evolved from the natural relationship that beginning researchers had with the creative process and their trust that following the creative process and letting it unfold would produce not only an artistic artifact but also a research outcome.

Lawrence-Lightfoot (1997) wrote about the evolution of an arts-based method. She described her life-long love of the arts:

The music that makes my heart sing, the poetry that soothes my soul, the dance that releases my rage, the novel that takes me to distant lands and brings me home, and the painting that offers me a new angle of vision. (p. 3)

It was this love, along with a deep appreciation of science and intellectual debate, that led her to combine art and science into a method that she called "portraiture" (p. 3). She defined this as a method that "combines systematic, empirical descriptions with aesthetic expressing, blending art and science, humanistic sensibilities and scientific rigor" (p. 3). She went on to say: "The portraits are designed to capture the richness complexity and dimensionality of human experience in social and cultural context, conveying the perspectives of the people who are negotiating those experiences" (p. 3).

This combination of appreciation for the power of art along with the need for systematic and thorough study is crucial in arts-based research. It also stresses the essential role of the arts and the attitude expressed in the title of Blumenfeld-Jones' (2002) study, "If I Could Have Said It, I Would Have."

Metaphor and metaphoric analysis help researchers bridge the conscious and unconscious worlds in order to access new insights and deepen the understanding of the data. Poems capture the essence of an experience; they "condense the story into images that pack the data into one scene" (Ely, Vinz, Downing, & Anzul, 1997, p. 135).

Pastiche allows for multiple perspectives simultaneously. Pastiche was defined by Ely et al. (1997) as "various textual experiments that interweave or link data, descriptions, analysis, or multiple genre into diverse configurations. . . . Pastiche assumes that the pieces. . . that make up the whole communicate particular messages above and beyond the parts" (pp. 96–97). Sometimes this form resembles a collage made up of poetry and images.

Art can be an organic process that engages the body, mind, and creative sprit and allows the researcher to revisit the data from another vantage point. Painting, sculpture, and photography allow the researcher a visual form of expression for statements more difficult to convey in words.

The recursive nature of performing can keep the research process alive as new insights often emerge with each presentation. The performance piece invites the audience to engage with the research study on a more direct visceral and emotional level than the written word.

History of Use in Music Therapy

Arts-based research has not been widely used in music therapy. Austin's study presented below is one of the only examples of arts-based research in music therapy, although two other arts-based studies using music will be discussed here.

Jenoure's (2002) "Sweeping the Temple: A Performance Collage" described the performance outcome of what began as a study in which African-American artists who taught in traditionally white colleges and universities were interviewed. As part of the research, Jenoure interviewed a close friend and colleague with whom she had performed for years. The colleague, Patti, was a dancer and teacher and was battling advanced breast cancer at the time of the interview. When she finished the research, Jenoure published a book (2000) but was also left with what she termed "leftover" bits of information that made her feel the research process was "untidy" (p. 76). After much soul searching regarding these leftover yet powerful parts of her research, as well the death of her colleague and fellow performer, she states:

The book was published and Patti's story was featured as one of four portraits that I developed from the interview data. However, that project was not complete and I knew it and the next step would be to breathe even more life into her portrait than I had been able to do through this narrative profile. *Sweeping the Temple,* a performance of my research, derives from several objectives. I had a desire to make Patti's experience more tangible to an audience—more sensual—more real. I wanted others to feel her tempo and anger and humor and vibrancy and sarcasm. I was also intent on honoring Patti, and one of my challenges would be to give her portrait a memorial quality while avoiding histrionics or any romanticizing of her death. Another concern was that of accessibility. It was important to communicate some key issues pertaining to the experience of at least this one African American teacher to an audience that might not read the published research. (p. 78)

Using a combination of an audiotape of an interview with Patti, spoken words by the author, sung vocals, and violin, the author presented her performance, honoring Patti's voice and experience as an African-American teacher in traditionally white institutions.

Summarizing, Jenoure (2002) stated:

To turn research into art, I had to first let go of expectations that this project would in any way replicate or even represent my initial study, although, certainly, the art is intended to report some aspects of it. In the case of this work, the performance became a vehicle for further examining specific details of Patti's experience. In fact, the notion of performing the data became a research project in its own right. (p. 87)

As we see in this example, the author felt there was information that could only be presented in this artistic form. Using an artistic method to present the findings gives us a sense of experience unavailable through any other means.

In an example where music is used in the analysis of the data, Blumenfeld-Jones and Barone (1997) studied students as they went through a teacher preparation program with a focus on diversity. They cited a need to connect the relationships "between data display and forms of expression" (p. 84). In other words, they sought a stronger connection between the data collected and how it is presented. They used four forms of data display. The first form was *linear chronological,* which presented the data from the interview in a linear manner, as it actually occurred in time between the participants. The second form was *conversational analysis* in which the vocal production patterns of the interview conversation were analyzed. The third form was *musical score* in which the interview conversation was analyzed in "in terms of musical qualities" (p. 96) such as pitch, tempo, rhythm, and harmony. The final form was *soliloquy* that focuses on the expressions of the participant as if he or he was speaking uninterrupted as a soliloquy. Again, in this example, we gain an insight into the topic that is unique and only available through an artistic process.

Methodology

The Arts and the Formulation of the Research Question

In teaching research, I (Michele Forinash) often encounter students who are trying to determine which burning issue to pursue in their research and I often ask that they provide an artistic response (McNiff, 1998) to several of their possible topics. By creating an artistic response in the form of drawing, sculpture, song, dance, or story to their potential topic, they gain a deeper level of awareness and new understanding and felt experience of the potential of their research topic. This artistic level of awareness can and usually does offer insight that is unavailable through other methods. Likewise, when students are stuck at various steps in their research process, using an artistic response can help them gain insight into how to move forward.

In a study of the culture of Alcoholics Anonymous (AA; discussed below), Austin (1997a, 1997b, 1998, 1999a, 1999b, 2000) began with an initial guiding question, "What's going on here?" To refine her guiding question, she engaged in a process of writing poetry and rap music in order to explore her thoughts and reactions to the research question. Through the process of writing poetry and rap music she refined her research question and it became: "What keeps people coming back to Alcoholics Anonymous meetings?"

The Arts and the Generation of Data

Ely et al. (1997) described Austin's process of interviewing a person who considered himself a recovering alcoholic. Prior to listening to the tape or transcribing the interview, Austin wrote a poem as a creative response to the interview. The poem incorporated quotes she remembered from the interview and became part of her data from the study. The poem is called "Parallel Process."

> "No judgment" he says.
> Yeah, I think—don't we all long for that?
> "Somebody to understand" he says.
> Yeah, I think—don't we all long for that?
> "Watching people grow and recover."
> I know just what he means.
> "Keep it simple, saved my life."
> And I think about how complicated my life is.
> "I've got to tend my garden," he says.
> And I think about the weeds in mine. (Austin in Ely et al., 1997, pp. 136–137)

The artistic response at this step in the research process yielded an experience of the interview process from Austin's perspective. It allows us to gain access to some of her feelings that were evoked as part of the interview process. This is vital data, which emerged from the creation of the poem and was unattainable from either the interview process or the transcription of the interview.

The Arts and the Analysis of Data

In the above discussion of Blumenfeld-Jones and Barone's (1997) study, we saw how music was used to provide a new level of analysis of the data, in this case from verbal interviews. By creating a score that included rhythm, tempo, pitch, and harmony, we not only heard the words of the interviewer and interviewees, but we also heard the musical nature of the interview. We heard dissonance and consonance, harmony and solo, rhythmic intensity and reverie, all of which contributed a vital element to our understanding of the meaning of the interview.

It is important to distinguish the difference between the arts as analysis from analyzing the arts. Many studies analyze the artistic process. Kasayka (1991) analyzed music from the Bonny Method of Guided Imagery in Music programs, in particular the *Peak Experience* program. This provided the reader with an important new level of understanding of the music in the program. She used accepted methods of musical analysis that involved examining notes, harmonies, dynamics, tempi, and so forth. Art as analysis would have used an artistic process like creating a poetic voice to the music or perhaps a visual artistic response to the program to analyze the program. We cite this example to clarify the difference between using the arts for analysis of data and analyzing the arts. In fact, arts-based research would not have been a good fit for Kasayka's stated research focus, which was to examine and analyze the *Peak Experience* tape and the session material measure by measure.

The Arts and Presentation of the Results

Presenting the research results in a performance piece leaves room for ambiguity and space for the emergence of images, thoughts, and insights that are grounded in the body and facilitate a connection between cognitive, kinesthetic, and emotional processes. The example above cited by Jenoure demonstrates the performance aspect of arts-based inquiry. In this example, Jenoure had completed her research and published her results in a book. Yet, after publication, the author felt that something was missing. It was this sense of incompletion that led to the creation of the performance aspect of her research, through which she came to other levels of awareness regarding her research that were only uncovered through the performance aspect. She took one of the four portraits of the people she interviewed for her research and created a performance piece based on this portrait.

Again, we must distinguish between research studies that incorporate music and the arts in the presentation of the data and studies in which the results are an artistic creation. Many studies include music in the form of musical excerpts that support the author's findings. For example, Lee (1996), in his seminal case study of a musician with AIDS, included many moving excerpts of improvisations from the music therapy sessions. Lee used the arts to provide the reader with raw data to support his discussion of the music therapy experiences. While hearing the actual music of the sessions provides the reader with new insights into the process, it is still the raw data from the sessions. Had Lee gone a step further and created a piece of music as a whole from the various excerpts or woven together these excerpts with his own improvisations or even suggested that the reader first listen to the CD as a whole before reading the text, it would have been closer to being arts-based research. This is in no way a criticism of Lee's work, rather a way of making a distinction between presenting the research findings and discussion as an artistic event versus presenting musical examples to support one's discussion.

Relationship to Other Types of Research

Ely's (Ely et al., 1997, 1991) method of naturalistic inquiry, which encourages the use of narrative forms, can be closely linked to arts-based research. Her method emphasizes the use of poetry, vignettes, layered stories, pastiche, and songs to enhance the research process by generating creative methods to enrich the analysis and interpretation of data.

Arnason's (1998) study of music therapists' experiences in group improvisation is a quintessential example of Ely's (Ely et al., 1997) method of naturalistic inquiry incorporating narrative forms. Arnason found that the use of narrative forms helped her to

meet a primary purpose of this research report which was to allow the reader into this group's particular process and musical experience. . . in writing up this study it was difficult to textually connect verbal and musical data. When I read or wrote words, they seemed to create a world of their own, with a particular language and meaning that did not necessarily or fully represent the experience of improvising music . . . musical improvisation in a therapy group is a dynamic fluctuating phenomenon that tends to elude the rational voice of written word. However, utilizing a variety of creative textual forms in order to capture and convey the spontaneous and ambiguous nature of improvisation, and people's experience in music, was an indispensable and creative research tool. (pp. 44–45)

Narrative inquiry is the use of the narrative form as the focus or the raw data of the research or as a means to study another question (Clandinin & Connelly, 1999; Kenny, 2002). Narrative inquiry tends to begin with lived experience as told in a story. The data can be collected in a story or in another narrative form such as a journal or letters. Narrative forms include stories, so there is a connection between narrative inquiry and arts-based research that utilizes story to respond to raw data and create another level of analysis.

Examples in Music Therapy

Austin's study of Alcoholics Anonymous (1997a, 1997b, 1998, 1999a, 1999b, 2000) provides us with an example of arts-based inquiry that utilized music, poetry, metaphoric analysis, and pastiche, and culminated in a performance of a musical play called "Grace Street." The recursive nature of the performance process allowed for opportunities to further examine and analyze the data. The research process fueled the creative process and the creative process illuminated aspects of the research so that both the play and the research evolved as new songs were added with each performance.

Austin recognized the ethical issues involved in studying an anonymous group in which there was no official gatekeeper or authority that could grant permission for the study. She attended an open meeting (which in AA means that it was not confined to alcoholics but open to anyone) for 4 months and identified herself to the chairperson at the first meeting in an attempt to explain her intentions. Members at the meeting who were standing nearby pointed out that this meeting was open to anyone and she need not explain her presence or intentions. Her research advisors felt that the open and anonymous nature of the meetings, along with her initial attempt to identify her intentions, provided her with implicit permission to conduct the study.

The composition of the group varied from week to week. Austin, like others at the meeting who were not alcoholics, was not allowed to speak during meetings. She did request and receive written consent from the group members she interviewed, and the confidentiality of those she interviewed was respected.

She kept a log that contained a transcription of her interview with Harry and one with Pam, a record of her experience of the meetings she attended, and analytic memos. She wrote about her personal feelings and reactions in a reflexive journal. Categories, bins, and themes emerged from the notes, memos, poetry, songs, metaphors, collage, and layered stories in her log. As discussed above, Austin was able to refine her original research question through the use of poetry and by composing a rap song.

From one bin of metaphors, she created a poem that led to the discovery of three major themes: In the Darkness, Beginning the Journey, and Heading for the Light. An excerpt follows:

> trapped in a void
> a black hole
> wearing a mask
> in the darkness
> a lizard self
> living in a glass cage
> lighting the fireworks
> hitting bottom

Playing with the data led to the emergence of nine more themes and a meta-metaphor (or meta-theme), The Hero's Journey in which the 12 themes were metaphors for the 12 steps of AA and compared the recovery process to the stages in the archetypal hero's journey in mythology.

Austin used this mythological form of analysis along with songs, poetry, layered stories, and reflections from her log to create a musical play as a method to further analyze the data and present her findings in a dramatic form. Rather that representing specific individuals, she created four composite characters from the interviews, along with her own experience of being a participant-observer for 4 months. These characters gave voice and breathed life into the research findings.

Excerpts from the musical production *Grace Street* follow:[1]

(Opening rap song sung by Willy, accompanied on the drums by Peter)

> The pain, the pain
> Hey, it's driving me insane
> I'm sitting here and watching
> My life go down the drain
> I'm drugging and I'm drinking
> My thinking is stinking
> And the ship I've been on has been hit
> And I'm sinking
> It's time to get down on my knees and pray
> Hey, hey, gotta get to AA
> Hey, hey, gotta get to AA
> *(All four characters)*
> Hey, hey, gotta get to AA
> AA AA AA AA (slowly fade out)

Voice One

Hi, my name is Katie and I'm an alcoholic.

Voice Two

Hi, my name is Peter and I'm an alcoholic and an addict.

Voice Three

Hi, my name is Hank and I'm a slow recovering alcoholic.

Voice Four

Hi, my name is Willy, I'm an alcoholic and addict, and I'm counting days.

Katie

I've been sober for ten years now.

---

[1] This song was first performed at the Annual Conference of the American Association of Music Therapy, Monticello, NY (Austin, 1997a).

Peter
Two years now.

Hank
Three months.

Willy
Three days.

Katie
I started drinking when I was thirteen. I used to carry vodka and orange juice to school in my thermos bottle. I went to performing arts high school and when the pressure was too much I'd drink—and there was a lot of pressure.

Peter
I began smoking marijuana at seven years old. I dropped acid in high school then moved on to freebasing coke. I drank alcohol to come down. I used to get high when I felt anything. I wanted to numb out—it was easier that way.

Hank
I drank beer when I was a baby. They said that I loved the taste of it. I started drinking seriously at fourteen. I drank out of fear. I was shy and insecure. I had a lot more fun with a few beers in me and people liked me. I wanted people to like me.

Willy
I started doing drugs in high school. I liked to experiment—mix things—alcohol, pot, ups, downs—now my drug of choice is cocaine—but last week somebody gave me some heroin. It takes the edge off the coke crash and with the smack, it takes a couple of weeks before it gets sloppy.

Katie
I used to drink with my mother and grandmother.

Peter
My friends

Hank
My boss

Willy
My father

(Katie and Willy speak the following together)

Katie
My mother is an alcoholic.

Willy
My father is an alcoholic.

Peter
My whole family is f---ed up.
I left home at sixteen—I raised myself.

Hank
My parents divorced when I was nine. My mother never recovered. She stayed in bed all day and cried a lot. I hated it when she cried. She's doing better now—we talk a lot. Her father was an alcoholic.

Katie, Willy, Peter, & Hank (together)
It's a family disease.

Katie
I was a blank page.

Peter
A lizard

Hank
Wearing a mask

Willy
Trapped in a glass cage

Katie, Willy, Peter & Hank (together)
But I didn't have a problem.

The next excerpt identified a major theme, hitting bottom, and began to give the audience a sense of how and why people come to Alcoholics Anonymous meetings.

All four
I lost

Peter
My job

Hank and Willy
My wife

Katie
My self. . . . I was in the darkness—a black hole

Peter
A void

Hank
Empty

Willy
I had band-aids on my soul

All Four
I hit bottom

(Silence—then. . .)

Willy
(sings the blues)
The rain keeps falling
Falling all night and day
The rain keeps falling
Falling all night and day
I was on my way home
And got lost along the way.

Hank
I was seriously depressed. It was hard to cross streets. I'd see a big truck coming and want to walk in front of it. I eventually went to see a therapist—I was drunk at the time—the therapist told me to go to AA . . . The amazing thing is—I went!

Peter
I had a lot of f---ed up friends who sold drugs and got high I thought my friends were the problem. I finally realized *I* was the f---ing problem. Then a friend of mine joined AA. He seemed different—like there was a light in his eyes or something. I don't know, maybe it was divine intervention—but I started coming to meetings with him.

Willy
I remember when I first came here to check it out. I raised my hand to speak and didn't get called on. I decided this place was for losers . . . When I got fired from my job I came back. My wife threw me out—I couldn't stop using—I had nowhere else to go.

Katie
When I moved back to New York I met this guy who was a recovering alcoholic. He told me about Grace Street. I took an apartment across the street and went to a few meetings and I "got it." The solution was "one day at a time," "take little steps." My sobriety lasted a few months and then I went home for Christmas. I got drunk every day. I came back to New York and kept drinking. I used to look out my window and watch people going into the meeting. I didn't feel I deserved to get sober. And then one morning I woke up still dressed from the night before and feeling very disoriented. It wasn't a particularly horrible drunk. I was just tired of feeling lost and afraid. So I got up, washed my face and walked across the street.

(Katie sings "Somewhere In the Darkness," see pages 467–469.)

Somewhere in the Darkness

Conclusion

Arts-based research, being multilayered and multidimensional, can capture subtleties and enrich the rendering of experiences in ways that do justice to the complexities of the research subject (Knowles & Thomas, 2002). Artistic forms are closer to the irrational world of the unconscious and the source of creativity and therefore come closer to capturing experience than the more rational world of words. The playfulness and spontaneity that are accessed through the art forms open up our imagination so that we can view something familiar in a new way and add other dimensions of awareness to what we are studying.

We recently participated in an arts-based research group at the Fifth International Qualitative Research Symposium hosted by Mechtild Jahn-Langenberg and the Institute of the Arts in Berlin, Germany. One of the conclusions we reached through this experience and others is that arts-based research is not for everyone. A member of our research group made the point that one must be cautious when working so deeply in the arts, for the researcher could get stuck in the primary process and experience infinite regressions without producing any tangible results. My (Diane Austin) experience, however, has been different. I have found that even though you are working deeply within the primary process, you are creating a musical, poetic, or artistic form and the form is self-organizing and can prevent fragmentation. You can step back, look at, listen to, and dialogue with the creative form. This process creates distance, brings in the cognitive piece, and facilitates a differentiation between conscious and unconscious processes, protecting the researcher from becoming overwhelmed by the primary process.

We believe arts-based research can provide a rich experience for those who want to keep the research process closely connected to their creative process. Arts-based inquiry has much to offer qualitative research methods in music therapy. Whether used as the sole method or as a step or steps in a particular method, arts-based inquiry provides us with the opportunity to use the arts forms that provide the foundation of our clinical work as a foundation in our research endeavors. It is our sincere hope that researchers will continue to explore the possibilities inherent in this method and share their results with the music therapy community.

References

Aigen, K. (1998) *Paths of development in Nordoff-Robbins music therapy.* Gilsum, NH: Barcelona Publishers.

Arnason, C. (1998). The experience of music therapists in an improvisational music therapy group. (Doctoral dissertation, New York University, 1998). *Dissertation Abstracts International, 59*(09), 3386.

Austin, D. (1997a, June). *Grace Street: A qualitative study of Alcoholics Anonymous.* Presentation at the Annual Conference of the American Association of Music Therapy, Monticello, NY.

Austin, D. (1997b, November). *Narrative forms in qualitative research.* Presentation at the 48th Annual Conference of the National Association for Music Therapy, Los Angeles, CA.

Austin, D. (1998, November). *Grace Street: A qualitative study of Alcoholics Anonymous.* Presentation at the Inaugural Conference of the American Music Therapy Association, Cleveland, OH.

Austin, D. (1999a, October). *Grace Street: A qualitative study of Alcoholics Anonymous.* Presentation at the Conference of the New York Coalition of Creative Arts Therapists, New York, NY.

Austin D. (1999b, November). *A qualitative study of Alcoholics Anonymous.* Presentation at the 9th World Congress of Music Therapy, Washington, DC.

Austin, D. (2000, November). *Qualitative research in music therapy.* Presentation at the American Music Therapy Association Conference, St. Louis, MO (with B. L. Wheeler).

Bagley, C., & Cancienne, M. B. (2002) *Dancing the data.* New York: Peter Lang Publishers.

Blumenfeld-Jones, D. S. (2002). If I could have said it, I would have. In C. Bagley & M. B. Cancienne (Eds.), *Dancing the data* (pp. 90–104). New York: Peter Lang Publishers.

Blumenfeld-Jones, D. S., & Barone, T. E. (1997). Interrupting the sign: The aesthetics of research texts. In J. Jipson & N. Paley (Eds.), *Daredevil research: Recreating analytic practice.* New York: Peter Lang Publishers.

Diaz, G. (2002). Artistic inquiry: On lighthouse hill. In C. Bagley & M. B. Cancienne (Eds.), *Dancing the data* (pp. 147–161). New York: Peter Lang Publishers.

Clandinin, D. J., & Connelly, F. M. (1999). *Narrative inquiry: Experience and story in qualitative research.* West Sussex, UK: Jossey-Bass Publications.

Ely, M., Vinz, R., Downing, M., & Anzul, M. (1997). *On writing qualitative research: Living by words.* Bristol, PA: The Falmer Press.

Ely, M., with Anzul, M., Friedman, T., Garner, D., & Steinmetz, A. M. (1991). *Circles within circles: Doing qualitative research.* London: The Falmer Press.

Forinash, M. (1992). A phenomenological analysis of Nordoff-Robbins approach to music therapy: The lived experience of clinical improvisation. *Music Therapy, 11,* 120–141.

Hervey, L. W. (2000). *Artistic inquiry in dance/movement therapy: Creative alternatives for research.* Springfield, IL: Charles C. Thomas.

Jenoure, T. (2000). *Navigators: African American musicians, dancers, and visual artists in academe.* Albany: State University of New York Press.

Jenoure, T. (2002). Sweeping the temple: A performance collage. In C. Bagley & M. B. Cancienne (Eds.), *Dancing the data* (pp. 73–89). New York: Peter Lang Publishers.

Jipson, J., & Paley, N. (1997). *Daredevil research: Recreating analytic practice.* New York: Peter Lang Publishers.

Kasayka, R. E. (1991). To meet and match the moment of hope: Transpersonal elements of the Guided Imagery and Music experience. *Dissertation Abstracts International, 52*(06), 2062A. (UMI No. DEY9134754)

Kenny, C. B. (2002) Blue Wolf says goodbye for the last time. *American Behavioral Scientist, 45,* 1214–1222.

Knowles, G., & Thomas, S. M. (2002). Artistry, inquiry, and sense of place: Secondary school students portrayed in context. In C. Bagley & M. B. Cancienne (Eds.), *Dancing the data* (pp. 121–132). New York: Peter Lang Publishers.

Lawrence-Lightfoot, S. (1997). The view of the whole: Origins and purposes. In S. Lightfoot-Lawrence & J. H. Davis (Eds.) *The art and science of portraiture.* San Francisco, CA: Jossey-Bass.

Lawrence-Lightfoot, S., & Davis, J. H. (1997). *The art and science of portraiture.* San Francisco, CA: Jossey-Bass.

Lee, C. (1996). *Music at the edge: The music therapy experiences of a musician with AIDS.* London: Routledge.

McNiff, S. (1998). *Art-based research.* Philadelphia: Jessica Kingsley Publishers.

Olsen, A. J. (1995). Moving the question: Authentic movement as research. *A Moving Journal,* Fall-Winter, 7–8.

Chapter 37
Personal Construct Psychology and the Repertory Grid Technique
Brian Abrams and Anthony Meadows

Cultivating a deeper understanding of the music therapy field, music therapy researchers have recently devoted increased efforts to examining, explicating, and building theories concerning the internal experiences and perceptions of clients and therapists (for example, B. Abrams, 2002; Bruscia, 1995; Hibben, 1999; Meadows, 2002; Wheeler, 1999). Recently, music therapy researchers have begun to utilize a technique known as the *repertory grid technique* (Kelly, 1955), an interactive data collection and analysis instrument designed to elicit the inner experiences and perceptions of the participant. The repertory grid technique is rooted within the philosophical and theoretical principles of *Personal Construct Psychology* (Kelly). This chapter will discuss the history, principles, and methods of Personal Construct Psychology (including an in-depth account of the repertory grid technique as well as consideration of other techniques), relationships between the repertory grid technique and other research methods, and applications of the repertory grid technique in music therapy.

Overview and Definition

Personal Construct Psychology was developed in the mid-1950s by George Kelly (1905–1967), a psychotherapist who did extensive clinical work with children and adults. Kelly felt that neither behaviorism nor Freudian theory, the two prevalent theories of the time, adequately explained the complex behavior of his clients, nor did they provide the necessary framework from which to contextualize his clients' problems. As a result, Kelly (1955) developed a theory of personality built upon the premises that all of one's living experiences are based upon the way that all aspects of one's world interrelate, and that all of one's current interpretations of the universe are subject to ongoing revision or replacement. Rooted in this theory, he also developed an approach to therapy and a research method. Kelly documented these theoretical, clinical, and research components of Personal Construct Psychology in his seminal two-volume work, *The Psychology of Personal Constructs* (1955).

Central to Kelly's theory of personality and approach to therapy was his notion of how human experience is constructed. Kelly noticed that his clients tended to perceive or experience any given quality of their lives in terms of its implicit opposite. Kelly called this pair of opposite qualities a *construct*. Take, for example, a client who began therapy because he felt stuck, unable to live the life he imagined for himself. When asked what he would like to feel (the opposite of being stuck), he said that he wanted to be fluid. So for this client, a construct of importance was *stuck* ↔ *fluid*, where each pole gives information about the nature of the problem and, in this case, the client's solution. When prompted for more constructs related to *stuck* ↔ *fluid*, this client added *tired* ↔ *energized*, *foggy* ↔ *clear vision*, *isolated* ↔ *connected*, and so on. Thus, according to Kelly, clients naturally contextualize their problems in terms of a system of constructs that both define and differentiate those problems.

Although it is easy to imagine constructs as cognitive schemas, or structures of how one thinks about her or his world, Kelly (1955) emphasized that this was only partially true. In spite of their verbal labels, constructs contain affective and experiential components, both of which can have equal and sometimes greater importance than their cognitive components (Kelly). Furthermore, Kelly understood that while some experiences are easily labeled, others are not, and therefore the construct is merely an approximation of the experience. In this way, Kelly was anticipating both phenomenology, with his emphasis on experience (Warren, 1998), and hermeneutics, with his interest in helping clients to explicate and understand their own meaning-making structures (Taylor, 1990).

Kelly placed a great deal of emphasis on the individual, both in her or his quest for meaning making, and on the assumption that people naturally develop, test, alter, and expand upon their own unique and idiosyncratic construct systems. He assumed that an individual's knowledge of the world is more or less structured and ordered in the form of a construct system, and that his clients' problems were the result of a construct system that was out of step with their current circumstances. Therefore, Kelly helped his clients articulate their construct systems around particular problems, using approaches such as the repertory grid technique, described in detail later in this chapter. He found that this served to illuminate and subsequently recontextualize client problems. This carried direct implications for research on therapy, in that the internal experiences and perceptions of clients or therapists can best be understood by explicating the construct system relevant to the phenomenon under consideration.

Whatever the research phenomenon, an individual's perceptions and experiences concerning that phenomenon are unique. This is not to say that there are not similarities in experiences or, indeed, similarities in the construct systems of two people when examining the same phenomenon. Kelly's emphasis, however, was on the ways in which each person experienced and perceived something and on explicating the relevant construct system. Interpretation of this construct system, once elicited, could be undertaken quantitatively or qualitatively, or both, depending on the specific research question asked and the nature of the data.

Historical Roots and Theoretical Premises

Historical Roots

After receiving his PhD in psychology in 1931, Kelly moved to rural Kansas to take up an academic position. "Faced with a sea of human suffering aggravated by bank foreclosures and economic suffering" (Fransella & Neimeyer, 2003, p. 21) during the Great Depression, Kelly found that his training in physiological psychology was of little use to him. Instead, he began to turn his attention to what he saw was needed, the assessment of school-age children and adults. It was during this period that he started to develop his thinking about the psychology of personal constructs and his techniques of therapy. Informing these developments was Kelly's view that "persons have created themselves and therefore can re-create themselves if they have the courage and imagination to do so" (Fransella & Neimeyer, p. 23). Finding himself largely alone in his efforts to help the troubled students under his care, Kelly turned to Freud's ideas for guidance. According to Fransella and Neimeyer, although Kelly developed a respect for Freud's idea of "listening to the language of distress" (p. 23), he ultimately rejected the idea that offering correct therapist interpretations of client experiences was the key to change. Instead, he began to realize that it was what the clients did with his interpretations that really mattered, and "the only criterion for a useful therapist-offered conceptualization was that it should be relevant to the client's problem and carry novel implications for a possible solution" (Fransella & Neimeyer, p. 23).

The Psychology of Personal Constructs was Kelly's first attempt to synthesize and articulate his comprehensive theory. Although generally positively reviewed, his work was largely ignored in the United States, perhaps aggravated by his own ambivalence about promoting his work and his untimely death in 1967. His students, particularly Don Bannister and Fay Fransella in England, continued to promote and develop Kelly's work. Bannister published the first research using the repertory grid in the 1960s (Bell, 2003), examining the thought processes of people with schizophrenia. Subsequently, the repertory grid technique gained widespread use in England throughout the 1970s, with a scoring service provided by Patrick Slater at the Institute of Psychiatry. According to Bell (2003), Slater reported that by the mid-1970s, 10,000 grids were being processed each year, and, in the decade that followed, the repertory grid was seen as dominating published research in Personal Construct Theory (Neimeyer, 1985). Although grid research has subsequently declined, it is still seen as integral to Personal Construct Theory, research, and clinical practice.

The field of Personal Construct Psychology has developed in several related ways in recent times, particularly in the United States, England, and Australia. Although the work of Kelly still underpins all research and writing in the field, developments have occurred on several levels. Of particular interest to readers of this chapter, the repertory grid technique has developed enormously since Kelly's original hand-scored system. Numerous methods of construct elicitation and analysis have been developed (Bell, 2003; Denicolo, 2003; Fransella, 2003; Shaw &

Gaines, 1990) and are now all based on computer programs of varying levels of complexity. Kelly's method of therapy, commonly called *personal construct therapy*, has been comprehensively described and discussed (Fransella; Neimeyer & Neimeyer, 1987; Winter, 1992). Recently, attention has also been paid to locating Kelly's theory in a broader historical and theoretical context (Fransella; Neimeyer & Mahoney, 1995; Warren, 1998), which has helped increase public awareness of the theory, particularly in the United States.

Theoretical Premises

Kelly based his notion of constructs and construct systems on the philosophical assumption of *constructive alternativism* (Kelly, 1955). Constructive alternativism falls within the area of epistemology that is sometimes called *gnosiology*—the systematic analysis of the concepts employed by ordinary and scientific thought in exploring the world (Brown & Chiesa, 1990). As summarized by Adams-Webber (1977), "This principle asserts that reality does not directly reveal itself to us, but rather it is subject to as many alternative ways of construing it as we can invent" (p. 1). Kelly also assumed that "all of our present interpretations of the world are subject to revision or replacement" (Kelly, p. 7). Any theory is an invented abstraction from the observations of the perceived patterns of events that are formed through ongoing experiences. While providing structure and meaning to these experiences, they reflexively constrain thought and are therefore constantly subject to change.

Kelly (1969) used the term *man-the-scientist* to describe the proactive way in which each person predicts, interprets, and makes meaning of her or his experiences. Referring to people as *scientists*, Kelly states:

> A scientist's inventions assist him in two ways: they tell him what to expect and they help him to see it when it happens. Those that tell him what to expect are theoretical inventions and those that help him to observe outcomes are instrumental inventions. The two types are never wholly independent of each other, and they usually stem from the same assumptions. This is unavoidable. Moreover, without his inventions, both theoretical and instrumental, Man would be disoriented and blind. He would not know where to look, or how to see. (p. 94)

Thus for Kelly, the construct and the individual's construct system provide the structure from which to *know where to look and how to see.* These constructs, in turn, give meaning to experience and provide the framework from which to predict future experiences. Kelly therefore felt that each person was a scientist in the ways they were constantly constructing meaning based on their ongoing experiences.

In his writings, Kelly was clearly anticipating *constructivism*, and in recent years, Personal Construct Psychology has come to be seen as closely related to constructivist meta-theory (Mahoney, 1988a; Rosen & Kuehlwein, 1996). As defined by Mahoney, "psychological constructivism refers to a family of theories that share the assertion that knowledge and experience entail a (pro)active participation of the individual" (p. 2). There are three broad and overlapping themes central to constructivism: proactive cognition, morphogenic nuclear structure, and self-organizing development (Mahoney). Each of these will be briefly discussed in the following section.

The first basic feature central to constructivism is *proactive cognition*, a view that human knowing is active, anticipatory, and constructive. Within this context, *constructive* is defined as "form giving" (Mahoney, 1988b, p. 300) and focuses the knowledge-developing strategies of the individual on building cognitive structures based on ongoing experiences.

The second basic feature of constructivism is closely related to the first and, in fact, expands upon it. *Morphogenic structure* "refers to the assertion that human systems are organized such that (a) central, core, or nuclear processes dictate and constrain the contents and particulars of ongoing activity, and (b) core ordering processes operate at predominantly tacit (unconscious) levels and are less accessible and less amenable to change than the more peripheral activities" (Mahoney, 1988b, p. 300). In other words, one's momentary, everyday experiences are influenced more or less consciously by deeper structures that organize one's life. Likewise, one's ongoing experiences serve to deepen, challenge, and alter one's deeper structures. Human activity and, over time, psychological development thus reflects deep and powerful *self organizing processes*, the third basic feature of constructivism. Thus, everyday experiences not only serve to perpetuate and refine these deep structures but also appear to involve repeated episodes of "discrepancy-enhancement, disequilibrium, and organizational deterioration" (Mahoney, p. 300). In healthy individuals this leads to the redevelopment of core or deep structures, whereas in individuals who lack the ability to adjust deeper structures to their experiences, it may lead to a level of disequilibrium that can warrant therapeutic intervention and even the development of a clinical disorder.

Methodology

Methods of Construct Elicitation and Analysis

With Kelly's (1955) emphasis on the construct and his theoretical focus on the construct system as being integral to the individual and her or his functioning in the world, it is easy to understand that he began to develop various ways of explicating, mapping, analyzing, and interpreting construct systems. He did so for two interrelated reasons. The first was to understand the construct system that was operating in a particular situation (for example, to elicit constructs related to a person's marriage), and the second was to gain clarity into what was not working, based on the constructs that were developed by the client. It is important to note that Kelly would do this with his clients. In the 1950s, when Freudian principles and behaviorism were the two primary psychological modalities operating clinically, this was a major step away from the objectification of clients (Smith, 1995) and a significant shift toward the idea that clients could be actively involved in their own treatment.

Repertory Grid Technique

Kelly developed several methods of construct analysis, all of which were based on the repertory grid technique. The *repertory grid technique* is a structured interview designed to elicit constructs on a particular topic and is based on the Role Construct Repertory Test, also known as the Rep Test (Winter, 1992), developed earlier by Kelly (1955). In its original form, Kelly developed the Rep Test to understand significant relationships in the client's life (such as mother, father, partner, friend, someone disliked), and it was used to focus the early stages of therapy. After the development of the Rep Test, Kelly expanded the use of the repertory grid technique to include much broader experiences of clients, such as facets of the self, types of jobs, pictures, or virtually any object or experience in the person's world relevant to her or his therapy. Winter provided a thorough summary of the diverse ways in which Kelly's original method of grid elicitation and analysis has been adapted and developed for both clinical and research purposes.

A number of computer-generated programs have also been developed to expand upon Kelly's basic idea of construct elicitation. Sewell, Mitterer, Adams-Webber, and Cromwell (1991) provided a comprehensive summary of these programs. Music therapy research has incorporated one particular computer-based method for construct elicitation and development known as RepGrid (signifying *repertory grid*), based upon the work of Shaw and Gaines (1990). RepGrid is a menu-driven, interactive system that guides the user through the various stages of construct elicitation and development. It is easy to operate, yet allows for each person's construct system to be developed as fully as the person wishes. RepGrid is one component of the computer software suite called Rep IV (2004). In the overview that follows, only those aspects of RepGrid pertinent to its use in the music therapy literature will be described. For a complete description of RepGrid's features, as well as information on accessing and utilizing RepGrid, consult the Centre for Person-Computer Studies[1] or go to www.repgrid.com.

---

[1] Centre for Person-Computer Studies, 3635 Ocean View Crescent, Cobble Hill, BC V0R 1L1, Canada.

RepGrid Process

The RepGrid process is flexible and can be tailored according to specific purposes. Generally, however, the process involves these four interrelated stages: (a) establishing a domain of inquiry, (b) construct development, (c) data analysis, and (d) data interpretation.

Establishing a Domain of Inquiry. The entire RepGrid process is structured like an interview in which a user interacts directly with the RepGrid computer interface (via the screen, keyboard, and mouse), supplying certain information and making various comparisons among aspects of the information provided. The user can be anyone whose experiences and perceptions are being explicated through RepGrid; in research applications, the user is typically the research participant. The user may work by herself or himself or in conjunction with a therapist, researcher, or some other person helping to guide the process.

RepGrid begins by prompting the user for a domain to be explored. This domain may involve experiential events or processes (client's or therapist's experiences of therapy sessions, client's or therapist's experiences of music-making or music-listening, and so forth), persons (clients, therapists, family members, peers, and so forth), or objects (music, musical instruments, other media, and so forth). RepGrid then prompts the user to enter labels for at least six specific examples of events/processes, persons, or objects pertaining to the selected domain. Each of these is known as an *element*. For example, given a research study designed to explore a research participant's perceptions of improvisational sound portraits of different family members, elements would stand for individual, recorded improvisations and might be labeled *Self, Mother, Father, Sister, Brother*, and *Grandmother* (this would meet the minimum requirement of six elements; more could be utilized if necessary or preferred). Depending upon the nature and purpose of the inquiry, one or more elements may be pre-specified for the user (as *givens*). Thus, in the above example, if the researcher's primary interest centered around relationships among one's self, one's mother, and one's father, then the researcher could provide *Self, Mother*, and *Father* as common, core elements for all research participants.

Construct Development. Once a basic pool of elements has been identified, RepGrid prompts the user to differentiate among the elements according to various continua between pairs of contrasting characteristics, applicable in some way to each of the elements. These continua are known as *constructs*. To create a construct, the user identifies a pair of contrasting characteristics that distinguishes some of the elements from the others and enters a term or phrase for each of these characteristics as labels for the two poles of a continuum that forms the basis of the construct. In order to establish a continuum, the contrasting characteristics must relate to one another in such a way that gradations between them are possible. For example, given a grid exploring a user's perceptions of recorded, improvisational sound portraits of different family members, the user may feel that some of the improvisations are simple, that some are complex, and that some are moderately simple or complex. The user could therefore identify the construct *simple* ←→ *complex* by entering the terms *simple* and *complex* as opposing ends of a construct row in the two-column construct spreadsheet. In this particular case, for the most active and thorough comparison process the user may opt to listen to various recordings of the improvisations in the midst of construct development.

To help facilitate the process of identifying constructs, the user can select a randomized elicitation option. In this option, three elements at a time are randomly selected from the overall pool of elements and are presented on the computer screen (see Figure 1). Upon considering each triad of elements, the user identifies some way in which two of the three are similar to one another and different from the third. The user then enters a term or phrase expressing the characteristic that is the basis of the similarity, as well as a term or phrase expressing the contrasting characteristic that is the basis for the corresponding difference. For example, given a random triad of element labels for improvisations of *Self, Sister*, and *Brother*, the user may feel that the *Sister* and *Brother* improvisations sound quiet whereas the *Self* improvisation sounds loud, thereby establishing the construct, *quiet* ←→ *loud* (see Figure 2).

Research Participant is considering "Family Member Improvisations"

Elicit construct from a triad

Can you choose two of this triad of elements which are in some way alike and different from the other one?

Self
Sister
Brother

Click in the element which is different, or here if you cannot do this.

Figure 1. A Random Triad of Elements, From Which the User Will Identify a Construct

---

Research Participant is considering "Family Member Improvisations"

Name the poles of your construct

Now I want you to think what you have in mind when you separate the pair from the other one. Just type one or two words for each pole to remind you what you are thinking or feeling when you use this construct.

Left pole rated 1 {Sister, Brother}: Quiet
Right pole rated 9 {Self}: Loud

Figure 2. Naming the Poles of the Newly-Elicited Construct

As in the case of elements, depending upon the nature and purpose of the inquiry one or more constructs may be pre-specified. After a construct has been identified, the user rates each of the elements from the overall pool according to how strongly or clearly each possesses one of the construct's polar characteristics over the other. The rating is based upon a numerical scale range specified by the user at the outset of the RepGrid session, according to the desired level of precision. For example, given the user has selected a rating scale of 1 to 9, once the *quiet* ←→ *loud* construct has been established, the user would have the opportunity to rate each improvisation on a scale from simple (1) to complex (9), including the option of any gradation in between the polar extremes (2–8; see Figure 3). Note that when a construct has been elicited by a random triad, RepGrid pre-rates the elements from that triad at the polar extremes by default— thus, *Brother* and *Sister* are both rated at 1 for *quiet* and *Self* is rated at 9 for *loud*; however, the user has the option to edit any of these values for greater specificity (see Figure 4). In Figure 4, the featured construct is indicated in the upper right of the chart diagram. Each row of the chart represents an element, with its number in the left column, its name in the middle column, and its polarity rating on the featured construct in the right column. Here, the user changes the polarity rating of the element Sister along the *quiet* ←→ *loud* construct from 1 (its default value as most quiet) to 2 (the user's sense of the improvisation being slightly less quiet than originally assigned) by clicking in the box containing this rating value and simply entering a new rating.

Research Participant is considering "Family Member Improvisations"

Name the poles of your construct

Now I want you to think what you have in mind when you separate the pair from the other one. Just type one or two words for each pole to remind you what you are thinking or feeling when you use this construct.

Left pole rated 1 {Sister, Brother}: Quiet
Right Pole rated 9 {Self}: Loud

According to how you feel about them, please assign to each of the other elements in turn a provisional value from 1 to 9 (by entering a number or clicking to use a popup menu)

Brother: 1
Sister: 1
Self: 9
Mother: 8
Father: 7
Grandmother: 4

Figure 3. Rating Each Element Along the Newly Elicited *Quiet* ←→ *Loud* Construct

Elements		Construct: Quiet ←→ Loud
#	Name	1 to 9
1	Self	9
2	Mother	8
3	Father	7
4	Sister	2
5	Brother	1
6	Grandmother	4

Figure 4. Editing the *Quiet* ←→ *Loud* Construct

The orientation of scale values in relation to particular polar attributes is arbitrary; thus, the actual scale values serve as reference points only and are not intrinsically related to the meaning of the polar attributes. For example, it is arbitrary in the *quiet* ←→ *loud* construct that quiet is represented by a 1, the low numerical polarity; the construct would be equally meaningful if the user had initially entered the characteristics in reverse polarity, since the ratings of the elements along that construct would be identical relative to the position of the characteristics. Moreover, because the scale range is the same for all constructs within a given RepGrid session, a common reference system is created in which each construct's element rating profile represents the construct's individual character as well as its relationship to all other constructs. Elicitation of constructs continues until the desired number or diversity of constructs has been reached.

As rating profiles of each construct are generated, corresponding profiles of each element are simultaneously created, based upon their ratings along constructs. This cross-reference of profiles represents a matrix known as a *repertory grid*, from which the term RepGrid was derived. The user can display this matrix as a rectangular table made up of cells. Each cell contains the rating of a particular element, identified by column, along a particular construct, identified by row. Lesser versus greater cell values indicate element polarities toward attributes on the left versus the right end of construct rows, respectively. For an illustration of a repertory grid, refer to Figure 5.

The diagram in Figure 5 is a graphic representation of elements and constructs in a grid matrix. The elements in this case are improvisational sound portraits of six members of the user's family. Each numerical value within the box represents the polarity of a particular improvisation, identified by column, along a particular construct, identified by row. Extending from each column at the bottom of the box are the names of the improvisations, while on either side of each row are the polar attributes of corresponding constructs. Within the box, lesser versus greater values indicate improvisation polarities toward attributes on the left versus the right end of construct rows, respectively. In this case, the scale range is 1–9; a 1 indicates extreme left polarity whereas a 9 indicates extreme right polarity—thus, along the *quiet ←→ loud* construct, the *Brother* improvisation is quietest whereas *Self* is loudest.

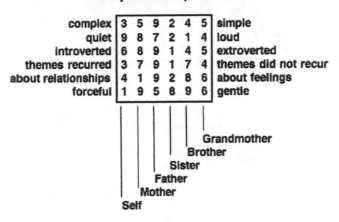

Display Research Participant (Example Grid)
"Family Member Improvisations"

Figure 5. A Repertory Grid

Data Analysis. The completed user's grid is raw data; that is, the grid represents a table of individual values prior to any analysis of those values according to their interrelationships. To analyze these grid data, the user can invoke one or more algorithmic tools built into RepGrid, each designed to perform mathematical computations resulting in a structural expression of the grid as a single, composite whole known as a *construction*. The user's construction represents her or his way of viewing the phenomenon under investigation in its entirety, involving all of its various parts in relationship to one another simultaneously. RepGrid provides the user with the option of partial grid analysis, in which certain constructs or elements are held in abeyance in order to explore the nature of constructions with and without selected parts.

One of RepGrid's analytical tools designed to produce a representation of the user's construction is the *Focus* algorithm. Focus calculates the percentage to which each construct's profile (that is, each row of grid values) matches the profiles of each of the other constructs (and likewise for the profiles of the elements). Results of Focus can be displayed as a diagram of the user's repertory grid, reorganized so that constructs are positioned according to how closely they match one another (and likewise with elements). In the diagram, the relative way that constructs and elements cluster together by virtue of their similarities reflects the nature of the user's overall construction. For an example of a Focus results diagram, refer to Figure 6.

The diagram in Figure 6 illustrates elements and constructs juxtaposed according to relative similarity by the Focus algorithm. The order of improvisations (elements) and constructs is reorganized from the original grid orientation so that degree of adjacency corresponds with degree of numerical similarity. For example, the construct rows *complex ←→ simple* and *introverted ←→ extroverted*, which match at around 85%, are placed directly next to one another; in addition, their poles are reversed to accommodate an optimal matching scheme—thus, *forceful ←→ gentle* has become *gentle ←→ forceful*. Tree diagrams above the improvisation labels and to the right of the construct labels indicate the relative levels of matching according to the location of each branch point with respect to the percentile scale along each diagram. Note that the lines extending from *complex ←→ simple* and *introverted ←→ extroverted* converge into a common branch at around the 85 mark under the scale.

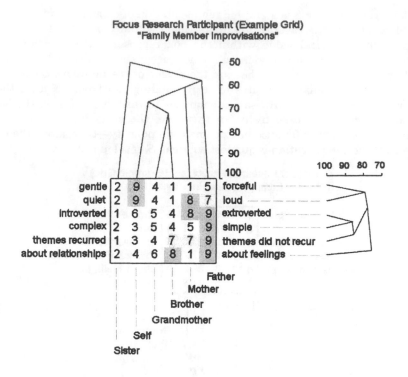

Figure 6. Results of a Grid Processed by the Focus Algorithm

Another analytical tool is the PrinGrid (or *principal components*) algorithm, closely related to a multiple-factor ANOVA. PrinGrid identifies ways in which all of the user's constructs can be combined into larger groups of constructs known as *components*. Each component carries a certain degree of overall importance with respect to the nature of the user's construction. The first component always carries the most importance, the second component the next most importance, and so on. The specific distribution of importance varies, but typically the first and second components are adequate for a basic understanding of the user's construction. Each component consists of a particular set of relative weights, or *loadings*, for every construct, indicating how centrally that construct defines the component's character.

PrinGrid results are displayed as a diagram in which constructs are represented as straight lines (labeled at each end with the construct's polar attributes) passing directly through the center of the diagram space, collectively forming a starburst pattern. Components are represented by the axes of the diagram, so that the first component involves the distinction between all construct poles on the left side versus those on the right side of the diagram, and the second component involves the distinction between all construct poles on the top versus those on the bottom of the diagram. Each component axis is labeled with the specific percentage of mathematical variance for which the component accounts, with respect to all grid values. The degree to which a construct is loaded on a component is expressed by its degree of alignment with the axis representing that component; likewise, the alignment between constructs indicates their relative similarity to one another. Unlike in the Focus diagram, however, the PrinGrid diagram does not represent individual similarities between constructs, but rather the relative interrelationships among all constructs simultaneously—in other words, with respect to the construction as a singular whole. Because components beyond the second cannot be represented as axes in the two-dimensional diagram, construct line lengths are shortened to the extent that they are loaded on components beyond the second. Thus, similarity in line lengths is another indicator of similarities among constructs. Moreover, because each construct line passes through the diagram center at a point representing that construct's mean element ratings values, off-center line placement indicates asymmetrical ratings relative to that construct's two poles (such as ratings that favor one end over the other). Elements, too, are represented in the diagram as labeled points positioned according to their polarity ratings on all constructs. For an illustration of this diagram, refer to Figure 7.

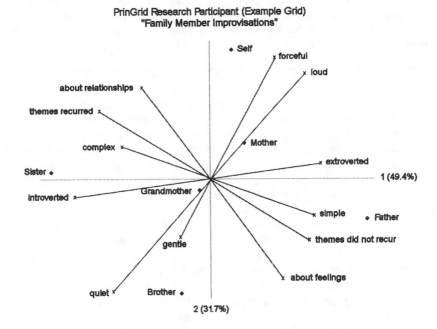

PrinGrid Research Participant (Example Grid)
"Family Member Improvisations"

Figure 7. Results of a Grid Processed by the PrinGrid Algorithm

The diagram in Figure 7 illustrates elements and constructs organized according to their composite interrelationships by the PrinGrid algorithm. Note that, although the constructs *complex ←→ simple* and *introverted ←→ extroverted* are among the most closely matched on an individual basis (as revealed through the Focus algorithm), their construct lines in the PrinGrid diagram are not the two that are most closely aligned. This implies that the meaning of any construct is suggested by its interrelationship with all others within the scheme of the larger construction as a whole. Lines with relatively short lengths such as *complex ←→ simple* and *forceful ←→ gentle* indicate pronounced loadings on components beyond the second, and thus appear as vanishing lines, rotating into unseen dimensions. Also note that the *forceful ←→ gentle* construct line is markedly off-center, indicating a low mean value of element ratings along that construct and thus dramatically heavier ratings toward the *gentle* polarity of the construct. Finally, note that in the overall construction, the improvisations of *Grandmother* and *Mother* are most closely related, carrying implications about the perceived relatedness of these two family members for the user (depending upon the theoretical basis for the analysis).

In addition, RepGrid allows the user to perform comparisons among grids when there are common constructs, common elements, or both, across those grids. This comparison feature utilizes the same basic algorithmic procedure as Focus. When only constructs or only elements are common across grids, the output is a list of paired constructs or elements with percentage matching indicated, as well as an indication of the total portion of construct pairs that fall at or above the threshold of each pair's match level. When both elements and constructs are common to two grids, the output can also include a graphic consensus diagram. This resembles the Focus diagram but with numerical values within the cells representing the numerical profile differences on the same item, between grids. To the side of this matrix are vertical line plots indicating percentage agreement across grids as well as match threshold indicators. The comparison feature can be useful because its results can be understood as the similarities and differences in meaning across multiple constructions (of one or more persons). Revealing these shared meanings can help to bring to light some of the more profound or subtle dimensions of a study phenomenon, which hold significance on a collective (or aggregate) level but which might otherwise appear incidental or inconsequential on an individual basis.

Data Interpretation. Representations of the user's construction generated by RepGrid's analytical tools do not carry any specific, intrinsic meanings. Thus, the user's construction must be interpreted in a manner consistent with the particular purposes and theoretical orientations underlying the given application of RepGrid. In research applications, the researcher typically performs the interpretation, although research participants or peers may also play a role in the interpretation process. In classifying approaches to interpretation in research applications, a core distinction can be made between quantitative and qualitative approaches.

Quantitative approaches are utilized when research questions involve measuring specific degrees of significance or verifying hypotheses concerning the study phenomenon (for example, Meadows, 2002). In these cases, the numerical results of analysis are treated as direct representations of the user's construction and are compared against threshold values that determine significance or support for hypothesis verification. A research hypothesis could be supported by substantial clustering among constructs revealed through the Focus algorithm or substantial loading values on principal components across a significant number of participants. The study's particular sample size, design, and so forth would determine threshold values for statistical significance as well as whether descriptive or inferential statistical computations would be appropriate.

Qualitative approaches, by contrast, are utilized when research questions entail the exploration of a study phenomenon without measurement or verification based upon precise numerical values and mathematical relationships (B. Abrams, 2002). In these cases, the visual/spatial expressions of the user's construction (that is, the graphic output of RepGrid's algorithmic tools) would serve as the core material for interpretation. Specifically, the researcher could extract possible meanings based upon the prominent clusters of constructs depicted in the graphic expression of the Focus algorithm as well as the major groupings of construct lines around the axes of the graphic PrinGrid diagram. For example, on the PrinGrid diagram, groupings of spatially aligned construct lines can be interpreted as *meta-components,* or composite structures of meaning accounting for the overall character of the user's entire construction across all of its various dimensions (B. Abrams). In qualitative studies, the researcher would seek both similarities and variations in constructions across participants, as even aspects unique to one participant would be treated with equal weight in developing an understanding of the phenomenon.

Relationship to Other Research Methods

The repertory grid technique was developed in an era when psychologically oriented research was overwhelmingly quantitative and where qualitative methods of data collection and analysis were in their infancy. As discussed by Fransella (1995), Kelly was consciously trying to distinguish his theory and research method from the prevailing theories and methods of the time (the 1940s and 1950s). Therefore, first and foremost the repertory grid technique must been seen as historically distinct. As previously discussed in this chapter, the repertory grid technique is based upon Kelly's theory of constructive alternativism and, while the technicalities of his data collection and analysis tool have changed (for example, through the use of computers to gather and analyze data), there have been no attempts to replace the underlying principles of RepGrid with any other theoretical orientation. In an era when objectivism was prominent in research, particularly because of the emphasis on behaviorism, Kelly sought a far more subjective approach to data collection, relying on the client her- or himself to create the construct system for the phenomenon under investigation. He was also instrumental in shifting the emphasis in what was meaningful in any experience back to the client her- or himself by asking the client and listening to the responses. Thus, Kelly employed interview techniques than are more commonly seen as qualitative long before qualitative research was in mainstream awareness. Furthermore, with its emphasis on the experiences of clients and the meaning given to experience, the repertory grid technique appears to share many characteristics with phenomenology (Fransella). It is therefore somewhat surprising that Kelly sought to distance his theory from the early phenomenological movement (Butt, 2003), because he interpreted phenomenology as far too subjective. It has only been recently that reviewers of Kelly's life and work interpret this as a misunderstanding on Kelly's part of the nature of phenomenology (Fransella) and are realigning personal construct psychology with phenomenology, particularly with the work of Merleau-Ponty (Butt).

While the repertory grid technique can been seen as historically distinct, it shares characteristics with both quantitative and qualitative methods that are commonly used in current research. Perhaps the most obvious commonality that the repertory grid technique shares with quantitative research is the ability to analyze grid data using descriptive and inferential statistics. For example, RepGrid has the capacity for correlational and principal components analyses so that any grid can be understood in terms of direct, numerical relationships among constructs. And even when the researcher does not use these types of analyses, any data analysis is limited by the ways in which the research participant has rated and related the constructs under investigation.

However, the extent to which the resulting data are used quantitatively varies considerably. Some researchers choose to use statistical analyses as the only form of data analysis (Bannister's [1960] grid intensity score), whereas others have used the data in a more post-positivistic sense (Meadows, 2002) and even qualitatively (B. Abrams, 2002). Thus, although any data analysis is framed within the grid developed by the research participant, there are multiple ways of analyzing the actual relationships among constructs and elements.

It is not surprising that renewed attention has been paid to the relationship of RepGrid to qualitative methods of data analysis, particularly phenomenology (Butt, 2003). Butt argues that Personal Construct Psychology and phenomenology share many similarities philosophically, and that the repertory grid technique can be seen as a kind of "phenomenological seeing" (p.384). While there is not agreement among personal construct psychologists as to the extent to which personal construct psychology is a member of the phenomenological family as suggested by Butt (p. 386) and a distinct theory and methodology (Warren, 1998), there are no doubt many philosophical similarities. Differences appear in research method. Whereas phenomenology is based primarily in verbal interview, the repertory grid technique is a systematized, computer-driven interview that generates distinct data based on constructs. In this way, there is an inherent relational hierarchy in the RepGrid interview that is not provided in a phenomenological interview. Furthermore, while phenomenological data analyses are based on verbal transcripts of interviews (see Chapter 26, Phenomenological Inquiry, in this book), RepGrid is based on the relationships among constructs and elements that are determined by the research participant.

While little has been said about the relationship of personal construct psychology to other qualitative methods of data analysis, the repertory grid technique appears to be a method of data collection that could be used for first-person research (see Chapter 30 in this book), where such research is defined as "any method in which researchers and/or participants gather data for themselves, using processes such as introspection, retrospection, self-perception. . . and so forth" (Bruscia, 2005, p. 379). Aldridge (1996) outlined several examples of first-person research using RepGrid in which music therapists examined their perceptions of clients and musical materials for the purpose of deepening self-awareness and understanding. While Bruscia outlines numerous methods of first-person research in Chapter 30, RepGrid again stands alone in the unique ways in which data can be collected and analyzed.

Thus, RepGrid holds a unique place amongst research methods because of the precise ways in which data can be collected and because subsequent analyses of this data can be conducted quantitatively or qualitatively.

Applications in Music Therapy

Personal construct inquiry has been widely utilized in various research applications within the psychology literature. However, only five applications specifically within music therapy can be found (B. Abrams, 2002; J. Abrams, 1999; Aldridge, 1996; Aldridge & Aldridge, 1996; Meadows, 2002). In each of these cases, personal construct inquiry was conducted using RepGrid software[2] to explicate various experiences and perceptions of clients, therapists, or both.

Aldridge (1996) utilized RepGrid in four individual cases to compare constructions involving music therapy clinical work and music therapy supervision. The first two cases

---

[2] The researchers utilized a previous version of RepGrid, *RepGrid 2.1b* (1993), a stand-alone computer program, not part of a suite as in *Rep IV;* however, the older and newer systems utilize the same principles and procedures and differ only in terms of several minor operating features.

involved a music therapist's perceptions of child clients and a music therapist's perceptions of adult clients. The second two cases involved a music therapy student's perceptions of music instruments and a music therapy supervisor's perceptions of those same musical instruments. In this latter pair of cases, both elements (musical instruments) and constructs (qualities of instruments) were the same for the two different participants (the supervisor was presented with the set of constructs identified by the student, who participated in the study first). Utilizing the Focus algorithm, the researcher identified major groupings of elements and constructs in *cluster* diagrams, which revealed various participant experiences of different clients as well as variations in experiences between student and supervisor of the same instruments (in these cases, carrying implications for how music therapy students and supervisors construe musical meaning according to personal and cultural differences).

Aldridge and Aldridge (1996) utilized RepGrid to examine one music therapist's perceptions of her clients who had participated in music improvisation in therapy, as well as the ways in which a music therapist constructed melody in a number of recorded classical compositions and, in turn, how these two types of perceptions related to one another. In this study, the research participant was also one of the researchers. Recorded music excerpts, pre-selected by the researchers, were presented at the time of the RepGrid comparisons. The participant explicated her construction of melody on two separate occasions separated by a year (using the same elements and constructs) to examine the stability of her construction over an extended period of time (most constructs maintained similar meanings, although several did shift). Categories of the participant's perceptions of clients and music were based upon major groupings in Focus cluster diagrams and revealed that the participant's construction of clients with whom she had worked included a number of categories meaningfully linked to the participant's constructions of melody. For example, constructions of both melody and clients included constructs with the basic properties of *openness* versus *being closed* and *intimacy* versus *distance*, although not all constructs with similar meanings had precisely the same labels.

J. Abrams (1999) utilized RepGrid to investigate relationships between two different music therapists' experiences of one pre-selected set of recorded musical compositions, presented at the time of RepGrid comparison. One of the two research participants was the researcher herself. Comparison between the two participants' Focus diagrams revealed that they construed recorded music excerpts similarly to one another; however, principal components diagrams revealed that one participant organized experiences of the music primarily according to sensory-emotional qualities, whereas the other utilized primarily musical and emotional qualities. In addition, a comparison between the two participants' grids revealed that the two participants identified several constructs that appeared to have similar meanings across their two grids in spite of apparently unrelated verbal labels. Because both participants in this study were music therapists, these findings carry potentially significant implications about how music therapists experience music in similar and different ways, as well as how one might go about exploring these similarities and differences through personal construct inquiry.

Meadows (2002) utilized RepGrid to examine Bonny Method of Guided Imagery and Music (BMGIM) guides' perceptions of gender qualities in their male and female BMGIM clients and how these perceptions are implicated in BMGIM therapy. Meadows had participants make comparisons among both male and female BMGIM clients, yielding a set of distinct constructs for each participant. All participants, however, were provided the given constructs *most male-like qualities* ←→ *no male-like qualities* and *most female-like qualities* ←→ *no female-like qualities*. These were given in order to explore the question of how gender is constructed by BMGIM therapists, independent of the actual sex of each client. Pearson r correlation and principal components values revealed that each participant did perceive their BMGIM clients according to gender constructs (that is, what it meant for clients to be male-like or female-like). Across all participant constructions, male-like and female-like qualities were generally construed as two very different constructs, yet these qualities were not necessarily related to the sex of the clients. Through further examination of participant data, the researcher also discovered that male-like qualities were generally seen as less conducive to effective therapy, whereas female-like qualities were seen as more conducive. These findings carry implications for how therapists in BMGIM and other music therapy methods do and do not construe their clients and the effectiveness of their work according to client gender qualities.

In contrast to explicating therapists' experiences of their clients, B. Abrams (2002) utilized RepGrid to explicate defining elements of clients' transpersonal experiences of BMGIM.

The study participants were experienced BMGIM guides exploring their own BMGIM experiences as clients. Participants made comparisons among their own BMGIM experiences (as clients) that included both those that participants considered transpersonal and those that they did not consider transpersonal. In addition to unique sets of constructs derived through this comparison, each participant was provided with the given construct *transpersonal* ←→ *not transpersonal*. The given construct allowed participants to qualify each of their BMGIM experiences in terms of the *transpersonal* ←→ *not transpersonal* distinction based solely upon their implicit sense of these qualities, without having to articulate the very defining qualities that the study itself was designed to illuminate. The relative position of the *transpersonal* ←→ *not transpersonal* construct among the meta-components (major groupings) displayed on the principal components diagram revealed a variety of individual definitions of transpersonal BMGIM experience. The researcher then identified some of the common themes across all of these individual variations (for example, body/physicality, self, music) that participants used as core bases for differentiating BMGIM experiences that were and were not transpersonal. Each of these themes carries implications for the meaning of transpersonal BMGIM experiences, their clinical value, and approaches to identifying them when they occur.

Summary

The repertory grid technique, specifically *Rep IV,* allows the researcher to explore the inner experiences and perceptions of a research participant using a structured, computer-driven interview. These inner experiences are characterized as opposites, commonly called constructs (Kelly, 1955). When completed, the interview technique allows for all the constructs created by the research participant to be compared and contrasted using either qualitative or quantitative methods of data analysis. The repertory grid technique was originally developed by George Kelly, a clinical psychologist. He developed a theory of personality, approach to therapy, and basic notion of how human experience is constructed, of which the repertory grid technique is an integral part. While only used in limited ways in music therapy research, *Rep IV* and programs like it show great potential in deepening our understanding of the inner experiences of both therapists and clients.

References

Abrams, B. (2002). Definitions of transpersonal BMGIM experience. *Nordic Journal of Music Therapy, 11,* 103–126.

Abrams, J. (1999). *An exploration of the RepGrid in revealing how music therapists experience music.* Unpublished manuscript, Temple University, Philadelphia.

Adams-Webber, J. R. (1977). *Personal construct theory: Concepts and applications.* London: John Wiley and Sons.

Aldridge, D. (1996). *Music therapy research and practice in medicine: From out of the silence.* Bristol, PA: Jessica Kingsley Publishers.

Aldridge, D., & Aldridge, G. (1996). A personal construct methodology for validating subjectivity in qualitative research. *The Arts in Psychotherapy, 23,* 225–236.

Bannister, D. (1960). Conceptual structure in thought-disordered schizophrenics. *Journal of Mental Science, 106,* 1230–1249.

Bell, R. C. (2003). The repertory grid technique. In F. Fransella (Ed.), *International handbook of Personal Construct Psychology* (pp. 95–104). London: John Wiley and Sons.

Brown, R., & Chiesa, M. (1990). George Kelly and repertory grids in psychotherapy. *British Journal of Psychotherapy, 6,* 411–419.

Bruscia, K. E. (1995). Modes of consciousness in Guided Imagery and Music (GIM): A therapist's experience of guiding. In C. B. Kenny (Ed.), *Listening, playing, creating: Essays in the power of sound* (pp. 165–198). Albany, NY: State University of New York Press.

Bruscia, K. E. (2005). First-person research. In B. L. Wheeler (Ed.), *Music therapy research* (2nd ed., pp. 379–391). Gilsum, NH: Barcelona Publishers.

Butt, T. (2003). The phenomenological context of Personal Construct Psychology. In F. Fransella (Ed.), *International handbook of Personal Construct Psychology* (pp. 379–386). London: John Wiley and Sons.

Denicolo, P. (2003). Elicitation methods to fit different purposes. In F. Fransella (Ed.), *International handbook of Personal Construct Psychology* (pp. 379–386). London: John Wiley and Sons.

Fransella, F. (1995). *George Kelly*. London: Sage Publications.

Fransella, F. (Ed.). (2003). *International handbook of Personal Construct Psychology*. London: John Wiley and Sons.

Fransella, F., & Neimeyer, R. A. (2003). George Alexander Kelly: The man and his theory. In F. Fransella (Ed.). *International handbook of Personal Construct Psychology* (pp. 21–32). London: John Wiley and Sons.

Hibben, J. (1999). *Inside music therapy: Client experiences*. Gilsum, NH. Barcelona Publishers.

Kelly, G. A. (1955). *The psychology of personal constructs*. New York: W. W. Norton.

Kelly, G.A. (1969). Ontological acceleration. In B. Maher (Ed.), *Clinical psychology and personality* (pp. 7–45). San Diego, CA: Academic Press.

Mahoney, M. J. (1988a). Constructive metatheory: I. Basic features and historical foundations. *International Journal of Personal Construct Psychology, 1,* 1–35.

Mahoney, M. J. (1988b). Constructive metatheory. II. Implications for psychotherapy. *International Journal of Personal Construct Psychology, 1,* 299–315.

Meadows, A. (2002). Gender implications in therapists' constructs of their clients. *Nordic Journal of Music Therapy, 11,* 127–141.

Neimeyer, R. A. (1985). *The development of Personal Construct Psychology*. Lincoln: University of Nebraska Press.

Neimeyer, R. A., & Mahoney, M. J. (Eds.). (1995). *Constructivism in psychotherapy*. Washington, DC: American Psychological Association.

Neimeyer, R. A., & Neimeyer, M. J. (1987). *Personal construct therapy casebook*. New York: Springer.

Rep IV [Computer software]. (2004). Cobble Hill, British Columbia, Canada: Centre for Person-Computer Studies.

RepGrid 2.1b [Computer software]. (1993). Calgary, Canada: Centre for Person-Computer Studies.

Rosen, H., & Kuehlwein, K. T. (Eds.). (1996). *Constructing realities: Meaning-making perspectives for psychotherapists*. San Francisco, CA: Jossey-Bass Publishers.

Sewell, K. W., Mitterer, J., Adams-Webber, J, & Cromwell, R. L. (1991). Omnigrid-PC: A new development in computerized repertory grids. *International Journal of Personal Construct Psychology, 4,* 175–192.

Shaw, M. L. G., & Gaines, B. L. (1990). *RepGrid manual: Version 2*. Calgary, Canada: Centre for Person-Computer Studies.

Smith, J. A. (1995). Repertory grids: An interactive, case-study perspective. In J. A. Smith, R. Harre, & L. van Langenhove (Eds.), *Rethinking methods in psychology* (pp. 162–177). London: Sage Publications.

Taylor, D. S. (1990). Making the most of your matrices: Hermeneutics, statistics, and the repertory grid. *International Journal of Personal Construct Psychology, 3,* 105–119.

Warren, B. (1998). *Philosophical dimensions of Personal Construct Psychology*. London: Routledge.

Wheeler, B. L. (1999). Experiencing pleasure in working with severely disabled children. *Journal of Music Therapy, 36,* 56–80.

Winter, D. A. (1992). *Personal Construct Psychology: Theory, research and clinical practice*. London: Routledge.

Part V

Types of Other Research:

Researching Music
Philosophical Inquiry
Developing Theory
Historical Research

Chapter 38
Approaches to Researching Music
Lars Ole Bonde

Music research is defined here as any method within music therapy in which researchers gather data concerning the relationship between music—improvised or composed, recorded or performed live—and client experiences and behavior. The focus may be on *material properties* of music (stimulus or effect); on *intentional properties* of music (description, analysis, and interpretation of meaning); or on *musical processes* (interactions and relationships). This chapter examines these perspectives, including their theoretical premises and methodologies. The chapter includes a presentation of how quantitative researchers operationalize music, that is, how they transform a target musical parameter, behavior, or preference into a specific and well-defined observable and measurable unit or variable, and how they measure music, for example, as independent and dependent variables in experimental or behavioral research. The chapter also presents ways that qualitative researchers have chosen to describe, analyze, and interpret music and music experiences in various ways.[1]

When and why is it relevant for music therapists and music therapy researchers to focus on analyzing the musical material, the meaning of music, or musical processes in music therapy? This simple but important question must be answered before a decision is made on how to focus the music research. Surprisingly few research studies in music therapy include in-depth investigations of the music itself or the musical interactions or processes between therapist and clients. Transcriptions of music (whether exact transcriptions and scores or other types of notation, such as graphic) do not appear very often in the literature. This is largely due to the questions and interests of the researcher. If the research focuses on effects of a specific music or sound stimulus or on aspects of the therapeutic relationship, it may not be relevant to give more than factual or broad descriptions of the music involved. The stance of the present author, however, is that the validity of a music therapy research study will always be enhanced by precise information on what music was used how, when, by whom, and in what context.

Researching the music is a different endeavor for a music therapist than for a musicologist. The traditional musicological dichotomy of autonomy and referentialism (or heteronomy)[2] is not very relevant for a music therapist or researcher, for whom it does not make much sense to consider music as a purely autonomous, aesthetic phenomenon, even if the music may have what one considers to be excellent aesthetic qualities. It makes more sense in music therapy to focus on musical experience as based on different aspects or properties of music. Researching the music (whether as a material or intentional phenomenon, or as a psychological or cultural process) should thus be based on a broad concept of music and music experience in order to cover the different properties (Bruscia, 1998; Ruud, 1990; Wigram, Pedersen, & Bonde, 2002).

A well-known model suggests that music may influence the human body, the human mind, and the human spirit. Adding the social and cultural context of the human being, we may talk about the music as a phenomenon influencing four levels or aspects of human existence. Correspondingly, Ruud (1990, 1998, 2001) has proposed a definition of music addressing four main properties or encompassing four levels of experience:[3]

Music as a sound phenomenon: The physiological and biomedical level, corresponding to music as a material, physical sound phenomenon with measurable, describable, and observable properties.

Music as a structural phenomenon: The level of music as nonreferential meaning, that is, a language with specific musico-linguistic and aesthetic rules and principles,

---

[1] The history of music research in music therapy, such as psychoanalytic explorations in music in the 20th century, falls outside the framework of the chapter.

[2] The core problem of music aesthetics is whether music expresses or is expressive of something other than the musical sounds and events themselves. Absolutists answer no; referentialists, yes. The question of the meaning of music in music therapy is discussed by Ruud (1998, Chapter 5) and Pavlicevic (1997).

[3] This model has many similarities with the model suggested by Sloboda (1985, Chapter 2, Music, Language and Meaning) who identifies three levels or properties: music as phonology, syntax, and semantics.

corresponding to music as structure or interplay of specific musical elements and parameters.

Music as a semantic phenomenon: The level of music as referential meaning and cultural marker, as metaphor, symbol, icon or index in a person's experience and in a culture, corresponding to music as a means of cultural and individual, culturally framed expression and meaning.

Music as a pragmatic phenomenon: The level of interpersonal communication and interaction, corresponding to music as a specific form of social and cultural interaction or practice (what Small [1998] calls *contextualized musicking*).

Researching the music in music therapy means addressing one or more of these levels and properties, with each posing different epistemological and methodological problems. Research on music may be conducted within any of several different paradigms, including positivist, postpositivist, and nonpositivist or constructivist. It is likely that a researcher with a positivist perspective will focus on sound and structure, whereas a researcher with a constructivist perspective will focus on semantics and pragmatics. Researching music within any of these traditions may involve observing, analyzing, evaluating, and interpreting human behavior and may study how music therapy functions as a treatment. All research demands rigor and all approaches have rules and methods that need to be understood and used appropriately. However, research within the positivist and postpositivist traditions is more likely to investigate the influence of music on external behavior, while research within the constructivist tradition often addresses internal phenomena like meaning and understanding of musical experiences. When determining the methodology that is most appropriate, it will be most helpful "to establish the focus of the research question first, before deciding on an appropriate research method" (Wigram, Pedersen, & Bonde, 2002, p. 225).

Music research within the positivist-postpositivist paradigm is often closely connected to research questions about the measurable outcomes of music therapy (questions of who, what, why, how much, how often, how many) and seeks results that may be generalized, while research within a constructivist paradigm is often connected with nonmeasurable but describable process questions (how, when, under what circumstances) and seeks specific or local results. But, of course, a constructivist researcher can be interested in outcome and a positivist or postpositivist researcher in process. Extending these paradigmatic concerns to quantitative and qualitative research methodologies means that a researcher, independent of paradigm, may choose to investigate some research questions using quantitative methods while addressing other research questions with qualitative methods.

In most quantitative music research, *music* is understood and defined as either a stimulus or a response—as independent or dependent variables operationalized for the specific study. In principle, it is possible to operationalize any element or parameter (or changes in the element) of music for observation or measurement: dynamics (loudness), tempo, melody, rhythm and meter, harmony and timbre (wave form), and texture. Many elements of music performance or behavior can also be categorized for observational purposes.

Nonmusical Responses

This section gives a brief presentation and discussion of research on nonmusical responses to musical stimuli, such as effects of music on different types of nonmusical behavior, on imagery, on immune system responses, on affective and aesthetic responses, and on mood and emotional responses. The study of nonmusical responses is not the focus of this chapter, as it is covered well in the music psychology literature (Hodges, 1996; Juslin & Sloboda, 2001; Thaut, 2002a). However, the problems connected with identifying discrete or complex responses to music are also relevant in music therapy research.

Nonmusical responses of interest to the researcher may include psychophysiological and emotional responses that are based on the operationalization of defined musical stimuli (independent variables) and measurement of their effect on a specific population (dependent variables). Experimental and behavioral designs can be applied: single case designs, multiple case designs, clinical effect, and pre-post designs are all common. Other studies in this area are descriptive research, intended to describe the area or response.

Gregory (2002) analyzed behavioral research designs (such as reversal, changing criterion, or multiple baseline designs) reported in 96 of 607 articles (15.8%) published in the

Journal of Music Therapy from 1964–1999. She found the use of music as an independent variable to include the following categories: music as background, music as stimulus, music activity, contingency, structure (reward), group contingency, cue, reinforcement, and lullabies. She found behavioral responses to include mostly nonmusical responses such as verbal interaction or response, tactile threshold, preference, pegboard task, cooperation, attention to therapist, participation, discrimination, imitation, compliance, memory, self-stimulation, head posture, movement, eye contact, gross motor, relaxation, agitation, participation, and so forth.

The challenge for the researcher is to select and operationalize a relevant musical stimulus. As described above, any musical parameter may be operationally defined, categorized, and measured or rated. These might include the following:

- Pitch/frequency (measured in Hz),
- Loudness (measured in dB),
- Wave form/timbre/harmonic spectrum (spectrum analysis of voice/acoustic/ electronic instruments/sounds; attack can also be measured),
- Duration (hours/minutes/seconds or smaller, from video analysis down to frames),
- Style (classical, jazz, rock, folk, and so forth, and subdivisions of the styles when appropriate),
- Tempo (measured exactly in BpM, or in categories such as slow-medium-fast or adagio-andante-allegro-presto),
- Rating of musical stimulus quality (such as stimulative, neutral, sedative),
- Frequency of selected musical events (such as melodic gestalt, rhythmic motive, breaks, change of texture and other parameters, musical interaction types).

Instruments for measurement include metronomes, tuning forks or electronic tuners, clocks, spectographs, audio and video recording and analysis systems, and expert knowledge on musical features that cannot be measured exactly, such as style. Many software programs are available for computer processing of data. Gregory (2000) gathered information on one aspect of measuring responses, namely the tests that are used in music therapy research. She examined 183 research articles in the *Journal of Music Therapy*, 92 of which included a test instrument. Only 20 of these were concerned with evaluating musical functions, and only 10 included evaluation of musical skills or musical performance.

Effects of Music on Nonmusical Behavior

Two studies included in Gregory's (2002) article may serve as examples of how effects of musical stimuli on nonmusical behavior have been studied with different client groups using behavioral designs.

Cohen (1992) studied the effect of singing instruction on the speech production of eight adults with neurological impairments and expressive speech disorders. The nine group sessions of singing instruction included physical exercises, vocal warm-up, chanting rhythmic speech drills, and singing songs that had been learned before their injuries. The five dependent measures included speaking fundamental frequency, and fundamental frequency variability, vocal intensity, rate of speech, and verbal intelligibility of the subjects. The audio-recorded pretest and posttest samples were analyzed by specialized computer programs, measuring fundamental frequency in Hz, variability in semitones, intensity in dB, and rate of speech in pause time; six independent judges rated the intelligibility.

Brotons and Pickett-Cooper (1996) studied the effects of five sessions of live music therapy on agitation behaviors of 47 patients with Alzheimer's before and after music therapy, and the influence of musical background on the patients' responses. The music therapy sessions included at least one of each of the following activities in the same order: singing, playing instruments, dance/movement, musical games, and composition/improvisation. The dependent measures included scores on the Agitation Behavior Scale, an observational checklist comprised of seven agitation behaviors, rated by staff members and caregivers on a 5-point severity index; and number of dosages of PRN (given as needed) psychotropic medications, reported by staff members. Musical background was determined by a questionnaire with nine questions on music education received and involvement in musical activities, completed by family members.

A methodological problem in this type of research is that it is not possible to control the independent variables in great detail, as even a firmly structured group music therapy session will inevitably include a number of uncontrolled elements, such as spontaneous group member interactions, misunderstandings, participant resistance, and so forth.

Using a different behavioral design, Elefant (2001, 2002, 2005) investigated whether songs in music therapy intervention could enhance the communication skills of seven girls with Rett syndrome. She used a single case multiple baseline (multiple probe), time series, within-subjects design, noteworthy for its flexibility and applicability to clinical work, enabling a clinician to research his or her own work. The independent variable was a selection of 18 songs chosen and sung by the therapist, divided into three sets and represented by picture symbols attached to a communication board, enabling the girls to indicate a preferred song. Parameters under control were familiarity (well-known vs. new songs), tempo (slow-medium-fast), meter (even, uneven), dynamics (*piano* to *forte*), vocal play (included or not included), and more. The dependent measures were choice making, response time, song preferences, affective responses, expressive vocalization, intentional speech, eye contact, and stereotypical hand movements.

Various types of experimental studies also focus on the effects of music on nonmusical responses. These are often inspired by experimental music psychology and do not always connect with clinical music therapy practice. However, they may present foundational information on responses to music that are relevant to music therapists' practice, for example, on how a normal population reacts to selected musical stimuli. Experimental studies of a specific music therapy intervention, vibroacoustic therapy (VAT; Skille & Wigram, 1995; Wigram, 1996, 1997) have demonstrated how low frequency sounds, usually between 30 and 80 Hz, alone or combined with selected music, influence somatic and functional variables in both clinical and nonclinical populations. VAT research has demonstrated beneficial influence on nonmusical variables such as stress, muscle tension and spasms, and alleviation of pain.

Effects of Music on Imagery and Hemispheric Processing

In one study of the effect of selected classical music on imagery, McKinney and Tims (1995) investigated the effects of two different pieces of music (Vaughan Williams' *Rhosymedre* and Ravel's *Introduction and Allegro*) on the imagery of 110 subjects, classified as low imagers or high imagers (as determined by the Creative Imagination Scale). A 2 x 2 factorial design was used to examine the different effects of these pieces of music on the imagery of the two groups. The two compositions were chosen as different in most musical parameters: duration (3'55 vs. 10'+), style (neo-Baroque vs. Impressionist), tempo (andante vs. allegro), rhythm (stable vs. fluid), form (clearly structured vs. loose/free), mood, timbre, and so forth.

Lem (1998, 1999, 2002) investigated the flow of imagery evoked by GIM music during unguided music imaging using *neurophenomenology*, a method combining systematic observation of participants with physical measurement. Electroencephalography (EEG) was used to investigate potential connections between the structural variability or psychoacoustic qualities of selected GIM music (Pierné's *Concertstück*), the listener's imagery, and brainwave activity (Lem, 1999). The analysis included a correlation of EEG activity (amplitude and frequency recording) and a structural analysis of the music, including the profile of affective expression in the 26 segments of the piece identified by music analysis.

Hemispheric processing of music experiences is a rapidly growing area of research, although it has only been applied to nonclinical populations up to this time. Peretz (2001) stated that current evidence from cognitive neuroscience points to the existence of a specific neural arrangement for certain musical emotions. She reviewed research showing that subjects exhibit greater left frontal EEG activity to music expressing joy and happiness and greater relative right frontal EEG activity to music expressing fear and sadness. New measurement technologies such as functional Magnetic Resonance Imaging (fMRI) enable a more detailed study of what brain activity can be perceived when subjects are listening to music. This may be of great relevance to music therapy researchers in the area of neurological impairments, although researchers state that there is a long way to go before accurately music perception can be measured.

Effects of Music on Affective Responses

Four basic approaches to the study of affective response to music can be identified in music psychology: psychophysiological research, adjective descriptor research, philosophical inquiry, and psychological aesthetics research (Radocy & Boyle 1997, p. 306). The most common measurement strategies are physiological measures, used in psychophysiological research, and verbal reports, used in adjective descriptor research, while empirical aesthetics are used in psychological aesthetics research. Philosophical inquiry is a qualitative method that will not be addressed here.

Physiological measures include heart rate, pulse rate, respiration rate, galvanic skin response, brain waves, blood pressure, and muscular response. The music psychology literature lists numerous studies of physiological responses (Bartlett, 1996; Thaut 2002b; Vink 2001). All types may be relevant for research on responses in music therapy, but the results of response studies with nonclinical participants cannot always be applied to clinical populations (D. Aldridge, 1996; Vink, 2001). However, the effects of music stimuli on muscular activity are clearly relevant in music therapy and can be measured by electromyography (EMG; Thaut). A newer type of physiological measure is immune system responses, as studied in psychoneuroimmunology. The influence of music—listening or playing—on relevant endocrine markers such as cortisol, prolactin, or melatonin can be studied by blood samples collected by venipuncture (McKinney, Clark, & Kumar, in preparation), and the influence on immune system markers such as salivary immunoglobulin A (sIgA) can be studied by saliva testing before and after the music therapy experience (Bunt, Burns, & Turton, 2000; Rider, 1997). For instance, sIgA and cortisol levels are widely accepted and validated as measures of stress (Bunt & Hoskyns, 2002). As mentioned above, hemispheric specialization and neural networks for processing musical stimuli can be studied with measuring technologies like computed tomography (CT or CAT) scanning, EEG, positron emission tomography (PET), and fMRI (Peretz, 2001).

Verbal reports include mood adjective checklists (such as Hevner's [1936] mood wheel; Farnsworth's [1954, 1958] adjective list; the University of Wales Institute of Science and Technology [UWIST] test [Matthews, Jones, & Chamberlain, 1990]; and the Ortony, Clore, & Collins [1988] Scale) where the participant chooses among a sorted or unsorted list of descriptive adjectives characterizing the music. Another verbal report is the semantic differential, where the participants indicate on a polarity profile with five or more steps whether he or she considers the music powerful-gentle, stimulating-calming, dark-light, dissonant-melodious, and so forth.

Empirical aesthetics involves the study of affective responses to music through observation of aesthetic behavior involving three basic methods: (a) correlational studies of the variation of two or more factors or collative properties of the musical stimulus in relation to one another, (b) content analysis of selected musical artifacts, and (c) experimental aesthetics based on systematic variation of factors influencing affective response. Berlyne's theory of the positive hedonic value of a musical stimulus as a function of arousal is based on research applying all three methods (Berlyne 1971; Radocy & Boyle, 1997).

Methodological problems in this area of musical response research are numerous. Vink (2001) and Thaut (2002b) mentioned some of them: The relationship between musical stimuli and physiological responses and between musical emotions and physiological responses is not simple and causal. Psychophysiological responses are idiosyncratic and often influenced by individual reactivity variables such as preference. The responses of nonclinical participants in experimental studies cannot be automatically transferred to the clinical situation. Results based on the use of classical music cannot be generalized to areas or situations where popular or folk music is used. It is difficult to decide whether an affective response is induced directly by the music, related to associations and connotations of the participant, or simply attributed by idiosyncratic cognitive or affective responses. The complexity of the relationship between properties of the musical stimuli, neurological and perceptual processes, and evoked client responses were highlighted in Thaut's theoretical model of "music perception in the music therapy process" (Thaut, 2002a, pp. 24–25).

A serious methodological problem is the interactive nature of affective and aesthetic response with an aesthetic object. In most research studies evaluation is made in retrospect, using one or more of the self-reports mentioned above after the interaction. But since music moves and changes in real time, it is a problem to measure responses retrospectively. However, it is possible to assess and measure affective and aesthetic responses in real time, during the presentation of the stimulus. In a study of the experience of musical tension, Nielsen (1983) used a pair of *tension tongs* enabling (nonclinical) participants to squeeze them to express their experience of tension while listening to Haydn's *Symphony No. 104.*

Another means of allowing a respondent to share responses to music in real time is the *Continuous Response Digital Interface (CRDI),* developed by the Center for Music Research at

Florida State University in the 1980s and used in many research studies of listeners' aesthetic responses to music as well as in music therapy (Gregory, 1989; Madsen & Frederickson, 1993). It was also used to replicate Nielsen's study mentioned above, indicating a strong and definite similarity independent of methodology (Madsen & Frederickson). A listener using CRDI uses a dial allowing movements of a visual pointer cross a 255-degree arc, which may be labeled with the words *positive* along the right side and *negative* along the left side of the arc. The dial pointer is positioned in the middle of the arc at the beginning of the session. An important point is that *aesthetic response* is not predefined for the participants. The standard dial may also be combined with a second dial, for example, a 180-degree dial adaptation of Hevner's mood wheel (Goins, 1998), enabling a correlation of aesthetic and affective response.

Geringer and Madsen (2003) described the background and lines of research using the CRDI:

> The first line of research is more "qualitative" and concerns what musicians as well as non-musicians consider to be the emotional content of music and their own "aesthetic response." The second and third research lines are more "quantitative" in nature. The second concerns the focus of the listener attention to aspects of ongoing music such as salient musical elements. The third line uses the CRDI to determine response latencies of discriminations or perceived magnitudes of changes in ongoing music stimuli. (p. 4)

Studies using the CRDI for music therapy purposes may address accurate assessment of moods expressed in the music and mood states of clients as influenced by the music. The CRDI and other self-report formats for measuring emotional response to music were reviewed by Schubert (2001).

How patients respond emotionally to music is a fundamental aspect of music therapy, and research based knowledge on how emotions are experienced, judged, and expressed musically is a complex yet important research theme. However, only a few of the studies reviewed in the *Handbook of Music Psychology* (Hodges, 1996) used real music and focused on musical factors (such as form and structural elements) affecting emotional responses; rather, many used single tones, scales, or simple sounds, selected, controlled and manipulated in the context of an experiment. Four such studies were reviewed (pp. 310–312), all with nonclinical subjects as participants. Hevner's early work (1935, 1936, 1937) on the impact of rhythm, harmony, tonality, and the structure of the melodic line on emotional or mood response has been influential for decades, and her *mood wheel,* an adjective checklist categorizing musically expressed moods in polarities, is still in use. Baker and Wigram (2004) discussed the classic studies of Hevner and another pioneer, Rigg (1937), with the conclusions summarized in Table 1.

Table 1
Early Established Musical Parameters Affecting Mood States
Baker & Wigram (2004). Used with permission.

Musical Component	Mood State Evoked
Major tonality	Happy, graceful, playful moods
Minor tonality	Sad, dreamy, sentimental moods
Firm rhythms	Vigorous and dignified moods
Flowing rhythms	Happy, graceful, dreamy and tender moods
Complex dissonant harmonies	Excitement, agitation, vigor or sadness
Simple consonant harmonies	Happiness, grace, serenity
Rising and falling melodic lines	No clear-cut, distinct, or constant mood
Slow tempos	Dignity, calmness, and sadness
Fast tempos	Restlessness and happiness
High pitches	Sprightly and humorous moods
Low pitches	Sadness, dignity and majesty
Ascending 4ths in the melody	Joyful moods
Descending minor 2nds	Sadness

Baker and Wigram (2004) remarked that the conclusions for some components are in conflict with later research, especially concerning rhythm and melodic direction. Radocy and Boyle (1997) stated, "the collative variables of a musical stimulus (complexity, novelty/familiarity, uncertainty/redundancy) are relativistic" (p. 307). A literature review by Abeles and

Chung (1996) and Thaut's (2002a) theoretical model, mentioned above, revealed the complex nature of musical and nonmusical factors' influence on emotional response in nonclinical populations. Adding clinical problems to a study only enhances the complexity.

Theories on how music induces or influences emotion may connect music psychology and music therapy (Gfeller, 2002; Vink, 2001). The most influential and therapeutically relevant theories on how music influences cognitive and affective responses of nonclinical persons were proposed by Meyer (1956, 2001), Berlyne (1971), and Mandler (1984). Vink (2001) gave an overview of Meyer's theory of how musical expectations influence response; of Berlyne's theory on the influence of musical complexity, familiarity, and redundancy on music's *hedonic value*; and of Mandler's theory of musical emotion as a cognitive appraisal of bodily experiences. Gfeller presented additional information on Kreitler and Kreitler's Cognitive Theory of Aesthetic Response (1972, as cited in Gfeller) and Bregman's Auditory Scene Analysis (1990, as cited in Gfeller). Although arousal plays an important role in all of the theories mentioned, it is difficult to conduct empirical studies of the relationship between musical emotion and arousal. This is because the psychophysiological properties of the musical stimulus as well as two classes of variables influencing the response—those related to the collative characteristics of the musical stimulus and those related to the experience of the listener (labeled *ecological properties* by Thaut [2002a])—must be controlled.

In a recent study, Rickard (2004) investigated the thesis that music that elicited intense emotions produces higher levels of physiological arousal than less emotional powerful music. Twenty-one nonclinical participants were "exposed to relaxing music, arousing (but not emotionally powerful) music, an emotionally powerful film scene, and a music piece selected by participants as 'emotionally powerful.' A range of physiological and subjective measures of arousal was recorded before and during the treatments" (p. 371).

Classical empirical studies as well as more recent empirical studies and theories are reviewed in the anthology *Music and Emotion* (Juslin & Sloboda, 2001). The book includes a review by Gabrielsson and Lindström (2001) of empirical research on the influence of musical structure on perceived emotional expression. This research included different methodological approaches of three types: free phenomenological descriptions, subject to content analysis; choice among descriptive terms, subject to frequency analysis; and rating of descriptive terms, analyzed by multivariate techniques such as factor analysis. The authors concluded that our knowledge in the area is still limited and ambiguous.

Sloboda and Juslin (2001) discussed the definition of emotion and how the influence of music on emotions can be approached. To the categorical, the dimensional, and the prototype approaches they added Stern's concept of *vitality affects*[4] as an "additional class. . . which. . . could be useful in explaining listeners' responses to music" (p. 76). Vitality affects appears to be a core concept in music therapy research (Hannibal, 1999, 2001; Pavlicevic, 1997; Smeijsters, 2003; Trevarthen & Malloch, 2000) and is also relevant when researching the music empirically. In the words of Ruud (1998): "The contour of the melodic line [of Dido's Lament], along with the tempo, points not to a categorical feeling, such as sadness, but to a 'vitality affect' in Daniel Stern's sense" (p. 77).

Wosch (2001, 2002, 2004) discussed emotional responses to music. He suggested a categorical approach with fives classes of basic emotion (interest, anxiety, rejection, sorrow, joy) and used this model in his own empirical research. In a study of four selected dyadic improvisations, Wosch (2002) developed a computer-based respondent interview (a continuous measurement self-report questionnaire) focusing on emotional qualities as experienced by the 41 participants. They listened to the improvisations using headphones and used mouse clicks to indicate when they experienced a shift in emotional quality (five categories corresponding to basic emotions, as mentioned above). Analysis included cluster analysis of the density of mouse clicks (presented in dendograms) and correlations with episodes identified as emotionally different, and with modified IAP analysis (autonomy profile, see below).

Bunt and Pavlicevic (2001) investigated music therapists' abilities to express and make judgments of emotions from musical improvisations made by music therapists. Improvisers randomly chose one of five basic emotions—happy, sad, tender, angry, fearful—and expressed the

---

4 Stern's (1985) concept of vitality affects was described by Sloboda and Juslin (2001) as "a set of elusive qualities related to intensity, shape, contour, and movement. . . . These qualities are not emotions but rather abstract 'forms' of feeling." They go on to say that "they are common to all forms of expression" (p. 79).

emotion using an instrument of their choice or voice. Listening participants rated the emotional state of the improvisation and gave comments on musical and other reasons for their judgment.

Problems With Research on Nonmusical Responses to Music

The literature shows a wide variety of results from many of the studies of nonmusical responses to music. Over a number of years of research, there have been few clear results from these studies, with results varying from study to study. As mentioned above, Abeles and Chung (1996), Juslin and Sloboda (2001), Thaut (2002a), Vink (2001), Sloboda and Juslin (2001), and many others have discussed the reasons for these problems. In the context of this chapter, the crucial problem is that research in responses of nonclinical populations cannot be applied indiscriminately to clinical music therapy research. The relevance of this research must therefore be considered by the researcher as related to the specific clinical context.

Sharing similar concerns but coming to a different conclusion, McMullen (1996) stated that popular theoretical explanations of affective/aesthetic responses to music have never provided and still do not provide empirical researchers with effective guidelines for their studies. His assumption was that this is closely related to the question of research paradigm. Most research into the relationship between music and aesthetic/affective behavior "has been undertaken within the causal perspective (or paradigm) when the answer might lie within an alternative interpretative framework" (McMullen, p. 388). McMullen suggested that an interpretative (non- or post-positivist) framework for the study of affective/aesthetic responses would be formed by two dimensions or polarities—perceived stimulus activation (plus-minus) and evaluation (acceptance-rejection)—facilitating research that can be integrated with philosophy, psychology, and related disciplines. This is an ambition shared in many of the qualitative methodologies described later in the chapter.

Musical Responses

Musical response studies are based on the operationalization of defined musical responses—musical behaviors or expressions—as dependent variables and measurements of their frequencies or qualities within a specific population and experimental condition. Music is most often both independent and dependent variables in such studies. Experimental and behavioral designs can be applied: applied behavior analysis, pre-post designs (single or multiple case), continuous response designs, and microanalysis (such as time series analysis).

Again, the challenge for the researcher is how to select and operationalize a relevant musical response. Any musical response may be operationally defined and measured, in most cases through observation (assessment, systematic live observation, audio and video analysis). Examples are:

- Changes in target musical parameters: pitch, loudness, timbre, duration, tempo,
- Frequency and duration of specific musical responses (such as formulation of melodic or rhythmic motives, respecting and using breaks, changes of texture or other parameters),
- Changes in general musical behavior (presence/frequency/duration of turn-taking, imitation, elaboration, or free improvisation),
- Changes in musical preferences.

Instruments for measurement include the same devices as mentioned above plus standardized or nonstandardized self-report questionnaires, tests, rating scales, assessment tools, real-time interface techniques, and expert knowledge on or analysis of musical and other relevant features that cannot be measured exactly (such as style, imagery, mandala drawings).

In the context of general music psychology research, Berlyne (1971) studied the relationship between liking and preference and informational properties of the musical stimulus, such as complexity, expectedness, and familiarity, and suggested that aesthetic success of a work of art is in part a function of its capacity to evoke emotional arousal. The most successful works of music are those that evoke an optimal level of arousal (as described with the *inverted U* curve). Berlyne's work has been influential on studies of aesthetic responses to music in therapy (see Gfeller, 2002; McMullen, 1974; Thaut, 2002a). Again, a problem of connecting to this general research is that the responses of nonclinical populations cannot be generalized to include clinical populations. This is probably the main reason why music therapists have often developed specific rating scales and assessment procedures to include children, adolescents, and adults with physical, emotional, and mental problems.

One of the first attempts to standardize observed musical responses was the two scales developed by Nordoff and Robbins (1971, 1977; see also Graham, 2000) to assess musical responses of children with disabilities. The scales were based on the study of improvisational music therapy with 52 children, more than half of these diagnosed as having autism. Scale 1 rated the client-therapist relationship in musical activity in two areas: Levels of Participation (seven levels, from unresponsiveness to stable musical relationship) and Qualities of Resistiveness (seven levels, from active rejection to resistance of own regressive tendencies). Scale 2 rated the child's musical communicativeness in three areas of activity: instrumental, voice, and body movement (nine levels, from no communicative responsiveness to freely functioning musical intelligence and skills).

Merle-Fishman and Marcus (1982) studied similarities and differences in musical behaviors and preferences of children with and without emotional disturbances. Sixteen children, ranging in age from 7 to 10 years, were distributed in two groups and placed into a clinical and a nonclinical group, matched for age. The two groups had seven weekly music therapy sessions that were unstructured and nondirective in order to allow spontaneous responses. Responses were operationally defined within five main categories adapted from Nordoff and Robbins (1971): instrument choice, interaction style, rhythmic behavior, verbal behavior, and vocal behavior. Frequency of responses was recorded by two independent observers on data sheets for the first three categories and by analysis of audio recordings for the last two.

Gibbons (1983) focused on rhythmic responses as a specific aspect of the musical responses of children with emotional disturbances. She studied how the ability to imitate rhythm patterns was related to the following independent variables: age, gender, motor coordination skills, tempo skills (as measured by Gordon's Musical Aptitude Profile Tempo Subtest), and need for structure to control behavior (rated by independent observers). Twenty-four children, ranging from 11 to 15 years and rated as belonging to one of three categories (children with mild, moderate, and severe needs for structure to control behavior) had five weekly sessions where they were instructed to imitate on conga drums rhythm patterns presented on audiotape. The rhythm test was highly structured and consisted of two sets of rhythm patterns, with one measure (which had to be reproduced exactly as presented to be considered correct) as the scoring unit. Independent observers viewed videotapes to rate the imitation.

Clair, Bernstein, and Johnson (1995) sought to describe rhythm playing characteristics of 28 people in the late stages of dementia. The design was ABCA (B and C being the first and last experimental sessions in a series of 16), with participants serving as their own controls. One observer rated the baseline and experimental sessions. For most areas of interest, the number of 5-second intervals in which criteria behaviors occurred was recorded; a frequency count of correct rhythmic pattern imitations was also included. Independent variables were: (a) types of drums and frequency and duration of participation, (b) rhythm patterns of changing complexity, (c) modeled drum strokes on a frame drum, and (d) structure of the session. Five dependent variables were measured through repeated video observation: overall participation duration, participation on four different types of drums, entrained playing over time, correct imitation of drum strokes, and imitation of progressively more complex rhythm patterns over time.

Various types of experimental studies in addition to the behavioral designs focus on the effect of music on musical response. These include factorial designs, rank order or two-group studies, and pretest-posttest experimental designs with repeated measures. These experimental studies of music variables are often inspired by experimental music psychology and do not always connect with clinical music therapy practice. However they may present relevant background or reference information on, for example, how a normal population responds musically to selected musical stimuli.

Musical Preferences

Common strategies in studies of musical preferences and tastes are assessment, paired comparisons, rating scales, questionnaires (sounding or silent), and behavioral measures:

- Assessment of general attitudes can be done by standardized or specially constructed surveys.

- Paired comparisons are used to investigate the categorical nature of short-term musical preference judgments: Two pieces, previously rated, may be played in AB or BA order, or the same piece may be heard in two slightly differing versions, so that people can indicate the preferred version or comment on various properties of the versions.

- Rating scales and questionnaires give participants the choice of ranking their musical preferences, often on a Likert scale. Large sample studies may use *sounding questionnaires* (structured/multiple choice; unstructured/open-end), in which people can hear specific selections and can rate or comment on them.

- Behavioral measures let the participants choose between a number of music stimuli by using channel shifters in a sound system or special devices like the Operant Music Listening Recorder (OMLR) that not only shift channel, input, and stimulus but also record the time spent listening to the stimulus. These types of behavioral measures are especially suited for the study of musical preferences of children or nonverbal populations.

Researching musical preferences has a long history in music psychology, music education, and music media research. The development of musical preference and taste is a complex, multifactorial process (Hargreaves, 1986), as musical preference is a function of many variables, including short- and long-term variables in the music, in the listener, and in the context (Radocy & Boyle, 1997).

However, in music therapy research the main goal of researching music preferences of clients is rather pragmatic: In music medicine or in receptive music therapy, it is important to identify the music a specific client or population may experience as helpful, enjoyable, sedative, relaxing, stimulating, or imagery evoking. "Musical preferences result from a complex mixture of musical and human characteristics" (Radocy & Boyle, 1997, p. 329), thus they are highly individual, even idiosyncratic, and closely related to culture and context. Thaut (2002b, p. 34) mentioned that *response specificity* or *response stereotype* of an individual has replaced the idea of *intersubject response stereotypes.* This is very important in clinical work, where the music therapist must always determine a client's personal arousal response. Nevertheless, it is possible to create more generally applicable music selections or programs for relaxation/stimulation, and general properties of sedative/stimulative music, as experienced by a majority of listeners, can be defined. Wigram, Pedersen, and Bonde (2002, p. 138) synthesized research-based knowledge of potential elements in physiologically stimulative versus relaxing music. Relaxing music is characterized by stability (or minor or gradual changes), clarity and predictability in all musical parameters, while stimulating music is characterized by sudden or unpredictable changes and variations in tempo, volume, rhythm, timbre, pitch harmony, texture, and unclear musical form.

Spintge (1993) defined *anxiolytic* music (music used to reduce anxiety, distress, and pain during surgical procedures) as different from *relaxing music.* Both types tend to be stable in dynamics, melody, and tempo, but while relaxing music has a rather limited frequency range (600–900 Hz), slow to medium tempo (60–80 BpM), and stable rhythm with little contrast, anxiolytic music has a large, ambient soundscape-like frequency range (20–10,000 Hz), a slower tempo (50–70 BpM), and floating rhythm with no contrast. Bonny (1983/2002c) created music programs to be used in coronary heart care. Participants chose individually between programs with selected, mostly relaxing classical music, and a program with popular music. The present author wishes to underline that this research points at the importance of the patient's free choice, both from a scientific and from an ethical point of view.

Wolfe, O'Connell, and Waldon (2002) compared musicians' and nonmusicians' ratings of selected recordings for musical relaxation within a pediatric setting. A panel of six experts rated 98 selected recordings expected or reported to be sedative/relaxing music (duration 90′). Ten of these were chosen for presentation to a group of nonmusicians who rated the relaxation quality of each piece and specified qualities that enhanced or distracted from relaxation. The categories of the content analysis were predetermined (and very traditional): dynamics, tempo, instrumentation, rhythm, harmony, melody extra musical, and other.

The music therapy literature only includes a few examples of research of musical preferences of specific clinical populations.

Wasserman, Plutchik, Deutsch, and Taketomo (1973a) developed a detailed questionnaire (24 items) of the musical preferences and musical aptitudes of 16 people with mental retardation and psychosis upon entering a ward music therapy program at a state mental hospital. Preferences were recorded by family members in eight genres or styles: popular, classical, show music, spiritual, rock and roll, folk song, country western, and religious music.

Lathom, Petersen, and Havlicek (1982) investigated the musical preferences of older people attending nutrition sites. Musical excerpts of eight musical styles were presented to 104 subjects, aged 55 years or older.

Wilson and Smith (2000) reviewed the availability of music therapy assessments and the feasibility of standardizing an assessment instrument for music therapists to use in school settings. Music preferences were assessed in only 12% of the 41 studies reviewed. Subject populations covered were predominantly children with developmental disabilities or mental retardation, children with autism, children with hearing impairments, and clients with psychiatric problems and emotional disturbance.

Included in the study by Elefant (2001, 2002, 2005) mentioned above was a structural analysis of 10 of the songs, the five most and the five least preferred by the participants, including the features mentioned as controlled, independent musical variables.

In a different context, Bonde (1997) reported on a large-scale music preference study of Danish radio listeners. Several aspects are relevant for music therapy research, both in design and in conclusions. A panel of seven music experts developed a theoretically informed model of seven important parameters potentially influencing preference: power (intensity), mood (using a modified version of Hevner's mood wheel), rhythm versus melody/harmony (understood as the balance/dominance of the rhythmic versus the melodic-harmonic element), text, performance (level of individuality), style and genre, and tempo. After that they rated many hundreds of examples in order to reach interrater reliability of all selections to be used in a sounding questionnaire of 70 items (3–5 selections within each genre/style, duration 0'25–0'30 per selection). The selections in the sounding questionnaire encompassed an optimum mix of qualities within the parameters (such as jazz selections with differences in tempo, mood, power). Selections were rated by 519 participants aged 14–80+ on two Likert scales, one on familiarity (How well do you know this kind of music?) and the other on preference (How do you like the music?). The result of the study indicated that only two parameters—power, and rhythm versus melody/harmony—had a significant influence on preference. Performance and text had only a marginal influence while mood, tempo, and style had no influence.

Nonmusical Features Exhibited Musically

Many music-based assessments focus also on nonmusical features. Music therapy assessment typically looks at the musical behavior of those being assessed and then uses some system to determine what those musical behaviors mean nonmusically, such as how they may be expressions of personality, developmental characteristics, and social functioning.

Although quantitative tools for musical assessment are sparse, ideas can be found in the literature. Wasserman, Plutchik, Deutsch, and Taketomo (1973b) developed three rating scales for musical aptitude and social behavior in adult patients with mental retardation and emotional illness. Individual participation was rated by independent observers in all three components of the sessions: (a) rhythm group participation (19 items, including rhythm skills and instrument choice), (b) singing group (22 items, including vocal skills and affects expressed when singing), and (c) vocal dynamics (15 items, including affects expressed). Edgerton (1994) used musical interactiveness in improvised music making when rating communicative and social behaviors in children with autism. Layman, Hussey, and Laing (2002) piloted an assessment instrument for children with severe emotional disturbances, including four domains: behavioral/social functioning, emotional responsiveness, language/communication abilities, and music skills. Included under music skills are musical awareness, response to music, response to cue, imitation, and vocal inflection. Functioning is measured "along a continuum anchored by defensive/ withdrawn behavior on one pole, and disruptive/intrusive behavior at the other pole. In the middle of the continuum are target behaviors" (p. 173). An example of a target behavior in the middle of the imitation category under musical awareness is "consistently imitated simple body movements when first shown" (p. 177). Musical data used in other quantitative assessments includes vocal range and different musical responses, behaviors, and preferences.

One of the most important factors in music therapy is the musical relationship between client and therapist. However, it is difficult to operationalize the level of contact (behavior) in music. Descriptive systems or scales have been designed by Schumacher (1999), Møller (2000), and Plahl (2000). These scales are based on theories or principles of developmental psychology and thus are appropriate for assessment or research with children with developmental disabilities or delays, while they may be of limited usefulness in working with children and adults with psychiatric problems (Moreau, 2003).

The Nordoff-Robbins scales mentioned above include several categories and levels of response in child-therapist relationship during musical activity, and in musical communicativeness. A third musical response scale was developed to assess musical expressivity. The use (and revision) of the Nordoff-Robbins scales in assessment of a wider range of client groups, including adults with learning disabilities, challenging behavior, or psychotic illnesses, is described by Graham (2000).

A quantitative assessment procedure that can also be used in research with developmental delays or other problems is the Analysis System to Evaluate the Quality of Relationship during Music Therapy (AQR; Schumacher & Calvet-Kruppa, 2001). The method was developed for the assessment and documentation of music therapy with children with profound disturbances within the autistic spectrum. Seven levels of contact/relationship were identified: 0 = lack of contact, 1 = contact-reaction, 2 = functional-sensory contact, 3 = contact to self/self-awareness, 4 = contact to others/intersubjectivity, 5 = relationship to others/interactivity, 6 = joint experience/interaffectivity. The levels are operationalized for observation. AQR can be used as a method of video analysis in several ways: whole sessions, activities, or episodes can be recorded, analyzed, and processed statistically.

Moreau (2003) developed the seven-point Scale for Measurement of Expressive and Musical Behavior (MAKS) in order to provide a valid and objective method for "detailed description of a patient's experience, perceptive abilities, expressive potential or communicative skills." Video episodes of patients (adolescents who had psychiatric problems) playing solo or in dyads were rated by trained raters using two scales: an expression scale with 14 items (such as formal shaping, sound quality, vigor) and four generic terms (handling of instrument, shaping/interpretation, vitality and dynamic expression, expressive quality); and a communication scale with 13 items (such autonomy, involvement, playful quality) and three generic terms (general engagement, relation to partner, expressive quality). MAKS was evaluated in a study with 52 raters, with measures for objectivity, reliability, and validity. It has been used in some studies since then, and Moreau concluded that "with a slight modification of the scale and an intensive rater training prior to application, the scale may describe nonverbal expressive and communicative behavior in an objective and reliable manner."

Pavlicevic and her colleagues (Pavlicevic & Trevarthen, 1989; Pavlicevic, Trevarthen, & Duncan, 1994) developed a specific rating scale, the Index of Music Experience and Music Improvisation Rating scale (MIR), for the study of joint musical improvisation of the therapist and patient as a framework for spontaneous and intimate nonverbal interaction. The scale was developed through a comparison of 15 people with schizophrenia, 15 people with depression, and 15 clinically normal controls (age 17–55 years). Loewy (2000) developed a qualitative model for music psychotherapy assessment, with 13 areas of inquiry looking at the awareness of the self, others, and the moment; thematic expression; listening and performing; collaboration between client and therapist; degrees of concentration; range of affect; investment and motivation; the use of structure; integration; self-esteem, risk-taking, and independence. Hintz (2000) developed an assessment procedure for geriatric patients involving scoring and addressing five areas: expressive musical skills, receptive musical skills, behavioral and psychosocial skills, motor skills, and cognitive memory skills. Scheiby (2002) described an assessment procedure in which the first step involved data with the following musical parameters: rhythm, melody, harmony, tempo, phrasing, themes, dynamics, and choice and use of instruments (pp. 130–132). In the second step the following categories are identified and described, based on musical and verbal interactions: affective, relational, cognitive, and developmental information; music-released fantasies and images; transpersonal, aesthetic, kinesthetic, creativity, and energetic information. D. Aldridge (1996, Chapter 9) discussed how assessment of musical improvisations may be a supplement to mental state examinations in areas where those examinations are lacking, and he presented two tables comparing features of medical and musical elements of assessment. He said that "intentionality, attention to, concentration on and perseverance with the task in hand are important features of producing musical improvisations and susceptible to be heard in the musical playing" (p. 204).

The most systematic and elaborated music assessment procedure was developed by Bruscia (1987, 1994, 2002) in his Improvisation Assessment Profiles (IAPs). The analogy between the elements of music and the existential themes and qualities of human existence is a core construction in Bruscia's IAPs. When developing this method for description and interpretation of clinical improvisations, Bruscia looked for concepts that would give the six profiles—each being a specific listening perspective or a way a music therapist or researcher may listen to client music—also psychological relevance:

- *Salience* (with five scales forming a spectrum: compliant, conform, attending, controlling, dominating),
- *Integration* (with the spectrum: undifferentiated, synchronized, integrated, differentiated, overdifferentiated),
- *Variability* (rigid, stable, variable, contrasting, random),
- *Tension* (hypo-tense, calm, cyclic, tense, hyper-tense),
- *Congruence* (unengaged, congruent, centered, incongruent, polarized),
- *Autonomy* (dependent, following, partner, leader, competitor/resister).

Through one, more, or all of these profiles it is possible to analyze the relationship of different elements of music, and scales of musical parameters are used to identify important aspects in music making. The IAPs also exist in an abridged form (Bruscia, 2002, pp. 80–82): Initial questions are formulated within the profiles of salience and tension, followed by an examination of the musical elements of rhythm, timbre, volume, phrasing, texture, with questions connected to the profiles of integration, variability, and autonomy. The final questions address physical elements, tonal elements, and the question of congruence. Table 2 presents the IAPs in an abridged form.

Wigram (2000, 2004) made an adapted version of the IAPs for event-based analysis of musical improvisations. This version of the IAPs is based on the profiles of autonomy and variability, which Wigram found most relevant for diagnostic assessment of communication disorder. Other researchers may choose other profiles as especially suited to their research questions, as Wosch (2002) did. In a recent review, Bruscia (2002) stated that, although they were developed for qualitative research, the IAPs can be used fruitfully also in quantitative research if measurable events are defined carefully (see also Wigram, 2004).

In the preface to the Norwegian translation of the IAPs, Bruscia (1994) wrote, that the method gives guidelines for how the musical elements and the process of an improvisation can be interpreted, based on psychoanalytic and humanistic-existential theories. The IAPs are an assessment tool based on two basic assumptions:

1. Improvised music is a sound reflection of the improviser's way of "being-in-the-world," not only in the here and now world of the improvisatory moment itself, but also of the more expanded context of the person's life world.
2. Each musical element provides a universal metaphor—or perhaps archetype—for expressing a particular aspect of "being-in-the-world." Thus each musical element has its own range of possibilities for expressive meanings which are different from the other elements. (p. 3)

The IAPs are used in the *Bruscia Method of Improvisation Analysis*, a research procedure in a maximum of 13 steps (Bruscia, 1987):

1. Plan analysis (participants, steps to be followed);
2. Contextualize improvisation (musical, extramusical);
3. Do open listenings (as improviser, as uninformed listener-reactor, as informed listener-analyzer);
4. Identify salient musical features;
5. Focus the analysis (what should be included);
6. Describe musical unfolding (as a narrative, plus a summary of the form);
7. Analyze salient musical elements (IAP profiles of integration, variability, and tension);
8. Analyze musical interactions between improvisers (IAP for autonomy);
9. Find extramusical metaphors;
10. Ground analyses in focused listenings;
11. Compare with other analyzed improvisations;
12. Synthesize findings in a report;
13. Ground analyses and extramusical meanings with participant.

Table 2
Improvisation Assessment Profiles—Abridged
Bruscia (2005). Used with permission

Basic Information

Improvisers and Instruments:
Title:
Given:
Length:
Situational context:
Overall impressions:
Form of improvisation:
How clearly formed are phrases?
Salience: Which musical elements are most salient?
Tension: Which musical elements have the most tension?
Tension: Any other tension (body, program lyrics, discussion)?

Rhythmic Elements

Integration: How related are rhythm and basic beat?
Integration: How related are simultaneous rhythmic parts?
Variability: How much do tempo, subdivision, meter change?
Variability: How much do rhythm patterns change?
Autonomy: Does client lead and/or follow with tempo/beat?
Autonomy: Does client lead and/or follow with rhythm?

Timbre

Integration: How closely related are simultaneous timbres?
Variability: How much does timbre change?
Autonomy: Does client lead and/or follow with timbre?

Volume

Integration: How closely related in volume are simultaneous parts?
Variability: How much does volume change?
Autonomy: Does client lead and/or follow with volume?

Texture

Integration: How different are simultaneous parts in role?
Integration: How different are simultaneous parts in register?
Variability: How much does texture change?
Autonomy: Does client lead and/or follow with texture

Phrasing

Integration: How do simultaneous phrases compare in length/shape?
Variability: How much does phrasing change?
Autonomy: Does client lead and/or follow with phrasing?

Physical Elements

Integration: How well do simultaneous movements fit together?
Variability: How much does body expression change?

Tonal Elements

Integration: How well does melody fit into the scale and key?
Integration: How closely related are simultaneous melodies?
Integration: How closely related is melody to harmony?
Integration: How closely related is harmony to scale/key?
Variability: How much do scale and key change?
Variability: How much do melodies change?
Variability: How much does harmony change?
Autonomy: Does client lead and/or follow with scale and key?
Autonomy: Does client lead and/or follow with melody?

Congruence

Any incongruent musical elements?
Any physical incongruence?
Any incongruence between improvisation and verbal materials?
Any incongruence between music and interpersonal relationships?

In this method, as in many of the following, the combination of open listenings, focused analyses, and contextualized interpretation are key figures. However, there are also many differences between this and phenomenological music analysis.

Understanding the Musical Experience

In qualitative, post-positivist music research, music is no longer considered a variable that can be manipulated within experimental or behavioral research designs. Studying music as an intentional, semantic, or pragmatic phenomenon is studying how music interacts with the body, mind, and spirit of a whole person. In the case of music therapy research, this is usually a client in music therapy. Philosophical and methodological inspiration can be found in musicology, but with caution, since musicologists have different interests than do music therapists. However, music therapy and the so-called New Musicology—the emergent musicology that is influenced by post-modern ideas—do share some important basic assumptions (see Ansdell, 1997, 2001; Ruud, 2000).

A great deal of music therapy research looks at understanding the musical experience, expanding upon it, and grasping its meaning. Much of this is qualitative research and this area of inquiry might be said to have been the focus of qualitative research in music therapy in the first 20 years of its development. Music therapy research studies using qualitative methods often include description, analysis, and interpretation of the music as part of the research. The following overview of selected methods will be divided into two sections: (a) methods to analyze (primarily) improvisations in active music therapy, and (b) methods to analyze (primarily) composed music used in receptive music therapy. While all of the methods do not divide neatly into one or the other focus, this is thought to be a reasonable approach to follow in presenting them. Table 3 provides an overview of methods for music analysis reviewed in the chapter, indicating whether or not they include the following components in the procedure: description of sound; music analysis (segmentation, transcription, graphic notation, phenomenological description, other types of description, structural analysis); open listening(s); client's comments; therapist's comments; comments by external consultants (lay or expert); the musical relationship; interpretation of meaning; psychological interpretation; and the use of narrative.

The challenge of music research is the attempt to connect the personal and the musical worlds of the client and the therapist (Lee, 2000). How can they be connected or bridged through music research? Theoretically, much qualitative music research is often based on the axiom that a client's music (experience) reflects his or her personality and pathology or problem (Bruscia, 1994; Wigram, Pedersen, & Bonde, 2002). Smeijsters (1999, 2003) has formulated a theory of music as analogy used within the framework of the double conceptualization of *pathological-musical processes* and *therapeutic-musical processes*. Bruscia (1987, 1994) has explored the analogies of musical expression and existential-psychological themes and has transformed (even operationalized) them to the listening perspectives of the IAPs and Heuristic Music Analysis (the former discussed above, the latter below).

Semiological Distinctions. It is important to distinguish among *description, analysis,* and *interpretation* of music. The Canadian music semiologist Nattiez (1990) has introduced a model of semiological process levels. He defined the *semiological tripartition* as an analytic process covering three dimensions of a symbolic phenomenon (music): (a) the poietic dimension, which is to say the symbolic form as a result of a process of creation; (b) the aesthesic dimension, or the assignment of meaning to the form by the receivers; and (c) the trace, or the physical and material form in which the symbolic form is accessible to the five senses (Nattiez 1990, pp. 11–12). D. Aldridge (1996) and Ansdell (1999) have demonstrated the relevance of the model and of Nattiez' concepts of trace, poietic, and aesthesic analysis for music therapy research.

Nattiez operates with six analytical situations:

1. Immanent analysis (the neutral ground, the trace),
2. Inductive poietics (internal observations of musical procedures),
3. External poietics (external documents are used to highlight procedures),
4. Inductive aesthesis (perceptive introspection, researcher as listener),
5. External aesthesis (information on other listeners' perception),
6. A final complex synthesis.

Table 3
Components in Qualitative Methods of Music Analysis

METHODS / COMPONENTS	Description of Sound	Open Listening(s)	Segmentation	Transcription	Graphic notation	Phenomenological description	Other types of description	Structural analysis	Client's Comments	Therapist's Comments	External Consultants (lay)	External Consultants (expert)	Musical Relationship	Interpretation of Meaning	Psychological Interpretation	Narrative
Bruscia Heuristic		X	X	X		X	X	X	(x)	(x)		(x)		X		
Bonny Dynamics			X	(x)		X		(x)						X		
Bonny Body		X					X							X		
Bonde & Pedersen			X	X		X	X	X	X					X		
Bergstrøm-Nielsen	X	X	X		X		X							X		
Grocke			X													
G. Aldridge		X	X	X	(x)		X		X	X			X	X		
Aigen Individual		X	X				X						X	X		X
Ansdell		X	X	X			X				(x)	X	X	X		
Metzner		X					X						X	X	X	
Skewes		X	X			X		X	X	X		X	X	X		X
Aigen Group			X				X	X	X	X			X			X
Arnason		X	X	(x)			X	X					X	X		X
Tüpker		X					X	X	(x)	(x)	(x)	X	X			X
Langenberg	X			X	(x)		X	X		X		X	X	X	X	
Lee		X	X	X			X	X	X	X		X	X	X		X
Trondalen	X	X	X	X	(x)	X	X	X	X	X			X	X	X	
Forinash & Gonzalez		X	X	X			X	X	X	X			X	X	X	
Ruud	X	X	X					X	X	X			X	X		
Ferrara	X	X	X			X	X	X					X	X		
Bruscia IAP	X		X				X						X	(x)	(x)	

X = included in the method; (x) = optional component or variant

D. Aldridge (1996, pp. 163–172) distinguishes among three levels of constitutive rules and one level of regulative rules. These levels may be specified in the following way:

- Level 1 (preceding Nattiez' analytical situations) is the sound, the performance, and the music experience itself.
- Level 2 (corresponding to Nattiez' situations 1–3) is the descriptive level of the *trace* (for example, an audio or video recording of an improvisation) and our dialogue on, or indexing of, the music. It is no longer the experience itself but our language-bound description of it, meant for verification and lexical labeling: What happened in the music and in the relationship, as observed by the researcher and documented by the client and other participants?
- Level 3 (corresponding to Nattiez' situations 4–5) is the level of interpretation and discourse. We try to understand and explain what happened, both through introspection and through interpretation systems with specific concepts and epistemology (for example, clinical psychology or psychodynamic theory). Conclusions are drawn on the meaning of the music.
- Level 4 (corresponding to Nattiez' situation 6) is the level of regulative rules where a synthesis is made, or in Aldridge's words, "therapeutic interpretation from a fixed point, but intuitively used in the therapeutic explanation" (p. 165).

The implications of these analytical distinctions for music research are discussed below.

Description is never without influences, no matter how exact and objective the researcher tries to be: Just as the map is not the territory, the score, transcription, or even the recording is not the music, only a representation of some of its features within the framework of a chosen language or symbol/coding/recording system. A transcription may be accompanied by a verbal description or indexes of the episodes, events as they unfold in time. A phenomenological description is an attempt to describe the *music as heard* (Clifton, 1983), as an intentional phenomenon unfolding here and now, as a virtual musical timespace (Christensen, 1996) in the listener's consciousness. The language may use musical terminology; however, the important point is the attempt to describe the music as a process unfolding in time and its salient features as experienced by or in a listener's consciousness.

Analysis goes beyond here and now and the real-time description. Analysis seeks to identify and classify observable and describable events and their relationship across the timespan: What is figure and ground; what is the role of a specific part in the whole? This is done through the study of similarities and differences: identification of musical patterns (in all elements and parameters), repetitions, and variations; types of interaction between parts or performers; the presentation and development of themes, motives, and roles. According to Cook (1987), the purpose of music analysis (of art music) is "to discover, or decide, how it works (p. xx)."[5] Analysis is an act of re-creation, asking the music the right questions to make it reveal its secrets. Within musicology there are a large number of analytic methods, but in spite of their apparent differences the basic questions are very similar: Is it possible to divide the whole "in a series of more-or-less independent sections. . . how do components relate to each other and which relationships are more important than other. . . and how is the influence of context?" (Cook, p. 2). In principle the questions are the same when analyzing improvisations, songs, or compositions in music therapy—the big difference is found in the answers since we, in most cases, are not dealing with composed musical masterpieces in elaborate form or with subtle harmonic or rhythmic properties. However, some extra questions must be added: How is the musical relationship of the players (in active music therapy), or how is the interplay of music and the (client) listener's music experience (in receptive music therapy)?

Interpretation is another important consideration. In traditional musicology of the 19th and 20th centuries (usually called formalism or structuralism, see Ansdell, 2001), researchers often had a positivist scientific ambition that made analysis of the artwork as an independent universe the ideal, while interpretation of some sort of meaning of the work was not considered

---

[5] Cook's book is a presentation of the most important types of musicological analysis, some of which are also used occasionally by music therapy researchers: traditional methods (focusing on elements like form, melody, harmony, and rhythm), Schenkerian analysis (including both Schenker's own method and later American applications of his ideas, focusing on *essential structures of music*), psychological approaches (for example, Meyer, Reti), formal approaches (set-theoretical analysis, semiotic analysis), and techniques of comparative analysis. In other words: music as syntax/structure can be analyzed in a number of ways.

proper. Kretzchmar's *musical hermeneutics,* an early attempt to address the narrative meaning of classical music, was not taken seriously. The critical musicology of the 1970s and 1980s and the postmodern new musicology of the last 20 years has changed the picture: It is not enough to analyze the syntax. Meaning and context must be integrated (see Ansdell, 1997). In music therapy this has always been obvious: Any description or analysis of the music must be related to the context—the client's personality, life story, culture, and, of course, pathology or problem area. However, as we shall see, this can be done in many ways and the re-creation or construction of the meaning of an improvisation will come to very different conclusions—one researcher using, for example, object relations theory, another using Jungian analytical psychology, a third cultural anthropology as framework of the interpretation.[6]

Analyzing Improvisations in Active Music Therapy. Methods focusing on improvisations have been an important area for music therapy research. The analytic traditions within musicology have not been suited for clinical purposes, as they were aimed at analyzing musical artifacts, thus inspiration has been found in procedures developed to describe and analyze contemporary music that was not fixed in scores and traditional Western notation practices.

Ferrara, a music theorist, published an article "Phenomenology as a Tool for Music Analysis," in 1984. Ferrara did not analyze improvisations, rather the object of his study was Varese's avant garde composition *Poeme Electronique* (1958). For this untraditional piece, one of the early electronic compositions, Ferrara suggested an eclectic analytic procedure labeled *Phenomenological Music Analysis.* The method incorporated phenomenological description, formal analysis, and hermeneutic interpretation. It included procedures in the following steps: (a) open listening, (b) syntactical level, (c) semantic level, (d) ontological level, and (e) final open listening, followed by (f) a meta-critique.[7]

Forinash and Gonzalez (1989) developed Ferrara's procedure into a method for analyzing and understanding the experience of music therapy, especially as focused on improvisation. They developed a seven-step procedure for clinically based research:

1. Compile data on the client's background (psychosocial history);
2. Describe the session (transcription from audiotape and log);
3. Study the syntax (analyze the musical elements, such as chord progressions of improvisations and songs, describe tempo as related to breathing);
4. Analyze sound as such (describe the qualities of the sounds. Add statements about the client's emotional, physical, and psychic states);
5. Analyze semantics (describe the referential meaning of the session);
6. Use ontology (try to become aware of the client's life world);
7. Do a metacritical evaluation (review the data collected in the previous steps).

Amir (1990) used this procedure for her study on meaning in improvised songs in two music therapy sessions with a young adult with a traumatic spinal cord injury. Many other researchers have modified or further developed phenomenological techniques, implicitly or explicitly referring to Ferrara's original contribution (Arnason, 2002; Bonde & Pedersen, 2001; Grocke, 1999; Kasayka, 1991; Ruud, 1990, 1998; Trondalen, 2003).

Ruud (1990) substituted structure for syntax and pragmatism for ontology, and recommended an analytic procedure where the steps 1–4 are preceded by the following preparations:

1. Information and associations concerning the session and its context are provided, including participants' comments;
2. The session is divided into segments or episodes, and a summary of significant features is written (for example, musical aspects, verbal comments, interpersonal elements);
3. Segments of particular clinical relevance are selected for musical microanalysis.

---

[6] This is illustrated clearly in a series of articles published in the *Nordic Journal of Music Therapy* (1998–2000), where the first session of the well-known Nordoff-Robbins case, Edward, is reinterpreted in several discourses. The series of reinterpretations included the original case study by Nordoff and Robbins (1977) and contributions from the following authors: Rolvsjord, Aigen, Bergstrøm-Nielsen, Neugebauer, Robarts, Forinash, and Ansdell. See also Ruud (1998), Chapter 7.

[7] Ferrara later developed an elaborated version of his method (Ferrara, 1991). This method, a procedure in 10 steps, may also be suitable for receptive music therapy research.

Common features in the music therapy variations on Ferrara's original model, including Ruud's substitutions, are summarized and discussed by Trondalen (2003, 2004), who suggested a revised seven-step procedure focusing on musical and interpersonal levels:

1. Contextual level (introducing the client's personal, social, biological, musical, and clinical history),
2. Structural level (a. characterization of the sound as such; b. structural analysis of the music (Grocke's SMMA, see below),
3. Semantic level (first, description of musical structures in relation to other information from the session → referential/explicit meaning, then interpretation of codes and symbols in the music → metaphor and analogy/implicit meaning),
4. Pragmatic level (potential outcome of the improvisation),
5. Phenomenological horizonalization (listing important issues, musical cues and events),
6. Phenomenological matrix (a descriptive summary of music, meaning and effect),
7. Meta-discussion (including also interviews with the client, therapist's self-reflection, and theoretical discussion).

In phenomenological procedures, music analysis, including elements of syntax/structure as well as semantics, is considered part of a complex whole. It is debatable whether we can talk about a specific phenomenological framework.[8] Trondalen mentions SMMA (Structural Model for Music Analysis) as a method on the structural level, based on a transcription or score, and she finds the method applicable for the analysis of clinical improvisations. However, since SMMA was developed for the analysis of composed music it is presented in the next section.

Langenberg (1988; Langenberg, Frommer, & Tress, 1992, 1993) developed a psycho-analytically based method aimed at uncovering the latent content of improvisations. Through what she called *resonator function,* observers can gain access to the hidden meaning of an improvisation. Triangulation of perspectives is used in the following procedure:

1. An improvisation is selected for analysis, based on clinical relevance, and the therapist writes a log;
2. A group of (3–5) observers (untrained in music therapy) listen without information and describe their feelings thoughts, images, and so forth;
3. The client does the same;
4. Analysis of the three accounts, divided into qualities concerning the musical aspects (sounds, expressions, and so forth) and qualities referring to the reactions of the observers; a synthesis of motifs is identified;
5. Music analysis by musical expert(s), including transcription;
6. Comparison and summary of all data;
7. Presentation of the analysis as a case study.

Morphological music analysis (Tüpker, 1988; see also Chapter 34 of this book, Morphological Research) has some similar features, although the theoretical background is different. A group of researchers (music therapists and lay people) listens to a selected improvisation. Their discussion has four steps:

1. *Wholeness:* Open listening to the whole, common summary.
2. *Internal regulation:* The music is analyzed in detail, and details are related to the whole.
3. *Transformation:* External information about the client is provided and music is *translated* into psychology: How is the life world of the client present in the improvisation?
4. *Reconstruction:* A *local theory* of the client is formulated. The morphological model can also be used with informants or co-researchers who are not music therapists.

The gestalt factors of *arrangement* and *effect* do not form a complementary relationship with each other but create a short circuit, as it were. The beginnings of formation are incessantly subjected to sorting procedures; these seem unachievable by any other limiting tendency. Thus,

---

[8] The relationship between phenomenology as a philosophy and as a specific research method (for example, to study clients' experiences of music therapy) will not be discussed here. See Chapter 26, Phenomenological Inquiry, for additional information.

actions are initiated but then inhibited but cannot be completed. At the same time, the sorting tendency does not unfold because no distinctive gestalt is formed, leading to disorganization.

An eclectic approach to the analysis of improvisations was developed by Arnason (2002). She gave guidelines for the examination of different levels of musical meaning through a series of reflections or listenings:

1. Open listening,
2. Listening to the musical parameters and their combinations, especially with focus on the client's way of playing,
3. Description of thoughts and feelings of the listener,
4. Imagery and metaphors elicited by the music,
5. Becoming aware of the client's life world and external influences on his/her musical experiences,
6. Final open listening (synthesis).

Corresponding to Ferrara's meta-critique, Arnason included two reflections: one on the client-therapist relationship (before Step 5) and one on the integration of musical and referential analysis with clinical context (after Step 6). The presentation format is an *improvisation narrative,* a type of interpretive musical description using "a mix of free verse poetry, prose, and abbreviated sentences to represent in words the dynamic and creative nature of improvised music" (p. 7).

The analytic methods reviewed can in principle be used for solo, dyadic, and group improvisations. However, group improvisations present specific challenges, as they are difficult to record, transcribe or represent, describe, analyze, and interpret.

Aigen (1992, 1997) used the following steps in his study of an adolescent creative music therapy group:

1. Video recording of a number of sessions (the therapist not being the observer),
2. Chronological summary of the sessions and discussion of the summary with the therapist(s),
3. Construction of *monologues* describing each participant (client); the monologues are based on client quotes, the therapist's description of the client at the observer/researchers assumptions concerning the inner world of the client,
4. Identification and detailed description of significant therapeutic episodes,
5. Identification and analysis of significant musical episodes in relation to the session as a whole,
6. Synthesis of Steps 1–5 in a narrative case study.

A psychoanalytically informed method to analyze group improvisations was developed by Metzner (2000). Theoretically, the *description protocol* method is based on especially Lorenzer's *scenic understanding* of the complex and ambiguous situations of one or more person's unknown and unconscious life, as represented by dreams, daydreams, and in this case by musical improvisations, and the accompanying guidelines for text analysis. The basic procedure is that the clinician or researcher listens to a selected improvisation one time with evenly suspended attention and writes a text during the music listening, including all sorts of observations, images, emotions, associations, and fantasies. Not the music, but this text is subject to a protocol administered in five steps of description, analysis, and hermeneutic interpretation, all five including specific guiding questions:

1. Logical understanding,
2. Psychological understanding,
3. Scenic understanding,
4. Deep hermeneutic understanding,
5. Reconstruction.

Reliability and validity have been examined through the analysis of 18 different protocols. The texts were analyzed by either the clinician or independent observers, by one or more observers, right after the improvisation or much later. According to Metzner, all protocols made therapeutic sense and there was good inter-observer correspondence. The method is time-consuming, but with proper training and theoretical foundation in Lorenzer's thinking a protocol can be completed in about 1 hour plus the duration of the improvisation.

A phenomenologically based model was developed by Skewes (2001, 2002). Her *Music Therapy Group Improvisation (MTGI) Listening Model* focuses on the musical dynamics and material of the group and the musical strategies of the group leader. A basic distinction between description and interpretation is made, incorporating multi-leveled narrative descriptions of musical properties that can be identified by musical listening. The model has five levels of listening and description, with the first four aiming at investigating a range of possible descriptions of the material, while the final distillation presents a consistent understanding of the complete data. The steps are as follows:

1. Open listening/narrative description focusing on the improvisation as a whole;
2. Focus on the musical properties/narrative description of musical properties and changes;
3. Focus on dynamic properties, directed by Bruscia's IAPs and narrative description about the scores within the relevant IAP profiles;
4. Focus on the group leader, identifying and describing materials, techniques and interactions used;
5. Final focus on the whole improvisation, but directed by material gathered in steps 1–4, distillation of meaning by exploration of the material from the four narrative descriptions.

Two independent expert listeners verified the researcher's descriptions, thus providing empirical support to the notion that the dynamics of group music interactions can be articulated and described in a valid way.

The methods to follow have special research purposes and contexts.

Ansdell (1996) developed a listening test for the analysis of music discourses as he did a reflexive metatheoretical study on the relationship between praxis (what music therapists do), discourse (what they say), and epistemology (what they know). The study was based on a simple yet elegant qualitative experiment, where a group of listeners (with different musical and therapeutic backgrounds) individually described a music therapy improvisation (Ansdell, 1995). The procedure followed three steps:

1. Open listening to the improvisation as a whole → free comments,
2. Second listening with stops every time the listener hears something significant or important → specific comments,
3. Final listening to the whole → additional comments.

All comments are recorded, enabling a comparative analysis of stop points (identification of significant moments), and transcribed for the purpose of discourse analysis. This test procedure can be used in all cases where the researcher wants to establish trustworthiness by comparing his or her own description, analysis, and interpretation to that of other people (colleagues, lay people, experts, and so forth) or when a triangulation of listening perspectives is useful (Ansdell & Pavlicevic, 2001). The procedure also addresses the *music therapist's dilemma*: the problems connected with using language to describe music and music knowledge within a more or less consciously chosen verbal discourse (Ansdell, 1999).

Aigen (1998) studied the work of Nordoff and Robbins with eight children during the years 1961–1962. The study was designed as a comparative analysis in four parts: (a) form and structure of the sessions, (b) detailed analysis of the use of music, (c) discussion of underlying philosophy and rationale of the model, and (d) examination of the therapeutic relationship in order to discuss the Nordoff-Robbins approach as music psychotherapy. The study was accompanied by two audio CDs, and the music analyses included verbal descriptions of these episodes. The music study included the use of idioms, styles, and scales, the "objectivity of the music without universality or singularity" (p. 259), the role and importance of personal expression in music, "establishing a musical world," and the importance of singing. Aigen discussed when a musical description is salient in considering clinical process, and he emphasized that this can only be determined empirically.

G. Aldridge (1998a, 1998b, 1999) investigated the processes leading to melody formation in Nordoff-Robbins based improvisational therapy. She selected episodes from two case studies (one with an oncology patient and one with a psychosomatic patient) and analyzed them with musical description and interpretation of therapeutic meaning as poles in a special format developed for the study. The analysis was based on transcriptions of the episodes, using traditional notation for the melodic line and special graphic notation for some rhythmic features and for the musical relationship between patient and therapists (see Figure 1). The focus was not on the final melodic *product,* as it would have been in a musicological study, but on the musical and therapeutic processes leading to the facilitation of melodic expressivity. The qualitative research design enabled the researcher to formulate a theory on the formation of expressive melody, based on the interpretations. One of the case studies (G. Aldridge, 1999) is also available in an electronic format (on CD-Rom), allowing the music to be heard while the score is studied.

Analyzing Composed Music in Receptive Music Therapy. A *Structural Model for Music Analysis* (SMMA) was developed by Grocke (1999) as part of her study of *pivotal moments* in the Bonny Method of Guided Imagery and Music (BMGIM). Inspired by Bonny's unpublished sheet of "Musical Elements to Listen for in the GIM Tapes," Grocke developed a means for systematic investigation of influential musical elements and parameters. Using this procedure, Grocke identified the music selections from GIM music programs that accompanied and supported pivotal experiences of clients. She found that strong, structured music in a musical form and from the romantic period provided the musical support necessary. (Complementarily, Lewis [1998–1999] found that transformative GIM experiences of a spiritual nature were more likely supported by impressionist music.) The SMMA allows the researcher to make systematic comments and descriptions of the following 15 elements and parameters: style and form, texture, time, rhythmic features, tempo, tonal features, melody, embellishments, harmony, timbre/quality of instrumentation, volume, intensity, mood, symbolism/association, and performance. SMMA analysis of four musical selections underpinning the pivotal moments of four clients allowed Grocke to identify the following common features:

> There was a formal structure in which repetition was evident; they were predominantly slow in speed and tempos were consistent; there was predictability in melodic, harmonic and rhythmic elements, and there was dialogue between solo instruments and orchestra, between groups of instruments, or in vocal parts. (pp. ii–iii)

The SMMA can also be applied to the analysis of improvisations. Wigram (2004) explained how the SMMA may be used as a checklist when describing music therapy improvisations. Grocke also introduced the *Event Structure Analysis* (ESA; Tesch, 1990) as a format facilitating the study of the relationship between music and imagery (coded as temporal or emotional events) as both unfold in time. An example of an Event Structure Analysis is shown in Table 4.

SMMA and ESA were used by Marr (2000, 2001) in her analysis of the GIM music program *Grieving,* She correlated the results of the SMMA analysis with the imagery of four clients, using the ESA format illustrated in Table 4. A similar procedure was used by Bonde in an analysis of the imagery of oncology patients in recovery to Brahms' *Violin Concerto,* 2nd Movement (Bonde, 2004b).

Phenomenological Description of music is used by many researchers as part of their music research method. Examples are provided by Bonny and Grocke (see Appendix 6 and 7 in Grocke, 1999).

Affective-Intuitive Listening or *Body Listening* is another method developed by Bonny (1993/2002b). It was designed to facilitate analysis from an experiential-embodied perspective, and consequently it is presented as a form of *Embodied Phenomenology* in Chapter 30, First-Person Research, of this book. *Creative Music Analyses* inspired by Bonny's affective-intuitive perspective may use other modalities to gather information on the researcher's or the therapist's experiences with the music, for instance, by making artwork, poetry, narratives, or dramatic forms as interpretations of a music program (also see Chapter 36, Arts-Based Research).

Bruscia developed two methods of music analysis, especially designed for research in music experiences in BMGIM. *Heuristic Music Analysis* and *Collaborative Heuristic Analysis of Music* are aimed at understanding how the GIM music programs are experienced and used by client and therapist during a session. The analysis involves the researcher exploring the music in four experiential spaces: focusing on the music or the imagery in both an alert and a deeply relaxed state. In the collaborative method, the group of researchers experiences the music program in all four spaces, both as guide and as imager. For additional information on the two methods, see Chapter 30, First-Person Research.

Bonny (1978, 1987/2002d) developed an intuitive method called *Dynamics of Experience* to describe the *affective-expressive contour* (or *inner morphology*) of the specially sequenced GIM music programs. These graphic charts, one of which is illustrated in Figure 2, give the reader an overview of how the music is sequenced to facilitate a specific dynamic affective experience. Bonde and Pedersen (2001) elaborated the method into a graphic description applicable to single selections. The graph includes specific levels of experience and precise indications of salient musical feature (with reference to the score) on a timeline of how the music unfolds affectively-

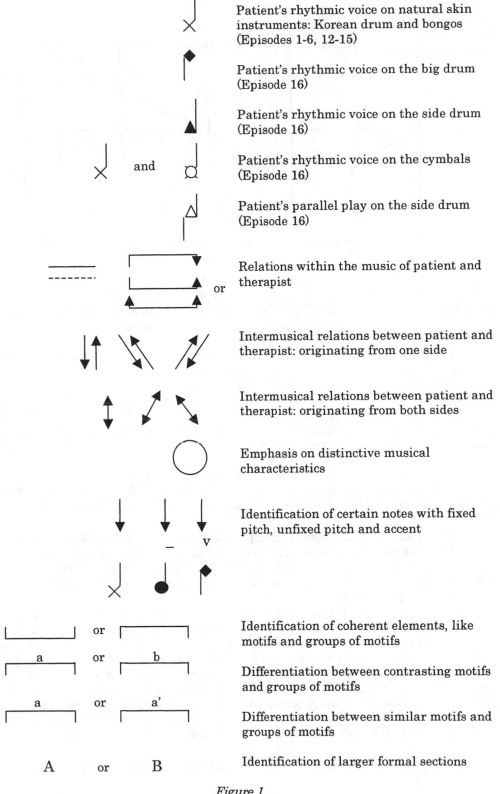

Figure 1
Special Notation of Rhythmic Features and Intermusical Relationships
in Clinical Improvisations
G. Aldridge (1998a). Used with permission.

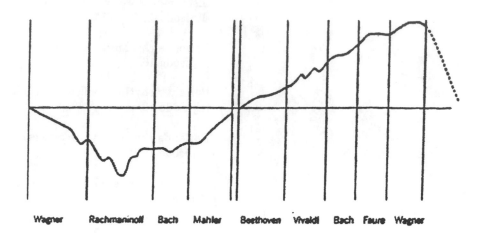

Figure 2
Affective-Expressive Contour of GIM Music Program, *Death-Rebirth and Peak Experience*
Bonny (1978/2002a). Used with permission.

dynamically, thus indicating an important aspect of the music's image potential. A less complex version of such a graph, called an *intensity profile,* can be used to capture the experiential intensity potential of a musical selection (Bonde, 2004a, 2004b; an example is given in Figure 3) or the experienced intensity of an improvisation (Trondalen, 2004). Figure 3 shows the experiential potential of a specific music selection and the most important changes in the music as heard. The timeline corresponds to the specific recording, while the comments on specific musical elements and parameters refer to the score. The analysis is based on collaborative heuristic analysis.

A survey of these and other methods especially designed for the analysis of music programs used in the Bonny Method is presented by Abrams (2002). A number of the methods presented above are further described and discussed in Mahns (1998, 2004) and Smeijsters (1997).

Additional Techniques. Some of the technical devices described as being useful for understanding nonmusical responses can also be used to research musical responses. Hevner's Mood wheel and other adjective checklists can be used to investigate the mood profile of composed as well as improvised music, as can the *polarity profile* (semantic differential) and free descriptions by the participants.

Repertory grid analysis, based on Kelly's Personal Construct Theory, can be used to find out how "music therapists organize their world of musical experience in one particular realm of activity" (D. Aldridge, 1996, p. 127), for instance, by eliciting the researcher's *tacit knowledge,* musical bias, or preunderstanding, thus enhancing the credibility of the research. This device was used by G. Aldridge (1998a) to examine her own understanding of melody, the basic construct in her music research. D. Aldridge (1996, Chapter 6) provides examples of how the repertory grid analysis, using the RepGrid software, may be used to elicit constructs such as the properties of musical instruments. This technique is discussed further in Chapter 37 of this book, Personal Construct Psychology and the Repertory Grid Technique.

Musical Representation: Traditional and Graphic Notation

When qualitative researchers choose to include representations of the music analyzed, they may use *traditional notation,* made either by hand or using software programs like Finale, Cubase, or Sibelius. It is even possible to combine a keyboard used for improvisation with a computer, using MIDI interface enabling an instant *computer notation* of the music (Lee, 1996, 2000).

Table 4
Event Structure Analysis
Marr (2000). Used with permission.

Code	Music	Greg	Joe	Ann	Kate	Comments
T1	Bar 15: Major changes to minor; new theme ascends, then descends, expected cadence	Dressing table; windows; the house was happy, now sad				Shift in the music: Major to minor; theme ascends and descends reflects shift in imagery; description of the house to emotion and feeling of the house
E2	Bar 25: Oboe line is embellished; weaves in and out	Stairwell; steep and worn			A bird in flight	Melody line reflected in the shape of the stairwell (Greg) and the visual line of the bird in flight (Kate)
T2 E1 (Ann)	Bar 33: Climax; final cadence; resolution.	House was home made; people in it.	Stairwell; a window; level with very large tree.	Water dripping off trees.		Ostinato pulse like dripping water. Music texture is thick, like not allowing light through the trees (Ann). Climax matches climax of house image—homemade and people in it (Greg), and the window is level with large tree—looking out (Joe).
T2	Bar 39: Violins break from ostinato and bring melodic material to final closure.	Look around the foyer—bright; guests come; black and white floor.	Got up 3 times to look at tree. Leaves are large, mapley, orange and rusty brown.			The oboe has stopped; melody is drawn into accompaniment—one room; bright; guests come. Foyer as entrance to house is like the start of the session (Greg), and a reminder of the previous day (Joe).

Marcello, *Concerto No. 2 in C minor for Oboe, Stings, and Basso Continuo—Adagio*
Code: T = temporal event
       E = emotional event
       1–4 = number of participants involved in an event

    Structural Analysis of Post-Tonal Therapeutic Improvisatory Music was developed by Lee (1990) before the availability of the MIDI technology. Inspired by Schenkerian constructs in musicological analysis, Lee demonstrated how microanalysis of, for example, metrical hierarchies, rhythmic and melodic patterns, and pitch classes can be used in the analysis of free clinical improvisations. Lee (1995, 1996, 2000) has continued to develop the method in several publications. He has labeled it *A Method of Analyzing Improvisations in Music Therapy* (2000) and included the aid of MIDI in his analyses. While other methods focus on exterior influences on the music, Lee wants to examine "the music building blocks of improvisation as a means to better understand the intricacies of the process" (p. 147). Lee worked with verbal clients in a type of collaborative inquiry, although the method can be adapted to nonverbal clients also. The method is a nine-stage procedure, including microanalysis inspired by musicological procedures:

Levels of Intensity:

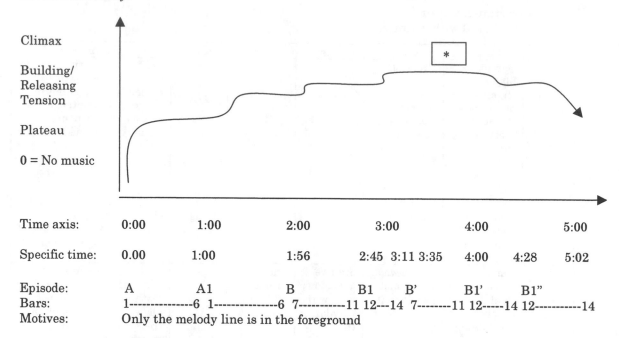

Time axis: 0:00   1:00   2:00   3:00   4:00   5:00

Specific time: 0.00   1:00   1:56   2:45 3:11 3:35 4:00   4:28   5:02

Episode: A   A1   B   B1   B'   B1'   B1"
Bars: 1---------------6 1---------------6 7-----------11 12---14 7--------11 12-----14 12-----------14
Motives: Only the melody line is in the foreground

Note: The original figure includes additional cues on the development of the following musical elements: Key, Instrument(s), Melody, Mood, Tempo, and Dynamics.

Figure 3
Example of an Intensity Profile (Bonde, 2004a)
Music selection: J. S. Bach: *Mein Jesu! was vor Seelenweh* BWV 487
Orchestral arrangement by L. Stokowski; Recording: *Music for the Imagination*

1. *Holistic listening.* A non-referential procedure focusing on the identification of the musically most significant features, structures and elements (referencing the Nordoff-Robbins approach to session review; see Figure 4 for an example of one of the ways that is suggested for doing this, a description of significant elements that are heard).
2. *Reactions of therapist to music as process.* Therapist writes a narrative on how he or she perceives the musical and therapeutic experience.
3. *Client listening.* A conversation on listening to the improvisation is recorded and later transcribed.
4. *Consultant listening.* One or more external experts in different fields comments (as in 3).
5. *Transcription into notation.* Many notation formats may be used: computer representation through MIDI and notation software, aural notation, or diagrammatic representation.
6. *Segmentation into musical components.* This is based on clear criteria and dividing the whole into manageable components.
7. *Verbal description.* Components are described concisely, creating a catalog of events or an inventory of musical constructs.
8. *In-depth analysis of segments and comparison of data.* In this stage musicological methods may be applied to answer questions such as: Is there a harmonic cell? Are there tonal centers? Are there melodic or rhythmic motifs or cells? Then follows a comparison of verbal data from stages 3 and 4 with the music analysis—a triangulation linking observations from separate areas. Convergences and divergences between verbal and music material are made clear.
9. *Synthesis.* Integration of all data and formulation of clinical conclusions.

An example of Lee's analysis is shown in Figure 4. It belongs to stage 1 of the method, where the third of a total of four listenings is aimed at creating a musical inventory of the improvisation, based on an exact transcription of the most significant musical elements and a description of their relationship. In the example, Lee identifies the two predominant melodic motives and chords and indicates the succession of musical events on a time line.

As was illustrated in Figure 1, the researcher can also develop *specific musical notation* suited for the analytic purpose.

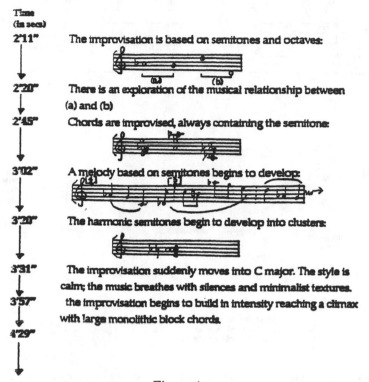

Figure 4
Musical Themes and Motives in an Improvisation, Presented as an Inventory
Lee, C. (2000). Used with permission.

Video documentation opens a new vista also when researching the music. Aigen (2002) published the first case study combining verbal description and video examples on an accompanying CD-Rom, thus creating a mixed-media narrative.

The dynamics of a piece of music can also be represented graphically by *digitized waveform* (DW, as analyzed by a computer program for sound analysis and editing). This enables correlations with stimulus responses as, for example, EEG amplitude and frequency (Lem, 1999). The DW is not identical with the so-called Intensity Profile (Bonde, 2004a, 2004b; Trondalen, 2004), however a comparison of the DW in the IP may part of an elaborated music analysis, including SMMA or other score based analytic methods.

The music may also be represented by *graphic notation* (Bergstrøm-Nielsen, 1993, 1999), enabling a graphic overview, using specific notation symbols of otherwise nontranscribable music interactions (see Figure 5).

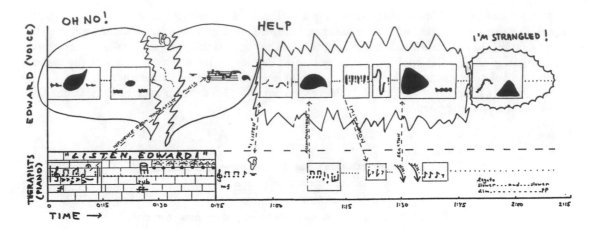

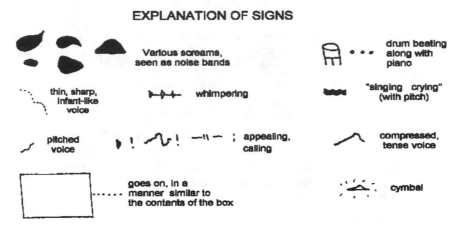

I perceived Edward's sounds as expressing emotional states of pain/sorrow, frustration/anger, and exhaustion/feeling deserted. They are probably typical of his life experience.

The therapists meet Edward with a firm "wall of sound." Later, a dialogue is opened. Edward shows faith at an unconscious level, indicated by the increasing degree of interchange in the music.

Figure 5
Example of Graphic Notation, Edward Score
Bergstrøm-Nielsen (1993, 1999). Used with permission.

Christensen (1996) developed a theoretical model of the *musical timespace* (see Figure 6). He made suggestions on how to describe music verbally, including verbal constructs (often polarities) appropriate for attentive listening. Examples are:

- Foreground-middle ground-background,
- Movement with or without direction,
- Density-opacity,
- Physical space-virtual space,
- Simplicity-complexity, expectation-surprise,
- Order-chaos,
- Close-distant,
- Soft-hard,
- Rigid-flexible.

These principles for theory-based verbal description can be used together with both traditional and graphic notation. In the final chapter of Christensen's (1996) book, the complete model illustrates the interrelationships between the musical time and space dimensions. The model identifies five basic listening dimensions that provide a basis for aural/auditory orientation in the natural environment—including music listening. They are *timbre,* and *pitch height* (space; microtemporal), *movement,* and *pulse* (macrotemporal), with *intensity* as a resulting complex dimension. In the interplay with the traditional elements of melody, rhythm, and harmony, which Christensen calls "secondary listening dimensions," a virtual musical timespace is constructed. The axioms of the musical timespace theory can be formulated in the following caption quotes: "Timbre is the substance of music" (p. 68). "Pitch height is a focused aspect of timbre" (p. 74). "Harmony is an emergent quality of timbre" (p. 75). "Rhythm is the temporal shape of movement" (p. 91). "Melody is the spatial shape of movement" (p. 98). "Movement represents macrotemporal change, and Pulse represents macrotemporal regularity" (p. 115). "Timbre represents microtemporal change, Pitch height represents microtemporal regularity" (p. 116). "The soundscape is a multi-layered pattern of timbres" (p. 142). "Micromodulation creates a microspace in the musical macrospace" (p. 149).

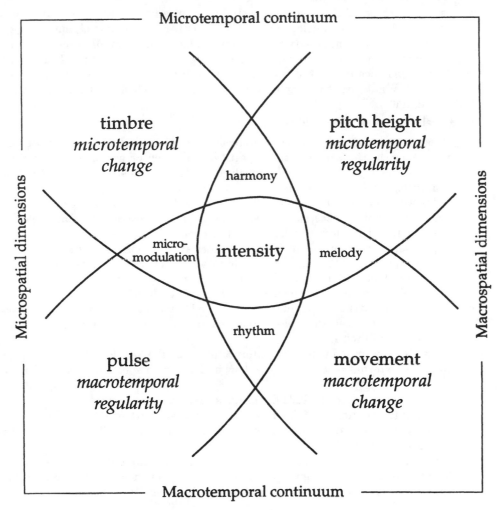

Figure 6
Model of *The Musical Timespace*
Christensen (1996). Used with permission.

Conclusion

Researching the music can never be an end in itself in a music therapy research context. It must always be part of a comprehensive methodology, for instance, as one or more steps or levels in a systematic procedure or as part of a methodological triangulation (Smeijsters, 1997). The researcher may also reflect on the properties or levels of music suggested by Ruud, and the analytical situations and levels suggested by Nattiez and D. Aldridge, and how they may be relevant for the research. Many cycles of listening and many types of reflection are needed in order to describe, analyze, and interpret the therapeutic significance of the music (G. Aldridge, 2002; Lee, 2000).

The researcher should examine his or her aims with researching the music and answer some basic questions before choosing one or more of the many methods described in this chapter (or developing his or her own):

- Is the purpose of the research to study a specific music intervention as stimulus and response? If yes: how can the music be operationalized for this purpose as independent and dependent variables? Is an experimental or a behavioral design appropriate? What limitations does it give the study if a positivist paradigm (or causal perspective) is chosen? What are the implications of mixing methods within a post-positivist paradigm?
- Is the purpose of the research to study the meaning of the music (improvised or composed) and the musical interaction process for the participants? If yes: Is it appropriate or necessary to study music as sound/structure, and can meaning/semantics be studied without going into a more technical analysis? What limitations does it give the study if a non-positivist (or interpretative perspective) is chosen? What are the implications of mixing methods within a post-positivist paradigm?

Other relevant questions could be:

- What is the trace, the object of analysis, and what was and is the position of the researcher in the semiological tripartition? Was he or she involved in the poietic process, or is he or she only involved in the aesthesic process? What are the limitations and implications?
- Is the audio or video recording sufficient and self evident as a trace or is some form of verbal description necessary? If so, what music experience data are relevant, and how can they be collected, selected, and analyzed?
- Is it necessary or convenient to make a musical notation/transcription? If yes, should it be complete or partial (selection criteria and procedures for identification of events or episodes should be given)? Should a transcription use traditional or graphic notation? Is (verbal) phenomenological description sufficient?
- How can the structure (syntax) be analyzed? How can the analysis be presented? How can the music therapist's dilemma (representing the musical experience in words) be dealt with?
- Does the research include an interpretation of the results of the music analysis (internal/external poietics)? If yes, how and why is a specific theoretical framework chosen?
- How can the research include the pragmatics and/or the context?
- How can the credibility of the music research be strengthened?
- What problems—analytical as well as meta-analytical—does the analysis and interpretation raise?
- And finally, how can the music research be integrated in a presentation format facilitating the reader's multi-modal experience and thorough understanding of the research questions, data, and procedures, and the results of the study?

References

Abeles, H. F., & Chung, J. W. (1996). Responses to music. In D. A. Hodges (Ed.), *Handbook of music psychology* (2nd ed.; pp. 285–342). San Antonio, TX: Institute for Music Research.

Abrams, B. (2002). Methods of analyzing music programs used in the Bonny Method. In K. E. Bruscia & D. E. Grocke (Eds.), *Guided Imagery and Music: The Bonny Method and beyond* (pp. 317–335). Gilsum, NH: Barcelona Publishers.

Aigen, K. (1992). Ongoing qualitative research at the Nordoff-Robbins Music Therapy Clinic at New York University. In *Body, mind, spirit: AAMT coming of age:* Proceedings of the 21st Annual Conference of the American Association for Music Therapy.

Aigen, K. (1997). *Here we are in music: One year with an adolescent creative music therapy group.* St. Louis, MO: MMB Music.

Aigen, K. (1998). *Paths of development in Nordoff-Robbins music therapy.* Gilsum, NH: Barcelona Publishers.

Aigen, K. (2002). *Playin' in the band: A qualitative study of popular music styles as clinical improvisation.* New York: Nordoff-Robbins Center for Music Therapy, New York University.

Aldridge, D. (1996). *Music therapy research and practice in medicine: From out of the silence.* London: Jessica Kingsley Publishers.

Aldridge, G. (1998a). *Die Entwicklung einer Melodie im Kontext improvisatorischer Musiktherapie* [The development of a melody in the context of improvisational music therapy]. Unpublished doctoral dissertation, Aalborg University/University Witten-Herdecke, Herdecke, Germany. Available at http://www.musictherapyworld.net/modules/archive/dissertations/list_all.php

Aldridge, G. (1998b). The implications of melodic expression for music therapy with a breast cancer patient. In D. Aldridge (Ed.), *Music therapy in palliative care: New voices* (pp. 135–153). London: Jessica Kingsley Publishers.

Aldridge, G. (1999). The development of melody: Four hands, two minds, one music. In D. Aldridge (Ed.), *Music therapy info CD-ROM* (Vol. 2, p. 13). Herdecke: Witten-Herdecke University.

Aldridge, G. (2002, August). Cycles of listening for identifying incidents of therapeutic significance in clinical improvisation. *Music Therapy Today.* Available at http://musictherapyworld.net

Amir, D. (1990). A song is born: Discovering meaning in improvised songs through phenomenological analysis of two music therapy sessions with a traumatic spinal-cord injured young adult. *Music Therapy, 9,* 62–81.

Ansdell, G. (1995). *Music for life: Aspects of Creative Music Therapy with adult clients.* London: Jessica Kingsley Publishers.

Ansdell, G. (1996). Talking about music therapy: A dilemma and a qualitative experiment. *British Journal of Music Therapy, 10,* 4–15.

Ansdell, G. (1997). Musical elaborations: What has New Musicology to say to music therapy? *British Journal of Music Therapy, 11,* 36–44.

Ansdell, G. (1999). *Music therapy as discourse and discipline: A study of music therapist's dilemma.* Unpublished doctoral dissertation, City University, London.

Ansdell, G. (2001). Musicology: Misunderstood guest at the music therapy feast? In G. diFranco, E. Ruud, T. Wigram, & D. Aldridge (Eds.), *Music therapy in Europe: The 5th European Music Therapy Congress* (pp. 17–34). Rome: ISMEZ.

Ansdell, G., & Pavlicevic, M. (2001). *Beginning research in the arts therapies: A practical guide.* London: Jessica Kingsley Publishers.

Arnason, C. L. R. (2002). An eclectic approach to the analysis of improvisations in music therapy sessions. *Music Therapy Perspectives, 20,* 4–12.

Baker, F., & Wigram, T. (2004). The immediate and long-term effects of singing on the mood states of people with traumatic brain injury. *British Journal of Music Therapy, 18,* 55–64.

Bartlett, D. L. (1996). Physiological responses to music and sound stimuli. In D. A. Hodges (Ed.), *Handbook of music psychology* (2nd ed., pp. 343–385). San Antonio, TX: Institute for Music Research.

Bergstrøm-Nielsen, C. (1993). Graphic notation as a tool in describing and analyzing music therapy improvisations. *Music Therapy, 12,* 40–58.

Bergstrøm-Nielsen, C. (1999). The music of Edward, session one, as graphic notation. *Nordic Journal of Music Therapy, 8,* 96–99.

Berlyne, D. E. (1971). *Aesthetics and psychobiology.* New York: Appleton-Century-Crofts.

Bonde, L. O. (1997). Music analysis and image potentials in classical music. *Nordic Journal of Music Therapy, 6,* 121–129.

Bonde, L. O. (2004a). *The Bonny Method of Guided Imagery and Music (BMGIM) with cancer survivors. A psychosocial study with focus on the influence of BMGIM on mood and quality of life.* Unpublished doctoral dissertation, Aalborg University, Aalborg, Denmark.

Bonde, L. O. (2004b). Musik als Co-Therapeutin. Gedanken zum Verhältnis zwischen Musik und Inneren Bildern in The Bonny Method of Guided Imagery and Music (BMGIM) [Music as co-therapist: Reflections on the relationship between music and imagery in BMGIM]. In I. Frohne-Hagemann (Ed.), *Rezeptive Musiktherapie. Theorie und Praxis* (pp. 111–139). Wiesbaden, Germany: Reichert Verlag.

Bonde, L. O., & Pedersen, I. N. (2001). Grounding image potentials in the musical experience: Reflections on a tape analysis of "Creativity I." *Col legno.* Available at http://www.musik.aau.dk/collegno/collegno.dk.html

Bonny, H. (1978). *GIM monograph #2: The role of taped music programs in the GIM process.* Salina, KS: Bonny Foundation. (Portions reprinted in *Music consciousness: The evolution of Guided Imagery and Music,* pp. 301-321, L. Summer, Ed., 2002a. Gilsum, NH: Barcelona Publishers)

Bonny, H. (1993). Body listening: A new way to review the GIM tapes. *Journal of the Association for Music and Imagery, 2,* 3–13. (Reprinted in *Nordic Journal of Music Therapy,* 2002b, *11,* 173–177)

Bonny, H. L. (2002c). Music listening for intensive coronary care units: A pilot project. In L. Summer (Ed.), *Music consciousness: The evolution of Guided Imagery and Music* (pp. 247–261). Gilsum, NH: Barcelona Publishers. (Reprinted from *Music Therapy,* 1983, *3,* 4–16)

Bonny, H. L. (2002d). Music: The language of immediacy. In L. Summer (Ed.), *Music consciousness: The evolution of Guided Imagery and Music* (pp. 103–115). Gilsum, NH: Barcelona Publishers. (Reprinted from *The Arts in Psychotherapy,* 1987, *14,* 255–261)

Brotons, M., & Pickett-Cooper, P. K. (1996). The effects of music therapy intervention on agitation behaviors of Alzheimer's disease patients. *Journal of Music Therapy, 33,* 2–18.

Bruscia, K. E. (1987). *Improvisational models of music therapy.* Springfield, IL: Charles C. Thomas.

Bruscia, K. E. (1994). *IAP. Improvisational Assessment Profiles. Kartlegging gjennom musikkterapeutisk improvisasion* [Improvisation Assessment Profiles: Assessment through improvisational music therapy]. Sandane, Norway: Høgskula på Sandane.

Bruscia, K. E. (1998). *Defining music therapy* (2nd ed.). Gilsum, NH: Barcelona Publishers.

Bruscia, K. E. (1999). *A method of analyzing music program in GIM: Manual for GIM training.* Unpublished manuscript.

Bruscia, K. E. (2002). Response to the Forum discussion of the "IAPs" in the *Nordic Journal* website. *Nordic Journal of Music Therapy, 11,* 72–82.

Bruscia, K. E. (2005). *Improvisation assessment profiles—Abridged.* Philadelphia, PA: Unpublished manuscript.

Bunt, L., & Pavlicevic, M. (2001). Music and emotion: Perspectives from music therapy. In P. N. Juslin & H. A. Sloboda (Eds.), *Music and emotion: Theory and research* (pp. 181–201). Oxford: Oxford University Press.

Bunt, L., & Hoskyns, S. (Eds.). (2002). *The handbook of music therapy.* New York: Brunner-Routledge.

Bunt, L., Burns, S., & Turton, P. (2000). Variations on a theme: The evolution of a music therapy research programme at the Bristol Cancer Help Centre. *British Journal of Music Therapy, 14,* 62–69.

Christensen, E. (1996). *The musical timespace: A theory of music listening.* Aalborg, Denmark: Aalborg University Press.

Clair, A. A., Bernstein, B., & Johnson, G. (1995). Rhythm playing characteristics in persons with severe dementia including those with probable Alzheimer's type. *Journal of Music Therapy, 32,* 113–131.

Clifton, T. (1983). *Music as heard: A study in applied phenomenology.* New Haven, CT: Yale University Press.

Cohen, N. S. (1992). The effect of singing instruction on the speech production of neurologically impaired persons. *Journal of Music Therapy, 29,* 87–102.

Cook, N. (1987). *A guide to musical analysis.* London: Norton.

Edgerton, C. L. (1994). The effect of improvisational music therapy on the communicative behaviors of autistic children. *Journal of Music Therapy, 31,* 31–62.

Elefant, C. (2001). Speechless yet communicative: Revealing the person behind the disability of Rett syndrome through clinical research on songs in music therapy. In G. diFranco, E.

Ruud, T. Wigram, & D. Aldridge (Eds.), *Music therapy in Europe: The 5th European Music Therapy Congress* (pp. 113–128). Rome: ISMEZ.

Elefant, C. (2002). *Enhancing communication in girls with Rett syndrome through songs in music therapy.* Unpublished doctoral dissertation, Aalborg University, Aalborg. Available at http://www.musictherapyworld.de/

Elefant, C. (2005). The use of single case designs in testing a specific hypothesis. In D. Aldridge (Ed.), *Case study designs in music therapy* (pp. 145–162). London: Jessica Kingsley Publishers.

Farnsworth, P. R. (1954). A study of the Hevner adjective list. *Journal of Aesthetics and Art Criticism 13:* 97–103.

Farnsworth, P. R. (1958). *The social psychology of music.* New York: Dryden Press.

Ferrara, L. (1984). Phenomenology as a tool for musical analysis. *The Musical Quarterly 70,* 355–373.

Ferrara, L. (1991). *Philosophy and the analysis of music: Bridges to musical sound, form, and reference* (Vol. 24). New York: Greenwood Press.

Forinash, M. (1990). A phenomenology of music therapy with the terminally ill (Doctoral dissertation, New York University, 1990). *Dissertation Abstracts International, 51*(09), 2915A.

Forinash, M., & Gonzalez, D. (1989). A phenomenological perspective of music therapy. *Music Therapy, 8,* 35–46.

Gabrielsson, A., & Lindström, E. (2001). The influence of musical structure on emotional expression. In P. N. Juslin & J. A. Sloboda (Eds.), *Music and emotion: Theory and research* (pp. 223–248). Oxford: Oxford University Press.

Geringer, J. M., & Madsen, C. K. (2003). Gradual tempo change and aesthetic responses of music majors. *International Journal of Music Education, 40,* 3–15.

Gfeller, K. (2002). The function of aesthetic stimuli in the therapeutic process. In R. Unkefer & M. H. Thaut (Eds.), *Music therapy in the treatment of adults with mental disorders* (2nd ed., pp. 68–84). St. Louis, MO: MMB Music.

Gibbons, A. C. (1983). Rhythm responses in emotionally disturbed children with differing needs for external structure. *Music Therapy, 3,* 94–102.

Goins, W. E. (1998). The effect of moodstates: Continuous versus summative responses. *Journal of Music Therapy, 35,* 241–258.

Graham, J. (2000). Assessment and evaluation: An approach for initial clinical assessment and on-going treatment in music therapy. In T. Wigram (Ed.), *Assessment and evaluation in the arts therapies: Art therapy, music therapy & dramatherapy* (pp. 63–76). Radlett, Hertfordshire, UK: Harper House.

Gregory, D. (1989). Using computers to measure continuous music response. *Psychomusicology, 8,* 127–134.

Gregory, D. (2000). Test instruments used by *Journal of Music Therapy* authors from 1984–1997. *Journal of Music Therapy, 37,* 79–94.

Gregory, D. (2002). Four decades of music therapy behavioral research designs: A content analysis of *Journal of Music Therapy* articles. *Journal of Music Therapy, 39,* 56–71.

Grocke, D.E. (1999). *A phenomenological study of pivotal moments in Guided Imagery and Music therapy.* Unpublished doctoral dissertation, University of Melbourne, Melbourne. Available at www.musictherapyworld.net

Hannibal, N. (1999). The client's potential for therapeutic insight assessed through the ability to reflect verbally and musically. *Nordic Journal of Music Therapy, 8,* 36–46.

Hannibal, N. (2001). *Præverbal overføring i musikterapi* [Preverbal transference in music therapy]. Unpublished doctoral dissertation, Aalborg University, Aalborg.

Hargreaves, D. (1986). *The developmental psychology of music.* Newcastle, UK: Cambridge University Press.

Hevner, K. (1935). The affective character of the major and minor modes in music. *American Journal of Psychology, 47,* 103–118.

Hevner, K. (1936). Experimental studies of the elements of expression in music. *American Journal of Psychology, 48,* 246–268.

Hevner, K. (1937). The affective value of pitch and tempo in music. *American Journal of Psychology, 49,* 621–630.

Hintz, M. R. (2000). Geriatric music therapy clinical assessment: Assessment of musical skills and related behaviors. *Music Therapy Perspectives, 18,* 31–40.

Hodges, D. A. (Ed.). (1996). *Handbook of music psychology.* San Antonio, TX: Institute for Music Research.

Juslin, P. N., & Sloboda, J. A. (Eds.). (2001). *Music and emotion: Theory and research.* Oxford: Oxford University Press.

Kasayka, R. E. (1991). To meet and match the moment of hope: Transpersonal elements of the Guided Imagery and Music experience. *Dissertation Abstracts International, 52*(06), 2062A. (UMI No. DEY9134754)

Langenberg, M. (1988). *Vom Handeln zu Behandeln* [From handling to treatment]. Stuttgart, Germany: Gustav Fischer Verlag.

Langenberg, M., Frommer, J., & Tress, W. (1992). Qualitative Methodik zur Beschreibung und Interpretation musiktherapeutischer Behandlungswerke [Qualitative method of describing and interpreting works created in music therapy treatment]. *Musiktherapeutische Umschau, 13*, 258–278.

Langenberg, M., Frommer, J., & Tress, W. (1993). A qualitative research approach to Analytical Music Therapy. *Music Therapy, 12*, 59–84.

Lathom, W. B., Petersen, M., & Havlicek, L. (1982). Musical preferences of older people attending nutrition sites. *Educational Gerontology, 8*, 155–165.

Layman, D. L., Hussey, D. L., & Laing, S. J. (2002). Music therapy assessment for severely emotionally disturbed children: A pilot study. *Journal of Music Therapy, 39*, 164–187.

Lee, C. (1990). Structural analysis of post-tonal therapeutic improvisatory music. *Journal of British Music Therapy, 4*, 6–20.

Lee, C. (1995). The analysis of therapeutic improvisatory music. In A. Gilroy & C. Lee. (Eds.), *Art and music: Therapy and research* (pp. 35–50). New York: Routledge.

Lee, C. (1996). *Music at the edge: Music therapy experiences of a musician with AIDS.* London: Routledge.

Lee, C. (2000). A method of analyzing improvisations in music therapy. *Journal of Music Therapy, 37*, 147–167.

Lem, A. (1998). EEG reveals potential connections between the structural variability of music and the listeners' imagery. *Australian Journal of Music Therapy, 9*, 3–17.

Lem, A. (1999). Selected patterns of brainwave activity point to the connection between imagery experiences and the psychoacoustic qualities of music. In R. R. Pratt & D. E. Grocke (Eds.), *MusicMedicine 3: Music medicine and music therapy: Expanding horizons* (pp. 75–87). Melbourne: Faculty of Music, University of Melbourne.

Lem, A. (2002, September). The flow of imagery evoked by GIM music: Preliminary findings relating to attributes of music, the listener's report and ANS arousal (SC). Australian Music & Psychology Presentation. Abstract at http://marcs.uws.edu.au/links/amps/

Lewis, K. (1998–1999). The Bonny Method of Guided Imagery and Music: Matrix for transpersonal experience. *Journal of The Association for Music and Imagery, 6*, 63–85.

Loewy, J. (2000). Music psychotherapy assessment. *Music Therapy Perspectives, 18*, 47–58.

Madsen, C. K., & Frederickson, W. E. (1993). The experience of musical tension: A replication of Nielsen's research using the continuous response digital interface. *Journal of Music Therapy, 30*, 46–63.

Mahns, W. (1998). *Symbolbildungen in der analytischen Kindermusiktherapie: Eine qualitative Studie über die Bedeutung der musikalischen Improvisation in der Musiktherapie mit Schulkindern* [Symbol development in analytical music therapy with children: A qualitative study of the meaning of improvisation in music therapy with school children]. Unpublished doctoral dissertation, Aalborg University, Aalborg.

Mahns, W. (2004). Symbolbildung in der analytischen Kindermusiktherapie: Eine qualitative Studie über die Bedeutung der musikalischen Improvisation in der Musiktherapie mit Schulkindern [Symbol development in analytical music therapy with children: A qualitative study of the meaning of improvisation in music therapy with school children]. Series: *Materialien zur Musiktherapie* (Vol. 6). Münster, Germany: Lit-Verlag.

Mandler, G. (1984). *Mind and body: Psychology of emotion and stress.* New York: W. W. Norton.

Marr, J. (2000). *The effects of music on imagery sequence in the Bonny Method of Guided Imagery and Music.* Unpublished master's thesis. University of Melbourne, Melbourne.

Marr, J. (2001). The effects of music on imagery sequence in the Bonny Method of Guided Imagery and Music (GIM). *Australian Journal of Music Therapy, 12*, 39–45.

Matthews, G., Jones, D. & Chamberlain, A. (1990) Refining the measurement of mood: the UWIST Mood Adjective checklist. *British Journal of Psychology, 81,* 17–42.

McKinney, C. H., & Tims, F. C. (1995). Differential effects of selected classical music on the imagery of high versus low imagers: Two studies. *Journal of Music Therapy, 32,* 22–45.

McKinney, K., Clark, M., & Kumar, M. (in preparation). *The effect of the Bonny Method of Guided Imagery and Music on distress, life quality, and endocrine hormone levels in women with non-metastatic breast cancer: A pilot study.*

McMullen, P. T. (1974). The influence of complexity in pitch sequence on preference responses of college-age subjects. *Journal of Music Therapy, 9,* 226–233.

McMullen, P. T. (1996). The musical experience and affective/aesthetic responses: A theoretical framework for empirical research. In D. A. Hodges (Ed.), *Handbook of music psychology* (2nd ed., pp. 387–400). San Antonio, TX: Institute for Music Research.

Merle-Fishman, C. R., & Marcus, M. L. (1982). Musical behaviors and preferences in emotionally disturbed and normal children: An exploratory study. *Music Therapy, 2,* 1–11.

Metzner, S. (2000). Eine Traum: Eine fremde Sprache kennen, ohne sie zu verstehen. Zur Evaluation von gruppenimprovisationen [A dream: Knowing a foreign language without understanding it. Evaluation of group improvisations]. *Musiktherapeutische Umschau, 21,* 234–246.

Meyer, L. B. (1956). *Emotion and meaning in music.* Chicago: University of Chicago Press.

Meyer, L. B. (2001). Music and emotions: Distinctions and uncertainties. In P. N. Juslin & J. A. Sloboda (Eds.), *Music and emotion: Theory and research* (pp. 341–360). Oxford: Oxford University Press.

Møller, A. S. (2000). Kontaktebenen—Ein Modell zur darstellung musik-therapeutischer Prozesse in der Arbeit mit stark entwicklungsverzögerten Patienten [Levels of contact. A model of processes in music therapy with developmentally delayed patients]. *Musiktherapeutische Umschau, 23,* 259–270.

Moreau, D. v. (2003, September). MAKS—A scale for measurement of expressive and musical behaviour. *Music Therapy Today, 4*(4). Available at http://www.musictherapyworld.net

Nattiez, J.-J. (1990). *Music and discourse: Towards a semiology of music.* Princeton, NJ: Princeton University Press.

Nielsen, F. V. (1983). *Oplevelse af musikalsk spænding* [The experience of musical tension]. Copenhagen, Denmark: Akademisk Forlag.

Nordoff, P., & Robbins, C. (1971). *Therapy in music for handicapped children.* New York: St. Martin's Press.

Nordoff, P., & Robbins, C. (1977). *Creative music therapy.* New York: John Day Co.

Ortony, A., Clore, G. L., & Collins, A. (1988) *The cognitive structure of emotions.* New York: Cambridge University Press.

Pavlicevic, M., & Trevarthen, C. (1989). A musical assessment of psychiatric states in adults. *Psychopathology, 22,* 325–334.

Pavlicevic, M., Trevarthen, C., & Duncan, J. (1994). Improvisational music therapy and the rehabilitation of persons suffering from chronic schizophrenia. *Journal of Music Therapy, 31,* 86–104.

Pavlicevic, M. (1997). *Music therapy in context: Music, meaning and relationship.* London: Jessica Kingsley Publishers.

Peretz, I. (2001). Listen to the brain: a biological perspective on musical emotions. In P. N. Juslin & J. A. Sloboda (Eds.), *Music and emotion: Theory and research* (pp. 105–134). Oxford: Oxford University Press.

Plahl, C. (2000). *Entwicklung fördern durch Musik. Evaluation musiktherapeutischer Behandlung* [Enhancing development through music. Evaluation of music therapy treatment procedures]. Münster: Waxman.

Radocy, R. E., & Boyle, J. D. (1997). *Psychological foundations of musical behavior* (3rd ed.). Springfield, IL: Charles C. Thomas.

Rickard, N. S. (2004). Intense emotional responses to music: A test of the physiological arousal hypothesis. *Psychology of Music, 32,* 371–388.

Rider, M. (1997). *The rhythmic language of health and disease.* St. Louis, MO: MMB Music.

Rigg, M. G. (1937). Musical expression: An investigation of the theories of Erich Sorantin. *Journal of Experimental Psychology, 21,* 223–229.

Ruud, E. (1990). *Musikk som kommunikasjon og samhandling. Teoretiske perspektiv på musikkterapien* [Music as communication and interaction. Theoretical perspectives of music therapy]. Oslo, Norway: Solum Forlag.

Ruud, E. (1998). *Music therapy: Improvisation, communication, and culture.* Gilsum, NH, Barcelona Publishers.

Ruud, E. (2000, August 18). *New Musicology, music education and music therapy.* Paper presented at the 13th Nordic Musicological Congress, Musikvidenskabeligt Institut, Århus, Denmark.

Ruud, E. (2001). *Varme øyeblikk : om musikk, helse og livskvalitet* [Hot moments: On music, health and quality of life]. Oslo: Unipub.

Scheiby, B. (2002). Improvisation as a musical healing tool and life approach—Theoretical and clinical applications of Analytical Music Therapy (AMT) improvisation in a short- and long-term rehabilitation facility. In J. T. Eschen (Ed.), *Analytical Music Therapy* (pp. 115–153). London: Jessica Kingsley Publishers.

Schubert, E. (2001). Continuous measurement of self-report emotional response to music. In P. N. Juslin & J. A. Sloboda (Eds.), *Music and emotion: Theory and research* (pp. 393–414). Oxford: Oxford University Press.

Schumacher, K. (1999). *Musiktherapie und Säuglingsforschung: Zusammenspiel; Einschätzung der Beziehungsqualität am Beispiel des instrumentalen Ausdrucks eines autistischen Kindes* [Music therapy and infant research: Interplay, assessment of relational qualities illustrated by the example of the instrumental play of an autistic child]. Frankfurt, Germany: P. Lang.

Schumacher, K., & Calvet-Kruppa, C. (2001). Die Relevanz entwicklungspsychologischer Erkenntnisse für die Musiktherapie [The relevance of developmental psychology for music therapy]. In H.-H.Decker-Voigt (Ed.), *Schulen der Musiktherapie* (pp. 102–124). Munich, Germany: Ernst Reinhardt Verlag.

Skewes, K. (2001). *The experience of group music therapy for six bereaved adolescents.* Unpublished doctoral dissertation, University of Melbourne, Melbourne. Available at www.musictherapyworld.net

Skewes, K. (2002, July). *Articulating the dynamics of music therapy group improvisations.* Paper presented at the 10th World Congress of Music Therapy, Oxford. Available at http://www.musictherapyworld.de/modules/wfmt/stuff/oxford2002.pdf

Skille, O., & Wigram, T. (1995). The effects of music, vocalization and vibration on brain and muscle tissue: Studies in vibroacoustic therapy. In T. Wigram, B. Saperston, & R. West (Eds.), *The art and science of music therapy: A handbook* (pp. 23–57). London: Harwood Academic Publications.

Sloboda, J. A. (1985). *The musical mind: The cognitive psychology of music.* Oxford: Clarendon Press.

Sloboda, J. A., & Juslin, P. N. (2001). Psychological perspectives on music and emotion. In P. N. Juslin & J. A. Sloboda (Eds.), *Music and emotion: Theory and research* (pp. 71–104). Oxford: Oxford University Press.

Small, C. (1998). *Musicking.* Hanover, NH: Wesleyan University Press.

Smeijsters, H. (1997). *Multiple perspectives: A guide to qualitative research in music therapy.* Gilsum, NH: Barcelona Publishers.

Smeijsters, H. (1999). *Grundlagen der Musiktherapie. Theorie und Praxis der Behandlung psychischer Störungen und Behinderungen* [The foundations of music therapy. Theory and practice in the treatment of mental disorders and disabilities]. Göttingen, Germany: Hogrefe.

Smeijsters, H. (2003). Forms of feeling and forms of perception: The fundamentals of analogy in music therapy. *Nordic Journal of Music Therapy, 12,* 71–85.

Spintge, R. (1993). Musik in der klinischen Medizin [Music in clinical medicine]. In H. Bruhn et al., *Musikpsychologie—ein Handbuch* (pp. 397–405). Reinbek, Germany: Rowohlt.

Stern, D. N. (1985). *The interpersonal world of the infant.* New York: Basic Books.

Tesch, R. (1990). *Qualitative research: Analysis types & software tools.* New York: The Falmer Press.

Thaut, M. H. (2002a). Neuropsychological processes in music perception and their relevance in music therapy. In R. Unkefer & M. H. Thaut (Eds.), *Music therapy in the treatment of adults with mental disorders* (2nd ed., pp. 2–32). St. Louis, MO: MMB Music.

Thaut, M. H. (2002b). Physiological and motor responses to music stimuli. In R. Unkefer & M. H. Thaut (Eds.), *Music therapy in the treatment of adults with mental disorders* (2nd ed., pp. 33–41). St. Louis, MO: MMB Music.

Trevarthen, C., & Malloch, S. N. (2000). The dance of wellbeing: Defining the musical therapeutic effect. *Nordic Journal of Music Therapy, 9*(2), 3–17.

Trondalen, G. (2003). Self-listening in music therapy with a young woman suffering from Anorexia nervosa. *Nordic Journal of Music Therapy, 12*, 3–17.

Trondalen, G. (2004). *Klingende relasjoner. En musikkterapistudie av "signifikante øyeblikk" i musikalsk samspill med unge mennesker med anoreksi* [Sounding relationships. A study of "significant moments" in musical interplay of adolescents with anorexia nervosa]. Oslo: Oslo University

Tüpker, R. (1988). *Ich singe, was ich nicht sagen kann. Zu einer morphologischen Grundlegung der Musiktherapie* [I sing, what I cannot say. A morphological foundation for music therapy]. Bosse, Germany: Regensburg.

Vink, A. (2001). Music and emotion. Living apart together: a relationship between music psychology and music therapy. *Nordic Journal of Music Therapy, 10*, 144–158.

Wasserman, N., Plutchik, R., Deutsch, R., & Taketomo, Y. (1973a). The musical background of a group of mentally retarded psychotic patients: Implications for music therapy. *Journal of Music Therapy, 10*, 78–82.

Wasserman, N., Plutchik, R., Deutsch, R., & Taketomo, Y. (1973b). A music therapy evaluation scale and its clinical application to mentally retarded adult patients. *Journal of Music Therapy, 10*, 64–77.

Wigram, T. (1996). *The effect of vibroacoustic therapy on clinical and non-clinical populations.* Unpublished doctoral dissertation, St. George's Medical School. University of London, London. Available at www.musictherapyworld.net

Wigram, T. (1997). Development of vibroacoustic therapy. In T. Wigram & C. Dileo (Eds.), *Music, vibration and health* (pp. 11–26). Cherry Hill, NJ: Jeffrey Books.

Wigram, T. (2000). A model of diagnostic assessment and analysis of musical data in music therapy. In T. Wigram (Ed.), *Assessment and evaluation in the arts therapies: Art therapy, music therapy and dramatherapy* (pp. 77–91). Radlett, Hertfordshire, UK: Harper House.

Wigram, T. (2004). *Improvisation. Methods and techniques for music therapy clinicians, educators and students.* London: Jessica Kingsley Publishers.

Wigram, T., Pedersen, I. N., & Bonde, L. O. (2002). *A comprehensive guide to music therapy.* London: Jessica Kingsley Publishers.

Wilson, B., & Smith, D. S. (2000). Music therapy assessment in school settings: A preliminary investigation. *Journal of Music Therapy, 37*, 95–117.

Wolfe, D. E., O'Connell, A. S., & Waldon, E. G. (2002). Music for relaxation: A comparison of musicians and nonmusicians on ratings of selected musical recordings. *Journal of Music Therapy, 39*, 40–55.

Wosch, T. (2001). Psychiatrische Einzelmusiktherapie als Modifikation von Leipziger Schule und Verstehender Psychiatrie [Individual psychiatric music therapy as a modification of the Leipzig model and hermeneutic psychiatry]. In H.-H. Decker-Voigt (Ed.), *Schulen der Musiktherapie* (pp. 183–207). Munich: Ernst Reinhardt Verlag.

Wosch, T. (2002). *Emotionale Mikroprozesse musikalischer Interaktionen. Eine Einzelfallanalyse zur Untersuchung musiktherapeutischer Improvisationen* (Emotional micro-processes in musical interaction. A single-case analysis of improvisational music therapy). Münster: Waxmann.

Wosch, T. (2004). Emotionspsychologie und ihre Bedeutung bei Regulativer Musiktherapie (RMT) und Guided Imagery and Music nach Helen Bonny (GIM) [Emotion psychology and its relevance for RMT and BMGIM]. In I. Frohne-Hagemann, *Rezeptive Musitherapie. Theorie und Praxis* (pp. 111–139). Wiesbaden: Reichert Verlag.

Acknowledgments

The author wishes to thank Jane Edwards, Tony Wigram, Ken Bruscia, and Barbara Wheeler warmly for their comments and suggestions at various points in the writing process.

Chapter 39
Philosophical Inquiry
Kenneth Aigen

The fierce controversies between contending philosophies disturb not a single leaf and cast not a troubling shadow over the world as we live in it as cognitive beings. As we shall see over and over again. . . philosophical differences seem at once momentous and negligible.

Danto[1]

What comes to mind when you hear the word *philosophy*? Perhaps you have some of the following images: dusty medieval texts being pored over by socially isolated beings known as philosophers; disputes over seemingly inconsequential questions such as whether a tree falling in the woods makes a sound if no one is there to hear it; Plato's account of Socrates' passion about virtue, truth, and beauty, a passion so great that he was willing to die for it; the famous dictum of Descartes, *Cogito Ergo Sum*, I think therefore I am; or, a discipline which has been described by philosophers themselves as both the queen of all sciences and completely irrelevant to science and the acquisition of human knowledge. In short, whether you consider philosophy to be essential to a morally, spiritually, and intellectually meaningful life or irrelevant to such a life, you will find yourself with ample company.

Why does the discipline of philosophy engender such differences of opinion regarding its nature? One answer can be seen in Arthur Danto's (1989) observation that "the issues of philosophy must be settled on some basis other than that of possible cognitions" (p. 13). This means that the traditional problems of philosophy cannot be solved by a particular discovery or experience. If the issue is solvable in this manner, then the question is not a truly philosophical one but rightly belongs to another discipline, such as history or science.

For example, the implementation of certain medical procedures—such as abortion or the sustaining of life through mechanical means—can bring up questions that are philosophical in nature. In the former procedure, the question relates to when life begins; the latter stimulates us to consider when life ends. We have much of the relevant scientific knowledge needed to answer such questions. That is, we can ascertain things like the viability of the fetus outside of the mother and the brain activity of the comatose individual, yet these facts do not answer the questions of when human life begins and when it ceases. In principle, no increase in our knowledge of physiology will provide an answer to the ethical dilemmas posed by these two medical situations. Instead, we are required to make value judgments in answering them. Hence, these questions of utmost importance in contemporary society are inherently philosophical, and philosophical thinking can be useful in helping us to identify the problems and to clarify the ethical dilemmas they represent.

I am a strong believer in the importance and usefulness of having a philosophical understanding of things, even in an applied discipline such as music therapy. Philosophy provides the foundation for all forms of knowledge. Using the metaphor of a tree, Carolyn Kenny (1998) suggests that philosophy provides the roots, theory the trunk, method the branches, and data the leaves, which eventually return to the ground, nourishing and influencing the roots.

Even among philosophers, there is no agreement on exactly what philosophy is. In fact, any definition *of* philosophy involves taking a particular position *in* philosophy. Similarly, there is no general agreement among philosophers on the nature of philosophical method. However, the notion that "in philosophy speculation is controlled by critical discussion" (Passmore, 1967, p. 218) provides a good starting point, not because it provides a definition but because it reminds us that all forms of critical inquiry—including scientific research—grew out of philosophy. Thus, becoming acquainted with philosophical modes of thinking and areas of inquiry can provide a foundation for intellectual explorations of all types.

Although it may not be possible to define philosophy, it nonetheless remains important to be able to provide a working, pragmatic definition of philosophical inquiry for the purpose of the present book, which is to demonstrate how different types of systematic inquiry can be applied to music therapy. Philosophical inquiry involves the use of philosophical procedures to "analyze and

---

[1] This quotation is from Danto (1989), p. xv.

contextualize theory, research, and practice within the history of ideas" (K. E. Bruscia, personal communication, March 4, 2003).[2]

Jorgensen (1992) distinguishes three characteristic procedures that philosophers follow in accomplishing their aims: clarifying terms, exposing and evaluating underlying assumptions of other philosophical and theoretical stances, and relating ideas as a systematic theory and showing their connection to other conceptual and theoretical systems. I would add a fourth characteristic: using argument as a primary mode of inquiry and a presentational device. The contexts in which philosophizing arises include presenting a philosophy; evaluating and comparing theories, theoretical systems, and comprehensive philosophical systems of thought; and addressing typically philosophical questions.

Characteristic Procedures of Philosophy

Clarifying Terms

Verbal language has *connotative* and *denotative* meanings. The former term refers to the implications and images stimulated by a word and the latter refers to its literal referent. While connotative uses are relevant for poetry, literature, and certain types of qualitative research, the activity of philosophy requires the precision of denotative meanings. Unless one can be precise about the meanings of words and the ideas they express, it is "difficult to compare ideas and systems of thought because one is uncertain of what is being compared" (Jorgensen, 1992, p. 91). Clarifying terms is of primary importance for two reasons: First, although our everyday use of the language of ideas tends to be good enough for most practical problems we encounter, it is inadequate when applied to philosophical problems. Second, some problems in philosophy result from an imprecise or improper use of language.

A music therapy study where the clarification of terms was the central purpose and procedure is *Defining Music Therapy* (2nd Edition) by Kenneth Bruscia (1998). The text is devoted to clarifying the term *music therapy,* defining areas and levels of music therapy, and distinguishing among the various types of clinical practice. The author provides a rationale for the practical benefits of addressing definitional concerns:

> Every definition sets boundaries for the field. Having such boundaries is crucial, for without them, it is impossible to know which types of clients and problems are best served by music therapy, which goals and methods are legitimately part of clinical practice, which topics are relevant for theory and research, and what kinds of ethical standards must be upheld. Furthermore, without these boundaries, it is impossible to design curricula and field training programs for preparing music therapists, and to establish meaningful requirements for earning credentials in the field. (p. 3)

At first glance, it may not be apparent why creating definitions is an example of philosophizing. Is not the applying of labels to entities a mechanical operation undertaken in all uses of language? In actuality, as Bruscia (1998) explains, "definitions are always more than factual statements or objective descriptions," something that is particularly true when the term being explained has no obvious logical or formal boundary. In studying definitions of music therapy drawn from all over the world, Bruscia observed how each definition reflected different "philosophies about music, therapy, health, illness, and even life" (p. 3). When we realize how

---

[2] Editor's note: In Chapter 40, Developing Theory, Bruscia provides further information as he clarifies the relationship of theories in music therapy to philosophy. He says:

> Theories in music therapy are also closely related to philosophy. Philosophy lays the foundation for all forms of knowledge. It is the discipline of disciplines. Every theory, regardless of domain or discipline, has its deepest roots in an entire philosophy of life, knowledge, reason, values, and ethics. Philosophy deals with fundamental questions about what exists, how we come to know what is and what is not, how we go about determining what is right and wrong, and what has value and beauty. It is not concerned with particularized areas of knowledge unless they relate in some way to these fundamental questions. In contrast, a theory deals with a particular topic, or domain, or discipline like physics, or mathematics, or music. (p. 541)

much variation there is in the terms we encounter in our professional activities—and that these differences reflect of deeply held worldviews, value systems, and philosophies—it gives us a newfound respect for the various definitions we encounter and the work that goes into crafting them.

Exposing and Evaluating Underlying Assumptions

Understanding this type of philosophical inquiry is to understand why philosophy is relevant to the concrete world of human actions. As Jorgensen (1992) avers:

> Assumptions predicate and underlie action. They consist of beliefs held to be true, taken for granted and acted on. . . . The philosopher makes explicit that which otherwise may remain implicit, and clarifies aspects that are prior to and deeper than the actions to which they give rise." (p. 93)

Because all human actions stem from the implementation of an implicit philosophy or belief system, it is necessary to articulate and understand the philosophy in order to understand the actions. Critical and analytical thinking are used in drawing inferences regarding belief systems:

> Critical thinking involves the capacity to judge the relative worth of actions and ideas. Analytical thinking entails the ability to take a situation or an idea apart. . . . One separates its constituent elements, makes judgments about the significance of those elements, and speculates about the various causes that might have le d to a particular thing. (Jorgensen, 1992, p. 93)

Once underlying beliefs are made apparent, the music therapist can choose a treatment, training, or research approach based on the values and beliefs that he or she would like to implement.

An important study by Even Ruud (1980) fits into this category of inquiry. He observed that clinical theories in music therapy have traditionally been built upon theories drawn from psychology. Hence, the focus of his study was to

> clarify the relation between music therapy and different approaches within the field of mental health, to see how different procedures in music therapy are related to general trends in treatment thought, and to see how these trends correspond to various philosophical orientations. (p. i)

This was done by considering the primary psychological orientations—psychoanalytic, behavioral, and humanistic-existential—and the music therapy theories derived from each, examining their underlying foundations, and comparing them to one another. The clinical procedures, goals, and rationales of various music therapists are compared to those typical of the various psychological orientations in order to draw parallels between them.

So, for example, Ruud (1980) describes psychoanalytic theory as including the following characteristics: (a) increased insight, (b) the resolution of disabling conflicts, (c) increased self-acceptance, (d) more efficient techniques for coping with problems, and (e) the general strengthening of the ego structure of the patient (pp. 21–22). Ruud then describes and analyzes the techniques of music therapists Wright and Priestley (1972) to show their relationship to psychoanalytic thought:

> The patient who has been avoiding unconscious conflicts and painful emotions is now allowed to express these conflicts and emotions. . . . Following this emotional expression (catharsis), the body is relaxed and it is easier for the patient to examine the causes of the anger and to find out other possible ways of dealing with the situation. This . . . could be considered as a general strengthening of the ego structure of the patient along lines of adequacy and security. (Ruud, pp. 22–23)

In another type of analysis, Freudian thought is revealed as deterministic as a consequence of its biological emphasis. This characteristic is considered by Ruud (1980) to place limitations on psychoanalytic investigations that look at humans in relation to their own selves and to others; it only accounts well for humans in relation to their biological environments. Ruud completes the analysis by saying that the overreliance on determinism leads to a restricted view of the human ego that is incompatible with music therapy practice. Yet, it is observed, modifying this view too much means leaving the familiar frame of reference of psychoanalysis and establishing a new one (Ruud, p. 25).

Relating Ideas as Systematic Theory

A body of philosophic thought should be coherent, consistent, systematically organized, and have explanatory value. It connects to other systems of thought as well as to human practices and beliefs. Evidence used in assessing the value of philosophies includes "logical argument, appeals to authority, precedent, example, or analogy" (Jorgensen, 1992, p. 94). Jorgensen notes that philosophy can be differentiated from science because in science "empirical data constitute the most persuasive evidence. In the philosophical worldview, however, other nonscientific ways of knowing may be equally or more persuasive" (p. 94). As a result of this epistemological tolerance, philosophy can connect the "various ways of knowing, be they scientific, artistic, religious, philosophical, or otherwise" (p. 94).

Kenny (1985) presents a philosophy in her introduction of systems theory as consisting of a holistic methodology, a view of nature as unified, and a humanistic perspective on the responsibilities of science. She uses this philosophy to create a larger context in which to understand music and healing, thus expanding the consciousness of the reader regarding what music therapy is and what it can be. In fact, she presents an entire world view based on music and connects this to processes that support health and human development:

> Music is no longer merely a metaphor to help us describe a phenomenon. Music, according to many physicists and systems theorists, is the way things are. . . . Music is what happens when things are created, when things become what they are, and particularly when things change. Music helps us to come home to the natural rhythms and patterns of our being, so that we can change. (p. 5)

She then connects this view to the clinical reality of the music therapist through understanding musical improvisation as a form of ritual that allows access to experiences that facilitate growth and transformation.

Using Argument as a Primary Mode of Inquiry

Of all the characteristics of philosophical inquiry, the use of argument is quite possibly the most important. This is because philosophical thinking appeals to our capacity for deductive, inductive, and retroductive reasoning. Our ability to evaluate philosophical claims is based on the evidence and chain of reasoning provided by the philosopher. In this sense, argument performs the same function in philosophy as method does in quantitative research and an inquiry audit does in qualitative research.

An argument consists of a premise whose truth value is assumed, a series of assertions deduced or inferred by this premise, and conclusions whose truth value is determined by how well the rules of logic were followed throughout the chain of the argument. In philosophic writing, a good argument will consider alternative points of view to the one promoted by the author and offer various forms of evidence to dispute them, often in the form of counterexamples.

It is common in philosophy for authors to sketch out the form of the argument before delving deeply into it. This prepares the readers for what follows, and they are in a better position to follow the argument. Because this type of analysis can be complex, it is helpful to see it in its most bare form before plunging in. There is also a rhetorical function to encountering the argument initially, meeting it again in a more developed form, and reviewing it one final time in conclusion. We can compare this to the aesthetic function of a sonata form with an exposition, development, and recapitulation of a theme. Both the aesthetic and the rhetorical forms have evolved because they help us to better assimilate information.

In order to understand how philosophical arguments are constructed we will examine in detail a study by the present author (Aigen, 1991) in the final section of this chapter.

Contexts in Which Philosophizing Arises

Presenting a Philosophy

Philosophy was discussed earlier as a coherent system of beliefs to guide human action. Philosophical systems can be presented directly by their authors, or they can be inferred from the observation and gathering of data.

As an example of the former approach, Barbara Hesser (1985) presents a philosophy for music therapy training, a rationale for having a philosophy, and a means for its promulgation.[3] She believes that the skills of a music therapist cannot be taught in an ethical vacuum, and that the attitudes held by instructors, whether implicit or explicit, will be transmitted to students and internalized as part of their training. She says: "The essential attitudes communicated to students during training are fundamental to the effectiveness of any course work or clinical training. These attitudes must be considered the core of the program" (p. 67). There is a variety of essential components to her philosophy: the process of becoming a music therapist is an in-depth, lifelong process; academic training should contain opportunities for the student's personal growth; participating in shared music-making is an important component of the teaching community; the training should be noncompetitive; and, each student's unique skills and interests should be emphasized. Because the training involves self-exploration on the part of students, establishing a safe and supportive atmosphere is essential.

The entire community—students, academic staff, and internship and fieldwork supervisors—"works together to be a reflection of the basic attitudes and values which are fundamental" to clinical work (p. 67). The student-teacher relationship characterizing the program parallels the client-therapist relationship in that members are considered to be learning from one another. Hence, the treatment philosophy taught is intimately tied to the educational procedures and human relationships comprising the program. Education, therapy, and a model for human relationships in general are integrated within this philosophy.

Evaluating and Comparing Theories, Theoretical Systems, and Comprehensive Philosophical Systems of Thought

This type of endeavor can have a number of different rationales: (a) facilitating communication between individuals from different theoretical traditions, (b) evaluating the theoretical development of a discipline, (c) stimulating the development of sophisticated theory, (d) remediating practical problems, and (e) organizing disparate theoretical elements into a unified whole.

When we consider the diversity of theoretical orientations within the music therapy profession and between music therapy and related professions, it becomes apparent that philosophic efforts at comparing different systems can translate concepts and facilitate communication, both among music therapists and between music therapists and other professionals. This enables adherents of one tradition to understand the ideas of others and to become less bound to one way of looking at things. This interchange of ideas stimulates the theoretical development of music therapy, since theoretical constructs that are relevant across different traditions tend to be more sophisticated and useful because their application is that much broader.

Moreover, this type of analysis can also show if the type of translation to which I am referring is even possible to do in an integral way. For example, there are traditions of both psychoanalytic and transpersonal orientations in music therapy. A possible philosophical inquiry would be to examine the theories from these traditions to see if they share similar underlying

---

[3] Editor's note: Since Hesser's philosophy of music therapy relates to the discipline of music therapy, it is an illustration of a theory rather than a philosophy, using Bruscia's distinction between a philosophy and a theory. In this chapter, however, Aigen uses it as an example of a philosophy. Thus, this appears to be an illustration of Aigen's statement in this chapter, "Even among philosophers, there is no agreement on exactly what philosophy is. In fact, any definition *of* philosophy involves taking a particular position *in* philosophy. Similarly, there is no general agreement among philosophers on the nature of philosophical method" (p. 526).

mechanisms or constructs, even though their surface languages may be quite different from one another. A positive finding would facilitate the convergence of theory, something that is characteristic of more developed disciplines. On the other hand, such an analysis might just as easily have the opposite result, showing that the underlying premises from the different systems are so different that it is impossible to translate concepts from one orientation to the other without sacrificing something essential.

An historically important publication of this type in music therapy is by William Sears (1968), as it illustrates the function of organizing disparate theoretical elements into a unified whole. His strategy was to organize, classify, and describe processes in music therapy so that a complete system would emerge that would enhance the scientific status of music therapy. Sears's intent was to express his system in a language which was theoretically neutral regarding particular personality theories or theories of psychotherapy, so that it could be applied by individuals working within a variety of orientations.

This system was presented in terms of three realms of experience in music: experience within structure, experience in self-organization, and experience in relating to others. As an example of experience within structure, consider how music "demands time-ordered behavior" and "permits ability-ordered behavior" (Sears, 1968, p. 33). As experience in self-organization, "music provides for self-expression" and "for the enhancement of pride in self" (p. 33). Last, as experience in relating to others, music "provides means by which self-expression is socially acceptable" (p. 33) and "enhances verbal and nonverbal social interaction and communication" (p. 34).

Sears saw his own work as constituting a working theory that summarized in "one system the best knowledge and thought presently available concerning the function of music in therapy" (p. 44). Interestingly, the tone he strikes appears to straddle different dichotomies on contemporary theoretical issues in music therapy. For example, he discusses his preference for expressing his system free of connections to any one school of thought, and yet frequently refers to music therapy as a behavioral science, seemingly not realizing the theoretical commitment that this implies. Also, at the beginning of his article, Sears avers that he is taking this strategy specifically not "to claim any special status for music therapy" (p. 31), yet he concludes that "processes in music therapy take place by uniquely involving the individual" (p. 44) in the three realms of experience mentioned above. In this light, Sears can be seen as an important transitional figure, someone whose writings reflected the underlying contradictions inherent in pioneering theoretical developments indigenous to music therapy while remaining within existing systems of thought.

Addressing Typically Philosophical Questions

Jorgensen divides the questions created into the subdisciplines of philosophy: *ontology,* the study of the nature of existence; *epistemology,* the study of knowledge; *axiology,* or matters of value; *ethics;* and *aesthetics,* the study of beauty and art. Music therapists who discuss questions such as the following are focusing on the typically philosophic: What is music therapy and what conditions must be present for a given activity to be a bona fide example of music therapy practice? What constitutes ethical music therapy practice? And, are aesthetic considerations relevant to clinical practice?

Ontological Issues. Ontological questions deal with ultimate issues of existence and essence. The following types of questions are considered to be ontological ones: What is the nature of reality? What, if anything, exists independently of human consciousness? Is the ultimate reality material? What is space and time? What is the nature of a cause-effect relationship?

In music therapy, ontological concerns can be formulated more specifically: What is music? Where does the impetus for harmonic or melodic motion originate? What is music therapy? What is the nature of the world in which the music therapist practices? We will look at two studies in this vein that illustrate contrasting approaches.

First is Charles Eagle's (1991) "Steps to a Theory of Quantum Therapy," in which he uses the procedure of relating his ideas as a systematized theory in relation to other theoretical systems. In this case, he presents a conception of clinical music therapy practice based upon four principles from quantum physics. His premise is that the universe is based upon quantum principles, and that music therapists who consider these aspects of their working reality will be more effective clinicians. Eagle's view is that quantum physics represents the highest, most well-verified achievement of modern science, and that music therapists should follow the lead of physiologists and psychologists in formulating theories based on these principles.

Here are two examples: For Eagle, the concept of complementarity, which holds that matter exhibits properties of both particle and wave phenomena and cannot be comprehensively described by either one, manifests in music therapy in the duality of process and product. Also, an implication of Heisenberg's uncertainty principle is that the observer unavoidably affects what is observed through the act of observation. The duality of observer and observed breaks down here and the traditional scientific notion of objective observation is thereby challenged. Eagle takes this to mean that "what we know about our universe is due to the observations made by us; we participate in creating our observed universes" (p. 58). For the music therapist, the connection is that we change a client merely by our presence in a therapy session. We do not merely observe our clinical reality, but we help create it through our presence in it.

While Eagle's purpose was to increase the awareness of music therapists through presenting an alternative way of considering music therapy, David Aldridge (1989) pursues a contrasting strategy. In "Music as Identity: A Phenomenological Comparison of the Organization of Music and the Self," he seeks to establish a conception of the individual person and of biological health based upon music. Aldridge sees a strong connection between form in music and form in biology:

> By regarding the identity of a person as a musical form that is continually being composed in the world, a surface appears on which to project our understanding of a person as a physiological and psychological whole being. The thrust of this endeavor is to view people as "symphonic" rather than "mechanic." (p. 1)

Aldridge reverses the traditional notion of basing the contribution of music to health on conceptions gleaned from a medical frame of reference, instead seeking to establish a sense of individual identity and health from considerations of the nature of music. This also contrasts with Eagle, who begins with conceptions from another discipline and attempts to develop music therapy correlates. Instead, Aldridge begins with musical phenomena and seeks to build the bridge in the other direction.

Aldridge establishes the connection between music and individual identity when he observes that "the perception of music requires an holistic strategy where the play of patterned frequencies is recognized within a matrix of time. People may be described in similar terms as beings in the world who are patterned frequencies in time" (p. 7). His perspective is that through improvised music we perceive a direct expression of a person that requires no verbal translation in order to be grasped. Because "musical form and biological form are isomorphic" (p. 7), improvised music can reveal the individual's state of health, and well-being can be directly assessed.

Epistemological Issues. Epistemological issues relate to questions of what it is possible to know. Do we have knowledge of the external world or only of the contents of our own minds? Can we gain knowledge with certainty or just probability? What does it mean to know that something is true? Are there different types of knowledge? These are traditional epistemological questions. Although not commonly addressed in the music therapy literature, we can conceive of some important questions for music therapy in this area. One concern of the study discussed in the final section of the present chapter (Aigen, 1991) is to support the articulation of an epistemology, or theory of knowledge, for music therapy. The rationale is as follows:

> Musical interaction is a unique way of gaining information about ourselves, other people, and our physical, social, and psychological environment. Through music therapy techniques like clinical improvisation, a therapist can engage in a musical interaction with a client and help to create music which facilitates a fundamental transformation in the inner being of the client. In some way, the inner world of the client becomes manifest to the therapist; clinical results render this judgment undeniable. Rather than [force] the knowledge gained in this manner into categories derived from purely verbal modes of thought. . . we [should] allow the musically obtained knowledge to suggest its own epistemology. (p. 374)

The thrust of this argument is that, because musical thought and interaction may be fundamentally different from verbal modes of thought, music therapists should create a theory of knowledge based upon what is suggested by what they experience as clinicians.

Clive Robbins and Michele Forinash (1991) utilize this strategy in presenting a multilevel theory of time that is stimulated by and illustrated through experiences in music therapy. They present four levels of time experience: physical time or clock time, characterized by sameness and fixity; growth time, "perceived in the process of growth or development of any living organism as it occurs over a period of time" (p. 51) and characterized by stability; emotional time, "the personal time of feeling" (p. 53), characterized by impulsiveness and mobility; and creative time or now time, "the moment of intuition" (p. 53), characterized by spontaneity and newness. These concepts are offered to music therapists in order to provide them with concepts within which they can understand their clinical experiences. The authors believe that "a clinician can gain security from a supportive conceptual perspective, one that provides a realistic framework for the artistic processes. . . and that can differentiate and elucidate the ongoing phenomena of creative music therapy" (p. 56). Thus the various concepts of time provide an orientation point for clinicians in therapy and also open new possibilities to consider how time is experienced in the clinical as well as the nonclinical milieu.

Axiological Issues. Axiological issues relate to questions of value: What is the role of music therapy in society? Who should receive services? What level or type of work is most appropriate for various populations? Should the type of music therapy—rehabilitative, psychotherapeutic, medical, or educational—offered to an individual be determined by that individual's condition or inherent need or by the specific training of the treating music therapist? What type of music therapy is more appropriate for what type of client and is this even the right way of approaching the question? Indeed, what is the purpose and ultimate significance of music therapy for the lives of individuals as well as for society as whole?

In a study of this type, "Beyond Healing to 'Whole-ing': A Voice for the Deinstitutionalization of Music Therapy," Marcia Broucek (1987) argues for an expanded concept of the nature and role of music therapy practice. While traditional concepts of music therapy have regarded it as an institutional service for individuals in exacerbated states of need, Broucek would like to see music therapy deinstitutionalized and its benefits offered to the population at large and to music therapists themselves.

Further, she offers the concept of the life spirit and articulates a conception of clients and types of therapeutic work in terms of it:

> Our tasks as therapists vary in light of our clients' life positions. For persons who are against life, our challenge is to revive the life spirit, to tap into each person's health and restore belief in the value of life. For clients who are indifferent to life, our challenge is to sustain the life spirit, to feed and encourage a suppressed or dormant belief in the creative potential of life. For those who embrace life, our challenge is to nurture the life spirit, to offer avenues for expansion, learning, and growth. (p. 51)

For each of these three categories of individuals, Broucek offers four types of personal need that music therapy can specifically address. She also challenges music therapists to determine where they stand on this continuum and to decide how their view of the profession relates to it. This translates to the question: "What roles do we see for music therapy in the larger world's struggle for life?" (p. 58). This type of value-laden question challenges music therapists to expand their conception of the profession and its possibilities for application outside the realm of pathology and disability.

Ethical Issues. In traditional philosophy, ethics is a prime area of concern. It deals with the following types of questions: What is good? What is moral? How should human beings relate to one another? What do we owe each other, if anything? What constitutes moral actions, and how are they determined? Who is entitled to make such judgments?

In music therapy, it has fallen primarily to professional associations to establish standards for ethical practice; indeed, establishing such standards for the protection of clients is one of the prime motivations for professionals to organize. In addition to providing guidelines for equitable and ethical relationships between clients and therapists, associations also address questions of ethical research, training, and publication practices.

Important questions for music therapists to address in this area include the following: What values underlie different treatment or research approaches? Are these values consistent with professional standards as well as those espoused by the practitioners of such approaches? What happens when client need conflicts with articulated standards? What obligations do practitioners have to articulate their value systems?

Cheryl Dileo Maranto and Madelaine Ventre (1985) discuss the ethical dimension of the principle of confidentiality, considered as the "client's right to privacy [which has] both ethical and legal implications" (p. 62). This proscription against revealing information regarding the client's treatment is seen as having clinical importance as well as reflecting a legal right. In order to benefit from therapy, a client must reveal him- or herself, something that would be unlikely without the guarantee that what is expressed in the therapy session remains between client and therapist. The establishment of trust, essential to therapy, is dependent upon the principle of confidentiality.

Client rights in this regard are not absolute and can come into conflict with both the rights of others and considerations of what is in the client's own best interests. For example, when a client is considered to present "an immediate danger to himself or others" (p. 62), the music therapist must act to protect the endangered party, regardless of whether or not this violates confidentiality. Certainly there is much that philosophical analysis can provide in helping to determine the proper course of action and ethical guidelines when aspects of an ethics code conflict. Another important study in this area is by Maranto (1987).

Aesthetic Issues. Aesthetic questions relate to issues of beauty, art, and the nature of aesthetic experience: What is the essence of art? Are aesthetic judgments objective? Are these judgments universal or culturally relative? What is beauty and what is its relationship to art?

This is perhaps the one area of philosophy that is most obviously relevant to music therapy. We can conceive of the following questions regarding aesthetic issues that are relevant to clinical practice: Are aesthetic considerations relevant in determining either clinical interventions or client outcome? How and when do they come into play? Which conceptions of aesthetics are consonant with clinical music therapy practice or clinical theory? What are the healing properties of aesthetic experiences? Are they essential or incidental to clinical music therapy process?

Considering that music is an aesthetic medium, it is surprising that music therapists have not pursued this area of inquiry extensively. In one of the earliest studies of aesthetics and music therapy, E. Thayer Gaston (1964) notes that "research in aesthetics is difficult, and there appears to be not much interest in it" (p. 2). For Gaston, the desire for aesthetic experience is universally present, a defining characteristic of human nature, and has a physiological basis. Moving through a long argument based upon mammalian biology, the need for early sensory stimulation, and the development of the uniquely human capacities of the brain, Gaston concludes that aesthetic experience is necessary for "health and normality" because it encompasses "the whole realm of feelings, values, [and] sentiments" (p. 5), essentially human qualities. His attitude is that "the significance of the aesthetic experience of music for the individual is, that without it, he would be less complete as a human being" (p. 5).

In a study applying the aesthetic thought of the philosopher John Dewey to music therapy (Aigen, 1995), I speculate that the dearth of published studies on the relevance of aesthetics to music therapy may be due to the fact that music therapists have traditionally based their clinical theories on medical and psychological models which, as Gaston noted, tend not to place much emphasis on the remedial properties of aesthetic experience. This tendency is exacerbated by the common feeling that aesthetic judgments are subjective, arbitrary, and not relevant in determining clinical interventions or outcome. I correlate Dewey's aesthetic thought with aspects of the creative music therapy approach of Nordoff and Robbins (1977). Also presented is the notion of improvised music as a clinical-aesthetic object whose clinical importance is aesthetically perceived by the therapist, much in the way a trained eye or ear can perceive the aesthetic properties of a nonclinical work of art. If music therapists can perceive the clinical significance of a client's music based upon properties of the music itself, rather than upon their own subjective preferences, this exploration can have implications for creating an epistemology for music therapy, as described above.

A Detailed Examination of One Philosophical Study

In order to understand how philosophical arguments are constructed, we will examine in detail the present author's study, *The Roots of Music Therapy: Towards an Indigenous Research Paradigm* (Aigen, 1991). It is a detailed analysis of the philosophy of science that had traditionally guided much of the research in music therapy from its origins until the time the study was conducted. It evaluates the philosophy for its suitability in guiding research on creative and improvisational clinical approaches in music therapy.

Because of its focus and structure, this study illustrates many of the procedures and topics constituting philosophical inquiry, and it demonstrates how these facets are integrated to further the purposes behind this type of inquiry: First, the study includes a detailed philosophical clarification of terms such as paradigm and theory; second, the primary focus is to expose and evaluate underlying the assumptions of a philosophical stance; third, a new philosophy of science is related in a systematic way; fourth, the entire study takes the form of an extended argument; fifth, the analysis includes the evaluation of a comprehensive philosophical system of thought; sixth, some typically philosophical questions are considered in the area of epistemology, the theory of knowledge.

The Argument

The argument of this study includes the following steps typical of this type of inquiry: defining the problem, considering possible explanations, presenting the argument, and operationalizing the argument.

Problem. The focus of this study originated in a concern regarding the schism between research and clinical practice in music therapy. Empirical evidence was presented to document that clinicians have continually observed that the research base of the field has been of limited applicability and relevance to clinical work.

Possible Explanations. After noting the problem, the first step was to articulate possible explanations for this state of affairs. Philosophical inquiry demands that we consider alternatives to our own points of view and establish that they are not viable. One could say that the philosopher has an ethical responsibility to make these alternatives clear, represent them in a fair light, and present convincing and uncontrived evidence regarding their deficiencies. I formulated five logically plausible alternatives: (a) The evidence documenting clinicians' opinions was either not valid or not representative of the profession as a whole; (b) the research actually was useful, but clinicians lacked the interest or expertise to apply it; (c) the research had value, but researchers failed to make the applications evident; (d) the philosophy of research guiding the work was sound, but its realization had serious flaws; and (e) the philosophy of research was fundamentally flawed, and a new research approach would need to be articulated.

Prior to beginning this study, I was convinced that the fifth reason (e) was correct, and that music therapy would benefit from a new research approach or paradigm. This is one important way in which philosophizing differs from empirical inquiry or research. Here, it is permissible to know the conclusion we want to reach rather than discovering it through our inquiry.

I discounted the first possible explanation (a) because my evidence for the dissatisfaction with research included surveys of music therapists and statements by prominent authors and theorists. The second explanation (b) was discounted because I presented evidence that clinicians were predisposed toward favorably receiving and applying research reports if the reports related to the issues and problems that they faced in their functioning as music therapists. I did not address the third possible explanation (c) directly, instead focusing my efforts on the fourth (d). My reasoning was that, if I could show that the basic research approach was flawed on a conceptual level, I would not need to address the researchers' inability to make the applications clear.

This strategy illustrates another important aspect of philosophical argument: It is not necessary to counter each and every point of an opposing position. At times, it is more economical to aggregate certain points and show that they are dependent upon a more fundamental notion. Then, if the fundamental notion can be discredited, all of the points resting on this notion are similarly discredited.

Form of the Argument. The argument comprising the inquiry was as follows:

1. Research in music therapy theory has been traditionally guided by the paradigm of medical and behavioral research as employed in psychology and the medical professions;
2. This research theory was devised to investigate other types of phenomena and has conceptual roots antithetical to those underlying the salient aspects of music therapy practice utilizing creative and improvisational methods;
3. Continuing to utilize this research paradigm limits the applicability of research theory and findings and inhibits the overall development of the profession;
4. Music therapy will become more theoretically developed when theory is drawn from concerns indigenous to the discipline;
5. It is necessary to develop a new research paradigm for music therapy, the conceptual bases of which should be congruent with clinical practice and allow for the development of indigenous theory.

Tasks. Once the basic argument was delineated, it was necessary to operationalize the argument in terms of specific tasks whose sequence reflected the logical form of what I was attempting to demonstrate. The goal of offering conceptual support for a new research paradigm was approached through answering the following questions:

1. What are the theoretical and methodological constraints, as well as the pragmatic professional considerations, that have guided traditional research in music therapy?
2. What are the indigenous elements of creative music therapy practice and the metatheoretical implications of these elements for research?
3. Are the guidelines that come to light in Task 1 congruent with the implications that arise in Task 2? If not, what is the nature of the conflict between them?
4. What are the elements of a conceptual framework or paradigm that will reflect the aspects of creative and improvisational music therapy practice iterated in Task 2?

We can look at each of these four tasks in terms of the characteristic procedures of philosophical inquiry: (a) Task 1 involves exposing the underlying assumptions of traditional research; (b) Task 2 is akin to the creation of a philosophy whose parts comprise a systematized whole based solely upon the author's experience; (c) Task 3 involves evaluating the underlying assumptions of Task 1; and (d) Task 4 is the creation of a philosophy based upon the analysis arising in Task 3.

This last task brings us full circle. The problem that stimulated the study is that research is music therapy has not been applicable to clinical practice. The solution, reached in Task 4, is to create an approach to research that reflects the principles underlying clinical practice.

The Findings

The findings of the study were developed in four areas sequentially: characterizing the nature of traditional research in music therapy; distilling the conceptual foundations of creative and improvisational music therapy practice; demonstrating the incompatibility of traditional research for examining this latter type of music therapy practice; and, developing a more suitable research philosophy.

Traditional Research in Music Therapy. Three primary components were focused on in this section. These included (a) collecting statements by important theoreticians regarding of what they considered legitimate research to consist; (b) inferring or deducing the underlying philosophy of science from which their advocacy of specific procedures was derived; and (c) determining the social, political, or methodological reasons behind their advocacy of these positions.

The investigation showed that the philosophy of science traditionally adhered to in music therapy consists of the following elements:

1. Belief in the doctrine of the unity of science that holds that there is a single scientific method whose components do not vary according to subject matter—the psychologist should be held to the same standards as the physicist;
2. Scientific data is objectively determined, theory neutral, and publicly observable. One's prior beliefs should not influence how one perceives data and cognitions of any

kind; thoughts, feelings, intuitions, and so forth, must be operationalized in terms of observable behaviors to figure in scientific activity;

3. The focus of research in music therapy should be on generating scientific laws to account for musical behavior;

4. Progress in science requires adherence to the reductionist program of explanation which holds that terms in the softer sciences should be translated or reduced to explanations in the more fundamental ones; that is, psychological explanations should not invoke constructs, for example, superego or self-esteem, that are not explainable based upon purely biological ones;

5. The purpose of science is to allow for prediction and control over phenomena, and music therapy research should be oriented to giving experimenters and clinicians the ability to predict and control client behaviors based on specific interventions.

Indigenous Elements of Music Therapy: Implications for Research. The next step was to present the salient aspects of creative and improvisational music therapy practice through a set of principles whose function was to provide "a meta-theoretical perspective from which models, theories, criteria for explanation and research designs" could be derived (Aigen, 1991, p. 201). I described the portrait as "a constellation of mutually supportive beliefs, adherence to which. . . will generate a meaningful, clinically-relevant research program" (p. 277).

All of the principles were examined in great detail, related to one another, and defended against criticism. For example, I discussed how the music therapist can, at times, abandon conscious and deliberate action and place trust in the external, creative process of musical creation. I then anticipated three possible objections to this statement: (a) that it implied an abrogation of professional responsibility, (b) that it would discredit the practice of music therapy as a legitimate treatment form, and (c) that it might lessen the importance of theory and training in music therapy practice.

These anticipated objections were directly answered. First, I asserted that the use of music therapy treatment is validated by client outcome, not by having a step-by-step, rule-based model for how treatment proceeds. Second, even if the inner processes of accomplished therapists are not formally determined according to verbalizable guidelines, there is still an important role for theory in training in the same way that all artists and creative professionals learn their craft through studying the work of more proficient practitioners.

In philosophical inquiry, one must anticipate possible objections and answer them in order to keep the reader engaged. If a reader comes up with an objection that you do not answer, he or she has a lessened motivation to follow your argument to its end conclusion.

Clash of Paradigms: The Nature of the Conflict. My analysis—that is, the evaluation of the appropriateness of the philosophy of science comprising traditional research in music therapy for investigating the indigenous elements of practice—demonstrated in what ways the five elements of the traditional research approach were not conceptually congruent with creative and improvisational music therapy practice.

The Elements of a New Research Approach. The final step of the study was to "provide a conceptual framework for studying aspects of music therapy process that lie outside the domain of traditional research." Because "the limitations of traditional methods stem from their philosophical bases," I felt that it was "apparent that new methods will require a new philosophical justification." The intent was to offer standards for observation and explanation that would "preserve the structure and salient elements of scientific practice" and yet formulate a research program that would maintain a high degree of clinical relevance (Aigen, 1991, p. 382).

The following areas of research activity were discussed with a focus on the considerations that would enhance the ability to create indigenous theory: (a) the use of language, (b) theory building, (c) the use of models, and (d) research design and methods.

In the area of the use of language, I discussed how a new paradigm for music therapy must recognize that translating clinical music to verbal language necessarily alters the salient content, treat music as a bona fide medium for the acquisition and communication of knowledge, and expand the traditional use of verbal language in science to allow it to carry the meaning and expressive value of music.

In the area of model building, two perspectives on the use of models in science were articulated. In the fictionalist view, the model is merely a calculating device, much as describing an automobile's power in terms of horsepower allows for measuring and comparing the capacities of different cars. This position contrasts with the position of realism, which holds that models reflect actual processes or entities and that scientists want their models to reflect reality.

I argued that by using medical, behavioral, or psychoanalytic models for treatment and clinical process, music therapists unwittingly adopted fictionalist criteria for models. While "these models can adequately represent music therapy phenomena in the language and constructs of their respective systems," they may only incidentally represent the salient properties of musical processes (Aigen, 1991, p. 416). Imported models are evaluated based upon their adequacy to the imported conceptual context, not to the actual musical phenomena. In contrast, the realist approach holds that models should be evaluated according to how well they represent the actual phenomena, independent of preexisting theoretical constraints. The realist view of models is thus more conducive to building indigenous theory.

The last set of suggestions in this study related to issues of research design and methods. The conclusion was that designs should be patterned after procedures of clinical practice. For example, some experimental researchers comparing music therapy to other treatment forms may feel compelled to predetermine the techniques or activities comprising the sessions. Yet if this does not reflect actual practice, there will be a serious question regarding the applicability of a research study so constructed. Moreover, one of the axioms of creative clinical practice presented in the study held that the therapeutic "relationship is the context from which the meaning of the events in a music therapy session is derived" (Aigen, 1991, p. 437). Therefore, to apply to clinical practice, research designs must allow for and account for the establishment of such a relationship and explore its manifestations and effects upon treatment outcome.

Conclusion

In sum, I would like to reiterate some of the concrete tasks that philosophical inquiry can help accomplish in music therapy:

1. Provide a suitable epistemology and value system for practice, training, and research;
2. Evaluate current theories and paradigms by distilling them into their underlying assumptions;
3. Allow for interdisciplinary dialogue by comparing concepts and theories;
4. Contribute to the general communal wisdom of humankind by drawing the implications of music therapy practice for areas such as epistemology, aesthetics, and education;
5. Diagnose the reasons for practical problems in music therapy and suggest solutions when these problems are of a conceptual nature;
6. Analyze and discuss the relationship between the artistic and scientific aspects of music therapy.

References

Aigen, K. (1991). The roots of music therapy: Towards an indigenous research paradigm. (Doctoral dissertation, New York University, 1990). *Dissertation Abstracts International, 52*(6), 1933A.

Aigen, K. (1995). The aesthetic foundation of clinical theory: An underlying foundation of Nordoff-Robbins music therapy. In C. B. Kenny (Ed.), *Listening, playing, creating: Essays on the power of sound* (pp. 233–258). Albany, NY: State University of New York Press.

Aldridge, D. (1989). Music as identity: A phenomenological comparison of the organization of music and the self. *The Arts in Psychotherapy, 16,* 91–97.

Broucek, M. (1987). Beyond healing to "whole-ing": A voice for the deinstitutionalization of music therapy. *Music Therapy, 6,* 50–58.

Bruscia, K. E. (1998). *Defining music therapy* (2nd ed.). Gilsum, NH: Barcelona Publishers.

Danto, A. C. (1989). *Connections to the world.* New York: Harper & Row.

Eagle, C. T. (1991). Steps to a theory of quantum therapy. *Music Therapy Perspectives, 9,* 56–60.

Gaston, E. T. (1964). The aesthetic experience and biological man. *Journal of Music Therapy, 1*, 1–7.

Hesser, B. (1985). Advanced clinical training in music therapy. *Music Therapy, 5*, 66–73.

Jorgensen, E. R. (1992) On philosophical method. In R. Colwell (Ed.), *Handbook of research on music teaching and learning* (pp. 91–101). New York: Schirmer Books.

Kenny, C. (1985). Music: A whole systems approach. *Music Therapy, 5*, 3–11.

Kenny, C. (1998). Embracing complexity: The creation of a comprehensive research culture in music therapy. *Journal of Music Therapy, 35*, 201–217.

Maranto, C. D. (1987). Continuing concerns in music therapy ethics. *Music Therapy, 6*, 59–63.

Maranto, C. D., & Ventre, M. (1985). Confidentiality and the music therapist: Ethical considerations. *Music Therapy, 5*, 61–65.

Nordoff, P., & Robbins, C. (1977). *Creative music therapy.* New York: John Day.

Passmore, J. (1967). Philosophy. In P. Edwards (Ed.), *The encyclopedia of philosophy* (Vol. 5, pp. 216–226). New York: Macmillan.

Robbins, C., & Forinash, M. (1991) A time paradigm: Time as a multilevel phenomenon in music therapy. *Music Therapy, 10*, 46–57.

Ruud, E. (1980). *Music therapy and its relationship to current treatment theories.* St. Louis, MO: MMB Music.

Sears, W. W. (1968). Processes in music therapy. In E. T. Gaston (Ed.), *Music in therapy* (pp. 30–44). New York: Macmillan.

Wright, P., & Priestley, M. (1972). Analytical Music Therapy. *British Journal of Music Therapy, 3*(2), 20–25.

Chapter 40
Developing Theory
Kenneth E. Bruscia

A theory is way of thinking about what we do or what we know. It usually consists of propositions, theorems, or constructs that give the theorist's conceptualization about phenomena within a particular domain. A proposition or theorem is a fundamental assertion that the theorist makes about the topic, whereas a construct is usually a single-standing idea or metaphor that the theorist uses to describe a particular aspect of the topic. In a complete, formal theory, the theorist generally presents a set of propositions and theorems that are logically related to one another so that, when considered together, they provide an integrated and comprehensive way of thinking about the target phenomena. In less formal theoretical writings, the theorist usually presents a construct or two or informally discusses theoretical ideas and relationships in a more limited way.

A theory is always created. The propositions or constructs are always constructed by the theorist based on how that theorist views what we do or what we know. Thus, a theory may be both descriptive and interpretive, empirical and speculative, depending upon how much the theorist adds his or her own perspective.

The purposes of theory may be: (a) to define or delimit practice or knowledge so as to gain greater clarity on boundaries; (b) to describe practice or knowledge in a way that changes perspectives on them; (c) to explicate patterns or structures that underpin practice or knowledge, so as to gain new insights; (d) to identify cause-effect relationships in practice or knowledge in a way that allows prediction and control of the phenomenon; or (d) to evaluate practice or knowledge so as to establish priorities.

A theory is always concerned with phenomena within a particular domain. In music therapy, the theories may be concerned with the disciplinary domain (music therapy assessment, treatment, and evaluation), the professional domain (phenomena related to music therapists, their training, credentialing, employment, characteristics, socio-economic and cultural aspects of music therapy, and so forth), and the foundational domain (phenomena pertaining to music, health, therapy, other health professions). This chapter focuses only on disciplinary theories.

The Place of Theory

Theory has a central place in music therapy—it shapes and is shaped by practice and research. Regardless of whether the theory has been clearly articulated by the therapist or theorist, theory provides a foundational structure for all clinical work. Conversely, practice is often the basis upon which a theory is developed. Similarly, research may be the foundation for theory, or it may be the result of theory. Theory in music therapy is also closely related to practice and knowledge in other disciplines. Often ideas from other disciplines are imported into music therapy and then expanded to accommodate the unique character of music therapy. For example, Ansdell (1997) proposed that the latest developments in musicology have important ramifications for music therapists, and at the same time, the new musicologists could learn much from music therapists. Similarly, importing the constructs of transference and countertransference from psychology has been influential in shaping how music therapists describe the client-music and therapist-music relationships in music psychotherapy (Bruscia, 1998b), and conversely, the myriad ways that music therapists have expanded these constructs to include musical phenomena have very important implications for psychology.

One might say that all the disciplines related to music therapy provide a way of thinking about practice and knowledge in music therapy, and conversely, that music therapy provides the same for these disciplines. Thus, for example, psychology provides a way of thinking about and knowing human beings, and this *epistemology* can be useful to how music therapists understand what they do and what they want to know. At the same time, music therapy has its own way of thinking and knowing about human beings, or its own epistemology, that can be useful to psychology. The same can be said about music, medicine, the social sciences, education, communications, humanities, the other arts, and all of their subdisciplines. In short, every discipline has its own epistemology, its own culture and focus of knowing, and this epistemology can be fruitfully applied to theory in other disciplines.

Theories in music therapy are also closely related to philosophy. Philosophy lays the foundation for all forms of knowledge.[1] It is the discipline of disciplines. Every theory, regardless of domain or discipline, has its deepest roots in an entire philosophy of life, knowledge, reason, values, and ethics. Philosophy deals with fundamental questions about what exists, how we come to know what is and what is not, how we go about determining what is right and wrong, and what has value and beauty. It is not concerned with particularized areas of knowledge unless they relate in some way to these fundamental questions. In contrast, a theory deals with a particular topic, domain, or discipline like physics, mathematics, or music.

Of course, philosophy and theory also have many similarities. They both have the same aim: understanding. In that, they relate to practice and research in the same way. Philosophy and theory focus on what practice and knowledge mean rather than on what constitutes effective action (practice), and on what is known or unknown (research). Philosophy and theory are also alike in that they both involve thinking activities, such as reflection, reasoning, criticism, speculation, and intuition. In a sense, philosophizing is theorizing, and theorizing is philosophizing.

Every theory has a metatheory. A metatheory is a theory of theories. For example, this chapter is a metatheory because it presents the author's constructions of what theories are, what they do, and so forth; and because there as many conceptions of theory as there are theorists, there is no one truth about the nature of theory. Often, a metatheory is a philosophical or theoretical perspective that underpins or overlays a theory. For example, every theory makes certain philosophical assumptions about the nature of existence, knowledge, and human values. Thus, this deeper layer of a theory is a metatheory or a reflection upon the theory. Similarly, if a theory in one discipline, say physics, is applied to a theory in another discipline such as music therapy, a metatheory is being developed. Or if an epistemology of another discipline, such as psychology, is applied to music therapy, it yields what might be called a psychological metatheory on a music therapy theory.

Methods of Developing Theory

One can create a theory in many different ways, depending upon the objective. The following sections describe some of the main methods of developing theory. Each method can be used alone; however, often they are used in combination. Thus, the examples given below may belong in more than one category.

Explication

A theory is developed by identifying, differentiating, defining, classifying, organizing, and naming concepts, practices, and terms found in music therapy. The focus may be on what clinicians, researchers, and theorists do, how they conceptualize what they do, and what terminology they use to describe their work. Explication requires a clearly delimited focus on a particular aspect of music therapy and what is already known or done in relation to it. As suggested by the name for this method, the theorist makes explicit what is implicit; or the theorist describes what is, or what is done, based on his or her perceptions and perspectives.

An example of this method of theory building is the inventory of 64 clinical techniques used in improvisational music therapy (Bruscia, 1987, pp. 533–558). After surveying several models of improvisational music therapy, the author identified, compared, and named all techniques used by the originators of these models. For purposes of this inventory, a technique was defined as "an operation or interaction initiated by the therapist to elicit and immediate response from the client, or to shape his/her immediate experience" (p. 533). The techniques were classified according to: (a) their focus (what aspect of the client was addressed); (b) their objective (what the therapist was trying to do with regard to the focus); and (c) their implementation (how the therapist went about achieving the objective). The techniques were then named and put into the following categories: empathy, structuring, intimacy, elicitation, redirection, procedural, emotional exploration, referential, and discussion.

---

[1] For additional information on philosophy and philosophical inquiry, see Chapter 39, Philosophical Inquiry.

Other examples include Aigen (1998), Bruscia (1995, 1998a, 2002a), Maranto (1993, 1991), and Wheeler (1983).

Integration

A theory is developed by relating concepts or practices in music therapy to those in another field. Most often this is done by importing theory, research, and practice from an outside field into music therapy, then using the joint processes of accommodation and assimilation. In the accommodation process, phenomena in music therapy are fit into theories or constructs imported from other fields. In the process, some aspect of music therapy is expanded, limited, revised, or modified to accommodate the other field. In the assimilation process, theories or constructs outside the field are modified to fit into music therapy. Here the external model is expanded, limited, revised, or modified to accommodate music therapy phenomena. Theories that integrate music therapy with other fields can vary greatly according to the relative emphasis given to accommodation and assimilation; however, in all cases, the outcome is a mutual fertilization of both fields. Ideas in music therapy are fertilized and expanded by the other field, and ideas in the other field are fertilized and expanded by music therapy.

Integration theories, then, are intrinsically interdisciplinary—they invariably deal with topics of shared interest among different disciplines, and through the process of accommodation and assimilation, they invariably integrate different disciplinary perspectives on the same topic. It is not surprising, then, that integration theories are most prominent in those fields of knowledge that are interdisciplinary by nature—like music therapy.

In surveying the literature, one finds that integration theories in music therapy cover a variety of topics and are drawn from many different but related disciplines. A distinction can be made between integration theories that apply the broad perspective of another discipline to music therapy and those that borrow specific constructs from another discipline around a topic of common interest. A few of the many integration theories that draw upon the broad perspective of another discipline includes Hadsell's (1974) theory of music therapy based on sociology, Eagle's (1991) theory of music therapy based on physics, and Thaut's (2000) scientific theory of music therapy based on the integrated perspectives of the psychology, physiology, and neurology of music, along with experimental aesthetics.

In addition to these more broadly based theories are those that borrow specific ideas about a shared topic. Curiously, these theories seem to cluster around four main interdisciplinary topics: health and pathology, human development, therapy, and music.

Health and Pathology. Music therapy theories that import ideas about health and pathology usually offer a model of practice based on ideas in other fields about what constitutes health or pathology. For example, the present author drew upon ideas about health from Antonovsky (1987), a medical sociologist, and Wilber (1995), a philosopher, to develop a definition of health for specific use in music therapy. As a result, health was defined as "the process of becoming one's fullest potential for individual and ecological wholeness" (Bruscia, 1998a, p. 84), and the fundamental aim of music therapy was defined as promoting this process. There are also integration theories that import knowledge about a specific pathology to further inform music therapy practice. For example, models of music therapy practice have been formulated based on outside theories on learning disability (Gfeller, 1994), anorexia (Smeijsters, 1996), pain (Eagle & Harsh, 1988), and problems in sensory integration (James, 1984), to name a few.

Human Development. Ideas about human development have been imported into music therapy from many sources, including the work of Piaget (Lehtonen, 1993, 1995; Rider, 1977; Robb, 1999), Erikson (Robb), Freud (Lehtonen, 1993), Wilber (Rugenstein, 1996), Winnicott (Barclay, 1987; Nolan, 1989; Summer, 1992; Tyler, 1998), Stern (Lehtonen, 1995; Wigram, Pedersen, & Bonde, 2002), and Basch-Kahre (Erkkilä, 1997; Lehtonen, 1995). In these theories, isomorphic aspects of nonmusical and musical development are identified, and information about how the human being develops in essentially nonmusical domains is used as a template for understanding developmental phenomena in music therapy.

Proceeding from the opposite direction, Briggs (1991) and Bruscia (1991) began with research on stages of musical development and linked them to stages of psychological development as outlined by Piaget, Freud, Mahler, and Wilber. These links then were used to build a foundation for the developmental assessment, treatment, and evaluation of clients in music therapy. Similarly, Loewy (1995) identified the musical stages of speech development and related these to simultaneous stages of development in cognitive, physical, and emotional domains.

Nature of Therapy. Ideas about the nature of therapy have been imported into music therapy from many different schools of clinical practice (Ruud, 1980; Wheeler, 1981), such as psychodynamic theory (Priestley, 1994; Bruscia, 1998b, 2002b), Jungian theory (Priestley, 1987; Ward, 2002), and humanistic theory (Bonny, 2002; Broucek, 1987), to name a few.

Notice that the theories in this category start from the question: What is the nature of therapy that leads us to think that it can be accomplished effectively through music? One might say that the main purpose is to identify isomorphic aspects between therapy and music, starting from what defines or characterizes the therapy.

Nature of Music. In the next category, the question about what is isomorphic between therapy and music is posed from the opposite direction than in the previous section; that is, rather than starting from what defines or characterizes therapy and applying it to music, here the starting point is what defines or characterizes music. Specifically, what is the nature of music that leads us to think that it can be used therapeutically? Here the theorist looks at music with therapy in mind.

The music therapy literature abounds in theoretical papers that identify the therapeutic potentials of music and then describe how these potentials can be or have been utilized within the music therapy process. Ideas about what makes music therapeutic emanate from many disciplines and particularly those hybrid disciplines that combine music with another field, such as psychology of music, sociology of music, anthropology of music, biology of music, neurology of music, physics of music (acoustics), and philosophy of music. Examples include the following theoretical writings:

- In a series of articles, Noy (1966, 1967) reviewed the psychoanalytic literature on music to identify issues in formulating a psychodynamic understanding of music—what it is, what properties it has, and what it does. Implicit in presenting such a review was the need to clarify the psychological and psychotherapeutic foundations of music therapy.
- Aigen (1991a) examined shamanic conceptions of music, and used these conceptions to define wellness and to articulate the role of music and music therapy in promoting and maintaining health.
- Deschênes (1995) examined the symbolic and semantic components of music and then related these to music therapy.
- Bruscia (1998a) defined and classified clinical practices in music therapy according to six models of music experience. The models are based on the extent to which the therapist focuses the client's experience on the (a) objective, (b) subjective, (c) collective, (d) universal, (e) aesthetic, and/or (f) transpersonal properties of music.
- Weisethaunet (1999) evaluated theoretical ideas about the nature of improvisation in terms of their relevance to clinical practice in music therapy.
- Weyman (2000) considered multi-faceted aspects of the experience of improvising, and implicitly suggested its therapeutic values.
- Grinde (2000) used a biological, evolutionary perspective to understand how music serves as a form of human adaptation, which in turn implies its therapeutic value.
- Trevarthen and Malloch (2000) identified and contextualized the therapeutic properties of music in terms of the therapeutic needs of human beings.
- Daveson and Skewes (2002) examined theoretical ideas about the nature of rhythm in terms of how it is used and conceptualized in music therapy.
- Marshman (2003) examined Jung's theory of artistic creation and its inherent aesthetic implications for music and, based on this, offered a theoretical explanation for why music is so powerful as a therapy.

Philosophical Analysis

A theory is developed by relating fundamental concerns of philosophy (ontology, epistemology, logic, ethics, aesthetics) to music therapy practice, theory, or research. There are two approaches, one that starts from philosophy and one that starts from music therapy.

The first approach is to import a philosophical theory or construct into music therapy and then apply it to a particular theory, practice, or research. In most cases, the aim is to enlarge upon or expand existing notions in music therapy. For example, Salas (1990) drew upon the philosophical notions of Gregory Bateson regarding aesthetic experience, and within that experience, the meaning of beauty. She then proposed that aesthetic experience, and the beauty that is derived within it, is an affirmation of ontological meaning, that is, the very meaning of one's existence. The value of music therapy, then, is that by providing aesthetic experiences through music, clients are able to explore and find beauty and meaning in their lives. Mereni (1996, 1997) sketched out the African philosophy of music and how music relates to the African causal theory of ailments. The close relationship between music and medicine and healing in Africa, and the rationale for this relationship, was then compared to modern music therapy in Western cultures. Other philosophical theories and constructs that have been applied to music therapy include: Dewey's aesthetic theory (Aigen, 1995), Heidegger's concept of lifeworld (Nagler, 1995), Buber's I-Thou ontology (Garred, 1996), Wittgenstein's language games (Stige, 2002), and Wilber's spectrum model (Bonde, 2001).

Notice there is some overlap between theories built upon philosophical analysis of the nature of music and earlier integration theories based on the nature of music. The main distinction is whether the nature of music is being analyzed philosophically or according to another discipline, such as sociology or psychology.

The second approach is to analyze existing music therapy theory, research, or practice so as to identify or further clarify its philosophical underpinnings. For example, Aigen (1991b) uncovered and evaluated the philosophical assumptions underlying the predominant view of music therapy at the time and provided arguments for a change in paradigm. Hadley (1999) analyzed the philosophical premises underlying Creative Music Therapy and Analytical Music Therapy and compared them with regard to what constitutes health versus pathology and how the relational dynamics of therapy are configured.

Empirical Analysis

A theory is developed based on the analysis of research data of some kind. The data may exist already, or they may be gathered through any form of empirical research. This method varies according to whether the research used to build the theory is quantitative or qualitative.

In quantitative research, an empirical theory is an attempt to evaluate or explain a body of existing research findings, so that deductions can be made from them. A method of increasing relevance to music therapy is meta-analysis (see Chapter 23 of this book). Typically, a meta-analysis in music therapy shows whether the effect of music or music therapy found in many different studies can be considered significant. This is done by statistically analyzing the size of the effect found in all of the studies examined, taking into consideration differences in dependent and independent variables. For example, Standley (1986, 1992, 1996, 2000; Standley & Whipple, 2003) has used meta-analytic procedures to examine the effectiveness of music and music therapy in medical and dental treatment. Other meta-analyses have been conducted by Koger, Chapin, and Brotons (1999), Silverman (2003), and Dileo and Bradt (in press).

In qualitative research, an empirical theory is an attempt to *conceptualize* a phenomenon based on some form of systematic observation, inquiry, or research investigation. Unlike in quantitative research where empirical theory comes from previous research, empirical theory in qualitative research comes from data specifically gathered for the purpose of theory building. A common method used is *grounded theory,* as developed by Strauss and Corbin (1990), and as described in Chapter 29 of this book. In this method, the theory is developed incrementally, while gathering and analyzing the data. Initial theoretical formulations are constantly compared with incoming data, and then meticulously elaborated, modified, and reinterpreted until the theory is fully grounded in the data. Data sources may include interviews, field observations, and various kinds of arts works or documents. An example is Amir's (1996a) study of meaningful moments in music therapy.

Another method of theory building through empirical analysis employs the RepGrid technique, a computerized program for analyzing the constructs of individuals (see Chapter 37 of this book). An example in music therapy is the study by Abrams (2002), who interviewed practitioners of Guided Imagery and Music (GIM) about their own GIM experiences as clients, and based on their construct systems, developed a theory on the nature of transpersonal experiences.

Reflective Synthesis

A theory is developed by reflecting on one's own experiences with a phenomenon, relating these reflections to existing ideas or perspectives of other theorists, looking at research, and intuitively synthesizing all these sources of insight into an original theory or vision. The theory may start from any of the sources.

Gaston (1968) and Sears (1968) were probably the first Americans to present general theories of music therapy, that is, ones that might account for most, if not all, music therapy practices. Gaston based his theory on an interdisciplinary analysis of music and what contributes to its universality. Bringing in biology, genetics, anthropology, and the behavioral sciences, he identified several basic premises regarding the therapeutic potential of music. Sears' (1968) theory delved into what he called the *processes* of music therapy, focusing on three kinds of experiences that music affords the client: experience within structure, experience with self-organization, and experience in relating to others.

Carolyn Kenny has devoted much of her career to the development of music therapy theory. In her first book, *The Mythic Artery,* Kenny (1982) built connections between music, myth, and nature, and then showed how the death-rebirth cycle is indigenous to them all. In her 1985 article, Kenny expanded and further organized her ideas by exploring the relevance of systems theory and proposing that the whole system is made up of different *fields* within fields and *spaces* within the fields, where the quest for wholeness (healing) unfolds and is reenacted through their dynamic interplay. These notions then provide the foundation for examining how music is a model of the whole system, as well as a field and space within it. *The Field of Play* (1989) can be seen as the culmination of many of Kenny's previous ideas, as well as the beginning of a newly organized direction for her theorizing. So far, she had identified the regenerative experience as a core process in music and nature, with wholeness and healing as the ultimate quest, and through her lens of systems theory, she had begun to identify many of the interdependent elements, fields, and spaces that interact in the ongoing process of reconnecting to this quest. Now, she was to organize these ideas into a formal theory and find a language that was closer to her understanding of the music therapy process. Briefly, Kenny's field of play theory proposed that there are seven fields essential to music therapy.

1. The aesthetic: A field or environment containing the conditions of beauty, including the human being. This is the loving and supportive field that resources all others.
2. The musical space: The contained space that arises out of the aesthetic when therapist and client relate to one another through music.
3. The field of play: The open field that arises out of the aesthetic field and the musical space, and that expands into a field of experimentation, play, and modeling. The field of play contains four interactive fields, as in the following points.
4. Ritual: Any repeatable form created through the conditions present at the time.
5. A particular state of consciousness: A field of relaxation, concentration, and playfulness.
6. Power: The field of energy that motivates receptivity and induces action
7. Creative process: The process and field that results from the interplay and overlaps of the previous fields.

These fields are environments that have varying conditions, each of which operates in an organic ecology according to certain principles. When the fields overlap, or when elements or conditions interact, a relationship emerges and a new field is created. In 1996, Kenny introduced a new element in her theory by identifying various qualities of the seven fields. The qualities are helpful in recognizing and distinguishing the fields, without operationally defining or limiting them.

There are many more theories built through reflective synthesis. Examples include Amir (1996b), Bruscia (2000), Goldberg (2002), and Perilli (2002).

The Nature of Theory

Theories vary in nature according to several dimensions. The first dimension is its objective or aim. A theory that aims at explaining cause-effect relationships in practice or research is quite different from a theory that aims at enlarging the way practice or research is construed. Thus, theories may vary according to how explanatory and how constructive they are, with the former emanating from positivistic paradigms, and the latter from nonpositivistic ones. Along with this, explanatory theories focus on what is or what was in order to predict what will be; whereas constructive theories focus on how the past and present can be re-visioned, in order to create yet unknown possibilities for the future. Thus, the objective or aim of a theory provides three different but related continua for describing a theory: (a) from explanatory to constructive aims, (b) from positivistic to nonpositivistic paradigms, and (c) from predictive versus visionary foci.

The second important dimension of theory is method. As discussed above, there are many different ways of creating a theory, and each theorist finds his or her own way of using and combining these methods, depending upon his or her own metatheory and epistemology. Method has an important impact on the nature of the theory created because it determines the kind of foundation that is laid for the theory. Thus, those who want a factual foundation for theory will gravitate toward theories based on empirical analysis, whereas those who want reason as the foundation for theory will gravitate toward philosophical analysis and those who want intuition combined with reason and experience will gravitate toward reflective synthesis, and so forth. In short, the method of theory building establishes its trustworthiness in combination with the epistemology of the person reading or using the theory. In the end, the creator of a theory and the user of a theory have to be on the same wavelength with regard to both metatheory and epistemology. Essentially, the method of developing a theory influences the extent to which the theory has objective or subjective foundations.

The third important dimension is outcome. If the theory is useful in guiding actions or decision-making, it can be described as practical. The practical theory helps people to do research or to do practice. If the theory is useful in understanding something or if it can help to gain insight about something, without immediately obvious implications for what to do, the theory can be described as more reflective. Thus, theories may be described along a continuum from practical to reflective.

The fourth important dimension is form, which involves completeness and coherence. A complete theory is one that has as many propositions as needed to deal with the all of the most important aspects of the target phenomenon, whereas an incomplete theory has one or more constructs that deal with only a few aspects. For example, consider the difference between a theory that covers the entire relationship between developmental theory and music therapy, and one that looks only at a particular period of development (0–2 years) or a particular developmental phenomenon, such as transitional objects. Thus, theories vary according to whether they are complete in their treatment of a topic, or whether they consist of only a few constructs.

Theories that have the most coherence describe the relationships between all parts and levels of the theory, for example propositions and corollaries, whereas theories with less coherence relate only some, if any, part of the theory. Thus, theories vary along a continuum ranging from less to more coherent.

The fifth dimension is disciplinary scope, that is, whether the theory was created to deal with the entire discipline or to only a part or dimension of it. For example, the theories of Sears (1968), Kenny (1989), and Amir (1996b) were meant to apply to all of music therapy and are thus more *general* in disciplinary scope. In contrast, the theories of Perilli (2002), Goldberg (2002), and Körlin (2002) were intended to apply to only Guided Imagery and Music, just as theories by Aigen (1996, 1998) and Robbins and Forinash (1991) were intended to apply to only Nordoff-Robbins Music Therapy. In these cases, the theory is specific to a particular approach within music therapy but not all of the discipline (which of course does not mean that the theories have no implications or value for the entire discipline). A theory can also be specific to a particular orientation. For example, a developmental theory or a behavioral theory of music therapy is specific in that it applies to only one orientation within the field and has less applicability than a theory that is orientation free. Thus, theories may be general or specific, depending upon whether their scope covers larger or smaller areas of music therapy, as differentiated by both method and clinical orientation.

Notice that disciplinary scope is different from completeness. A theory examining the significance of metaphor in GIM, for example, may be quite complete in its coverage of the topic; however, it cannot be considered a general theory because it is not applicable to all practices within the discipline of music therapy. In this case, then, the theory is complete but specific. Conversely, the iso principle is a construct rather than a complete theory, but since it was meant to apply to the entire discipline, it would be considered incomplete as a theory but general in its scope.

Closely linked to the generality and completeness of a theory is the dimension of relevance. Here the question is how well the theory covers the most significant aspects of the target phenomenon or domain, regardless of whether the theory is general or specific in scope and regardless of how completely developed the theory is. Is the theory pertinent? Does it deal with the topics and issues that are essential to consider in understanding or explaining the phenomenon or domain? For example, compare the relevance of a theory on the role of metaphors in GIM with a theory on the role of contingent reinforcement in GIM. Both theories are specific in scope and both could be equally complete, but obviously, the theory on metaphor is more relevant to the intrinsic nature of GIM than a theory on reinforcement. Thus, in addition to generality and completeness, theories vary along a continuum from less to more relevant.

The problem with relevance is that it is a matter of opinion. What is relevant to one person may not be so to another. This is usually not so much of a problem in determining the relevance of specific theories where the phenomenon or domain are clearly defined and delimited by the theorist. In these kinds of theories, the boundaries are more carefully delineated, and this makes relevance easier to evaluate. In general theories, however, this is not the case. The reason is that it is more difficult to draw the boundaries for an entire discipline. One person's idea of what the full scope of music therapy is may be different from another person's. Thus, for someone who defines music therapy as only this method, or only this approach, or only this orientation, relevance is limited to only his or her definition of the discipline. Thus, people with narrower views of music therapy will tend to see more theories as irrelevant than relevant, and those with broader views will tend to see more theories as relevant than irrelevant.

Certainly, a major factor in sketching out the full scope of music therapy is its interdisciplinary nature. As soon as there are two disciplines to balance or integrate, differences of opinion arise. If, for example, we simply say that music therapy is an amalgam of music disciplines and therapy disciplines, at least two polarities are already implicit. One camp will say that music therapy is a music-centered discipline, and therefore, for theory to be relevant, it must be music-centered; while the other camp will say that it is therapy-centered, and that for theory to be relevant, it must be therapy-centered. And then, there is what lies in the middle of these two polarities—the true integration and equal balance of music disciplines and therapy disciplines to form a new discipline that has its own unique identity, which is intrinsically different from either the music or therapy side or any of their subsidiary disciplines. For this camp, a theory is relevant only if it is centered on music therapy itself. A metaphor may be helpful. A cake is not flour-centered or egg-centered, based on relative proportions used; it is a cake—a unique combination of ingredients that undergoes a metamorphosis that leads to a new entity altogether. This in no way undermines the importance of understanding the flour or the egg; it only emphasizes that understanding either the flour or the egg or both is not sufficient for understanding the cake.

For purposes of our discussion, then, theories can be music-centered, therapy-centered, or music therapy-centered. The music-centered theory gives greater emphasis to understanding the nature of music and its role in therapy; the therapy-centered theory gives greater emphasis to understanding the nature of therapy and how music can contribute to it; a music therapy-centered theory gives greater emphasis to how music therapy itself works—how both music and therapist work equally and in tandem, how the client-music and the client-therapist relationships are used equally and integratively, how music and therapy processes unfold together, and so forth.

This entire discussion leads us to the last dimension that defines the nature of any theory: whether it is indigenous or imported. Based on the above distinctions and definitions, an imported theory is a theory that emanates from or gives precedence to music (and any of its subdisciplines) or therapy (and any of its subdisciplines). An imported theory is one of the two polarities: it is either music-centered or therapy-centered. A music-centered theory tends to describe and explain music therapy in musical terms; a therapy-centered theory tends to describe or explain music therapy in therapy terms. Both are imported views, with neither being more indigenous to music therapy than the other. Imported theories make sense to people in outside disciplines, because they often use their language.

An indigenous theory is music therapy-centered. It deals with phenomena as they appear in music therapy settings, as they unfold through music therapy intervention, as they change through music therapy processes, as they make sense within a music therapy context, as they are perceived and languaged by music therapists, and as they can be understood by other music therapists. Indigenous theories describe and explain what music therapists do and think through their theory, research, and practice. Because of this, indigenous theories make sense to people inside the field because they have first-hand knowledge of the experiences being described. Thus, the final dimension to be considered in understanding the nature of any theory is the extent to which the information is imported from music or therapy disciplines or is indigenous to music therapy.

It is hoped that these descriptions of the various dimensions of theory, and the distinctions that have been made, will enable readers to be more discerning when reading a theory and evaluating its integrity or usefulness.

References

Abrams, B. (2002). Transpersonal dimensions of the Bonny Method. In K. Bruscia & D. Grocke (Eds.), *Guided Imagery and Music: The Bonny Method and beyond* (pp. 339–358). Gilsum, NH: Barcelona Publishers.

Aigen, K. (1991a). The voice of the forest: A conception of music for music therapy. *Music Therapy, 10,* 77–98.

Aigen, K. (1991b). *The roots of music therapy: Towards an indigenous research paradigm.* Unpublished doctoral dissertation, New York University (University Microfilms 9134717).

Aigen, K. (1995). An aesthetic foundation of clinical theory: An underlying basis of Creative Music Therapy. In C. Kenny (Ed.), *Listening, playing, creating: Essays on the power of sound* (pp. 233–257). Albany NY: State University of New York Press.

Aigen, K. (1996). *Being in music: Foundations of Nordoff-Robbins Music Therapy.* St. Louis, MO: MMB Music.

Aigen, K. (1998). *Paths of development in Nordoff-Robbins Music Therapy.* Gilsum, NH: Barcelona Publishers.

Amir, D. (1996a). Experiencing music therapy: Meaningful moments in the music therapy process. In M. Langenberg, K. Aigen, & J. Frommer (Eds.), *Qualitative music therapy research: Beginning dialogues* (pp. 109–130). Gilsum, NH: Barcelona Publishers.

Amir, D. (1996b). Music therapy—Holistic model. *Music Therapy, 14,* 44–60.

Ansdell, G. (1997). Musical elaborations: What has the New Musicology to say to music therapy? *British Journal of Music Therapy, 11,* 36–44.

Antonovsky, A. (1987). *Unraveling the mystery of health: How people manage stress and stay well.* San Francisco: Jossey-Bass.

Barclay, M. (1987). A contribution to a theory of music therapy: Additional phenomenological perspectives on GestaltQualitat and transitional phenomena. *Journal of Music Therapy, 24,* 224–238.

Bonde, L. O. (2001). Steps towards a meta-theory of music therapy? An introduction to Ken Wilber's Integral Psychology and a discussion of its relevance to music therapy. *Nordic Journal of Music Therapy, 19,* 176–187.

Bonny, H. L. (L. Summer, Ed.). (2002). *Music and consciousness: The evolution of Guided Imagery and Music.* Gilsum, NH: Barcelona Publishers.

Briggs, C. (1991). A model for understanding musical development. *Music Therapy, 10,* 1–21.

Broucek, M. (1987). Beyond healing to "whole-ing": A voice for the deinstitutionalization of music therapy. *Music Therapy, 6,* 50–58.

Bruscia, K. (1987). *Improvisational models of music therapy.* Springfield, IL: Charles C Thomas Publishers.

Bruscia, K. (1991). Musical origins: Developmental foundations for music therapy. *Proceedings of the Eighteenth Annual Conference of the Canadian Association for Music Therapy* (pp. 2–10). Regina, Saskatchewan, Canada: Canadian Association for Music Therapy.

Bruscia, K. (1995). Modes of consciousness in Guided Imagery and Music (GIM): A therapist's experience of the guiding process. In C. B. Kenny (Ed.), *Listening, playing, and creating: Essays on the power of sound* (pp. 165–197). Albany NY: State University of New York Press.

Bruscia, K. (1998a). *Defining music therapy* (2nd ed.). Gilsum, NH: Barcelona Publishers.

Bruscia, K. (Ed.). (1998b). *The dynamics of music psychotherapy.* Gilsum, NH: Barcelona Publishers.

Bruscia, K. (2000). The nature of meaning in music therapy: Kenneth Bruscia interviewed by Brynjulf Stige. *Nordic Journal of Music Therapy, 9,* 84–96.

Bruscia, K. (2002a). The boundaries of Guided Imagery and Music and the Bonny method. In K. Bruscia & D. Grocke (Eds.), *Guided Imagery and Music: The Bonny Method and beyond* (pp. 37–62). Gilsum, NH: Barcelona Publishers.

Bruscia, K. (2002b). A psychodynamic orientation to the Bonny Method. In K. Bruscia & D. Grocke (Eds.), *Guided Imagery and Music: The Bonny Method and beyond* (pp. 225–244). Gilsum, NH: Barcelona Publishers.

Daveson, B., & Skewes, K. (2002). A philosophical inquiry into the role or rhythm in music therapy. *The Arts in Psychotherapy, 29,* 265–270.

Deschênes, B. (1995). Music and symbols. *Music Therapy Perspectives, 13,* 40–45.

Dileo, C., & Bradt, J. (Eds.). (in press). *Music therapy and medicine: A meta-analysis of the literature according to medical specialty.* Cherry Hill, NJ: Jeffrey Books.

Eagle, C. (1991). Steps to a quantum therapy. *Music Therapy Perspectives, 9,* 56–60.

Eagle, C., & Harsh, M. (1988). Elements of pain and music: The aio connection. *Music Therapy, 7,* 15–27.

Erkkilä, J. (1997). From the unconscious to the conscious: Musical improvisation and drawings as tools in the music therapy of children. *Nordic Journal of Music Therapy, 6,* 112–120.

Garred, R. (1996). Improvisational music therapy as encounter. *Nordic Journal of Music Therapy, 5,* 76–86.

Gaston, E. T. (1968). Man and music. In E. T. Gaston (Ed.), *Music in therapy* (pp. 6–29). New York: Macmillan Publishing Co.

Gfeller, K. (1994). Prominent theories in learning disabilities and implications for music therapy methodology. *Music Therapy Perspectives, 2,* 9–13.

Goldberg, F. (2002). A holographic field theory model of the Bonny Method of Guided Imagery and Music (BMGIM). In K. Bruscia & D. Grocke (Eds.), *Guided Imagery and Music: The Bonny Method and beyond* (pp. 359–378). Gilsum, NH: Barcelona Publishers.

Grinde, B. (2000). A biological perspective on musical appreciation. *Nordic Journal of Music Therapy, 9,* 18–27.

Hadley, S. (1999). A comparative analysis of the philosophical premises underlying Creative Music Therapy and Analytical Music Therapy. *Australian Journal of Music Therapy, 10,* 3–19.

Hadsell, N. (1974). A sociological theory and approach to music therapy with adult psychiatric patients. *Journal of Music Therapy, 11,* 113–124.

James, M. R. (1984). Sensory integration: A theory for therapy and research. *Journal of Music Therapy, 21,* 79–88.

Kenny, C. (1982). *The mythic artery: The magic of music therapy.* Atascadero CA: Ridgeview Publishing Co.

Kenny, C. (1985). Music: A whole systems approach. *Music Therapy, 5,* 3–11.

Kenny, C. (1989). *The field of play: A guide for the theory and practice of music therapy.* Atascadero, CA: Ridgeview Publishing Co.

Kenny, C. (1996). The dilemma of uniqueness: An essay on consciousness and qualities. *Nordic Journal of Music Therapy, 5,* 87–96.

Koger, S., Chapin, K., & Brotons, M. (1999). Is music therapy an effective intervention for dementia? A meta-analytic review of literature. *Journal of Music Therapy, 36,* 2–15.

Körlin, D. (2002). A neuropsychological theory of traumatic imagery in the Bonny Method of Guided Imagery and Music (BMGIM). In K. Bruscia & D. Grocke (Eds.), *Guided Imagery and Music: The Bonny Method and beyond* (pp. 379–415). Gilsum, NH: Barcelona Publishers.

Lehtonen, K. (1993). Reflections on music therapy and developmental psychology. *Nordic Journal of Music Therapy, 2,* 3–12.

Lehtonen, K. (1995). Is music an archaic form of thinking? *British Journal of Music Therapy, 9,* 20–26.

Loewy, J. (1995). The musical stages of speech: A developmental model of pre-verbal sound making. *Music Therapy, 13,* 47–73.

Maranto, C. Dileo (1991). A classification model for music and medicine. In C. Dileo Maranto (Ed.), *Applications of music in medicine* (pp. 1–6). Washington, DC: National Association for Music Therapy.

Maranto, C. Dileo (1993). *Music therapy: International perspectives.* Pipersville, PA: Jeffrey Books.

Marshman, A. (2003). The power of music: A Jungian aesthetic. *Music Therapy Perspectives, 21,* 21–26.

Mereni, A. (1996). "Kinesis und Katharsis": The African traditional concept of sound/motion (music): Its application in, and implications for, music therapy, Part II. *British Journal of Music Therapy, 10,* 17–23.

Mereni, A. (1997). "Kinesis und Katharsis": The African traditional concept of sound/motion (music): Its application in, and implications for, music therapy, Part III. *British Journal of Music Therapy, 11,* 20–23.

Nagler, J. (1995). Toward the aesthetic lifeworld. *Music Therapy, 13,* 75–91.

Nolan, P. (1989). Music as a transitional object in the treatment of bulimia. *Music Therapy Perspectives,* 6, 49–51.

Noy, P. (1966). The psychodynamic meaning of music, Part I. *Journal of Music Therapy, 3,* 126–134.

Noy, P. (1967). The psychodynamic meaning of music, Parts II–V. *Journal of Music Therapy, 4,* 7–23, 45–51, 81–94, 117–125.

Perilli, G. (2002). A theory of metaphor in the Bonny Method of Guided Imagery and Music. In K. Bruscia & D. Grocke (Eds.), *Guided Imagery and Music: The Bonny Method and beyond* (pp. 417–448). Gilsum, NH: Barcelona Publishers.

Priestley, M. (1987). Music and the shadow. *Music Therapy, 6,* 20–27.

Priestley, M. (1994). *Essays on Analytical Music Therapy.* Gilsum, NH: Barcelona Publishers.

Rider, M. (1977). The relationship between auditory and visual perception on tasks employing Piaget's concept of conservation. *Journal of Music Therapy, 14,* 126–138.

Robb, S. (1999). Piaget, Erikson, and coping styles: Implications for music therapy and the hospitalized preschool child. *Music Therapy Perspectives, 17,* 14–19.

Robbins, C., & Forinash, M. (1991). A time paradigm: Time as a multilevel phenomenon in music therapy. *Music Therapy, 19,* 46–57.

Rugenstein, L. (1996). Wilber's spectrum model of transpersonal psychology and its application to music therapy. *Music Therapy, 14,* 9–28.

Ruud, E. (1980). *Music therapy and its relationship to current treatment theories.* St. Louis, MO: MMB Music.

Salas, J. (1990). Aesthetic experience in music therapy. *Music Therapy, 9,* 1–15.

Sears, W. (1968). Processes in music therapy. In E. T. Gaston (Ed.), *Music in therapy* (pp. 30–44). New York: Macmillan Publishing Co.

Silverman, M. (2003). The influence of music on the symptoms of psychosis: A meta-analysis. *Journal of Music Therapy, 40,* 27–40.

Smeijsters, H. (1996). Music therapy with anorexia nervosa: An integrative theoretical and methodological perspective. *British Journal of Music Therapy, 10,* 3–13.

Standley, J. (1986). Music research in medical/dental treatment: Meta-analysis and clinical applications. *Journal of Music Therapy, 23,* 56–122.

Standley, J. (1992). Meta-analysis of research in music and medical treatment: Effect size as a basis for comparison across multiple dependent and independent variables. In R. Spintge & R. Droh (Eds.), *MusicMedicine* (pp. 364–378). St. Louis, MO: MMB Music.

Standley, J. (1996). Meta-analysis of research in music and medical treatment: Effect size as a basis for comparison across multiple dependent and independent variables. In R. Spintge & R. Droh (Eds.), *MusicMedicine* (pp. 364–378). St. Louis, MO: MMB Music.

Standley, J. (2000). Music research in medical treatment. In *Effectiveness of music therapy procedures: Documentation of research and clinical practice* (3rd ed., pp. 1–64). Silver Spring, MD: American Music Therapy Association.

Standley, J. M., & Whipple, J. (2003). Music therapy with pediatric patients: A meta-analysis. In S. L. Robb (Ed.), *Music therapy in pediatric healthcare: Research and evidence-based practice* (pp. 1–18). Silver Spring, MD: American Music Therapy Association.

Stige, B. (2002). *Culture-centered music therapy.* Gilsum, NH: Barcelona Publishers.

Strauss, A., & Corbin, J. (1990). *Basics of qualitative research: Grounded theory procedures.* Thousand Oaks, CA: Sage Publications.

Summer, L. (1992). Music: The aesthetic elixir. *Journal of the Association for Music and Imagery, 1,* 43–54.

Thaut, M. (2000). *A scientific model of music in therapy and medicine.* San Antonio, TX: IMR Press, University of Texas.

Trevarthen, C., & Malloch, S. (2000). The dance of wellbeing: Defining the musical therapeutic effect. *Nordic Journal of Music Therapy,* 9, 3–17.

Tyler, H. (1998). Behind the mask: An exploration of the true and false self as revealed in music therapy. *British Journal of Music Therapy, 12,* 60–66.

Ward, K. (2002). A Jungian orientation to the Bonny Method. In K. Bruscia & D. Grocke (Eds.), *Guided Imagery and Music: The Bonny Method and beyond* (pp. 207–224). Gilsum, NH: Barcelona Publishers.

Weisethaunet, H. (1999). Critical remarks on the nature of improvisation. *Nordic Journal of Music Therapy, 8,* 143–155.

Weymann, E. (2000). Sensitive suspense—Experiences with musical improvisation. *Nordic Journal of Music Therapy, 9,* 38–45.

Wheeler, B. (1981). The relationship between music therapy and theories of psychotherapy. *Music Therapy, 1,* 9–16.

Wheeler, B. (1983). A psychotherapeutic classification of music therapy practices: A continuum of procedures. *Music Therapy Perspectives, 1,* 8–16.

Wigram, T., Pedersen, I. N., & Bonde, L. O. (2002). *A comprehensive guide to music therapy: Theory, clinical practice, research and training.* London: Jessica Kingsley Publishers.

Wilber, K. (1995). *Sex, ecology, spirituality.* Boston: Shambhala.

Chapter 41
Historical Research in Music Therapy
Alan L. Solomon

History is the story of things worthy of being remembered.

French Academy

In their classic text, *The Lessons of History*, Will and Ariel Durant (1968) define history as "the events or record of the past" (p. 14). Renier (1961) enhances this simple pronouncement by indicating that history is "the story of the experiences" of men and women "living in civilized societies" (p. 79). These definitions may surprise the reader who understands history to be the study of the past. The distinction between these definitions and the study of the past is important. History is not generally defined as the study of the past because the past has, well, passed. That is, it no longer exists and cannot be studied directly. It is through the study of the evidence of the past that we develop historical knowledge:

> Since time is irreversible, the historian knows the past only by the remains left over. These traces are presumed valid evidence of the past, although just what they indicate is interpreted variously and disputed vigorously by historians. But in the end, historians do not doubt that a part of the past can be known and must be known. . . from this evidence. (Berkhofer, 1969, pp. 11–12)

The immediate purpose of historical research is, of course, "to save the facts of the past from oblivion" (Halphen, as quoted by Renier, p. 258). As Renier writes: "For every human being the memory of his childhood is a matter of supreme importance. To it he owes his sense of identity and possibly his consciousness, without it he can take no important decision, he cannot improve his condition, he cannot survive" (p. 13). If this statement is true for individuals, can it be no less true for society in general or specific professions like music therapy?

The word *history* is derived from the Latin *histore* which means "narrative." A narrative is a story and, in the case of history, a true story, based on evidence, that brings us knowledge about the past. This is why Barzun and Graff (1992) refer to history as "the story of past facts" (p. 44). Questions of historical truth are important as historian Paul Ricoeur (1984) indicates when he asks: "What does the term 'real' signify when it is applied to the historical past?" and "What do we mean when we say that something really happened?" (p. 1). Ricoeur describes these questions as the most troublesome facing historical thinking, and yet, "if it is difficult to find a reply, the question itself is inevitable: it makes the difference between history and fiction" (p. 1). The historian, however, is constrained by "*what once was*. He owes a *debt* to the past, a debt of *gratitude* with respect to the dead, which makes him an *insolvent debtor*" (p. 2).

Interestingly, history is also what James Hoopes (2000) describes as "an exercise of the imagination" (p. 3):

> History, like life, is a test of our ability imaginatively to place ourselves in the positions of other people, so that we can understand the reasons for their actions. Through research and study we learn facts about those other people. But we can never know everything about anyone, living or dead. The historical record is always incomplete. Imagination must fill in the gaps of our knowledge, though of course our imaginings must derive from facts and be consistent with them. (p. 3)

So the term *history* is commonly used in four distinct, but related, ways referring to: (a) the events of the past; (b) that which has been written about the past; (c) the ideas, images, or memories of the past that exist in people's minds; and (d) an area of scholarly inquiry, that is, a way of knowing about the past. If *research* is systematic inquiry, the purpose of which is to gain knowledge, then *historical research* is gaining knowledge about the past by systematically studying the evidence of the past. Historical research in music therapy, then, is the systematic study of the past practices, materials, institutions, and people involved in therapeutic applications of music (Solomon & Heller, 1982).

Topic Selection

The first category of topics to consider for historical research in music therapy pertains to the history of people, otherwise known as biography. Who were the important personalities in the development of music therapy as a profession and what were their contributions?

During the 20th century people like Ruth Boxberger, Dorothy Brin Crocker, Arthur Flagler Fultz, Esther Goetz Gilliland, Ray Green, Wilhelmina Harbert, Betty Isern Howery, Erwin Schneider, Sister Josepha Schorsch, William Sears, Myrtle Fish Thompson, Roy Underwood, and others made essential contributions to the developing field of music therapy, yet their contributions are largely unknown to most of us. And what of earlier centuries? The 19th century contributions of Edwin Atlee, D. Hector Chomet, and Samuel Mathews, and the 18th century contributions of Richard Brocklesby and Richard Browne similarly need study (Heller & Solomon, 1982; Solomon, Davis, & Heller, 2002).

Recent examples of music therapy biography include Darlene Brooks' (2002) "Charles E. Braswell: A Man With Vision," Sherri Robb's (1999) "Marian Erdman: Contributions of an American Red Cross Hospital Recreation Worker," and Jennifer Miller's (1988) "The Contributions of Wayne Ruppenthal to the Field of Music Therapy."

The second category of topics is the history of places, which may include geographical areas, such as cities, states, regions, or countries, as well as specific institutions, such as the history of the music therapy program at an individual treatment facility. Examples include Dena Condron's (2000) *The American Association for Music Therapy: From Inception to Unification* and Alan L. Solomon's (1985) "A Historical Study of the National Association for Music Therapy: 1960–1980," a documentary history of the 2nd and 3rd decades of the National Association for Music Therapy (NAMT).

The third category is the history of events and ideas, that is, the ways that music therapy has been used and the clientele that has benefited from music therapy. Important questions in this category may deal with issues such as treatment trends, technological advances, and treatment philosophies. Recent examples include Margaret Ann Rorke's (2001) "Music Therapy in the Age of Enlightenment," Shannon de l'Etoile's (2000) "The History of the Undergraduate Curriculum in Music Therapy," and Bryan C. Hunter's (1999) "Singing as a Therapeutic Agent, in *The Etude*."

Other Issues in Topic Selection

There are other important issues in topic selection, beyond the perceived need for the study, which must be considered when a student undertakes a historical research project. Interest is essential; a student must have an interest in the proposed topic of study. Nothing is more distressing to the student, and ultimately worthless, than research that is not approached with dedication, discipline, and motivation. One thing is certain in any research undertaking—there will be problems to confront and obstacles to overcome. Without the drive to successfully conclude the project, the results will fall far short of expectations.

Other important factors include time, financial considerations, and practicality. Is it reasonable to expect that the historical research project can be concluded within the available time? What are the financial considerations? It is the nature of historical evidence that it is not always conveniently located in one site close to the residence of the investigator. One may have to travel to a distant location to study an important artifact or to interview one of the principals.

Finally, how practical is the topic? Is it practical to think that someone can write a history of music therapy west of the Mississippi, for example, before the histories of regions, states, cities, and institutions in that geographical area have been written? One way to avoid these pitfalls is to properly delimit the topics to be studied.

Delimitation of Topics

Delimitation refers to the process whereby the researcher sets the boundaries for the study. In other words, it is here that the researcher decides what will and what will not be included in the proposed study. It is the failure to properly focus the study that often presents the most significant problem for the student attempting a historical research project for the first time.

There are many ways, including time, geography, and subject matter, to delimit historical studies in music therapy.

In selecting an initial topic, there is a tendency for students, in their eagerness to make a significant contribution to the field or earn a good grade, to choose a topic that is so broad that the necessary infrastructure for such a topic does not exist and will result in failure despite the best intentions and efforts of the student.

For example, a student may decide to study the history of music therapy in Indiana. From the point of view of time, is it reasonable to think that someone could write a history spanning approximately 300 years when no historical studies of music therapy in Indiana communities have been conducted to date? Perhaps a good first step would be to delimit this topic chronologically, say a history of music therapy in Indiana since 1951 (a landmark year which saw the first meeting of music therapists in the state at Logansport State Hospital on November 29).

Even with this chronological delimitation, the topic is still so broad that it should be the source of serious concern for the student, as it surely will be for the faculty member supervising the study. Another option would be to delimit the study geographically. For example, if the study were delimited to a history of music therapy in Evansville, IN, since 1951, the study would finally begin to take on reasonable proportions.

For the student researcher, however, this topic may still be too broad given the time and resources available to conduct the study. Another option would be to delimit the study by subject matter, such as the use of music therapy with a specific clientele. An example of a workable solution might be a history of the use of music therapy with the developmentally disabled in Evansville, IN, since 1951. For a student located in Evansville, such a topic would certainly be a possibility because collecting the evidence that would form the basis for the study would not cause unreasonable hardship for the student in terms of the time, travel, or financial resources that would be required. And this study, if well done, would benefit the profession by helping to build the infrastructure required for projects of larger scope.

Sources of Evidence

There are many different types of evidence that are useful in conducting historical research, but all evidence is initially categorized as either primary or secondary sources. A *primary source* is a firsthand witness of the historical event under study. A *secondary source* is any source that is not primary. For example, Ray Green, the first president of NAMT, is a primary source for the organizational meeting that was held on June 2, 1950, resulting in the founding of NAMT, because he was present at that meeting. Whether that evidence is in the form of his notes from that meeting, a picture he took at the meeting, or his memories of that meeting, they are all considered primary sources for this event.

It is important to note that whether a source is primary or secondary depends on the questions you ask of the source, not the source itself. For example, Ruth Boxberger was a pioneer and early leader in music therapy. Her doctoral dissertation was a history of the first 10 years of NAMT. That dissertation is a primary source of the life of Ruth Boxberger because she wrote it, and would be essential for anyone writing her biography. But Boxberger was not a witness to all the events she described in her 10-year history of NAMT, so, if you are asking questions regarding the history of NAMT, her dissertation would be a secondary source. In other words, one cannot tell if a source is primary or secondary just by looking at it. One must know what information the source is being used for in order to determine whether the source is primary or secondary.

Historical research in music therapy uses many different sources of evidence. One is pictorial records, that is, photographs or drawings that provide evidence of historical events. In "Music in Special Education Before 1930: Hearing and Speech Development," Solomon (1980) presented several pictures providing evidence of the way music was used in 19th century institutions for people with hearing impairments. One picture showed a classroom at the Clarke Institution for Deaf-Mutes in Northampton, MA (circa 1890), with the students sitting in a semicircle in front of the teacher and one of the students standing beside the teacher. The class is looking at what appears to be a small model of a cow or horse. But what was important for the purpose of this study appeared in the background of the photo. Clearly situated in the background of the photo, leaning up against the wall, is a guitar. It is not hanging on the wall, like a decoration, but leaning next to the teacher's position in front of the class where it could be easily accessed by the teacher (Solomon, p. 238). Photographs do not speak, never mind sing, but the presence and location of the guitar in the classroom suggest that the guitar was used in some manner.

Another photograph shows how music was used at the McCowen Oral School in Chicago (circa 1890). In this picture an older student is playing the piano while one student is leaning against the piano with his ear pressed to the instrument. Also in the room are two teachers who are singing to students through ear trumpets (Solomon, 1980, p. 239). In this case, we see not only music instruments but also how they are being used.

Another source of evidence is official records. By analyzing the minutes of meetings, for example, we can often reconstruct the events that took place and come to an understanding of what happened, what the issues were, and who was responsible. In the previously mentioned study of the history of the first 10 years of NAMT, Boxberger (1963) used the minutes of the June 2, 1950, meeting conducted by Ray Green as evidence of the events that led to the founding of NAMT.

Personal correspondence is another method of obtaining evidence of historical events. Boxberger (1964) cited a letter from E. Thayer Gaston in describing the development of music therapy internship programs in Topeka, KS, at the Winter Veterans Administration Hospital, Topeka State Hospital, and the Menninger Foundation, and the impact that these programs had on the establishment of a graduate program in music therapy at The University of Kansas.

Interviews are a unique and significant way of obtaining historical evidence (the emergence of oral history as a major research technique will be discussed later). Interviews allow for the collection of historical evidence that may not exist in any other form than the memories that people hold of the past. While investigating the development of NAMT's Central Office in the 1960s, for example, this writer found little evidence in the form of official documentation but was able to learn details not otherwise available by interviewing one of the principals, Ruth Boxberger, NAMT's first executive secretary.

Other forms of historical evidence in music therapy include artifacts and handwritten materials. *Artifacts* are physical objects that are the results of human behavior from the past. Examples in music therapy might be tape recordings, such as the recordings of Wayne County General Hospital psychiatric patients who performed over a local radio station under the guidance of Ira Altshuler, MD, or musical instruments constructed by music therapy clients. Handwritten materials might take the form of a diary or journal of events recorded by an eyewitness.

Analysis of Evidence

Once evidence is obtained, it must be analyzed for credibility and accuracy. After all, just because someone remembers something does not mean that this memory is factual or accurate. Anyone who has witnessed an event that happened suddenly and passed quickly, such as an automobile accident, knows that several eyewitnesses can have different perceptions and understandings of what they witnessed. And often their recollections of the event directly contradict one another (this points out why primary sources are not necessarily more accurate than secondary sources— ideally one can corroborate a point with both primary and secondary sources). The process by which historical researchers determine the credibility and accuracy of evidence is called *criticism*.[1]

External criticism authenticates evidence—that is, it helps us determine whether the evidence is what we think it is, what it appears to be, or what someone claims it to be. There is no test that is administered to determine credibility beyond the judgment, common sense, and knowledge of the subject matter possessed by the researcher and, ultimately, the consensus of other informed researchers. Some of the questions that might be addressed to the evidence in the process of external criticism involve the location and age of the evidence, the existence of corroboratory evidence, and any reason to suspect that the item might not be genuine (Phelps, Ferrara, & Goolsby, 1993).

---

[1] Editor's note: As discussed in other chapters of this book, people's constructions or interpretations of events may also differ. This awareness has led to constructivism and other nonpositivistic approaches to examining evidence and to research. See Chapter 5, Principles of Qualitative Research, and Chapter 28, Naturalistic Inquiry, for discussion of these perspectives.

Internal criticism becomes an issue after the credibility and integrity of the evidence have been established through external criticism. Internal criticism, which deals only with written (and perhaps electronically recorded) information, seeks to determine the truthfulness of the information provided by the evidence. Is the information accurate, at least in light of other known facts? After all, just because an item is genuine does not mean that all the information it contains is accurate. A letter or the minutes of a meeting may contain inaccuracies that could lead to erroneous conclusions if not discovered. Questions the researcher might ask in applying internal criticism typically deal with real meaning versus literal meaning, how the evidence was reported, whether the information seems improbable or conflicts with what we know, internal inconsistencies, and bias on the part of the reporter (Shafer, 1998).

An example of determining the consistency of a source recently came to the attention of this writer while analyzing an article titled "Music in Medicine" by B. H. Larson, MD, from the May 1928 issue of the *Journal of the Michigan State Medical Society*. Larson lists an entry in his bibliography from *The Lancet*, written by "Dr. J. T. R. Davidson." Attempts to track down this article were fruitless. We always expect that bibliographies in published articles are accurate, but this writer began to wonder if the editorial standards in 1928 were as rigorous as they are now when this writer found the word "rhythmic" misspelled in the article as "rythmic." The misspelling only occurred once and was obviously a typographical error, but created some doubt as to whether or not the difficulty in finding the article by Davidson might also be the result of an error. After altering the spelling to what seemed to be the most obvious alternative, "Davison," the article was retrieved without difficulty.

Oral History

Oral history is often a good, first historical research project because it can be conducted on a small scale while still being of interest to others; it does not necessarily require expensive equipment, travel, and extensive knowledge of a new research methodology; and it teaches basic skills (such as organization and critical analysis) that are useful in other historical research endeavors. An individual's first experience with oral history often happens when he or she interviews a relative while preparing a family history.

Unlike the broader field of oral traditions, which are verbal stories passed from one generation to another, oral history is the verbal memories that a person has of his or her life and includes the individuals a person has known, the events in which a person has participated or observed, and the places a person has visited.

In his book *The Voice of the Past*, Paul Thompson (2000) correctly states that oral history is as old as history itself; in fact, oral history was the first kind of history. He also points out that some of the world's most famous historians have relied heavily, sometimes exclusively, on oral evidence.

Oral history is not a substitute for, but a complement to, written records. Although oral history does not compensate for the loss of written evidence, it does allow for the accumulation of information that might otherwise be permanently lost. One of the great advantages of oral history, and also one of its biggest attractions to historians, is that the historian actively participates in the creation of the evidence. While uncovering new evidence previously unknown or thought lost is exciting, oral history also allows for the opportunity to obtain the exact information that one seeks.

Conducting Oral History in Music Therapy

The first step in conducting an oral history project, as with any research project, is careful planning. The researcher must decide what information needs to be obtained and who is most likely to have that information.

The researcher must then decide which type of interview is appropriate for the situation at hand. One type of interview is, by nature, more like a friendly, informal conversation. An example occurred in this writer's own work in 1982 while studying the history of NAMT. This writer found little written evidence concerning the establishment if the Association's Central Office in Lawrence, KS, but knew, for example, that Ruth Boxberger had been appointed as the Association's first executive. This writer was able to speak with Dr. Boxberger at the 1982 NAMT conference in Baltimore, MD, where we met in a quiet corner of the hotel lobby. During this impromptu interview, this writer was able to gather all the information needed and was even able to draw some new leads.

The second type of interview is the structured, formal interview such as one might see on television. This type of interview requires much advance planning and thought if it is to be successful (see Hoopes, 2000).

The next step is to arrange for the interview. One must request and obtain permission for the interview in advance, request permission to tape record the interview if that is being considered, be well prepared by conducting considerable background research on the interviewee and the topics to be discussed, prepare a written interview guide, and so forth. Only after all this has been successfully accomplished can the researcher consider conducting the interview. After concluding the interview, the researcher must analyze the results, summarize, and draw conclusions. Ken Metzler's (1997) book *Creative Interviewing: The Writer's Guide to Gathering Information by Asking Questions* is an excellent guide and contains helpful information on all aspects of interviewing.

Historiography

Historiography is the process and product of presenting historical facts in a narrative based on a critical examination of the sources. Or, as George Heller (2003) writes: "Having gathered all the available evidence and criticized the sources, the historical researcher is ready to become a historian, that is to write a narrative" (p. 21). The writer of historical research is bound by the same rules and traditions that are the hallmark of all good writing: organization; the avoidance of jargon and clichés; clearly written sentences; and appropriate use of quotations, footnotes, and bibliography (Barzun & Graff, 1992). Unlike novelists, however, the historical narrative must be true to the evidence and, hopefully, be written in a style that engages the reader and brings the past to life.

Barzun and Graff (1992), in their monumental work *The Modern Researcher*, titled part II of that work "Writing, Speaking, and Publishing." There is simply no substitute for mastering this material for anyone seriously interested in becoming a good writer of research literature.

Ethical Precautions

Historical researchers adhere to the same ethical guidelines and precautions that are common in the general research community. The American Historical Association publishes a comprehensive "Statement on Standards of Professional Conduct," which "addresses dilemmas and concerns about the practice of history that historians have regularly brought to the American Historical Association seeking guidance and counsel" and which includes:

- A description of the "shared values" that historian's hold including trust and respect,
- Integrity of the historical record,
- Leaving a clear trail for subsequent historians to follow,
- Acknowledging one's debts to the work of other historians,
- Recognizing that multiple, conflicting perspectives are among the truths of history,
- Awareness of one's own biases and a readiness to follow sound method and analysis wherever they may lead,
- Acknowledging the receipt of any financial support or assistance from others.

The document closes with the admonition to "encourage all historians to uphold and defend their professional responsibilities with the utmost seriousness, and to advocate for integrity and fairness and high standards throughout the historical profession" (American Historical Association, 2005).

Ethical standards in scholarship, the area most pertinent to this discussion, establish the expectation that historians maintain scholarly integrity, including utilizing sound research methods and awareness of bias. Historians have the additional ethical responsibility to preserve sources and advocate their availability to others as well as encouraging intellectual diversity within the discipline.

Finally, historians are expected to maintain "standards of civility" that govern relationships between historians: "The preeminent value of all intellectual communities is reasoned discourse—the continuous colloquy among historians of diverse points of view. A commitment to such discourse makes possible the fruitful exchange of views, opinions, and knowledge" (American Historical Association, 2005).

Consequences of Historical Research

The consequences of historical research in music therapy affect the field of music therapy as well as the individual researcher. Benefits to the field include the ability of historical research to educate and inform, to inspire and motivate, and to unify and organize:

> The education or information provided by the results of historical research may benefit the general public, therapists, clients, students, and researchers in music therapy. . . . Increasing the public's knowledge about the problems, processes, and products of music therapy in the past and the present could benefit the field in important and tangible ways.
>
> Therapists, clients, and students also have a vital interest in the results of historical research in music therapy. Little is known, but much more can be known about how music has been used in therapy. Methods and materials, techniques and literature, skills and concepts have not been defined overnight. They represent the accumulated wisdom of many past labors. Therapists do not need to "reinvent the wheel" at each moment of the therapeutic process. Trends in music therapy have a demonstrated propensity to recur, sometimes with alarming frequency and intensity. Music therapists have been known to jump on the nearest bandwagon and head relentlessly for a previously experienced extreme of a pendulum swing. (Solomon & Heller, 1982, pp. 171–172)

As pointed out earlier, historical researchers, no matter how young and enthusiastic, inevitably come to the realization that historians cannot know everything about everyone or anything. But the attempt, and what is gained in the attempt, is invaluable, as Hoopes (2000) points out:

> Because history is an act of our minds, historical knowledge can lead to self-knowledge. To test or verify historical thought we must check not only the data or facts but also our thinking itself. We therefore learn not only about history but about the quality of our minds. The process is no different from that followed in the exact sciences, except that the qualities revealed in historical thinking include those of human and imaginative sympathy. Biases, prejudices, predispositions, all manner of attitudes and likes and dislikes, which we may not even have known we had, are revealed when we study a discipline like history, with its human content. History should be one of the most interesting, personally challenging, of all disciplines. (pp. 3–4)

And finally, history offers the possibility of hope:

> The mere fact that something has occurred holds within it the possibility that it could occur again, that, as the saying goes, history might repeat itself. Hope does not require probability; it does not even demand plausibility. Possibility is sufficient. People who know history have reason to hope. That may well be its greatest contribution to human existence. (Heller, 2003)

Conclusion

History teaches us many things about the world in which we live. To enliven history through historical narrative "may reveal human nature and thereby make a future possible" (Heller, 2003, p. 35).

An underpinning of all philosophies of history involves the regularity with which events occur in human history. One particular postulate predicts "the inevitable appearance of senseless interruptions which prevent orderly progress or evolution" (Renier, 1961, p. 221). Such a scenario presents an ever-strengthening rationale for additional historical research in music therapy to increase our collective sense of identity and purpose and to ensure our future and the continued progress and evolution of our discipline.

References

American Historical Association. (2005). *Statement on standards of professional conduct.* Available at http://www.historians.org/pubs/free/professionalstandards.cfm.

Barzun, J., & Graff, H. F. (1992). *The modern researcher* (5th ed.). Ft. Worth: Harcourt Brace Jovanovich College Publishers.

Berkhofer, R. F., Jr. (1969). *A behavioral approach to historical analysis.* New York: The Free Press.

Boxberger, R. (1964). A historical study of the National Association for Music Therapy (Doctoral dissertation, The University of Kansas, 1963). *Dissertation Abstracts International, 24,* 5449.

Brooks, D. M. (2002). Charles E. Braswell: A man with vision. *Journal of Music Therapy, 39,* 74–100.

Condron, D. (2000). *The American Association for Music Therapy: From inception to unification.* Unpublished master's thesis, Temple University, Philadelphia.

de l'Etoile, S. (2000). The history of the undergraduate curriculum in music therapy. *Journal of Music Therapy, 37,* 51–69.

Durant, W., & Durant, A. (1968). *The lessons of history.* New York: Simon and Schuster.

Heller, G. N. (2000). History, celebrations, and the transmission of hope: The American Music Therapy Association, 1950–2000. *Journal of Music Therapy, 37,* 245–246.

Heller, G. N. (2003). *Reading, researching, writing, and publishing history in music education and music therapy.* Unpublished manuscript, University of Kansas, Lawrence, KS.

Hoopes, J. (2000). *Oral history: An introduction for students.* Chapel Hill: University of North Carolina Press.

Hunter, B. C. (1999). Singing as a therapeutic agent, in *The Etude. Journal of Music Therapy, 36,* 125–143.

Metzler, K. (1997). *Creative interviewing: The writer's guide to gathering information by asking questions* (3rd ed.). Boston: Allyn & Bacon.

Miller, J. J. (1998). The contributions of Wayne Ruppenthal to the field of music therapy. *Journal of Music Therapy, 35,* 105–118.

Phelps, R. P., Ferrara, L. & Goolsby, T. W. (1993). *A guide to research in music education* (4th ed.). Metuchen, NJ: The Scarecrow Press.

Renier, G. J. (1961). *History: Its purpose and method.* London: George Allen & Unwin, Ltd.

Ricoeur, P. (1984). *The reality of the historical past.* Milwaukee, WI: Marquette University Press.

Robb, S. L. (1999). Marian Erdman: Contributions of an American Red Cross hospital recreation worker. *Journal of Music Therapy, 36,* 314–329.

Rorke, M. A. (2001). Music therapy in the Age of Enlightenment. *Journal of Music Therapy, 38,* 66–73.

Shafer, R. J. (Ed). (1998). *A guide to historical method* (3rd ed.). Homewood, IL: Dorsey Press.

Solomon, A. L. (1985). A historical study of the National Association for Music Therapy, 1960–1980 (Doctoral dissertation, The University of Kansas, 1984). *Dissertation Abstracts International, 46,* 2957-A.

Solomon, A. L. (1980). Music in special education before 1930: Hearing and speech development. *Journal of Research in Music Education, 28,* 236–242.

Solomon, A. L., Davis, W. B., & Heller, G. N. (2002). *Historical research in music therapy: A bibliography* (4th ed.). Silver Spring, MD: American Music Therapy Association.

Solomon, A. L., & Heller, G. N. (1982). Historical research in music therapy: An important avenue for studying the profession. *Journal of Music Therapy, 19,* 161–178.

Thompson, P. (2000). *The voice of the past: Oral history* (3rd ed.). New York: Oxford University Press.

Additional Readings

Ankersmit, F. R. (2001). *Historical representation*. Stanford, CA: Stanford University Press.

Arnold, J. H. (2000). *History: A very short introduction*. Oxford, UK: Oxford University Press.

Bentley, M. (1999). *Modern historiography: An introduction*. New York: Routledge.

Burke, P. (Ed.). (2001). *New perspectives on historical writing* (2nd ed.). University Park, PA: Pennsylvania State University Press.

Davis, W. B. (1993). Keeping the dream alive: Profiles of three early twentieth century music therapists. *Journal of Music Therapy, 30*, 34–45.

Heller, G. N. (1987). Ideas, initiatives, and implementations: Music therapy in America, 1789–1848. *Journal of Music Therapy, 24*, 35–46.

Heller, G. N., & Wilson, B. D. (1992). Historical research. In R. J. Colwell (Ed.), *Handbook of research on music teaching and learning* (pp. 102–114). New York: Schirmer Books.

Howell, M. C., & Prevenier, W. (2001). *From reliable sources: An introduction to historical methods*. Ithaca, NY: Cornell University Press.

Johnson, R. E. (1981). E. Thayer Gaston: Leader in scientific thought on music therapy and education. *Journal of Research in Music Education, 29*, 279–286.

Keene, J. A. (1987). *A history of music education in the United States*. Hanover, NH: University Press of New England.

Lukacs, J. (2000). *A student's guide to the study of history*. Wilmington, DE: ISI Books.

Wineburg, S. S. (2001). *Historical thinking and other unnatural acts: Charting the future of teaching the past*. Philadelphia: Temple University Press.

Indexes

Author Index

Topic Index

Author Index

Subject Index